continued on back inside cover

E-commerce

business. technology. society.

TENTH EDITION

Kenneth C. Laudon
New York University

Carol Guercio Traver
Azimuth Interactive, Inc.

PEARSON

Boston   Columbus   Indianapolis   New York   San Francisco   Upper Saddle River
Amsterdam   Cape Town   Dubai   London   Madrid   Milan   Munich   Paris   Montreal   Toronto
Delhi   Mexico City   São Paulo   Sydney   Hong Kong   Seoul   Singapore   Taipei   Tokyo

Editor In Chief: Stephanie Wall
Executive Editor: Bob Horan
Program Manager Team Lead: Ashley Santora
Program Manager: Denise Vaughn
Editorial Assistant: Kaylee Rotella
Executive Marketing Manager: Anne K. Fahlgren
Project Manager Team Lead: Judy Leale
Project Manager: Karalyn Holland
Operations Specialist: Michelle Klein
Creative Director: Blair Brown

Sr. Art Director: Janet Slowik
Cover Designer: DePinho Design
Cover Image: Shutterstock VLADGRIN
Media Project Manager: Lisa Rinaldi
Full Service Project Management: Azimuth Interactive, Inc.
Composition: Azimuth Interactive, Inc.
Printer/Binder: Edwards Brothers Malloy
Cover Printer: Lehigh-Phoenix Color/Hagarstown
Text Font: ITC Veljovic Std. Book, 9.5pt

Credits and acknowledgements borrowed from other sources and reproduced, with permission, in this textbook appear on page C-1.

Library of Congress Cataloging-in-Publication Information Is Available

10 9 8 7 6 5 4 3 2

ISBN 10: 0-13-302444-X
ISBN 13: 978-0-13-302444-9

PREFACE

E-commerce. Business. Technology. Society. 10E provides you with an in-depth introduction to the field of e-commerce. We focus on concepts that will help you understand and take advantage of the evolving world of opportunity offered by e-commerce, which is dramatically altering the way business is conducted and driving major shifts in the global economy.

Just as important, we have tried to create a book that is thought-provoking and current. We use the most recent data available, and focus on companies that you are likely to encounter on a daily basis in your everyday life, such as Facebook, Google, Twitter, Amazon, YouTube, Pinterest, eBay, and many more that you will recognize, as well as some exciting startups that may be new to you. We also have up-to-date coverage of the key topics in e-commerce today, from privacy and piracy, to government surveillance, cyberwar, social, local, and mobile marketing, Internet sales taxes, intellectual property, and more. You will find here the most up-to-date and comprehensive overview of e-commerce today.

The e-commerce concepts you learn in this book will make you valuable to potential employers. The e-commerce job market is expanding rapidly. Many employers expect new employees to understand the basics of e-commerce, social and mobile marketing, and how to develop an e-commerce presence. Every industry today is touched in at least some way by e-commerce. The information and knowledge you find in this book will be valuable throughout your career, and after reading this book, we expect that you will be able to participate in, and even lead, management discussions of e-commerce for your firm.

WHAT'S NEW IN THE TENTH EDITION

New Chapter on Social, Mobile, and Local Marketing

Given the growing importance of social, mobile, and local marketing in e-commerce, we have written an entirely new chapter devoted to providing an in-depth examination of these topics. In this new chapter, you will learn how companies are using Facebook, Twitter, and Pinterest for social marketing, how to begin a social marketing campaign and how to measure results for each of these platforms. We provide similar examination of mobile and local and location-based marketing as well.

New Infographics

A variety of infographics throughout the book provide a more visual and intuitive access to concepts and information. Infographics make it easier to see and remember patterns and relationships than traditional charts and graphs.

Currency

The 10th edition features all new or updated opening, closing, and "Insight on" cases. The text, as well as all of the data, figures, and tables in the book, have been updated through October 2013 with the latest marketing and business intelligence available from eMarketer, Pew Internet & American Life Project, Forrester Research, comScore, Gartner Research, and other industry sources.

What's New in E-commerce 2014

E-commerce today is greatly different from e-commerce only five years ago. The iPhone was introduced in 2007. The iPad tablet was first introduced in 2010 and has already gone through several generations! The smartphone and tablet devices have changed e-commerce into a social, local, and mobile experience. The 10th edition spotlights the following themes and content:

Headlines
- Social, Mobile, Local: We have included an entirely new chapter describing social, mobile, and local marketing. Content about social networks, the mobile platform and local e-commerce appears throughout the book.
  - » Social networks such as Facebook, Twitter, Pinterest, and LinkedIn continue their rapid growth, laying the groundwork for a social network marketing platform
  - » The mobile platform composed of smartphones and tablet computers takes off and becomes a major factor in search, marketing, payment, retailing and services, and online content. Mobile device use poses new security and privacy issues as well.
  - » Location-based services lead to explosive growth in local advertising and marketing.
- Online privacy continues to deteriorate, driven by a culture of self-revelation and powerful technologies for collecting personal information online without the knowledge or consent of users.
- Internet security risks increase; cyberwarfare becomes a new way of conducting warfare among nation-states and a national security issue.

Business
- E-commerce revenues surge after the recession.
- Internet advertising growth resumes, at a faster rate than traditional advertising.
- Social marketing grows faster than traditional online marketing like search and display advertising.
- E-books take off and expand the market for text, supported by the iPad, Kindle, Nook, and iPhone.
- Streaming of popular TV shows and movies (Netflix, Amazon, and Hulu.com) becomes a reality, as Internet distributors and Hollywood and TV producers strike deals for Web distribution that also protects intellectual property.

- "Free" and "freemium" business models compete to support digital content.
- New mobile payment platforms emerge to challenge PayPal.
- B2B e-commerce exceeds pre-recession levels as firms become more comfortable with digital supply chains.

Technology

- Smartphones, tablets, and e-book readers, along with associated software applications, and coupled with 4G cellular network expansion, fuel rapid growth of the mobile platform.
- Investment in cloud computing increases, providing the computing infrastructure for a massive increase in online digital information and e-commerce.
- Cloud-based streaming services for music and video challenge sales of downloads and physical product.
- Software apps fuel growth in app sales, marketing, and advertising; transforming software production and distribution.
- Touch interface operating systems dominate mobile devices. Windows 8 introduced with a touch screen interface, mimicking Apple's iOS and Google Android smartphones.
- The cost of developing sophisticated Web sites continues to drop due to declining software and hardware prices and open source software tools.
- Internet and cellular network capacity is challenged by the rapid expansion in digital traffic generated by mobile devices; the use of bandwidth caps tier-pricing expands.
- Internet telecommunications carriers support differential pricing to maintain a stable Internet; opposed by Net neutrality groups pushing non-discriminatory pricing.

Society

- The mobile, "always on" culture in business and family life continues to grow.
- Congress considers legislation to regulate the use of personal information for behavioral tracking and targeting consumers online.
- States heat up the pursuit of taxes on Internet sales by Amazon and others.
- Intellectual property issues remain a source of conflict with significant movement toward resolution in some areas, such as Google's deals with Hollywood and the publishing industry, and Apple's and Amazon's deals with e-book and magazine publishers.
- P2P piracy traffic declines as paid streaming music and video gains ground, although digital piracy of online content remains a significant threat to Hollywood and the music industry.
- Governments around the world increase surveillance of Internet users and Web sites in response to national security threats; Google continues to tussle with China and other countries over censorship and security issues.

- Venture capital investing in e-commerce explodes for social, mobile, and local software applications. Crowdfunding becomes a new source of funding for e-commerce start-ups.

WELCOME TO THE NEW E-COMMERCE

Since it began in 1995, electronic commerce has grown in the United States from a standing start to a $419 billion retail, travel, and media business and a $4.7 trillion business-to-business juggernaut, bringing about enormous change in business firms, markets, and consumer behavior. Economies and business firms around the globe are being similarly affected. During this relatively short time, e-commerce has itself been transformed from its origin as a mechanism for online retail sales into something much broader. Today, e-commerce has become the platform for media and new, unique services and capabilities that aren't found in the physical world. There is no physical world counterpart to Facebook, Twittter, Google search, or a host of other recent online innovations from Pinterest and iTunes to Tumblr. Welcome to the new e-commerce!

Although e-commerce today has been impacted by the worldwide economic recession, in the next five years, e-commerce in all of its forms is still projected to continue growing at high single-digit rates, becoming the fastest growing form of commerce. Just as automobiles, airplanes, and electronics defined the twentieth century, so will e-commerce of all kinds define business and society in the twenty-first century. The rapid movement toward an e-commerce economy and society is being led by both established business firms such as Walmart, Ford, IBM, Macy's, and General Electric, and newer entrepreneurial firms such as Google, Amazon, Apple, Facebook, Yahoo, Twitter, YouTube, and Photobucket. Students of business and information technology need a thorough grounding in electronic commerce in order to be effective and successful managers in the next decade. This book is written for tomorrow's managers.

While newer firms such as Facebook, Tumblr, YouTube, Twitter, Pinterest, Flickr, and Square have grown explosively in the last two years and grab our attention, the traditional forms of retail e-commerce and services also remain vital and have proven to be more resilient than traditional retail channels in facing the economic recession. The experience of these firms from 1995 to the present is also a focus of this book. The defining characteristic of these firms is that they are profitable, sustainable, efficient, and innovative, with powerful brand names. Many of these now-experienced retail and service firms, such as eBay, Amazon, E*Trade, Priceline, and Expedia, are survivors of the first era of e-commerce, from 1995 to spring 2000. These surviving firms have evolved their business models, integrated their online and offline operations, and changed their revenue models to become profitable. Students must understand how to build these kinds of e-commerce businesses in order to help the business firms they manage to succeed in the e-commerce era.

It would be foolish to ignore the lessons learned in the early period of e-commerce. Like so many technology revolutions in the past—automobiles, electricity, telephones, television, and biotechnology—there was an explosion of entrepreneurial efforts, followed by consolidation. By 2005, the survivors of the early period were

moving to establish profitable businesses while maintaining rapid growth in revenues. In 2013, e-commerce is entering a new period of explosive entrepreneurial
activity focusing on social networks and the mobile digital platform created by smartphones and tablet computers. These technologies and social behaviors are bringing
about extraordinary changes to our personal lives, markets, industries, individual
businesses, and society as a whole. In 2012–2013, the stock values of Apple, Google,
and Amazon hit new highs, along with many start-ups. E-commerce is generating
thousands of new jobs for young managers in all fields from marketing to management, entrepreneurial studies, and information systems. Today, e-commerce has
moved into the mainstream life of established businesses that have the market brands
and financial muscle required for the long-term deployment of e-commerce technologies and methods. If you are working in an established business, chances are the
firm's e-commerce capabilities and Web presence are important factors for its success.
If you want to start a new business, chances are very good that the knowledge you
learn in this book will be very helpful.

BUSINESS. TECHNOLOGY. SOCIETY.

We believe that in order for business and technology students to really understand
e-commerce, they must understand the relationships among e-commerce business
concerns, Internet technology, and the social and legal context of e-commerce. These
three themes permeate all aspects of e-commerce, and therefore, in each chapter, we
present material that explores the business, technological, and social aspects of that
chapter's main topic.

Given the continued growth and diffusion of e-commerce, all students—regardless of their major discipline—must also understand the basic economic and business
forces driving e-commerce. E-commerce has created new electronic markets where
prices are more transparent, markets are global, and trading is highly efficient,
though not perfect. E-commerce has a direct impact on a firm's relationship with suppliers, customers, competitors, and partners, as well as how firms market products,
advertise, and use brands. Whether you are interested in marketing and sales, design,
production, finance, information systems, or logistics, you will need to know how
e-commerce technologies can be used to reduce supply chain costs, increase production efficiency, and tighten the relationship with customers. This text is written to
help you understand the fundamental business issues in e-commerce.

We spend a considerable amount of effort analyzing the business models and
strategies of "pure-play" online companies and established businesses now employing
"bricks-and-clicks" business models. We explore why e-commerce firms fail and the
strategic, financial, marketing, and organizational challenges they face. We also discuss how e-commerce firms learned from the mistakes of early firms, and how established firms are using e-commerce to succeed. Above all, we attempt to bring a strong
sense of business realism and sensitivity to the often exaggerated descriptions of
e-commerce. As founders of a dot.com company and participants in the e-commerce
revolution, we have learned that the "e" in e-commerce does not stand for "easy."

The Web and e-commerce have caused a major revolution in marketing and
advertising in the United States. We spend two chapters discussing online marketing

and advertising. Chapter 6 discusses "traditional" online marketing formats like search engine marketing, display advertising, and e-mail, as well as various Internet marketing technologies underlying those efforts, and metrics for measuring marketing success. Chapter 7 provides an in-depth examination of social, mobile, and local marketing, which relies on mobile devices and social networks.

E-commerce is driven by Internet technology. Internet technology, and information technology in general, is perhaps the star of the show. Without the Internet, e-commerce would be virtually nonexistent. Accordingly, we provide three chapters specifically on the Internet and e-commerce technology, and in every chapter we provide continuing coverage by illustrating how the topic of the chapter is being shaped by new information technologies. For instance, Internet technology drives developments in security and payment systems, marketing strategies and advertising, financial applications, media distribution, business-to-business trade, and retail e-commerce. We discuss the rapid growth of the mobile digital platform, the emergence of cloud computing, new open source software tools and applications that enable Web 2.0, and new types of Internet-based information systems that support electronic business-to-business markets.

E-commerce is not only about business and technology, however. The third part of the equation for understanding e-commerce is society. E-commerce and Internet technologies have important social consequences that business leaders can ignore only at their peril. E-commerce has challenged our concepts of privacy, intellectual property, and even our ideas about national sovereignty and governance. Google, Facebook, Apple, Amazon, and assorted advertising networks maintain profiles on millions of shoppers and consumers worldwide. The proliferation of illegally copied music and videos on the Internet, and the growth of social networking sites often based on displaying copyrighted materials without permission, are challenging the intellectual property rights of record labels, Hollywood studios, and artists. And many countries—including the United States—are demanding to control the content of Web sites displayed within their borders for political and social reasons. Tax authorities in the United States and Europe are demanding that e-commerce sites pay sales taxes just like ordinary brick and mortar stores on mainstreet. As a result of these challenges to existing institutions, e-commerce and the Internet are the subject of increasing investigation, litigation, and legislation. Business leaders need to understand these societal developments, and they cannot afford to assume any longer that the Internet is borderless, beyond social control and regulation, or a place where market efficiency is the only consideration. In addition to an entire chapter devoted to the social and legal implications of e-commerce, each chapter contains material highlighting the social implications of e-commerce.

FEATURES AND COVERAGE

Strong Conceptual Foundation The book emphasizes the three major driving forces behind e-commerce: business development and strategy, technological innovations, and social controversies and impacts. Each of these driving forces is represented in every chapter, and together they provide a strong and coherent conceptual framework for understanding e-commerce. We analyze e-commerce, digital markets, and e-business firms just as we would ordinary businesses and markets using concepts from economics, marketing, finance, sociology, philosophy, and information systems. We strive to maintain a critical perspective on e-commerce and avoid industry hyperbole.

Some of the important concepts from economics and marketing that we use to explore e-commerce are transaction cost, network externalities, information asymmetry, social networks, perfect digital markets, segmentation, price dispersion, targeting, and positioning. Important concepts from the study of information systems and technologies play an important role in the book, including Internet standards and protocols, client/server computing, multi-tier server systems, cloud computing, mobile digital platform and wireless technologies, and public key encryption, among many others. From the literature on ethics and society, we use important concepts such as intellectual property, privacy, information rights and rights management, governance, public health, and welfare.

From the literature on business, we use concepts such as business process design, return on investment, strategic advantage, industry competitive environment, oligopoly, and monopoly. We also provide a basic understanding of finance and accounting issues, and extend this through an "E-commerce in Action" case that critically examines the financial statements of Amazon. One of the witticisms that emerged from the early years of e-commerce and that still seems apt is the notion that e-commerce changes everything except the rules of business. Businesses still need to make a profit in order to survive in the long term.

Currency Important new developments happen almost every day in e-commerce and the Internet. We try to capture as many of these important new developments in each annual edition. You will not find a more current book for a course offered for the 2014 academic year. Many other texts are already six months to a year out of date before they even reach the printer. This text, in contrast, reflects extensive research through October 2013, just weeks before the book hits the press.

Real-World Business Firm Focus and Cases From Akamai Technologies to Google, Microsoft, Apple, and Amazon, to Facebook, Twitter, and Tumblr, to Netflix, Pandora, and Elemica, this book contains hundreds of real-company examples and over 60 more extensive cases that place coverage in the context of actual dot.com businesses. You'll find these examples in each chapter, as well as in special features such as chapter-opening, chapter-closing, and "Insight on" cases. The book takes a realistic look at the world of e-commerce, describing what's working and what isn't, rather than presenting a rose-colored or purely "academic" viewpoint.

In-depth Coverage of Marketing and Advertising The text includes two chapters on marketing and advertising, both traditional online marketing and social, mobile, and local marketing. Marketing concepts, including market segmentation, personalization, clickstream analysis, bundling of digital goods, long-tail marketing, and dynamic pricing, are used throughout the text.

In-depth Coverage of B2B E-commerce We devote an entire chapter to an examination of B2B e-commerce. In writing this chapter, we developed a unique and easily understood classification schema to help students understand this complex arena of e-commerce. This chapter covers four types of Net marketplaces (e-distributors, e-procurement companies, exchanges, and industry consortia) as well as the development of private industrial networks and collaborative commerce.

Current and Future Technology Coverage Internet and related information technologies continue to change rapidly. The most important changes for e-commerce include dramatic price reductions in e-commerce infrastructure (making it much less expensive to develop sophisticated Web sites), the explosive growth in the mobile platform such as iPhones, iPads, tablet computers, and expansion in the development of social technologies, which are the foundation of online social networks. What was once a shortage of telecommunications capacity has now turned into a surplus, PC prices have continued to fall, smartphone and tablet sales have soared, Internet high-speed broadband connections are now typical and are continuing to show double-digit growth, and wireless technologies such as Wi-Fi and cellular broadband are transforming how, when, and where people access the Internet. While we thoroughly discuss the current Internet environment, we devote considerable attention to describing Web 2.0 and emerging technologies and applications such as the advanced network infrastructure, fiber optics, wireless Web and 4G technologies, Wi-Fi, IP multicasting, and future guaranteed service levels.

Up-to-Date Coverage of the Research Literature This text is well grounded in the e-commerce research literature. We have sought to include, where appropriate, references and analysis of the latest e-commerce research findings, as well as many classic articles, in all of our chapters. We have drawn especially on the disciplines of economics, marketing, and information systems and technologies, as well as law journals and broader social science research journals including sociology and psychology.

We do not use references to Wikipedia in this text, for a variety of reasons. Most colleges do not consider Wikipedia a legitimate or acceptable source for academic research and instruct their students not to cite it. Material found on Wikipedia may be out of date, lack coverage, lack critical perspective, and cannot necessarily be trusted. Our references are to respected academic journals; industry sources such as eMarketer, comScore, Hitwise, Nielsen, and Gartner; newspapers such as the *New York Times* and *Wall Street Journal*; and industry publications such as *Computerworld* and *InformationWeek*, among others. Figures and tables sourced to "authors' estimates" reflect analysis of data from the U.S. Department of Commerce, estimates from various research firms, historical trends, revenues of major online retailers, consumer online buying trends, and economic conditions.

Special Attention to the Social and Legal Aspects of E-commerce We have paid special attention throughout the book to the social and legal context of e-commerce. Chapter 8 is devoted to a thorough exploration of four ethical dimensions of e-commerce: information privacy, intellectual property, governance, and protecting public welfare on the Internet. We have included an analysis of the latest Federal Trade Commission and other regulatory and nonprofit research reports, and their likely impact on the e-commerce environment.

A major theme throughout this chapter, and the remainder of the book, is the impact of social, mobile, and local commerce on how consumers use the Internet.

Writing That's Fun to Read Unlike some textbooks, we've been told by many students that this book is actually fun to read and easy to understand. This is not a book written by committee—you won't find a dozen different people listed as authors, co-authors, and contributors on the title page. We have a consistent voice and perspective that carries through the entire text and we believe the book is the better for it.

OVERVIEW OF THE BOOK

The book is organized into four parts.

Part 1, "Introduction to E-commerce," provides an introduction to the major themes of the book. Chapter 1 defines e-commerce, distinguishes between e-commerce and e-business, and defines the different types of e-commerce. Chapter 2 introduces and defines the concepts of business model and revenue model, describes the major e-commerce business and revenue models for both B2C and B2B firms, and introduces the basic business concepts required throughout the text for understanding e-commerce firms including industry structure, value chains, and firm strategy.

Part 2, "Technology Infrastructure for E-commerce," focuses on the technology infrastructure that forms the foundation for all e-commerce. Chapter 3 traces the historical development of the Internet I and thoroughly describes how today's Internet works. A major focus of this chapter is mobile technology, Web 2.0 applications, and the near-term future Internet that is now under development and will shape the future of e-commerce. Chapter 4 builds on the Internet chapter by focusing on the steps managers need to follow in order to build a commercial Web site. This e-commerce infrastructure chapter covers the systems analysis and design process that should be followed in building an e-commerce Web presence; the major decisions regarding outsourcing site development and/or hosting; and how to choose software, hardware, and other tools that can improve Web site performance. Chapter 5 focuses on Internet security and payments, building on the e-commerce infrastructure discussion of the previous chapter by describing the ways security can be provided over the Internet. This chapter defines digital information security, describes the major threats to security, and then discusses both the technology and policy solutions available to business managers seeking to secure their firm's sites. This chapter concludes with a section on Internet payment systems. We identify the stakeholders in payment systems, the dimensions to consider in creating payment systems, and the various types of online payment systems (credit cards, stored value payment systems such as PayPal, digital wallets such as Google Wallet and others), and the development of mobile payment systems.

Part 3, "Business Concepts and Social Issues," focuses directly on the business concepts and social-legal issues that surround the development of e-commerce. Chapter 6 focuses on e-commerce consumer behavior, the Internet audience, and introduces the student to the basics of online marketing and branding, including traditional browser-based online marketing technologies and marketing strategies. Topics include the Web site as a marketing platform, search engine marketing and advertising, display ad marketing, e-mail campaigns, affiliate and lead generation marketing programs, multichannel marketing, and various customer retention strategies such as personalization (including interest-based advertising, also known as behavioral targeting) and customer service tools. The chapter also covers other marketing strategies such as pricing and long-tail marketing. Internet marketing technologies (Web transaction logs, tracking files, data mining and big data) and CRM are also explored. The chapter concludes with a section on understanding the costs and benefits of various types of online marketing, including a new section on Web analytics software. Chapter 7 is devoted to an in-depth analysis of social, mobile, and local marketing. Topics include Facebook, Twitter, and Pinterest marketing platforms, the evolution of mobile marketing away from browsers and towards in-app marketing, and the growing use of geo-aware technologies to support geo-fencing and in-store geo-marketing.

Part 4, "E-commerce in Action," focuses on real-world e-commerce experiences in retail and services, online media, auctions, portals, and social networks, and business-to-business e-commerce. These chapters take a sector approach rather than the conceptual approach used in the earlier chapters. E-commerce is different in each of these sectors. Chapter 9 takes a close look at the experience of firms in the retail marketplace for both goods and services. Chapter 9 also includes an "E-commerce in Action" case that provides a detailed analysis of the business strategies and financial operating results of Amazon, which can be used as a model to analyze other e-commerce firms. Additional "E-commerce in Action" cases will be available online at the authors' Web site for the text, www.azimuth-interactive.com/ecommerce10e. Chapter 10 explores the world of online content and digital media and examines the enormous changes in online publishing and entertainment industries that have occurred over the last two years, including streaming movies, e-books, and online newspapers and magazines. Chapter 11 explores the online world of social networks, auctions, and portals. Chapter 12 concentrates on the world of B2B e-commerce, describing both electronic Net marketplaces and the less-heralded, but very large arena of private industrial networks and the movement toward collaborative commerce.

PEDAGOGY AND CHAPTER OUTLINE

The book's pedagogy emphasizes student cognitive awareness and the ability to analyze, synthesize, and evaluate e-commerce businesses. While there is a strong data and conceptual foundation to the book, we seek to engage student interest with lively writing about e-commerce businesses and the transformation of business models at traditional firms.

Each chapter contains a number of elements designed to make learning easy as well as interesting.

Learning Objectives A list of learning objectives that highlights the key concepts in the chapter guides student study.

Chapter-Opening Cases Each chapter opens with a story about a leading e-commerce company that relates the key objectives of the chapter to a real-life e-commerce business venture.

Pinterest:
A Picture Is Worth a Thousand Words

Like all of the most successful e-commerce companies, Pinterest taps into a simple truth. In Pinterest's case, the simple truth is that people love to collect things, and show off their collections to others. And like other Internet firms that have goals of global scope, such as Google, Facebook, and Amazon, Pinterest also has a global mission: to connect everyone in the world through the things they find interesting. How? Founded in 2009 by Ben Silbermann, Evan Sharp, and Paul Sciarra and launched in March 2010, Pinterest allows you to create virtual scrapbooks of images, video, and other content that you "pin" to a virtual bulletin board or pin board on the Web site. Categories range from Animals to Videos, with Food & Drink, DIY & Crafts, and Women's Fashion among the most popular. Find something that you particularly like? In addition to "liking" and perhaps commenting on it, you can re-pin it to your own board, or follow a link back to the original source. Find someone whose taste you admire or who shares your passions? You can follow one or more of that pinner's boards to keep track of everything she or he pins.

Reportedly the fastest Web site in history to reach 10 million visitors a month, Pinterest currently has more than 50 million unique visitors a month, more than double its traffic in the previous year. According to some tracking services, it is now the third most visited social network in the United States, behind Facebook and Twitter. It is also one of the "stickiest" sites on the Web—according to comScore, users spend an average of 80 minutes per session on Pinterest, and almost 60% of users with accounts visit once or more a week. Jeff Jordan, a partner at Andreessen Horowitz, a venture capital firm and investor in Pinterest, says he has seen only one other site with similar numbers—Facebook. And like Facebook before it, Pinterest has begun a transition toward monetizing that appeal. The first step, in November 2012, was to offer business accounts that provide additional resources for brands. Currently, there is no charge for a business account, but that clearly may change in the future. In March 2013, Pinterest introduced a new Web analytics tool, also currently free, that helps Web site owners understand how people are using pinned material that has originated from their Web sites. Shortly

© Blaize Pascall / Alamy

"Insight on" Cases Each chapter contains three real-world cases illustrating the themes of technology, business, and society. These cases take an in-depth look at relevant topics to help describe and analyze the full breadth of the field of e-commerce. The cases probe such issues as the ability of governments to regulate Internet content, how to design Web sites for accessibility, the challenges faced by luxury marketers in online marketing, and smartphone security.

Margin Glossary Throughout the text, key terms and their definitions appear in the text margin where they are first introduced.

Real-Company Examples Drawn from actual e-commerce ventures, well over 100 pertinent examples are used throughout the text to illustrate concepts.

Chapter-Closing Case Studies Each chapter concludes with a robust case study based on a real-world organization. These cases help students synthesize chapter concepts and apply this knowledge to concrete problems and scenarios such as evaluating Pandora's freemium business model, ExchangeHunterJumper's efforts to build a brand, and the fairness of the Google Books settlement.

Chapter-Ending Pedagogy Each chapter contains extensive end-of-chapter materials designed to reinforce the learning objectives of the chapter.

Key Concepts Keyed to the learning objectives, Key Concepts present the key points of the chapter to aid student study.

Review Questions Thought-provoking questions prompt students to demonstrate their comprehension and apply chapter concepts to management problem solving.

2.6 CASE STUDY

Pandora and the Freemium Business Model

Case Study | 97

Projects At the end of each chapter are a number of projects that encourage students to apply chapter concepts and to use higher level evaluation skills. Many make use of the Internet and require students to present their findings in an oral or electronic presentation or written report. For instance, students are asked to evaluate publicly available information about a company's financials at the SEC Web site, assess payment system options for companies across international boundaries, or search for the top 10 cookies on their own computer and the sites they are from.

Web Resources Web resources that can extend students' knowledge of each chapter with projects, exercises, and additional content are available at www.azimuth-interactive.com/ecommerce10e. The Web site contains the following content provided by the authors:

- Additional projects, exercises, and tutorials
- Information on how to build a business plan and revenue models
- Essays on careers in e-commerce

SUPPORT PACKAGE

The following supplementary materials are available to qualified instructors through the Online Instructor Resource Center. Contact your Pearson sales representative for information about how to access them.

- **Instructor's Manual with solutions** This comprehensive manual pulls together a wide variety of teaching tools so that instructors can use the text easily and effectively. Each chapter contains an overview of key topics, a recap of the key learning objectives, additional topics for class discussion and debate, lecture tips, discussion of the chapter-ending case, and answers to the Case Study Questions, Review Questions, and Student Projects.

- **Test Bank** For quick test preparation, the author-created Test Bank contains multiple-choice, true/false, and short-essay questions that focus both on content and the development of critical/creative thinking about the issues evoked by the chapter. The Test Bank is available in Microsoft Word and TestGen format. The TestGen is also available in WebCT and BlackBoard-ready format. TestGen allows instructors to view, edit, and add questions.

- **PowerPoint lecture presentation slides** These slides illustrate key points, tables, and figures from the text in lecture-note format. The slides can be easily converted to transparencies or viewed electronically in the classroom. The slides also include additional questions for the opening cases and the "Insight on" vignettes throughout the book. These questions are very useful for in-class discussions, or quizzes.

- **Learning Tracks** These additional essays, created by the authors, provide instructors and students with more in-depth content on selected topics in e-commerce.

  Chapter 1
  1.1 Global E-commerce Europe
  1.2 Global E-commerce Latin America
  1.3 Global E-commerce China

  Chapter 6
  6.1 Basic Marketing Concepts
  6.2 Consumer Behavior: Cultural, Social, and Psychological Background Factors
  6.3 Social Media Marketing - Blogging

- **Video Cases** The authors have created a collection of video case studies that integrate short videos, supporting case study material, and case study questions. Video cases can be used in class to promote discussion or as written assignments.

  Chapter 1
  1.1 The Future of E-commerce

  Chapter 2
  2.1 Deals Galore at Groupon

ACKNOWLEDGMENTS

Pearson Education sought the advice of many excellent reviewers, all of whom strongly influenced the organization and substance of this book. The following individuals provided extremely useful evaluations of this and previous editions of the text:

Deniz Aksen, Koç University (Istanbul)

Carrie Andersen, Madison Area Technical College

Dr. Shirley A. Becker, Northern Arizona University

Prasad Bingi, Indiana-Purdue University, Fort Wayne

Christine Barnes, Lakeland Community College

Cliff Butler, North Seattle Community College

Joanna Broder, University of Arizona

James Buchan, College of the Ozarks

Ashley Bush, Florida State University

Mark Choman, Luzerne City Community College

Andrew Ciganek, Jacksonville State University

Daniel Connolly, University of Denver

Tom Critzer, Miami University

Dursan Delen, Oklahoma State University

Abhijit Deshmukh, University of Massachusetts

Brian L. Dos Santos, University of Louisville

Robert Drevs, University of Notre Dame

Akram El-Tannir, Hariri Canadian University, Lebanon

Kimberly Furumo, University of Hawaii at Hilo

John H. Gerdes, University of California, Riverside

Philip Gordon, University of California at Berkeley

Allan Greenberg, Brooklyn College

Bin Gu, University of Texas at Austin

Peter Haried, University of Wisconsin- La Crosse

Sherri Harms, University of Nebraska at Kearney

Sharon Heckel, St. Charles Community College

David Hite, Virginia Intermont College

Gus Jabbour, George Mason University

Ellen Kraft, Georgian Court University

Gilliean Lee, Lander University

Zoonky Lee, University of Nebraska, Lincoln

Andre Lemaylleux, Boston University, Brussels

Haim Levkowitz, University of Massachusetts, Lowell

Yair Levy, Nova Southeastern University

Richard Lucic, Duke University

John Mendonca, Purdue University

Dr. Abdulrahman Mirza, DePaul University

Kent Palmer, MacMurray College

Karen Palumbo, University of St. Francis

Wayne Pauli, Dakota State University

Jamie Pinchot, Thiel College

Kai Pommerenke, University of California at Santa Cruz

Barry Quinn, University of Ulster, Northern Ireland

Michelle Ramim, Nova Southeastern University

Jay Rhee, San Jose State University

Jorge Romero, Towson University

John Sagi, Anne Arundel Community College

Patricia Sendall, Merrimack College

Dr. Carlos Serrao, ISCTE/DCTI, Portugal

Neerja Sethi, Nanyang Business School, Singapore

Amber Settle, DePaul CTI

Vivek Shah, Texas State University-San Marcos

Seung Jae Shin, Mississippi State University

Sumit Sircar, University of Texas at Arlington

Hongjun Song, University of Memphis

Pamela Specht, University of Nebraska at Omaha

Esther Swilley, Kansas State University

Tony Townsend, Iowa State University

Bill Troy, University of New Hampshire

Susan VandeVen, Southern Polytechnic State University

Hiep Van Dong, Madison Area Technical College

And Michael Van Hilst, Nova Southeastern University

Mary Vitrano, Palm Beach Community College

Andrea Wachter, Point Park University

Catherine Wallace, Massey University, New Zealand

Biao Wang, Boston University

Haibo Wang, Texas A&M International University

Harry Washington, Lincoln University

Rolf Wigand, University of Arkansas at Little Rock

Erin Wilkinson, Johnson & Wales University

Alice Wilson, Cedar Crest College

Dezhi Wu, Southern Utah University

Gene Yelle, SUNY Institute of Technology

David Zolzer, Northwestern State University

We would like to thank eMarketer, Inc. and David Iankelevich for their permission to include data and figures from their research reports in our text. eMarketer is one of the leading independent sources for statistics, trend data, and original analysis covering many topics related to the Internet, e-business, and emerging technologies. eMarketer aggregates e-business data from multiple sources worldwide.

In addition, we would like to thank all those at Pearson who have worked so hard to make sure this book is the very best it can be. We want to thank Bob Horan, Executive Editor of the Pearson MIS list, and Karalyn Holland, Senior Production Project Manager, for their support; Judy Leale for overseeing production of this project; and DePinho Design for the outstanding cover design. Very special thanks to Robin Pickering, Megan Miller, and Will Anderson at Azimuth Interactive, Inc., for all their hard work on the production of, and supplements for, this book.

A special thanks also to Susan Hartman, Executive Editor for the first and second editions and to Frank Ruggirello, Publisher at Addison-Wesley when we began this project, and now Vice President and Editorial Director at Benjamin-Cummings.

Finally, last but not least, we would like to thank our family and friends, without whose support this book would not have been possible.

Kenneth C. Laudon
Carol Guercio Traver

Brief Contents

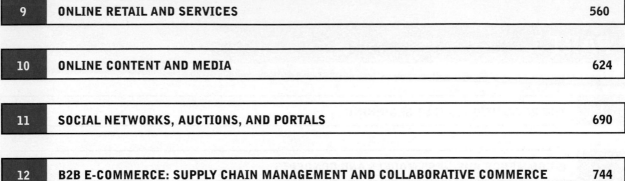

Contents

PART 2 Technology Infrastructure for E-commerce

| **5** | **E-COMMERCE SECURITY AND PAYMENT SYSTEMS** | **244** |

PART 3 Business Concepts and Social Issues

6	E-COMMERCE MARKETING AND ADVERTISING CONCEPTS	324

PART 4 E-commerce in Action

9   ONLINE RETAIL AND SERVICES   560

---

11   SOCIAL NETWORKS, AUCTIONS, AND PORTALS   690

---

12   B2B E-COMMERCE: SUPPLY CHAIN MANAGEMENT AND COLLABORATIVE COMMERCE   744

Introduction to E-commerce

CHAPTER 1

The Revolution Is Just Beginning

LEARNING OBJECTIVES

After reading this chapter, you will be able to:

- Define e-commerce and describe how it differs from e-business.
- Identify and describe the unique features of e-commerce technology and discuss their business significance.
- Recognize and describe Web 2.0 applications.
- Describe the major types of e-commerce.
- Understand the evolution of e-commerce from its early years to today.
- Identify the factors that will define the future of e-commerce.
- Describe the major themes underlying the study of e-commerce.
- Identify the major academic disciplines contributing to e-commerce.

Pinterest:

A Picture Is Worth a Thousand Words

Like all of the most successful e-commerce companies, Pinterest taps into a simple truth. In Pinterest's case, the simple truth is that people love to collect things, and show off their collections to others. And like other Internet firms that have goals of global scope, such as Google, Facebook, and Amazon, Pinterest also has a global mission: to connect everyone in the world through the things they find interesting. How? Founded in 2009 by Ben Silbermann, Evan Sharp, and Paul Sciarra and launched in March 2010, Pinterest allows you to create virtual scrapbooks of images, video, and other content that you "pin" to a virtual

© Blaize Pascall / Alamy

bulletin board or pin board on the Web site. Categories range from Animals to Videos, with Food & Drink, DIY & Crafts, and Women's Fashion among the most popular. Find something that you particularly like? In addition to "liking" and perhaps commenting on it, you can re-pin it to your own board, or follow a link back to the original source. Find someone whose taste you admire or who shares your passions? You can follow one or more of that pinner's boards to keep track of everything she or he pins.

Reportedly the fastest Web site in history to reach 10 million users, Pinterest currently has more than 50 million users, more than double from the previous year. According to some tracking services, it is now the third most visited social network in the United States, behind Facebook and Twitter. It is also one of the "stickiest" sites on the Web—according to comScore, users spend an average of 80 minutes per session on Pinterest, and almost 60% of users with accounts visit once or more a week. Jeff Jordan, a partner at Andreessen Horowitz, a venture capital firm and investor in Pinterest, says he has seen only one other site with similar numbers—Facebook. And like Facebook before it, Pinterest has begun a transition toward monetizing that appeal. The first step, in November 2012, was to offer business accounts that provide additional resources for brands. Currently, there is no charge for a business account, but that clearly may change in the future. In March 2013, Pinterest introduced a new Web analytics tool, also currently free, that helps Web site owners understand how people are using pinned material that has originated from their Web sites. Shortly thereafter,

SOURCES: "Stick with Pinterest," by Thad Rueter, Internet-Retailer.com, May 22, 2013; "Pinterest (Officially) Jumps the Pond," by Zak Stambor, Internet-Retailer.com, May 10, 2013; "Why Is Pinterest a $2.5 Billion Company? An Early Investor Explains," by J.J. Colao, Forbes.com, May 8, 2013; "Pinterest Gets a New Look," by Zac Stambor, InternetRetailer.com, March 19, 2013; "Introducing Pinterest Web Analytics," blog.Pinterest.com, March 12, 2013; "Meet Django," Djangoproject.com, accessed August 13, 2012; "Going Mobile with Pinterest," Pinterestinvite.org, accessed August 13, 2012; "Pinterest Gives Copyright Credit to Etsy, Kickstarter, SoundCloud," by Sarah Kessler, Mashable.com, July 19, 2012; "Whole Foods: The King of Pinterest?," by Vicky Garza, *Austin Business Journal*, July 13, 2012; "Pinterest on Wish List of Rakuten, Japan's Amazon," by Evelyn M. Rusli, *New York Times*, July 12, 2012; "A Mobile Shopping App Takes an Interest in Pinterest," by Katie Deatsch, InternetRetailer.com, July 11, 2012; "Pinterest Tops Tumblr in National Popularity?," by Stephanie Mlot, *PC Magazine*, June 28, 2012; "Pinterest Whets Consumer Desire with Images that Turn Window Shoppers into Online Buyers," by Matt Butter, *Forbes*, June 6, 2012; "Gemvara Raises $25 Million," by Stefany Moore, InternetRetailer.com, June 5, 2012; "Pinterest Raises $100 Million with $1.5 Billion Valuation," by Pui-Wing Tam, *Wall Street Journal*, May 17, 2012; "Japanese E-commerce Company Rakuten Invests in Pinterest," by Zak Stambor, InternetRetailer.com, May 17, 2012; "Now on Pinterest: Scams," by Riva Richmond, *New York Times*, May 16, 2012; "Real Simple is First Print Mag to Reach 100K Pinterest Followers," *Advertising Age*, May 11, 2012; "Pinterest Plagued by More Scams, Fake Android Apps," by Fahmida Y. Rashid, PCMag.com, April 30, 2012; "Nearly 1/3 Online Shoppers Have Made Purchases from What They've Seen on Pinterest," by Zak Stambor, InternetRetailer.com, April 25, 2012; "E-commerce Giants Amazon and eBay Add Pinterest Buttons," by Kate Kaye,

it began a revamp of its look, in an effort to help users discover new content more effectively and interact with it and other Pinterest users. In May 2013, it introduced its first localized site, for the United Kingdom, with another localized site for France reportedly in the wings.

Whole Foods, the natural foods supermarket chain, was one of the first companies to develop a presence on Pinterest, and now has more than 120,000 followers. It doesn't use Pinterest to advertise its own products in an overt way. Instead, it uses Pinterest as a way to communicate Whole Foods' core values through carefully curating and presenting images relevant to those values. Pinterest is also having an impact on the magazine world. For instance, Time Inc.'s *Real Simple,* also an early adopter, is one of the most-followed brands on Pinterest, with more than 300,000 followers. Pinterest has become a leading source of traffic to the Real Simple Web site, providing twice as many referrals as Facebook and Twitter combined. Other publishers are experiencing similar results.

For consumers, Pinterest can function both as a source of inspiration and aspiration. It has proven to be very popular for creating shopping wish lists and a great way to get ideas. Retailers, in particular, have taken notice and for good reason: several reports have shown that Pinterest helps drive shoppers to make purchases. For example, a study of 25,000 online stores using the Shopify e-commerce platform found there was as much traffic originating from Pinterest as from Twitter, and that Pinterest users spent an average of $80 each time they made an online purchase, twice the amount of Facebook users. Bizrate Insights found that almost a third of online shoppers surveyed had made a purchase based on what they had seen on Pinterest and other image-sharing sites; an even higher percentage (37%) had seen items they wanted to buy but had not yet purchased. There clearly remains room for growth, however. According to *Internet Retailer*, almost half of the retailers it surveyed in 2013 did not yet have a presence on Pinterest.

Pinterest's Web site was created using Django, an open source Web 2.0 framework that uses the Python programming language, which enables rapid development and reusability of components, coupled with elegant design. As with Facebook and Twitter, many third-party developers have also joined the party, with additional apps, browser extensions, and other third-party content that leverage off of the Pinterest platform. For instance, Zoomingo offers both a Web site and a mobile shopping app that allows you to find and get sale alerts for items you and others have pinned. Pinterest is also aggressive about leveraging ties to other social networks such as Facebook and Twitter—when you register, you can do so via Facebook, Twitter, or e-mail. Once you've registered, you can easily add Pinterest to your Facebook Timeline or link to your Twitter account.

On the mobile front, Pinterest introduced its own iPhone app in March 2011 and has frequently updated it since then, and an iPad app is also available. However, rather than develop additional stand-alone apps for Android, BlackBerry, or Windows smartphones, Pinterest chose a different route: to create a mobile version of its Web site using HTML5. Unlike an app, Pinterest Mobile runs inside the smartphone's browser rather than as a stand-alone program, and is able to serve multiple platforms.

Despite all the good news for Pinterest, there are some significant issues lurking just behind the scenes that may cloud its future; chief among them is copyright infringement. The basis of Pinterest's business model involves users potentially violating others' copyrights by posting images without permission and/or attribution. Although Pinterest's Terms of Service puts the onus on its users to avoid doing so, the site knowingly facilitates such actions by, for example, providing a "Pin it" tool embedded in the user's browser toolbar. Much of the content on the site reportedly violates its Terms of Service. Pinterest has provided an opt-out code to enable other sites to bar its content from being shared on Pinterest, but some question why they should have to take action when Pinterest is creating the problem. Further, the code does not necessarily resolve the issue, since it does not prevent someone from downloading an image and then uploading it to Pinterest. Another thing Pinterest has done to try to ameliorate the problem is to automatically add citations (attribution) to content coming from certain specified sources, such as Flickr, YouTube, Vimeo, Etsy, Kickstarter, and SlideShare, among others. It also complies with the Digital Millenium Copyright Act, which requires sites to remove images that violate copyright, but this too requires the copyright holder to be proactive and take action to demand the images be removed. Although no major copyright cases have been filed against it so far, how Pinterest resolves this issue may have a major impact on its ultimate success.

Pinterest is also not immune to the spam and scams that plague many e-commerce initiatives. Security analysts believe Pinterest will have to adapt its systems to deal with scammers and warn users to be wary of requests to pin content before viewing it and to be suspicious of "free" offers, surveys, and links with questionable titles. Pinterest has acknowledged the problem and has promised to improve its technology.

Another issue facing Pinterest is competition. Will Pinterest be like MySpace, destined to be eclipsed by a later entrant? Although some similar firms preceded Pinterest into the "visual collection" space, such as Polyvore and StyleCaster, Pinterest can be considered a first mover and as such has some significant advantages. However, other competitors have sprung up, such as Juxtapost (which allows private boards), Manteresting (aimed at the male demographic), Wanelo, and Fancy. Fancy has a revenue model based on linking its users to transactions, taking a 10% cut of purchases in the process, and has backing from co-founders of both Twitter and Facebook. The Fancy could become a formidable rival to Pinterest.

ClickZ.com, April 11, 2012; "Many Magazines Racing to Capitalize on Pinterest," *Advertising Age*, April 7, 2012; Interest in Pinterest Skyrockets," by Zak Stambor, InternetRetailer.com, March 23, 2012; "Is Pinterest the Next Napster?" by Therese Poletti, *Wall Street Journal*, March 14, 2012; "A Site That Aims to Unleash the Scrapbook Maker in All of Us," by Jenna Wortham, *New York Times*, March 11, 2012; "What Marketers Can Learn from Whole Foods' Organic Approach to Pinterest," by Lauren Drell, Mashable.com, February 23, 2012; "Pinterest Releases Optional Code to Prevent Unwanted Image Sharing," by Andrew Webster, Theverge.com, February 20, 2012; "A Scrapbook on the Web Catches Fire," by David Pogue, *New York Times*, February 15, 2012.

In 1994, e-commerce as we now know it did not exist. In 2013, less than 20 years later, around 155 million American consumers are expected to spend about $419 billion, and businesses more than $4.8 trillion, purchasing goods and services online or via a mobile device. A similar story has occurred throughout the world. And in this short period of time, e-commerce has been reinvented not just once, but twice.

The early years of e-commerce, during the late 1990s, were a period of business vision, inspiration, and experimentation. It soon became apparent, however, that establishing a successful business model based on those visions would not be easy. There followed a period of retrenchment and reevaluation, which led to the stock market crash of 2000–2001, with the value of e-commerce, telecommunications, and other technology stocks plummeting. After the bubble burst, many people were quick to write off e-commerce. But they were wrong. The surviving firms refined and honed their business models, ultimately leading to models that actually produced profits. Between 2002–2008, retail e-commerce grew at more than 25% per year.

Today, we are in the middle of yet another transition: a new and vibrant social, mobile, and local model of e-commerce growing alongside the more traditional e-commerce retail sales model exemplified by Amazon. Social network sites such as Facebook, Twitter, YouTube, and Pinterest, which enable users to distribute their own content (such as videos, music, photos, personal information, blogs, and software applications), have rocketed to prominence. Spurred by the explosive growth in smartphones such as iPhones and Androids, tablet computers, and ultra-lightweight laptops, a new e-commerce platform has emerged called "social e-commerce" that is closely intertwined with social networks, mobile computing, and heretofore private social relationships. Never before in the history of media have such large audiences been aggregated and made so accessible. Businesses are grappling with how best to approach this audience from an advertising and marketing perspective. Governments, private groups, and industry players are trying to understand how to protect privacy on this new e-commerce platform. Social networks and user-generated content sites are also examples of technology that is highly disruptive of traditional media firms. The movement of eyeballs towards these sites means fewer viewers of cable and broadcast television and Hollywood movies, and fewer readers of printed newspapers and magazines, and so those industries are also facing a transition. It's probably safe to predict that this will not be the last transition for e-commerce, either.

1.1 E-COMMERCE: THE REVOLUTION IS JUST BEGINNING

Table 1.1 describes the major trends in e-commerce in 2013–2014. Social networks have become a new e-commerce platform rivaling traditional e-commerce platforms by providing search, advertising, and payment services to vendors and customers. Who needs Google when you can have a swarm of friends recommend music, clothes, cars, and videos on a social network site where you spend most of your time online? The mobile platform based on smartphones and tablet computers has also finally arrived with a bang, making true mobile e-commerce a reality.

TABLE 1.1	MAJOR TRENDS IN E-COMMERCE 2013–2014

BUSINESS

- Retail e-commerce in the United States continues double-digit growth (over 15%), with global growth rates even higher in Europe and emerging markets such as China, India, and Brazil.
- A new "social e-commerce" platform, based on social networks and supported by advertising, emerges, growing to an estimated $5 billion in 2013 in the United States, and $8 billion worldwide.
- Mobile retail e-commerce explodes, and is estimated to reach almost $40 billion in the United States in 2013.
- A new app-based online economy grows alongside traditional Internet e-commerce, generating an estimated $25 billion in revenue worldwide in 2013.
- Local e-commerce, the third dimension of the social, mobile, local e-commerce wave, also is growing in the United States, to an estimated $4.4 billion in 2013.
- Facebook continues to grow, with more than 1.1 billion active users worldwide.
- Twitter continues to grow, with more than 200 million active users worldwide.
- Search engine marketing continues to challenge traditional marketing and advertising media.
- Social and mobile advertising platforms show strong growth and begin to challenge search engine marketing.
- The number of people of all ages online in the United States continues to increase, to an estimated 243 million, although the rate of growth is slowing.
- The global population using the Internet continues to expand, to over 2.5 billion, with around 33% of the world's population now online.
- Online businesses continue to strengthen profitability by refining their business models and leveraging the capabilities of the Internet.
- The breadth of e-commerce offerings grows, especially in entertainment, retail apparel, luxury goods, appliances, and home furnishings.
- Small businesses and entrepreneurs continue to flood into the e-commerce marketplace, often riding on the infrastructures created by industry giants such as Apple, Facebook, Amazon, Google, and eBay.
- Brand extension through the Internet continues to grow as large firms such as Walmart and Target pursue integrated, multi-channel bricks-and-clicks strategies.
- B2B e-commerce in the United States continues to strengthen and grow beyond the $4.7 trillion mark.

TECHNOLOGY

- A mobile computing and communications platform based on smartphones and tablet computers (the "new client") becomes a reality and begins to rival the PC platform.
- More than 1.5 million apps in Apple's and Google's app stores create a new platform for online transactions, marketing, and advertising.
- Computing and networking component prices continue to fall dramatically.
- As firms track the trillions of online interactions that occur each day, a flood of data, typically referred to as "Big Data," is being produced.

TABLE 1.1	MAJOR TRENDS IN E-COMMERCE 2013–2014 (CONT.)

- In order to make sense out of Big Data, firms turn to sophisticated software called business analytics (or Web analytics) that can identify purchase patterns as well as consumer interests and intentions in milliseconds.
- Cloud computing completes the transformation of the mobile platform by storing consumer content and software on Internet servers and making it available to any consumer-connected device from the desktop to a smartphone.

SOCIETY

- Consumer- and user-generated content, and syndication in the form of social networks, tweets, blogs, and wikis, continue to grow and provide an entirely new self-publishing forum that engages millions of consumers.
- The amount of data the average American consumes (estimated to be more than 34 gigabytes per day) continues to increase.
- Social networks encourage self-revelation, while threatening privacy.
- Participation by adults in social networks on the Internet increases; Facebook becomes ever more popular in all demographic categories.
- E-books finally gain wide acceptance and today account for about half of all book sales.
- Conflicts over copyright management and control continue, but there is substantial agreement among Internet distributors and copyright owners that they need one another.
- Explosive growth continues in online and mobile viewing of video and television programs.
- Taxation of Internet sales becomes more widespread and accepted by large online merchants.
- Surveillance of Internet communications by both repressive regimes and Western democracies grows.
- Concerns over commercial and governmental privacy invasion increase as firms provide government agencies with access to private personal information.
- Internet security continues to decline as major sites are hacked and lose control over customer information.
- Spam remains a significant problem despite legislation and promised technology fixes.
- Invasion of personal privacy expands as marketers extend their capabilities to track users.

More and more people and businesses are using the Internet to conduct commerce; smaller, local firms are learning how to take advantage of the Internet as Web services and Web site tools become very inexpensive. New e-commerce brands emerge while traditional retail brands such as Walmart and Target further extend their multi-channel, bricks-and-clicks strategies and retain their dominant retail positions by strengthening their Internet operations. At the societal level, other trends are apparent. The Internet has created a platform for millions of people to create and share content, establish new social bonds, and strengthen existing ones through social networks, blogging, and photo- and video-posting sites. These same social networks have created significant privacy issues. The major digital copyright owners have increased their pursuit of online file-swapping services with mixed success, while reaching broad agreements with the big technology players like Apple, Amazon, and Google to protect intellectual property rights. States have successfully moved toward taxation of Internet sales, while Internet gaming sites have been severely curtailed through criminal prosecutions in the United States. Sovereign nations have expanded their surveillance of, and control over, Internet communications and content as a part of their anti-terrorist activities and their traditional interest in snooping on citizens. Privacy seems to have lost some of its meaning in an age when millions create public online personal profiles.

THE FIRST 30 SECONDS

It is important to realize that the rapid growth and change that has occurred in the first 19 years of e-commerce represents just the beginning—what could be called the first 30 seconds of the e-commerce revolution. Technology continues to evolve at exponential rates. This underlying ferment presents entrepreneurs with new opportunities to both create new businesses and new business models in traditional industries, and also to destroy old businesses. Business change becomes disruptive, rapid, and even destructive, while offering entrepreneurs new opportunities and resources for investment.

Improvements in underlying information technologies and continuing entrepreneurial innovation in business and marketing promise as much change in the next decade as was seen in the last decade. The twenty-first century will be the age of a digitally enabled social and commercial life, the outlines of which we can barely perceive at this time. Analysts estimate that by 2017, consumers will be spending about $637 billion and businesses about $6.6 trillion in online transactions. By 2020, some industry analysts believe e-commerce may account for 20% of all retail sales (eMarketer, Inc., 2013a). It appears likely that e-commerce will eventually impact nearly all commerce, and that most commerce will be e-commerce by the year 2050.

Can e-commerce continue to grow indefinitely? It's possible that at some point, e-commerce growth may slow simply as a result of overload: people may just not have the time to watch yet another online video, open another e-mail, or read another blog, tweet, or Facebook update. However, currently, there is no foreseeable limit to the continued rapid development of Internet and e-commerce technology, or limits on the inventiveness of entrepreneurs to develop new uses for the technology. Therefore, for now at least, it is likely that the disruptive process will continue.

Business fortunes are made—and lost—in periods of extraordinary change such as this. The next five years hold out extraordinary opportunities—as well as risks—for new and traditional businesses to exploit digital technology for market advantage. For society as a whole, the next few decades offer the possibility of extraordinary gains in social wealth as the digital revolution works its way through larger and larger segments of the world's economy, offering the possibility of high rates of productivity and income growth in an inflation-free environment.

As a business or technology student, this book will help you perceive and understand the opportunities and risks that lie ahead. By the time you finish, you will be able to identify the technological, business, and social forces that have shaped the growth of e-commerce and extend that understanding into the years ahead.

WHAT IS E-COMMERCE?

e-commerce

the use of the Internet, the Web, and apps to transact business. More formally, digitally enabled commercial transactions between and among organizations and individuals

Our focus in this book is **e-commerce**—the use of the Internet, the World Wide Web (Web), and mobile apps to transact business. Although the terms Internet and Web are often used interchangeably, they are actually two very different things. The Internet is a worldwide network of computer networks, and the Web is one of the Internet's most popular services, providing access to billions of Web pages. An app (short-hand for application) is a software application. The term is typically used when referring to mobile applications, although it is also sometimes used to refer to desktop computer applications as well. (We describe the Internet, Web, and apps more fully later in this chapter and in Chapters 3 and 4.) More formally, we focus on digitally enabled commercial transactions between and among organizations and individuals. Each of these components of our working definition of e-commerce is important. *Digitally enabled transactions* include all transactions mediated by digital technology. For the most part, this means transactions that occur over the Internet, the Web, and/or via mobile apps. *Commercial transactions* involve the exchange of value (e.g., money) across organizational or individual boundaries in return for products and services. Exchange of value is important for understanding the limits of e-commerce. Without an exchange of value, no commerce occurs.

The professional literature sometimes refers to e-commerce as "digital commerce" in part to reflect the fact that in 2013, apps account for a growing amount of e-commerce revenues. For our purposes, we consider "e-commerce" and "digital commerce" to be synonymous.

THE DIFFERENCE BETWEEN E-COMMERCE AND E-BUSINESS

There is a debate about the meaning and limitations of both e-commerce and e-business. Some argue that e-commerce encompasses the entire world of electronically based organizational activities that support a firm's market exchanges—including a firm's entire information system's infrastructure (Rayport and Jaworski, 2003). Others argue, on the other hand, that e-business encompasses the entire world of internal and external electronically based activities, including e-commerce (Kalakota and Robinson, 2003).

e-business

the digital enabling of transactions and processes within a firm, involving information systems under the control of the firm

We think it is important to make a working distinction between e-commerce and e-business because we believe they refer to different phenomena. E-commerce is not "anything digital" that a firm does. For purposes of this text, we will use the term **e-business** to refer primarily to the digital enabling of transactions and processes *within* a firm, involving information systems under the control of the firm. For the most part, in our view, e-business does not include commercial transactions involving an exchange of value across organizational boundaries. For example, a company's online inventory control mechanisms are a component of e-business, but such internal processes do not directly generate revenue for the firm from outside businesses or consumers, as e-commerce, by definition, does. It is true, however, that a firm's e-business infrastructure provides support for online e-commerce exchanges; the same infrastructure and skill

FIGURE 1.1   **THE DIFFERENCE BETWEEN E-COMMERCE AND E-BUSINESS**

E-commerce primarily involves transactions that cross firm boundaries. E-business primarily involves the application of digital technologies to business processes within the firm.

sets are involved in both e-business and e-commerce. E-commerce and e-business systems blur together at the business firm boundary, at the point where internal business systems link up with suppliers or customers (see **Figure 1.1**). E-business applications turn into e-commerce precisely when an exchange of value occurs (see Mesenbourg, U.S. Department of Commerce, 2001, for a similar view). We will examine this intersection further in Chapter 12.

WHY STUDY E-COMMERCE?

Why are there college courses and textbooks on e-commerce when there are no courses or textbooks on "TV Commerce," "Radio Commerce," "Railroad Commerce," or "Highway Commerce," even though these technologies had profound impacts on commerce in the twentieth century and account for far more commerce than e-commerce?

The reason for the interest specifically in e-commerce is that e-commerce technology (discussed in detail in Chapters 3 and 4) is different and more powerful than any of the other technologies we have seen in the past century. E-commerce technologies—and the digital markets that result—have brought about some fundamental, unprecedented shifts in commerce. While these other technologies transformed economic life in the twentieth century, the evolving Internet and other information technologies are shaping the twenty-first century.

Prior to the development of e-commerce, the marketing and sale of goods was a mass-marketing and sales force–driven process. Marketers viewed consumers as passive targets of advertising campaigns and branding "blitzes" intended to influence their long-term product perceptions and immediate purchasing behavior. Companies sold their products via well-insulated channels. Consumers were trapped by geographical and social boundaries, unable to search widely for the best price and quality. Information about prices, costs, and fees could be hidden from the consumer, creating profitable "information asymmetries" for the selling firm. **Information asymmetry** refers to any disparity in relevant market information among parties in a transaction. It was so expensive to change national or regional prices in traditional retailing (what are called *menu costs*) that "one national price" was the norm, and dynamic pricing to the marketplace let alone to individuals in the marketplace—changing prices in real time—was unheard of. In this environment, manufacturers prospered by relying on huge production runs of products that could not be customized or personalized. One of the shifts that e-commerce is bringing about is a reduction in information asymmetry among market participants (consumers and merchants). Preventing consumers from learning about costs, price discrimination strategies, and profits from sales becomes more difficult with e-commerce, and the entire marketplace potentially becomes highly price competitive. At the same time, online merchants gain considerable market power over consumers by using consumer personal information in ways inconceivable 10 years ago to maximize their revenues.

EIGHT UNIQUE FEATURES OF E-COMMERCE TECHNOLOGY

Figure 1.2 illustrates eight unique features of e-commerce technology that both challenge traditional business thinking and explain why we have so much interest in e-commerce. These unique dimensions of e-commerce technologies suggest many new possibilities for marketing and selling—a powerful set of interactive, personalized, and rich messages are available for delivery to segmented, targeted audiences. E-commerce technologies make it possible for merchants to know much more about consumers and to be able to use this information more effectively than was ever true in the past. Online merchants can use this new information to develop new information asymmetries, enhance their ability to brand products, charge premium prices for high-quality service, and segment the market into an endless number of subgroups, each receiving a different price. To complicate matters further, these same technologies make it possible for merchants to know more about other merchants than was ever true in the past. This presents the possibility that merchants might collude on prices rather than compete and drive overall average prices up. This strategy works especially well when there are just a few suppliers (Varian, 2000a). We examine these different visions of e-commerce further in Section 1.2 and throughout the book.

Each of the dimensions of e-commerce technology illustrated in Figure 1.2 deserves a brief exploration, as well as a comparison to both traditional commerce and other forms of technology-enabled commerce.

Ubiquity

In traditional commerce, a **marketplace** is a physical place you visit in order to transact. For example, television and radio typically motivate the consumer to go someplace to make a purchase. E-commerce, in contrast, is characterized by its **ubiquity**: it is available just about everywhere, at all times. It liberates the market from being restricted to a physical space and makes it possible to shop from your desktop, at home, at work, or even from your car, using mobile e-commerce. The result

FIGURE 1.2   **EIGHT UNIQUE FEATURES OF E-COMMERCE TECHNOLOGY**

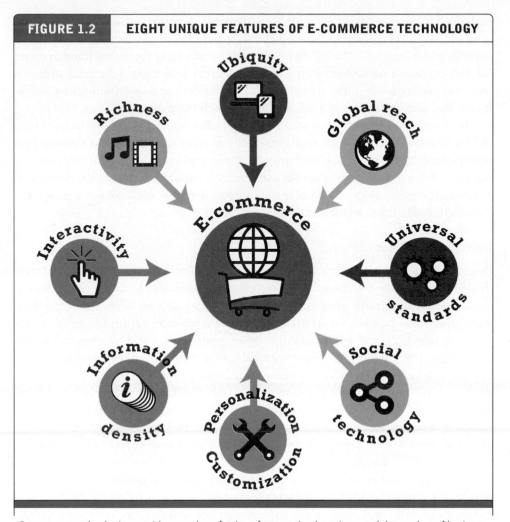

E-commerce technologies provide a number of unique features that have impacted the conduct of business.

is called a **marketspace**—a marketplace extended beyond traditional boundaries and removed from a temporal and geographic location. From a consumer point of view, ubiquity reduces *transaction costs*—the costs of participating in a market. To transact, it is no longer necessary that you spend time and money traveling to a market. At a broader level, the ubiquity of e-commerce lowers the cognitive energy required to transact in a marketspace. *Cognitive energy* refers to the mental effort required to complete a task. Humans generally seek to reduce cognitive energy outlays. When given a choice, humans will choose the path requiring the least effort—the most convenient path (Shapiro and Varian, 1999; Tversky and Kahneman, 1981).

marketspace
marketplace extended beyond traditional boundaries and removed from a temporal and geographic location

Global Reach

E-commerce technology permits commercial transactions to cross cultural, regional, and national boundaries far more conveniently and cost-effectively than is true in traditional commerce. As a result, the potential market size for e-commerce merchants is roughly equal to the size of the world's online population (an estimated 2.56 billion in 2013) (eMarketer, Inc., 2013b). More realistically, the Internet makes it much easier for start-up online merchants within a single country to achieve a national audience than was ever possible in the past. The total number of users or customers an e-commerce business can obtain is a measure of its **reach** (Evans and Wurster, 1997).

reach
the total number of users or customers an e-commerce business can obtain

In contrast, most traditional commerce is local or regional—it involves local merchants or national merchants with local outlets. Television and radio stations, and newspapers, for instance, are primarily local and regional institutions with limited but powerful national networks that can attract a national audience. In contrast to e-commerce technology, these older commerce technologies do not easily cross national boundaries to a global audience.

Universal Standards

One strikingly unusual feature of e-commerce technologies is that the technical standards of the Internet, and therefore the technical standards for conducting e-commerce, are **universal standards**—they are shared by all nations around the world. In contrast, most traditional commerce technologies differ from one nation to the next. For instance, television and radio standards differ around the world, as does cell phone technology. The universal technical standards of the Internet and e-commerce greatly lower *market entry costs*—the cost merchants must pay just to bring their goods to market. At the same time, for consumers, universal standards reduce *search costs*—the effort required to find suitable products. And by creating a single, one-world marketspace, where prices and product descriptions can be inexpensively displayed for all to see, *price discovery* becomes simpler, faster, and more accurate (Banerjee, et al., 2005; Bakos, 1997; Kambil, 1997). Users of the Internet, both businesses and individuals, also experience *network externalities*—benefits that arise because everyone uses the same technology. With e-commerce technologies, it is possible for the first time in history to easily find many of the suppliers, prices, and delivery terms of a specific product anywhere in the world, and to view them in a coherent, comparative environment. Although this is not necessarily realistic today for all or even many products, it is a potential that will be exploited in the future.

universal standards
standards that are shared by all nations around the world

Richness

Information **richness** refers to the complexity and content of a message (Evans and Wurster, 1999). Traditional markets, national sales forces, and small retail stores have great richness: they are able to provide personal, face-to-face service using aural and visual cues when making a sale. The richness of traditional markets makes them a powerful selling or commercial environment. Prior to the development of the Web, there was a trade-off between richness and reach: the larger the audience reached, the less rich the message. The Internet has the potential for offering considerably more information richness than traditional media such as printing presses, radio, and television because it is interactive and can adjust the message to individual users. Chatting with an online sales person, for instance, comes very close to the customer

richness
the complexity and content of a message

experience in a small retail shop. The richness enabled by the Internet allows retail and service merchants to market and sell "complex" goods and services that heretofore required a face-to-face presentation by a sales force to a much larger audience.

Interactivity

Unlike any of the commercial technologies of the twentieth century, with the possible exception of the telephone, e-commerce technologies allow for **interactivity**, meaning they enable two-way communication between merchant and consumer and among consumers. Traditional television, for instance, cannot ask viewers questions or enter into conversations with them, or request that customer information be entered into a form. In contrast, all of these activities are possible on an e-commerce site and are now commonplace with smartphones, social networks, and Twitter. Interactivity allows an online merchant to engage a consumer in ways similar to a face-to-face experience.

interactivity
technology that allows for two-way communication between merchant and consumer

Information Density

E-commerce technologies vastly increase **information density**—the total amount and quality of information available to all market participants, consumers, and merchants alike. E-commerce technologies reduce information collection, storage, processing, and communication costs. At the same time, these technologies greatly increase the currency, accuracy, and timeliness of information—making information more useful and important than ever. As a result, information becomes more plentiful, less expensive, and of higher quality.

information density
the total amount and quality of information available to all market participants

A number of business consequences result from the growth in information density. In e-commerce markets, prices and costs become more transparent. *Price transparency* refers to the ease with which consumers can find out the variety of prices in a market; *cost transparency* refers to the ability of consumers to discover the actual costs merchants pay for products (Sinha, 2000). But there are advantages for merchants as well. Online merchants can discover much more about consumers; this allows merchants to segment the market into groups willing to pay different prices and permits them to engage in *price discrimination*—selling the same goods, or nearly the same goods, to different targeted groups at different prices. For instance, an online merchant can discover a consumer's avid interest in expensive exotic vacations, and then pitch expensive exotic vacation plans to that consumer at a premium price, knowing this person is willing to pay extra for such a vacation. At the same time, the online merchant can pitch the same vacation plan at a lower price to more price-sensitive consumers. Merchants also have enhanced abilities to differentiate their products in terms of cost, brand, and quality.

Personalization/Customization

E-commerce technologies permit **personalization**: merchants can target their marketing messages to specific individuals by adjusting the message to a person's name, interests, and past purchases. Today this is achieved in a few milliseconds and followed by an advertisement based on the consumer's profile. The technology also permits

personalization
the targeting of marketing messages to specific individuals by adjusting the message to a person's name, interests, and past purchases

customization

changing the delivered product or service based on a user's preferences or prior behavior

customization—changing the delivered product or service based on a user's preferences or prior behavior. Given the interactive nature of e-commerce technology, much information about the consumer can be gathered in the marketplace at the moment of purchase. With the increase in information density, a great deal of information about the consumer's past purchases and behavior can be stored and used by online merchants. The result is a level of personalization and customization unthinkable with traditional commerce technologies. For instance, you may be able to shape what you see on television by selecting a channel, but you cannot change the contents of the channel you have chosen. In contrast, the online version of the *Wall Street Journal* allows you to select the type of news stories you want to see first, and gives you the opportunity to be alerted when certain events happen. Personalization and customization allow firms to precisely identify market segments and adjust their messages accordingly.

Social Technology: User Content Generation and Social Networking

In a way quite different from all previous technologies, e-commerce technologies have evolved to be much more social by allowing users to create and share content with a worldwide community. Using these forms of communication, users are able to create new social networks and strengthen existing ones. All previous mass media in modern history, including the printing press, use a broadcast model (one-to-many) where content is created in a central location by experts (professional writers, editors, directors, actors, and producers) and audiences are concentrated in huge aggregates to consume a standardized product. The telephone would appear to be an exception but it is not a "mass communication" technology. Instead the telephone is a one-to-one technology. The Internet and e-commerce technologies have the potential to invert this standard media model by giving users the power to create and distribute content on a large scale, and permit users to program their own content consumption. The Internet provides a unique, many-to-many model of mass communication.

Table 1.2 provides a summary of each of the unique features of e-commerce technology and their business significance.

WEB 2.0: PLAY MY VERSION

Many of the unique features of e-commerce technology and the Internet come together in a set of applications and social media technologies referred to as **Web 2.0**. The Internet started out as a simple network to support e-mail and file transfers among remote computers. The Web started out as a way to use the Internet to display simple pages and allow the user to navigate among the pages by linking them together electronically. You can think of this as Web 1.0. By 2007 something else was happening. The Internet and the Web had evolved to the point where users could create, edit, and distribute content to others; share with one another their preferences, bookmarks, and online personas; participate in virtual lives; and build online communities. This "new" Web is called by many Web 2.0, and while it draws heavily on the "old" Web 1.0, it is nevertheless a clear evolution from the past.

Web 2.0

a set of applications and technologies that allows users to create, edit, and distribute content; share preferences, bookmarks, and online personas; participate in virtual lives; and build online communities

TABLE 1.2	BUSINESS SIGNIFICANCE OF THE EIGHT UNIQUE FEATURES OF E-COMMERCE TECHNOLOGY
E-COMMERCE TECHNOLOGY DIMENSION	**BUSINESS SIGNIFICANCE**
Ubiquity—Internet/Web technology is available everywhere: at work, at home, and elsewhere via mobile devices, anytime.	The marketplace is extended beyond traditional boundaries and is removed from a temporal and geographic location. "Marketspace" is created; shopping can take place anywhere. Customer convenience is enhanced, and shopping costs are reduced.
Global reach—The technology reaches across national boundaries, around the earth.	Commerce is enabled across cultural and national boundaries seamlessly and without modification. "Marketspace" includes potentially billions of consumers and millions of businesses worldwide.
Universal standards—There is one set of technology standards, namely Internet standards.	There is a common, inexpensive, global technology foundation for businesses to use.
Richness—Video, audio, and text messages are possible.	Video, audio, and text marketing messages are integrated into a single marketing message and consuming experience.
Interactivity—The technology works through interaction with the user.	Consumers are engaged in a dialog that dynamically adjusts the experience to the individual, and makes the consumer a co-participant in the process of delivering goods to the market.
Information density—The technology reduces information costs and raises quality.	Information processing, storage, and communication costs drop dramatically, while currency, accuracy, and timeliness improve greatly. Information becomes plentiful, cheap, and accurate.
Personalization/Customization—The technology allows personalized messages to be delivered to individuals as well as groups.	Personalization of marketing messages and customization of products and services are based on individual characteristics.
Social technology—User content generation and social networks.	New Internet social and business models enable user content creation and distribution, and support social networks.

Let's take a quick look at some examples of Web 2.0 applications and sites:

- Twitter is a social network/micro-blogging service that encourages users to enter 140-character messages ("tweets") in answer to the question "What are you doing?" Twitter has more than 200 million active users worldwide, sending around 400 million tweets per day and more than 12 billion tweets a month. Twitter has begun to monetize its subscribers by developing an ad platform and providing marketing services to firms that want to stay in instant contact with their customers.

- YouTube, owned by Google after a $1.65 billion purchase, is the world's largest online consumer-generated video-posting site. YouTube is now morphing into a premium video content distributor and video producer, offering feature-length movies, television series, and its own original content. In March 2013, YouTube had over 150 million unique viewers in the United States, and more than 1 billion a month worldwide. According to Google, 72 hours of video are posted to the site every minute! YouTube reportedly streams more than 4 billion videos per day, including more than 600 million a day on mobile devices (YouTube, 2013; comScore, 2013a).

- Instagram is a mobile photo-sharing application that allows users to easily apply a variety of different photo filters and borders, and then post the photos to social networks such as Facebook, Twitter, Foursquare, Tumblr, and Flickr. Launched in November 2010, Instagram quickly attracted more than 50 million users and in April 2012 was purchased by Facebook for $1 billion (Buck, 2012).

- Wikipedia allows contributors around the world to share their knowledge and in the process has become the most successful online encyclopedia, far surpassing "professional" encyclopedias such as Encarta and Britannica. Wikipedia is one of the largest collaboratively edited reference projects in the world, with more than 4.2 million articles available in English and more than 26 million in total, in 286 languages. Wikipedia relies on volunteers, makes no money, and accepts no advertising. Wikipedia is consistently ranked as one of the top 10 most visited sites on the Web (Wikipedia.org, 2013; Wikimedia Foundation, 2011; comScore, 2013b).

- Tumblr is a combination of blog platform and social network. It allows users to easily post text, photos, links, music, videos and more. As of May 2013, Tumblr hosts almost 110 million blogs, containing over 50 billion posts. On a typical day, users make over 70 million posts (Tumblr.com, 2013). Tumblr has more than doubled in size since September 2011.

What do these Web 2.0 applications and sites have in common? First, they rely on user- and consumer-generated content. "Regular" people (not just experts or professionals) are creating, sharing, modifying, and broadcasting content to huge audiences. Second, easy search capability is a key to their success. Third, they are inherently highly interactive, creating new opportunities for people to socially connect to others. They are "social" sites because they support interactions among users. Fourth, they rely on broadband connectivity. Fifth, many of them are currently only marginally profitable, and their business models are unproven despite considerable investment. Nevertheless, the potential monetary rewards for social sites with huge audiences is quite large. Sixth, they attract extremely large audiences when compared to traditional Web 1.0 applications, exceeding in many cases the audience size of national broadcast and cable television programs. These audience relationships are intensive and long-lasting interactions with millions of people. In short, they attract eyeballs in very large numbers. Hence, they present marketers with extraordinary opportunities for targeted marketing and advertising. They also present consumers with the opportunity to rate and review products, and entrepreneurs with ideas for future business ventures. Last, these sites act as application development platforms where users can contribute and use software applications for free. Briefly, it's a whole new world from what has gone before.

TYPES OF E-COMMERCE

There are several different types of e-commerce and many different ways to characterize them. **Table 1.3** lists the major types of e-commerce discussed in this book.[1] For the most part, we distinguish different types of e-commerce by the nature of the market relationship—who is selling to whom. Social, mobile, and local e-commerce can be looked at as subsets of these types of e-commerce.

Business-to-Consumer (B2C) E-commerce

The most commonly discussed type of e-commerce is **business-to-consumer (B2C) e-commerce**, in which online businesses attempt to reach individual consumers. B2C commerce includes purchases of retail goods, travel services, and online content. Even though B2C is comparatively small (about $419 billion in 2013 in the United States),

business-to-consumer (B2C) e-commerce
online businesses selling to individual consumers

TABLE 1.3	MAJOR TYPES OF E-COMMERCE
TYPE OF E-COMMERCE	EXAMPLE
B2C—business-to-consumer	Amazon is a general merchandiser that sells consumer products to retail consumers.
B2B—business-to-business	Go2Paper.com is an independent third-party marketplace that serves the paper industry.
C2C—consumer-to-consumer	On a large number of auction sites such as eBay, and listing sites such as Craigslist, consumers can auction or sell goods directly to other consumers.
Social e-commerce	Facebook is both the leading social network and social e-commerce site.
M-commerce—mobile e-commerce	Mobile devices such as tablet computers and smartphones can be used to conduct commercial transactions.
Local e-commerce	Groupon offers subscribers daily deals from local businesses in the form of "Groupons," discount coupons that take effect once enough subscribers have agreed to purchase.

[1] For the purposes of this text, we subsume business-to-government (B2G) e-commerce within B2B e-commerce, viewing the government as simply a form of business when it acts as a procurer of goods and/or services.

it has grown exponentially since 1995, and is the type of e-commerce that most consumers are likely to encounter (see **Figure 1.3**). Within the B2C category, there are many different types of business models. Chapter 2 has a detailed discussion of seven different B2C business models: portals, online retailers, content providers, transaction brokers, market creators, service providers, and community providers.

Business-to-Business (B2B) E-commerce

business-to-business (B2B) e-commerce

online businesses selling to other businesses

Business-to-business (B2B) e-commerce, in which businesses focus on selling to other businesses, is the largest form of e-commerce, with about $4.7 trillion in transactions in the United States in 2013 (see **Figure 1.4**). There is an estimated $12.9 trillion in business-to-business exchanges of all kinds, online and offline, suggesting that B2B e-commerce has significant growth potential. The ultimate size of B2B e-commerce is potentially huge. There are two primary business models used within the B2B arena: Net marketplaces, which include e-distributors, e-procurement companies, exchanges and industry consortia, and private industrial networks.

Consumer-to-Consumer (C2C) E-commerce

consumer-to-consumer (C2C) e-commerce

consumers selling to other consumers

Consumer-to-consumer (C2C) e-commerce provides a way for consumers to sell to each other, with the help of an online market maker such as eBay or Etsy, or the

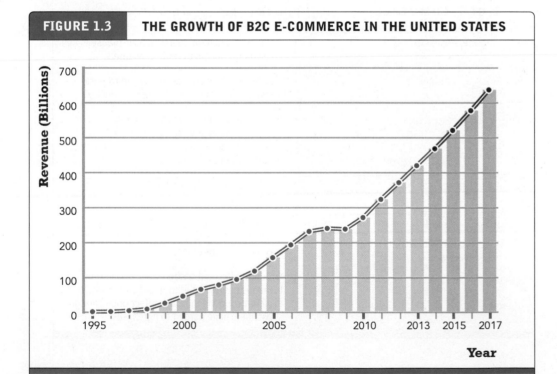

| FIGURE 1.3 | THE GROWTH OF B2C E-COMMERCE IN THE UNITED STATES |

In the early years, B2C e-commerce was doubling or tripling each year. Although B2C e-commerce growth in the United States slowed in 2008–2009 due to the economic recession, it resumed growing at about 13% in 2010 and since then, has continued to grow at double-digit rates.

SOURCES: Based on data from eMarketer, Inc., 2013a; authors' estimates.

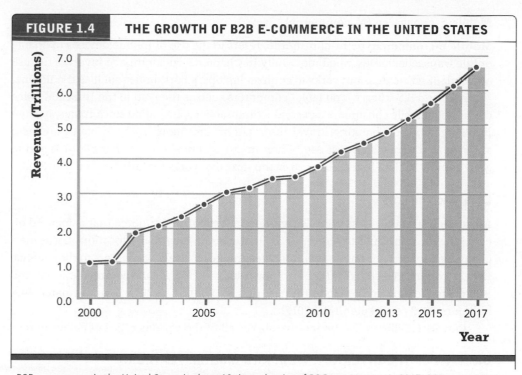

FIGURE 1.4   **THE GROWTH OF B2B E-COMMERCE IN THE UNITED STATES**

B2B e-commerce in the United States is about 10 times the size of B2C e-commerce. In 2017, B2B e-commerce is projected to be about $6.6 trillion. (Note: Does not include EDI transactions.)

SOURCES: Based on data from U.S. Census Bureau, 2013; authors' estimates.

classifieds site Craigslist. Given that in 2013, eBay is likely to generate around $75 billion in gross merchandise volume around the world, it is probably safe to estimate that the size of the global C2C market in 2013 is more than $90 billion (eBay, 2013). In C2C e-commerce, the consumer prepares the product for market, places the product for auction or sale, and relies on the market maker to provide catalog, search engine, and transaction-clearing capabilities so that products can be easily displayed, discovered, and paid for.

Social E-commerce

Social e-commerce is e-commerce that is enabled by social networks and online social relationships. It is sometimes also referred to as Facebook commerce, but in actuality is a much larger phenomenon that extends beyond just Facebook. The growth of social e-commerce is being driven by a number of factors, including the increasing popularity of social sign-on (signing onto Web sites using your Facebook or other social network ID), network notification (the sharing of approval or disapproval of products, services, and content via Facebook's Like button or Twitter tweets), online collaborative shopping tools, and social search (recommendations from online trusted friends). Social e-commerce is still in its infancy, but is estimated to generate about $5 billion in the United States in 2013, and about $8 billion in the rest of the world (eMarketer, Inc., 2012a).

social e-commerce
e-commerce enabled by social networks and online social relationships

Mobile E-commerce (M-commerce)

**mobile e-commerce
(m-commerce)**
use of mobile devices to
enable online transactions

Mobile e-commerce, or m-commerce, refers to the use of mobile devices to enable online transactions. Described more fully in Chapter 3, m-commerce involves the use of cellular and wireless networks to connect laptops, smartphones such as the iPhone, Android, and BlackBerry, and tablet computers such as the iPad to the Internet. Once connected, mobile consumers can conduct transactions, including stock trades, in-store price comparisons, banking, travel reservations, and more. Mobile retail purchases are expected to reach almost $40 billion in 2013 (almost double that of 2012) and to grow rapidly in the United States over the next five years (eMarketer, Inc., 2013a).

Local E-commerce

local e-commerce
e-commerce that is focused
on engaging the consumer
based on his or her current
geographic location

Local e-commerce, as its name suggests, is a form of e-commerce that is focused on engaging the consumer based on his or her current geographic location. Local merchants use a variety of online marketing techniques to drive consumers to their stores. Local e-commerce is the third prong of the social, mobile, local e-commerce wave, and is expected to grow in the United States from $3.6 billion in 2011 to an estimated $4.4 billion in 2013 (eMarketer, Inc., 2012b).

Figure 1.5 illustrates the relative size of all of the various types of e-commerce.

GROWTH OF THE INTERNET, WEB, AND MOBILE PLATFORM

The technology juggernauts behind e-commerce are the Internet, the Web, and increasingly, the mobile platform. We describe the Internet, Web, and mobile platform in some detail in Chapter 3. The **Internet** is a worldwide network of computer networks built on common standards. Created in the late 1960s to connect a small number of mainframe computers and their users, the Internet has since grown into the world's largest network. It is impossible to say with certainty exactly how many computers and other wireless access devices such as smartphones are connected to the Internet worldwide at any one time, but the number is clearly more than 1 billion. The Internet links businesses, educational institutions, government agencies, and individuals together, and provides users with services such as e-mail, document transfer, shopping, research, instant messaging, music, videos, and news.

Internet
worldwide network of
computer networks built
on common standards

One way to measure the growth of the Internet is by looking at the number of Internet hosts with domain names. (An *Internet host* is defined by the Internet Systems Consortium as any IP address that returns a domain name in the in-addr.arpa domain, which is a special part of the DNS namespace that resolves IP addresses into domain names.) In July 2013, there were almost 1 billion Internet hosts in over 245 countries, up from just 70 million in 2000 (Internet Systems Consortium, 2013).

The Internet has shown extraordinary growth patterns when compared to other electronic technologies of the past. It took radio 38 years to achieve a 30% share of U.S. households. It took television 17 years to achieve a 30% share. It took only 10 years for the Internet/Web to achieve a 53% share of U.S. households once a graphical user interface was invented for the Web in 1993.

**World Wide Web (the
Web)**
provides easy access to
Web pages

The **World Wide Web (the Web)** is one of the most popular services that runs on the Internet infrastructure. The Web was the original "killer app" that made the

FIGURE 1.5 | **THE RELATIVE SIZE OF DIFFERENT TYPES OF E-COMMERCE**

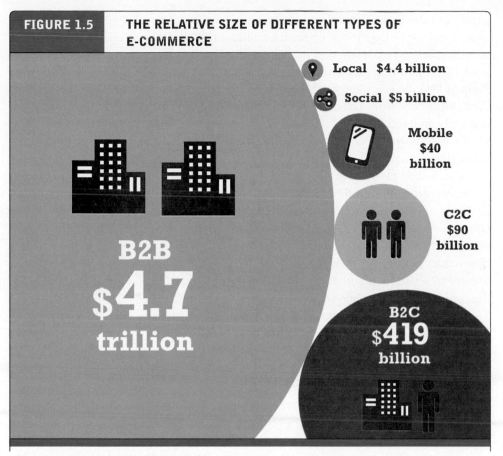

Local $4.4 billion

Social $5 billion

Mobile $40 billion

C2C $90 billion

B2B $4.7 trillion

B2C $419 billion

B2B e-commerce dwarfs all other forms of e-commerce; mobile, social, and local e-commerce, although growing rapidly, are still relatively small in comparison to "traditional" e-commerce.

Internet commercially interesting and extraordinarily popular. The Web was developed in the early 1990s and hence is of much more recent vintage than the Internet. We describe the Web in some detail in Chapter 3. The Web provides access to billions of Web pages indexed by Google and other search engines. These pages are created in a language called *HTML (HyperText Markup Language)*. HTML pages can contain text, graphics, animations, and other objects. You can find an exceptionally wide range of information on Web pages, ranging from the entire collection of public records from the Securities and Exchange Commission, to the card catalog of your local library, to millions of music tracks and videos. The Internet prior to the Web was primarily used for text communications, file transfers, and remote computing. The Web introduced far more powerful and commercially interesting, colorful multimedia capabilities of direct relevance to commerce. In essence, the Web added color, voice, and video to the Internet, creating a communications infrastructure and information storage system that rivals television, radio, magazines, and even libraries.

There is no precise measurement of the number of Web pages in existence, in part because today's search engines index only a portion of the known universe of Web pages, and also because the size of the Web universe is unknown. Google has identified over 30 trillion unique URLs, up from 1 trillion in 2008, although many of these pages do not necessarily contain unique content. Today, it is likely that Google indexes at least 120 billion Web pages, if not more. In addition to this "surface" or "visible" Web, there is also the so-called "deep Web" that is reportedly 1,000 to 5,000 times greater than the surface Web. The deep Web contains databases and other content that is not routinely indexed by search engines such as Google. Although the total size of the Web is not known, what is indisputable is that Web content has grown exponentially since 1993.

The mobile platform is the newest "latest and greatest" development in Internet infrastructure. The **mobile platform** provides the ability to access the Internet from a variety of mobile devices such as smartphones, tablets, and other ultra-lightweight laptop computers via wireless networks or cell phone service. In 2013, there are over 363 million mobile devices in the United States that can be connected to the Internet (more than 1 device for each person in the United States), and that number is expected to grow to almost 400 million by 2017 (eMarketer, Inc., 2013b). **Figure 1.6** illustrates the rapid growth of mobile Internet access.

Read *Insight on Technology: Will Apps Make the Web Irrelevant?* for a look at the challenge that apps and the mobile platform pose to the Web's dominance of the Internet ecosphere.

mobile platform

provides the ability to access the Internet from a variety of highly mobile devices such as smartphones, tablets, and other ultra-lightweight laptop computers

ORIGINS AND GROWTH OF E-COMMERCE

It is difficult to pinpoint just when e-commerce began. There were several precursors to e-commerce. In the late 1970s, a pharmaceutical firm named Baxter Healthcare initiated a primitive form of B2B e-commerce by using a telephone-based modem that permitted hospitals to reorder supplies from Baxter. This system was later expanded during the 1980s into a PC-based remote order entry system and was widely copied throughout the United States long before the Internet became a commercial environment. The 1980s saw the development of Electronic Data Interchange (EDI) standards that permitted firms to exchange commercial documents and conduct digital commercial transactions across private networks.

In the B2C arena, the first truly large-scale digitally enabled transaction system was deployed in France in 1981. The Minitel was a French videotext system that combined a telephone with an 8-inch screen. By the mid-1980s, more than 3 million Minitels were deployed, and more than 13,000 different services were available, including ticket agencies, travel services, retail products, and online banking. The Minitel service continued in existence until December 31, 2006, when it was finally discontinued by its owner, France Telecom.

However, none of these precursor systems had the functionality of the Internet. Generally, when we think of e-commerce today, it is inextricably linked to the Internet. For our purposes, we will say e-commerce begins in 1995, following the appearance of the first banner advertisements placed by AT&T, Volvo, Sprint, and others on Hotwired.com in late October 1994, and the first sales of banner ad space by Netscape and Infoseek in early 1995. Since then, e-commerce has been the fastest growing form of commerce in the United States.

FIGURE 1.6 — MOBILE INTERNET ACCESS IN THE UNITED STATES

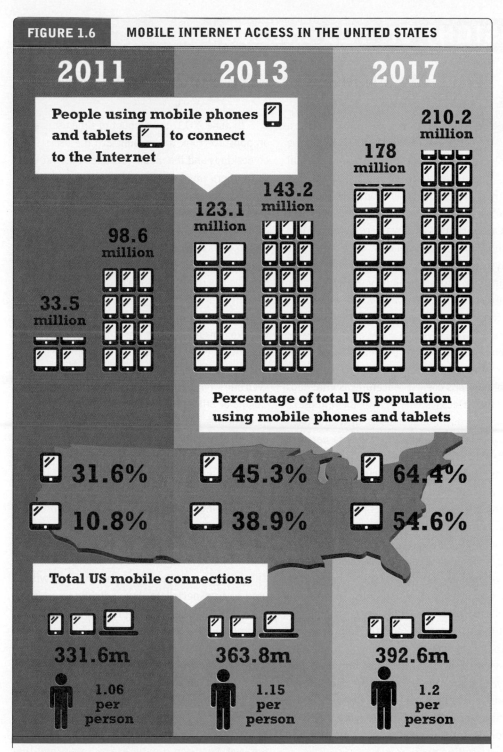

Continued growth in the number of people using mobile phones and tablets to connect to the Internet will provide a significant stimulus to mobile e-commerce.

SOURCES: Based on data from eMarketer, Inc., 2013c, 2013d, 2013e.

INSIGHT ON TECHNOLOGY

WILL APPS MAKE THE WEB IRRELEVANT?

Nowadays, it's hard to recall a time before the Web. How did we get along without the ability to pull up a Web browser and search for any item, learn about any topic, or play just about any type of game? Though the Web has come a remarkably long way from its humble beginnings, many experts claim that the Web's best days are behind it, and that there's a new sheriff in town: apps. Opinions vary widely over the future role of the Web in a world where apps have become an ever larger portion of the Internet marketspace. In 10 years, will Web browsers be forgotten relics, as we rely entirely on apps to do both our work and our play on the Internet? Will the Web and apps coexist peacefully as vital cogs in the Internet ecosystem? Or will the app craze eventually die down as tech users gravitate back towards the Web as the primary way to perform Internet-related tasks?

Apps have grown into a disruptive force ever since Apple launched its App Store in 2008. The list of industries apps have disrupted is wide-ranging: communications, media and entertainment, logistics, education, and healthcare. The average U.S. consumer spends over 2 and a half hours per day on smartphones and tablets, 80% of which is spent within apps. Despite not even existing prior to 2008, apps account for $25 billion in revenues, and the app economy is continuing to show robust growth, suggesting it is nowhere near saturated. Not only that, but the growth is not coming from more users trying the same small number of apps. Consumers are trying new apps all the time, leaving plenty of room for new app developers to innovate and create best-selling apps.

In June 2011, the amount of time users spent on apps overtook the amount of time users spent on desktops and the mobile Web for the first time. Consumers have gravitated to apps for several reasons. First, smartphones and tablet computers enable users to use apps anywhere, instead of being tethered to a desktop or having to lug a heavy laptop around. Of course, smartphones and tablets enable users to use the Web too, but apps are often more convenient and boast more streamlined, elegant interfaces than mobile Web browsers.

Not only are apps more appealing in certain ways to consumers, they are much more appealing to content creators and media companies. Apps are much easier to control and monetize than Web sites, not to mention they can't be crawled by Google or other services. On the Web, the average price of ads per thousand impressions is falling, and after twenty years, many content providers are still mostly struggling to turn the Internet into a profitable content delivery platform. Much of software and media companies' focus has shifted to developing mobile apps for this reason.

These trends are why some pundits boldly proclaim that "the Web is dead," and that the shift from the Web to apps has only just started. These analysts believe that the Internet will be used to transport data, but individual app interfaces will replace the Web browser as the most common way to access and display content. Even the creator of the Web, Tim Berners-Lee, feels that the Web as we know it is being threatened. That's not a good sign.

But there is no predictive consensus about the role of the Web in our lives in the next decade and beyond. Many analysts believe the demise of the Web has been greatly exaggerated, and that

(continued)

the Web boasts many advantages over today's apps that users will be unwilling to relinquish. Although apps may be more convenient than the Web in many respects, the depth of the Web browsing experience trumps that of apps. The Web is a vibrant, diverse array of sites, and browsers have an openness and flexibility that apps lack. The connections between Web sites enhance their usefulness and value to users, and apps that instead seek to lock users in cannot offer the same experience.

Other analysts who are more optimistic about the Web's chances to remain relevant in an increasingly app-driven online marketplace feel this way because of the emergence of HTML5. HTML5 is a new markup language that will enable more dynamic Web content and allow for browser-accessible Web apps that are as appealing as device-specific apps. In fact, there is another group of analysts who believe that apps and the Web are going to come together, with HTML5 bringing the best of the app experience to the Web, and with apps developing new Web-like capabilities. Already, work is underway to create more "smart" apps that handle a wider array of

tasks than today's apps can handle, such as Google Glasses or apps with Siri integration.

A shift towards apps and away from the Web would have a ripple effect on e-commerce firms. As the pioneer of apps and the market leader in apps, smartphones, and tablet computers, Apple stands to gain from a shift towards apps, and although they will also face increasing opposition from other companies, including Google, the established success of the App Store will make it next to impossible to dethrone them. Google's search business is likely to suffer from all of the "walled garden" apps that it cannot access, but it also has a major stake in the world of smartphones, tablets, and apps itself with its fleet of Android-equipped devices. Facebook has already seen its members make the transition from using its site on the Web to using its mobile app, but it has yet to determine how it will monetize the app platform effectively. Web-based companies that fail to find an answer to this problem may eventually fall by the wayside. The one sure bet is that nobody knows for sure exactly what the future holds for apps, the Web, and the Internet.

SOURCES: "Convergence of User Experiences," Savas.me, April 4, 2013; Simon Khalaf, "Flurry Five-Year Report: It's an App World. The Web Just Lives in It," Flurry.com, April 3, 2013; Eric Jackson, "Here's Why Google and Facebook Might Completely Disappear in the Next 5 Years," Forbes.com, April 30, 2012; Gabe Knuth, "Is The Web Dead In the Face of Native Apps? Not Likely, But Some Think So," Brianmadden.com, March 28, 2012; Janna Quitney Anderson and Lee Rainie, "Imagining the Internet," Pew Internet and American Life Project, March 23, 2012; Chris Anderson and Michael Wolff, "The Web is Dead. Long Live the Internet," Wired.com, August 17, 2010; Chris Anderson, "The Web is Dead? A Debate," Wired.com, August 17, 2010.

The data suggests that, over the next five years, B2C e-commerce in the United States will grow by about 14% annually, much faster than traditional retail sales (which are growing at only about 4% a year). There is tremendous upside potential. Today, for instance, B2C retail e-commerce is still a very small part (around 6–7%) of the overall $3.8 trillion retail market in the United States, and under current projections, will still be less than Walmart's fiscal 2013 revenue ($466 billion) in 2017. There is obviously much room to grow (see **Figure 1.7**). However, it's not likely that B2C e-commerce revenues will continue to expand forever at double-digit rates. As online sales become a larger percentage of all sales, online sales growth will likely eventually decline to that growth level. This point still appears to be a long way off. Online content sales, everything from

FIGURE 1.7	ROOM TO GROW

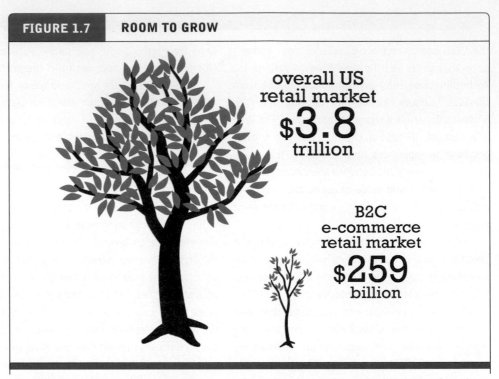

overall US
retail market
$3.8
trillion

B2C
e-commerce
retail market
$259
billion

The B2C e-commerce retail market is still just a small part of the overall U.S. retail market, but with much room to grow in the future.

SOURCES: Bureau of Economic Analysis, U.S. Department of Commerce, 2013; eMarketer, Inc., 2013a.

music, to video, medical information, games, and entertainment, have an even longer period to grow before they hit any ceiling effects.

1.2 E-COMMERCE: A BRIEF HISTORY

Although e-commerce is not very old, it already has a tumultuous history. The history of e-commerce can be usefully divided into three periods: 1995–2000, the period of invention; 2001–2006, the period of consolidation; and 2007–present, a period of reinvention with social, mobile, and local expansion. The following examines each of these periods briefly, while **Figure 1.8** places them in context along a timeline.

E-COMMERCE 1995–2000: INVENTION

The early years of e-commerce were a period of explosive growth and extraordinary innovation, beginning in 1995 with the first widespread use of the Web to advertise products. During this Invention period, e-commerce meant selling retail goods, usually quite simple goods, on the Internet. There simply was not enough bandwidth for more complex products. Marketing was limited to unsophisticated static display ads and not very powerful search engines. The Web policy of most large firms, if they

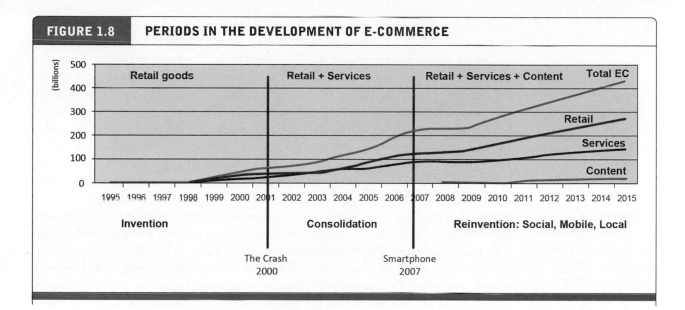

| FIGURE 1.8 | PERIODS IN THE DEVELOPMENT OF E-COMMERCE |

had one at all, was to have a basic static Web site depicting their brands. The rapid growth in e-commerce was fueled by over $125 billion in venture capital. This period of e-commerce came to a close in 2000 when stock market valuations plunged, with thousands of companies disappearing (the "dot-com crash").

The early years of e-commerce were also one of the most euphoric of times in American commercial history. It was also a time when key e-commerce concepts were developed. For computer scientists and information technologists, the early success of e-commerce was a powerful vindication of a set of information technologies that had developed over a period of 40 years—extending from the development of the early Internet, to the PC, to local area networks. The vision was of a universal communications and computing environment that everyone on Earth could access with cheap, inexpensive computers—a worldwide universe of knowledge stored on HTML pages created by hundreds of millions of individuals and thousands of libraries, governments, and scientific institutes. Technologists celebrated the fact that the Internet was not controlled by anyone or any nation, but was free to all. They believed the Internet— and the e-commerce that rose on this infrastructure—should remain a self-governed, self-regulated environment.

For economists, the early years of e-commerce raised the realistic prospect of a nearly perfect competitive market: where price, cost, and quality information are equally distributed, a nearly infinite set of suppliers compete against one another, and customers have access to all relevant market information worldwide. The Internet would spawn digital markets where information would be nearly perfect— something that is rarely true in other real-world markets. Merchants in turn would have equal direct access to hundreds of millions of customers. In this near-perfect information marketspace, transaction costs would plummet because search costs— the cost of searching for prices, product descriptions, payment settlement, and order fulfillment—would all fall drastically (Bakos, 1997). For merchants, the cost of searching for customers would also fall, reducing the need for wasteful advertising. At the same time, advertisements could be personalized to the needs of every customer. Prices and even costs would be increasingly transparent to the consumer, who could now know exactly and instantly the worldwide best price, quality, and availability of most products. Information asymmetry would be greatly reduced. Given the instant nature of Internet communications, the availability of powerful sales information systems, and the low cost involved in changing prices on a Web site (low menu costs), producers could dynamically price their products to reflect actual demand, ending the idea of one national price, or one suggested manufacturer's list price. In turn, market middlemen—the distributors and wholesalers who are intermediaries between producers and consumers, each demanding a payment and raising costs while adding little value—would disappear (**disintermediation**). Manufacturers and content originators would develop direct market relationships with their customers. The resulting intense competition, the decline of intermediaries, and the lower transaction costs would eliminate product brands, and along with it, the possibility of *monopoly profits* based on brands, geography, or special access to factors of production. Prices for products and services would fall to the point where prices covered costs of production plus a fair, "market rate" of return on capital, plus additional small payments for entrepreneurial effort (that would not last long). Unfair competitive advantages (which occur when one competitor has an advantage others cannot purchase) would be eliminated, as would extraordinary returns on invested capital. This vision was called **friction-free commerce** (Smith et al., 2000).

For real-world entrepreneurs, their financial backers, and marketing professionals, e-commerce represented an extraordinary opportunity to earn far above normal returns on investment. The e-commerce marketspace represented access to millions of consumers worldwide who used the Internet and a set of marketing communications technologies (e-mail and Web pages) that was universal, inexpensive, and powerful. These new technologies would permit marketers to practice what they always had done—segmenting the market into groups with different needs and price sensitivity, targeting the segments with branding and promotional messages, and positioning the product and pricing for each group—but with even more precision. In this new marketspace, extraordinary profits would go to **first movers**—those firms who were first to market in a particular area and who moved quickly to gather market share. In a "winner take all" market, first movers could establish a large customer base quickly, build brand name recognition early, create an entirely new distribution channel, and then inhibit competitors (new entrants) by building in *switching costs* for their customers through proprietary interface designs and features available only at one site. The idea for entrepreneurs was to create near monopolies online based on size, convenience, selection, and brand. Online businesses using the new technology could create informative, community-like features unavailable to traditional merchants. These "communities of consumption" also would add value and be difficult for traditional merchants to imitate. The thinking was that once customers became accustomed to using a company's unique Web interface and feature set, they could not easily be switched to competitors. In

disintermediation

displacement of market middlemen who traditionally are intermediaries between producers and consumers by a new direct relationship between producers and consumers

friction-free commerce

a vision of commerce in which information is equally distributed, transaction costs are low, prices can be dynamically adjusted to reflect actual demand, intermediaries decline, and unfair competitive advantages are eliminated

first mover

a firm that is first to market in a particular area and that moves quickly to gather market share the best case, the entrepreneurial firm would invent proprietary technologies and techniques that almost everyone adopted, creating a network effect. A **network effect** occurs where all participants receive value from the fact that everyone else uses the same tool or product (for example, a common operating system, telephone system, or software application such as a proprietary instant messaging standard or an operating system such as Windows), all of which increase in value as more people adopt them.[2]

To initiate this process, entrepreneurs argued that prices would have to be very low to attract customers and fend off potential competitors. E-commerce was, after all, a totally new way of shopping that would have to offer some immediate cost benefits to consumers. However, because doing business on the Web was supposedly so much more efficient when compared to traditional "bricks-and-mortar" businesses (even when compared to the direct mail catalog business) and because the costs of customer acquisition and retention would supposedly be so much lower, profits would inevitably materialize out of these efficiencies. Given these dynamics, market share, the number of visitors to a site ("eyeballs"), and gross revenue became far more important in the earlier stages of an online firm than earnings or profits. Entrepreneurs and their financial backers in the early years of e-commerce expected that extraordinary profitability would come, but only after several years of losses.

Thus, the early years of e-commerce were driven largely by visions of profiting from new technology, with the emphasis on quickly achieving very high market visibility. The source of financing was venture capital funds. The ideology of the period emphasized the ungoverned "Wild West" character of the Web and the feeling that governments and courts could not possibly limit or regulate the Internet; there was a general belief that traditional corporations were too slow and bureaucratic, too stuck in the old ways of doing business, to "get it"—to be competitive in e-commerce. Young entrepreneurs were therefore the driving force behind e-commerce, backed by huge amounts of money invested by venture capitalists. The emphasis was on *deconstructing* (destroying) traditional distribution channels and disintermediating existing channels, using new pure online companies who aimed to achieve impregnable first-mover advantages. Overall, this period of e-commerce was characterized by experimentation, capitalization, and hypercompetition (Varian, 2000b).

E-COMMERCE 2001–2006: CONSOLIDATION

In the second period of e-commerce, from 2000 to 2006, a sobering period of reassessment of e-commerce occurred, with many critics doubting its long-term prospects. Emphasis shifted to a more "business-driven" approach rather than being technology driven; large traditional firms learned how to use the Web to strengthen their market positions; brand extension and strengthening became more important than creating new brands; financing shrunk as capital markets shunned start-up firms; and traditional bank financing based on profitability returned.

network effect
occurs where users receive value from the fact that everyone else uses the same tool or product

---

[2] The network effect is quantified by Metcalfe's Law, which argues that the value of a network grows by the square of the number of participants.

During this period of consolidation, e-commerce changed to include not just retail products but also more complex services such as travel and financial services. This period was enabled by widespread adoption of broadband networks in American homes and businesses, coupled with the growing power and lower prices of personal computers that were the primary means of accessing the Internet, usually from work or home. Marketing on the Internet increasingly meant using search engine advertising targeted to user queries, rich media and video ads, and behavioral targeting of marketing messages based on ad networks and auction markets. The Web policy of both large and small firms expanded to include a broader "Web presence" that included not just Web sites, but also e-mail, display, and search engine campaigns; multiple Web sites for each product; and the building of some limited community feedback facilities. E-commerce in this period was growing again by more than 10% a year.

E-COMMERCE 2007—PRESENT: REINVENTION

Beginning in 2007 with the introduction of the iPhone, to the present day, e-commerce has been transformed yet again by the rapid growth of online social networks, widespread adoption of consumer mobile devices such as smartphones and tablet computers, and the expansion of e-commerce to include local goods and services. The defining characteristics of this period are often characterized as the "social, mobile, local" online world. In this period, entertainment content begins to develop as a major source of e-commerce revenues and mobile devices become entertainment centers, as well as on-the-go shopping devices for retail goods and services. Marketing is transformed by the increasing use of social networks, word-of-mouth, viral marketing, and much more powerful data repositories and analytic tools for truly personal marketing. Firms' online policies expand in the attempt to build a digital presence that surrounds the online consumer with coordinated marketing messages based on their social network memberships, use of search engines and Web browsers, and even their personal e-mail messages, social networks, the mobile platform, and local commerce. This period is as much a sociological phenomenon as it is a technological or business phenomenon. Not many of the social, mobile, and local e-commerce companies have been able to monetize their huge audiences into profitable operations yet, but many eventually will. The *Insight on Business* case, *Start-up Boot Camp*, takes a look at Y-Combinator, which has mentored a number of these new social, mobile, and local e-commerce ventures.

Table 1.4 summarizes e-commerce in each of these three periods.

ASSESSING E-COMMERCE: SUCCESSES, SURPRISES, AND FAILURES

Looking back at the early years of e-commerce, it is apparent that e-commerce has been, for the most part, a stunning technological success as the Internet and the Web ramped up from a few thousand to billions of e-commerce transactions per year, and this year will generate an estimated $419 billion in total B2C revenues and around $4.7 trillion in B2B revenues, with around 155 million online buyers in the United States. With enhancements and strengthening, described in later chapters, it is clear that e-commerce's digital infrastructure is solid enough to sustain significant growth in e-commerce during the next decade. The Internet scales well. The "e" in e-commerce has been an overwhelming success.

INSIGHT ON BUSINESS

START-UP BOOT CAMP

By now we've all heard the story of some lines of code written by Mark Zuckerberg in a Harvard dorm room blossoming into a multi-billion dollar business. These days, it's harder than ever to keep track of all the tech start-ups being bought for millions and even billions of dollars, often even without a cent of revenue to show for themselves. A number of them have something in common—they have been nurtured, and in some cases, whipped into shape, with the help of an "incubator."

As entrepreneurs continue to launch a growing number of e-commerce companies, incubators have come to occupy a vital role in Silicon Valley, helping new businesses move from little more than a great idea to an established, vibrant business. Founded in 2005 by programmer and venture capitalist Paul Graham, Y Combinator is Silicon Valley's best known incubator. Twice a year the company provides a three-month boot camp, complete with seed funding and mentorship from an extensive network of highly regarded tech entrepreneurs, like Gmail creator Paul Buchheit. Every boot camp ends with a demonstration day, known as "D Day," where all of the entrepreneurs, known as "founders," pitch their fledgling businesses to a group of wealthy venture capitalists hoping to unearth the next Facebook or Google.

When companies are admitted to Y Combinator after a rigorous selection progress, they are given $100,000 or more in exchange for a 7% stake in the company. Founders have regular meetings with Y Combinator partners, and have free access to technical advice, emotional support, and lessons in salesmanship. Through 2013, Y Combinator has helped launch 511 start-up companies, which together have a net worth of $11.5 billion. Y Combinator proudly touts that the average

value of a company that it helps launch is about $22.4 million, but these numbers are inflated by Y Combinator's biggest successes: Dropbox and Airbnb. Dropbox, an increasingly popular file hosting service, is worth approximately $4 billion, and Airbnb, an online vacation rental marketplace, comes in at $2.5 billion. Other well-known graduates include Reddit, a social news site, and Stripe, which offers Web-based credit card payment software. Another somewhat surprising success from a recent boot camp is Teespring. Started in 2012 by two students at Brown University, Teespring is a crowdfunding Web site that sells custom-made T-shirts and hoodies. Teespring raised $1.3 million in early 2013.

Not every company that makes it through Y Combinator's boot camps is this successful, or successful at all. Companies that fail to attract sufficient investor interest at D Day can try again with a different company, go their own way and "grow organically," which is practically a death sentence in today's Silicon Valley, or resign themselves to work at Google or Facebook. Y Combinator has had to reduce its class sizes from over 80 to less than 50 because the quality of companies had been less appealing to investors. Still, that number is likely to increase again, and there is no shortage of entrepreneurs with visions of guiding their companies to becoming the next billion dollar business. A Y Combinator company with a successful pitch on D Day is likely to garner at least $1 million in investment money.

The most recent spate of incredibly lucrative start-up companies have been social media-related services. The image hosting service Instagram was purchased by Facebook for a cool billion dollars, despite not having any revenue. Other similar companies include TweetDeck (bought by Twitter for $40 million), GroupMe (bought by Skype, $85

(continued)

million), and Siri (bought by Apple, $200 million). Pinterest is likely to be next, and it already carries a $2.5 billion valuation from early 2013. These companies have such enormous valuations not because of their current revenues, which are often nonexistent, but because they are perceived as having some small, but realistic, chance of becoming the next Facebook or Google. As one venture capital investor explained it, a company with a 1% chance of being a hundred-billion company might be worth a billion dollars.

Social network fever appears to be dying down somewhat, however. After the lukewarm reception to the IPOs of Groupon, Zynga, and Facebook, social media start-ups are no longer in as high demand. The demographics of Y Combinator's latest class reflects this change. In past years, start-ups focused on developing sweeping projects to attract billions of eyeballs without much concern about revenue, but more recent Y Combinator participants are focused on revenue charts instead of eyeballs, and on services and technology that solve concrete, even 'boring' problems. Examples include CircuitLab, a digital service that helps people design electrical circuits, Thalmic Labs, maker of a device that allows people to use physical gestures to control technology, and Wevorce, a technology platform that helps couples navigate amicable divorce.

Some skeptics believe that incubators like Y Combinator might not be the best idea for every start-up. For start-ups with solid, but not eye-popping peripherals, Y Combinator's D Day might actually hurt their chances of getting funding. Having to compete against an extremely qualified field of start-up companies diminishes the appeal for less flashy businesses. Once you've failed at acquiring funding at Y Combinator, other prospective investors might become concerned. There is also the concern that many companies raise too much money early on, and grow to a size that makes it more difficult to develop the product. Lastly, some tech investors worry that Y Combinator relies too much on Graham for its success, and would struggle to duplicate its results without him.

Graham dismisses these concerns, and both enrollment and investment numbers indicate that Y Combinator and its fledgling companies are becoming more and more successful. Though Dropbox and Airbnb are its biggest success stories, 37 other companies that Y Combinator has funded have a current valuation of over $40 million, which is good news both for those companies and for Y Combinator, which owns a stake in all of them. As the business world continues its shift towards technology, Y Combinator and other incubators stand ready to ease the transition.

SOURCES: Joshua Reeves, "Don't Raise Capital Until You Know How to Spend It," *Wall Street Journal*, June 3, 2013; Cromwell Schubarth, "Y Combinator Tally: 511 Startups, $11.5B Valuation," bizjournals.com, May 28, 2013; Leena Rao, "Paul Graham: 37 Y Combinator Companies Have Valuations of or Sold for At Least $40M," *TechCrunch*, May 26, 2013; Rebecca Grant, "Y Combinator Adds Five New Partners to Guide Its Startups Towards Success," *VentureBeat*, May 16, 2013; Nathaniel Rich, "Silicon Valley's Start-up Machine," *New York Times*, May 2, 2013; Charles Moldow, "For Y Combinator Graduates, Timing Should Be Everything," allthingsd.com, April 30, 2013; Amir Efrati, "At Y Combinator, Social is Out, Revenue is In," *Wall Street Journal*, March 26, 2013; Drew Hansen, "What's the Secret Behind Y Combinator's Success?" www.forbes.com, February 18, 2013

From a business perspective, though, the early years of e-commerce were a mixed success, and offered many surprises. Only about 10% of dot-coms formed since 1995 have survived as independent companies in 2013. Only a very tiny percentage of these survivors are profitable. Yet online B2C sales of goods and services are still growing. Consumers have learned to use the Web as a powerful source of information about products they actually purchase through other channels, such as at a traditional bricks-and-mortar store. This is especially true of expensive consumer durables such

TABLE 1.4	EVOLUTION OF E-COMMERCE	
1995–2000 INVENTION	2001–2006 CONSOLIDATION	2007–PRESENT RE-INVENTION
Technology driven	Business driven	Mobile technology enables social, local, and mobile commerce
Revenue growth emphasis	Earnings and profits emphasis	Audience and social network connections emphasis
Venture capital financing	Traditional financing	Smaller VC investments; early small-firm buyouts by large online players
Ungoverned	Stronger regulation and governance	Extensive government surveillance
Entrepreneurial	Large traditional firms	Entrepreneurial social and local firms
Disintermediation	Strengthening intermediaries	Proliferation of small online intermediaries renting business processes of larger firms
Perfect markets	Imperfect markets, brands, and network effects	Continuation of online market imperfections; commodity competition in select markets
Pure online strategies	Mixed "bricks-and-clicks" strategies	Return of pure online strategies in new markets; extension of bricks-and-clicks in traditional retail markets
First-mover advantages	Strategic-follower strength; complementary assets	First-mover advantages return in new markets as traditional Web players catch up
Low-complexity retail products	High-complexity retail products and services	Retail, services, and content

as appliances, automobiles, and electronics. This "Internet-influenced" commerce is very difficult to estimate, but is believed to have been somewhere around $1.3 trillion in 2013 (Forrester Research, 2012). Altogether then, B2C retail e-commerce (both actual purchases and purchases influenced by online shopping but actually buying in a store) are expected to amount to over $1.5 trillion in 2013, or over 45% of total retail sales in the United States. The "commerce" in e-commerce is basically very sound, at least in the sense of attracting a growing number of customers and generating revenues.

Although e-commerce has grown at an extremely rapid pace in customers and revenues, it is clear that many of the visions, predictions, and assertions about e-commerce developed in the early years have not have been fulfilled. For instance, economists' visions of "friction-free" commerce have not been entirely realized. Prices are sometimes lower online, but the low prices are sometimes a function of entrepreneurs selling products below their costs. Consumers are less price sensitive than expected; surprisingly, the Web sites with the highest revenue often have the highest prices. There remains considerable persistent and even increasing price dispersion: online competition has lowered prices, but price dispersion remains pervasive in many markets despite lower search costs (Levin, 2011; Ghose and Yao, 2010). The concept of one world, one market, one price has not occurred in reality as entrepreneurs discover new ways to differentiate their products and services. While for the most part Internet prices save consumers about 20% on average when compared to in-store prices, sometimes online prices are higher than for similar products purchased offline, especially if shipping costs are considered. For instance, prices on books and CDs vary by as much as 50%, and prices for airline tickets as much as 20% (Alessandria, 2009; Aguiar and Hurst, 2008; Baye, 2004; Baye et al., 2004; Brynjolfsson and Smith, 2000; Bailey, 1998a, b). Merchants have adjusted to the competitive Internet environment by engaging in "hit-and-run pricing" or changing prices every day or hour (using "flash pricing" or "flash sales") so competitors never know what they are charging (neither do customers); by making their prices hard to discover and sowing confusion among consumers by "baiting and switching" customers from low-margin products to high-margin products with supposedly "higher quality." Finally, brands remain very important in e-commerce—consumers trust some firms more than others to deliver a high-quality product on time (Rosso and Jansen, 2010).

The "perfect competition" model of extreme market efficiency has not come to pass. Merchants and marketers are continually introducing information asymmetries. Search costs have fallen overall, but the overall transaction cost of actually completing a purchase in e-commerce remains high because users have a bewildering number of new questions to consider: Will the merchant actually deliver? What is the time frame of delivery? Does the merchant really stock this item? How do I fill out this form? Many potential e-commerce purchases are terminated in the shopping cart stage because of these consumer uncertainties. Some people still find it easier to call a trusted catalog merchant on the telephone than to order on a Web site. Finally, intermediaries have not disappeared as predicted. Most manufacturers, for instance, have not adopted the Dell model of online sales (direct sales by the manufacturer to the consumer), and Dell itself has moved towards a mixed model heavily reliant on in-store sales where customers can "kick the tires" by trying the keyboard and viewing the screen. Apple stores are among the most successful stores in the world, with sales of about $5,600 per square foot, about 20 times the average for retail stores. People still like to shop in a physical store.

If anything, e-commerce has created many opportunities for middlemen to aggregate content, products, and services into portals and search engines and thereby introduce themselves as the "new" intermediaries. Yahoo, MSN, and Amazon, along with third-party travel sites such as Travelocity, Orbitz and Expedia, are all examples of this kind of intermediary. As illustrated in **Figure 1.9**, e-commerce has not driven existing retail chains and catalog merchants out of business, although it has created opportunities for entrepreneurial Web-only firms to succeed.

The visions of many entrepreneurs and venture capitalists for e-commerce have not materialized exactly as predicted either. First-mover advantage appears to have succeeded only for a very small group of sites. Historically, first movers have been long-term losers, with the early-to-market innovators usually being displaced by established "fast-follower" firms with the right complement of financial, marketing, legal, and production assets needed to develop mature markets, and this has proved true for

FIGURE 1.9	SHARE OF ONLINE RETAIL SALES BY TYPE OF COMPANY

- Retail chain
- Web only
- Catalog/ call center
- Consumer brand manufacturer

Web-only firms account for the largest share of online retail sales, followed closely by online sales by traditional retail chain stores.

SOURCE: Based on data from Internet Retailer, 2013.

e-commerce as well. Many e-commerce first movers, such as eToys, FogDog (sporting goods), Webvan (groceries), and Eve.com (beauty products) are out of business. Customer acquisition and retention costs during the early years of e-commerce were extraordinarily high, with some firms, such as E*Trade and other financial service firms, paying up to $400 to acquire a new customer. The overall costs of doing business online—including the costs of technology, site design and maintenance, and warehouses for fulfillment—are often no lower than the costs faced by the most efficient bricks-and-mortar stores. A large warehouse costs tens of millions of dollars regardless of a firm's online presence. The knowledge of how to run the warehouse is priceless, and not easily moved. The start-up costs can be staggering. Attempting to achieve or enhance profitability by raising prices has often led to large customer defections (as can be seen from Netflix's recent experience). From the e-commerce merchant's perspective, the "e" in e-commerce does not stand for "easy."

PREDICTIONS FOR THE FUTURE: MORE SURPRISES

Given that e-commerce has changed greatly in the last several years, its future cannot be predicted except to say "Watch for more surprises." There are several factors that will help define the future of e-commerce. First, there is little doubt that the technology of e-commerce—the Internet, the Web, and the growing number of mobile devices, including smartphones and tablet computers—will continue to propagate through all commercial activity. The overall revenues from e-commerce (goods and services) in the United States rose in 2012 by around 16% and are expected to continue to rise, most likely at an annualized rate of about 14% per year through 2017. The number of products and services sold online and the size of the average purchase order both will continue to grow at near double-digit rates. The number of online shoppers in the United States will also continue to grow, although at a much more modest rate of about 1% per year. There has also been a significant broadening of the online product mix compared to the early years when books, computer software, and hardware dominated e-commerce (see **Figure 1.10**). This trend will continue. (See Chapter 9 for changes in retail products and services.)

Second, traditional, well-endowed, experienced Fortune 500 companies will continue to play a dominant role in e-commerce, while new start-up ventures will quickly gain large online audiences for new products and services not dominated by the large players. There will also be a continuation of audience consolidation on the Internet in general, with the top 100 sites garnering over 80% of all online

FIGURE 1.10   ONLINE RETAIL SALES BY CATEGORY, 2012

The mix of products sold online has significantly broadened, although computers and other electronics remain the leading category, with $56.8 billion in sales.

SOURCES: Based on data from U.S. Department of Commerce, 2013; eMarketer, Inc., 2013a; Internet Retailer, 2013; authors' estimates.

TABLE 1.5	TOP 15 ONLINE RETAILERS RANKED BY ONLINE SALES
ONLINE RETAILER	ONLINE SALES (2012) (IN BILLIONS)
Amazon	$61.1
Staples	$10.3
Apple	$8.8
Walmart	$7.7
Liberty Interactive (QVC, etc.)	$4.3
Sears	$4.2
Office Depot	$4.1
Dell	$3.9
Netflix	$3.6
Best Buy	$3.3
OfficeMax	$3.2
Macy's	$3.2
CDW	$3.1
Newegg	$2.8
W.W. Grainger	$2.7

SOURCES: Based on data from Internet Retailer, 2013; company reports on Form 10-K filed with the Securities and Exchange Commission.

sales (Internet Retailer, 2013). **Table 1.5** lists the top 15 online retailers, as ranked by 2012 online sales. The table shows an unmistakable trend toward well-known, traditional brands from strong traditional retail chains, with Staples, Walmart, Office Depot, Sears, Best Buy, OfficeMax, and Macy's all in the top 15.

Third, the number of successful purely online companies will remain smaller than integrated online/offline stores that combine traditional sales channels such as physical stores and printed catalogs with online efforts. For instance, traditional catalog sales firms such as L.L.Bean have transformed themselves into integrated online and direct mail firms with more than half of their sales coming from the online channel.

The future of e-commerce will include the continued growth of regulatory activity both in the United States and worldwide. Governments around the world have challenged the early vision of computer scientists and information technologists that the Internet should be a self-regulating and self-governing phenomenon. The Internet and e-commerce have been so successful and powerful, so all-pervasive, that they directly involve the social, cultural, and political life of entire nations and cultures. Throughout history, whenever technologies have risen to this level of social importance, power, and visibility, they become the target of efforts to regulate and control the technology to ensure that positive social benefits result from their use and to guarantee the public's health and welfare. Radio, television, automobiles, electricity, and railroads are all the subject of regulation and legislation. Likewise, with e-commerce. In the U.S. Congress, there have already been a number of bills passed (as well as hundreds proposed) to control various facets of the Internet and e-commerce, from consumer privacy to pornography, gambling, and encryption. We can expect these efforts at regulation in the United States and around the world to increase as e-commerce extends its reach and importance.

A relatively new factor that will influence the growth of e-commerce is the cost of energy, in particular gasoline and diesel. As fuel costs rise, traveling to shop at physical locations can be very expensive. Buying online can save customers time and energy costs. There is growing evidence that shoppers are changing their shopping habits and locales because of fuel costs, and pushing the sales of online retailers to higher levels.

In summary, the future of e-commerce will be a fascinating mixture of traditional retail, service, and media firms extending their brands to online markets; early-period e-commerce firms such as Amazon and eBay strengthening their financial results and dominant positions; and a bevy of entirely new entrepreneurial firms with the potential to rocket into prominence by developing huge new audiences in months. Firms that fit this pattern include Facebook, Twitter, Pinterest, and Tumblr.

1.3 UNDERSTANDING E-COMMERCE: ORGANIZING THEMES

Understanding e-commerce in its totality is a difficult task for students and instructors because there are so many facets to the phenomenon. No single academic discipline is prepared to encompass all of e-commerce. After teaching the e-commerce course for several years and writing this book, we have come to realize just how difficult it is to "understand" e-commerce. We have found it useful to think about e-commerce as involving three broad interrelated themes: technology, business, and society. We do not mean to imply any ordering of importance here because this book and our thinking freely range over these themes as appropriate to the problem we are trying to understand and describe. Nevertheless, as in previous technologically driven commercial revolutions, there is a historic progression. Technologies develop first, and then those developments are exploited commercially. Once commercial exploitation of the technology becomes widespread, a host of social, cultural, and political issues arise.

TECHNOLOGY: INFRASTRUCTURE

The development and mastery of digital computing and communications technology is at the heart of the newly emerging global digital economy we call e-commerce. To understand the likely future of e-commerce, you need a basic understanding of the information technologies upon which it is built. E-commerce is above all else a technologically driven phenomenon that relies on a host of information technologies as well as fundamental concepts from computer science developed over a 50-year period. At the core of e-commerce are the Internet and the Web, which we describe in detail in Chapter 3. Underlying these technologies are a host of complementary technologies: cloud computing, personal computers, smartphones, tablet computers, local area networks, relational and non-relational databases, client/server computing, data mining, and fiber-optic switches, to name just a few. These technologies lie at the heart of sophisticated business computing applications such as enterprise-wide computing systems, supply chain management systems, manufacturing resource planning systems, and customer relationship management systems. E-commerce relies on all these basic technologies—not just the Internet. The Internet, while representing a sharp break from prior corporate computing and communications technologies, is nevertheless just the latest development in the evolution of corporate computing and part of the continuing chain of computer-based innovations in business. **Figure 1.11** illustrates the major stages in the development of corporate computing and indicates how the Internet and the Web fit into this development trajectory.

To truly understand e-commerce, you will need to know something about packet-switched communications, protocols such as TCP/IP, client/server and cloud

| FIGURE 1.11 | THE INTERNET AND THE EVOLUTION OF CORPORATE COMPUTING |

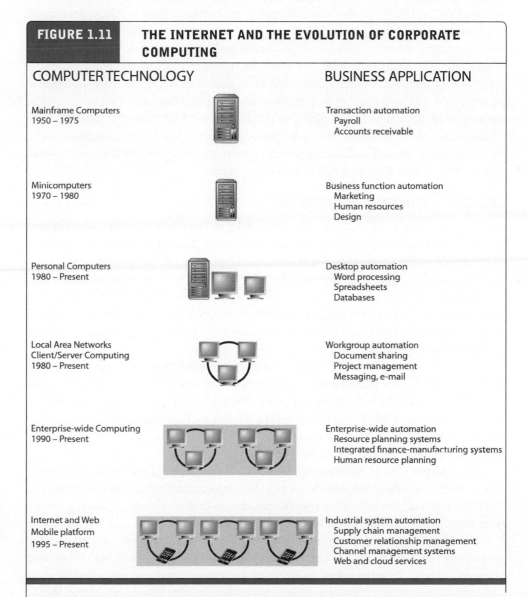

COMPUTER TECHNOLOGY | BUSINESS APPLICATION

Mainframe Computers
1950 – 1975

Transaction automation
  Payroll
  Accounts receivable

Minicomputers
1970 – 1980

Business function automation
  Marketing
  Human resources
  Design

Personal Computers
1980 – Present

Desktop automation
  Word processing
  Spreadsheets
  Databases

Local Area Networks
Client/Server Computing
1980 – Present

Workgroup automation
  Document sharing
  Project management
  Messaging, e-mail

Enterprise-wide Computing
1990 – Present

Enterprise-wide automation
  Resource planning systems
  Integrated finance-manufacturing systems
  Human resource planning

Internet and Web
Mobile platform
1995 – Present

Industrial system automation
  Supply chain management
  Customer relationship management
  Channel management systems
  Web and cloud services

The Internet and Web, and the emergence of a mobile platform held together by the Internet cloud, are the latest in a chain of evolving technologies and related business applications, each of which builds on its predecessors.

computing, mobile digital platforms, Web servers, HTML5, CSS, and software programming tools such as Flash and JavaScript on the client side, and Java, PHP, Ruby on Rails, and ColdFusion on the server side. All of these topics are described fully in Part 2 of the book (Chapters 3–5).

BUSINESS: BASIC CONCEPTS

While technology provides the infrastructure, it is the business applications—the potential for extraordinary returns on investment—that create the interest and excitement in e-commerce. New technologies present businesses and entrepreneurs with new ways of organizing production and transacting business. New technologies change the strategies and plans of existing firms: old strategies are made obsolete and new ones need to be invented. New technologies are the birthing grounds where thousands of new companies spring up with new products and services. New technologies are the graveyard of many traditional businesses, such as record stores. To truly understand e-commerce, you will need to be familiar with some key business concepts, such as the nature of digital markets, digital goods, business models, firm and industry value chains, value webs, industry structure, digital disruption, and consumer behavior in digital markets, as well as basic concepts of financial analysis. We'll examine these concepts further in Chapters 2, 6, 7, and 9 through 12.

SOCIETY: TAMING THE JUGGERNAUT

With more than 243 million Americans now using the Internet, many for e-commerce purposes, and more than 2.5 billion users worldwide, the impact of the Internet and e-commerce on society is significant and global. Increasingly, e-commerce is subject to the laws of nations and global entities. You will need to understand the pressures that global e-commerce places on contemporary society in order to conduct a successful e-commerce business or understand the e-commerce phenomenon. The primary societal issues we discuss in this book are individual privacy, intellectual property, and public welfare policy.

Since the Internet and the Web are exceptionally adept at tracking the identity and behavior of individuals online, e-commerce raises difficulties for preserving privacy—the ability of individuals to place limits on the type and amount of information collected about them, and to control the uses of their personal information. Read the *Insight on Society* case, *Facebook and the Age of Privacy,* to get a view of some of the ways e-commerce sites use personal information.

Because the cost of distributing digital copies of copyrighted intellectual property—tangible works of the mind such as music, books, and videos—is nearly zero on the Internet, e-commerce poses special challenges to the various methods societies have used in the past to protect intellectual property rights.

The global nature of e-commerce also poses public policy issues of equity, equal access, content regulation, and taxation. For instance, in the United States, public telephone utilities are required under public utility and public accommodation laws to make basic service available at affordable rates so everyone can have telephone service. Should these laws be extended to the Internet and the Web? If goods are purchased by a New York State resident from a Web site in California, shipped from a center in Illinois, and

INSIGHT ON SOCIETY

FACEBOOK AND THE AGE OF PRIVACY

In a January 2010 interview, Mark Zuckerberg, the founder of Facebook, proclaimed that the "age of privacy" had to come to an end. According to Zuckerberg, social norms had changed and people were no longer worried about sharing their personal information with friends, friends of friends, or even the entire Web. This view is in accordance with Facebook's broader goal, which is, according to Zuckerberg, to make the world a more open and connected place. Supporters of Zuckerberg's viewpoint believe the twenty-first century is an age of "information exhibitionism," a new era of openness and transparency.

However, not everyone is a true believer. Privacy—limitations on what personal information government and private institutions can collect and use—is a founding principle of democracies. A decade's worth of privacy surveys in the United States show that well over 80% of the American public fear the Internet is a threat to their privacy.

With more than 1.1 billion users worldwide, and about 230 million in North America, Facebook's privacy policies are going to shape privacy standards on the Internet for years to come. The economic stakes in the privacy debate are quite high, involving billions in advertising and transaction dollars. Social network sites such as Facebook use a model based on building a database of hundreds of millions of users who post personal information, preferences, and behaviors, and who are encouraged, or deceived, into relinquishing control over their information, which is then sold to advertisers and outside third parties. The less privacy Facebook's users want or have, the more Facebook profits.

Facebook's current privacy policies are quite a flip-flop from its original policy in 2004, which promised users near complete control over who could see their personal profile. Only immediate friends whom you invited were given access. Other users in your network could not get much information about you at all. People outside that network could find nothing about you. However, every year since 2004, Facebook has attempted to extend its control over user information and content, usually without notice.

For instance, in 2007, Facebook introduced the Beacon program, which was designed to broadcast users' activities on participating Web sites to their friends. After a public outcry, Facebook terminated the Beacon program in 2009, and paid $9.5 million to settle a host of class action lawsuits.

In 2009, undeterred by the Beacon fiasco, Facebook unilaterally decided that it would publish users' basic personal information on the public Internet, and announced that whatever content users had contributed belonged to Facebook, and that its ownership of that information never terminated. However, as with the Beacon program, Facebook's efforts to take permanent control of user information resulted in users joining online resistance groups and it was ultimately forced to withdraw this policy as well.

In 2009, Facebook also introduced the Like button, and in 2010 extended it to third-party Web sites to alert Facebook users to their friends' browsing and purchases. In 2011, it began publicizing users' "likes" of various advertisers in Sponsored Stories (i.e., advertisements) that included the users' names and profile pictures without their explicit consent, without paying them, and without giving them a way to opt out. This resulted in yet another class action lawsuit, which Facebook settled for $20 million in June 2012. As part of the settlement, Facebook agreed to make it clear to users that information like

(continued)

their names and profile pictures might be used in Sponsored Stories. In 2011, Facebook enrolled all Facebook subscribers into its facial recognition program without notice. This too raised the privacy alarm, forcing Facebook to make it easier for users to opt out. In 2012, Facebook, under pressure from European regulators, promised that it would not use the "tag suggestion" feature, which allows photos to be automatically matched with particular users.

In May 2012, Facebook went public, creating even more pressure to increase revenues and profits to justify its stock market value. Shortly thereafter, Facebook announced that it was launching a mobile advertising product that pushes ads to the mobile news feeds of users based on the apps they use through the Facebook Connect feature, without explicit permission from the user to do so. It also announced Facebook Exchange, a program that allows advertisers to serve ads to Facebook users based on their browsing activity while not on Facebook. Privacy advocates have raised the alarm yet again and more lawsuits have been filed by users who claim that Facebook has invaded their privacy by tracking their Internet use even after they have logged off from Facebook. Although Facebook is not yet combining this data with its own database of user personal information, there are concerns that it may do so in the future. In February 2013, Facebook agreed to partner with Acxiom, Epsilon, and Datalogix—all data marketing companies that deliver targeted ads based on offline data. The firms will reportedly provide customer lists to Facebook, who will match them to its users. In June 2013, Facebook also announced it was introducing searchable hashtags, whose use has been popularized by Twitter, Tumblr, and other social media sites. This is just one further step moving Facebook away from its initial origins as a place for friends to connect and toward a public platform where what one posts becomes part of a public conversation.

In June 2013, a further threat became apparent, this time emanating from a somewhat different source. The National Security Agency's PRISM program allegedly required Facebook and many other online service providers to give it access to data on users for investigations into national security issues. An uproar ensued, pushing Internet privacy issues to the forefront of the national consciousness.

It appears that Zuckerberg's proclamation that the age of privacy is over was premature. Instead, privacy issues may turn out to be an enduring headache and perhaps ultimately Facebook's Achilles heel. As Facebook itself noted in its S-1 filing with the Securities and Exchange Commission, if it adopts "policies or procedures related to areas such as sharing or user data that are perceived negatively by our users or the general public," its revenue, financial results, and business may be significantly harmed. And this, more than anything else, may be the savior for privacy at Facebook.

■■ SOURCES: "Facebook Introduces Hashtags, Moving Away From Friends," by Bianca Bosker, HuffingtonPost.com, June 16, 2013; "Facebook Shares Numbers on Government Data Requisitions In Response to PRISM Reports," HuffingtonPost.com, June 15, 2013; "Facebook To Partner With Data Brokers," by Bob Sullivan, Redtape.NBCNews.com, February 26, 2013; "Facebook Seeks Dismissal of $15 Billion Privacy Suit," by Joel Rosenblatt, Bloomberg.com, October 5, 2012; "Facebook Can ID Faces, But Using Them Grows Tricky," by Somini Sengupta and Kevin J. O'Brien, *New York Times*, September 12, 2012; "Facebook to Face Senate Hearing on Facial Recognition," by Katy Bachman, AdWeek.com, July 16, 2012; "Facebook to Target Ads Based on App Usage," by Shayndi Raice, *Wall Street Journal*, July 6, 2012; "Facebook's Facial-Recognition Acquisition Raises Privacy Concerns," by Samantha Murphy, Mashable.com, June 25, 2012; "Facebook Exchange Ads Raise Privacy Concerns," by Mikal E. Belicove, CNBC.com, June 21, 2012; "Facebook About to Launch Facebook Exchange, Real-Time Ad Bidding," by Jessica Guynn, *Los Angeles Times*, June 13, 2012; "Facebook Suit Over Subscriber Tracking Seeks $15 Billion," by Kit Chellel and Jeremy Hodges, Bloomberg.com, May 19, 2012; Facebook Inc. Form S-1/A filed with the Securities and Exchange Commission, May 16, 2012; "Facebook and Your Privacy," by Consumer Reports Staff, ConsumerReports.org, May 3, 2012; "Facebook Offers More Disclosure to Users," by Kevin J. O'Brien, *New York Times*, April 12, 2012; "German State to Sue Facebook over Facial Recognition Feature," by Emil Protalinski, ZDnet.com, November 10, 2011; "Facebook Aims to Simplify Privacy Settings," by Somini Sengupta, *New York Times*, August 23, 2011; "Facebook Again in Spotlight on Privacy," by Geoffrey Fowler, *Wall Street Journal*, June 8, 2011; "Facebook Redesigns Privacy Controls," by Ben Worthen, *Wall Street Journal*, May 27, 2010; "How Facebook Pulled a Privacy Bait and Switch," by Dan Tynan, *PC World*, May 2010.

delivered to New York, what state has the right to collect a sales tax? Should some heavy Internet users who consume extraordinary amounts of bandwidth be charged extra for service, or should the Internet be neutral with respect to usage? What rights do nation-states and their citizens have with respect to the Internet, the Web, and e-commerce? We address issues such as these in Chapter 8, and also throughout the text.

ACADEMIC DISCIPLINES CONCERNED WITH E-COMMERCE

The phenomenon of e-commerce is so broad that a multidisciplinary perspective is required. There are two primary approaches to e-commerce: technical and behavioral.

Technical Approaches

Computer scientists are interested in e-commerce as an exemplary application of Internet technology. They are concerned with the development of computer hardware, software, and telecommunications systems, as well as standards, encryption, and database design and operation. Management scientists are primarily interested in building mathematical models of business processes and optimizing these processes. They are interested in e-commerce as an opportunity to study how business firms can exploit the Internet to achieve more efficient business operations.

Behavioral Approaches

In the behavioral area, information systems researchers are primarily interested in e-commerce because of its implications for firm and industry value chains, industry structure, and corporate strategy. The information systems discipline spans the technical and behavioral approaches. For instance, technical groups within the information systems specialty also focus on data mining, search engine design, and artificial intelligence. Economists have focused on online consumer behavior, pricing of digital goods, and on the unique features of digital electronic markets. The marketing profession is interested in marketing, brand development and extension, online consumer behavior, and the ability of e-commerce technologies to segment and target consumer groups, and differentiate products. Economists share an interest with marketing scholars who have focused on e-commerce consumer response to marketing and advertising campaigns, and the ability of firms to brand, segment markets, target audiences, and position products to achieve above-normal returns on investment.

Management scholars have focused on entrepreneurial behavior and the challenges faced by young firms who are required to develop organizational structures in short time spans. Finance and accounting scholars have focused on e-commerce firm valuation and accounting practices. Sociologists—and to a lesser extent, psychologists—have focused on general population studies of Internet usage, the role of social inequality in skewing Internet benefits, and the use of the Web as a social network and group communications tool. Legal scholars are interested in issues such as preserving intellectual property, privacy, and content regulation.

No one perspective dominates research about e-commerce. The challenge is to learn enough about a variety of academic disciplines so that you can grasp the significance of e-commerce in its entirety.

The Pirate Bay:
Searching for a Safe Haven

The Pirate Bay (TPB) is one of the world's most popular pirated music and content sites, offering free access to millions of copyrighted songs and thousands of copyrighted Hollywood movies. It claims it is the world's largest BitTorrent tracker. In June 2013, TPB reported that it had over 6 million registered users. It is in the top 500 Web sites in the world in terms of global traffic, with about 20% of the visitors coming from the United States. It even has a Facebook page and Twitter feed. This despite the fact that TPB has been subjected to repeated legal efforts to shut it down. In fact, the authorities pursuing TPB must feel as if they are engaged in a never-ending game of Whack-a-mole, as each time they "whack" TPB, it somehow manages to reappear. But the battle is far from over. The Internet is becoming a tough place for music and video pirates to make a living in part because of enforcement actions, but more importantly because of new mobile and wireless technologies that enable high-quality content to be streamed for just a small fee.

TPB is part of a European social and political movement that opposes copyrighted content and demands that music, videos, TV shows, and other digital content be free

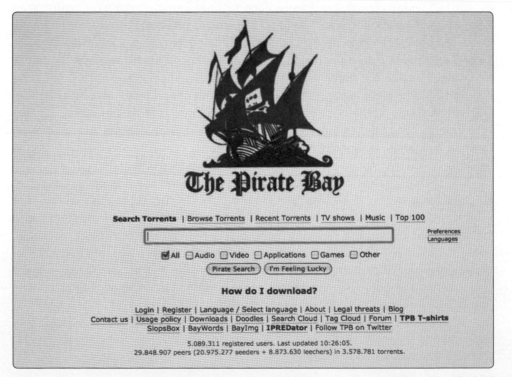

© Tommy (Louth) / Alamy

and unrestricted. TPB does not operate a database of copyrighted content. Neither does it operate a network of computers owned by "members" who store the content, nor does it create, own, or distribute software (like BitTorrent and most other so-called P2P networks) that permit such networks to exist in the first place. Instead, TPB simply provides a search engine that responds to user queries for music tracks, or specific movie titles, and generates a list of search results that include P2P networks around the world where the titles can be found. By clicking on a selected link, users gain access to the copyrighted content, but only after downloading software and other files from that P2P network.

TPB claims it is merely a search engine providing pointers to existing P2P networks that it does not itself control. It says that it cannot control what content users ultimately find on those P2P networks, and that it is no different from any other search engine, such as Google or Bing, which are not held responsible for the content found on sites listed in search results. From a broader standpoint, TPB's founders also claim that copyright laws in general unjustly interfere with the free flow of information on the Internet, and that in any event, they were not violating Swedish copyright law, which they felt should be the only law that applied. And they further claimed they did not encourage, incite, or enable illegal downloading. Nevertheless, the defendants have never denied that theirs was a commercial enterprise. Despite all the talk calling for the free, unfettered spread of culture, TPB was a money-making operation from the beginning, designed to produce profits for its founders, with advertising as the primary source of revenue.

However, the First Swedish Court in Stockholm declared TPB's four founders guilty of violating Swedish copyright law, and sentenced each to one year in prison and payment of $3.5 million in restitution to the plaintiffs, all Swedish divisions of the major record firms (Warner Music, Sony, and EMI Group among them). The court found that the defendants had incited copyright infringement by providing a Web site with search functions, easy uploading and storage possibilities, and a tracker. The court also said that the four defendants had been aware of the fact that copyrighted material was shared with the help of their site and that the defendants were engaged in a commercial enterprise, the basis of which was encouraging visitors to violate the copyrights of owners. In fact, the primary purpose of TPB was to violate copyrights in order to make money for the owners (commercial intent).

Meanwhile, the U.S. government pressured the Swedish government to strengthen its copyright laws to discourage rampant downloading. In Sweden, downloading music and videos from illegal sites was very popular, engaged in by 43% of the Swedish Internet population. To strengthen its laws, Sweden adopted the European Union convention on copyrights, which allows content owners to receive from Internet providers the names and addresses of people suspected of sharing pirated files. In France, participating in these pirate sites will result in banishment from the Internet for up to three years. As a result, Internet traffic in Sweden declined by 40%, and has stayed there.

TPB has appealed the court judgment, has paid no fine, and its founders have, as yet, never spent a night in jail. TPB continues to operate much as before. Well, almost. In 2011, the firm moved its servers into caves in Sweden, and dispersed multiple

SOURCES: "The Pirate Bay Moves to .SX as Prosecutor Files Motion to Seize Domains," Torrentfreak.com, April 30, 2013; thepiratebay.sx, accessed May 25, 2013; alexa.com/siteinfo/ thepiratebay.sx, May 25, 2013; "Pirate Bay Founder Submits Emotional Plea for Pardon," by Ernesto, TorrentFreak, July 7, 2012; "The Pirate Bay Evades ISP Blockade with IPv6, Can Do It 18 Quintillion More Times," by Sebastian Anthony, Extremetech. com, June 8, 2012; "World's Biggest Ad Agency Keelhauls 2,000 Pirate Sites," by Natalie Apostolu, *The Register*, June 14, 2011; "Internet Piracy and How to Stop It," *New York Times*, June 8, 2011; "The Pirate Bay: Five Years After the Raid," by Ernesto, Torrentfreak.com, May 31, 2011; "Why Google Would Defend Pirate Bay?," by Parmy Olson, *Forbes*, May 19, 2011; "The Protect IP Act: COICA Redux," by Abigail Phillips, Electronic Frontier Foundation, May 12, 2011; "Preventing Real Online Threats to Economic Creativity and Theft of Intellectual Property (Protect IP Act) of 2011," United States Senate, 112th Congress, 1st Session, 2011; "Pirate Bay Keeps Sinking: Another Law Suit Coming," by Stan Schroeder, mashable.com, June 22, 2010; "Idea Man of LimeWire at a Crossroads," by Joseph Plambeck, *New York Times*, May 23, 2010; "Pirate Bay Sunk by Hollywood Injunction For Now," by Charles Arthur, *The Guardian*, May 17, 2010; "British Put Teeth in Anti-Piracy Proposal," by Eric Pfanner, *New York Times,* March 14, 2010.

copies of its program to other countries just in case Swedish police tried to confiscate its servers again. Since then, like the fight against the original Caribbean pirates of the seventeenth century, global forces continue to marshal against TPB. Not the British Navy this time, but a loose coalition of a number of European countries and the United States. The firm has been hounded by lawsuits, police raids, and confiscation of servers in France, Finland, Italy, Germany, Denmark, Ireland, the U.K., and Greece. These countries have in some cases refused to allow Internet service providers in their countries to host TPB, or link to TPB, no matter where in the world its servers are located, although TPB has in some cases been able to circumvent this by frequently changing its IP address. In 2013, authorities shut down TPB's top-level domains in Sweden, Greenland, and Iceland. For the time being at least, it has found a safe haven in the the Caribbean island Saint Maarten, a fitting location for a latter-day pirate organization.

TPB has caused England, France, Malaysia, Finland, and most recently the United States to consider strong intellectual property protection laws that will prevent domestic search engines and ISPs from linking to infringing sites, or resolving their domain names. Meanwhile, the world's largest advertising agency, GroupM, keelhauled TPB and 2,000 other sites worldwide in 2011 by putting the sites on its blacklist of copyright infringing sites where it will not buy advertising space. Pirating intellectual property is, above all, about the money, as any good pirate knows.

The TPB case is just the latest in a saga of court cases involving the record industry, which wants to preserve its dominance of copyrighted music, and Internet users who want free music. In 2005, after several years of heated court battles, the case of *Metro-Goldwyn-Mayer Studios v. Grokster, et al.* finally reached the U.S. Supreme Court. In June 2005, the Court handed down its unanimous decision: Internet file-sharing services such as Grokster, StreamCast, BitTorrent, and Kazaa could be held liable for copyright infringement because they intentionally sought to induce, enable, and encourage users to share music that was owned by record companies. Indeed, it was their business model: steal the music, gather a huge audience, and monetize the audience by advertising or through subscription fees. Since the court ruling, Kazaa, Morpheus, Grokster, BearShare, iMesh, and many others have either gone out of business or settled with the record firms and converted themselves into legal file-sharing sites by entering into relationships with music industry firms. In May 2010, Mark Gorton, founder of the largest U.S. pirate site, LimeWire, lost a copyright infringement case. In May 2011, admitting his guilt ("I was wrong"), and having facilitated the mass piracy of billions of songs over a 10-year period, Gorton and his file-sharing company agreed to compensate the four largest record labels by paying them $105 million.

These legal victories, and stronger government enforcement of copyright laws, have not proven to be the magic bullet that miraculously solves all the problems facing the music industry. The music industry has had to drastically change its business model and decisively move towards digital distribution platforms. They have made striking progress, and, for the first time, in 2011 sales of music in a purely digital format accounted for more revenue than sales of music in a physical format. To do so, the music industry employed a number of different business models and online delivery platforms, including Apple's iTunes pay-per-download model, subscription models, streaming models and now music in the cloud.

In each of these new media delivery platforms, the copyright owners—record companies, artists, and Hollywood studios—have struck licensing deals with the technology platform owners and distributors (Apple, Amazon, and Google). These new platforms offer a win-win solution. Consumers are benefitted by having near instant access to high-quality music tracks and videos without the hassle of P2P software downloads. Content owners get a growing revenue stream and protection for their copyrighted content. And the pirates? TPB and other pirate sites may not be able to compete with new and better ways to listen to music and view videos. Like the real pirates of the Caribbean, who are now just a footnote in history books, technology and consumer preference for ease of use may leave them behind.

Case Study Questions

1. Why did TPB believe it was not violating copyright laws? What did the Swedish court rule?

2. How has TPB managed to continue operating despite being found in violation of copyright laws?

3. How has the music industry reacted to the problems created by pirates like TPB?

1.5   REVIEW

KEY CONCEPTS

■ Define e-commerce and describe how it differs from e-business.

- E-commerce involves digitally enabled commercial transactions between and among organizations and individuals. Digitally enabled transactions include all those mediated by digital technology, meaning, for the most part, transactions that occur over the Internet, the Web, and/or via mobile apps. Commercial transactions involve the exchange of value (e.g., money) across organizational or individual boundaries in return for products or services.

- E-business refers primarily to the digital enabling of transactions and processes within a firm, involving information systems under the control of the firm. For the most part, e-business does not involve commercial transactions across organizational boundaries where value is exchanged.

■ Identify and describe the unique features of e-commerce technology and discuss their business significance.

There are eight features of e-commerce technology that are unique to this medium:
- *Ubiquity*—available just about everywhere, at all times, making it possible to shop from your desktop, at home, at work, or even from your car.

- *Global reach*—permits commercial transactions to cross cultural and national boundaries far more conveniently and cost-effectively than is true in traditional commerce.
- *Universal standards*—shared by all nations around the world, in contrast to most traditional commerce technologies, which differ from one nation to the next.
- *Richness*—enables an online merchant to deliver marketing messages in a way not possible with traditional commerce technologies.
- *Interactivity*—allows for two-way communication between merchant and consumer and enables the merchant to engage a consumer in ways similar to a face-to-face experience, but on a much more massive, global scale.
- *Information density*—is the total amount and quality of information available to all market participants. The Internet reduces information collection, storage, processing, and communication costs while increasing the currency, accuracy, and timeliness of information.
- *Personalization* and *customization*—the increase in information density allows merchants to target their marketing messages to specific individuals and results in a level of personalization and customization unthinkable with previously existing commerce technologies.
- *Social technology*—provides a many-to-many model of mass communications. Millions of users are able to generate content consumed by millions of other users. The result is the formation of social networks on a wide scale and the aggregation of large audiences on social network platforms.

■ **Recognize and describe Web 2.0 applications.**

- A set of applications has emerged on the Internet, loosely referred to as Web 2.0. These applications attract huge audiences and represent significant opportunities for e-commerce revenues. Web 2.0 applications such as social networks, photo- and video-sharing sites, and blog platforms support very high levels of interactivity compared to other traditional media.

■ **Describe the major types of e-commerce.**

There are five major types of e-commerce:
- *B2C e-commerce* involves businesses selling to consumers and is the type of e-commerce that most consumers are likely to encounter.
- *B2B e-commerce* involves businesses selling to other businesses and is the largest form of e-commerce.
- *C2C e-commerce* is a means for consumers to sell to each other. In C2C e-commerce, the consumer prepares the product for market, places the product for auction or sale, and relies on the market maker to provide catalog, search engine, and transaction clearing capabilities so that products can be easily displayed, discovered, and paid for.
- *Social e-commerce* is e-commerce that is enabled by social networks and online social relationships.
- *M-commerce* involves the use of wireless digital devices to enable online transactions.
- *Local e-commerce* is a form of e-commerce that is focused on engaging the consumer based on his or her current geographic location.

■ Understand the evolution of e-commerce from its early years to today.

E-commerce has gone through three stages: innovation, consolidation, and reinvention. The early years of e-commerce were a period of explosive growth, beginning in 1995 with the first widespread use of the Web to advertise products and ending in 2000 with the collapse in stock market valuations for dot-com ventures.

• The early years of e-commerce were a technological success, with the digital infrastructure created during the period solid enough to sustain significant growth in e-commerce during the next decade, and a mixed business success, with significant revenue growth and customer usage, but low profit margins.

• E-commerce during its early years did not fulfill economists' visions of perfect friction-free commerce, or fulfill the visions of entrepreneurs and venture capitalists for first-mover advantages, low customer acquisition and retention costs, and low costs of doing business.

• E-commerce entered a period of consolidation beginning in 2001 and extending into 2006.

• E-commerce entered a period of reinvention in 2007 with the emergence of the mobile digital platform, social networks, and Web 2.0 applications that attracted huge audiences in a very short time span.

■ Identify the factors that will define the future of e-commerce.

Factors that will define the future of e-commerce include the following:

• E-commerce technology (the Internet, the Web, and the mobile platform) will continue to propagate through all commercial activity, with overall revenues from e-commerce and the number of products and services sold all rising.

• Traditional well-endowed and experienced Fortune 500 companies will continue to play a dominant role.

• The number of successful purely online companies will continue to decline, and most successful e-commerce firms will adopt an integrated, multi-channel bricks-and-clicks strategy.

• Regulation of the Internet and e-commerce by government will grow both in the United States and worldwide.

■ Describe the major themes underlying the study of e-commerce.

E-commerce involves three broad interrelated themes:

• *Technology*—To understand e-commerce, you need a basic understanding of the information technologies upon which it is built, including the Internet, the Web, and mobile platform, and a host of complementary technologies—cloud computing, personal computers, smartphones, tablet computers, local area networks, client/server computing, packet-switched communications, protocols such as TCP/IP, Web servers, HTML, and relational and non-relational databases, among others.

• *Business*—While technology provides the infrastructure, it is the business applications—the potential for extraordinary returns on investment—that create the interest and excitement in e-commerce. Therefore, you also need to understand some key business concepts such as electronic markets, information goods, business models, firm and industry value chains, industry structure, and consumer behavior in digital markets.

- *Society*—Understanding the pressures that global e-commerce places on contemporary society is critical to being successful in the e-commerce marketplace. The primary societal issues are intellectual property, individual privacy, and public policy.

■ **Identify the major academic disciplines contributing to e-commerce.**

There are two primary approaches to e-commerce: technical and behavioral. Each of these approaches is represented by several academic disciplines. On the technical side:

- Computer scientists are interested in e-commerce as an application of Internet technology.
- Management scientists are primarily interested in building mathematical models of business processes and optimizing them to learn how businesses can exploit the Internet to improve their business operations.
- Information systems professionals are interested in e-commerce because of its implications for firm and industry value chains, industry structure, and corporate strategy.
- Economists have focused on online consumer behavior and on the features of digital electronic markets.

On the behavioral side:

- Sociologists have focused on studies of Internet usage, the role of social inequality in skewing Internet benefits, and the use of the Web as a personal and group communications tool.
- Finance and accounting scholars have focused on e-commerce firm valuation and accounting practices.
- Management scholars have focused on entrepreneurial behavior and the challenges faced by young firms that are required to develop organizational structures in short time spans.
- Marketing scholars have focused on consumer response to online marketing and advertising campaigns, and the ability of firms to brand, segment markets, target audiences, and position products to achieve higher returns on investment.

QUESTIONS

1. What is e-commerce? How does it differ from e-business? Where does it intersect with e-business?
2. What is information asymmetry?
3. What are some of the unique features of e-commerce technology?
4. What is a marketspace?
5. What are three benefits of universal standards?
6. Compare online and traditional transactions in terms of richness.
7. Name three of the business consequences that can result from growth in information density.
8. What is Web 2.0? Give examples of Web 2.0 sites and explain why you included them in your list.
9. Give examples of B2C, B2B, C2C, and social, mobile, and local e-commerce besides those listed in the chapter materials.

10. How are e-commerce technologies similar to or different from other technologies that have changed commerce in the past?
11. Describe the three different stages in the evolution of e-commerce.
12. Define disintermediation and explain the benefits to Internet users of such a phenomenon. How does disintermediation impact friction-free commerce?
13. What are some of the major advantages and disadvantages of being a first mover?
14. Discuss the ways in which the early years of e-commerce can be considered both a success and a failure.
15. What are five of the major differences between the early years of e-commerce and today's e-commerce?
16. What factors will help define the future of e-commerce over the next five years?
17. Why is a multidisciplinary approach necessary if one hopes to understand e-commerce?

PROJECTS

1. Define "social e-commerce" and describe why it is a new form of advertising, search, and commerce.

2. Search the Web for an example of each of the major types of e-commerce described in Section 1.1. Create an electronic slide presentation or written report describing each Web site (take a screenshot of each, if possible), and explain why it fits into the category of e-commerce to which you have assigned it.

3. Choose an e-commerce Web site and assess it in terms of the eight unique features of e-commerce technology described in Table 1.2. Which of the features does the site implement well, and which features poorly, in your opinion? Prepare a short memo to the president of the company you have chosen detailing your findings and any suggestions for improvement you may have.

4. Given the development and history of e-commerce in the years from 1995–2013, what do you predict we will see during the next five years of e-commerce? Describe some of the technological, business, and societal shifts that may occur as the Internet continues to grow and expand. Prepare a brief electronic slide presentation or written report to explain your vision of what e-commerce will look like in 2017.

5. Follow up on events at Pinterest since June 2013 (when the opening case was prepared). Prepare a short report on your findings.

CHAPTER 2

E-commerce Business Models and Concepts

After reading this chapter, you will be able to:

- Identify the key components of e-commerce business models.
- Describe the major B2C business models.
- Describe the major B2B business models.
- Understand key business concepts and strategies applicable to e-commerce.

Tweet Tweet:

Twitter's Business Model

Twitter, the social network phenomenon based on 140-character text messages, continues in the long tradition of Internet developments that appear to spring out of nowhere and take the world by storm. Twitter provides a platform for users to express themselves by creating content and sharing it with followers, who sign up to receive "tweets."

Twitter began as a Web-based version of popular text messaging services provided by cell phone carriers. The basic idea was to marry short text messaging on cell phones with the Web

© Kennedy Photography / Alamy

and its ability to create social groups. You start by establishing a Twitter account online. By typing a short message called a tweet online or to a code on your cell phone (40404), you can tell your followers what you are doing, your location, or whatever else you might want to say. You are limited to 140 characters, but there is no installation required and no charge.

Coming up with solid numbers for Twitter is not easy. By 2013, Twitter had an estimated 550 million registered users worldwide, although it is not clear how many continue to actively use the service after signing up. According to Twitter itself, it had 200 million "active" users worldwide as of July 2013. Industry observers believe Twitter is the third largest social network worldwide, behind Facebook and Google+.

What started out in 2006 with 5,000 tweets has turned into a deluge of 400 million daily tweets worldwide. There were more than 150 million tweets about the 2012 Olympics, and more than 80,000 tweets per minute about Usain Bolt's 200-meter victory. Between October 27 and November 1, 2012, there were more than 20 million tweets sent about the impact and aftermath of Superstorm Sandy. Some celebrities, such as Justin Bieber, have millions of followers (in Justin Bieber's case, 42 million as of mid-2013). On the other hand, research indicates that the vast majority of tweets are generated by a small percentage of users: one study found that the top 15% of users account for 85% of all tweets. Another study found that Twitter had only a 40% retention rate: 60% of users failed to return the following month.

Since its founding, Twitter is reported to have raised more than $1.1 billion in venture capital funding, and as of mid-2013, the company is valued at close to $10 billion. This might seem somewhat preposterous given that Twitter has not yet generated a profit. Like many social network firms, Twitter began operating without any revenue stream. Over a period of about five years, however, it has developed a business model based primarily on advertising revenue that is finally taking off. It more than doubled ad revenue in 2012 to an estimated $288 million, with more than 50% coming from mobile advertising. Analysts estimate that Twitter's ad revenue could top $1 billion by 2015.

Twitter's main asset is user attention and audience size (eyeballs per day). An equally important asset is the database of tweets that contains the comments, observations, and opinions of the audience, and the search engine that mines those tweets for patterns. These are real-time and spontaneous observations.

Yet another asset has emerged: Twitter is a powerful alternative media platform for the distribution of news, videos, and pictures. Twitter has become like a global town square and was among the first to report on terrorist attacks in Mumbai, the Iranian rebellion in June 2009, the political violence in Bangkok and Kenya in May 2010, and the uprisings in Egypt, Tunisia, and other areas in the Mideast and Africa in 2011.

How can these assets be monetized? Not surprisingly, as noted previously, Twitter's revenue model is based primarily on advertising. In April 2010, Twitter announced its first foray into the big-time ad marketplace with Promoted Tweets. Promoted Tweets are Twitter's version of Google's text ads. In response to a query to Twitter's search function for tablet computers, for example, a Best Buy tweet about tablets will be displayed. Promoted Tweets look like all other tweets, are part of the tweet stream of messages, and are offered on a "cost-per-click" basis of between $.50 to $1.50 per click. Twitter has since expanded the display of Promoted Tweets to other sites in the Twitter ecosystem, such as HootSuite. Twitter also offers geo-targeted Promoted Tweets. Many companies are now using the service, ranging from Best Buy, to Ford, to Starbucks, to Virgin America. According to Twitter, Promoted Tweets are producing greater engagement with viewers than are traditional Web advertisements. In April 2013, Twitter added keyword targeting in timelines functionality for Promoted Tweets, which enables advertisers to send Promoted Tweets to specific users based on keywords in their recent tweets or tweets with which they have interacted. Twitter's research indicates that users are much more likely to engage with such Promoted Tweets.

A second Twitter monetization effort is called Promoted Trends. "Trends" is a section of the Twitter home page that lets users know what's hot, what a lot of people are talking about. A company can place a Promoted Trends banner at the top of the Trends section, and when users click on the banner, they are taken to the follower page for that company or product. A Promoted Trend must be purchased for an entire market for a day (for example, the United States) for a flat fee. In the United States, the fee is now $200,000, up from $80,000 when Promoted Trends were first introduced in June 2010. Promoted Trends are available for purchase in 50 different countries, enabling Twitter to increase its revenue stream.

In October 2010, Twitter launched Promoted Accounts, which are suggestions to follow various advertiser accounts based on the list of accounts that the user already

SOURCES: "Twitter Stats," Business.twitter.com/basics/ what_is_twitter," July 15, 2013; "Twitter Amplify Partnerships: Great Content, Great Brands, Great Engagement," by Glenn Brown, blog.twitter.com, May 23, 2013; "TV Ad Targeting Uses 'Video Fingerprinting'," by Christopher Heine, Adweek.com, May 23, 2013; "Twitter's Latest Buy: Big Data Startup Lucky Sort," by Daniel follows. Like Promoted Tweets, Promoted Accounts can be geo-targeted at both the country level and the Nielsen DMA (Designated Marketing Area, roughly equivalent to a city and its suburb) level. Promoted Accounts are priced on a cost-per-follower basis, with advertisers only paying for new followers gained. Prices range from $.50 to a maximum of $2.50. Twitter added Enhanced Profile Pages for brands in February 2012. For a reported $15,000 to $25,000, companies get their own banner to display images, and the ability to pin a tweet to the top of the company's Twitter stream. In March 2012, Twitter began testing Promoted Tweets and Promoted Accounts on iOS and Android devices, and by June 2012 was reporting that it was generating the majority of its revenues from ads on mobile devices rather than on its Web site. This is one of the reasons why investors are so "bullish" on Twitter's prospects.

In 2013, Twitter began a natural progression into the video ad market. Video clips that include video ads can now be embedded within tweets. Known as the Twitter Amplify program, in May 2013, Twitter announced an extension of the program that will include a number of major advertisers, including Conde Nast, MLB.com, Warner Music, and others. In May 2013, Twitter launched a beta version of a television ad targeting product that allows marketers to show Promoted Tweets to people who have been tweeting about a television show. The product leverages "video fingerprinting" technology created by Bluefin Labs, which Twitter acquired in February 2013 for $90 million.

Another monetizing service is real-time search. If there's one thing Twitter has uniquely among all the social network sites, it's real-time information. In 2010, Twitter entered into agreements with Google, Microsoft, and Yahoo to permit these search engines to index tweets and make them available to the entire Internet. This service gives free real-time content to the search engines as opposed to archival content. It is unclear who's doing whom a service here, and the financial arrangements are not public. Microsoft extended the deal for two years in September 2011, but Google let its deal with Twitter expire.

Other large players are experimenting. Dell created a Twitter outlet account, @DellOutlet, and is using it to sell open-box and discontinued computers. Dell also maintains several customer service accounts. Twitter could charge such accounts a commission on sales because Twitter is acting like an e-commerce sales platform similar to Amazon. Other firms have used their Twitter follower fan base to market discount air tickets (JetBlue) and greeting cards (Someecards).

Freemium is another possibility. Twitter could ask users to pay a subscription fee for premium services such as videos and music downloads. However, it may be too late for this idea because users have come to expect the service to be free.

But perhaps the biggest treasure trove that Twitter has still not quite figured out how to monetize is its database of billions of real-time tweets. Twitter is a fabulous listening post on the Internet frontier, and helping firms understand how their customers are reacting to products, services, and marketing efforts could provide a bonanza. In May 2013, Twitter purchased big data start-up Lucky Sort, hoping that it would help it in that effort.

Terdiman, News.cnet.com, May 13, 2013; "A Guide to the Twitter Advertising Ecosystem," by Alex Cocotas, *Business Insider*, May 9, 2013; "Mapping the Global Twitter Heartbeat: The Geography of Twitter," by Kalev H. Leetaru et al., *First Monday*, May 6, 2013; "Twitter's New Video Plan: Ads, Brought to You by Ads," by Peter Kafka, Allthingsd.com, April 16, 2013; "Twitter Forecast Up After Strong Mobile Showing," eMarketer.com, March 28, 2013; "Report: Twitter Now Charges $200,000 for Promoted Trends," by Seth Fiegerman, Mashable.com, February 11, 2013; "Twitter Embraces Changing Identity," by Nick Bilton, *New York Times*, July 30, 2012; "Analyst: Twitter Passed 500M Users in June 2012, 140M of Them in US; Jakarta 'Biggest Tweeting' City," by Ingrid Lunden, Techcrunch.com, July 30, 2012; "Apple Officials Said to Consider Stake in Twitter," by Evelyn M. Rusli and Nick Bilton, *New York Times*, July 27, 2012; "Twitter's Mobile Ads Begin to Click," by Shira Ovide, *Wall Street Journal*, June 28, 2012; "Microsoft's Bing Extends Twitter Search Deal," by David Roe, Cmswire.com, September 2011; "40 Fast Facts on Twitter," by Jennifer Lawinski, August 8, 2011; "Twitter Raises Big Bucks to Buy Back Shares," Denverpost.com, July 23, 2011; "How Twitter Makes Money," by Harry Gold, ClickZ.com, April 26, 2011; "Twitter to Launch Geo-targeted Promoted Tweets and Data for Marketers," by Sarah Shearnman, Brandrepublic.com, April 7, 2011; "Twitter Users: A Vocal Minority," by Paul Verna, eMarketer, March 2011; "Twitter as Tech Bubble Barometer," by Spencer E. Ante, Amir Efrati, and Anupreeta Das, *Wall Street Journal*, February 10, 2011; "Promoted Promotions," Blog.twitter.com, October 4, 2010; "The Blogosphere: Colliding with Social and Mainstream Media," by Paul Verna, eMarketer, September 21, 2010; "Will Twitter's Ad Strategy Work," by Erica Naone, *Technology Review*, April 15, 2010; "Twitter Rolls Out Ads," by Jessica Vascellaro and Emily Steel, *Wall Street Journal*, April 14, 2010.

The story of Twitter illustrates the difficulties of turning a good business idea with a huge audience into a successful business model that produces revenues and even profits.

Thousands of firms have discovered that they can spend other people's invested capital much faster than they can get customers to pay for their products or services. In most instances of failure, the business model of the firm is faulty from the beginning. In contrast, successful e-commerce firms have business models that are able to leverage the unique qualities of the Internet, the Web, and the mobile platform, provide customers real value, develop highly effective and efficient operations, avoid legal and social entanglements that can harm the firm, and produce profitable business results. In addition, successful business models must scale. The business must be able to achieve efficiencies as it grows in volume. But what is a business model, and how can you tell if a firm's business model is going to produce a profit?

In this chapter, we focus on business models and basic business concepts that you must be familiar with in order to understand e-commerce.

2.1   E-COMMERCE BUSINESS MODELS

INTRODUCTION

business model
a set of planned activities designed to result in a profit in a marketplace

business plan
a document that describes a firm's business model

e-commerce business model
a business model that aims to use and leverage the unique qualities of the Internet and the World Wide Web

A **business model** is a set of planned activities (sometimes referred to as *business processes*) designed to result in a profit in a marketplace. A business model is not always the same as a business strategy, although in some cases they are very close insofar as the business model explicitly takes into account the competitive environment (Magretta, 2002). The business model is at the center of the business plan. A **business plan** is a document that describes a firm's business model. A business plan always takes into account the competitive environment. An **e-commerce business model** aims to use and leverage the unique qualities of the Internet, the Web, and the mobile platform.

EIGHT KEY ELEMENTS OF A BUSINESS MODEL

If you hope to develop a successful business model in any arena, not just e-commerce, you must make sure that the model effectively addresses the eight elements listed in **Figure 2.1**. These elements are value proposition, revenue model, market opportunity, competitive environment, competitive advantage, market strategy, organizational development, and management team. Many writers focus on a firm's value proposition and revenue model. While these may be the most important and most easily identifiable aspects of a company's business model, the other elements are equally important when evaluating business models and plans, or when attempting to understand why a particular company has succeeded or failed (Kim and Mauborgne, 2000). In the following sections, we describe each of the key business model elements more fully.

FIGURE 2.1 THE EIGHT KEY ELEMENTS OF A BUSINESS MODEL

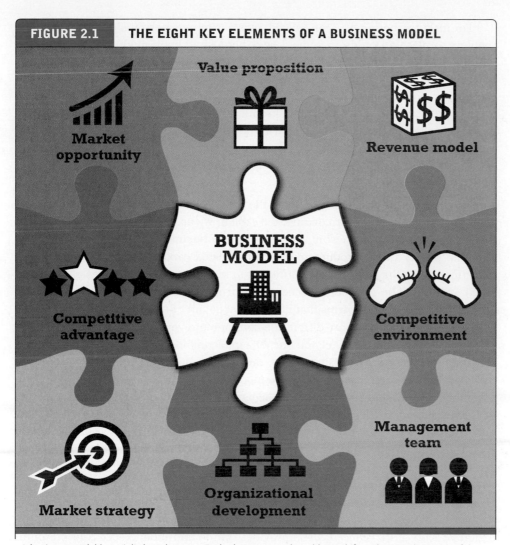

A business model has eight key elements. Each element must be addressed if you hope to be successful.

Value Proposition

A company's value proposition is at the very heart of its business model. A **value proposition** defines how a company's product or service fulfills the needs of customers (Kambil, Ginsberg, and Bloch, 1998). To develop and/or analyze a firm's value proposition, you need to understand why customers will choose to do business with the firm instead of another company and what the firm provides that other firms do not and cannot. From the consumer point of view, successful e-commerce value propositions include personalization and customization of product offerings, reduction of product search costs, reduction of price discovery costs, and facilitation of transactions by managing product delivery (Kambil, 1997; Bakos, 1998).

value proposition
defines how a company's product or service fulfills the needs of customers

For instance, before Amazon existed, most customers personally traveled to book retailers to place an order. In some cases, the desired book might not be available, and the customer would have to wait several days or weeks, and then return to the bookstore to pick it up. Amazon makes it possible for book lovers to shop for virtually any book in print from the comfort of their home or office, 24 hours a day, and to know immediately whether a book is in stock. Amazon's Kindle takes this one step further by making e-books instantly available with no shipping wait. Amazon's primary value propositions are unparalleled selection and convenience.

Revenue Model

revenue model

describes how the firm will earn revenue, produce profits, and produce a superior return on invested capital

A firm's **revenue model** describes how the firm will earn revenue, generate profits, and produce a superior return on invested capital. We use the terms *revenue model* and *financial model* interchangeably. The function of business organizations is both to generate profits and to produce returns on invested capital that exceed alternative investments. Profits alone are not sufficient to make a company "successful" (Porter, 1985). In order to be considered successful, a firm must produce returns greater than alternative investments. Firms that fail this test go out of existence.

Although there are many different e-commerce revenue models that have been developed, most companies rely on one, or some combination, of the following major revenue models: the advertising model, the subscription model, the transaction fee model, the sales model, and the affiliate model.

advertising revenue model

a company provides a forum for advertisements and receives fees from advertisers

In the **advertising revenue model**, a company that offers content, services, and/or products also provides a forum for advertisements and receives fees from advertisers. Companies that are able to attract the greatest viewership or that have a highly specialized, differentiated viewership and are able to retain user attention ("stickiness") are able to charge higher advertising rates. Yahoo, for instance, derives a significant amount of revenue from display and video advertising.

subscription revenue model

a company offers its users content or services and charges a subscription fee for access to some or all of its offerings

In the **subscription revenue model**, a company that offers content or services charges a subscription fee for access to some or all of its offerings. For instance, the digital version of *Consumer Reports* provides online and mobile access to premium content, such as detailed ratings, reviews, and recommendations, only to subscribers, who have a choice of paying a $6.95 monthly subscription fee or a $30.00 annual fee. Experience with the subscription revenue model indicates that to successfully overcome the disinclination of users to pay for content, the content offered must be perceived as a high-value-added, premium offering that is not readily available elsewhere nor easily replicated. Companies successfully offering content or services online on a subscription basis include Match.com and eHarmony (dating services), Ancestry.com (see **Figure 2.2**) and Genealogy.com (genealogy research), Microsoft's Xboxlive.com (video games), Rhapsody.com (music), and Hulu.com.

transaction fee revenue model

a company receives a fee for enabling or executing a transaction

In the **transaction fee revenue model**, a company receives a fee for enabling or executing a transaction. For example, eBay provides an auction marketplace and receives a small transaction fee from a seller if the seller is successful in selling the item. E*Trade, a financial services provider, receives transaction fees each time it executes a stock transaction on behalf of a customer.

FIGURE 2.2 **ANCESTRY.COM SUBSCRIPTION SERVICES**

Ancestry.com offers a variety of different membership options for different subscription fees.
SOURCE: Ancestry.com, 2012.

In the **sales revenue model**, companies derive revenue by selling goods, content, or services to customers. Companies such as Amazon (which sells books, music, and other products), LLBean.com, and Gap.com all have sales revenue models.

In the **affiliate revenue model**, companies that steer business to an "affiliate" receive a referral fee or percentage of the revenue from any resulting sales. For example, MyPoints makes money by connecting companies with potential customers by offering special deals to its members. When they take advantage of an offer and make a purchase, members earn "points" they can redeem for freebies, and MyPoints receives a fee. Community feedback companies such as Epinions receive much of their revenue from steering potential customers to Web sites where they make a purchase.

Table 2.1 on page 64 summarizes these major revenue models. The *Insight on Society* case, *Foursquare: Check Your Privacy at the Door,* examines some of the issues associated with Foursquare's business and revenue model.

Market Opportunity

The term **market opportunity** refers to the company's intended **marketspace** (i.e., an area of actual or potential commercial value) and the overall potential financial opportunities available to the firm in that marketspace. The market opportunity is

sales revenue model
a company derives revenue by selling goods, information, or services

affiliate revenue model
a company steers business to an affiliate and receives a referral fee or percentage of the revenue from any resulting sales

market opportunity
refers to the company's intended marketspace and the overall potential financial opportunities available to the firm in that marketspace

marketspace
the area of actual or potential commercial value in which a company intends to operate

INSIGHT ON SOCIETY

FOURSQUARE: CHECK YOUR PRIVACY AT THE DOOR

Foursquare is one of a host of companies that combine a social network business model with location-based technology. Foursquare's niche: a mobile social application that allows you to check in to a restaurant or other location, and automatically lets friends on Facebook and other programs learn where you are. If you're in a new town, the app transmits your location and sends you information about popular spots close by, with reviews from other Foursquare users. After starting up Foursquare on a smartphone, you'll see a list of local bars and restaurants based on your cell phone's GPS position. Select a location, "check in," and a message is sent to your friends. Enhancements to the original Foursquare app allow you to be directed to a new location, browse locations by category, conduct specific searches, and discover recently opened locations in your area. Foursquare also has a widely accepted loyalty program. Each check-in awards you points and badges. Visitors compete to become "Mayors" of a venue based on how many times they have checked in over a month's time. Mayors receive special offers.

Foursquare was founded by Dennis Crowley and Naveen Selvadurai. They began building the first version of the application in Fall 2008, originally working in the kitchen of Crowley's East Village New York apartment. They debuted the application at the South by Southwest Interactive Festival in March 2009, and soon attracted venture capital. As of July 2013, Foursquare had over 33 million members worldwide, split fairly evenly between the United States and the rest of the world, who have checked in over 3.5 billion times.

Foursquare shares many similarities with other social networks like Facebook and Twitter, which began operating without a revenue model in place. Like those companies, Foursquare has been able to command high valuations from venture capital investors (reportedly as high as $760 million at one point), despite its lack of significant revenue or profit. How is this possible? The answer lies in the coupling of its social network business model with smartphone-based technology that can identify where you are located within a few yards. There's potentially a great deal of money to be made from knowing where you are. Location-based data has extraordinary commercial value because advertisers can then send you advertisements, coupons, and flash bargains, based on where you are located. The revenue from location-based marketing and advertising is expected to rise to 6.5 billion by 2017.

Just as Facebook and Twitter are monetizing their user bases with an advertising-based, social retail-based revenue model, so too is Foursquare. In June 2011, Foursquare partnered with American Express to offer discounts to cardholders when they check in on their cell phone to certain shops and restaurants. In July 2012, Foursquare announced the next steps in the monetization of its business model: Local Updates and Promoted Updates (now called Foursquare Ads). Local Updates allow retailers to deliver geo-targeted offers and messages to customers, while Foursquare Ads, similar to Twitter's Promoted Tweets, are geo-targeted paid advertisements. People are shown ads based on their location and how likely they are to become customers, based on their previous check-in behavior. In April 2013, Foursquare announced it was working on a new ad product that will use its location and behavioral data to retarget ads to users on third-party Web sites. Foursquare claims it will not target users on an individual basis, but rather place users into various consumer segments, such as "luxury"

(continued)

or "business traveler," allowing advertisers to serve those users display and video ads based on those segments. Foursquare hopes this new initiative will help increase its revenue beyond the $2 million it reportedly earned in 2012.

As the popularity of location-based services like Foursquare has grown, so too have concerns about privacy. The revelations by the *Wall Street Journal* in Spring 2011 that Apple and Google were surreptitiously and continuously collecting personal, private location data from iPhone and Android phones spurred privacy groups and Congress to launch investigations. In June 2011, the Federal Communications Commission, in cooperation with the Federal Trade Commission, sponsored a forum to discuss the social impact of location-based services, both positive and negative. Industry representatives from Facebook, Google, and Foursquare argued that existing apps as well as corporate policies were adequate to protect personal privacy because they rely on user permissions to share location (opt-in services). The industry argued as well that consumers get real benefits from sharing location data, otherwise they would not voluntarily give this data. Privacy advocates pointed out that many apps have no privacy policy, that most of the popular apps transmit location data to their developers after which the information is not well controlled, and that these services are creating a situation where government, marketers, creditors, and telecommunications firms will end up knowing nearly everything about citizens, including their whereabouts.

As a case in point, in April 2012, Foursquare was hit by a privacy landmine when an app called Girls Around Me surfaced that used Foursquare's application programming interface to show photos of women currently checked in around a particular neighborhood by pulling public photos of the women from their Facebook profiles linked to their Foursquare accounts. Foursquare quickly shut down the app and shortly thereafter made changes to its API to eliminate the ability of users to see strangers checked into a venue without being checked into the same place themselves. Illustrating the continuing issues Foursquare faces on the privacy front, the version of its mobile app introduced in June 2012 allowed users to see all of their friends' check-ins from the prior two weeks. As the ACLU noted, historical location data can reveal far more about a person than can individual location records. Many users may not truly understand how much of their location history is available to their friends. Nor is there an easy way for users to control the visibility of their location history—users are limited to either deleting specific check-ins individually or being off the grid completely.

In December 2012, Foursquare announced further changes to its privacy policy. It now shows a user's full name and also allows businesses to access data logs for individuals for a longer period of time. These changes tie into its monetization efforts—the more data Foursquare collects on its users, the more attractive its advertising products are likely to be. Although Foursquare does make it possible to customize privacy settings, its revenue model relies on the fact that most users will not.

SOURCES: "About Foursquare," Foursquare.com, accessed July 31, 2013; "Foursquare Selling Its Location Data Through Ad Targeting Firm Turn," Adage.com, July 31, 2013; "Location-Based Advertising and Marketing—2nd Edition, by Berg Insight AB, April 18, 2013; "Foursquare Planning to Offer Check-in Data to Target Ads on Other Platforms," Adage.com, April 12, 2013; "Foursquare to Start Using Full Names, Sharing More of Your Data with Venues from January 28, According to New Privacy Policy," by Ingrid Lunden, Techcrunch.com, December 30, 2012; "Three Reasons Why Foursquare's New Advertising Model Might Work," by Anne Marie Kelly, *Forbes*, August 22, 2012; "Foursquare Will Test Paid Ads," by Stuart Elliott, *New York Times*, July 25, 2012; "Wrap Up on Privacy and Location Based Services," by Prof. Peter Swire, Ohio State University, FCC Forum: Helping Consumers Harness the Potential of Location Based Services, June 28, 2011; "Technology and Privacy," by Prof. Matt Blaze, University of Pennsylvania, FCC Forum: Helping Consumers Harness the Potential of Location Based Services, June 28, 2011; "Companies Try to Allay Fears at FCC-FTC Hearing," by Brad Reed, *Network World*, June 28, 2011; "A Start-Up Matures, Working With AmEx," by Jenna Wortham, *New York Times*, June 22, 2011; "Apple, Google Collect User Data," by Julia Angwin and Jennifer Valentino-Devries, *Wall Street Journal*, April 22, 2011; "Telling Friends Where You Are (or Not)," by Jenna Wortham, *New York Times*, March 14, 2010.

TABLE 2.1	FIVE PRIMARY REVENUE MODELS	
REVENUE MODEL	EXAMPLES	REVENUE SOURCE
Advertising	Yahoo	Fees from advertisers in exchange for advertisements
Subscription	WSJ.com Consumerreports.org	Fees from subscribers in exchange for access to content or services
Transaction Fee	eBay E*Trade	Fees (commissions) for enabling or executing a transaction
Sales	Amazon L.L.Bean Gap iTunes	Sales of goods, information, or services
Affiliate	MyPoints	Fees for business referrals

usually divided into smaller market niches. The realistic market opportunity is defined by the revenue potential in each of the market niches where you hope to compete.

For instance, let's assume you are analyzing a software training company that creates online software-learning systems for sale to businesses. The overall size of the software training market for all market segments is approximately $70 billion. The overall market can be broken down, however, into two major market segments: instructor-led training products, which comprise about 70% of the market ($49 billion in revenue), and computer-based training, which accounts for 30% ($21 billion). There are further market niches within each of those major market segments, such as the Fortune 500 computer-based training market and the small business computer-based training market. Because the firm is a start-up firm, it cannot compete effectively in the large business, computer-based training market (about $15 billion). Large brand-name training firms dominate this niche. The start-up firm's real market opportunity is to sell to the thousands of small business firms that spend about $6 billion on computer-based software training. This is the size of the firm's realistic market opportunity (see **Figure 2.3**).

Competitive Environment

competitive environment

refers to the other companies operating in the same marketspace selling similar products

A firm's **competitive environment** refers to the other companies selling similar products and operating in the same marketspace. It also refers to the presence of substitute products and potential new entrants to the market, as well as the power of customers and suppliers over your business. We discuss the firm's environment later in the chapter. The competitive environment for a company is influenced by several factors: how many competitors are active, how large their operations are, what the market share of each competitor is, how profitable these firms are, and how they price their products.

Firms typically have both direct and indirect competitors. Direct competitors are companies that sell products and services that are very similar and into the same

FIGURE 2.3 | **MARKETSPACE AND MARKET OPPORTUNITY IN THE SOFTWARE TRAINING MARKET**

Small Business
$19 Billion

Small Business
$6 Billion

Instructor-Led
Training
$49 Billion

Computer-Based
Training
$21 Billion

Fortune 500
$15 Billion

Fortune 500
$30 Billion

Marketspaces are composed of many market segments. Your realistic market opportunity will typically focus on one or a few market segments.

market segment. For example, Priceline and Travelocity, both of whom sell discount airline tickets online, are direct competitors because both companies sell identical products—cheap tickets. Indirect competitors are companies that may be in different industries but still compete indirectly because their products can substitute for one another. For instance, automobile manufacturers and airline companies operate in different industries, but they still compete indirectly because they offer consumers alternative means of transportation. CNN.com, a news outlet, is an indirect competitor of ESPN.com, not because they sell identical products, but because they both compete for consumers' time online.

The existence of a large number of competitors in any one segment may be a sign that the market is saturated and that it may be difficult to become profitable. On the other hand, a lack of competitors could either signal an untapped market niche ripe for the picking, or a market that has already been tried without success because there is no money to be made. Analysis of the competitive environment can help you decide which it is.

Competitive Advantage

Firms achieve a **competitive advantage** when they can produce a superior product and/or bring the product to market at a lower price than most, or all, of their competitors (Porter, 1985). Firms also compete on scope. Some firms can develop global markets, while other firms can develop only a national or regional market. Firms that can provide superior products at the lowest cost on a global basis are truly advantaged.

Firms achieve competitive advantages because they have somehow been able to obtain differential access to the factors of production that are denied to their competitors—at least in the short term (Barney, 1991). Perhaps the firm has been

competitive advantage
achieved by a firm when it can produce a superior product and/or bring the product to market at a lower price than most, or all, of its competitors

asymmetry

exists whenever one participant in a market has more resources than other participants

first-mover advantage

a competitive market advantage for a firm that results from being the first into a marketplace with a serviceable product or service

complementary resources

resources and assets not directly involved in the production of the product but required for success, such as marketing, management, financial assets, and reputation

unfair competitive advantage

occurs when one firm develops an advantage based on a factor that other firms cannot purchase

perfect market

a market in which there are no competitive advantages or asymmetries because all firms have equal access to all the factors of production

leverage

when a company uses its competitive advantages to achieve more advantage in surrounding markets

able to obtain very favorable terms from suppliers, shippers, or sources of labor. Or perhaps the firm has more experienced, knowledgeable, and loyal employees than any competitors. Maybe the firm has a patent on a product that others cannot imitate, or access to investment capital through a network of former business colleagues or a brand name and popular image that other firms cannot duplicate. An **asymmetry** exists whenever one participant in a market has more resources—financial backing, knowledge, information, and/or power—than other participants. Asymmetries lead to some firms having an edge over others, permitting them to come to market with better products, faster than competitors, and sometimes at lower cost.

For instance, when Apple announced iTunes, a service offering legal, downloadable individual song tracks for 99 cents a track that would be playable on any digital device with iTunes software, the company had better-than-average odds of success simply because of Apple's prior success with innovative hardware designs, and the large stable of music firms that Apple had meticulously lined up to support its online music catalog. Few competitors could match the combination of cheap, legal songs and powerful hardware to play them on.

One rather unique competitive advantage derives from being a first mover. A **first-mover advantage** is a competitive market advantage for a firm that results from being the first into a marketplace with a serviceable product or service. If first movers develop a loyal following or a unique interface that is difficult to imitate, they can sustain their first-mover advantage for long periods (Arthur, 1996). Amazon provides a good example. However, in the history of technology-driven business innovation, most first movers often lack the **complementary resources** needed to sustain their advantages, and often follower firms reap the largest rewards (Rigdon, 2000; Teece, 1986). Indeed, many of the success stories we discuss in this book are those of companies that were slow followers—businesses that gained knowledge from failure of pioneering firms and entered into the market late.

Some competitive advantages are called "unfair." An **unfair competitive advantage** occurs when one firm develops an advantage based on a factor that other firms cannot purchase (Barney, 1991). For instance, a brand name cannot be purchased and is in that sense an "unfair" advantage. Brands are built upon loyalty, trust, reliability, and quality. Once obtained, they are difficult to copy or imitate, and they permit firms to charge premium prices for their products.

In **perfect markets**, there are no competitive advantages or asymmetries because all firms have access to all the factors of production (including information and knowledge) equally. However, real markets are imperfect, and asymmetries leading to competitive advantages do exist, at least in the short term. Most competitive advantages are short term, although some can be sustained for very long periods. But not forever. In fact, many respected brands fail every year.

Companies are said to **leverage** their competitive assets when they use their competitive advantages to achieve more advantage in surrounding markets. For instance, Amazon's move into the online grocery business leverages the company's huge customer database and years of e-commerce experience.

Market Strategy

No matter how tremendous a firm's qualities, its marketing strategy and execution are often just as important. The best business concept, or idea, will fail if it is not properly marketed to potential customers.

Everything you do to promote your company's products and services to potential customers is known as marketing. **Market strategy** is the plan you put together that details exactly how you intend to enter a new market and attract new customers.

For instance, Twitter, YouTube, and Pinterest have a social network marketing strategy that encourages users to post their content on the sites for free, build personal profile pages, contact their friends, and build a community. In these cases, the customer becomes part of the marketing staff!

market strategy
the plan you put together that details exactly how you intend to enter a new market and attract new customers

Organizational Development

Although many entrepreneurial ventures are started by one visionary individual, it is rare that one person alone can grow an idea into a multi-million dollar company. In most cases, fast-growth companies—especially e-commerce businesses—need employees and a set of business procedures. In short, all firms—new ones in particular—need an organization to efficiently implement their business plans and strategies. Many e-commerce firms and many traditional firms that attempt an e-commerce strategy have failed because they lacked the organizational structures and supportive cultural values required to support new forms of commerce (Kanter, 2001).

Companies that hope to grow and thrive need to have a plan for **organizational development** that describes how the company will organize the work that needs to be accomplished. Typically, work is divided into functional departments, such as production, shipping, marketing, customer support, and finance. Jobs within these functional areas are defined, and then recruitment begins for specific job titles and responsibilities. Typically, in the beginning, generalists who can perform multiple tasks are hired. As the company grows, recruiting becomes more specialized. For instance, at the outset, a business may have one marketing manager. But after two or three years of steady growth, that one marketing position may be broken down into seven separate jobs done by seven individuals.

organizational development
plan describes how the company will organize the work that needs to be accomplished

For instance, eBay founder Pierre Omidyar started an online auction site, according to some sources, to help his girlfriend trade Pez dispensers with other collectors, but within a few months the volume of business had far exceeded what he alone could handle. So he began hiring people with more business experience to help out. Soon the company had many employees, departments, and managers who were responsible for overseeing the various aspects of the organization.

Management Team

Arguably, the single most important element of a business model is the **management team** responsible for making the model work. A strong management team gives a model instant credibility to outside investors, immediate market-specific knowledge, and experience in implementing business plans. A strong management team may not

management team
employees of the company responsible for making the business model work

be able to salvage a weak business model, but the team should be able to change the model and redefine the business as it becomes necessary.

Eventually, most companies get to the point of having several senior executives or managers. How skilled managers are, however, can be a source of competitive advantage or disadvantage. The challenge is to find people who have both the experience and the ability to apply that experience to new situations.

To be able to identify good managers for a business start-up, first consider the kinds of experiences that would be helpful to a manager joining your company. What kind of technical background is desirable? What kind of supervisory experience is necessary? How many years in a particular function should be required? What job functions should be fulfilled first: marketing, production, finance, or operations? Especially in situations where financing will be needed to get a company off the ground, do prospective senior managers have experience and contacts for raising financing from outside investors?

Table 2.2 summarizes the eight key elements of a business model and the key questions that must be answered in order to successfully develop each element.

RAISING CAPITAL

seed capital

typically, an entrepreneur's personal funds derived from savings, credit card advances, home equity loans, or from family and friends

Raising capital is one of the most important functions for a founder of a start-up business and its management team. Not having enough capital to operate effectively is a primary reason why so many start-up businesses fail. Many entrepreneurs initially "bootstrap" to get a business off the ground, using personal funds derived from savings, credit card advances, home equity loans, or from family and friends. Funds of this type are often referred to as **seed capital**. Once such funds are exhausted, if the

TABLE 2.2	KEY ELEMENTS OF A BUSINESS MODEL
COMPONENTS	KEY QUESTIONS
Value proposition	Why should the customer buy from you?
Revenue model	How will you earn money?
Market opportunity	What marketspace do you intend to serve, and what is its size?
Competitive environment	Who else occupies your intended marketspace?
Competitive advantage	What special advantages does your firm bring to the marketspace?
Market strategy	How do you plan to promote your products or services to attract your target audience?
Organizational development	What types of organizational structures within the firm are necessary to carry out the business plan?
Management team	What kinds of experiences and background are important for the company's leaders to have?

company is not generating enough revenue to cover operating costs, additional capital will be needed. Traditional sources of capital include incubators, commercial banks, angel investors, venture capital firms, and strategic partners.

Incubators (sometimes also referred to as accelerators) such as Y-Combinator (profiled in Chapter 1's Insight on Business case) typically provide a small amount of funding, but more importantly, also provide an array of services to start-up companies that they select to participate in their programs, such as business, technical, and marketing assistance, as well as introductions to other sources of capital. Well-known incubator programs include TechStars, DreamIt Ventures, and Capital Factory.

Obtaining a loan from a commercial bank is often difficult for a start-up company without much revenue, but it may be worthwhile to investigate programs offered by the U.S. Small Business Administration, and its state or local equivalents. The advantage of obtaining capital in the form of a loan (debt) is that, although it must be repaid, it does not require an entrepreneur to give up any ownership of the company.

Angel investors are typically wealthy individuals (or a group of individuals) who invest their own money in an exchange for an equity share in the stock in the business. In general, angel investors make smaller investments (typically $1 million or less) than venture capital firms, are interested in helping a company grow and succeed, and invest on relatively favorable terms compared to later stage investors. The first round of external investment in a company is sometimes referred to as Series A financing.

Venture capital investors typically become more interested in a start-up company once it has begun generating some revenue, even if it is not profitable. **Venture capital investors** invest funds they manage for other investors such as investment banks, pension funds, insurance companies, or other businesses, and usually want to obtain a larger stake in the business and exercise more control over the operation of the business. Venture capital investors also typically want a well-defined "exit strategy," such as a plan for an initial public offering or acquisition of the company by a more established business within a relatively short period of time (typically 3 to 7 years), that will enable them to obtain an adequate return on their investment. Venture capital investment often ultimately means that the founder(s) and initial investors will no longer control the company at some point in the future.

A new method for start-ups to raise capital is just around the corner. **Crowdfunding** involves using the Internet to enable individuals to collectively contribute their money to support various projects. The concepts behind crowdfunding have been popularized by Kickstarter and Indiegogo (see the *Insight on Business* case, *Crowdfunding Takes Off*), but they were not able to be used for equity investments in for-profit companies in the United States due to securities regulations. However, the passage of the Jumpstart Our Business Startups (JOBS) Act in 2012 and issuance of enabling regulations by the Securities and Exchange Commission in July 2013 will now enable companies to begin to use the Internet to solicit wealthy ("accredited") investors to invest in small and early-stage start-ups in exchange for stock. Equity crowdfunding investments by non-accredited investors, although approved by the JOBS Act in concept, will not be allowed until the SEC passes further implementing regulations.

incubators
typically provide a small amount of funding and also an array of services to start-up companies

angel investors
typically wealthy individuals or a group of individuals who invest their own money in exchange for an equity share in the stock of a business; often are the first outside investors in a start-up

venture capital investors
typically invest funds they manage for other investors; usually later-stage investors

crowdfunding
involves using the Internet to enable individuals to collectively contribute their money to support a project

INSIGHT ON BUSINESS

CROWDFUNDING TAKES OFF

Think you have the next big idea but lack the resources to make it happen? Crowdfunding sites might be your best shot. Sites such as Kickstarter, Indiegogo, RocketHub, and Crowdrise have led the growth of crowdfunding from $530 million in 2009 to almost $2.7 billion in 2012, and will reach $5 billion and beyond by the start of 2014. The Internet is the ideal medium for crowdfunding because it allows individuals and organizations in need of funds and investors to reach one another from all over the globe.

How do sites like Kickstarter and Indiegogo work? The idea is simple—an inventor, artist, or activist looking to raise money for a cause uses the site to create a page for that project. People can pledge to support the project, but the money actually only changes hands once a project fully reaches its goal. Otherwise, prospective donors lose nothing out of pocket. The sites take a small commission, usually about 5 percent, on completed projects. Active campaigns are placed on the front pages of each site.

The applications for crowdfunding are diverse, from art installations, to movies, to political action projects, to inventions. All you need is an idea that investors believe is worth their money. Crowdfunding is quickly becoming a mainstay in nearly all of these fields. Kickstarter has financed more installation art projects than the National Endowment for the Arts in Washington, and several of the biggest Kickstarter projects to date have been movie projects that have struggled to gain traction at Hollywood studios, like the Veronica Mars movie project ($5.7 million) and Zach Braff's prospective film "Wish I Was Here" (3.1 million). Contributors receive special rewards corresponding to the size of their investment in the project.

Protest movements like Occupy Wall Street have also used crowdfunding to great effect, raising funds to distribute newsletters and publish print advertisements in major newspapers. Turkish protesters crowdfunded a full-page ad in the *New York Times* to raise awareness of their dissatisfaction with Prime Minister Tayyip Erdogan. They reached their set goal of $53,800 on Indiegogo with almost a full month to spare, making it the fastest political fundraising campaign in the site's history.

Not every crowdfunding project gets off the ground—Kickstarter reports that only about 44% of its projects have reached their funding goals. Sometimes projects that do get off the ground simply flame out, disappointing all of their investors. Although this is no different than investing in stocks or other equities, Kickstarter has sought to ease investor fears by improving its communication and handling of the risk inherent in the projects hosted on its site. They introduced a section where fundraisers are required to disclose the risks inherent in their project, and for inventions, the site now requires photos of prototype products instead of simply drawings, simulations, or renderings.

There also is some worry that the lack of privacy involved with donating to crowdfunding sites has a negative effect on the process. In the art world, many artists are concerned that they will make enemies within their industry if they ignore requests for crowdfunding donations, not to mention the possibility of the focus on fundraising corrupting the artistic process. However,

(continued)

the biggest donors to the Turkish protest movement were able to keep their identities secret to avoid detection by their government, and other companies have emerged that facilitate private crowdfunding investments. Some critics have also argued that those who need Kickstarter the least are the ones benefiting the most. The Veronica Mars producers and Zach Braff are well established in Hollywood, for example. Kickstarter counters that a high-profile project draws attention to the site and helps lesser-known artists in their own fundraising efforts.

The applications for crowdfunding are limited only by imagination. Kickstarter and Indiegogo have helped people pay for adoptions and fertility treatments, have enabled Olympic athletes to raise money towards their competition expenses, and have helped video game entrepreneurs get their passion projects off the ground. A cottage industry has also sprung up around crowdfunding and specific crowdfunding Web sites, including consultants who bill themselves as experts in attracting funding for Kickstarter projects via social media campaigns. Infomercial mainstay As Seen on TV is also hoping to cash in on crowdfunding, unveiling a new site where its customers can pick the products they are most interested in buying. The next Snuggie or ShamWow might be developed using crowdfunding.

A new use of crowdfunding is to provide seed capital for startup companies. Under the JOBS Act passed by Congress in 2012, a company will be able to crowdfund up to $1 million over a 12-month period. Many expect the use of crowdfunding for this purpose to skyrocket once regulations allowing it are fully implemented in 2013. Some critics worry that there will be a steep learning curve and that a period of chaos is likely to ensue, until all participants (entrepreneurs, investors, crowdfunding platforms, and regulators) become familiar with all the potential benefits and risks of equity crowdfunding. In the meantime, however, many companies, such as Crowdfunder, AngelList, and CircleUp are already laying the groundwork for an expected explosion of activity. For example, during a test period from December 2012 through April 2013, 18 start-ups raised $6.7 million in funding commitments from 620 investors via AngelList's AngelList Invest service. Niche companies are also springing up. For instance, SeedInvest is a company that caters to investors who may have privacy concerns about crowdfunding. Sometimes, when a new startup company attracts big name backers, inexperienced investors join in and cause the start-up's valuation to balloon beyond a reasonable level. With more privacy, SeedInvest argues, valuations become accurate and investing in startups becomes more orderly. SoMoLend is another niche company, focused on debt lending for small business. CircleUp is focused on consumer products. AlumniFinder is aimed at bringing alumni together to back college entrepreneurs. These are just a few of the many companies specializing in equity crowdfunding right now, but ultimately, as with most new marketspaces, these are likely to be boiled down to just a handful of survivors.

SOURCES: "SEC Finally Moves on Equity Crowdfunding, Phase 1," by Chance Barnett, Forbes.com, July 19, 2013; "Preparing for the Chaos of Equity Crowdfunding," Phys.org, July 18, 2013; Kickstarter.com, "What is Kickstarter?", accessed July 12, 2013; Indiegogo.com, "FAQ," accessed July 12, 2013; "Why Crowdfunding Hasn't Caught on in Asia," by Kurt Wagner, Tech.Fortune.com, July 8, 2013; "SeedInvest Raises $1M to Help Angels Invest Online — Privately," by Lora Kolodny, *Wall Street Journal*, June 28, 2013; "Infomercial Maker Seeks Next Snuggie Using Crowdfunding Site," by Lora Kolodny, *Wall Street Journal*, June 24, 2013; "The Trouble with Kickstarter," by Ellen Gamerman, *Wall Street Journal*, June 21, 2013; Crowdfunding Finds a Creative Outlet," by Ella Delany, *New York Times*, June 11, 2013; "Turkish Protesters Are Crowdfunding a Full-Page Ad in the New York Times," by Brian Fung, *National Journal*, June 4, 2013; "Top 10 Crowdfunding Sites for Fundraising," by Chance Barnett, Forbes.com, May 8, 2013; "AngelList Commits to Crowdfunding," by Lora Kolodny, *Wall Street Journal*, April 24, 2013; "2013 and the Evolution of Crowdfunding," Ryan Caldbeck, Forbes.com, December 26, 2012.

CATEGORIZING E-COMMERCE BUSINESS MODELS: SOME DIFFICULTIES

There are many e-commerce business models, and more are being invented every day. The number of such models is limited only by the human imagination, and our list of different business models is certainly not exhaustive. However, despite the abundance of potential models, it is possible to identify the major generic types (and subtle variations) of business models that have been developed for the e-commerce arena and describe their key features. It is important to realize, however, that there is no one correct way to categorize these business models.

Our approach is to categorize business models according to the different major e-commerce sectors—B2C and B2B—in which they are utilized. You will note, however, that fundamentally similar business models may appear in more than one sector. For example, the business models of online retailers (often called e-tailers) and e-distributors are quite similar. However, they are distinguished by the market focus of the sector in which they are used. In the case of e-tailers in the B2C sector, the business model focuses on sales to the individual consumer, while in the case of the e-distributor, the business model focuses on sales to another business. Many companies use a variety of different business models as they attempt to extend into as many areas of e-commerce as possible. We look at B2C business models in Section 2.2 and B2B business models in Section 2.3.

A business's technology platform is sometimes confused with its business model. For instance, "mobile e-commerce" refers to the use of mobile devices and cellular and wide area networks to support a variety of business models. Commentators sometimes confuse matters by referring to mobile e-commerce as a distinct business model, which it is not. All of the basic business models we discuss below can be implemented on both the traditional Internet/Web and mobile platforms. Likewise, although they are sometimes referred to as such, social e-commerce and local e-commerce are not business models in and of themselves, but rather subsectors of B2C and B2B e-commerce in which different business models can operate.

Finally, you will also note that some companies use multiple business models. For instance, Amazon has multiple business models: it is an e-retailer, content provider, market creator, e-commerce infrastructure provider, and more. eBay is a market creator in the B2C and C2C e-commerce sectors, using both the traditional Internet/Web and mobile platforms, as well as an e-commerce infrastructure provider. Firms often seek out multiple business models as a way to leverage their brands, infrastructure investments, and assets developed with one business model into new business models.

2.2 MAJOR BUSINESS-TO-CONSUMER (B2C) BUSINESS MODELS

Business-to-consumer (B2C) e-commerce, in which online businesses seek to reach individual consumers, is the most well-known and familiar type of e-commerce. **Table 2.3** illustrates the major business models utilized in the B2C arena.

TABLE 2.3	**B2C BUSINESS MODELS**			
BUSINESS MODEL	VARIATIONS	EXAMPLES	DESCRIPTION	REVENUE MODEL
E-tailer	Virtual Merchant	Amazon iTunes Bluefly	Online version of retail store, where customers can shop at any hour of the day or night without leaving their home or office	Sales of goods
	Bricks-and-Clicks	Walmart.com Sears.com	Online distribution channel for a company that also has physical stores	Sales of goods
	Catalog Merchant	LLBean.com LillianVernon.com	Online version of direct mail catalog	Sales of goods
	Manufacturer-Direct	Dell.com Mattel.com SonyStyle.com	Manufacturer uses online channel to sell direct to customer	Sales of goods
Community Provider		Facebook LinkedIn Twitter Pinterest	Sites where individuals with particular interests, hobbies, common experiences, or social networks can come together and "meet" online	Advertising, subscription, affiliate referral fees
Content Provider		WSJ.com CBSSports.com CNN.com ESPN.com Rhapsody.com	Information and entertainment providers such as newspapers, sports sites, and other online sources that offer customers up-to-date news and special interest how-to guidance and tips and/or information sales	Advertising, subscription fees, affiliate referral fees
Portal	Horizontal/General	Yahoo AOL MSN Facebook	Offers an integrated package of content, content-search, and social network services: news, e-mail, chat, music downloads, video streaming, calendars, etc. Seeks to be a user's home base	Advertising, subscription fees, transaction fees
	Vertical/Specialized (Vortal)	Sailnet	Offers services and products to specialized marketplace	Advertising, subscription fees, transaction fees
	Search	Google Bing Ask.com	Focuses primarily on offering search services	Advertising, affiliate referral
Transaction Broker		E*Trade Expedia Monster Travelocity Hotels.com Orbitz	Processors of online sales transactions, such as stockbrokers and travel agents, that increase customers' productivity by helping them get things done faster and more cheaply	Transaction fees
Market Creator		eBay Etsy Amazon Priceline	Businesses that use Internet technology to create markets that bring buyers and sellers together	Transaction fees
Service Provider		VisaNow.com Carbonite RocketLawyer	Companies that make money by selling users a service, rather than a product	Sales of services

E-TAILER

e-tailer
online retail store

Online retail stores, often called **e-tailers**, come in all sizes, from giant Amazon to tiny local stores that have Web sites. E-tailers are similar to the typical bricks-and-mortar storefront, except that customers only have to connect to the Internet or use their smartphone to place an order. Some e-tailers, which are referred to as "bricks-and-clicks," are subsidiaries or divisions of existing physical stores and carry the same products. REI, JCPenney, Barnes & Noble, Walmart, and Staples are examples of companies with complementary online stores. Others, however, operate only in the virtual world, without any ties to physical locations. Amazon, Blue Nile, and Drugstore.com are examples of this type of e-tailer. Several other variations of e-tailers—such as online versions of direct mail catalogs, online malls, and manufacturer-direct online sales—also exist.

Given that the overall retail market in the United States in 2013 is estimated to be around $3.9 trillion, the market opportunity for e-tailers is very large (Bureau of Economic Analysis, 2013). Every Internet and smartphone user is a potential customer. Customers who feel time-starved are even better prospects, since they want shopping solutions that will eliminate the need to drive to the mall or store (Bellman, Lohse, and Johnson, 1999). The e-tail revenue model is product-based, with customers paying for the purchase of a particular item.

barriers to entry
the total cost of entering a new marketplace

This sector, however, is extremely competitive. Since **barriers to entry** (the total cost of entering a new marketplace) into the e-tail market are low, tens of thousands of small e-tail shops have sprung up. Becoming profitable and surviving is very difficult, however, for e-tailers with no prior brand name or experience. The e-tailer's challenge is differentiating its business from existing competitors.

Companies that try to reach every online consumer are likely to deplete their resources quickly. Those that develop a niche strategy, clearly identifying their target market and its needs, are best prepared to make a profit. Keeping expenses low, selection broad, and inventory controlled are keys to success in e-tailing, with inventory being the most difficult to gauge. Online retail is covered in more depth in Chapter 9.

COMMUNITY PROVIDER

community provider
creates an online environment where people with similar interests can transact (buy and sell goods); share interests, photos, and videos; communicate with like-minded people; and receive interest-related information

Although community providers are not a new phenomenon, the Internet has made such sites for like-minded individuals to meet and converse much easier, without the limitations of geography and time to hinder participation. **Community providers** create an online environment where people with similar interests can transact (buy and sell goods); share interests, photos, videos; communicate with like-minded people; receive interest-related information; and even play out fantasies by adopting online personalities called avatars. The social network sites Facebook, LinkedIn, Twitter, and Pinterest, and hundreds of other smaller, niche sites all offer users community-building tools and services.

The basic value proposition of community providers is to create a fast, convenient, one-stop site where users can focus on their most important concerns and interests, share the experience with friends, and learn more about their own interests. Community providers typically rely on a hybrid revenue model that includes subscription fees, sales revenues, transaction fees, affiliate fees, and advertising fees from other firms that are attracted by a tightly focused audience.

Community sites such as iVillage make money through affiliate relationships with retailers and from advertising. For instance, a parent might visit RightStart.com for tips on diapering a baby and be presented with a link to Huggies.com; if the parent clicks the link and then makes a purchase from Huggies.com, RightStart gets a commission. Likewise, banner ads also generate revenue. Some of the oldest online communities are The Well (Well.com), which provides a forum for technology and Internet-related discussions, and The Motley Fool (Fool.com), which provides financial advice, news, and opinions. The Well offers various membership plans ranging from $10 to $15 a month. Motley Fool supports itself through ads and selling products that start out "free" but turn into annual subscriptions.

Consumers' interest in communities is mushrooming. Community is, arguably, the fastest growing online activity. While many community sites have had a difficult time becoming profitable, many have succeeded over time, with advertising as their main source of revenue. Both the very large social network sites such as Facebook, Twitter, and LinkedIn, as well as niche sites with smaller dedicated audiences, are ideal marketing and advertising territories. Traditional online communities such as The Well, iVillage, and WebMD (which provides medical information to members) find that breadth and depth of knowledge at a site is an important factor. Community members frequently request knowledge, guidance, and advice. Lack of experienced personnel can severely hamper the growth of a community, which needs facilitators and managers to keep discussions on course and relevant. For the newer community social network sites, the most important ingredients of success appear to be ease and flexibility of use, and a strong customer value proposition. For instance, Facebook leapfrogged over its rival MySpace by encouraging the development of third-party revenue-producing applications.

Online communities benefit significantly from offline word-of-mouth, viral marketing. Online communities tend to reflect offline relationships. When your friends say they have a profile on Facebook, and ask you to "friend" them, you are encouraged to build your own online profile.

CONTENT PROVIDER

Content providers distribute information content, such as digital video, music, photos, text, and artwork. It is estimated that U.S. consumers will spend more than $24 billion for online content such as movies, music, videos, television shows, e-books, and newspapers during 2013.

Content providers make money by charging a subscription fee. For instance, in the case of Rhapsody.com, a monthly subscription fee provides users with access to thousands of music tracks. Other content providers, such as WSJ.com (the *Wall Street Journal* online newspaper), *Harvard Business Review*, and many others, charge customers for content downloads in addition to, or in place of, a subscription fee.

Of course, not all online content providers charge for their information: just look at CBSSports.com, CIO.com, CNN.com, and the online versions of many newspapers and magazines. Users can access news and information at these sites without paying a

content provider
distributes information content, such as digital news, music, photos, video, and artwork

cent, although sometimes they may be required to register as a member. These popular sites make money in other ways, such as through advertising and partner promotions on the site. Increasingly, however, "free content" may be limited to headlines and text, whereas premium content—in-depth articles or videos—is sold for a fee.

Generally, the key to becoming a successful content provider is owning the content. Traditional owners of copyrighted content—publishers of books and newspapers, broadcasters of radio and television content, music publishers, and movie studios—have powerful advantages over newcomers who simply offer distribution channels and must pay for content, often at very high prices.

Some content providers, however, do not own content, but syndicate (aggregate) and then distribute content produced by others. *Syndication* is a major variation of the standard content provider model. Aggregators, who collect information from a wide variety of sources and then add value to that information through post-aggregation services, are another variation. For instance, Shopping.com collects information on the prices of thousands of goods online, analyzes the information, and presents users with tables showing the range of prices and links to the sites where the products can be purchased. Shopping.com adds value to content it aggregates, and resells this value to advertisers who advertise on its site.

Any e-commerce start-up that intends to make money by providing content is likely to face difficulties unless it has a unique information source that others cannot access. For the most part, this business category is dominated by traditional content providers. The *Insight on Technology* case, *Battle of the Titans: Music in the Cloud,* discusses how changes in Internet technology are driving the development of new business models in the online content market by Internet titans Apple, Google, and Amazon.

Online content is discussed in further depth in Chapter 10.

PORTAL

portal
offers users powerful search tools as well as an integrated package of content and services all in one place

Portals such as Yahoo, MSN, and AOL offer users powerful search tools as well as an integrated package of content and services, such as news, e-mail, instant messaging, calendars, shopping, music downloads, video streaming, and more, all in one place. Initially, portals sought to be viewed as "gateways" to the Internet. Today, however, the portal business model is to be a destination site. They are marketed as places where consumers will hopefully stay a long time to read news, find entertainment, and meet other people (think of destination resorts). Portals do not sell anything directly—or so it seems—and in that sense they can present themselves as unbiased. The market opportunity is very large: in 2013, around 243 million people in the United States accessed the Internet at work or home. Portals generate revenue primarily by charging advertisers for ad placement, collecting referral fees for steering customers to other sites, and charging for premium services.

Although there are numerous portal/search engine sites, the top five sites (Google, Yahoo, MSN/Bing, AOL, and Ask.com) gather more than 95% of the search engine traffic because of their superior brand recognition (comScore, 2013). Many of the top sites were among the first to appear on the Web and therefore had first-mover advantages. Being first confers advantage because customers come to trust a reliable

INSIGHT ON TECHNOLOGY

BATTLE OF THE TITANS: MUSIC IN THE CLOUD

Business models are closely related to the technologies available to produce and distribute products and services. Nowhere is this more apparent than the recorded music business, whose foundations since the early 20th century have been based on the technology on hand, from sheet music, to records, tape cassettes, CDs, and DVDs. And now, the Internet has enabled two new business models: the online store download-and-own model used by Amazon and Apple's iTunes, where you purchase songs and store them on a computer or devices, and the subscription service model used by Rhapsody, Pandora, and many others, where for a monthly fee you can listen to an online library of songs streamed to your devices. In this business model you don't own the music, and if you miss a payment, it's gone.

Both the download-and-own and subscription service models have significant shortcomings that detract from the customer experience. If you download music to a computer, you need cables and software to get the music to your smartphone, and you will be limited as to how many devices you can use. You may download using different devices and then face a problem coordinating them. Subscription services have confusing pricing schemes, typically cost $15 a month or more, and require you to have Internet access. Many services don't allow you to store songs locally on a device for off-the-Net play, while others allow local storage of music that will not be playable if you miss the monthly payment. Many of the inconveniences of these existing business models were created by record companies who feared, legitimately, that their music would be ripped off and their revenue decimated.

Changes in technology have introduced yet a third recorded music business model: cloud streaming. Here, you own the music and you can store it on a single online cloud drive and play it from any device you choose—one music collection, no coordination issues, and local storage for offline playback. The technology behind this business model is cloud computing, a model of computing where software and files are stored on servers located on the Internet rather than on local devices like PCs and local servers in an office or corporate headquarters. While cloud computing started out as a new and less-expensive method of information processing for large corporations, it is spreading to consumer services such as music, file storage, productivity software, and calendars. What makes cloud computing possible is mammoth data centers stocked with hundreds of thousands of computer processors, and cheap broadband networks that can move files and software instructions rapidly back and forth from local devices to cloud servers.

In 2012, Apple, Amazon, and Google, three of the largest Internet players, introduced their cloud-based music models. The resulting competition is a battle royale among Internet titans to preserve existing advantages for each firm, and to dominate the future of music distribution.

Amazon was the first to announce its cloud music service, in March 2011. Using a "music locker" business model, Amazon's Cloud Player allows you to upload MP3 and ACC music files, store the music on Cloud Player, and play the music on any number of supported digital devices, such as your PC, Mac, Kindle Fire, Android Phone, iPhone, or iPod Touch. If you are a paid subscriber of Amazon's Cloud Drive storage service, you can access Cloud Player at no additional cost. If not, you can subscribe for $24.99 a year, which entitles you to import up to 250,000 songs. Presto: your music is no longer tied to a single digital device or platform. Amazon also sells music; it is the second largest

(continued)

music retailer in the world, with more than 20 million songs for sale.

Amazon's announcement was followed by Google's announcement in May 2011 of its own music locker service, now known as Google Play. This is another music locker service based on cloud computing. You download a Google music uploader app called Music Manager and it searches your hard drive or smartphone for music files, and automatically uploads them to the Google cloud. You get free storage for 20,000 songs, for $9.99 a month, you can enjoy unlimited listening to millions of songs and create a personalized radio station similar to that offered by Pandora based on any song or artist. In addition, the Google Play store has over 18 million songs available for purchase.

In June 2011, Apple finally joined the party, announcing its own cloud service player and storage system, iCloud. Apple is the largest retailer of music in the world with an inventory of more than 26 million songs. Apple's iCloud service allows you to store all your digital files, including music files, on Apple's cloud drive, and then play your music on any Apple device or PC connected to the Internet. Apple's approach is a "matching service" where you do not need to upload any of your music files. In a unique agreement with the four largest music firms, Apple's iCloud software identifies the music titles stored on your device and places high-quality copies into your iCloud drive automatically. iTunes Match is available on a subscription basis for the same price as Amazon's Cloud Player, $24.99 a year. Without it, you are limited only to the music you have purchased through iTunes. You can also upload digital documents, from photos and calendars to spreadsheets and papers, to the iCloud.

Apple provides 5 gigabytes of storage for free, with additional amounts available for purchase. Apple's iCloud drive service is coordinated with its iOS 5 operating system for smartphones and i-devices. The operating system does not require a PC or Mac base station, and you can manage all your digital content online using just an iPhone.

It's still too early to tell which of these giants will prevail in the music distribution business, but all will continue to be the dominant players. While there are mostly similarities among the various cloud services (they all play on any device you choose), some differences may have business significance. For instance, Google and Amazon require users to upload their music, which can take many hours or even days, and some of your music tracks might be very low quality. Apple's service matches your local collection and places high-quality versions of the music online automatically. It's unclear if this is a permanent advantage because both Google and Amazon could negotiate similar deals with the music companies. Google and Apple can sell users expensive smartphones to play cloud music, whereas Amazon has no proprietary music player.

Music is just the first online content to go onto cloud servers. It will soon be followed by movies, television shows, books, and magazines. In addition, the presence of all this content will drive consumers to buy mobile devices. None of the titans plan to miss out on this opportunity. There's also money for the content producers. The streaming music cloud services promise to provide a rich and stable stream of revenue for the content producers and artists. Instead of fighting each other, for once it appears the content owners and the Internet content distributors have reached a consensus on a mutually profitable business model for content.

SOURCES: "iTunes Match," Apple.com, accessed August 1, 2013; "Google Play/Music," Play.google.com, accessed August 1, 2013; "Get Started with the Amazon MP3 Store and Cloud Player," Amazon.com, accessed August 1, 2013; "Web Services to Drive Future Growth for Amazon," by Trefis Team, Forbes. com, August 21, 2012; "Top Cloud Services for Storing and Streaming Music," by Paul Lilly, *PCWorld*, July 29, 2012; "The Cloud That Ate Your Music," by Jon Pareles, *New York Times*, June 22, 2011; "Amazon's and Google's Cloud Services Compared," by Paul Boutin, *New York Times*, June 6, 2011; "For a Song, Online Giants Offer Music in a Cloud," by Walter Mossberg, *Wall Street Journal*, May 19, 2011; "Apple's Cloud Music Service Might Crush the Competition," by Mikko Torikka, VentureBeat.com, May 19, 2011; "Amazon Beats Apple and Google to Cloud Music," by Dean Takahashi, VentureBeat.com, March 28, 2011.

provider and experience switching costs if they change to late arrivals in the market. By garnering a large chunk of the marketplace, first movers—just like a single telephone network—can offer customers access to commonly shared ideas, standards, and experiences (something called *network externalities* that we describe in later chapters).

The traditional portals have company. Facebook and other social network sites are now the initial start or home page (portal) for millions of Internet users in the United States.

Yahoo, AOL, MSN, and others like them are considered to be horizontal portals because they define their marketspace to include all users of the Internet. Vertical portals (sometimes called vortals) attempt to provide similar services as horizontal portals, but are focused around a particular subject matter or market segment. For instance, Sailnet specializes in the consumer sailboat market that contains about 8 million Americans who own or rent sailboats. Although the total number of vortal users may be much lower than the number of portal users, if the market segment is attractive enough, advertisers are willing to pay a premium in order to reach a targeted audience. Also, visitors to specialized niche vortals spend more money than the average Yahoo visitor. Google and Ask.com can also be considered portals of a sort, but focus primarily on offering search and advertising services. They generate revenues primarily from search engine advertising sales and also from affiliate referral fees.

TRANSACTION BROKER

Companies that process transactions for consumers normally handled in person, by phone, or by mail are **transaction brokers**. The largest industries using this model are financial services, travel services, and job placement services. The online transaction broker's primary value propositions are savings of money and time. In addition, most transaction brokers provide timely information and opinions. Companies such as Monster.com offer job searchers a national marketplace for their talents and employers a national resource for that talent. Both employers and job seekers are attracted by the convenience and currency of information. Online stock brokers charge commissions that are considerably less than traditional brokers, with many offering substantial deals, such as cash and a certain number of free trades, to lure new customers.

Given rising consumer interest in financial planning and the stock market, the market opportunity for online transaction brokers appears to be large. However, while millions of customers have shifted to online brokers, some are still wary about switching from their traditional broker who provides personal advice and a brand name. Fears of privacy invasion and the loss of control over personal financial information also contribute to market resistance. Consequently, the challenge for online brokers is to overcome consumer fears by emphasizing the security and privacy measures in place, and, like physical banks and brokerage firms, providing a broad range of financial services and not just stock trading. This industry is covered in greater depth in Chapter 9.

Transaction brokers make money each time a transaction occurs. Each stock trade, for example, nets the company a fee, based on either a flat rate or a sliding scale related to the size of the transaction. Attracting new customers and encouraging them

transaction broker
site that processes transactions for consumers that are normally handled in person, by phone, or by mail

to trade frequently are the keys to generating more revenue for these companies. Travel sites generate commissions from travel books and job sites generate listing fees from employers up front, rather than charging a fee when a position is filled.

MARKET CREATOR

market creator
builds a digital environment where buyers and sellers can meet, display products, search for products, and establish a price for products

Market creators build a digital environment in which buyers and sellers can meet, display products, search for products, and establish prices. Prior to the Internet and the Web, market creators relied on physical places to establish a market. Beginning with the medieval marketplace and extending to today's New York Stock Exchange, a market has meant a physical space for transacting business. There were few private digital network marketplaces prior to the Web. The Web changed this by making it possible to separate markets from physical space. Prime examples are Priceline, which allows consumers to set the price they are willing to pay for various travel accommodations and other products (sometimes referred to as a reverse auction), and eBay, the online auction site utilized by both businesses and consumers. Market creators make money by either charging a percentage of every transaction made, or charging merchants for access to the market.

For example, eBay's auction business model is to create a digital electronic environment for buyers and sellers to meet, agree on a price, and transact. This is different from transaction brokers who actually carry out the transaction for their customers, acting as agents in larger markets. At eBay, the buyers and sellers are their own agents. Each sale on eBay nets the company a commission based on the percentage of the item's sales price, in addition to a listing fee. eBay is one of the few e-commerce companies that has been profitable virtually from the beginning. Why? One answer is that eBay has no inventory or production costs. It is simply a middleman.

The market opportunity for market creators is potentially vast, but only if the firm has the financial resources and marketing plan to attract sufficient sellers and buyers to the marketplace. As of June 30, 2013, eBay had more than 132 million active registered users, and this makes for an efficient market (eBay, 2013). There are many sellers and buyers for each type of product, sometimes for the same product, for example, laptop computer models. Many other digital auctions have sprung up in smaller, more specialized vertical market segments such as jewelry and automobiles.

In addition to marketing and branding, a company's management team and organization can make a difference in creating new markets, especially if some managers have had experience in similar businesses. Speed is often the key in such situations. The ability to become operational quickly can make the difference between success and failure.

SERVICE PROVIDER

service provider
offers services online

While e-tailers sell products online, **service providers** offer services online. There's been an explosion in online services that is often unrecognized. Web 2.0 applications such as photo sharing, video sharing, and user-generated content (in blogs and social network sites) are all services provided to customers. Google has led the way in developing online applications such as Google Maps, Google Docs, and Gmail. Other personal services such as online medical bill management, financial and pension planning, and travel recommendation are showing strong growth.

Service providers use a variety of revenue models. Some charge a fee, or monthly subscriptions, while others generate revenue from other sources, such as through advertising and by collecting personal information that is useful in direct marketing. Some services are free but are not complete. For instance, Google Apps' basic edition is free, but a business edition with advanced tools costs $5/user/month or $50/user/year. Much like retailers who trade products for cash, service providers trade knowledge, expertise, and capabilities for revenue.

Obviously, some services cannot be provided online. For example, dentistry, medical services, plumbing, and car repair cannot be completed via the Internet. However, online arrangements can be made for these services. Online service providers may offer computer services, such as information storage (as does Carbonite), provide legal services (RocketLawyer), or offer advice and services to high-net-worth individuals, such as at HarrisMyCFO.com. Grocery shopping sites such as FreshDirect and Peapod are also providing services.[1] To complicate matters a bit, most financial transaction brokers (described previously) provide services such as college tuition and pension planning. Travel brokers also provide vacation-planning services, not just transactions with airlines and hotels. Indeed, mixing services with your products is a powerful business strategy pursued by many hard-goods companies (for example, warranties are services).

The basic value proposition of service providers is that they offer consumers valuable, convenient, time-saving, and low-cost alternatives to traditional service providers or—in the case of search engines and most Web 2.0 applications—they provide services that are truly unique. Where else can you search 50 billion Web pages, or share photos with as many people instantly? Research has found, for instance, that a major factor in predicting online buying behavior is *time starvation*. Time-starved people tend to be busy professionals who work long hours and simply do not have the time to pick up packages, buy groceries, send photos, or visit with financial planners (Bellman, Lohse, and Johnson, 1999). The market opportunity for service providers is as large as the variety of services that can be provided and potentially is much larger than the market opportunity for physical goods. We live in a service-based economy and society; witness the growth of fast-food restaurants, package delivery services, and wireless cellular phone services. Consumers' increasing demand for convenience products and services bodes well for current and future online service providers.

Marketing of service providers must allay consumer fears about hiring a vendor online, as well as build confidence and familiarity among current and potential customers. Building confidence and trust is critical for service providers just as it is for retail product merchants.

---

[1] FreshDirect and other e-commerce businesses can also be classified as online retailers insofar as they warehouse commonly purchased items and make a profit based on the spread between their buy and sell prices.

2.3 MAJOR BUSINESS-TO-BUSINESS (B2B) BUSINESS MODELS

In Chapter 1, we noted that business-to-business (B2B) e-commerce, in which businesses sell to other businesses, is more than 10 times the size of B2C e-commerce, even though most of the public attention has focused on B2C. For instance, it is estimated that revenues for all types of B2B e-commerce in the United States will total around $4.8 trillion in 2013, compared to about $419 billion for all types of B2C e-commerce. Clearly, most of the dollar revenues in e-commerce involve B2B e-commerce. Much of this activity is unseen and unknown to the average consumer.

B2B e-commerce relies overwhelmingly on a technology called *electronic data interchange (EDI)* (U.S. Census Bureau, 2013). EDI is useful for one-to-one relationships between a single supplier and a single purchaser, and originally was designed for proprietary networks, although it is migrating rapidly to the Internet. Many firms have supplemented their EDI systems, however, with more powerful Internet technologies that can enable many-to-one and many-to-many market relationships where there are many suppliers selling to a single or small group of very large purchasers, or, in the case of independent exchanges, where there are many sellers and many buyers simultaneously in the marketplace. EDI is not designed for these types of relationships. **Table 2.4** lists the major business models utilized in the B2B arena.

TABLE 2.4	B2B BUSINESS MODELS		
BUSINESS MODEL	EXAMPLES	DESCRIPTION	REVENUE MODEL
(1) NET MARKETPLACE			
E-distributor	Grainger.com Partstore.com	Single-firm online version of retail and wholesale store; supply maintenance, repair, operation goods; indirect inputs	Sales of goods
E-procurement	Ariba PerfectCommerce	Single firm creating digital markets where sellers and buyers transact for indirect inputs	Fees for market-making services, supply chain management, and fulfillment services
Exchange	OceanConnect	Independently owned vertical digital marketplace for direct inputs	Fees and commissions on transactions
Industry Consortium	Exostar Elemica	Industry-owned vertical digital market open to select suppliers	Fees and commissions on transactions
(2) PRIVATE INDUSTRIAL NETWORK			
	Walmart Procter & Gamble	Company-owned network that coordinates supply chains with a limited set of partners	Cost absorbed by network owner and recovered through production and distribution efficiencies

E-DISTRIBUTOR

Companies that supply products and services directly to individual businesses are **e-distributors**. W.W. Grainger, for example, is the largest distributor of maintenance, repair, and operations (MRO) supplies. MRO supplies are thought of as indirect inputs to the production process—as opposed to direct inputs. In the past, Grainger relied on catalog sales and physical distribution centers in metropolitan areas. Its catalog of equipment went online in 1995 at Grainger.com, giving businesses access to more than 1 million items. Company purchasing agents can search by type of product, such as motors, HVAC, or fluids, or by specific brand name.

E-distributors are owned by one company seeking to serve many customers. However, as with exchanges (described on the next page), critical mass is a factor. With e-distributors, the more products and services a company makes available on its site, the more attractive that site is to potential customers. One-stop shopping is always preferable to having to visit numerous sites to locate a particular part or product.

e-distributor
a company that supplies products and services directly to individual businesses

E-PROCUREMENT

Just as e-distributors provide products to other companies, **e-procurement firms** create and sell access to digital electronic markets. Firms such as Ariba, for instance, have created software that helps large firms organize their procurement process by creating mini-digital markets for a single firm. Ariba creates custom-integrated online catalogs (where supplier firms can list their offerings) for purchasing firms. On the sell side, Ariba helps vendors sell to large purchasers by providing software to handle catalog creation, shipping, insurance, and finance. Both the buy and sell side software is referred to generically as "value chain management" software.

e-procurement firm
creates and sells access to digital electronic markets

B2B service providers make money through transaction fees, fees based on the number of workstations using the service, or annual licensing fees. They offer purchasing firms a sophisticated set of sourcing and supply chain management tools that permit firms to reduce supply chain costs. In the software world, firms such as Ariba are sometimes also called **application service providers (ASPs)**; they are able to offer firms much lower costs of software by achieving scale economies. **Scale economies** are efficiencies that result from increasing the size of a business, for instance, when large, fixed-cost production systems (such as factories or software systems) can be operated at full capacity with no idle time. In the case of software, the marginal cost of a digital copy of a software program is nearly zero, and finding additional buyers for an expensive software program is exceptionally profitable. This is much more efficient than having every firm build its own supply chain management system, and it permits firms such as Ariba to specialize and offer their software to firms at a cost far less than the cost of developing it.

B2B service provider
sells business services to other firms

application service provider (ASP)
a company that sells access to Internet-based software applications to other companies

scale economies
efficiencies that arise from increasing the size of a business

EXCHANGES

Exchanges have garnered most of the B2B attention and early funding because of their potential market size even though today they are a small part of the overall B2B picture. An **exchange** is an independent digital electronic marketplace where hun-

exchange
an independent digital electronic marketplace where suppliers and commercial purchasers can conduct transactions

dreds of suppliers meet a smaller number of very large commercial purchasers (Kaplan and Sawhney, 2000). Exchanges are owned by independent, usually entrepreneurial start-up firms whose business is making a market, and they generate revenue by charging a commission or fee based on the size of the transactions conducted among trading parties. They usually serve a single vertical industry such as steel, polymers, or aluminum, and focus on the exchange of direct inputs to production and short-term contracts or spot purchasing. For buyers, B2B exchanges make it possible to gather information, check out suppliers, collect prices, and keep up to date on the latest happenings all in one place. Sellers, on the other hand, benefit from expanded access to buyers. The greater the number of sellers and buyers, the lower the sales cost and the higher the chances of making a sale. The ease, speed, and volume of transactions are summarily referred to as *market liquidity*.

In theory, exchanges make it significantly less expensive and time-consuming to identify potential suppliers, customers, and partners, and to do business with each other. As a result, they can lower transaction costs—the cost of making a sale or purchase. Exchanges can also lower product costs and inventory-carrying costs—the cost of keeping a product on hand in a warehouse. In reality, as will be discussed in Chapter 12, B2B exchanges have had a difficult time convincing thousands of suppliers to move into singular digital markets where they face powerful price competition, and an equally difficult time convincing businesses to change their purchasing behavior away from trusted long-term trading partners. As a result, the number of exchanges has fallen significantly.

INDUSTRY CONSORTIA

industry consortia
industry-owned vertical marketplaces that serve specific industries

Industry consortia are industry-owned *vertical marketplaces* that serve specific industries, such as the automobile, aerospace, chemical, floral, or logging industries. In contrast, *horizontal marketplaces* sell specific products and services to a wide range of companies. Vertical marketplaces supply a smaller number of companies with products and services of specific interest to their industry, while horizontal marketplaces supply companies in different industries with a particular type of product and service, such as marketing-related, financial, or computing services. For example, Exostar is an online trading exchange for the aerospace and defense industry, founded by BAE Systems, Boeing, Lockheed Martin, Raytheon, and Rolls-Royce in 2000. Exostar connects with more than 300 procurement systems and has registered more than 70,000 trading partners in 95 countries around the world.

Industry consortia have tended to be more successful than independent exchanges in part because they are sponsored by powerful, deep-pocketed industry players, and also because they strengthen traditional purchasing behavior rather than seek to transform it.

PRIVATE INDUSTRIAL NETWORKS

private industrial network
digital network designed to coordinate the flow of communications among firms engaged in business together

Private industrial networks constitute about 75% of all B2B expenditures by large firms and far exceed the expenditures for all forms of Net marketplaces. A **private industrial network** (sometimes referred to as a private trading exchange or PTX) is a digital network (often but not always Internet-based) designed to coordinate the flow of communications among firms engaged in business together. The network is owned by a single large purchasing firm. Participation is by invitation only to trusted long-term suppliers of direct inputs. These networks typically evolve out of a firm's own enterprise resource planning (ERP) system, and are an effort to include key suppliers in the firm's own business decision making. For instance, Walmart operates one of the largest private industrial networks in the world for its suppliers, who on a daily basis use Walmart's network to monitor the sales of their goods, the status of shipments, and the actual inventory level of their goods.

We discuss the nuances of B2B e-commerce in more detail in Chapter 12.

2.4 E-COMMERCE ENABLERS: THE GOLD RUSH MODEL

Of the nearly 500,000 miners who descended on California in the Gold Rush of 1849, less than 1% ever achieved significant wealth. However, the banking firms, shipping companies, hardware companies, real estate speculators, and clothing companies such as Levi Strauss built long-lasting fortunes. Likewise in e-commerce. No discussion of e-commerce business models would be complete without mention of a group of companies whose business model is focused on providing the infrastructure necessary for e-commerce companies to exist, grow, and prosper. These are the e-commerce enablers: the Internet infrastructure companies. They provide the hardware, operating system software, networks and communications technology, applications software, Web design, consulting services, and other tools that make e-commerce (see **Table 2.5** on page 86). While these firms may not be conducting e-commerce per se (although in many instances, e-commerce in its traditional sense is in fact one of their sales channels), as a group they have perhaps profited the most from the development of e-commerce. We discuss many of these players in the following chapters.

2.5 HOW E-COMMERCE CHANGES BUSINESS: STRATEGY, STRUCTURE, AND PROCESS

Now that you have a clear grasp of the variety of business models used by e-commerce firms, you also need to understand how e-commerce has changed the business environment in the last decade, including industry structures, business strategies, and industry and firm operations (business processes and value chains). We return to these concepts throughout the book as we explore the e-commerce phenomenon. In general, the Internet is an open standards system available to all players, and this fact inherently makes it easy for new competitors to enter the marketplace and offer substitute products or channels of delivery. The Internet tends to intensify competition. Because information becomes available to everyone, the Internet inherently shifts power to buyers who can quickly discover the lowest-cost provider. On the other hand, the

TABLE 2.5	E-COMMERCE ENABLERS
INFRASTRUCTURE	PLAYERS
Infrastructure	Players
Hardware: Web Servers	IBM, HP, Dell, Oracle
Software: Server Software	Microsoft, Red Hat Linux, Apple
Cloud Providers	Amazon Web Services, Rackspace, Google, IBM,
Hosting Services	Rackspace, Webintellects, 1&1 Internet, HostGator, Hostway
Domain Name Registration	Go Daddy, Network Solutions, Dotster
Content Delivery Networks	Akamai, Limelight
Site Design	GSI Commerce, Fry, Oracle
E-commerce Platform Providers	GSI Commerce, Magento, IBM, ATG, Demandware
Mobile Commerce Hardware Platform	Apple, Samsung, Google
Mobile Commerce Software Platform	Apple, Google, Adobe, Usablenet, Unbound Commerce, Branding Brand
Streaming, Rich Media, Online Video	Adobe, Apple, Easy 2 Technologies, Channel Advisor
Security and Encryption	VeriSign, Checkpoint, GeoTrust, Entrust, EMC, Thawte, McAfee
Payment Systems	PayPal, Authorize.net, Chase Paymentech, Cybersource
Web Performance Management	Compuware Gomez, Smartbear, Keynote Systems
Comparison Engine Feeds/Marketplace Management	Channel Advisor, Mercent, CPC Strategy
Customer Relationship Management	Oracle, SAP, GSI Commerce, Salesforce.com, NetSuite
Order Management	JDA Software, GSI Commerce, Stone Edge
Fulfillment	JDA Software, GSI Commerce, CommerceHub
Social Marketing	Buffer, HootSuite, SocialFlow
Search Engine Marketing	iProspect, Channel Advisor, Rimm-Kaufman Group
E-mail Marketing	Constant Contact, Experian CheetahMail, Bronto Software, MailChimp
Affiliate Marketing	Commission Junction, Google Affiliate Network, LinkShare
Customer Reviews and Forums	Bazaarvoice, PowerReviews, BizRate
Live Chat/Click-to-Call	LivePerson, BoldChat, Oracle
Web Analytics	Google Analytics, Adobe Omniture, IBM Coremetrics

Internet presents many new opportunities for creating value, for branding products and charging premium prices, and for enlarging an already powerful offline physical business such as Walmart or Sears.

Recall Table 1.2 in Chapter 1 that describes the truly unique features of e-commerce technology. **Table 2.6** suggests some of the implications of each unique feature

TABLE 2.6	EIGHT UNIQUE FEATURES OF E-COMMERCE TECHNOLOGY
FEATURE	**SELECTED IMPACTS ON BUSINESS ENVIRONMENT**
Ubiquity	Alters industry structure by creating new marketing channels and expanding size of overall market. Creates new efficiencies in industry operations and lowers costs of firms' sales operations. Enables new differentiation strategies.
Global reach	Changes industry structure by lowering barriers to entry, but greatly expands market at same time. Lowers cost of industry and firm operations through production and sales efficiencies. Enables competition on a global scale.
Universal standards	Changes industry structure by lowering barriers to entry and intensifying competition within an industry. Lowers costs of industry and firm operations by lowering computing and communications costs. Enables broad scope strategies.
Richness	Alters industry structure by reducing strength of powerful distribution channels. Changes industry and firm operations costs by reducing reliance on sales forces. Enhances post-sales support strategies.
Interactivity	Alters industry structure by reducing threat of substitutes through enhanced customization. Reduces industry and firm costs by reducing reliance on sales forces. Enables differentiation strategies.
Personalization/ Customization	Alters industry structure by reducing threats of substitutes, raising barriers to entry. Reduces value chain costs in industry and firms by lessening reliance on sales forces. Enables personalized marketing strategies.
Information density	Changes industry structure by weakening powerful sales channels, shifting bargaining power to consumers. Reduces industry and firm operations costs by lowering costs of obtaining, processing, and distributing information about suppliers and consumers.
Social technologies	Changes industry structure by shifting programming and editorial decisions to consumers. Creates substitute entertainment products. Energizes a large group of new suppliers.

for the overall business environment—industry structure, business strategies, and operations.

INDUSTRY STRUCTURE

E-commerce changes industry structure, in some industries more than others. **Industry structure** refers to the nature of the players in an industry and their relative bargaining power. An industry's structure is characterized by five forces: *rivalry among*

industry structure
refers to the nature of the players in an industry and their relative bargaining power

industry structural analysis

an effort to understand and describe the nature of competition in an industry, the nature of substitute products, the barriers to entry, and the relative strength of consumers and suppliers

existing competitors, the *threat of substitute products, barriers to entry into the industry*, the *bargaining power of suppliers*, and the *bargaining power of buyers* (Porter, 1985). When you describe an industry's structure, you are describing the general business environment in an industry and the overall profitability of doing business in that environment. E-commerce has the potential to change the relative strength of these competitive forces (see **Figure 2.4**).

When you consider a business model and its potential long-term profitability, you should always perform an industry structural analysis. An **industry structural analysis** is an effort to understand and describe the nature of competition in an industry, the nature of substitute products, the barriers to entry, and the relative strength of consumers and suppliers.

FIGURE 2.4	HOW E-COMMERCE INFLUENCES INDUSTRY STRUCTURE

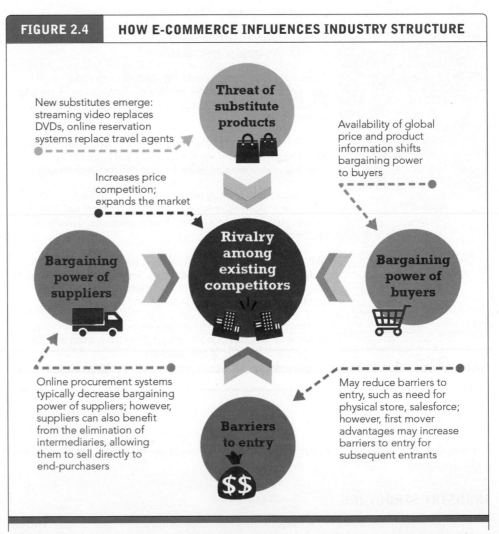

E-commerce has many impacts on industry structure and competitive conditions. From the perspective of a single firm, these changes can have negative or positive implications depending on the situation. In some cases, an entire industry can be disrupted, while at the same time, a new industry is born. Individual firms can either prosper or be devastated.

E-commerce can affect the structure and dynamics of industries in very different ways. Consider the recorded music industry, an industry that has experienced significant change because of e-commerce. Historically, the major record companies owned the exclusive rights to the recorded music of various artists. With the entrance into the marketplace of substitute providers such as Napster and Kazaa, millions of consumers began to use the Internet to bypass traditional music labels and their distributors entirely. In the travel industry, entirely new middlemen such as Travelocity entered the market to compete with traditional travel agents. After Travelocity, Expedia, CheapTickets, and other travel services demonstrated the power of e-commerce marketing for airline tickets, the actual owners of the airline seats—the major airlines—banded together to form their own Internet outlet for tickets, Orbitz, for direct sales to consumers (although ultimately selling the company to a private investor group). Clearly, e-commerce creates *new industry dynamics* that can best be described as the give and take of the marketplace, the changing fortunes of competitors.

Yet in other industries, e-commerce has strengthened existing players. In the chemical and automobile industries, e-commerce is being used effectively by manufacturers to strengthen their traditional distributors. In these industries, e-commerce technology has not fundamentally altered the competitive forces—bargaining power of suppliers, barriers to entry, bargaining power of buyers, threat of substitutes, or rivalry among competitors—within the industry. Hence, each industry is different and you need to examine each one carefully to understand the impacts of e-commerce on competition and strategy.

New forms of distribution created by new market entrants can completely change the competitive forces in an industry. For instance, consumers gladly substituted free access to Wikipedia for a $699 set of World Book encyclopedias, or a $40 DVD, radically changing the competitive forces in the encyclopedia industry. As we describe in Chapter 10, the content industries of newspapers, books, movies, games, and television have been transformed by the emergence of new distribution platforms.

Inter-firm rivalry (competition) is one area of the business environment where e-commerce technologies have had an impact on most industries. In general, e-commerce has increased price competition in nearly all markets. It has been relatively easy for existing firms to adopt e-commerce technology and attempt to use it to achieve competitive advantage vis-à-vis rivals. For instance, e-commerce inherently changes the scope of competition from local and regional to national and global. Because consumers have access to global price information, e-commerce produces pressures on firms to compete by lowering prices (and lowering profits). On the other hand, e-commerce has made it possible for some firms to differentiate their product or services from others. Amazon patented one-click purchasing, for instance, while eBay created a unique, easy-to-use interface and a differentiating brand name. Therefore, although e-commerce has increased emphasis on price competition, it has also enabled businesses to create new strategies for differentiation and branding so that they can retain higher prices.

It is impossible to determine if e-commerce technologies have had an overall positive or negative impact on firm profitability in general. Each industry is unique, so it is necessary to perform a separate analysis for each one. Clearly, e-commerce has shaken the foundations of some industries, in particular, information product industries (such as the music, newspaper, book, and software industries) as well as other information-intense industries such as financial services. In these industries, the power of consumers has grown relative to providers, prices have fallen, and overall profitability has been challenged. In other industries, especially manufacturing, e-commerce has not greatly changed relationships with buyers, but has changed relationships with suppliers. Increasingly, manufacturing firms in entire industries have banded together to aggregate purchases, create industry exchanges or marketplaces, and outsource industrial processes in order to obtain better prices from suppliers. Throughout this book, we document these changes in industry structure and market dynamics introduced by e-commerce.

INDUSTRY VALUE CHAINS

value chain

the set of activities performed in an industry or in a firm that transforms raw inputs into final products and services

While an industry structural analysis helps you understand the impact of e-commerce technology on the overall business environment in an industry, a more detailed industry value chain analysis can help identify more precisely just how e-commerce may change business operations at the industry level. One of the basic tools for understanding the impact of information technology on industry and firm operations is the value chain. The concept is quite simple. A **value chain** is the set of activities performed in an industry or in a firm that transforms raw inputs into final products and services. Each of these activities adds economic value to the final product; hence, the term *value chain* as an interconnected set of value-adding activities. **Figure 2.5** illustrates the six generic players in an industry value chain: suppliers, manufacturers, transporters, distributors, retailers, and customers.

By reducing the cost of information, e-commerce offers each of the key players in an industry value chain new opportunities to maximize their positions by lowering costs and/or raising prices. For instance, manufacturers can reduce the costs they pay for goods by developing Internet-based B2B exchanges with their

FIGURE 2.5   E-COMMERCE AND INDUSTRY VALUE CHAINS

Every industry can be characterized by a set of value-adding activities performed by a variety of actors. E-commerce potentially affects the capabilities of each player as well as the overall operational efficiency of the industry.

suppliers. Manufacturers can develop direct relationships with their customers, bypassing the costs of distributors and retailers. Distributors can develop highly efficient inventory management systems to reduce their costs, and retailers can develop highly efficient customer relationship management systems to strengthen their service to customers. Customers in turn can search for the best quality, fastest delivery, and lowest prices, thereby lowering their transaction costs and reducing prices they pay for final goods. Finally, the operational efficiency of the entire industry can increase, lowering prices and adding value for consumers, and helping the industry to compete with alternative industries.

FIRM VALUE CHAINS

The concept of value chain can be used to analyze a single firm's operational efficiency as well. The question here is: How does e-commerce technology potentially affect the value chains of firms within an industry? A **firm value chain** is the set of activities a firm engages in to create final products from raw inputs. Each step in the process of production adds value to the final product. In addition, firms develop support activities that coordinate the production process and contribute to overall operational efficiency. **Figure 2.6** illustrates the key steps and support activities in a firm's value chain.

firm value chain
the set of activities a firm engages in to create final products from raw inputs

E-commerce offers firms many opportunities to increase their operational efficiency and differentiate their products. For instance, firms can use the Internet's communications efficiency to outsource some primary and secondary activities to specialized, more efficient providers without such outsourcing being visible to the consumer. In addition, firms can use e-commerce to more precisely coordinate the steps in the value chains and reduce their costs. Finally, firms can use e-commerce to provide users with more differentiated and high-value products. For instance, Amazon

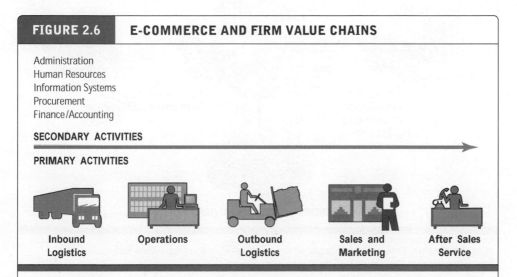

| **FIGURE 2.6** | **E-COMMERCE AND FIRM VALUE CHAINS** |

Administration
Human Resources
Information Systems
Procurement
Finance/Accounting

SECONDARY ACTIVITIES

PRIMARY ACTIVITIES

Inbound Logistics   Operations   Outbound Logistics   Sales and Marketing   After Sales Service

Every firm can be characterized by a set of value-adding primary and secondary activities performed by a variety of actors in the firm. A simple firm value chain performs five primary value-adding steps: inbound logistics, operations, outbound logistics, sales and marketing, and after sales service.

provides consumers with a much larger inventory of books to choose from, at a lower cost, than traditional book stores. It also provides many services—such as instantly available professional and consumer reviews, and information on buying patterns of other consumers—that traditional bookstores cannot.

FIRM VALUE WEBS

While firms produce value through their value chains, they also rely on the value chains of their partners—their suppliers, distributors, and delivery firms. E-commerce creates new opportunities for firms to cooperate and create a value web. A **value web** is a networked business ecosystem that uses e-commerce technology to coordinate the value chains of business partners within an industry, or at the first level, to coordinate the value chains of a group of firms. **Figure 2.7** illustrates a value web.

A value web coordinates a firm's suppliers with its own production needs using an Internet-based supply chain management system. We discuss these B2B systems in Chapter 12. Firms also use the Internet to develop close relationships with their logistics partners. For instance, Amazon relies on UPS tracking systems to provide its

value web

networked business ecosystem that coordinates the value chains of several firms

| FIGURE 2.7 | INTERNET-ENABLED VALUE WEB |

Internet technology enables firms to create an enhanced value web in cooperation with their strategic alliance and partner firms, customers, and direct and indirect suppliers.

customers with online package tracking, and it relies on the U.S. Postal Service systems to insert packages directly into the mail stream. Amazon has partnership relations with hundreds of firms to generate customers and to manage relationships with customers. In fact, when you examine Amazon closely, you realize that the value it delivers to customers is in large part the result of coordination with other firms and not simply the result of activities internal to Amazon. The value of Amazon is, in large part, the value delivered by its value web partners. This is difficult for other firms to imitate in the short run.

BUSINESS STRATEGY

A **business strategy** is a set of plans for achieving superior long-term returns on the capital invested in a business firm. A business strategy is therefore a plan for making profits in a competitive environment over the long term. **Profit** is simply the difference between the price a firm is able to charge for its products and the cost of producing and distributing goods. Profit represents economic value. Economic value is created anytime customers are willing to pay more for a product than it costs to produce. Why would anyone pay more for a product than it costs to produce? There are multiple answers. The product may be unique (there are no other suppliers), it may be the least costly product of its type available, consumers may be able to purchase the product anywhere in the world, or it may satisfy some unique needs that other products do not. Each of these sources of economic value defines a firm's strategy for positioning its products in the marketplace. There are four generic strategies for achieving a profitable business: differentiation, cost, scope, and focus. We describe each of these below. The specific strategies that a firm follows will depend on the product, the industry, and the marketplace where competition is encountered.

Although the Internet is a unique marketplace, the same principles of strategy and business apply. As you will see throughout the book, successful e-commerce strategies involve using the Internet and mobile platform to leverage and strengthen existing business (rather than destroy your business), and to provide products and services your competitors cannot copy (in the short term anyway). That means developing unique products, proprietary content, distinguishing processes (such as Amazon's one-click shopping), and personalized or customized services and products (Porter, 2001). There are five generic business strategies: product/service differentiation, cost competition, scope, focus, and customer/supplier intimacy. Let's examine these ideas more closely.

Differentiation refers to all the ways producers can make their products or services unique and distinguish them from those of competitors. The opposite of differentiation is **commoditization**—a situation where there are no differences among products or services, and the only basis of choosing is price. As economists tell us, when price alone becomes the basis of competition and there are many suppliers and many customers, eventually the price of the good/service falls to the cost to produce

business strategy
a set of plans for achieving superior long-term returns on the capital invested in a business firm

profit
the difference between the price a firm is able to charge for its products and the cost of producing and distributing goods

differentiation
refers to all the ways producers can make their products or services unique and different to distinguish them from those of competitors

commoditization
a situation where there are no differences among products or services, and the only basis of choosing is price

it (marginal revenues from the nth unit equal marginal costs). And then profits are zero! This is an unacceptable situation for any business person. The solution is to differentiate your product or service and to create a monopoly-like situation where you are the only supplier.

There are many ways businesses differentiate their products or services. A business may start with a core generic product or service, but then create expectations among users about the "experience" of consuming the product or using the service—"Nothing refreshes like a Coke!" or "Nothing equals the experience of driving a BMW." Businesses may also augment products and services by adding features to make them different from those of competitors. And businesses can differentiate their products and services further by enhancing their abilities to solve related consumer problems. For instance, tax programs such as TurboTax can import data from spreadsheet programs, as well as be used to electronically file tax returns. These capabilities are enhancements to the product that solve a customer's problems. The purpose of marketing is to create these differentiation features and to make the consumer aware of the unique qualities of products and services, creating in the process a "brand" that stands for these features. We discuss marketing and branding in Chapters 6 and 7.

In their totality, the differentiation features of a product or service constitute the customer value proposition we described in earlier sections of this chapter. E-commerce offers some unique ways to differentiate products and services, such as the ability to personalize the shopping experience and to customize the product or service to the particular demands of each consumer. E-commerce businesses can also differentiate products and services by making it possible to purchase the product from home, work, or on the road (ubiquity); by making it possible to purchase anywhere in the world (global reach); by creating unique interactive content, videos, stories about users, and reviews by users (richness and interactivity); and by storing and processing information for consumers of the product or service, such as warranty information on all products purchased through a site or income tax information online (information density).

strategy of cost competition

offering products and services at a lower cost than competitors

Adopting a **strategy of cost competition** means a business has discovered some unique set of business processes or resources that other firms cannot obtain in the marketplace. Business processes are the atomic units of the value chain. For instance, the set of value-creating activities called Inbound Logistics in Figure 2.6 is in reality composed of many different collections of activities performed by people on the loading docks and in the warehouses. These different collections of activities are called *business processes*—the set of steps or procedures required to perform the various elements of the value chain.

When a firm discovers a new, more efficient set of business processes, it can obtain a cost advantage over competitors. Then it can attract customers by charging a lower price, while still making a handsome profit. Eventually, its competitors go out of business as the market decisively tilts toward the lowest-cost provider. Or, when a business discovers a unique resource, or lower-cost supplier, it can also compete effectively on cost. For instance, switching production to low-wage-cost areas of the world is one way to lower costs.

Competing on cost can be a short-lived affair and very tricky. Competitors can also discover the same or different efficiencies in production. And competitors can also move production to low-cost areas of the world. Also, competitors may decide to lose money for a period as they compete on cost.

E-commerce offers some ways to compete on cost, at least in the short term. Firms can leverage ubiquity by lowering the costs of order entry (the customer fills out all the forms, so there is no order entry department); leverage global reach and universal standards by having a single order entry system worldwide; and leverage richness, interactivity, and personalization by creating customer profiles online and treating each individual consumer differently—without the use of an expensive sales force that performed these functions in the past. Finally, firms can leverage information intensity by providing consumers with detailed information on products, without maintaining either expensive catalogs or a sales force.

While e-commerce offers powerful capabilities for intensifying cost competition, which makes cost competition appear to be a viable strategy, the danger is that competitors have access to the same technology. The *factor markets*—where producers buy supplies—are open to all. Assuming they have the skills and organizational will to use the technology, competitors can buy many of the same cost-reducing techniques in the marketplace. Even a skilled labor force can be purchased, ultimately. However, self-knowledge, proprietary tacit knowledge (knowledge that is not published or codified), and a loyal, skilled workforce are in the short term difficult to purchase in factor markets. Therefore, cost competition remains a viable strategy.

Two other generic business strategies are scope and focus. A **scope strategy** is a strategy to compete in all markets around the globe, rather than merely in local, regional, or national markets. The Internet's global reach, universal standards, and ubiquity can certainly be leveraged to assist businesses in becoming global competitors. Yahoo, for instance, along with all of the other top 20 e-commerce companies, has readily attained a global presence. A **focus/market niche strategy** is a strategy to compete within a narrow market segment or product segment. This is a specialization strategy with the goal of becoming the premier provider in a narrow market. For instance, L.L.Bean uses e-commerce to continue its historic focus on outdoor sports apparel; and W.W. Grainger—the Web's most frequently visited B2B site—focuses on the narrow MRO market segment. E-commerce offers some obvious capabilities that enable a focus strategy. Firms can leverage richness and interactivity to create highly focused messages to different market segments; information intensity makes it possible to focus e-mail and other marketing campaigns on small market segments; personalization—and related customization—means the same product can be customized and personalized to fulfill the very focused needs of specific market segments and consumers.

Another generic strategy is **customer intimacy**, which focuses on developing strong ties with customers. Strong linkages with customers increase *switching costs* (the costs of switching from one product or service to a competing product or service) and thereby enhance a firm's competitive advantage. For example, Amazon's one-click shopping that retains customer details and recommendation services based on

scope strategy
competing in all markets around the globe, rather than just local, regional, or national markets

focus/market niche strategy
competing within a narrow market or product segment

customer intimacy
focuses on developing strong ties with customers in order to increase switching costs

TABLE 2.7	BUSINESS STRATEGIES	
STRATEGY	DESCRIPTION	EXAMPLE
Differentiation	Making products and services unique and different in order to distinguish them from those of competitors	Warby Parker (Vintage-inspired prescription eyeglasses)
Cost competition	Offering products and services at a lower cost than competitors	Walmart.com
Scope	Competing in all markets around the globe, rather than merely in local, regional, or national markets	Apple iDevices
Focus/market niche	Competing within a narrow market or product segment	Bonobos.com (Men's clothing)
Customer intimacy	Developing strong ties with customers	Amazon; Netflix

previous purchases makes it more likely that customers will return to make subsequent purchases.

Table 2.7 summarizes the five basic business strategies.

Industry structure, industry and firm value chains, value webs, and business strategy are central business concepts used throughout this book to analyze the viability of and prospects for e-commerce sites. In particular, the signature case studies found at the end of each chapter are followed by questions that may ask you to identify the competitive forces in the case, or analyze how the case illustrates changes in industry structure, industry and firm value chains, and business strategy.

Pandora
and the Freemium Business Model

Pandora is the Internet's most successful subscription radio service. As of June 2013, it had over 200 million registered users (140 million of which access the service via a mobile device) and over 70 million active listeners. Pandora now accounts for more than 70% of all Internet radio listening hours and a 7% share of total U.S. radio listening (both traditional and Internet).

At Pandora, users select a genre of music based on a favorite musician, and a computer algorithm puts together a personal radio station that plays not only the music of the selected artist but also closely related music by different artists. A team of professional musicians listens to new songs each day and classifies the music according to more than 400 musical criteria including male or female vocal, electric vs. acoustical guitar, distortion of instruments, presence of background vocals, strings, and various other instruments. These criteria are used in a computer algorithm to classify new songs into five genres: Pop/Rock, Hip-Hop/Electronica, Jazz, World Music, and Classical. Within each of these genres are hundreds of sub-genres. Like Taylor Swift? Create a radio station on Pandora with Taylor Swift as the artist and you can listen all

© NetPhotos / Alamy

day not only to some Taylor Swift tracks but also to musically related artists such as Carrie Underwood, Rascal Flatts, Anna Nalick, and others.

Pandora's founders, Will Glaser and Tim Westergren, launched Pandora in 2005. Their biggest challenge was how to make a business out of a totally new kind of online radio station when competing online stations were making music available for free, many without advertising, and online subscription services were streaming music for a monthly fee and finding some advertising support as well. Online music illegally downloaded from P2P networks for free was also a significant factor, as was iTunes, which by 2005 was a roaring success, charging 99 cents a song with no ad support, and 20 million users at that time. The idea of a "personal" radio station playing your kind of music was very new.

Facing stiff odds, Pandora's first business model was to give away 10 hours of free access, and then ask subscribers to pay $36 a month for a year after they used up their free 10 hours. The result: 100,000 people listened to their 10 hours for free and then refused to use their credit cards to pay for the annual service. People loved Pandora but were unwilling to pay for it, or so it seemed in the early years.

Facing financial collapse, in November 2005 Pandora introduced an ad-supported option. Subscribers could listen to a maximum of 40 hours of music in a calendar month for free. After the 40 hours were used up, subscribers had three choices: (a) pay 99 cents for the rest of the month, (b) sign up for a premium service offering unlimited usage, or (c) do nothing. If they chose (c), the music would stop, but users could sign up again the next month. The ad-supported business model was a risky move because Pandora had no ad server or accounting system, but it attracted so many users that in a few weeks they had a sufficient number of advertisers (including Apple) to pay for their infrastructure. In 2006, Pandora added a "Buy" button to each song being played and struck deals with Amazon, iTunes, and other online retail sites. Pandora now gets an affiliate fee for directing listeners to Amazon where users can buy the music. In 2008, Pandora added an iPhone app to allow users to sign up from their smartphones and listen all day if they wanted. This added 35,000 new users a day. By 2009, this "free" ad-supported model had attracted 20 million users. All of Pandora's plans come with restrictions required by the music companies that own the music, including the inability to hear a song on demand, no replay, and a skip limit of six skips per hour per station. Also, the music cannot be used commercially or outside the United States. After struggling for years showing nothing but losses, threatened by the music companies who wanted to raise their Internet radio rates, Pandora finally had some breathing room.

Still not giving up on its premium service, in late 2009, the company launched Pandora One, a premium service that offered no advertising, higher quality streaming music, a desktop app, and fewer usage limits. The service cost $36 a year. By July 2010, Pandora had 600,000 subscribers to its premium service, about 1% of its then 60 million users. Pandora reported $55 million in annual revenue for 2009 and $137 million for 2010. Pandora's "new" business model proved so successful that it went public in June 2011. Revenues again doubled in 2011, to $274 million, and in 2012, to $427 million with about 88% ($375 million) coming from advertising and the remainder from subscriptions and other sources. However, Pandora has not yet shown a profit, and does face competition from services such as Spotify, which also is using the freemium strategy.

Pandora is an example of the "freemium" business revenue model. The model is based on giving away some services for free to 99% of the customers, and relying on the other 1% of the customers to pay for premium versions of the same service. As Chris Anderson, author of *Free: The Future of a Radical Price,* has pointed out, since the marginal cost of digital products is typically close to zero, providing free product does not cost much, and potentially enables you to reach many more people, and if the market is very large, even getting just 1% of that market to purchase could be very lucrative. There are many other examples of successful freemium model companies. For many traditional print media like newspapers and magazines, the freemium model may be their path to survival. But it won't work for every online business.

While it clearly has worked for Pandora, there is ongoing debate among e-commerce CEOs and venture capitalists about the effectiveness of the freemium model. The crux of the issue is that while freemium can be an efficient way to gather a large group of potential customers, companies have found that it's a challenge to convert eyeballs into those willing to pay. Absent subscriber revenue, firms need to rely on advertising revenues.

MailChimp's story is both a success and a cautionary tale. The company lets anyone send e-mail newsletters to customers, manage subscriber lists, and track the performance of an e-mail marketing campaign. Despite the powerful tools it gives marketers, and its open applications programming interface, after 10 years in business, the company had only 85,000 paid subscribers.

In 2009, CEO Ben Chestnut decided that it was time to implement new strategies to attract additional customers. MailChimp began giving away its basic tools and charging subscription fees for special features. The concept was that as those customers' e-mail lists grew, they would continue using MailChimp and be willing to pay for enhanced services. These services included more than just the ability to send e-mails to a greater number of people. Clients would pay to use sophisticated analytics to help them target their e-marketing campaigns more efficiently and effectively.

In just over a year, MailChimp went from 85,000 to 450,000 users. E-mail volume went from 200 million a month to around 700 million. Most importantly, the number of paying customers increased more than 150%, while profit increased more than 650%! Sounds great, but there was also a price to pay. Although the company also saw a significant increase in abuse of its system, they developed an algorithm that has helped them to find and eliminate spammers using their service.

For MailChimp, freemium has been worth the price. It currently supports more than 3 million subscribers worldwide, sending 35 billion e-mails a year. However, Ning, a company that enables users to create their own social networks, tried freemium and came to a different conclusion. They abandoned it in July 2010.

Marc Andreessen, co-author of Mosaic, the first Web browser, and founder of Netscape, launched Ning in 2004. With his assistance, the company has raised $119 million in funding. Despite being the market's leading social network infrastructure

SOURCES: "Pandora Announces June 2013 Audience Metrics," July 9, 2013; "Happy 5th Birthday, Evernote!," by Seth Fiegerman, Mashable.com, June 27, 2013; Pandora Media, Inc., Quarterly Report on Form 10-Q, May 29, 2013; "How MailChimp Learned to Treat Data Like Orange Juice and Rethink the Email in the Process," by Derrick Harris, Gigaom.com, May 5, 2013; "Pandora Now Has 200 Million Registered Users," by Seth Fiegerman, Mashable.com, April 9, 2013; "Evernote's Capital-Intensive Freemium Model Works," by Sraman Mitra, Sramanamitra.com, April 9, 2013; "Remember Ning? Once-buzzy Social Network Has Relaunched Again as a Publishing Platform," by Eliza Kern, Gigaom.com, March 25, 2013; "As Evernote's Cult Grows, the Business Market Beckons," by Rob Walker, Businessweek.com, February 28, 2013; "When Freemium Fails," by Sarah E. Needleman and Angus Loten, *Wall Street Journal*, August 22, 2012; "An Interview with Phil Libin (Evernote)," Doeswhat.com, February 25, 2012; "Glam Media Completes Ning Acquisition," press release, December 5, 2011; "Pandora IPO Prices at $16; Valuation $2.6 Billion," by Eric Savitz, Blogs.forbes.com, June 14, 2011; "Social-Networking Site Ning: Charging Users Works for Us," by Jennifer Valentino-DeVries, *Wall Street Journal*, April 13, 2011; "Explainer: What Is the Freemium Business Model," by Pascal-Emmanuel Gobry, *San Francisco Chronicle*, April 8, 2011; "Shattering Myths About 'Freemium' Services: Mobility is Key," by Martin Scott, *WirelessWeek*, April 7, 2011; "Going Freemium: One Year Later," by Ben Chestnut, Blog.mailchimp.com, September 27, 2010; "How To Avoid The Traps and Make a 'Freemium' Business Model Pay," Anna Johnson, Kikabink.com, June 14th, 2010; "6 Ways for Online Business Directories to Convert More Freemium to Premium," BusinessWeek.com, April 14, 2010; "Case Studies in Freemium: Pandora, Dropbox, Evernote, Automattic and MailChimp," by Liz Gannes, Gigacom.com, Mar. 26, 2010; *Free: The Future of a Radical Price*, by Chris Anderson, Hyperion, 2009.

platform, Ning was having a common problem—converting eyeballs into paying customers. While 13% of customers were paying for some premium services, the revenue was not enough. The more free users Ning acquired, the more it cost the company.

In May 2010, Ning announced the impending end of the freemium model. The company shed staff, going from 167 to 98, and began using 100% of its resources to capture premium users. Since shifting to a three-tier paid subscription model, Ning has experienced explosive growth, increasing the number of paying customers from 17,000 to more than 100,000 and growing revenue by more than 500%. By September 2011, Ning had more than 100 million registered user social profiles and its social networks reached more than 60 million monthly unique users. In December 2011, Ning was acquired by Glam Media, a leading social media company, for $200 million. In March 2013, Glam relaunched Ning as a personal blogging platform for brands and individuals to bring all of their social media followers together in one place. This version of Ning will attempt to intertwine content publishing with community. Glam intends to charge users a fee, rather than returning to a free or freemium strategy.

So when does it make sense to include freemium in a business plan? It makes sense when the product is easy to use and has a very large potential audience, preferably in the millions. A solid customer value proposition is critical. It's helpful if a large user network increases the perceived value of the product (i.e., a dating service). Freemium may work when a company has good long-term customer retention rates and the product produces more value over time. An extremely important part of the equation is that the variable costs of providing the product or service to additional customers for free must be low.

For example, Evernote, a personal note-taking service, added freemium to its business model and has since grown its user base to over 65 million, adding about 100,000 users a day. The company has over 1.4 million paying users. Evernote reportedly has a conversion rate of about 3.7%, which is considered to be quite high in the freemium business world. Evernote has also discovered that the longer a subscriber remains an active user, the more likely he or she is to convert to a premium subscription. For instance, 12% of those who continue to use Evernote for at least two years become premium subscribers. Evernote currently is taking in about $75–$80 million in revenues and has raised over $250 million in funding, the most recent round of which has valued the company at $1 billion, clear proof that the freemium model can add tremendous value.

Companies also face challenges in terms of what products and/or services to offer for free versus what to charge for (this may change over time), the cost of supporting free customers, and how to price premium services. Further, it is difficult to predict attrition rates, which are highly variable at companies using freemium. So, while freemium can be a great way to get early users and to provide a company with a built-in pool for upgrades, it's tough to determine how many users will be willing to pay and willing to stay.

A freemium strategy makes sense for companies such as Pandora, where there is a very low marginal cost, approaching zero, to support free users. It also makes sense for a company where the value to its potential customers depends on a large network, like

Facebook. Freemium also works when a business can be supported by the percentage of customers who are willing to pay, like Evernote and Pandora, especially when there are other revenues like affiliate and advertising fees that can make up for shortfalls in subscriber revenues. Freemium has also become the standard model for most apps, with over 75% of the top 100 apps in Apple's app store using a freemium strategy.

Case Study Questions

1. Compare Pandora's original business model with its current business model. What's the difference between "free" and "freemium" revenue models?

2. What is the customer value proposition that Pandora offers?

3. Why did MailChimp ultimately succeed with a freemium model but Ning did not?

4. What's the most important consideration when considering a freemium revenue model?

2.7 REVIEW

KEY CONCEPTS

■ Identify the key components of e-commerce business models.

A successful business model effectively addresses eight key elements:

- *Value proposition*—how a company's product or service fulfills the needs of customers. Typical e-commerce value propositions include personalization, customization, convenience, and reduction of product search and price delivery costs.
- *Revenue model*—how the company plans to make money from its operations. Major e-commerce revenue models include the advertising model, subscription model, transaction fee model, sales model, and affiliate model.
- *Market opportunity*—the revenue potential within a company's intended marketspace.
- *Competitive environment*—the direct and indirect competitors doing business in the same marketspace, including how many there are and how profitable they are.
- *Competitive advantage*—the factors that differentiate the business from its competition, enabling it to provide a superior product at a lower cost.
- *Market strategy*—the plan a company develops that outlines how it will enter a market and attract customers.
- *Organizational development*—the process of defining all the functions within a business and the skills necessary to perform each job, as well as the process of recruiting and hiring strong employees.
- *Management team*—the group of individuals retained to guide the company's growth and expansion.

■ **Describe the major B2C business models.**

There are a number of different business models being used in the B2C e-commerce arena. The major models include the following:
- *Portal*—offers powerful search tools plus an integrated package of content and services; typically utilizes a combined subscription/advertising revenue/transaction fee model; may be general or specialized (vortal).
- *E-tailer*—online version of traditional retailer; includes virtual merchants (online retail store only), bricks-and-clicks e-tailers (online distribution channel for a company that also has physical stores), catalog merchants (online version of direct mail catalog), and manufacturers selling directly to the consumer.
- *Content provider*—information and entertainment companies that provide digital content; typically utilizes an advertising, subscription, or affiliate referral fee revenue model.
- *Transaction broker*—processes online sales transactions; typically utilizes a transaction fee revenue model.
- *Market creator*—uses Internet technology to create markets that bring buyers and sellers together; typically utilizes a transaction fee revenue model.
- *Service provider*—offers services online.
- *Community provider*—provides an online community of like-minded individuals for networking and information sharing; revenue is generated by advertising, referral fees, and subscriptions.

■ **Describe the major B2B business models.**

The major business models used to date in the B2B arena include:
- *E-distributor*—supplies products directly to individual businesses.
- *E-procurement*—single firms create digital markets for thousands of sellers and buyers.
- *Exchange*—independently owned digital marketplace for direct inputs, usually for a vertical industry group.
- *Industry consortium*—industry-owned vertical digital market.
- *Private industrial network*—industry-owned private industrial network that coordinates supply chains with a limited set of partners.

■ **Understand key business concepts and strategies applicable to e-commerce.**

E-commerce has had a major impact on the business environment in the last decade, and have affected:
- *Industry structure*—the nature of players in an industry and their relative bargaining power by changing the basis of competition among rivals, the barriers to entry, the threat of new substitute products, the strength of suppliers, and the bargaining power of buyers.
- *Industry value chains*—the set of activities performed in an industry by suppliers, manufacturers, transporters, distributors, and retailers that transforms raw inputs into final products and services by reducing the cost of information and other transaction costs.
- *Firm value chains*—the set of activities performed within an individual firm to create final products from raw inputs by increasing operational efficiency.

- *Business strategy*—a set of plans for achieving superior long-term returns on the capital invested in a firm by offering unique ways to differentiate products, obtain cost advantages, compete globally, or compete in a narrow market or product segment.

QUESTIONS

1. What is a business model? How does it differ from a business plan?
2. What are the eight key components of an effective business model?
3. What are Amazon's primary customer value propositions?
4. Describe the five primary revenue models used by e-commerce firms.
5. Why is targeting a market niche generally smarter for a community provider than targeting a large market segment?
6. Would you say that Amazon and eBay are direct or indirect competitors? (You may have to visit the Web sites to answer.)
7. What are some of the specific ways that a company can obtain a competitive advantage?
8. Besides advertising and product sampling, what are some other market strategies a company might pursue?
9. How do venture capitalists differ from angel investors?
10. Why is it difficult to categorize e-commerce business models?
11. Besides the examples given in the chapter, what are some other examples of vertical and horizontal portals in existence today?
12. What are the major differences between virtual storefronts, such as Drugstore.com, and bricks-and-clicks operations, such as Walmart.com? What are the advantages and disadvantages of each?
13. Besides news and articles, what other forms of information or content do content providers offer?
14. What is a reverse auction? What company is an example of this type of business?
15. What are the key success factors for exchanges? How are they different from portals?
16. How have the unique features of e-commerce technology changed industry structure in the travel business?
17. Who are the major players in an industry value chain and how are they impacted by e-commerce technology?
18. What are four generic business strategies for achieving a profitable business?
19. What is the difference between a market opportunity and a marketspace?

PROJECTS

1. Select an e-commerce company. Visit its Web site and describe its business model based on the information you find there. Identify its customer value proposition, its revenue model, the marketspace it operates in, who its main competitors are, any comparative advantages you believe the company possesses, and what its market strategy appears to be. Also try to locate

information about the company's management team and organizational structure. (Check for a page labeled "the Company," "About Us," or something similar.)

2. Examine the experience of shopping on the Web versus shopping in a traditional environment. Imagine that you have decided to purchase a digital camera (or any other item of your choosing). First, shop for the camera in a traditional manner. Describe how you would do so (for example, how you would gather the necessary information you would need to choose a particular item, what stores you would visit, how long it would take, prices, etc.). Next, shop for the item on the Web. Compare and contrast your experiences. What were the advantages and disadvantages of each? Which did you prefer and why?

3. Visit eBay and look at the many types of auctions available. If you were considering establishing a rival specialized online auction business, what are the top three market opportunities you would pursue, based on the goods and auction community in evidence at eBay? Prepare a report or electronic slide presentation to support your analysis and approach.

4. During the early days of e-commerce, first-mover advantage was touted as one way to success. On the other hand, some suggest that being a market follower can yield rewards as well. Which approach has proven to be more successful—first mover or follower? Choose two e-commerce companies that prove your point, and prepare a brief presentation to explain your analysis and position.

5. Prepare a research report (3 to 5 pages) on the current and potential future impacts of e-commerce technology, including mobile devices, on the book publishing industry.

6. Select a B2C e-commerce retail industry segment such as pet products, online gaming, or gift baskets, and analyze its value chain and industry value chain. Prepare a short presentation that identifies the major industry participants in that business and illustrates the move from raw materials to finished product.

7. The ringtone industry is a profitable segment of the music industry. Research the ringtone industry in terms of industry structure, value chains, and competitive environment. Is there room in this industry for another competitor, and if so, what kind of business model and market strategy would it follow?

Technology Infrastructure for E-commerce

CHAPTER 3

E-commerce Infrastructure: The Internet, Web, and Mobile Platform

LEARNING OBJECTIVES

After reading this chapter, you will be able to:

- Discuss the origins of the Internet.
- Identify the key technology concepts behind the Internet.
- Discuss the impact of the mobile platform and cloud computing.
- Describe the role of Internet protocols and utility programs.
- Explain the current structure of the Internet.
- Understand the limitations of today's Internet.
- Describe the potential capabilities of the Internet of the future.
- Understand how the Web works.
- Describe how Internet and Web features and services support e-commerce.
- Understand the impact of m-commerce applications.

Google Glass:

Augment My Reality

Walk down the street in any major city and count the number of people pecking away at their iPhones or Androids. Roam your campus—how many of your friends are texting, tweeting, or watching a YouTube video on their smartphone? Ride the train and observe how many fellow travelers are reading an online newspaper on their phone or tablet computer. Today, the primary means of accessing the Internet, both in the United States and worldwide, is through smartphones and tablet computers. Traditional desktop and laptop PCs will, of course, remain important e-commerce and Internet tools, but the action has shifted to the mobile platform. Rather than being just another channel to the Internet, mobile devices are becoming THE channel. This means the primary platform for e-commerce products and services will also change to the mobile platform. The number of mobile Internet users is expected to grow to more than 80% of all Internet users in the United States, about 210 million people, by 2017.

© REUTERS/Carlo Allegri

The mobile platform provides the foundation for a number of unique new services. One of the most exciting examples is augmented reality: content (text, video, and sound) that is superimposed over live images in order to enrich the user's experience. The technology brings together location and context, helping the user understand his or her environment better. Only recently have mobile devices and their associated networks improved to the point where augmented reality tools are feasible, but a growing number of businesses are investing in augmented reality services for their mobile clients. Many companies are already exploring the wealth of possible applications for augmented reality. Though some are smaller software companies, you've probably heard of at least one of them: Google.

In 2012, Google began releasing information about its prototype augmented reality glasses, and co-founder Sergey Brin began regularly sporting trial versions to public events including the annual Technology, Entertainment, Design (TED) conference and the Oscars. The small, wrap-around, lens-less glass frames have a clear display mounted above the eye and a camera that can snap pictures or record video. A full-fledged augmented reality display that incorporates 3D and virtual reality, overlaying graphics and other images on top of the wearer's current view and adjusting as the line of sight shifts is at least five years away, however.

The 2013 beta version, Glass Explorer, distributed (for $1500 each) to 8,000 lucky app developers and consumers who submitted a winning 50-word response to the hashtag #ifihadglass, focuses on functionality. Commands are issued via either a microphone or touchpad, both of which reside on one arm of the glasses frame. Headphones are unnecessary due to bone-induction technology, which transmits sound via skull vibrations. A viewfinder is likewise unnecessary since video and pictures record what the wearer is actually seeing. Data ranging from calendar notifications to tweets to real-time transcriptions and translations displays on a prism screen in the upper right corner of the field of vision. Directions can be viewed or listened to through the MyGlass companion app when Glass is tethered to a GPS-enabled smartphone. Voice-to-text functionality enables hands-free message response. A quiet chime in the right ear announces the arrival of new texts or events. The computer is awoken from sleep/standby mode with either a tap or an upward nod. To preserve the battery it returns to standby 15 seconds after a tap and three seconds after a nod if no further instructions are given.

The major concerns raised by critics ahead of Glass's 2014 full launch are safety and privacy. In response to the former, Google counters that because the wearer must look slightly upward and to the right to view the screen, vision remains unobstructed. Furthermore, because Glass quickly enters standby mode when not in use, the screen is often dimmed. Still, a West Virginia state representative introduced legislation to amend the existing law prohibiting texting while driving to include the use of a "wearable computer with a head mounted display." While the bill must be reintroduced in the next session, other states are sure to follow.

While Google scoffs at the idea of Glass being used as a surveillance device, emphasizing the use of spoken commands ("OK Glass. Take a picture."), the glow emitted by the active screen, and the fact that the subject of a photo or video must be stared at, at least one reviewer notes that it is rare for bystanders to notice when the button is pushed rather than using the voice command. The bone-induction speaker technology, similar to some hearing aids, conducts the sound to your ear, giving the impression that it is more audible to surrounding people than it actually is. But with many casinos and bars preemptively banning Glass, further design changes may be in the offing. Google must ensure that onlookers feel comfortable in the presence of Glass wearers. Some analysts speculated that product launch postponement from late 2013 to 2014 might be due to addressing these concerns. Meanwhile, Google has actively worked to assuage public apprehension, announcing that facial recognition apps would not be permitted—at least not until strong privacy protections have been developed. But at least one facial recognition app, aimed at helping people remember the names of those to whom they have been introduced, has already been developed. And an alternative operating system that bypasses Glass' swiping and voice commands, allowing a picture to be snapped with a wink, also has emerged. What's more, fears about warrantless access to everything a user sees and records, as well as the government's ability to remotely turn on Glass, as it does with OnStar systems in cars, are not unfounded.

An arguably easier obstacle is Glass' geeky image, which Google took a step towards reversing in the September 2013 issue of *Vogue*. Models sport Glass as a futuristic high-fashion accessory in a spread entitled, "The Final Frontier." Seven months earlier, Google was reportedly in talks with affordable, designer-quality, online prescription eyewear newcomer Warby Parker. If these talks did not result in a more fashionable design for the initial Glass release, they may bear fruit in tackling yet another challenge: how the 64% of the U.S. population that wears prescription glasses can integrate Glass with their eyewear. A prototype into which a lens can be fit has been developed, but widespread adoption may depend on input from a fashion-conscious partner.

In August 2013, Niantic Labs, an independent start-up owned by Google, released the first Glass app (Glassware) to move towards augmented reality. Called Field Trip, it uses GPS data and location descriptions from more than 130 online sources to augment sightseeing trips. Cards with pictures and facts about the historical sites, tourist attractions, and landmarks pop up along with options for finding out about nearby restaurants, local merchants, sales, and specials. While Field Trip had already been released for Android and iOS, a Glassware version was always the objective. Glass "recognizes" what the wearer is viewing in Field Trip. The advantage lies not only in eliminating looking down at a handheld device, but in having instant information without performing any tasks. What's more, Glass can narrate the information, acting as a personal tour guide.

It's not hard to figure out where the e-commerce might reside in these tools. How would you like your business to show up on the Google Glasses of users visiting or searching for points of interest in your neighborhood? Google currently does not allow ad serving on Glass, but in August 2013, the U.S. Patent and Trademark Office approved a patent Google had filed two years previously for a head-mounted eye-tracking system. Analysts speculated that recognition software would identify images and generate a log of viewed items that could be used to develop a "pay-per-gaze" advertising model. Advertisers could be charged each time an image, either online or in the real world, including billboards, posters, and bus ads, is viewed. What's more, pupil dilation may be used to gauge the viewer's reaction and emotional state upon viewing the advertisement. Online ads could be triggered when a positive response is recorded to a real world ad and feedback provided to the advertiser about which images and messages are most effective. Length of gaze and which image within a scene draws the gaze also will be measurable. While further privacy concerns are raised, not to mention whether Glass wearers are going to accept automatic ad serving based on their reactions to images, the patent suggests that personally identifying data may be removed, opt-in or opt-out options offered, and anonymous analytics provided to advertisers.

Consumers will have to opt-in on a wide range of other variables including social etiquette, fashion, comfort, ease-of-use, and superiority to handheld devices before they conclude that Glass is the platform to augment their reality.

SOURCES: "Google Glass Release Date and Price: Is Field Trip Glass's Killer App?" by Robert Schoon, Latinospost.com, Aug 21, 2013; "Is This the Way Google Will Monetize Google Glass?" by Tony Danova, *Business Insider*, Aug. 20, 2013; "Google Patents System for Tracking What You See," by Brandon Bailey, Mercurynews.com, August 19, 2013; "Fashion Models put on Google Glass for Vogue," by Paresh Dave, *Los Angeles Times*, August 19, 2013; "Google Pushes Glass Release Date Back to 2014," by Sharon Gaudin, Computerworld.com, August 19, 2013; "Google Glass Sees All—and That Raises Privacy Concerns," by Jessica Guynn, *Los Angeles Times*, August 9, 2013; "Google Glass: What You Need to Know," by James Rivington, Techradar.com, August 8, 2013; "Google Glass 'Winners' Can Buy Glass Now," by Bianca Bosker, Huffingtonpost.com, May 22, 2013, "Google Glass: What Do You Want to Know About Google's Internet Eyewear?" by Taylor Hatmaker, Readwrite.com, May 8, 2013; "Google Glass Picks Up Early Signal: Keep Out," by David Streitfeld, *New York Times*, May 6, 2013; "Revenues for Augmented Reality in Consumer Electronics Industry to Approach $600 billion by 2016, Forecasts Semico Research," Reuters, August 16, 2012.

This chapter examines the Internet, Web, and mobile platform of today and tomorrow, how it evolved, how it works, and how its present and future infrastructure enables new business opportunities.

The opening case illustrates how important it is for business people to understand how the Internet and related technologies work, and to be aware of what's new. Operating a successful e-commerce business and implementing key e-commerce business strategies such as personalization, customization, market segmentation, and price discrimination require that business people understand Internet technology and keep track of Web and mobile platform developments.

The Internet and its underlying technology is not a static phenomenon in history, but instead continues to change over time. Computers have merged with cell phone services; broadband access in the home and broadband wireless access to the Internet via smartphones, tablet computers, and laptops are expanding rapidly; self-publishing on the Web via blogging, social networking, and podcasting now engages millions of Internet users; and software technologies such as Web services, cloud computing, and smartphone apps are revolutionizing the way businesses are using the Internet. Looking forward a few years, the business strategies of the future will require a firm understanding of these technologies to deliver products and services to consumers. **Table 3.1** summarizes some of the most important developments in e-commerce infrastructure for 2013–2014.

3.1 THE INTERNET: TECHNOLOGY BACKGROUND

What is the Internet? Where did it come from, and how did it support the growth of the Web? What are the Internet's most important operating principles? How much do you really need to know about the technology of the Internet?

Let's take the last question first. The answer is: it depends on your career interests. If you are on a marketing career path, or general managerial business path, then you need to know the basics about Internet technology, which you'll learn in this and the following chapter. If you are on a technical career path and hope to become a Web designer, or pursue a technical career in Web infrastructure for businesses, you'll need to start with these basics and then build from there. You'll also need to know about the business side of e-commerce, which you will learn about throughout this book.

Internet

an interconnected network of thousands of networks and millions of computers linking businesses, educational institutions, government agencies, and individuals

As noted in Chapter 1, the **Internet** is an interconnected network of thousands of networks and millions of computers (sometimes called *host computers* or just *hosts*) linking businesses, educational institutions, government agencies, and individuals. The Internet provides approximately 2.56 billion people around the world (including about 243 million people in the United States) with services such as e-mail, apps, newsgroups, shopping, research, instant messaging, music, videos, and news (eMarketer, Inc., 2013a, 2013b). No single organization controls the Internet or how it functions, nor is it owned by anybody, yet it has provided the infrastructure for a transformation in commerce, scientific research, and culture. The word Internet is

TABLE 3.1	TRENDS IN E-COMMERCE INFRASTRUCTURE 2013–2014

BUSINESS

- Mobile devices become the primary access point to social network services and a rapidly expanding social marketing and advertising platform, and create a foundation for location-based Web services and business models.
- Explosion of Internet content services and mobile access devices strains the business models of Internet backbone providers (the large telecommunication carriers).
- The growth in cloud computing and bandwidth capacity enables new business models for distributing music, movies, and television.
- Search becomes more social and local, enabling social and local commerce business models.
- Internet backbone carriers initiate differential pricing models so that users pay for bandwidth usage.
- "Big data" produced by the Internet creates new business opportunities for firms with the analytic capability to understand it.

TECHNOLOGY

- Mobile devices such as smartphones and tablet computers are well on their way to becoming the dominant mode of access to the Internet. The new client is mobile.
- The explosion of mobile apps threatens the dominance of the Web as the main source of online software applications and leads some to claim "the Web is dead."
- HTML5 grows in popularity among publishers and developers and makes possible Web applications that are just as visually rich and lively as so-called native mobile apps.
- Cloud computing reshapes computing and storage, and becomes an important force in the delivery of software applications and online content.
- The Internet runs out of IPv4 addresses; transition to IPv6 begins.
- The shipment of tablet computers exceeds the shipment of PCs.
- The decreased cost of storage and advances in database software leads to explosion in online data collection known as "big data," and creates new business opportunities for firms with the analytic capability to understand it.
- The Internet of Things, with millions of sensor-equipped devices connecting to the Internet, starts to become a reality.

SOCIETY

- ICANN, which manages the Internet's domain name system, okays vast expansion of top-level domain names.
- Governance of the Internet becomes more involved with conflicts between nations.
- Government control over, and surveillance of, the Internet is expanded in most advanced nations, and in many nations the Internet is nearly completely controlled by government agencies.
- The growing Web-based infrastructure for tracking online and mobile consumer behavior conflicts with individual claims to privacy and control over personal information.

derived from the word *internetwork*, or the connecting together of two or more computer networks. The **Web** is one of the Internet's most popular services, providing access to billions, perhaps trillions, of Web pages, which are documents created in a programming language called HTML that can contain text, graphics, audio, video, and other objects, as well as "hyperlinks" that permit users to jump easily from one page to another. Web pages are navigated using browser software.

the Web
one of the Internet's most popular services, providing access to more than 100 billion Web pages

THE EVOLUTION OF THE INTERNET: 1961—THE PRESENT

Today's Internet has evolved over the last 50 or so years. In this sense, the Internet is not "new;" it did not happen yesterday. Although journalists talk glibly about "Internet" time—suggesting a fast-paced, nearly instant, worldwide global change mechanism—in fact, it has taken about 50 years of hard work to arrive at today's Internet.

The history of the Internet can be segmented into three phases (see **Figure 3.1**). In the first phase, the *Innovation Phase,* from 1961 to 1974, the fundamental building blocks of the Internet were conceptualized and then realized in actual hardware and software. The basic building blocks are packet-switching hardware, a communications protocol called TCP/IP, and client/server computing (all described more fully later in this section). The original purpose of the Internet, when it was conceived in the 1960s, was to link large mainframe computers on different college campuses. This kind of one-to-one communication between campuses was previously only possible through the telephone system or private networks owned by the large computer manufacturers.

In the second phase, the *Institutionalization Phase*, from 1975 to 1995, large institutions such as the Department of Defense (DoD) and the National Science Foundation (NSF) provided funding and legitimization for the fledging invention called the Internet. Once the concepts behind the Internet had been proven in several government-supported demonstration projects, the DoD contributed $1 million to further develop them into a robust military communications system that could withstand nuclear war. This effort created what was then called ARPANET (Advanced Research Projects Agency Network). In 1986, the NSF assumed responsibility for the development of a civilian Internet (then called NSFNET) and began a 10-year-long $200 million expansion program.

In the third phase, the *Commercialization Phase*, from 1995 to the present, government agencies encouraged private corporations to take over and expand both the

| FIGURE 3.1 | STAGES IN THE DEVELOPMENT OF THE INTERNET |

Innovation
1961 – 1974

Institutionalization
1975 – 1995

Commercialization
1995 →

The Internet has developed in three stages over approximately a 50-year period from 1961 to the present. In the Innovation stage, basic ideas and technologies were developed; in the Institutionalization stage, these ideas were brought to life; in the Commercialization stage, once the ideas and technologies had been proven, private companies brought the Internet to millions of people worldwide.

Internet backbone and local service to ordinary citizens—families and individuals across America and the world who were not students on campuses. By 2000, the Internet's use had expanded well beyond military installations and research universities. See **Table 3.2** on pages 114–116 for a closer look at the development of the Internet from 1961 on.

THE INTERNET: KEY TECHNOLOGY CONCEPTS

In 1995, the Federal Networking Council (FNC) passed a resolution formally defining the term *Internet* as a network that uses the IP addressing scheme, supports the Transmission Control Protocol (TCP), and makes services available to users much like a telephone system makes voice and data services available to the public (see **Figure 3.2**).

Behind this formal definition are three extremely important concepts that are the basis for understanding the Internet: packet switching, the TCP/IP communications protocol, and client/server computing. Although the Internet has evolved and changed dramatically in the last 30 years, these three concepts are at the core of the way the Internet functions today and are the foundation for the Internet of the future.

Packet Switching

Packet switching is a method of slicing digital messages into discrete units called **packets**, sending the packets along different communication paths as they become

packet switching
a method of slicing digital messages into packets, sending the packets along different communication paths as they become available, and then reassembling the packets once they arrive at their destination

packets
the discrete units into which digital messages are sliced for transmission over the Internet

FIGURE 3.2	RESOLUTION OF THE FEDERAL NETWORKING COUNCIL

"The Federal Networking Council (FNC) agrees that the following language reflects our definition of the term 'Internet.'

'Internet' refers to the global information system that—

(i) is logically linked together by a globally unique address space based on the Internet Protocol (IP) or its subsequent extensions/follow-ons;

(ii) is able to support communications using the Transmission Control Protocol/Internet Protocol (TCP/IP) suite or its subsequent extensions/follow-ons, and/or other IP-compatible protocols; and

(iii) provides, uses or makes accessible, either publicly or privately, high level services layered on the communications and related infrastructure described herein."

Last modified on October 30, 1995.

SOURCE: Federal Networking Council, 1995

TABLE 3.2	DEVELOPMENT OF THE INTERNET TIMELINE

YEAR	EVENT	SIGNIFICANCE
INNOVATION PHASE 1961–1974		
1961	Leonard Kleinrock (MIT) publishes a paper on "packet switching" networks.	The concept of packet switching is born.
1962	J.C.R. Licklider (MIT) writes memo calling for an "Intergalatic Computer Network."	The vision of a global computer network is born.
1969	BBN Technologies awarded ARPA contract to build ARPANET.	The concept of a packet-switched network moves closer toward physical reality.
1969	The first packet-switched message is sent on ARPANET from UCLA to Stanford.	The communications hardware underlying the Internet is implemented for the first time. The initial ARPANET consisted of 4 routers (then called Interface Message Processors (IMPs)) at UCLA, Stanford, UCSB, and the University of Utah.
1972	E-mail is invented by Ray Tomlinson of BBN. Larry Roberts writes the first e-mail utility program permitting listing, forwarding, and responding to e-mails.	The first "killer app" of the Internet is born.
1973	Bob Metcalfe (XeroxParc Labs) invents Ethernet and local area networks.	**Client/server computing is invented.** Ethernet permitted the development of local area networks and client/server computing in which thousands of fully functional desktop computers could be connected into a short-distance (<1,000 meters) network to share files, run applications, and send messages.
1974	"Open architecture" networking and TCP/IP concepts are presented in a paper by Vint Cerf (Stanford) and Bob Kahn (BBN).	**TCP/IP invented.** The conceptual foundation for a single common communications protocol that could potentially connect any of thousands of disparate local area networks and computers, and a common addressing scheme for all computers connected to the network, are born. Prior to this, computers could communicate only if they shared a common proprietary network architecture. With TCP/IP, computers and networks could work together regardless of their local operating systems or network protocols.
INSTITUTIONALIZATION PHASE 1975–1995		
1977	Lawrence Landweber envisions CSNET (Computer Science Network)	CSNET is a pioneering network for U.S. universities and industrial computer research groups that could not directly connect to ARPANET, and was a major milestone on the path to the development of the global Internet.
1980	TCP/IP is officially adopted as the DoD standard communications protocol.	The single largest computing organization in the world adopts TCP/IP and packet-switched network technology.
1980	Personal computers are invented.	Altair, Apple, and IBM personal desktop computers are invented. These computers become the foundation for today's Internet, affording millions of people access to the Internet and the Web.

(continued)

TABLE 3.2	DEVELOPMENT OF THE INTERNET TIMELINE (CONTINUED)	
YEAR	EVENT	SIGNIFICANCE
1984	Apple Computer releases the HyperCard program as part of its graphical user interface operating system called Macintosh.	The concept of "hyperlinked" documents and records that permit the user to jump from one page or record to another is commercially introduced.
1984	Domain Name System (DNS) introduced.	DNS provides a user-friendly system for translating IP addresses into words that people can easily understand.
1989	Tim Berners-Lee of CERN in Switzerland proposes a worldwide network of hyperlinked documents based on a common markup language called HTML—HyperText Markup Language.	**The concept of an Internet-supported service called the World Wide Web based on HTML pages is born.** The Web would be constructed from "pages" created in a common markup language, with "hyperlinks" that permitted easy access among the pages.
1990	NSF plans and assumes responsibility for a civilian Internet backbone and creates NSFNET.[1] ARPANET is decommissioned.	The concept of a "civilian" Internet open to all is realized through nonmilitary funding by NSF.
1993	The first graphical Web browser called Mosaic is invented by Marc Andreessen and others at the National Center for Supercomputing at the University of Illinois.	Mosaic makes it very easy for ordinary users to connect to HTML documents anywhere on the Web. The browser-enabled Web takes off.
1994	Andreessen and Jim Clark form Netscape Corporation.	The first commercial Web browser—Netscape—becomes available.
1994	The first banner advertisements appear on Hotwired.com in October 1994.	**The beginning of e-commerce.**
COMMERCIALIZATION PHASE 1995–PRESENT		
1995	NSF privatizes the backbone, and commercial carriers take over backbone operation.	**The fully commercial civilian Internet is born.** Major long-haul networks such as AT&T, Sprint, GTE, UUNet, and MCI take over operation of the backbone. Network Solutions (a private firm) is given a monopoly to assign Internet addresses.
1995	Jeff Bezos founds Amazon; Pierre Omidyar forms AuctionWeb (eBay).	E-commerce begins in earnest with pure online retail stores and auctions.
1998	The U.S. federal government encourages the founding of the Internet Corporation for Assigned Names and Numbers (ICANN).	Governance over domain names and addresses passes to a private nonprofit international organization.
1999	The first full-service Internet-only bank, First Internet Bank of Indiana, opens for business.	Business on the Web extends into traditional services.
2003	The Internet2 Abilene high-speed network is upgraded to 10 Gbps.	A major milestone toward the development of ultra-high-speed transcontinental networks several times faster than the existing backbone is achieved.

[1] "Backbone" refers to the U.S. domestic trunk lines that carry the heavy traffic across the nation, from one metropolitan area to another. Universities are given responsibility for developing their own campus networks that must be connected to the national backbone.

(continued)

TABLE 3.2	DEVELOPMENT OF THE INTERNET TIMELINE (CONTINUED)	
YEAR	EVENT	SIGNIFICANCE
2005	NSF proposes the Global Environment for Network Innovations (GENI) initiative to develop new core functionality for the Internet.	Recognition that future Internet security and functionality needs may require the thorough rethinking of existing Internet technology.
2006	The U.S. Senate Committee on Commerce, Science, and Transportation holds hearings on "Network Neutrality."	The debate grows over differential pricing based on utilization that pits backbone utility owners against online content and service providers and device makers.
2007	The Apple iPhone is introduced.	The introduction of the iPhone represents the beginning of the development of a viable mobile platform that will ultimately transform the way people interact with the Internet.
2008	The Internet Society (ISOC) identifies Trust and Identity as a primary design element for every layer of the Internet, and launches an initiative to address these issues.	The leading Internet policy group recognizes the current Internet is threatened by breaches of security and trust that are built into the existing network.
2008	Internet "cloud computing" becomes a billion-dollar industry.	Internet capacity is sufficient to support on-demand computing resources (processing and storage), as well as software applications, for large corporations and individuals.
2009	Internet-enabled smartphones become a major new Web access platform.	Smartphones extend the reach and range of the Internet to more closely realize the promise of the Internet anywhere, anytime, anyplace.
2009	Broadband stimulus package and Broadband Data Improvement Act enacted.	President Obama signs stimulus package containing $7.2 billion for the expansion of broadband access in the United States.
2011	ICANN expands domain name system.	ICANN agrees to permit the expansion of generic top-level domain names from about 300 to potentially thousands using any word in any language.
2012	World IPv6 Launch day.	Major ISPs, home networking equipment manufacturers, and Web companies begin to permanently enable IPv6 for their products and services as of June 6, 2012.
2013	The Internet of Things (IoT) starts to become a reality.	Internet technology spreads beyond the computer and mobile device to anything that can be equipped with sensors, leading to predictions that up to 100 billion uniquely identifiable objects will be connected to the Internet by 2020.

SOURCES: Based on Leiner, et al., 2000; Zakon, 2005; Gross, 2005; Geni.net, 2007; ISOC.org, 2010; arstechnica.com, 2010; ICANN, 2011a; Internet Society, 2012; IEEE Computer Society, 2013.

available, and then reassembling the packets once they arrive at their destination (see **Figure 3.3**). Prior to the development of packet switching, early computer networks used leased, dedicated telephone circuits to communicate with terminals and other computers. In circuit-switched networks such as the telephone system, a complete point-to-point circuit is put together, and then communication can proceed. However, these "dedicated" circuit-switching techniques were expensive and wasted available communications capacity—the circuit would be maintained regardless of whether any data was being sent. For nearly 70% of the time, a dedicated voice circuit is not being fully used because of pauses between words and delays in assembling the circuit

FIGURE 3.3	PACKET SWITCHING

I want to communicate with you.	Original text message
00101101100010011011110001101	Text message digitized into bits
01100010 10101100 11000011	Digital bits broken into packets
0011001 10101100 11000011	Header information added to each packet indicating destination, and other control information, such as how many bits are in the total message and how many packets

In packet switching, digital messages are divided into fixed-length packets of bits (generally about 1,500 bytes). Header information indicates both the origin and the ultimate destination address of the packet, the size of the message, and the number of packets the receiving node should expect. Because the receipt of each packet is acknowledged by the receiving computer, for a considerable amount of time, the network is not passing information, only acknowledgments, producing a delay called latency.

segments, both of which increase the length of time required to find and connect circuits. A better technology was needed.

The first book on packet switching was written by Leonard Kleinrock in 1964 (Kleinrock, 1964), and the technique was further developed by others in the defense research labs of both the United States and England. With packet switching, the communications capacity of a network can be increased by a factor of 100 or more. (The communications capacity of a digital network is measured in terms of bits per second.[2]) Imagine if the gas mileage of your car went from 15 miles per gallon to 1,500 miles per gallon—all without changing too much of the car!

In packet-switched networks, messages are first broken down into packets. Appended to each packet are digital codes that indicate a source address (the origination point) and a destination address, as well as sequencing information and error-control information for the packet. Rather than being sent directly to the destination address, in a packet network, the packets travel from computer to computer until they reach their destination. These computers are called routers. A **router** is a special-purpose computer that interconnects the different computer networks that make up the Internet and routes packets along to their ultimate destination as they travel. To ensure that packets take the best available path toward their destination, routers use a computer program called a **routing algorithm**.

Packet switching does not require a dedicated circuit, but can make use of any spare capacity that is available on any of several hundred circuits. Packet switching

router
special-purpose computer that interconnects the computer networks that make up the Internet and routes packets to their ultimate destination as they travel the Internet

routing algorithm
computer program that ensures that packets take the best available path toward their destination

---

[2] A bit is a binary digit, 0 or 1. A string of eight bits constitutes a byte. A home telephone dial-up modem connects to the Internet usually at 56 Kbps (56,000 bits per second). Mbps refers to millions of bits per second, whereas Gbps refers to billions of bits per second.

protocol
a set of rules and standards for data transfer

Transmission Control Protocol/Internet Protocol (TCP/IP)
the core communications protocol for the Internet

TCP
protocol that establishes the connections among sending and receiving Web computers and handles the assembly of packets at the point of transmission, and their reassembly at the receiving end

IP
protocol that provides the Internet's addressing scheme and is responsible for the actual delivery of the packets

Network Interface Layer
responsible for placing packets on and receiving them from the network medium

Internet Layer
responsible for addressing, packaging, and routing messages on the Internet

Transport Layer
responsible for providing communication with the application by acknowledging and sequencing the packets to and from the application

Application Layer
provides a wide variety of applications with the ability to access the services of the lower layers

makes nearly full use of almost all available communication lines and capacity. Moreover, if some lines are disabled or too busy, the packets can be sent on any available line that eventually leads to the destination point.

Transmission Control Protocol/Internet Protocol (TCP/IP)

While packet switching was an enormous advance in communications capacity, there was no universally agreed-upon method for breaking up digital messages into packets, routing them to the proper address, and then reassembling them into a coherent message. This was like having a system for producing stamps but no postal system (a series of post offices and a set of addresses). The answer was to develop a **protocol** (a set of rules and standards for data transfer) to govern the formatting, ordering, compressing, and error-checking of messages, as well as specify the speed of transmission and means by which devices on the network will indicate they have stopped sending and/or receiving messages.

Transmission Control Protocol/Internet Protocol (TCP/IP) has become the core communications protocol for the Internet (Cerf and Kahn, 1974). **TCP** establishes the connections among sending and receiving Web computers, and makes sure that packets sent by one computer are received in the same sequence by the other, without any packets missing. **IP** provides the Internet's addressing scheme and is responsible for the actual delivery of the packets.

TCP/IP is divided into four separate layers, with each layer handling a different aspect of the communication problem (see **Figure 3.4**). The **Network Interface Layer** is responsible for placing packets on and receiving them from the network medium, which could be a LAN (Ethernet) or Token Ring network, or other network technology. TCP/IP is independent from any local network technology and can adapt to changes at the local level. The **Internet Layer** is responsible for addressing, packaging, and routing messages on the Internet. The **Transport Layer** is responsible for providing communication with the application by acknowledging and sequencing the packets to and from the application. The **Application Layer** provides a wide variety of applications with the ability to access the services of the lower layers. Some of the best-known applications are HyperText Transfer Protocol (HTTP), File Transfer Protocol (FTP), and Simple Mail Transfer Protocol (SMTP), all of which we will discuss later in this chapter.

IP Addresses

The IP addressing scheme answers the question "How can billions of computers attached to the Internet communicate with one another?" The answer is that every computer connected to the Internet must be assigned an address—otherwise it cannot send or receive TCP packets. For instance, when you sign onto the Internet using a dial-up, DSL, or cable modem, your computer is assigned a temporary address by your Internet Service Provider. Most corporate and university computers attached to a local area network have a permanent IP address.

FIGURE 3.4 — THE TCP/IP ARCHITECTURE AND PROTOCOL SUITE

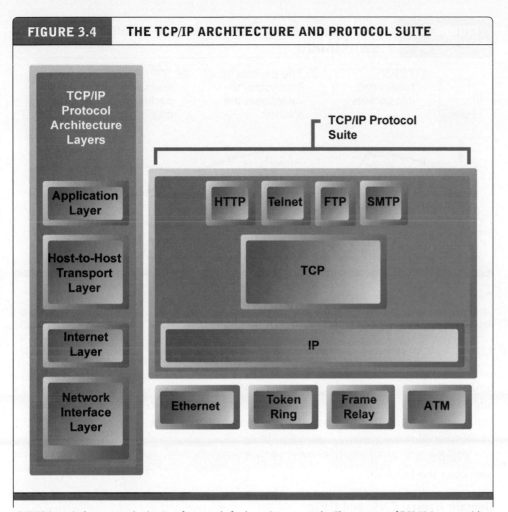

TCP/IP is an industry-standard suite of protocols for large internetworks. The purpose of TCP/IP is to provide high-speed communication network links.

There are two versions of IP currently in use: IPv4 and IPv6. An **IPv4 Internet address** is a 32-bit number that appears as a series of four separate numbers marked off by periods, such as 64.49.254.91. Each of the four numbers can range from 0–255. This "dotted quad" addressing scheme supports up to about 4 billion addresses (2 to the 32nd power). In a typical Class C network, the first three sets of numbers identify the network (in the preceding example, 64.49.254 is the local area network identification) and the last number (91) identifies a specific computer.

Because many large corporate and government domains have been given millions of IP addresses each (to accommodate their current and future work forces), and with all the new networks and new Internet-enabled devices requiring unique IP addresses

IPv4 Internet address
Internet address expressed as a 32-bit number that appears as a series of four separate numbers marked off by periods, such as 64.49.254.91

| FIGURE 3.5 | ROUTING INTERNET MESSAGES: TCP/IP AND PACKET SWITCHING |

The Internet uses packet-switched networks and the TCP/IP communications protocol to send, route, and assemble messages. Messages are broken into packets, and packets from the same message can travel along different routes.

being attached to the Internet, by 2011, there were only an estimated 76 million IPv4 addresses left, declining at the rate of 1 million per week. IPv6 was created to address this problem. An **IPv6 Internet address** is 128 bits, so it can support up to 2^{128} (3.4×10^{38}) addresses, many more than IPv4.

Figure 3.5 illustrates how TCP/IP and packet switching work together to send data over the Internet.

Domain Names, DNS, and URLs

Most people cannot remember 32-bit numbers. An IP address can be represented by a natural language convention called a **domain name**. The **Domain Name System (DNS)** allows expressions such as Cnet.com to stand for a numeric IP address (cnet. com's numeric IP is 216.239.113.101).[3] A **Uniform Resource Locator (URL)**, which is the address used by a Web browser to identify the location of content on the Web, also uses a domain name as part of the URL. A typical URL contains the protocol to be used when accessing the address, followed by its location. For instance, the URL http://www.azimuth-interactive.com/flash_test refers to the IP address 208.148.84.1 with the domain name "azimuth-interactive.com" and the protocol being used to access the address, HTTP. A resource called "flash_test" is located on the server directory path /flash_test. A URL can have from two to four parts; for example, name1.name2.name3.org. We discuss domain names and URLs further in Section 3.4.

IPv6 Internet address
Internet address expressed as a 128-bit number

domain name
IP address expressed in natural language

Domain Name System (DNS)
system for expressing numeric IP addresses in natural language

Uniform Resource Locator (URL)
the address used by a Web browser to identify the location of content on the Web

[3] You can check the IP address of any domain name on the Internet. In Windows 7 or Vista, use Start/ cmd to open the DOS prompt. Type ping < Domain Name >. You will receive the IP address in return.

FIGURE 3.6   THE HIERARCHICAL DOMAIN NAME SYSTEM

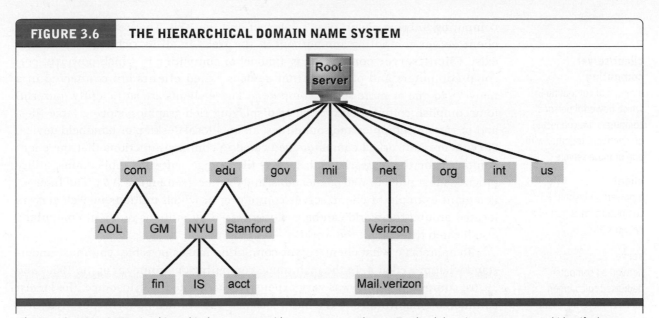

The Domain Name System is a hierarchical namespace with a root server at the top. Top-level domains appear next and identify the organization type (such as .com, .gov, .org, etc.) or geographic location (such as .uk [Great Britain] or .ca [Canada]). Second-level servers for each top-level domain assign and register second-level domain names for organizations and individuals such as IBM.com, Microsoft. com, and Stanford.edu. Finally, third-level domains identify a particular computer or group of computers within an organization, e.g., www.finance.nyu.edu.

Figure 3.6 illustrates the Domain Name System and **Table 3.3** summarizes the important components of the Internet addressing scheme.

Client/Server Computing

While packet switching exploded the available communications capacity and TCP/IP provided the communications rules and regulations, it took a revolution in

TABLE 3.3	PIECES OF THE INTERNET PUZZLE: NAMES AND ADDRESSES
IP addresses	Every device connected to the Internet must have a unique address number called an Internet Protocol (IP) address.
Domain names	The Domain Name System allows expressions such as Pearsoned.com (Pearson Education's Web site) to stand for numeric IP locations.
DNS servers	DNS servers are databases that keep track of IP addresses and domain names on the Internet.
Root servers	Root servers are central directories that list all domain names currently in use for specific domains; for example, the .com root server. DNS servers consult root servers to look up unfamiliar domain names when routing traffic.

client/server computing
a model of computing in which powerful personal computers are connected in a network together with one or more servers

client
a powerful personal computer that is part of a network

server
networked computer dedicated to common functions that the client computers on the network need

computing to bring about today's Internet and the Web. That revolution is called client/server computing and without it, the Web—in all its richness—would not exist. **Client/server computing** is a model of computing in which powerful personal computers and other Internet devices called **clients** are connected in a network to one or more server computers. These clients are sufficiently powerful to accomplish complex tasks such as displaying rich graphics, storing large files, and processing graphics and sound files, all on a local desktop or handheld device. **Servers** are networked computers dedicated to common functions that the client computers on the network need, such as file storage, software applications, utility programs that provide Web connections, and printers (see **Figure 3.7**). The Internet is a giant example of client/server computing in which millions of Web servers located around the world can be easily accessed by millions of client computers, also located throughout the world.

To appreciate what client/server computing makes possible, you must understand what preceded it. In the mainframe computing environment of the 1960s and 1970s, computing power was very expensive and limited. For instance, the largest commercial mainframes of the late 1960s had 128k of RAM and 10-megabyte disk drives, and occupied hundreds of square feet. There was insufficient computing capacity to support graphics or color in text documents, let alone sound files, video, or hyperlinked documents.

With the development of personal computers and local area networks during the late 1970s and early 1980s, client/server computing became possible. Client/server computing has many advantages over centralized mainframe computing. For instance, it is easy to expand capacity by adding servers and clients. Also, client/server networks are less vulnerable than centralized computing architectures. If one server goes down, backup or mirror servers can pick up the slack; if a client computer is inoperable, the rest of the network continues operating. Moreover, processing load is balanced over many powerful smaller computers rather than

FIGURE 3.7   **THE CLIENT/SERVER COMPUTING MODEL**

In the client/server model of computing, client computers are connected in a network together with one or more servers.

being concentrated in a single huge computer that performs processing for everyone. Both software and hardware in client/server environments can be built more simply and economically.

Today there are more than 1.6 billion personal computers in existence worldwide (Deloitte, 2013). Personal computing capabilities have also moved to smart phones and tablet computers (all much "thinner" clients with a bit less computing horsepower, and limited memory, but which rely on Internet servers to accomplish their tasks). In the process, more computer processing will be performed by central servers.

THE NEW CLIENT: THE MOBILE PLATFORM

There's a new client in town. In a few years, the primary means of accessing the Internet both in the United States and worldwide will be through highly portable smartphones and tablet computers, and not traditional desktop or laptop PCs. This means that the primary platform for e-commerce products and services will also change to a mobile platform.

The change in hardware has reached a tipping point. The form factor of PCs has changed from desktops to laptops and tablet computers such as the iPad (and more than 100 other competitors). Tablets are lighter, do not require a complex operating system, and rely on the Internet cloud to provide processing and storage. And, while there are an estimated 1.6 billion PCs in the world, the number of cell phones long ago exceeded the population of PCs. In 2013, there are an estimated 4.3 billion worldwide mobile phone users, with 247 million in the United States, around 1 billion in China, and 525 million in India. The population of mobile phone users is almost three times that of PC owners. About 33%, or 1.4 billion, of the world's mobile phone users are smartphone users. In the United States, about 143 million people access the Internet using mobile devices, mostly smartphones and tablets (eMarketer, Inc., 2013c, 2013d, 2013e). Briefly, the Internet world is turning into a lighter, mobile platform. The tablet is not replacing PCs so much as supplementing PCs for use in mobile situations.

Smartphones are a disruptive technology that radically alters the personal computing and e-commerce landscape. Smartphones involve a major shift in computer processors and software that is disrupting the 40-year dual monopolies established by Intel and Microsoft, whose chips, operating systems, and software applications have dominated the PC market since 1982. Few cell phones use Intel chips, which power 90% of the world's PCs; only a small percentage of smartphones use Microsoft's operating system (Windows Mobile). Instead, smartphone manufacturers either purchase operating systems such as Symbian, the world leader, or build their own, such as Apple's iPhone iOS and BlackBerry's OS, typically based on Linux and Java platforms. Cell phones do not use power-hungry hard drives but instead use flash memory chips with storage up to 32 megabytes that also require much less power.

The mobile platform has profound implications for e-commerce because it influences how, where, and when consumers shop and buy.

FIGURE 3.8 | **THE CLOUD COMPUTING MODEL**

THE INTERNET

Software and
hardware services
Collaboration
Social networking
Integration of devices

In the cloud computing model, hardware and software services are provided on the Internet by vendors operating very large server farms and data centers.

THE INTERNET "CLOUD COMPUTING" MODEL: SOFTWARE AND HARDWARE AS A SERVICE

The growing bandwidth power of the Internet has pushed the client/server model one step further, towards what is called the "cloud computing model" (**Figure 3.8**). **Cloud computing** refers to a model of computing in which firms and individuals obtain computing power and software applications over the Internet, rather than purchasing the hardware and software and installing it on their own computers. Currently, cloud computing is the fastest growing form of computing, with an estimated market size in 2013 of over $130 billion (Gartner, Inc., 2013a).

Hardware firms such as IBM, HP, and Dell have built very large, scalable cloud computing centers that provide computing power, data storage, and high-speed Internet connections to firms that rely on the Internet for business software applications. Amazon, the Internet's largest retailer, is also one of the largest providers of cloud infrastructure and software services.

Software firms such as Google, Microsoft, SAP, Oracle, and Salesforce.com sell software applications that are Internet-based. Instead of software as a product, in the cloud computing model, software is a service provided over the Internet (referred to as SaaS—software as a service). For instance, Google claims there are around 40 million active users and 4 million businesses that use Google Apps, its suite of office software applications such as word processing, spreadsheets, and calendars, that users access over the Internet. More than 100,000 firms and organizations use Salesforce.com's customer relationship management software.

Microsoft, which in the past has depended on selling boxed software to firms and individuals, is adapting to this new marketplace with its own "software plus service" (buy the boxed version and get "free" online services), Windows Live, and online technology initiatives.

cloud computing
model of computing in which firms and individuals obtain computing power and software over the Internet

Cloud computing has many significant implications for e-commerce. For e-commerce firms, cloud computing radically reduces the cost of building and operating Web sites because the necessary hardware infrastructure and software can be licensed as a service from Internet providers at a fraction of the cost of purchasing these services as products. This means firms can adopt "pay-as-you-go" and "pay-as-you-grow" strategies when building out their Web sites. For instance, according to Amazon, hundreds of thousands of customers use Amazon's Web Services arm, which provides storage services, computing services, database services, messaging services, and payment services. For individuals, cloud computing means you no longer need a powerful laptop or desktop computer to engage in e-commerce or other activities. Instead, you can use much less-expensive tablet computers or smartphones that cost a few hundred dollars. For corporations, cloud computing means that a significant part of hardware and software costs (infrastructure costs) can be reduced because firms can obtain these services online for a fraction of the cost of owning, and they do not have to hire an IT staff to support the infrastructure. These benefits come with some risks: firms become totally dependent on their cloud service providers.

OTHER INTERNET PROTOCOLS AND UTILITY PROGRAMS

There are many other Internet protocols and utility programs that provide services to users in the form of Internet applications that run on Internet clients and servers. These Internet services are based on universally accepted protocols—or standards—that are available to everyone who uses the Internet. They are not owned by any organization, but they are services that have been developed over many years and made available to all Internet users.

Internet Protocols: HTTP, E-mail Protocols, FTP, Telnet, and SSL/TLS

HyperText Transfer Protocol (HTTP) is the Internet protocol used to transfer Web pages (described in the following section). HTTP was developed by the World Wide Web Consortium (W3C) and the Internet Engineering Task Force (IETF). HTTP runs in the Application Layer of the TCP/IP model shown in Figure 3.4 on page 119. An HTTP session begins when a client's browser requests a resource, such as a Web page, from a remote Internet server. When the server responds by sending the page requested, the HTTP session for that object ends. Because Web pages may have many objects on them—graphics, sound or video files, frames, and so forth—each object must be requested by a separate HTTP message. For more information about HTTP, you can consult RFC 2616, which details the standards for HTTP/1.1, the version of HTTP most commonly used today (Internet Society, 1999). (An RFC is a document published by the Internet Society [ISOC] or one of the other organizations involved in Internet governance that sets forth the standards for various Internet-related technologies. You will learn more about the organizations involved in setting standards for the Internet later in the chapter.)

E-mail is one of the oldest, most important, and frequently used Internet services. Like HTTP, the various Internet protocols used to handle e-mail all run in the Application Layer of TCP/IP. **Simple Mail Transfer Protocol (SMTP)** is the Internet protocol used to send e-mail to a server. SMTP is a relatively simple, text-based protocol that

HyperText Transfer Protocol (HTTP)
the Internet protocol used for transferring Web pages

Simple Mail Transfer Protocol (SMTP)
the Internet protocol used to send mail to a server

Post Office Protocol 3 (POP3)

a protocol used by the client to retrieve mail from an Internet server

Internet Message Access Protocol (IMAP)

a more current e-mail protocol that allows users to search, organize, and filter their mail prior to downloading it from the server

File Transfer Protocol (FTP)

one of the original Internet services. Part of the TCP/IP protocol that permits users to transfer files from the server to their client computer, and vice versa

Telnet

a terminal emulation program that runs in TCP/IP

Secure Sockets Layer (SSL) /Transport Layer Security (TLS)

protocols that secure communications between the client and the server

Ping

a program that allows you to check the connection between your client and the server

was developed in the early 1980s. SMTP handles only the sending of e-mail. To retrieve e-mail from a server, the client computer uses either **Post Office Protocol 3 (POP3)** or **Internet Message Access Protocol (IMAP)**. You can set POP3 to retrieve e-mail messages from the server and then delete the messages on the server, or retain them on the server. IMAP is a more current e-mail protocol supported by all browsers and most servers and ISPs. IMAP allows users to search, organize, and filter their mail prior to downloading it from the server.

File Transfer Protocol (FTP) is one of the original Internet services. FTP runs in TCP/IP's Application Layer and permits users to transfer files from a server to their client computer, and vice versa. The files can be documents, programs, or large database files. FTP is the fastest and most convenient way to transfer files larger than 1 megabyte, which some e-mail servers will not accept. More information about FTP is available in RFC 959 (Internet Society, 1985).

Telnet is a network protocol that also runs in TCP/IP's Application Layer and is used to allow remote login on another computer. The term Telnet also refers to the Telnet program, which provides the client part of the protocol and enables the client to emulate a mainframe computer terminal. (The industry-standard terminals defined in the days of mainframe computing are VT-52, VT-100, and IBM 3250.) You can then attach yourself to a computer on the Internet that supports Telnet and run programs or download files from that computer. Telnet was the first "remote work" program that permitted users to work on a computer from a remote location.

Secure Sockets Layer (SSL)/Transport Layer Security (TLS) are protocols that operate between the Transport and Application Layers of TCP/IP and secure communications between the client and the server. SSL/TLS helps secure e-commerce communications and payments through a variety of techniques, such as message encryption and digital signatures, that we will discuss further in Chapter 5.

Utility Programs: Ping and Tracert

Packet InterNet Groper (Ping) allows you to check the connection between a client computer and a TCP/IP network (see **Figure 3.9**). Ping will also tell you the time it takes for the server to respond, giving you some idea about the speed of the server

FIGURE 3.9	THE RESULT OF A PING

A ping is used to verify an address and test the speed of the round trip from a client computer to a host and back.

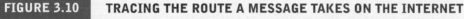

FIGURE 3.10   **TRACING THE ROUTE A MESSAGE TAKES ON THE INTERNET**

VisualRoute and other tracing programs provide some insight into how the Internet uses packet switching. This particular message traveled from a computer in Ashburn, Virginia, to San Antonio, Texas.

SOURCE: Visualware, Inc., 2011.

and the Internet at that moment. You can run Ping from the DOS prompt on a personal computer with a Windows operating system by typing: ping < domain name >. We will discuss Ping further in Chapter 5, because one way to slow down or even crash a domain server is to send it millions of ping requests.

Tracert is one of several route-tracing utilities that allow you to follow the path of a message you send from your client to a remote computer on the Internet. **Figure 3.10** shows the result of a message sent to a remote host using a visual route-tracing program called VisualRoute (available from Visualware).

Tracert
one of several route-tracing utilities that allow you to follow the path of a message you send from your client to a remote computer on the Internet

3.2   THE INTERNET TODAY

In 2013, there are an estimated 2.56 billion Internet users worldwide, up from 100 million users at year-end 1997. While this is a huge number, it represents only about 36% of the world's population (Internetworldstats.com, 2012). Although Internet user growth has slowed in the United States to about 1% annually, in Asia, Internet growth is about 10% annually, and by 2017, it is expected that there will be about 3.2 billion Internet users worldwide. One would think the Internet would be overloaded with such incredible growth; however, this has not been true for several reasons. First, client/server computing is highly extensible. By simply adding servers and clients, the population of Internet users can grow indefinitely. Second, the Internet architecture is built in layers so that each layer can change without disturbing developments in other layers. For instance, the technology used to move messages through the Internet can go through radical changes to make service faster without being disruptive to your desktop applications running on the Internet.

Figure 3.11 illustrates the "hourglass" and layered architecture of the Internet. The Internet can be viewed conceptually as having four layers: Network Technology

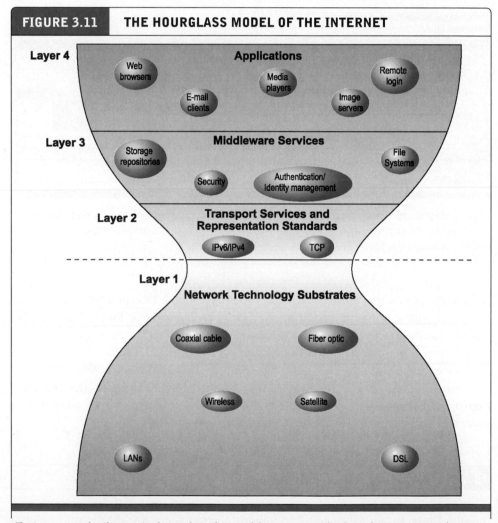

FIGURE 3.11   THE HOURGLASS MODEL OF THE INTERNET

Layer 4 **Applications**
Web browsers · E-mail clients · Media players · Image servers · Remote login

Layer 3 **Middleware Services**
Storage repositories · Security · Authentication/Identity management · File Systems

Layer 2 **Transport Services and Representation Standards**
IPv6/IPv4 · TCP

Layer 1 **Network Technology Substrates**
Coaxial cable · Fiber optic · Wireless · Satellite · LANs · DSL

The Internet can be characterized as an hourglass modular structure with a lower layer containing the bit-carrying infrastructure (including cables and switches) and an upper layer containing user applications such as e-mail and the Web. In the narrow waist are transportation protocols such as TCP/IP.

Substrates, Transport Services and Representation Standards, Middleware Services, and Applications.[4] The **Network Technology Substrate layer** is composed of telecommunications networks and protocols. The **Transport Services and Representation Standards layer** houses the TCP/IP protocol. The **Applications layer** contains client applications such as the World Wide Web, e-mail, and audio or video playback. The **Middleware Services layer** is the glue that ties the applications to the communications networks and includes such services as security, authentication, addresses, and storage repositories. Users work with applications (such as e-mail) and rarely become aware of middleware that operates in the background. Because all layers use TCP/IP and other common standards linking all four layers, it is possible for there to be significant changes in the Network layer without forcing changes in the Applications layer.

THE INTERNET BACKBONE

Figure 3.12 illustrates some of the main physical elements of today's Internet. Originally, the Internet had a single backbone, but today's Internet has several backbones

| FIGURE 3.12 | INTERNET NETWORK ARCHITECTURE |

Today's Internet has a multi-tiered open network architecture featuring multiple national backbones, regional hubs, campus area networks, and local client computers.

---

[4] Recall that the TCP/IP communications protocol also has layers, not to be confused with the Internet architecture layers.

Network Technology Substrate layer

layer of Internet technology that is composed of telecommunications networks and protocols

Transport Services and Representation Standards layer

layer of Internet architecture that houses the TCP/IP protocol

Applications layer

layer of Internet architecture that contains client applications

Middleware Services layer

the "glue" that ties the applications to the communications networks and includes such services as security, authentication, addresses, and storage repositories

Network Service Provider (NSP)
owns and controls one of the major networks comprising the Internet's backbone

backbone
high-bandwidth fiber-optic cable that transports data across the Internet

bandwidth
measures how much data can be transferred over a communications medium within a fixed period of time; is usually expressed in bits per second (bps), kilobits per second (Kbps), megabits per second (Mbps),or gigabits per second (Gbps)

redundancy
multiple duplicate devices and paths in a network

Internet Exchange Point (IXP)
hub where the backbone intersects with local and regional networks and where backbone owners connect with one another

campus area network (CAN)
generally, a local area network operating within a single organization that leases access to the Web directly from regional and national carriers

that are physically connected with each other and that transfer information from one private network to another. These private networks are referred to as **Network Service Providers (NSPs)**, which own and control the major backbone networks (see **Table 3.4**). For the sake of clarity we will refer to these networks of backbones as a single "backbone." The **backbone** has been likened to a giant pipeline that transports data around the world in milliseconds. In the United States, the backbone is composed entirely of fiber-optic cable with bandwidths ranging from 155 Mbps to 2.5 Gbps. **Bandwidth** measures how much data can be transferred over a communications medium within a fixed period of time and is usually expressed in bits per second (bps), kilobits (thousands of bits) per second (Kbps), megabits (millions of bits) per second (Mbps), or gigabits (billions of bits) per second (Gbps).

Connections to other continents are made via a combination of undersea fiber-optic cable and satellite links. The backbones in foreign countries typically are operated by a mixture of private and public owners. The backbone has built-in redundancy so that if one part breaks down, data can be rerouted to another part of the backbone. **Redundancy** refers to multiple duplicate devices and paths in a network.

INTERNET EXCHANGE POINTS

In the United States, there are a number of hubs where the backbone intersects with regional and local networks, and where the backbone owners connect with one another (see **Figure 3.13**). These hubs were originally called Network Access Points (NAPs) or Metropolitan Area Exchanges (MAEs), but now are more commonly referred to as **Internet Exchange Points (IXPs)**. IXPs use high-speed switching computers to connect the backbone to regional and local networks, and exchange messages with one another. The regional and local networks are owned by private telecommunications firms; they generally are fiber-optic networks operating at more than 100 Mbps. The regional networks lease access to ISPs, private companies, and government institutions.

CAMPUS AREA NETWORKS

Campus area networks (CANs) are generally local area networks operating within a single organization—such as New York University or Microsoft Corporation. In fact, most large organizations have hundreds of such local area networks.

TABLE 3.4	MAJOR U.S. INTERNET BACKBONE OWNERS
AT&T	Verio (NTT Communications)
AOL Transit Data Network (ATDN)	CenturyLink
Cable & Wireless	Sprint
Level 3 Communications	Verizon

FIGURE 3.13	SOME MAJOR U.S. INTERNET EXCHANGE POINTS (IXPs)		
Region	**Name**	**Location**	**Operator**
EAST	MAE East	Virginia and Miami	MCI
	New York International Internet Exchange (NYIIX)	New York	Telehouse
	Peering and Internet Exchange (PAIX)	New York, Philadelphia, and Northern Virginia	Switch and Data
	NAP of the Americas	Miami	Terremark
CENTRAL	MAE Chicago	Chicago	MCI
	Chicago NAP	Chicago	SBC
	MAE Central	Dallas and Atlanta	MCI
	Peering and Internet Exchange (PAIX)	Atlanta	Switch and Data
WEST	MAE West	San Jose and Los Angeles	MCI
	Peering and Internet Exchange (PAIX)	Palo Alto, San Jose, and Seattle	Switch and Data
	Los Angeles International Internet Exchange (LAIIX)	Los Angeles	Telehouse

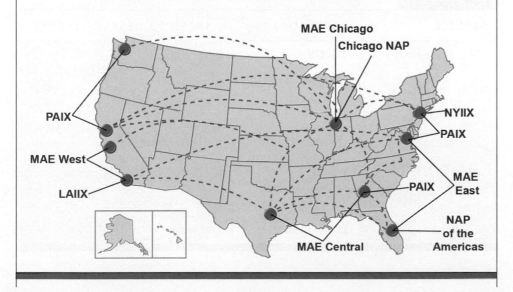

These organizations are sufficiently large that they lease access to the Web directly from regional and national carriers. These local area networks generally are running Ethernet (a local area network protocol) and have network operating systems such as Windows Server or Linux that permit desktop clients to connect to the Internet through a local Internet server attached to their campus networks. Connection speeds in campus area networks are in the range of 10–100 Mbps to the desktop.

INTERNET SERVICE PROVIDERS

Internet Service Provider (ISP)

firm that provides the lowest level of service in the multi-tiered Internet architecture by leasing Internet access to home owners, small businesses, and some large institutions

The firms that provide the lowest level of service in the multi-tiered Internet architecture by leasing Internet access to home owners, small businesses, and some large institutions are called **Internet Service Providers (ISPs)**. ISPs are retail providers. They deal with "the last mile of service" to the curb—homes and business offices. ISPs typically connect to IXPs with high-speed telephone or cable lines (45 Mbps and higher).

There are a number of major ISPs, such as AT&T, Comcast, Cablevision (Optimum), Cox, Time Warner Cable, Verizon, Sprint, and CenturyLink (formerly Qwest), as well as thousands of local ISPs in the United States, ranging from local telephone companies offering dial-up and DSL telephone access to cable companies offering cable modem service, to small "mom-and-pop" Internet shops that service a small town, city, or even county with mostly dial-up phone access. If you have home or small business Internet access, an ISP likely provides the service to you. Satellite firms also offer Internet access, especially in remote areas where broadband service is not available.

narrowband

the traditional telephone modem connection, now operating at 56.6 Kbps

Table 3.5 summarizes the variety of services, speeds, and costs of ISP Internet connections. There are two types of ISP service: narrowband and broadband. **Narrowband** service is the traditional telephone modem connection now operating at 56.6

TABLE 3.5	ISP SERVICE LEVELS AND BANDWIDTH CHOICES	
SERVICE	COST/MONTH	SPEED TO DESKTOP (KBPS)
Telephone modem	$10–$25	30–56 Kbps
DSL	$15–$50	768 Kbps–7 Mbps
FiOS	$90–$130	15 Mbps–50 Mbps
Cable modem	$20–$50	1 Mbps–20 Mbps
Satellite	$20–$50	768 Kbps–5 Mbps
T1	$300–$1,200	1.54 Mbps
T3	$2,500–$10,000	45 Mbps

Kbps (although the actual throughput hovers around 30 Kbps due to line noise that causes extensive resending of packets). This used to be the most common form of connection worldwide but is quickly being replaced by broadband connections in the United States, Europe, and Asia. Broadband service is based on DSL, cable modem, telephone (T1 and T3 lines), and satellite technologies. **Broadband**, in the context of Internet service, refers to any communication technology that permits clients to play streaming audio and video files at acceptable speeds—generally anything above 100 Kbps. In the United States, broadband users surpassed dial-up users in 2004, and in 2013, there are an estimated 84.5 million broadband households (about 70% of all households) (eMarketer, Inc., 2013f).

The actual throughput of data will depend on a variety of factors including noise in the line and the number of subscribers requesting service. Service-level speeds quoted are typically only for downloads of Internet content; upload speeds tend to be much slower. T1 lines are publicly regulated utility lines that offer a guaranteed level of service, but the actual throughput of the other forms of Internet service is not guaranteed.

Digital Subscriber Line (DSL) service is a telephone technology that provides high-speed access to the Internet through ordinary telephone lines found in a home or business. Service levels range from about 768 Kbps up to 7 Mbps. DSL service requires that customers live within two miles (about 4,000 meters) of a neighborhood telephone switching center.

Cable modem refers to a cable television technology that piggybacks digital access to the Internet using the same analog or digital video cable providing television signals to a home. Cable Internet is a major broadband alternative to DSL service, generally providing faster speeds and a "triple play" subscription: telephone, television, and Internet for a single monthly payment. Cable modem services range from 1 Mbps up to 15 Mbps. Comcast, Time Warner Road Runner, Cox, and Cablevision are some of the major cable Internet providers.

T1 and T3 are international telephone standards for digital communication. **T1** lines offer guaranteed delivery at 1.54 Mbps, while T3 lines offer delivery at a whopping 45 Mbps. T1 lines cost about $300–$1,200 per month, and **T3** lines between $2,500 and $10,000 per month. These are leased, dedicated, guaranteed lines suitable for corporations, government agencies, and businesses such as ISPs requiring high-speed guaranteed service levels.

Satellite companies provide high-speed broadband Internet access, primarily to homes and offices located in rural areas where DSL or cable access is not available. Access speeds and monthly costs are comparable to DSL and cable, but typically require a higher initial payment for installation of a small (18-inch) satellite dish. Satellite providers typically have policies that limit the total megabytes of data that a single account can download within a set period, usually 24 hours. The major satellite providers are HughesNet, WildBlue, and StarBand.

Nearly all large business firms and government agencies have broadband connections to the Internet. Demand for broadband service has grown so rapidly because it greatly speeds up the process of downloading Web pages and increasingly, large

broadband
refers to any communication technology that permits clients to play streaming audio and video files at acceptable speeds—generally anything above 100 Kbps

Digital Subscriber Line (DSL)
delivers high-speed access through ordinary telephone lines found in homes or businesses

cable modem
piggybacks digital access to the Internet on top of the analog video cable providing television signals to a home

T1
an international telephone standard for digital communication that offers guaranteed delivery at 1.54 Mbps

T3
an international telephone standard for digital communication that offers guaranteed delivery at 45 Mbps

TABLE 3.6	TIME TO DOWNLOAD A 10-MEGABYTE FILE BY TYPE OF INTERNET SERVICE
TYPE OF INTERNET SERVICE	TIME TO DOWNLOAD
NARROWBAND SERVICES	
Telephone modem	25 minutes
BROADBAND SERVICES	
DSL @ 1 Mbps	1.33 minutes
Cable modem @ 10 Mbps	8 seconds
T1	52 seconds
T3	2 seconds

video and audio files located on Web pages (see **Table 3.6**). As the quality of Internet service offerings expands to include Hollywood movies, music, games, and other rich media-streaming content, the demand for broadband access will continue to swell. In order to compete with cable companies, telephone companies provide an advanced form of DSL called FiOS (fiber-optic service) that provides up to 50 Mbps speeds for households, which is much faster than cable systems.

INTRANETS

intranet
a TCP/IP network located within a single organization for purposes of communications and information processing

The very same Internet technologies that make it possible to operate a worldwide public network can also be used by private and government organizations as internal networks. An **intranet** is a TCP/IP network located within a single organization for purposes of communications and information processing. Internet technologies are generally far less expensive than proprietary networks, and there is a global source of new applications that can run on intranets. In fact, all the applications available on the public Internet can be used in private intranets. The largest provider of local area network software is Microsoft, followed by open source Linux, both of which use TCP/IP networking protocols.

WHO GOVERNS THE INTERNET?

Aficionados and journalists often claim that the Internet is governed by no one, and indeed cannot be governed, and that it is inherently above and beyond the law. What these people forget is that the Internet runs over private and public telecommunications facilities that are themselves governed by laws, and subject to the same pressures as all telecommunications carriers. In fact, the Internet is tied into a complex web of governing bodies, national governments, and international professional societies. There is no one single governing organization that controls activity on the Internet. Instead, there are a number of organizations that influence the system and monitor its operations. Among the governing bodies of the Internet are:

- The *Internet Corporation for Assigned Names and Numbers (ICANN)*, which coordinates the Internet's systems of unique identifiers: IP addresses, protocol parameter registries, and the top-level domain systems. ICANN was created in 1998 by the U.S. Department of Commerce.
- The *Internet Assigned Numbers Authority (IANA)*, which is based at ICANN and in charge of IP addresses.
- The *Internet Engineering Task Force (IETF)*, which is an open international community of network operators, vendors, and researchers concerned with the evolution of the Internet architecture and operation of the Internet. The IETF has a number of working groups, organized into several different areas, that develop and promote Internet standards, which influence the way people use and manage the Internet.
- The *Internet Research Task Force (IRTF)*, which focuses on the evolution of the Internet. The IRTF has a number of long-term research groups working on various topics such as Internet protocols, applications, applications, and technology.
- The *Internet Engineering Steering Group (IESG)*, which is responsible for technical management of IETF activities and the Internet standards process.
- The *Internet Architecture Board (IAB)*, which helps define the overall architecture of the Internet and oversees the IETF and IRTF.
- The *Internet Society (ISOC)*, which is a consortium of corporations, government agencies, and nonprofit organizations that monitors Internet policies and practices.
- The *Internet Governance Forum (IGF)*, which is a multi-stakeholder open forum for debate on issues related to Internet governance.
- The *World Wide Web Consortium (W3C)*, which is a largely academic group that sets HTML and other programming standards for the Web.
- The *Internet Network Operators Groups (NOGs)*, which are informal groups that are made up of ISPs, IXPs, and others that discuss and attempt to influence matters related to Internet operations and regulation.

While none of these organizations has actual control over the Internet and how it functions, they can and do influence government agencies, major network owners, ISPs, corporations, and software developers with the goal of keeping the Internet operating as efficiently as possible. ICANN comes closest to being a manager of the Internet and reflects the powerful role that the U.S. Department of Commerce has played historically in Internet governance.

In addition to these professional bodies, the Internet must also conform to the laws of the sovereign nation-states in which it operates, as well as the technical infrastructures that exist within each nation-state. Although in the early years of the Internet there was very little legislative or executive interference, this situation is changing as the Internet plays a growing role in the distribution of information and knowledge, including content that some find objectionable.

The U.S. Department of Commerce originally created ICANN with the intent that it take temporary control of the Domain Name System and the 13 root servers that are at the heart of the Internet addressing scheme. Beginning in 2000, ICANN and the Department of Commerce suggested they would turn over control of the DNS to some unspecified international body. However, this is no longer the case. The United States changed its policy in June 2005, when the Department of Commerce announced it would retain oversight over the root servers. There were several reasons for this move, including the use of the Internet for basic communications services by terrorist groups, and the uncertainty that might be caused should an international body take over. In 2008, the Department of Commerce reaffirmed this stance, stating that it "has no plans to transition management of the authoritative root zone file to ICANN" (U.S. Department of Commerce, 2008). At the same time, growing Internet powers China and Russia are lobbying for more functions of the Internet to be brought under the control of the United Nations, raising fears that governance of the Internet could become even more politicized (Pfanner, 2012).

Read *Insight on Society: Government Regulation and Surveillance of the Internet* for a further look at the issue of censorship of Internet content and substance.

3.3 THE FUTURE INTERNET INFRASTRUCTURE

The Internet is changing as new technologies appear and new applications are developed. The next era of the Internet is being built today by private corporations, universities, and government agencies. To appreciate the potential benefits of the Internet of the future, you must first understand the limitations of the Internet's current infrastructure.

LIMITATIONS OF THE CURRENT INTERNET

Much of the Internet's current infrastructure is several decades old (equivalent to a century in Internet time). It suffers from a number of limitations, including:

- *Bandwidth limitations*. There is insufficient capacity throughout the backbone, the metropolitan switching centers, and most importantly, the "last mile" to the house and small businesses. The result is slow peak-hour service (congestion) and a limited ability to handle high volumes of video and voice traffic.

latency
delays in messages caused by the uneven flow of information packets through the network

- *Quality of service limitations*. Today's information packets take a circuitous route to get to their final destinations. This creates the phenomenon of **latency**—delays in messages caused by the uneven flow of information packets through the network. In the case of e-mail, latency is not noticeable. However, with streaming video and synchronous communication, such as a telephone call, latency is noticeable to the user and perceived as "jerkiness" in movies or delays in voice communication. Today's Internet uses "best-effort" quality of service (QOS), which makes no guarantees about when or whether data will be delivered, and provides each packet with the same level of service, no matter who the user is or what type of data is contained in the packet. A higher level of service quality is required if the Internet is to keep expanding into new services, such as video on demand and telephony.

- *Network architecture limitations*. Today, a thousand requests for a single music track from a central server will result in a thousand efforts by the server to download the music to each requesting client. This slows down network performance, as the

INSIGHT ON SOCIETY

GOVERNMENT REGULATION AND SURVEILLANCE OF THE INTERNET

On December 17, 2010, a Tunisian street vendor named Mohamed Bouazizi set himself on fire to protest police confiscation of his wares and long-term harassment and humiliation. Within hours, news of the incident spread throughout Tunisia and the rest of world through Internet services such as Twitter and Facebook, and cell phone networks. Within days, tens of thousands of Tunisians took to the streets in what they called the "Jasmine Revolution." By January, President Ben Ali resigned and fled the country after 23 years in power. In the following weeks and months, the news of the Tunisian uprising spread throughout the Arab world, leading hundreds of thousands of protestors to take on their respective dictatorships in Egypt, Syria, Libya, Bahrain, and Yemen, along with smaller protests in other Arab countries. Called the "Arab Spring," the Internet and cell phone–based message services like Twitter played a critical role in helping young protestors discover one another, organize, and act together.

Events like the Jasmine Revolution and the Arab Spring, along with many earlier incidents, encourage us all to think of the Internet and the Web as an extraordinary technology unleashing torrents of human creativity, innovation, expression, and sometimes, popular rebellion. On a scale much larger than the invention of movable type by Gutenberg in fifteenth-century Germany, the Internet allows hundreds of millions of people to e-mail, Facebook, Twitter, and Google (all verbs that are new to our age, the Internet age). How ironic then that the same Internet has spawned an explosion in government control and surveillance of individuals on the Internet! Totalitarian dictators of the twentieth century

would have given their eyeteeth for such a marvelous technology that can track what millions of people do, say, think, and search for in billions of e-mails, searches, blogs, and Facebook posts.

Many people assume that because the Internet is so widely dispersed, it must be difficult to control or monitor. Legions of music and video pirates believe they are anonymous on the Internet and cannot possibly be held accountable for what they do. Unfortunately, with contemporary surveillance technologies, these beliefs are either false or misleading. In reality, just about all governments assert some kind of control and surveillance over Internet content and messages. There's a tug of war going on between sophisticated users of the Internet and state-sponsored censors and security police around the world.

Internet traffic in all countries runs through large fiber-optic trunk lines. In China, there are three such lines, and China requires the companies that own these lines to configure their routers for both internal and external service requests. When a request originates in China for a Web page in Chicago, Chinese routers examine the request to see if the site is on a blacklist, and then examine words in the requested Web page to see if it contains blacklisted terms. Blacklisted terms include "falun" (a suppressed religious group in China) and "Tiananmen Square massacre" (or any symbols that might lead to such results such as "198964" which signifies June 4, 1989, the date of the massacre), among many others. The system is often referred to as "The Great Firewall of China" and is implemented with the assistance of Cisco Systems (the U.S. firm that is the largest manufacturer of routers in the world). Other U.S. Internet firms are also involved in China's censorship and surveillance

(continued)

efforts, including Yahoo, Microsoft, and Juniper Networks, among many others.

When U.S. search engines (Microsoft, Google, and Yahoo) moved into China in 2002, the firms agreed to censor the search results of Chinese citizens according to criteria dictated by China's Internet agency in return for access to the China market. For instance, in 2002, the Chinese government summarily shut off access from inside China to Google's offshore servers in Hong Kong, which did not exercise self-censorship. Even before this action, Google's results were often slowed by the Great Firewall. After this incident, Google decided in 2006 to locate its servers on Chinese soil (Google.cn), where they became directly subject to China's censorship regime, which bans from the Internet anything that damages the honor or interests of the state, disturbs the public order, or infringes upon national customs and habits.

Flash forward to January 2010: Google announced it was leaving China after a massive cyber assault was launched from Taiwan but that was allegedly instigated by the Chinese government in an effort to steal user information (such as what Chinese citizens were searching for). Thirty-four other U.S. companies were targeted, all high-tech Internet-related concerns. Google claimed it could no longer abide by China's growing demands for censorship and surveillance although the attack was also a direct threat to Google's business algorithms and proprietary technology. In other words, this attack was aimed at Google's jugular. Google began automatically redirecting all Chinese mainland traffic to its uncensored Hong Kong servers. The Chinese government objected. Google, in a minor compromise, stopped the automatic redirect and instead put a button on the screen that users could click to search the Hong Kong site, otherwise they would default to the censored Chinese site. The Chinese government objected again and threatened to withdraw Google's license to operate in China. In March 2011, Google

accused the Chinese government of disrupting Gmail service inside China and making it appear like a technical problem with Google. And as the Arab Spring spread throughout the Middle East and Africa, China strengthened its efforts to censor the Internet. The word "freedom" is now censored on Chinese search engines, along with "Jasmine" and "Arab Spring."

China is hardly the only government that exercises powerful controls over its citizens' use of the Internet. In June 2009, the video of Neda Agha-Soltan, who had been shot by a squad of Iranian riot police and was bleeding to death on the streets of Tehran, quickly raced around the world via the Internet and cell phone networks despite the efforts of the Iranian government, which had completely shut down text messaging in the country; blocked access to selected sites such as YouTube, MySpace, and Facebook; and slowed all Internet traffic in Iran by 90% so it could sift through e-mail messages. In the protests that followed the disputed Iranian election of June 2009, Twitter became the primary organizing tool of the protestors, and an important source of information for the rest of the world, along with YouTube and other social sites to which protestors were able to connect, despite the best efforts of Iranian government censors.

Iran's Internet surveillance of its citizens is considered by security experts to be one of the world's most sophisticated mechanisms for controlling and censoring the Internet, allowing it to examine the content of individual online communications on a massive scale, far more sophisticated than even China's Internet surveillance activities. The Iranian system goes far beyond preventing access to specific sites such as BBC World News, Google, and Facebook. Because the techniques for getting around government site access censorship are widely known (generally find a proxy server in another country that will allow you access to a forbidden site), governments need to do much more to control access and to figure out what

(continued)

their citizens are really thinking. One technique is deep packet inspection of every e-mail, text, or tweet. Deep packet inspection allows governments to read messages, alter their contents for disinformation purposes, and identify senders and recipients. It is accomplished by installing computers in the line between users and ISPs, opening up every digitized packet, inspecting for keywords and images, reconstructing the message, and sending it on. This is done for all Internet traffic including Skype, Facebook, e-mail, tweets, and messages sent to proxy servers. These operations can slow down Internet service, but this delay can be avoided by installing additional servers. Iran's Internet Monitoring Center is located in the government telecommunications monopoly, a central choke point for all Internet traffic in the country. Iran has some of the world's finest deep packet monitoring equipment supplied by a joint venture called Nokia Siemens Networks. There are, of course, reasons why Iran's government did not simply shut down the Internet entirely. Some traffic is required for business purposes, and keeping the Internet functioning allows the state to identify its enemies and critics.

Not to be outdone, both Europe and the United States have at various times taken steps to control access to Internet sites, censor Web content, and engage in extensive surveillance of communications, although not to the extent of Iran, China, and many other nations. For instance, Britain has a list of blocked sites, as does Germany and France. The Australian Communications and Media Authority has developed a list of several hundred Web sites that have been refused registration in Australia, mostly violent video game and online pornography sites. The United States and European countries generally ban the sale, distribution, and/or possession of online child pornography. Both France and Germany bar online Nazi memorabilia. Even in South Korea, one of the world's most wired countries, reports have surfaced that

the government is monitoring its citizens' Internet usage and cracking down on freedoms.

In response to terrorism threats and other crimes, European governments and the U.S. government have also initiated deep packet inspection of e-mail and text communications. This surveillance is not limited to cross-border international data flows and includes large-scale domestic surveillance and analysis of "ordinary" e-mail, tweets, and other messages. For instance, the FBI has recently created a secret Internet surveillance unit, the National Domestic Communications Assistance Center, in a collaborative effort with the U.S. Marshals Service and the Drug Enforcement Agency. The NDCAC's mission is to assist in the development of new surveillance technologies that will allow authorities to increase the interception of Internet, wireless, and VoIP communications. Although it may seem preposterous that any U.S. government agency could read an estimated 150 billion daily e-mails, this task is, in reality, only slightly more complicated than Google's handling of 10 to 12 billion search queries per month. Governments and private technology companies are partnering to use software to analyze millions of e-mails, tweets, and other messages in an effort to preemptively fight terror and stop other crimes. Governments and telecommunications companies are also increasingly working together to monitor Internet users.

For instance, in 2013, NSA contractor Edward Snowden made headlines by leaking classified NSA documents shedding light on the NSA's PRISM program, which grants the agency unauthorized access to the servers of major Internet companies such as Facebook, Google, Apple, Microsoft, and many others. Additionally, the documents revealed the existence of the NSA's XKeyscore program, which allows analysts to search databases of e-mails, chats, and browsing histories of individual citizens without any authorization. Warrants, court clearance, or other forms of legal documentation are not required

(continued)

for analysts to use the technology. The NSA claims that the program was only used to monitor foreign intelligence targets and that it has assisted in apprehending hundreds of terrorists. However, in August 2013, the NSA declassified several documents that show the collection of 56,000 Internet communications by Americans with no connection to terrorism and without legal consent to do so.

The NSA technologies leaked by Snowden appear to be the most wide-reaching and all-encompassing Internet surveillance technologies that are currently in use by any government. If Snowden had not come forward, it is unclear whether the existence of these programs would have come to public light. The NSA claims that it has begun putting safeguards in place to prevent the accidental collection of data on lawful U.S. citizens not suspected of any terror connections. As surveillance technologies become more and more sophisticated, the need for such controls on the scope and usage of each program will become ever more important.

▬ SOURCES: "NSA Surveillance Covers 75 Percent of U.S. Internet Traffic: WSJ," by Reuters, News.Yahoo.com, August 20, 2013; "New Snowden Leak: NSA Program Taps All You Do Online," by Amanda Wills, Mashable.com, August 1, 2013; "Report: Snowden Says NSA Can Tap E-mail, Facebook Chats," by Doug Stanglin, USAToday.com, July 31, 2013; "Snowden: NSA Collects 'Everything,' Including Content of Emails," by Eyder Peralta, NPR.org, June 17, 2013; "Sir Tim Berners-Lee Accuses Government of 'Draconian' Internet Snooping," by Lucy Kinder, *The Telegraph*, September 6, 2012; "Korea Policing the Net. Twist? It's South Korea," by Choe Sang-Hun, *New York Times*, August 12, 2012; "How Governments and Telecom Companies Work Together on Surveillance Laws," by Ryan Gallagher, Slate.com, August 14, 2012; "FBI Quietly Forms Secret Net-Surveillance Unit," by Declan McCullagh, News.Cnet.com, May 22, 2012; "Catching Scent of Revolution, China Moves to Snip Jasmine," by Andrew Jacobs and Jonathon Ansfield, *New York Times*, May 10, 2011; "Google Accuses Chinese of Blocking Gmail Service," by David Barboza and Claire Cain Miller, *New York Times*, March 20, 2011; "Bullets Stall Youthful Push for Arab Spring," by Michael Slackman, *New York Times*, March 17, 2011; "OpenNet Initiative Releases 2010 Year in Review," Berkman Center for Internet and Society, Harvard University, March 22, 2011; "Google Co-founder Sergey Brin Urges US to Act Over China Web Censorship," by Bobbie Johnson, TheGuardian.co.uk, May 10, 2010; "Journalists' E-mails Hacked in China," by Andrew Jacobs, *New York Times*, March 31, 2010; "Enemies of the Internet. Countries Under Surveillance," Reporters Without Borders, www.rsf.org, March 12, 2010; "Google Hack Smells More and More Like Chinese Government Job," by Katherine Noyes, Technewsworld.com, February 22, 2010; "Google Warns of China Exit Over Hacking," by Jessica Vascellaro, *Wall Street Journal*, January 13, 2010; "Foreign Intelligence Surveillance Act (FISA)," *New York Times*, July 23, 2009.

same music track is sent out a thousand times to clients that might be located in the same metropolitan area. This is very different from television, where the program is broadcast once to millions of homes.

- *Wired Internet.* The Internet is still largely based on cables—fiber-optic and coaxial copper cables. Copper cables use a centuries-old technology, and fiber-optic cable is expensive to place underground. The wired nature of the Internet restricts mobility of users although it is changing rapidly as Wi-Fi hotspots proliferate, and cellular phone technology advances. However, cellular systems are often overloaded due to the growth in the number of smartphones.

Now imagine an Internet at least 1,000 times as powerful as today's Internet, one that is not subjected to the limitations of bandwidth, protocols, architecture, physical connections, and language detailed previously. Welcome to the world of the future Internet, and the next generation of e-commerce services and products!

THE INTERNET2® PROJECT

Internet2®
advanced networking consortium of more than 350 member institutions working in partnership to facilitate the development, deployment, and use of revolutionary Internet technologies

Internet2® is an advanced networking consortium of more than 350 member institutions including universities, corporations, government research agencies, and not-for-profit networking organizations, all working in partnership to facilitate the development, deployment, and use of revolutionary Internet technologies. The broader

Internet2 community includes more than 66,000 institutions across the United States and international networking partners in more than 50 countries. Internet2's work is a continuation of the kind of cooperation among government, private, and educational organizations that created the original Internet.

The advanced networks created and in use by Internet2 members provide an environment in which new technologies can be tested and enhanced. For instance, Internet2 provides a next-generation, nationwide 100 gigabit-per-second network that not only makes available a reliable production services platform for current high-performance needs but also creates a powerful experimental platform for the development of new network capabilities. The fourth generation of this network, built through a federal stimulus grant from the National Telecommunications and Information Administration's Broadband Technology Opportunities Program, began to be deployed in 2011 (see **Figure 3.14**). The hybrid optical and packet network provides 8.8 terabits of capacity with the ability to seamlessly scale as requirements grow, includes over 15,000 miles of owned fiber optic cable, and will reach into underserved areas of the country, supporting connectivity for approximately 200,000 U.S. community anchor institutions (schools, local libraries, and museums), and enabling them to provide citizens across the country with telemedicine, distance learning, and other advanced applications not possible with consumer-grade Internet services. The infrastructure

---

FIGURE 3.14 | **INTERNET2 100 GIGABIT NETWORK**

Internet2 is in the process of deploying a 100 gigabit-per-second network. The network represents the first national implementation of 100 gigabit Ethernet capabilities across the entire network.

SOURCE: Internet2.edu, 2011.

supports a wide range of IP and optical services already available today and also will stimulate a new generation of innovative services. The goal is to create an intelligent global ecosystem that will enable researchers, scientists, and others to "turn on" high-capacity network connections whenever and wherever they are needed. Other initiatives involve science and engineering (advanced network applications in support of distributed lab environments, remote access to rare scientific instruments, and distributed large-scale computation and data access), health sciences and health networks (telemedicine, medical and biological research, and health education and awareness), and arts and humanities (collaborative live performances, master classes, remote auditions, and interactive performing arts education and media events).

THE FIRST MILE AND THE LAST MILE

The Internet2 project is just the tip of the iceberg when it comes to future enhancements to the Internet. In 2007, the NSF began work on the Global Environment for Network Innovations (GENI) initiative. GENI is a unique virtual laboratory for exploring future internets at scale. GENI aims to promote innovations in network science, security technologies, services, and applications. GENI is a partnership of leading academic centers and private corporations such as Cisco, IBM, and HP, among many others. To date, awards have been made to 83 academic/industry teams for various projects to build, integrate, and operate early prototypes of the GENI virtual laboratory (Geni.net, 2013). In June 2012, the NSF announced that it would be building on the GENI project as part of US Ignite, a White House initiative aimed at realizing the potential of fast, open, next-generation networks. GENI will underlie US Ignite and provide a virtual laboratory for experiments that the NSF hopes will transform cybersecurity, network performance, and cloud computing research (National Research Foundation, 2012).

The most significant privately initiated (but often government-influenced) changes are coming in two areas: fiber-optic trunk line bandwidth and wireless Internet services. Fiber optics is concerned with the first mile or backbone Internet services that carry bulk traffic long distances. Wireless Internet is concerned with the last mile—from the larger Internet to the user's smartphone, tablet computer, or laptop.

Fiber Optics and the Bandwidth Explosion in the First Mile

fiber-optic cable
consists of up to hundreds of strands of glass or plastic that use light to transmit data

Fiber-optic cable consists of up to hundreds of strands of glass that use light to transmit data. It often replaces existing coaxial and twisted pair cabling because it can transmit much more data at faster speeds, with less interference and better data security. Fiber-optic cable is also thinner and lighter, taking up less space during installation. The hope is to use fiber optics to expand network bandwidth capacity in order to prepare for the expected increases in Web traffic once next-generation Internet services are widely adopted.

Telecommunication firms have made substantial investments in fiber optic cross-country and regional cable systems in the last decade. This installed base of fiber optic cable represents a vast digital highway that is currently being exploited by YouTube (Google), Facebook, and other high-bandwidth applications. Telecommunications companies are recapitalizing and building new business models based on market prices for digital traffic. The net result is that society ultimately benefited from extraordinarily low-cost, long-haul, very high-bandwidth communication facilities that are already paid for.

Demand for fiber-optic cable has begun to strengthen as consumers demand integrated telephone, broadband access, and video from a single source. In 2011, around 19 million miles of optical fiber were installed in the United States, the most since 2000. Verizon has spent over $23 billion since 2004 building and expanding its FIOS fiber-optic Internet service. In 2013, there are about 5 million Verizon FiOS broadband customers. FiOS provides download speeds of up to 50 Mbps and upload speeds of up to 10 Mbps. In 2011, Google joined the fray with Google Fiber, a 1 Gbps fiber optic network. Currently, Google Fiber is available in Kansas City, Kansas and Missouri, with plans to expand to Austin, Texas and Provo, Utah. **Table 3.7** illustrates several optical bandwidth standards and compares them to traditional T lines.

The Last Mile: Mobile Internet Access

Fiber-optic networks carry the long-haul bulk traffic of the Internet—and in the future will play an important role in bringing BigBand to the household and small business. The goal of the Internet2 and GENI projects is to bring gigabit and ultimately terabit bandwidth to the household over the next 20 years. But along with fiber optics, arguably the most significant development for the Internet and Web in the last five years has been the emergence of mobile Internet access.

Wireless Internet is concerned with the last mile of Internet access to the user's home, office, car, smartphone, or tablet computer, anywhere they are located. Up until 2000, the last-mile access to the Internet—with the exception of a small satellite Internet connect population—was bound up in land lines of some sort: copper coaxial TV cables or telephone lines or, in some cases, fiber-optic lines to the office. Today, in comparison, high-speed cell phone networks and Wi-Fi network hotspots provide a major alternative.

In 2012, more tablet and laptop computers with wireless networking functionality built in were sold in the United States than desktop computers. More smartphones were sold than PCs of any kind in 2012 as well. Smartphones are the fastest growing mobile devices with respect to Internet access. Clearly, a large part of the future Internet will be mobile, access-anywhere broadband service for the delivery of video, music, and Web search. According to eMarketer, there are already 143 million mobile

TABLE 3.7	HIGH-SPEED OPTICAL BANDWIDTH STANDARDS
STANDARD	SPEED
T1	1.544 Mbps
T3	43.232 Mbps
OC-3	155 Mbps
OC-12	622 Mbps
OC-48	2.5 Gbps
OC-192	9.6 Gbps

Note: "OC" stands for Optical Carrier and is used to specify the speed of fiber-optic networks conforming to the SONET standard. SONET (Synchronous Optical Networks) includes a set of signal rate multiples for transmitting digital signals on optical fiber. The base rate (OC-1) is 51.84 Mbps.

Internet users in the United States in 2013, and more than 1.88 billion worldwide (eMarketer, Inc., 2013e; 2013g).

Telephone-based versus Computer Network-based Wireless Internet Access There are two different basic types of wireless Internet connectivity: telephone-based and computer network-based systems.

Telephone-based wireless Internet access connects the user to a global telephone system (land, satellite, and microwave) that has a long history of dealing with thousands of users simultaneously and already has in place a large-scale transaction billing system and related infrastructure. Cellular telephones and the telephone industry are currently the largest providers of wireless access to the Internet today. In 2012, there were more than 1.7 billion mobile phones sold worldwide, with a similar amount expected to be sold in 2013. The percentage of smartphones sold exceeded regular mobile phones for the first time during the second quarter of 2013, accounting for over 51% of all mobile phone sales (Gartner, Inc., 2013b). **Table 3.8** summarizes the various telephone technologies used for wireless Internet access.

Smartphones, such as an iPhone, Android, or BlackBerry, combine the functionality of a cell phone with that of a laptop computer with Wi-Fi capability. This makes it possible to combine in one device music, video, Web access, and telephone service.

Wireless local area network (WLAN)-based Internet access derives from a completely different background from telephone-based wireless Internet access. Popularly known as **Wi-Fi**, WLANs are based on computer local area networks where the task is to connect client computers (generally stationary) to server computers within local areas of, say, a few hundred meters. WLANs function by sending radio signals that are broadcast over the airwaves using certain radio frequency ranges (2.4 GHz to 5.875 GHz, depending on the type of standard involved). The major technologies here are the various versions of the Wi-Fi standard, WiMax, and Bluetooth (see **Table 3.9**).

Wi-Fi
Wireless standard for Ethernet networks with greater speed and range than Bluetooth

TABLE 3.8	WIRELESS INTERNET ACCESS TELEPHONE TECHNOLOGIES		
TECHNOLOGY	SPEED	DESCRIPTION	PLAYERS
3G (THIRD GENERATION)			
CDMA2000 EV-DO HSPA (W-CDMA)	144 Kbps–2 Mbps	High-speed, mobile, always on for e-mail, browsing, instant messaging. Implementing technologies include versions of CDMA2000 EV-DO (used by CDMA providers) and HSPDA (used by GSM providers). Nearly as fast as Wi-Fi.	Verizon, Sprint, AT&T, T-Mobile, Vodafone
3.5G (3G+)			
CDMA2000 EV-DO, Rev.B	Up to 14.4 Mbps	Enhanced version of CDMA 2000 EV-DO.	Verizon, Sprint
HSPA+	Up to 11 Mbps	Enhanced version of HSPA.	AT&T, T-Mobile
4G (FOURTH GENERATION)			
Long-Term Evolution (LTE)	Up to 100 Mbps	True broadband on cell phone.	AT&T, Verizon, Sprint, T-Mobile (in 2013)

TABLE 3.9	WIRELESS INTERNET ACCESS NETWORK TECHNOLOGIES		
TECHNOLOGY	RANGE/ SPEED	DESCRIPTION	PLAYERS
Wi-Fi (IEEE 802.11 a/b/g/n)	300 feet/ 11–70 Mbps	Evolving high-speed, fixed broadband wireless local area network for commercial and residential use	Linksys, Cisco, and other Wi-Fi router manufacturers; entrepreneurial network developers
WiMax (IEEE 802.16)	30 miles/ 50–70 Mbps	High-speed, medium-range, broadband wireless metropolitan area network	Clearwire, Sprint, Fujitsu, Intel, Alcatel, Proxim
Bluetooth (wireless personal area network)	1–30 meters/ 1–3 Mbps	Modest-speed, low-power, short-range connection of digital devices	Sony Ericsson, Nokia, Apple, HP, and other device makers

In a Wi-Fi network, a *wireless access point* (also known as a "hot spot") connects to the Internet directly via a broadband connection (cable, DSL telephone, or T1 line) and then transmits a radio signal to a transmitter/receiver installed in a laptop computer or PDA, either as a PC card or built-in at manufacture (such as Intel's Centrino processor, which provides built-in support for Wi-Fi in portable devices). **Figure 3.15** illustrates how a Wi-Fi network works.

FIGURE 3.15	WI-FI NETWORKS

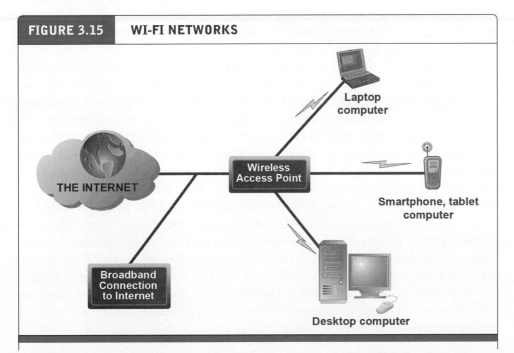

In a Wi-Fi network, wireless access points connect to the Internet using a land-based broadband connection. Clients, which could be laptops, desktops, or tablet computers, connect to the access point using radio signals.

Wi-Fi offers high-bandwidth capacity from 11 Mbps to 70 Mbps—far greater than any 3G or 4G service currently in existence—but has a limited range of 300 meters, with the exception of WiMax discussed below. Wi-Fi is also exceptionally inexpensive. The cost of creating a corporate Wi-Fi network in a single 14-story building with an access point for each floor is less than $100 an access point. It would cost well over $500,000 to wire the same building with Ethernet cable.

While initially a grass roots, "hippies and hackers" public access technology, billions of dollars have subsequently been poured into private ventures seeking to create for-profit Wi-Fi networks. The most prominent network has been created by Boingo Wireless with more than 700,000 hot spots around the globe. AT&T Wi-Fi Services (formerly Wayport) created another large network that provides Wi-Fi service at hotels, airports, McDonald's, and IHOP restaurants, and Hertz airport rental offices, with around 30,000 hot spots in the United States. T-Mobile and Sprint have also established nationwide Wi-Fi services at 2,000 Starbucks coffee shops and thousands of other public locations. Apple, in turn, has made Wi-Fi automatically available to iPhone and iPad devices as an alternative to the more expensive and much slower 3G and 4G cellular systems.

Will WLAN compete directly against far more expensive telephone 4G services? The answer is "eventually, but not right now." Wi-Fi was originally a local area network technology of limited range, for stationary client computers, but with high capacity suitable for most Web surfing and some corporate uses with modest bandwidth demands. Cellular phone systems are wide area networks of nearly unlimited range, for mobile client computers and handhelds, and with modest but rapidly increasing capacity suitable for e-mail, photos, and Web browsing (on very small screens). However, the rock-bottom price of Wi-Fi coupled with ambitious plans for a 30-mile-range WiMax (802.16) service suggests that Wi-Fi could drain significant business from far more capital-intensive cellular systems.

A second WLAN technology for connecting to the Internet, and for connecting Internet devices to one another, is called Bluetooth. **Bluetooth** is a personal connectivity technology that enables links between mobile computers, mobile phones, PDAs, and connectivity to the Internet (Bluetooth.com, 2013). Bluetooth is the universal cable cutter, promising to get rid of the tangled mess of wires, cradles, and special attachments that plague the current world of personal computing. With Bluetooth, users can wear a cell phone wireless earbud, share files in a hallway or conference room, synchronize their smartphone with their laptop without a cable, send a document to a printer, and even pay a restaurant bill from the table to a Bluetooth-equipped cash register. Bluetooth is also an unregulated media operating in the 2.4 GHz spectrum but with a very limited range of 30 feet or less. It uses a frequency hopping signal with up to 1,600 hops per second over 79 frequencies, giving it good protection from interference and interception. Bluetooth-equipped devices—which could be cell phones or laptops—constantly scan their environments looking for connections to compatible devices. Today, almost all cell phones and mobile devices are Bluetooth-enabled.

Bluetooth
technology standard for short-range wireless communication under 30 feet

THE FUTURE INTERNET

The increased bandwidth and expanded wireless network connectivity of the Internet of the future will result in benefits beyond faster access and richer communications. First-mile enhancements created by fiber-optic networks will enhance reliability and quality of Internet transmissions and create new business models and opportunities. Some of the major benefits of these technological advancements include latency solutions, guaranteed service levels, lower error rates, and declining costs. Widespread wireless access to the Internet will also essentially double or even triple the size of the online shopping marketspace because consumers will be able to shop and make purchases just about anywhere. This is equivalent to doubling the physical floor space of all shopping malls in America. We describe some of these benefits in more detail in the following sections.

Latency Solutions

One of the challenges of packet switching, where data is divided into chunks and then sent separately to meet again at the destination, is that the Internet does not differentiate between high-priority packets, such as video clips, and those of lower priority, such as self-contained e-mail messages. Because the packets cannot yet be simultaneously reassembled, the result can be distorted audio and video streams.

Differentiated quality of service (**diffserv**) is a technology that assigns levels of priority to packets based on the type of data being transmitted. Video conference packets, for example, which need to reach their destination almost instantaneously, receive much higher priority than e-mail messages. In the end, the quality of video and audio will skyrocket without undue stress on the network. Differential service is very controversial because it means some users may get more bandwidth than others, and potentially they may have to pay a higher price for more bandwidth.

differentiated quality of service (diffserv)
a new technology that assigns levels of priority to packets based on the type of data being transmitted

Guaranteed Service Levels and Lower Error Rates

In today's Internet, there is no service-level guarantee and no way to purchase the right to move data through the Internet at a fixed pace. Today's Internet promises only "best effort." The Internet is democratic—it speeds or slows everyone's traffic alike. In the future, it will be possible to purchase the right to move data through the network at a guaranteed speed in return for higher fees.

Declining Costs

As the Internet pipeline is upgraded, the availability of broadband service will expand beyond major metropolitan areas, significantly reducing the cost of access. More users means lower cost, as products and technology catch on in the mass market. Higher volume usage enables providers to lower the cost of both access devices, or clients, and the service required to use such products. Both broadband and wireless service fees are expected to decline as geographic service areas increase, in part due to competition for that business.

The Internet of Things

Internet of Things (IoT)

Use of the Internet to connect a wide variety of devices, machines, and sensors

No discussion of the future Internet would be complete without mentioning the **Internet of Things (IoT)**, also sometimes referred to as the Industrial Internet. Internet technology is spreading beyond the desktop, laptop, and tablet computer, and beyond the smartphone, to consumer electronics, electrical appliances, cars, medical devices, utility systems, machines of all types, even clothing—just about anything that can be equipped with sensors that collect data and connect to the Internet, enabling the data to be analyzed with data analytics software. The Internet of Things builds on a foundation of existing technologies, such as RFID, and is being enabled by the availability of low-cost sensors, the drop in price of data storage, the development of "Big Data" analytics software that can work with trillions of pieces of data, as well as implementation of IPV6, which will allow Internet addresses to be assigned to all of these new devices. Funding and research for the Internet of Things is being spearheaded by the European Union and China (where it is known as the Sensing Planet), and in the United States by companies such as IBM's Smarter Planet initiative. Although challenges remain before the Internet of Things is fully realized, it is coming closer and closer to fruition, and predictions indicate that there could be up to 100 billion uniquely identifiable objects connected to the Internet by 2020. (IEEE Computer Society, 2013).

3.4 THE WEB

Without the Web, there would be no e-commerce. The invention of the Web brought an extraordinary expansion of digital services to millions of amateur computer users, including color text and pages, formatted text, pictures, animations, video, and sound. In short, the Web makes nearly all the rich elements of human expression needed to establish a commercial marketplace available to nontechnical computer users worldwide.

While the Internet was born in the 1960s, the Web was not invented until 1989–1991 by Dr. Tim Berners-Lee of the European Particle Physics Laboratory, better known as CERN (Berners-Lee et al., 1994). Several earlier authors—such as Vannevar Bush (in 1945) and Ted Nelson (in the 1960s)—had suggested the possibility of organizing knowledge as a set of interconnected pages that users could freely browse (Bush, 1945; Ziff Davis Publishing, 1998). Berners-Lee and his associates at CERN built on these ideas and developed the initial versions of HTML, HTTP, a Web server, and a browser, the four essential components of the Web.

First, Berners-Lee wrote a computer program that allowed formatted pages within his own computer to be linked using keywords (hyperlinks). Clicking on a keyword in a document would immediately move him to another document. Berners-Lee created the pages using a modified version of a powerful text markup language called Standard Generalized Markup Language (SGML).

Berners-Lee called this language HyperText Markup Language, or HTML. He then came up with the idea of storing his HTML pages on the Internet. Remote client computers could access these pages by using HTTP (introduced earlier in Section 3.1

and described more fully in the next section). But these early Web pages still appeared as black and white text pages with hyperlinks expressed inside brackets. The early Web was based on text only; the original Web browser only provided a line interface.

Information being shared on the Web remained text-based until 1993, when Marc Andreessen and others at the National Center for Supercomputing Applications (NCSA) at the University of Illinois created a Web browser with a graphical user interface (GUI) called **Mosaic** that made it possible to view documents on the Web graphically—using colored backgrounds, images, and even primitive animations. Mosaic was a software program that could run on any graphically based interface such as Macintosh, Windows, or Unix. The Mosaic browser software read the HTML text on a Web page and displayed it as a graphical interface document within a GUI operating system such as Windows or Macintosh. Liberated from simple black and white text pages, HTML pages could now be viewed by anyone in the world who could operate a mouse and use a Macintosh or PC.

Mosaic
Web browser with a graphical user interface (GUI) that made it possible to view documents on the Web graphically

Aside from making the content of Web pages colorful and available to the world's population, the graphical Web browser created the possibility of **universal computing**, the sharing of files, information, graphics, sound, video, and other objects across all computer platforms in the world, regardless of operating system. A browser could be made for each of the major operating systems, and the Web pages created for one system, say, Windows, would also be displayed exactly the same, or nearly the same, on computers running the Macintosh or Unix operating systems. As long as each operating system had a Mosaic browser, the same Web pages could be used on all the different types of computers and operating systems. This meant that no matter what kind of computer you used, anywhere in the world, you would see the same Web pages. The browser and the Web have introduced us to a whole new world of computing and information management that was unthinkable prior to 1993.

universal computing
the sharing of files, information, graphics, sound, video, and other objects across all computer platforms in the world, regardless of operating system

In 1994, Andreessen and Jim Clark founded Netscape, which created the first commercial browser, **Netscape Navigator**. Although Mosaic had been distributed free of charge, Netscape initially charged for its software. In August 1995, Microsoft Corporation released its own free version of a browser, called **Internet Explorer**. In the ensuing years, Netscape fell from a 100% market share to less than .5% in 2009. The fate of Netscape illustrates an important e-commerce business lesson. Innovators usually are not long-term winners, whereas smart followers often have the assets needed for long-term survival. Much of the Netscape browser code survives today in the Firefox browser produced by Mozilla, a nonprofit heavily funded by Google.

Netscape Navigator
the first commercial Web browser

Internet Explorer
Microsoft's Web browser

HYPERTEXT

Web pages can be accessed through the Internet because the Web browser software on your PC can request Web pages stored on an Internet host server using the HTTP protocol. **Hypertext** is a way of formatting pages with embedded links that connect documents to one another and that also link pages to other objects such as sound, video, or animation files. When you click on a graphic and a video clip plays, you have clicked on a hyperlink. For example, when you type a Web address in your browser such as http://www.sec.gov, your browser sends an HTTP request to the sec.gov server requesting the home page of sec.gov.

hypertext
a way of formatting pages with embedded links that connect documents to one another, and that also link pages to other objects such as sound, video, or animation files

HTTP is the first set of letters at the start of every Web address, followed by the domain name. The domain name specifies the organization's server computer that is housing the document. Most companies have a domain name that is the same as or closely related to their official corporate name. The directory path and document name are two more pieces of information within the Web address that help the browser track down the requested page. Together, the address is called a Uniform Resource Locator, or URL. When typed into a browser, a URL tells it exactly where to look for the information. For example, in the following URL:

http://www.megacorp.com/content/features/082602.html

http = the protocol used to display Web pages

www.megacorp.com = domain name

content/features = the directory path that identifies where on the domain Web server the page is stored

082602.html = the document name and its format (an HTML page)

The most common domain extensions (known as general top-level domains, or gTLDs) currently available and officially sanctioned by ICANN are shown in **Table 3.10**. Countries also have domain names, such as .uk, .au, and .fr (United Kingdom, Australia, and France, respectively). These are sometimes referred to as country-code top-level domains, or ccTLDs. In 2008, ICANN approved a significant expansion of gTLDs, with potential new domains representing cities (such as .berlin), regions (.africa), ethnicity (.eus), industry/activities (such as .health), and even brands (such as .deloitte). In 2009, ICANN began the process of implementing these guidelines. In 2011, ICANN removed nearly all restrictions on domain names, thereby greatly expanding the number of different domain names available. More than 2000 applications for new gTLDs have been filed and ICANN has begun the process of implementing the program. The first new gTLDs may be ready to "go live" in late 2013 or early 2014.

MARKUP LANGUAGES

Although the most common Web page formatting language is HTML, the concept behind document formatting actually had its roots in the 1960s with the development of Generalized Markup Language (GML).

HyperText Markup Language (HTML)

HyperText Markup Language (HTML) is a GML that is relatively easy to use. HTML provides Web page designers with a fixed set of markup "tags" that are used to format a Web page (see **Figure 3.16** on page 152). When these tags are inserted into a Web page, they are read by the browser and interpreted into a page display. You can see the source HTML code for any Web page by simply clicking on the "Page Source" command found in all browsers. In Figure 3.16, the HTML code in the first screen produces the display in the second screen.

HyperText Markup Language (HTML)
GML that is relatively easy to use in Web page design. HTML provides Web page designers with a fixed set of markup "tags" that are used to format a Web page

TABLE 3.10	**TOP-LEVEL DOMAINS**		
GENERAL TOP-LEVEL DOMAIN (GTLD)	YEAR(S) INTRODUCED	PURPOSE	SPONSOR/ OPERATOR
.com	1980s	Unrestricted (but intended for commercial registrants)	VeriSign
.edu	1980s	U.S. educational institutions	Educause
.gov	1980s	U.S. government	U.S. General Services Administration
.mil	1980s	U.S. military	U.S. Department of Defense Network Information Center
.net	1980s	Unrestricted (but originally intended for network providers, etc.)	VeriSign
.org	1980s	Unrestricted (but intended for organizations that do not fit elsewhere)	Public Interest Registry (was operated by VeriSign until December 31, 2002)
.int	1998	Organizations established by international treaties between governments	Internet Assigned Numbers Authority (IANA)
.aero	2001	Air-transport industry	Societé Internationale de Telecommunications Aeronautiques SC (SITA)
.biz	2001	Businesses	NeuLevel
.coop	2001	Cooperatives	DotCooperation LLC
.info	2001	Unrestricted use	Afilias LLC
.museum	2001	Museums	Museum Domain Name Association (MuseDoma)
.name	2001	For registration by individuals	Global Name Registry Ltd.
.pro	2002	Accountants, lawyers, physicians, and other professionals	RegistryPro Ltd
.jobs	2005	Job search	Employ Media LLC
.travel	2005	Travel search	Tralliance Corporation
.mobi	2005	Web sites specifically designed for mobile phones	mTLD Top Level Domain, Ltd.
.cat	2005	Individuals, organizations, and companies that promote the Catalan language and culture	Fundació puntCAT
.asia	2006	Regional domain for companies, organizations, and individuals based in Asia	DotAsia Organization
.tel	2006	Telephone numbers and other contact information	ICM Registry
.xxx	2010	New top-level domain for pornographic content	None yet approved

SOURCE: Based on data from ICANN, 2011b.

FIGURE 3.16	EXAMPLE HTML CODE (A) AND WEB PAGE (B)

(a)   (b)

HTML is a text markup language used to create Web pages. It has a fixed set of "tags" that are used to tell the browser software how to present the content on screen. The HTML shown in Figure 3.17 (a) creates the Web page seen in Figure 3.17 (b).

HTML defines the structure and style of a document, including the headings, graphic positioning, tables, and text formatting. Since its introduction, the major browsers have continuously added features to HTML to enable programmers to further refine their page layouts. Unfortunately, some browser enhancements may work only in one company's browser. Whenever you build an e-commerce site, you should take care that the pages can be viewed by the major browsers, even outdated versions of browsers. HTML Web pages can be created with any text editor, such as Notepad or WordPad, using Microsoft Word (simply save the Word document as a Web page), or any one of several Web page development tools such as Microsoft Expression Web or Adobe Dreamweaver.[5]

The most recent version of HTML is HTML5. HTML5 introduces features like video playback and drag-and-drop that in the past were provided by plug-ins like Adobe Flash. HTML5 applications have many of the rich interactive features found in smartphone apps. The *Insight on Technology* case, *Is HTML5 Ready for Prime Time?* examines some of the issues associated with use of HTML5.

eXtensible Markup Language (XML)

a markup language specification developed by the World Wide Web Consortium (W3C) that is designed to describe data and information

eXtensible Markup Language (XML)

eXtensible Markup Language (XML) takes Web document formatting a giant leap forward. XML is a markup language specification developed by the W3C that is similar to HTML, but has a very different purpose. Whereas the purpose of HTML is to control

---

[5] A detailed discussion of how to use HTML is beyond the scope of this text.

INSIGHT ON TECHNOLOGY

IS HTML5 READY FOR PRIME TIME?

Can HTML5 save businesses billions of dollars in development costs and bring about the demise of the native app? Possibly! The newest standard for how Web pages should be rendered by a browser has been welcomed by developers far in advance of its scheduled 2014 ratification by the W3C. Advocated by Apple founder Steve Jobs as the preferred method for displaying video on the Web, HTML5's video element replaces plug-ins such as Flash, QuickTime, and RealPlayer, and represents a dramatic breakthrough in Web page design. As a result, Adobe has abandoned development of mobile Flash and agreed to use HTML5 to develop future tools.

HTML5 has become a catch-all term that encompasses not only the video element but also the use of the newest versions of Cascading Style Sheets (CSS3) and JavaScript, and another new tool, HTML5 Canvas. Also intended to replace plug-ins, it is used with a set of JavaScript functions to render simple animations, which reduces page load time. Multi-platform Web developers began using HTML5 because these new elements provided device independence, but soon discovered that they could do even more. The built-in functionality of mobile devices, including GPS and swiping, can be accessed, enabling m-commerce sites to build Web-based mobile apps that can replicate the native app experience. Web-based mobile apps (HTML5 apps) work just like Web pages. When a user navigates to the page containing the mobile app, the page content, including graphics, images, and video, are loaded into the browser from the Web server, rather than residing in the mobile device hardware like a native app. This concept has been embraced by mobile developers who naturally dream of being able to reach all platforms with a single product.

For businesses, the cost savings of HTML5 are obvious. A single HTML5 app requires far less effort to build than multiple native apps for the iOS, Android, Windows Phone, and other platforms. HTML5 apps can more easily be linked to and shared on social networks, encouraging viral distribution. Some HTML5 apps can even be designed so that they can be run on mobile devices when they are offline. Differences in how apps run across different platforms and workarounds are eliminated.

One company quick to capitalize on the Web-based mobile app trend was Usablenet, a software platform provider. Usablenet released an HTML5 mobile platform in April 2011. The Usablenet Mobile 2.0 system provides m-commerce proprietors with a set of tools for building HTML5 sites that are optimized for touch-based browsers and can exploit mobile device functionality. Photo galleries can be swiped through, individual photos can be double-tapped to zoom in, scrolling promotions and expanding and collapsing menus can be incorporated, and consumers can search for nearby store locations based on their current whereabouts. Amtrak, Delta, Expedia, FedEx, Hilton, Marks & Spencer, Sprint, JCPenney, and Victoria's Secret are among the Fortune 1000 companies who have already discovered the advantages of an HTML5 m-commerce site built with Usablenet Mobile 2.0.

An April 2012 Usablenet study examined the experiences of 50 retail and travel companies who had built HTML5 m-commerce sites using its system and found that 28% enjoyed increased site traffic as well as an 11% increase in the number of page views per visit. ShopNBC, one of the top 100 m-commerce proprietors according to Internet Retailer, found that mobile customers not only spent more time on their site but also began streaming their broadcast channel in greater numbers. What's more, ShopNBC and other study participants' users were 15% less likely to enter the site and immediately leave, a statistic referred to as the bounce rate.

(continued)

Another company that is delighted with its HTML5 revamp is ideeli.com, a members-only discount fashion flash-sales site that offers sales from as many as 40 designers at a time, beginning at noon each day and lasting for 40 hours. Because its iPad traffic had increased 70% over the previous year, ideeli wanted an upgrade to optimize for small screen size and speed load time. The results were impressive. iPad visitors increased by 70% and now comprise between 10% and 20% of its customers. What's more, this translated to a 25% increase in average order value. Ideeli achieved increased page-load times because HTML5 can cache data in the mobile browser. After a user has visited the site, part of ideeli's database is stored there, decreasing the number of times the browser must ping the database. This boosts site responsiveness, particularly between 12:00 and 12:15 PM when flash sales are just taking off and ideeli records 15% of its daily traffic. HTML5 has also enabled ideeli to maintain just one Web site for all users, both desktop and mobile. This is yet another huge cost-savings benefit for some retailers, who can go back to creating just one Web site by incorporating contact points for HTML5 apps.

The *Financial Times*'s HTML5 app has also proven to be an important driver for FT's business. FT first switched from a native app to HTML5 in 2011, in part to make maintaining the app across multiple platforms and devices easier. In 2013, FT rolled out a redesign of the app, featuring even more videos and personalization features. FT's managing director, Robert Grimshaw, believes that those who have chosen to develop native apps in parallel will struggle with the overhead of maintaining and developing them.

The biggest challenge of HTML5 apps is to meet and then attempt to surpass the user experience and performance level of native apps. Although HTML5 sites load faster than first-generation mobile commerce sites, native apps generally still trump HTML5 apps on speed because a great deal of the interface already resides on the mobile device. Only newly requested data must be loaded. The mobile device platform also provides a standard user interface that native app developers can exploit to provide ease of execution for the user.

According to Tim Berners-Lee, founder and chief of the W3C and an ardent opponent of native apps because they remove functionality from the Web, HTML5 security and access control issues are currently being addressed. For instance, HTML5 does not support digital rights management (DRM). In the past, media companies developed their own copy protection standards based on geographical region and/or whether payment had been proffered. These were enforced through their own media players. Because HTML5 does not require plug-ins to play video (or audio), and further, because HTML5 is an official W3C standard charged with remaining vendor neutral, this presents a challenge to the HTML5 working group.

Although HTML5 is being widely adopted on e-commerce and m-commerce sites, native apps aren't going anywhere. Instead, developers are incorporating HTML5 code into native apps, creating a kind of hybrid or mixed mode app. While the lure of reaching all platforms with a single product is potent, if developers cannot produce a product that equals the performance of native apps, they will stick with the side their bread is buttered on and continue to develop native apps for the top sellers.

SOURCES: "Financial Times: 'There is No Drawback to Working in HTML5'," by Stuart Dredge, TheGuardian.com, April 29, 2013; "The HTML5 Promise: Responsive Web Design for Any Screen," by Tom Foremski, Siliconvalleywatcher.com, April 16, 2013; "Why HTML5 Is in Trouble on the Mobile Front," by David Meyer, ZDNet, September 5, 2012; "A Technology Switch Bears Mobile Commerce Fruit," by Kevin Woodward, Internet Retailer, August 30, 2012; "HTML5: Don't Believe the Hype Cycle," by Dan Rowinski, ReadWriteWeb.com, August 21, 2012; "Is HTML5 the End of Native Mobile Apps?," by Hernán Gonzalez, ClickZ.com, August 17, 2012; "ShopNBC.com Targets More App-like Features in its Mobile Site Update," by Kevin Woodward, Internet Retailer, July 2, 2012; "What Do You Get by Adding HTML5 to Your Mobile Site?," by Bill Siwicki, Internet Retailer, April 12, 2012; "HTML5 Mobile Sites Give Apps a Run for their Money," by Bill Siwicki, Internet Retailer, February 3, 2012; "HTML5 Is Popular, Still Unfinished," by Don Clark, *Wall Street Journal*, November 11, 2011; "Adobe's Flash Surrender Proves Steve Jobs And Apple Were Right All Along With HTML5," by Nigam Arora, *Forbes*, November, 9, 2011.

FIGURE 3.17   **A SIMPLE XML DOCUMENT**

```
<?xml version="1.0"?>
<note>
<to>George</to>
<from>Carol</from>
<heading>Just a Reminder</heading>
<body>Don't forget to order the groceries from FreshDirect!</body>
</note>
```

The tags in this simple XML document, such as <note>, <to>, and <from>, are used to describe data and information, rather than the look and feel of the document.

the "look and feel" and display of data on the Web page, XML is designed to describe data and information. For example, consider the sample XML document in **Figure 3.17**. The first line in the sample document is the XML declaration, which is always included; it defines the XML version of the document. In this case, the document conforms to the 1.0 specification of XML. The next line defines the first element of the document (the root element): < note >. The next four lines define four child elements of the root (to, from, heading, and body). The last line defines the end of the root element. Notice that XML says nothing about how to display the data, or how the text should look on the screen. HTML is used for information display in combination with XML, which is used for data description.

Figure 3.18 on page 156 shows how XML can be used to define a database of company names in a company directory. Tags such as < Company >, < Name >, and < Specialty > can be defined for a single firm, or an entire industry. On an elementary level, XML is extraordinarily easy to learn and is very similar to HTML except that you can make up your own tags. At a deeper level, XML has a rich syntax and an enormous set of software tools, which make XML ideal for storing and communicating many types of data on the Web.

XML is "extensible," which means the tags used to describe and display data are defined by the user, whereas in HTML the tags are limited and predefined. XML can also transform information into new formats, such as by importing information from a database and displaying it as a table. With XML, information can be analyzed and displayed selectively, making it a more powerful alternative to HTML. This means that business firms, or entire industries, can describe all of their invoices, accounts payable, payroll records, and financial information using a Web-compatible markup language. Once described, these business documents can be stored on intranet Web servers and shared throughout the corporation.

WEB SERVERS AND CLIENTS

We have already described client/server computing and the revolution in computing architecture brought about by client/server computing. You already know that a server is a computer attached to a network that stores files, controls peripheral devices,

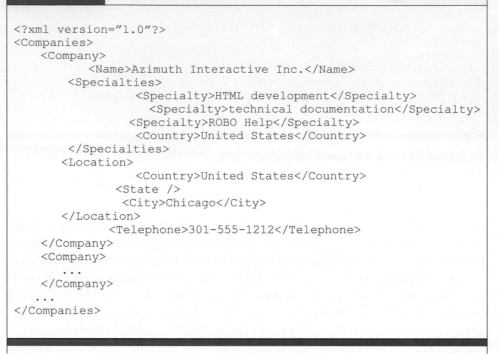

FIGURE 3.18   **SAMPLE XML CODE FOR A COMPANY DIRECTORY**

```xml
<?xml version="1.0"?>
<Companies>
    <Company>
          <Name>Azimuth Interactive Inc.</Name>
        <Specialties>
                  <Specialty>HTML development</Specialty>
                    <Specialty>technical documentation</Specialty>
                  <Specialty>ROBO Help</Specialty>
                  <Country>United States</Country>
        </Specialties>
        <Location>
                  <Country>United States</Country>
              <State />
                <City>Chicago</City>
        </Location>
                <Telephone>301-555-1212</Telephone>
    </Company>
    <Company>
        ...
    </Company>
    ...
</Companies>
```

This XML document uses tags to define a database of company names.

interfaces with the outside world—including the Internet—and does some processing for other computers on the network.

But what is a Web server? **Web server software** refers to the software that enables a computer to deliver Web pages written in HTML to client computers on a network that request this service by sending an HTTP request. The two leading brands of Web server software are Apache, which is free Web server shareware that accounts for about 52% of the market, and Microsoft's Internet Information Services (IIS), which accounts for about 20% of the market (Netcraft, 2013).

Aside from responding to requests for Web pages, all Web servers provide some additional basic capabilities such as the following:

- *Security services*—These consist mainly of authentication services that verify that the person trying to access the site is authorized to do so. For Web sites that process payment transactions, the Web server also supports SSL and TLS, the protocols for transmitting and receiving information securely over the Internet. When private information such as names, phone numbers, addresses, and credit card data needs to be provided to a Web site, the Web server uses SSL to ensure that the data passing back and forth from the browser to the server is not compromised.

- *FTP*—This protocol allows users to transfer files to and from the server. Some sites limit file uploads to the Web server, while others restrict downloads, depending on the user's identity.

Web server software

software that enables a computer to deliver Web pages written in HTML to client computers on a network that request this service by sending an HTTP request

- *Search engine*—Just as search engine sites enable users to search the entire Web for particular documents, search engine modules within the basic Web server software package enable indexing of the site's Web pages and content and permit easy keyword searching of the site's content. When conducting a search, a search engine makes use of an index, which is a list of all the documents on the server. The search term is compared to the index to identify likely matches.

- *Data capture*—Web servers are also helpful at monitoring site traffic, capturing information on who has visited a site, how long the user stayed there, the date and time of each visit, and which specific pages on the server were accessed. This information is compiled and saved in a log file, which can then be analyzed. By analyzing a log file, a site manager can find out the total number of visitors, the average length of each visit, and the most popular destinations, or Web pages.

The term *Web server* is also used to refer to the physical computer that runs Web server software. Leading manufacturers of Web server computers include IBM, Dell, and Hewlett-Packard. Although any personal computer can run Web server software, it is best to use a computer that has been optimized for this purpose. To be a Web server, a computer must have the Web server software installed and be connected to the Internet. Every public Web server computer has an IP address. For example, if you type http://www.pearsonhighered.com/laudon in your browser, the browser software sends a request for HTTP service to the Web server whose domain name is pearsonhighered.com. The server then locates the page named "laudon" on its hard drive, sends the page back to your browser, and displays it on your screen. Of course, firms also can use Web servers for strictly internal local area networking in intranets.

Aside from the generic Web server software packages, there are actually many types of specialized servers on the Web, from **database servers** that access specific information within a database, to **ad servers** that deliver targeted banner ads, to **mail servers** that provide e-mail messages, and **video servers** that provide video clips. At a small e-commerce site, all of these software packages might be running on a single computer, with a single processor. At a large corporate site, there may be hundreds or thousands of discrete server computers, many with multiple processors, running specialized Web server functions. We discuss the architecture of e-commerce sites in greater detail in Chapter 4.

A **Web client**, on the other hand, is any computing device attached to the Internet that is capable of making HTTP requests and displaying HTML pages. The most common client is a Windows or Macintosh computer, with various flavors of Unix/Linux computers a distant third. However, the fastest growing category of Web clients are not computers at all, but smartphones, tablets, and netbooks outfitted with wireless Web access software. In general, Web clients can be any device—including a printer, refrigerator, stove, home lighting system, or automobile instrument panel—capable of sending and receiving information from Web servers.

WEB BROWSERS

A Web browser is a software program whose primary purpose is to display Web pages. Browsers also have added features, such as e-mail and newsgroups (an online discussion group or forum). The leading Web browser is Microsoft Internet Explorer, with

database server
server designed to access specific information within a database

ad server
server designed to deliver targeted banner ads

mail server
server that provides e-mail messages

video server
server that serves video clips

Web client
any computing device attached to the Internet that is capable of making HTTP requests and displaying HTML pages, most commonly a Windows PC or Macintosh

about 54% of the market as of August 2013. Mozilla Firefox is currently the second most popular Web browser, with about 20% of the U.S. Web browser market. First released in 2004, Firefox is a free, open source Web browser for the Windows, Linux, and Macintosh operating systems, based on Mozilla open source code (which originally provided the code for Netscape). It is small and fast and offers many features such as pop-up blocking and tabbed browsing. The third most popular browser, with about a 19% market share, is Google's Chrome, a small, yet technologically advanced open source browser. Apple's Safari browser is fourth, with about 5% of the market (Marketshare.hitslink.com, 2013).

3.5 THE INTERNET AND THE WEB: FEATURES AND SERVICES

The Internet and the Web have spawned a number of powerful software applications upon which the foundations of e-commerce are built. You can think of all these as Web services, and it is interesting as you read along to compare these services to other traditional media such as television or print media. If you do, you will quickly realize the richness of the Internet environment.

E-MAIL

electronic mail (e-mail)

the most-used application of the Internet. Uses a series of protocols to enable messages containing text, images, sound, and video clips to be transferred from one Internet user to another

Since its earliest days, **electronic mail**, or **e-mail**, has been the most-used application of the Internet. Worldwide, there are an estimated 3.9 billion e-mail accounts, sending an estimated 145 billion e-mails a day. About 76% of these e-mail accounts (2.97 billion) are consumer accounts and about 24% (929 million) are corporate e-mail accounts (Radicati Group, 2013). Estimates vary on the amount of spam, ranging from 40% to 90%. E-mail marketing and spam are examined in more depth in Chapter 6.

E-mail uses a series of protocols to enable messages containing text, images, sound, and video clips to be transferred from one Internet user to another. Because of its flexibility and speed, it is now the most popular form of business communication—more popular than the phone, fax, or snail mail (the U.S. Postal Service). In addition to text typed within the message, e-mail also allows **attachments**, which are files inserted within the e-mail message. The files can be documents, images, sounds, or video clips.

attachment

a file inserted within an e-mail message

INSTANT MESSAGING

instant messaging (IM)

displays words typed on a computer almost instantaneously. Recipients can then respond immediately to the sender the same way, making the communication more like a live conversation than is possible through e-mail

Instant messaging (IM) allows you to send messages in real time, one line at a time, unlike e-mail. E-mail messages have a time lag of several seconds to minutes between when messages are sent and received. IM displays lines of text entered on a computer almost instantaneously. Recipients can then respond immediately to the sender the same way, making the communication more like a live conversation than is possible through e-mail. To use IM, users create a buddy list they want to communicate with, and then enter short text messages that their buddies will receive instantly (if they are online at the time). And although text remains the primary communication mechanism in IM, users can insert audio clips or photos into their instant messages, and even participate in video conferencing. Instant messaging over the Internet competes with wireless phone Short Message Service (SMS) texting, which is far more expensive than IM.

The major IM systems are Microsoft's Windows Live Messenger, Skype, Yahoo Messenger, Google Talk, and AIM (AOL Instant Messenger). Facebook also offers instant messaging services via Facebook Chat. IM systems were initially developed as proprietary systems, with competing firms offering versions that did not work with one another. In 2011, there still is no built-in interoperability among the major IM systems. The number of worldwide IM accounts is around 2.9 billion (Radicati Group, 2013).

SEARCH ENGINES

Search engines identify Web pages that appear to match keywords, also called queries, entered by a user and then provide a list of the best matches (search results). Almost 60% of all adult American Internet users use a search engine on any given day, generating over 19 billion queries a month (Pew Internet & American Life Project, 2013; comScore, 2013a). There are hundreds of different search engines, but the vast majority of the search results are supplied by the top five providers (see **Figure 3.19**).

search engine
identifies Web pages that appear to match keywords, also called queries, entered by the user and then provides a list of the best matches

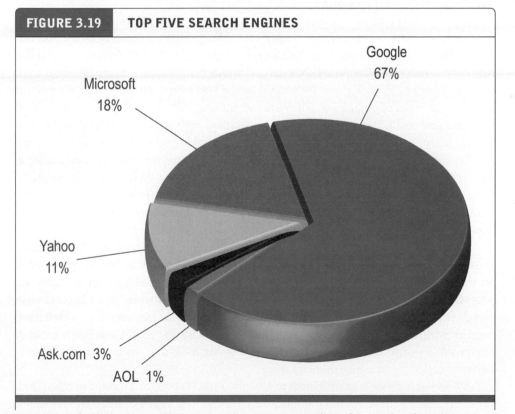

FIGURE 3.19	TOP FIVE SEARCH ENGINES

Google 67%

Microsoft 18%

Yahoo 11%

Ask.com 3%

AOL 1%

Google is, by far, the leading search engine based on its percentage share of the number of searches.
SOURCE: Based on data from comScore, 2013a.

Web search engines started out in the early 1990s shortly after Netscape released the first commercial Web browser. Early search engines were relatively simple software programs that roamed the nascent Web, visiting pages and gathering information about the content of each Web page. These early programs were called variously crawlers, spiders, and wanderers; the first full-text crawler that indexed the contents of an entire Web page was called WebCrawler, released in 1994. AltaVista (1995), one of the first widely used search engines, was the first to allow "natural language" queries such as "history of Web search engines" rather than "history + Web + search engine."

The first search engines employed simple keyword indexes of all the Web pages visited. They would count the number of times a word appeared on the Web page, and store this information in an index. These search engines could be easily fooled by Web designers who simply repeated words on their home pages. The real innovations in search engine development occurred through a program funded by the Department of Defense called the Digital Library Initiative, designed to help the Pentagon find research papers in large databases. Stanford, Berkeley, and three other universities became hotbeds of Web search innovations in the mid-1990s. At Stanford in 1994, two computer science students, David Filo and Jerry Yang, created a hand-selected list of their favorite Web pages and called it "Yet Another Hierarchical Officious Oracle," or Yahoo!. Yahoo initially was not a real search engine, but rather an edited selection of Web sites organized by categories the editors found useful. Yahoo later developed "true" search engine capabilities.

In 1998, Larry Page and Sergey Brin, two Stanford computer science students, released their first version of the Google search engine. This search engine was different: not only did it index each Web page's words, but Page had discovered that the AltaVista search engine not only collected keywords from sites but also calculated what other sites linked to each page. By looking at the URLs on each Web page, they could calculate an index of popularity. AltaVista did nothing with this information. Page took this idea and made it a central factor in ranking a Web page's appropriateness to a search query. He patented the idea of a Web page ranking system (PageRank System), which essentially measures the popularity of the Web page. Brin contributed a unique Web crawler program that indexed not just keywords on a Web page, but combinations of words (such as authors and their article titles). These two ideas became the foundation for the Google search engine (Brandt, 2004). **Figure 3.20** illustrates how Google works.

Initially, few understood how to make money from search engines. That changed in 2000 when Goto.com (later Overture) allowed advertisers to bid for placement on their search engine results, and Google followed suit in 2003 with its AdWords program, which allowed advertisers to bid for placement of short text ads on Google search results. The spectacular increase in Internet advertising revenues (which have been growing at around 20%–25% annually over the last few years), has helped search engines transform themselves into major shopping tools and created an entire new industry called "search engine marketing."

When users enter a search term at Google, Bing, Yahoo, or any of the other Web sites serviced by these search engines, they receive two types of listings: sponsored links, for which advertisers have paid to be listed (usually at the top of the search

FIGURE 3.20   HOW GOOGLE WORKS

1. A user enters a search query.

6. Results delivered to user, 10 to a page.

5. Small text summaries are prepared for each Web page.

4. Using Google's PageRank software, the system measures the "importance" or popularity of each page by solving an equation with millions of variables and terms. These are likely the "best" pages for the query.

2. Google's Web servers receive the search request. Google uses an estimated 1 to 2 million PCs linked together and connected to the Internet to handle incoming queries and produce search results.

3. The search request is sent to Google's index servers, which maintain data about the Web pages that contain the keywords matching the query, and the location of those pages.

The Google search engine is continuously crawling the Web, indexing the content of each page, calculating its popularity, and caching the pages so that it can respond quickly to your request to see a page. The entire process takes about one-half of a second.

results page), and unsponsored "organic" search results. In addition, advertisers can purchase small text ads on the right side of the search results page. Although the major search engines are used for locating general information of interest to users, search engines have also become a crucial tool within e-commerce sites. Customers can more easily search for the product information they want with the help of an internal search program; the difference is that within Web sites, the search engine is limited to finding matches from that one site. In addition, search engines have extended their services to include news, maps, satellite images, computer images, e-mail, group calendars, group meeting tools, and indexes of scholarly papers. In 2012, Google and Bing added social search terms to their search results. Whatever these search engines can glean from your e-mails and social network posts they can use in response to your searches to make the results more "personal" and social. Outside of e-mail, search engines are the most common online daily activity and produce the largest online audiences.

ONLINE FORUMS AND CHAT

An **online forum** (also referred to as a message board, bulletin board, discussion board, discussion group, or simply a board or forum) is a Web application that enables Internet users to communicate with each other, although not in real time. A forum provides a container for various discussions (or "threads") started (or "posted") by members of the forum, and depending on the permissions granted to forum members by the forum's administrator, enables a person to start a thread and reply to other people's threads. Most forum software allows more than one forum to be created. The forum administrator typically can edit, delete, move, or otherwise modify any

online forum
a Web application that allows Internet users to communicate with each other, although not in real time

thread on the forum. Unlike an electronic mailing list (such as a listserv), which automatically sends new messages to a subscriber, an online forum typically requires that the member visit the forum to check for new posts. Some forums offer an "e-mail notification" feature that notifies users that a new post of interest to them has been made.

Online chat differs from an online forum in that, like IM, chat enables users to communicate via computer in real time, that is, simultaneously. However, unlike IM, which works only between two people, chat can occur among several users. Typically, users log in to a "chat room" where they can text message others. Some chat rooms offer virtual chat, which enables users to incorporate 2-D and 3-D graphics along with avatars (an icon or representation of the user) into their chat, or offers the ability to communicate via audio and/or video. Chat systems include Internet Relay Chat (IRC), Jabber, Yahoo, and MSN chat, and a number of proprietary systems based on the Microsoft Windows or Java platform. E-commerce firms typically use online forums and online chat to help develop community and as customer service tools. We will discuss the use of online forums as a community-building tool further in Chapter 11.

STREAMING MEDIA

Streaming media enables live Web video, music, video, and other large-bandwidth files to be sent to users in a variety of ways that enable the user to play back the files. In some situations, such as live Web video, the files are broken into chunks and served by specialized video servers to users in chunks. Client software puts the chunks together and plays the video. In other situations, such as YouTube, a single large file is downloaded from a standard Web server to users who can begin playing the video before the entire file is downloaded. Streamed files must be viewed "live"; they cannot be stored on client hard drives without special software. Streamed files are "played" by a software program such as Windows Media Player, Apple QuickTime, Flash, and RealMedia Player. There are a number of tools used to create streaming files, but one of the most common is Adobe's Flash program. The Flash player has the advantage of being built into most client browsers; no plug-in is required to play Flash files.

Sites such as YouTube, Metacafe, and Facebook have popularized user-generated video streaming. Web advertisers increasingly use video to attract viewers. Streaming audio and video segments used in Web ads and news stories are perhaps the most frequently used streaming services. As the capacity of the Internet grows, streaming media will play an even larger role in e-commerce.

COOKIES

A **cookie** is a tool used by a Web site to store information about a user. When a visitor enters a Web site, the site sends a small text file (the cookie) to the user's computer so that information from the site can be loaded more quickly on future visits. The cookie can contain any information desired by the Web site designers, including customer number, pages visited, products examined, and other detailed information about the behavior of the consumer at the site. Cookies are useful to consumers because the Web site will recognize returning patrons and not ask them to register again. Cookies are also used by advertisers to ensure visitors do not receive the same

---

online chat

enables users to communicate via computer in real time, that is, simultaneously. Unlike IM, chat can occur among several users

streaming media

enables music, video, and other large files to be sent to users in chunks so that when received and played, the file comes through uninterrupted

cookie

a tool used by Web sites to store information about a user. When a visitor enters a Web site, the site sends a small text file (the cookie) to the user's computer so that information from the site can be loaded more quickly on future visits. The cookie can contain any information desired by the site designers advertisements repeatedly. Cookies can also help personalize a Web site by allowing the site to recognize returning customers and make special offers to them based on their past behavior at the site. Cookies allow Web marketers to customize products and segment markets—the ability to change the product or the price based on prior consumer information (described more fully in later chapters). As we will discuss throughout the book, cookies also can pose a threat to consumer privacy, and at times they are bothersome. Many people clear their cookies at the end of every day. Some disable them entirely using tools built into most browsers.

WEB 2.0 FEATURES AND SERVICES

Today's broadband Internet infrastructure has greatly expanded the services available to users. These new capabilities have formed the basis for new business models. Digital content and digital communications are the two areas where innovation is most rapid. Web 2.0 applications and services are "social" in nature because they support communication among individuals within groups or social networks.

Online Social Networks

Online social networks are services that support communication within networks of friends, colleagues, and entire professions. Online social networks have developed very large worldwide audiences and form the basis for new advertising platforms and for social e-commerce (see Chapters 6, 7, and 11). The largest social networks are Facebook (1.1 billion members worldwide), LinkedIn (more than 235 million members worldwide), Twitter (more than 200 million active users worldwide), and Pinterest (more than 70 million members). These networks rely on user-generated content (messages, photos, and videos) and emphasize sharing of content. All of these features require significant broadband Internet connectivity and equally large cloud computing facilities to store content.

Blogs

A **blog** (originally called a **weblog**) is a personal Web page that typically contains a series of chronological entries (newest to oldest) by its author, and links to related Web pages. The blog may include a blogroll (a collection of links to other blogs) and trackbacks (a list of entries in other blogs that refer to a post on the first blog). Most blogs allow readers to post comments on the blog entries as well. The act of creating a blog is often referred to as "blogging." Blogs are either hosted by a third-party site such as Blogger.com (owned by Google), LiveJournal, TypePad, Xanga, WordPress, and Tumblr, or prospective bloggers can download software such as Movable Type to create a blog that is hosted by the user's ISP. Blog pages are usually variations on templates provided by the blogging service or software and hence require no knowledge of HTML. Therefore, millions of people without HTML skills of any kind can post their own Web pages, and share content with friends and relatives. The totality of blog-related Web sites is often referred to as the "blogosphere."

Blogs have become hugely popular. Tumblr, Wordpress, and LiveJournal together hosted over 225 million blogs as of April 2013, so it is likely that the total number is significantly higher. According to eMarketer, there are an estimated 26 million active U.S. bloggers, and 74 million U.S. blog readers (eMarketer, Inc., 2013h, 2013i). No one

blog
personal Web page that is created by an individual or corporation to communicate with readers

knows how many of these blogs are kept up to date or are just yesterday's news. And no one knows how many of these blogs have a readership greater than one (the blog author). In fact, there are so many blogs you need a blog search engine just to find them (such as Google's or Technorati's search engine), or you can just go to a list of the most popular 100 blogs and dig in. We discuss blogs further in Chapters 6 and 7 as a marketing and advertising mechanism, and in Chapter 10 as a part of the significant growth in user-generated content.

Really Simple Syndication (RSS)

Really Simple Syndication (RSS)

program that allows users to have digital content, including text, articles, blogs, and podcast audio files, automatically sent to their computers over the Internet

The rise of blogs is correlated with a distribution mechanism for news and information from Web sites that regularly update their content. **Really Simple Syndication (RSS)** is an XML format that allows users to have digital content, including text, articles, blogs, and podcast audio files, automatically sent to their computers over the Internet. An RSS aggregator software application that you install on your computer gathers material from the Web sites and blogs that you tell it to scan and brings new information from those sites to you. Sometimes this is referred to as "syndicated" content because it is distributed by news organizations and other syndicators (or distributors). Users download an RSS aggregator and then "subscribe" to the RSS "feeds." When you go to your RSS aggregator's page, it will display the most recent updates for each channel to which you have subscribed. RSS has rocketed from a "techie" pastime to a broad-based movement. Although Google has closed down Google Reader, a popular RSS product, a number of other RSS reader options remain, including Feedly, Reeder, and NewsBlur.

Podcasting

podcast

an audio presentation— such as a radio show, audio from a movie, or simply a personal audio presentation—stored as an audio file and posted to the Web

A **podcast** is an audio presentation—such as a radio show, audio from a movie, or simply a personal audio presentation—stored as an audio file and posted to the Web. Listeners download the files from the Web and play them on their players or computers. While commonly associated with Apple's iPod portable music player, you can listen to MP3 podcast files with any MP3 player. Podcasting has transitioned from an amateur independent producer media in the "pirate radio" tradition to a professional news and talk content distribution channel.

Wikis

wiki

Web application that allows a user to easily add and edit content on a Web page

A **wiki** is a Web application that allows a user to easily add and edit content on a Web page. (The term wiki derives from the "wiki wiki" (quick or fast) shuttle buses at Honolulu Airport.) Wiki software enables documents to be written collectively and collaboratively. Most wiki systems are open source, server-side systems that store content in a relational database. The software typically provides a template that defines layout and elements common to all pages, displays user-editable source code (usually plain text), and then renders the content into an HTML-based page for display in a Web browser. Some wiki software allows only basic text formatting, whereas others allow the use of tables, images, or even interactive elements, such as polls and games.

Since wikis by their very nature are very open in allowing anyone to make changes to a page, most wikis provide a means to verify the validity of changes via a "Recent Changes" page, which enables members of the wiki community to monitor and review the work of other users, correct mistakes, and hopefully deter "vandalism."

The most well-known wiki is Wikipedia, an online encyclopedia that contains more than 4.2 million English-language articles on a variety of topics, appears in 286 languages, and has 365 million readers worldwide. It is more popular than iTunes. The Wikimedia Foundation, which operates Wikipedia, also operates a variety of related projects, including Wikibooks, a collection of collaboratively written free textbooks and manuals; Wikinews, a free content news source; and Wiktionary, a collaborative project to produce a free multilingual dictionary in every language, with definitions, etymologies, pronunciations, quotations, and synonyms.

Music and Video Services

With the low-bandwidth connections of the early Internet, audio and video files were difficult to download and share, but with the huge growth in broadband connections, these files are not only commonplace but today constitute the majority of Web traffic. Spurred on by the worldwide sales of more than 600 million iOS devices (iPhones, iPads, and iPod Touches) through June 2013, as well as millions of other smartphones and MP3 players, the Internet has become a virtual digital river of music files (Smith, 2013). Today, the iTunes Store has a catalog with more than 26 million tracks, 190,000 television episodes, and 45,000 movies, including more than 3,000 in high definition (Apple, 2012).

Online video viewing has also exploded in popularity. In July 2013, around 187 million Americans watched 48 billion videos for an average of 22.6 hours per viewer (comScore, 2013b). By far, the most common type of Internet video is provided by YouTube, with more than 4 billion videos streamed and viewed each a day (120 billion a month), and 6 billion hours of video watched each month, most of it short clips taken from television shows, or user-generated content. The largest sources of legal, paid television content are the iTunes Store, where you can purchase specific episodes or entire seasons of TV shows, and Hulu, which is owned by major television producers NBCUniversal, News Corp., The Walt Disney Company, and Providence Equity Partners.

Internet advertising makes extensive use of streaming video ads: in July 2013, Americans watched 19.6 billion video ads, more than double the amount in the previous year! Companies that want to demonstrate use of their products have found video clips to be extremely effective. And audio reports and discussions also have become commonplace, either as marketing materials or customer reports.

Future digital video networks will be able to deliver better-than-broadcast-quality video over the Internet to computers and other devices in homes and on the road. High-quality interactive video and audio makes sales presentations and demonstrations more effective and lifelike and enables companies to develop new forms of customer support. The Internet is well on its way to becoming a major distribution channel for movies, television shows, and sporting events (see Chapter 10).

Internet Telephony

If the telephone system were to be built from scratch today, it would be an Internet-based, packet-switched network using TCP/IP because it would be less expensive and more efficient than the alternative existing system, which involves a mix of circuit-switched legs with a digital backbone. Likewise, if cable television systems were built from scratch today, they most likely would use Internet technologies for the same reasons.

Already, nearly all prepaid phone cards use the Internet for the long distance portion of calls. About 30% of the international calls from or to the United States use the Internet. **IP telephony** is a general term for the technologies that use **Voice over Internet Protocol (VoIP)** and the Internet's packet-switched network to transmit voice, fax, and other forms of audio communication over the Internet. VoIP can be used over a traditional handset as well as over a mobile device. VoIP avoids the long distance charges imposed by traditional phone companies.

There were about 175 million residential VoIP subscribers worldwide in 2012, and this number is expanding rapidly as cable systems provide telephone service as part of their "triple play": voice, Internet, and TV as a single package. This number is dwarfed, however, by the number of mobile VoIP subscribers, which quintupled in 2012 to over 640 million (Burger, 2012; 2013).

VoIP is a disruptive technology. In the past, voice and fax were the exclusive provenance of the regulated telephone networks. With the convergence of the Internet and telephony, however, this dominance is already starting to change, with local and long distance telephone providers and cable companies becoming ISPs, and ISPs getting into the phone market. Key players in the VoIP market include independent service providers such as VoIP pioneers Vonage and Skype (now owned by Microsoft), as well as traditional players such as telephone and cable companies that have moved aggressively into the market.

Video Conferencing, Video Chatting, and Telepresence

Internet video conferencing is accessible to anyone with a broadband Internet connection and a Web camera (webcam). The most widely used Web conferencing suite of tools is WebEx (now owned by Cisco). VoIP companies such as Skype and ooVoo also provide more limited Web conferencing capabilities, commonly referred to as video chatting. Apple's FaceTime is another video chatting technology available for iOS mobile devices with a forward-facing camera and Macintosh computers equipped with Apple's version of a Webcam, called a FaceTime camera.

Telepresence takes video conferencing up several notches. Rather than single persons "meeting" by using webcams, telepresence creates an environment in a room using multiple cameras and screens, which surround the users. The experience is uncanny and strange at first because as you look at the people in the screens, they are looking directly at you. Broadcast quality and higher screen resolutions help create the effect. Users have the sensation of "being in the presence of their colleagues" in a way that is not true for traditional webcam meetings. Providers of telepresence software and hardware include Cisco, HP, and Teliris.

IP telephony

a general term for the technologies that use VoIP and the Internet's packet-switched network to transmit voice and other forms of audio communication over the Internet

Voice over Internet Protocol (VoIP)

protocol that allows for transmission of voice and other forms of audio communication over the Internet

Online Software and Web Services: Web Apps, Widgets, and Gadgets

We are all used to installing software on our PCs. But as the Web and e-commerce move towards a service model, applications increasingly will be running off Web servers. Instead of buying a "product" in a box, you will be paying for a Web service instead. There are many kinds of Web services now available, many free, all the way from full-function applications, such as Microsoft Office 365, to much smaller chunks of code called "widgets" and "gadgets."

Widgets pull content and functionality from one place on the Web to a place where you want it, such as on your Web page, blog, or Facebook page. You can see Web widget services most clearly in photo sites such as Picnik.com, which offers a free photo-editing application that is powerful and simple to use. Facebook's Like button is a widget that is used by more than 50 million people a day in the United States. Walmart, eBay, and Amazon, along with many other retailers, are creating shopping widgets that users can drag to their blogs or profile pages on various social networks so visitors can shop at a full-function online store without having to leave the page. Yahoo, Google, MSN, and Apple all have collections of hundreds of widgets available on their Web sites.

Gadgets are closely related to widgets. They are small chunks of code that usually supply a single limited function such as a clock, calendar, or diary. You can see a collection of gadgets at http://www.google.com/ig/directory?synd=open.

Intelligent Personal Assistants

The idea of having a conversation with a computer, having it understand you and be able to carry out tasks according to your direction, has long been a part of science fiction, from the 1968 Hollywood movie *2001: A Space Odyssey*, to an old Apple promotional video depicting a professor using his personal digital assistant to organize his life, gather data, and place orders at restaurants. That was all fantasy. But Apple's Siri, billed as an intelligent personal assistant and knowledge navigator and released in October 2011 for the iPhone 4S, has many of the capabilities of the computer assistants found in fiction. Siri has a natural language, conversational interface, situational awareness, and is capable of carrying out many tasks based on verbal commands by delegating requests to a variety of different Web services. For instance, you can ask Siri to find a restaurant nearby that serves Italian food. Siri may show you an ad for a local restaurant in the process. Once you have identified a restaurant you would like to eat at, you can ask Siri to make a reservation using OpenTable. You can also ask Siri to place an appointment on your calendar, search Google (or Bing) for airline flights, and figure out what's the fastest route between your current location and a destination using public transit. The answers are not always completely accurate, but critics have been impressed with its uncanny abilities. Siri is currently available on the iPhone 4S, the iPhone 5, the third and fourth generation iPad, iPad Mini, and the fifth generation iPod Touch.

In July, 2012, Google released its version of an intelligent assistant for Android-based smartphones, which it calls Google Now. Google Now is part of the Google Search application. While Google Now has many of the capabilities of Apple's Siri, it attempts to go further by predicting what users may need based on situational awareness, including physical location, time of day, previous location history, calendar, and expressed interests based on previous activity, as described in its patent application (United States Patent Office, 2012). For instance, if you often search for a particular musician or style of music, Google Now might provide recommendations for similar music. If it knows that you go to a health club every other day, Google Now will remind you not to schedule events during these periods. If it knows that you typically read articles about health issues, the system might monitor Google News for similar articles and make recommendations.

3.6 MOBILE APPS: THE NEXT BIG THING IS HERE

The use of mobile Internet access devices such as smartphones, iPads and other tablet computers, and laptops in e-commerce has truly exploded. From nearly zero mobile commerce prior to 2007, today, mobile commerce revenue in the United States is expected to be over $38 billion, representing around 15% of all retail e-commerce sales in 2013. According to market research firm eMarketer, over 60% of all online shoppers are mobile shoppers as well, and this number is expected to increase to over 80% by 2016. In addition, eMarketer also believes that 72 million people in the United States will make a purchase through a mobile device in 2013, and this number will increase by almost 65% to 120 million in 2016 (eMarketer, Inc., 2013j). While mobile commerce is more widespread among younger consumers, there is evidence that even those over 55 are beginning to use this channel more frequently.

Tablets are being added into the mix. More than 50% of tablet owners have reported using their tablets at least once a week to shop, particularly on nights and weekends, and often from the comfort of couch or bed. More than 40% have made a purchase using their tablet (eMarketer, Inc., 2012). As a result, companies are rapidly increasing their investment in mobile commerce technologies. An Internet Retailer survey found that almost 90% of merchants surveyed believed mobile commerce is important to their future online business, and that around 70% are planning to increase the size of the mobile commerce budgets. As with many other aspects of e-commerce, Amazon is a leader, with more than $4 billion in mobile sales worldwide in 2012 (Internet Retailer, 2013). More than $13 billion in mobile sales worldwide were transacted using eBay (Walsh, 2013).

Mobile capabilities include making sure Web sites are compatible with mobile browsers, are optimized for use on various devices (discussed further in Chapter 4), and provide downloadable mobile apps. Although both are important, right now, mobile apps appear to be attracting most of the attention. According to Nielsen, in March 2013, smartphone users spent 87% of their time using mobile apps, and only 13% of their time using the mobile Web. iPad users showed a similar pattern: 76% of their time was spent using mobile apps and only 24% of their time was spent using the mobile Web (Nielsen, 2013). *Insight on Technology: Apps For Everything: The App Ecosystem* gives you some further background on mobile apps.

INSIGHT ON BUSINESS

APPS FOR EVERYTHING: THE APP ECOSYSTEM

When Steve Jobs introduced the iPhone in January 2007, no one—including himself—envisioned that the device would launch a revolution in consumer and business software, or become a major e-commerce platform, let alone a game platform, advertising platform, and general media platform for television shows, movies, videos, and e-books. In short, it's become the personal computer all over again, just in a much smaller form factor.

The iPhone's original primary functions, beyond being a cell phone, were to be a camera, text messaging device, and Web browser. What Apple initially lacked for the iPhone were software applications that would take full advantage of its computing capabilities. The solution was software developed by outside developers—tens of thousands of outside developers—who were attracted to the mission by potential profits and fame from the sale or free distribution of their software applications on a platform approved by the leading innovator in handheld computing and cellular devices. More than two-thirds of apps are free. Every month, Apple receives more than 25,000 new apps from independent developers who may be teenagers in a garage, major video game developers, or major publishers, as well as Fortune 500 consumer products firms using apps for marketing and promotion.

In July 2008, Apple introduced the App Store, which provides a platform for the distribution and sale of apps by Apple as well as by independent developers. Following in the footsteps of the iTunes music store, Apple hoped that the software apps—most free—would drive sales of the iPhone device. It was not expecting the App Store itself to become a major source of revenue. Fast forward to 2013: there are now an estimated 880,000 approved apps available for download from the App Store. Other smartphone developers also followed suit: there are also thousands of apps available for Android phones, BlackBerrys, and Windows phones. As of May 2013, Apple reported that more than 50 billion apps had been downloaded, and over 2 billion are downloaded each month. Apple does not report its app revenues separately, but it does report the amount of money it pays out to app developers, which allows analysts to guess at how much money Apple makes on app sales. Analysts now believe the App Store is generating over $1 billion in profit for Apple per year. Even so, Apple's primary goal in offering apps is not to make money from them, but instead to drive sales of devices—the iPhones, iPads, and iPods that need software to become useful. It's the reverse of printer companies who make cheap printers in order to sell expensive ink. At the same time, apps tie the customer to a hardware platform: as you add more and more apps to your phone, the cost of switching to, say, an Android, rises with each new app installed.

The app phenomenon, equally virulent on Android and BlackBerry operating system platforms, has spawned a new digital ecosystem: tens of thousands of developers, a wildly popular hardware platform, and millions of consumers looking for a computer in their pocket that can replace their now clunky desktop-laptop Microsoft Windows computers, do a pretty good job as a digital media center while on the road, and, by the way, serve as a cell phone.

The range of applications among the 880,000 or so apps on the Apple platform is staggering and defies brief description. You can use the Genius feature to recommend new apps based on ones you already have. There are so many apps that searching for a particular app can be a problem unless you know the name of the app or the developer. Google is probably the best search engine for apps. Enter a search term like "Kraft app" and you'll find that Kraft has an app called iFood Assistant that provides recipes

(continued)

using Kraft products. The most popular app categories are games, education, entertainment, books, and lifestyle.

The implications of the app ecosystem for e-commerce are significant. The smartphone in your pocket becomes not only a general-purpose computer, but also an always-present shopping tool for consumers, as well as an entirely new marketing and advertising platform for vendors. Early e-commerce applications using desktops and laptops were celebrated by pundits as allowing people to shop in their pajamas. Smartphones extend this range from pajamas to office desktops to trains, planes, and cars, all fully clothed. You can shop anywhere, shop everywhere, and shop all the time, in between talking, texting, watching video, and listening to music.

Almost all of the top 100 brands have a presence in at least one of the major app stores, and more than 85% have an app in the Apple App Store. Here are a few examples of how some different firms are using apps to advance and support their brands:

- Converse's Sampler: Allows users to take a picture and "try on" a pair of shoes to see how they look in the clothes they're wearing, as well as to immediately purchase the shoes
- Benjamin Moore's Color Capture: Enables users to match colors and paints
- Colgate-Palmolive's Max White Photo Recharger: Enables users to whiten their teeth in photos
- Tiffany's Engagement Ring Finder: Lets users view diamonds by size, shape, setting, metal, and design
- Charmin's SitOrSquat: Restroom Finder: Provides users with locations of nearest public bathrooms, including cleanliness reviews, availability of changing tables, and handicapped access.

There are, of course, dangers in any ecosystem dominated by a single company. The Apple iOS platform is closed and proprietary, a walled garden, a limiting sandbox. The apps you buy there can play nowhere else. Many apps are incredibly single-purposed and limited in applicability. The apps don't come with any warranty. Because Apple controls who can play in the sandbox, there is the possibility, even the likelihood, that Apple acts as a censor of content, or as a monopolist that prevents certain applications from entering the marketplace, or more likely, as an arbitrary, inscrutable bureaucratic machine that decides which apps will play and which will not. For instance, Apple has removed applications because of sexually themed content. Such programs often appear on the store's list of most-downloaded apps. Clearly Apple is concerned the App Store might become an adult digital theme park that would turn off parents and families who are the target audience for iPhone and iPad sales. In 2012, for the first time, Apple was forced to remove malware from its App Store. A Russian app entitled "Find and Call" purported to simplify users' contacts lists, but instead stole those contacts and uploaded the address book to a remote server, spamming those addresses. In 2013, researchers at Georgia Tech created an app that was able to elude all of Apple iOS's most current security tools, including sandboxing, code signing, and various anti-exploit technologies. Clearly, the app ecosystem is not immune to many of the same issues that apply to the Internet and e-commerce at large.

SOURCES: "App Store Metrics," 148Apps.biz, accessed August 20, 2013; "Researchers Outwit Apple, Plant Malware in App Store," by Gregg Keizer, *Computerworld*, August 20, 2013; "Apple Gives Away 10 Apps to Celebrate App Store's 5th Birthday," by Gregg Keizer, *Computerworld*, July 9, 2013; "Apple: App Store Now Makes Over $1 Billion in Profits Per Year," SeekingAlpha.com, May 30, 2013; "First Instance of iOS App Store Malware Detected, Removed," by Christina Bonnington, Wired.com, July 5, 2012; "The Apps Strategies of the Top 100 Brands," by Haydn Shaughnessy, Forbes.com, October 27, 2011; "The State of Mobile Apps," by The Nielsen Company, June 1, 2010; "Mobile Apps and Consumer Product Brands," by Tobi Elkin, eMarketer, March 2010; "Apple Bans Some Apps for Sex-Tinged Content," by Jenna Wortham, *New York Times*, February 22, 2010; "Inside the App Economy," by Douglas MacMillan, *BusinessWeek*, October 22, 2009.

PLATFORMS FOR MOBILE APPLICATION DEVELOPMENT

Unlike mobile Web sites, which can be accessed by any Web-enabled mobile device, apps are platform-specific. Applications for the iPhone, iPad, and other iOS devices are written in the Objective-C programming language using the iOS SDK (software developer kit). Applications for Android operating system–based phones typically are written using Java, although portions of the code may be in the C or C++ programming language. BlackBerry apps also are written in Java. Applications for Windows mobile devices are written in C or C++.

APP MARKETPLACES

Once written, applications are distributed through various marketplaces. Android apps for Android-based phones are distributed through Google Play, which is controlled by Google. iPhone applications are distributed through Apple's App Store. BlackBerry applications can be found in RIM's App World, while Microsoft operates the Windows Phone Marketplace for Windows mobile devices. Apps can also be purchased from third-party vendors such as Amazon's Appstore. It is important to distinguish "native" mobile apps, which run directly on a mobile device and rely on the device's internal operating system, from Web apps referred to in Section 3.5, which install into your browser, although these can operate in a mobile environment as well.

3.7 CASE STUDY

Akamai Technologies:
Attempting to Keep Supply Ahead of Demand

In 2013, the amount of Internet traffic generated by YouTube alone is greater than the amount of traffic on the entire Internet in 2000. In the last two years, Netflix's subscriber base jumped by 18 million to more than 29 million subscribers, most of whom are now streaming movies over the Internet. In 2013, analysts estimate that between 9 PM and midnight, Netflix takes up a full third of bandwidth in the United States. Because of video streaming and the explosion in mobile devices demanding high-bandwidth applications, Internet traffic has increased 800% since 2007 and is predicted to triple by the end of 2016. Internet video is now a majority of Internet traffic and will reach 55% by 2016, according to networking giant

Cisco Systems. Mobile platform traffic from smartphones and Wi-Fi devices is growing at 60% and will soon push cellular networks and the Internet to their capacities. Cisco estimates that annual global Internet traffic will be around 1.4 zettabytes in 2017: that's 1,400 exabytes, or, in other words, 14 with 19 zeroes behind it!

Experts call services like YouTube, Netflix, and high definition streaming video "net bombs" because they threaten the effective operation of the Internet. At some point, demand will exceed capacity, and there will be either "brownouts," where everyone's connection speed slows down, or "capping" of bandwidth hogs (those 10% of Internet users who consume 60% of the Internet's capacity because of extensive video downloading).

Analysts differ on how fast Internet capacity is growing. Large telecommunication companies (AT&T, Verizon, Comcast, and Level3) argue that demand will soon overwhelm capacity, while other experts argue that Internet bandwidth can double every year for a very long time and easily keep up with demand. Perhaps they're both right: Internet capacity can expand to keep up with demand if sufficient capital is invested in backbone and local networks. That's a big "if." As a result, and in order to raise capital, nearly all the large ISPs such as Comcast, Charter, Cox, and AT&T have bandwidth caps in place where heavy users of video are charged more for their Internet service. More charges based on usage are in the pipeline.

Is Internet bandwidth capacity doubling every year? The proof is in the pudding. How much faster has your home or office bandwidth connection become in the last year? Chances are, your Internet connection speed has not changed in several years, and you may be seeing the effects online. For instance, in 2012, millions of viewers streamed the summer Olympics, including 1.5 million users watching the women's gymnastics team final live. Throughout the first week of events, online viewers reported an avalanche of dropped connections, choppy frame rates, and other technical problems. Even on a regular Friday or Saturday night, the average Internet home viewer will experience stuttering video and sound. This is hardly the stuff of a bright future for mass audience video over the Web.

In today's broadband environment, the threshold of patience is probably much lower than even a few seconds. Increased video and audio customer expectations are bad news for anyone seeking to use the Web for delivery of high-quality multimedia content such as CD-quality music and high definition video. If you are SiriusXM Radio and you want to stream online music to several million users a day, you will definitely need some help. If you are Apple iTunes and want to provide music and video downloads to your 500 million online customers, you also will need some help. Akamai is one of the Web's major helpers, and each of the preceding companies, along with an overwhelming majority of the Web's top companies, use Akamai's services to speed the delivery of content. Akamai serves more than 10 terabits of Web traffic per second.

Slow-loading Web pages and Web content—from music to video—sometimes result from poor design, but more often than not, the problem stems from the underlying infrastructure of the Internet. As you have learned in this chapter, the Internet was originally developed to carry text-based e-mail messages among a relatively small group of researchers, not bandwidth-hogging graphics, sound, and video files to tens of millions of people all at once. The Internet is a collection of networks that has to pass information from one network to another. Sometimes the handoff is not smooth. Every 1,500-byte packet of information sent over the Internet must be verified by the receiving server and an acknowledgment sent to the sender. This slows down not only the distribution of content such as music, but also slows down interactive requests, such as purchases, that require the client computer to interact with an online shopping cart. Moreover, each packet may go through many different servers on its way to its final destination, multiplying by several orders of magnitude the number of acknowledgments required to move a packet from New York to San Francisco. The Internet today spends much of its time and capacity verifying packets, contributing to a problem called "latency" or delay. For this reason, a single e-mail with a 1-megabyte attached PDF file can create more than 50 megabytes of Internet traffic and data storage on servers, client hard drives, and network backup drives.

Akamai (which means intelligent, clever, or "cool" in Hawaiian) Technologies was founded by Tom Leighton, an MIT professor of applied mathematics, and Daniel Lewin, an MIT grad student, with the idea of expediting Internet traffic to overcome these limitations. When Timothy Berners-Lee, founder of the World Wide Web, realized that congestion on the Internet was becoming an enormous problem, he issued a challenge to Leighton's research group to invent a better way to deliver Internet content. The result was a set of breakthrough algorithms that became the basis for Akamai. Lewin received his master's degree in electrical engineering and computer science in 1998. His master's thesis was the theoretical starting point for the company. It described storing copies of Web content such as pictures or video clips at many different locations around the Internet so that one could always retrieve a nearby copy, making Web pages load faster.

Officially launched in August 1998, Akamai's current products are based on the Akamai Intelligent Platform, a cloud platform made up of over 137,000 servers in 87 countries within over 1,150 networks around the world, and all within a single network hop of 90% of all Internet users. Akamai software on these servers allows the platform to identify and block security threats and provide comprehensive knowledge of network conditions, as well as instant device-level detection and optimization. Specific products include Aqua Web Solutions for site performance, mobile performance, and data collection and online marketing; Terra Enterprise Solutions that enable businesses to leverage Akamai's cloud platform; Kona Security Solutions and Sola Media Solutions that focus on the delivery of interactive HD quality video on multiple devices; and Aura Network Solutions. Akamai's site performance products allow customers to move their Web content closer to end users so a user in New York City, for instance, will be served L.L.Bean pages from the New York Metro area Akamai servers, while users of the L.L.Bean site in San Francisco will be served pages from Akamai servers in San Francisco. Akamai has a wide range of large corporate and government clients: 1 out of every 3 global Fortune 500 companies, the top 30 media and entertainment companies, 96 of the top 100 online U.S. retailers, all branches of the U.S. military, all the top Internet portals, all the major U.S. sports leagues, and so on. In 2013, Akamai delivers between 15% and 30% of all Web traffic, and over 2 trillion daily Internet interactions. Other competitors in the content delivery network (CDN) industry include Blue Coat, Limelight, Savvis, and Mirror Image Internet.

Accomplishing this seemingly simple task requires that Akamai monitor the entire Internet, locating potential sluggish areas and devising faster routes for information to travel. Frequently used portions of a client's Web site, or large video or audio files that would be difficult to send to users quickly, are stored on Akamai's servers. When a user requests a song or a video file, his or her request is redirected to an Akamai server nearby and the content served from this local server. Akamai's servers are placed in Tier 1 backbone supplier networks, large ISPs, universities, and other networks. Akamai's software determines which server is optimum for the user and then transmits the "Akamaized" content locally. Web sites that are "Akamaized" can be delivered anywhere from 4 to 10 times as fast as non-Akamaized content. Akamai has developed a number of other business services based on its Internet savvy, including targeted advertising based on user location and zip code, content security, business intelligence, disaster recovery, on-demand bandwidth and computing capacity during spikes in Internet traffic, storage, global traffic management, and streaming services. Akamai also offers a product called Advertising Decision Solutions, which provides companies with intelligence generated by the Internet's most accurate and comprehensive knowledge base of Internet network activity. Akamai's massive server deployment and relationships with networks throughout the world enable optimal collection of geography and bandwidth-sensing information. As a result, Akamai provides a highly accurate knowledge base with worldwide coverage. Customers integrate a simple program into their Web server or application server. This program communicates with the Akamai database to retrieve the very latest information. The Akamai network of servers is constantly mapping the Internet, and at the same time, each company's software is in continual communication with the Akamai network. The result: data is always current. Advertisers can deliver ads based on country, region, city, market area, area code, county, zip code, connection type, and speed. You can see several interesting visualizations of the Internet that log basic real-time Web activity by visiting the Akamai Web site.

The shift towards cloud computing and the mobile platform as well as the growing popularity of streaming video have provided Akamai with new growth opportunities. As more businesses and business models are moving to the Web, Akamai has seen its client base continue to grow beyond the most powerful Internet retailers and online content providers. In 2013, Akamai unveiled a new series of features for its Aqua Mobile Accelerator service, which automatically senses the quality of a wireless Internet connection and optimizes it continuously. It also detects the type of device submitting a request for data, whether a PC-based browser, smartphone, or tablet, and optimizes content delivery for that platform. Akamai customers report that Aqua Mobile Accelerator has equalized the performance of mobile Web sites and traditional desktop-accessible Web sites. Akamai has also continued to develop the Akamai Intelligent Platform as an alternative to traditional content delivery methods.

Akamai is also acutely aware of the increase in cybercrime as more traffic migrates to the Internet. Growth in Internet traffic is good news for Akamai, but the company must also now deal with politically motivated cyberattacks, organized crime online, and state-sponsored cyberwarfare. In 2013, Akamai improved its Kona Site Defender tool, which offers a variety of security measures for Akamai clients. The tool protects

SOURCES: "Facts & Figures," Akamai.com, accessed August 19, 2013; "Akamai in 60 Seconds," Akamai.com, accessed August 19, 2013; "The State of the Internet, 1st Quarter 2013 Report," by Akamai Technologies, Inc., July 23, 2013; "Cisco Visual Networking Index, 2012–2017," by Cisco Systems, Inc., May 29, 2013; "Akamai Shares Jump on Cloud-Computing Profit Boost," by Sarah Frier, Bloomberg.com, July 26, 2012; "Olympics Website Leans on Open Source, Akamai for Winning Results," by Bernard Golden, CIO. com, June 26, 2012; "You Think the Internet is Big Now? Akamai Needs to Grow 100-Fold," by Mathew Ingram, GigaOM.com, June 20, 2012; "Akamai Eyes Acceleration Boost for Mobile Content," by Stephen Lawson, *Computerworld*, March 20, 2012; "To Cash In on Wave of Web Attacks, Akamai Launches Stand-alone Security Business," by Andy Greenberg, Forbes.com, February 21, 2012; "Internet Data Caps Cometh," by Holman Jenkins, *Wall Street Journal*, May 11, 2011; "Wider Streets for Internet Traffic," by Anne Eisenberg, *New York Times*, October 9, 2010; "Google TV, Apple TV, and Roku's Biggest Enemy: A Lack of Internet Bandwidth," by Steven Vaughan-Nichols, zdnet.com, October 8, 2010.

against Distributed Denial of Service (DDoS) attacks and includes a firewall for Web applications. Akamai also upgraded Site Defender's Web Application Firewall feature and developed modifications to the tool that make it easier for its users to use. Analysts also expect Akamai to acquire Web security companies to bolster that aspect of their business, with a focus on companies offering the ability to block viruses, prevent data loss, and control bandwidth through the Internet rather than with traditional software or hardware. With so many businesses now dependent on the uninterrupted flow of content over the Internet, Akamai is in a very strong position to sell security services to its customers. However, as impressive as Akamai's operation has become, it may not be nearly enough to cope with the next 5 to 10 years of Internet growth.

Case Study Questions

1. Why does Akamai need to geographically disperse its servers to deliver its customers' Web content?

2. If you wanted to deliver software content over the Internet, would you sign up for Akamai's service? What alternatives exist?

3. What advantages does an advertiser derive from using Akamai's service? What kinds of products might benefit from this kind of service?

4. Why don't major business firms distribute their videos using P2P networks like BitTorrent?

5. Do you think Internet users should be charged based on the amount of bandwidth they consume, or on a tiered plan where users would pay in rough proportion to their usage?

3.8 REVIEW

KEY CONCEPTS

■ **Discuss the origins of the Internet.**

The Internet has evolved from a collection of mainframe computers located on a few U.S. college campuses to an interconnected network of thousands of networks and millions of computers worldwide. The history of the Internet can be divided into three phases:

- During the *Innovation Phase* (1961–1974), the Internet's purpose was to link researchers nationwide via computer.
- During the *Institutionalization Phase* (1975–1995), the Department of Defense and National Science Foundation provided funding to expand the fundamental building blocks of the Internet into a complex military communications system and then into a civilian system.

- During the *Commercialization Phase* (1995 to the present), government agencies encouraged corporations to assume responsibility for further expansion of the network, and private business began to exploit the Internet for commercial purposes.

■ **Identify the key technology concepts behind the Internet.**

The Internet's three key technology components are:
- *Packet switching*, which slices digital messages into packets, routes the packets along different communication paths as they become available, and then reassembles the packets once they arrive at their destination.
- *TCP/IP*, which is the core communications protocol for the Internet. TCP establishes the connections among sending and receiving Web computers and makes sure that packets sent by one computer are received in the correct sequence by the other, without any packets missing. IP provides the addressing scheme and is responsible for the actual delivery of the packets.
- *Client/server technology*, which makes it possible for large amounts of information to be stored on Web servers and shared with individual users on their client computers (which may be desktop PCs, laptops, netbooks, tablets, or smartphones).

■ **Discuss the impact of the mobile platform and cloud computing.**

- The mobile platform is becoming the primary means for accessing the Internet.
- The number of cellphone subscribers worldwide far exceeds the number of PC owners.
- The form factor of PCs has changed from desktops to laptops and tablet computers such as the iPad.
- Smartphones are a disruptive technology that radically alters the personal computing and e-commerce landscape.
- Cloud computing refers to a model of computing in which firms and individuals obtain computing power and software applications over the Internet, rather than purchasing the hardware and software and installing it on their own computers. Cloud computing is the fastest growing form of computing.

■ **Describe the role of Internet protocols and utility programs.**

Internet protocols and utility programs make the following Internet services possible:
- *HTTP* delivers requested Web pages, allowing users to view them.
- *SMTP* and *POP* enable e-mail to be routed to a mail server and then picked up by the recipient's server, while *IMAP* enables e-mail to be sorted before being downloaded by the recipient.
- *SSL* and *TLS* ensure that information transmissions are encrypted.
- *FTP* is used to transfer files from servers to clients and vice versa.
- *Telnet* is a utility program that enables work to be done remotely.
- *Ping* is a utility program that allows users to verify a connection between client and server.
- *Tracert* lets you track the route a message takes from a client to a remote computer.

■ Explain the current structure of the Internet.

The main structural elements of the Internet are:
- The *backbone*, which is composed primarily of high-bandwidth fiber-optic cable operated by a variety of providers.
- *IXPs*, which are hubs that use high-speed switching computers to connect the backbone with regional and local networks.
- *CANs*, which are local area networks operating within a single organization that connect directly to regional networks.
- *ISPs*, which deal with the "last mile" of service to homes and offices. ISPs offer a variety of types of service, ranging from dial-up service to broadband DSL, cable modem, T1 and T3 lines, and satellite link service.
- *Governing bodies*, such as IAB, ICANN, IESG, IETF, ISOC, and W3C. Although they do not control the Internet, they have influence over it and monitor its operations.

■ Understand the limitations of today's Internet.

To envision what the Internet of tomorrow will look like, we must first look at the limitations of today's Internet:
- *Bandwidth limitations*. Today's Internet is slow and incapable of effectively sharing and displaying large files, such as video and voice files.
- *Quality of service limitations*. Data packets don't all arrive in the correct order, at the same moment, causing latency; latency creates jerkiness in video files and voice messages.
- *Network architecture limitations*. Servers can't keep up with demand. Future improvements to Internet infrastructure will improve the way servers process requests for information, thus improving overall speed.
- *Language development limitations*. The nature of HTML restricts the quality of "rich" information that can be shared online. Future languages will enable improved display and viewing of video and graphics.
- *Limitations arising from the "wired" nature of the Internet*. The Internet is based primarily on physical cables, which restricts the mobility of users.

■ Describe the potential capabilities of the Internet of the future.

Internet2 is a consortium working together to develop and test new technologies for potential use on the Internet. In addition to the Internet2 project, other groups are working to expand Internet bandwidth via improvements to fiber optics. Wireless LAN and 4G technologies are providing users of smartphones and tablet computers with increased access to the Internet and its various services. The increased bandwidth and expanded connections will result in a number of benefits, including latency solutions; guaranteed service levels; lower error rates; and declining costs. The Internet of Things will be a big part of the Internet of the future, with more and more sensor-equipped machines and devices connected to the Internet.

■ Understand how the Web works.

The Web was developed during 1989–1991 by Dr. Tim Berners-Lee, who created a computer program that allowed formatted pages stored on the Internet to be linked using keywords (hyperlinks). In 1993, Marc Andreessen created the first graphical Web browser, which made it possible to view documents on the Web graphically and created the possibility of universal computing. The key concepts you need to be familiar with in order to understand how the Web works are the following:

- *Hypertext*, which is a way of formatting pages with embedded links that connect documents to one another and that also link pages to other objects.
- *HTTP*, which is the protocol used to transmit Web pages over the Internet.
- *URLs*, which are the addresses at which Web pages can be found.
- *HTML*, which is the programming language used to create most Web pages and which provides designers with a fixed set of tags that are used to format a Web page.
- *XML*, which is a newer markup language that allows designers to describe data and information.
- *Web server software*, which is software that enables a computer to deliver Web pages written in HTML to client computers that request this service by sending an HTTP request. Web server software also provides security services, FTP, search engine, and data capture services. The term Web server also is used to refer to the physical computer that runs the Web server software.
- *Web clients*, which are computing devices attached to the Internet that are capable of making HTTP requests and displaying HTML pages.
- *Web browsers*, which display Web pages and also have added features such as e-mail and newsgroups.

■ **Describe how Internet and Web features and services support e-commerce.**

Together, the Internet and the Web make e-commerce possible by allowing computer users to access product and service information and to complete purchases online. Some of the specific features that support e-commerce include:

- *E-mail*, which uses a series of protocols to enable messages containing text, images, sound, and video clips to be transferred from one Internet user to another. E-mail is used in e-commerce as a marketing and customer support tool.
- *Instant messaging*, which allows messages to be sent between two users almost instantly, allowing parties to engage in a two-way conversation. In e-commerce, companies are using instant messaging as a customer support tool.
- *Search engines*, which identify Web pages that match a query submitted by a user. Search engines assist users in locating Web pages related to items they may want to buy.
- *Online forums* (message boards), which enable users to communicate with each other, although not in real time, and online chat, which allows users to communicate in real time (simultaneously), are being used in e-commerce as community-building tools.
- *Streaming media*, which enables music, video, and other large files to be sent to users in chunks so that when received and played, the file comes through uninterrupted. Like standard digital files, streaming media may be sold as digital content and used as a marketing tool.
- *Cookies*, which are small text files that allow a Web site to store information about a user, are used by e-commerce as a marketing tool. Cookies allow Web sites to personalize the site to the user and also permit customization and market segmentation.

Web 2.0 features and services include:

- *Social networks*, which are online services that support communication within networks of friends, colleagues, and even entire professions.
- *Blogs*, which are personal Web pages that typically contain a series of chronological entries (newest to oldest) by the author and links to related Web pages.
- *RSS*, which is an XML format that allows users to have digital content, including text, articles, blogs, and podcast audio files, automatically sent to their computers over the Internet.
- *Podcasts*, which are audio presentations—such as a radio show, audio from a movie, or simply personal audio presentations—stored as audio files and posted to the Web.
- *Wikis*, which are Web applications that allow a user to easily add and edit content on a Web page.
- *Music and video services*, such as iTunes and digital video on demand.
- *Internet telephony*, which uses VoIP to transmit audio communication over the Internet.
- *Online software and services*, such as Web apps, widgets, and gadgets.

■ **Understand the impact of m-commerce applications.**

- M-commerce applications are part of the larger $38 billion m-commerce market.
- Smartphone and tablet users spent the majority of their time using mobile apps rather than the mobile Web.
- There are a variety of different platforms for mobile application development including Objective-C (for iOS devices), Java (BlackBerrys and Android smartphones), and C and C++ (Windows mobile devices and some BlackBerry coding).
- Mobile apps for the iPhone are distributed through Apple's App Store, for BlackBerrys through RIM's App World, for Android devices through Google Play, and for Windows mobile devices through Microsoft's Windows Phone Marketplace. There are also third-party vendors such as Amazon's Appstore.

QUESTIONS

1. What are the three basic building blocks of the Internet?
2. What is latency, and how does it interfere with Internet functioning?
3. Explain how packet switching works.
4. How is the TCP/IP protocol related to information transfer on the Internet?
5. What technological innovation made client/server computing possible?
6. What is cloud computing, and how has it impacted the Internet?
7. Why are smartphones a disruptive technology?
8. What types of companies form the Internet backbone today?
9. What function do the IXPs serve?
10. What is the goal of the Internet2 project?
11. Compare and contrast intranets, extranets, and the Internet as a whole.
12. What are some of the major limitations of today's Internet?
13. What are some of the challenges of policing the Internet? Who has the final say when it comes to content?
14. Compare and contrast the capabilities of Wi-Fi and 3G/4G wireless networks.
15. What are the basic capabilities of a Web server?

16. What are the major technological advancements that are anticipated to accompany the Internet of the future? Discuss the importance of each.
17. Why was the development of the browser so significant for the growth of the Web?
18. What advances and features does HTML5 offer?
19. Name and describe five services currently available through the Web.
20. Why are mobile apps the next big thing?

PROJECTS

1. Review the opening case on augmented reality. What developments have occurred since this case was written in September 2013?

2. Locate where cookies are stored on your computer. (They are probably in a folder entitled "Cookies" within your browser program.) List the top 10 cookies you find and write a brief report describing the kinds of sites that placed the cookies. What purpose do you think the cookies serve? Also, what do you believe are the major advantages and disadvantages of cookies? In your opinion, do the advantages outweigh the disadvantages, or vice versa?

3. Call or visit the Web sites of a cable provider, DSL provider, and satellite provider to obtain information on their Internet services. Prepare a brief report summarizing the features, benefits, and costs of each. Which is the fastest? What, if any, are the downsides of selecting any of the three for Internet service (such as additional equipment purchases)?

4. Select two countries (excluding the United States) and prepare a short report describing their basic Internet infrastructure. Are they public or commercial? How and where do they connect to backbones within the United States?

5. Investigate the Internet of Things. Select one example and describe what it is and how it works.

CHAPTER 4

Building an E-commerce Presence: Web Sites, Mobile Sites, and Apps

LEARNING OBJECTIVES

After reading this chapter, you will be able to:

- Understand the questions you must ask and answer, and the steps you should take, in developing an e-commerce presence.
- Explain the process that should be followed in building an e-commerce presence.
- Describe the major issues surrounding the decision to outsource site development and/or hosting.
- Identify and understand the major considerations involved in choosing Web server and e-commerce merchant server software.
- Understand the issues involved in choosing the most appropriate hardware for an e-commerce site.
- Identify additional tools that can improve Web site performance.
- Understand the important considerations involved in developing a mobile Web site and building mobile applications.

USA Today

Redesigns

More than a year ahead of its 30th anniversary, *USA Today* began an ambitious overhaul of its Web site and mobile apps, as well as its print product. Between 2008 and 2012, digital jumped from the fourth most popular news medium to second (behind only television), switching places with traditional newspapers. Parent company Gannett decided that "the nation's newspaper," packed with color photos and graphics from its inception, needed to update its signature format to keep ahead of the competition, which—after initial ridicule—had adopted many of its features. The goal was to capitalize on *USA Today*'s core competency—visual storytelling—to breathe new life into the print product and modernize its digital offerings. More original reporting, both written and video, from the over 5,000 Gannett and *USA Today* journalists would both benefit from and enhance the new design.

While global brand consultancy firm Wolff Olins crafted a twenty-first-century logo, digital advertising agency Fi (formerly Fantasy Interactive) experimented through various iterations to arrive at the optimal combination of images, info-graphics, video, live news feeds, and scan-ability. David Payne, Chief Digital Officer for Gannett and project supervisor, stressed that a quick scan had to be sufficient for readers to locate all top stories. A horizontal navigation scheme was another nonnegotiable so that the design would transfer from desktops and laptops to tablets. Fi focused on making the Web site experience simulate scrolling through an iPad app. Payne also wanted to separate advertising from content while above all ensuring that readers using any device would be served the correct mixed media news content for each story.

Across all digital platforms including a Facebook app, iOS and Android apps, and a tablet app, larger photos and graphic-driven stories had to be accommodated. Interactive weather mapping, live video, and page customization were included in the Web and tablet versions. The Fi team decided that the Web site, though keeping the same color scheme and logo, needed to have its own unique design tailored to a digital space. Rather than mimicking newsprint texture and typography and the long scrollable pages of the typical above the fold/below the fold format of most newspaper sites, they wanted to fill the screen with visual content and snippets of stories to grab the reader's attention. Reinvigorating the Web site, which, like Web sites in general, was losing viewership to apps, was a key objective.

Another objective was to integrate advertising unconstrained by the traditional Interactive Advertising Bureau (IAB) suite standards that had been used by most news Web sites since 2002. The standard IAB banner ads limit advertisers to a specific space and use outdated screen resolutions. Payne gave Fi free rein to allow the entire browser window to be used for ads that simulated a television commercial break or an ad encountered while turning the pages in a magazine. The Fi team strove to integrate ads into the content flow. Gannett-owned PointRoll created many of these high-impact ads using HTML5 so that they would be compatible across all platforms.

On the other hand, certain features simulating the reading of a newspaper were embraced because they promoted intuitive navigation. Each of the nine sections was color-coded just like the print product. A navigation bar at the top of the home page allows direct access to a section. The featured news story image and headline grace the right side, while a list of the other top news stories of the day occupies the left top. Below are images and headlines for the featured story in each section, each of which is marked with a section bar. When a story is opened it appears as an overlay on top of the Home page. Left and right arrows lead to other articles in the section. This was done so that a hard refresh would not be necessary in order to go deeper into the site. The flat architecture, with just two layers for the entire site, gives readers the sense on the Home page that nine papers have been correlated, but as stories are opened, it appears as if a single page has been placed on top. The designers suspect that much like *USA Today*'s once ridiculed graphics-heavy design, elements of the new Web site design will be adopted by its competitors. While they fretted a bit that they might be nudging readers out of their comfort zone, they drew on *USA Today*'s brash heritage, adopting full use of all screen real estate and rejecting the IAB banner ad format in favor of full screen ads.

A highly publicized, complete relaunch of the Web site in September 2012, accompanied by reintroductions of every digital channel, was well received. AIGA (formerly the American Institute of Graphic Arts), a professional organization for the design community, praised the horizontal interface, simple three-column layouts, rich colors, large gridded images, layered articles, and separation of ads and news content. The use of the latest responsive design tools, HTML5, Cascading Style Sheets (CSS), and JavaScript, was also lauded. A responsive template adapts to tablet-sized screens, subtracting a column of news present for wider browsers. *USA Today* decided, however, to adopt a separate mobile theme rather than use more browser detection techniques, which do not always work. Focusing on just tablet and desktop maximized their ability to use all available screen space, while the mobile design provides a cleaner, less-cluttered view of the same news stories for the smaller screen. Full-page advertisements, available for all digital formats, were praised by business magazine *Fast Company*, which referred to them as a luxury. One of the foremost authorities in journalism education, the nonprofit Poynter Institute, posited that the redesign could raise *USA Today*'s value in a time of journalistic upheaval. The site received a Site of the Day award from the Favourite Website Awards (FWA) program and The Cutting Edge Award from Adobe. What's more, Web Designer Magazine featured it in a five-page spread, and .net Magazine featured the single-page app format in its How We Built section.

Seven months later, at the end of April 2013, *USA Today* publisher Larry Kramer sent out a staff announcement heralding the success of the project. Prompted by the release of circulation numbers from the Alliance for Audited Media (AAM) showing yet another drop in readership for the print edition, Kramer wanted to reassure his employees that overall readership—with the digital editions taken into account—had registered substantial gains. He boasted that readership had surpassed 50 million, up from 38.7 million the month preceding the launch (August 2012). By his reckoning this placed *USA Today* above both the *New York Times* (48 million, including the *Boston Globe*) and the *Wall Street Journal* (25 million, including Marketwatch and AllThingsD).

While designing for optimum reading conditions across all platforms was a key objective, the driving force behind *USA Today*'s upgrade was boosting its ad-based business model. CDO Payne believes that sound- and motion-rich ads that directly engage the viewer are the future of Web advertising. With the new digital canvas, ads do not require a user to click them to reach multimedia content. With a click-through rate of only 1–2%, advertisers are spending money on rich content that is rarely consumed. If this content simply appears in the information stream, ROI will undoubtedly soar. The question is, will readers accept automatic ad serving as they move between newspaper sections?

USA Today is betting that by reducing the number of ads per page to just one on article pages and allowing users to close it, the full-page interstitials between sections will be acceptable. Both the larger-format single ads and the multimedia interstitials allow it to charge a premium for ad placement. The gamble is that by balancing user preferences and advertiser desires, both parties will experience enhanced quality. The quality over quantity approach will, in turn, drive more revenue.

SOURCES: "USA Today Memo: 'Our Strategy Is Working….We Are Moving in the Right Direction'," by Jim Romenesko, Jimromenesko. com, April 30, 2013; "USAToday. com: Redesigning One of America's Most Popular News Sites," blog.f-i. com, April 15, 2013; "Check Out These USA Today Homepage Design Concepts That Didn't Make the Cut," by Kirsten Acuna, *Business Insider*, September 20, 2012; "New USA Today Website 'Very, Very influenced by iPad Design'," by Sam Kirkland, poynter. com, September 19, 2012; "It's a New Website Rethink for USA TODAY, Too," by Dr. Mario R. Garcia, Garciamedia.com, September 17, 2012; "In USA Today Redesign, Hope for a New Canvas for Web Advertisers," by Jason Del Rey, Adage.com, September 13, 2012; "USA TODAY Unveils Redesigned Newspaper, Website, Apps," Usatoday.com, September 13, 2012.

I n Chapter 3, you learned about e-commerce's technological foundation: the Internet, Web, and the mobile platform. In this chapter, you will examine the important factors that a manager needs to consider when building an e-commerce presence. The focus will be on the managerial and business decisions you must make before you begin, and that you will continually need to make. Although building a sophisticated e-commerce presence isn't easy, today's tools are much less expensive and far more powerful than they were during the early days of e-commerce. You do not have to be Amazon or eBay to create a successful Web e-commerce presence. In this chapter, we focus on both small and medium-sized businesses as well as much larger corporate entities that serve thousands of customers a day, or even an hour. As you will see, although the scale may be very different, the principles and considerations are basically the same.

4.1 IMAGINE YOUR E-COMMERCE PRESENCE

Before you begin to build a Web site or app of your own, there are some important questions you will need to think about and answer. The answers to these questions will drive the development and implementation of your online presence.

WHAT'S THE IDEA? (THE VISIONING PROCESS)

Before you can plan and actually build a Web presence, you need to have a vision of what you hope to accomplish and how you hope to accomplish it. The vision includes not just a statement of mission, but also identification of the target audience, characterization of the market space, a strategic analysis, an Internet marketing matrix, and a development timeline. It starts with a dream of what's possible, and concludes with a timeline and preliminary budget for development of the Web presence.

If you examine any successful Web site, you can usually tell from the home page what the vision that inspires the site is. If the company is a public company, you can often find a succinct statement of its vision or mission in the reports it files with the Securities and Exchange Commission. For Amazon, it's to become the largest marketplace on earth. For Facebook, it's to make the world more open and connected. For Google, it's to organize the world's information and make it universally accessible and useful. The Web presence you want to build may not have such all-encompassing ambitions, but a succinct statement of mission, purpose, and direction is the key factor in driving the development of your project. For instance, Texture Media, which operates NaturallyCurly.com, described in the Insight on Business case later in this chapter, describes itself as a social media company empowering, embracing, and connecting the world of curls, kinks, and waves. The NaturallyCurly Web site is clearly aimed at creating a community of women surrounding the topics of hair, fashion, and health. The mission of Theknot.com is to be the Internet's comprehensive, one-stop wedding planning solution.

WHERE'S THE MONEY: BUSINESS AND REVENUE MODEL

Once you have defined a mission statement, a vision, you need to start thinking about where the money will be coming from. You will need to develop a preliminary idea of your business and revenue models. You don't need detailed revenue and cost projections at this point. Instead, you need a general idea of how your business will generate revenues. The basic choices have been described in Chapter 2. Basic business models are portal, e-tailer, content provider, transaction broker, market creator, service provider, and community provider (social network).

The basic revenue model alternatives are advertising, subscriptions, transaction fees, sales, and affiliate revenue. There's no reason to adopt a single business or revenue model, and in fact, many firms have multiple models. For instance, the New York Times digital business model is to both sell subscriptions and sell ad space. In addition, they sell unique photographs and gifts. At Theknot.com, a vertical portal for the wedding industry, you will find ads, affiliate relationships, and sponsorships from major creators of wedding products and services, including a directory to local wedding planners, all of which produce revenue for Theknot.com. Petsupplies.com and Petsmart.com, the most popular pet Web sites in the United States, have more focused sales revenue models, and present themselves almost entirely as e-tailers of pet supplies.

WHO AND WHERE IS THE TARGET AUDIENCE

Without a clear understanding of your target audience, you will not have a successful Web presence. There are two questions here: who is your target audience and where are they on the Web? Your target audience can be described in a number of ways: demographics, behavior patterns (lifestyle), current consumption patterns (online vs. offline purchasing), digital usage patterns, content creation preferences (blogs, social networks, sites like Pinterest), and buyer personas (profiles of your typical customer). Understanding the demographics of your target audience is usually the first step. Demographic information includes age, income, gender, and location. In some cases, this may be obvious and in others, much less so. For instance, Harley-Davidson sells motorcycles to a very broad demographic range of varying ages, incomes, and locations, from 34-year-olds to 65-year-olds. Although most of the purchasers are middle-aged men, with middle incomes, many of the men ride with women, and the Harley-Davidson Web site has a collection of women's clothing and several Web pages devoted to women riders. While the majority of men who purchase Harley-Davidsons have modest incomes, a significant group of purchasers are professionals with above-average incomes. Hence, the age and income demographic target is quite broad. What ties Harley-Davidson riders together is not their shared demographics, but their love of the motorcycles and the brand, and the lifestyle associated with touring the highways of America on a powerful motorcycle that sounds like a potato popper. In contrast, a site like Theknot.com is aimed at women in the 18–34-year-old range who are in varying stages of getting married, with lifestyles that include shopping online, using smartphones and tablets, downloading apps, and using Facebook. This audience is technologically hip. These women read and contribute to blogs, comment on forums, and use Pinterest to find ideas for fashion. A "typical" visitor to Theknot.com would be a 28-year-old woman who has an engagement ring, is just starting the wedding planning process, has an income of $45,000, lives in the Northeast, and is interested in a beach wedding. There are, of course, other "typical" profiles. For each profile for your Web site you will need to develop a detailed description.

WHAT IS THE BALLPARK? CHARACTERIZE THE MARKETPLACE

The chances of your success will depend greatly on the characteristics of the market you are about to enter, and not just on your entrepreneurial brilliance. Enter into a declining market filled with strong competitors, and you will multiply your chances of failure. Enter into a market that is emerging, growing, and has few competitors, and you stand a better chance. Enter a market where there are no players, and you will either be rewarded handsomely with a profitable monopoly on a successful product no one else thought of (Apple) or you will be quickly forgotten because there isn't a market for your product at this point in time (the Franklin e-book reader circa 1999).

Features of the marketplace to focus on include the demographics of the market and how a Web presence fits into the market. In addition, you will want to know about the structure of the market: competitors and substitute products.

What are the features of the marketplace you are about to enter? Is the market growing, or receding in size? If it's growing, among which age and income groups? Is the marketplace shifting from offline to online delivery? If so, is the market moving towards traditional Web sites, mobile, and/or tablets? Is there a special role for a mobile presence in this market? What percentage of your target audience uses a Web site, smartphone, or tablet? What about social networks? What's the buzz on products like yours? Are your potential customers talking about the products and services you want to offer on Facebook, Twitter, or blogs? How many blogs focus on products like yours? How many Twitter posts mention similar offerings? How many Facebook Likes (signs of customer engagement) are attached to products you want to offer?

The structure of the market is described in terms of your direct competitors, suppliers, and substitute products. You will want to make a list of the top five or ten competitors and try to describe their market share, and distinguishing characteristics. Some of your competitors may offer traditional versions of your products, while others will offer new renditions or versions of products that have new features. You need to find out everything you can about your competitors. What's the market buzz on your competitors? How many unique monthly visitors (UMVs) do they have? How many Facebook Likes, Twitter followers, and/or Pinterest followers? How are your competitors using social sites and mobile devices as a part of their online presence. Is there something special you could do with social networks that your competitors do not? Do a search on customer reviews of their products. You can find online services (some of them free) that will measure the number of online conversations about your competitors, and the total share of Internet voice each of your competitors receives. Do your competitors have a special relationship with their suppliers that you may not have access to? Exclusive marketing arrangements would be one example of a special supplier relationship. Finally, are there substitutes for your products and services? For instance, your site may offer advice to the community of pet owners, but local pet stores or local groups may be a more trusted source of advice on pets.

WHERE'S THE CONTENT COMING FROM?

Web sites are like books: they're composed of a lot of pages that have content ranging from text, to graphics, photos, and videos. This content is what search engines catalog as they crawl through all the new and changed Web pages on the Internet. The content is why your customers visit your site and either purchase things or look at ads that generate revenue for you. Therefore, the content is the single most important foundation for your revenue and ultimate success.

There are generally two kinds of content: static and dynamic. Static content is text and images that do not frequently change, such as product descriptions, photos, or text that you create to share with your visitors. Dynamic content is content that changes regularly, say, daily or hourly. Dynamic content can be created by you, or increasingly, by bloggers and fans of your Web site and products. User-generated content has a number of advantages: it's free, it engages your customer fan base, and search engines are more likely to catalog your site if the content is changing. Other sources of content, especially photos, are external Web sites that aggregate content such as Pinterest, discussed in the opening case in Chapter 1.

KNOW YOURSELF: CONDUCT A SWOT ANALYSIS

A **SWOT analysis** is a simple but powerful method for strategizing about your business and understanding where you should focus your efforts. In a SWOT analysis you describe your strengths, weaknesses, threats, and opportunities. In the example SWOT analysis in **Figure 4.1**, you will see a profile of a typical start-up venture that includes a unique approach to an existing market, a promise of addressing unmet needs in this market, and the use of newer technologies (social and mobile platforms) that older competitors may have overlooked. There are many opportunities to address a large market with unmet needs, as well as the potential to use the initial Web site as a home base and spin-off related or nearby sites, leveraging the investment in design and technology. But there are also weaknesses and threats. Lack of financial and human resources are typically the biggest weakness of start-up sites. Threats include

SWOT analysis
describes a firm's strengths, weaknesses, opportunities, and threats

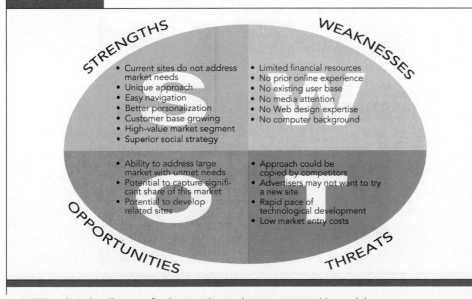

FIGURE 4.1   SWOT ANALYSIS

A SWOT analysis describes your firm's strengths, weaknesses, opportunities, and threats.

competitors that could develop the same capabilities as you, and low market entry costs, which might encourage many more start-ups to enter the marketplace.

Once you have conducted a SWOT analysis, you can consider ways to overcome your weaknesses and build on your strengths. For instance, you could consider hiring or partnering to obtain technical and managerial expertise, and looking for financing opportunities (including friends and relatives).

DEVELOP AN E-COMMERCE PRESENCE MAP

E-commerce has moved from being a PC-centric activity on the Web to a mobile and tablet-based activity as well. While 80% or more of e-commerce today is conducted using PCs, increasingly smartphones and tablets will be used for purchasing. Currently, smartphones and tablets are used by a majority of Internet users in the United States to shop for goods and services, explore purchase options, look up prices, and access social sites. Your potential customers use these various devices at different times during the day, and involve themselves in different conversations depending on what they are doing—touching base with friends, tweeting, or reading a blog. Each of these are "touch points" where you can meet the customer, and you have to think about how you develop a presence in these different virtual places. **Figure 4.2** provides a roadmap to the platforms and related activities you will need to think about when developing your e-commerce presence.

Figure 4.2 illustrates four different kinds of e-commerce presence: Web sites, e-mail, social media, and offline media. For each of these types there are different platforms that you will need to address. For instance, in the case of Web site presence, there are three different platforms: traditional desktop, tablets, and smartphones,

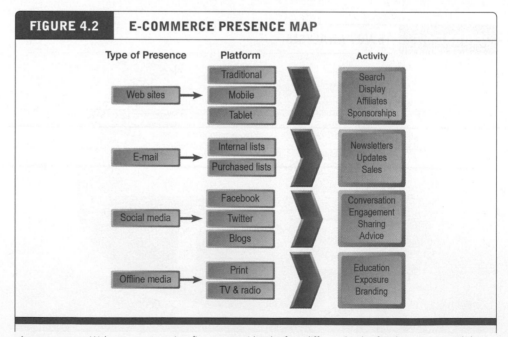

| FIGURE 4.2 | E-COMMERCE PRESENCE MAP |

An e-commerce Web presence requires firms to consider the four different kinds of Web presence, and the platforms and activities associated with each type of presence.

each with different capabilities. And for each type of e-commerce presence there are related activities you will need to consider. For instance, in the case of Web sites, you will want to engage in search engine marketing, display ads, affiliate programs, and sponsorships. Offline media, the fourth type of e-commerce presence, is included here because many firms use multiplatform or integrated marketing where print ads refer customers to Web sites. The marketing activities in Figure 4.2 are described in much greater detail in Chapters 6 and 7.

DEVELOP A TIMELINE: MILESTONES

Where would you like to be a year from now? It's a good idea for you to have a rough idea of the time frame for developing your e-commerce presence when you begin. You should break your project down into a small number of phases that could be completed within a specified time. Six phases are usually enough detail at this point. **Table 4.1** illustrates a one-year timeline for the development of a start-up Web site.

HOW MUCH WILL THIS COST?

It's too early in the process to develop a detailed budget for your e-commerce presence, but it is a good time to develop a preliminary idea of the costs involved. How much you spend on a Web site depends on what you want it to do. Simple Web sites can be built and hosted with a first-year cost of $5,000 or less if all the work is done in-house by yourself and others willing to work without pay. A more reasonable budget for a small Web start-up would be $25,000 to $50,000. Here the firm owner would develop all the content at no cost, and a Web designer and programmer would be hired to implement the initial Web site. As discussed later, the Web site would be hosted on a cloud-based server. The Web sites of large firms that offer high levels of interactivity

TABLE 4.1	E-COMMERCE PRESENCE TIMELINE	
PHASE	ACTIVITY	MILESTONE
Phase 1: Planning	Envision Web presence; determine personnel	Web mission statement
Phase 2: Web site development	Acquire content; develop a site design; arrange for hosting the site	Web site plan
Phase 3: Web Implementation	Develop keywords and metatags; focus on search engine optimization; identify potential sponsors	A functional Web site
Phase 4: Social media plan	Identify appropriate social platforms and content for your products and services	A social media plan
Phase 5: Social media implementation	Develop Facebook, Twitter, and Pinterest presence	Functioning social media presence
Phase 6: Mobile plan	Develop a mobile plan; consider options for porting your Web site to smartphones	A mobile media plan

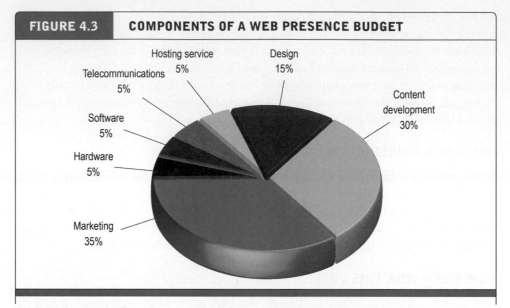

| FIGURE 4.3 | COMPONENTS OF A WEB PRESENCE BUDGET |

While hardware and software costs have fallen dramatically, Web sites face significant design, content development, and marketing costs.

and linkage to corporate systems can cost several hundred thousand to millions of dollars a year to create and operate.

While how much you spend to build a Web site depends on how much you can afford, and, of course, the size of the opportunity, **Figure 4.3** provides some idea of the relative size of various Web site costs. In general, the cost of hardware, software, and telecommunications for building and operating a Web site has fallen dramatically (by over 50%) in the last decade, making it possible for very small entrepreneurs to build fairly sophisticated sites. At the same time, while technology has lowered the costs of system development, the costs of marketing, content development, and design have risen to make up more than half of typical Web site budgets. The longer-term costs would also have to include site and system maintenance, which are not included here.

4.2 BUILDING AN E-COMMERCE PRESENCE: A SYSTEMATIC APPROACH

Once you have developed a vision of the Web presence you want to build, it's time to start thinking about how to build and implement the Web presence. Building a successful e-commerce presence requires a keen understanding of business, technology, and social issues, as well as a systematic approach. E-commerce is just too important to be left totally to technologists and programmers.

The two most important management challenges are (1) developing a clear understanding of your business objectives and (2) knowing how to choose the right technology to achieve those objectives. The first challenge requires you to build a plan for developing your firm's presence. The second challenge requires you to understand some of the basic elements of e-commerce infrastructure. Let the business drive the technology.

Even if you decide to outsource the development effort and operation to a service provider, you will still need to have a development plan and some understanding of the basic e-commerce infrastructure issues such as cost, capability, and constraints. Without a plan and a knowledge base, you will not be able to make sound management decisions about e-commerce within your firm.

Let's assume you are a manager for a medium-sized industrial parts firm in the United States. You have been given a budget of $100,000 to develop an e-commerce presence for the firm. The purpose will be to sell and service the firm's customers, who are mostly small machine and metal fabricating shops, and to engage your customers through a blog and user forum. Where do you start? In the following sections, we will examine developing an e-commerce Web site, and then, at the end of the chapter, discuss some of the considerations involved in developing a mobile site and building mobile applications.

First, you must be aware of the main areas where you will need to make decisions (see **Figure 4.4**). On the organizational and human resources fronts, you will have to bring together a team of individuals who possess the skill sets needed to build and manage a successful e-commerce Web site. This team will make the key decisions about business objectives and strategy, technology, site design, and social and information policies. The entire development effort must be closely managed if you hope to avoid the disasters that have occurred at some firms.

You will also need to make decisions about hardware, software, and telecommunications infrastructure. The demands of your customers should drive your choices of technology. Your customers will want technology that enables them to find what they want easily, view the product, purchase the product, and then receive the product from your warehouses quickly. You will also have to carefully consider design. Once you have identified the key decision areas, you will need to think about a plan for the project.

| **FIGURE 4.4** | **PIECES OF THE E-COMMERCE SITE-BUILDING PUZZLE** |

Building an e-commerce Web site requires that you systematically consider the many factors that go into the process.

FIGURE 4.5 WEB SITE SYSTEMS DEVELOPMENT LIFE CYCLE

PLANNING: THE SYSTEMS DEVELOPMENT LIFE CYCLE

Your second step in building an e-commerce Web site will be creating a plan document. In order to tackle a complex problem such as building an e-commerce site, you will have to proceed systematically through a series of steps. One methodology is the systems development life cycle. The **systems development life cycle (SDLC)** is a methodology for understanding the business objectives of any system and designing an appropriate solution. Adopting a life cycle methodology does not guarantee success, but it is far better than having no plan at all. The SDLC method also helps in creating documents that communicate objectives, important milestones, and the uses of resources to management. **Figure 4.5** illustrates the five major steps involved in the systems development life cycle for an e-commerce site:

systems development life cycle (SDLC)

a methodology for understanding the business objectives of any system and designing an appropriate solution

- Systems analysis/planning
- Systems design
- Building the system
- Testing
- Implementation

SYSTEMS ANALYSIS/PLANNING: IDENTIFY BUSINESS OBJECTIVES, SYSTEM FUNCTIONALITY, AND INFORMATION REQUIREMENTS

In the systems analysis/planning step of the SDLC, you try to answer the question, "What do we want this e-commerce site to do for our business?" The key point is to let the business decisions drive the technology, not the reverse. This will ensure that your technology platform is aligned with your business. We will assume here that you have identified a business strategy and chosen a business model to achieve your strategic objectives (see Chapter 2). But how do you translate your strategies, business models, and ideas into a working e-commerce Web site?

One way to start is to identify the specific business objectives for your site, and then develop a list of system functionalities and information requirements. **Business objectives** are simply capabilities you want your site to have.

System functionalities are types of information systems capabilities you will need to achieve your business objectives. The **information requirements** for a system are the information elements that the system must produce in order to achieve the business objectives. You will need to provide these lists to system developers and programmers so they know what you as the manager expect them to do.

Table 4.2 describes some basic business objectives, system functionalities, and information requirements for a typical e-commerce site. As shown in the table, there are nine basic business objectives that an e-commerce site must deliver. These objectives must be translated into a description of system functionalities and ultimately into a set of precise information requirements. The specific information requirements for a system typically are defined in much greater detail than Table 4.2 indicates. To a large extent, the business objectives of an e-commerce site are not that different from those of an ordinary retail store. The real difference lies in the system functionalities

business objectives
capabilities you want your site to have

system functionalities
types of information systems capabilities you will need to achieve your business objectives

information requirements
the information elements that the system must produce in order to achieve the business objectives

TABLE 4.2	SYSTEM ANALYSIS: BUSINESS OBJECTIVES, SYSTEM FUNCTIONALITIES, AND INFORMATION REQUIREMENTS FOR A TYPICAL E-COMMERCE SITE	
BUSINESS OBJECTIVE	**SYSTEM FUNCTIONALITY**	**INFORMATION REQUIREMENTS**
Display goods	Digital catalog	Dynamic text and graphics catalog
Provide product information (content)	Product database	Product description, stocking numbers, inventory levels
Personalize/customize product	Customer on-site tracking	Site log for every customer visit; data mining capability to identify common customer paths and appropriate responses
Engage customers in conversations	On-site blog	Software with blogging and community response functionality
Execute a transaction	Shopping cart/payment system	Secure credit card clearing; multiple payment options
Accumulate customer information	Customer database	Name, address, phone, and e-mail for all customers; online customer registration
Provide after-sale customer support	Sales database	Customer ID, product, date, payment, shipment date
Coordinate marketing/advertising	Ad server, e-mail server, e-mail, campaign manager, ad banner manager	Site behavior log of prospects and customers linked to e-mail and banner ad campaigns
Understand marketing effectiveness	Site tracking and reporting system	Number of unique visitors, pages visited, products purchased, identified by marketing campaign
Provide production and supplier links	Inventory management system	Product and inventory levels, supplier ID and contact, order quantity data by product

and information requirements. In an e-commerce site, the business objectives must be provided entirely in digital form without buildings or salespeople, 24 hours a day, 7 days a week.

SYSTEM DESIGN: HARDWARE AND SOFTWARE PLATFORMS

system design specification

description of the main components in a system and their relationship to one another

Once you have identified the business objectives and system functionalities, and have developed a list of precise information requirements, you can begin to consider just how all this functionality will be delivered. You must come up with a **system design specification**—a description of the main components in the system and their relationship to one another. The system design itself can be broken down into two components: a logical design and a physical design. A **logical design** includes a data flow diagram that describes the flow of information at your e-commerce site, the processing functions that must be performed, and the databases that will be used. The logical design also includes a description of the security and emergency backup procedures that will be instituted, and the controls that will be used in the system.

logical design

describes the flow of information at your e-commerce site, the processing functions that must be performed, the databases that will be used, the security and emergency backup procedures that will be instituted, and the controls that will be used in the system

A **physical design** translates the logical design into physical components. For instance, the physical design details the specific model of server to be purchased, the software to be used, the size of the telecommunications link that will be required, the way the system will be backed up and protected from outsiders, and so on.

Figure 4.6(a) presents a data flow diagram for a simple high-level logical design for a very basic Web site that delivers catalog pages in HTML in response to HTTP requests from the client's browser, while **Figure 4.6(b)** shows the corresponding physical design. Each of the main processes can be broken down into lower-level designs that are much more precise in identifying exactly how the information flows and what equipment is involved.

physical design

translates the logical design into physical components

BUILDING THE SYSTEM: IN-HOUSE VERSUS OUTSOURCING

Now that you have a clear idea of both the logical and physical designs for your site, you can begin considering how to actually build the site. You have many choices, and much depends on the amount of money you are willing to spend. Choices range from outsourcing everything (including the actual systems analysis and design) to building everything yourself (in-house). **Outsourcing** means that you will hire an outside vendor to provide the services involved in building the site rather than using in-house personnel. You also have a second decision to make: will you host (operate) the site on your firm's own servers or will you outsource the hosting to a Web host provider? These decisions are independent of each other, but they are usually considered at the same time. There are some vendors who will design, build, and host your site, while others will either build or host (but not both). **Figure 4.7** on page 198 illustrates the alternatives.

outsourcing

hiring an outside vendor to provide the services you cannot perform with in-house personnel

Build Your Own versus Outsourcing

Let's take the building decision first. If you elect to build your own site, there are a range of options. Unless you are fairly skilled, you should use a pre-built template to create the Web site. For example, Yahoo Merchant Solutions, Amazon Stores, and eBay

FIGURE 4.6	A LOGICAL AND A PHYSICAL DESIGN FOR A SIMPLE WEB SITE

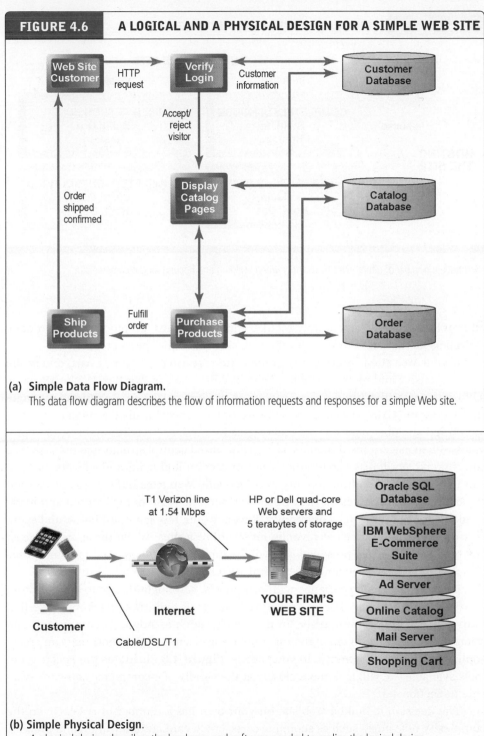

(a) Simple Data Flow Diagram.
This data flow diagram describes the flow of information requests and responses for a simple Web site.

(b) Simple Physical Design.
A physical design describes the hardware and software needed to realize the logical design.

You have a number of alternatives to consider when building and hosting an e-commerce site.

all provide templates that merely require you to input text, graphics, and other data, as well as the infrastructure to run the Web site once it has been created.

If your Web site is not a sales-oriented site requiring a shopping cart, one of the least expensive and most widely used site building tools is WordPress. **WordPress** is a blogging tool with a sophisticated content management system. A **content management system (CMS)** is a database software program specifically designed to manage structured and unstructured data and objects in a Web site environment. A CMS provides Web managers and designers with a centralized control structure to manage Web site content. WordPress also has thousands of user-built plug-ins and widgets that you can use to extend the functionality of a Web site. Web sites built in WordPress are treated by search engines like any other Web site: their content is indexed and made available to the entire Web community. Revenue-generating ads, affiliates, and sponsors are the main sources of revenue for WordPress sites. While these are the least costly sources of a Web presence, you will be limited to the "look and feel" and functionality provided by the template and infrastructure supplied by these vendors.

If you have some experience with computers, you might decide to build the site yourself "from scratch." There are a broad variety of tools, ranging from those that help you build everything truly "from scratch," such as Adobe Dreamweaver and Microsoft Expression, to top-of-the-line prepackaged site-building tools that can create sophisticated sites customized to your needs. **Figure 4.8** illustrates the spectrum of tools available. We will look more closely at the variety of e-commerce software available in Section 4.3.

The decision to build a Web site on your own has a number of risks. Given the complexity of features such as shopping carts, credit card authentication and processing, inventory management, and order processing, the costs involved are high, as are the risks of doing a poor job. You will be reinventing what other specialized firms have already built, and your staff may face a long, difficult learning curve, delaying your entry to market. Your efforts could fail. On the positive side, you may be better

WordPress
open source content management and blog Web site design tool

content management system (CMS)
organizes, stores, and processes Web site content

FIGURE 4.8 — THE SPECTRUM OF TOOLS FOR BUILDING YOUR OWN E-COMMERCE SITE

Build from Scratch

HTML
Dreamweaver
Expression
CGI Scripts
SQL Database

Use Packaged Site-Building Tools

Commerce Server 10
(Commerce-Server.net)
IBM WebSphere

Use Prebuilt Templates

Google Sites
Yahoo! Merchant Solutions
Amazon Webstore
WordPress

able to build a site that does exactly what you want, and, more importantly, develop the in-house knowledge to allow you to change the site rapidly if necessary due to a changing business environment.

If you choose more expensive site-building packages, you will be purchasing state-of-the art software that is well tested. You could get to market sooner. However, to make a sound decision, you will have to evaluate many different packages, and this can take a long time. You may have to modify the packages to fit your business needs and perhaps hire additional outside vendors to do the modifications. Costs rise rapidly as modifications mount. A $4,000 package can easily become a $40,000 to $60,000 development project (see **Figure 4.9**). If you choose the template route, you will be limited to the functionality already built into the templates, and you will not be able to add to the functionality or change it.

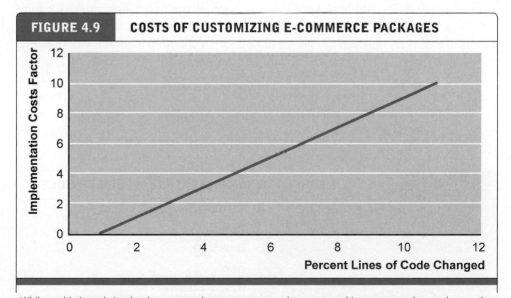

FIGURE 4.9 — COSTS OF CUSTOMIZING E-COMMERCE PACKAGES

While sophisticated site development packages appear to reduce costs and increase speed to market, as the modifications required to fit the package to your business needs rise, costs rise rapidly.

In the past, bricks-and-mortar retailers in need of an e-commerce site typically designed the site themselves (because they already had the skilled staff in place and had extensive investments in information technology capital such as databases and telecommunications). However, as Web applications have become more sophisticated, larger retailers today rely heavily on vendors to provide sophisticated Web site capabilities, while also maintaining a substantial internal staff. Small start-ups may build their own sites from scratch using in-house technical personnel in an effort to keep costs low. Medium-size start-ups will often purchase a Web site design and programming expertise from vendors. Very small mom-and-pop firms seeking simple storefronts will use templates or blogging tools like WordPress. For e-commerce sites, the cost of building has dropped dramatically in the last five years, resulting in lower capital requirements for all players (see *Insight on Business: Curly Hair and Appillionaires*.)

Host Your Own versus Outsourcing

Now let's look at the hosting decision. Most businesses choose to outsource hosting and pay a company to host their Web site, which means that the hosting company is responsible for ensuring the site is "live," or accessible, 24 hours a day. By agreeing to a monthly fee, the business need not concern itself with many of the technical aspects of setting up a Web server and maintaining it, telecommunications links, nor with staffing needs.

co-location

when a firm purchases or leases a Web server (and has total control over its operation) but locates the server in a vendor's physical facility. The vendor maintains the facility, communications lines, and the machinery

You can also choose to *co-locate*. With a **co-location** agreement, your firm purchases or leases a Web server (and has total control over its operation) but locates the server in a vendor's physical facility. The vendor maintains the facility, communications lines, and the machinery. Co-location has expanded with the spread of virtualization where one server has multiple processors (4 to 16) and can operate multiple Web sites at once with multiple operating systems. In this case, you do not buy the server but rent its capabilities on a monthly basis, usually at one-quarter of the cost of owning the server itself. See **Table 4.3** for a list of some of the major hosting/co-location providers. There is an extraordinary range of prices for co-location, ranging from $4.95 a month, to several hundred thousands of dollars per month depending on the size of the Web site, bandwidth, storage, and support requirements.

While co-location involves renting physical space for your hardware, you can think of using a cloud service provider as renting virtual space in your provider's infrastructure. Cloud services are rapidly replacing co-location because they are less expensive, and arguably more reliable. Unlike with co-location, your firm does not own

TABLE 4.3	KEY PLAYERS: HOSTING/CO-LOCATION/CLOUD SERVICES
Amazon EC2	IBM Global Services
Bluehost	Rackspace
CenturyLink	ServerBeach
GoDaddy	Verio
GSI Commerce	Verizon/Terremark

INSIGHT ON BUSINESS

CURLY HAIR AND APPILLIONAIRES

With so many big companies dominating the e-commerce scene, you may wonder if there's a chance for the little guy anymore. The answer is yes: there are still billions left in potential online retail sales, with additional money to be made from advertising revenues. In fact, there's an e-commerce frenzy going on that nearly rivals the dot-com era with one exception: the start-ups have much leaner development models made possible in part by much cheaper technology, and social media that can provide inexpensive marketing and sales.

NaturallyCurly.com is a good example of a low-entry-cost, niche-oriented site that created an online community where none existed before. Gretchen Heber and Michelle Breyer started the site with $500 in 1998. Both had naturally curly hair and often had long discussions about the difficulty of dealing with it on muggy days. Or they'd talk about how good it looked on other days. Based on a hunch that other people also needed help coping with curly hair issues, they launched NaturallyCurly.com. They spent $200 on the domain name, and bought some curly hair products to review on the site. The site was built with a simple Web server and the help of a 14-year-old Web page designer. The idea was to act as a content site with community feedback. They added a bulletin board for users to send in their comments.

There were no competitors at first, and even without advertising on Google, they started showing up in Google searches for "curly hair" near or at the top of the search results list. In 2000, after a year of operation, they got an e-mail from Procter & Gamble, the world's largest personal care products company, asking if they would accept advertising for $2,000 a month

for two years. From there, the site grew by adding additional advertising from leading hair care products companies and now generates revenue in excess of $1 million from advertising and sales of products on Curlmart.com, its online boutique for curly hair products, which they launched in 2004. In 2005, it obtained its first round of outside funding, from an angel network in Texas. Since then the company has gone through three rounds of additional funding.

In September 2010, NaturallyCurly unveiled a new Web site, one that offers a more personalized experience for its users. The revamp included hair-type–specific content, an upgraded geo-targeted Salon and Stylist finder, and an upgraded "Frizz Forecast." The firm has also moved aggressively into social marketing by establishing a Facebook page and a Twitter account. Curlmart. com, its e-commerce site, now showcases 60 different brands and 550 community-vetted products. In 2011, NaturallyCurly moved into mobile apps. Curls on-the-Go is a free app that personalizes advice to its users based on their hair characteristics and preferred styles. The app is designed to sell products, provide reviews from visitors to its Web sites, and to help users find local salons. Other apps include CurlTalk and CurlyNikki. In 2011, NaturallyCurly also added TextureTrends, an annual market intelligence briefing that helps advance the site as a community of experts and influencers.

In 2012, Naturally Curly Network became TextureMedia Inc., which sells ad space for its network of six related, branded Web sites: CurlMart, TextureTrends, Curlniki, curlStylist, Curls on-the Go (mobile app), and the mother ship Naturallycurly.com. The combined sites generate more than 2.7 million unique visitors a month, and the firm is profitable.

(continued)

Other start-up firms are finding that cloud computing and social marketing greatly reduce the costs of building a Web site and starting a company. Christian Gheorghe started Tidemark Systems on a shoestring, but not by buying his own computers or building the IT infrastructure of a typical company. Tidemark Systems produces a Web-based business analytic software package that client companies use to track and analyze everything from sales to employee benefits. Rather than purchase office productivity software, he used Google Docs and open source alternatives for databases. For a phone system, he used Skype for free, and Gmail for his e-mail system. Instead of buying his own servers, he rented computing time from Amazon's cloud service for roughly twelve cents an hour. With cloud services, he had to pay only for the computer power he actually used. Storing 100 gigabytes of data in the cloud cost Tidemark $10 a month. Fast forward a few years: Tidemark has now raised almost $50 million in venture capital, and hopes to go public by 2015. Although Gheorghe no longer needs to pinch pennies, the "lean and mean" vision upon which he founded Tidemark continues to this day.

Like cloud computing and social networks, the app economy has changed the economics of software production and e-commerce and has led to Appillionaires—a very small group of app creators who make it big. One of the best known appillionaires is Chris Stevens, author of the *Alice for the iPad* app, an interactive rendering of Lewis Carroll's *Alice in Wonderland*. Within a few months of its release, *Alice for iPad* was reviewed on Oprah Winfrey's television show and rose to the top ranks of apps in the iTunes store. What kind of infrastructure did Chris Stevens need to build this interactive book (and a series of related apps in the interactive book format)? An iMac and an iPhone, along with three months of 15-hour days. Stevens has been a reporter, graphic designer, and a writer for CNET. Along with a friend, who like Stevens had been recently fired from their jobs, he co-founded Atomic Antelope Inc., an interactive app book publisher. His friend provided the programming. In March 2012, Atomic Antelope's second hit app, *Alice in New York*, won a Kirkus Star Award, the second for the company.

It isn't just hardware that's getting so inexpensive, but other services as well that are vital for the success of small start-ups. Market intelligence, public relations, and even design services can be found online for a fraction of the cost of traditional service firms. For instance, 99Designs.com bills itself as the fastest growing design marketplace in the world. It crowdsources design projects to participating designers and artists. Typical projects have six to ten designers submitting several designs each for a $300 job. Successful bidders on recent projects have come from Italy, Indonesia, Slovakia, and New Zealand.

The moral of the story: its never been cheaper to start an e-commerce company. In fact, a slow economy may be an entrepreneur's best friend. Failures are not so noticeable, which creates a better environment for risk-taking, which encourages innovation.

▬ **SOURCES:** "Tidemark Raises $13 Million for Cloud Analytics," by Andrew Nusca, ZDNet.com, August 1, 2013; "How NaturallyCurly Co-Founder Turned a Niche Community into a Multi-Million Dollar Brand," Empowerlounge.com, July 2013; "TextureMedia's Story—How a Forum Blossomed," by Crista Bailey, viglink.com, May 15, 2013; "As Boom Lures App Creators, Tough Part is Making a Living," by David Streitfeld, *New York Times*, November 17, 2012; "Behind the Curls: TextureMedia Becomes a Big Hairy Deal," by Sandra Zaragoza, *Austin Business Journal*, August 12, 2012; "Community and the Value of a Kinky Idea," by Laura Lorber, Entrepreneur.com, August 2012; "How to Launch a Billion Dollar Startup on a Shoestring," by George Anders, Forbes.com, May 2, 2012; "Chris Stevens on Alice for the iPad, Book Apps, and Toronto," *Toronto Review*, January 9, 2012; "Striking It Rich In The App Store: For Developers, It's More Casino Than Gold Mine," by Chris Stevens, *FastCompany*, November 2, 2011; *Appillionaires: Secrets from Developers Who Struck It Rich on the App Store*, by Chris Stevens, Wiley, September 2011; "World's Leading Social Media Company for Curly-, Kinky- and Wavy-Haired Women Relaunches as Texture-Media, Inc.," TextureMedia Inc., September 27, 2011; "The NaturallyCurly Network Captures $1.2 Million in Additional Angel Investment," Naturallycurly.com, June 22, 2011; "NaturallyCurly.com Unveils New Look," NaturallyCurly.com, September 27, 2010; "NaturallyCurly Expands Network and Content Coverage with Acquisition of CurlyNikki.com," NaturallyCurly.com, September 16, 2010; "The New Internet Startup Boom: Get Rich Slow," by Josh Quittner, Time.com, April 9, 2009.

the hardware. Cloud service providers offer a standardized infrastructure, virtualization technology, and usually employ a pay-as-you-go billing system.

Hosting, co-location, and cloud services have become a commodity and a utility: costs are driven by very large providers (such as IBM) who can achieve large economies of scale by establishing huge "server farms" located strategically around the country and the globe. This means the cost of pure hosting has fallen as fast as the fall in server prices, dropping about 50% every year! Telecommunications costs have also fallen. As a result, most hosting services seek to differentiate themselves from the commodity hosting business by offering extensive site design, marketing, optimization, and other services. Small, local ISPs also can be used as hosts, but service reliability is an issue. Will the small ISP be able to provide uninterrupted service, 24 hours a day, 7 days a week, 365 days a year? Will they have service staff available when you need it?

There are several disadvantages to outsourcing hosting. If you choose a vendor, make sure the vendor has the capability to grow with you. You need to know what kinds of security provisions are in place for backup copies of your site, internal monitoring of activity, and security track record. Is there a public record of a security breach at the vendor? Most Fortune 500 firms have their own private cloud data centers so they can control the Web environment. On the other hand, there are risks to hosting your own site if you are a small business. Your costs will be higher than if you had used a large outsourcing firm because you don't have the market power to obtain low-cost hardware and telecommunications. You will have to purchase hardware and software, have a physical facility, lease communications lines, hire a staff, and build security and backup capabilities yourself.

TESTING THE SYSTEM

Once the system has been built and programmed, you will have to engage in a testing process. Depending on the size of the system, this could be fairly difficult and lengthy. Testing is required whether the system is outsourced or built in-house. A complex e-commerce site can have thousands of pathways through the site, each of which must be documented and then tested. **Unit testing** involves testing the site's program modules one at a time. **System testing** involves testing the site as a whole, in the same way a typical user would when using the site. Because there is no truly "typical" user, system testing requires that every conceivable path be tested. Final **acceptance testing** requires that the firm's key personnel and managers in marketing, production, sales, and general management actually use the system as installed on a test Internet or intranet server. This acceptance test verifies that the business objectives of the system as originally conceived are in fact working. It is important to note that testing is generally under-budgeted. As much as 50% of the software effort can be consumed by testing and rebuilding (usually depending on the quality of the initial design).

unit testing
involves testing the site's program modules one at a time

system testing
involves testing the site as a whole, in a way the typical user will use the site

acceptance testing
verifies that the business objectives of the system as originally conceived are in fact working

IMPLEMENTATION AND MAINTENANCE

Most people unfamiliar with systems erroneously think that once an information system is installed, the process is over. In fact, while the beginning of the process is over, the operational life of a system is just beginning. Systems break down for a variety of reasons—most of them unpredictable. Therefore, they need continual checking, testing, and repair. Systems maintenance is vital, but sometimes not budgeted for. In general, the annual system maintenance cost will roughly parallel the development cost. A $40,000 e-commerce site will likely require a $40,000 annual expenditure to maintain. Very large e-commerce sites experience some economies of scale, so that, for example, a $1 million site will likely require a maintenance budget of $500,000 to $700,000.

Why does it cost so much to maintain an e-commerce site? Unlike payroll systems, for example, e-commerce sites are always in a process of change, improvement, and correction. Studies of traditional systems maintenance have found 20% of the time is devoted to debugging code and responding to emergency situations (for example, a new server was installed by your ISP, and all your hypertext links were lost and CGI scripts disabled—the site is down!) (Lientz and Swanson, 1980; Banker and Kemerer, 1989). Another 20% of the time is concerned with changes in reports, data files, and links to backend databases. The remaining 60% of maintenance time is devoted to general administration (making product and price changes in the catalog) and making changes and enhancements to the system. E-commerce sites are never finished: they are always in the process of being built and rebuilt. They are dynamic—much more so than payroll systems.

The long-term success of an e-commerce site will depend on a dedicated team of employees (the Web team) whose sole job is to monitor and adapt the site to changing market conditions. The Web team must be multi-skilled; it will typically include programmers, designers, and business managers drawn from marketing, production, and sales support. One of the first tasks of the Web team is to listen to customers' feedback on the site and respond to that feedback as necessary. A second task is to develop a systematic monitoring and testing plan to be followed weekly to ensure all the links are operating, prices are correct, and pages are updated. A large business may have thousands of Web pages, many of them linked, that require systematic monitoring. Other important tasks of the Web team include **benchmarking** (a process in which the site is compared with those of competitors in terms of response speed, quality of layout, and design) and keeping the site current on pricing and promotions. The Web is a competitive environment where you can very rapidly frustrate and lose customers with a dysfunctional site.

benchmarking

a process in which the site is compared with those of competitors in terms of response speed, quality of layout, and design

FACTORS IN OPTIMIZING WEB SITE PERFORMANCE

The purpose of a Web site is to deliver content to customers and to complete transactions. The faster and more reliably these two objectives are met, the more effective the Web site is from a commerce perspective. If you are a manager or marketing executive, you will want the Web site operating in a way that fulfills customers' expectations. You'll have to make sure the Web site is optimized to achieve this business objective. The optimization of Web site performance is more complicated than it seems and involves at least three factors: page content, page generation, and page delivery (see **Figure 4.10**). In this chapter, we describe the software and hardware choices you will need to make in building an e-commerce site; these are also important factors in Web site optimization.

Using efficient styles and techniques for *page design* and *content* can reduce response times by two to five seconds. Simple steps include reducing unnecessary

FIGURE 4.10   **FACTORS IN WEB SITE OPTIMIZATION**

Page Delivery

Content delivery networks
Edge caching
Bandwidth

Page Generation

Server response time
Device-based accelerators
Efficient resource allocation
Resource utilization thresholds
Monitoring site performance

Page Content

Optimize HTML
Optimize images
Site architecture
Efficient page style

Web site optimization requires that you consider three factors: page content, page generation, and page delivery.

HTML comments and white space, using more efficient graphics, and avoiding unnecessary links to other pages in the site. *Page generation* speed can be enhanced by segregating computer servers to perform dedicated functions (such as static page generation, application logic, media servers, and database servers), and using various devices from vendors to speed up these servers. Using a single server or multiple servers to perform multiple tasks reduces throughput by more than 50%. *Page delivery* can be speeded up by using edge-caching services such as Akamai, or specialized content delivery networks such as RealNetworks, or by increasing local bandwidth. We will discuss some of these factors throughout the chapter, but a full discussion of Web site optimization is beyond the scope of this text.

4.3   CHOOSING SOFTWARE AND HARDWARE

Much of what you are able to do at an e-commerce site is a function of the software and hardware. Along with telecommunications, hardware and software constitute the infrastructure of a Web presence. As a business manager in charge of building the site, you will need to know some basic information about both.

SIMPLE VERSUS MULTI-TIERED WEB SITE ARCHITECTURE

Prior to the development of e-commerce, Web sites simply delivered Web pages to users who were making requests through their browsers for HTML pages with content of various sorts. Web site software was appropriately quite simple—it consisted of a

system architecture
the arrangement of software, machinery, and tasks in an information system needed to achieve a specific functionality

server computer running basic Web server software. We might call this arrangement a single-tier system architecture. **System architecture** refers to the arrangement of software, machinery, and tasks in an information system needed to achieve a specific functionality (much like a home's architecture refers to the arrangement of building materials to achieve a particular functionality). The NaturallyCurly Web site started this way—there were no monetary transactions. Tens of thousands of dot-com sites still perform this way. Orders can always be called in by telephone and not taken online.

However, the development of e-commerce required a great deal more interactive functionality, such as the ability to respond to user input (name and address forms), take customer orders for goods and services, clear credit card transactions on the fly, consult price and product databases, and even adjust advertising on the screen based on user characteristics. This kind of extended functionality required the development of Web application servers and a multi-tiered system architecture to handle the processing loads. *Web application servers*, described more fully later in this section, are specialized software programs that perform a wide variety of transaction processing required by e-commerce.

In addition to having specialized application servers, e-commerce sites must be able to pull information from and add information to pre-existing corporate databases. These older databases that predate the e-commerce era are called *backend* or *legacy* databases. Corporations have made massive investments in these systems to store their information on customers, products, employees, and vendors. These backend systems constitute an additional layer in a multi-tiered site.

two-tier architecture
e-commerce system architecture in which a Web server responds to requests for Web pages and a database server provides backend data storage

Figure 4.11 illustrates a simple two-tier and a more complex multi-tier e-commerce system architecture. In **two-tier architecture**, a Web server responds to requests for Web pages and a database server provides backend data storage. In a **multi-tier architecture**, in contrast, the Web server is linked to a middle-tier layer that typically includes a series of application servers that perform specific tasks, as well as to a backend layer of existing corporate systems containing product, customer, and pricing information. A multi-tiered site typically employs several physical computers, each running some of the software applications and sharing the workload across many physical computers.

multi-tier architecture
e-commerce system architecture in which the Web server is linked to a middle-tier layer that typically includes a series of application servers that perform specific tasks as well as a backend layer of existing corporate systems

The remainder of this section describes basic Web server software functionality and the various types of Web application servers.

WEB SERVER SOFTWARE

All e-commerce sites require basic Web server software to answer requests from customers for HTML and XML pages.

When you choose Web server software, you will also be choosing an operating system for your site's computers. Looking at all servers on the Web, the leading Web server software, with about 52% of the market, is Apache, which works with Linux and Unix operating systems. Unix is the original programming language of the Internet and Web, and Linux is a derivative of Unix designed for the personal computer. Apache was developed by a worldwide community of Internet innovators. Apache is free and can be downloaded from many sites on the Web; it also comes installed on most IBM

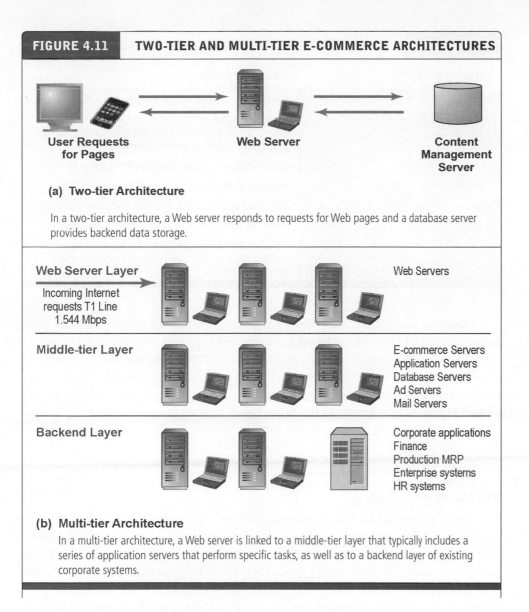

FIGURE 4.11   **TWO-TIER AND MULTI-TIER E-COMMERCE ARCHITECTURES**

User Requests for Pages   **Web Server**   **Content Management Server**

(a) Two-tier Architecture

In a two-tier architecture, a Web server responds to requests for Web pages and a database server provides backend data storage.

Web Server Layer   Web Servers

Incoming Internet requests T1 Line 1.544 Mbps

Middle-tier Layer   E-commerce Servers
Application Servers
Database Servers
Ad Servers
Mail Servers

Backend Layer   Corporate applications
Finance
Production MRP
Enterprise systems
HR systems

(b) Multi-tier Architecture

In a multi-tier architecture, a Web server is linked to a middle-tier layer that typically includes a series of application servers that perform specific tasks, as well as to a backend layer of existing corporate systems.

Web servers. Literally thousands of programmers have worked on Apache over the years; thus, it is extremely stable. There are thousands of utility software programs written for Apache that can provide all the functionality required for a contemporary e-commerce site. In order to use Apache, you will need staff that is knowledgeable in Unix or Linux.

Microsoft Internet Information Services (IIS) is the second major Web server software available, with about 20% of the market. IIS is based on the Windows operating system and is compatible with a wide selection of Microsoft utility and support programs. These numbers are different among the Fortune 1000 firms, and different again if you include blogs, which are served up by Microsoft and Google at their own proprietary sites.

TABLE 4.4	BASIC FUNCTIONALITY PROVIDED BY WEB SERVERS
FUNCTIONALITY	DESCRIPTION
Processing of HTTP requests	Receive and respond to client requests for HTML pages
Security services (Secure Sockets Layer)/ Transport Layer Security	Verify username and password; process certificates and private/public key information required for credit card processing and other secure information
File Transfer Protocol	Permits transfer of very large files from server to server
Search engine	Indexing of site content; keyword search capability
Data capture	Log file of all visits, time, duration, and referral source
E-mail	Ability to send, receive, and store e-mail messages
Site management tools	Calculate and display key site statistics, such as unique visitors, page requests, and origin of requests; check links on pages

There are also at least 100 other smaller providers of Web server software, most of them based on the Unix or Sun Solaris operating systems. Note that the choice of Web server has little effect on users of your system. The pages they see will look the same regardless of the development environment. There are many advantages to the Microsoft suite of development tools—they are integrated, powerful, and easy to use. The Unix operating system, on the other hand, is exceptionally reliable and stable, and there is a worldwide open software community that develops and tests Unix-based Web server software.

Table 4.4 shows the basic functionality provided by all Web servers.

Site Management Tools

site management tools
verify that links on pages are still valid and also identify orphan files

In Chapter 3, we described most of the basic functionality of the Web servers listed in Table 4.4. Another functionality not described previously is site management tools. **Site management tools** are essential if you want to keep your site working, and if you want to understand how well it is working. Site management tools verify that links on pages are still valid and also identify orphan files, or files on the site that are not linked to any pages. By surveying the links on a Web site, a site management tool can quickly report on potential problems and errors that users may encounter. Your customers will not be impressed if they encounter a "404 Error: Page Does Not Exist" message on your Web site. Links to URLs that have moved or been deleted are called dead links; these can cause error messages for users trying to access that link. Regularly checking that all links on a site are operational helps prevent irritation and frustration in users who may decide to take their business elsewhere to a better functioning site.

Even more importantly, site management tools can help you understand consumer behavior on your Web site. Site management software and services, such as those provided by Webtrends, can be purchased in order to more effectively monitor customer purchases and marketing campaign effectiveness, as well as keep track of standard hit counts and page visit information. **Figure 4.12** shows a screenshot that illustrates WebTrends Analytics 10.

Dynamic Page Generation Tools

One of the most important innovations in Web site operation has been the development of dynamic page generation tools. Prior to the development of e-commerce, Web sites primarily delivered unchanging static content in the form of HTML pages. While this capability might be sufficient to display pictures of products, consider all the elements of a typical e-commerce site today by reviewing Table 4.2 (on page 195), or visit what you believe is an excellent e-commerce site. The content of successful

FIGURE 4.12   WEBTRENDS ANALYTICS

Using a sophisticated Web analytics solution such as Webtrends Analytics, managers can quickly understand the return on investment of their online marketing efforts and determine how to improve conversion by drilling down into abandonment paths, product preferences, and successful campaign elements for different types of customers.

SOURCE: Webtrends, Inc., 2011.

e-commerce sites is always changing, often day by day. There are new products and promotions, changing prices, news events, and stories of successful users. E-commerce sites must intensively interact with users who not only request pages but also request product, price, availability, and inventory information. One of the most dynamic sites is eBay—the auction site. There, the content is changing minute by minute. E-commerce sites are just like real markets—they are dynamic. News sites, where stories change constantly, also are dynamic.

The dynamic and complex nature of e-commerce sites requires a number of specialized software applications in addition to static HTML pages. Perhaps one of the most important is dynamic page generation software. With **dynamic page generation**, the contents of a Web page are stored as objects in a database, rather than being hard-coded in HTML. When the user requests a Web page, the contents for that page are then fetched from the database. The objects are retrieved from the database using Common Gateway Interface (CGI), Active Server Pages (ASP), Java Server Pages (JSP), or other server-side programs. CGI, ASP, and JSP are described in the last section of this chapter. This technique is much more efficient than working directly in HTML code. It is much easier to change the contents of a database than it is to change the coding of an HTML page. A standard data access method called *Open Database Connectivity (ODBC)* makes it possible to access any data from any application regardless of what database is used. ODBC is supported by most of the large database suppliers such as Oracle, Sybase, and IBM. ODBC makes it possible for HTML pages to be linked to backend corporate databases regardless of who manufactured the database. Web sites must be able to pull information from, and add information to, these databases. For example, when a customer clicks on a picture of a pair of boots, the site can access the product catalog database stored in a DB2 database, and access the inventory database stored in an Oracle database to confirm that the boots are still in stock and to report the current price.

Dynamic page generation gives e-commerce several significant capabilities that generate cost and profitability advantages over traditional commerce. Dynamic page generation lowers *menu costs* (the costs incurred by merchants for changing product descriptions and prices). Dynamic page generation also permits easy online *market segmentation*—the ability to sell the same product to different markets. For instance, you might want variations on the same banner ad depending on how many times the customer has seen the ad. In the first exposure to a car ad, you might want to emphasize brand identification and unique features. On the second viewing you might want to emphasize superlatives like "most family friendly" to encourage comparison to other brands. The same capability makes possible nearly cost-free *price discrimination*—the ability to sell the same product to different customers at different prices. For instance, you might want to sell the same product to corporations and government agencies but use different marketing themes. Based on a cookie you place on client computers, or in response to a question on your site that asks visitors if they are from a government agency or a corporation, you would be able to use different marketing and promotional materials for corporate clients and government clients. You might want to reward loyal customers with lower prices, say on DVDs or musical tracks, and

dynamic page generation

the contents of a Web page are stored as objects in a database, rather than being hard-coded in HTML. When the user requests a Web page, the contents for that page are then fetched from the database charge full price to first-time buyers. Dynamic page generation allows you to approach different customers with different messages and prices.

Dynamic page generation also enables the use of a content management system (CMS). As previously described, a CMS is used to create and manage Web content. A CMS separates the design and presentation of content (such as HTML documents, images, video, audio) from the content creation process. The content is maintained in a database and dynamically linked to the Web site. A CMS usually includes templates that can be automatically applied to new and existing content, WYSIWYG editing tools that make it easy to edit and describe (tag) content, and collaboration, workflow, and document management tools. Typically, an experienced programmer is needed to install the system, but thereafter, content can be created and managed by non-technical staff. There are a wide range of commercial CMSs available, from top-end enterprise systems offered by Autonomy, EMC/Documentum, OpenText, IBM, and Oracle, to mid-market systems by Ixiasoft, PaperThin, and Ektron, as well as hosted software as a service (SaaS) versions by Clickability, CrownPeak Technology, and OmniUpdate. There are also several open source content management systems available, such as WordPress, Joomla, Drupal, OpenCms, and others.

APPLICATION SERVERS

Web application servers are software programs that provide the specific business functionality required of a Web site. The basic idea of application servers is to isolate the business applications from the details of displaying Web pages to users on the front end and the details of connecting to databases on the back end. Application servers are a kind of middleware software that provides the glue connecting traditional corporate systems to the customer as well as all the functionality needed to conduct e-commerce. In the early years, a number of software firms developed specific separate programs for each function, but increasingly, these specific programs are being replaced by integrated software tools that combine all the needed functionality for an e-commerce site into a single development environment, a packaged software approach.

Table 4.5 on page 212 illustrates the wide variety of application servers available in the marketplace. The table focuses on "sell-side" servers that are designed to enable selling products on the Web. So-called "buy-side" and "link" servers focus on the needs of businesses to connect with partners in their supply chains or find suppliers for specific parts and assemblies. These buy-side and link servers are described more fully in Chapter 12. There are several thousand software vendors that provide application server software. For Linux and Unix environments, many of these capabilities are available free on the Internet from various sites. Most businesses—faced with this bewildering array of choices—choose to use integrated software tools called merchant server software.

E-COMMERCE MERCHANT SERVER SOFTWARE FUNCTIONALITY

E-commerce merchant server software provides the basic functionality needed for online sales, including an online catalog, order taking via an online shopping cart, and online credit card processing.

Web application server
software programs that provide specific business functionality required of a Web site

e-commerce merchant server software
software that provides the basic functionality needed for online sales, including an online catalog, order taking via an online shopping cart, and online credit card processing

TABLE 4.5	APPLICATION SERVERS AND THEIR FUNCTION
APPLICATION SERVER	**FUNCTIONALITY**
Catalog display	Provides a database for product descriptions and prices
Transaction processing (shopping cart)	Accepts orders and clears payments
List server	Creates and serves mailing lists and manages e-mail marketing campaigns
Proxy server	Monitors and controls access to main Web server; implements firewall protection
Mail server	Manages Internet e-mail
Audio/video server	Stores and delivers streaming media content
Chat server	Creates an environment for online real-time text and audio interactions with customers
News server	Provides connectivity and displays Internet news feeds
Fax server	Provides fax reception and sending using a Web server
Groupware server	Creates workgroup environments for online collaboration
Database server	Stores customer, product, and price information
Ad server	Maintains Web-enabled database of advertising banners that permits customized and personalized display of advertisements based on consumer behavior and characteristics
Auction server	Provides a transaction environment for conducting online auctions
B2B server	Implements buy, sell, and link marketplaces for commercial transactions

Online Catalog

online catalog
list of products available on a Web site

A company that wants to sell products on the Web must have a list, or **online catalog**, of its products, available on its Web site. Merchant server software typically includes a database capability that will allow for construction of a customized online catalog. The complexity and sophistication of the catalog will vary depending on the size of the company and its product lines. Small companies, or companies with small product lines, may post a simple list with text descriptions and perhaps color photos. A larger site might decide to add sound, animations, or videos (useful for product demonstrations) to the catalog, or interactivity, such as customer service representatives available via instant messaging to answer questions. Today, larger firms make extensive use of streaming video.

Shopping Cart

shopping cart
allows shoppers to set aside desired purchases in preparation for checkout, review what they have selected, edit their selections as necessary, and then actually make the purchase by clicking a button

Online **shopping carts** are much like their real-world equivalent; both allow shoppers to set aside desired purchases in preparation for checkout. The difference is that the online variety is part of a merchant server software program residing on the Web server, and allows consumers to select merchandise, review what they have selected, edit their selections as necessary, and then actually make the purchase by clicking a button. The merchant server software automatically stores shopping cart data.

Credit Card Processing

A site's shopping cart typically works in conjunction with credit card processing software, which verifies the shopper's credit card and then puts through the debit to the card and the credit to the company's account at checkout. Integrated e-commerce software suites typically supply the software for this function. Otherwise, you will have to make arrangements with a variety of credit card processing banks and intermediaries.

MERCHANT SERVER SOFTWARE PACKAGES (E-COMMERCE SUITES)

Rather than build your site from a collection of disparate software applications, it is easier, faster, and generally more cost-effective to purchase a **merchant server software package** (also called an **e-commerce server suite**). Merchant server software/e-commerce suites offer an integrated environment that promises to provide most or all of the functionality and capabilities you will need to develop a sophisticated, customer-centric site. An important element of merchant sofware packages is a built-in shopping cart that can display merchandise, manage orders, and clear credit card transactions. E-commerce suites come in three general ranges of price and functionality.

Basic packages for elementary e-commerce business applications are provided by Bizland, HyperMart, and Yahoo Merchant Solutions. Webs.com also offers free Web building tools and hosting services. OSCommerce is a free, open source e-commerce suite used by many small start-up sites. PayPal can be used as a payment system on simple Web sites, and widgets can add interesting capabilities.

Midrange suites include IBM WebSphere Commerce Express Edition and Commerce Server (formerly Microsoft Commerce Server). High-end enterprise solutions for large global firms are provided by IBM WebSphere's Commerce on Cloud, Professional, and Enterprise Editions, Oracle ATG Web Commerce, GSI Commerce, Demandware, Magento, and others. There are several hundred software firms that provide e-commerce suites, which raises the costs of making sensible decisions on this matter. Many firms simply choose vendors with the best overall reputation. Quite often this turns out to be an expensive but ultimately workable solution.

Choosing an E-commerce Suite

With all of these vendors, how do you choose the right one? Evaluating these tools and making a choice is one of the most important and uncertain decisions you will make in building an e-commerce site. The real costs are hidden—they involve training your staff to use the tools and integrating the tools into your business processes and organizational culture. The following are some of the key factors to consider:

- Functionality
- Support for different business models

merchant server software package (e-commerce server suite)
offers an integrated environment that provides most or all of the functionality and capabilities needed to develop a sophisticated, customer-centric site

- Business process modeling tools
- Visual site management tools and reporting
- Performance and scalability
- Connectivity to existing business systems
- Compliance with standards
- Global and multicultural capability
- Local sales tax and shipping rules

For instance, although e-commerce suites promise to do everything, your business may require special functionality—such as streaming audio and video. You will need a list of business functionality requirements. Your business may involve several different business models—such as a retail side and a business-to-business side; you may run auctions for stock excess as well as fixed-price selling. Be sure the package can support all of your business models. You may wish to change your business processes, such as order taking and order fulfillment. Does the suite contain tools for modeling business process and work flows? Understanding how your site works will require visual reporting tools that make its operation transparent to many different people in your business. A poorly designed software package will drop off significantly in performance as visitors and transactions expand into the thousands per hour, or minute. Check for performance and scalability by stress-testing a pilot edition or obtaining data from the vendor about performance under load. You will have to connect the e-commerce suite to your traditional business systems. How will this connection to existing systems be made, and is your staff skilled in making the connection? Because of the changing technical environment—in particular, changes in mobile commerce platforms—it is important to document exactly what standards the suite supports now, and what the migration path will be toward the future. Finally, your e-commerce site may have to work both globally and locally. You may need a foreign language edition using foreign currency denominations. And you will have to collect sales taxes across many local, regional, and national tax systems. Does the e-commerce suite support this level of globalization and localization?

WEB SERVICES AND OPEN SOURCE OPTIONS

While existing firms often have the financial capital to invest in commercial merchant server software suites, many small firms and start-up firms do not. They have to build their own Web sites, at least initially. There are really two options here, the key factor being how much programming experience and time you have. One option is to utilize the e-commerce merchant services provided by hosting sites such as Yahoo Merchant Solutions. For a $50 setup fee, and a starter plan of $39.95, the service will walk you through setting up your Web site and provide Web hosting, a shopping cart, technical help by phone, and payment processing. Entrabase and Tripod provide easy-to-use site-building tools and e-commerce templates for e-commerce sites. An e-commerce template is a predesigned Web site that allows users to customize the look and feel of the site to fit their business needs and provides a standard set of functionalities.

Most templates today contain ready-to-go site designs with built-in e-commerce suite functionality like shopping carts, payment clearance, and site management tools.

One of the most popular low-cost tools for creating a Web site without having to have any programming skills is Homestead.com. Building a Web site at Homestead involves three steps: choosing a design from over 2,000 templates, customizing the design with logos and content, and publishing it on the Web on Homestead servers with your own unique IP address, and e-mail. Once you build the Web site, Homestead provides a comprehensive set of services such as PayPal and credit card payment clearing, online catalog, shopping cart, real-time transaction processing, and custom shipping tables. Marketing support is available in the form of search engine optimization for your site, and advertising on Google, Amazon, and MSN. There is a 30-day free trial, and basic service for $4.99 a month, with charges for additional services.

If you have considerable, or at least some, programming background, you can consider open source merchant server software. **Open source software** is software developed by a community of programmers and designers, and is free to use and modify. **Table 4.6** provides a description of some open source options.

open source software
software that is developed by a community of programmers and designers, and is free to use and modify

TABLE 4.6	OPEN SOURCE SOFTWARE OPTIONS
MERCHANT SERVER FUNCTIONALITY	**OPEN SOURCE SOFTWARE**
Web server	Apache (the leading Web server for small and medium businesses)
Shopping cart, online catalog	Many providers: Zen-Cart.com, AgoraCart.com, X-Cart.com, osCommerce.com
Credit card processing	Many providers, such as ASPDotNetStorefront. Credit card acceptance is typically provided in shopping cart software but you may need a merchant account from a bank as well.
Database	MySQL (the leading open source SQL database for businesses)
Programming/scripting language	PHP (a scripting language embedded in HTML documents but executed by the server, providing server-side execution with the simplicity of HTML editing). Perl is an alternative language. JavaScript programs are client-side programs that provide user interface components. Ruby on Rails (RoR, Rails) is another popular open source Web application framework.
Analytics	Analytics keep track of your site's customer activities and the success of your Web advertising campaign. You can also use Google Analytics if you advertise on Google, which provides good tracking tools; most hosting services will provide these services as well. Other open source analytic tools include Piwik, CrawlTrack, and Open Web Analytics.

The advantage of using open source Web building tools is that you get exactly what you want, a truly customized unique Web site. The disadvantage is that it will take several months for a single programmer to develop the site and get all the tools to work together seamlessly. How many months do you want to wait before you get to market with your ideas?

One alternative to building a Web site first is to create a blog first, and develop your business ideas and a following of potential customers on your blog. Once you have tested your ideas with a blog, and attract a Web audience, you can then move on to developing a simple Web site.

THE HARDWARE PLATFORM

hardware platform
refers to all the underlying computing equipment that the system uses to achieve its e-commerce functionality

Whether you host your own site or outsource the hosting and operation of your site, you will need to understand certain aspects of the computing hardware platform. The **hardware platform** refers to all the underlying computing equipment that the system uses to achieve its e-commerce functionality. Your objective is to have enough platform capacity to meet peak demand (avoiding an overload condition), but not so much platform that you are wasting money. Failing to meet peak demand can mean your site is slow, or actually crashes. How much computing and telecommunications capacity is enough to meet peak demand? How many hits per day can your site sustain?

To answer these questions, you will need to understand the various factors that affect the speed, capacity, and scalability of an e-commerce site.

RIGHT-SIZING YOUR HARDWARE PLATFORM: THE DEMAND SIDE

The most important factor affecting the speed of your site is the demand that customers put on the site. **Table 4.7** lists the most important factors to consider when estimating the demand on a site.

Demand on a Web site is fairly complex and depends primarily on the type of site you are operating. The number of simultaneous users in peak periods, the nature of customer requests, the type of content, the required security, the number of items in inventory, the number of page requests, and the speed of legacy applications that may be needed to supply data to the Web pages are all important factors in overall demand on a Web site system.

stateless
refers to the fact that the server does not have to maintain an ongoing, dedicated interaction with the client

Certainly, one important factor to consider is the number of simultaneous users who will likely visit your site. In general, the load created by an individual customer on a server is typically quite limited and short-lived. A Web session initiated by the typical user is **stateless**, meaning that the server does not have to maintain an ongoing, dedicated interaction with the client. A Web session typically begins with a page request, then a server replies, and the session is ended. The sessions may last from tenths of a second to a minute per user. Nevertheless, system performance does degrade as more and more simultaneous users request service. Fortunately, degradation (measured as "transactions per second" and "latency" or delay in response) is fairly graceful over a wide range, up until a peak load is reached and service quality becomes unacceptable (see **Figure 4.13** on page 218).

TABLE 4.7	FACTORS IN RIGHT-SIZING AN E-COMMERCE PLATFORM				
SITE TYPE	PUBLISH/ SUBSCRIBE	SHOPPING	CUSTOMER SELF- SERVICE	TRADING	WEB SERVICES/ B2B
Examples	WSJ.com	Amazon	Travelocity	E*Trade	Ariba e-procurement exchanges
Content	Dynamic Multiple authors High volume Not user-specific	Catalog Dynamic items User profiles with data mining	Data in legacy applications Multiple data sources	Time sensitive High volatility Multiple suppliers and consumers Complex transactions	Data in legacy applications Multiple data sources Complex transactions
Security	Low	Privacy Nonrepudiation Integrity Authentication Regulations	Privacy Nonrepudiation Integrity Authentication Regulations	Privacy Nonrepudiation Integrity Authentication Regulations	Privacy Nonrepudiation Integrity Authentication Regulations
Percent secure pages	Low	Medium	Medium	High	Medium
Cross session information	No	High	High	High	High
Searches	Dynamic Low volume	Dynamic High volume	Nondynamic Low volume	Nondynamic Low volume	Nondynamic Moderate volume
Unique items (SKUs)	High	Medium to high	Medium	High	Medium to high
Transaction volume	Moderate	Moderate to high	Moderate	High to extremely high	Moderate
Legacy integration complexity	Low	Medium	High	High	High
Page views (hits)	High to very high	Moderate to high	Moderate to low	Moderate to high	Moderate

Serving up static Web pages is **I/O intensive**, which means it requires input/ output (I/O) operations rather than heavy-duty processing power. As a result, Web site performance is constrained primarily by the server's I/O limitations and the telecommunications connection, rather than the speed of the processor.

Other factors to consider when estimating the demand on a Web site are the user profile and the nature of the content. If users request searches, registration forms, and order taking via shopping carts, then demands on processors will increase markedly.

I/O intensive
requires input/output operations rather than heavy-duty processing power

| FIGURE 4.13 | DEGRADATION IN PERFORMANCE AS NUMBER OF USERS INCREASES |

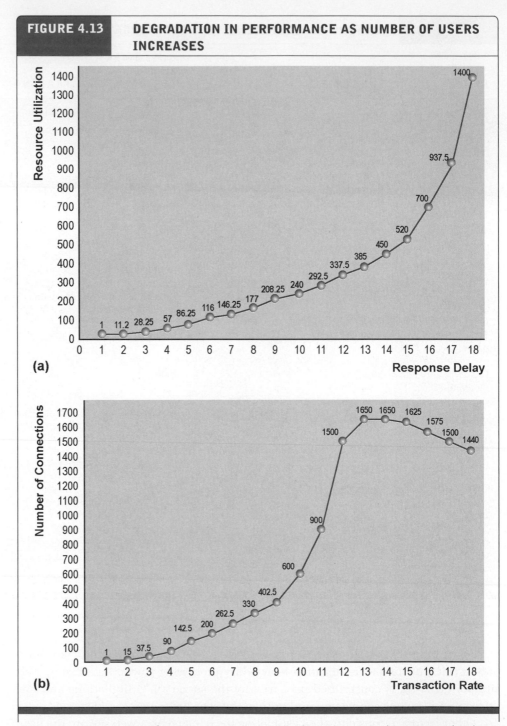

(a)

(b)

Degradation in Web server performance occurs as the number of users (connections) increases, and as the system's resources (processors, disk drives) become more utilized. In (a), user-experienced delay rises gracefully until an inflection point is reached, and then delay rises exponentially to an unacceptable level. In (b), the transaction rate rises gracefully until the number of users rapidly escalates the transaction rate, and at a certain inflection point, the transaction rate starts declining as the system slows down or crashes.

RIGHT-SIZING YOUR HARDWARE PLATFORM: THE SUPPLY SIDE

Once you estimate the likely demand on your site, you will need to consider how to scale up your site to meet demand. We have already discussed one solution that requires very little thought: outsource the hosting of your Web site to a cloud-based service. See Chapter 3 for a discussion of cloud-based computing services. However, if you decide to host your own Web site, scalability is an important consideration. **Scalability** refers to the ability of a site to increase in size as demand warrants. There are three steps you can take to meet the demands for service at your site: scale hardware vertically, scale hardware horizontally, and/or improve the processing architecture of the site (see **Table 4.8**). **Vertical scaling** refers to increasing the processing power of individual components. **Horizontal scaling** refers to employing multiple computers to share the workload and increase the "footprint" of the installation (IBM, 2002).

You can scale your site vertically by upgrading the servers from a single processor to multiple processors. You can keep adding processors to a computer depending on the operating system and upgrade to faster chip speeds as well.

There are two drawbacks to vertical scaling. First, it can become expensive to purchase additional processors with every growth cycle, and second, your entire site becomes dependent on a small number of very powerful computers. If you have two such computers and one goes down, half of your site, or perhaps your entire site, may become unavailable.

scalability
the ability of a site to increase in size as demand warrants

vertical scaling
increasing the processing power of individual components

horizontal scaling
employing multiple computers to share the workload

TABLE 4.8	**VERTICAL AND HORIZONTAL SCALING TECHNIQUES**
TECHNIQUE	APPLICATION
Use a faster computer	Deploy edge servers, presentation servers, data servers, etc.
Create a cluster of computers	Use computers in parallel to balance loads.
Use appliance servers	Use special-purpose computers optimized for their task.
Segment workload	Segment incoming work to specialized computers.
Batch requests	Combine related requests for data into groups, process as group.
Manage connections	Reduce connections between processes and computers to a minimum.
Aggregate user data	Aggregate user data from legacy applications in single data pools.
Cache	Store frequently used data in cache rather than on the disk.

TABLE 4.9	IMPROVING THE PROCESSING ARCHITECTURE OF YOUR SITE
ARCHITECTURE IMPROVEMENT	DESCRIPTION
Separate static content from dynamic content	Use specialized servers for each type of workload.
Cache static content	Increase RAM to the gigabyte range and store static content in RAM.
Cache database lookup tables	Use cache tables used to look up database records.
Consolidate business logic on dedicated servers	Put shopping cart, credit card processing, and other CPU-intensive activity on dedicated servers.
Optimize ASP code	Examine your code to ensure it is operating efficiently.
Optimize the database schema	Examine your database search times and take steps to reduce access times.

Horizontal scaling involves adding multiple single-processor servers to your site and balancing the load among the servers. You can then partition the load so some servers handle only requests for HTML or ASP pages, while others are dedicated to handling database applications. You will need special load-balancing software (provided by a variety of vendors such as Cisco, Microsoft, and IBM) to direct incoming requests to various servers.

There are many advantages to horizontal scaling. It is inexpensive and often can be accomplished using older PCs that otherwise would be disposed of. Horizontal scaling also introduces redundancy—if one computer fails, chances are that another computer can pick up the load dynamically. However, when your site grows from a single computer to perhaps 10 to 20 computers, the size of the physical facility required (the "footprint") increases and there is added management complexity.

A third alternative—improving the processing architecture—is a combination of vertical and horizontal scaling, combined with artful design decisions. **Table 4.9** lists some of the more common steps you can take to greatly improve performance of your site. Most of these steps involve splitting the workload into I/O-intensive activities (such as serving Web pages) and CPU-intensive activities (such as taking orders). Once you have this work separated, you can fine-tune the servers for each type of load. One of the least expensive fine-tuning steps is to simply add RAM to a few servers and store all your HTML pages in RAM. This reduces load on your hard drives and increases speed dramatically. RAM is thousands of times faster than hard disks, and RAM is inexpensive. The next most important step is to move your CPU-intensive activities, such as order taking, onto a high-end, multiple processor server that is dedicated to handling orders and accessing the necessary databases. Taking these steps can permit you to reduce the number of servers required to service 10,000 concurrent users from 100 down to 20, according to one estimate.

4.4 OTHER E-COMMERCE SITE TOOLS

Now that you understand the key factors affecting the speed, capacity, and scalability of your Web site, we can consider some other important requirements. You will need a coherent Web site design that makes business sense—not necessarily a site to wow visitors or excite them, but to sell them something. You will also need to know how to build active content and interactivity into your site—not just display static HTML pages. You must be able to track customers who come, leave, and return to your site in order to be able to greet return visitors ("Hi Sarah, welcome back!"). You will also want to track customers throughout your site so you can personalize and customize their experience. You will definitely want the ability for customers to generate content and feedback on your site to increase their engagement with your brand. Finally, you will need to establish a set of information policies for your site—privacy, accessibility, and access to information policies.

In order to achieve these business capabilities, you will need to be aware of some design guidelines and additional software tools that can cost-effectively achieve the required business functionality.

WEB SITE DESIGN: BASIC BUSINESS CONSIDERATIONS

This is not a text about how to design Web sites. (In Chapter 6, we discuss Web site design issues from a marketing perspective.) Nevertheless, from a business manager's perspective, there are certain design objectives you must communicate to your Web site designers to let them know how you will evaluate their work. At a minimum, your customers will need to find what they need at your site, make a purchase, and leave. A Web site that annoys customers runs the risk of losing the customer forever. See **Table 4.10** for a list of the most common consumer complaints about Web sites.

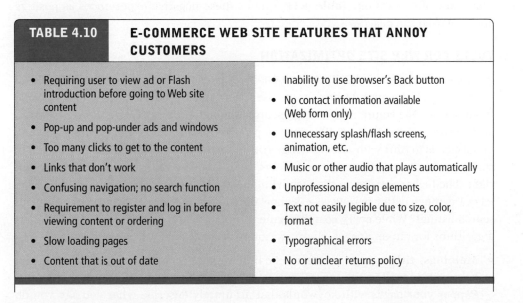

TABLE 4.10	E-COMMERCE WEB SITE FEATURES THAT ANNOY CUSTOMERS
• Requiring user to view ad or Flash introduction before going to Web site content	• Inability to use browser's Back button
• Pop-up and pop-under ads and windows	• No contact information available (Web form only)
• Too many clicks to get to the content	• Unnecessary splash/flash screens, animation, etc.
• Links that don't work	• Music or other audio that plays automatically
• Confusing navigation; no search function	• Unprofessional design elements
• Requirement to register and log in before viewing content or ordering	• Text not easily legible due to size, color, format
• Slow loading pages	• Typographical errors
• Content that is out of date	• No or unclear returns policy

TABLE 4.11	THE EIGHT MOST IMPORTANT FACTORS IN SUCCESSFUL E-COMMERCE SITE DESIGN
FACTOR	**DESCRIPTION**
Functionality	Pages that work, load quickly, and point the customer toward your product offerings
Informational	Links that customers can easily find to discover more about you and your products
Ease of use	Simple foolproof navigation
Redundant navigation	Alternative navigation to the same content
Ease of purchase	One or two clicks to purchase
Multi-browser functionality	Site works with the most popular browsers
Simple graphics	Avoids distracting, obnoxious graphics and sounds that the user cannot control
Legible text	Avoids backgrounds that distort text or make it illegible

Some critics believe poor design is more common than good design. It appears easier to describe what irritates people about Web sites than to describe how to design a good Web site. The worst e-commerce sites make it difficult to find information about their products and make it complicated to purchase goods; they have missing pages and broken links, a confusing navigation structure, and annoying graphics or sounds that you cannot turn off. **Table 4.11** restates these negative experiences as positive goals for Web site design.

TOOLS FOR WEB SITE OPTIMIZATION

A Web site is only as valuable from a business perspective as the number of people who visit. Web site optimization (as we use it here) means how to attract lots of people to your site. One solution is through search engines such as Google, Bing, Ask.com, and several hundred others. The first stop for most customers looking for a product or service is to start with a search engine, and follow the listings on the page, usually starting with the top three to five listings, then glancing to the sponsored ads to the right. The higher you are on the search engine pages, the more traffic you will receive. Page 1 is much better than Page 2. So how do you get to Page 1 in the natural (unpaid) search listings? While every search engine is different, and none of them publish their algorithms for ranking pages, there are some basic ideas that work well:

- **Metatags, titles, page contents:** Search engines "crawl" your site and identify keywords as well as title pages and then index them for use in search arguments. Pepper your pages with keywords that accurately describe what you say you do in your metatag site "description" and "keywords" sections of your source code.

Experiment: use different keywords to see which work. "Vintage cars" may attract more visitors than "antique cars" or "restored cars."

- **Identify market niches:** Instead of marketing "jewelry," be more specific, such as "Victorian jewelry," or "1950s jewelry" to attract small, specific groups who are intensely interested in period jewelry and closer to purchasing.

- **Offer expertise:** White papers, industry analyses, FAQ pages, guides, and histories are excellent ways to build confidence on the part of users and to encourage them to see your Web site as the place to go for help and guidance.

- **Get linked up:** Encourage other sites to link to your site; build a blog that attracts people and who will share your URL with others and post links in the process. List your site with Yahoo Directory for $300 a year. Build a Facebook page for your company, and think about using Twitter to develop a following or fan base for your products.

- **Buy ads:** Complement your natural search optimization efforts with paid search engine keywords and ads. Choose your keywords and purchase direct exposure on Web pages. You can set your budget and put a ceiling on it to prevent large losses. See what works, and observe the number of visits to your site produced by each keyword string.

- **Local e-commerce:** Developing a national market can take a long time. If your Web site is particularly attractive to local people, or involves products sold locally, use keywords that connote your location so people can find you nearby. Town, city, and region names in your keywords can be helpful, such as "Vermont cheese" or "San Francisco blues music."

TOOLS FOR INTERACTIVITY AND ACTIVE CONTENT

The more interactive a Web site is, the more effective it will be in generating sales and encouraging return visitors. Although functionality and ease of use are the supreme objectives in site design, you will also want to interact with users and present them with a lively, "active" experience. You will want to personalize the experience for customers by addressing their individual needs, and customize the content of your offerings based on their behavior or expressed desires. In order to achieve these business objectives, you will need to consider carefully the tools necessary to build these capabilities. Simple interactions such as a customer submitting a name, along with more complex interactions involving credit cards, user preferences, and user responses to prompts, all require special programs. The following sections provide a brief description of some commonly used software tools for achieving high levels of site interactivity.

Common Gateway Interface (CGI)

Common Gateway Interface (CGI) is a set of standards for communication between a browser and a program running on a server that allows for interaction between the user and the server. CGI permits an executable program to access all the information within incoming requests from clients. The program can then generate all the output required to make up the return page (the HTML, script code, text, etc.), and send it back

Common Gateway Interface (CGI)
a set of standards for communication between a browser and a program running on a server that allows for interaction between the user and the server

to the client via the Web server. For instance, if a user clicks the My Shopping Cart button, the server receives this request and executes a CGI program. The CGI program retrieves the contents of the shopping cart from the database and returns it to the server. The server sends an HTML page that displays the contents of the shopping cart on the user's screen. Notice that all the computing takes place on the server side (this is why CGI programs and others like it are referred to as "server-side" programs).

CGI programs can be written in nearly any programming language as long as they conform to CGI standards. Currently, Perl is the most popular language for CGI scripting. Generally, CGI programs are used with Unix servers. CGI's primary disadvantage is that it is not highly scalable because a new process must be created for each request, thereby limiting the number of concurrent requests that can be handled. CGI scripts are best used for small to medium-sized applications that do not involve a high volume of user traffic. There are also Web server extensions available, such as FastCGI, that improve CGI's scalability (Doyle and Lopes, 2005).

Active Server Pages (ASP and ASP.NET)

Active Server Pages (ASP) is Microsoft's original version of server-side programming for Windows. Invented by Microsoft in late 1996, ASP grew rapidly to become the major technique for server-side Web programming in the Windows environment. ASP enables developers to easily create and open records from a database and execute programs within an HTML page, as well as handle all the various forms of interactivity found on e-commerce sites. Like CGI, ASP permits an interaction to take place between the browser and the server. ASP uses the same standards as CGI for communication with the browser. ASP programs are restricted to use on Windows servers running Microsoft's IIS Web server software. ASP.NET, first released in January 2002, and part of Microsoft's .NET framework, is the successor to ASP.

Java, Java Server Pages (JSP), and JavaScript

Java is a programming language that allows programmers to create interactivity and active content on the client computer, thereby saving considerable load on the server. Java was invented by Sun Microsystems in 1990 as a platform-independent programming language for consumer electronics. The idea was to create a language whose programs (so-called Write Once Run Anywhere [WORA] programs) could operate on any computer regardless of operating system. This would be possible if every operating system at the time (Macintosh, Windows, Unix, DOS, and mainframe MVS systems) had a Java Virtual Machine (VM) installed that would interpret the Java programs for that environment.

By 1995, it had become clear, however, that Java was more applicable to the Web than to consumer electronics. Java programs (known as Java applets) could be downloaded to the client over the Web and executed entirely on the client's computer. Applet tags could be included in an HTML page. To enable this, each browser would have to include a Java VM. Today, the leading browsers do include a VM to run Java programs. When the browser accesses a page with an applet, a request is sent to the server to download and execute the program and allocate page space to display the results of the program. Java can be used to display interesting graphics, create interactive environments (such as a mortgage calculator), and directly access the Web server.

Java Server Pages (JSP), like CGI and ASP, is a Web page coding standard that allows developers to use a combination of HTML, JSP scripts, and Java to dynamically generate Web pages in response to user requests. JSP uses Java "servlets," small Java programs that are specified in the Web page and run on the Web server to modify the Web page before it is sent to the user who requested it. JSP is supported by most of the popular application servers on the market today.

JavaScript is a programming language invented by Netscape that is used to control the objects on an HTML page and handle interactions with the browser. It is most commonly used to handle verification and validation of user input, as well as to implement business logic. For instance, JavaScript can be used on customer registration forms to confirm that a valid phone number, zip code, or even e-mail address has been given. Before a user finishes completing a form, the e-mail address given can be tested for validity. JavaScript appears to be much more acceptable to corporations and other environments in large part because it is more stable and also it is restricted to the operation of requested HTML pages.

ActiveX and VBScript

Microsoft—not to be outdone by Sun Microsystems and Netscape—invented the **ActiveX** programming language to compete with Java and **VBScript** to compete with JavaScript. When a browser receives an HTML page with an ActiveX control (comparable to a Java applet), the browser simply executes the program. Unlike Java, however, ActiveX has full access to all the client's resources—printers, networks, and hard drives. VBScript performs in the same way as JavaScript. ActiveX and VBScript work only if you are using Internet Explorer. Otherwise, that part of the screen is blank.

ColdFusion

ColdFusion is an integrated server-side environment for developing interactive Web applications. Originally developed by Macromedia and now offered by Adobe, ColdFusion combines an intuitive tag-based scripting language and a tag-based server scripting language (CFML) that lowers the cost of creating interactive features. ColdFusion offers a powerful set of visual design, programming, debugging, and deployment tools.

Web 2.0 Design Elements

One easy way to pump up the energy on your Web site is to include some appropriate widgets (sometimes called gadgets, plug-ins, or snippets). **Widgets** are small chunks of code that execute automatically in your HTML Web page. They are prebuilt and many are free. Social networks and blogs use widgets to present users with content drawn from around the Web (news headlines from specific news sources, announcements, press releases, and other routine content), calendars, clocks, weather, live TV, games, and other functionality. You can copy the code to an HTML Web page. You can find widgets at Apple's Dashboard Widgets, Widgetbox.com, and Yahoo WidgetEngine and Widgets.

Java Server Pages (JSP)
like CGI and ASP, a Web page coding standard that allows developers to dynamically generate Web pages in response to user requests

JavaScript
a programming language invented by Netscape that is used to control the objects on an HTML page and handle interactions with the browser

ActiveX
a programming language created by Microsoft to compete with Java

VBScript
a programming language invented by Microsoft to compete with JavaScript

ColdFusion
an integrated server-side environment for developing interactive Web applications

widget
a small, prebuilt chunk of code that executes automatically in your HTML Web page; capable of performing a wide variety of tasks

Mashups are a little more complicated and involve pulling functionality and data from one program and including it in another. The most common mashup involves using Google Maps data and software and combining it with other data. For instance, if you have a local real estate Web site, you can download Google Maps and satellite image applications to your site so visitors can get a sense of the neighborhood. There are thousands of Google Map mashups, from maps of Myanmar political protests, to maps of the Fortune 500 companies, all with associated news stories and other content. Other mashups involve sports, photos, video, shopping, and news.

The point of these Web 2.0 applications is to enhance user interest and engagement with your Web site and brand.

PERSONALIZATION TOOLS

You will definitely want to know how to treat each customer on an individual basis and emulate a traditional face-to-face marketplace. *Personalization* (the ability to treat people based on their personal qualities and prior history with your site) and *customization* (the ability to change the product to better fit the needs of the customer) are two key elements of e-commerce that potentially can make it nearly as powerful as a traditional marketplace, and perhaps even more powerful than direct mail or shopping at an anonymous suburban shopping mall. Speaking directly to the customer on a one-to-one basis, and even adjusting the product to the customer is quite difficult in the usual type of mass marketing, one-size-fits-all commercial transaction that characterizes much of contemporary commerce.

There are a number of methods for achieving personalization and customization. For instance, you could personalize Web content if you knew the personal background of the visitor. You could also analyze the pattern of clicks and sites visited for every customer who enters your site. We discuss these methods in later chapters on marketing. The primary method for achieving personalization and customization is through the placement of cookie files on the user's client computer. As we discussed in Chapter 3, a cookie is a small text file placed on the user's client computer that can contain any kind of information about the customer, such as customer ID, campaign ID, or purchases at the site. And then, when the user returns to the site, or indeed goes further into your site, the customer's prior history can be accessed from a database. Information gathered on prior visits can then be used to personalize the visit and customize the product.

For instance, when a user returns to a site, you can read the cookie to find a customer ID, look the ID up in a database of names, and greet the customer ("Hello Mary! Glad to have you return!"). You could also have stored a record of prior purchases, and then recommend a related product ("How about the wrench tool box now that you have purchased the wrenches?"). And you could think about customizing the product ("You've shown an interest in the elementary training programs for Word. We have a special 'How to Study' program for beginners in Office software. Would you like to see a sample copy online?").

We further describe the use of cookies and their effectiveness in achieving a one-to-one relationship with the customer in Chapter 8.

THE INFORMATION POLICY SET

In developing an e-commerce site, you will also need to focus on the set of information policies that will govern the site. You will need to develop a **privacy policy**—a set of public statements declaring to your customers how you treat their personal information that you gather on the site. You also will need to establish **accessibility rules**—a set of design objectives that ensure disabled users can effectively access your site. There are more than 50 million Americans who are disabled and require special access routes to buildings as well as computer systems (see *Insight on Society: Designing for Accessibility*). E-commerce information policies are described in greater depth in Chapter 8.

privacy policy
a set of public statements declaring to your customers how you treat their personal information that you gather on the site

accessibility rules
a set of design objectives that ensure disabled users can effectively access your site

4.5	**DEVELOPING A MOBILE WEB SITE AND BUILDING MOBILE APPLICATIONS**

Today, building a Web site is just one part of developing an e-commerce presence. Given that 143 million U.S. Internet users (almost 60% of all Internet users) access the Web at least part of the time from mobile devices, firms today need to develop mobile Web sites, mobile Web apps, as well as native apps, in order to interact with customers, suppliers, and employees. Deciding which of these extended Web presence tools to use is a first step.

There are three kinds of mobile e-commerce software offerings to consider, each with unique advantages and costs. A **mobile Web site** is a version of a regular Web site that is scaled down in content and navigation so that users can find what they want and move quickly to a decision or purchase. You can see the difference between a regular Web site and a mobile site by visiting the Amazon Web site from your desktop computer and then a smartphone or tablet computer. Amazon's mobile site is a cleaner, more interactive site suitable for finger navigation, and efficient consumer decision making. Like traditional Web sites, mobile Web sites run on a firm's servers, and are built using standard Web tools such as server-side HTML, Linux, PHP, and SQL. Like all Web sites, the user must be connected to the Web and performance will depend on bandwidth. Generally, mobile Web sites operate more slowly than traditional Web sites viewed on a desktop computer connected to a broadband office network. Most large firms today have mobile Web sites.

mobile Web site
version of a regular desktop Web site that is scaled down in content and navigation

A new trend in the development of mobile Web sites is the use of **responsive Web design** tools and design techniques, which make it possible to design a Web site that automatically adjusts its layout and display according to the user's screen resolution, whether a desktop, tablet, or smartphone. Responsive design tools include HTML5 and CSS3 and its three key design principles involve using flexible grid-based layouts, flexible images and media, and media queries.

responsive Web design
tools and design principles that automatically adjust the layout of a Web site depending on user screen resolution

A **mobile Web app** is an application built to run on the mobile Web browser built into a smartphone or tablet computer. In the case of Apple, the native browser is Safari. Generally it is built to mimic the qualities of a native app using HTML5 and Java.

mobile Web app
application built to run on the mobile Web browser built into a smartphone or tablet computer

INSIGHT ON SOCIETY

DESIGNING FOR ACCESSIBILITY

There are approximately 38 million Americans with hearing loss and 25 million with significant vision loss. These and other disabilities often can be addressed with intelligent software and hardware design. But, for the most part, this has not yet occurred. As a result, the Internet and mobile devices are unfriendly places for many disabled.

To begin to remedy some of these issues, in October 2010, the 21st Century Communications and Video Accessibility Act was signed into law. The act requires that services using broadband must be fully accessible to people with disabilities and that programs on television and the Internet include closed captioning. The FCC is currently in the process of issuing regulations and pilot programs to implement the act, and the act is expected to take full effect over the next three years. September 30, 2012 was the deadline for online video services to implement closed captioning as part of the act.

Disability advocates are also using lawsuits to move the ball forward. In January 2010, Arizona State University (ASU) reached an agreement with blind plaintiffs represented by the National Federation of the Blind and the American Council of the Blind. In July 2009, both had sued ASU to stop ASU's planned use of Kindle e-book reading devices in a pilot program that would be inaccessible to blind students. Amazon is working on changes to the Kindle that make it more friendly for disabled persons. In 2013, Amazon has continued to introduce improved accessibility features, including a reference guide of gestures for blind and visually impaired customers.

In 1998, Congress amended the Rehabilitation Act to require U.S. agencies, government contractors, and others receiving federal money to make electronic and information technology services accessible to people with disabilities. Known as Section 508, this legislation requires Web sites of federally funded organizations to be accessible to users who are blind, deaf, blind and deaf, or unable to use a mouse. Early court decisions with respect to Section 508 have ruled that the regulations apply only to physical spaces, and not virtual spaces. Since then, however, both the interpretation of the law and public sentiment have resulted in many well-known Web sites attempting to conform to the spirit of Section 508, sometimes voluntarily and sometimes under threat from advocacy groups.

Meanwhile, the National Federation of the Blind (NFB) brought a class-action suit against Target for failing to make its Web site accessible for the blind. In September 2006, a federal district court ruled that the Americans with Disabilities Act (ADA) did indeed apply to Web sites. In August 2008, Target and the NFB settled the suit. Target made no admission or concession that its Web site violated the ADA, but agreed to bring it into compliance with certain online assistive technology guidelines. In addition, Target agreed to pay damages of $6 million.

However, in 2012, a federal district court in Massachusetts did rule that Web sites can be considered "public accommodation," and as such fall under the jurisdiction of the ADA (*National Association of the Deaf, et al., v. Netflix Inc.*). For example, Netflix's "Watch Instantly" feature does not provide equal access, which it must do as a "place of exhibition or entertainment." In October 2012, Netflix settled the case, agreeing to caption all of its streaming videos by 2014.

In the meantime, companies are anxiously awaiting the issuance of new regulations by the U.S. Department of Justice on Web site accessibility, which are now expected to be issued by the end of 2013.

So how does a blind person access the Web, and how should designers build in accessibility for the blind? One tool is screen-reader software that

(continued)

translates text information on the screen into synthesized speech or Braille. A blind person navigates a Web page by checking the hypertext links on the page, usually by jumping from link to link with the Tab key; the screen-reader software automatically reads the highlighted text as the focus moves from link to link. The screen-reader software is looking for ASCII text, which it can convert to speech or Braille. Once the desired hypertext link has been located, the blind person presses the Enter key (clicks on the link) to go where the link points.

There are also several simple strategies Web designers can use to improve accessibility. Embedding text descriptions behind images is one example that allows screen readers to announce those descriptions. So instead of hearing "Image," when a screen reader passes over an image, the visually impaired user can hear "Photo of a cruise ship sitting in a harbor." Allowing users to set the color and font schemes also can make a difference for the visually impaired. Adding screen magnification tools and sound labels where hyperlinks appear are two additional ways to increase accessibility.

These are examples of "equivalent alternatives" to visual content that disability advocates suggest should be required, both for visual and auditory content, to ensure individuals with disabilities have equal access to information that appears on-screen. Guidelines for creating accessible Web pages include ensuring that text and graphics are understandable when viewed without color, using features that enable activation of page elements via a variety of input devices (such as keyboard, head wand, or Braille reader), and providing clear navigation mechanisms (such as navigation bars or a site map) to aid users.

The World Wide Web Consortium (W3C) issued Web Content Accessibility Guidelines (WCAG) 2.0 in June 2010 (final draft form) that provide all organizations with strategies in Web design for accommodating people with many different kinds of disabilities.

Ensuring accessibility of mobile devices has its own set of issues, in many instances ones that are even more challenging than those associated with the Web. There is only a limited selection of mobile devices with built-in accessibility features. The small size of the device, screen, and keypad presents its own problems. Third-party applications, such as text-to-speech/screen readers and screen magnifiers, are starting to become available, but much work still needs to be done. For instance, many mobile devices come equipped with voice control capabilities and audio alerts, which could be helpful to those with vision or motor difficulties, but in most cases, these are still limited to simple tasks, and do not provide access to the full functionality of the device. In addition, the deaf community cannot rely on audio content or alerts, so developers need to provide text or other alternatives for auditory information. Those with impaired motor functionality also face great challenges in dealing with input to mobile devices. To deal with these challenges, the WC3 recommends that mobile content developers follow Section 508, WCAG 2.0, and its guidelines on mobile Web best practices.

■■■ **SOURCES:** "Justice Department Pushes Back Date for Proposed Website Accessibility Rules—Yet Again," by Minh N. Vu, Lexology.com, July 30, 2013; "Disabled Sue Over Web Shopping," by Joe Palazzolo, *Wall Street Journal*, March 21, 2013; "Netflix and Deaf-Rights Group Settle Suit Over Video Captions," by Dara Kerr, Cnn.com, October 11, 2012; "A New Mobile View," by Amy Dusto, Internetretailer.com, September 5, 2012; "FCC: Online Video Caption Requirements Go Forward," by Chris Tribbey, Homemediamagazine.com, August 29, 2012; "FCC tells Web TV Providers to Start Using Online Captions Next Month," by Jim Barthold, Fierceonlinevideo.com, August 22, 2012; *National Association of the Deaf, et al. ("NAD"), versus Netflix Inc.* 2012; United States District Court of Massachusetts, June 19, 2012; "Can A Web Site be a Public Accommodation Under the ADA?," Timothy Springer, webaccessibility.com, June 5, 2012; "Mobile Web Accessibility," by Tim Shelton, Accessibletech.com, July 2011; "For the Disabled, Just Getting Online is a Struggle," by Wilson Rotham, Technolog.msnbc.msn.com, January 21, 2011; "W3C Web Accessibility Initiative [Final Draft]," WC3.org, June 2010; "A Giant Leap and a Big Deal: Delivering on the Promise of Equal Access to Broadband for People with Disabilities," Federal Communications Commission, April 23, 2010; "21st Century Communications and Video Accessibility Act of 2009," Hearings, 111th Congress, House of Representatives, H.R. 3101, April 2010; "Blindness Organizations and Arizona State University Resolve Litigation Over Kindle," National Federation of the Blind, Press Release, January 11, 2010; "Web Accessibility: Making Your Site Accessible to the Blind," by Curtis Chong, National Federation of the Blind, accessed August 14, 2009.

Mobile Web apps are specifically designed for the mobile platform in terms of screen size, finger navigation, and graphical simplicity. Mobile Web apps can support complex interactions used in games and rich media, perform real-time, on-the-fly calculations, and can be geo-sensitive using the smartphone's built-in global positioning system (GPS) function. Mobile Web apps typically operate faster than mobile Web sites but not as fast as native apps.

native app
application designed specifically to operate using the mobile device's hardware and operating system

A **native app** is an application designed specifically to operate using the mobile device's hardware and operating system. These stand-alone programs can connect to the Internet to download and upload data, and can operate on this data even when not connected to the Internet. Download a book to an app reader, disconnect from the Internet, and read your book. Because the various types of smartphones have different hardware and operating systems, apps are not "one size fits all" and therefore need to be developed for different mobile platforms. An Apple app that runs on an iPhone cannot operate on Android phones. As you learned in Chapter 3, native apps are built using different programming languages depending on the device for which they are intended, which is then compiled into binary code, and which executes extremely fast on mobile devices, much faster than HTML or Java-based mobile Web apps. For this reason, native apps are ideal for games, complex interactions, on-the-fly calculations, graphic manipulations, and rich media advertising.

PLANNING AND BUILDING A MOBILE WEB PRESENCE

What is the "right" mobile Web presence for your firm? The answer depends on identifying the business objectives, and from these, deriving the information requirements of your mobile presence. The same kind of systems analysis and design (SAD) reasoning described earlier in the chapter is needed for planning and building a mobile presence, although there are important differences.

The first step is to identify the business objectives you are trying to achieve. **Table 4.12** illustrates the thought process for the analysis stage of building a mobile presence. Why are you developing a mobile presence? Is it to drive sales by creating an easily browsed catalog where users can shop and purchase? Strengthen your brand by creating an engaging, interactive experience? Enable customers to interact with your customer community? How are your competitors using their mobile presence? Once you have a clear sense of business objectives, you will be able to describe the kind of system functionality that is needed and specify the information requirements for your mobile presence.

After you have identified the business objectives, system functionality, and information requirements, you can think about how to design and build the system. Now is the time to consider which to develop: a mobile Web site, a mobile Web app, or a native app. From our previous discussion, if your objective is branding or building community, then a native app is recommended because you can display rich interactive media and highly interactive, efficient games. If your objective is to drive sales, advertise, or gather feedback on specific products, all of which require an online database of products, then a mobile Web site or mobile Web app is recommended because high-speed interactions are not needed, and these objectives are really just an extension of your main desktop Web site.

TABLE 4.12	SYSTEMS ANALYSIS FOR BUILDING A MOBILE PRESENCE	
BUSINESS OBJECTIVE	**SYSTEM FUNCTIONALITY**	**INFORMATION REQUIREMENTS**
Drive sales	Digital catalog; product database	Product descriptions, photos, SKUs, inventory
Branding	Showing how customers use your products	Videos and rich media; product and customer demonstrations
Building customer community	Interactive experiences, games with multiple players	Games, contests, forums, social sign-up to Facebook
Advertising and promotion	Coupons and flash sales for slow-selling items	Product descriptions, coupon management, and inventory management
Gathering customer feedback	Ability to retrieve and store user inputs including text, photos, and video	Customer sign-in and identification; customer database

MOBILE WEB PRESENCE: DESIGN CONSIDERATIONS

Designing a mobile presence is somewhat different from traditional desktop Web site design because of different hardware, software, and consumer expectations. **Table 4.13** describes some of the major differences.

Designers need to take mobile platform constraints into account when designing for the mobile platform. File sizes should be kept smaller and the number of files sent to the user reduced. Focus on a few, powerful graphics, and minimize the number of images sent to the user. Simplify choice boxes and lists so the user can easily scroll and touch-select the options.

TABLE 4.13	UNIQUE FEATURES THAT MUST BE TAKEN INTO ACCOUNT WHEN DESIGNING A MOBILE WEB PRESENCE
FEATURE	**IMPLICATIONS FOR MOBILE PLATFORM**
Hardware	Mobile hardware is smaller, and there are more resource constraints in data storage and processing power.
Connectivity	The mobile platform is constrained by slower connection speeds than desktop Web sites.
Displays	Mobile displays are much smaller and require simplification. Some screens are not good in sunlight.
Interface	Touch-screen technology introduces new interaction routines different from the traditional mouse and keyboard. The mobile platform is not a good data entry tool but can be a good navigational tool.

MOBILE WEB PRESENCE: PERFORMANCE AND COST CONSIDERATIONS

If you don't have an existing Web site, the most efficient process is to build a site in the first instance using responsive Web design, as previously described. If you already have a Web site that you don't want to totally redevelop, the least expensive path is to resize it to create a smartphone-friendly mobile site. Doing so typically will not require a complete redesign effort. You will need to reduce the graphics and text, simplify the navigation, and focus on improving the customer experience so you do not confuse people. Because your customers might still use a relatively slow 3G cell connection, you will need to lighten up the amount of data you send. Also, given the difficulty of customer data entry on a mobile device, you cannot expect customers to happily enter long strings of numbers or text characters. For marketing clarity, make sure the brand images used on the mobile Web site match those on the traditional Web site. Small companies can develop a mobile Web site for under $10,000 using the same consultants and servers as their existing Web site.

Building a mobile Web app that uses the mobile device's browser requires more effort and cost than developing a mobile Web site, suffers from the same limitations as any browser-based application, but does offer some advantages such as better graphics, more interactivity, and faster local calculations as, for instance, in mobile geo-location applications like Foursquare that require local calculations of position and then communication with the site's Web server.

The most expensive path to a mobile presence is to build a native app. Native apps can require more extensive programming expertise. In addition, virtually none of the elements used in your existing Web site can be reused, and you will need to redesign the entire logic of the interface and carefully think out the customer experience. For instance, there is a fairly stable HTML traditional Web site interface with buttons, graphics, videos, and ads that has developed over the last decade. This is not true for apps. There is no set of standards or expectations even on the part of users—every app looks different from every other app. This means the user confronts large variations in app design, so your interface must be quite simple and obvious. Many of the bells and whistles found on the large desktop Web site screen cannot be used in mobile apps. You'll need even greater simplification and focus. These weaknesses are also native apps' greatest strength: you have the opportunity to create a really stunning, unique customer experience where users can interact with your brand. If you want an intense branding experience with your customers, where interaction between your brand and customers is effortless and efficient, then native apps are the best choice.

The *Insight on Technology* case, *Building a Mobile Presence,* takes a further look at some of the considerations involved for two very different companies—Deckers Outdoors Corporation and USAA.

INSIGHT ON TECHNOLOGY

BUILDING A MOBILE PRESENCE

Today, almost every company with a Web presence is thinking about or developing mobile applications and mobile Web sites. Customers expect, and even demand, to be able to use a mobile device of their choice to obtain information or perform a transaction anywhere and at any time. So, if a company wants to stay connected to its customers, it needs a mobile presence.

Developing mobile apps or a mobile Web site has some special challenges. The user experience on a mobile device is fundamentally different from that on a PC. There are special features on mobile devices such as location-based services that give firms the potential to interact with customers in new ways. Firms need to be able to take advantage of those features while delivering an experience that is appropriate to a small screen. You can't just port a Web site or desktop application to a smartphone or tablet. There are multiple mobile platforms to work with—iPhone, Android, BlackBerry, and Windows—and a firm may need a different version of an application to run on each of these.

It's important to understand how, why, and where customers use mobile devices and how these mobile experiences change business interactions and behavior. For example, do customers who use an app conduct a greater number of transactions (like purchasing) on apps when compared to a mobile browser? When compared to a tablet computer, do customers spend more or less time researching products and shopping from a smartphone?

Deckers Outdoor Corporation is the parent company of brands such as UGG Australia and Teva. Deckers launched a mobile Web site in 2011 and also offers an iPhone app. Deckers has spent considerable time studying its customers'

mobile behavior. It looked at how customers use their mobile devices while browsing and shopping to find out how consumers connect with its brand through the mobile channel. When people use mobile devices, how do they research products? Are they looking for information about product features, product reviews, or retail store locations?

Deckers' customer analysis showed that when consumers use mobile devices inside a Deckers store, what is most important is a seamless interaction. Customers want to be able to look at a product on their phones and see the same information inside the store, plus some additional information, such as consumer reviews.

Deckers is clearly doing something right. Its mobile sales have grown by over 50% from 2011 to 2012, from $1 million to $1.5 million, helping to fuel an overall increase in sales of over 12%. Its 2013 sales appear to be following a similar trend, with e-commerce sales once again leading the way with a 22.6% increase.

A mobile strategy involves more than selecting mobile devices, operating systems, and applications. It also involves changes to the way a firm interacts with its customers. Mobile technology can streamline processes, make them more portable, and enhance them with capabilities such as touch interfaces, location and mapping features, alerts, texting, cameras, and video functionality. The technology can also create less efficient processes or fail to deliver benefits if the mobile application is not properly designed.

USAA is a giant financial services company serving over 9.4 million members of the U.S. military and their families, which not surprisingly, is a highly mobile population. About 90% of USAA's interactions with its customers take place through its Web site and mobile presence. As a result,

(continued)

USAA is acutely aware of the importance of mobile and is using mobile technology to provide simpler and more powerful ways for customers to interact with the company. By the end of 2012, more than 5.2 million members had downloaded its mobile apps, representing a more than 60% increase since 2011. In addition, the number of times members accessed their accounts using USAA's iPad app increased by almost 200%.

USAA has a strong reputation for innovation, and has over 100 developers dedicated to its mobile site and writing apps for Apple, Android, BlackBerry, and Windows Phone mobile devices. Since its launch in 2009, USAA members have made over 24.6 million deposits, totaling $13.8 billion, using USAA's Deposit@Mobile service, including 13.3 million deposits totaling $4.7 billion in 2012 alone, up more than 70% from 2011. Deposit@Mobile enables photo deposits: a customer can capture an image of a check with a smartphone and automatically submit it to the bank. The money is instantly deposited in the customer's account. This system eliminates the labor and expense of processing paper checks, and the time required to mail the check and wait for the deposit to clear. A new version of Deposit@Mobile launched in 2013 allows members to use imaging to deposit up to 10 checks into multiple accounts at a time. In 2013, USAA also piloted an app that lets consumers take a photo of a blank check to help speed the process of creating a new USAA deposit account, an industry first.

USAA continually adds functionality to its mobile presence. For instance, USAA has developed an accident report and claims service that enables customers to snap a photo and submit a claim directly from the site of an accident using their phones. The app is also able to send geographic information system (GIS) data to a towing service and display nearby car rental locations. It launched an accident animation function in November 2012 that allows members to explain and add narration about an accident using animation and voice capture technology.

The ability to apply for life insurance via a mobile app also become available in December 2012. A new Investment Center that launched in August 2012 gives members the ability to trade stocks, mutual funds, and CDs, create and monitor watchlists, access real-time quotes and market research, and deposit checks directly into investment accounts. Other products and services that are available through mobile include auto insurance, auto loans, property insurance, renter's insurance, and credit cards.

In May 2013, USAA launched a voice command service, called the Virtual Mobile Assistant, which supports over 200 navigational commands, and allows members to transfer funds, check stocks, file auto insurance claims, and pay bills, among other actions, on their iPhones, and in the near future, on other mobile devices. The functionality is based on Nuance's virtual assistant Nina software, which combines speech recognition, text-to-speech, voice biometrics, and natural language understanding, and is expected to be particularly useful for the disabled and military members who are deployed in the field. Never one to rest, USAA plans to add the new feature to USAA apps for iPad and Android and undoubtedly has a number of plans for future mobile enhancements up its sleeve.

SOURCES: "USAA Adds Voice Technology to Mobile App," by Minya Liang, USAA.com, June 14, 2013; "USAA Launches Voice Command Mobile Banking," by Marilyn Moritz, Ksat.com, May 2, 2013; "USAA Readies Voice Recognition for its iPhone App," by Mary Wisniewski, *American Banker*, February 22, 2013; "USAA Surpasses 5 Million Mobile App Downloads," by Mary Wisniewski, *American Banker*, February 13, 2013; "USAA App Hits Five Million Downloads," USAA.com, February 13, 2013; "USAA Pilots Use of Mobile Check Capture to Fund New Accounts," by John Adams, *American Banker*, January 9, 2013; "Mobility Transforms the Customer Relationship," by Samuel Greengard, *Baseline*, February 2012; "Going Mobile: A Portable Approach to Process Improvement," *Business Agility Insights*, June 2012; "How USAA Innovates Online Banking," by John Adams, *American Banker*, September 1, 2012; "How Deckers Used a Mobile Application to Build Customer Traffic," by William Atkinson, *CIO Insight*, November 9, 2011.

CASE STUDY

Orbitz Charts
Its Mobile Trajectory

When it comes to mobile apps and gauging their impact on consumers and business, there's no better industry to look at than the online travel industry and its airline and hotel reservation systems. And there's no better company in this industry in developing mobile apps than Orbitz Worldwide Inc., the leading online travel site. Orbitz connects consumers to plane tickets from 400 airlines, hotel rooms from 80,000 hotels worldwide, rental cars from 13 rental car agencies, as well as cruises and vacation packages. On a busy day, consumers will make an estimated 2 million searches for airline reservations and more than 1 million hotel reservations.

As early as 1999, fledgling Internet travel companies such as Priceline, Expedia, and Travelocity were already transforming the travel industry. Recognizing the threat, and the opportunity, five major airlines—United, Delta, Continental, Northwest, and American—banded together to form a new venture that would become Orbitz. By the time the site launched in 2001, six other airlines had invested and anti-trust objections from consumer groups and competitors had been rejected by the U. S. Department of Transportation. Even at that early date, the Orbitz management team was forward-thinking, providing the capability for consumers to access flight updates and cancellations via pagers and mobile phones. By the time the Department of Justice had completely cleared Orbitz for takeoff and it had completed its IPO in November 2003, Orbitz had recruited more than 100 independent hotels in addition to its initial TravelWeb syndicate, which included the big players such as Marriott, Hilton, and Hyatt.

In 2006, Orbitz became the first Internet travel company to offer a WML-only (Wireless Markup Language) mobile Web site in the United States. (Expedia had a mobile site for its UK customers.) Users could check flight statuses for 27 airlines, some of which did not yet have a mobile site, and search for hotels in the 19 largest destination markets in the United States and in Cancun, Mexico. They also had access to a personal page dedicated to itineraries for Orbitz-booked trips and links to autodial Orbitz customer service. Additional services added in 2007 included enabling mobile users to view average wait times to get through security and available Wi-Fi services for a particular airport. A data feedback system was instituted to compute check-in delays and taxi line wait-times based on customer-inputted experiences. In 2008, Orbitz added an iPhone/iPod–specific app with the same capabilities for itinerary, flight status, WiFi availability, and wait-time checking as well as the ability to view weather and traffic conditions, reports from other travelers, and information about where to park and ground transportation. Customers could also now use technology specifically designed for touch-based Safari browsers to book a hotel room during inclement weather.

By 2010, market research had pushed Orbitz to increase its investment in mobile technology. It launched a redesigned mobile Web site in July, and a smartphone app for Google Inc.'s Android operating system in November, along with an updated iPhone app. Users of any Web-enabled device could now access a tool set comparable to the one available on its regular Web site to purchase flights, book car rentals, and secure hotel accommodations, including same-day reservations, as well as Orbitz's Price Assurance service, which guarantees consumers an automatic refund if another Orbitz customer books the same service for less. The native apps and redesigned mobile site were developed in-house with input from an unnamed outside vendor.

In Spring 2011, Orbitz was first-to-market with an m-commerce site designed specifically for business users. Orbitz knew that since most business travelers were already carrying a smartphone or other Web-enabled mobile device, and mobile Internet access was overtaking conventional desktop access, there was no time to waste. Since corporate travel managers typically must adhere to company-specific rules about preferred vendors, cost prerequisites, mandatory services, and compulsory documentation, the platform had to be able to store and abide by those rules and be customizable for each firm. Orbitz decided that the optimal solution was to construct a mobile Web site that could be accessed from any Web-enabled device rather than build native apps for multiple different devices. The goals were to provide a uniform and yet native app-like experience for each type of device, and deliver full travel policy compliance for business clients. The Orbitz for Business mobile Web site delivers the same set of tools enjoyed by the consumer market, applies saved policy controls to new reservations, and delivers both global and company-specific messages on both the home page and in search results to assist business travelers in adhering to company guidelines. Business-specific tools include the ability to enter and modify the trip purpose, search results that give precedence to preferred vendors, and access company-specific reference data. Orbitz is sure that converting business customers from passive viewers of travel updates and weather conditions to active mobile purchasers of all facets of a professional trip is dependent only upon the short juncture it will take for them to become at ease with the technology and familiar with the integration possible between Orbitz for Business and their corporate travel policy. New customer acquisition can be triggered, at least initially, by offering last-minute promotions and deals to a customer base that is often searching for same-day reservations.

In July 2011, Orbitz added a hotel-booking app for iPad users. When launched, the GPS-enabled app displays a map of the user's current location. Pins dot the map to indicate hotel locations, which can be touched to display the establishment name, address, phone number, and cost, providing instant price comparison. Hotels can also be selected from a scrolling list to the left of the map. Expanding a tile supplies additional details including pictures, reviews, and lists of room features and establishment amenities. Users can also toggle to a data table view, enabling comparisons based on multiple features and amenities in addition to price. If the user's current location is not the desired target, a search by city, address, zip code, or landmark can be conducted instead. Lodging choices can be filtered and sorted according to various criteria including price, user-rated review score, distance from destination, and a star-based rating. The full complement of hotels available on Orbitz's regular Web site is offered at the same rate on the m-commerce site, including all special offers. Chris Brown, Orbitz's vice president of product strategy, explained that native touch-based apps appeal to a set of consumers who prefer this style of interaction, at that time not available on the Web, and in particular to those searching for same-day accommodations. While only 12 to 14% of traditional e-commerce Web site shoppers want to reserve a room for the day on which they are searching, smartphone and other Web-enabled device users book for that night between 60 and 65% of the time. Barney Harford, CEO of Orbitz Worldwide, touted the ability to book a hotel room in just three taps.

Despite all of these changes, upgrades, and additions to their mobile platforms in what would normally be considered a narrow business time frame, the rapidly expanding and changing mobile environment called for further investments. When the m-commerce site was redesigned to support transactions, Orbitz had pursued a minimalist approach. According to Brown, the m-commerce site, as well as the initial rollouts of the Android and iPhone apps, were valuable learning experiences for the company that enabled them to assemble skilled teams. This prepared them to create second-generation applications that could meet evolving consumer expectations. Three main improvements were made to the second-generation m-commerce site. First, it was optimized to accommodate the small screen size of any Web-enabled mobile device. Second, it was updated to accommodate swiping gestures, and third, it was revamped to expedite touch screen transactions.

Swiping, once the exclusive province of apps, can now be accomplished using HTML5. What's more, HTML5 enables m-commerce sites to incorporate capabilities identical to mobile apps simply by tapping into the built-in functionality of mobile devices, including GPS. Orbitz employed HTML5 to enable customers to swipe through pictures of hotels. Mobile transaction speed was given a boost through the implementation of a new proprietary global online travel agency platform. The platform speeds up page loading by essentially creating mobile Web pages on the fly from the standard e-commerce Web page and eliminating redirects. The standard Web page is passed through a page-rendering framework tool that instantly produces an HTML5 version that can exploit inherent smartphone capabilities. Faster browsing is not the only advantage, however. Brown stressed the reduced labor hours required in contrast to having to create mobile-optimized counterparts for each standard Web page.

Consumers could also now book vacation packages, view the savings accrued from the simultaneous booking of a flight and hotel room, and create an online profile linked to their credit card to speed the check-out process. GPS capabilities enabled consumers to locate nearby hotels and conduct price, distance, and rating comparisons. Likewise, improved search and sorting and filtering capabilities enabled consumers to compare flights and car rentals based on various criteria, including traveler type, and to access customer reviews. Looking to capitalize on the market research findings that highlighted the burgeoning role of Web-enabled mobile devices in securing same-day accommodations, Orbitz also instituted mobile-exclusive same-day deals. These specials, called Mobile Steals, are available both on the m-commerce site and through the Hotels by Orbitz app, which was also released

SOURCES: "Orbitz.com Rolls Out Major Update to Orbitz Flights, Hotels, Cars App for Android," marketwatch.com, Orbitz.com, August 21, 2013; "Anticipated Earnings Increase for Orbitz Worldwide (OWW)," Forbes.com, August 6, 2013; "Orbitz Releases the First Native App for iPad that Allows Consumers to Book Flights, Hotels, and Rental Cars," Orbitz.com, February 25, 2013; "Orbitz, Inc. History," Funding-Universe.com, accessed September 2, 2012; "How to Embark upon an M-commerce Redesign," by Kevin Woodward, *Internet Retailer*, August 10, 2012; "Top 10 Mobile Commerce Apps of Q2," by Rimma Kats, *Mobile Commerce Daily*, July 6, 2012; "Orbitz Revamps iPhone App with Focus on Streamlined Booking, Deals," by Lauren Johnson, *Mobile Commerce Daily*, June 22, 2012; "Orbitz Rolls Out Major Update to App for iPhone and iPod Touch," Orbitz, June 21, 2012; "Orbitz Releases New Travel App," by Emily Brennan, *New York Times*, June 21, 2012; "Orbitz Launches New iPhone App, Bets on Mobile Growth," by Erica Ogg, Gigaom.com, June 21, 2012; "Orbitz: Mobile Searches May Yield Better Hotel Deals," by Barbara De Lollis, *USA Today*, May 10, 2012; Orbitz Worldwide Inc., Form 10-K for the fiscal year ended December 31, 2011, Securities and Exchange Commission, filed March 31, 2012; "Orbitz Launches Revamped Mobile Site, Daily Deals to Capitalize on Last-Minute Travel," by Lauren Johnson, *Mobile Commerce Daily*, December 13, 2011; "Orbitz Travels the M-commerce Site Redesign Route," by Bill Siwicki, *Internet Retailer*, December 13, 2011; "Orbitz Unveils Powerful New Mobile Website and Introduces New 'Mobile Steals' Program Offering Discounted Mobile-only Rates on Hotels," Orbitz, December 12, 2011; "Orbitz Creates Intuitive Search-and-Book Experience via iPad App," by Rimma Kats, *Mobile Commerce Daily*, July 7, 2011; "Get a Room," by Kevin Woodward, *Internet Retailer*, July 7, 2011; "Orbitz Launches New 'Orbitz Hotels' App for iPad®," Orbitz, July 6, 2011; "Orbitz for Business Debuts Mobile Booking

for the Android and iPhone. Last-minute perishable goods are available in more than 50 markets worldwide, benefitting both lodging proprietors and consumers. Proprietors are able to fill rooms that might otherwise remain vacant, and consumers enjoy savings of up to 50% off the standard rate.

Even so, with mobile transaction customers doubling in one year's time, Orbitz decided that an overhaul of its native iPhone app was also in order. When relaunched in June 2012, the iOS app included an improved filtering tool that enabled users to search and compare offerings by cost, distance from destination, and star ratings. Like Hotels by Orbitz, an improved GPS-enabled mapping function displayed nearby hotels and Mobile Steals, providing instant price comparisons. Securing flight, lodging, and car rental reservations was simplified, eliminating browser screens and data entry repetition, and allowing users to perform all three operations in a continuous in-app stream unassociated with a mobile Web site. This was the heart of the redesign: to eliminate the mobile Web site and consolidate the entire search and reservation process within the native app so that users would no longer experience disruptive and time-consuming redirects either to Orbitz's mobile site or to an airline, hotel, or car rental agency site to complete the booking. The goal was to trump its competitors on speed and ease of use.

Brown believed that although mobile transactions in 2012 still represented less than 10% of Orbitz's total bookings, the investment would be rewarded by the broad opportunity presented by the rapidly escalating m-commerce market. New customer acquisition was expected as users discovered the increased transaction speed provided by the app. Increased speed is particularly attractive to consumers looking to book same-day reservations, which also comprise about 50% of Orbitz's mobile car rental purchases.

In order to verify that its goals for the app had been achieved, Orbitz commissioned a speed comparison study with Atmosphere Research Group and C + R Research. The travel apps, m-commerce sites, and e-commerce sites of its major competitors, including Kayak, Expedia, Priceline, and Travelocity, were pitted against the Orbitz iPhone app. The study found that Orbitz iPhone app users were able to book a round-trip flight to Hilton Head, South Carolina, a hotel reservation, and a car rental in slightly more than seven minutes, twice as fast as people using its iPhone app competitors. Only 60% of study participants using a competitor's product (aggregated) were able to complete the task as quickly. The Orbitz iPhone app transaction speed also surpassed comparable iPad and Android apps as well as desktop e-commerce site experiences. Study participants overwhelmingly awarded positive marks to the completely in-house–built Orbitz iPhone app in comparison to its competitors, 92% and 30%, respectively.

To speed the identification and fulfillment of future needs, customers' search history, personal information, frequent flyer program data, and travel preferences are saved within the app, enabling one-tap access to recent searches and automatic search suggestions. Itineraries can be accessed even while offline, and flight status and gate change data can be accessed with a single tap. Trips can also be easily added to the Apple Calendar app, formerly called iCal, used by many iPhone and iPod touch users.

In 2013, Orbitz continued to expand its array of apps across different operating systems and platforms. It launched a full version of its *Flights, Hotels, Cars* app optimized for iPad, the first of its kind among travel service providers. Orbitz also fully overhauled the same app for Android, marking the third generation of its Android native app. Orbitz plans to continue its mobile development across all platforms. Thus far, the approach is working, as Orbitz has posted better than expected earnings in 2013 and projects continued growth going forward.

Case Study Questions

1. When compared to traditional desktop customers, why are mobile phone users much more likely to book a room or airline reservation for the same day?

2. In the mobile design project of 2011, why did Orbitz management decide to construct a mobile Web site for corporate users rather than a native app?

3. What is "business logic" and why was it important for corporate travelers to have online reservation systems that included business logic?

4. Why did Orbitz reverse policy in 2012 and build native apps for each mobile platform (iOS and Android) instead of a single mobile Web site?

Site Targeting Corporate Travelers," by Dan Butcher, *Mobile Commerce Daily*, April 15, 2011; "Two Travel Providers Make Mobile Moves," by Katie Deatsch, *Internet Retailer*, November 16, 2010; "Orbitz Launches Native iPhone® and Android™ Applications That Allow Consumers to Shop and Book Flight, Hotel and Car Rental Options," Orbitz, November 15, 2010; "Orbitz for iPhone Review," by Joe Seifi, AppSafari.com, November 13th, 2008; "Orbitz Goes Mobile," by Russell Buckley, MobHappy.com, September 6, 2007; "Orbitz Mobile," by Dennis Bournique, WAPReview.com, August 15, 2006.

4.7 REVIEW

KEY CONCEPTS

■ Understand the questions you must ask and answer, and the steps you should take, in developing an e-commerce presence.

Questions you must ask and answer when developing an e-commerce presence include:

- What is your vision and how do you hope to accomplish it?
- What is your business and revenue model?
- Who and where is the target audience?
- What are the characteristics of the marketplace?
- Where is the content coming from?
- Conduct a SWOT analysis.
- Develop an e-commerce presence map.
- Develop a timeline.
- Develop a detailed budget.

■ Explain the process that should be followed in building an e-commerce presence.

Factors you must consider when building an e-commerce site include:

- Hardware architecture
- Software
- Telecommunications capacity
- Site design
- Human resources
- Organizational capabilities

The systems development life cycle (a methodology for understanding the business objectives of a system and designing an appropriate solution) for building an e-commerce Web site involves five major steps:

- Identify the specific business objectives for the site, and then develop a list of system functionalities and information requirements.
- Develop a system design specification (both logical design and physical design).
- Build the site, either by in-house personnel or by outsourcing all or part of the responsibility to outside contractors.
- Test the system (unit testing, system testing, and acceptance testing).
- Implement and maintain the site.

The basic business and system functionalities an e-commerce site should contain include:

- *Digital catalog*—allows a site to display goods using text and graphics.
- *Product database*—provides product information, such as a description, stocking number, and inventory level.
- *Customer on-site tracking*—enables a site to create a site log for each customer visit, aiding in personalizing the shopping experience and identifying common customer paths and destinations.
- *Shopping cart/payment system*—provides an ordering system, secure credit card clearing, and other payment options.
- *On-site blog*—engages customers in conversation
- *Customer database*—includes customer information such as the name, address, phone number, and e-mail address.
- *Sales database*—contains information regarding the customer ID, product purchased, date, payment, and shipment to be able to provide after-sale customer support.
- *Ad server*—tracks the site behavior of prospects and customers that come through e-mail or banner ad campaigns.
- *Site tracking and reporting system*—monitors the number of unique visitors, pages visited, and products purchased.
- *Inventory management system*—provides a link to production and suppliers in order to facilitate order replenishment.

■ **Describe the major issues surrounding the decision to outsource site development and/or hosting.**

Advantages of building a site in-house include:
- The ability to change and adapt the site quickly as the market demands
- The ability to build a site that does exactly what the company needs

Disadvantages of building a site in-house include:
- The costs may be higher.
- The risks of failure may be greater, given the complexity of issues such as security, privacy, and inventory management.
- The process may be more time-consuming than if you had hired an outside specialist firm to manage the effort.
- Staff may experience a longer learning curve that delays your entry into the market.

Using design templates cuts development time, but preset templates can also limit functionality.

A similar decision is also necessary regarding outsourcing the hosting of the site versus keeping it in-house. Relying on an outside vendor to ensure that the site is live 24 hours a day places the burden of reliability on someone else, in return for a monthly hosting fee. The downside is that if the site requires fast upgrades due to heavy traffic, the chosen hosting company may or may not be capable of keeping up. Reliability versus scalability is the issue in this instance.

■ Identify and understand the major considerations involved in choosing Web server and e-commerce merchant server software.

Early Web sites used single-tier system architecture and consisted of a single-server computer that delivered static Web pages to users making requests through their browsers. The extended functionality of today's Web sites requires the development of a multi-tiered systems architecture, which utilizes a variety of specialized Web servers, as well as links to pre-existing backend or legacy corporate databases.

All e-commerce sites require basic Web server software to answer requests from customers for HTML and XML pages. When choosing Web server software, companies are also choosing what operating system the site will run on. Apache, which runs on the Unix system, is the market leader.

Web servers provide a host of services, including:
• Processing user HTML requests
• Security services
• File transfer
• Search engine
• Data capture
• E-mail
• Site management tools

Dynamic server software allows sites to deliver dynamic content, rather than static, unchanging information. Web application server programs enable a wide range of e-commerce functionality, including creating a customer database, creating an e-mail promotional program, and accepting and processing orders, as well as many other services.

E-commerce merchant server software is another important software package that provides catalog displays, information storage and customer tracking, order taking (shopping cart), and credit card purchase processing. E-commerce suites can save time and money, but customization can significantly drive up costs. Factors to consider when choosing an e-commerce suite include its functionality, support for different business models, visual site management tools and reporting systems, performance and scalability, connectivity to existing business systems, compliance with standards, and global and multicultural capability.

■ Understand the issues involved in choosing the most appropriate hardware for an e-commerce site.

Speed, capacity, and scalability are three of the most important considerations when selecting an operating system, and therefore the hardware that it runs on.

To evaluate how fast the site needs to be, companies need to assess the number of simultaneous users the site expects to see, the nature of their requests, the type of information requested, and the bandwidth available to the site. The answers to these questions will provide guidance regarding the processors necessary to meet customer demand. In some cases, additional processing power can increase capacity, thereby improving system speed.

Scalability is also an important issue. Increasing processing supply by scaling up to meet demand can be done through:

- *Vertical scaling*—improving the processing power of the hardware, but maintaining the same number of servers
- *Horizontal scaling*—adding more of the same processing hardware
- *Improving processing architecture*—identifying operations with similar workloads and using dedicated, tuned servers for each type of load

■ **Identify additional tools that can improve Web site performance.**

In addition to providing a speedy Web site, companies must also strive to have a well-designed site that encourages visitors to buy. Building in interactivity improves site effectiveness, as do personalization techniques that provide the ability to track customers while they are visiting the site. Commonly used software tools for achieving high levels of Web site interactivity and customer personalization include:

- *Common Gateway Interface (CGI) scripts*—a set of standards for communication between a browser and a program on a server that allows for interaction between the user and the server
- *Active Server Pages (ASP)*—a Microsoft tool that also permits interaction between the browser and the server
- *Java applets*—programs written in the Java programming language that also provide interactivity
- *JavaScript*—used to validate user input, such as an e-mail address
- *ActiveX and VBScript*—Microsoft's version of Java and JavaScript, respectively
- *Cookies*—text files stored on the user's hard drive that provide information regarding the user and his or her past experience at a Web site

■ **Understand the important considerations involved in developing a mobile Web site and building mobile applications.**

- When developing a mobile presence, it is important to understand the difference between a mobile Web site, mobile Web apps, and native apps.
- The first step is to identify business objectives, since they help determine which type of mobile presence is best.
- Design should take into account mobile platform constraints.
- Developing a mobile Web site is likely to be the least expensive option; mobile Web apps require more effort and cost; native apps are likely to be the most expensive to develop.

QUESTIONS

1. Name the main pieces of the e-commerce site-building puzzle.
2. Define the systems development life cycle and discuss the various steps involved in creating an e-commerce site.
3. Discuss the differences between a simple logical and a simple physical Web site design.
4. Why is system testing important? Name the types of testing and their relation to each other.
5. Compare the costs for system development and system maintenance. Which is more expensive, and why?
6. Why is a Web site so costly to maintain? Discuss the main factors that impact cost.

7. What are the main differences between single-tier and multi-tier site architecture?
8. Name the basic functionalities a Web server should provide.
9. What are the main factors to consider when choosing the best hardware platform for your Web site?
10. Why is Web server bandwidth an important issue for e-commerce sites?
11. Compare and contrast the various scaling methods. Explain why scalability is a key business issue for Web sites.
12. What are the eight most important factors impacting Web site design, and how do they affect a site's operation?
13. What are Java and JavaScript? What role do they play in Web site design?
14. Name and describe three methods used to treat customers individually. Why are they significant to e-commerce?
15. What are some of the policies e-commerce businesses must develop before launching a site, and why must they be developed?

PROJECTS

1. Go to Webs.com or NetworkSolutions.com. Both sites allow you to create a simple e-tailer Web site for a free trial period. Create a Web site. The site should feature at least four pages, including a home page, product page, shopping cart, and contact page. Extra credit will be given for additional complexity and creativity. Come to class prepared to present your e-tailer concept and Web site.

2. Visit several e-commerce sites, not including those mentioned in this chapter, and evaluate the effectiveness of the sites according to the eight basic criteria/functionalities listed in Table 4.11. Choose one site you feel does an excellent job on all the aspects of an effective site and create an electronic presentation, including screen shots, to support your choice.

3. Imagine that you are the head of information technology for a fast-growth e-commerce start-up. You are in charge of development of the company's Web site. Consider your options for building the site in-house with existing staff, or outsourcing the entire operation. Decide which strategy you believe is in your company's best interest and create a brief presentation outlining your position. Why choose that approach? And what are the estimated associated costs, compared with the alternative? (You'll need to make some educated guesses here—don't worry about being exact.)

4. Choose two e-commerce suite software packages and prepare an evaluation chart that rates the packages on the key factors discussed in the section "Choosing an E-commerce Suite." Which package would you choose if you were developing a Web site of the type described in this chapter, and why?

5. Choose one of the open source Web content management systems such as WordPress, Joomla, or Drupal or another of your own choosing and prepare an evaluation chart similar to that required by Project 4. Which system would you choose and why?

CHAPTER 5

E-commerce Security and Payment Systems

After reading this chapter, you will be able to:

- Understand the scope of e-commerce crime and security problems.
- Describe the key dimensions of e-commerce security.
- Understand the tension between security and other values.
- Identify the key security threats in the e-commerce environment.
- Describe how technology helps protect the security of messages sent over the Internet.
- Identify the tools used to establish secure Internet communications channels and protect networks, servers, and clients.
- Appreciate the importance of policies, procedures, and laws in creating security.
- Describe the features of traditional payment systems.
- Identify the major e-commerce payment systems in use today.
- Describe the features and functionality of electronic billing presentment and payment systems.

Cyberwar:

MAD 2.0

From the earliest of days, humans have warred against each other, with the tools of warfare evolving over time from sticks and stones, to arrows and spears, to artillery and bombs. Physical warfare and weaponry are familiar and readily recognizable. But today, there is also another type of warfare that is becoming increasingly common, a type that is conducted by a hidden army of hackers wielding weaponry that consists of algorithms and computer code. Cyberspace has become a new battlefield, one that often involves other targets, such as financial systems and communications networks, as collateral objectives.

The phrase "shot heard round the world" is sometimes used to identify the start of a chain of events of historic import, such as the Revolutionary War and World War I. Although certainly not "heard" in the

© Rafal Olechowski / Fotolia

traditional sense, the release of the Stuxnet worm can be viewed as the first shot in a cyberwar between the United States and Iran that is still ongoing today. Thought to have been created by a secret joint U.S./Israeli task force that began while President George W. Bush was in office, Stuxnet was first discovered in June 2010. Stuxnet was designed to disable the software and computers that controlled the centrifuges in Iran's uranium enrichment process, and reportedly delayed Iran's ability to make nuclear arms for as many as five years. Stuxnet is the first cyberweapon believed to have caused significant physical damage to its target.

Another piece of malware, the Duqu worm, emerged in September 2011. Believed to have been created by Stuxnet's developers, Duqu was designed to collect passwords, take desktop screenshots to monitor users' actions, and pilfer various kinds of documents. It is believed that Duqu was intended to further gauge the status of Iran's nuclear program. In another strike against Iran, in April 2012, a Trojan named Flame hit computers in the Iranian Oil Ministry and the National Iranian Oil Company. Flame used a fraudulent digital certificate and spread via USB flash drives and other methods. It could sniff network traffic and record audio, screenshots, Skype conversations, and keystrokes, as well as download information from other devices via Bluetooth. Flame was suspected of pursuing multiple Iranian objectives including key oil export hubs. It shared some key characteristics with both Stuxnet and Duqu.

In August 2012, security experts Kaspersky Labs announced the detection of another cyberwarfare tool. Called Gauss, it was likely used to "follow the money" in Middle

SOURCES: "Budget Documents Detail Extent of U.S. Cyberoperations," by David E. Sanger, *New York Times*, August 31, 2013; "Silent War," by Michael Joseph Gross, *Vanity Fair*, July 2013; "U.S. Helps Allies Trying to Battle Iranian Hackers," by Thom Shanker and David E. Sanger, *New York Times*, June 8, 2013; "Cyberattacks Against U.S. Corporations Are on the Rise," by David E. Sanger and Nicole Perlroth, *New York Times*, May 12, 2013; "Cyberattacks Seem Meant to Destroy, Not Just Disrupt," by Nicole Perlroth and David E. Sanger, *New York Times*, March 28, 2013; "Experts: NKorea training teams of 'cyber warriors'," by Rachael King and Youkyung Lee, Associated Press, March 24, 2013; "Why China Is Reading Your Email," by David Feith, *Wall Street Journal*, March 19, 2013; "New Clue in South Korea Cyberattack Reveals Link to Chinese Criminals," by Mark Clayton, *Christian Science Monitor*, March 21, 2013; "Computer Networks in South Korea Are Paralyzed in Cyberattacks," by Choe Sang-Hun, *New York Times*, March 20, 2013; "U.S. Steps Up Alarm Over Cyberattacks," by Siobhan Gorman and Siobhan Hughes, *Wall Street Journal*, March 12, 2013; "As Hacking Against U.S. Rises, Experts Try to Pin Down Motive," by Nicole Perlroth, David E. Sanger, and Michael S. Schmidt, *New York Times*, March 3, 2013; "U.S., China Ties Tested in Cyberspace," by Julian E. Barnes, Siobhan Gorman, and Jeremy Page, *Wall Street Journal*, February 19, 2013; "Obama Order Gives Firms Cyberthreat Information," by Michael S. Schmidt and Nicole Perlroth, *New York Times*, February 12, 2013; "Bank Hacking Was the Work of Iranians, Officials Say," by Nicole Perlroth and Quentin Hardy, *New York Times*, January 8, 2013; "Iran Blamed for Cyberattacks: U.S. Officials Say Iranian Hackers Behind Electronic Assaults on U.S. Banks, Foreign Energy Firms," by Siobhan Gorman and Julian E. Barnes, *Wall Street Journal*, October 12, 2012; "Wiper Malware Could Be Connected to Stuxnet and Duqu, Researchers Say," by Lucian Constantin, *Computerworld*, August 30, 2012; "Analysis Shows Traces of Wiper Malware,

Eastern banking transactions. With an online banking module, and laden with encrypted malicious code, the Trojan was designed to collect the banking credentials of patrons of multiple Lebanon-based banks, Citibank, and PayPal. Gauss was built on the same platform as Flame and appears closely related to, and probably built in the same laboratory as, Stuxnet. Added together, the evidence suggests a possible effort by the U.S. government to root out terrorist group funding networks.

Around the same time, a virus named Shamoon appeared. It wiped out the data on 75% (30,000) of the computers on the main computer network of Saudi Arabia's Aramco, in what was termed one of the most destructive private sector attacks to that date. U.S. and Israeli officials felt that this strike at an American ally likely originated from Iran. Not long after, in September 2012, another wave of cyberattacks began, this time focusing on U.S. financial institutions. Thought to be another Iranian effort in response to the U.S.'s previous cyberattacks, the Web sites of a number of banks were knocked offline by distributed denial of service (DDoS) attacks. The severity of the attacks was unprecedented: although no account information was stolen, nor financial gain sought, the financial institutions spent millions dealing with the attacks, which continued through March 2013.

North Korea is another budding cyberwarfare adversary. In March 2013, it was accused of launching its most damaging attack to date on South Korean and American commercial, educational, governmental, and military institutions. Over 30,000 computers at three major South Korean banks and the two largest television broadcasters were affected. Internet banking sites were temporarily blocked, computer screens went blank, ATM machines failed, and commerce was disrupted. The attackers used the Chinese-written Gondad exploit kit to infect PCs with a Trojan that provides an entryway for an attacker to take control of the machine, creating a bot or zombie computer. Once the digital backdoor is created, the controller can deposit a malware payload, in this case, a wiper agent named Dark Seoul. Like Shamoon, Dark Seoul overwrites the master boot record (MBR). U.S. and South Korean security experts at South Korea's newly formed cyber security command center believe North Korea has been assembling and training a cyberwarrior team of thousands. For North Korea, the threat of cyber-retaliation is negligible. Internet access is only now extending beyond a privileged few, businesses are just beginning to adopt online banking, and worthwhile targets are virtually nonexistent.

Although cyberattacks tend to be reported as discrete incidents, they are in fact ongoing activities punctuated by major events. In July 2010, after 10 years of debate, 15 nations including the United States and Russia agreed on a set of recommendations that it was hoped would lead to an international treaty banning computer warfare. It never materialized. Kaspersky Labs founder, Eugene Kaspersky, has continued to advocate for its passage. As Kaspersky points out, cyberweapons are both cheap and potent, and today more than 100 nations have cyberwarfare capabilities and programs. Digital security companies can discover only a fraction of the existing malware. And because telecommunications security necessarily requires inspecting content, democratic nations' attempts to pass cybersecurity legislation usually meets opposition from privacy groups. An international treaty seems the best hope of avoiding MAD 2.0, the modern version of the Cold War era "mutually assured destruction," in which cyber-offensive actions are engaged in to destroy aggressors' Internet and other critical infrastructure. In the absence of a treaty, individual nations are building up their arsenals and offensive capabilities. In the United States, that includes the U.S. CyberCommand, commanded by General Keith B. Alexander, the director of the National Security Association. Alexander has spoken publicly of having 40 cyberteams, including 13 focused on offensive operations.

Industrial cyberespionage is closely related to cyberwarfare. Google has been battling Chinese cyberespionage for some time. In January 2010, it was the victim of a phishing attack that enabled China to steal some of its proprietary code. In March 2011, Google blamed the Chinese government for manipulating and disrupting Gmail and Google Talk. In June 2012, Google detected a possible Chinese-sponsored cyberattack against its users' Gmail accounts. Google is not the only company that has been targeted. At least 17 cyberespionage rings based in China have been identified. Their modus operandi is to insert spyware through phishing e-mails. Evidence suggests that it is a well-financed, centralized effort. The seven economic objectives in China's 12th Five-Year Plan (2011–2015) parallel the corporate and research targets. For example, in the biotechnology sector, drug manufacturers Wyeth and Abbott Laboratories and medical device maker Boston Scientific were hit. The computing center for the Food and Drug Administration, where sensitive information including chemical formulas and drug trial documents are stored, also was infiltrated. In the manufacturing sector, the networks of Cypress Semiconductor Corp, Aerospace Corp, and Environmental Systems Research Institute were compromised, possibly yielding China data regarding the manufacture of telecommunication chips, semiconductors, mapping software, and documents pertaining to national security space programs. Small strategic targets such as iBahn, the company that provides Internet access to business travelers at the Marriott and other large hotel chains, have exposed access points into numerous corporate networks as well as access to millions of confidential, and possibly encrypted, e-mail messages.

According to 2012 congressional testimony, over the past 12 years, China has penetrated the networks of at least 760 ISPs, corporations, research universities, and government agencies. Cyberespionage is a far quicker and cheaper path to economic dominance than independent research and development. Representative Mike Rogers estimated that China had garnered $500 billion worth of U.S. corporate assets. The magnitude of this wealth transfer is difficult to quantify because there are so many unknown variables. How quickly can source code, blueprints, chemical formulas, and other data be translated into products that can outcompete?

In response to these revelations, the Obama administration has publicly castigated the Chinese government, naming it the top cyberthreat to U.S. firms. Efforts to pass the Cyber Intelligence Sharing and Protection Act (CISPA), which would allow ISPs and other Internet companies to collect, analyze, and share with the National Security Agency (NSA) and other agencies activities perceived as possible threats, have thus far failed, in part because of concerns about privacy. With CISPA stalled in Congress, President Obama signed an executive order in February 2013 that allows companies associated with the supervision of electrical grids, dams, and financial institutions to voluntarily join a program to receive classified and other cybersecurity threat information previously available only to government contractors, and to develop and implement a cybersecurity framework.

But No Links to Flame," by Dennis Fisher, ThreatPost.com, August 29, 2012; "Nation-backed Surveillance Malware Monitors Middle East Bank Accounts," by Gregg Keizer, *Computerworld*, August 9, 2012; "Google to Warn Users of Possible State-Sponsored Cyber Attacks," by Jason Ryan, ABCNews.com, June, 5, 2012; "Attacks on Iranian Oil industry Led to Flame Malware Find," by Gregg Keizer, *Computerworld*, May 29, 2012; "Virus Linked to State-Sponsored Cyber Espionage," by Doug Isenberg, GigaLaw.com, May 28, 2012; "Iran Probes Cyberattack on Oil Ministry," by Doug Isenberg, GigaLaw.com, April 23, 2012; "How China Steals Our Secrets," by Richard A. Clarke, *New York Times*, April 2, 2012; "China-Based Hacking of 760 Companies Shows Cyber Cold War," by Michael Riley and John Walcott, Bloomberg.com, December 14, 2011.

As *Cyberwar: MAD 2.0* illustrates, the Internet and Web are increasingly vulnerable to large-scale attacks and potentially large-scale failure. Increasingly, these attacks are led by organized gangs of criminals operating globally—an unintended consequence of globalization. Even more worrisome is the growing number of large-scale attacks that are funded, organized, and led by various nations against the Internet resources of other nations. Currently there are few if any steps that individuals or businesses can take to prevent these kinds of attacks. However, there are several steps you can take to protect your business Web sites, your mobile devices, and your personal information from routine security attacks. Reading this chapter, you should also start thinking about how your business could survive in the event of a large-scale "outage" of the Internet.

In this chapter, we will examine e-commerce security and payment issues. First, we will identify the major security risks and their costs, and describe the variety of solutions currently available. Then, we will look at the major payment methods and consider how to achieve a secure payment environment. **Table 5.1** highlights some of the major trends in online security in 2013–2014.

TABLE 5.1	WHAT'S NEW IN E-COMMERCE SECURITY 2013–2014

- Mobile malware presents a tangible threat as smartphones and other mobile devices become more common targets of cybercriminals.
- Politically motivated, targeted attacks by hacktivist groups continue, in some cases merging with financially motivated cybercriminals to target financial systems with advanced persistent threats.
- Hackers and cybercriminals continue to focus their efforts on social network sites to exploit potential victims.
- Nations continue to engage in cyberwarfare and cyberespionage.
- Large-scale data breaches continue to expose data about individuals to hackers and other cybercriminals.
- Certificate authorities and the digital encryption regime that provides a basis for trust within the Internet infrastructure tighten standards in an attempt to prevent further attacks after several high-profile hacks.
- Malicious attacks targeting Mac computers increase.
- The amount of spam continues to decrease as a result of the demise of Rustock, the largest spam-sending botnet in the world and better detection techniques by e-mail providers.

5.1 THE E-COMMERCE SECURITY ENVIRONMENT

For most law-abiding citizens, the Internet holds the promise of a huge and convenient global marketplace, providing access to people, goods, services, and businesses worldwide, all at a bargain price. For criminals, the Internet has created entirely new—and lucrative—ways to steal from the more than 1 billion Internet consumers worldwide in 2013. From products and services to cash to information, it's all there for the taking on the Internet.

It's also less risky to steal online. Rather than rob a bank in person, the Internet makes it possible to rob people remotely and almost anonymously. Rather than steal a CD at a local record store, you can download the same music for free and almost without risk from the Internet. The potential for anonymity on the Internet cloaks many criminals in legitimate-looking identities, allowing them to place fraudulent orders with online merchants, steal information by intercepting e-mail, or simply shut down e-commerce sites by using software viruses and swarm attacks. The Internet was never designed to be a global marketplace with a billion users, and lacks many basic security features found in older networks such as the telephone system or broadcast television networks. By comparison, the Internet is an open, vulnerable-design network. The actions of cybercriminals are costly for both businesses and consumers, who are then subjected to higher prices and additional security measures. However, the overall security environment is strengthening as business managers and government officials make significant investments in security equipment and business procedures.

THE SCOPE OF THE PROBLEM

Cybercrime is becoming a more significant problem for both organizations and consumers. Bot networks, DDoS attacks, Trojans, phishing, data theft, identity fraud, credit card fraud, and spyware are just some of the threats that are making daily headlines. Social networks also have had security breaches. But despite the increasing attention being paid to cybercrime, it is difficult to accurately estimate the actual amount of such crime, in part because many companies are hesitant to report it due to the fear of losing the trust of their customers, and because even if crime is reported, it may be difficult to quantify the actual dollar amount of the loss.

One source of information is a survey conducted by Ponemon Institute of 56 representative U.S. companies in various industries. The 2012 survey found that the average annualized cost of cybercrime for the organizations in the study was $8.9 million per year, representing a 6% increase over 2011, and a 38% increase over 2010. The average cost per attack was around $600,000, an over 40% increase from the previous year. The number of cyberattacks also increased, by over 40%. The most costly cybercrimes were those caused by denial of service, malicious insiders, and Web-based attacks. The most prevalent types of attacks were viruses, worms, and Trojans, experienced by 100% of the companies surveyed, followed by malware (95%), botnets (71%), and Web-based attacks (64%) (Ponemon Institute, 2012).

Reports issued by security product providers, such as Symantec, are another source of data. Symantec issues a semi-annual *Internet Security Threat Report*, based on 69 million sensors monitoring Internet activity in more than 150 countries. Advances in technology have greatly reduced the entry costs and skills required to enter the cybercrime business. According to Symantec, low-cost and readily available Web attack kits, which enable hackers to create malware without having to write software from scratch, are responsible for more than 60% of all malicious activity. In addition, there has been a surge in polymorphic malware, which enables attackers to generate a unique version of the malware for each victim, making it much more difficult for pattern-matching software used by security firms to detect. Other findings indicate that targeted attacks are increasing (by 40% in 2012); social networks are helping criminals identify individual targets; and mobile platforms and applications are increasingly vulnerable. According to Symantec, mobile malware presented a tangible and significant threat, with a 58% increase in the number of mobile malware families identified compared to 2011 (Symantec, 2013a). However, Symantec does not attempt to quantify actual crimes and/or losses related to these threats.

Online credit card fraud and phishing attacks are perhaps the most high-profile form of e-commerce crimes. Although the average amount of credit card fraud loss experienced by any one individual is typically relatively small, the overall amount is substantial. The research firm CyberSource estimates online credit card fraud in the United States amounted to about $3.5 billion in 2012. Online fraud peaked in 2008 at $4 billion, suggesting that merchants are managing their credit card payment risks much better than in the past (CyberSource, 2013). The overall rate of online credit card fraud is estimated to be about 0.8% of all online card transactions. As a percentage of all e-commerce revenues, credit card fraud is declining as merchants and credit companies expand security systems to prevent the most common types of low-level fraud. But the nature of credit card fraud has changed greatly from the theft of a single credit card number and efforts to purchase goods at a few sites, to the simultaneous theft of millions of credit card numbers and their distributions to thousands of criminals operating as gangs of thieves. The emergence of identity fraud, described in detail later in this chapter, as a major online/offline type of fraud may well increase markedly the incidence and amount of credit card fraud, since identity fraud often includes the use of stolen credit card information and the creation of phony credit card accounts.

The Underground Economy Marketplace: The Value of Stolen Information

Criminals who steal information on the Internet do not always use this information themselves, but instead derive value by selling the information to others on so-called underground economy servers. For example, in 2013, Vladislav Horohorin (alias "BadB") was sentenced to over 7 years in federal prison for using online criminal forums to sell stolen credit and debit card information (referred to as "dumps"). At the time of his arrest, Horohorin possessed over 2.5 million stolen credit and debit card numbers. There are several thousand known underground economy servers around the world that sell stolen information (about half of these are in the United States). **Table 5.2** lists some recently observed prices, which typically vary depending on the quantity being purchased. Experts believe the cost of stolen information has fallen as the tools of harvesting have increased the supply. On the demand side, the same efficiencies and opportunities provided by new technology have increased the number of people who want to use stolen information. It's a robust marketplace.

Finding these servers is difficult for the average user (and for law enforcement agencies), and you need to be vetted by other criminals before gaining access. This

TABLE 5.2	THE CYBER BLACK MARKET FOR STOLEN DATA
Credit card	$2–$90
A full identity (U.S. bank account, credit card, date of birth, social security, etc.)	$3–$20
Bank account	$80–$700
Online accounts (PayPal, eBay, Facebook, Twitter, etc)	$10–$1500
E-mail accounts	$5–$12
Botnet rental	$15
A single compromised computer	$6–$20
Social security number	$5–$7
Attack toolkits	$120 per month
1,000 fake Instagram "followers"	$15

SOURCES: Based on data from Finkle, 2013; PandaSecurity, 2012; Danchev, 2011; Symantec, Inc., 2011, 2010.

vetting process takes place through e-mail exchanges of information, money, and reputation. Criminals have fairly good, personalized security!

Not every cybercriminal is necessarily after money. In some cases, such criminals aim to just deface, vandalize, and/or disrupt a Web site, rather than actually steal goods or services. The cost of such an attack includes not only the time and effort to make repairs to the site but also damage done to the site's reputation and image, as well as revenues lost as a result of the attack. Ponemon Institute estimates that the average loss to corporations for a breach of data security in 2012 was $5.4 million (Ponemon Institute, 2013).

So, what can we can conclude about the overall size of cybercrime? Cybercrime against e-commerce sites is dynamic and changing all the time, with new risks appearing often. The amount of losses to businesses appears to be significant but stable, and may represent a declining percentage of overall sales because firms have invested in security measures to protect against the simplest crimes. Individuals face new risks of fraud, many of which (unlike credit cards where federal law limits the loss to $50 for individuals) involve substantial uninsured losses involving debit cards and bank accounts. The managers of e-commerce sites must prepare for an ever-changing variety of criminal assaults, and keep current in the latest security techniques.

WHAT IS GOOD E-COMMERCE SECURITY?

What is a secure commercial transaction? Anytime you go into a marketplace you take risks, including the loss of privacy (information about what you purchased). Your prime risk as a consumer is that you do not get what you paid for. As a merchant in the market, your risk is that you don't get paid for what you sell. Thieves take merchandise and then either walk off without paying anything, or pay you with a fraudulent instrument, stolen credit card, or forged currency.

E-commerce merchants and consumers face many of the same risks as participants in traditional commerce, albeit in a new digital environment. Theft is theft, regardless of whether it is digital theft or traditional theft. Burglary, breaking and entering, embezzlement, trespass, malicious destruction, vandalism—all crimes in a traditional commercial environment—are also present in e-commerce. However, reducing risks in e-commerce is a complex process that involves new technologies, organizational policies and procedures, and new laws and industry standards that empower law enforcement officials to investigate and prosecute offenders. **Figure 5.1** illustrates the multi-layered nature of e-commerce security.

To achieve the highest degree of security possible, new technologies are available and should be used. But these technologies by themselves do not solve the problem. Organizational policies and procedures are required to ensure the technologies are not subverted. Finally, industry standards and government laws are required to enforce payment mechanisms, as well as to investigate and prosecute violators of laws designed to protect the transfer of property in commercial transactions.

The history of security in commercial transactions teaches that any security system can be broken if enough resources are put against it. Security is not absolute. In addition, perfect security of every item is not needed forever, especially in the

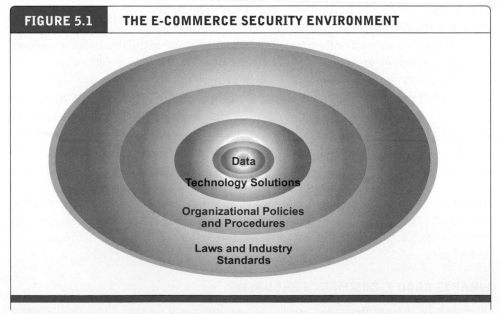

FIGURE 5.1	THE E-COMMERCE SECURITY ENVIRONMENT

E-commerce security is multi-layered, and must take into account new technology, policies and procedures, and laws and industry standards.

information age. There is a time value to information—just as there is to money. Sometimes it is sufficient to protect a message for a few hours, days, or years. Also, because security is costly, we always have to weigh the cost against the potential loss. Finally, we have also learned that security is a chain that breaks most often at the weakest link. Our locks are often much stronger than our management of the keys.

We can conclude then that good e-commerce security requires a set of laws, procedures, policies, and technologies that, to the extent feasible, protect individuals and organizations from unexpected behavior in the e-commerce marketplace.

DIMENSIONS OF E-COMMERCE SECURITY

There are six key dimensions to e-commerce security: integrity, nonrepudiation, authenticity, confidentiality, privacy, and availability.

Integrity refers to the ability to ensure that information being displayed on a Web site, or transmitted or received over the Internet, has not been altered in any way by an unauthorized party. For example, if an unauthorized person intercepts and changes the contents of an online communication, such as by redirecting a bank wire transfer into a different account, the integrity of the message has been compromised because the communication no longer represents what the original sender intended.

Nonrepudiation refers to the ability to ensure that e-commerce participants do not deny (i.e., repudiate) their online actions. For instance, the availability of free e-mail accounts with alias names makes it easy for a person to post comments or send a message and perhaps later deny doing so. Even when a customer uses a real name and e-mail address, it is easy for that customer to order merchandise online and then later deny doing so. In most cases, because merchants typically do not obtain a physical copy of a signature, the credit card issuer will side with the customer because the merchant has no legally valid proof that the customer ordered the merchandise.

Authenticity refers to the ability to identify the identity of a person or entity with whom you are dealing on the Internet. How does the customer know that the Web site operator is who it claims to be? How can the merchant be assured that the customer is really who she says she is? Someone who claims to be someone he is not is "spoofing" or misrepresenting himself.

Confidentiality refers to the ability to ensure that messages and data are available only to those who are authorized to view them. Confidentiality is sometimes confused with **privacy**, which refers to the ability to control the use of information a customer provides about himself or herself to an e-commerce merchant.

E-commerce merchants have two concerns related to privacy. They must establish internal policies that govern their own use of customer information, and they must protect that information from illegitimate or unauthorized use. For example, if hackers break into an e-commerce site and gain access to credit card or other information, this violates not only the confidentiality of the data, but also the privacy of the individuals who supplied the information.

Availability refers to the ability to ensure that an e-commerce site continues to function as intended.

integrity
the ability to ensure that information being displayed on a Web site or transmitted or received over the Internet has not been altered in any way by an unauthorized party

nonrepudiation
the ability to ensure that e-commerce participants do not deny (i.e., repudiate) their online actions

authenticity
the ability to identify the identity of a person or entity with whom you are dealing on the Internet

confidentiality
the ability to ensure that messages and data are available only to those who are authorized to view them

privacy
the ability to control the use of information about oneself

availability
the ability to ensure that an e-commerce site continues to function as intended

TABLE 5.3	CUSTOMER AND MERCHANT PERSPECTIVES ON THE DIFFERENT DIMENSIONS OF E-COMMERCE SECURITY	
DIMENSION	**CUSTOMER'S PERSPECTIVE**	**MERCHANT'S PERSPECTIVE**
Integrity	Has information I transmitted or received been altered?	Has data on the site been altered without authorization? Is data being received from customers valid?
Nonrepudiation	Can a party to an action with me later deny taking the action?	Can a customer deny ordering products?
Authenticity	Who am I dealing with? How can I be assured that the person or entity is who they claim to be?	What is the real identity of the customer?
Confidentiality	Can someone other than the intended recipient read my messages?	Are messages or confidential data accessible to anyone other than those authorized to view them?
Privacy	Can I control the use of information about myself transmitted to an e-commerce merchant?	What use, if any, can be made of personal data collected as part of an e-commerce transaction? Is the personal information of customers being used in an unauthorized manner?
Availability	Can I get access to the site?	Is the site operational?

Table 5.3 summarizes these dimensions from both the merchants' and customers' perspectives. E-commerce security is designed to protect these six dimensions. When any one of them is compromised, overall security suffers.

THE TENSION BETWEEN SECURITY AND OTHER VALUES

Can there be too much security? The answer is yes. Contrary to what some may believe, security is not an unmitigated good. Computer security adds overhead and expense to business operations, and also gives criminals new opportunities to hide their intentions and their crimes.

Ease of Use

There are inevitable tensions between security and ease of use. When traditional merchants are so fearful of robbers that they do business in shops locked behind security gates, ordinary customers are discouraged from walking in. The same can be true with respect to e-commerce. In general, the more security measures added to an e-commerce site, the more difficult it is to use and the slower the site becomes.

As you will discover reading this chapter, digital security is purchased at the price of slowing down processors and adding significantly to data storage demands on storage devices. Security is a technological and business overhead that can detract from doing business. Too much security can harm profitability, while not enough security can potentially put you out of business.

Public Safety and the Criminal Uses of the Internet

There is also an inevitable tension between the desires of individuals to act anonymously (to hide their identity) and the needs of public officials to maintain public safety that can be threatened by criminals or terrorists. This is not a new problem, or even new to the electronic era. The U.S. government began informal tapping of telegraph wires during the Civil War in the mid-1860s in order to trap conspirators and terrorists, and the first police wiretaps of local telephone systems were in place by the 1890s—20 years after the invention of the phone (Schwartz, 2001). No nation-state has ever permitted a technological haven to exist where criminals can plan crimes or threaten the nation-state without fear of official surveillance or investigation. In this sense, the Internet is no different from any other communication system. Drug cartels make extensive use of voice, fax, the Internet, and encrypted e-mail; a number of large international organized crime groups steal information from commercial Web sites and resell it to other criminals who use it for financial fraud. Over the years, the U.S. government has successfully pursued various "carding forums" (Web sites that facilitate the sale of stolen credit card and debit card numbers), such as Shadowcrew, Carderplanet, and Cardersmarket resulting in the arrest and prosecution of a number of their members and the closing of the sites. However, other criminal organizations have emerged to take their place.

Terrorists are also fond users of the Internet and have been for many years. Encrypted files sent via e-mail were used by Ramzi Yousef—a member of the terrorist group responsible for bombing the World Trade Center in 1993—to hide plans for bombing 11 U.S. airliners. The Internet was also used to plan and coordinate the subsequent attacks on the World Trade Center on September 11, 2001. The case of Umar Farouk Abdulmutallab further illustrates how terrorists make effective use of the Internet to radicalize, recruit, train, and coordinate youthful terrorists. Abdulmutallab allegedly attempted to blow up an American airliner in Detroit on Christmas Day 2009. He was identified, contacted, recruited, and trained, all within six weeks, according to a Pentagon counterterrorism official. In an effort to combat such terrorism, the U.S. government has significantly ramped up its surveillance of communications delivered via the Internet over the past several years. The extent of that surveillance has created a major controversy with National Security Administration contractor Edward Snowden's release of classified NSA documents that revealed that the NSA had obtained access to the servers of major Internet companies such as Facebook, Google, Apple, Microsoft, and others, as well as that NSA analysts have been searching e-mail, online chats, and browsing histories of U.S. citizens without any court approval. The proper balance between public safety and privacy in the effort against terrorism has proven to be a very thorny problem for the U.S. government.

<table>
<tr><td>**5.2**</td><td>**SECURITY THREATS IN THE E-COMMERCE ENVIRONMENT**</td></tr>
</table>

From a technology perspective, there are three key points of vulnerability when dealing with e-commerce: the client, the server, and the communications pipeline. **Figure 5.2** illustrates a typical e-commerce transaction with a consumer using a credit card to purchase a product. **Figure 5.3** illustrates some of the things that can go wrong at each major vulnerability point in the transaction—over Internet communications channels, at the server level, and at the client level.

In this section, we describe a number of the most common and most damaging forms of security threats to e-commerce consumers and site operators: malicious code, potentially unwanted programs, phishing, hacking and cybervandalism, credit card fraud/theft, spoofing, pharming, and spam (junk) Web sites (link farms), identity fraud, Denial of Service (DoS) and DDoS attacks, sniffing, insider attacks, poorly designed server and client software, social network security issues, mobile platform security issues, and finally, cloud security issues.

FIGURE 5.2	**A TYPICAL E-COMMERCE TRANSACTION**

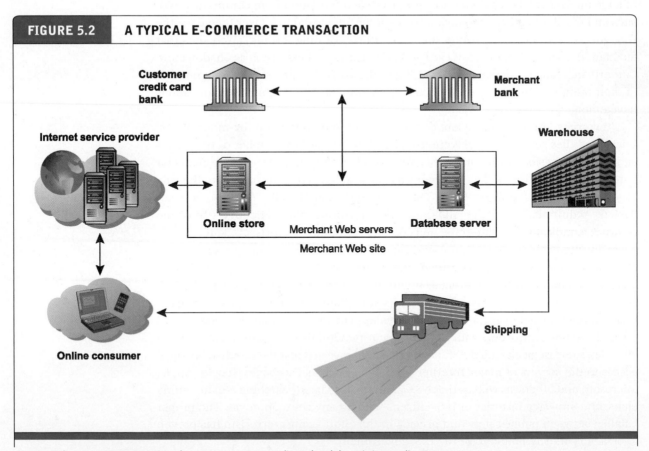

In a typical e-commerce transaction, the customer uses a credit card and the existing credit payment system.

FIGURE 5.3   **VULNERABLE POINTS IN AN E-COMMERCE TRANSACTION**

There are three major vulnerable points in e-commerce transactions: Internet communications, servers, and clients.

MALICIOUS CODE

Malicious code (sometimes referred to as "malware") includes a variety of threats such as viruses, worms, Trojan horses, ransomware, and bots. Some malicious code, sometimes referred to as an *exploit,* is designed to take advantage of software vulnerabilities in a computer's operating system, Web browser, applications, or other software components. For example, Microsoft reported that the Blackhole exploit kit available for purchase or rent from various hacker forums was the most commonly detected exploit family in the second half of 2012. Java exploits, those that affected Adobe products, and those aimed at the Windows operating system were also quite common. Overall, according to Microsoft, exploits comprised 14.5% of the worldwide malware threats in the fourth quarter of 2012 (Microsoft, 2013). According to Panda Security, 27 million new strains of malware were created in 2012, an average of about 74,000 every day (PandaLabs, 2013). In the past, malicious code was often intended to simply impair computers, and was often authored by a lone hacker, but increasingly the intent is to steal e-mail addresses, logon credentials, personal data, and financial information. Malicious code is also used to develop integrated malware networks that organize the theft of information and money.

One of the latest innovations in malicious code distribution is to embed it in the online advertising chain, including in Google and other ad networks. As the ad network

malicious code (malware)

includes a variety of threats such as viruses, worms, Trojan horses, and bots chain becomes more complicated, it becomes more and more difficult for Web sites to vet ads placed on their sites to ensure they are malware-free. Favorite targets are social media sites and large government agencies. In fact, according to Cisco's 2013 Annual Security Report, online advertisements are the second most likely origin of malicious content online, comprising about 16% of total Web malware encounters (Cisco, 2013). More than 1.5 million malicious ads are served every day, including "drive-by downloads" and fake anti-virus campaigns. A **drive-by download** is malware that comes with a downloaded file that a user intentionally or unintentionally requests. Drive-by is now one of the most common methods of infecting computers. For instance, Web sites as disparate as eWeek.com (a technology site) to MLB.com (Major League Baseball) to AmericanIdol.com have experienced instances where ads placed on their sites either had malicious code embedded or directed clickers to malicious sites. Malicious code embedded in PDF files also is common. Malware authors are also increasingly using links embedded within e-mail instead of the more traditional file attachments to infect computers. The links lead directly to a malicious code download or Web sites that include malicious JavaScript code. Equally important, there has been a major shift in the writers of malware from amateur hackers and adventurers to organized criminal efforts to defraud companies and individuals. In other words, it's now more about the money than ever before.

A **virus** is a computer program that has the ability to replicate or make copies of itself, and spread to other files. In addition to the ability to replicate, most computer viruses deliver a "payload." The payload may be relatively benign, such as the display of a message or image, or it may be highly destructive—destroying files, reformatting the computer's hard drive, or causing programs to run improperly. According to Microsoft, viruses comprised 7.7% of the worldwide malware threats in the fourth quarter of 2011.

Viruses are often combined with a worm. Instead of just spreading from file to file, a **worm** is designed to spread from computer to computer. A worm does not necessarily need to be activated by a user or program in order for it to replicate itself. The Slammer worm is one of the most notorious. Slammer targeted a known vulnerability in Microsoft's SQL Server database software, infected more than 90% of vulnerable computers worldwide within 10 minutes of its release on the Internet; crashed Bank of America cash machines, especially in the southwestern part of the United States; affected cash registers at supermarkets such as the Publix chain in Atlanta, where staff could not dispense cash to frustrated buyers; and took down most Internet connections in South Korea, causing a dip in the stock market there. The Conficker worm, which first appeared in November 2008, is the most significant worm since Slammer, and reportedly infected 9 to 15 million computers worldwide (Symantec, 2010). In the fourth quarter of 2012, worms accounted for 17.6% of the worldwide malware threats, according to Microsoft.

Ransomware (scareware) is a type of malware (often a worm) that locks your computer or files to stop you from accessing them. Ransomware will often display a notice that says an authority such as the FBI, Department of Justice, or IRS has detected illegal activity on your computer and demands that you pay a fine in order to unlock the computer and avoid prosecution.

---

drive-by download
malware that comes with a downloaded file that a user requests

virus
a computer program that has the ability to replicate or make copies of itself, and spread to other files

worm
malware that is designed to spread from computer to computer

ransomware (scareware)
malware that prevents you from accessing your computer or files and demands that you pay a fine

A **Trojan horse** appears to be benign, but then does something other than expected. The Trojan horse is not itself a virus because it does not replicate, but is often a way for viruses or other malicious code such as bots or *rootkits* (a program whose aim is to subvert control of the computer's operating system) to be introduced into a computer system. The term *Trojan horse* refers to the huge wooden horse in Homer's *Iliad* that the Greeks gave their opponents, the Trojans—a gift that actually contained hundreds of Greek soldiers. Once the people of Troy let the massive horse within their gates, the soldiers revealed themselves and captured the city. In today's world, a Trojan horse may masquerade as a game, but actually hide a program to steal your passwords and e-mail them to another person. Miscellaneous Trojans and Trojan downloaders and droppers (Trojans that install malicious files to a computer they have infected by either downloading them from a remote computer or from a copy contained in their own code) were found on almost 45% of computers around the world reporting malware threats to Microsoft in the fourth quarter of 2012. According to PandaLabs, Trojans accounted for over 75% of all malware created in 2012, and over 75% of all malware infections. In May 2011, Sony experienced the largest data breach in history when a Trojan horse took over the administrative computers of Sony's Play-Station game center and downloaded personal and credit card information involving 77 million registered users (Wakabayashi, 2011). Zeus is another example of a Trojan horse. Zeus steals information from users by keystroke logging. It is distributed through the Zeus botnet, which has millions of slave computers, and utilizes drive-by downloads and phishing tactics to persuade users to download files with the Trojan horse.

A **backdoor** is a feature of viruses, worms, and Trojans that allows an attacker to remotely access a compromised computer. Downadup is an example of a worm with a backdoor, while Virut, a virus that infects various file types, also includes a backdoor that can be used to download and install additional threats. According to GData Security Labs, the number of backdoors increased steadily in 2012 (GData SecurityLabs, 2013).

Bots (short for robots) are a type of malicious code that can be covertly installed on your computer when attached to the Internet. Around 90% of the world's spam, and 80% of the world's malware, is delivered by botnets. Once installed, the bot responds to external commands sent by the attacker; your computer becomes a "zombie" and is able to be controlled by an external third party (the "bot-herder"). **Botnets** are collections of captured computers used for malicious activities such as sending spam, participating in a DDoS attack, stealing information from computers, and storing network traffic for later analysis. The number of botnets operating worldwide is not known but is estimated to be well into the thousands. Bots and bot networks are an important threat to the Internet and e-commerce because they can be used to launch very large-scale attacks using many different techniques. In March 2011, federal marshals accompanied members of Microsoft's digital crimes unit in raids designed to disable the Rustock botnet, the leading source of spam in the world with nearly 500,000 slave PCs under the control of its command and control servers located at six Internet hosting services in the United States. Officials confiscated the Rustock control servers at the hosting sites, which claimed they had no idea what the Rustock servers were doing. The actual spam e-mails were sent by the slave PCs under the command of the Rustock servers (Wingfield, 2011). In 2013, Microsoft and the FBI

Trojan horse
appears to be benign, but then does something other than expected. Often a way for viruses or other malicious code to be introduced into a computer system

backdoor
feature of viruses, worms and Trojans that allows an attacker to remotely access a compromised computer

bot
type of malicious code that can be covertly installed on a computer when connected to the Internet. Once installed, the bot responds to external commands sent by the attacker

botnet
collection of captured bot computers

engaged in another aggressive botnet operation, targeting 1,400 of Zeus-derived Citadel botnets, which had been used in 2012 to raid bank accounts at major banks around the world, netting over $500 million (Chirgwin, 2013). However, illustrating the difficulty of the task, new Citadel botnets resurfaced within several months, once again stealing banking credentials, this time from Japanese banks (Muncaster, 2013).

Malicious code is a threat at both the client and the server levels, although servers generally engage in much more thorough anti-virus activities than do consumers. At the server level, malicious code can bring down an entire Web site, preventing millions of people from using the site. Such incidents are infrequent. Much more frequent malicious code attacks occur at the client level, and the damage can quickly spread to millions of other computers connected to the Internet. **Table 5.4** lists some well-known examples of malicious code.

POTENTIALLY UNWANTED PROGRAMS (PUPS)

potentially unwanted program (PUP)
program that installs itself on a computer, typically without the user's informed consent

In addition to malicious code, the e-commerce security environment is further challenged by **potentially unwanted programs (PUPs)** such as adware, browser parasites, spyware, and other applications that install themselves on a computer, such as rogue security software, typically without the user's informed consent. Such programs are increasingly found on social network and user-generated content sites where users are fooled into downloading them. Once installed, these applications are usually exceedingly difficult to remove from the computer. One example of a PUP is Vista Antispyware 2013, which infects PCs running the Vista operating system. Vista Antispyware poses as a legitimate anti-spyware program when in fact it is malware that, when installed, disables the user's security software, alters the user's Web browser, and diverts users to scam Web sites where more malware is downloaded.

adware
a PUP that serves pop-up ads to your computer

Adware is typically used to call for pop-up ads to display when the user visits certain sites. While annoying, adware is not typically used for criminal activities. ZangoSearch and PurityScan are examples of adware programs that open a partner site's Web pages or display the partner's pop-up ads when certain keywords are used in Internet searches. Adware was found on around 20% of all computers reporting threats to Microsoft in the fourth quarter of 2012. A **browser parasite** is a program that can monitor and change the settings of a user's browser, for instance, changing the browser's home page, or sending information about the sites visited to a remote computer. Browser parasites are often a component of adware. For example, Websearch is an adware component that modifies Internet Explorer's default home page and search settings.

browser parasite
a program that can monitor and change the settings of a user's browser

spyware
a program used to obtain information such as a user's keystrokes, e-mail, instant messages, and so on

Spyware, on the other hand, can be used to obtain information such as a user's keystrokes, copies of e-mail and instant messages, and even take screenshots (and thereby capture passwords or other confidential data). Spyware constituted the least reported PUP, with less than 1% of computers reporting it. Other miscellaneous PUPs were reported by around 33% of computers worldwide.

PHISHING

social engineering
exploitation of human fallibility and gullibility to distribute malware

Social engineering relies on human curiosity, greed, and gullibility in order to trick people into taking an action that will result in the downloading of malware. Kevin Mitnick, until his capture and imprisonment in 1999, was one of America's most

TABLE 5.4	NOTABLE EXAMPLES OF MALICIOUS CODE	
NAME	TYPE	DESCRIPTION
Citadel	Trojan/botnet	Variant of Zeus Trojan, focuses on the theft of authentication credentials and financial fraud. Botnets spreading Citadel were targets of Microsoft/FBI action in 2012.
Zeus	Trojan/botnet	Sometimes referred to as king of financial malware. May install via drive-by download and evades detection by taking control of Web browser and stealing data that is exchanged with bank servers.
Reventon	Ransomware worm/Trojan	Based on Citadel/Zeus Trojans. Locks computer and displays warning from local police alleging illegal activity on computer; demands payment of fine to unlock.
Ramnit	Virus/worm	One of the most prevalent malicious code families still active in 2013. Infects various file types, including executable files, and copies itself to removable drives, executing via AutoPlay when the drive is accessed on other computers
Sality.AE	Virus/worm	Most common virus in 2012. Disables security applications and services, connects to a botnet, then downloads and installs additional threats. Uses polymorphism to evade detection.
Downadup	Worm/ backdoor	Disables security software, copies itself to all drives at a location, and connects to a P2P botnet to download other malware.
Conficker	Worm	First appeared November 2008. Targets Microsoft operating systems. Uses advanced malware techniques. Largest worm infection since Slammer in 2003. Still considered a major threat.
Netsky.P	Worm/Trojan horse	First appeared in early 2003. It spreads by gathering target e-mail addresses from the computers, then infects and sends e-mail to all recipients from the infected computer. It is commonly used by bot networks to launch spam and DoS attacks.
Storm (Peacomm, NuWar)	Worm/Trojan horse	First appeared in January 2007. It spreads in a manner similar to the Netsky.P worm. May also download and run other Trojan programs and worms.
Nymex	Worm	First discovered in January 2006. Spreads by mass mailing; activates on the 3rd of every month, and attempts to destroy files of certain types.
Zotob	Worm	First appeared in August 2005. Well-known worm that infected a number of U.S. media companies.
Mydoom	Worm	First appeared in January 2004. One of the fastest spreading mass-mailer worms.
Slammer	Worm	Launched in January 2003. Caused widespread problems.
CodeRed	Worm	Appeared in 2001. It achieved an infection rate of over 20,000 systems within 10 minutes of release and ultimately spread to hundreds of thousands of systems.
Melissa	Macro virus/ worm	First spotted in March 1999. At the time, the fastest spreading infectious program ever discovered. It attacked Microsoft Word's Normal.dot global template, ensuring infection of all newly created documents. It also mailed an infected Word file to the first 50 entries in each user's Microsoft Outlook Address Book.
Chernobyl	File-infecting virus	First appeared in 1998. It wipes out the first megabyte of data on a hard disk (making the rest useless) every April 26, the anniversary of the nuclear disaster at Chernobyl.

wanted computer criminals. Mitnick used simple deceptive techniques to obtain pass-words, social security, and police records all without the use of any sophisticated technology (Mitnick, 2011).

phishing

any deceptive, online attempt by a third party to obtain confidential infor-mation for financial gain

Phishing is any deceptive, online attempt by a third party to obtain confidential information for financial gain. Phishing attacks typically do not involve malicious code but instead rely on straightforward misrepresentation and fraud, so-called "social engi-neering" techniques. One of the most popular phishing attacks is the e-mail scam letter. The scam begins with an e-mail: a rich former oil minister of Nigeria is seeking a bank account to stash millions of dollars for a short period of time, and requests your bank account number where the money can be deposited. In return, you will receive a million dollars. This type of e-mail scam is popularly known as a "Nigerian letter" scam (see **Figure 5.4**).

Thousands of other phishing attacks use other scams, some pretending to be eBay, PayPal, or Citibank writing to you for "account verification" (known as "spear phishing," or targeting a known customer of a specific bank or other type of busi-ness). Click on a link in the e-mail and you will be taken to a Web site controlled by the scammer, and prompted to enter confidential information about your accounts, such as your account number and PIN codes. On any given day, millions of these phishing attack e-mails are sent, and, unfortunately, some people are fooled and disclose their personal account information. For instance, in April 2011, the Oak Ridge National Laboratory (a highly classified atomic energy facility) was forced to disconnect Internet access for workers after the lab's computers were hacked as a

| FIGURE 5.4 | AN EXAMPLE OF A NIGERIAN LETTER E-MAIL SCAM |

This is an example of a typical Nigerian letter e-mail scam.
© keith morris / Alamy

result of a phishing attack. The intrusion resulted from a spear-phishing e-mail sent to lab employees purportedly from the Human Resources Department discussing their benefits, and included a link to a malicious Web page. Only two employees were ensnared, but that was enough to start a malicious data breach (Zetter, 2011).

Phishers rely on traditional "con man" tactics, but use e-mail to trick recipients into voluntarily giving up financial access codes, bank account numbers, credit card numbers, and other personal information. Often, phishers create (or "spoof") a Web site that purports to be a legitimate financial institution and cons users into entering financial information, or the site downloads malware such as a keylogger to the victim's computer. Phishers use the information they gather to commit fraudulent acts such as charging items to your credit cards or withdrawing funds from your bank account, or in other ways "steal your identity" (identity fraud). Phishing attacks are a common form of e-commerce crime and reached record-setting highs in 2012, according to the Anti-Phishing Working Group (APWG, 2013). Symantec reported that in 2012, about 1 in every 400 e-mails contained a phishing attack (Symantec, 2013). In 2013, two Romanians and one Nigerian who were found to have servers containing the details of over 30,000 bank customers in 14 different countries, and 70 million customer e-mail addresses to be used in phishing scams, were sentenced to jail terms in the United Kingdom totaling 21 years (Dunn, 2013). In the United States, men from Romania, Bulgaria, Croatia, and Canada also were sentenced to federal prison terms for their involvement in a phishing scheme that targeted customers of a number of banks, eBay, and PayPal (Federal Bureau of Investigation, 2013).

To combat phishing, in January 2012, leading e-mail service providers, including Google, Microsoft, Yahoo, and AOL, as well as financial services companies such as PayPal, Bank of America, and others, joined together to form DMARC.org, an organization aimed at dramatically reducing phishing e-mail. By January 2013, e-mail providers who had implemented DMARC represented around 80% of consumer in-boxes in the United States, and around 60% globally (DMARC.org, 2013). It appears as if some of this effort is having an effect, as the APWG reports that in the first quarter of 2013, phishing e-mail report numbers declined significantly during the quarter.

HACKING, CYBERVANDALISM, HACKTIVISM, AND DATA BREACHES

A **hacker** is an individual who intends to gain unauthorized access to a computer system. Within the hacking community, the term **cracker** is typically used to denote a hacker with criminal intent, although in the public press, the terms hacker and cracker tend to be used interchangeably. Hackers and crackers gain unauthorized access by finding weaknesses in the security procedures of Web sites and computer systems, often taking advantage of various features of the Internet that make it an open system that is easy to use. In the past, hackers and crackers typically were computer aficionados excited by the challenge of breaking into corporate and government Web sites. Sometimes they were satisfied merely by breaking into the files of an e-commerce site. Today, hackers have malicious intentions to disrupt, deface, or destroy sites (**cybervandalism**) or to steal personal or corporate information they can use for financial gain (data breach). In one of the most brazen hacking crimes to occur to date, hackers on two separate occasions infiltrated the systems of credit-card

hacker
an individual who intends to gain unauthorized access to a computer system

cracker
within the hacking community, a term typically used to denote a hacker with criminal intent

cybervandalism
intentionally disrupting, defacing, or even destroying a site

processing companies that handle prepaid debit cards, raised the withdrawal limits on the cards, and were able to steal over $45 million from automated teller machines (Santora, 2013).

hacktivism

cybervandalism and data theft for political purposes

Hacktivism adds a political twist. Hacktivists typically attack governments, organizations, and even individuals for political purposes, employing the tactics of cybervandalism, distributed denial of service attacks, data thefts, doxing (gathering and exposing personal information of public figures, originating from the term "documents" or "docx"), and more. LulzSec and Anonymous are two prominent hacktivist groups. See the *Insight on Business* case, *We Are Legion*, for a further look at some recent hacktivism incidents.

Groups of hackers called *tiger teams* are sometimes used by corporate security departments to test their own security measures. By hiring hackers to break into the system from the outside, the company can identify weaknesses in the computer system's armor. These "good hackers" became known as **white hats** because of their role in helping organizations locate and fix security flaws. White hats do their work under contract, with agreement from clients that they will not be prosecuted for their efforts to break in.

white hats

"good" hackers who help organizations locate and fix security flaws

black hats

hackers who act with the intention of causing harm

In contrast, **black hats** are hackers who engage in the same kinds of activities but without pay or any buy-in from the targeted organization, and with the intention of causing harm. They break into Web sites and reveal the confidential or proprietary information they find. These hackers believe strongly that information should be free, so sharing previously secret information is part of their mission.

grey hats

hackers who believe they are pursuing some greater good by breaking in and revealing system flaws

Somewhere in the middle are the **grey hats**, hackers who believe they are pursuing some greater good by breaking in and revealing system flaws. Grey hats discover weaknesses in a system's security, and then publish the weakness without disrupting the site or attempting to profit from their finds. Their only reward is the prestige of discovering the weakness. Grey hat actions are suspect, however, especially when the hackers reveal security flaws that make it easier for other criminals to gain access to a system.

data breach

occurs when an organization loses control over its information to outsiders

A **data breach** occurs whenever organizations lose control over corporate information to outsiders. According to Symantec, data about more than 230 million people were exposed in 2011 as a result of data breaches. Breaches caused by hacker attacks were responsible for exposing more than 187 million identities. Many of the data breaches resulted from a hacking campaign called Operation AntiSec run by the hacker collectives Anonymous and LulzSec, which began in the spring of 2011, and which continued into 2012, despite some arrests. In 2012, the total number of publicized data breaches declined by over 25%, with the number of individual identities declining by 60% to "only" 93 million. According to Symantec, the decline can be attributed in part to the fact that Anonymous and LulzSec were not as active in publicizing hacks in 2012 as they had been in 2011. Significant breaches that did occur included a data breach at Zappos.com that affected 24 million customers, the compromise of a payment processor for Visa and Mastercard, and a breach at LinkedIn, exposing the data of 6.5 million members. (Symantec, 2013, 2012a, 2012b).

INSIGHT ON BUSINESS

WE ARE LEGION

As more of the world's data and services migrate to the Internet, hackers are empowered to do more damage than ever before. Some of today's hackers are more than just the online equivalent of vandals—they have agendas and often are seeking to effect some kind of social change. Known as "hacktivists," this new breed of hacker has presented a major challenge for law enforcement agencies worldwide.

One of the highest-profile instances of hacktivism in recent history, and to date still the largest data breach in Internet history, took place in April 2011. System administrators at Sony's online gaming service PlayStation Network (PSN) discovered that personal information of its 77 million users, as well as credit card information from 12 million of those users, had likely been transferred from its servers to outside computers.

The attack continued across other Sony sites and properties, including Sony Online Entertainment and Sony Pictures Entertainment. The attacks represented an instance of "revenge hacking," the use of the Internet to destroy or disrupt political opponents, or to punish organizations for their public behavior. The hackers left a text file named Anonymous on Sony's server with the words "We are legion." Later, LulzSec, an offshoot group of Anonymous, claimed responsibility for both attacks. Anonymous is the name of an Internet collective of hackers and vigilantes. Sony and others believe the attack, which followed weeks of DoS attacks on the same Sony servers, was retaliation for Sony's civil suit against George Hotz, one of the world's best-known hackers. Hotz cracked the iPhone operating system in 2008; in 2010, he cracked the Sony PlayStation client operating system and later published the procedures on his Web site.

Sony argued publicly that it had been the victim of a sophisticated cyberattack. In fact, most computer security breaches are the result of fairly simple tactics, management failures to anticipate well-known security risks, unwillingness to spend resources on expensive security measures, sloppy procedures, lack of training, carelessness, and outdated software. LulzSec itself claimed Sony's lax security allowed it to perform a standard SQL injection attack on a primitive security hole that allowed it to access whatever information it wanted.

In 2012, the attacks on Sony by Anonymous and in particular LulzSec spurred law enforcement agencies in the United States and other countries to begin working together to curtail further Anonymous attacks. After arrests of key LulzSec members began in 2011, the group vowed to "retire," stating that the risk had become greater than the benefits of continuing their attacks. This was likely in response to the 2011 arrest of a LulzSec leader, Hector Xavier Monsegur, known online as Sabu. The FBI used the prospect of heavy jail time to force Sabu to cooperate with further investigations, allowing them to continue tracking down and apprehending other LulzSec members. But the phenomenon of hacktivism is much bigger than one individual or group, and targeted attacks have continued.

In 2013, hacktivists continued to strike frequently, often with geopolitical motives. The Syrian Electronic Army (SEA) executed a series of strikes on sites controlled by the United States, such as the Marine Corps recruitment site and the *New York Times*' site. In each case, the SEA's goal was to spread messages supporting Syrian President Bashar Al-Assad in the country's civil war. The SEA's attack on the Times' site crippled it for nearly an entire day, and its attack on the Marine Corps recruitment site redirected visitors to a separate site with a pro-Syrian government message and several pictures of people

(continued)

wearing U.S. military uniforms displaying anti-war messages. Other sites like the *Washington Post*, the Huffington Post, CNN, Thompson Reuters, and Twitter all reported being the target of attacks as well. In each of these cases, the SEA targeted a domain name systems provider used by the main site, gained access to that provider, and used their access to attack the main site. The domain name system service compromised in the Times attack was an Australian-based company called Melbourne IT, which was first the target of an SEA phishing attack, and was then used by the hacktivist group to bring down the main Times site. The inflammatory video "The Innocence of Muslims" has also spurred hacktivist attacks against U.S. financial institutions intended to force the removal of the video from YouTube.

Although hacktivist attacks continue seemingly unabated, and the cost of launching an attack has dropped and is continuing to drop, there is some hope for law enforcement going forward. As agencies become more familiar with the techniques used by hacktivist groups, and as they develop methods of surveillance that make it increasingly difficult to remain anonymous on the Internet, hackers may find it tougher than ever to execute series of attacks like those made by LulzSec or by the SEA. Also, arrests of high-profile hackers like Sabu have served as a deterrent to would-be members of hacktivist groups. In 2013, a London judge sentenced four members of LulzSec who helped execute attacks on Sony and other gaming companies to jail time.

There is still some debate about whether all hacktivism is necessarily bad, or whether hacktivism serves a social good, preventing technology from exerting undue power over society. Hacktivists also generally believe that all information should be freely available on the Internet. Aaron Swartz, a well-known Internet activist, was arrested in 2012 for downloading and distributing academic articles that were behind the pay wall of the online repository JSTOR. Swartz had been a co-founder of the social news site Reddit, had helped to develop RSS, and was very prominent in technological circles. Facing the prospect of decades of jail time, Swartz committed suicide and immediately became a martyr to hacktivists and other tech innovators. Bradley Manning, regarded as a criminal by law enforcement for his role in the WikiLeaks data breach, is also viewed as a hacktivist hero for his commitment to freedom of information.

As data breaches rise in significance and frequency, the Obama administration and Congress have proposed the Data Accountability and Trust Act, which would require firms to establish security requirements and policies, notify potential victims of a data loss without unreasonable delay, and notify a major media outlet and all major credit-reporting agencies within 60 days if the credit card data on more than 5,000 individuals is at risk. The Act has been passed by the House of Representatives, but remains stalled in the Senate as of September 2013. Currently, 49 states and U.S. territories have such legislation. However, it is unclear if the proposed legislation, even if passed, would reduce the incidence of data breaches and hacktivism.

■ SOURCES: "Syrian Group Cited as New York Times Outage Continues," by Heather Kelly, CNN.com August 29, 2013; "New York Times' Website Back Up After Cyberattack," by Roger Yu, *USA Today*, August 28, 2013; "Syrian Hacktivists Target Thompson Reuters," by Warwick Ashford, ComputerWeekly.com, July 30, 2013; "A Short History of Hacktivism," by Ty McCormick, theage.com, May 10, 2013; "Social Media and Hacktivism: Two Ideas Made for Each Other?," by Hon Lau, Symantec.com, May 1, 2013; "'Funded Hacktivism' or Cyber-terrorists, AmEx Attackers Have Big Bankroll," by Sean Gallagher, ArsTechnica.com, March 30, 2013; "What is a 'Hacktivist,'" by Peter Ludlow, *New York Times*, January 13, 2013; "9 Ways Hacktivists Shocked the World in 2012," by Mathew J. Schwartz, Informationweek.com, December 21, 2012; "Second Accused LulzSec Hacker Arrested in US," by Charlie Osborne, ZDNet.com, August 29, 2012; "Hacker Group Claims Responsibility for New Sony Break-In," by Riva Richmond, *New York Times*, June 2, 2011; "Expert: Sony Had Outdated Software, Lax Security," by Jesse Emspak, IBtimes.com, May 5, 2011; "Anonymous Press Release," Anonymous Enterprises LLC Bermuda, May 4, 2011; "Hackers Breach Second Sony Service," by Ian Sherr, *Wall Street Journal*, May 2, 2011.

CREDIT CARD FRAUD/THEFT

Theft of credit card data is one of the most feared occurrences on the Internet. Fear that credit card information will be stolen prevents users from making online purchases in many cases. Interestingly, this fear appears to be largely unfounded. Incidences of stolen credit card information are much lower than users think, around 0.8% of all online card transactions (CyberSource, 2013). Several surveys have documented a slow drift downwards in the frequency and value of online credit card fraud due to better merchant screening systems and security improvements. Nevertheless, online credit card fraud is twice as common as offline card fraud.

There is substantial credit card fraud in traditional commerce, but the consumer is largely insured against losses by federal law. In the past, the most common cause of credit card fraud was a lost or stolen card that was used by someone else, followed by employee theft of customer numbers and stolen identities (criminals applying for credit cards using false identities). Federal law limits the liability of individuals to $50 for a stolen credit card. For amounts more than $50, the credit card company generally pays the amount, although in some cases, the merchant may be held liable if it failed to verify the account or consult published lists of invalid cards. Banks recoup the cost of credit card fraud by charging higher interest rates on unpaid balances, and by merchants who raise prices to cover the losses.

But today, the most frequent cause of stolen cards and card information is the systematic hacking and looting of a corporate server where the information on millions of credit card purchases is stored. For instance, in March 2010, Albert Gonzalez was sentenced to 20 years in prison for organizing the largest theft of credit card numbers in American history. Along with several Russian co-conspirators, Gonzalez broke into the central computer systems of TJX, BJs, Barnes & Noble, and other companies, stealing over 160 million card numbers and costing these firms over $200 million in losses (Fox and Botelho, 2013).

International orders have been particularly prone to repudiation. If an international customer places an order and then later disputes it, online merchants often have no way to verify that the package was actually delivered and that the credit card holder is the person who placed the order. Most online merchants will not process international orders.

A central security issue of e-commerce is the difficulty of establishing the customer's identity. Currently there is no technology that can identify a person with certainty. Until a customer's identity can be guaranteed, online companies are at a much higher risk of loss than traditional offline companies. The federal government has attempted to address this issue through the Electronic Signatures in Global and National Commerce Act (the "E-Sign" law), which gives digital signatures the same authority as hand-written signatures in commerce. This law also intended to make digital signatures more commonplace and easier to use. Except for large businesses conducting transactions over the Internet, the law has had little impact on B2C e-commerce, but that may be changing.

SPOOFING, PHARMING, AND SPAM (JUNK) WEB SITES

spoofing
involves attempting to hide a true identity by using someone else's e-mail or IP address.

Spoofing involves attempting to hide a true identity by using someone else's e-mail or IP address. For instance, a spoofed e-mail will have a forged sender e-mail address designed to mislead the receiver about who sent the e-mail. IP spoofing involves the creation of TCP/IP packets that use someone else's source IP address, indicating that the packets are coming from a trusted host. Most current routers and firewalls can offer protection against IP spoofing. Spoofing a Web site sometimes involves **pharming**, automatically redirecting a Web link to an address different from the intended one, with the site masquerading as the intended destination. Links that are designed to lead to one site can be reset to send users to a totally unrelated site—one that benefits the hacker.

pharming
automatically redirecting a Web link to an address different from the intended one, with the site masquerading as the intended destination

Although spoofing and pharming do not directly damage files or network servers, they threaten the integrity of a site. For example, if hackers redirect customers to a fake Web site that looks almost exactly like the true site, they can then collect and process orders, effectively stealing business from the true site. Or, if the intent is to disrupt rather than steal, hackers can alter orders—inflating them or changing products ordered—and then send them on to the true site for processing and delivery. Customers become dissatisfied with the improper order shipment, and the company may have huge inventory fluctuations that impact its operations.

In addition to threatening integrity, spoofing also threatens authenticity by making it difficult to discern the true sender of a message. Clever hackers can make it almost impossible to distinguish between a true and a fake identity or Web address.

spam (junk) Web sites
also referred to as link farms; promise to offer products or services, but in fact are just collections of advertisements

Spam (junk) Web sites (also sometimes referred to as *link farms*) are a little different. These are sites that promise to offer some product or service, but in fact are just a collection of advertisements for other sites, some of which contain malicious code. For instance, you may search for "[name of town] weather," and then click on a link that promises your local weather, but then discover that all the site does is display ads for weather-related products or other Web sites. Junk or spam Web sites typically appear on search results, and do not involve e-mail. These sites cloak their identities by using domain names similar to legitimate firm names, and redirect traffic to known spammer-redirection domains such as topsearch10.com.

IDENTITY FRAUD

identity fraud
involves the unauthorized use of another person's personal data for illegal financial benefit

Identity fraud involves the unauthorized use of another person's personal data, such as social security, driver's license, and/or credit card numbers, as well as user names and passwords, for illegal financial benefit. Criminals can use such data to obtain loans, purchase merchandise, or obtain other services, such as mobile phone or other utility services. Cybercriminals employ many of the techniques described previously, such as spyware, phishing, data breaches, and credit card theft, for the purpose of identity fraud. Data breaches, in particular, often lead to identity fraud: in 2012, one in four data breach notification recipients later became a victim.

Identity fraud is a significant problem in the United States. In 2012, according to Javelin Strategy & Research, identity fraud increased by over 8%, with the total number of victims increasing to almost 13 million people. The total dollar losses as a result of identity fraud also increased by over 15%, to almost $21 million (Javelin Research & Strategy, 2013).

DENIAL OF SERVICE (DOS) AND DISTRIBUTED DENIAL OF SERVICE (DDOS) ATTACKS

In a **Denial of Service (DoS) attack**, hackers flood a Web site with useless pings or page requests that inundate and overwhelm the site's Web servers. Increasingly, DoS attacks involve the use of bot networks and so-called "distributed attacks" built from thousands of compromised client computers. DoS attacks typically cause a Web site to shut down, making it impossible for users to access the site. For busy e-commerce sites, these attacks are costly; while the site is shut down, customers cannot make purchases. And the longer a site is shut down, the more damage is done to a site's reputation. Although such attacks do not destroy information or access restricted areas of the server, they can destroy a firm's online business. Often, DoS attacks are accompanied by attempts at blackmailing site owners to pay tens or hundreds of thousands of dollars to the hackers in return for stopping the DoS attack.

A **Distributed Denial of Service (DDoS) attack** uses hundreds or even thousands of computers to attack the target network from numerous launch points. DoS and DDoS attacks are threats to a system's operation because they can shut it down indefinitely. Major Web sites such as Yahoo and Microsoft have experienced such attacks, making the companies aware of their vulnerability and the need to continually introduce new measures to prevent future attacks. In August 2012, WikiLeaks, a site dedicated to the release of classified information, was hit by a massive DDoS attack that left its Web site effectively inoperable. According to WikiLeaks, the amount of bandwidth consumed by the attacks was in the 10 gigabits per second range, and the range of IP addresses used was so large that it is believed whoever was running the attack either controlled thousands of computers or was able to simulate them. In an interesting twist, previously, one of the largest DDoS attacks had occurred in December 2010 when the hacker group Anonymous launched simultaneous attacks on MasterCard, Visa, PayPal, and other firms that had refused to handle online donations to WikiLeaks. The systems were slowed but none were forced to shut down. All told, over 750 separate DDoS attacks were reported to Akamai in 2012, and Akamai anticipates that this number will continue to grow in 2013. During the period from September 2012 through March 2013, many of the attacks were against U.S. banks, as described in the opening case (Akamai, 2013). In another measure of the prevalence of DDoS attacks, in an Arbor Networks survey of 130 ISP and network operators around the world, over 75% of participants reported that customers had experienced DDoS attacks in the previous year, with over 40% experiencing actual infrastructure outages as a result (Arbor Networks, 2013).

SNIFFING

A **sniffer** is a type of eavesdropping program that monitors information traveling over a network. When used legitimately, sniffers can help identify potential network troublespots, but when used for criminal purposes, they can be damaging and very difficult to detect. Sniffers enable hackers to steal proprietary information from anywhere on a network, including passwords, e-mail messages, company files, and confidential reports.

E-mail wiretaps are a variation on the sniffing threat. An e-mail wiretap is a method for recording or journaling e-mail traffic generally at the mail server level from any

Denial of Service (DoS) attack
flooding a Web site with useless traffic to inundate and overwhelm the network

Distributed Denial of Service (DDoS) attack
using numerous computers to attack the target network from numerous launch points

sniffer
a type of eavesdropping program that monitors information traveling over a network

individual. E-mail wiretaps are used by employers to track employee messages, and by government agencies to surveil individuals or groups. E-mail wiretaps can be installed on servers and client computers. The USA PATRIOT Act permits the FBI to compel ISPs to install a black box on their mail servers that can impound the e-mail of a single person or group of persons for later analysis. In the case of American citizens communicating with other citizens, an FBI agent or government lawyer need only certify to a judge on the secret 11-member U.S. Foreign Intelligence Surveillance Court (FISC) that the information sought is "relevant to an ongoing criminal investigation" to get permission to install the program. Judges have no discretion. They must approve wiretaps based on government agents' unsubstantiated assertions. In the case of suspected terrorist activity, law enforcement does not have to inform a court prior to installing a wire or e-mail tap. A 2007 amendment to the 1978 Foreign Intelligence Surveillance Act, known as FISA, provided new powers to the National Security Agency to monitor international e-mail and telephone communications where one person is in the United States, and where the purpose of such interception is to collect foreign intelligence (Foreign Intelligence Surveillance Act of 1978; Protect America Act of 2007). In September 2012, the U.S. House of Representatives voted in favor of the FISA Amendments Reauthorization Act, which, if also passed by the Senate, will extend the provisions of FISA for five more years, until 2017. NSA's XKeyscore program, revealed by Edward Snowden, is a form of "wiretap" that allows NSA analysts to search through vast databases containing not only e-mail, but online chats, and browsing histories of millions of individuals (Wills, 2013).

The Communications Assistance for Law Enforcement Act (CALEA) requires all communications carriers (including ISPs) to provide near-instant access to law enforcement agencies to their message traffic. Many Internet services (such as Facebook and LinkedIn) that have built-in ISP services technically are not covered by CALEA. One can only assume these non-ISP e-mail operators cooperate with law enforcement. Unlike the past where wiretaps required many hours to physically tap into phone lines, in today's digital phone systems, taps are arranged in a few minutes by the large carriers at their expense.

INSIDER ATTACKS

We tend to think of security threats to a business as originating outside the organization. In fact, the largest financial threats to business institutions come not from robberies but from embezzlement by insiders. Bank employees steal far more money than bank robbers. The same is true for e-commerce sites. Some of the largest disruptions to service, destruction to sites, and diversion of customer credit data and personal information have come from insiders—once trusted employees. Employees have access to privileged information, and, in the presence of sloppy internal security procedures, they are often able to roam throughout an organization's systems without leaving a trace. Research from Carnegie Mellon University documents the significant damage insiders have done to both private and public organizations. (Software Engineering Institute, 2012). Survey results also indicate that insiders are more likely to be the source of cyberattacks than outsiders, and to cause more damage to an organization than external attacks (PWC, 2013). In some instances, the insider might not have criminal intent, but inadvertently exposes data that can then be exploited by others. For instance, a Ponemon Institute study found that negligent insiders are a top cause of data breaches.

POORLY DESIGNED SERVER AND CLIENT SOFTWARE

Many security threats prey on poorly designed server and client software, sometimes in the operating system and sometimes in the application software, including browsers. The increase in complexity and size of software programs, coupled with demands for timely delivery to markets, has contributed to an increase in software flaws or vulnerabilities that hackers can exploit. For instance, **SQL injection attacks** take advantage of vulnerabilities in poorly coded Web application software that fails to properly validate or filter data entered by a user on a Web page to introduce malicious program code into a company's systems and networks. An attacker can use this input validation error to send a rogue SQL query to the underlying database to access the database, plant malicious code, or access other systems on the network. Large Web applications have hundreds of places for inputting user data, each of which creates an opportunity for an SQL injection attack. A large number of Web-facing applications are believed to have SQL injection vulnerabilities, and tools are available for hackers to check Web applications for these vulnerabilities.

Each year, security firms identify thousands of software vulnerabilities in Internet browsers, PC, Macintosh, and Linux software, as well as mobile device operating systems and applications. For instance, in its most recent semi-annual *Internet Security Threat Report,* Symantec identified over 5,000 different software vulnerabilities. Browser vulnerabilities in particular are a popular target, as well as browser plug-ins such as for Adobe Reader. According to Kaspersky Labs, the number of browser-based attacks in 2012 increased to almost 1.6 billion, 1.7 times greater than in 2011. Java vulnerabilities on both PC and Mac computers accounted for 50% of detected attacks, with Adobe Acrobat Reader the second most common target, at 28% (Kaspersky Labs, 2012). A **zero-day vulnerability** is one that has been previously unreported and for which no patch yet exists. In 2012, 14 zero-day vulnerabilities were reported, up from 8. The trend continues in 2013. Not surprisingly, Java has been the target of several zero-day attacks during 2013. For instance, in January 2013, just a day after Oracle had patched two previous zero-day vulnerabilities, it learned that an exploit kit for yet another zero-day vulnerability was being marketed on a hacker forum (Schwartz, 2013). The very design of the personal computer includes many open communication ports that can be used, and indeed are designed to be used, by external computers to send and receive messages. The port most frequently attacked is TCP port 445 (Microsoft-DS); attacks on port 80 (WWW/HTTP) and 443 (SSL/HTTPS) also are common. Given their complexity and design objectives, all operating systems and application software, including Linux and Macintosh, have vulnerabilities.

SOCIAL NETWORK SECURITY ISSUES

Social networks like Facebook, Twitter, LinkedIn, Pinterest, and Tumblr provide a rich and rewarding environment for hackers. Viruses, site takeovers, identity fraud, malware-loaded apps, click hijacking, phishing, and spam are all found on social networks (US-CERT, 2011). For instance, the Ramnit worm stole account information from more than 45,000 Facebook users in 2012. Also in 2012, LinkedIn revealed that Russian hackers had obtained almost 6.5 million user passwords and posted them online and Twitter was hit by a widespread spam attack involving malicious tweets

SQL injection attack
takes advantage of poorly coded Web application software that fails to properly validate or filter data entered by a user on a Web page

zero-day vulnerability
software vulnerability that has been previously unreported and for which no patch yet exists

that included a user's Twitter name, which ultimately redirected the user to a Russian Web site containing the Blackhole exploit kit. The first widespread account takeover accounts in Pinterest also occurred in 2012. These attacks sent image spam to other social networks such as Facebook and Twitter from the victimized users' Pinterest accounts. Tumblr suffered similar attacks as well. By sneaking in among our friends, hackers can masquerade as friends and dupe users into scams.

Social network firms have thus far been relatively poor policemen because they have failed to aggressively weed out accounts that send visitors to malware sites (unlike Google, which maintains a list of known malware sites and patrols its search results looking for links to malware sites). Social networks are open: anyone can set up a personal page, even criminals. Most attacks are social engineering attacks that tempt visitors to click on links that sound reasonable. Social apps downloaded from either the social network or a foreign site are not certified by the social network to be clean of malware. It's "clicker beware."

MOBILE PLATFORM SECURITY ISSUES

The explosion in mobile devices has broadened opportunities for hackers. Mobile users are filling their devices with personal and financial information, and using them to conduct an increasing number of transactions, from retail purchases to mobile banking, making them excellent targets for hackers. In general, mobile devices face all the same risks as any Internet device as well as some new risks associated with wireless network security. For instance, public Wi-Fi networks that are not secured are very susceptible to hacking. While most PC users are aware their computers and Web sites may be hacked and contain malware, most cell phone users believe their cell phone is as secure as a traditional landline phone. As with social network members, mobile users are prone to think they are in a shared, trustworthy environment.

Mobile cell phone malware was developed as early as 2004 with Cabir, a Bluetooth worm affecting Symbian operating systems (Nokia phones) and causing the phone to continuously seek out other Bluetooth-enabled devices, quickly draining the battery. The iKee.B worm infected jailbroken iPhones, turning the phones into botnet-controlled devices. An iPhone in Europe could be hacked by an iPhone in the United States, and all its private data sent to a server in Poland. Ikee.B established the feasibility of cell phone botnets. The first malicious iPhone app was discovered and removed from the iTunes Store. Many—if not most—apps written for Android phones have poor protection for user information, and the number of malicious and high-risk Android apps detected by TrendMicro skyrocketed to 350,000 in 2012, an exponential increase when compared to just the 1,000 detected in 2011. This trend has continued in 2013, with the number of malicious and high-risk apps doubling to over 700,000 in the second quarter. Examples include rogue version or "trojanized" versions of popular apps such as Angry Birds and Bad Piggies (TrendMicro Incorporated, 2013a, 2013b). And it is not just rogue applications that are dangerous, but also popular legitimate applications that simply have little protection from hackers (Kolesnikov-Jessup, 2011; US-CERT 2010). ViaForensics, a mobile security firm in Chicago, found in a study of 50 popular iPhone apps that only three had adequate protection for usernames, passwords, and other sensitive data.

Vishing attacks target gullible cell phone users with verbal messages to call a certain number and, for example, donate money to starving children in Haiti. *Smish-*

ing attacks exploit SMS/text messages. Compromised text messages can contain e-mail and Web site addresses that can lead the innocent user to a malware site. Criminal SMS spoofing services have emerged, which conceal the cybercriminal's true phone number, replacing it with a false alpha-numeric name. SMS spoofing can also be used by cybercriminals to lure mobile users to a malicious Web site by sending a text that appears to be from a legitimate organization in the From field, and suggesting the receiver click on a malicious URL hyperlink to update an account or obtain a gift card. A small number of downloaded apps from app stores have also contained malware. *Madware*—innocent-looking apps that contain adware that launches pop-up ads and text messages on your mobile device—is also becoming an increasing problem.

Read the *Insight on Technology* case, *Think Your Smartphone Is Secure?* for a further discussion of some of the issues surrounding smartphone security.

CLOUD SECURITY ISSUES

The move of so many Internet services into the cloud also raises security risks. From an infrastructure standpoint, DDoS attacks threaten the availability of cloud services on which more and more companies are relying. Safeguarding data being maintained in a cloud environment is also a major concern. For example, researchers identified several ways data could be accessed without authorization on Dropbox, which offers a popular cloud file-sharing service. Dropbox has also experienced several security snafus, including leaving all of its users' files publicly accessible for four hours in June 2011 due to a software bug, the discovery of a security hole in its iOS app that allowed anyone with physical access to the phone to copy login credentials, and the theft of usernames and passwords in August 2012. To combat some of these issues, Dropbox has implemented a number of measures, including two-factor authentication, which relies on two separate elements—something you know, such as a password, coupled with a separately generated code. Around the same time, a hack into writer Mat Honan's Apple iCloud account using social engineering tactics allowed the hackers to wipe everything from his Mac computer, iPhone, and iPad, which were linked to the cloud service, as well as take over his Twitter and Gmail accounts (Honan, 2012). In March 2013, an unknown intruder gained access to usernames, e-mail addresses, and encrypted passwords used by customers of Evernote, a cloud note-taking service. Evernote was forced to reset 50 million passwords. These incidents highlight the risks involved as devices, identities, and data become more and more interconnected in the cloud.

5.3   TECHNOLOGY SOLUTIONS

At first glance, it might seem like there is not much that can be done about the onslaught of security breaches on the Internet. Reviewing the security threats in the previous section, it is clear that the threats to e-commerce are very real, potentially devastating for individuals, businesses, and entire nations, and likely to be increasing in intensity along with the growth in e-commerce. But in fact a great deal of progress has been made by private security firms, corporate and home users, network administrators, technology firms, and government agencies. There are two lines of defense:

INSIGHT ON TECHNOLOGY

THINK YOUR SMARTPHONE IS SECURE?

So far, there have been few publicly identified, large-scale, smartphone security breaches, but just because it hasn't happened yet doesn't mean it won't. With about 140 million smartphone users in the United States, 143 million people accessing the Internet from mobile devices, business firms increasingly switching their employees to the mobile platform, and consumers using their phones for financial transactions and even paying bills, the size and richness of the smartphone target for hackers is growing.

Have you ever purchased anti-virus software for your smartphone? Probably not. Many users believe their smartphones are unlikely to be hacked because Apple and Google are protecting them from malware, and that Verizon and AT&T can keep the cell phone network secure just as they do the land-line phone system. Telephone systems are "closed" and therefore not subject to the kinds of attacks that occur on the open Internet.

Hackers can do to a smartphone just about anything they can do to any Internet device: request malicious files without user intervention, delete files, transmit files, install programs running in the background that can monitor user actions, and potentially convert the smartphone into a robot that can be used in a botnet to send e-mail and text messages to anyone.

Apps are one avenue for potential security breaches. Apple, Google, and RIM (BlackBerry) now offer over 1.75 million apps collectively. Apple claims that it examines each and every app to ensure that it plays by Apple's iTunes rules, but risks remain. Most of the known cases that occurred thus far have involved jailbroken phones. The first iPhone app confirmed to have embedded malware made it past Apple into the iTunes store in July 2012. However, security company Kaspersky expects the iPhone to face an onslaught of malware over the course of the next year. Apple iTunes app rules make some user information available to all apps by default, including the user's GPS position and name. However, a rogue app could easily do much more. Nicolas Seriot, a Swiss researcher, built a test app called "SpyPhone" that was capable of tracking users and all their activities, then transmitting this data to remote servers, all without user knowledge. The app harvested geolocation data, passwords, address book entries, and e-mail account information. Apple removed the app once it was identified. That this proof-of-concept app was accepted by the iTunes staff of reviewers suggests Apple cannot effectively review new apps prior to their use. Thousands of apps arrive each week. Also, Apple's 'walled garden' approach means that only Apple is truly qualified to defend iOS devices from attacks. Until it changes this policy, third parties won't be able to develop services to protect Apple devices as they may be able to with Android.

The amount of malware on the Android platform has skyrocketed over the past year. In part this was due to the fact that security on that platform was much less under the control of Google because it employs "open" app model compared to Apple's "walled garden" approach. In addition, in the past, Google did not review Android apps, instead relying on user input and technical hurdles to limit malware. However, in 2013, in response to the growing malware problem, Google launched a universal app-scanning system that instantly checks each app for malicious code at the device level.

Android apps run in a "sandbox," where they cannot affect one another or manipulate device

(continued)

features without user permission. Android apps can use any personal information found on a Droid phone but they must also inform the user what each app is capable of doing, and what personal data it requires. Google removes any apps that break its rules against malicious activity. One problem: users may not pay attention to permission requests and simply click "Yes" when asked to grant permissions. Apple's iPhone does not inform users what information apps are using, but does restrict the information that can be collected by any app.

Google can perform a remote wipe of offending apps from all Droid phones without user intervention. This is a wonderful capability, but is itself a security threat if hackers gain access to the remote wipe capability at Google. In one incident, Google pulled down dozens of mobile banking apps made by a developer called "09Droid." The apps claimed to give users access to their accounts at many banks throughout the world. In fact, the apps were unable to connect users to any bank, and were removed before they could do much harm. Google does take preventive steps to reduce malware apps such as vetting the backgrounds of developers, and requiring developers to register with its Google Wallet payment service (both to encourage users to pay for apps using their service but also to force developers to reveal their identities and financial information).

Beyond the threat of rogue apps, smartphones of all stripes are susceptible to browser-based malware that takes advantage of vulnerabilities in all browsers. In addition, most smartphones, including the iPhone, permit the manufacturers to remotely download configuration files to update operating systems and security protections. Unfortunately, flaws in the public key encryption procedures that permit remote server access to iPhones have been discovered, raising further questions about the security of such operations. Attackers have also developed methods of hijacking phones using weaknesses in SIM cards. There are at least 500 million vulnerable SIM cards in use today, and the defects allow hackers to obtain the encryption key that guards users' personal information, granting them nearly complete access over the phone in the process.

In 2013, internal NSA documents indicated that the law enforcement agency had developed the capability to tap into sensitive personal data held on all major smartphone devices, even the BlackBerry mail system, which is considered the most secure of any smartphone. In 2011, the NSA was also granted the ability to conduct warrantless searches of American communications in a way that had previously been reserved only for foreigners. While the NSA had devoted entire teams to individual smartphone operating systems in order to make this breakthrough, their success is proof-of-concept for other more malicious organizations to develop similar capabilities.

Suddenly, our smartphones and tablets don't seem quite as safe anymore. Some commentators dismiss these concerns as more hype than reality. But reality is catching up with the hype.

SOURCES: "NSA Secretly Broke Smartphone Security," by Cory Doctorow, BoingBoing.com, September 8, 2013; "Obama Administration Had Restrictions on NSA Reversed in 2011," by Ellen Nakashima, September 7, 2013; "How Google Just Quietly Made Your Android Phone More Secure," by JR Raphael, *Computerworld*, July 26, 2013; "Crypto Flaw Makes Millions of Smartphone Susceptible to Hijacking," by Dan Goodin, ArsTechnica.com, July 22, 2013; "Android Will Account for 58% of Smartphone App Downloads in 2013, with iOS Commanding a Market Share of 75% in Tablet Apps," ABI Research, March 4, 2013; "Smartphone Cyberattacks to Grow This Year," by David Goldman, money.cnn.com, January 8, 2013; "iPhone Malware: Spam App 'Find and Call' Invades App Store," by Zach Epstein, BGR.com, July 5, 2012; "iPhone Malware: Kaspersky Expects Apple's iOS to be Under Attack by Next Year," by Sara Gates, Huffington Post, May 15, 2012; "Android, Apple Face Growing Cyberattacks," by Byron Acohido, *USA Today*, June 3, 2011; "Security to Ward Off Crime on Phones," by Riva Richmond, *New York Times*, February 23, 2011; "AT&T Plans Smartphone Security Service for 2012," "Smartphone Security Follies: A Brief History," by Brad Reed, *Network World*, April 18, 2011.

| FIGURE 5.5 | TOOLS AVAILABLE TO ACHIEVE SITE SECURITY |

There are a number of tools available to achieve site security.

technology solutions and policy solutions. In this section, we consider some technology solutions, and in the following section, we look at some policy solutions that work.

The first line of defense against the wide variety of security threats to an e-commerce site is a set of tools that can make it difficult for outsiders to invade or destroy a site. **Figure 5.5** illustrates the major tools available to achieve site security.

PROTECTING INTERNET COMMUNICATIONS

Because e-commerce transactions must flow over the public Internet, and therefore involve thousands of routers and servers through which the transaction packets flow, security experts believe the greatest security threats occur at the level of Internet communications. This is very different from a private network where a dedicated communication line is established between two parties. A number of tools are available to protect the security of Internet communications, the most basic of which is message encryption.

ENCRYPTION

Encryption is the process of transforming plain text or data into **cipher text** that cannot be read by anyone other than the sender and the receiver. The purpose of encryption is (a) to secure stored information and (b) to secure information transmission. Encryption can provide four of the six key dimensions of e-commerce security referred to in Table 5.3 on page 254:

encryption

the process of transforming plain text or data into cipher text that cannot be read by anyone other than the sender and the receiver. The purpose of encryption is (a) to secure stored information and (b) to secure information transmission

cipher text

text that has been encrypted and thus cannot be read by anyone other than the sender and the receiver

- *Message integrity*—provides assurance that the message has not been altered.
- *Nonrepudiation*—prevents the user from denying he or she sent the message.
- *Authentication*—provides verification of the identity of the person (or computer) sending the message.
- *Confidentiality*—gives assurance that the message was not read by others.

This transformation of plain text to cipher text is accomplished by using a key or cipher. A **key** (or **cipher**) is any method for transforming plain text to cipher text.

Encryption has been practiced since the earliest forms of writing and commercial transactions. Ancient Egyptian and Phoenician commercial records were encrypted using substitution and transposition ciphers. In a **substitution cipher**, every occurrence of a given letter is replaced systematically by another letter. For instance, if we used the cipher "letter plus two"—meaning replace every letter in a word with a new letter two places forward—then the word "Hello" in plain text would be transformed into the following cipher text: "JGNNQ." In a **transposition cipher**, the ordering of the letters in each word is changed in some systematic way. Leonardo Da Vinci recorded his shop notes in reverse order, making them readable only with a mirror. The word "Hello" can be written backwards as "OLLEH." A more complicated cipher would (a) break all words into two words and (b) spell the first word with every other letter beginning with the first letter, and then spell the second word with all the remaining letters. In this cipher, "HELLO" would be written as "HLO EL."

Symmetric Key Encryption

In order to decipher these messages, the receiver would have to know the secret cipher that was used to encrypt the plain text. This is called **symmetric key encryption** or **secret key encryption**. In symmetric key encryption, both the sender and the receiver use the same key to encrypt and decrypt the message. How do the sender and the receiver have the same key? They have to send it over some communication media or exchange the key in person. Symmetric key encryption was used extensively throughout World War II and is still a part of Internet encryption.

The possibilities for simple substitution and transposition ciphers are endless, but they all suffer from common flaws. First, in the digital age, computers are so powerful and fast that these ancient means of encryption can be broken quickly. Second, symmetric key encryption requires that both parties share the same key. In order to share the same key, they must send the key over a presumably *insecure* medium where it could be stolen and used to decipher messages. If the secret key is lost or stolen, the entire encryption system fails. Third, in commercial use, where we are not all part of the same team, you would need a secret key for each of the parties with whom you transacted, that is, one key for the bank, another for the department store, and another for the government. In a large population of users, this could result in as many as $n^{(n-1)}$ keys. In a population of millions of Internet users, thousands of millions of keys would be needed to accommodate all e-commerce customers (estimated at about 156 million in the United States). Potentially, 156^2 million different keys would be needed. Clearly this situation would be too unwieldy to work in practice.

key (cipher)
any method for transforming plain text to cipher text

substitution cipher
every occurrence of a given letter is replaced systematically by another letter

transposition cipher
the ordering of the letters in each word is changed in some systematic way

symmetric key encryption (secret key encryption)
both the sender and the receiver use the same key to encrypt and decrypt the message

Modern encryption systems are digital. The ciphers or keys used to transform plain text into cipher text are digital strings. Computers store text or other data as binary strings composed of 0s and 1s. For instance, the binary representation of the capital letter "A" in ASCII computer code is accomplished with eight binary digits (bits): 01000001. One way in which digital strings can be transformed into cipher text is by multiplying each letter by another binary number, say, an eight-bit key number 0101 0101. If we multiplied every digital character in our text messages by this eight-bit key and sent the encrypted message to a friend along with the secret eight-bit key, the friend could decode the message easily.

The strength of modern security protection is measured in terms of the length of the binary key used to encrypt the data. In the preceding example, the eight-bit key is easily deciphered because there are only 2^8 or 256 possibilities. If the intruder knows you are using an eight-bit key, then he or she could decode the message in a few seconds using a modern desktop PC just by using the brute force method of checking each of the 256 possible keys. For this reason, modern digital encryption systems use keys with 56, 128, 256, or 512 binary digits. With encryption keys of 512 digits, there are 2^{512} possibilities to check out. It is estimated that all the computers in the world would need to work for 10 years before stumbling upon the answer.

The **Data Encryption Standard (DES)** was developed by the National Security Agency (NSA) and IBM in the 1950s. DES uses a 56-bit encryption key. To cope with much faster computers, it has been improved by *Triple DES*—essentially encrypting the message three times, each with a separate key. Today, the most widely used symmetric key encryption algorithm is **Advanced Encryption Standard (AES)**, which offers key sizes of 128, 192, and 256 bits. AES had been considered to be relatively secure, but in August 2011, researchers from Microsoft and a Belgian university announced that they had discovered a way to break the algorithm, and with this work, the "safety margin" of AES continues to erode. There are also many other symmetric key systems that are currently less widely used, with keys up to 2,048 bits.[1] Google announced in May 2013 that it was planning to upgrade the security of its SSL certificates to 2,048-bit keys and has reportedly accelerated other programs to encrypt data in the wake of the controversy over the NSA's PRISM program (Kirk, 2013; Rosenblatt, 2013).

Public Key Encryption

In 1976, a new way of encrypting messages called **public key cryptography** was invented by Whitfield Diffie and Martin Hellman. Public key cryptography solves the problem of exchanging keys. In this method, two mathematically related digital keys are used: a public key and a private key. The private key is kept secret by the owner, and the public key is widely disseminated. Both keys can be used to encrypt and decrypt a message. However, once the keys are used to encrypt a message, the same key cannot be used to unencrypt the message. The mathematical algorithms used to produce the keys are one-way functions. A *one-way irreversible mathematical function*

Data Encryption Standard (DES)

developed by the National Security Agency (NSA) and IBM. Uses a 56-bit encryption key

Advanced Encryption Standard (AES)

the most widely used symmetric key encryption algorithm, offering 128-, 192-, and 256-bit keys

public key cryptography

two mathematically related digital keys are used: a public key and a private key. The private key is kept secret by the owner, and the public key is widely disseminated. Both keys can be used to encrypt and decrypt a message. However, once the keys are used to encrypt a message, that same key cannot be used to unencrypt the message

[1] For instance: DESX and RDES with 168-bit keys; the RC Series: RC2, RC4, and RC5 with keys up to 2,048 bits; and the IDEA algorithm, the basis of PGP, e-mail public key encryption software described later in this chapter, which uses 128-bit keys.

is one in which, once the algorithm is applied, the input cannot be subsequently derived from the output. Most food recipes are like this. For instance, it is easy to make scrambled eggs, but impossible to retrieve whole eggs from the scrambled eggs. Public key cryptography is based on the idea of irreversible mathematical functions. The keys are sufficiently long (128, 256, and 512 bits) that it would take enormous computing power to derive one key from the other using the largest and fastest computers available. **Figure 5.6** illustrates a simple use of public key cryptography and takes you through the important steps in using public and private keys.

FIGURE 5.6	PUBLIC KEY CRYPTOGRAPHY—A SIMPLE CASE
STEP	**DESCRIPTION**
1. The sender creates a digital message.	The message could be a document, spreadsheet, or any digital object.
2. The sender obtains the recipient's public key from a public directory and applies it to the message.	Public keys are distributed widely and can be obtained from recipients directly.
3. Application of the recipient's key produces an encrypted cipher text message.	Once encrypted using the public key, the message cannot be reverse-engineered or unencrypted using the same public key. The process is irreversible.
4. The encrypted message is sent over the Internet.	The encrypted message is broken into packets and sent through several different pathways, making interception of the entire message difficult (but not impossible).
5. The recipient uses his/her private key to decrypt the message.	The only person who can decrypt the message is the person who has possession of the recipient's private key. Hopefully, this is the legitimate recipient.

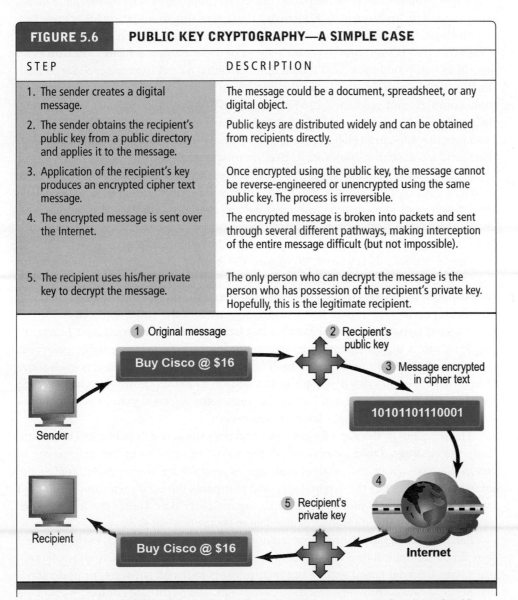

In the simplest use of public key cryptography, the sender encrypts a message using the recipient's public key, and then sends it over the Internet. The only person who can decrypt this message is the recipient, using his or her private key. However, this simple case does not ensure integrity or an authentic message.

Public Key Encryption Using Digital Signatures and Hash Digests

In public key encryption, some elements of security are missing. Although we can be quite sure the message was not understood or read by a third party (message confidentiality), there is no guarantee the sender really is the sender; that is, there is no authentication of the sender. This means the sender could deny ever sending the message (repudiation). And there is no assurance the message was not altered somehow in transit. For example, the message "Buy Cisco @ $16" could have been accidentally or intentionally altered to read "Sell Cisco @ $16." This suggests a potential lack of integrity in the system.

A more sophisticated use of public key cryptography can achieve authentication, nonrepudiation, and integrity. **Figure 5.7** illustrates this more powerful approach.

hash function

an algorithm that produces a fixed-length number called a hash or message digest

To check the integrity of a message and ensure it has not been altered in transit, a hash function is used first to create a digest of the message. A **hash function** is an algorithm that produces a fixed-length number called a *hash* or *message digest*. A hash function can be simple, and count the number of digital 1s in a message, or it can be more complex, and produce a 128-bit number that reflects the number of 0s and 1s, the number of 00s and 11s, and so on. Standard hash functions are available (MD4 and MD5 produce 128- and 160-bit hashes) (Stein, 1998). These more complex hash functions produce hashes or hash results that are unique to every message. The results of applying the hash function are sent by the sender to the recipient. Upon receipt, the recipient applies the hash function to the received message and checks to verify the same result is produced. If so, the message has not been altered. The sender then encrypts both the hash result and the original message using the recipient's public key (as in Figure 5.6 on page 279), producing a single block of cipher text.

digital signature (e-signature)

"signed" cipher text that can be sent over the Internet

One more step is required. To ensure the authenticity of the message and to ensure nonrepudiation, the sender encrypts the entire block of cipher text one more time using the sender's private key. This produces a **digital signature** (also called an *e-signature*) or "signed" cipher text that can be sent over the Internet.

A digital signature is a close parallel to a handwritten signature. Like a handwritten signature, a digital signature is unique—only one person presumably possesses the private key. When used with a hash function, the digital signature is even more unique than a handwritten signature. In addition to being exclusive to a particular individual, when used to sign a hashed document, the digital signature is also unique to the document, and changes for every document.

The recipient of this signed cipher text first uses the sender's public key to authenticate the message. Once authenticated, the recipient uses his or her private key to obtain the hash result and original message. As a final step, the recipient applies the same hash function to the original text, and compares the result with the result sent by the sender. If the results are the same, the recipient now knows the message has not been changed during transmission. The message has integrity.

Early digital signature programs required the user to have a digital certificate, and were far too difficult for an individual to use. Newer programs from several small companies are Internet-based and do not require users to install software, or understand digital certificate technology. DocuSign, EchoSign, and Sertifi are companies offering online digital signatures. Many insurance, finance, and surety companies now permit customers to electronically sign documents.

FIGURE 5.7	PUBLIC KEY CRYPTOGRAPHY WITH DIGITAL SIGNATURES

STEP	DESCRIPTION
1. The sender creates an original message.	The message can be any digital file.
2. The sender applies a hash function, producing a 128-bit hash result.	Hash functions create a unique digest of the message based on the message contents.
3. The sender encrypts the message and hash result using recipient's public key.	This irreversible process creates a cipher text that can be read only by the recipient using his or her private key.
4. The sender encrypts the result, again using his or her private key.	The sender's private key is a digital signature. There is only one person who can create this digital mark.
5. The result of this double encryption is sent over the Internet.	The message traverses the Internet as a series of independent packets.
6. The receiver uses the sender's public key to authenticate the message.	Only one person can send this message, namely, the sender.
7. The receiver uses his or her private key to decrypt the hash function and the original message. The receiver checks to ensure the original message and the hash function results conform to one another.	The hash function is used here to check the original message. This ensures the message was not changed in transit.

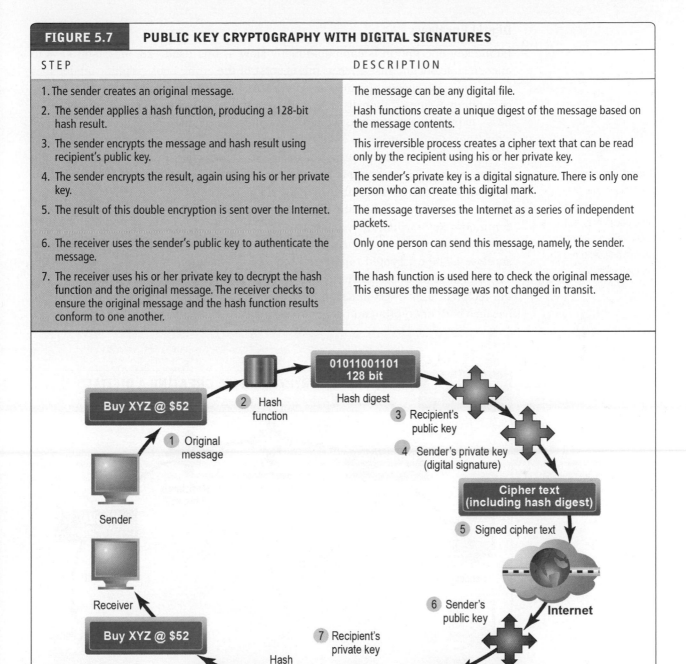

A more realistic use of public key cryptography uses hash functions and digital signatures to both ensure the confidentiality of the message and authenticate the sender. The only person who could have sent the above message is the owner or the sender using his/her private key. This authenticates the message. The hash function ensures the message was not altered in transit. As before, the only person who can decipher the message is the recipient, using his/her private key.

Digital Envelopes

Public key encryption is computationally slow. If one used 128- or 256-bit keys to encode large documents—such as this chapter or the entire book—significant declines in transmission speeds and increases in processing time would occur. Symmetric key encryption is computationally faster, but as we pointed out previously, it has a weakness—namely, the symmetric key must be sent to the recipient over insecure transmission lines. One solution is to use the more efficient symmetric encryption and decryption for large documents, but public key encryption to encrypt and send the symmetric key. This technique is called using a **digital envelope**. See **Figure 5.8** for an illustration of how a digital envelope works.

In Figure 5.8, a diplomatic document is encrypted using a symmetric key. The symmetric key—which the recipient will require to decrypt the document—is itself encrypted, using the recipient's public key. So we have a "key within a key" (a *digital envelope*). The encrypted report and the digital envelope are sent across the Web. The recipient first uses his/her private key to decrypt the symmetric key, and then the recipient uses the symmetric key to decrypt the report. This method saves time because both encryption and decryption are faster with symmetric keys.

digital envelope
a technique that uses symmetric encryption for large documents, but public key encryption to encrypt and send the symmetric key

| FIGURE 5.8 | PUBLIC KEY CRYPTOGRAPHY: CREATING A DIGITAL ENVELOPE |

A digital envelope can be created to transmit a symmetric key that will permit the recipient to decrypt the message and be assured the message was not intercepted in transit.

Digital Certificates and Public Key Infrastructure (PKI)

There are still some deficiencies in the message security regime described previously. How do we know that people and institutions are who they claim to be? Anyone can make up a private and public key combination and claim to be someone they are not. Before you place an order with an online merchant such as Amazon, you want to be sure it really is Amazon.com you have on the screen and not a spoofer masquerading as Amazon. In the physical world, if someone asks who you are and you show a social security number, they may well ask to see a picture ID or a second form of certifiable or acceptable identification. If they really doubt who you are, they may ask for references to other authorities and actually interview these other authorities. Similarly, in the digital world, we need a way to know who people and institutions really are.

Digital certificates, and the supporting public key infrastructure, are an attempt to solve this problem of digital identity. A **digital certificate** is a digital document issued by a trusted third-party institution known as a **certification authority (CA)** that contains the name of the subject or company, the subject's public key, a digital certificate serial number, an expiration date, an issuance date, the digital signature of the certification authority (the name of the CA encrypted using the CA's private key), and other identifying information (see **Figure 5.9**).

In the United States, private corporations such as VeriSign, browser manufacturers, security firms, and government agencies such as the U.S. Postal Service and the

digital certificate
a digital document issued by a certification authority that contains the name of the subject or company, the subject's public key, a digital certificate serial number, an expiration date, an issuance date, the digital signature of the certification authority, and other identifying information

certification authority (CA)
a trusted third party that issues digital certificates

| FIGURE 5.9 | DIGITAL CERTIFICATES AND CERTIFICATION AUTHORITIES |

The PKI includes certification authorities that issue, verify, and guarantee digital certificates that are used in e-commerce to assure the identity of transaction partners.

Federal Reserve issue CAs. Worldwide, thousands of organizations issue CAs. A hierarchy of CAs has emerged with less-well-known CAs being certified by larger and better-known CAs, creating a community of mutually verifying institutions. **Public key infrastructure (PKI)** refers to the CAs and digital certificate procedures that are accepted by all parties. When you sign into a "secure" site, the URL will begin with "https" and a closed lock icon will appear on your browser. This means the site has a digital certificate issued by a trusted CA. It is not, presumably, a spoof site.

public key infrastructure (PKI)
CAs and digital certificate procedures that are accepted by all parties

To create a digital certificate, the user generates a public/private key pair and sends a request for certification to a CA along with the user's public key. The CA verifies the information (how this is accomplished differs from CA to CA). The CA issues a certificate containing the user's public key and other related information. Finally, the CA creates a message digest from the certificate itself (just like a hash digest) and signs it with the CA's private key. This signed digest is called the *signed certificate*. We end up with a totally unique cipher text document—there can be only one signed certificate like this in the world.

There are several ways the certificates are used in commerce. Before initiating a transaction, the customer can request the signed digital certificate of the merchant and decrypt it using the merchant's public key to obtain both the message digest and the certificate as issued. If the message digest matches the certificate, then the merchant and the public key are authenticated. The merchant may in return request certification of the user, in which case the user would send the merchant his or her individual certificate. There are many types of certificates: personal, institutional, Web server, software publisher, and CAs themselves.

Pretty Good Privacy (PGP)
a widely used e-mail public key encryption software program

You can easily obtain a public and private key for personal, noncommercial use at the International PGP Home Page Web site, Pgpi.org. **Pretty Good Privacy (PGP)** was invented in 1991 by Phil Zimmerman, and has become one of the most widely used e-mail public key encryption software tools in the world. Using PGP software installed on your computer, you can compress and encrypt your messages as well as authenticate both yourself and the recipient. There are also a number of Firefox, Chrome, Internet Explorer, and Safari add-ons, extensions, or plug-ins that enable you to encrypt your e-mail.

Limitations to Encryption Solutions

PKI is a powerful technological solution to security issues, but it has many limitations, especially concerning CAs. PKI applies mainly to protecting messages in transit on the Internet and is not effective against insiders—employees—who have legitimate access to corporate systems including customer information. Most e-commerce sites do not store customer information in encrypted form. Other limitations are apparent. For one, how is your private key to be protected? Most private keys will be stored on insecure desktop or laptop computers.

There is no guarantee the person using your computer—and your private key—is really you. For instance, you may lose your laptop or smartphone, and therefore lose the private key. Likewise, there is no assurance that someone else in the world cannot use your personal ID papers, such as a social security card, to obtain a PKI authenticated online ID in your name. If there's no real world identification system, there can be no Internet identification system. Under many digital signature laws, you are responsible for whatever your private key does even if you were not the person using the key. This is very different from mail-order or telephone order credit card rules, where you have a right to dispute the credit card charge. Second, there is no guarantee the verifying computer of the merchant is secure. Third, CAs are self-selected organizations seeking to gain access to the business of authorization. They may not be authorities on the corporations or individuals they certify. For instance, how can a CA know about all the corporations within an industry to determine who is or is not legitimate? A related question concerns the method used by the CA to identify the certificate holder. Was this an e-mail transaction verified only by claims of the applicants who filled out an online form? For instance, VeriSign acknowledged in one case that it had mistakenly issued two digital certificates to someone fraudulently claiming to represent Microsoft. Digital certificates have been hijacked by hackers, tricking consumers into giving up personal information. For example, in 2011, the CA-granting firm Comodo was hacked by an Iranian hacker and lost control of its CA-granting process. The hacker issued hundreds of CAs to servers that appeared to the user to be legitimate sites operated by Google, Yahoo, and others. The Dutch company DigiNotar was hit by a similar attack, and hackers were thought to have obtained more than 200 digital certificates, including ones for Google, Mozilla, and Yahoo, among others. Last, what are the policies for revoking or renewing certificates? The expected life of a digital certificate or private key is a function of the frequency of use and the vulnerability of systems that use the certificate. Yet most CAs have no policy or just an annual policy for reissuing certificates. If Microsoft, Apple, or Cisco ever rescinded a number of CAs, millions of users would not be able to access sites. The CA system is difficult and costly to police.

SECURING CHANNELS OF COMMUNICATION

The concepts of public key encryption are used routinely for securing channels of communication.

Secure Sockets Layer (SSL) and Transport Layer Security (TLS)

The most common form of securing channels is through the *Secure Sockets Layer (SSL)* and *Transport Layer Security (TLS)* protocols. When you receive a message from a server on the Web with which you will be communicating through a secure channel, this means you will be using SSL/TLS to establish a secure negotiated session. (Notice that the URL changes from HTTP to HTTPS.) A **secure negotiated session** is a client-server session in which the URL of the requested document, along with the contents, contents of forms, and the cookies exchanged, are encrypted (see **Figure 5.10**). For instance, your credit card number that you entered into a form would be encrypted. Through a series of handshakes and communications, the browser and the server establish one another's identity by exchanging digital certificates, decide on the strongest shared form of encryption, and then proceed to communicate using an agreed-upon session key. A **session key** is a unique symmetric encryption key chosen just for this single secure session. Once used, it is gone forever. Figure 5.10 shows how this works.

secure negotiated session
a client-server session in which the URL of the requested document, along with the contents, contents of forms, and the cookies exchanged, are encrypted

session key
a unique symmetric encryption key chosen for a single secure session

FIGURE 5.10	SECURE NEGOTIATED SESSIONS USING SSL/TLS

Certificates play a key role in using SSL/TLS to establish a secure communications channel.

In practice, most private individuals do not have a digital certificate. In this case, the merchant server will not request a certificate, but the client browser will request the merchant certificate once a secure session is called for by the server.

SSL/TLS provides data encryption, server authentication, optional client authentication, and message integrity for TCP/IP connections. SSL/TLS addresses the issue of authenticity by allowing users to verify another user's identity or the identity of a server. It also protects the integrity of the messages exchanged. However, once the merchant receives the encrypted credit and order information, that information is typically stored in unencrypted format on the merchant's servers. While SSL/TLS provides secure transactions between merchant and consumer, it only guarantees server-side authentication. Client authentication is optional.

In addition, SSL/TLS cannot provide irrefutability—consumers can order goods or download information products, and then claim the transaction never occurred. Recently, social network sites such as Facebook and Twitter have begun to use SSL/TLS to thwart account hijacking using Firesheep over wireless networks. Firesheep, an add-on for Firefox, can be used by hackers to grab unencrypted cookies used to "remember" a user and allow the hacker to immediately log on to a Web site as that user. SSL/TLS can thwart such an attack because it encrypts the cookie.

Virtual Private Networks (VPNs)

A **virtual private network (VPN)** allows remote users to securely access a corporation's local area network via the Internet, using a variety of VPN protocols. VPNs use both authentication and encryption to secure information from unauthorized persons (providing confidentiality and integrity). Authentication prevents spoofing and misrepresentation of identities. A remote user can connect to a remote private local network using a local ISP. The VPN protocols will establish the link from the client to the corporate network as if the user had dialed into the corporate network directly. The process of connecting one protocol through another (IP) is called *tunneling,* because the VPN creates a private connection by adding an invisible wrapper around a message to hide its content. As the message travels through the Internet between the ISP and the corporate network, it is shielded from prying eyes by an encrypted wrapper.

A VPN is "virtual" in the sense that it appears to users as a dedicated secure line when in fact it is a temporary secure line. The primary use of VPNs is to establish secure communications among business partners—larger suppliers or customers, and employees working remotely. A dedicated connection to a business partner can be very expensive. Using the Internet and VPN as the connection method significantly reduces the cost of secure communications.

virtual private network (VPN)
allows remote users to securely access internal networks via the Internet, using the Point-to-Point Tunneling Protocol (PPTP)

Wireless (Wi-Fi) Networks

Accessing the Internet via a wireless (Wi-Fi) network has its own particular security issues. Early Wi-Fi networks used a security standard called Wired Equivalent Privacy (WEP) to encrypt information. WEP was very weak, and easy for hackers to crack. A new standard, Wi-Fi Protected Access (WPA) was developed that provided a higher standard of protection, but this too soon became vulnerable to intrusion. Today, the current standard is **WPA2**, which uses the AES algorithm for encryption and CCMP, a more advanced authentication code protocol.

PROTECTING NETWORKS

Once you have protected communications as well as possible, the next set of tools to consider are those that can protect your networks, as well as the servers and clients on those networks.

WPA2
wireless security standard that uses the AES algorithm for encryption and CCMP, a more advanced authentication code protocol

Firewalls

Firewalls and proxy servers are intended to build a wall around your network and the attached servers and clients, just like physical-world firewalls protect you from fires for a limited period of time. Firewalls and proxy servers share some similar functions, but they are quite different.

A **firewall** refers to either hardware or software that filters communication packets and prevents some packets from entering or exiting the network based on a security policy. The firewall controls traffic to and from servers and clients, forbidding communications from untrustworthy sources, and allowing other communications from trusted sources to proceed. Every message that is to be sent or received from the network is processed by the firewall, which determines if the message meets security

firewall
refers to either hardware or software that filters communication packets and prevents some packets from entering the network based on a security policy

guidelines established by the business. If it does, it is permitted to be distributed, and if it doesn't, the message is blocked. Firewalls can filter traffic based on packet attributes such as source IP address, destination port or IP address, type of service (such as WWW or HTTP), the domain name of the source, and many other dimensions. Most hardware firewalls that protect local area networks connected to the Internet have default settings that require little if any administrator intervention and employ simple but effective rules that deny incoming packets from a connection that does not originate from an internal request—the firewall only allows connections from servers that you requested service from. A common default setting on hardware firewalls (DSL and cable modem routers) simply ignores efforts to communicate with TCP port 445, the most commonly attacked port. The increasing use of firewalls by home and business Internet users has greatly reduced the effectiveness of attacks, and forced hackers to focus more on e-mail attachments to distribute worms and viruses.

There are two major methods firewalls use to validate traffic: packet filters and application gateways. *Packet filters* examine data packets to determine whether they are destined for a prohibited port or originate from a prohibited IP address (as specified by the security administrator). The filter specifically looks at the source and destination information, as well as the port and packet type, when determining whether the information may be transmitted. One downside of the packet filtering method is that it is susceptible to spoofing, since authentication is not one of its roles.

Application gateways are a type of firewall that filters communications based on the application being requested, rather than the source or destination of the message. Such firewalls also process requests at the application level, farther away from the client computer than packet filters. By providing a central filtering point, application gateways provide greater security than packet filters but can compromise system performance.

Proxy Servers

proxy server (proxy)
software server that handles all communications originating from or being sent to the Internet, acting as a spokesperson or bodyguard for the organization

Proxy servers (proxies) are software servers (often a dedicated computer) that handle all communications originating from or being sent to the Internet by local clients, acting as a spokesperson or bodyguard for the organization. Proxies act primarily to limit access of internal clients to external Internet servers, although some proxy servers act as firewalls as well. Proxy servers are sometimes called *dual-home systems* because they have two network interfaces. To internal computers, a proxy server is known as the *gateway*, while to external computers it is known as a *mail server* or *numeric address*.

When a user on an internal network requests a Web page, the request is routed first to the proxy server. The proxy server validates the user and the nature of the request, and then sends the request onto the Internet. A Web page sent by an external Internet server first passes to the proxy server. If acceptable, the Web page passes onto the internal network Web server and then to the client desktop. By prohibiting users from communicating directly with the Internet, companies can restrict access to certain types of sites, such as pornographic, auction, or stock-trading sites. Proxy servers also improve Web performance by storing frequently requested Web pages locally, reducing upload times, and hiding the internal network's address, thus making

FIGURE 5.11 **FIREWALLS AND PROXY SERVERS**

The primary function of a firewall is to deny access by remote client computers to local computers. The primary purpose of a proxy server is to provide controlled access from local computers to remote computers.

it more difficult for hackers to monitor. **Figure 5.11** illustrates how firewalls and proxy servers protect a local area network from Internet intruders and prevent internal clients from reaching prohibited Web servers.

Intrusion Detection and Prevention Systems

In addition to a firewall and proxy server, an intrusion detection and/or prevention system can be installed. An **intrusion detection system (IDS)** examines network traffic, watching to see if it matches certain patterns or preconfigured rules indicative of an attack. If it detects suspicious activity, the IDS will set off an alarm alerting administrators and log the event in a database. An IDS is useful for detecting malicious activity that a firewall might miss. An **intrusion prevention system (IPS)** has all the functionality of an IDS, with the additional ability to take steps to prevent and block suspicious activities. For instance, an IPS can terminate a session and reset a connection, block traffic from a suspicious IP address, or reconfigure firewall or router security controls.

PROTECTING SERVERS AND CLIENTS

Operating system features and anti-virus software can help further protect servers and clients from certain types of attacks.

Operating System Security Enhancements

The most obvious way to protect servers and clients is to take advantage of automatic computer security upgrades. The Microsoft, Apple, and Linux/Unix operating systems

intrusion detection system (IDS)
examines network traffic, watching to see if it matches certain patterns or preconfigured rules indicative of an attack

intrusion prevention system (IPS)
has all the functionality of an IDS, with the additional ability to take steps to prevent and block suspicious activities

are continuously updated to patch vulnerabilities discovered by hackers. These patches are autonomic; that is, when using these operating systems on the Internet, you are prompted and informed that operating system enhancements are available. Users can easily download these security patches for free. The most common known worms and viruses can be prevented by simply keeping your server and client operating systems and applications up to date. Application vulnerabilities are fixed in the same manner. For instance, most popular Internet browsers are updated automatically with little user intervention.

Anti-Virus Software

The easiest and least-expensive way to prevent threats to system integrity is to install anti-virus software. Programs by McAfee, Symantec (Norton AntiVirus), and many others provide inexpensive tools to identify and eradicate the most common types of malicious code as they enter a computer, as well as destroy those already lurking on a hard drive. Anti-virus programs can be set up so that e-mail attachments are inspected before you click on them, and the attachments are eliminated if they contain a known virus or worm. It is not enough, however, to simply install the software once. Since new viruses are developed and released every day, daily routine updates are needed in order to prevent new threats from being loaded. Some premium-level anti-virus software is updated hourly.

Anti-virus suite packages and stand-alone programs are available to eliminate intruders such as bot programs, adware, and other security risks. Such programs work much like anti-virus software in that they look for recognized hacker tools or signature actions of known intruders.

5.4 MANAGEMENT POLICIES, BUSINESS PROCEDURES, AND PUBLIC LAWS

Worldwide, in 2013, companies are expected to spend over $65 billion on security hardware, software, and services (Gartner, 2013). However, most CEOs and CIOs believe that technology is not the sole answer to managing the risk of e-commerce. The technology provides a foundation, but in the absence of intelligent management policies, even the best technology can be easily defeated. Public laws and active enforcement of cybercrime statutes also are required to both raise the costs of illegal behavior on the Internet and guard against corporate abuse of information. Let's consider briefly the development of management policy.

A SECURITY PLAN: MANAGEMENT POLICIES

In order to minimize security threats, e-commerce firms must develop a coherent corporate policy that takes into account the nature of the risks, the information assets that need protecting, and the procedures and technologies required to address the risk, as well as implementation and auditing mechanisms. **Figure 5.12** illustrates the key steps in developing a solid security plan.

FIGURE 5.12	DEVELOPING AN E-COMMERCE SECURITY PLAN

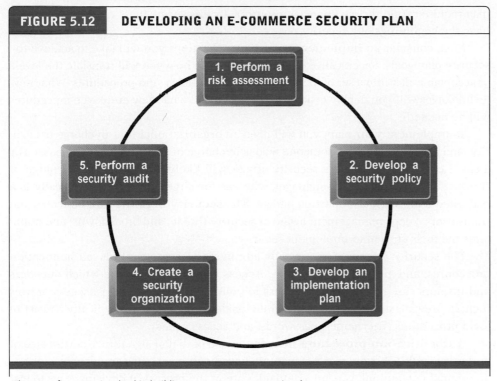

There are five steps involved in building an e-commerce security plan.

A security plan begins with **risk assessment**—an assessment of the risks and points of vulnerability. The first step is to inventory the information and knowledge assets of the e-commerce site and company. What information is at risk? Is it customer information, proprietary designs, business activities, secret processes, or other internal information, such as price schedules, executive compensation, or payroll? For each type of information asset, try to estimate the dollar value to the firm if this information were compromised, and then multiply that amount by the probability of the loss occurring. Once you have done so, rank order the results. You now have a list of information assets prioritized by their value to the firm.

Based on your quantified list of risks, you can start to develop a **security policy**—a set of statements prioritizing the information risks, identifying acceptable risk targets, and identifying the mechanisms for achieving these targets. You will obviously want to start with the information assets that you determined to be the highest priority in your risk assessment. Who generates and controls this information in the firm? What existing security policies are in place to protect the information? What enhancements can you recommend to improve security of these most valuable assets? What level of risk are you willing to accept for each of these assets? Are you willing, for instance, to lose customer credit card data once every 10 years? Or will you pursue a 100-year hurricane strategy by building a security edifice for credit card data that can withstand the once-in-100-year disaster? You will need to estimate how much it will cost to achieve this level of acceptable risk. Remember, total and complete security

risk assessment
an assessment of the risks and points of vulnerability

security policy
a set of statements prioritizing the information risks, identifying acceptable risk targets, and identifying the mechanisms for achieving these targets

implementation plan
the action steps you will take to achieve the security plan goals

security organization
educates and trains users, keeps management aware of security threats and breakdowns, and maintains the tools chosen to implement security

access controls
determine who can gain legitimate access to a network

authentication procedures
include the use of digital signatures, certificates of authority, and public key infrastructure

biometrics
the study of measurable biological or physical characteristics

security token
physical device or software that generates an identifier that can be used in addition to or in place of a password

authorization policies
determine differing levels of access to information assets for differing levels of users

authorization management system
establishes where and when a user is permitted to access certain parts of a Web site

may require extraordinary financial resources. By answering these questions, you will have the beginnings of a security policy.

Next, consider an **implementation plan**—the steps you will take to achieve the security plan goals. Specifically, you must determine how you will translate the levels of acceptable risk into a set of tools, technologies, policies, and procedures. What new technologies will you deploy to achieve the goals, and what new employee procedures will be needed?

To implement your plan, you will need an organizational unit in charge of security, and a security officer—someone who is in charge of security on a daily basis. For a small e-commerce site, the security officer will likely be the person in charge of Internet services or the site manager, whereas for larger firms, there typically is a dedicated team with a supporting budget. The **security organization** educates and trains users, keeps management aware of security threats and breakdowns, and maintains the tools chosen to implement security.

The security organization typically administers access controls, authentication procedures, and authorization policies. **Access controls** determine which outsiders and insiders can gain legitimate access to your networks. Outsider access controls include firewalls and proxy servers, while insider access controls typically consist of login procedures (usernames, passwords, and access codes).

Authentication procedures include the use of digital signatures, certificates of authority, and PKI. Now that e-signatures have been given the same legal weight as an original pen-and-ink version, companies are in the process of devising ways to test and confirm a signer's identity. Companies frequently have signers type their full name and click on a button indicating their understanding that they have just signed a contract or document.

Biometric devices can also be used to verify physical attributes associated with an individual, such as a fingerprint or retina (eye) scan or speech recognition system. (**Biometrics** is the study of measurable biological, or physical, characteristics.) A company could require, for example, that an individual undergo a fingerprint scan before being allowed access to a Web site, or before being allowed to pay for merchandise with a credit card. Biometric devices make it even more difficult for hackers to break into sites or facilities, significantly reducing the opportunity for spoofing. Security tokens are used by millions of corporation and government workers to log on to corporate clients and servers. Apple's new iPhone 5S features a unique fingerprint sensor called the Touch ID built into the iPhone's home button to unlock the phone and authorize purchases from the iTunes, iBooks, and App stores without requiring users to enter a PIN or other security code. According to Apple, the system does not store an actual fingerprint, but rather biometric data, which will be encrypted and stored only on a chip within the iPhone, and will not be made available to third parties.

Security tokens are physical devices or software that generate an identifier that can be used in addition to or in place of a password. One example is RSA's SecurID token, which continuously generates six-digit passwords.

Authorization policies determine differing levels of access to information assets for differing levels of users. **Authorization management systems** establish where and when a user is permitted to access certain parts of a Web site. Their primary function is to restrict access to private information within a company's Internet infrastructure. Although there are several authorization management products currently available, most operate in the same way: the system encrypts a user session to function like a passkey that follows the user from page to page, allowing access only to those areas that the user is permitted to enter, based on information set at the system database. By establishing entry rules up front for each user, the authorization management system knows who is permitted to go where at all times.

The last step in developing an e-commerce security plan is performing a security audit. A **security audit** involves the routine review of access logs (identifying how outsiders are using the site as well as how insiders are accessing the site's assets). A monthly report should be produced that establishes the routine and nonroutine accesses to the systems and identifies unusual patterns of activities. As previously noted, tiger teams are often used by large corporate sites to evaluate the strength of existing security procedures. Many small firms have sprung up in the last five years to provide these services to large corporate sites.

security audit
involves the routine review of access logs (identifying how outsiders are using the site as well as how insiders are accessing the site's assets)

THE ROLE OF LAWS AND PUBLIC POLICY

The public policy environment today is very different from the early days of e-commerce. The net result is that the Internet is no longer an ungoverned, unsupervised, self-controlled technology juggernaut. Just as with financial markets in the last 70 years, there is a growing awareness that e-commerce markets work only when a powerful institutional set of laws and enforcement mechanisms are in place. These laws help ensure orderly, rational, and fair markets. This growing public policy environment is becoming just as global as e-commerce itself. Despite some spectacular internationally based attacks on U.S. e-commerce sites, the sources and persons involved in major harmful attacks have almost always been uncovered and, where possible, prosecuted.

Voluntary and private efforts have played a very large role in identifying criminal hackers and assisting law enforcement. Since 1995, as e-commerce has grown in significance, national and local law enforcement activities have expanded greatly. New laws have been passed that grant local and national authorities new tools and mechanisms for identifying, tracing, and prosecuting cybercriminals. For instance, a majority of states now require companies that maintain personal data on their residents to publicly disclose when a security breach affecting those residents has occurred. **Table 5.5** on page 294 lists the most significant federal e-commerce security legislation and regulation.

Following passage of the National Information Infrastructure Protection Act of 1996, which makes DoS attacks and virus distribution federal crimes, the FBI and the Department of Justice established the National Infrastructure Protection Center (NIPC). Now subsumed within the National Cyber Security Division of the Department of Homeland Security, this organization's sole mission is to identify and combat threats against the United States' technology and telecommunications infrastructure.

By increasing the punishment for cybercrimes, the U.S. government is attempting to create a deterrent to further hacker actions. And by making such actions federal crimes, the government is able to extradite international hackers and prosecute them within the United States.

TABLE 5.5	E-COMMERCE SECURITY LEGISLATION AND REGULATION
LEGISLATION/REGULATION	SIGNIFICANCE
Computer Fraud and Abuse Act (1986)	Primary federal statute used to combat computer crime.
Electronic Communications Privacy Act (1986)	Imposes fines and imprisonment for individuals who access, intercept, or disclose the private e-mail communications of others.
National Information Infrastructure Protection Act (1996)	Makes DoS attacks illegal; creates NIPC in the FBI.
Health Insurance Portability and Accountability Act (1996)	Requires certain health care facilities to report data breaches.
Financial Modernization Act (Gramm-Leach-Bliley Act) (1999)	Requires certain financial institutions to report data breaches.
Cyberspace Electronic Security Act (2000)	Reduces export restrictions.
Computer Security Enhancement Act (2000)	Protects federal government systems from hacking.
Electronic Signatures in Global and National Commerce Act (the "E-Sign Law") (2000)	Authorizes the use of electronic signatures in legal documents.
USA PATRIOT Act (2001)	Authorizes use of computer-based surveillance of suspected terrorists.
Homeland Security Act (2002)	Authorizes establishment of the Department of Homeland Security, which is responsible for developing a comprehensive national plan for security of the key resources and critical infrastructures of the United States; DHS becomes the central coordinator for all cyberspace security efforts.
CAN-SPAM Act (2003)	Although primarily a mechanism for civil and regulatory lawsuits against spammers, the CAN-SPAM Act also creates several new criminal offenses intended to address situations in which the perpetrator has taken steps to hide his or her identity or the source of the spam from recipients, ISPs, or law enforcement agencies. Also contains criminal sanctions for sending sexually explicit e-mail without designating it as such.
U.S. SAFE WEB Act (2006)	Enhances FTC's ability to obtain monetary redress for consumers in cases involving spyware, spam, Internet fraud, and deception; also improves FTC's ability to gather information and coordinate investigations with foreign counterparts.
Improving Critical Infrastructure Cybersecurity Executive Order (2013)	After Congress failed to pass cybersecurity legislation in 2012, this executive order issued by the Obama administration directs federal agenices to share cybersecurity threat intelligence with private sector companies that may be targets, and the development and implementation of a cybersecurity framework for private industry, incorporating best practices and voluntary standards.

After September 11, 2001, Congress passed the USA PATRIOT Act, which broadly expanded law enforcement's investigative and surveillance powers. The act has provisions for monitoring e-mail and Internet use. The Homeland Security Act of 2002 also attempts to fight cyberterrorism and increases the government's ability to compel information disclosure by computer and ISP sources. Recent proposed legislation that focuses on requiring firms to report data breaches to the FTC, protection of the national electric grid, and cybersecurity has all failed to pass.

Private and Private-Public Cooperation Efforts

The good news is that e-commerce sites are not alone in their battle to achieve security on the Internet. Several organizations—some public and some private—are devoted to tracking down criminal organizations and individuals engaged in attacks against Internet and e-commerce sites. One of the better-known private organizations is the **CERT Coordination Center** (formerly known as the Computer Emergency Response Team) at Carnegie Mellon University. CERT monitors and tracks online criminal activity reported to it by private corporations and government agencies that seek out its help. CERT is composed of full-time and part-time computer experts who can trace the origins of attacks against sites despite the complexity of the Internet. Its staff members also assist organizations in identifying security problems, developing solutions, and communicating with the public about widespread hacker threats. The CERT Coordination Center also provides product assessments, reports, and training in order to improve the public's knowledge and understanding of security threats and solutions. The U.S. Department of Homeland Security (DHS) operates the **United States Computer Emergency Readiness Team (US-CERT)**, which coordinates cyber incident warnings and responses across both the government and private sectors.

CERT Coordination Center
monitors and tracks online criminal activity reported to it by private corporations and government agencies that seek out its help

US-CERT
division of the U.S. Department of Homeland Security that coordinates cyber incident warnings and responses across government and private sectors

Government Policies and Controls on Encryption Software

In the United States, both Congress and the executive branch have sought to regulate the uses of encryption and to restrict availability and export of encryption systems as a means of preventing crime and terrorism. At the international level, four organizations have influenced the international traffic in encryption software: the Organization for Economic Cooperation and Development (OECD), G-7/G-8 (the heads of state of the top eight industrialized countries in the world), the Council of Europe, and the Wassenar Arrangement (law enforcement personnel from the top 33 industrialized counties in the world). Various governments have proposed schemes for controlling encryption software or at least preventing criminals from obtaining strong encryption tools (see **Table 5.6**). The U.S. and U.K. governments are also devoting a large amount of resources to cryptography-related programs that will enable them to break encrypted communications collected on the Internet. Documents leaked by former NSA contractor Edward Snowden indicate that both the NSA and its U.K. counterpart, the GCHQ, may be able to break encryption schemes used by SSL/TLS, VPNs, and on 4G smartphones (Vaughan-Nichols, 2013).

TABLE 5.6	GOVERNMENT EFFORTS TO REGULATE AND CONTROL ENCRYPTION
REGULATORY EFFORT	IMPACT
Restricted export of strong security systems	Supported primarily by the United States. Widespread distribution of encryption schemes weakens this policy. The policy is changing to permit exports except to pariah countries.
Key escrow/key recovery schemes	France, the United Kingdom, and the United States supported this effort in the late 1990s but now have largely abandoned it. There are few trusted third parties.
Lawful access and forced disclosure	Growing support in U.S. legislation and in OECD countries.
Official hacking	All countries are rapidly expanding budgets and training for law enforcement "technical centers" aimed at monitoring and cracking computer-based, encryption activities of suspected criminals.

5.5 PAYMENT SYSTEMS

TYPES OF PAYMENT SYSTEMS

In order to understand e-commerce payment systems, you first need to be familiar with the various types of generic payment systems. Then you will be able to clarify the different requirements that e-commerce payment systems must meet and identify the opportunities provided by e-commerce technology for developing new types of payment systems. There are five main types of payment systems: cash, checking transfer, credit cards, stored value, and accumulating balance.

Cash

cash

legal tender defined by a national authority to represent value

Cash, which is legal tender defined by a national authority to represent value, is the most common form of payment in terms of number of transactions. The key feature of cash is that it is instantly convertible into other forms of value without the intermediation of any other institution. For instance, free airline miles are not cash because they are not instantly convertible into other forms of value—they require intermediation by a third party (the airline) in order to be exchanged for value (an airline ticket). Private organizations sometimes create a form of private cash called scrip that can be instantly redeemed by participating organizations for goods or cash. Examples include trading stamps, "point" programs, and other forms of consumer loyalty currency.

Why is cash still so popular today? Cash is portable, requires no authentication, and provides instant purchasing power for those who possess it. Cash allows for micropayments (payments of small amounts). The use of cash is "free" in that neither merchants nor consumers pay a transaction fee for using it. Using cash does not require any complementary assets, such as special hardware or the existence of an account, and it puts very low cognitive demands on the user. Cash is anonymous and difficult to trace, and in that sense it is "private." Other forms of payment require significant use of third parties and leave an extensive digital or paper trail.

On the other hand, cash is limited to smaller transactions (you can't easily buy a car or house with cash), it is easily stolen, and it does not provide any **float** (the period of time between a purchase and actual payment for the purchase); when it is spent, it is gone. With cash, purchases tend to be final and irreversible (i.e., they are irrefutable) unless otherwise agreed by the seller.

float
the period of time between a purchase and actual payment for the purchase

Checking Transfer

A **checking transfer**, which represents funds transferred directly via a signed draft or check from a consumer's checking account to a merchant or other individual, is the second most common form of payment in the United States in terms of number of transactions, and the most common in terms of total amount spent.

checking transfer
funds transferred directly via a signed draft or check from a consumer's checking account to a merchant or other individual

Checks can be used for both small and large transactions, although typically they are not used for micropayments (less than $1). Checks have some float (it can take up to 10 days for out-of-state checks to clear), and the unspent balances can earn interest. Checks are not anonymous and require third-party institutions to work. Checks also introduce security risks for merchants: They can be forged more easily than cash, so authentication is required. For merchants, checks also present some additional risk compared to cash because they can be canceled before they clear the account or they may bounce if there is not enough money in the account.

Credit Card

A **credit card** represents an account that extends credit to consumers, permits consumers to purchase items while deferring payment, and allows consumers to make payments to multiple vendors with one instrument. **Credit card associations** such as Visa and MasterCard are nonprofit associations that set standards for the **issuing banks**—such as Citibank—that actually issue the credit cards and process transactions. Other third parties (called **processing centers** or **clearinghouses**) usually handle verification of accounts and balances. Credit card issuing banks act as financial intermediaries, minimizing the risk to transacting parties.

credit card
represents an account that extends credit to consumers, permits consumers to purchase items while deferring payment, and allows consumers to make payments to multiple vendors at one time

credit card association
nonprofit association that sets standards for issuing banks

issuing bank
bank that actually issues credit cards and processes transactions

processing center (clearinghouse)
institution that handles verification of accounts and balances

Credit cards offer consumers a line of credit and the ability to make small and large purchases instantly. They are widely accepted as a form of payment, reduce the risk of theft associated with carrying cash, and increase consumer convenience. Credit cards also offer consumers considerable float. With a credit card, for instance, a consumer typically need not actually pay for goods purchased until receiving a credit card bill 30 days later. There were around 540 million credit cards in circulation in the United States in 2012 (Nilson Report, 2013). Merchants benefit from increased consumer spending resulting from credit card use, but they pay a hefty transaction fee of 3% to 5% of the purchase price to the issuing banks. In addition, federal Regulation Z places the risks of the transaction (such as credit card fraud, repudiation of the transaction, or nonpayment) largely on the merchant and credit card issuing bank. Regulation Z limits cardholder liability to $50 for unauthorized transactions that occur before the card issuer is notified. Once a card is reported stolen, consumers are not liable for any subsequent charges.

Credit cards have less finality than other payment systems because consumers can refute or repudiate purchases under certain circumstances, and they limit risk for consumers while raising risk for merchants and bankers.

Stored Value

stored value payment system
account created by depositing funds into an account and from which funds are paid out or withdrawn as needed

Accounts created by depositing funds into an account and from which funds are paid out or withdrawn as needed are **stored value payment systems**. Stored value payment systems are similar in some respects to checking transfers—which also store funds—but do not involve writing a check. Examples include debit cards, gift certificates, prepaid cards, and smart cards (described in greater detail later in the chapter). **Debit cards** immediately debit a checking or other demand-deposit account. For many consumers, the use of a debit card eliminates the need to write a paper check. There were 560 million debit cards in use nationwide in 2012 (The Nilson Report, 2013). However, because debit cards are dependent on funds being available in a consumer's bank account, larger purchases are still typically paid for by credit card, and their use in the United States still lags behind that of other developed nations, in part because they do not have the protections provided by Regulation Z and they do not provide any float.

debit card
immediately debits a checking or other demand-deposit account

Peer-to-peer (P2P) payment systems such as PayPal (discussed further in Section 5.6) are variations on the stored value concept. P2P payment systems do not insist on prepayment but do require an account with a stored value, either a checking account with funds available or a credit card with an available credit balance. PayPal is often referred to as a P2P payment system because it allows small merchants and individuals to accept payments without using a merchant bank or processor to clear the transaction.

Accumulating Balance

accumulating balance payment system
account that accumulates expenditures and to which consumers make periodic payments

Accounts that accumulate expenditures and to which consumers make periodic payments are **accumulating balance payment systems**. Traditional examples include utility, phone, and American Express accounts, all of which accumulate balances, usually over a specified period (typically a month), and then are paid in full at the end of the period.

PAYMENT SYSTEMS STAKEHOLDERS

The main stakeholders in payment systems are consumers, merchants, financial intermediaries, and government regulators. Each of these stakeholders has different preferences. Consumers are interested primarily in low-risk, low-cost, refutable (able to be repudiated or denied), convenient, and reliable payment mechanisms. Consumers have demonstrated they will not use new payment mechanisms unless they are equally or more beneficial to them than existing systems. In general, most consumers use cash, checks, and/or credit cards. The specific payment system chosen will change depending on the transaction situation. For instance, cash may be preferred to keep certain transactions private and anonymous, but the same consumer may want a record of transaction for the purchase of a car.

Merchants are interested primarily in low-risk, low-cost, irrefutable (i.e., final), secure, and reliable payment mechanisms. Merchants currently carry much of the risk of checking and credit card fraud, refutability of charges, and much of the hardware cost of verifying payments. Merchants typically prefer payments made by cash, check, and to a lesser extent credit cards, which usually carry high fees and allow transactions to be repudiated after the fact by consumers.

Financial intermediaries, such as banks and credit card networks, are primarily interested in secure payment systems that transfer risks and costs to consumers and merchants, while maximizing transaction fees payable to themselves. The preferred payment mechanisms for financial intermediaries are checking transfers, debit cards, and credit cards.

Government regulators are interested in maintaining trust in the financial system. Regulators seek to protect against fraud and abuse in the use of payment systems; ensure that the interests of consumers and merchants are balanced against the interests of the financial intermediaries whom they regulate; and enforce information reporting laws. The most important regulations of payment systems in the United States are Regulation Z, Regulation E, and the Electronic Funds Transfer Act (EFTA) of 1978, regulating ATM machines. Regulation Z limits the risk to consumers when using credit cards. In contrast, EFTA and Regulation E place more risk on consumers when using debit or ATM cards. For instance, if you lose an ATM card or debit card, you are potentially liable for any losses to the account. However, in reality, Visa and MasterCard have issued policies that limit consumer risk for loss of debit cards to the same $50 that applies to credit cards.

5.6   E-COMMERCE PAYMENT SYSTEMS

For the most part, existing payment mechanisms have been able to be adapted to the online environment, albeit with some significant limitations that have led to efforts to develop alternatives. In addition, new types of purchasing relationships, such as between individuals online, and new technologies, such as the development of the mobile platform, have also created both a need and an opportunity for the development of new payment systems. In this section, we provide an overview of the major e-commerce payment systems in use today. **Table 5.7** lists some of the major trends in e-commerce payments in 2013–2014.

TABLE 5.7	MAJOR TRENDS IN E-COMMERCE PAYMENTS 2013–2014

- Payment by credit and/or debit card remains the dominant form of online payment.
- Mobile retail payment volume skyrockets.
- PayPal remains the most popular alternative payment method online.
- Start-up Square begins to gain traction with a smartphone app, credit card reader, and credit card processing service that permits anyone to accept credit card payments.
- Google introduces Google Wallet, a mobile payment system based on near field communication (NFC) chips; Apple continues to go its own way, releasing iPhone 5S with fingerprint sensing technology but without NFC chips.

U.S. online payments represent a market of almost $420 billion in 2013, and are expect to grow an additional $220 million to around $640 billion by 2017. Institutions and business firms that can handle this volume of transactions (mostly the large banking and credit firms) generally extract 2%–3% of the transactions in the form of fees, or about $8 to $13 billion a year in revenue. Given the size of the market, competition for online payments is spirited.

In the United States, the primary form of online payment is still the existing credit card system. Although credit card usage slipped somewhat during the recession, the total payments volume for online use of credit cards by U.S. consumers is expected to remain steady through 2017, while usage of debit cards decline. Alternative payment methods, although currently representing around 16% of e-commerce transactions, are expected to continue to make inroads into traditional payment methods, growing to around 20% of all online payment transactions by 2017. Mobile payments are also expected to grow significantly by 2017 (Javelin Strategy & Research, 2012; Digital Transactions, 2012). **Figure 5.13** illustrates the approximate usage of various payment types. **Figure 5.14** illustrates the percentage of consumers that use various alternative payment methods.

In other parts of the world, e-commerce payments can be very different depending on traditions and infrastructure. Credit cards are not nearly as dominant a form of online payment as they are in the United States. If you plan on operating a Web site in Europe, Asia, or Latin America, you will need to develop different payment

FIGURE 5.13	ONLINE PAYMENT METHODS IN THE UNITED STATES

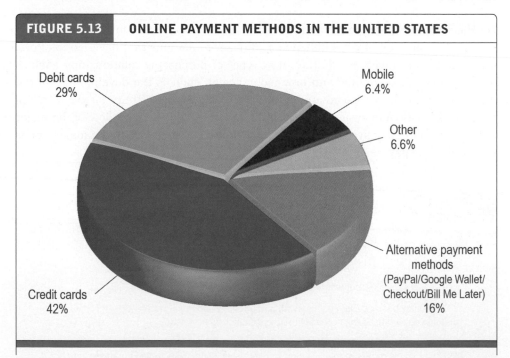

Traditional credit cards are still the dominant method of payment for online purchases, although alternative methods such as PayPal and mobile payments are faster growing.

SOURCES: Based on data from Javelin Strategy & Research, 2012; Digital Transactions, 2012; industry sources.

FIGURE 5.14	ALTERNATIVE PAYMENT METHODS USED BY CONSUMERS IN THE UNITED STATES, 2012

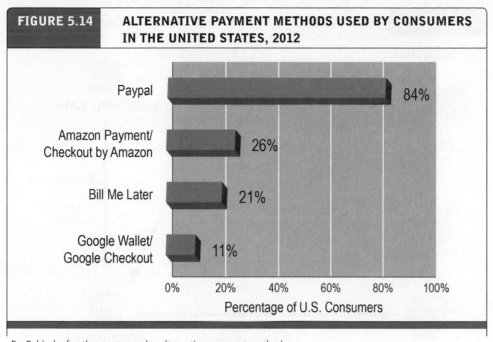

PayPal is, by far, the most popular alternative payment method.

SOURCES: Based on data from Javelin Strategy & Research, 2012; Digital Transactions, 2012.

systems for each region. Consumers in Europe rely for the most part on bank debit cards (especially in Germany) and some credit cards. Online purchases in China are typically paid for by check or cash when the consumer picks up the goods at a local store. In Japan, consumers use postal and bank transfers and CODs, using local convenience stores (konbini) as the pickup and payment point. Japanese consumers also use accumulated balance accounts with the telephone company for Internet purchases made from their home computers. Japan and some European countries make extensive use of mobile phones for payment of small purchases (and even parking tickets).

ONLINE CREDIT CARD TRANSACTIONS

Because credit and debit cards are the dominant form of online payment, it is important to understand how they work and to recognize the strengths and weaknesses of this payment system. Online credit card transactions are processed in much the same way that in-store purchases are, with the major differences being that online merchants never see the actual card being used, no card impression is taken, and no signature is available. Online credit card transactions most closely resemble Mail Order-Telephone Order (MOTO) transactions. These types of purchases are also called Cardholder Not Present (CNP) transactions and are the major reason that charges can be disputed later by consumers. Since the merchant never sees the credit card, nor receives a hand-signed agreement to pay from the customer, when disputes arise, the merchant faces the risk that the transaction may be disallowed and reversed, even though he has already shipped the goods or the user has downloaded a digital product.

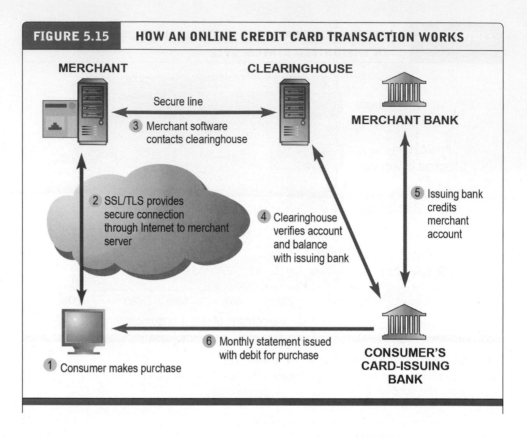

FIGURE 5.15 — **HOW AN ONLINE CREDIT CARD TRANSACTION WORKS**

MERCHANT

CLEARINGHOUSE

Secure line

③ Merchant software contacts clearinghouse

MERCHANT BANK

② SSL/TLS provides secure connection through Internet to merchant server

④ Clearinghouse verifies account and balance with issuing bank

⑤ Issuing bank credits merchant account

① Consumer makes purchase

⑥ Monthly statement issued with debit for purchase

CONSUMER'S CARD-ISSUING BANK

merchant account

a bank account that allows companies to process credit card payments and receive funds from those transactions

Figure 5.15 illustrates the online credit card purchasing cycle. There are five parties involved in an online credit card purchase: consumer, merchant, clearinghouse, merchant bank (sometimes called the "acquiring bank"), and the consumer's card-issuing bank. In order to accept payments by credit card, online merchants must have a merchant account established with a bank or financial institution. A **merchant account** is simply a bank account that allows companies to process credit card payments and receive funds from those transactions.

As shown in Figure 5.15, an online credit card transaction begins with a purchase (1). When a consumer wants to make a purchase, he or she adds the item to the merchant's shopping cart. When the consumer wants to pay for the items in the shopping cart, a secure tunnel through the Internet is created using SSL/TLS. Using encryption, SSL/TLS secures the session during which credit card information will be sent to the merchant and protects the information from interlopers on the Internet (2). SSL does not authenticate either the merchant or the consumer. The transacting parties have to trust one another.

Once the consumer credit card information is received by the merchant, the merchant software contacts a clearinghouse (3). As previously noted, a clearinghouse is a financial intermediary that authenticates credit cards and verifies account balances. The clearinghouse contacts the issuing bank to verify the account information (4). Once verified, the issuing bank credits the account of the merchant at the merchant's bank (usually this occurs at night in a batch process) (5). The debit to the consumer account is transmitted to the consumer in a monthly statement (6).

Credit Card E-commerce Enablers

Companies that have a merchant account still need to buy or build a means of handling the online transaction; securing the merchant account is only step one in a two-part process. Today, Internet payment service providers (sometimes referred to as payment gateways) can provide both a merchant account and the software tools needed to process credit card purchases online.

For instance, Authorize.net is an Internet payment service provider. The company helps a merchant secure an account with one of its merchant account provider partners and then provides payment processing software for installation on the merchant's server. The software collects the transaction information from the merchant's site and then routes it via the Authorize.net "payment gateway" to the appropriate bank, ensuring that customers are authorized to make their purchases. The funds for the transaction are then transferred to the merchant's merchant account. CyberSource is another well-known Internet payment service provider.

Limitations of Online Credit Card Payment Systems

There are a number of limitations to the existing credit card payment system. The most important limitations involve security, merchant risk, administrative and transaction costs, and social equity.

The existing system offers poor security. Neither the merchant nor the consumer can be fully authenticated. The merchant could be a criminal organization designed to collect credit card numbers, and the consumer could be a thief using stolen or fraudulent cards. The risk facing merchants is high: consumers can repudiate charges even though the goods have been shipped or the product downloaded. The banking industry attempted to develop a secure electronic transaction (SET) protocol, but this effort failed because it was too complex for consumers and merchants alike.

The administrative costs of setting up an online credit card system and becoming authorized to accept credit cards are high. Transaction costs for merchants also are significant—roughly 3.5% of the purchase plus a transaction fee of 20–30 cents per transaction, plus other setup fees.

Credit cards are not very democratic, even though they seem ubiquitous. Millions of young adults do not have credit cards, along with almost 100 million other adult Americans who cannot afford cards or who are considered poor risks because of low incomes.

ALTERNATIVE ONLINE PAYMENT SYSTEMS

The limitations of the online credit card system have opened the way for the development of a number of alternative online payment systems. Chief among them is PayPal. PayPal (purchased by eBay in 2002) enables individuals and businesses with e-mail accounts to make and receive payments up to a specified limit. Paypal is an example of an **online stored value payment system**, which permits consumers to make instant, online payments to merchants and other individuals based on value stored in

online stored value payment system
permits consumers to make instant, online payments to merchants and other individuals based on value stored in an online account

an online account. In 2012, PayPal processed $145 billion in payments ($48 billion of which were generated on eBay, and $97 billion elsewhere on the Web), and had 132 million active registered users. PayPal builds on the existing financial infrastructure of the countries in which it operates. You establish a PayPal account by specifying a credit, debit, or checking account you wish to have charged or paid when conducting online transactions. When you make a payment using PayPal, you e-mail the payment to the merchant's PayPal account. PayPal transfers the amount from your credit or checking account to the merchant's bank account. The beauty of PayPal is that no personal credit information has to be shared among the users, and the service can be used by individuals to pay one another even in small amounts. Issues with PayPal include its high cost (in addition to paying the credit card fee of 3.5%, PayPal tacks on a variable fee of 1.5%–3% depending on the size of the transaction) and its lack of consumer protections when a fraud occurs or a charge is repudiated. PayPal is discussed in further depth in the case study at the end of the chapter.

Although PayPal is by far the most well-known and commonly used online credit/debit card alternative, there are a number of other alternatives as well. Amazon Payments is aimed at consumers who have concerns about entrusting their credit card information to unfamiliar online retailers. Consumers can purchase goods and services at non-Amazon Web sites using the payment methods stored in their Amazon accounts, without having to reenter their payment information at the merchant's site. Amazon provides the payment processing. Google Checkout (now merged into Google Wallet, described further in the following section on mobile payment systems) offers similar functionality, enabling consumers to sign in once and then shop online at thousands of different stores without having to reenter account information.

Bill Me Later (owned by eBay as well) also appeals to consumers who do not wish to enter their credit card information online. Bill Me Later describes itself as an open-ended credit account. Users select the Bill Me Later option at checkout and are asked to provide their birth date and the last four digits of their social security number. They are then billed for the purchase by Bill Me Later within 10 to 14 days. Bill Me Later is currently offered by more than 1,000 online merchants.

WUPay (formerly eBillme, and now operated by Western Union) offers a similar service. WUPay customers who select the WUPay option at firms such as Sears, Kmart, Buy.com, and other retailers do not have to provide any credit card information. Instead they are e-mailed a bill, which they can pay via their bank's online bill payment service, or in person at any Western Union location. Dwolla is a similar cash-based payment network for both individuals and merchants. It bypasses the credit card network and instead connects directly into a bank account. Dwolla is free for transactions under $10 and only 25 cents per transaction for those over $10, and is currently available at more than 15,000 merchants.

Like Dwolla, Stripe is another company that is attempting to provide an alternative to the traditional online credit card system. Stripe focuses on the merchant side of the process. It provides simple software code that enables companies to bypass much of the administrative costs involved in setting up an online credit card system, and instead lets companies begin accepting credit card payments almost immediately without the need to obtain a merchant account or use a gateway provider. Unlike

PayPal, the customer doesn't need a Stripe account to pay, and all payments are made directly to the company rather than being routed through a third party.

MOBILE PAYMENT SYSTEMS: YOUR SMARTPHONE WALLET

The use of mobile devices as payment mechanisms is already well established in Europe, Japan, and South Korea and is now exploding in the United States, where the infrastructure to support mobile payment is finally being put in place. Mobile retail payments in the United States totalled over $20 billion in 2012 (Javelin Strategy & Research, 2012).

Near field communication (NFC) is one of the enabling technologies for mobile payment systems. **Near field communication (NFC)** is a set of short-range wireless technologies used to share information among devices within about 2 inches of each other (50 mm). NFC devices are either powered or passive. A connection requires one powered unit (the initiator), and one target unpowered unit that can respond to requests from the powered unit. NFC targets can be very simple forms such as tags, stickers, key fobs, or readers. NFC peer-to-peer communication is possible where both devices are powered. An NFC-equipped smartphone, for instance, can be swiped by a merchant's reader to record a payment wirelessly and without contact. In September 2011, Google introduced Google Wallet, a mobile app designed to work with NFC chips. Google Wallet currently works with the MasterCard PayPass contactless payment card system. It is also designed to work with Android smartphones that are equipped with NFC chips. About 20 million smartphones in the United States are now equipped with NFC, and over 140 million were sold worldwide in 2012. Almost all high-end smartphones now include NFC support, with the exception of the iPhone. Apple's iPhone 5S, introduced in September 2013, included a fingerprint sensor with technology it calls Touch ID, which will enable it to be used to authorize payments at the iTunes, iBooks, and App Stores without requiring users to enter a separate PIN or security code. However, Apple's failure thus far to include an NFC chip in the iPhone has slowed the adoption of NFC-based mobile wallet technology in the United States. PayPal and Square are attacking the mobile payment market from a different direction, with apps and credit card readers that attach to smartphones.

near field communication (NFC)
a set of short-range wireless technologies used to share information among devices

The promise of riches beyond description to a firm that is able to dominate the mobile payments marketplace has set off what one commentator has called a goat rodeo surrounding the development of new technologies and methods of mobile payment. The end-of-chapter case study, *Online Payment Marketplace: Goat Rodeo,* provides a further look at the future of online and mobile payment in the United States, including the efforts of PayPal, Google, Square, and others.

DIGITAL CASH AND VIRTUAL CURRENCIES

Although the terms digital cash and virtual currencies are often used synonymously, they actually refer to two separate types of alternative payment systems. **Digital cash** typically is based on an algorithm that generates unique authenticated tokens representing cash value that can be used "in the real world." Examples of digital cash include Bitcoin and Ukash. Bitcoins are encrypted numbers (sometimes referred to as cryptocurrency) that are generated by a complex algorithm using a peer-to-peer network in

digital cash
an alternative payment system in which unique, authenticated tokens represent cash value

a process referred to as "mining," that requires extensive computing power. Like real currency, Bitcoins have a fluctuating value tied to open-market trading. Like cash, Bitcoins are anonymous—they are exchanged via a 34-character alphanumeric address that the user has, and do not require any other identifying information. Bitcoins have recently attracted a lot of attention as a potential money laundering tool for cyber-criminals, and have also been plagued by security issues, with some high-profile heists. Nonetheless, there are companies, such as BitPay, that are touting Bitcoins as a legit-imate alternative payment system, and trying to make it easier for merchants to accept them. Read the *Insight on Society* case, *Bitcoin*, for a further look at Bitcoin and some of the issues surrounding it. Ukash is another digital cash system that uses a unique 19-digit code, and can be stored online in an eWallet. Ukash can be purchased at more than 460,000 retail locations around the globe, and used wherever it is accepted.

virtual currency

typically circulates within an internal virtual world community or is issued by a specific corporate entity, and used to purchase virtual goods

Virtual currencies, on the other hand, typically circulate primarily within an internal virtual world community, such as Linden Dollars, created by Linden Lab for use in its virtual world, Second Life, or are associated with a specific corporation, such as Facebook Credits, which can be used to purchase Facebook gift cards. Both types are typically used for purchasing virtual goods.

5.7 ELECTRONIC BILLING PRESENTMENT AND PAYMENT

In 2007, for the first time, the number of bill payments made online exceeded the number of physical checks written (Fiserv, 2007). In the $16 trillion U.S. economy with an $11.4 trillion consumer sector for goods and services, there are a lot of bills to pay—an average of 30 billion of them a year, according to Western Union. No one knows for sure, but some experts believe the life-cycle cost of a paper bill for a busi-ness, from point of issuance to point of payment, ranges from $3 to $7. This calcula-tion does not include the value of time to consumers, who must open bills, read them, write checks, address envelopes, stamp, and then mail remittances. The billing market represents an extraordinary opportunity for using the Internet as an electronic billing and payment system that potentially could greatly reduce both the cost of paying bills and the time consumers spend paying them. Estimates vary, but online payments are believed to cost between only 20 to 30 cents to process.

electronic billing presentment and payment (EBPP) system

form of online payment system for monthly bills

Electronic billing presentment and payment (EBPP) systems are systems that enable the online delivery and payment of monthly bills. EBPP services allow consumers to view bills electronically and pay them through electronic funds transfers from bank or credit card accounts. More and more companies are choosing to issue statements and bills electronically, rather than mailing out paper versions. But even those businesses that do mail paper bills are increasingly offering online bill payment as an option to customers, allowing them to immediately transfer funds from a bank or credit card account to pay a bill somewhere else.

MARKET SIZE AND GROWTH

In 2002, 61% of bill payments were made by check, and only 12% by online bill payment. In 2012, in contrast, bill payments now account for half of all bill payments,

INSIGHT ON SOCIETY

BITCOIN

In recent years, a number of countries around the world have experienced banking crises, eroding trust in the system. As globalization has continued and the world's banking systems have grown more unified, the debt crises of individual nations have had a ripple effect on the rest of the world, more so than in the past. Enter Bitcoin, a form of electronic currency that does not exist in physical form and can be transferred from one person to another via peer-to-peer networks, without the need for a bank or other financial institution as intermediary. Bitcoin is more complicated than traditional currencies, but is accepted by a growing number of merchants, some reputable, and some not.

Because Bitcoin requires no intermediaries to conduct transactions, it is out of the control of bankers and politicians. Bitcoin is a decentralized currency, and although it's not a physical currency that you can put in your pocket, its supporters believe that it requires less trust than traditional currency. There is no need to trust the qualifications of central banks to monitor the currency, to hold money and transfer it, to lend money responsibly, and to safeguard our personal information.

Bitcoin also allows businesses to take and make payments much more easily than through channels like PayPal and credit cards. Bitcoin allows merchants to avoid the fees associated with these services, enabling frictionless transactions. On the other hand, with Bitcoin, all transactions are irreversible, and if Bitcoins are somehow stolen, the victim has no recourse. Still, purchasers who use Bitcoin receive other benefits, such as not being required to provide personal information to merchants. With the proliferation of security breaches experienced by major companies seemingly every week, this is now an important advantage. Bitcoin also allows people without access to traditional banking services to conduct financial transactions more easily.

Bitcoin has many unique attributes that differentiate it from traditional currencies. For starters, Bitcoins are not minted, but have been generated at a predetermined rate beginning in 2009. The program that is used to generate Bitcoins runs on a peer-to-peer network and requires very powerful computer systems to operate. "Mining" a Bitcoin is the result of these powerful computers solving cryptographic problems in tandem with other similar computers—the computer that hits upon the solution is awarded the coin, and a record of all of the involved computers' attempts at mining the coin is logged jointly, as "proof-of-work." Because Bitcoins take time and computing energy from a host of machines to mine, they are considered to have value. At this point, several years after the launch of Bitcoin, only a very powerful computer system is capable of unearthing new Bitcoins before the rest of the nodes on the network.

The process is designed to simulate mining for gold and to slowly increase the supply in the market. A finite amount of coins are "built into the software," such that in the year 2140, all of the coins will be mined and present in the market. Each time a coin is spent, the chain of ownership is verified on all of the thousands of nodes on the network. This prevents coins from being spent multiple times, since no coin can be exchanged without the authentication of thousands of node computers. The widely distributed nature of the Bitcoin mining network makes it nearly impervious to hacking, because a would-be hacker is forced to gain access to thousands of independent computer systems at the same time.

Despite these advantages, there are many reasons to be skeptical of Bitcoin. Law enforcement agencies and governments are justifiably

(continued)

concerned about the emergence of a new currency whose purpose is to avoid regulation. A newly mined Bitcoin has no origin, purchase history, or any data associated with it, and could be used with nearly complete anonymity for any purchase. Many supporters of Bitcoin are using it for criminal or illegal purposes. One report found that a full 5% percent of Bitcoins that were in circulation were collected by the online black market Silk Road, which sells illegal drugs. Pornographic Web sites also are staunch supporters of Bitcoin. Still, studies of Bitcoin released in 2013 indicate that once a user attempts to spend or cash out his Bitcoin holdings, remaining anonymous becomes more difficult. By using Bitcoin addresses in tandem with the services used by the individuals in charge of those addresses, law enforcement may in fact be able to catch thieves and apprehend anyone making illegal purchases.

Benefits of traditionally regulated currencies include making it difficult to effectively launder money or to engage in criminal activities with complete anonymity. From a law enforcement perspective, the increasing popularity of Bitcoin is a troubling development. For now, regulatory agencies only require that "virtual currency" trading entities register as Money Services Businesses and be subject to the regulations required of those businesses—using Bitcoins to buy products and services is fully legal. However, in the future, governments might see fit to take a firmer stand against virtual currencies. Bitcoin supporters know that without support from governments, it will never gain mainstream acceptance.

Economists also are skeptical of Bitcoin for several reasons. Many critics observe that for a system intended to reduce the need for trust in external institutions like banks, Bitcoin requires an awful lot of trust itself. Bitcoin users must accept the risks that the currency will not catch on with a significant enough number of individuals and businesses, that governments may eventually intervene to halt the proliferation and use of Bitcoins, and that Bitcoin won't be replaced by superior virtual currencies in the future, rendering Bitcoins nearly worthless. Bitcoin has also demonstrated tremendous volatility in its first few years of use, which hinders its chances for widespread adoption. At the start of 2013, Bitcoins was valued at $13, and by April 10, $266. The way Bitcoins are generated also encourages hoarding, because the computing power required to mine Bitcoins is likely to increase, making each coin worth more. "Man in the middle" attacks may also be effective for stealing Bitcoins that are sent from user to user, and the perpetrators may be difficult to apprehend.

Nevertheless, the number of high-profile online businesses accepting Bitcoins is growing, including WordPress and Reddit, and Bitcoin has the backing of a number of high-profile figures in tech, including the Winklevoss twins, famous for their legal entanglements with Facebook. The Winklevosses are aiming to create the first exchange-traded fund for Bitcoins only. The proposal is far from a done deal, as other Bitcoin-related organizations, like Mt. Gox, the most famous Bitcoin exchange, are currently in the crosshairs of federal regulators for money laundering and other similar issues. This early into the life of Bitcoin, it's too early to say whether digital currencies are here to stay or whether skeptics are correct.

SOURCES: "How Bitcoin Spreads Violate Fundamental Economic Laws," by Donald Marron, Forbes.com, September 3, 2013; "Is Digital Currency Catching On?," by Ariella Brown, CFO.com, September 3, 2013; "Bitcoin Offers Privacy—As Long As You Don't Cash Out or Spend It," by Jeremy Kirk, Pcworld.com, August 28, 2013; "Following the Bitcoin Trail," Economist.com, August 28, 2013; "Government Eyes Regulation of 'Bitcoins,'" by Kavya Sukumar, *USA Today*, August 26, 2013; "Nine Trust-Based Problems with Bitcoin," by Steven Strauss, HuffingtonPost.com, April 4, 2013; "The Bitcoin Boom," by Maria Bustillos, *The New Yorker*, April 2, 2013; "Bitcoin: The Cryptoanarchists' Answer to Cash," by Morgen E. Peck, *IEEE Spectrum*, May 30, 2012.

while paper checks now account for less than 25%. Among online households, almost three-quarters pay at least one bill online each month, and almost half receive at least one bill electronically each month. Mobile bill payments are made by only 8% of online households, but that number is growing quickly, as the number of smartphone users making mobile bill payments jumped over 40% in the last year (Fiserv, 2013).

One major reason for the surge in EBPP usage is that companies are starting to realize how much money they can save through online billing. Not only is there the savings in postage and processing, but payments can be received more quickly (3 to 12 days faster, compared to paper bills sent via regular mail), thereby improving cash flow. In order to realize these savings, many companies are becoming more aggressive in encouraging their customers to move to EBPP by instituting a charge for the privilege of continuing to receive a paper bill.

Financials don't tell the whole story, however. Companies are discovering that a bill is both a sales opportunity and a customer retention opportunity, and that the electronic medium provides many more options when it comes to marketing and promotion. Rebates, savings offers, cross-selling, and upselling are all possible in the digital realm.

Consumers are also becoming more receptive to online bill payment, particularly via mobile device. A survey by Fiserv found that nearly a third of respondents indicated that they were very interested in viewing and paying bills from their smartphone (Fiserv, 2013).

EBPP BUSINESS MODELS

There are two main competing business models in the EBPP marketspace: biller-direct and consolidator. The biller-direct system was originally created by utility companies that send millions of bills each month. Their purpose is to make it easier for their customers to pay their utility bills routinely online. Today, telephone and credit card companies also frequently offer this service, as well as a number of individual stores. Companies implementing a biller-direct system can either develop their own system in-house (usually only an option for the very largest companies), install a system acquired from a third-party EBPP software vendor, use a third-party EBPP service bureau (the service bureau hosts a biller-branded Web site that enables consumers to view and pay bills and handles all customer enrollment, bill presentment, and payment processing), or use an application service provider (similar to a service bureau, but runs on the biller's Web site rather than being hosted on the service provider's Web site).

In the consolidator model, a third party, such as a financial institution or a focused portal such as Intuit's Paytrust.com, Fiserv's MyCheckFree, Pageonce, and others, aggregates all bills for consumers and ideally permits one-stop bill payment (pay anyone). Currently, financial institutions have been more successful than portals in attracting online bill payers. The consolidator model faces several challenges. For billers, using the consolidator model means an increased time lag between billing and payment, and also inserts an intermediary between the company and its customer. For

FIGURE 5.16	MAJOR PLAYERS IN THE EBPP MARKETSPACES

EBPP Systems

Biller-Direct

Telephone
Utilities
Credit Card Companies

Consolidators

Financial Institutions
Intuit Paytrust
MyCheckFree
Pageonce

Infrastructure Providers

Fiserv
Yodlee
FIS
Online Resources
MasterCard RPPS

The main business models in the EBPP marketspace are biller-direct and consolidator. Infrastructure providers support both of these competing models and sometimes operate their own online payment portals.

consumers, security continues to be a major issue. Most consumers are unwilling to pay any kind of fee to pay bills online, and many are concerned about sharing personal financial information with nonfinancial institutions. Today, more and more banks are offering online bill payment free to some or all of their customers as an enticement.

Supporting these two primary business models are infrastructure providers such as Fiserv, Yodlee, FIS, Online Resources Corporation, MasterCard RPPS (Remote Payment and Presentment Service), and others that provide the software to create the EBPP system or handle billing and payment collection for the biller. **Figure 5.16** categorizes the major players in the EBPP marketspace.

Online Payment Marketplace:
Goat Rodeo

Nearly every day, it seems, a new online or mobile payment system is announced. The online payment marketplace is experiencing an explosion of innovative ideas, plans, and announcements, which one commentator has likened to a goat rodeo, a chaotic situation in which powerful players with different agendas compete with one another for public acceptance, and above all, huge potential revenues.

Others liken the payment marketplace to a battle among the titans of online payment and retailing: PayPal, credit card companies, telecommunications carriers like Verizon, AT&T, and T-Mobile, mobile hardware and software companies like Apple and Google, and even large retailers like Walmart and Target are all working to develop their very own online and mobile payment systems.

Each of these titans has its own version of a future payment system that challenges the other players. They all want to help us spend money and increase the convenience of shopping. They all want to not only gather the fees that such systems can produce, but also use it to gather oceans of personal consumer information and display ads throughout the payment transaction process, along with coupons, daily deals, and flash sales based on their knowledge of the consumer.

The continuing double-digit growth of e-commerce is certainly one factor driving market participants, but a more important factor is the emergence of the mobile platform of smartphones and tablets that opens the door for new firms to enter the online payment marketplace based on new technologies and control of the mobile platform itself. The future growth of online payment is mobile because that's where consumers are increasingly making their purchases and because the market is not yet dominated by any single player.

The overall online payment market in the United States is estimated to be worth about $420 billion in 2013 and is growing at more than 12% a year. While small compared to the total e-commerce picture, mobile commerce, driven by smartphones, tablets, and cellular networks, is growing at more than 40% a year. In 2013, mobile commerce is expected to generate $39 billion in revenue. While most of these mobile commerce transactions are occurring through the use of credit cards (just as desktop e-commerce), there is a rapidly growing segment of so-called "proximity" or "contactless" payments which amounts to an estimated $1 billion in 2013 but which are expected to grow to $58 billion by 2017. And according to the Federal Reserve, U.S. consumers spent an estimated $3.3 trillion on 60 billion credit and debit card transactions in 2010 (the latest year for which data is available). Even if a small percentage of these transactions move from plastic to mobile payments, the potential revenue is very large. This is enough to drive even old goats into a frenzy.

While credit and debit cards remain the dominant method of online payment, PayPal is currently the most successful alternative. Founded in 1998, PayPal was initially aimed at individuals buying and selling goods on eBay. PayPal allowed account holders to both receive and make payments in eBay auctions without revealing their credit card numbers, and without having to establish a credit card processing account with the credit card companies or merchant banks. Merchants did not have to purchase an expensive credit card swiping device or pay additional monthly fees. Sometimes called a "peer-to-peer" payment system, PayPal permitted users to e-mail payments to one another. Users established accounts by giving PayPal either a credit card number or a bank account number. PayPal offered security and convenience for both consumers and merchants. PayPal charged users a fee of 2%–3% for a retail transaction and 4% for a money transfer. eBay purchased PayPal in 2002, and PayPal has since expanded from its eBay foundation to the larger world of online payments at e-commerce sites. around the globe.

PayPal is currently the largest alternative online payment service and accounts for about 78% of the alternative payment market. In 2012, PayPal cleared about $145 billion in payments worldwide. In the mobile payment marketplace, PayPal cleared about $14 billion in payments, more than thee times as much as in 2011, and about 30% of the overall mobile payment market. In mobile payments, PayPal is a much smaller player than in the larger alternative payment market. This situation gives competitors an opening to challenge PayPal.

Until March 2012, PayPal's mobile payment solution consisted of using an existing PayPal account with a mobile phone browser, just like paying from a desktop computer. While this system worked for purchasing goods while shopping online, it was of little use paying for coffee at the local Starbucks or purchasing goods and services from a local merchant. In March 2012, PayPal introduced PayPal Here, a card reader that plugs into a cell phone and can accept credit card payments, as well as check payments by taking a photo of the check. The card reader device and local accounting for payments is powered by a free smartphone app. PayPal charges 2.7% of each mobile transaction.

PayPal was late to the smartphone mobile payment market, beaten to the punch by a start-up firm called Square. Square started in 2009 with a smartphone app, credit card reader, and credit card processing service that allows anyone—businesses and individuals--to accept credit card payments. Square is one of the fastest growing e-commerce payment firms. Co-founder Jack Dorsey is a serial entrepreneur: he is a co-founder of Twitter. Initial funding for Square was provided by its founders and a $10 million investment led by Khosla Ventures in December 2009. The company was valued at $45 million and had 25 employees. In January 2011, Square received a $27.5 million venture investment led by Sequoia Capital, which valued the company at $240 million. In June 2011, Square received a $100 million investment from Kleiner Perkins Caufield and Byers, which valued the company at $1 billion. Finally, in September 2012, the company raised $200 million from Citibank, Visa, and Starbucks. In late 2012, Square lined up another $200 million in financing from Citi Ventures, Starbucks, and others, valuing the company at $3 billion. Square currently has 500 employees.

Today analysts estimate that more than a million merchants accept credit card payments using a Square device in North America although these numbers cannot be easily verified. The technology is quite simple: a square-shaped credit card reader plugs into smartphones and tablet computers loaded with a Square app that processes the credit card information. Versions are available for iOS and Android devices. Users can sign up online by registering a credit card with Square. Square charges merchants 2.75% of each transaction for the service, and there are no additional fees, minimums, or financial statements to file. In contrast, credit card fees for merchants typically range from 3% to 5%. Analysts believe that Square loses money on transactions less than $10, given that it must pay credit companies over 2% for their payment clearance. The future of Square will depend on the revenues it can derive from selling consumer information and placing ads on its payment system.

Square's initial credit card reader product was aimed at a market that was poorly served by credit card companies: small businesses like coffee shops, news stands, small retailers, and farmers' market merchants, as well as piano teachers, baby sitters, and taxi drivers. A poll by the National Retail Federation found that 50% of businesses planned to use a mobile device as a cash register in the next 18 months. How many "small businesses" are there? There are 7.6 million businesses in the United States, and 6.5 million have fewer than 20 employees. These small firms employ about 30 million people and generate about $1 trillion in revenues. Mobile payment systems are aimed directly at this large, underserved marketplace.

In March 2011, Square introduced its second product: Square Register, an app for the iPad that turns the iPad into a cash register. Voila: restaurants and small shops no longer needed to buy an expensive digital cash register or a credit card swiping machine from Verifone. What's more, the merchant can take the iPad home to watch movies when not used as a cash register! In May 2012, Square released the second version of Square Register, which has a more sophisticated business suite of accounting, inventory, and analytics software that allows merchants to identify best-selling items and time-of-day purchase patterns.

With a new app called Pay With Square, introduced in July 2012, Square plans to make contactless payments possible by simply entering the premises of a business, and using a photo as a personal ID in combination with a Square Register. In this system, there's no need to swipe a credit card. Here's how it will work. You enter your name, photo, and credit card number into your smartphone's Pay With Square app. Using the phone's GPS, the app identifies merchants nearby that use Pay With Square. On entering the shop, you press an icon and the app sends your payment information and photo to the Square Register. After ordering your sandwich, you pay by saying your name to the merchant, who checks your photo on the Square Register to ensure it's really you. So far this app has not caught on with merchants or consumers.

Square claims that 150,000 merchants now use Square Registers and that the company clears more than $15 billion in transactions annually. PayPal, Groupon, and Intuit have developed copycat versions of the same idea: payments for very small businesses based on smartphone and tablet card readers. Groupon's card reader system is linked to its daily deals. In March 2013, PayPal introduced an iPad app that accepts its card reader, PayPal Here. The iPad app is optimized for a larger tablet screen. In 2013, Square introduced Square Stand, an integrated collection of devices including Square Register, a cash box, receipt printer, and barcode scanner—like a traditional cash register rather than just a credit card reader. This digitally enabled cash register is, however, connected to the Internet and to users in the shop via Bluetooth. Going further in the direction of commerce and not just mobile payments, Square announced in June 2013 an online marketplace where merchants can list their products online at a Web site hosted by Square, which will also process all payments online. This is the first time Square has offered online payments and a marketplace. Before this, Square offered only face-to-face payments in physical stores.

The key for all these payment systems is scale: getting enough consumers and merchants to adopt the Square dongle and purchase the iPads needed for the Square Register. Square received a tremendous boost in achieving scale in August 2012 when Starbucks agreed to use Square for all its credit card transactions in the United States. Starbucks has plenty of scale: 17,000 stores worldwide and 11,000 in the United States. Analysts believe that with Starbucks as a partner, Square will come to dominate the card swiping marketplace, and potentially play a large role in other contactless payment schemes.

While PayPal and Square duke it out in the card swiping payment market for small merchants, other payment schemes and plans that take advantage of the full capabilities of mobile devices are being announced monthly, if not daily. The greatest potential in the next five years for mobile payment systems is systems based on NFC. So-called "swipe and pay" systems, NFC enables a direct secure communication link between the consumer's smartphone and the merchant's cash register. All that's needed is to bring the smartphone in close proximity (six inches) to the cash register. The two biggest players in the NFC payment market are the telecommunication carriers' Isis system and Google's Google Wallet. A third stealth player is Merchant Customer Exchange (MCX), which is being created by some of the largest retailers in the United States.

Isis is a mobile swipe and pay venture backed by Verizon, AT&T, and T-Mobile, originally announced in 2010. To date, Isis has lined up Chase, Visa, MasterCard, Capital One, and American Express to process credit card transactions. Implementation of Isis is difficult when compared to Square's payment system because merchants need to purchase NFC terminals, and consumers need smartphones with NFC chips installed. Isis conducted a test of its payment system in September 2012 in Salt Lake City and Austin. Why Salt Lake City? Its metro transit system already uses NFC terminals to accept payment from riders' smartphones. Based on the market test, Isis will launch its payment system nationwide in late 2013.

Google Wallet is an online payment system originally designed for desktop PCs, but Google has now extended it to include a mobile component in partnership with Sprint, Citibank, and MasterCard. Google has included support for the operation of NFC chips into the latest version of its Android smartphone operating system. Samsung's Galaxy phones are the only phones sold in the United States that have a built-in NFC chip. Google Wallet is the only NFC system that is operational, and Google claims that it is available at 150,000 merchants. In Google's system, customers tap the merchant's NFC terminal at checkout. Called Tap & Go, Google offers its payment system with no charge to credit card companies and will not take a slice of transactions like Isis and other mobile payment systems. Instead, Google will retain the right to display ads, coupons, loyalty programs, and daily deals by local merchants nearby on the user's mobile screen. As with the Isis program, widespread use of Google Wallet will require cooperation from handset makers and merchants, who will be required to invest in new hardware. So far in 2013, Google Wallet has not been a market success.

Merchant Customer Exchange (MCX) is an NFC payment system being developed by Walmart, Target, Sears, 7-Eleven Inc., Sunoco, and 10 other national pharmacies, supermarkets, and restaurant chains. Announced in March 2012, the backers of this effort have annual sales of more than $1 trillion dollars. That's enough to make everyone involved in mobile payments stand up and listen, even Google.

So far, MCX has not released a system, but when it does, it reportedly will use NFC. Customers will be able to download an app to their smartphone and make purchases by tapping the phone against an NFC reader by the cash register. Why are these nationwide merchants willing to invest billions in a mobile payment system when financial service firms and technology players also are investing billions in competing systems? The answer is control over the customer during the transaction, and the information on customer purchase history that the apps will be recording. The merchants do not want this valuable marketing asset to flow to financial service firms or Google.

SOURCES: "PayPal Device Allows Automatic Smartphone Payments," by Greg Bensinger, *Wall Street Journal*, September 9, 2013; "Isis to Launch NFC Mobile Payments Across US in 2013," by Sarah Clark, NFCworld.com, July 31, 2013; "Square Stand Now Available Online and in Apple Retail and Bestbuy Stores," Squareup.com, July 9, 2013; "Mobile Payments: An Updated Forecast," by Bryan Yeager, eMarketer, July 2013; "Square Takes on PayPal Online," by Greg Bensinger, *Wall Street Journal*, June 26, 2013; "Square Leaps Beyond Payments to Commerce With Online Marketplace," by Jessica Guyn, *Los Angeles Times*, June 25, 2013; "PayPal Takes on Square Register With New iPad Payments App," by Leena Rao, Techcrunch.com, March 13, 2013; "Groupon Launches Credit Card Payment Business," by Alistair Barr and Nivedita Bhattachrjee, Reuters, September 19, 2012; "Delays Strike Mobile-Payments Test," by Robin Sidel, *Wall Street Journal*, September 13, 2012; "Square Closes Financing Round," by Evelyn M. Rusli, *New York Times*, September 17, 2012; "Can Square Remain Hip?" by Petere Eavis, *New York Times*, August 31, 2012; "Big Retailers Team Up On Mobile Payments Plan," Reuters, August 15, 2012; "Payments Network Takes on Google," by Robin Sidel, *Wall Street Journal*, August 15, 2012; "Square Gets a Jolt From Starbucks," by Rolfe Winkler and Andrew R. Johnson, *Wall Street Journal*, August 8, 2012; "Starbucks and Square to Team Up" by Claire Cain Miller, *New York Times*, August 8, 2012; "Pay By Voice? So Long Wallet," by David Pogue, *New York Times*, July 18, 2012; "Consumers and Mobile Financial Services," Board of Governors, Federal Reserve System, March 2012; "The 2010 Federal Reserve Payments Study," Federal Reserve System, 2011.

The future for smartphone mobile payments is assured given the size of the players involved, the potential rewards for successful players, and the demands of consumers for a payment system that does not involve swiping plastic cards and dealing with slips of paper. But it is unlikely that all the payment systems described above will survive, and also quite likely that consumers will remain confused by all their payment options for some time yet to come.

Case Study Questions

1. What is the value proposition that Square offers consumers? How about merchants? What are some of the weaknesses of Square's system?

2. Why would telecommunications carriers like AT&T and Verizon want to move into the payments business? What chance do they have to compete against Google? What's their advantage?

3. What advantages does PayPal have in the mobile payment market? What are its weaknesses?

4. What strategies would you recommend that PayPal pursue in order to translate its dominance in alternative online payments into a strong position in the emerging mobile payment market, especially in on-premise payments?

5.9   REVIEW

KEY CONCEPTS

■ **Understand the scope of e-commerce crime and security problems.**

While the overall size of cybercrime is unclear at this time, cybercrime against e-commerce sites is growing rapidly, the amount of losses is growing, and the management of e-commerce sites must prepare for a variety of criminal assaults.

■ **Describe the key dimensions of e-commerce security.**

There are six key dimensions to e-commerce security:
- *Integrity*—ensures that information displayed on a Web site or sent or received via the Internet has not been altered in any way by an unauthorized party.
- *Nonrepudiation*—ensures that e-commerce participants do not deny (repudiate) their online actions.
- *Authenticity*—verifies an individual's or business's identity.
- *Confidentiality*—determines whether information shared online, such as through e-mail communication or an order process, can be viewed by anyone other than the intended recipient.
- *Privacy*—deals with the use of information shared during an online transaction. Consumers want to limit the extent to which their personal information can be

divulged to other organizations, while merchants want to protect such information from falling into the wrong hands.
- *Availability*—determines whether a Web site is accessible and operational at any given moment.

■ **Understand the tension between security and other values.**

Although computer security is considered necessary to protect e-commerce activities, it is not without a downside. Two major areas where there are tensions between security and Web site operations are:
- *Ease of use*—The more security measures that are added to an e-commerce site, the more difficult it is to use and the slower the site becomes, hampering ease of use. Security is purchased at the price of slowing down processors and adding significantly to data storage demands. Too much security can harm profitability, while not enough can potentially put a company out of business.
- *Public safety*—There is a tension between the claims of individuals to act anonymously and the needs of public officials to maintain public safety that can be threatened by criminals or terrorists.

■ **Identify the key security threats in the e-commerce environment.**

The most common and most damaging forms of security threats to e-commerce sites include:
- *Malicious code*—viruses, worms, Trojan horses, ransomware, and bot networks are a threat to a system's integrity and continued operation, often changing how a system functions or altering documents created on the system.
- *Potentially unwanted programs (adware, spyware, etc.)*—a kind of security threat that arises when programs are surreptitiously installed on your computer or computer network without your consent.
- *Phishing*—any deceptive, online attempt by a third party to obtain confidential information for financial gain.
- *Hacking and cybervandalism*—intentionally disrupting, defacing, or even destroying a site.
- *Credit card fraud/theft*—one of the most-feared occurrences and one of the main reasons more consumers do not participate in e-commerce. The most common cause of credit card fraud is a lost or stolen card that is used by someone else, followed by employee theft of customer numbers and stolen identities (criminals applying for credit cards using false identities).
- *Spoofing*—occurs when hackers attempt to hide their true identities or misrepresent themselves by using fake e-mail addresses or masquerading as someone else.
- *Pharming*—involves redirecting a Web link to an address different from the intended one, with the site masquerading as the intended destination.
- *Identity fraud*—involves the unauthorized use of another person's personal data, such as social security, driver's license, and/or credit card numbers, as well as user names and passwords, for illegal financial benefit.
- *Denial of Service (DoS) and Distributed Denial of Service (DDoS) attacks*—hackers flood a Web site with useless traffic to inundate and overwhelm the network, frequently causing it to shut down and damaging a site's reputation and customer relationships.

- *Sniffing*—a type of eavesdropping program that monitors information traveling over a network, enabling hackers to steal proprietary information from anywhere on a network, including e-mail messages, company files, and confidential reports. The threat of sniffing is that confidential or personal information will be made public.
- *Insider jobs*—although the bulk of Internet security efforts are focused on keeping outsiders out, the biggest threat is from employees who have access to sensitive information and procedures.
- *Poorly designed server and client software*—the increase in complexity and size of software programs has contributed to an increase in software flaws or vulnerabilities that hackers can exploit.
- *Social network security issues*—malicious code, PUPs, phishing, data breaches, identity fraud, and other e-commerce security threats have all infiltrated social networks.
- *Mobile platform security issues*—the mobile platform presents an alluring target for hackers and cybercriminals, and faces all the same risks as other Internet devices, as well as new risks associated with wireless network security.
- *Cloud security issues*—as devices, identities, and data become more and more intertwined in the cloud, safeguarding data in the cloud becomes a major concern.

■ **Describe how technology helps protect the security of messages sent over the Internet.**

Encryption is the process of transforming plain text or data into cipher text that cannot be read by anyone other than the sender and the receiver. Encryption can provide four of the six key dimensions of e-commerce security:

- *Message integrity*—provides assurance that the sent message has not been altered.
- *Nonrepudiation*—prevents the user from denying that he or she sent a message.
- *Authentication*—provides verification of the identity of the person (or computer) sending the message.
- *Confidentiality*—gives assurance that the message was not read by others.

There are a variety of different forms of encryption technology currently in use. They include:

- *Symmetric key encryption*—Both the sender and the receiver use the same key to encrypt and decrypt a message. Advanced Encryption Standard (AES) is the most widely used symmetric key encryption system on the Internet today.
- *Public key cryptography*—Two mathematically related digital keys are used: a public key and a private key. The private key is kept secret by the owner, and the public key is widely disseminated. Both keys can be used to encrypt and decrypt a message. Once the keys are used to encrypt a message, the same keys cannot be used to unencrypt the message.
- *Public key encryption using digital signatures and hash digests*—This method uses a mathematical algorithm called a hash function to produce a fixed-length number called a hash digest. The results of applying the hash function are sent by the sender to the recipient. Upon receipt, the recipient applies the hash function to the received message and checks to verify that the same result is produced. The sender then encrypts both the hash result and the original message using the recipient's public key, producing a single block of cipher text. To ensure both the authenticity of the message and nonrepudiation, the sender

encrypts the entire block of cipher text one more time using the sender's private key. This produces a digital signature or "signed" cipher text that can be sent over the Internet to ensure the confidentiality of the message and authenticate the sender.

- *Digital envelope*—This method uses symmetric encryption to encrypt and decrypt the document, but public key encryption to encrypt and send the symmetric key.
- *Digital certificates and public key infrastructure*—This method relies on certification authorities who issue, verify, and guarantee digital certificates (a digital document that contains the name of the subject or company, the subject's public key, a digital certificate serial number, an expiration date, an issuance date, the digital signature of the certification authority, and other identifying information).

■ Identify the tools used to establish secure Internet communications channels and protect networks, servers, and clients.

In addition to encryption, there are several other tools that are used to secure Internet channels of communication, including:

- *Secure Sockets Layer (SSL)/Transport Layer Security (TLS)*—This is the most common form of securing channels. The SSL protocol provides data encryption, server authentication, client authentication, and message integrity for TCP/IP connections.
- *Virtual private networks (VPNs)*—These allow remote users to securely access internal networks via the Internet, using PPTP, an encoding mechanism that allows one local network to connect to another using the Internet as the conduit.
- *WPA2*—the most current wireless security standard uses the AES algorithm for encryption and CCMP, a more advanced authentication code protocol.

After communications channels are secured, tools to protect networks, the servers, and clients should be implemented. These include:

- *Firewalls*—software applications that act as filters between a company's private network and the Internet itself, preventing unauthorized remote client computers from attaching to your internal network.
- *Proxies*—software servers that act primarily to limit access of internal clients to external Internet servers and are frequently referred to as the gateway.
- *Intrusion detection and prevention systems (IDS/IDP)*—an IDS examines network traffic, watching to see if it matches certain patterns or preconfigured rules indicative of an attack, while an IPS has all of the funcationality of an IDS with the additional ability to take steps to prevent and block suspicious activities.
- *Operating system controls*—built-in username and password requirements that provide a level of authentication. Some operating systems also have an access control function that controls user access to various areas of a network.
- *Anti-virus software*—a cheap and easy way to identify and eradicate the most common types of viruses as they enter a computer, as well as to destroy those already lurking on a hard drive.

■ Appreciate the importance of policies, procedures, and laws in creating security.

In order to minimize security threats:

- E-commerce firms must develop a coherent corporate policy that takes into account the nature of the risks, the information assets that need protecting, and the procedures and technologies required to address the risk, as well as implementation and auditing mechanisms.
- Public laws and active enforcement of cybercrime statutes also are required to both raise the costs of illegal behavior on the Internet and guard against corporate abuse of information.

The key steps in developing a security plan are:
- *Perform a risk assessment*—an assessment of the risks and points of vulnerability.
- *Develop a security policy*—a set of statements prioritizing the information risks, identifying acceptable risk targets, and identifying the mechanisms for achieving these targets.
- *Create an implementation plan*—a plan that determines how you will translate the levels of acceptable risk into a set of tools, technologies, policies, and procedures.
- *Create a security team*—the individuals who will be responsible for ongoing maintenance, audits, and improvements.
- *Perform periodic security audits*—routine reviews of access logs and any unusual patterns of activity.

■ **Describe the features of traditional payment systems.**

Traditional payment systems include:
- *Cash*, whose key feature is that it is instantly convertible into other forms of value without the intermediation of any other institution.
- *Checking transfers*, which are funds transferred directly through a signed draft or check from a consumer's checking account to a merchant or other individual; these are the second most common forms of payment.
- *Credit card accounts*, which are accounts that extend credit to a consumer and allow consumers to make payments to multiple vendors at one time.
- *Stored value systems*, which are created by depositing funds into an account and from which funds are paid out or are withdrawn as needed. Stored value payments systems include debit cards, phone cards, and smart cards.
- *Accumulating balance systems*, which accumulate expenditures and to which consumers make periodic payments.

■ **Identify the major e-commerce payment systems in use today.**

The major types of e-commerce payment systems in use today include:
- *Online credit card transactions,* which are the primary form of online payment system. There are five parties involved in an online credit card purchase: consumer, merchant, clearinghouse, merchant bank (sometimes called the "acquiring bank"), and the consumer's card-issuing bank. However, the online credit card system has a number of limitations involving security, merchant risk, cost, and social equity.
- *PayPal*, which is an example of an online stored value payment system that permits consumers to make instant, online payments to merchants and other individuals based on value stored in an online account.
- *Alternative payment services* such as Amazon Payments, Google Checkout/ Google Wallet, and Bill Me Later, which enable consumers to shop online at a

wide variety of merchants without having to provide credit card information each time they make a purchase.

- *Mobile payment systems*, using either credit card readers attached to a smartphone (Square, PayPal Here) or near field communication (NFC) chips, which enable contactless payment.
- *Digital cash* such as Bitcoin, which is based on an algorithm that generates unique authenticated tokens representing cash value, and virtual currencies, that typically circulate within an internal virtual world or are issued by a corporation, and usually used for the purchase of virtual goods.

■ **Describe the features and functionality of electronic billing presentment and payment systems.**

Electronic billing presentment and payment (EBPP) systems are a form of online payment systems for monthly bills. EBPP services allow consumers to view bills electronically and pay them through electronic funds transfers from bank or credit card accounts. Major players in the EBPP marketspace include:

- *Biller-direct systems*, which were originally created by large utilities to facilitate routine payment of utility bills, but which are increasingly being used by other billers.
- *Consolidators*, which attempt to aggregate all bills for consumers in one place and ideally permit one-stop bill payment.
- *Infrastructure providers,* which support the biller-direct and consolidator business models.

QUESTIONS

1. Why is it less risky to steal online? Explain some of the ways criminals deceive consumers and merchants.
2. Explain why an e-commerce site might not want to report being the target of cybercriminals.
3. Give an example of security breaches as they relate to each of the six dimensions of e-commerce security. For instance, what would be a privacy incident?
4. How would you protect your firm against a Denial of Service attack?
5. Explain why the U.S. government wants to restrict the export of strong encryption systems. Why would other countries be against it?
6. Name the major points of vulnerability in a typical online transaction.
7. How does spoofing threaten a Web site's operations?
8. Why is adware or spyware considered to be a security threat?
9. What are some of the steps a company can take to curtail cybercriminal activity from within a business?
10. Explain some of the modern-day flaws associated with encryption. Why is encryption not as secure today as it was earlier in the century?
11. Briefly explain how public key cryptography works.
12. Compare and contrast firewalls and proxy servers and their security functions.
13. Is a computer with anti-virus software protected from viruses? Why or why not?
14. Identify and discuss the five steps in developing an e-commerce security plan.

15. How do biometric devices help improve security? What particular type of security breach do they reduce?
16. What are tiger teams, who uses them, and what are some of the tactics they use in their work?
17. How do the interests of the four major payment systems stakeholders impact each other?
18. Compare and contrast stored value payment systems and checking transfers.
19. Why is a credit card not considered an accumulating balance payment system?
20. Name some advantages and disadvantages of using cash as a form of payment.
21. Describe the relationship between credit card associations and issuing banks.
22. What is Regulation Z, and how does it protect the consumer?
23. Briefly discuss the disadvantages of credit cards as the standard for online payments. How does requiring a credit card for payment discriminate against some consumers?
24. Describe the major steps involved in an online credit card transaction.
25. Why is Bitcoin so controversial?
26. What is NFC and how does it work?
27. Discuss why EBPP systems are becoming increasingly popular.
28. How are the two main types of EBPP systems both alike and different from each other?

PROJECTS

1. Imagine you are the owner of an e-commerce Web site. What are some of the signs that your site has been hacked? Discuss the major types of attacks you could expect to experience and the resulting damage to your site. Prepare a brief summary presentation.

2. Given the shift toward mobile commerce, do a search on "mobile commerce crime." Identify and discuss the new security threats this type of technology creates. Prepare a presentation outlining your vision of the new opportunities for cybercrime.

3. Find three certification authorities and compare the features of each company's digital certificates. Provide a brief description of each company as well, including number of clients. Prepare a brief presentation of your findings.

4. Research the challenges associated with payments across international borders and prepare a brief presentation of your findings. Do most e-commerce companies conduct business internationally? How do they protect themselves from repudiation? How do exchange rates impact online purchases? What about shipping charges? Summarize by describing the differences between a U.S. customer and an international customer who each make a purchase from a U.S. e-commerce merchant.

PART **3**

Business Concepts and Social Issues

E-commerce Marketing and Advertising Concepts

After reading this chapter, you will be able to:

- Identify the key features of the Internet audience.
- Discuss the basic concepts of consumer behavior and purchasing decisions.
- Understand how consumers behave online.
- Identify and describe the basic digital commerce marketing and advertising strategies and tools.
- Identify and describe the main technologies that support online marketing.
- Understand the costs and benefits of online marketing communications.

Video Ads:

Shoot, Click, Buy

I he age of online video ads is upon us, just in case you haven't noticed. Improvements in video production tools, higher bandwidth, and better streaming quality have fueled an online video surge. Video production is no longer the exclusive province of just a few major players in New York and Hollywood, but instead has expanded to a much larger group of potential creators, including users themselves. In addition, the ways online video can be viewed have also expanded, from desktop PCs and laptops to smartphones, tablet computers, netbooks, and Web-enabled television sets.

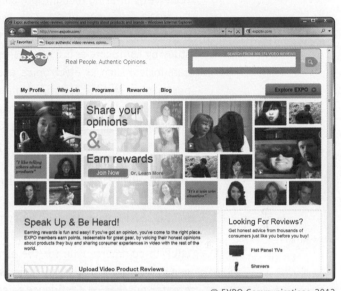

© EXPO Communications, 2012

The online audience for videos is huge. In July 2013, 187 million U.S. Internet users watched online video content during the month, with each viewer spending an average of 22.5 hours! Because this is where the eyeballs are, video is an obvious advertising medium. And just in time: Internet users have learned how to avoid traditional banner ads by instinctively moving their eyes to a different part of the screen. Click-throughs on banner ads are miniscule but videos are another story: next to search engine advertising and focused e-mail campaigns, videos have the highest click-through rate. In addition, nearly 100% of online spenders are video viewers, and they provide a highly desirable demographic with strong buying power. Research by comScore has also found that retail site viewers who view videos are 64% more likely to purchase. As a result, advertisers are jumping on the bandwagon. Americans viewed nearly 19.6 billion video ads in July 2013, more than double the amount in July 2012. Video ads reached 55% of the total U.S population. Google Sites (YouTube) delivered the highest number of video ads, with 3.4 billion, followed by the BrightRoll Platform (a video ad network) with 2.1 billion, and Adap.tv (a video ad exchange) also with 2.1 billion. Hulu served about 1.2 billion video ads.

Firms are using online video for marketing in a variety of ways. Many companies produce their own videos to promote their brands and sell products. User-generated video reviews are another effective marketing mechanism. EXPO is a consumer network that aggregates hundreds of thousands of video reviews created by over 200,000 members on its Web site, ExpoTV.com. EXPO also distributes the product review videos to retailers such as Amazon, Walmart, and Target, to social media sites such as Facebook and YouTube, to manufacturer Web sites and mobile apps, and as paid media, including pre-roll, rich media campaigns, and newsletters via such firms as WebCollege, a leading provider of rich product information to a network of more than 1,000 retailers in North America and Europe. EXPO has created a trusted database of videos that can be used as advertising by accepting reviews for any nationally available product and publishing all videos received, regardless of positive or negative opinion, as long as they meet quality standards. EXPO screens each video for relevance and quality, and rewards members who submit quality reviews by offering recognition, contests, loyalty points, and special consumer programs. By 2013, over 400,000 videos related to over 200,000 different products have been produced by EXPO members, and these videos have generated over 50 million views. A study by comScore and EXPO using a sample of 25 video product reviews across various categories, such as electronics and consumer packaged goods, found that the highest performing reviews contained many of the same effective elements seen in professionally produced television commercials, and that the rates of presence of many of these elements were greater than those seen in regular online display ads. comScore research indicates that after seeing a video product review, 40% more consumers considered the product unique and differentiated, and willingness to pay more for the product rose by 30%. EXPO's clients include consumer packaged goods brands such as Nabisco, Clairol, Febreze, and many others, as well as consumer electronics firms such as LG. For example, for LG, EXPO collected 720 video product reviews of LG products that were viewed over 280,000 times, totaling over 6,000 hours of engagement. On ExpoTV, there is an 11% click-to-commerce rate for the electronics category, which EXPO believes is driven by genuine and credible video reviews posted by peers that provide deeper knowledge and greater purchasing confidence to consumers.

Many large firms are moving into the online video advertising marketplace with sophisticated campaigns and big budgets. For instance, Rite Aid was searching for ways to boost sales in a recessionary period. One idea was to use its Web site to drive sales at its 4,600 retail stores. In 2010, Rite Aid introduced its Video Values program. Online visitors who watch videos about Rite Aid products receive a coupon that can be redeemed at the store. If you watch 20 videos, you receive a $5 bonus coupon in addition to product coupons. Currently, Rite Aid is streaming 500,000 videos a month, which are generating a 20% coupon redemption rate. The coupons are personalized and participants have to register. Rite Aid generates extensive demographic data on its most engaged customers who can later be contacted in e-mail campaigns. In turn, bargain hunting sites and blogs add a social component to the effort by driving bargain hunters to Rite Aid's site.

As of July 2013, the top 100 global brands collectively have about 1,400 YouTube channels with over 250,000 videos that have attracted 9.6 billion views. Brands with over 40 channels include 3M, Disney, Nike, IBM, and Google. The top 100 brands have invested over $4 billion in the creation of video assets. Disney, Google, and Sony have achieved over 1 billion total views, and 15 out of the 100 brands had more than 100 million views. Media and consumer technology companies are by far the most active producers of online videos.

Smaller firms are also using video. Online fashion retailer KarmaLoop offers KarmaLoopTV, with the objective of creating a community focused on Verge Culture, a demographic of young people heavily involved in music, fashion, sports, and the arts. The videos feature exclusive interviews with fashion designers, brands, artists, and musicians.

As of September 2013, KarmaLoopTV has more than 40,000 subscribers and over 21 million video views on YouTube, as well as a dedicated Web site, KarmaloopTV.com, with 5 million unique visitors and 16 million page views per month.

Orabrush is another small firm that has successfully used video ads on YouTube, in its case, to build its business from the ground up. Dr. Robert Wagstaff, a dentist who invented a breath-freshening tongue cleaner, was unsuccessful marketing it through traditional channels. Jeffrey Harmon, an MBA student at nearby Brigham Young University, whom Wagstaff had hired on a part-time basis, convinced him to give video ads a try. He initially posted a YouTube video called "How to tell if you have bad breath" on Orabrush's landing page, and found that it tripled Orabrush's conversion rate. From there, they decided to create Orabrush's own YouTube video channel. Today the channel has more than 100 videos, over 190,000 subscribers, and more than 50 million video views, and more importantly, has resulted in sales of over 3 million units. YouTube continues to account for 80% of Orabrush's marketing effort, although it now also has a Facebook page.

People care and get excited about videos far more than banner ads and e-mail. This makes videos an ideal advertising medium. Several changes in the underlying technology of video advertising are helping to increase the effectiveness of these ads. For instance, it is now possible to make video ads interactive so viewers can click on a product and add it to their shopping cart as the video is playing. It's sort of like "streaming e-commerce." These "interactive video ads" are appearing throughout the Web, especially at newspaper sites as an alternative to display ads that are increasingly ignored. Video ads can also be optimized, allowing retailers to change elements of the videos and measure the impact in near real time. The introduction of the iPad in 2010 made viewing videos much more pleasant and mobile. Interaction rates with videos displayed on iPads are six times higher than desktop PCs. The challenge is figuring out how to package advertising messages more directly with the videos, and how to piggyback advertising onto millions of user-generated videos and measure the impact on sales. Google, Yahoo, AOL, and literally hundreds of smaller firms are hard at work trying to attach the right ads to the right videos, a tricky process since computers cannot "understand" the content of videos (although they can "understand" the audio script—sort of). One start-up firm, YuMe.com, specializes in matching ads to popular online videos. One risk: your ad is attached to a perfectly inappropriate video. No one wants their product ads attached to stolen, pornographic, or inappropriate videos.

Another challenge is to figure out how to show the ad while the video plays without destroying the viewing experience. The final challenge is to avoid turning the viewer off, and causing a kind of video blindness on a mass scale, which is the fate of display ads today. One solution: YouTube now offers the TrueView ad format, which provides "skippable" ads that allow users to skip the pre-roll ad embedded in videos and which doesn't charge the advertiser for skipped ads. Skippable ads offer the prospect that the video ad marketplace will be self-cleansing with really unpopular, annoying, frequently skipped ads disappearing. And for those ads where "the creative" works, as they say in the ad industry, the rewards are potentially huge. For instance, Toyota's Swagger Wagon campaign, featuring a couple of unhip GenX parents rapping, went a long way toward advancing the Toyota brand in a demographic that they otherwise had difficulty reaching.

SOURCES: Corp.ExpoTV.com, accessed September 14, 2013; Karmalooptv.com, accessed September 14, 2013; "comScore Releases July 2013 U.S. Online Video Rankings," comscore.com, August 19, 2013; "The Top 100 Global Brands on YouTube," Pixability TV 30 Webinar, June 19, 2013; "Rethinking the Brand-Retailer-Consumer Ecosystem," by Adam Paul, News.expotv.com, April 24, 2013; "Orabrush Surpasses 50 Million Views on Its YouTube Channel," Orabrush.com, November 15, 2012; "Global Social Media Check-Up 2012," Burson-Marsteller, July 2012; "As Seen on YouTube! Orabrush Reinvents the Infomercial," by Joseph Flaherty, Wired.com, May 21, 2012; "YouTube Sees 'TrueView' Boosting Best Ads, eMarketer, Inc., December 28, 2011; "Yahoo Study Shows Changes in Online Video Audience," Zacks.com, June 29, 2011; "The Video Viewing Audience," eMarketer, Inc., (Lisa Phillips), February 2011; "Persuasive Potential of Consumer Produced Content," comScore, December 2010; "YouTube to Introduce 'Skippable' Ads," *Wall Street Journal*, June 29, 2010; "Video E-Commerce: Innovative Models Drive Sales," by Jeffrey Grant, eMarketer, Inc., May, 2010; "How EXPO Helped LG Learn More about Their Customers," EXPO, February 17, 2010; "Video Ad Start-Up YuMe Raises $25 Million," by Brad Stone, *New York Times*, February 17, 2010.

Perhaps no area of business has been more affected by Internet and mobile platform technologies than marketing and marketing communications. As a communications tool, the Internet affords marketers new ways of contacting millions of potential customers at costs far lower than traditional media. The Internet also provides new ways—often instantaneous and spontaneous—to gather information from customers, adjust product offerings, and increase customer value. The Internet has spawned entirely new ways to identify and communicate with customers, including search engine marketing, social network marketing, behavioral targeting, and targeted e-mail, among others.

The Internet was just the first transformation. Today, the mobile platform based on smartphones and tablet computers is transforming online marketing and communications yet again. The key changes in 2013 involve social networks, mobile marketing, and location-based services, including local marketing, as well as the increasing prevalence of digital video ads, as discussed in the opening case. **Table 6.1** summarizes some of the significant new developments in online marketing and advertising for 2013–2014.

The subject of online marketing, branding, and market communications is very broad and deep. We have created two chapters to cover the material. In this chapter, we begin by examining consumer behavior on the Web, the major types of online marketing and branding, and the technologies that support advances in online marketing. We then focus on understanding the costs and benefits of online marketing communications. In Chapter 7, we focus on the social, mobile, and local marketing phenomenon in greater depth.

6.1 CONSUMERS ONLINE: THE INTERNET AUDIENCE AND CONSUMER BEHAVIOR

Before firms can begin to sell their products online, they must first understand what kinds of people they will find online and how those people behave in the online marketplace. In this section, we focus primarily on individual consumers in the business-to-consumer (B2C) arena. However, many of the factors discussed apply to the B2B arena as well, insofar as purchasing decisions by firms are made by individuals. For readers who have no background in marketing, we have created an online Learning Track, Learning Track 6.1, that discusses basic marketing and branding concepts.

INTERNET TRAFFIC PATTERNS: THE ONLINE CONSUMER PROFILE

We will start with an analysis of some basic background demographics of Web consumers in the United States. The first principle of marketing and sales is "know thy customer." Who is online, who shops online and why, and what do they buy? In 2013, around 243 million people of all ages had access to the Internet. Almost 85 million households in the United States (over 70% of all households) have broadband access to the Internet. By comparison, 98% of all U.S. households currently have televisions and 94% have telephones. Worldwide, around 2.56 billion people are online.

TABLE 6.1	WHAT'S NEW IN ONLINE MARKETING AND ADVERTISING 2013–2014

BUSINESS

- Online marketing and advertising spending increases by 15%, compared to only about 3% for traditional media marketing and advertising.
- Social media marketing and advertising channels expand, but search and display marketing remains dominant.
- Mobile marketing and advertising grows at twice the rate of traditional online marketing.
- Local marketing and advertising based on geolocation services like Groupon and LivingSocial take off.
- Video advertising continues to be one of the fastest growing formats.
- Search engine marketing and advertising continues its dominance, but its rate of growth is slowing somewhat compared to other formats.

TECHNOLOGY

- Powerful, low-power, handheld mobile devices challenge the PC as the major online marketing and advertising platform. Smartphones and tablet computers become prevalent Web access devices.
- Big data: online tracking produces oceans of data, challenging business analytics programs.
- Cloud computing makes rich marketing content and multi-channel, cross-platform marketing a reality.
- The Twitter, Facebook, and Pinterest platforms grow into valuable social customer relationship management tools, enabling businesses to connect with customers on social network sites.

SOCIETY

- Targeted advertising based on behavioral tracking on leads to growing privacy awareness and fears.
- Social network sites are accused of abusing customer profile information without providing sufficient user controls over profile distribution.
- Mobile GPS tracking of individual location information built into smartphones and other mobile devices raises privacy concerns.

Although the number of new online users increased at a rate of 30% a year or higher in the early 2000s, over the last several years, this growth rate has slowed to about 2%–3% a year in the United States. E-commerce businesses can no longer count on a double-digit growth rate in the online population to fuel their revenues. The days of extremely rapid growth in the U.S. Internet population are over.

Intensity and Scope of Usage

The slowing rate of growth in the U.S. Internet population is compensated for, in part, by an increasing intensity and scope of use. Overall, over 80% of adult users of the Internet report logging on on a typical day (Pew Internet & American Life Project, 2013a). Several studies also show that a greater amount of time is being spent online by Internet users—over 2 hours a day (eMarketer, Inc., 2013a). In 2013, mobile smartphones and tablets are major access points to the Internet and online commerce. About 143 million people, almost 60% of all U.S. Internet users, access the Internet using a mobile device. Owners of mobile devices spend over 2 hours a day using them for nontelephone activities. In 2013, around 125 million mobile users played games, around 75 million viewed videos, around 100 million visited a social site, and millions of others listened to music, shopped, and texted (eMarketer, Inc., 2013b). The more time users spend online, becoming more comfortable and familiar with Internet features and services, the more services they are likely to explore, according to the Pew Internet & American Life Project.

Demographics and Access

The demographic profile of the Internet—and e-commerce—has changed greatly since 1995. Up until 2000, single, white, young, college-educated males with high incomes dominated the Internet. This inequality in access and usage led to concerns about a possible "digital divide." However, in recent years, there has been a marked increase in Internet usage by females, minorities, seniors, and families with modest incomes, resulting in a notable decrease—but not elimination—in the earlier inequality of access and usage (Pew Internet & American Life Project, 2013b).

An roughly equal percentage (about 85%) of men and women use the Internet today. Young adults (18–29) form the age group with the highest percentage of Internet use, at 98%. Adults in the 30–49 group (92%) are also strongly represented. Another fast-growing group online is the 65 and over segment, 56% of whom now use the Internet. Teens (12–17) also have a very high percentage of their age group online (97%). The percentage of very young children (1–11 years) online has also spurted, to 45% of that age group (eMarketer, Inc., 2013c, 2013d). Variation across ethnic groups is not as wide as across age groups. Ten years ago, there were significant differences among ethnic groups, but this has receded. In 2012, user participation by whites is 86%, African Americans, 85%, and Hispanics, 76%.

About 96% of households with income levels above $75,000 have Internet access, compared to only 76% of households earning less than $30,000. Over time, income differences have declined but they remain significant with a 20% gap between the highest category of household income and the lowest. Amount of education also makes a significant difference when it comes to online access. Of those individuals with less than a high school education, only 59% were online in 2013, compared to 96% of individuals with a college degree or more. Even a high school education boosted Internet usage, with that segment reaching 78%. In general, educational disparities far exceed other disparities in Internet access and usage (Pew Internet & American Life Project, 2013b; eMarketer, Inc., 2013c, 2013d).

Overall, there remains a strong relationship between age, income, ethnicity, and education on one hand and Internet usage on the other. The so-called "digital divide" has indeed moderated, but it still persists along the income, education, age, and ethnic dimensions. Gender, income, education, age, and ethnicity also impact online behavior. According to the Pew Internet & American Life Project, adults over the age of 65, those who have not completed high school, those who make less than $30,000 a year, and Hispanics are all less likely to purchase products online. Women are slightly more likely to purchase online than men, but not significantly so. With respect to online banking, the demographics are similar—those 65 and older are less likely than any age group to bank online, while those with at least some college are more likely than those with a high school diploma or less. Online banking is also more popular with men than women. No significant differences were found in terms of ethnicity (Pew Internet & American Life Project, 2012). Other commentators have observed that children of poorer and less educated families are spending considerably more time using their access devices for entertainment (movies, games, Facebook, and texting) than children from wealthier households. For all children and teenagers, the majority of time spent on the Internet has been labeled "wasted time" because the majority of online use is for entertainment, and not education or learning (Richtel, 2012).

Type of Internet Connection: Broadband and Mobile Impacts

While a great deal of progress has been made in reducing glaring gaps in access to the Internet, there are significant inequalities in access to broadband service. In 2013, around 85 million households had broadband service in their homes—70% of all households (eMarketer, Inc., 2013e). Research suggests the broadband audience is different from the dial-up audience: the broadband audience is more educated and affluent. The Federal Communications Commission reports that only 50% of Hispanic and African American homes have broadband, and only 40% of those homes with less than $20,000 in annual income (Federal Communications Commission, 2012). The broadband audience is much more intensely involved with the Internet and much more capable of using the Internet. For marketers, this audience offers unique opportunities for the use of multimedia marketing campaigns, and for the positioning of products especially suited for this audience. On the other hand, the dial-up households still buy products online, visit news sites, and use social network sites—just not as frequently or intensely as broadband households. The explosive growth of smartphones and tablet computers connected to broadband cellular and Wi-Fi networks is the foundation for a truly mobile e-commerce and marketing platform, which did not exist a few years ago. Marketers are now beginning to use this new platform for brand development.

Community Effects: Social Contagion in Social Networks

For a physical retail store, the most important factor in shaping sales is location, location, location. If you are located where thousands of people pass by every day, you will tend to do well. But for Internet retailers, physical location has almost no consequence as long as customers can be served by shipping services such as UPS or the post office or their services can be downloaded to anywhere. What does make a difference for consumer purchases on the Internet is whether or not the consumer is located in "neighborhoods" where others purchase on the Internet. These neighborhoods can be either face-to-face and truly personal, or digital. These so-called neighborhood effects, and the role of social emulation in consumption decisions, are well known for goods such as personal computers. In general, there is a relationship between being a member of a social network and purchasing decisions. Research on an Internet grocery found that being located near other users of the online grocery increased the likelihood of purchasing at the site by 50% (Bell and Song, 2004). Yet the relationship between "connectedness" (either offline or online) and purchase decisions is not straightforward or simple. People who score in the top 10%–15% of connectedness "do their own thing" to differentiate themselves and often do not share purchase decisions with friends. In fact, highly connected users often stop purchasing what their friends purchase. One can think of them as iconoclasts. The middle 50% of connected people very often share purchase patterns of their friends. One can think of these people as "keeping up with the Joneses" (Iyengar, et al., 2009). A Forrester Research study found that less than 2% of online purchases could be traced back to social networks, although for short-term, flash sales, the percentage rises to 6% (Forrester Research, 2011a). Other research reported by Goldman Sachs shows that social networks account for about 5% of online purchase activity, compared to search engines (31%) and recommendation engines (27%) (Dyer, 2011).

Membership in social networks has a large influence on discovering new independent music, but less influence on already well-known products (Garg, 2009). Membership in an online brand community like Ford's Facebook page and community has a direct effect on sales (Adjei, et al., 2009). Amazon's recommender systems ("Consumers who bought this item also bought ...") create co-purchase networks where people do not know one another personally, but nevertheless triple the influence of complementary products (Oestreicher-Singer and Sundararajan, 2008). The value of social networks to marketers rests on the proposition that brand strength and purchase decisions are closely related to network membership, rank, prominence, and centrality. At this point, the strength and scope of the relationship between social network membership, brand awareness, and purchase decisions is not completely understood, although all researchers agree that it exists in a variety of contexts and in varying degrees (Guo, et al., 2011).

CONSUMER BEHAVIOR MODELS

consumer behavior
a social science discipline that attempts to model and understand the behavior of humans in a marketplace

Once firms have an understanding of who is online, they need to focus on how consumers behave online. The study of **consumer behavior** is a social science discipline that attempts to model and understand the behavior of humans in a marketplace. Several social science disciplines play roles in this study, including sociology, psychology, and economics. Models of consumer behavior attempt to predict or "explain" what consumers purchase and where, when, how much, and why they buy. The expectation is that if the consumer decision-making process can be understood, firms will have a much better idea how to market and sell their products. **Figure 6.1** illustrates a general consumer behavior model that takes into account a wide range of factors that influence a consumer's marketplace decisions. Learning Track 6.2 contains further information about the cultural, social, and psychological background factors that influence consumer behavior.

PROFILES OF ONLINE CONSUMERS

Online consumer behavior parallels that of offline consumer behavior with some obvious differences. It is important to first understand why people choose the Internet channel to conduct transactions. **Table 6.2** lists the main reasons consumers choose the online channel.

While price appears on this list, overwhelmingly, consumers shop on the Web because of convenience, which in turn is produced largely by saving them time. Overall transaction cost reduction appears to be the major motivator for choosing the online channel, followed by other cost reductions in the product or service.

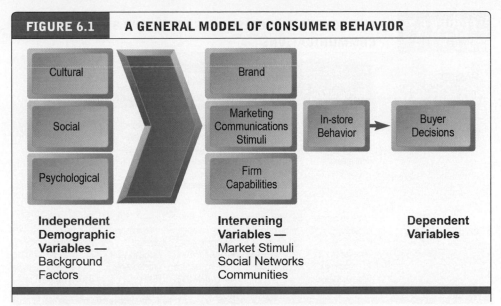

| FIGURE 6.1 | A GENERAL MODEL OF CONSUMER BEHAVIOR |

Consumer behavior models try to predict the decisions that consumers make in the marketplace.
SOURCE: Adapted from Kotler and Armstrong, 2009.

THE ONLINE PURCHASING DECISION

Once online, why do consumers actually purchase a product or service at a specific site? Among the most important are price and the availability of free shipping. That the seller is someone whom the purchaser trusts is also a very important factor. The ability to make a purchase without paying tax and the availability of an online coupon are also significant factors.

TABLE 6.2	WHY CONSUMERS CHOOSE THE ONLINE CHANNEL
REASON	PERCENTAGE OF RESPONDENTS
24-hour shopping convenience	35.1%
Easier to compare prices	33.1%
Free shipping offers	31.5%
No crowds like in mall/traditional stores	30.8%
More convenient to shop online	29.2%
Easier to find items online than in stores	17.5%
Better variety online	17.4%
No sales tax	14.9%
Direct shipping to gift recipients	13.8%
Easier to compare products	11.4%

SOURCE: Based on data from eMarketer, Inc., 2011a.

FIGURE 6.2	THE CONSUMER DECISION PROCESS AND SUPPORTING COMMUNICATIONS				
MARKET COMMUNICATIONS	**Awareness—Need Recognition**	**Search**	**Evaluation of Alternatives**	**Purchase**	**Post-purchase Behavior—Loyalty**
Offline Communications	Mass media TV Radio Print media Social networks	Catalogs Print ads Mass media Sales people Product raters Store visits Social networks	Reference groups Opinion leaders Mass media Product raters Store visits Social networks	Promotions Direct mail Mass media Print media	Warranties Service calls Parts and repair Consumer groups Social networks
Online Communications	Targeted banner ads Interstitials Targeted event promotions Social networks	Search engines Online catalogs Site visits Targeted e-mail Social networks	Search engines Online catalogs Site visits Product reviews User evaluations Social networks	Online promotions Lotteries Discounts Targeted e-mail Flash sales	Communities of consumption Newsletters Customer e-mail Online updates Social networks

You also need to consider the process that buyers follow when making a purchase decision, and how the Internet environment affects consumers' decisions. There are five stages in the consumer decision process: awareness of need, search for more information, evaluation of alternatives, the actual purchase decision, and post-purchase contact with the firm. **Figure 6.2** shows the consumer decision process and the types of offline and online marketing communications that support this process and seek to influence the consumer before, during, and after the purchase decision.

The stages of the consumer decision process are basically the same whether the consumer is offline or online. On the other hand, the general model of consumer behavior requires modification to take into account new factors, and the unique features of the Internet that allow new opportunities to interact with the customer online also need to be accounted for. In **Figure 6.3**, we have modified the general model of consumer behavior to focus on user characteristics, product characteristics, and Web site features, along with traditional factors such as brand strength and specific market communications (advertising) and the influence of both online and offline social networks.

In the online model, Web site features, along with consumer skills, product characteristics, attitudes towards online purchasing, and perceptions about control over the Web environment come to the fore. Web site features include latency (delay in downloads), navigability, and confidence in a Web site's security. There are parallels in the analog world. For instance, it is well known that consumer behavior can be influenced by store design, and that understanding the precise movements of consumers through a physical store can enhance sales if goods and promotions are arranged along the most likely consumer tracks. Consumer skills refers to the knowledge that consumers have about how to conduct online transactions (which increases with experience). Product characteristics refers to the fact that some products can be easily

FIGURE 6.3	A MODEL OF ONLINE CONSUMER BEHAVIOR

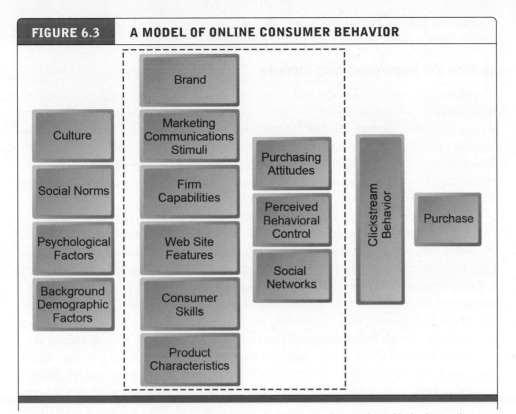

In this general model of online consumer behavior, the decision to purchase is shaped by background demographic factors, several intervening factors, and, finally, influenced greatly by clickstream behavior very near to the precise moment of purchase.

described, packaged, and shipped over the Internet, whereas others cannot. Combined with traditional factors, such as brand, advertising, and firm capabilities, these factors lead to specific attitudes about purchasing at a Web site (trust in the Web site and favorable customer experience) and a sense that the consumer can control his or her environment on the Web site.

Clickstream behavior refers to the transaction log that consumers establish as they move about the Web, from search engine to a variety of sites, then to a single site, then to a single page, and then, finally, to a decision to purchase. These precious moments are similar to "point-of-purchase" moments in traditional retail. A study of over 10,000 visits to an online wine store found that detailed and general clickstream behavior were as important as customer demographics and prior purchase behavior in predicting a current purchase (Van den Poel and Buckinx, 2005). Clickstream marketing takes maximum advantage of the Internet environment. It presupposes no prior "deep" knowledge of the customer (and in that sense is "privacy-regarding"), and can be developed dynamically as customers use the Internet. For instance, the success of search engine marketing (the display of paid advertisements on Web search pages) is based in large part on what the consumer is looking for at the moment and how they go about looking (detailed clickstream data). After examining the detailed data, general

clickstream behavior
the transaction log that consumers establish as they move about the Web

clickstream data is used (days since last visit, past purchases). If available, demographic data is used (region, city, and gender).

SHOPPERS: BROWSERS AND BUYERS

The picture of Internet use sketched in the previous section emphasizes the complexity of behavior online. Although the Internet audience still tends to be concentrated among the well educated, affluent, and youthful, the audience is increasingly becoming more diverse. Clickstream analysis shows us that people go online for many different reasons. Online shopping is similarly complex. Beneath the surface of the $362 billion B2C e-commerce market in 2012 are substantial differences in how users shop online.

For instance, as shown in **Figure 6.4**, about 73% of U.S. Internet users, age 14 and older, are "buyers" who actually purchase something entirely online. Another 16% research products on the Web ("browsers"), but purchase them offline. With the teen and adult U.S. Internet audience (14 years or older) estimated at about 213 million in 2013, online shoppers (the combination of buyers and browsers, totalling 89%) add up to a market size of almost 190 million consumers. Most marketers find this number exciting.

The significance of online browsing for offline purchasing should not be underestimated. Although it is difficult to precisely measure the amount of offline sales that occur because of online product research, several different studies have found that about one-third of all offline retail purchasing is influenced by online product research, blogs, banner ads, and other Internet exposure. The offline influence varies by product. This amounts to about $1.3 trillion in annual retail sales, a truly extraordinary number. By 2015, Forrester predicts that more than 50% of all retail commerce in the United States will be influenced by the Web (Forrester Research, 2012a).

E-commerce is a major conduit and generator of offline commerce. The reverse is also true: online traffic is driven by offline brands and shopping. While online

| FIGURE 6.4 | ONLINE SHOPPERS AND BUYERS |

Did not shop or buy online 11%

Shopped online but did not buy 16%

Online buyers 73%

About 89% of U.S Internet users, age 14 and older, shop online, either by researching products or by purchasing products online. The percentage of those actually purchasing has increased to about 73%. Only about 11% do not buy or shop online.

SOURCE: Based on data from eMarketer, Inc., 2013g.

research influences offline purchases, it is also the case that offline marketing media heavily influence online behavior including sales. Traditional print media (magazines and newspapers) and television are by far the most powerful media for reaching and engaging consumers with information about new products and directing them to the Web. Online communities and blogging are also very influential but not yet as powerful as traditional media. This may be surprising to many given the attention to social networks as marketing vehicles, but it reflects the diversity of influences on consumer behavior and the real-world marketing budgets of firms that are still heavily dominated by traditional media. Even more surprising in the era of Facebook, face-to-face interactions are a more powerful influence than participation in online social communities.

These considerations strongly suggest that e-commerce and traditional commerce are coupled and should be viewed by merchants (and researchers) as part of a continuum of consuming behavior and not as radical alternatives to one another. Commerce is commerce; the customers are often the same people. Customers use a wide variety of media, sometimes multiple media at once. The significance of these findings for marketers is very clear. Online merchants should build the information content of their sites to attract browsers looking for information, build content to rank high in search engines, put less attention on selling per se, and promote services and products (especially new products) in offline media settings in order to support their online stores.

WHAT CONSUMERS SHOP FOR AND BUY ONLINE

You can look at online sales as divided roughly into two groups: small-ticket and big-ticket items. Big-ticket items include computer equipment and consumer electronics, where orders can easily be more than $1,000. Small-ticket items include apparel, books, health and beauty supplies, office supplies, music, software, videos, and toys, where the average purchase is typically less than $100. In the early days of e-commerce, sales of small-ticket items vastly outnumbered those of large-ticket items. But the recent growth of big-ticket items such as computer hardware, consumer electronics, furniture, and jewelry has changed the overall sales mix. Consumers are now much more confident spending online for big-ticket items. Although furniture and large appliances were initially perceived as too bulky to sell online, these categories have rapidly expanded in the last few years. Free shipping offered by Amazon and other large retailers has also contributed to consumers buying many more expensive and large items online such as air conditioners. The types of purchases made also depend on levels of experience with the Web. New Web users tend primarily to buy small-ticket items, while experienced Web users are more willing to buy large-ticket items in addition to small-ticket items. Refer to Figure 1.10 to see how much consumers spent online for various categories of goods in 2012.

INTENTIONAL ACTS: HOW SHOPPERS FIND VENDORS ONLINE

Given the prevalence of "click here" banner ads, one might think customers are "driven" to online vendors by spur-of-the-moment decisions. In fact, only a tiny percentage of shoppers click on banners to find vendors. E-commerce shoppers are highly intentional. Typically, they are focused browsers looking for specific products, companies, and services. Once they are online, a majority of consumers use a search engine as their preferred method of research for purchasing a product. Many will go directly to a online marketplace, such as Amazon or eBay, and some will go directly to a specific retail Web site. Merchants can convert these "goal-oriented," intentional shoppers into buyers if the merchants can target their communications to the shoppers and design their sites in such a way as to provide easy-to-access and useful product information, full selection, and customer service, and do this at the very moment the customer is searching for the product. This is no small task.

WHY MORE PEOPLE DON'T SHOP ONLINE

A final consumer behavior question to address is: Why don't more online Web users shop online? About 27% of Internet users do not buy online. Why not?

Probably the largest factor preventing more people from shopping online is the "trust factor," the fear that online merchants will cheat you, lose your credit card information, or use personal information you give them to invade your personal privacy, bombarding you with unwanted e-mail and pop-up ads. Secondary factors can be summarized as "hassle factors," like shipping costs, returns, and inability to touch and feel the product.

TRUST, UTILITY, AND OPPORTUNISM IN ONLINE MARKETS

A long tradition of research shows that the two most important factors shaping the decision to purchase online are utility and trust (Brookings Institute, 2011; Kim, et al., 2009; Ba and Pavlou, 2002). Consumers want good deals, bargains, convenience, and speed of delivery. In short, consumers are looking for utility. On the other hand, in any seller-buyer relationship, there is an asymmetry of information. The seller usually knows a lot more than the consumer about the quality of goods and terms of sale. This can lead to opportunistic behavior by sellers (Akerlof, 1970; Williamson, 1985; Mishra, 1998). Consumers need to trust a merchant before they make a purchase. Sellers can develop trust among online consumers by building strong reputations of honesty, fairness, and delivery of quality products—the basic elements of a brand. Feedback forums such as Epinions.com (now part of Shopping.com), Amazon's book reviews from reviewers, and eBay's feedback forum are examples of trust-building online mechanisms (NielsenWire, 2012; Opinion Research Corporation, 2009). Online sellers who develop trust among consumers are able to charge a premium price for their online products and services (Kim and Benbasat, 2006, 2007; Pavlou, 2002). A review of the literature suggests that the most important factors leading to a trusting online relationship are perception of Web site credibility, ease of use, and perceived risk (Corritore, et al., 2006). An important brake on the growth of e-commerce is lack of trust. Newspaper and television ads are far more trusted than online ads (Nielsen, 2011). Personal friends and family are far more powerful determinants of online purchases than membership in social networks (eMarketer, Inc., 2010a). These attitudes have grown more positive over time, but new concerns about the use of personal information by Web marketers is raising trust issues among consumers again.

6.2   DIGITAL COMMERCE MARKETING AND ADVERTISING STRATEGIES AND TOOLS

Internet marketing has many similarities to, and differences from, ordinary marketing. (For more information on basic marketing concepts, see Learning Tracks 6.1 and 6.2). The objective of Internet marketing—as in all marketing—is to build customer relationships so that the firm can achieve above-average returns (both by offering superior products or services and by communicating the brand's features to the consumer). These relationships are a foundation for the firm's brand. But Internet marketing, including all forms of digital marketing, is also very different from ordinary marketing because the nature of the medium and its capabilities are so different from anything that has come before.

There are four features of Internet marketing that distinguish it from traditional marketing channels. Compared to traditional print and television marketing, Internet marketing can be more personalized, participatory, peer-to-peer, and communal. Not all types of Internet marketing have these four features. For instance, there's not much difference between a marketing video splashed on your computer screen without your consent and watching a television commercial. However the same marketing video can be targeted to your personal interests, community memberships, and allow you to share it with others using a Like or + tag. Marketers are learning that the most effective Internet marketing has all four of these features.

STRATEGIC ISSUES AND QUESTIONS

In the past, from 2000 to 2010, the first step in building an online brand was to build a Web site, and then try to attract an audience. The most common "traditional" marketing techniques for establishing a brand and attracting customers were search engine marketing, display ads, e-mail campaigns, and affiliate programs. This is still the case: building a Web site is still a first step, and the "traditional" online marketing techniques are still the main powerhouses of brand creation and online sales revenue in 2013. But today, marketers need to take a much broader view of the online marketing challenge, and to consider other media channels for attracting an audience such as social network sites and mobile devices, in concert with traditional Web sites.

The five main elements of a comprehensive multi-channel marketing plan are: Web site, traditional online marketing, social marketing, mobile marketing, and offline marketing. **Table 6.3** illustrates these five main platforms, central elements within each type, some examples, and the primary function of marketing in each situation. Each of the main types of online marketing are discussed in this section and throughout the chapter in greater detail.

Immediately, by examining Table 6.3, you can understand the management complexity of building brands online. There are five major types of marketing, and a variety of different platforms that perform different functions. If you're a manager of a start-up, or the Web site manager of an existing commercial Web site, you face a number of strategic questions. Where should you focus first? Build a Web site, develop a blog, or jump into developing a Facebook presence? If you have a successful Web

TABLE 6.3	THE DIGITAL MARKETING ROADMAP		
TYPE OF MARKETING	**PLATFORMS**	**EXAMPLES**	**FUNCTION**
Web Site	Traditional Web site	Ford.com	Anchor site
Traditional Online Marketing	Search engine marketing	Google; Bing; Yahoo	Query-based intention marketing
	Display advertising	Yahoo; Google; MSN	Interest- and context-based marketing; targeted marketing
	E-mail	Major retailers	Permission marketing
	Affiliates	Amazon	Brand extension
Social Marketing	Social networks	Facebook/Google +1	Conversations; sharing
	Micro blogging sites	Twitter	News, quick updates
	Blogs/forums	Pinterest; TheFancy	Communities of interest; sharing
	Video marketing	YouTube	Engage; inform
	Game marketing	Farmville; SimCity	Identification
Mobile Marketing	Smartphone site	m.ford.com	Quick access; news; updates
	Tablet site	t.ford.com	Visual engagement
	Apps	Ford Mustang Customerizer	Visual engagement
		Vehicle Brochure Apps	Visual engagement
Offline Marketing	Television	Cadillac CTS Olympics 2012	Brand anchoring; inform
	Newspapers	Nike Olympics ambush campaign	Brand anchoring; inform
	Magazines	BMW Expression of Joy print and video campaign	Brand anchoring; inform

site that already uses search engine marketing and display ads, where should you go next: develop a social network presence or use offline media? Does your firm have the resources to maintain a social media marketing campaign?

A second strategic management issue involves the integration of all these different marketing platforms into a single coherent branding message. Often, there are different groups with different skill sets involved in Web site design, search engine and display marketing, social media marketing, and offline marketing. Getting all these different specialties to work together and coordinate their campaigns can be very difficult. The danger is that a firm ends up with different teams managing each of the four platforms rather than a single team managing the digital online presence, or for that matter, marketing for the entire firm including retail outlets.

A third strategic management question involves resource allocation. There are actually two problems here. Each of the different major types of marketing, and each of the different platforms, has different metrics to measure its effectiveness. In some cases, for new social marketing platforms, there is no commonly accepted metric, and few that have withstood critical scrutiny or have a deep experience base providing empirical data. For instance, in Facebook marketing, an important metric is how many Likes your Facebook page produces. The connection between Likes and sales is still being explored. In search engine marketing, effectiveness is measured by how many clicks your ads are receiving; in display advertising, by how many impressions of your ads are served. Second, each of these platforms has different costs for Likes, impressions, and clicks. In order to choose where your marketing resources should be deployed, you will have to link each of these activities to sales revenue. You will need to determine how much clicks, Likes, and impressions are worth. We address these questions in greater detail in Chapter 7.

THE WEB SITE AS A MARKETING PLATFORM: ESTABLISHING THE CUSTOMER RELATIONSHIP

A firm's Web site is a major tool for establishing the initial relationship with the customer. The Web site performs four important functions: establishing the brand identity and consumer expectations, informing and educating the consumer, shaping the customer experience, and anchoring the brand in an ocean of marketing messages coming from different sources. The Web site is the one place the consumer can turn to find the complete story. This is not true of apps, e-mails, or search engine ads.

The first function of a Web site is to establish the brand's identity and to act as an anchor for the firm's other Web marketing activities, thereby driving sales revenue. This involves identifying for the consumer the differentiating features of the product or service in terms of quality, price, product support, and reliability. Identifying the differentiating features of the product on the Web site's home page is intended to create expectations in the user of what it will be like to consume the product. For instance, Coke's Web site creates the expectation that the consumer will experience happiness by opening a Coke. Ford's Web site focuses on automobile technology and high miles per gallon. The expectation created by Ford's Web site is that if you buy a Ford, you'll be experiencing the latest automotive technology and the highest mileage. At the location-based social network Web site for Foursquare, the focus is on meeting friends, discovering local places, and saving money with coupons and rewards.

Web sites also function to anchor the brand online, acting as a central point where all the branding messages that emanate from the firm's multiple digital presences, such as Facebook, Twitter, mobile apps, or e-mail, come together at a single online location. Aside from branding, Web sites also perform the typical functions of any commercial establishment by informing customers of the company's products and services. Web sites, with their online catalogs and associated shopping carts, are important elements of the online customer experience. **Customer experience** refers to the totality of experiences that a customer has with a firm, including the search, informing, purchase, consumption, and after-sales support for the product. The concept "customer experience" is broader than the traditional concept of "customer satisfaction" in that a much broader range of

customer experience
the totality of experiences that a customer has with a firm, including the search, informing, purchase, consumption, and after-sales support for its products, services, and various retail channels

impacts is considered, including the customer's cognitive, affective, emotional, social, and physical relationship to the firm and its products. The totality of customer experiences will generally involve multiple retail channels. This means that, in the customer's mind, the Web site, Facebook page, Twitter feed, physical store, and television advertisements are all connected as part of his or her experience with the company.

TRADITIONAL ONLINE MARKETING AND ADVERTISING TOOLS

Below we describe the basic marketing and advertising tools for attracting e-commerce consumers: search engine marketing, display ad marketing (including banner ads, rich media ads, video ads, and sponsorships), e-mail and permission marketing, affiliate marketing, viral marketing, and lead generation marketing.

online advertising

a paid message on a Web site, online service, or other interactive medium

Companies will spend an estimated $171 billion on advertising in 2013, and an estimated $42 billion of that amount on **online advertising**, which includes display (banners, video, and rich media), search, mobile messaging, sponsorships, classifieds, lead generation, and e-mail, on desktop, laptop, and tablet computers, as well as mobile phones (see **Figure 6.5**) (eMarketer, Inc., 2013h).

In the last five years, advertisers have aggressively increased online spending and cut outlays on traditional channels such as newspapers and magazines while outdoor,

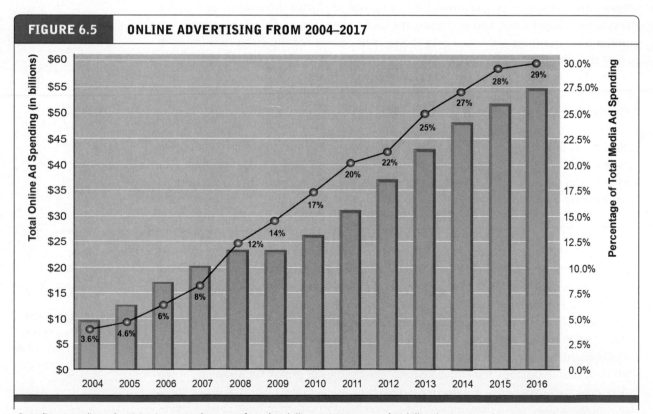

| FIGURE 6.5 | **ONLINE ADVERTISING FROM 2004–2017** |

Spending on online advertising is expected to grow from $43 billion in 2012 to over $60 billion by 2017, and comprise an increasing percentage of total media ad spending.

SOURCES: Based on data from eMarketer, Inc., 2013h.

TABLE 6.4	ONLINE ADVERTISING SPENDING FOR SELECTED FORMATS (IN BILLIONS)		
FORMAT	2013	2017	AVERAGE GROWTH RATE
Search	$19.6	$25.6	8.1%
Banner ads	$8.6	$12.2	7.4%
Video	$4.1	$9.2	26.6%
Classifieds	$2.7	$3.1	3.6%
Rich media	$2.0	$5.4	24.9%
Lead generation	$1.9	$2.3	6.5%
Sponsorships	$1.9	$3.1	15.4%
E-mail	$0.23	$0.26	3.4%

SOURCES: Based on data from eMarketer, Inc., 2013i.

television, and radio advertising have shown modest growth. Over the next five years, online advertising is expected to continue to be the fastest growing form of advertising, and by 2017, it is expected to be the second largest ad channel with over a 30% share.

Table 6.4 provides some comparative data on the amount of spending for certain advertising formats. The online advertising format that currently produces the highest revenue is paid search, followed by display ads, but the fastest growing online ad format is video ads. Note, however, that this does not include mobile ads, which are growing fastest of all.

Spending on online advertising among different industries is somewhat skewed. Retail accounts for the highest percentage (20%), followed by financial services (13%), automotive (12%), telecommunications (11%), leisure travel (9%), computing products (8%), consumer packaged goods (7%), pharmaceuticals and healthcare (6%), media (5%), and entertainment (4%) (Interactive Advertising Bureau/PricewaterhouseCoopers, 2013). Online advertising has both advantages and disadvantages when compared to advertising in traditional media, such as television, radio, and print (magazines and newspapers). One big advantage for online advertising is that the Internet is where the audience has moved, especially the very desirable 18–34 age group. A second big advantage for online advertising is the ability to target ads to individuals and small groups and to track performance of advertisements in almost real time. **Ad targeting**, the sending of market messages to specific subgroups in the population in an effort to increase the likelihood of a purchase, is as old as advertising itself, but prior to the Internet, it could only be done with much less precision, certainly not down to the level of individuals. Ad targeting is also the foundation of price discrimination: the ability to charge different types of consumers different prices for the same product or

ad targeting
the sending of market messages to specific subgroups in the population

service. With online advertising, it's theoretically possible to charge every customer a different price.

Theoretically, online advertising can personalize every ad message to precisely fit the needs, interests, and values of each consumer. In practice, as we all know from spam and constant exposure to pop-up ads that are of little interest, the reality is very different. Online advertisements also provide greater opportunities for interactivity—two-way communication between advertisers and potential customers. The primary disadvantages of online advertising are concerns about its cost versus its benefits, how to adequately measure its results, and the supply of good venues to display ads. For instance, the owners of Web sites who sell advertising space ("publishers") do not have agreed-upon standards or routine audits to verify their claimed numbers as do traditional media outlets. We examine the costs and benefits of online advertising as well as research on its effectiveness in Section 6.4.

Search Engine Marketing and Advertising

Search engines are the largest marketing and advertising platform on the Internet, and until recently, the fastest growing. In 2013, companies will spend an estimated $19.6 billion on search engine marketing and advertising, almost half of all spending for digital marketing. On an average day in the United States, around 116 million American adults (around 59% of the adult online population) will use a search engine (Pew Internet & American Life Project, 2013a). Briefly, this is where the eyeballs are (at least for a few moments) and this is where advertising can be very effective by responding with ads that match the interests and intentions of the user. The click-through rate for search engine advertising is generally 1%–5% and has been fairly steady over the years. The top three search engine providers (Google, Microsoft/Bing, and Yahoo) supply more than 95% of all online searches. **Search engine marketing (SEM)** refers to the use of search engines to build and sustain brands. **Search engine advertising** refers to the use of search engines to support direct sales to online consumers.

search engine marketing (SEM)
involves the use of search engines to build and sustain brands

search engine advertising
involves the use of search engines to support direct sales to online

Search engines are often thought of as mostly direct sales channels focused on making sales in response to advertisements. While this is a major use of search engines, they are also used more subtly to strengthen brand awareness, drive traffic to other Web sites or blogs to support customer engagement, to gain deeper insight into customers' perceptions of the brand, to support other related advertising (for instance, sending consumers to local dealer sites), and to support the brand indirectly. Search engines can also provide marketers insight into customer search patterns, opinions customers hold about their products, top trending search keywords, and what their competitors are using as keywords and the customer response. For example, Pepsico, home of mega brands like Pepsi and Doritos, makes no sales on the Web, but has several branding Web sites aimed at consumers, investors, and shareholders. The focus is on building, sustaining, and updating the Pepsi collection of branded consumer goods. A search on Pepsi will generate numerous search results that link to Pepsi marketing materials.

Types of Search Engine Advertising There are at least three different types of search engine advertising: keyword paid inclusion (so-called "sponsored links"), advertising keywords (such as Google's AdWords), and search engine context ads (such as Google's AdSense). Search engine sites originally performed unbiased searches of the Web's huge collection of Web pages and derived most of their revenue from banner advertisements. This form of search engine results is often called **organic search** because the inclusion and ranking of Web sites depends on a more or less "unbiased" application of a set of rules (an algorithm) imposed by the search engine. Since 1998, search engine sites slowly transformed themselves into digital yellow pages, where firms pay for inclusion in the search engine index, pay for keywords to show up in search results, or pay for keywords to show up in other vendors' ads.

Most search engines offer **paid inclusion** (also called sponsored link) programs, which, for a fee, guarantee a Web site's inclusion in its list of search results, more frequent visits by its Web crawler, and suggestions for improving the results of organic searching. Search engines claim that these payments—costing some merchants hundreds of thousands a year—do not influence the organic ranking of a Web site in search results, just inclusion in the results. However, it is the case that page inclusion ads get more hits, and the rank of the page appreciates, causing the organic search algorithm to rank it higher in the organic results.

Google claims that it does not permit firms to pay for their rank in the organic results, although it does allocate two to three sponsored links at the very top of their pages, albeit labeling them as "Sponsored Links." Merchants who refuse to pay for inclusion or for keywords typically fall far down on the list of results, and off the first page of results, which is akin to commercial death.

The two other types of search engine advertising rely on selling keywords in online auctions. In **keyword advertising**, merchants purchase keywords through a bidding process at search sites, and whenever a consumer searches for that word, their advertisement shows up somewhere on the page, usually as a small text-based advertisement on the right, but also as a listing on the very top of the page. The more merchants pay, the higher the rank and greater the visibility of their ads on the page. Generally, the search engines do not exercise editorial judgment about quality or content of the ads although they do monitor the use of language. In addition, some search engines rank the ads in terms of their popularity rather than merely the money paid by the advertiser so that the rank of the ad depends on both the amount paid and the number of clicks per unit time. Google's keyword advertising program is called AdWords, Yahoo's is called Sponsored Search, and Microsoft's is called adCenter.

Network keyword advertising (**context advertising**), introduced by Google as its AdSense product in 2002, differs from the ordinary keyword advertising described previously. Publishers (Web sites that want to show ads) join these networks and allow the search engine to place "relevant" ads on their sites. The ads are paid for by advertisers who want their messages to appear across the Web. Google-like text messages are the most common. The revenue from the resulting clicks is split between the search engine and the site publisher, although the publisher gets much more than half in some cases. About half of Google's revenue comes from AdWords and the rest comes from AdSense.

Search engine advertising is nearly an ideal targeted marketing technique: at precisely the moment that a consumer is looking for a product, an advertisement for

---

organic search
inclusion and ranking of sites depends on a more or less unbiased application of a set of rules imposed by the search engine

paid inclusion
for a fee, guarantees a Web site's inclusion in its list of sites, more frequent visits by its Web crawler, and suggestions for improving the results of organic searching

keyword advertising
merchants purchase keywords through a bidding process at search sites, and whenever a consumer searches for that word, their advertisement shows up somewhere on the page

network keyword advertising (context advertising)
publishers accept ads placed by Google on their Web sites, and receive a fee for any click-throughs from those ads

that product is presented. Consumers benefit from search engine advertising because ads for merchants appear only when consumers are looking for a specific product. There are no pop-ups, Flash animations, videos, interstitials, e-mails, or other irrelevant communications to deal with. Thus, search engine advertising saves consumers cognitive energy and reduces search costs (including the cost of cars or trains needed to do physical searches for products). In a recent study, the global value of search to both merchants and consumers was estimated to be more than $800 billion, with about 65% of the benefit going to consumers in the form of lower search costs and lower prices (McKinsey, 2011).

Because search engine marketing can be very effective, companies optimize their Web sites for search engine recognition. The better optimized the page is, the higher a ranking it will achieve in search engine result listings, and the more likely it will appear on the top of the page in search engine results. **Search engine optimization** is the process of improving the ranking of Web pages with search engines by altering the content and design of the Web pages and site. By carefully selecting key words used on the Web pages, updating content frequently, and designing the site so it can be easily read by search engine programs, marketers can improve the impact and return on investment in their Web marketing programs.

search engine optimization

techniques to improve the ranking of Web pages generated by search engine algorithms

social search

effort to provide fewer, more relevant, and trustworthy results based on the social graph

Social Search **Social search** is an attempt to use your social contacts (and your entire social graph) to provide search results. In contrast to the top search engines that use a mathematical algorithm to find pages that satisfy your query, social search reviews your friends' (and their friends') recommendations, past Web visits, and use of Like buttons. One problem with Google and mechanical search engines is that they are so thorough: enter a search for "smartphone" and in .28 second you will receive 504 million results, some of them providing helpful information and others that are suspect. Social search is an effort to provide fewer, more relevant, and trustworthy results based on the social graph. For instance, Google has developed Google +1 as a social layer on top of its existing search engine. Users can place a +1 next to Web sites they found helpful, and their friends will be automatically notified. Subsequent searches by their friends would list the +1 sites recommended by friends higher up on the page. Facebook's Like button is a similar social search tool. Facebook's Graph Search is a social search engine introduced by Facebook in March 2013. Graph Search produces information from within a user's network of friends supplemented with additional results provided by Bing.

Search Engine Issues While search engines have provided significant benefits to merchants and customers, they also present risks and costs. For instance, search engines have the power to crush a small business by placing its ads on the back pages of search results. Merchants are at the mercy of search engines for access to the online marketplace, and this access is dominated by a single firm, Google. How Google decides to rank one company over another in search results is not known. No one really knows how to improve in its rankings (although there are hundreds of firms who claim otherwise). Google editors intervene in unknown ways to punish certain Web sites and reward others. Using paid sponsored listings, as opposed to relying on organic search results, eliminates some, but not all, of this uncertainty.

Other practices that degrade the results and usefulness of search engines include:

- **Link farms** are groups of Web sites that link to one another, thereby boosting their ranking in search engines that use a PageRank algorithm to judge the "usefulness" of a site. For instance, in the 2010 holiday season, JCPenney was found to be the highest ranked merchant for a large number of clothing products. On examination, it was discovered that this resulted from Penney's hiring a search engine optimization company to create thousands of Web sites that linked to JCPenney's Web site. As a result, JCPenney's Web site became the most popular (most linked-to) Web site for products like dresses, shirts, and pants. No matter what popular clothing item people searched for, JCPenney came out on top. Experts believe this was the largest search engine fraud in history.

- **Content farms** are companies that generate large volumes of textual content for multiple Web sites designed to attract viewers and search engines. Content farms profit by attracting large numbers of readers to their sites and exposing them to ads. The content typically is not original but is artfully copied or summarized from legitimate content sites.

- **Click fraud** occurs when a competitor clicks on search engine results and ads, forcing the advertiser to pay for the click even though the click is not legitimate. Competitors can hire offshore firms to perform fraudulent clicks or hire botnets to automate the process. Click fraud can quickly run up a large bill for merchants, and not result in any growth in sales.

Display Ad Marketing

In 2013, companies spent around $17.6 billion on display ad marketing, over 40% of all spending for digital marketing. Over 5.3 trillion display ad impressions were served in 2012 (comScore, 2013). The top five display ad companies are Google, Facebook, Yahoo, Microsoft, and AOL, and together they account for over 50% of U.S. display ad revenue. The Interactive Advertising Bureau (IAB), an industry organization, has established voluntary industry guidelines for display ads. Publishers are not required to use these guidelines, but many do. One objective of IAB is to give the consumer a consistent experience across all Web sites. The various types of ads are designed to help advertisers break through the "noise" and clutter created by the high number of display ad impressions that a typical user is exposed to within a given day. **Figure 6.6** shows examples of the seven core standard ad units, as specified by the IAB. The top three ad formats—the medium rectangle, the leaderboard, and the wide skyscraper—account for nearly 80% of all display ad impressions served (Google, 2012). Eye-tracking research has found that for both desktop and tablet computers, leaderboard ads are the most effective in grabbing a user's attention and holding it (Tobii/Mediative, 2012). Display ads consist of four different kinds of ads: banner ads, rich media ads (animated ads), sponsorships, and video ads.

link farms
groups of Web sites that link to one another, thereby boosting their ranking in search engines

content farms
companies that generate large volumes of textual content for multiple Web sites designed to attract viewers and search engines

click fraud
occurs when a competitor clicks on search engine results and ads, forcing the advertiser to pay for the click even though the click is not legitimate

FIGURE 6.6 | **TYPES OF DISPLAY ADS**

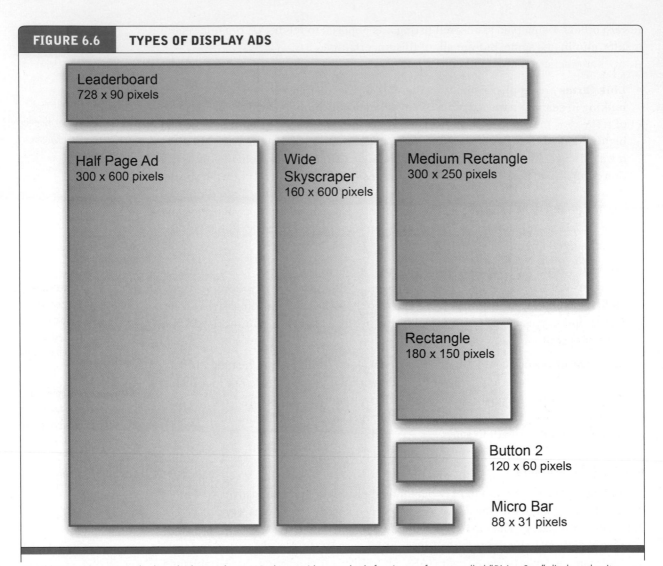

In addition to the various display ads shown above, IAB also provides standards for six new formats called "Rising Star" display ad units.
SOURCE: Based on data from Interactive Advertising Bureau, 2011.

banner ad

displays a promotional message in a rectangular box at the top or bottom of a computer screen

Banner Ads Banner ads are the oldest and most familiar form of display marketing. They are also the least effective and the lowest cost form of online marketing. A banner ad displays a promotional message in a rectangular box at the top or bottom of a computer screen. A **banner ad** is similar to a traditional ad in a printed publication but has some added advantages. When clicked, it brings potential customers directly to the advertiser's Web site, and the site where the ad appears can observe the user's behavior on the site. The ability to identify and track the user is a key feature of online advertising. Banner ads feature Flash video and other animations. It's important to note, although the terms banner ad and display ad are often used interchangeably, that banner ads are just one form of display ad.

Rich Media Ads **Rich media ads** are ads that employ animation, sound, and interactivity, using Flash, HTML5, Java, and JavaScript. Rich media ads are expected to account for about $2 billion in online advertising expenditures (about 5% of total online advertising) in 2013. They are far more effective than simple banner ads. For instance, one research report that analyzed 24,000 different rich media ads with more than 12 billion impressions served in North America between July and December 2011 found that exposure to rich media ads boosted advertiser site visits by nearly 300% compared to standard banner ads. Viewers of rich media ads that included video were six times more likely to visit the advertiser's Web site, by either directly clicking on the ad, typing the advertiser's URL, or searching (MediaMind, 2012a).

The IAB provides guidance for a number of different types of rich media ads, such as those that contain in-banner video, those that are expandable/retractable, pop-ups, floating versions, and interstitials. An **interstitial ad** (interstitial means "in between") is a way of placing a full-page message between the current and destination pages of a user. Interstitials are usually inserted within a single Web site, and displayed as the user moves from one page to the next. The interstitial is typically contained in its own browser window and moves automatically to the page the user requested after allowing enough time for the ad to be read. Interstitials can also be deployed over an advertising network and appear as users move among Web sites.

Since the Web is such a busy place, people have to find ways to cope with overstimulation. One means of coping is known as *sensory input filtering*. This means that people learn to filter out the vast majority of the messages coming at them. Internet users quickly learn at some level to recognize banner ads or anything that looks like a banner ad and to filter out most of the ads that are not exceptionally relevant. Interstitial messages, like TV commercials, attempt to make viewers a captive of the message. Typical interstitials last 10 seconds or less and force the user to look at the ad for that time period. IAB standards for pre-roll ads also limit their length. To avoid boring users, ads typically use animated graphics and music to entertain and inform them. A good interstitial will also have a "skip through" or "stop" option for users who have no interest in the message.

The IAB also provides mobile rich media ad interface definitions (MRAID) in an effort to provide a set of standards designed to work with HTML5 and JavaScript that developers can use to create rich media ads to work with apps running on different mobile devices. The hope is make it easier to display ads across a wide variety of devices without having to rewrite code (Interactive Advertising Bureau, 2012).

Video Ads **Video ads** are TV-like advertisements that appear as in-page video commercials or before, during, or after a variety of content. **Table 6.5** describes some of the IAB standards for video ads.

Although from a total spending standpoint, online video ads are still very small when compared to the amount spent on search engine advertising, video ads are one of the fastest growing forms of online advertisement, accounting for about $4.1 billion in online advertising spending, which is expected to more than double to $9.2 billion by 2017. The rapid growth in video ads is due in part to the fact that video ads are far more effective than other display ad formats. For instance, according to research analyzing

rich media ad
ad employing animation, sound, and interactivity, using Flash, HTML5 Java, and JavaScript

interstitial ad
a way of placing a full-page message between the current and destination page of a user

video ad
TV-like advertisement that appears as an in-page video commercial or before, during, or after content

TABLE 6.5	TYPES OF VIDEO ADS		
FORMAT	DESCRIPTION	WHEN USED	USED WITH
Linear video ad	Pre-roll; takeover; ad takes over video for a certain period of time	Before, between, or after video	Text, banners, rich media video player skins
Nonlinear video ad	Overlay; ad runs at same time as video content and does not take over full screen	During, over, or within video	
In-banner video ad	Rich media; ad is triggered within banner, may expand outside banner	Within Web page, generally surrounded by content	None
In-text video ad	Rich media; ad is delivered when user mouses over relevant text	Within Web page, identified as a highlighted word within relevant content	None

a variety of ad formats, in-stream video ads had click-through rates 12 times that of rich media and 27 times that of standard banner ads (MediaMind, 2012b). Exactly how to best take advantage of this opportunity is still somewhat a puzzle. Internet users are apparently willing to tolerate advertising in order to watch online as long as the ads are not too long and don't interfere too much with the viewing experience.

There are many formats for displaying ads with videos. The most widely used format is the "pre-roll" (followed by the mid-roll and the post-roll) where users are forced to watch a video ad either before, in the middle of, or at the end of the video they originally clicked on.

There are many specialized video advertising networks such as SAY Media, Advertising.com, and others who run video advertising campaigns for national advertisers and place these videos on their respective networks of Web sites. Firms can also establish their own video and television sites to promote their products. Retail sites are among the largest users of advertising videos. In 2011, Zappos, the largest online shoe retailer, created a video for every one of its products, adding 100,000 videos to its Web sites.

sponsorship
a paid effort to tie an advertiser's name to information, an event, or a venue in a way that reinforces its brand in a positive yet not overtly commercial manner

Sponsorships A **sponsorship** is a paid effort to tie an advertiser's name to particular information, an event, or a venue in a way that reinforces its brand in a positive yet not overtly commercial manner. In 2013, companies will spend about $1.9 billion for sponsorship marketing. Sponsorships typically are more about branding than immediate sales. A common form of sponsorship is targeted content (or advertorials), in which editorial content is combined with an ad message to make the message more valuable and attractive to its intended audience. For instance, WebMD.com, the leading medical information Web site in the United States, offers "sponsorship sites" on the WebMD Web site to companies such as Phillips to describe its home defibrillators, and Lilly to describe its pharmaceutical solutions for attention deficit disorders among children. Social media sponsorships, in which marketers pay for mentions in social media, such as blogs, tweets, or in online video, have also become a popular tactic. Sponsorships have also moved onto the mobile platform. For instance, Suburu sponsors an app called MapMyDogwalk, a GPS-enabled dog walking tool.

Advertising Networks In the early years of e-commerce, firms placed ads on the few popular Web sites in existence, but by early 2000, there were hundreds of thousands of sites where ads could be displayed, and it became very inefficient for a single firm to purchase ads on each individual Web site. Most firms, even very large firms, did not have the capability by themselves to place banner ads and marketing messages on thousands of Web sites and monitor the results. Specialized marketing firms called **advertising networks** appeared to help firms take advantage of the powerful marketing potential of the Internet, and to make the entire process of buying and selling online ads more efficient and transparent. These ad networks have proliferated and have greatly increased the scale and liquidity of online marketing.

Advertising networks represent the most sophisticated application of Internet database capabilities to date, and illustrate just how different Internet marketing is from traditional marketing. Advertising networks sell advertising and marketing opportunities (slots) to companies who wish to buy exposure to an online audience (advertisers). Advertising networks obtain their inventory of ad opportunities from a network of participating sites that want to display ads on their sites in return for receiving a payment from advertisers everytime a visitor clicks on an ad. These sites are usually referred to as Web publishers. Marketers buy audiences and publishers sell audiences by attracting an audience and capturing audience information. Ad networks are the intermediaries who make this market work efficiently.

Figure 6.7 illustrates how these systems work. Advertising networks begin with a consumer requesting a page from a member of the advertising network (1). A connection is established with the third-party ad server (2). The ad server identifies the user by reading the cookie file on the user's hard drive and checks its user profile database for the user's profile (3). The ad server selects an appropriate banner ad based on the user's previous purchases, interests, demographics, or other data in the profile (4). Whenever the user later goes online and visits any of the network member sites, the ad server recognizes the user and serves up the same or different ads regardless of the site content. The advertising network follows users from site to site through the use of Web tracking files (5).

Advertising Exchanges and Real-Time Bidding. **Ad exchanges** take the online advertising market a step further by aggregating the supply side of advertising slots available at publishers across several ad networks, and establishing a **real-time bidding process (RTB)** where marketers can bid for slots based on their marketing criteria. Want to contact males age 18 to 34, recent visitors to a car site, unmarried, high risk-taking profile, located in New York or California, urban home, and financial service industry employment? An ad exchange will allow you to bid in real time on this audience against other advertisers, and then manage the placement of ads, accounting, and measurement for your firm. Ad exchanges offer tremendous global scale and efficiency. About 60% of display ads are now placed through ad exchanges. One of the best known is Google's DoubleClick Ad Exchange, which is based on more than 100 ad networks (the supply side), and provides a computer-based market for buyers to

advertising networks
connect online marketers with publishers by displaying ads to consumers based on detailed customer information

ad exchanges
create a market where many ad networks sell ad space to marketers

real-time bidding process (RTB)
online auctions where advertisers bid for audience slots

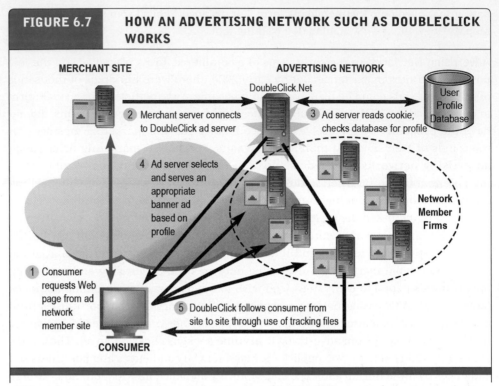

| FIGURE 6.7 | HOW AN ADVERTISING NETWORK SUCH AS DOUBLECLICK WORKS |

Millions of publishers have audiences to sell, and pages to fill with ads. Thousands of advertisers are looking for audiences. Ad networks are intermediaries that connect publishers with marketers.

purchase audiences (the demand side). This exchange sells audiences sliced into 1,600 interest categories. It displays more than 300 billion ad impressions a month across 2 million Web sites worldwide, and maintains or distributes more than 500 million user profiles of Internet users (AdAge.com, 2013). These profiles are based on Web tracking files, offline purchase information, and social network data. Marketing firms, the buyers from publishers of Web sites, can target their audience and control the frequency and timing of ads during the day. The case study at the end of the chapter, *Instant Ads: Real-Time Marketing on Exchanges*, provides you with a further look at ad exchanges and real-time bidding.

E-mail Marketing

direct e-mail marketing
e-mail marketing messages sent directly to interested users

When e-mail marketing began, unsolicited e-mail was not common. **Direct e-mail marketing** (e-mail marketing messages sent directly to interested users) was one of the first and most effective forms of online marketing communications. Direct e-mail marketing messages are sent to an opt-in audience of Internet users who, at one time or another, have expressed an interest in receiving messages from the advertiser. By sending e-mail to an opt-in audience, advertisers were targeting interested consumers. Response rates to legitimate, opt-in e-mail campaigns average just over 6%, depending on the targeting and freshness of the list. By far, in-house e-mail lists are more effective than purchased e-mail lists. Because of the comparatively high response rates and low cost, direct e-mail marketing remains a common form of online marketing communications. Other benefits of e-mail marketing include its mass reach, the ability to track and measure response, the ability to personalize content and tailor offers, the ability to drive traffic to Web sites for more interaction, the ability to test and optimize content and offers, and the ability to target by region, demographic, time of day, or other criteria. In 2013, U.S. companies will spend about $230 million on e-mail marketing, a relatively small amount when compared to search and display ad marketing. But these numbers can be deceiving. E-mail marketing still packs a punch with solid customer response. Click-through rates for legitimate e-mail depend on the promotion (the offer), the product, and the amount of targeting, but average over 7% for an in-house list, higher than postal mail response rates (3.5%) (Direct Marketing Association, 2012). Despite the deluge of spam mail, e-mail remains a highly cost-effective way of communicating with existing customers, and to a lesser extent, finding new customers. Data from the CMO Council shows that almost two-thirds of marketers surveyed rated e-mail as the most successful digital marketing tactic (eMarketer, Inc., 2012a). E-mail is also increasingly being accessed via mobile devices, which has the potential to create both opportunities and issues for marketers. About one-third of e-mails are opened on mobile devices, and mobile users have much higher e-mail utilization rates than do desktop users. Upwards of 88% of smartphone users check their e-mail daily.

E-mail marketing and advertising is inexpensive and somewhat invariant to the number of mails sent. The cost of sending 1,000 mails is about the same as the cost to send 1 million. The primary cost of e-mail marketing is for the purchase of the list of names to which the e-mail will be sent. This generally costs anywhere from 5 to 20 cents a name, depending on how targeted the list is. Sending the e-mail is virtually cost-free. In contrast, the cost to send a direct mail 5 x 7-inch post card is about 15 cents per name, but printing and mailing costs raise the overall cost to around 75 to 80 cents a name. While the cost of legitimate e-mail messages based on high-quality commercial opt-in e-mail lists is $5 to $10 per thousand, the direct mail cost is $500 to $700 per thousand.

While e-mail marketing often is sales oriented, it can also be used as an integral feature of a multi-channel marketing campaign designed to strengthen brand recognition. For instance, in 2012, Jeep created an e-mail campaign to a targeted audience of people who had searched on SUVs, and visited Chrysler and Jeep Facebook pages. The e-mail campaign announced a contest based on a game users could play online that involved tracking an arctic beast with a Jeep. Recipients could sign up on Facebook, Twitter, or the Jeep blog.

Although e-mail can still be an effective marketing and advertising tool, it faces three main challenges: spam, software tools used to control spam that eliminate much e-mail from user inboxes, and poorly targeted purchased e-mail lists. **Spam** is unsolicited commercial e-mail (sometimes referred to as "junk" e-mail) and *spammers* are people who send unsolicited e-mail to a mass audience that has not expressed any interest in the product. Spammers tend to market pornography, fraudulent deals and services, scams, and other products not widely approved in most civilized societies. Legitimate direct opt-in e-mail marketing is not growing as fast as behaviorally

spam
unsolicited commercial e-mail

targeted banners, pop-ups, and search engine advertising because of the explosion in spam. Consumer response to even legitimate e-mail campaigns has become more sophisticated. In general, e-mail works well for maintaining customer relationships but poorly for acquiring new customers.

While click fraud may be the Achilles' heel of search engine advertising, spam is the nemesis of effective e-mail marketing and advertising. The percentage of all e-mail that is spam is estimated at around 65–70% in 2013 (Symantec, 2013). Most spam originates from bot networks, which consist of thousands of captured PCs that can initiate and relay spam messages (see Chapter 5). Spam volume has declined somewhat since authorities took down the Rustock botnet in 2011. Spam is seasonally cyclical, and varies monthly due to the impact of new technologies (both supportive and discouraging of spammers), new prosecutions, and seasonal demand for products and services.

Legislative attempts to control spam have been mostly unsuccessful. Thirty-seven states in the United States have laws regulating or prohibiting spam (National Conference of State Legislatures, 2010). State legislation typically requires that unsolicited mail (spam) contain a label in the subject line ("ADV") indicating the message is an advertisement, require a clear opt-out choice for consumers, and prohibit e-mail that contains false routing and domain name information (nearly all spammers hide their own domain, ISP, and IP address).

Congress passed the first national anti-spam law ("Controlling the Assault of Non-Solicited Pornography and Marketing" or CAN-SPAM Act) in 2003, and it went into effect in January 2004. The act does not prohibit unsolicited e-mail (spam) but instead requires unsolicited commercial e-mail messages to be labeled (though not by a standard method) and to include opt-out instructions and the sender's physical address. It prohibits the use of deceptive subject lines and false headers in such messages. The FTC is authorized (but not required) to establish a "Do Not E-mail" registry. State laws that require labels on unsolicited commercial e-mail or prohibit such messages entirely are pre-empted, although provisions merely addressing falsity and deception may remain in place. The act imposes fines of $10 for each unsolicited pornographic e-mail and authorizes state attorneys general to bring lawsuits against spammers. The act obviously makes lawful legitimate bulk mailing of unsolicited e-mail messages (what most people call spam), yet seeks to prohibit certain deceptive practices and provide a small measure of consumer control by requiring opt-out notices. In this sense, critics point out, CAN-SPAM ironically legalizes spam as long as spammers follow the rules. For this reason, large spammers have been among the bill's biggest supporters, and consumer groups have been the act's most vociferous critics.

There have been a number of state and federal prosecutions of spammers, and private civil suits by large ISPs such as Microsoft. Volunteer efforts by industry are another potential control point. Notably, the Direct Marketing Association (DMA), an industry trade group that represents companies that use the postal mail system as well as e-mail for solicitations, is now strongly supporting legislative controls over spam, in addition to its voluntary guidelines. The DMA would like to preserve the legitimate use of e-mail as a marketing technique. The DMA has formed a 15-person anti-spam group and spends $500,000 a year trying to identify spammers. The DMA is also a supporter of the National Cyber-Forensics & Training Alliance (NCFTA), a nonprofit organization with "close ties" to the FBI. NCFTA operates a variety of initiatives aimed at combating cybercrime, including digital phishing via spam.

Affiliate Marketing

Affiliate marketing is a form of marketing where a firm pays a commission to other Web sites (including blogs) for sending customers to their Web site. Affiliate marketing generally involves pay-for-performance: the affiliate or affiliate network gets paid only if users click on a link or purchase a product. In 2012, companies spent about $2.5 billion on affiliate marketing (Forrester Research, 2012b). Industry experts estimate that around 10% of all retail online sales are generated through affiliate programs (as compared to search engine ads, which account for more than 30% of online sales).

Visitors to an affiliate Web site typically click on ads and are taken to the advertiser's Web site. In return, the advertiser pays the affiliate a fee, either on a per-click basis or as a percentage of whatever the customer spends on the advertiser's site. Paying commissions for referrals or recommendations long predated the Web.

For instance, Amazon has a strong affiliate program consisting of more than 1 million participant sites, called Associates, which receive up to 15% on sales their referrals generate. Affiliates attract people to their blogs or Web sites where they can click on ads for products at Amazon. Amazon pays affiliates a percentage on the sales generated within 24 hours of a visitor's click. Members of eBay's Affiliates Program can earn between $20 and $35 for each active registered user sent to eBay. Amazon, eBay, and other large e-commerce companies with affiliate programs typically administer such programs themselves. Smaller e-commerce firms who wish to use affiliate marketing often decide to join an affiliate network (sometimes called an affiliate broker), which acts as an intermediary. Bloggers often sign up for Google's AdSense program to attract advertisers to their sites. They are paid for each click on an ad and sometimes for subsequent purchases made by visitors.

affiliate marketing
commissions paid by advertisers to affiliate Web sites for referring potential customers to their Web site

Viral Marketing

Just as affiliate marketing involves using a trusted Web site to encourage users to visit other sites, **viral marketing** is a form of social marketing that involves getting customers to pass along a company's marketing message to friends, family, and colleagues. It's the online version of word-of-mouth advertising, which spreads even faster and further than in the real world. In the offline world, next to television, word of mouth is the second most important means by which consumers find out about new products. And the most important factor in the decision to purchase is the face-to-face recommendations of parents, friends, and colleagues. Millions of online adults in the United States are "influencers" who share their opinions about products in a variety of online settings. In addition to increasing the size of a company's customer base, customer referrals also have other advantages: they are less expensive to acquire since existing customers do all the acquisition work, and they tend to use online support services less, preferring to turn back to the person who referred them for advice. Also, because they cost so little to acquire and keep, referred customers begin to generate profits for a company much earlier than customers acquired through other marketing methods.

viral marketing
the process of getting customers to pass along a company's marketing message to friends, family, and colleagues

There are a number of online venues where viral marketing appears. E-mail used to be the primary online venue for viral marketing ("please forward this e-mail to your friends"), but venues such as Facebook, Google+, YouTube, blogs, and social game sites now play a major role. For example, as of August 2012, Blendtec's "Will It Blend" and Evian's "Live Young" videos headed up the top 10 viral video advertisements of all time, both with more than 100 million views on YouTube. Volkswagen's "The Force" video advertisement was in fourth place, with more than 58 million views.

Lead Generation Marketing

lead generation marketing

uses multiple e-commerce presences to generate leads for businesses who later can be contacted and converted into customers

Lead generation marketing uses multiple e-commerce presences to generate leads for businesses who later can be contacted and converted into customers through sales calls, e-mails, or other means. In one sense, all Internet marketing campaigns attempt to develop leads. But lead generation marketing is a specialized subset of the Internet marketing industry that provides consulting services and software tools to collect and manage leads for firms, and to convert these leads to customers. Companies will spend an estimated $1.9 billion on lead generation marketing in 2013. Sometimes called "inbound marketing," lead generation marketing firms help other firms build Web sites, launch e-mail campaigns, use social network sites and blogs to optimize the generation of leads, and then manage those leads by initiating further contacts, tracking interactions, and interfacing with customer relationship management systems to keep track of customer-firm interactions. One of the foremost lead generation marketing firms is Hubspot.com, which has developed a software suite for generating and managing leads.

Social, Mobile, and Local Marketing and Advertising

In this section we provide a brief overview of the social, mobile, and local marketing and advertising landscape. Then, in Chapter 7, we provide a much more in-depth examination of social, mobile, and local marketing and advertising tools.

social marketing/ advertising

the use of online social networks and communities to build brands and drive sales

Social Marketing and Advertising **Social marketing/advertising** involves the use of online social networks and communities to build brands and drive sales revenues. There are several kinds of social networks, from Facebook and Twitter, to social apps, social games, blogs, and forums (Web sites that attract people who share a community of interests or skills). In 2013, companies spent about $4.2 billion on social marketing and advertising, and this is expected to grow to about $6.45 billion by 2015. Next to mobile marketing, it is the fastest growing type of online marketing. Nevertheless, in 2013, it represented only 10% of all online marketing and is still dwarfed by the amount spent on search engine advertising and display advertising (eMarketer, Inc., 2013j).

Marketers cannot ignore the huge audiences that social networks such as Facebook, Twitter, and LinkedIn are gathering, which rival television and radio in size. In 2013, there were an estimated 1.1 billion Facebook members, 200 million active Twitter users, 50 million Pinterest members, and more than 225 million who have joined LinkedIn worldwide. In the United States, in July 2013, Facebook had around 140 million unique visitors. Around two-thirds of the U.S. Internet population visits social sites. It's little wonder that marketers and advertisers are joyous at the prospect of connecting with this large audience. Over 90% of U.S. companies are using social networks for marketing purposes in 2013, and research has found that social network users are more likely to talk about and recommend a company or product they follow on Facebook or Twitter (eMarketer, Inc., 2012a, 2012b).

There are four features of social marketing and advertising that are driving its growth:

- *Social sign-on:* Signing in to various Web sites through social network pages like Facebook. This allows Web sites to receive valuable social profile information from Facebook and use it in their own marketing efforts.

- *Collaborative shopping:* Creating an environment where consumers can share their shopping experiences with one another by viewing products, chatting, or texting. Instead of talking about the weather, friends can chat online about brands, products, and services.

- *Network notification:* Creating an environment where consumers can share their approval (or disapproval) of products, services, or content, or share their geolocation, perhaps a restaurant or club, with friends. Facebook's ubiquitous "Like" button is an example. Twitter tweets and followers are another example.

- *Social search (recommendation):* Enabling an environment where consumers can ask their friends for advice on purchases of products, services, and content. While Google can help you find things, social search can help you evaluate the quality of things by listening to the evaluations of your friends or their friends. For instance, Amazon's social recommender system can use your Facebook social profile to recommend products.

Social networks offer advertisers all the formats found on portal and search sites including banner ads (the most common), short pre-roll and post-roll ads associated with videos, and sponsorship of content. Having a corporate Facebook page is in itself an advertising portal for brands just like a Web page. Many firms, such as Coca-Cola, have shut down product-specific Web pages and instead use Facebook pages.

Blogs and online games can also be used for social marketing. Blogs have been around for a decade and are a part of the mainstream online culture (see Chapter 3 for a description of blogs). Around 26 million people write blogs, and around 74 million read blogs. Blogs play a vital role in online marketing. Around 43% of all U.S. companies used blogs for marketing in 2012. Although more firms use Twitter and Facebook, these sites have not replaced blogs, and in fact often point to blogs for long-form content. Because blog readers and creators tend to be more educated, have higher incomes, and be opinion leaders, blogs are ideal platforms for ads for many products and services that cater to this kind of audience. Because blogs are based on the personal opinions of the writers, they are also an ideal platform to start a viral marketing campaign. Advertising networks that specialize in blogs provide some efficiency in placing ads, as do blog networks, which are collections of a small number of popular blogs, coordinated by a central management team, and which can deliver a larger audience to advertisers. For more information on social marketing using blogs, see Learning Track 6.3.

The online gaming marketplace continues to expand rapidly as users are able to play games on smartphones and tablets, as well as PCs and consoles. The story of game advertising in 2013 is social, local, and mobile: social games are ascendant, mobile devices are the high-growth platform, and location-based local advertising is starting to show real traction. The objective of game advertising is both branding and driving customers to purchase moments at restaurants and retail stores. In 2013, over 125 million people played games on their mobile devices, another 43 million on consoles, and another 97 million played online games with a PC. Of the online gamers, about 80 million played social games, such as Zynga's FarmVille, CityVille, and Words With Friends. Between 2012 and 2017, gaming is expected to grow at nearly 40%, driven largely by mobile app games and social site games.

Mobile Marketing and Advertising Marketing on the mobile platform is growing rapidly although it remains a small part (7%) of the overall $43.3 billion online marketing spending. In 2013, spending on all forms of mobile marketing is estimated to be about $7.7 billion, and it is growing at over 50% a year (eMarketer, Inc., 2013j). A number of factors are driving advertisers to the mobile platform of smartphones and tablets, including much more powerful devices, faster networks, wireless local networks, rich media and video ads, and growing demand for local advertising by small business and consumers. Most important, mobile is where the eyeballs are now and increasingly will be in the future: 143 million people access the Internet at least some of the time from mobile devices.

Although still in its infancy, mobile marketing includes the use of display banner ads, rich media, video, games, e-mail, text messaging, in-store messaging, Quick Response (QR) codes, and couponing. Over 90% of retail marketing professionals had plans for mobile marketing campaigns in 2012, and mobile is now a required part of the standard marketing budget. In 2013, search engine advertising was the most popular mobile advertising format, accounting for over 50% of all mobile ad spending, and not surprising given that search is the second most common smartphone application (after voice and text communication). Search engine ads can be further optimized for the mobile platform by showing ads based on the physical location of the user. Display ads are also a popular format, accounting for about 45% of mobile ad spending. Display ads can be served as a part of a mobile Web site or inside apps and games. Mobile messaging generally involves SMS text messaging to consumers offering coupons or flash marketing messages. Messaging is especially effective for local advertising because consumers can be sent messages and coupons as they pass by or visit locations. Video advertising currently accounts for the smallest percentage of mobile ad spending, but it is one of the fastest growing formats. Ad networks such as Google's AdMob, Apple's iAd, and Millennial Media are the largest providers of mobile advertising.

Apps on mobile devices constitute a new marketing platform that did not exist a few years ago. Apps are a nonbrowser pathway for users to experience the Web and perform a number of tasks from reading the newspaper to shopping, searching, and buying. Apps provide users much faster access to content than do multi-purpose browsers. Apps are also starting to influence the design and function of traditional Web sites as consumers are attracted to the look and feel of apps, and their speed of operation. There are over a million apps on Apple iTunes and Google Apps Marketplace and another million apps provided by Internet carriers and third-party storefronts like GetJar and PocketGear, app portals like dev.appia.com, and the Amazon Appstore. An estimated 1.2 billion people use apps in 2013 worldwide (SocialMediaToday.com, 2013). By 2013, more than 100 billion apps had been downloaded.

Local Marketing: The Social-Mobile-Local Nexus Along with social marketing and mobile marketing, local marketing is the third major trend in e-commerce marketing in 2013–2014. The growth of mobile devices has accelerated the growth of local search and purchasing since 2007. According to Google, local searches represented about 25% of all searches, and 50% of all mobile searches in 2012 (Screenwerk, 2012; Searchengineland.com, 2012). New marketing tools like local advertisements on social networks and daily deal sites are also contributing to local marketing growth.

Spending on online local ads in the United States is estimated at around $27.6 billion in 2013 and is expected to grow to more than $48 billion by 2017 (BIA/Kelsey, 2013). In contrast, spending on traditional local advertising is expected to be flat during the same time period. The most common local marketing tools are geotargeting using Google Maps (local stores appearing on a Google map), display ads in hyperlocal publications like those created by Patch Properties, aimed at narrowly defined communities, daily deals, and coupons.

The most commonly used venues include Facebook, Google, Amazon Local, Groupon, LivingSocial, LinkedIn, Yahoo, Bing, and Twitter, as well as more specific location-based offerings such as Google Places, Yahoo Local, Citysearch, YellowBook, SuperPages, and Yelp. The "daily deal" coupon sites, Groupon and LivingSocial, and location-based mobile firms such as Foursquare are also a significant part of this trend.

We examine social, mobile, and local marketing in greater depth in Chapter 7.

MULTI-CHANNEL MARKETING: INTEGRATING ONLINE AND OFFLINE MARKETING

Without an audience, marketing is not possible. With the rapid growth of the Internet, media consumption patterns have changed greatly as consumers are more and more likely to engage with online media, from videos and news sites, to blogs, Twitter feeds, Facebook friends, and Pinterest posts. Increasingly, marketers are using multiple online channels to "touch" customers, from e-mail to Facebook, search ads, display ads on mobile devices, and affiliate programs. Forrester Research reports, for instance, that most customers purchased online following some Web marketing influence, and nearly half of online purchases followed multiple exposures to Web marketing efforts (Forrester Research, 2012a).

In 2013, for the first time ever, the average American will spend more time with digital media per day than the amount viewing TV (**Figure 6.8**). The average adult will spend more than 5 hours a day online and using a mobile device for something other than telephone calls, compared to about 4 and a half hours watching television (eMarketer, Inc., 2013a). An increasing percentage of American media consumers multitask by using several media at once in order to increase the total media exposure.

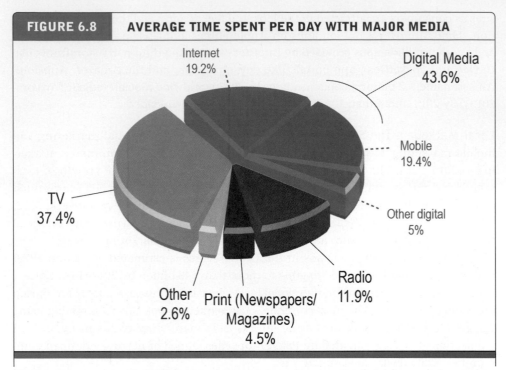

FIGURE 6.8	AVERAGE TIME SPENT PER DAY WITH MAJOR MEDIA

The Internet represents only 24% of consumer exposure to media, suggesting that online marketing needs to be coupled with offline marketing to achieve optimal effectiveness.
SOURCE: Based on data from eMarketer, Inc., 2013a.

In this environment, marketers increasingly are developing multi-channel marketing programs that can take advantage of the strengths of various media, and reinforce branding messages across media. Online marketing is not the only way, or by itself the best way, to engage consumers. Internet campaigns can be significantly strengthened by also using e-mail, TV, print, and radio. The marketing communications campaigns most successful at driving traffic to a Web site have incorporated both online and offline tactics, rather than relying solely on one or the other. Several research studies have shown that the most effective online advertisements are those that use consistent imagery with campaigns running in other media at the same time.

Insight on Business: Are the Very Rich Different from You and Me? examines how luxury goods providers use online marketing in conjunction with their offline marketing efforts.

OTHER ONLINE MARKETING STRATEGIES

In addition to the "traditional" online marketing and advertising tools we have previously discussed, such as search engine, display, and e-mail marketing, and the newer social, mobile, and local marketing and advertising tools, there are also a number of other, more focused online marketing strategies. Here we examine tools aimed at customer retention, pricing, and a strategy known as the "long tail."

INSIGHT ON BUSINESS

ARE THE VERY RICH DIFFERENT FROM YOU AND ME?

"Let me tell you about the very rich. They are different from you and me." So observed F. Scott Fitzgerald in the short story, "The Rich Boy." Palm Beach has its Worth Avenue, New York has its Fifth Avenue, Los Angeles has its Rodeo Drive, and Chicago has the Magnificent Mile. So where do the rich go on the Web to get that $5,000 cocktail dress, or that $3,000 Italian suit? Well, today, it turns out they may not be so different from the rest of us: they look for online deals. At Net-a-Porter, a leading fashion site that combines an online magazine with a strong sales component, you can find that Gucci silk crepe jumpsuit ($1,995) that looks smashing over a pair of Gucci stretch-suede over-the-knee boots ($2,495). Who could resist?

Even experts find it hard to define what it means to be affluent and who is affluent. After all, how high is up? There are 24 million households (20% of all households) where household income is in the $100,000 t0 $250,000 range. These are often referred to as HENRYs (High Earnings, Not Yet Rich). But the really affluent are those 2.4 million (2% of the 120 million households) that earn more than $250,000 a year. And then there are the 9 million households (.7% of households) that earn more than a million a year. Finally, we have arrived at a reasonable understanding of affluence: there are the "sort of rich" HENRYs, the affluent, and what the experts call "ultra rich."

Retail consumption in general is highly skewed: the wealthiest top 10% of households account for 50% of all retail spending, and 37% of all e-commerce retail spending. The recovery in consumer spending since 2009 has been largely driven by the 24 million affluent households, and this is especially true of luxury goods. Luxury goods markets worldwide expanded by 10% in

2012 and are on track for 8% growth in 2013. Luxury retail is growing three times faster than the general economy. The economy has bounced back for some, the stock market is touching new highs, and home sale prices have improved. Wealthy Americans are spending on expensive clothing, accessories, jewelry, and beauty products.

Yet even the rich are not immune to the lure of a good deal. The problem is that luxe retailers are typically loath to offer sales because they believe sales detract from their reputations for timeless quality. However, change is in the air (or online as it were). LVMH, the world's largest luxe brand holding company, has launched Nowness, a Web site featuring all manner of daily specials. Times are changing when Lacoste (the polo shirts with the crocodile logo) pulls the plug on print advertising and puts all its U.S. marketing dollars on the Internet. You know something is different when Faberge introduces its first new line of luxe jewelery in 90 years with a Web-only marketing effort on a single Web site. The site offers 100 pieces of jewelry ranging in price from $48,000 to $10 million. A Faberge marketing report found the rich like to buy online if they have plenty of personal attention. Shopping carts? Please, are you kidding? "No, thank you." A personal sales rep to walk you through the Web site? "Yes, of course."

It used to be that luxe brands either avoided the Web entirely or just put up sites with Flash videos and high-end photography. But when ordinary department stores are discounting even luxe-branded goods, the high-end brands are getting down and dirty on the Web, rebuilding their sites for active competition with the department stores.

Luxe retailers are in fact offering more discounts—but they're secret. How can a sale be secret? Whispered discounts at the physical stores

(continued)

("Shhhh! There's a special sale in the dress department!") have their online counterpart in flash e-mail campaigns and "private online sales" in which selected online customers are e-mailed alerts such as "A $3,000 handbag on sale for the next two hours for $800." Neiman Marcus calls them "Midday Dash" sales. Two-hour online-only sales promise 50% off on luxe goods that can be purchased only by clicking on a link in the e-mail. One week's "dash sale" featured a $697 Burberry handbag, marked down from $1,395.

Luxury retailers have a dilemma: they need to attract not just the ultra-affluent, but also the aspirational HENRYs who are far more numerous and anxious to display their wealth. They need to be both exclusive and accessible. One solution is the so-called Mercedes Benz strategy: build luxurious but affordable cars for the HENRYs while maintaining a focus on high-end truly luxe models for the ultra-affluent. Mercedes Benz combines a dual level product strategy with effective use of social and mobile media. Mercedes' Facebook page is a main hub of interaction between the brand and its customers, with 2.3 million followers entertained with sweepstakes, videos, images, news, and links to its blog, the Mercedes Reporter, for additional insight into why Mercedes is unique and worth all that money. Mercedes also uses Twitter and a dozen iPhone apps to engage a broader range of customers by providing personalized video tours of its cars.

Louis Vuitton and other luxury clothing retailers approach the ultra-affluent and HENRYs with similar tools. Louis Vuitton built its reputation on a line of less expensive canvas handbags that sell in the $500 range. In 2013 it has added a line of expensive leather bags to reposition itself as more upmarket to appeal to the ultra-affluent. The Capucine handbag in full-grain Taurillon calf leather sells for $4,600, and since introduction, it is usually sold out.

While luxury retails still rely on upscale retail stores offering personal attention and an unparalleled consumer experience, the action has moved to the Internet in part because that's where the wealthy shop. Wealthy consumers are much more likely to own iPads, spend on average twice as much, and aren't afraid to lay down serious money on a whim. In addition, luxe retailers can offer discreet sales to a select group of customers without tarnishing the brand, preserving exclusivity, and creating a sense of urgency by limiting the time to purchase. At the same time, they can deny they discount their items. If prices were public, customers would know that the $800 Marni skirt they bought today was on sale the next day for $400. They might conclude that none of these goods are worth the price charged, certainly not the retail price, no matter what it is. Online dash sales are sort of like impulse buying at Walmart, but instead of 20 batteries for $5, it's more like one Burberry bag for $1,000. Rich people can indulge bigger impulses. But like the rest of us, the rich just can't seem to get enough of a good thing, especially if it's half price.

The explosion of social media and the increasing investments in the online channel by luxury companies has reinforced and enlarged the community of those who explore, comment upon, and eventually purchase luxury goods. Luxury companies are more than doubling their "friends" on Facebook annually in recognition of the link between online and offline purchases. Burberry Group Plc, the U.K.'s largest luxury goods maker, reports that it obtains the most reach and most response from digital initiatives compared with other media. To promote the Burberry Body fragrance, the London-based company offered exclusive samples to its Facebook fans. It received more than 225,000 requests in little more than a week.

Tiffany, the quintessential luxe firm, experienced lower profits in the recession of 2008–2009, but never experienced a loss. Since then, however, revenues have expanded sharply worldwide, increasing by 4% in 2012, twice as fast as the economy as a whole. Tiffany's strategy is not to lower prices but to add more lower-priced items to the marketing mix. For instance, pendants are going for as little

(continued)

as $150 to "only" $15,000 (those are the ones with the big shiny things).

Yet some luxury retailers have had a difficult time developing an effective online presence for their wealthy customers. A recent report from the Luxury Institute found that online luxe goods retailers fall short in community building. Most sites do not track online customer comments on rating and review sites, or blogs (let alone Twitter), although most use search engine optimization. When you're really good and charging accordingly, why ask customers what they think?

Developing an online marketing approach that increases a company's access to consumers while retaining an image of exclusivity was the challenge faced by Tiffany & Co. The company is in the enviable position of being perhaps the most famous jewelry company in the United States. Tiffany's offline marketing communications seek to engender feelings of beauty, quality, and timeless style—all hallmarks of the Tiffany brand. How could Tiffany maintain its approach on the Web, a medium that often emphasizes speed and flashy graphics over grace and elegance, and low-cost bargains over high-priced exclusive fashion? The Web, for the most part, is all about low prices and great deals—concepts that are anathema to the high-fashion merchant. The answer is apparent in a visit to the Tiffany.com Web site. The site features limited inventory, with a focus on high-resolution images of its exclusive and original designs in jewelry and apparel. There are no sales, coupons, discounts, or other offers although visitors can choose jewelry in lower price ranges (less than $250 for instance). The Web site and Facebook brand page reflect custom service and design, calm, and simplicity. The prices are equally exclusive: an exquisite Atlas Hinged Bangle in 18k rose gold and round brilliant diamonds for $9,000, and sunglasses for $500.

Today, Tiffany has shifted more of its direct marketing effort from the offline catalog to the online catalog, a YouTube Channel, and a Facebook brand page with four million Likes. It has Web sites in 13 different countries, including Canada, the United Kingdom, Japan, and Australia. Tiffany sites carry over 2,100 products in six categories of goods: engagement, jewelry, watches, designers and collections, gifts, and accessories. In 2012, Tiffany's online sales were over $227 million, 6% of its $3.8 billion worldwide sales, placing it in second place in the online jewelry industry. (Blue Nile is first with $400 million in online sales.)

Other cutting-edge fashion houses such as Christian Dior, Armani, and Bottega Veneta have similarly launched aggressive Web and social marketing brand pages and selling platforms. In the case of Armani, Emporio Armani personally directed the online effort. To avoid the cheaper catalog look, he had his store design team hand over architectural plans to the flagship store in Milan so that they could be used as a metaphor and model for the Web site. Now visitors can turn left or right as they would at the Milan store, and take a virtual tour of the goods on display. Armani wanted a three-dimensional look, and the ability to shine bright lights on the products being examined, a trick used in his stores to impart the sense of elegance. The cost of opening the site has been a fraction of the cost of launching a new store, and less risky. A trip to the Armani Web site is a trip all unto itself: stunning video images of the latest seasonal collections, Armani Jeans, and the Armani Exchange, where you can actually buy something from the Emporio Armani retail collection.

SOURCES: "Worldwide Luxury Goods Continues Double-Digit Annual Growth," Bain & Company, Press Release, May 16, 2013; "Louis Vuitton Walks the Fine Luxury Line," by Renee Schultes, *Wall Street Journal*, April 14, 2013; "What Recession? Americans Regain a Craving for Luxury," by Nadya Masidlover, *Wall Street Journal*, February 13, 2013; "Luxury Report 2013: The Ultimate Five-Year Guide to the Luxury Consumer Market," Unity Marketing Inc. 2013; "Luxury Marketing: Recreating the One-on-One Experience With Mobile," [Patricia Orsini], eMarketer, Inc., September 2012; Tiffany & Co. Annual Report on 10-K, March 28, 2012; "Affluents: Demographic Profile and Marketing Approach," eMarketer, Inc. (Mark Dolliver), January 2012; "Affluent Shoppers and Luxury Brand Retailers Online," eMarketer, Inc. (Jeffrey Grau), September 2011; "High Fashion Relents to Web's Pull," by Stephanie Clifford, *New York Times*, July 11, 2010; "Luxury Brands Warming to the Web," by Mark Porter, Reuters, June 3, 2011; "Mr Porter to Test Men's Urge to Shop Online," by Ray Smith, *Wall Street Journal*, February 10, 2011.

Customer Retention Strategies

The Internet offers several extraordinary marketing techniques for building a strong relationship with customers and for differentiating products and services.

Personalization, One-to-One Marketing, and Interest-based Advertising (Behavioral Targeting) No Internet-based marketing technique has received more popular and academic comment than "one-to-one" or "personalized marketing." **One-to-one marketing (personalization)** segments the market on the basis of individuals (not groups), based on a precise and timely understanding of their needs, targeting specific marketing messages to these individuals, and then positioning the product vis-à-vis competitors to be truly unique. One-to-one marketing is the ultimate form of market segmentation, targeting, and positioning—where the segments are individuals.

The movement toward market segmentation has been ongoing since the development of systematic market research and mass media in the 1930s. However, e-commerce and the Internet are different in that they enable personalized one-to-one marketing to occur on a mass scale.

A good example of personalization at work is Amazon or Barnesandnoble.com. Both sites greet registered visitors (based on cookie files), recommend recent books based on user preferences (stored in a user profile in their database) as well as what other consumers purchased, and expedite checkout procedures based on prior purchases.

Behavioral targeting of ads involves using the online and offline behavior of consumers to adjust the advertising message delivered online, often in real time (milliseconds from the consumer's first URL entry). The intent is to increase the efficiency of marketing and advertising, and to increase the revenue streams of firms who are in a position to behaviorally target visitors. Because "behavioral targeting" as a label has somewhat unfavorable connotations, the online advertising industry, led by Google, has introduced a new name for behavioral targeting. They call it **interest-based advertising**.

One of the original promises of the Web has been that it can deliver a marketing message tailored to each consumer based on this data, and then measure the results in terms of click-throughs and purchases. If you are visiting a jewelry site, you would be shown jewelry ads. If you entered a search query like "diamonds," you would be shown text ads for diamonds and other jewelry. This was taken one step further by advertising networks composed of several thousand sites. An advertising network could follow you across thousands of Web sites and come up with an idea of what you are interested in as you browse, and then display ads related to those interests. For instance, if you visit a few men's clothing sites in the course of a few hours, you will be shown ads for men's clothing on most other sites you visit subsequently, regardless of their subject content. If you search for a certain pair of shoes at Zappos, and Like them to your friends on Facebook, you will be shown ads for the exact same shoes at other sites (including Facebook). Behavioral targeting combines nearly all of your online behavioral data into a collection of interest areas, and then shows you ads based on those interests, as well as the interests of your friends. What's new about today's behavioral targeting is the breadth of data collected: your e-mail content, social

one-to-one marketing (personalization)
segmenting the market based on a precise and timely understanding of an individual's needs, targeting specific marketing messages to these individuals, and then positioning the product vis-à-vis competitors to be truly unique

interest-based advertising (behavioral targeting)
using search queries and clicks on results to behaviorally target consumers

network page content, friends, purchases online, books read or purchased, newspaper sites visited, and many other behaviors. And finally, ad exchanges take the marketing of all this information one step further. Most popular Web sites have more than 100 tracking programs on their home pages that are owned by third-party data collector firms who then sell this information in real time to the highest bidding advertiser in real-time online auctions. Ad exchanges make it possible for advertisers to retarget ads at individuals as they roam across the Internet. **Retargeting ads** involves showing the same or similar ads to individuals across multiple Web sites. Retargeted ads are nearly as effective as the original ad (eMarketer, Inc., 2011a).

retargeting ads
showing the same ad to individuals across multiple Web sites

There are four methods that online advertisers use to behaviorally target ads: search engine queries, the collection of data on individual browsing history online (monitoring the clickstream), the collection of data from social network sites, and increasingly, the integration of this online data with offline data like income, education, address, purchase patterns, credit records, driving records, and hundreds of other personal descriptors tied to specific, identifiable persons. This level of integration of both "anonymous" as well as identifiable information is routinely engaged in by Google, Microsoft, Yahoo, Facebook, and legions of small and medium-sized marketing firms that use their data, or collect data from thousands of Web sites using Web beacons and cookies. On average, online information bureaus maintain 2,000 data elements on each adult person in their database. The currency and accuracy of this data are never examined, and the retention periods are not known. Currently, there are no federal laws or regulations governing this data.

Earlier in the chapter we described search engine advertising in some detail. Search engine advertising has turned out to be the most effective online advertising format by several orders of magnitude, and provides more than 95% of the revenue of Google, the world's largest online advertising agency. Why is search engine advertising so effective? Most agree that when users enter a query into a search engine, it reveals a very specific intention to shop, compare, and possibly purchase. When ads are shown at these very moments of customer behavior, they are 4 to 10 times as effective as other formats. The author John Battelle coined the phrase and the notion that the Web is a database of intentions composed of the results from every search ever made and every path that searchers have followed, since the beginning of the Web. In total, this database contains the intentions of all mankind. This treasure trove of intentions, desires, likes, wants, and needs is owned by only a few private business firms, namely, Google, Microsoft, and to a lesser extent, Yahoo, in massive, global databases (Battelle, 2003). Batelle later extended the concept of a database of intentions beyond search to include the social graph (Facebook and Google+), status updates (Twitter and Facebook), and the "check-in" (Foursquare and Yelp) (Battelle, 2010). The database of intentions can be exploited to track and target individuals and groups. Not only is this capability unprecedented, but it's growing exponentially into the foreseeable future. The potential for abuse is also growing exponentially.

The decline in the growth rate of search engine advertising, from the early days of double-digit growth to today's growth of high single digits, has caused the major search engine firms to seek out alternative forms of future growth, which include display, rich media, and video advertising on millions of Web publisher sites. Web publishers have responded by producing billions of pages of content. In this environment, the effectiveness of display ads has been falling in terms of response rates and prices for ads. Behavioral targeting is an effective way to solve this problem and increase response rates. Behavioral targeting of both search and display advertising is currently driving the expansion in online advertising.

Behavioral targeting seeks to optimize consumer response by using information that Web visitors reveal about themselves online, and if possible, to combine this with offline identity and consumption information gathered by companies such as Acxiom. Behavioral targeting is based on real-time information about visitors' use of Web sites, including pages visited, content viewed, search queries, ads clicked, videos watched, content shared, and products they purchased. Once this information is collected and analyzed on the fly, behavioral targeting programs attempt to develop profiles of individual users, and then show advertisements most likely to be of interest to the user. More than 75% of North American advertisers use some form of targeting in their online display ads (eMarketer, Inc., 2012a).

For a variety of technical and other reasons, this vision has, thus far, not been widely achieved. The percentage of ads that are actually targeted is unknown, but most display ads are not targeted. Instead, advertisers use less expensive context ads displayed to a general audience without any targeting, or very minimal demographic targeting. The quality of the data, largely owned by the online advertising networks, is quite good but hardly perfect. The ability to understand and respond—the business intelligence and real-time analytics—is still weak, preventing companies from being able to respond quickly in meaningful ways when the consumer is online. The firms who sell targeted ads to their clients claim the targeted ads are two or three times more effective than general ads. There is not very good data to support these claims from independent sources. Generally these claims confound the impact of brands on targeted audiences, and the impact of the ads placed to this targeted audience. Advertisers target groups that are most likely to buy their product even in the absence of targeting ads at them. The additional impact of a targeted ad is much smaller than ad platforms claim. A recent research report based on real data from 18 ad campaigns on Yahoo, involving 18.4 million users, found that brand interest is the largest single factor in determining targeted ad effectiveness, and not the targeted ad itself (Farahat and Bailey, 2012). And marketing companies are not yet prepared to accept the idea that there needs to be several hundred or a thousand variations on the same display ad depending on the customer's profile. Such a move would raise costs. Last, consumer resistance to targeting continues. In a recent Truste/Harris Interactive Poll, more than 58% of those surveyed said that they do not like online behavioral ads (TRUSTe, 2012). A survey found that the percentage of people who plan to opt for Do Not Track options has doubled from 27% in 2011 to 50% in 2012 (Gigaom, 2012). Behavioral tracking does not work very well if half the audience declines to be targeted. On average, consumers can expect that at least 80% of the ads they see online are not very well targeted at them. This situation will no doubt improve.

Nevertheless, firms are experimenting with more precise targeting methods, and ad budgets for targeting are expanding rapidly. Snapple used behavioral targeting methods (with the help of online ad firm Tacoda) to identify the types of people attracted to Snapple Green Tea. Answer: people who like the arts and literature, travel internationally, and visit health sites. Microsoft offers MSN advertisers access to personal data derived from nearly 500 million worldwide Windows Live users. Some advertisers have reported more than 50% increases in click-through rates. General Motors uses Digitas (a Boston-based online ad firm) to create several hundred versions of a single ad for its Acadia crossover vehicle. Viewers are initially shown ads that emphasize brand, features, and communities. On subsequent viewings, they are shown different ads based on demographics, lifestyle, and behavioral considerations. Men are shown versions of the ads emphasizing engines, specifications, and performance, while women are shown versions that emphasize comfort, accessibility, and families.

The growth of targeting continues to raise privacy issues. The public and congressional reaction to behavioral targeting is described more fully in Chapter 8.

Customization and Customer Co-Production

Customization is an extension of personalization. **Customization** means changing the product—not just the marketing message—according to user preferences. **Customer co-production** means the users actually think up the innovation and help create the new product.

Many leading companies now offer "build-to-order" customized products on the Internet on a large scale, creating product differentiation and, hopefully, customer loyalty. Customers appear to be willing to pay a little more for a unique product. The key to making the process affordable is to build a standardized architecture that lets consumers combine a variety of options. For example, Nike offers customized sneakers through its Nike iD program on its Web site. Consumers can choose the type of shoe, colors, material, and even a logo of up to eight characters. Nike transmits the orders via computers to specially equipped plants in China and Korea. The sneakers cost only $10 extra and take about three weeks to reach the customer. At the Shop M&M's Web site, customers can get their own message printed on custom-made M&Ms; Timberland. com also offers online customization of its boots.

Information goods—goods whose value is based on information content—are also ideal for this level of differentiation. For instance, the New York Times—and many other content distributors—allows customers to select the news they want to see on a daily basis. Many Web sites, particularly portal sites such as Yahoo, MSN, and AOL, allow customers to create their own customized version of the Web site. Such pages frequently require security measures such as usernames and passwords to ensure privacy and confidentiality.

Customer Service

A Web site's approach to customer service can significantly help or hurt its marketing efforts. Online customer service is more than simply following through on order fulfillment; it has to do with users' ability to communicate with a company and obtain desired information in a timely manner. Customer service can help reduce consumer frustration, cut the number of abandoned shopping carts, and increase sales.

Most consumers want to, and will, serve themselves as long as the information they need to do so is relatively easy to find. Online buyers largely do not expect or desire "high-touch" service unless they have questions or problems, in which case

customization

changing the product, not just the marketing message, according to user preferences

customer co-production

in the Web environment, takes customization one step further by allowing the customer to interactively create the product they want relatively speedy answers that are responsive to their individual issue. Researchers have found that online consumers strongly attach to brands when they have a problem with an order. Customer loyalty increases substantially when online buyers learn that customer service representatives are available online or at an 800-number and were willing and able to resolve the situation quickly. Conversely, online buyers who do not receive satisfaction at these critical moments often terminate their relationship with the business and switch to merchants that may charge more but deliver superior customer service (Ba, et al., 2010; Wolfinbarger and Gilly, 2001).

There are a number of tools that companies can use to encourage interaction with prospects and customers and provide customer service—FAQs, customer service chat systems, intelligent agents, and automated response systems—in addition to the customer relationship management systems described in the preceding section.

frequently asked questions (FAQs)

a text-based listing of common questions and answers

Frequently asked questions (**FAQs**), a text-based listing of common questions and answers, provide an inexpensive way to anticipate and address customer concerns. Adding an FAQ page on a Web site linked to a search engine helps users track down needed information more quickly, enabling them to help themselves resolve questions and concerns. By directing customers to the FAQs page first, Web sites can give customers answers to common questions. If a question and answer do not appear, it is important for sites to make contact with a live person simple and easy. Offering an e-mail link to customer service at the bottom of the FAQs page is one solution.

real-time customer service chat systems

a company's customer service representatives interactively exchange text-based messages with one or more customers on a real-time basis

Real-time customer service chat systems (in which a company's customer service representatives interactively exchange text-based messages with one or more customers on a real-time basis) are an increasingly popular way for companies to assist online shoppers during a purchase. Chats with online customer service representatives can provide direction, answer questions, and troubleshoot technical glitches that can kill a sale. Leading vendors of customer service chat systems include LivePerson and InstantService. Vendors claim that chat is significantly less expensive than telephone-based customer service. However, critics point out this conclusion may be based on optimistic assumptions that chat representatives can assist three or four customers at once, and that chat sessions are shorter than phone sessions. Also, chat sessions are text sessions, and not as rich as talking with a human being over the phone. On the plus side, chat has been reported to raise per-order sales figures, providing sales assistance by allowing companies to "touch" customers during the decision-making process. Evidence suggests that chat can lower shopping cart abandonment rates, increase the number of items purchased per transaction, and increase the dollar value of transactions. "Click to call" or "live call" is another version of a real-time online customer service system, in which the customer clicks a link or accepts an invitation to have a customer service representative call them on the telephone.

automated response system

sends e-mail order confirmations and acknowledgments of e-mailed inquiries

Intelligent agent technology is another way customers are providing assistance to online shoppers. Intelligent agents are part of an effort to reduce costly contact with customer service representatives. **Automated response systems** send e-mail order confirmations and acknowledgments of e-mailed inquiries, in some cases letting the customer know that it may take a day or two to actually research an answer to their question. Automating shipping confirmations and order status reports are also common.

Pricing Strategies

As we noted in Chapter 1, during the early years of e-commerce, many academics and business consultants predicted that the Web would lead to a new world of information symmetry and "frictionless" commerce. In this world, newly empowered customers, using intelligent shopping agents and the nearly infinite product and price information available on the Internet, would shop around the world (and around the clock) with minimal effort, driving prices down to their marginal cost and driving intermediaries out of the market as customers began to deal directly with producers (Wigand and Benjamin, 1995; Rayport and Sviokla, 1995; Evans and Wurster, 1999; Sinha, 2000). The result was supposed to be an instance of the **"Law of One Price"**: with complete price transparency in a perfect information marketplace, one world price for every product would emerge. "Frictionless commerce" would, of course, mean the end of marketing based on brands.

But it didn't work out this way. Firms still compete for customers through price as well as product features, scope of operations, and focus. **Pricing** (putting a value on goods and services) is an integral part of marketing strategy. Together, price and quality determine customer value. Pricing of e-commerce goods has proved very difficult for both entrepreneurs and investors to understand.

In traditional firms, the prices of traditional goods—such as books, drugs, and automobiles—are usually based on their fixed and variable costs as well as the market's **demand curve** (the quantity of goods that can be sold at various prices). *Fixed costs* are the costs of building the production facility. *Variable costs* are costs involved in running the production facility—mostly labor. In a competitive market, with undifferentiated goods, prices tend toward their *marginal costs* (the incremental cost of producing the next unit) once manufacturers have paid the fixed costs to enter the business.

Firms usually "discover" their demand curves by testing various price and volume bundles, while closely watching their cost structure. Normally, prices are set to maximize profits. A profit-maximizing company sets its prices so that the *marginal revenue* (the revenue a company receives from the next unit sold) from a product just equals its marginal costs. If a firm's marginal revenue is higher than its marginal costs, it would want to lower prices a bit and sell more product (why leave money on the table when you can sell a few more units?). If its marginal revenue for selling a product is lower than its marginal costs, then the company would want to reduce volume a bit and charge a higher price (why lose money on each additional sale?).

In the early years of e-commerce, something unusual happened. Sellers were pricing their products far below their marginal costs. Some sites were losing money on every sale. How could this be? New economics? New technology? The Internet age? No. Internet merchants could sell below their marginal costs (even giving away products for free) simply because a large number of entrepreneurs and their venture capitalist backers thought this was a worthwhile activity, at least in the short term. The idea was to attract "eyeballs" with free goods and services, and then later, once the consumer was part of a large, committed audience, charge advertisers enough money to make a profit, and (maybe) charge customers subscription fees for value-added services (the so-called *"piggyback" strategy* in which a small number of users can be

Law of One Price
with complete price transparency in a perfect information marketplace, there will be one world price for every product

pricing
putting a value on goods and services

demand curve
the quantity of goods that can be sold at various prices

convinced to pay for premium services that are piggybacked upon a larger audience that receives standard or reduced value services). To a large extent, social networking sites and user-generated content sites have resurrected this revenue model with a focus on the growth in audience size and not short-term profits. To understand the behavior of entrepreneurial firms, it is helpful to examine a traditional demand curve (see **Figure 6.9**).

A small number of customers are willing to pay a great deal for the product—far above P_1. A larger number of customers would happily pay P_1, and an even larger number of customers would pay less than P_1. If the price were zero, the demand might approach infinity! Ideally, in order to maximize sales and profits, a firm would like to pick up all the money in the market by selling the product at the price each customer is willing to pay. This is called **price discrimination**—selling products to different people and groups based on their willingness to pay. If some people really want the product, sell it to them at a high price. But sell it to indifferent people at a much lower price; otherwise, they will not buy. This only works if the firm can (a) identify the price each individual would be willing to pay, and (b) segregate the customers from one another so they cannot find out what the others are paying. Therefore, most firms adopt a fixed price for their goods (P_1), or a small number of prices for different versions of their products.

What if the marginal cost of producing a good is zero? What should the price be for these goods? It would be impossible then to set prices based on equalizing marginal revenue and marginal cost—because marginal cost is zero. The Internet is primarily filled with information goods—from music to research reports, to stock quotes, stories, weather reports, articles, pictures, and opinions—whose marginal cost of production

price discrimination
selling products to different people and groups based on their willingness to pay

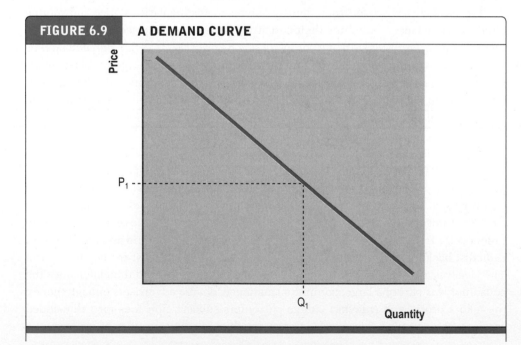

FIGURE 6.9 | **A DEMAND CURVE**

A demand curve shows the quantity of product (Q) that could be sold at various prices (P).

is zero when distributed over the Internet. Thus, another reason certain goods, such as some information goods, may be free on the Internet is that they are "selling" for what it costs to produce them—next to nothing. Content that is stolen from television, CDs, and Hollywood movies has zero production costs. Content that is contributed by users also has zero production costs for the Web sites themselves.

Free and Freemium Let's examine free pricing of Internet services. Everyone likes a bargain, and the best bargain is something for free. Businesses give away free PCs, free data storage, free music, free Web sites, free photo storage, and free Internet connections. Free is not new: banks used to give away "free" toasters to depositors in the 1950s. Google offers free office apps, free e-mail, and free collaboration sites. There can be a sensible economic logic to giving things away. Free content can help build market awareness (such as the free online *New York Times* that contains only the daily stories—not the archived stories) and can lead to sales of other follow-on products. Finally, free products and services knock out potential and actual competitors (the free browser Internet Explorer from Microsoft spoiled the market for Netscape's browser) (Shapiro and Varian, 1999).

Today, online "free" is increasingly being implemented as "freemium" to borrow a phrase from Chris Anderson's book *Free: The Future of a Radical Price*. The freemium pricing model is a cross-subsidy online marketing strategy where users are offered a basic service for free, but must pay for premium or add-on services. The people who pay for the premium services hopefully will pay for all the free riders on the service. Skype uses a freemium model: millions of users can call other Skype users on the Internet for free, but there's a charge for calling a land line or cell phone. Flickr, Google Sites, Yahoo, and a host of others offer premium services at a price in order to support "free" services. Even YouTube is launching a premium movie service where Hollywood movies are streamed for a price. Evernote.com offers online users a "universal memory drawer" that allows you to store any digital information (photos, videos, and documents) on the Evernote site, and then coordinate all of your digital devices from laptops, desktops, and smartphones. The basic service is free, but additional storage and special services cost $5 a month (Takahashi, 2010). Pandora offers free Internet radio, but it is restricted to a few hours a month. Premium unlimited service costs $36 a year.

"Free" and "freemium" as pricing strategies do have limits. In the past, many e-commerce businesses found it difficult to convert the eyeballs into paying customers. YouTube is still not profitable. Free sites attract hundreds of millions of price-sensitive "free loaders" who have no intention of ever paying for anything, and who switch from one free service to another at the very mention of charges. The piggyback strategy has not been a universal success. "Free" eliminates a rich price discrimination strategy. Clearly some of the free loaders would indeed pay a small amount each month, and this revenue is lost to the firms who offer significant services for free. Some argue that everything digital will one day be free in part because Internet users expect it to be so. But the history of "free" includes broadcast television, which used to be "free" (it was advertising-supported) but the public eventually had no problem moving to cable television and DVDs as paid services. The exceptions to "free" are really valuable streams of information that are exclusive, expensive to produce, not widely distributed, unique, and have immediate consumption or investment value. Even in the age of the Internet, these digital streams will sell for a price greater than zero. There probably is no free lunch after all, at least not one that's worth eating.

Versioning One solution to the problem of free information goods is **versioning**—creating multiple versions of the goods and selling essentially the same product to different market segments at different prices. In this situation, the price depends on the value to the consumer. Consumers will segment themselves into groups that are willing to pay different amounts for various versions (Shapiro and Varian, 1998). Versioning fits well with a modified "free" strategy. A reduced-value version can be offered for free, while premium versions can be offered at higher prices. What are characteristics of a "reduced-value version?" Low-priced—or in the case of information goods, even "free"—versions might be less convenient to use, less comprehensive, slower, less powerful, and offer less support than the high-priced versions. Just as there are different General Motors car brands appealing to different market segments (Cadillac, Buick, Chevrolet, and GMC), and within these divisions, hundreds of models from the most basic to the more powerful and functional, so can information goods be "versioned" in order to segment and target the market and position the products. In the realm of information goods, online magazines, music companies, and book publishers offer sample content for free, but charge for more powerful content. The *New York Times*, for instance, offers free daily content for several days after publication, but then charges per article for access to the more powerful archive of past issues. Writers, editors, and analysts are more than willing to pay for access to archived, organized content. Some Web sites offer "free services" with annoying advertising, but turn off the ads for a monthly fee.

Bundling "Ziggy" Ziegfeld, a vaudeville entrepreneur at the turn of the twentieth century in New York, noticed that nearly one-third of his theater seats were empty on some Friday nights, and during the week, matinee shows were often half empty. He came up with an idea for bundling tickets into "twofers": pay for one full-price ticket and get the next ticket free. Twofers are still a Broadway theater tradition in New York. They are based on the idea that (a) the marginal cost of seating another patron is zero, and (b) a great many people who would not otherwise buy a single ticket would buy a "bundle" of tickets for the same or even a slightly higher price.

Bundling of information goods online extends the concept of a twofer. **Bundling** offers consumers two or more goods for a price that is less than the goods would cost when purchased individually. The key idea behind the concept of bundling is that although consumers typically have very diverse ideas about the value of a single product, they tend to agree much more on the value of a bundle of products offered at a fixed price. In fact, the per-product price people are willing to pay for the bundle is often higher than when the products are sold separately. Bundling reduces the variance (dispersion) in market demand for goods.

Examples of bundling abound in the information goods marketplace. Microsoft bundles its separate Office tools (Word, Excel, PowerPoint, and Access) into a single Microsoft Office package. Even though many people want to use Word and Excel, far fewer want Access or PowerPoint. However, when all products are put into a single

versioning
creating multiple versions of information goods and selling essentially the same product to different market segments at different prices

bundling
offers consumers two or more goods for a reduced price

bundle, a very large number of people will agree that about $399 (or around $100 per tool) is a "fair" price for so many products. Likewise, the more software applications that Microsoft bundles with its basic operating system, the more the marketplace agrees that as a package of functionality, it is reasonably priced. On the Web, many content sites bundle as opposed to charging individual prices. Theoretically, bundlers have distinct competitive advantages over those who do not or cannot bundle. Specifically, on the supply side, bundler firms can pay higher prices for content, and on the demand side, bundlers can charge higher prices for their bundles than can single-good firms (Bakos and Brynjolfsson, 2000).

However, bundling of digital goods does not always work. It depends on the bundle and the price. For instance, Reed Elsevier, the world's largest publisher of scientific journals, created a bundle of 1,500 digital scientific journals for American universities, and priced the bundle at a substantial markup to what universities were paying for a much smaller number of journals. It then raised the price to universities that did not want the bundle. The result was a marketplace rebellion shaped in part by the fact that much of the research in these journals was paid for by taxpayers through government grants.

Dynamic Pricing and Flash Marketing The pricing strategies we have discussed so far are all fixed-price strategies. Versions and bundles are sold for fixed prices based on the firm's best effort at maximizing its profits. But what if there is product still left on the shelf along with the knowledge that someone, somewhere, would be willing to pay something for it? It might be better to obtain at least some revenue from the product, rather than let it sit on the shelf, or even perish. Imagine also that there are some people in every market who would pay a hefty premium for a product if they could have it right away. In other situations, such as for an antique, the value of the product has to be discovered in the marketplace (usually because there is a belief that the marketplace would value the product at a much higher price than its owner paid as a cost). In other cases, the value of a good is equal to what the market is willing to pay (and has nothing to do with its cost). Or let's say you want to build frequent visits to your site and offer some really great bargains for a few minutes each day, or the whole day with a set time limit. Here is where dynamic pricing mechanisms come to the fore, and where the strengths of the Internet can be seen.

There are three prevalent kinds of *dynamic pricing mechanisms:* auctions, yield management, and flash marketing. *Auctions* have been used for centuries to establish the instant market price for goods. Auctions are flexible and efficient market mechanisms for pricing unique or unusual goods, as well as commonplace goods such as computers, flower bundles, and cameras.

Yield management is quite different from auctions. In auctions, thousands of consumers establish a price by bidding against one another. In *yield management*, managers set prices in different markets, appealing to different segments, in order to sell excess capacity. Airlines exemplify yield management techniques. Every few minutes during the day, they adjust prices of empty airline seats to ensure at least some of the 50,000 empty airline seats are sold at some reasonable price—even below marginal cost of production. Frito-Lay, as mentioned earlier, also uses yield management techniques to ensure products move off the shelf in a timely fashion. Amazon and other large online retailers frequently use yield management techniques that involve changing prices hourly to stimulate demand and maximize revenues.

Yield management works under a limited set of conditions. Generally, the product is perishable (an empty airline seat perishes when the plane takes off without a full load); there are seasonal variations in demand; market segments are clearly defined; markets are competitive; and market conditions change rapidly (Cross, 1997). In general, only very large firms with extensive monitoring and database systems in place have been able to afford yield management techniques.

A third dynamic pricing technique is *flash marketing*, which has proved extraordinarily effective for travel services, luxury clothing goods, and other goods. Using e-mail or dedicated Web site features to notify loyal customers (repeat purchasers), merchants offer goods and services for a limited time (usually hours) at very low prices. JetBlue has offered $14 flights between New York and Los Angeles. Deluxe hotel rooms are flash marketed at $1 a night. Companies like Rue La La, HauteLook, and Gilt Groupe are based on flash marketing techniques. Blink and you can easily miss these great prices. Gilt.com purchases overstocked items from major fashion brands and then offers them to their subscribers at discounted prices via daily e-mail and SMS flash messages. Typically, the sale of an item lasts for two hours or until the inventory is depleted. On many occasions, Gilt.com rises to the top of most frequently visited Web sites when it conducts a sale. Critics point out that these sites take advantage of compulsive shoppers and lead to overshopping for unneeded goods. In another example of mass retail dynamic pricing, in May 2011, Amazon used its new cloud music service to offer a flash one-day sale of Lady Gaga's latest album for 99 cents. Response was so great that Amazon's cloud servers could not meet the demand, and the offer has not been repeated.

The Internet has truly revolutionized the possibilities to engage in dynamic, and even misleading, pricing strategies. With millions of consumers using a site every hour, and access to powerful databases, merchants can raise prices one minute and drop them another minute when a competitor threatens. Bait-and-switch tactics become more common: a really low price on one product is used to attract people to a site when in fact the product is not available.

We discuss dynamic pricing, auctions, and yield management techniques in greater detail in Chapter 11.

Long Tail Marketing

Consider that Amazon sells a larger number of obscure books than it does of "hit" books (defined as the top 20% of books sold). Nevertheless, the hit books generate 80% of Amazon's revenues. Consumers distribute themselves in many markets according to a power curve where 80% of the demand is for the hit products, and demand for nonhits quickly recedes to a small number of units sold. In a traditional market, niche products are so obscure no one ever hears about them. One impact of the Internet and e-commerce on sales of obscure products with little demand is that obscure products become more visible to consumers through search engines, recommendation engines, and social networks. Hence, online retailers can earn substantial revenue selling products for which demand and price are low. In fact, with near zero inventory costs, and a good search engine, the sales of obscure products can become a much larger percentage of total revenue. Amazon, for instance, has millions of book titles for sale at $2.99 or less, many written by obscure authors. Because of its search and recommendation engines, Amazon is able to generate profits from the sale of this large number of obscure titles. This is called the "**long tail**" effect. See *Insight on Technology: The Long Tail: Big Hits and Big Misses.*

long tail
a colloquial name given to various statistical distributions characterized by a small number of events of high amplitude and a very large number of events with low amplitude

6.3 | INTERNET MARKETING TECHNOLOGIES

Internet marketing has many similarities to and differences from ordinary marketing. The objective of Internet marketing—as in all marketing—is to build customer relationships so that the firm can achieve above-average returns (both by offering superior products or services and by communicating the product's features to the consumer). But Internet marketing is also very different from ordinary marketing because the nature of the medium and its capabilities are so different from anything that has come before. In order to understand just how different Internet marketing can be and in what ways, you first need to become familiar with some basic Internet marketing technologies.

THE REVOLUTION IN INTERNET MARKETING TECHNOLOGIES

In Chapter 1, we listed eight unique features of e-commerce technology. **Table 6.6** on page 378 describes how marketing has changed as a result of these new technical capabilities.

On balance, the Internet has had four very powerful impacts on marketing. First, the Internet, as a communications medium, has broadened the scope of marketing communications—in the sense of the number of people who can be easily reached as well as the locations where they can be reached, from desktops to mobile smartphones (in short, everywhere). Second, the Internet has increased the richness of marketing communications by combining text, video, and audio content into rich messages. Arguably, the Web is richer as a medium than even television or video because of the complexity of messages available, the enormous content accessible on a wide range of subjects, and the ability of users to interactively control the experience. Third, the Internet has greatly expanded the information intensity of the marketplace by providing marketers (and customers) with unparalleled fine-grained, detailed, real-time information about consumers as they transact in the marketplace.

Fourth, the always-on, always-attached, environment created by mobile devices results in consumers being much more available to receive marketing messages. One result is an extraordinary expansion in marketing opportunities for firms.

WEB TRANSACTION LOGS

How can e-commerce sites know more than a department store or the local grocery store does about consumer behavior? A primary source of consumer information on

INSIGHT ON TECHNOLOGY

THE LONG TAIL: BIG HITS AND BIG MISSES

The "Long Tail" is a name given to various statistical distributions characterized by a small group of events of high amplitude and a large group of events with low amplitude. Coined by *Wired Magazine* writer Chris Anderson in 2004, the Web's Long Tail has since gone on to fascinate academics and challenge online marketers. The concept is straightforward. Think Hollywood movies: there are big hits and also thousands of films that no one ever hears about. In economics, it's the Pareto principle: 20% of anything produces 80% of the effects. That means 20% of a product line produces 80% of the revenue, and by extension, 80% of the product line only returns 20% of the revenue. It's these nonhit misses that make up the Long Tail. Anderson claims to have discovered a new rule: no matter how much content you put online, someone, somewhere will show up to buy it. Rather than 20:80, Anderson suggests the Internet changes the Pareto principle. Internet search, recommendation engines, and online social networks all enable niche products to be discovered and purchased. eBay would seem to be a perfect example. The online tag sale contains millions of items drawn from every Aunt Tilly's closet in the world and still seems to find a buyer somewhere for just about anything, revenue that would not be realized without an online marketplace.

On the Internet, where search costs are tiny, and storage and distribution costs are near zero, Amazon is able to offer millions of books for sale compared to a typical large bookstore. The same is true of DVDs, digital cameras, e-books, and streaming videos. Wherever you look on the Web, you find huge inventories, and a great many items that few people are interested in buying. But someone is almost always searching for something. With 2.56 billion people online, even a one-in-a-million

product could find over 2,000 buyers. Researchers note that it isn't just that some people search for strange things, but rather that most shoppers have a taste for both popular as well as niche products. The strength of "infinite inventory" online retailers like Amazon is that they can satisfy the broadest range of individual tastes. Unlike physical stores, such as Walmart and Sears, online merchants have much lower overhead costs because they do not have physical stores and have lower labor costs. Therefore, they can load up on inventory, including items that rarely sell. Researchers argue that one impact of the Internet is to alter the 20:80 rule to something more like 30:70, where the niche products make up a larger share of the revenues than in traditional catalogs or stores.

There are several implications of the Long Tail phenomenon for Internet marketing. Some writers such as Anderson claim that the Internet revolutionizes digital content by making even niche products highly profitable, and that the revenues produced by small niche products will ultimately outweigh the revenues of hit movies, songs, and books. For content producers, this means less focus on the blockbusters that bust the budget, and more emphasis on the steady base, focusing on creating a quantity of titles that have at least some audience. The Long Tail is a democratizing phenomenon: even less well-known movies, songs, books, and apps can now find a market. For economists, the Long Tail represents a net gain for social welfare because customers can find exactly the niche content they really want rather than just accept the "big hits" on the shelf. The Long Tail makes more customers happy, and the possibility of making money on niche products should encourage more production of "indie" music and film.

One problem with the Long Tail in the past is that people sometimes have had difficulty finding

(continued)

these niche products because they are—by definition—largely unknown. In their native state, the revenue value of low-demand products is locked up in collective ignorance. Here's where recommender systems come into play: they can guide consumers to obscure but wonderful works based on the recommendations of others. Netflix has spent millions in recent years on improving its recommender system.

Long-Tail keywords are another way marketers are trying to unlock the power of the Long Tail. Long-Tail keywords are phrases that a small but significant number of people might use to find products. For instance, instead of investing in keywords such as "shoes" or "men's shoes," a marketer focused on the Long Tail might choose a keyword like "purple Adidas running shoes." Another way marketers tap into the Long Tail is to create highly specific blog or other content, that they then promote through social media.

Social networks also make the Long Tail phenomenon even stronger. One online person discovers an unheard-of niche product and shares his or her feelings with others. A recent study found that popularity information of the sort produced in a social network spurs sales of niche products more than mainstream products because of the higher perceived quality of the niche product. If a lot of people say they like an obscure product, it means more to consumers than if the same popularity attaches to a mainstream product.

But some research casts some doubt on the revenue potential in the Long Tail. In an odd twist, the number of DVD titles online that never get purchased is increasing. Solid best sellers have expanded and produce the vast part of online media revenues. A massive study of millions of digital downloads in England found that 75% of the digital titles were not downloaded even once. The Long Tail is a very lonely, quiet place. In reality, there seems to be more selling of less (the hits) than less selling of more (the misses). A U.S. study similarly found that 10% of the music titles at Rhapsody, a music site, produced 78% of the revenues. Researchers at Wharton examined over 17,000 movies at Netflix viewed by 480,000 users between 2000 and 2005. They found Long Tail effects missing: demand for the top 20% of movies actually expanded from 86% to 90%. While recommender systems are helpful for revealing niche content, they aren't very smart, and you still need several people to discover the niche product before alerting their friends. Recommender systems tend to recommend what the crowd likes. But niche products need serendipity to be discovered.

Both the Long Tail and the winner-take-all approaches have implications for marketers and product designers. In the Long Tail approach, online merchants, especially those selling digital goods such as content, should build up huge libraries of content because they can make significant revenues from niche products that have small audiences. In the winner-take-all approach, the niche products produce little revenue, and firms should concentrate on hugely popular titles and services. Surprisingly, contrary to what Anderson originally theorized, the evidence for online digital content increasingly supports a winner-take-all perspective. George Clooney: do not worry.

SOURCES: "Microsoft, Apps and the Long Tail," by Ben Bajarin, Time.com, July 8, 2013; "The Resurgence of Long-Tail Keywords in SEO," by Jayson DeMers, Searchenginewatch.com, March 18, 2013; "The State of SEO: What's Working Now," by Neil Patel, Quicksprout.com, January 21, 2013; "Article Marketing Tips: Using Long-Tail Keywords," by Steve Shaw, Internet Business, ezinearticles.com, August 26, 2012; "Goodbye Pareto Principle, Hello Long Tail: The Effect of Search Costs on the Concentration of Product Sales," by Eric Brynjolfsson, et al., *Management Science*, July 2012; "Recommendation Networks and the Long Tail of Electronic Commerce," by Gail Oestreicher-Singer, New York University, 2012; "Research Commentary - Long Tails vs. Superstars: The Effect of Information Technology on Product Variety and Sales Concentration Patterns" by Erik Brynjolfsson, Yu (Jeffrey) Hu, and Michael D. Smith, *Information Systems Research*, December 2010; "Anatomy of the Long Tail: Ordinary People With Extraordinary Tastes," by Sharad Goel, et al., Proceedings of the Third ACM Conference on Web Search and Data Mining, 2010; "How Does Popularity Affect Choices? A Field Experiment," by Catherine Tucker and Juanjuan Zhang, *Management Science,* May 2011; "Rethinking the Long Tail Theory: How to Define Hits and Misses," by Serguei Netessine and Tom Tan, Knowledge@Wharton, October 7, 2009; "Should You Invest in the Long Tail?," by Anita Elberse, *Harvard Business Review*, July–August 2008; "Superstars and Underdogs: An Examination of the Long Tail Phenomenon in Video Sales," by Anita Elberse and Felix Oberholzer-Gee, Harvard Business School Working Paper Series, No. 07-015, December, 2006; "From Niches to Riches: Anatomy of the Long Tail," by Eric Brynjolfsson, Yu Hu, and Michael Smith, *MIT Sloan Management Review*, Summer 2006; "The Long Tail," by Chris Anderson, *Wired Magazine*, October 2004.

TABLE 6.6	IMPACT OF UNIQUE FEATURES OF E-COMMERCE TECHNOLOGY ON MARKETING
E-COMMERCE TECHNOLOGY DIMENSION	**SIGNIFICANCE FOR MARKETING**
Ubiquity	Marketing communications have been extended to the home, work, and mobile platforms; geographic limits on marketing have been reduced. The marketplace has been replaced by "marketspace" and is removed from a temporal and geographic location. Customer convenience has been enhanced, and shopping costs have been reduced.
Global reach	Worldwide customer service and marketing communications have been enabled. Potentially hundreds of millions of consumers can be reached with marketing messages.
Universal standards	The cost of delivering marketing messages and receiving feedback from users is reduced because of shared, global standards of the Internet.
Richness	Video, audio, and text marketing messages can be integrated into a single marketing message and consuming experience.
Interactivity	Consumers can be engaged in a dialog, dynamically adjusting the experience to the consumer, and making the consumer a co-producer of the goods and services being sold.
Information density	Fine-grained, highly detailed information on consumers' real-time behavior can be gathered and analyzed for the first time. "Data mining" Internet technology permits the analysis of terabytes of consumer data every day for marketing purposes.
Personalization/ Customization	This feature potentially enables product and service differentiation down to the level of the individual, thus strengthening the ability of marketers to create brands.
Social technology	User-generated content and social networking sites, along with blogs, have created new, large, online audiences where the content is provided by users. These audiences have greatly expanded the opportunity for marketers to reach new potential customers in a nontraditional media format. Entirely new kinds of marketing techniques are evolving. These same technologies expose marketers to the risk of falling afoul of popular opinion by providing more market power to users who now can "talk back."

transaction log
records user activity at a Web site

registration forms
gather personal data on name, address, phone, zip code, e-mail address, and other optional self-confessed information on interests and tastes

shopping cart database
captures all the item selection, purchase, and payment data

the Web is the transaction log maintained by all Web servers. A **transaction log** records user activity at a Web site. The transaction log is built into Web server software. Transaction log data becomes even more useful when combined with two other visitor-generated data trails: registration forms and the shopping cart database. Users are enticed through various means (such as free gifts or special services) to fill out registration forms. **Registration forms** gather personal data on name, address, phone, zip code, e-mail address (usually required), and other optional self-confessed information on interests and tastes. When users make a purchase, they also enter additional information into the shopping cart database. The **shopping cart database** captures all the item selection, purchase, and payment data. Other potential additional sources of data are information users submit on product forms, contribute to chat groups, or send via e-mail messages using the "Contact Us" option on most sites.

For a Web site that has a million visitors per month, and where, on average, a visitor makes 15 page requests per visit, there will be 15 million entries in the log each month. These transaction logs, coupled with data from the registration forms and shopping cart database, represent a treasure trove of marketing information for both individual sites and the online industry as a whole. Nearly all the new Internet marketing capabilities are based on these data-gathering tools. For instance, here are just a few of the interesting marketing questions that can be answered by examining a site's Web transaction logs, registration forms, and shopping cart database:

- What are the major patterns of interest and purchase for groups and individuals?
- After the home page, where do most users go first, and then second and third?
- What are the interests of specific individuals (those we can identify)?
- How can we make it easier for people to use our site so they can find what they want?
- How can we change the design of the site to encourage visitors to purchase our high-margin products?
- Where are visitors coming from (and how can we optimize our presence on these referral sites)?
- How can we personalize our messages, offerings, and products to individual users?

Businesses can choke on the massive quantity of information found in a typical site's log file. We describe some technologies that help firms more effectively utilize this information below.

SUPPLEMENTING THE LOGS: TRACKING FILES

While transaction logs create the foundation of online data collection at a single Web site, marketers use tracking files to follow users across the entire Web as they visit other sites. There are four kinds of tracking files: cookies, beacons, Flash cookies, and apps (software programs used on smartphones and Web sites). As described in Chapter 3, a cookie is a small text file that Web sites place on the hard disk of visitors' client computers every time they visit, and during the visit, as specific pages are visited. Cookies allow a Web site to store data on a user's computer and then later retrieve it. The cookie typically includes a name, a unique ID number for each visitor that is stored on the user's computer, the domain (which specifies the Web server/domain that can access the cookie), a path (if a cookie comes from a particular part of a Web site instead of the main page, a path will be given), a security setting that provides whether the cookie can only be transmitted by a secure server, and an expiration date (not required). First-party cookies come from the same domain name as the page the user is visiting, while third-party cookies come from another domain, such as ad serving or adware companies, affiliate marketers, or spyware servers. On some Web sites, there are literally hundreds of tracking files on the main pages.

A cookie provides Web marketers with a very quick means of identifying the customer and understanding his or her prior behavior at the site. Web sites use cookies to determine how many people are visiting the site, whether they are new or repeat visitors, and how often they have visited, although this data may be somewhat inaccurate because people share computers, they often use more than one computer, and cookies may have been inadvertently or intentionally erased. Cookies make shopping carts and "quick checkout" options possible by allowing a site to keep track of a user as he or she adds to the shopping cart. Each item added to the shopping cart is stored in the site's database along with the visitor's unique ID value.

Ordinary cookies are easy to spot using your browser, but Flash cookies, beacons, and tracking codes are not easily visible. All common browsers allow users to see the cookies placed in their cookies file. Users can delete cookies, or adjust their settings so that third-party cookies are blocked, while first-party cookies are allowed.

With growing privacy concerns, over time the percentage of people deleting cookies has risen. The more cookies are deleted, the less accurate are Web page and ad server metrics, and the less likely marketers will be able to understand who is visiting their sites or where they came from. As a result, advertisers have sought other methods. One way is using Adobe Flash software, which creates its own cookie files, known as Flash cookies. Flash cookies can be set to never expire, and can store about 5 MB of information compared to the 1,024 bytes stored by regular cookies. A 2009 study by researchers at the University of California-Berkeley analyzed the use of Flash cookies at the top 100 Web sites, and found that 98% used regular cookies and 54% used Flash cookies, many to store the same information as the regular cookie. Some used the Flash cookies to re-create cookies that consumers had previously deleted.

Although cookies are site-specific (a Web site can only receive the data it has stored on a client computer and cannot look at any other cookie), when combined with Web beacons (also called "bugs"), they can be used to create cross-site profiles. Web beacons are tiny (1-pixel) graphic files embedded in e-mail messages and on Web sites. Web beacons are used to automatically transmit information about the user and the page being viewed to a monitoring server in order to collect personal browsing behavior and other personal information. For instance, when a recipient opens an e-mail in HTML format or opens a Web page, a message is sent to a server calling for graphic information. This tells the marketer that the e-mail was opened, indicating that the recipient was at least interested in the subject header. Web beacons are not visible to users. They are often clear or colored white so they are not visible to the recipient. You may be able to determine if a Web page is using Web beacons by using the View Source option of your browser and examining the IMG (image) tags on the page. As noted above, Web beacons are typically 1 pixel in size and contain the URL of a server that differs from the one that served the page itself. *Insight on Society: Every Move You Take, Every Click You Make, We'll Be Tracking You* examines the use of Web tracking files.

DATABASES, DATA WAREHOUSES, DATA MINING, AND BIG DATA

profiling
profiling uses a variety of tools to create a digital image for each consumer

Databases, data warehouses, data mining, and the variety of marketing decision-making techniques loosely called *profiling* are at the heart of the revolution in Internet marketing. **Profiling** uses a variety of tools to create a digital image for each consumer. This image can be quite inexact, even primitive, but it can also be as detailed as a

INSIGHT ON SOCIETY

EVERY MOVE YOU TAKE, EVERY CLICK YOU MAKE, WE'LL BE TRACKING YOU

Advertising-supported Web sites depend on knowing as much personal information as possible about you. One of the main ways ad firms discover your personal information is by placing so-called "tracking files" on your computer's browser. There are several kinds of third-party tracking files on Web pages. Cookies are the best known. These simple text files are placed in your browser and assign a unique number to your computer, which is then used by advertisers to track you across the Web as you move from one site to another (without telling you). Web beacons (sometimes also referred to as Web bugs) are a little more pernicious. Beacons are small software files that track your clicks, choices, and purchases, and even location data from mobile devices, and then send that information, often in real time, to advertisers tracking you. Beacons can also assign your computer a unique number and track you across the Web. A Flash cookie is a third kind of tracking file. Installed by Adobe Flash as you watch movies, these files can be used to install regular cookies on your computer and even restore cookies you have deleted. Recently, the use of Flash cookies has declined, replaced in part by Web sites using HTML5 local storage, which can be used for tracking the same way as Flash and regular cookies. Tracking can also be performed by apps on cell phones as well as Facebook. Most Facebook apps, for instance, all send personal information, including names, to dozens of advertising and Internet tracking companies.

So how common is Web tracking? In a trail-blazing series of articles in the *Wall Street Journal*, researchers examined the tracking files on 50 of the most popular U.S Web sites. What they found revealed a very widespread surveillance system.

Only one site, Wikipedia, had no tracking files. Two-thirds of the tracking files came from companies whose primary business is identifying and tracking Internet users to create consumer profiles that can be sold to advertising firms looking for specific types of customers. The other third came from database firms that gather and bundle the information and then sell it to marketers. Many of the tracking tools gather incredibly personal information such as age, gender, race, income, marital status, health concerns, TV shows and movies viewed, magazines and newspapers read, and books purchased. While tracking firms claim the information they gather is anonymous, this is true in name only. Scholars have shown that with just a few pieces of information, such as age, gender, zip code, and marital status, specific individuals can be easily identified. In October 2012, a Web Privacy Census conducted by the University of California Berkeley Center for Law and Technology found that the total number of cookies on the top 100 Web sites had increased by 80%, from 3,600 when first measured in 2009 to over 6,400. The vast majority of these cookies (about 85%) were third-party tracking cookies, from over 450 different third-party hosts. Google's DoubleClick was the top tracker, and the most frequently appearing cookie keys were those associated with Google Analytics. Similar results were observed when looking at the top 1,000 and top 25,000 Web sites. One cause: growth of online ad auctions where advertisers buy data about users' Web browsing behavior. When you visit a site, your visit is auctioned and the winner gets to show you some ads. All this takes place in a few milliseconds so you don't know its happening. Welcome to the brave new world of Internet marketing!

The Privacy Foundation has issued guidelines for Web beacon usage. The guidelines suggest that

(continued)

Web beacons should be visible as an icon on the screen, the icon should be labeled to indicate its function, and it should identify the name of the company that placed the Web beacon on the page. In addition, if a user clicks on the Web beacon, it should display a disclosure statement indicating what data is being collected, how the data is used after it is collected, what companies receive the data, what other data the Web beacon is combined with, and whether or not a cookie is associated with the Web beacon. Users should be able to opt out of any data collection done by the Web beacon, and the Web beacon should not be used to collect information from Web pages of a sensitive nature, such as medical, financial, job-related, or sexual matters. None of these ideas are found in current law.

In an effort to address growing congressional concerns about privacy, and build consumer trust online, an industry advertising group, the Network Advertising Initiative (NAI), released self-regulatory guidelines for the industry. Major advertising industry groups have adopted guidelines that emphasize transparency (tell consumers how you use their information) and choice (opt-in and opt-out). The NAI requires online firms to notify customers of Web beacon usage, state the purpose of their use, and disclose any data that could be released to third parties. The NAI also called for users to be given a choice (whether opt-in or opt-out) of any release of personally identifiable information (PII) to third parties, and to provide an opt-in choice for any release of information related to PII. In addition, the NAI provides a capability open to all Web users to opt out of online advertising networks collecting nonpersonal information on them. However, for this to work, users need to have a cookie downloaded to their browser that will inform the networks not to collect information on this user.

Currently, there are no laws or regulations in the United States that prevent firms from installing tracking files or using that information in any way they please. Although there has been considerable interest in protecting the privacy of consumers, thus far efforts to enact federal Do Not Track legislation have failed.

One roadblock involves the meaning of Do Not Track. Industry wants an opt-in, default Track Me feature on all Web sites, while the government and privacy groups are pushing for an opt-out Do Not Track feature in which the default is Do Not Track. In July 2013, a working group commissioned by the W3C proposed that Web users should be able to tell advertising networks not to show them targeted advertisements. Still unresolved, however, is whether those networks and data brokers should be allowed to collect the data in the first place.

Nearly all browsers now offer users the option of using a Do Not Track feature. But users have to remember to turn it on. A March 2013 survey by Forrester Research found that less than 20% of users used the Do Not Track setting on their browsers. In addition, not all Web sites honor the Do Not Track request, since they are not legally obligated to do so. Major Web sites and the online advertising industry insist their industry can self-regulate itself and preserve individual privacy. However, this solution has not worked in the past.

SOURCES: " 'Do Not Track' Rules Come a Step Closer to an Agreement," by Somini Sengupta and Natasha Singer, *New York Times,* July 15, 2013; "What Firefox's New Privacy Settings Mean for You," by Sarah A. Downey, Abine.com, March 29, 2013; "The Web Privacy Census," by Chris Jay Hoofnagle and Nathan Good, law.berkeley.edu/privacycensus.htm, October 2012; "Online Data Collection Explodes Year Over Year in US," eMarketer, Inc., July 19, 2012; "Online Tracking Ramps Up," by Julia Angwin, *Wall Street Journal,* June 17, 2012; "Microsoft's "Do Not Track" Move Angers Advertising Industry," by Julia Angwin, *Wall Street Journal,* May 31, 2012; "Opt-Out Provision Would Halt Some, but Not All, Web Tracking," by Tanzina Vega, *New York Times,* February 28, 2012; "How Companies Learn Your Secrets," by Charles Duhigg, *New York Times Magazine,* February 16, 2012; "Latest in Web Tracking: Stealthy 'Supercookies,'" by Julia Angwin, *Wall Street Journal,* August 18, 2011; "WPP Ad Unit Has Your Profile," by Emily Steel, *Wall Street Journal,* June 27, 2011; "Not Me Dot Com," by Luke O'Neil, *Wall Street Journal,* June 18, 2011; "Show Us the Data. (It's Ours, After All)," by Richard Thaler, *New York Times,* April 23, 2011; "What They Know About You," by Jennfier Valentino-Devries, *Wall Street Journal,* July 31, 2010; "Sites Feed Personal Details to New Tracking Industry," Julia Angwin and Tom McGinty, *Wall Street Journal,* July 30, 2010; "Study Finds Behaviorally-Targeted Ads More Than Twice As Valuable, Twice as Effective As Non-targeted Online Ads," Network Advertising Initiative, March 24, 2010.

character in a novel. The quality of a consumer profile depends on the amount of data used to create it, and the analytical power of the firm's software and hardware. Together, these techniques attempt to identify precisely who the online customer is and what they want, and then, to fulfill the customer's criteria exactly. These techniques are more powerful, far more precise, and more fine-grained than the gross levels of demographic and market segmentation techniques used in mass marketing media or by telemarketing.

In order to understand the data in transaction logs, registration forms, shopping carts, cookies, Web bugs, and other unstructured data sources like e-mails, Tweets, and Likes, Internet marketers need massively powerful and capacious databases, database management systems, and analytic tools.

Databases

The first step in interpreting huge transaction streams is to store the information systematically. A **database** is a software application that stores records and attributes. A telephone book is a physical database that stores records of individuals and their attributes such as names, addresses, and phone numbers. A **database management system** (**DBMS**) is a software application used by organizations to create, maintain, and access databases. The most common DBMS are DB2 from IBM and a variety of SQL databases from Oracle, Sybase, and other providers. **Structured query language** **(SQL)** is an industry-standard database query and manipulation language used in relational databases. **Relational databases** such as DB2 and SQL represent data as two-dimensional tables with records organized in rows, and attributes in columns, much like a spreadsheet. The tables—and all the data in them—can be flexibly related to one another as long as the tables share a common data element.

Relational databases are extraordinarily flexible and allow marketers and other managers to view and analyze data from different perspectives very quickly.

Data Warehouses and Data Mining

A **data warehouse** is a database that collects a firm's transactional and customer data in a single location for offline analysis by marketers and site managers. The data originate in many core operational areas of the firm, such as Web site transaction logs, shopping carts, point-of-sale terminals (product scanners) in stores, warehouse inventory levels, field sales reports, external scanner data supplied by third parties, and financial payment data. The purpose of a data warehouse is to gather all the firm's transaction and customer data into one logical repository where it can be analyzed and modeled by managers without disrupting or taxing the firm's primary transactional systems and databases. Data warehouses grow quickly into storage repositories containing terabytes (trillions of bytes) of data on consumer behavior at a firm's stores and Web sites. With a data warehouse, firms can answer such questions as: What products are the most profitable by region and city? What regional marketing campaigns are working? How effective is store promotion of the firm's Web site? Data warehouses can provide business managers with a more complete awareness of customers through data that can be accessed quickly.

database
a software application that stores records and attributes

database management system (DBMS)
a software application used by organizations to create, maintain, and access databases

structured query language (SQL)
industry-standard database query language used in relational databases

relational databases
represent data as two-dimensional tables with records organized in rows and attributes in columns; data within different tables can be flexibly related as long as the tables share a common data element

data warehouse
a database that collects a firm's transactional and customer data in a single location for offline analysis

data mining
a set of analytical techniques that look for patterns in the data of a database or data warehouse, or seek to model the behavior of customers

customer profile
a description of the typical behavior of a customer or a group of customers at a Web site

query-driven data mining
data mining based on specific queries

model-driven data mining
involves the use of a model that analyzes the key variables of interest to decision makers

Data mining is a set of analytical techniques that look for patterns in the data of a database or data warehouse, or seek to model the behavior of customers. Web site data can be "mined" to develop profiles of visitors and customers. A **customer profile** is simply a set of rules that describe the typical behavior of a customer or a group of customers at a Web site. Customer profiles help to identify the patterns in group and individual behavior that occur online as millions of visitors use a firm's Web site. For example, almost every financial transaction you engage in is processed by a data mining application to detect fraud. Phone companies closely monitor your cell phone use as well to detect stolen phones and unusual calling patterns. Financial institutions and cell phone firms use data mining to develop fraud profiles. When a user's behavior conforms to a fraud profile, the transaction is not allowed or is terminated (Mobasher, 2007).

There are many different types of data mining. The simplest type is **query-driven data mining**, which is based on specific queries. For instance, based on hunches of marketers who suspect a relationship in the database or who need to answer a specific question, such as "What is the relationship between time of day and purchases of various products at the Web site?", marketers can easily query the data warehouse and produce a database table that rank-orders the top 10 products sold at a Web site by each hour of the day. Marketers can then change the content of the Web site to stimulate more sales by highlighting different products over time or placing particular products on the home page at certain times of day or night.

Another form of data mining is model-driven. **Model-driven data mining** involves the use of a model that analyzes the key variables of interest to decision makers. For example, marketers may want to reduce the inventory carried on the Web site by removing unprofitable items that do not sell well. A financial model can be built showing the profitability of each product on the site so that an informed decision can be made.

A more fine-grained behavioral approach that seeks to deal with individuals as opposed to market segments derives rules from individual consumer behavior (along with some demographic information) (Adomavicius and Tuzhilin, 2001a; Chan, 1999; Fawcett and Provost, 1996, 1997). Here, the pages actually visited by specific users are stored as a set of conjunctive rules. For example, if an individual visits a site and typically ("as a rule") moves from the home page to the financial news section to the Asian report section, and then often purchases articles from the "Recent Developments in Banking" section, this person—based on purely past behavioral patterns—might be shown an advertisement for a book on Asian money markets. These rules can be constructed to follow an individual across many different Web sites.

There are many drawbacks to all these techniques, not least of which is that there may be millions of rules, many of them nonsensical, and many others of short-term duration. Hence, the rules need extensive validation and culling (Adomavicius and Tuzhilin, 2001b). Also, there can be millions of affinity groups and other patterns in the data that are temporal or meaningless. The difficulty is isolating the valid, powerful (profitable) patterns in the data and then acting on the observed pattern fast enough to make a sale that otherwise would not have been made. As we see later, there are practical difficulties and trade-offs involved in achieving these levels of granularity, precision, and speed.

Hadoop and the Challenge of Big Data

Up until about five years ago, most data collected by organizations consisted of structured transaction data that could easily fit into rows and columns of relational database management systems. Since then, there has been an explosion of data from Web traffic, e-mail messages, and social media content (tweets, status messages), even music playlists, as well as machine-generated data from sensors. These data may be unstructured or semi-structured and thus not suitable for relational database products that organize data in the form of columns and rows. The popular term "big data" refers to this avalanche of digital data flowing into firms around the world largely from Web sites and Internet click stream data. The volumes of data are so large that traditional DBMS cannot capture, store, and analyze the data in a reasonable time. Some examples of "big data" challenges are analyzing 12 terabytes of tweets created each day to improve your understanding of consumer sentiment towards your products; 100 million e-mails in order to place appropriate ads alongside the e-mail messages; or 500 million call detail records to find patterns of fraud and churn. Big data and the tools needed to deal with it really started with Google and other search engines. Google's problem: it has to deal with 500 million searches a day, and within milliseconds, display search results and place ads. For fun, do a search on "big data" and you'll see Google respond with more than 1 billion results in 38 milliseconds (about a third of a second). That's much faster than you can read this sentence!

Big data usually refers to data in the petabyte and exabyte range—in other words, billions to trillions of records, all from different sources. Big data are produced in much larger quantities and much more rapidly than traditional data. Even though "tweets" are limited to 140 characters each, Twitter generates more than 8 terabytes of data daily. According to the IDC technology research firm, data is more than doubling every two years, so the amount of data available to organizations is skyrocketing. Making sense out of it quickly in order to gain a market advantage is critical.

Businesses are interested in big data because they contain more patterns and interesting anomalies than smaller data sets, with the potential to provide new insights into customer behavior, weather patterns, financial market activity, or other phenomena. However, to derive business value from these data, organizations need new technologies and tools capable of managing and analyzing nontraditional data along with their traditional enterprise data.

To handle unstructured and semi-structured data in vast quantities, as well as structured data, organizations are using Hadoop. **Hadoop** is an open source software framework managed by the Apache Software Foundation that enables distributed parallel processing of huge amounts of data across inexpensive computers. It breaks a big data problem down into subproblems, distributes them among up to thousands of inexpensive computer processing nodes, and then combines the result into a smaller data set that is easier to analyze. You've probably used Hadoop to find the best airfare on the Internet, get directions to a restaurant, search on Google, or connect with a friend on Facebook.

Hadoop can process large quantities of any kind of data, including structured transactional data, loosely structured data such as Facebook and Twitter feeds, complex data such as Web server log files, and unstructured audio and video data. Hadoop runs on a cluster of inexpensive servers, and processors can be added or removed as

big data
big data refers to very large data sets in the petabyte and exabyte range

Hadoop
a software framework for working with various big data sets

needed. Companies use Hadoop to analyze very large volumes of data as well as for a staging area for unstructured and semi-structured data before they are loaded into a data warehouse. Facebook stores much of its data on its massive Hadoop cluster, which holds an estimated 100 petabytes, about 10,000 times more information than the Library of Congress. Yahoo uses Hadoop to track user behavior so it can modify its home page to fit user interests. Life sciences research firm NextBio uses Hadoop and HBase to process data for pharmaceutical companies conducting genomic research. Top database vendors such as IBM, Hewlett-Packard, Oracle, and Microsoft have their own Hadoop software distributions. Other vendors offer tools for moving data into and out of Hadoop or for analyzing data within Hadoop.

CUSTOMER RELATIONSHIP MANAGEMENT (CRM) SYSTEMS

customer relationship management (CRM) system
a repository of customer information that records all of the contacts that a customer has with a firm and generates a customer profile available to everyone in the firm with a need to "know the customer"

customer touchpoints
the ways in which customers interact with the firm

Customer relationship management systems are another important Internet marketing technology. A **customer relationship management (CRM) system** is a repository of customer information that records all of the contacts that a customer has with a firm (including Web sites) and generates a customer profile available to everyone in the firm with a need to "know the customer." CRM systems also supply the analytical software required to analyze and use customer information. Customers come to firms not just over the Web but also through telephone call centers, customer service representatives, sales representatives, automated voice response systems, ATMs and kiosks, in-store point-of-sale terminals, and mobile devices (m-commerce). Collectively, these are referred to as "**customer touchpoints**." In the past, firms generally did not maintain a single repository of customer information, but instead were organized along product lines, with each product line maintaining a customer list (and often not sharing it with others in the same firm).

In general, firms did not know who their customers were, how profitable they were, or how they responded to marketing campaigns. For instance, a bank customer might see a television advertisement for a low-cost auto loan that included an 800-number to call. However, if the customer came to the bank's Web site instead, rather than calling the 800-number, marketers would have no idea how effective the television campaign was because this Web customer contact data was not related to the 800-number call center data. **Figure 6.10** illustrates how a CRM system integrates customer contact data into a single system.

CRMs are part of the evolution of firms toward a customer-centric and marketing-segment–based business, and away from a product-line–centered business. CRMs are essentially a database technology with extraordinary capabilities for addressing the needs of each customer and differentiating the product or service on the basis of treating each customer as a unique person. Customer profiles can contain the following information:

- A map of the customer's relationship with the institution
- Product and usage summary data
- Demographic and psychographic data
- Profitability measures

- Contact history summarizing the customer's contacts with the institution across most delivery channels
- Marketing and sales information containing programs received by the customer and the customer's responses
- E-mail campaign responses
- Web site visits

With these profiles, CRMs can be used to sell additional products and services, develop new products, increase product utilization, reduce marketing costs, identify and retain profitable customers, optimize service delivery costs, retain high lifetime value customers, enable personal communications, improve customer loyalty, and increase product profitability.

For instance, Home Depot saw increased competition from online hardware stores and decided to emphasize e-commerce as part of its business strategy. The company sought a comprehensive CRM solution that could organize and analyze information

---

| FIGURE 6.10 | **A CUSTOMER RELATIONSHIP MANAGEMENT SYSTEM** |

Business intelligence
Data mining
Analysis and reporting
Modeling

Marketing campaign management
Advertising campaign management
Behavioral targeting

Data aggregation
Data cleaning
Customer database
Data warehouse

Transaction processing
Operational data collection

Telephone   Sales force   Web site   In-store   Social networks   Mail

Customer Touch Points

This is an example of a CRM system for a financial services institution. The system captures customer information from all customer touchpoints as well as other data sources, merges the data, and aggregates it into a single customer data repository or data warehouse where it can be used to provide better service, as well as to construct customer profiles for marketing purposes. Online analytical processing (OLAP) allows managers to dynamically analyze customer activities to spot trends or problems involving customers. Other analytical software programs analyze aggregate customer behavior to identify profitable and unprofitable customers as well as customer activities.

from both clicks and mortar. They used a CRM software package called Epiphany Insight to gain a better understanding of which Home Depot products were selling on the Web and enabled their customer service focus from their stores to exist on the Web as well. Epiphany has since been acquired by Infor. Other leading CRM vendors include SAP, SalesForce.com, Oracle, Kana, and eGain.

6.4 UNDERSTANDING THE COSTS AND BENEFITS OF ONLINE MARKETING COMMUNICATIONS

As we noted earlier, online marketing communications still comprise only a small part of the total marketing communications universe. While there are several reasons why this is the case, two of the main ones are concerns about how well online advertising really works and about how to adequately measure the costs and benefits of online advertising. We will address both of these topics in this section. But first, we will define some important terms used when examining the effectiveness of online marketing.

ONLINE MARKETING METRICS: LEXICON

In order to understand the process of attracting prospects to your firm's Web site or Facebook page via marketing communications and converting them into customers, you will need to be familiar with Web marketing terminology. **Table 6.7** lists some terms commonly used to describe the impacts and results of online marketing for display ads, social network ads, and e-mail campaigns.

impressions
number of times an ad is served

click-through rate (CTR)
the percentage of people exposed to an online advertisement who actually click on the banner

view-through rate (VTR)
measures the 30-day response rate to an ad

hits
number of http requests received by a firm's server

page views
number of pages requested by visitors

The first nine metrics focus primarily on the success of a Web site in achieving audience or market share by "driving" shoppers to the site. These measures often substitute for solid information on sales revenue as e-commerce entrepreneurs seek to have investors and the public focus on the success of the Web site in "attracting eyeballs" (viewers).

Impressions are the number of times an ad is served. **Click-through rate (CTR)** measures the percentage of people exposed to an online advertisement who actually click on the advertisement. Because not all ads lead to an immediate click, the industry has invented a new term for a long-term hit called **view-through rate (VTR)**, which measures the 30-day response rate to an ad. **Hits** are the number of HTTP requests received by a firm's server. Hits can be misleading as a measure of Web site activity because a "hit" does not equal a page. A single page may account for several hits if the page contains multiple images or graphics. A single Web site visitor can generate hundreds of hits. For this reason, hits are not an accurate representation of Web traffic or visits, even though they are generally easy to measure; the sheer volume of hits can be huge—and sound impressive—but not be a true measure of activity. **Page views** are the number of pages requested by visitors. However, with increased usage of Web frames that divide pages into separate sections, a single page that has three frames will generate three page views. Hence, page views per se are also not a very useful metric.

Stickiness (sometimes called *duration*) is the average length of time visitors remain at a Web site. Stickiness is important to marketers because the longer the

TABLE 6.7	MARKETING METRICS LEXICON

COMMON MARKETING DISPLAY AD METRICS	DESCRIPTION
Impressions	Number of times an ad is served
Click-through rate (CTR)	Percentage of times an ad is clicked
View-through rate (VTR)	Percentage of times an ad is not clicked immediately but the Web site is visited within 30 days
Hits	Number of HTTP requests
Page views	Number of pages viewed
Stickiness (duration)	Average length of stay at a Web site
Unique visitors	Number of unique visitors in a period
Loyalty	Measured variously as the number of page views, frequency of single-user visits to the Web site, or percentage of customers who return to the site in a year to make additional purchases
Reach	Percentage of Web site visitors who are potential buyers; or the percentage of total market buyers who buy at a site
Recency	Time elapsed since the last action taken by a buyer, such as a Web site visit or purchase
Acquisition rate	Percentage of visitors who indicate an interest in the Web site's products by registering or visiting product pages
Conversion rate	Percentage of visitors who become customers
Browse-to-buy ratio	Ratio of items purchased to product views
View-to-cart ratio	Ratio of "Add to cart" clicks to product views
Cart conversion rate	Ratio of actual orders to "Add to cart" clicks
Checkout conversion rate	Ratio of actual orders to checkouts started
Abandonment rate	Percentage of shoppers who begin a shopping cart purchase but then leave the Web site without completing a purchase (similar to above)
Retention rate	Percentage of existing customers who continue to buy on a regular basis (similar to loyalty)
Attrition rate	Percentage of customers who do not return during the next year after an initial purchase

SOCIAL MARKETING METRICS	
Gross rating points	Audience size times frequency of views (audience reach)
Applause ratio	Number of Likes per post
Conversation ratio	Ratio of number of comments per post
Amplification	Number of shares (or re-tweets) per post
Sentiment ratio	Ratio of positive comments to total comments
Duration of engagement	Average time on site

E-MAIL METRICS	
Open rate	Percentage of e-mail recipients who open the e-mail and are exposed to the message
Delivery rate	Percentage of e-mail recipients who received the e-mail
Click-through rate (e-mail)	Percentage of recipients who clicked through to offers
Bounce-back rate	Percentage of e-mails that could not be delivered
Unsubscribe rate	Percentage of recipients who click unsubscribe
Conversion rate (e-mail)	Percentage of recipients who actually buy

stickiness (duration)
average length of time visitors remain at a site

unique visitors
the number of distinct, unique visitors to a site

loyalty
percentage of purchasers who return in a year

reach
percentage of the total number of consumers in a market who will visit a site

recency
average number of days elapsed between visits

acquisition rate
percentage of visitors who register or visit product pages

conversion rate
percentage of visitors who purchase something

browse-to-buy ratio
ratio of items purchased to product views

view-to-cart ratio
ratio of "Add to cart" clicks to product views

cart conversion rate
ratio of actual orders to "Add to cart" clicks

checkout conversion rate
ratio of actual orders to checkouts started

abandonment rate
% of shoppers who begin a shopping cart, but then fail to complete it

retention rate
% of existing customers who continue to buy

attrition rate
% of customers who purchase once, but do not return within a year

amount of time a visitor spends at a Web site, the greater the probability of a purchase. For instance, while Facebook generates a great deal of stickiness, it's not the case that this translates directly into more sales and more revenue. Equally important is what people do when they visit a Web site and not just how much time they spend there. People don't go to Facebook to buy or research goods, whereas Google visitors are more likely to visit because they are searching for something to buy (Nielsen, 2012).

The number of unique visitors is perhaps the most widely used measure of a Web site's popularity. The measurement of **unique visitors** counts the number of distinct, unique visitors to a Web site, regardless of how many pages they view. **Loyalty** measures the percentage of visitors who return in a year. This can be a good indicator of a site's Web following, and perhaps the trust shoppers place in a site. **Reach** is typically a percentage of the total number of consumers in a market who visit a Web site; for example, 10% of all book purchasers in a year will visit Amazon at least once to shop for a book. This provides an idea of the power of a Web site to attract market share. **Recency**—like loyalty—measures the power of a Web site to produce repeat visits and is generally measured as the average number of days elapsed between shopper or customer visits. For example, a recency value of 25 days means the average customer will return once every 25 days.

The metrics described so far do not say much about commercial activity nor help you understand the conversion from visitor to customer. Several other measures are more helpful in this regard. **Acquisition rate** measures the percentage of visitors who register or visit product pages (indicating interest in the product). **Conversion rate** measures the percentage of visitors who actually purchase something. Conversion rates can vary widely, depending on the success of the site. Fireclick, a provider of Web analytics software, publishes conversion rate statistics, and cites a global conversion rate of around 3%–4% (Fireclick, 2013). The **browse-to-buy ratio** measures the ratio of items purchased to product views. The **view-to-cart ratio** calculates the ratio of "Add to cart" clicks to product views. **Cart conversion rate** measures the ratio of actual orders to "Add to cart" clicks. **Checkout conversion rate** calculates the ratio of actual orders to checkouts started. **Abandonment rate** measures the percentage of shoppers who begin a shopping cart form but then fail to complete the form and leave the Web site. Abandonment rates can signal a number of potential problems—poor form design, lack of consumer trust, or consumer purchase uncertainty caused by other factors. A recent study on shopping cart abandonment found that, on average, 65% of carts were abandoned in 2012 (Baymard, 2012). Among the reasons for abandonment were security concerns, customer just checking prices, couldn't find customer support, couldn't find preferred payment option, and the item being unavailable at checkout. Given that more than 80% of online shoppers generally have a purchase in mind when they visit a Web site, a high abandonment rate signals many lost sales. **Retention rate** indicates the percentage of existing customers who continue to buy on a regular basis. **Attrition rate** measures the percentage of customers who purchase once but never return within a year (the opposite of loyalty and retention rates).

Social network marketing differs from display ad marketing because the objective is to create word-of-mouth impact and alter the interaction among your visitors, and between your visitors and your brand. While unique visitors is important, it's even more important what they do when they arrive on-site. **Conversation ratio** measures the number of comments produced per post to your site. **Applause ratio** measures the number of Likes or Shares per post. **Amplification** measures the number of re-tweets or re-shares per post. All three of these measures are different dimensions of "word of mouth" advertising on social network sites. **Sentiment ratio** is the ratio of positive comments to total comments.

Facebook, Nielsen, and comScore are also measuring Facebook exposure using gross rating points, a traditional ad metric that multiplies the reach, or size, of an audience by the frequency with which that audience sees a brand. By using this metric, marketers can discuss online advertising in the same terms that they already use for TV, print, or outdoor ads (Raice, 2011; Nielsen, 2011). Facebook's application software development package provides extensive measures of user interactions and demographics. On the other hand, this metric does not measure dimensions of consumer engagement, which is the main strength of social network advertising. You will learn more about measuring the effectiveness of social, mobile, and local advertising in Chapter 7.

E-mail campaigns have their own set of metrics. **Open rate** measures the percentage of customers who open the e-mail and are exposed to the message. Generally, open rates are quite high, in the area of 50% or greater. However, some browsers open mail as soon as the mouse cursor moves over the subject line, and therefore this measure can be difficult to interpret. **Delivery rate** measures the percentage of e-mail recipients who received the e-mail. **Click-through rate (e-mail)** measures the percentage of e-mail recipients who clicked through to the offer. Finally, **bounce-back rate** measures the percentage of e-mails that could not be delivered.

There is a lengthy path from simple online ad impressions, Web site visits, and page views to the purchase of a product and the company making a profit (see **Figure 6.11**). You first need to make customers aware of their needs for your product and somehow drive them to your Web site. Once there, you need to convince them you have the best value—quality and price—when compared to alternative providers. You then must persuade them to trust your firm to handle the transaction (by providing a secure environment and fast fulfillment). Based on your success, a percentage of customers will remain loyal and purchase again or recommend your Web site to others.

HOW WELL DOES ONLINE ADVERTISING WORK?

What is the most effective kind of online advertising? How does online advertising compare to offline advertising? The answers depend on the goals of the campaign, the nature of the product, and the quality of the Web site you direct customers toward. The answers also depend on what you measure. Click-through rates are interesting, but ultimately it's the return on the investment in the ad campaign that counts. A broader understanding of the matter requires that you consider the cost of purchasing the promotional materials and mailing lists, and the studio production costs for radio and TV ads. Also, each media has a different revenue-per-contact potential because the products advertised differ. For instance, online purchases tend to be for smaller items when compared to newspaper, magazine, and television ads (although this too seems to be changing).

conversation ratio
number of comments produced per post

applause ratio
number of Likes or Shares per post

amplification
number of re-tweets or re-shares per post

sentiment ratio
ratio of positive comments to total comments

open rate
% of customers who open e-mail

delivery rate
% of e-mail recipients who received e-mail

click-through rate (e-mail)
% of e-mail recipients who clicked through to the offer

bounce-back rate
percentage of e-mails that could not be delivered

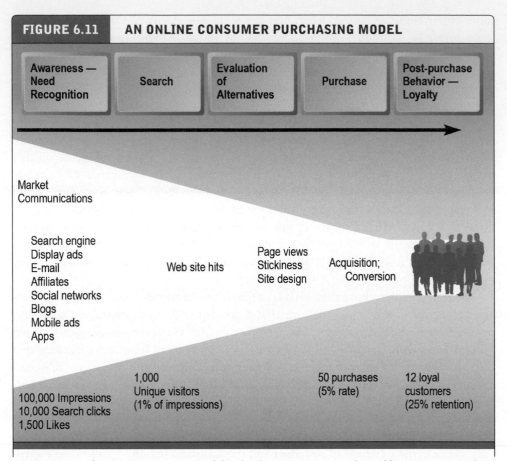

FIGURE 6.11   AN ONLINE CONSUMER PURCHASING MODEL

The conversion of visitors into customers, and then loyal customers, is a complex and long-term process that may take several months.

Table 6.8 lists the click-through rates for various types of online marketing communications tools. There is a great deal of variability within any of these types, so the figures should be viewed as general estimates. Click-through rates on all these formats are a function of personalization and other targeting techniques. For instance, several studies have found that e-mail response rates can be increased 20% or more by adding social sharing links. And while the average Google click-through rate is less than 1%, some merchants can hit 10% or more by making their ads more specific and attracting only the most interested people. Permission e-mail click-through rates have been fairly consistent over the last five years, in the 3%–5% range. Putting the recipient's name in the subject line can double the click-through rate. (For unsolicited e-mail and outright spam, response rates are much lower, even though about 20% of U.S. e-mail users report clicking occasionally on an unsolicited e-mail.)

The click-through rate for video ads may seem low, but it is twice as high as the rate for banner ads. The "interaction rate" (sometimes referred to as "dwell rate") with rich media ads and video ads is about 7%–8%. "Interaction" means the user clicks on the video, plays it, stops it, or takes some other action (possibly skips the ad altogether)

TABLE 6.8	ONLINE MARKETING COMMUNICATIONS: TYPICAL CLICK-THROUGH RATES

MARKETING METHODS	TYPICAL CLICK-THROUGH RATES
Banner ads	.03%–.30%
Google enhanced search ads (Product Listing Ads)	1.66%
Search engine keyword purchase	.70–5.0%
Video	.50%–1.5%
Rich media	.15–2.0%
Sponsorships	1.50%–3.00%
Affiliate relationships	.20%–.40%
E-mail marketing in-house list	3.0–5.0%
E-mail marketing purchased list	.01%–1.50%
Social site display ads	.15%–.25%
Mobile display ads	.15%–.50%

SOURCES: Based on data from The Search Agency, 2013; eMarketer, 2013k; PointRoll, 2013; Salesforce Social.com, 2013; VINDICO, 2013; industry sources; authors' estimates.

(eMarketer, Inc., 2009; Eyeblaster, 2009). Although click-through rate is an important metric for video ads, advertising agencies also focus on other metrics to assess the success of an online video campaign, such as number of unique viewers, target impressions, brand lift, sales impact, and conversions (Brightroll, 2012).

How effective is online advertising compared to offline advertising? In general, the online channels (e-mail, search engine, display ads, video, and social, mobile, and local marketing) compare very favorably with traditional channels. This explains in large part why online advertising has grown so rapidly in the last five years. Search engine advertising over the last five years has grown to be one of the most cost-effective forms of marketing communications and accounts for, in large part, the growth of Google, as well as other search engines. Surprisingly, direct opt-in e-mail is nearly twice as cost-effective as search engine advertising. This is, in part, because e-mail lists are so inexpensive compared to keywords, and because opt-in e-mail is a form of targeting people who are already interested in receiving more information.

A study of the comparative impacts of offline and online marketing concluded that the most powerful marketing campaigns used multiple forms of marketing, including online, catalog, television, radio, newspapers, and retail store. Traditional media like television and print media remain the primary means for consumers to find out about new products even though advertisers have reduced their budgets for print media ads. The consensus conclusion is that consumers who shop multiple channels are spending more than consumers who shop only with a single channel, in part because they have more discretionary income but also because of the combined number of "touchpoints" that marketers are making with the consumers. The fastest growing channel in consumer marketing is the multi-channel shopper.

THE COSTS OF ONLINE ADVERTISING

cost per thousand (CPM)
advertiser pays for impressions in 1,000 unit lots

cost per click (CPC)
advertiser pays prenegotiated fee for each click an ad receives

cost per action (CPA)
advertiser pays only for those users who perform a specific action

Effectiveness cannot be considered without an analysis of costs. Initially, most online ads were sold on a barter or **cost per thousand (CPM)** impressions basis, with advertisers purchasing impressions in 1,000-unit lots. Today, other pricing models have developed, including **cost per click (CPC)**, where the advertiser pays a prenegotiated fee for each click an ad receives; **cost per action (CPA)**, where the advertiser pays a prenegotiated amount only when a user performs a specific action, such as a registration or a purchase; and hybrid arrangements, combining two or more of these models (see **Table 6.9**).

While in the early days of e-commerce, a few online sites spent as much as $400 on marketing and advertising to acquire one customer, the average cost was never that high. While the costs for offline customer acquisition are higher than online, the offline items are typically far more expensive. If you advertise in the *Wall Street Journal,* you are tapping into a wealthy demographic that may be interested in buying islands, jets, other corporations, and expensive homes in France. A full-page black and white ad in the *Wall Street Journal* National Edition costs about $350,000, whereas other papers are in the $10,000 to $100,000 range. For these kinds of prices, you will need to either sell quite a few apples or a small number of corporate jet lease agreements.

One of the advantages of online marketing is that online sales can generally be directly correlated with online marketing efforts. If online merchants can obtain offline purchase data from a data broker, the merchants can measure precisely just how much revenue is generated by specific banners or e-mail messages sent to prospective customers. One way to measure the effectiveness of online marketing is by looking at the ratio of additional revenue received divided by the cost of the campaign (Revenue/Cost). Any positive whole number means the campaign was worthwhile.

TABLE 6.9	DIFFERENT PRICING MODELS FOR ONLINE ADVERTISEMENTS
PRICING MODEL	**DESCRIPTION**
Barter	Exchange of ad space for something of equal value
Cost per thousand (CPM)	Advertiser pays for impressions in 1,000-unit lots
Cost per click (CPC)	Advertiser pays prenegotiated fee for each click ad received
Cost per action (CPA)	Advertiser pays only for those users who perform a specific action, such as registering, purchasing, etc.
Hybrid	Two or more of the above models used together
Sponsorship	Term-based; advertiser pays fixed fee for a slot on a Web site

A more complex situation arises when both online and offline sales revenues are affected by an online marketing effort. A large percentage of the online audience uses the Web to "shop" but not buy. These shoppers buy at physical stores. Merchants such as Sears and Walmart use e-mail to inform their registered customers of special offers available for purchase either online or at stores. Unfortunately, purchases at physical stores cannot be tied precisely with the online e-mail campaign. In these cases, merchants have to rely on less precise measures such as customer surveys at store locations to determine the effectiveness of online campaigns.

In either case, measuring the effectiveness of online marketing communications—and specifying precisely the objective (branding versus sales)—is critical to profitability. To measure marketing effectiveness, you need to understand the costs of various marketing media and the process of converting online prospects into online customers.

In general, online marketing communications are more costly on a CPM basis than traditional mass media marketing, but are more efficient in producing sales. **Table 6.10** shows costs for typical online and offline marketing communications. For instance, a local television spot (30 seconds) can cost $4,000–$40,000 to run the ad

TABLE 6.10	TRADITIONAL AND ONLINE ADVERTISING COSTS COMPARED
TRADITIONAL ADVERTISING	
Local television	$4,000 for a 30-second commercial during a movie; $45,000 for a highly rated show
Network television	$80,000–$600,000 for a 30-second spot during prime time; the average is $120,000 to $140,000
Cable television	$5,000–$8,000 for a 30-second ad during prime time
Radio	$200–$1,000 for a 60-second spot, depending on the time of day and program ratings
Newspaper	$120 per 1,000 circulation for a full-page ad
Magazine	$50 per 1,000 circulation for an ad in a regional edition of a national magazine, versus $120 per 1,000 for a local magazine
Direct mail	$15–$20 per 1,000 delivered for coupon mailings; $25–$40 per 1,000 for simple newspaper inserts
Billboard	$5,000–$25,000 for a 1–3 month rental of a freeway sign
ONLINE ADVERTISING	
Banner ads	$2–$15 per 1,000 impressions on a Web site, depending on how targeted the ad is (the more targeted, the higher the price)
Video and rich media	$20–$25 per 1,000 ads, depending on the Web site's demographics
E-mail	$5–$15 per 1,000 targeted e-mail addresses
Sponsorships	$30–$75 per 1,000 viewers, depending on the exclusivity of the sponsorship (the more exclusive, the higher the price)
Social network ads	$0.50–$3.00 per 1,000 impressions, with news feed ads at the high end of the range

and an additional $40,000 to produce the ad, for a total cost of $44,000–$80,000. The ad may be seen by a population of, say, 2 million persons (impressions) in a local area for a CPM ranging from 2 to 4 cents, which makes television very inexpensive for reaching large audiences quickly. A Web site banner ad costs virtually nothing to produce and can be purchased at Web sites for a cost of from $2–$15 per thousand impressions. Direct postal mail can cost 80 cents to $1 per household drop for a post card, but e-mail can be sent for virtually nothing and costs only $5–$15 per thousand targeted names. Hence, e-mail is far less expensive than postal mail on a CPM basis.

WEB ANALYTICS: SOFTWARE FOR MEASURING ONLINE MARKETING RESULTS

A number of software programs are available to automatically calculate activities at a Web site. Other software programs and services assist marketing managers in identifying exactly which marketing initiatives are paying off and which are not.

Web analytics

software package that collects, stores, analyzes, and graphically presents data on each of the stages in the conversion of shoppers to customers process on e-commerce sites

The purpose of marketing is to convert shoppers into customers who purchase what you sell. The process of converting shoppers into customers is often called a "purchasing funnel." We have characterized this as a process rather than a funnel that is composed of several stages: awareness, engagement, interaction, purchase, and post-purchase service and loyalty. **Web analytics** is a software package that collects, stores, analyzes, and graphically presents data on each of the stages in the conversion of shoppers to customers process on e-commerce sites (see **Figure 6.12**).

Web analytics packages can tell business managers how people become *aware* of their site, and where they come from (e.g., search, self-entered URL, e-mail, social campaigns, or off-line traditional print and TV ads), along with demographic, behavioral, and geographic information. Are shoppers coming from mobile devices, from Facebook or Pinterest? This information can help managers decide the best ways to drive traffic to their sites, the so-called "in-bound" links to a site. Once on the Web site, analytics packages can record how *engaged* visitors are with the site's content, measured in terms of pages viewed and duration on site. This information can allow managers to change the design or their sites, or change the content viewers are seeing. For instance, video testimonials from product users may be much more engaging than expert reviews or user text comments. In a social network marketing world, where consumers' opinions and behavior can be harvested and broadcast to their friends, an important intermediate step in the consumer conversion process is to encourage visitors to *interact* with your content and share their experiences, opinions, preferences, and behaviors with their friends, as well as other visitors to the site. Web analytics packages can track visitor interaction and help managers decide what content leads to higher levels of visitor interaction with friends and other visitors. The *purchase activity* on the shopping car page is a major focus of analytics tools not just because this is where the revenue is generated, but also because this is where the customer frequently exits the entire site and the firm loses a potential sale. Current shopping cart abandonment at the top 500 retailer sites is about 60% in the United States, with little change over the last five years, and higher in other countries (eMarketer, Inc.,

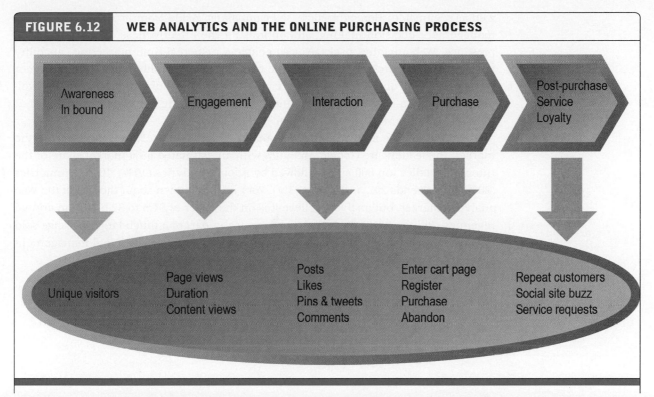

Web analytics help e-commerce firms to better understand consumer behavior at each stage of the online purchasing process.

2013l). This seems like an extraordinary rate but, like most of the indicators discussed in this chapter, abandonment is a complex phenomenon and often not what it seems. Consumers use carts like a shopping list, and don't complete the transaction immediately; they use it for price comparison and to know shipping costs, or taxes; they complete transactions later on a different device, such as a mobile phone. Another measure of near-purchase activity is the add-to-cart rate. Web analytics software can help managers tease out the meaning of behavior on a Web site's shopping cart page. Finally, Web analytics can help managers discover customer *loyalty and post-purchase* behavior. In an increasingly social marketing environment, marketing managers need to know how their products and services are being talked about on other sites, Facebook pages, or Twitter tweets, often called "buzz" or sentiment analysis. Are the comments positive or negative? What is the source of negative comments? Possible candidates are poor quality, high costs, poor warranty service, and shipping issues.

The end objective of Web analytics packages is to help business managers optimize the return on investment on their Web sites and social marketing efforts, and to do this by building a detailed understanding of how consumers behave when visiting their Web sites. Web analytics also allows managers to measure the impact of specific marketing campaigns involving, say, discounts, loyalty points, and special offers, as well as regional, or demographic-based campaigns. Aside from its role in enhancing management decision making, and optimizing the effectiveness of building a Web presence, Web analytics packages also enable a near real-time marketing capability where managers are able to change the content of a Web site, respond to customer complaints and comments, and align campaigns with trending topics or news developments, all in a near real-time manner (real-time may be a matter of minutes or at most 24 hours) (eMarketer, Inc., 2013m).

While there are a great many Web analytics firms and software packages on the market, the leaders are Google Analytics with an estimated 65% market share of the Internet Retailer top 500 sites, followed by Adobe Analytics (10%), IBM Coremetrics (20%), Web Trends 2%, and Others (3%). Very little is known about the size of the Web analytics market, but analysts believe it is on the order of $1.5 to $2 billion in annual revenues (Belisle, 2013). Web analytics is typically part of a much larger package sold to corporations from hardware, to Web design tools, cloud services, and management expertise.

Instant Ads:
Real-Time Marketing on Exchanges

The holy grail of advertising and marketing is to deliver the right message to the right person at the right time. If this were possible, no one would receive ads they did not want to see, and then no advertising dollars would be wasted, reducing the costs to end users and increasing the efficiency of each ad dollar. In the physical world, only a very rough approximation of this ideal is possible. Advertisers can buy television and radio spots, newspaper ads, and billboards based on broad demographics and interests of likely potential customers. The Internet promised to change this. On the Internet, ads supposedly could be targeted to individual consumers based on their personal characteristics, interests, and recent clickstream behavior. One early vision of e-commerce was a trade-off between privacy and efficiency: let us know a little more about you, and we will show you only the advertising and products you are interested in seeing, and even offer free content. E-commerce was supposed to end the mass advertising that exploded in the television era.

But contrary to popular impressions and the fears of privacy advocates, most of the display ads shown to site visitors are marvelously irrelevant to visitors' interests, both short term and long term. For this reason, the click-through rate for banner advertising is a stunningly low 0.03%, and the price of display ads has fallen to a few cents because of their poor performance. Check this out: point your browser at Yahoo (the largest display advertiser on earth), look at the prominent ads shown on the right, and ask yourself if you are really interested in the ad content at this moment in time. How about ever? Chances are slim you are interested at this moment even if the ad is somewhat appropriate to your demographics. Often, it's an ad for something you are totally not interested in and never have been. In 2013, only 20% of Internet users find that display ads on Web sites are relevant to their interests, up only slightly from previous years.

A part of the problem was (and still is) that online display ad publishers like Yahoo, and the advertising networks they ended up owning, did not know very much about you (until recently), and what they did know was quite general: gender, zip code, age, and perhaps some prior purchases. They could build a "profile" of you, but it was very imprecise, and not very predictive of how you would respond to any specific ad. The resulting ads displayed were frequently far off the mark of what you were interested in at the moment. And even if they knew everything about you, the advertising networks did not have the mechanism to sell that information instantly to a potential advertiser. For this reason, banner ads displayed on the Web sites you visited in the past rarely had anything to do with your interests at the time. Rather than achieve the holy grail of advertising, much of Web-based display advertising was extraordinarily ignorant of who you were or what you were looking for. Search engine advertising was typically better, since it was responding to search terms you yourself had entered, and reflected more accurately your intentions.

Behavioral targeting and tracking of online behavior have begun to improve the situation for display advertisers by expanding the scope, breadth, and depth of personal information, making it possible for advertisers to fine-tune their display ads and to develop a much finer-grained, digital image of individual customers—real people, not just profiles. Using beacons, Web bugs, cookies, and Flash cookies, almost all the top Web sites now install tracking software onto visitor computers. A *Wall Street Journal* study of the 50 top Web sites in the United States, accounting for 40% of U.S. page views, found these sites installed 3,180 tracking files on a test computer that visited each site. Only one top-50 site installed no tracking files: Wikipedia. Over two-thirds of the tracking files were installed by 131 companies. Guess who the biggest trackers were? Google, Microsoft, and Yahoo. The vast majority of these tracking files are third-party cookies and beacons. (They are not installed by the Web site you are visiting, but through a commercial arrangement with the Web site you are visiting, tracking firms are allowed to place cookies and beacons.) What the *Journal* stumbled onto was an entire ecosystem of firms ranging from Internet giants like Yahoo, Google, and Microsoft, to smaller data aggregators, and finally to huge advertising firms that pay for the data their clients want to use in targeting ads.

Today, when a user visits a site, a tracking number or cookie is assigned to the user. Often a "beacon" or Web bug is installed, which captures what people are typing on a Web site. For instance, a beacon will record your comments on automobiles, illness, or favorite movies, as well as the fact you like *Dancing With the Stars*, do cross-word puzzles, bought a Kindle, purchased romantic titles, have an iPad, and installed the *New York Times* reader. When the user visits other sites where the tracking firm has installed its software, the user is recognized, more behavior is observed, and this information is added to the original cookie file on the user's computer, or sent to the firm's tracking server using the installed beacon. The file keeps growing the more the user visits Web sites. Facebook has three tools in 2013 for targeting ads: it sells advertisers the topics you are interested in, the sites you follow as a fan, and profile information such as newlyweds, moving, college, as well as personal education and other data.

So what happens to all this information about you and others? The cookie and beacon owners collect all this information and sell it to advertisers. On the basis of all this personal and clickstream information, a profile of the individual user is developed by data exchange firms such as BlueKai Inc. and eXelate Media as well as the three big players. EXelate claims to have anonymous data on more than 400 million unique users who visit more than 500 of the most popular Web sites.

The information and the individual profiles are sold to advertisers usually for around 10 cents a piece. Advertisers specify the profiles they are looking for: male, 24 to 35 years old, urban, drives a sports sedan, sports fan, high income, and likes books (think possible BMW customer). Once individuals fitting this profile appear at a Web site, the advertiser pays to have a prefabricated ad displayed to that person. Voila! Targeting, personalization! A more efficient market communications process, happier Internet users who see what they are interested in looking at, and users who click more often.

Not quite yet. One thing is missing from this heady mix of behavioral tracking and targeting: immediacy. When you click on a search engine result, it's because you are interested in that product or service right now, this moment, this instant. Google, which is currently used by 75% of global Internet users, or approximately 1.5 billion people, is believed to be the largest and best repository of immediate user interests. For display ads, even targeted ones, this has not been possible until recently. Previously, online advertisers reserved slots (available pages, location on page, time of day/week) based on their best guesstimates of the types of people (i.e., profiles) who would show up to see those pages and be exposed to the ad. They really were clueless when it came to who you are and what you were interested in at the moment of opening a Web page. Advertisers could not make on-the-fly, instant decisions about ads to show Web site visitors based on what they were doing just before this instant, and just before they landed on a page.

In the last two years this situation is changing, and for the first time display advertisers, portals, and ad networks they own are building the capability to display banner ads that are based on the granular behavior of individuals just prior to displaying the ad, and to do so in real time, in milliseconds. There are two players here: the often small-fry data collection firms (the third-party owners of cookies and beacons) and the large players. Both are developing data exchanges where advertisers can purchase all the individual-level data available. The second part of the change is the really large Web advertisers like Google, Microsoft, Facebook, and Yahoo who have each developed real-time ad exchanges that permit advertisers to bid for ad spaces in the few milliseconds between a user entering a Web address (or clicking on a search query) and the page appearing, based on the data purchased from data exchanges. The inventory that ad exchanges sell comes from hundreds of thousands of Web site publishers who have Web pages that are initially empty and not producing revenue. Ad exchanges are middlemen who stand between Web site publishers who have ad space to sell and advertisers who want to display ads to highly targeted audiences. Operators of ad exchanges hold out the promise of maximizing the revenue publishers can receive for their ad space, and they promise ad buyers the most efficient way to buy audiences that precisely meet their needs. The exchange operators exact a fee for this service based on the size of the ad buy.

Generally, publishers prefer to sell most of their inventory directly to advertisers and avoid paying a middleman, like Google's Ad Exchange. But they often have excess inventory and use ad exchanges to sell this unused inventory. Ad exchanges use real-time bidding (RTB) to allocate publisher ad spaces to advertisers. Real Time Bidding refers to advertising technology that permits publishers to sell ad space on their sites (including banner, video, rich media, or mobile ads) on demand, and in real time. Both the publishers who sell ad space, and the advertisers who buy, need to be connected to the same ad exchange for transactions to occur.

The largest ad exchanges are Google's Double Click Ad Exchange (AdEx), Apple's iAd, Microsoft's Ad Exchange, and Yahoo's Right Media. Less well-known ad exchanges are Rubicon Project and Turn. What unites all these large players is the fact that they are the largest collectors of personal information on the Internet, and therefore, have access to an extraordinary amount of consumer data at their fingertips, and they have the analytics power and data mining capabilities to use this information. Rubicon, for instance, while hardly a household word, is the second most aggressive data collector on the Web with 2,470 cookies and tracking code on the top 1,000 Web sites, according to a study by the Berkeley Center for Law and Technology. BlueKai is the most aggressive data collector with 2,570 cookies on the top 1,000 sites. Rubicon and BlueKai have their own ad exchanges. The largest publishers are also beginning to create their ad exchanges rather than pay the large ad exchanges. For instance, the Wall Street Journal (DowJones) developed its own exchange, and the New York Times, Gannett, Tribune, and Hearst newspapers have launched their own exchanges.

Facebook launched its own ad exchange in September 2012 as a way to monetize its huge audience. Facebook Exchange (FBX) allows ad technology companies called "demand side platforms," which gather pools of targeted audiences, to sell these audiences to advertisers through automated systems that allow buyers to bid for targeted audiences. For instance, an airline with extra seats for flights from New York to Los Angeles could target an ad on Facebook to people who had searched for a Los Angeles flight but didn't buy a ticket, or an ad for a Los Angeles hotel for someone who booked a flight but not a hotel room. The Facebook Exchange will only sell standard Marketplace ads (small ads on the right side of a user's page). How does Facebook know what its users have searched for? There are two ways. Facebook can place a cookie on its users' browsers that records the users' searches, including search terms on Google or another search engine. A second way is to work with ad networks who have placed cookies on users' browsers prior to visiting Facebook. Facebook will not allow advertisers to gain access to users' Facebook data (Likes, friends, and content posts) and will not be selling user profiles. So for now, the Facebook Exchange is simply a way for advertisers to gain access to people when they are on Facebook. Because Facebook does not allow Google, or other content miners, to gain access to Facebook pages, Facebook is therefore a kind of walled garden that advertisers can reach only by going through Facebook Exchange or other ad services owned by Facebook. Not far behind Facebook is Twitter. Planning its own IPO in 2013, with the urgent need to somehow monetize its audience using ads, has launched its own ad exchange in 2013 called MoPub that will help mobile publishers manage their inventory of ad spaces.

Ad exchanges offer more than just an auction site for ads. In addition they offer access to huge databases of personal profiles (which are anonymously identified, the companies claim), and data mining analytics, which can help advertisers find the most cost-effective ad purchases. For instance, Turn, a well-known ad exchange and analytics firm helps advertisers make over 50 billion advertising decisions, analyzes over 1.5 trillion customer attributes, and provides instant access to billions of digital advertising impressions. The system is cloud-based, and clients pay fees for accessing the infrastructure, and are not required to purchase software or equipment. The Turn platform currently stores almost 1.2 billion stable and anonymous user profiles with their history—site visits, time of visits, frequency, recency, and relative velocity—before and after every single impression. These profiles are continuously updated and are available in real time for analysis, modeling, and action. Because people change, and personal information can degrade rapidly as life circumstances change, Turn seeks to maintain an up-to-the-minute snapshot of each user in the target target audience.

While not a large publisher, Facebook has one of the largest and most intensely engaged audiences on the Internet. Interestingly, Facebook pages cannot be searched by search engines, and Facebook controls access to all Facebook pages because you need an account to see other pages. This situation gives Facebook an extraordinary opportunity to sell access to its users. In September 2012 Facebook launched its own ad exchange as a way to monetize its huge audience. Facebook Exchange (FBX) allows ad technology companies called "demand side platforms," which gather pools of targeted audiences, to sell these audiences to advertisers through automated systems that allow buyers to bid for targeted audiences. For instance, an airline with extra seats for flights from New York to Los Angeles could target an ad on Facebook to people who had searched for a Los Angeles flight but didn't buy a ticket, or an ad for a Los Angeles hotel for someone who booked a flight but not a hotel room. The Facebook Exchange will only sell standard Marketplace ads (small ads on the right side of a user's page). How does Facebook know what its users have searched for? There are two ways. Facebook can place a cookie on its users' browsers that records the users' searches, including search terms on Google or another search engine. A second way is to work with ad networks who have placed cookies on users' browsers prior to visiting Facebook. Facebook will not allow advertisers to gain access to users' Facebook data (Likes, friends, and content posts) and will not be selling user profiles. So for now, the Facebook Exchange is simply a way for advertisers to gain access to people when they are on Facebook.

Advertisers will spend an estimated $3.3 billion in the United States on RTB advertising in 2013, more than three times the level of 2011. Roughly 19% of total display ad spending is now arranged through automated buying systems. These ad exchanges have moved closer to the ideal Web advertising environment by allowing advertisers to decide where to place their ads on the fly, based on fairly solid data on the people most likely to see the ad. This is far different from the traditional ad placement process, which placed ads weeks and months in advance of the ad being displayed.

Ad exchanges have several challenges and they raise a number of issues. Ghost web sites, sites that have no real audience or following, can offer pages that no one visits and receive payments from ad exchanges. There are no agreed-on audience measures to assure advertisers that the ads were really delivered to the target audience. For instance, when advertisers buy a 6 p.m. local news slot for a 60-second ad, a variety of audience measuring firms from Nielsen to comScore will verify the ads were actually delivered. But with instant ad selection and delivery, there is no direct way to ensure the target audience actually received the ads. Several firms have stepped into this market with tools for proving the intended audience really did receive the ads.

SOURCES: "Twitter Beefs Up Ad Presence," by Emily Wilson, Magnetmediafilms.com, September 11, 2013; "Automated Ad Exchanges Will Dominate If They Address Fraud, Privacy Issues," by Dorian Benkoil, PBS.org/mediashift, April 8, 2013; "Your Online Attention, Bought in an Instant," by Natasha Singer, *New York Times*, November 17, 2012; "Real Time Bidding: Ad Spending Forecast," [Lauren Fisher] eMarketer, Inc., November 2012; "Web Privacy Census," Berkeley Center for Law and Technology, November 2012; "Wall Street Journal Network Launches Private Ad Exchange," by Erik Sass, Mediapost.com, October 12, 2012; "Ad Tech Company eXelate Raises $12M," by Ted O'Hear, Techcrunch.com, September 24, 2012; "Facebook Efforts on Advertising Face a Day of Judgment," by Somini Sengupta, *New York Times*, July 22, 2012; "Facebook Exchange and the Rise of Real-Time Ad Bidding," by Michael Baker, *Forbes*, June 14, 2012; "Facebook to Debut Ad Exchange in Bid to Boost Revenues," by Robert Hof, *Forbes*, June 13, 2012; "What's a Facebook Ad Exchange?" by Peter Kafka, *All Things Digital*, June 13, 2012; "ComScore, eXelate Cleaning Up 'Garbage In, Garbage Out,'" by Erin Griffith, *Ad Week*, August 16, 2011; "Tracking the Trackers: Early Results," by Jonathan Mayer, Stanford Center for Internet and Society, July 12, 2011; "Real-Time Bidding Becomes a $832 Million Market in 2011," by Michael Barrett, AdAgeDigital, February 8, 2011; "Sites Feed Personal Details to New Tracking Industry," by Julia Angwin and Tom McGinty, *Wall Street Journal*, July 30, 2010; "Yahoo Finally Allows Real-Time Bidding on Network and Exchange," Kate Kaye, ClickZ.com, March 15, 2010; "Instant Ads Set the Pace on the Web," by Stephanie Clifford, *New York Times*, March 10, 2010; "Online Ad Auctions," by Hal Varian, Draft, University of California and Google, February 16, 2009.

Case Study Questions

1. Pay a visit to your favorite portal and count the total ads on the opening page. Count how many of these ads are (a) immediately of interest and relevant to you, (b) sort of interesting or relevant but not now, and (c) not interesting or relevant. Do this 10 times and calculate the percentage of the three kinds of situations. Describe what you find and explain the results using this case.

2. Advertisers use different kinds of "profiles" in the decision to display ads to customers. Identify the different kinds of profiles described in this case, and explain why they are relevant to online display advertising.

3. How can display ads achieve search-engine–like results?

4. Do you think instant display ads based on your immediately prior clickstream will be as effective as search engine marketing techniques? Why or why not?

6.6 REVIEW

KEY CONCEPTS

■ **Identify the key features of the Internet audience.**

Key features of the Internet audience include:

- *The number of users online in the United States.* In 2013, the total is around 243 million.
- *Intensity and scope of use.* Both are increasing, with over 80% of adult users in the United States logging on in a typical day and engaging in a wider set of activities.
- *Demographics and access.* Although the Internet population is growing increasingly diverse, some demographic groups have much higher percentages of online usage, and different patterns of usage exist across various groups.
- *Lifestyle impacts.* Intensive Internet use may cause a decline in traditional social activities. The social development of children who use the Internet intensively instead of engaging in face-to-face interactions or undirected play out of doors may also be negatively impacted.
- *Media choices.* The more time individuals spend using the Internet, the less time they spend using traditional media.

■ **Discuss the basic concepts of consumer behavior and purchasing decisions.**

Models of consumer behavior attempt to predict or explain what consumers purchase, and where, when, how much, and why they buy. Factors that impact buying behavior include:

- Cultural factors

- Social factors
- Psychological factors

There are five stages in the consumer decision process:
- Awareness of need
- Search for more information
- Evaluation of alternatives
- The actual purchase decision
- Post-purchase contact with the firm

The online consumer decision process is basically the same, with the addition of two new factors:
- *Web site capabilities*—the content, design, and functionality of a site.
- *Consumer clickstream behavior*—the transaction log that consumers establish as they move about the Web and through specific sites.

■ **Understand how consumers behave online.**

Clickstream analysis shows us that people go online for many different reasons, at different times, and for numerous purposes.
- About 73% of online users are "buyers" who actually purchase something entirely online. Another 16% of online users research products on the Web, but purchase them offline. This combined group, referred to as "shoppers," constitutes approximately 89% of the online Internet audience.
- Online sales are divided roughly into two groups: small-ticket and big-ticket items. In the early days of e-commerce, sales of small-ticket items vastly outnumbered those of large-ticket items. However, the recent growth of big-ticket items such as computer hardware and consumer electronics has changed the overall sales mix.
- There are a number of actions that e-commerce vendors could take to increase the likelihood that shoppers and nonshoppers would purchase online more frequently. These include better security of credit card information and privacy of personal information, lower shipping costs, and easier returns.

■ **Identify and describe the basic digital commerce marketing and advertising strategies and tools.**

The major digital commerce marketing and advertising strategies and tools include:
- A *Web site* is the major tool for establishing the initial relationship with the customer.
- *Search engine marketing and advertising* allows firms to pay search engines for inclusion in the search engine index (formerly free and based on "objective" criteria), receiving a guarantee that their firm will appear in the results of relevant searches.
- *Display ads* are promotional messages that users can respond to by clicking on the banner and following the link to a product description or offering. Display ads include banner ads, rich media, video ads, and sponsorships.
- *E-mail marketing* sends e-mail directly to interested users, and has proven to be one of the most effective forms of marketing communications.
- *Lead generation marketing* uses multiple e-commerce presences to generate leads for businesses who later can be contacted and converted into customers.

- *Affiliate marketing* involves a firm putting its logo or banner ad on another firm's Web site from which users of that site can click through to the affiliate's site.
- *Viral marketing* is form of social marketing that involves getting customers to pass along a company's marketing message to friends, family, and colleagues.
- *Social marketing and advertising* involves using the social graph to communicate brand images and directly promote sales of products and services.
- *Mobile and local marketing and advertising* involves using display ads, search engine advertising, video ads, and mobile messaging on mobile devices such as smartphones and tablet computers, often using the geographic location of the user.
- *Multi-channel marketing* (combining offline and online marketing efforts) is typically the most effective. Although many e-commerce ventures want to rely heavily on online communications, marketing communications campaigns most successful at driving traffic have incorporated both online and offline tactics.
- *Customer retention techniques* for strengthening customer relationships include personalization, one-to-one marketing, and interest-based advertising, customization and customer co-production, and customer service (such as CRMs, FAQs, live chat, intelligent agents, and automated response systems).
- *Online pricing strategies* include offering products and services for free, versioning, bundling, and dynamic pricing.

■ **Identify and describe the main technologies that support online marketing.**

- *Web transaction logs*—records that document user activity at a Web site. Coupled with data from the registration forms and shopping cart database, these represent a treasure trove of marketing information for both individual sites and the online industry as a whole.
- *Tracking files*—Various files, like cookies, Web beacons, Flash cookies, and apps, that follow users and track their behavior as they visit sites across the entire Web.
- *Databases, data warehouses, data mining, and profiling*—technologies that allow marketers to identify exactly who the online customer is and what they want, and then to present the customer with exactly what they want, when they want it, for the right price.
- *CRM systems*—a repository of customer information that records all of the contacts a customer has with a firm and generates a customer profile available to everyone in the firm who has a need to "know the customer."

■ **Understand the costs and benefits of online marketing communications.**

Key terms that one must know in order to understand evaluations of online marketing communications' effectiveness and its costs and benefits include:
- *Impressions*—the number of times an ad is served.
- *Click-through rate*—the number of times an ad is clicked.
- *View-through rate*—the 30-day response rate to an ad.
- *Hits*—the number of http requests received by a firm's server.
- *Page views*—the number of pages viewed by visitors.
- *Stickiness (duration)*—the average length of time visitors remain at a site.
- *Unique visitors*—the number of distinct, unique visitors to a site.
- *Loyalty*—the percentage of purchasers who return in a year.
- *Reach*—the percentage of total consumers in a market who will visit a site.

- *Recency*—the average number of days elapsed between visits.
- *Acquisition rate*—the percentage of visitors who indicate an interest in the site's product by registering or visiting product pages.
- *Conversion rate*—the percentage of visitors who purchase something.
- *Browse-to-buy ratio*—the ratio of items purchased to product views.
- *View-to-cart ratio*—the ratio of "Add to cart" clicks to product views.
- *Cart conversion rate*—the ratio of actual orders to "Add to cart" clicks.
- *Checkout conversion rate*—the ratio of actual orders to checkouts started.
- *Abandonment rate*—the percentage of shoppers who begin a shopping cart form, but then fail to complete the form.
- *Retention rate*—the percentage of existing customers who continue to buy on a regular basis.
- *Attrition rate*—the percentage of customers who purchase once, but do not return within a year.
- *Conversation ratio*—the number of comments produced per post to a site.
- *Applause ratio*—the number of Likes or Shares per post.
- *Amplification*—the number of re-tweets or re-shares per post.
- *Sentiment ratio*—the ratio of positive comments to total comments.
- *Open rate*—the percentage of customers who open the mail and are exposed to the message.
- *Delivery rate*—the percentage of e-mail recipients who received the e-mail.
- *Click-through rate (e-mail)*—the percentage of e-mail recipients who clicked through to the offer.
- *Bounce-back rate*—the percentage of e-mails that could not be delivered.

Studies have shown that low click-through rates are not indicative of a lack of commercial impact of online advertising, and that advertising communication does occur even when users do not directly respond by clicking. Online advertising in its various forms has been shown to boost brand awareness and brand recall, create positive brand perceptions, and increase intent to purchase.

Effectiveness cannot be considered without analysis of cost. Typical pricing models for online marketing communications include:
- *Barter*—the exchange of ad space for something of equal value.
- *Cost per thousand (CPM)*—the advertiser pays for impressions in 1,000-unit lots.
- *Cost per click (CPC)*—the advertiser pays a prenegotiated fee for each click an ad receives.
- *Cost per action (CPA)*—the advertiser pays only for those users who perform a specific action.
- *Hybrid models*—combines two or more other models.
- *Sponsorships*—the advertiser pays a fixed fee for a particular term.

Online marketing communications are typically less costly than traditional mass media marketing. Also, online sales can generally be directly correlated with online marketing efforts, unlike traditional marketing communications tactics.

QUESTIONS

1. Is growth of the Internet, in terms of users, expected to continue indefinitely? What, if anything, will cause it to slow?

2. Other than search engines, what are some of the most popular uses of the Internet?
3. Would you say that the Internet fosters or impedes social activity? Explain your position.
4. Research has shown that many consumers use the Internet to investigate purchases before actually buying, which is often done in a physical storefront. What implication does this have for online merchants? What can they do to entice more online buying, rather than pure research?
5. Describe a perfect market from the supplier's and customer's perspectives. Explain why an imperfect market is more advantageous for businesses.
6. Why have advertising networks become controversial? What, if anything, can be done to overcome any resistance to this technique?
7. Compare and contrast four marketing strategies used in mass marketing, direct marketing, micromarketing, and one-to-one marketing.
8. List the differences among databases, data warehouses, and data mining.
9. Name some of the drawbacks to the four data mining techniques used in Internet marketing.
10. What pricing strategy turned out to be deadly for many e-commerce ventures during the early days of e-commerce? Why?
11. Is price discrimination different from versioning? If so, how?
12. What are some of the reasons that freebies, such as free Internet service and giveaways, don't work to generate sales at a Web site?
13. Explain how versioning works. How is this different from dynamic pricing?
14. Why do companies that bundle products and services have an advantage over those that don't or can't offer this option?
15. What are some reasons why online advertising still constitutes only about 25% of the total advertising market?
16. What are some of the advantages of direct e-mail marketing?
17. Why is offline advertising still important?
18. What is the difference between hits and page views? Why are these not the best measurements of Web traffic? Which is the preferred metric for traffic counts?
19. Define CTR, CPM, CPC, CPA, and VTR.

PROJECTS

1. Go to www.strategicbusinessinsights.com/vals/presurvey.shtml. Take the survey to determine which lifestyle category you fit into. Then write a two-page paper describing how your lifestyle and values impact your use of e-commerce. How is your online consumer behavior affected by your lifestyle?

2. Visit Net-a-porter.com and create an Internet marketing plan for it that includes each of the following:
   • One-to-one marketing
   • Affiliate marketing
   • Viral marketing
   • Blog marketing
   • Social network marketing

Describe how each plays a role in growing the business, and create a slide presentation of your marketing plan.

3. Use the Online Consumer Purchasing Model (Figure 6.11) to assess the effectiveness of an e-mail campaign at a small Web site devoted to the sales of apparel to the ages 18–26 young adult market in the United States. Assume a marketing campaign of 100,000 e-mails (at 25 cents per e-mail address). The expected click-through rate is 5%, the customer conversion rate is 10%, and the loyal customer retention rate is 25%. The average sale is $60, and the profit margin is 50% (the cost of the goods is $30). Does the campaign produce a profit? What would you advise doing to increase the number of purchases and loyal customers? What Web design factors? What communications messages?

4. Surf the Web for at least 15 minutes. Visit at least two different e-commerce sites. Make a list describing in detail all the different marketing communication tools you see being used. Which do you believe is the most effective and why?

5. Do a search for a product of your choice on at least three search engines. Examine the results page carefully. Can you discern which results, if any, are a result of a paid placement? If so, how did you determine this? What other marketing communications related to your search appear on the page?

6. Examine the use of rich media and video in advertising. Find and describe at least two examples of advertising using streaming video, sound, or other rich media technologies. (Hint: Check the sites of Internet advertising agencies for case studies or examples of their work.) What are the advantages and/or disadvantages of this kind of advertising? Prepare a 3- to 5-page report on your findings.

7. Visit your Facebook page and examine the ads shown in the right margin. What is being advertised and how do you believe it is relevant to your interests or online behavior? You could also search on a retail product on Google several times, and related products, then visit Yahoo or another popular site to see if your past behavior is helping advertisers track you.

CHAPTER 7

Social, Mobile, and Local Marketing

After reading this chapter, you will be able to:

- Understand the difference between traditional online marketing and the new social-mobile-local marketing platforms.
- Describe the size and growth of social, local, and mobile marketing.
- Understand the relationships between social, mobile, and local marketing.
- Understand the social marketing process from fan acquisition to sales.
- Identify the marketing capabilities of social marketing platforms such as Facebook, Twitter, and Pinterest.
- Identify the key elements of a mobile marketing campaign including app and in-app marketing.
- Understand the capabilities of location-based local marketing including in-store messaging, geo-fencing, geo-social-based services, and geo-targeting.

Facebook:

Putting Social Marketing to Work

W hen Facebook issued its stock for sale in an initial public offering on May 18, 2012, it followed a very long build-up of excitement based on the belief that the company, with its then 190 million users in North America and its 1 billion global audience, would turn into a marketing behemoth to rival or exceed Google, Yahoo, and Amazon. Facebook was, according to some analysts, the next Google in terms of an advertising platform and possibly even an e-commerce platform that could compete with Amazon. Facebook raised $16 billion in the IPO, placing it in the "Big League" of e-commerce stock offerings. Offered at $38 a share, Facebook's share price fell dramatically in subsequent months to a low of $17.50 in September 2012 on investor fears that Facebook would be unable to increase

© Rafal Olechowski / Fotolia

its advertising revenues fast enough to justify its price. Flash forward to August 2013: Facebook's shares have doubled, rising back to the offering price. While its shares have not soared to higher levels as many high-flying start-ups have in the past, and market-ers are still not certain that Facebook's marketing machine really works, investors are willing to continue holding the shares in the hope that social marketing really will work. For its part, Facebook is furiously inventing new ways to put targeted ads in front of its increasingly mobile users. It appears to be succeeding, at least for now.

Most observers agree that Facebook initially flubbed the shift to mobile devices—smartphones and tablets. In 2011, Facebook had virtually no ad revenues from mobile devices and no mobile strategy. At the time of its botched IPO in 2012, Mark Zuckerberg, CEO of Facebook, was developing a mobile strategy that essentially depended on inserting ads into users' News Feeds. No one knew at that time if it would work. There is no side bar for ads on smartphones, and limited space on tablets, so the only ad marketing opportunity appeared to be in the News Feed. Throughout 2012, Facebook took a crash course on mobile by redesigning its Facebook app specifically for smartphones, introducing ads into users' News Feeds, and creating a new kind of ad called an "app-install ad," which are ads paid for by Facebook app developers that encourage users to download their apps (usually for free). App-install ads and in-app ads became Facebook's secret weapon that investors had not even heard about. Facebook was aided by a shift away from mobile browsers to apps: in 2013, more than half of mobile users worldwide regularly use brand, product, or store apps.

Advertisers display ads within these apps, and Facebook shares the ad fees with the app developers. App-install ads, and ads within apps, are the largest single source of Facebook mobile ads. There are an estimated 8,000 app developer firms in the United States alone, and they have created over 25,000 Facebook platform apps. Facebook users install about 20 million apps every day. These apps range from games like FarmVille, Words With Friends, and Mafia Wars, to music apps like Spotify and Pandora, to charity-oriented apps like Social Vibe and Charity Trivia. App ads, and in-app ads, have become central to Facebook's mobile strategy. In-app ads have an advantage over standard News Feed ads: they are not perceived to be as disruptive or annoying as News Feed ads, and users are more willing to experience the inconvenience of being exposed to ads in return for a free game.

In the first six months of 2013, 40% of Facebook users accessed the service from mobile devices (they also used desktop devices at work and home), and mobile ads generated 41% of Facebook's $1.6 billion revenue. Now, instead of being behind the mobile curve, it is at least on the curve, if not ahead of it. Another factor in Facebook's turnaround in social mobile marketing is its success with small local businesses. Facebook has more than 1 million active advertisers in 2013 in part because of its emphasis on local business advertising.

One such small business firm using Facebook is Pacific Rim, a winery in Portland, Oregon, that produces affordable Riesling wines. In 2010, Pacific Rim launched a Facebook page, Pacific Rim Riesling Rules, aimed at building an online community of Riesling lovers as well as creating a retail point of sale. The page used contests to drive Likes, videos to engage users, animations to illustrate the wine production process, and the ability to purchase the wine directly from Pacific Rim. When visitors clicked on a photo of a bottle they were taken to a shopping cart on the company's Web site. They also launched seasonal contests, asking visitors to write 150-word essays on why they loved Riesling. The Facebook community voted on the submissions, and the winner received $1,000. Pacific Rim gave away $15,000, and generated 15,000 Likes over a 15-week period. Currently, the winery sells 200,000 cases of wine a year.

But questions still remain about Facebook marketing. The question both investors and marketers face is straightforward: does Facebook's social marketing and advertising platform really work? Does it mean anything if millions of Facebook users Like your marketing campaign? Do Likes turn into sales? Is Facebook better for marketing (brand recognition and awareness) than it is for driving sales through advertisements? And, if Facebook's marketing platform does work, how well does it work when compared to other online marketing techniques such as search, e-mail, display ads, and affiliate programs? Facebook's marketing success on both the desktop and mobile devices is currently based on the insertion of ads in users' News Feeds. Currently an estimated 1 in 20 News Feed items are ads. When the ads reach 1 in 10 organic News Feed items, how will users react? How about 1 in 5? Zuckerberg, along with marketers, is concerned that putting more ads in the News Feed is not the answer to sustaining future growth. Facebook will have to come up with some other ad opportunities especially on the mobile platform. The most likely candidate: video advertising using short video clips.

Facebook's purchase of Instagram for $1 billion in April 2012 is another possible source of ad revenue. Since the purchase, Instagram has added 70 million new users to its existing 30 million, and today, active users post more than 40 million photos per day. Once Facebook fully integrates Instagram into user pages, a stream of photos and videos will appear on the screen, accompanied by ads laced into the stream.

Early market research raised questions about the effectiveness of social networks as marketing platforms. Research by Goldman Sachs found that social network sites were not very effective at driving purchases. Less than 5% of online purchasers in the study ranked social network sites as the most important factor in purchasing. Surveys by market research firm Compete found that social network sites were the least influential sources used by consumers prior to purchase, ranging from 2% to 7%. The most influential factors in purchasing appear to be the retailers' Web site, search engines, display ads, and e-mail. To counter this research, Facebook commissioned a study by comScore to demonstrate the value of marketing on Facebook. Among the findings was the claim that being a fan of a brand on Facebook leads to more frequent purchases of the brand. The study did not answer the question of whether other marketing channels had a larger effect on sales than a Facebook Like.

There are many marketing success stories, from both large Fortune 500 firms and small start-ups, that lend credibility to Facebook's claim that its social network marketing platform does, in fact, work. Currently, 88% of U.S. companies use Facebook for marketing purposes.

Despite having the largest online social audience in the world, and its recent success in mobile display ads, it remains unclear if Facebook can monetize its user base to the level expected by the stock market and continue growing revenues at double-digit rates as it has done in the past. It will require several years of experimentation by marketers and Facebook to discover if social marketing on Facebook really works the way Wall Street hopes it will.

SOURCES: "Facebook's Stock Soars Amid Rosy Growth Expectations," by Vindu Goel, *New York Times*, July 25, 2013; "Why Facebook's Mobile Ads are Working Better Than Google's," Timothy Senovec, HuffingtonPost.com, July 25, 2013; "Facebook is Erasing Doubts on Mobile," by Vindu Goel, *New York Times*, July 24, 2013; "Facebook's Ad Sales Surprise Investors, Sending Shares up 17%," by Evelyn M. Rusli, *Wall Street Journal*, July 24, 2013; "Google Results Show Struggle With Mobile," by Clair Cain Miller, *New York Times*, July 7, 2013; "The Facebook Ads Benchmark Report," by Salesforce.com, 2013; "The Power of Like: How Brands Reach and Influence Fans Through Social Marketing," by comScore and Facebook, October 21, 2012; "Facebook Marketing: Reaching Consumers in a Changing Environment," by eMarketer Inc., August 2012; "Likeonomics: The Unexpected Truth Behind Earning Trust, Influencing Behavior, and Inspiring Action," by Rohit Bhargava, Wiley, 2012; "Facebook's Growth Slows," by Shaynd Raice, *Wall Street Journal*, July 27, 2012; "Facebook Combats Criticism Over Ads," by Shayndi Raice, *Wall Street Journal*, June 12, 2012; "Facebook IPO Sputters," by Shayndi Raice, *New York Times*, May 18, 2012; "Big Brands Like Facebook, But They Don't Like to Pay," by Emily Steel and Geoffrey Fowler, *Wall Street Journal*, November 2, 2012; "The Facebook App Economy," by Il-Horn-Hann, Siva Viswanathan, and Byungwan Koh, Center for Digital Innovation Technology and Strategy, September 19, 2011.

7.1   INTRODUCTION TO SOCIAL, MOBILE, AND LOCAL MARKETING

Social, mobile, and local marketing have transformed the online marketing landscape. Before 2007, Facebook was a fledgling company limited to college students. Apple had not yet announced the iPhone. Online marketing consisted largely of creating a corporate Web site, buying display ads on Yahoo, purchasing Ad Words on Google, and sending e-mail. The workhorse of online marketing was the display ad that flashed brand messages to millions of users who were not expected to respond immediately, ask questions, or make observations. The primary measure of success was how many "eyeballs" (unique visitors) a Web site produced, and how many "impressions" a marketing campaign generated. An impression was one ad shown to one person. Both of these measures were carryovers from the world of television, which measures marketing in terms of audience size and ad views.

FROM EYEBALLS TO CONVERSATIONS

After 2007, everything began to change, with the rapid growth of Facebook and other social network sites, the explosive growth of smartphones beginning with Apple iPhone in 2007, and the growing interest in local marketing. What's different about the new world of social-mobile-local marketing and advertising are the related concepts of "conversations" and "engagement." Marketing today is based on businesses marketing themselves as partners in multiple online conversations with their customers, potential customers, and even critics. Your brand is being talked about on the Web and social media (that's the conversation part). Marketing your firm and building and, sometimes, restoring your brands requires you to locate, identify, and participate in these conversations. Social marketing means all things social: listening, discussing, interacting, empathizing, and engaging. Rather than bombarding your audience with fancier, louder ads, instead have a conversation with them and engage them in your brand. The emphasis in online marketing has shifted from a focus on eyeballs to a focus on participating in customer-oriented conversations. In this sense, social marketing and advertising is not simply a "new ad channel," but a collection of technology-based tools for communicating with shoppers.

In the past, businesses could tightly control their brand messaging and lead consumers down a funnel of cues that ended in a purchase. That is not true of social marketing. Consumer purchase decisions are increasingly driven by the conversations, choices, tastes, and opinions of the consumer's social network. Social marketing is all about businesses participating in and shaping this social process.

FROM THE DESKTOP TO THE SMARTPHONE AND TABLET

Today, social, mobile, and local marketing are the fastest growing forms of online marketing (**Figure 7.1**). It's taken five years for this new landscape to emerge, and firms are still learning how to use the new social and mobile marketing technologies.

By 2012, mobile marketing had already overtaken social marketing using traditional Web browsers on the Web. In 2013, spending on mobile marketing will be

FIGURE 7.1	SOCIAL, MOBILE, AND LOCAL MARKETING 2011–2015

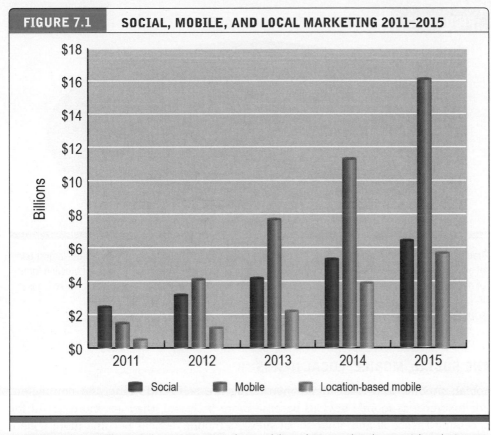

In 2013, marketers will spend almost twice as much on mobile marketing as they do on social marketing.
SOURCE: Based on data from eMarketer, Inc., 2013a.

almost double the amount spent on social marketing. By 2015, it is estimated that mobile marketing spending will account for around $16 billion annually, while social marketing will be just over $6 billion. While social marketing is growing at around 30% a year, mobile is growing at around 50% a year. Location-based marketing, estimated to be about $2.3 billion in 2013, is a rapidly expanding segment of mobile advertising. This figure underestimates the total social marketing spending because more than 25% of Facebook visits originate from a mobile device. A substantial part of the mobile marketing spending should be counted as "social" marketing. Nevertheless, the figure indicates the extraordinary impact that mobile devices are having on marketing expenditures.

Figure 7.2 puts the social-mobile-local forms of advertising into the context of the total online advertising market. Here you can see that traditional online marketing (browser-based search and display ads, and e-mail marketing) still constitutes the majority of all online marketing, but it is growing much more slowly than social-mobile-local marketing. By 2015, social-mobile-local marketing will be 50% or more of all online marketing. The marketing dollars are following customers and shoppers from the PC to mobile devices.

FIGURE 7.2 **ONLINE MARKETING PLATFORMS**

Traditional desktop marketing, including most of local marketing to local audiences, remains the largest part of all online marketing. Mobile marketing is aimed often at local audiences and is the fastest growing form of online marketing, followed closely by social marketing on social networks. Location-based marketing is in its infancy but it is also growing far faster than traditional desktop marketing.

SOURCE: Based on data from eMarketer, Inc., 2013a.

THE SOCIAL, MOBILE, LOCAL NEXUS

Social, mobile, and local digital marketing are self-reinforcing and connected. For instance, as mobile devices become more powerful, they are more useful for accessing Facebook and other social sites. As mobile devices become more widely adopted, they can be used by customers to find local merchants, and for merchants to alert customers in their neighborhood to special offers. Over time, these will become more overlapped as the three platforms become more tightly coupled.

Around 25% of all Facebook visits are from mobile devices, and 30% of its ad revenue is generated by its mobile audience. Likewise, local marketing and mobile are highly related: local advertisers most often target mobile devices. And a considerable amount of mobile ad spending comes from local advertisers. The strong ties among social, mobile, and local marketing has significant implications for managing your own marketing campaign in this new environment. The message is that when you design a social marketing campaign, you must also consider that your customers will be accessing the campaign using mobile devices, and often they will also be looking for local content. Social-mobile-local must be seen in an integrated management framework (comScore, 2013a).

7.2 SOCIAL MARKETING

Social marketing differs markedly from traditional online marketing. The objectives of traditional online marketing are to put your business's message in front of as many visitors as possible and hopefully encourage them to come to your Web site to buy products and services, or to find out more information. The more "impressions" (ad views) you get, and the more unique visitors to your site, the better. Traditional online marketing never expected to listen to customers, much less have a conversation with them, any more than TV advertisers expected to hear from viewers.

In social marketing, the objective is to encourage your potential customers to become fans of your company's products and services, and engage with your business by entering into a conversation with it. Your further objective is to encourage your business's fans to share their enthusiasm with their friends, and in so doing create a community of fans online. Ultimately, the point is to strengthen the brand and drive sales, and to do this by increasing your "share of online conversation." There is some reason to believe that social marketing is more cost effective than traditional marketing although this is still being explored.

SOCIAL MARKETING PLAYERS

There are hundreds of social network sites in the United States and worldwide, but the most popular sites account for over 90% of all visits. Unique visitors are one way to measure the reach (popularity) of social sites. **Figure 7.3** illustrates the highly skewed distribution of unique monthly visitors to social sites and the dominance of Facebook. At the same time, Figure 7.3 illustrates that Facebook has competition from rapidly growing sites that offer different marketing opportunities. LinkedIn, Twitter, Pinterest, Tumblr, and Instagram have more combined unique monthly visitors than

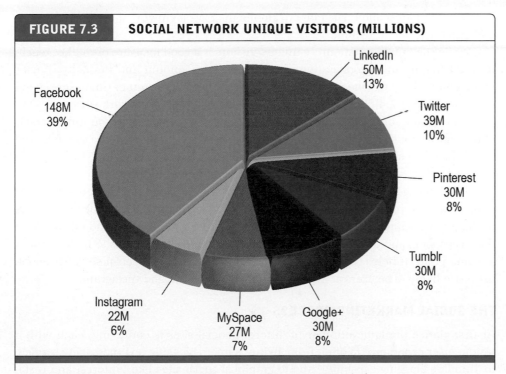

| FIGURE 7.3 | SOCIAL NETWORK UNIQUE VISITORS (MILLIONS) |

Among social networks, Facebook attracts the most monthly unique visitors by far.
SOURCE: Based on data from comScore, 2013b.

FIGURE 7.4   **ENGAGEMENT AT TOP SOCIAL SITES**

Visitors spend significantly more time on Facebook than any other social network site.
SOURCE: Based on data from eMarketer, Inc., 2013x.

Facebook. Pinterest and Instagram are among the fastest growing sites in Web history, and Tumblr is not far behind.

While the number of monthly unique visitors is a good measure of market reach, it is not helpful in understanding engagement—the amount and intensity of user involvement in a site. One measure of engagement is the amount of time users spend on a site. **Figure 7.4** illustrates engagement at the top social network sites.

On measures of engagement, Facebook once again dominates, accounting for 60% of user engagement with the average visitor spending 336 minutes on the site, followed by the blogging site Tumblr. In May 2013 Yahoo purchased Tumblr for $1 billion and picked up a 22% share of social marketing site engagement.

For a manager of a social marketing campaign, these findings suggest that in terms of reach and engagement, the place to start a social campaign is Facebook. Yet visitors to the other leading social sites collectively account for more reach and engagement than Facebook, and therefore, a social marketing campaign also has to include them at some point. It helps that social network users use multiple social sites. Facebook users are likely to be users at Twitter, Pinterest, LinkedIn, and Instagram.

THE SOCIAL MARKETING PROCESS

At first glance the large number of different social sites is confusing, each with a unique user experience to offer, from Twitter's micro blogging text messaging service, to Tumblr's blogging capability, and to graphical social sites like Pinterest and Insta-gram. Yet they can all be approached with a common framework. **Figure 7.5** illustrates

FIGURE 7.5   THE SOCIAL MARKETING PROCESS

Fan Acquisition   Engagement   Amplification   Community   Brand Strength (Sales)

The social marketing process has five steps.

a social marketing framework that can be applied to all social, mobile, and local marketing efforts.

There are five steps in the social marketing process: Fan acquisition, engagement, amplification, community, and brand strength (sales). Each of these steps in the process can be measured. The metrics of social marketing are quite different from those of traditional Web marketing or television marketing. This is what makes social marketing so different—the objectives and the measures. This will become more apparent as we describe marketing on specific social sites.

Social marketing campaigns begin with **fan acquisition**, which involves using any of a variety of means, from display ads to News Feed and page pop-ups, to attract people to your Facebook page, Twitter feed, or other platform like a Web page. It's getting your brand "out there" in the stream of social messages. Display ads on social sites have a social dimension (sometimes called "display ads with social features" or simply "social ads"). Social ads encourage visitors to interact and do something social, such as participate in a contest, obtain a coupon, or obtain free services for attracting friends.

The next step is to generate **engagement,** which involves using a variety of tools to encourage users to interact with your content and brand located on your Facebook or Web pages. You can think of this as "starting the conversation" around your brand. You want your fans to talk about your content and products. You can generate engagement through attractive photos, interesting text content, and blogger reports, with plenty of opportunities for users to express opinions. You can also provide links to Pinterest photos of your products or fan comments on blog sites like Tumblr.

Once you have engaged visitors, you can begin to use social site features to amplify your messages by encouraging users to tell their friends by clicking a Like or +1 button, or by sending a message to their followers on Twitter. **Amplification** involves using the inherent strength of social networks. On Facebook, the average user has 120 "friends." This includes all people they have ever friended, including people whom they don't really know (and who don't really know them). Facebook users typically have only three to four close friends with whom they can discuss confidential matters, and a larger set of around 20 friends with whom they have two-way communications (mutual friends). Let's use 20 as a reasonable number of

fan acquisition
attracting people to your marketing messages

engagement
encouraging visitors to interact with your content and brand

amplification
encouraging visitors to share their Likes and comments with their friends

mutual friends for marketing purposes. For marketers, this means that if they can attract one fan and encourage that fan to share his or her approval with his or her friends, the message can be amplified twenty times: 20 friends of the one fan can be influenced. Best of all: the friends of fans are free. Marketers pay to attract only the initial fan and they are not charged by social sites (currently) for the amplification that can result.

Once you have gathered enough engaged fans, you will have created the foundation for a **community**—a more or less stable group of fans who are engaged and communicating with one another over a substantial period of time (say several months or more). Marketers have a number of tactics to nurture these communities, including inside information on new products, price breaks for loyalty, and free gifts for bringing in new members. The ultimate goal is to enlarge your firm's "share of the online conversation." The process ends with strengthening the brand and, hopefully, additional sales of products and services. Brand strength can be measured in a variety of ways both online and offline, a subject that is beyond the boundaries of this text (Ailawadi, et al., 2003; Aaker, 1996; Simon and Sullivan, 1993; Keller, 1993).

Ultimately, the point of marketing is to drive sales revenue. Measuring the impact of a social marketing campaign on brand strength and sales is still being explored by marketers, social site managers, and researchers, but generally the results are positive: social marketing campaigns drive sales. Whether they drive sales better than alternative online marketing measures is still a matter of research.

In the sections that follow we will examine social, mobile, and local marketing more closely. The focus will be on describing the primary marketing tools of each platform and how to envision and manage a marketing campaign on each platform.

FACEBOOK MARKETING

Nearly everyone reading this book has a Facebook page. There are power users who spend hours a day on the site, some with thousands of "friends," and there are casual users who have a small set of perhaps 20 friends and relatives. While most have a basic understanding of Facebook, it's worthwhile to review the major features of Facebook before discussing its marketing potential.

Basic Facebook Features

Facebook describes itself as having three pillars: News Feed, Timeline (Profile), and the recently added Graph Search. Facebook also has many other features that are equally important to its potential as a marketing platform. **Table 7.1** describes these features.

Reviewing Table 7.1, it is clear that Facebook is built to encourage people to reveal as much personal information about themselves as feasible, including activities, behavior, photos, music, movies, purchases, and preferences. One result is that Facebook is the world's largest repository of deeply personal behavioral information on the Internet. Facebook knows a great deal more about its users than Google does about its users. Second, Facebook's features are built to maximize the connections among people in the form of notifications, tagging, messaging, posting, and sharing. In many instances, the movement of personal information is so widespread that it is beyond the

community

a stable group of fans engaged and communicating with one another over a substantial period of time about your brand

TABLE 7.1	BASIC FACEBOOK FEATURES
FEATURE	DESCRIPTION
Profile	As part of account creation, you create a profile that includes certain personal information. The profile may also include photos and other media. Establishes baseline information that will be shared with friends.
Friend search	Helps you find friends who are already using Facebook, as well as friends who are not, typically by searching your e-mail contact list. Creates your baseline social network based on prior contacts.
Timeline	A history of your actions on Facebook, including photos, history of posts, and comments to your News Feed, as well as life events that you post and want others to see as a part of your profile. Additions you make to your Timeline may appear on your friends' News Feed. Creates additional links with friends.
Tagging	Ability to tag photos, status updates, check-ins, or comments with the names of friends. Tagging links to that person's Timeline and News Feed. Your friends are notified they have been tagged, and you are linked to their Timeline. Friends of your friends may also be notified. Whenever Facebook detects the person in a new image, it notifies all those who have tagged the photo that this friend appears in a new photo that you can link to. The tagging tool is designed to create additional connections among users.
News Feed	The center of the action on Facebook Home pages, News Feed is a continuously updated list of stories from friends and Pages that you have liked on Facebook. News Feed stories include status updates, photos, videos, links, app activity, and Likes. Provides a continual stream of messages from friends and others.
Status update	A way to post your comments, observations, and location to all your friends.
Like button	The ubiquitous Like button communicates your support of comments, photos, activities, brands, articles, and products to your friends, and also to the Facebook social graph and third-party marketers. The Like button lives on virtually all Facebook content including status updates, photos, comments, brands, timelines, apps, and even ads. The Like button also appears on external sites, mobile and social apps, and ads. These sites are utilizing Facebook's Like social plug-in, and when you Like something outside of Facebook, it appears on your Timeline, where friends can comment on the activity.
Apps	Facebook apps are built by third-party developers, and add functionality to Facebook. Apps run the gamut from games (FarmVille) to photos (Instagram, now part of Facebook), music (Spotify), and publications (Washington Post Social Reader). Your personal information and that of your friends is shared with apps that you install. Most Facebook apps are free, and most rely on revenues from advertising that they expose you to.
Open Graph	A feature used by app developers to integrate their apps into the Facebook pages of users who sign up for the app, and in that sense, it opens the Facebook social graph to the developer, who can then use all the features of Facebook in the app. For instance, this feature allows your performance on game apps to be sent to your Friend's News Feeds. Supports the development of social apps and increases links among users.
Graph Search	A "social" search engine introduced in July 2013 that searches your social network, and potentially the entire Facebook social graph, for answers to your queries. It is a "semantic" search engine insofar as it provides a single answer rather than a list of links based on an algorithm's estimate of user intentions. It is also a "hybrid" search engine that relies on Bing to supplement results when your social network comes up empty. Graph Search indexes everyone's public posts, Likes, photos, and interests, and makes them available to all users of Facebook, friends or not. All of your information is available to Graph Search, and there is no opting out, and no editing of content is allowed. However, privacy controls can limit distribution, and you can delete personal information and photos from Facebook's social graph.

social density
refers to the number of interactions among members of a group and reflects the "connectedness" of a group, even if these connections are forced on users

understanding of users and outside observers. The effect of these two factors is to greatly magnify the social density of the Facebook audience. **Social density** refers to the number of interactions among members of a group and reflects the "connectedness" of a group, even if these connections are forced on users. For instance, some natural groups of people are not very "social" and few messages flow among members. Other natural groups are loquacious and chatty with many messages flowing among members. The scope, intensity, and depth of Facebook's repository of personal information and rich social network present extraordinary marketing opportunities.

Facebook Marketing Tools: A New Marketing Vocabulary

Facebook offers a large number of marketing opportunities and tools for branding and developing community on its site. Facebook is adding to its marketing platform every day in order to drive its revenue, and at times the various ways to market on Facebook can be confusing. But here are a few basic marketing features to focus on.

socially enabled ad
a display ad with options for viewers to announce their approval to their social network

Marketplace Ads. Like Yahoo, Google, and thousands of other sites, Facebook sells display ads. These are displayed in the right column of users' Home pages, and most other pages in the Facebook interface, such as Photos, Apps, and Profile. The purpose of these ads is to send users either to the business's Facebook page or Web site. Marketplace Ads are almost all "socially enabled." A **socially enabled ad** is a display ad with multiple opportunities for viewers to "Become a fan," "Like us on Facebook," share content with others, tweet, or pin a photo to Pinterest. While socially enabled ads seem ubiquitous, only about 30% of display ads are socially enabled. Facebook can target Marketplace Ads based on users' past behavior and their friends' past behavior. For instance, users who have demonstrated an interest in skiing, and who have many friends who ski, are likely to be shown ads for ski travel packages.

News Feed. The News Feed is where Facebook users spend most of their time because that is where posts about their friends appear. The News Feed is the center of the action for Facebook users. Industry analysts believe that Facebook users spend 27% of their time on the Home/News Feed section, followed by their Profiles (21%) and Photos (17%). There are several ways for a firm to appear in users' News Feeds. Unpaid "stories about friends" describe how a friend has actively engaged with a brand, for instance, "Sara Likes Southwest Airlines," followed by a story from Sara describing why she likes Southwest. However, paid brand messages can also be inserted into the News Feed or just to the right of the News Feed (these are also called "Premium Ads"), where they may receive more attention than Marketplace Ads.

Brand Pages. Facebook's early efforts at brand marketing focused on the development of brand pages as a means for firms to establish a direct relationship with their current and potential customers. Nearly all Fortune 1000 companies, and hundreds of thousands of smaller firms, have brand pages. Brand pages are similar to brand Web sites, but as the online audience has shifted towards Facebook as the primary online environment, firms have followed with brand pages on Facebook and other social networks as an adjunct to their "main" Web page on the Internet. The purpose of a brand page is to develop "fans" of the brand by providing users opportunities to interact with the brand through blogs, comments, contests, and offerings (Facebook Offers) on the brand page. Brand pages have "social" calls to action such as "Become a Fan," or "Like Us on Facebook." Using social calls to action, brand pages can escape their isolation and make it more easily into the users' social networks where friends can hear the message.

Social brand pages have many more social opportunities for fans to like and comment than are typical of traditional Web pages. However, corporate Web sites have, over time, adopted many social features and the two are now often indistinguishable. Brand pages on Facebook typically attract more visitors than a brand's Web site. For instance, the Skittles brand page on Facebook has attracted over 25 million Likes, while its Web site attracts only around 22,000 monthly unique visitors.

Promoted Posts. Promoted Posts are ads that begin as posts but for which businesses pay a fee to get additional distribution among fans, friends of fans, or nonfriends in their News Feeds. Promoted Posts can provide a link to a Facebook brand page for a company, or show videos, special offers, and photos.

Sponsored Stories. A Facebook "story" is not really a story in the conventional sense. It's a short message describing an action that someone has taken on Facebook. There are two kinds of stories: organic and sponsored (paid). Organic stories can appear on a user's News Feed, Ticker, or Timeline. Ticker is a real-time feed showing friends' activities, chats, and music listening. Some examples of stories that may appear on your News Feed, Ticker, or Timeline are a status update from a friend, a photo post from a page your friend likes, a friend liking something on Facebook, or the activity of a friend such as watching a TV show or listening to a music track. The relationship between a user and the story are maintained over time and entered into Facebook's Social Graph. Subsequently, advertisers looking to display ads to a particular group of people somehow involved with a product or topic can target ads to this entire group. These connections automatically opt users into further communications with the page, app, or Web site. In addition, Facebook is able to map the social relationships between users, other users (friends), and various objects like products, brands, photos, music, or videos.

Sponsored Stories are messages coming from friends (including businesses) about engaging with a page, post, app or event that a business, organization, or individual has paid for to increase the chance people will see them. For instance, if you have been on Ford Motor Company's Facebook page and Liked a story about a car, then Ford can sponsor stories to your News Feed.

Sponsored Stories
messages about friends' activities that advertisers pay to have distributed on user News Feeds

The reason why businesses pay for Sponsored Stories is that only about 16% of organic stories will reach their fan base. Stories compete with one another in Facebook's algorithm in terms of relevance to the user. Firms sponsor stories to ensure their posts and actions will reach a much larger percentage of their fan base. For instance, if Ford Motor Company posts an announcement of a new model to its Facebook brand page, only around 16% of its fans will see this post in their News Feed. However, if Ford pays to sponsor the story, it will appear in front of a much larger percentage of its fan base.

Generally, Sponsored Stories cannot be used to reach Facebook users who are not connected to the user. It wouldn't make sense to sponsor a story and place it in your News Feed if you were not related in any way to the story sponsor. This prevents users from being overwhelmed by irrelevant ads. But if the user has liked Walt Disney World, anything Walt Disney World does, or your friend does with respect to Walt Disney World, could be promoted to you.

Like Button. The Like button on Facebook and similar buttons, such as Share and +1 on other social sites, are perhaps the single most important element in the rise of social marketing. "Like" is the engine of social marketing. The Like button was introduced by Facebook on its own Web site in 2009 and rolled out as a plug-in to other Web sites in 2010. Unlike traditional Web advertising, the **Like button** gives users a chance to share their feelings about content and other objects they are viewing and Web sites they are visiting. It's a way for users to express their opinions to their friends about their Web experience. With Like buttons on millions of Web sites, Facebook can track user behavior on other sites and then sell this information to marketers. Like is also a plug-in that other Web sites install on their Web sites.

Like button
gives users a chance to share their feelings about content and other objects they are viewing

Like gives Big Data real meaning. Industry analysts estimate that there are 2.7 billion Likes every day, 2.5 billion content items shared, 300 million photos uploaded, and 500 TB (terabytes) of data received. This breaks down to each user Liking something three times a day and posting a photo every three days. Facebook does not know how many Web pages have a Like button, but analysts estimate the number is at least 2.5 million Web pages.

Mobile Ads. Around 65% of Facebook's users worldwide access Facebook using smartphones and tablets (about 40% in the United States). Worldwide, 700 million access Facebook from their smartphones. Mobile device users spend about 23% of their time on e-mail, and 15% of their time on Facebook (comScore/Facebook, 2012). Users download a Facebook app to their mobile devices to gain access to the mobile interface. Users can also access Facebook using their mobile browser although it is slower. In 2013, about 30% of Facebook ad revenue will come from its mobile ad platform, and it is the fastest growing revenue stream for Facebook. Therefore, Facebook has declared that mobile is its future (Hof, 2013). In 2012, Facebook introduced Facebook Home, which is an app that overlays the Android screen and becomes the smartphone interface for users. Facebook Home has not received widespread use. Mobile app install ads are those paid for by Facebook's 3,500 mobile app developers to persuade users to install their app.

Because the smartphone screen is much smaller than regular computer screens, there is no room for Marketplace Ads on the right, so all mobile ads need to be displayed in the users' News Feed. Mobile ads can include many of the ad formats described above, including Marketplace Ads, Sponsored Stories, and Promoted Posts. Critics complain that the number of ads in the mobile News Feed becomes distracting and annoying. Mobile ads often take up the entire screen. There also is far less targeting of mobile ads, which increases the likelihood users will see irrelevant ads. So far, despite the annoyance, Facebook mobile users continue to sign up and view the ads, and Facebook mobile ad revenue is growing an estimated 40% annually in 2013.

Facebook Exchange (FBX). **Facebook Exchange (FBX)** is a real-time bidding system that allows advertisers to target their ads based on personal information provided by Facebook. FBX competes with Google's display ad system DoubleClick and other real-time exchanges. Visitors to third-party Web sites are marked with a cookie, and can then be shown ads related to their Web browsing when they return to Facebook.

Table 7.2 summarizes the major tools used by marketers to build their brands on Facebook.

Starting a Facebook Marketing Campaign

Prior to starting a Facebook marketing campaign, there are some basic strategy questions you need to address. While every product presumably could benefit from a social marketing campaign, how is this true of your products? Who is your audience?

Facebook Exchange (FBX)

a real-time bidding system that allows advertisers to target their ads based on personal information provided by Facebook.

TABLE 7.2	BASIC FACEBOOK MARKETING TOOLS
MARKETING TOOL	DESCRIPTION
Marketplace Ads	Fan acquisition. Right-column socially enabled display ads similar to display ads elsewhere on the Web. Requires payment.
News Feed Premium Ads	Fan acquisition. Paid brand messages can be inserted into the News Feed, or just to the right of the News Feed (Premium Ads). Requires payment.
Brand Pages	Engagement and community building. Similar to a business Web page, but much more social by encouraging user interaction and response; ongoing discussions among the community of fans. Facebook Offers on a brand page are a way for firms to deliver offers to customers. Shoppers receive an e-mail that can be presented to the firm's Web site or Facebook page for redemption. Both brand pages and Offers are currently free.
Promoted Posts	Amplification. Ads that begin as posts on a fan page, which are given additional distribution among fans, friends of fans, or nonfriends. Requires payment.
Sponsored Stories	Amplification. Messages (stories) coming from your friends about their experience with a page, event, or app. Sponsored Stories are paid for by a business that wants to ensure their stories are displayed in your News Feed.
Like Button	Amplification. A feature that allows users to express support for content on social sites to their friends, and friends of friends. The one tool that marketers cannot control. Currently free.
Mobile Ads	Fan acquisition and engagement. Marketplace Ads, Promoted Posts, and Sponsored Stories delivered to smartphones and tablets. Requires payment.
Facebook Exchange (FBX)	Facebook's real-time ad exchange, which sells ads and retargets ads through online bidding. Advertisers place cookies on user browsers when they visit a site, and when they return to Facebook, they are shown ads on the right side from the site they visited. Requires payment.

How can you reach them? How have real-world social networks been used in the past to support sales in your industry? Can you be a "thought leader?" Once you have identified your audience, what content will get them excited and interested? Where are you going to get the content? What will it cost and what impact do you expect it to have on your brand and sales? At this point you do not need a detailed budget, but you should be able to develop estimates of the cost of such a campaign, as well as anticipated revenues.

If you're new to Facebook marketing, start simple and build on your fan base based on experience. A typical marketing campaign for Facebook might include the following elements:

- Establish a Facebook page for your brand. Content is king: have interesting, original content that visitors can be enthusiastic about. Acquire fans.
- Use comment and feedback tools to develop fan comments. You want visitors to engage with your content. You can also encourage bloggers to develop content for your page.
- Develop a community of users. Try to encourage fans to talk with one another, and develop new (free) content for your page.
- Encourage brand involvement through videos and rich media showing products being used by real customers.
- Use contests and competitions to deepen fan involvement.
- Develop display ads for use on other Facebook pages.
- Develop display ads for use in response to social search queries.
- Liberally display the Like button so fans share the experience with their friends.
- For more information on social marketing using Facebook, see Learning Track 7.1.

Table 7.3 provides some examples of Facebook marketing campaigns.

TABLE 7.3	SELECTED FACEBOOK MARKETING CAMPAIGNS
COMPANY	MARKETING CAMPAIGN
Target Stores	Promotes discounts across Facebook, Twitter, and mobile platforms providing access to the Cartwheel.Target.com Web site. Shoppers' Cartwheel interactions shared with their Facebook friends.
Domino's Pizza	Uses Marketplace Ads to offer discounts, along with Premium Ads in News Feeds on the day of the discounts to drive sales.
Expedia	Uses its fan base to enlist friends' help to win a free vacation package using both Marketplace and Premium Ads.
Jackson Hewitt	Tax preparation service anchored in Walmart stores used Facebook to increase engagement with its brand by placing Marketplace Ads promoting a dancing game. Winners were given a $25 gift certificate to use at Walmart.

Measuring Facebook Marketing Results

There are many ways to measure the success of a Facebook marketing campaign, some very sophisticated. This is a very new field that changes daily. Making matters more complicated is that industry sources sometimes use different names to refer to the same thing! Where this occurs we try to give both the most reasonable name and alternative names you might find in trade literature.

Table 7.4 describes some of the basic metrics to use when evaluating a social marketing campaign. It uses the five steps of the social marketing process found in Figure 7.5—fan acquisition, engagement, amplification, community, and ultimately brand strengthening and sales—as an organizing schema.

TABLE 7.4	MEASURING FACEBOOK MARKETING
SOCIAL MARKETING PROCESS	MEASUREMENT
Fan acquisition (impressions)	The number of people exposed to your Promoted Posts, Sponsored Stories, and Facebook brand page posts (impressions). The percentage of those exposed who become fans based on Likes or comments. The ratio of impressions to fans.
Engagement (conversation rate)	The number of posts, comments, and responses. The number of views of brand page content. The number of Likes generated per visitor. The number of users who responded to games, contests, and coupons (participation). The number of minutes on average that visitors stay on your page (duration). The rate of Likes per post or other content (applause rate).
Amplification (reach)	The percentage of Likes, shares, or posts to other sites (the rate at which fans share your content).
Community	The monthly interaction rate with your content (i.e., the monthly total of posts, comments, and actions on your Facebook brand page). The average monthly on-site minutes for all fans. The ratio of positive to negative comments.
Brand Strength/Sales	The percentage (or revenue) of your online sales that is generated by Facebook links compared to other platforms, such as e-mail, search engines, and display ads. The percentage of Facebook-sourced customer purchases compared to other sources of customers (conversion ratio). The conversion ratio for friends of fans.

While the ultimate goal of Facebook marketing is to drive sales (which typically will take place on your Web site), it is very important to understand what the elements of social marketing that produce these sales are, and how they can be improved.

At the most elementary level, the number of fans (or followers) generated is the beginning of all social marketing. Visitors become fans when they like your content. In the early days of social marketing, firms put a great deal of emphasis on the size of the fan base, and collecting Likes. This is less important today, as social marketing managers have become more sophisticated. Fan engagement in your content and brand is the first step towards developing a truly social experience, and arguably is more important than simply the number of impressions or the number of fans. Fans that you never hear from are not valuable. Engagement relates to how your fans are interacting with your content, how intensely, and how often. Understanding the kinds of content (videos, text, photos, or posts from fans) that create the highest levels of engagement is also very important.

The ability to amplify your marketing message by tapping into the social network of your fans is also at the core of social marketing. This can be measured very simply as the rate at which fans recommend your content to their friends, and how many of their friends further recommend your content to their friends.

Measuring the strength of a Facebook community is not that much different from measuring the strength of an offline community. In both cases you attempt to measure the collective activities of all in the community. Among your fans, how many actively participate? What is the total number of actions taken by fans in a month? How many minutes of involvement are generated each month? What is the percentage of favorable comments?

Finally, measuring sales that result from social campaigns is also straightforward. First, measure the percentage of sales you receive from the Facebook channel. You can easily measure the number of visits to your Web site that originate on Facebook, and the sales these visits generate. In addition, you can compare purchase rates (conversion rate) for fans and compare these to conversion rates for non-fans from Facebook. More important, you can compare the Facebook conversion rate to other visitors who come from different marketing channels, such as e-mail, display ads, and blogs.

Facebook marketing has entered its second generation even though it's only three years old. The emphasis today in social marketing has gone beyond collecting Likes and more towards building engagement with high-quality content that fans want to share with their friends; nurturing stable communities of intensely involved fans and friends of fans; and ultimately turning these communities of fans into communities of purchasers.

The experience of marketers is tantalizing but still unclear. E-mail and search easily drive more sales than Facebook or any social marketing today (eMarketer, Inc., 2013b). Facebook ads are much less likely to be clicked on than display ads on the Web, and sell for less than half the price of Web display ads. Facebook users join social networks to be social, not to buy or even shop. Despite these limitations, in the space of a few years, Facebook has been able to create a billion dollar business selling ads. Rather than replace other ad venues, Facebook may be creating a whole new venue that it dominates and that has unique value, but nevertheless does not diminish the role of e-mail or search in the marketing mix. However, Facebook still faces the challenge of monetizing its billion-person network and convincing marketers.

There are a variety of Facebook analytics tools that provide valuable information about your Facebook marketing efforts. Facebook Page Insights, provided by Facebook, tracks total Page Likes, People Talking About This (PTAT) (which tracks the number of unique people who have clicked on, Liked, commented on, or shared a post), Page Tags and Mentions, Page Checkins, and other interactions on a page. It also tracks something it calls Engagement Rate. People are considered to have engaged with a post if they Like it, comment on it, share it, or click it.

Social media management system HootSuite enables teams to execute marketing campaigns across multiple networks from one dashboard, and also provides custom reports. Major analytics providers, such as Google Analytics, Webtrends, and IBM Digital Analytics, also provide Facebook reporting modules. Read the *Insight on Technology* case study, *Fairmont Hotels: Using Google Analytics to Optimize Social and Mobile Marketing* for a further look at how one organization is using analytics tools to help them better understand social marketing.

TWITTER MARKETING

Twitter is a micro-blogging social network site that allows users to send and receive 140-character messages. Twitter has an estimated 40 million users in the United States (about 12% of Internet users) and an additional 160 million worldwide (eMarketer, Inc., 2013c). Analysts peg its 2013 revenues at $545 million, which is nearly double its 2012 revenue. Investors value the company at $10 billion in 2013. About 60% of Twitter's users access the service on mobile devices. Almost all of Twitter's revenue comes from pop-ads that appear in users' timelines (tweet stream), but Twitter also has many other marketing tools in its quiver. The real magic of Twitter, like Facebook, is that Twitter does not pay for the 400 million tweets sent each day. They are supplied for free by active users. Twitter sells ads based on the content of these user messages. Some analysts believe Twitter could easily become the next Google. See the opening case in Chapter 2 for more information on Twitter.

Twitter was designed from the start as a real-time text messaging service. Twitter offers advertisers and marketers a chance to interact and engage with their customers in real time and in a fairly intimate, one-on-one manner. Advertisers can buy ads that look like organic tweets (the kind you receive from friends), and these ads can tie into and enhance marketing events like new product announcements or pricing changes. Twitter is announcing new marketing tools every quarter in an effort to boost its revenues and do an IPO in the next year. On the other hand, users of Twitter are beginning to complain about the interruption of their tweet stream by ads, and there may be a limit to how many ads users will tolerate. Like other social networks, Twitter users use the service to send messages to one another, not to shop or purchase goods.

Basic Twitter Features

While most people probably know what a tweet is, Twitter offers marketers many other ways of communicating using Twitter. In fact, Twitter has introduced a whole

INSIGHT ON TECHNOLOGY

FAIRMONT HOTELS: USING GOOGLE ANALYTICS TO OPTIMIZE SOCIAL AND MOBILE MARKETING

In the global hotel business, customer acquisition and customer loyalty are the keys to success. Major hotel chains report that about 30% of bookings come from repeat customers. Identifying these loyal customers and targeting them with marketing messages has a very high return on investment. In the new world of multiple access points on different platforms, tracking visitors to digital properties is a herculean task for marketers. Visitors may come from a traditional Web site, from Facebook or another social site like Twitter or Pinterest, or from a mobile site or app. Complicating matters, visitors to any of these presence points can share their initial contact and engagement with your content, resulting in secondary and tertiary traffic to your site. The result is a flood of data points of moments when individuals are engaging with your content.

Fairmont Raffles Hotels International (FRHI) is a global operator of high-end hotels located in over 100 countries. The company also owns vacation ownership resorts and condominiums. The first Fairmont Hotel, the iconic Fairmont Hotel in San Francisco, is known for its luxury accommodations and wealthy clientele and is located on Nob Hill overlooking San Francisco Bay.

The travel industry of which hotels are a part generates an estimated $148 billion in bookings each year, nearly 35% of all e-commerce. The hotel booking segment generates about $60 billion annually. FRHI receives bookings requests from four different places: its branded Web site (Fairmont.com), merchant Web sites (Expedia.com or Hotels.com), opaque Web sites where the user does not know the hotel until they pay for the booking (Priceline.com), and retail Web sites (third-party distributors or portals like Hotel

Reservation System's HRS.com). Fairmont was an early Internet adopter, creating its first Web site in 1995, when marketing essentially involved putting the existing reservation system on the Internet to handle transactions, and posting pictures and other features of the hotel. Tracking visitors to the Web site was straightforward: visitors entered the site with a browser that revealed the customer's IP address, and interaction with online content was easily observable as page views. Cookies were used to identify frequent visitors and former customers, who could be offered discounts for their loyalty.

With the advent of mobile devices and social sites, the marketing equation has become much more complicated. Fairmont has branded content pages on the Web, as well as on Facebook, Twitter, and Pinterest. When a visitor Likes the firm's Facebook page, the message is sent to all the visitor's friends. The same is true for the company's Twitter and Pinterest pages. In addition, the Fairmont iPhone app replicates much of the functionality of the firm's Web site. Because marketing messages placed on Facebook, Twitter, Pinterest, or any social site can easily ricochet across a number of other social networks, or get passed from one individual to another by SMS text messaging or Facebook Chat, it's difficult for marketers to measure exactly how their social messaging is generating traffic. Who was the first visitor to click on the link, who did he or she share it with, and how did the first click lead to additional clicks, or posts, either on the original site or another platform entirely? The person who ultimately clicks on a post and ends up on the firm's Web site is often not the first person to receive the post.

The problem for Fairmont was how to integrate all these visitor touch points and interactions to enable marketing managers to understand which

(continued)

of their digital efforts were attracting visitors, how visitors were engaging with content once they entered the various sites, and if these diverse digital efforts were leading to sales. In 2010, Fairmont turned to Google Analytics to find solutions.

Google Analytics is an analytics product that is used by an estimated 50% of the top 1 million Web sites. Basic service is free and a premium package is available for a fee. Google Analytics for Mobile was introduced in 2010. Mobile analytics is a subset of Web analytics that seeks to understand how potential customers use a firm's apps and mobile Web sites—from discovery of the app (how did that happen), to download (who downloads and installs), and engagement (what did the visitor do). The service works across both tablets and smartphones, and is fully integrated with the regular Google Analytics package designed originally for analyzing Web site traffic.

Google cloud servers run the databases needed to process the streams of information produced by users on all platforms. At participating Web sites, Google Analytics downloads to every visitor's browser a short piece of code (also known as a beacon) that records user behavior and identifies the user by the IP address of the user's computer, and then sends this information back to Google's servers without user visibility, and without placing a noticeable load on a firm's own Web servers.

With this trove of information, Google Analytics can track visitors from all referral sources including direct visits to the Web site, social networks, search engines, referral sites, and mobile devices. Marketers identify key performance indicators (measures of critical performance), establish goals, optimize content and pages, and track users' from initial visit to online behavior to, ultimately, sales. Google Analytics provides dashboards and reports that can be viewed on desktops and mobile devices to marketing analysts; provides a single source of data on visitors; tracks the impact of various marketing campaigns; and develops information for managers on the impact of marketing on key performance indicators including purchases, site visits, length of time on site, engagement with all pieces of content such as downloading content, or sharing content on social networks.

Fairmont uses Google Analytics to track all the platforms users use to discover Fairmont and ultimately book a room. For instance, for visitors from Twitter's Web interface, the source is identified as a direct source "twitter.com." Visitors using one of several Twitter mobile apps are identified as other Twitter sources, or as referral traffic when, say, a user visits Fairmont from a Twitter referral site (Expedia.com). Fairmont also uses Google Analytics Campaign Tracking. Tracking tells marketers the source of the visitor (Facebook app); the medium (unpaid or paid search; referral site; or direct organic search engine); keywords the user may be responding to; the campaign name; and content features. Users can identify a specific link in a campaign.

Google Analytics allows Fairmont marketers to understand the growth in its social media campaigns and the viral traffic generated by visitors who post comments. Each Twitter tweet, Pinterest photo, or Facebook post is uniquely tagged, allowing Fairmont marketers to measure and compare the effectiveness of its campaigns regardless if they are on Facebook, Twitter, or Pinterest. Fairmont can now identify the most successful ads, campaigns, channels, and paths to conversion and then make faster and better investments with its marketing budget.

SOURCES: "Shop.com Analytics Transition," Blastam.com, August 2013; "Internet Travel Hotel Booking Statistics," Statisticsbrain.com, July 29, 2013; "Citrix ByteMobile Mobile Analytics Report," Citrix.com, June 2013; "Fairmont Hotels Harness the Power of Google Analytics to Optimize Social Media Marketing," Google Analytics, January 2013; "Streams: From Insight to Action," Webtrends.com, January 2013; "PUMA Kicks Up Order Rate 7% With Google Analytics," by Jesse Nichols, analytics.blogspot.com, 2012; "Mobile Analytics and Reporting," by Google, Google.com/analytics/features/mobile.html, undated.

TABLE 7.5	TWITTER FEATURES
FEATURE	DESCRIPTION
Tweet	140-character text message. Messages can be private (to a single person or one to one), public (to everyone, one to many), or to a group of followers.
Followers	You can follow someone's tweets and receive them as soon as they are made. Others can follow your tweets.
Message (DM)	A direct private message (DM) is like an e-mail that only you and the recipient can read.
Hashtag #<word>	Like a Twitter search engine, #<word> organizes the conversations on Twitter around a specific topic. Click on a hashtag and you are taken to the search results for that term.
Mention	A public Tweet that includes another user's name "@ username." You can click on mentions and link back to that person's profile. As a public tweet, your followers will be alerted as well.
Reply	A public response to a tweet using the Reply button. Replies show up on your timeline and that of the person you are responding to.
Timeline	Your timeline is your home page on Twitter listing the tweets you have received in chronological order, the most recent first. Click on a tweet in the timeline and it expands to reveal videos, and photos. Place your mouse over a tweet to reply, retweet, or make it a favorite (which is passed to your followers).
Retweet	Allows you to send along a tweet to all of your followers.
Links	Twitter has a link-shortening feature that allows you to paste in a URL of any link and it will be automatically shortened.

new vocabulary that is specific to Twitter's platform. **Table 7.5** describes the most common Twitter features.

Twitter Marketing Tools: A New Marketing Vocabulary

There are many kinds of Twitter marketing products, and the firm is creating new ones every few months. The current major Twitter marketing tools include the following.

Promoted Tweets. Advertisers pay to have their tweets appear in users' search results. Promoted Tweets are Twitter's version of Google's Ad Words. The tweets appear as "promoted" in the search results. Pricing is on a "cost-per-click" basis of between $.50 to $1.50 per click, and based on an auction run by Twitter on the Twitter ad platform. Promoted Tweets can be geo-targeted and also offer keyword targeting that enables advertisers to send the tweets to specific users based on keywords in their recent tweets or tweets with which they have interacted. For instance, if you are tweeting with a friend about a really cool new album, and the band has scheduled a concert in your area, Twitter can pass this information to marketers who will send a Promoted Tweet offering tickets. Twitter says this will not lead to more ads, but much better targeted ads close to the point of consumer purchase.

Promoted Trends. Advertisers pay to move their hashtags (# symbol used to mark keywords in a tweet) to the top of Twitter's Trends List. Otherwise, hashtags are found by the Twitter search engine, and only those that are organically popular make it to the Trends List. Promoted Trends cost about $200,000 a day in the United States in 2013, and are also available for purchase in 50 different countries.

Promoted Accounts. Advertisers pay to have their branded account suggested to users who are likely to be interested in the account in the "Who to Follow" list, Twitter's account recommendation engine, on the Twitter home page. Promoted Accounts can be targeted by interest, geography, and gender, and are priced on a cost-per-follower basis, with advertisers paying only for new followers gained.

Enhanced Profile Pages. Companies get their own banner and the ability to pin a tweet to the top of the company's timeline. The price reportedly ranges from $15,000 to $25,000.

Amplify. The Twitter Amplify program provides marketers with a real-time digital dashboard so they can see the resulting tweet activity about the show or the brand. Based on this information, marketers can send Promoted Tweets to users who tweeted about a show. They can alter the copy as well based on other information about the tweeters. For example, Jim Beam used Amplify in 2013 to promote its new Jim Beam Red Stag brand of premium bourbon. The intent was to increase brand awareness, purchase intent, and user engagement. The strength of Twitter, according to Jim Beam marketers, is that it allows the brand to be a part of a real-time conversation, as opposed to Facebook, which is better at reaching a mass audience but not at engaging consumers in real time. The power of social media, including Facebook, is finding consumer advocates who will speak on behalf of the brand.

Television Ad Retargeting. Millions of users tweet with their friends while watching television, and Twitter can follow the conversation to identify who is watching a particular show. Marketers displaying TV ads can retarget those ads or other messages to tweeters in real time to reinforce their marketing message. Advertisers with video content, like the National Basketball Association, insert in-tweet video clips, which are video replays. Advertisers can precede the video with an ad, or place an ad just below the video on screen. Companies can follow up with a Promoted Tweet.

Lead Generation Cards. Marketers can embed a "card" into business tweeters' standard Twitter messages. When users click on the message, a promotional offer appears and users are asked to sign up. Cards are different from display ads because they are used only by businesses who want to develop new leads, and they always include an offer, such as 50% off your next cup of coffee. This is a one-click process. The users' e-mail and Twitter account names are automatically obtained by Twitter and sent to marketers, who can then follow up with a tweet or an e-mail.

Table 7.6 summarizes these Twitter marketing tools.

Starting a Twitter Marketing Campaign

If you're new to Twitter marketing, start simple and build on your follower base using experience as a guide for what works. A typical marketing campaign for Twitter may include the following elements:

- Establish a Twitter account. Start following others you are interested in or conversations that you might want to participate with # < topic > . Don't expect any followers

TABLE 7.6	TWITTER MARKETING TOOLS
TWITTER MARKETING TOOLS	DESCRIPTION
Promoted Tweets	Advertisers pay to have their tweets appear in users' search results and timelines. The tweets appear as "promoted", and the pricing is on a per-click basis, based on an auction run on the Twitter ad platform. Promoted Tweets can be both keyword- and geo-targeted.
Promoted Trends	Advertisers pay to move their hashtags (# symbol used to mark keywords in a tweet) to the top of Twitter's Trends List. Otherwise, hashtags are found by the Twitter search engine, and only those that are organically popular make it to the Trends List.
Promoted Accounts	Advertisers pay to have their branded account suggested to users likely to be interested in the account in the "Who to Follow" list, Twitter's account recommendation engine, available on the Twitter home page. Promoted Accounts can be specifically targeted and are priced on a cost-per-follower basis.
Enhanced Profile Pages	Companies can get their own banner to display images and the ability to pin a tweet to the top of the company's timeline.
Amplify	A real-time digital dashboard connecting television commercials and tweet activity.
TV Ad Retargeting	Tweeting viewers of TV shows with the same ads targeted at them on a show they are watching.
Lead Generation Card	Promotional offers that appear in users' Twitter timeline of messages with a coupon or other offer. Used for lead generation.

at first. Your visibility rises as you follow others, who will begin to tweet back or retweet interesting content. Then start retweeting content you think the group would be interested in, and start encouraging ongoing conversations.

- Try a simple Promoted Tweet. Twitter has a very good online ad facility that will allow you to define an ad, establish the groups you would like to target, and understand the costs. You might start with a regional or metropolitan Promoted Tweet. Test various formats. You don't have to pay for Promoted Tweets unless someone clicks on the tweet, so it is up to you to make those clicks count. Direct users to your Web site and offer a coupon or discount.

- Promoted Trends can be very expensive—around $200,000. If your budget will allow, and your topic is of general interest to a large audience, you can try this tool. Geo-targeting is possible.

- TV ad retargeting is obviously a big business tool for media companies that have television content and television ads. Retargeting these to the Twitter community strengthens the overall brand image, and can direct people to the firm's Web site.

- Lead Generation Cards are something that small and medium-sized businesses can use. If you sell anything locally, from pizza to stationery, make up an offer and build a Lead Generation Card specifying the geo-location where your business is located.

As with Facebook, the objective is to establish your brand identity online and seek out engagement with users, not immediate sales. Encourage others to retweet your content and offers to their friends.

Table 7.7 describes some selected Twitter marketing campaigns.

TABLE 7.7	SELECTED TWITTER MARKETING CAMPAIGNS
COMPANY	MARKETING CAMPAIGN
ESPN/Ford	Used embedded replays of football games in posts sent to Twitter users who have shown an interest in sports. Ads for Ford shown before the video roll.
Starbucks	Used both Promoted Tweets and Lead Generation Cards. Users only need to hit the Submit button and their personal information flows to Starbucks to sign them up for special offers or coupons.
LG Electronics	Used hashtags and Promoted Tweets to promote a treasure hunt and drive awareness of a new smartphone.
Porsche	Used hashtags and Promoted Tweets to enhance awareness of its new 911 sports car launch and support television, newspaper, and magazine campaigns.
Airbnb	The community marketplace for unique accommodations used Promoted Tweets to stimulate interest in a new sublet program with a $200 discount offer.
HubSpot	The online marketing firm used Promoted Accounts and Promoted Tweets to target B2B decision-makers in online marketing.
Lord & Taylor	The luxury goods retail chain used Twitter to promote a giveaway of Rihanna tickets at one of its store locations, and in the process, drive traffic to its stores.

Measuring Twitter Marketing Results

Measuring the results of Twitter marketing is similar to measuring the results of Facebook and other social marketing platforms, with some minor changes to account for the unique qualities of Twitter. **Table 7.8** describes some basic ways to measure the results of a Twitter marketing campaign.

Tools provided by Twitter include a dashboard that provides real-time information on impressions, retweets, clicks, replies, and follows for Promoted Tweets and Promoted Accounts. Twitter's Timeline activity dashboard provides data on how every tweet performs in terms of mentions, follows, and reach. Twitter's Followers dashboard enables marketers to track the growth of the follower base, as well as information about their interests, geography, and engagement.

Third-party tools include TweetDeck, which enables you to track mentions, people, and keywords; Twitalyzer, which provides one-click access to Twitter metrics

TABLE 7.8	MEASURING TWITTER MARKETING RESULTS
SOCIAL MARKETING PROCESS	**MEASUREMENT**
Fan acquisition (impressions)	The number of people exposed to your Promoted Tweets, Promoted Trends, etc. (impressions).
	The number of followers and monthly growth.
Engagement (conversation rate)	The number of comments, responses to, and retweets of, your tweets.
	The number of views of brand page content.
	The number of users that responded to games, contests, and coupons (participation).
	The number of minutes on average that followers stay on your page (duration).
Amplification (reach)	The rate at which fans retweet or otherwise share your tweets.
Community	The monthly interaction rate (i.e., the monthly total of comments and responses to, and retweets of, your content).
	The average monthly onsite minutes for all followers.
	The ratio of positive to negative tweets.
Brand Strength/Sales	The number of leads generated (people who sign up for news or content).
	Visitor/lead rate: the number of visitors that become leads to compare campaigns.
	The percentage (or revenue) of your online sales generated by Twitter links compared to other platforms, such as e-mail, search engines, and display ads.
	The percentage of Twitter-sourced customer purchases compared to other sources of customers (conversion ratio).

that analyze followers, mentions, retweets, influencers, and their locations; and Back-Tweets, which allows you to search through a tweet archive for URLs sent via Twitter.

PINTEREST MARKETING

Pinterest is the social network site that provides users with an online board to which they can "pin" interesting pictures. The success of Pinterest is based in part on a shift in consumer behavior enabled by new technologies: people talk about brands using pictures rather than words. Large numbers of Web users are pinning and instagramming about their lives using pictures.

You can think of Pinterest as a highly interactive and social online magazine or "zine." One difference, of course, is that users contribute all the photos. The site currently has 36 categories of boards from gifts, animals, art, cars, and motorcycles to crafts, food, and men's and women's fashion. Users can pin to these boards, create their own boards, and follow other pinners and boards as well. Firms can create their own brand boards and product pins. See the opening case in Chapter 1 for more information on Pinterest.

Users who pin photos can alert Facebook and Twitter friends and followers who can access their pictures and boards on Pinterest. Pinned photos and photo boards are available to all Pinterest users at this time, although many marketers are pushing Pinterest to develop private boards that can allow marketers to require registration (customer information) as a condition of access to content. But the point of Pinterest, according to its cofounder Ben Silberman, is to share beautiful, interesting photos and graphics as widely as possible across the Web. Everyone can repin images they like to their own boards as well. Pinterest is therefore one of the largest image sharing sites on the Internet.

Pinterest is also one of the fastest growing sites in Web history. In 2010, Pinterest had 10,000 users, then 12 million by the end of 2011, and 50 million by June 2013. It regularly has around 25 million monthly unique visitors (in comparison, Facebook typically has around 150 million, LinkedIn around 40 million, and Twitter around 37 million). Today, 15% of online adults use Pinterest. Pinterest's visitors are overwhelmingly female: over 80% are women, but users cover a broad demographic range from grandparents to teenagers, with about a third between the ages of 18–34. There's no reason why participation of men cannot expand rapidly in the near future. The hope for marketers, and Pinterest, is that its "referral capacity" (the ability to direct users to retail Web sites where they can purchase something) will rapidly increase as its audience grows and intensity of use grows.

One way to look at the millions of pictures on Pinterest is as disguised display ads—click, and off you go to a brand Web site for a purchase. Other times you'll end up on another pinner's board without a clue about how to purchase the product. Pinterest is working on solving this problem. Pinterest pins are much better than display ads because they are unobtrusive, and because they don't look like display ads. Instead, they look like sumptuous catalog or magazine photos. In the future, analysts believe, Pinterest could charge an affiliate fee for any subsequent purchases. Pinterest could also charge businesses for creating brand sites or boards, which currently are free.

Basic Pinterest Features

Marketing on Pinterest requires that you understand the basic features and capabilities of Pinterest. While all users of Pinterest understand how to pin photos to an online scrapbook, many other capabilities are less well understood or used. **Table 7.9** provides a list of Pinterest features.

TABLE 7.9	PINTEREST FEATURES
FEATURE	DESCRIPTION
Pins	Used to post a photo to a Pinterest board.
Board	An online scrapbook where photos are organized by the user.
Repins	The ability to pin the photos of other users to your own boards, and to share with your friends.
Hashtags and keywords	Use <#hashtags> in the description of your pins, e.g., #style, #cars, #sports cars. Use keywords people are likely to use when searching for specific content.
Share	Sharing your pinned photos with friends. Options: Twitter, Facebook, e-mail, embed.
Image Hover	A widget you can add to your browser. When your mouse hovers over an online image, the Pin It button pops up and you can pin the photo automatically to your Pinterest boards.
Embed	Code that allows you to embed your pinned photos into your blog automatically.
Me+ Contributors	Allows others to contribute to your boards (only if they are already a follower of yours).
Follow	Users can choose to follow other pinners and boards and receive e-mail updates.
Number of Pins and Followers	A count of the number of pins and the number of followers visible at the top of the brand page.
Link to URL; Link to pinner	Click on the URL of the company who pinned a photo; click on a link to the person who pinned a photo.
Price display	Hover over a product and a display pops up with the price and model information.
Integration with Facebook and Twitter	Login from Facebook, Twitter, and other social sites. Your personal profile (but not your photo) information from Facebook comes over to Pinterest; your pins go onto your Facebook Timeline. Twitter and Pinterest profile pages are also integrated.
Pin It browser button (bookmarklet)	Browsers' red Pin It button. Users drag the button onto their browser screen, allowing them to instantly pin photos they see on the Web.
Pinterest app	Smartphone app that allows users to pin photos, browse pins and boards, get ideas while shopping, and display pins.
Pinterest widget	Pin It button on your brand page that makes it easy for people to pin images from your site.

Pinterest Marketing Tools: A New Marketing Vocabulary

Pinterest marketing tools are still in an early stage of development. The company is adding new tools every month as Pinterest begins the journey towards monetizing its large user audience. Pinterest insists that pinned photos from retail and other firms are not a form of advertising, and that Pinterest's main objective is to provide people with a tool for collecting and organizing the things they love. Instead of seeking profits, Pinterest's focus has been to attempt to become a very valuable service by providing users with the ability to easily find more information about the product in the photo, and where to buy it. Current users appear to appreciate the noncommercial look and experience of Pinterest. The challenge for management is to monetize Pinterest's audience through advertising and affiliate revenues without alienating its users. Pinterest faces the same issues in this regard as Facebook and Twitter. **Table 7.10** identifies and describes some of the primary Pinterest marketing tools.

For instance, Lands' End has several brand pages on Pinterest, one of which is Lands' End Canvas. Search for Lands' End Canvas and it takes you to the page that Lands' End Canvas created and where Lands' End has pinned some of its catalog

TABLE 7.10	PINTEREST MARKETING TOOLS
MARKETING TOOL	**DESCRIPTION**
Add Pin It or Follow button to your Web site (Pinterest widget)	Makes it easy for visitors to pin photos from your Web site, and be notified when you post new photos to your site.
Pin as display ad	The Pinned photo acts as a display ad by directing users back to a firm's Web site.
Create theme-based boards to reflect your brand messaging	Pinterest recommends that business boards not be strictly sales-oriented, but lifestyle-oriented instead.
Brand page	A new Pinterest feature that allows companies to create a corporate brand page. In the past, Pinterest did not distinguish between a personal page and a corporate brand page.
URL Link to stores	Makes it easier for consumers to click through links on brand pages and product pins so they can reliably purchase what they see. The goal is to integrate photos of inventory with Pinterest to make items more easily tracked. What this means is retailers can see a definite link between a sale and a photo they pinned. Currently, after thousands of repins, clicking on the URL sometimes leads to a broken link.
Retail brand Pins (Product Pin; Enhanced Pin)	A new kind of pin for food, retail, and movies. Click on a Retail Pin and you will see the price and where to buy it. Food Pins reveal recipes.
Integration with other social sites	Ask your Facebook fans and Twitter followers to pin photos of your products and tag you. Repin these photos to your brand page on Pinterest. Give a shout-out to your loyal users and fans to show potential customers how much current users like using your product.
Network with users, followers, and others	As with Facebook and Twitter, comment, mention, and communicate with others using Pinterest. Participate in the community and you will become better known, and learn more about potential customers and what they believe and to what they aspire.

photos. On this brand page, only Lands' End Canvas products are pinned, and the company is identified. You can see the number of people who have pinned these photos elsewhere, and the total number of others who follow this line of clothing and have posted their own photos. When you click on a photo, you get a larger version of the photo (sometimes called a photo landing page), and the chance to link to the Web site (canvas.landsend.com) where you can purchase the product and find similar ones. You will also see on this photo landing page a picture of the person who pinned the photo, other boards where it was pinned, and recommendations for related photos and products in a section titled "People who pinned this also pinned ...."

Table 7.11 provides a brief description of Pinterest marketing campaigns of selected retailers.

Starting a Pinterest Marketing Campaign

Before leaping into a Pinterest campaign, ask yourself some questions about your products and services, and then identify some strategic objectives for your Pinterest presence. First, sketch out a vision of what you hope to accomplish with a Pinterest presence. Are you an established brand trying to strengthen your brand? Are you the new kid on the block that no one knows and you want to start a marketing campaign? Are your products visual and can your brand be expressed in a set of pictures? Most products have a visual component, some more compelling than others. Today, most Pinterest marketing campaigns involve clothing, jewelry, home furnishings, food, and

TABLE 7.11	SELECTED PINTEREST MARKETING CAMPAIGNS
COMPANY	CAMPAIGN
Whole Foods	Natural and organic food stores with 55 boards, 2,100 pinned photos, and 128,000 followers.
West Elm	Home furnishing company emphasizing simple and elegant designs. 52 boards, 4,800 Pins, and 156,000 followers.
New York Times Styles Desk	New York Times Styles Desk provides inspirational lifestyle photos and articles from their food and drink, fashion and beauty, and garden and interior design sections. Curated by New York Times editors. 56 boards, 452 pins, 65,000 followers.
Bergdorf Goodman	New York's Fifth Avenue luxury goods department store. 38 boards, 2,400 pins, and 57,000 followers.
Lands' End	A clothing retailer that started as a mail order business and is now a successful multi-channel retailer of outerwear, footwear, home furnishings, and apparel. 45 boards, 820 pins, and 4,300 followers.
Etsy	Online-only Web site that sells handmade craft objects, vintage items, and arts and crafts supplies. Provides a platform for small firms to sell their goods on their own storefronts. 78 boards, 7,300 pins, 292,000 followers. Arts and Crafts Pinterest boards show both its products and how to use them in everyday life. The emphasis is on attaining a life style, and humanizing the Etsy products to form a deeper bond with their customers.

art/crafts. If your product is hip implants, for instance, it might be hard to portray your products to likely consumers (but not impossible if you are creative). Is the consumer accustomed to seeing the products in your industry expressed through photos? Food is increasingly a visual experience with the growth of food magazines and Web sites.

Next, consider the target demographic for your products and services, and compare it to the Pinterest demographic. Currently, Pinterest visitors are over 80% women, primarily in the 18–34 range, and while this might change over time, your offerings will have to be attractive to women. Do your products or services appeal to this demographic?

Think about strategy in your marketspace. What are your competitors doing? Are they on Pinterest? Do they have an effective presence? What types of people follow your competitors and what are the users pinning? How many followers, re-pinners, brand pages, and product pins are there? Because photos are central to a Pinterest presence, where will the photos for your brand pages come from? Are you, or a member of your team, a skilled photographer? You can pin photos from all over the Web, and from other Pinterest boards, but then you're just sharing content, not creating unique and unusual content.

Pinterest is an adjunct to a fully developed marketing plan, both online and offline. You will want to integrate your social and online marketing efforts with a Facebook and Twitter presence. You can share photos from your Web site, and send Web photos to your brand pages. The same photos can be used on your Facebook page and on Twitter. Your customers will be using all these platforms and you will have to follow them to keep up.

Once you have envisioned your Pinterest campaign and developed a marketing plan, you can start implementing your plan. In order to implement your Pinterest plan, you should have a traditional Web site where your products are displayed (a catalog) and can be purchased. Second, you should also have a Facebook brand page to develop followers and a method for informing your followers of new Pins. Once these are in place, you can begin your Pinterest campaign:

- Create a Pinterest brand page and start pinning photos of your products. Grow, and change your pins and board regularly. Be sure your photos are the same quality level or higher than those of your competitors. If necessary, hire a skilled photographer. Brand pages generally do not allow followers to pin photos but only to follow and comment. The idea here is to control the content of your brand page, and develop other boards where followers can pin pictures.

- Improve the quality of your photos. Computer screens limit the resolution that can be displayed to users, but the lighting, composition, and color in your pinned photos are under your control.

- Use URL links and keywords. Make sure your pins have a URL link to your store, or to vendor stores, so followers can easily buy as well as "see." Be sure to use keywords and hashtags to classify each of your photos so they show up in Pinterest searches. Remember, Pinterest cannot "see" a photo or understand its content. It only "knows" the content based on your tags.

- Create a Pinterest product pin. If you are in the food, retail, or movie distribution business, product pins are worth a try if you have a popular product at an attractive price, or if you want to use a specific product as a loss-leader to motivate people to come to your Web site (where you can expose them to your entire catalog of products).

- Use Pin It buttons. Add a Pin It button to your Web site and Facebook page to encourage fans and followers to pin your photos to their own boards, and to recommend them to friends.

- Create multiple theme-based life style boards. Develop several theme-based boards that emphasize life styles or fashions. Pinterest is not just, or even primarily, a selling site. It is also an entertainment and branding site. You want followers to adore your photos. On theme-based boards you will want others besides yourself to be able to pin.

- Use your Facebook and Twitter networks. Start using your Facebook and Twitter networks by adding a Pin It button to Facebook (also called a Pinterest tab), and start sharing your pinned photos with your followers.

- Integrate with Facebook and Twitter. Create Facebook and Twitter logins so that users can go to your pins and boards without leaving the Facebook and Twitter sites.

- Be social. Join the conversation. It's all about being social. Follow other pinners and boards and ask to receive e-mail and Facebook updates.

Measuring Pinterest Marketing Results

Because Pinterest is just beginning to introduce and test its marketing tools, learning how to measure the results of a Pinterest marketing campaign is also in the early stages. Nevertheless, like any social marketing platform, the key dimensions to measure are fan (follower) acquisition, engagement, amplification, community, and sales. **Table 7.12** describes some basic ways to measure the results of a Pinterest marketing campaign.

Pinterest provides a built-in Web Analytics service that offers insights into how people are interacting with pins that originate from their Web sites. There are several firms that will help produce the metrics referred to in Table 7.12. For instance, Curalate is an online service to measure the impact of Pinterest and other visual social media. It listens and measures visual conversations by seeing what pictures users pin and repin, and also analyzes the colors in the picture.

THE DOWNSIDE OF SOCIAL MARKETING

Social marketing is not without its disadvantages. One problem is that brands lose a substantial amount of control over where their ads appear in terms of other content and what people say about their brands on social sites. Ads placed on Facebook according to an algorithm can be placed near content that does not represent the values of the brand. This is not peculiar to social marketing, as advertising using Google's advertising platform faces the same problem. This is very different, however, from TV ads where brands maintain near complete control. Social sites are unique in that

TABLE 7.12	**MEASURING PINTEREST MARKETING RESULTS**
SOCIAL MARKETING PROCESS	MEASUREMENT
Fan acquisition (impressions)	The number of people exposed to your pins.
	The number of followers and the rate of growth.
	The number of people that have pinned your product photos.
	The percentage of those exposed to your pins who also pin them to their own or other boards.
Engagement (conversation rate)	The number of posts, comments, and responses to your brand or pins on Pinterest.
	The number of users who are responding to games, contests, and coupons (participation).
	The number of minutes on average fans stay on your brand or product pages (duration).
	The rate of pins per post or other content (applause rate).
Amplification	The rate at which fans share your pinned photos by sharing or repinning to their own or others' boards.
Community	The monthly interaction rate with your content (i.e., the monthly total of pins, comments, and actions on your Pinterest brand page).
	The average monthly onsite minutes for all fans.
	The ratio of positive to negative comments.
Brand Strength/Sales	The percentage of your online sales that are generated by Pinterest links (referrals) compared to other platforms, such as e-mail, search engines, and display ads.
	The percentage of Pinterest-sourced customer purchases, compared to other sources of customers (conversion ratio).
	The conversion ratio for users receiving repinned photos (friends of followers).

disgruntled consumers, or just malicious people, can post material that is inaccurate and/or embarrassing (Vega and Kaufman, 2013).

The *Insight on Society* case, *Marketing to Children of the Web in the Age of Social Networks,* illustrates some additional issues with respect to social marketing.

7.3 MOBILE MARKETING

Although still in its infancy, mobile marketing involves the use of mobile devices such as smartphones and tablet computers to display banner ads, rich media, video, games, e-mail, text messaging, in-store messaging, QuickResponse (QR) codes, and couponing. Over 90% of retail marketing professionals have plans for mobile marketing campaigns, and mobile is now a required part of the standard marketing budget. Mobile smartphones represent a radical departure from previous marketing technologies simply because the devices integrate so many human and consumer activities

INSIGHT ON SOCIETY

MARKETING TO CHILDREN OF THE WEB IN THE AGE OF SOCIAL NETWORKS

Children as young as three or four years old can often recognize brands and status items before they can even read, and almost 75% of four-year-olds generally ask their parents for specific brands. These findings are cause for celebration for some marketers. In the United States, estimates are that children influence over $1 trillion in overall family spending. In order to capture a portion of this spending and position themselves for future purchases as the child ages, marketers are becoming increasingly interested in advertising aimed at children.

Today, there are around 46 million children under the age of 18 online. Social and mobile marketing provides advertisers with an entirely new arsenal to influence children. What's in the arsenal? Here are some of the most common child-advertiser tools: mobile phone marketing, behavioral profiling, digital "360 buzz" campaigns, commercialized online communities, viral videos, game advertising, and avatar advertising. Using online custom banner ads, product characters, games, virtual worlds, and surveys, marketers are both influencing behaviors and gathering valuable data about purchasing preferences and family members. Coupled with in-bedroom televisions, video games, cell phones, and other digital paraphernalia, a children's digital culture has been created with built-in avenues to the psyche of young minds—in some cases, minds that are so young they are unlikely to know when they are being marketed to and when they are being given misleading or even harmful information.

Marketers have also moved aggressively to use online social networks and viral marketing to get kids hooked on brands early in life. For instance, Red Bull does little traditional TV advertising and instead uses Web-based contests, games, and apps such as Urban Futbol, an Angry Birds-like game app based on the Red Bull Balcony Shot events.

As another example, consider the Unilever product called AXE. AXE is a deodorant for young men. Unilever launched the product in the United States by posting online videos that supposedly showed the AXE effect: women chasing men who used AXE. The response was sensational: millions of people forwarded the videos to friends in a massive viral outpouring. Marketers also created an online game that allowed guys to indicate the kind of young woman they were interested in and get recommendations on which AXE fragrance to buy. You can bet that many of these postings and shared experiences were written by children. Using social networks, blogs, and YouTube, in a way much more powerful than earlier Web marketing to children, marketers are able to circumvent what few restrictions exist on marketing to children.

While such moves may be savvy marketing, are they ethical? Some people say no. Research has shown that young children cannot understand the potential effects of revealing their personal information; neither can they distinguish between substantive material on Web sites and the advertisements surrounding it. Experts argue that since children don't understand persuasive intent until they are eight or nine years old, it is unethical to advertise to them before they can distinguish between advertising and the real world. Others believe that fair advertising is an important and necessary part of the maturation process for future adults in today's society. But does that argument hold when children are gaining increased access to information about unhealthy activities, such as beer drinking through Web sites geared to a young adult audience? Although brewers admit they are targeting a younger market

(continued)

segment—twenty-somethings—they have set up warning screens and registration pages that require users to enter a birth date proving they are of legal drinking age. Of course, there is no process to verify such data, making it easy for underage consumers to gain access to, and be influenced by, entertaining content at drinking-oriented Web sites.

In 1998, Congress passed the Children's Online Privacy Protection Act (COPPA) after the FTC discovered that 80% of Web sites were collecting personal information from children, but only 1% required their parents' permission. Under COPPA, companies must post a privacy policy on their Web sites, detailing exactly how they collect information from consumers, how they'll use it, and the degrees to which they'll protect consumer privacy. Companies are not permitted to use personal information collected from children under 13 years of age without the prior, verifiable consent of parents. The FTC initially employed a sliding scale with respect to determining what constituted verifiable parental consent. If firms wanted to use the personal information of children for internal uses only, the FTC required an e-mail from the parent plus one other form of verification (such as a credit card or phone number). A stricter standard was required of firms who want to sell personal information about children. These Web sites were required to use one of the following means of verification in addition to an e-mail: a print-and-send consent form, credit card transaction, a toll-free number staffed by trained personnel, or an e-mail with a password or PIN.

Since the law took effect, the FTC has obtained a number of settlements and fined a number of companies for violations of COPPA. In October 2012, the operator of fan sites for Justin Bieber, Selena Gomez, Rihanna, and others agreed to pay a $1 million penalty for collecting personal information from children such as names, e-mail addresses, street addresses, and cell phone numbers without their parents' permission. Previously, in May 2011, Disney's Playdom was fined $3 million, the largest penalty to date, for collecting and disclosing children's information without parental approval. According to the FTC, many of Playdom's games, particularly Pony Stars, allowed children under the age of 13 to register at the site, and required that they share their ages and e-mail addresses during registration. The site then allowed those children to publicly post their full names, e-mail addresses, instant messenger IDs, and location on personal profile pages and in online community forums.

In August 2011, the FTC announced its first-ever COPPA enforcement action involving mobile apps. W3 Innovations, doing business as Broken Thumbs Apps, was fined $50,000 for collecting personal information such as e-mail addresses from children in connection with numerous apps, such as Emily's Girl World and Emily's Dress Up. Shortly thereafter, in response to the explosion in children's use of mobile devices, the proliferation of online social networks, and interactive gaming, the FTC announced long-awaited proposed revisions to its COPPA regulations , which finally took effect in July 2013. As the FTC chairman, Jon Leibowitz, noted, children may be "tech savvy, but judgment-poor." Privacy groups applaud the effort, but whether the new regulations will really affect the way Internet companies do business is not yet clear, and enforcement is likely to continue to be an issue.

SOURCES: "FTC to Better Define New COPPA 'Actual Knowledge' Standards," by John Eggerton, Broadcastingcable.com, July 8, 2013; "Child Privacy Online: FTC Updates COPPA Rules," by Mathew Schwartz, Informationweek.com, July 5, 2013; "Revised Children's Online Privacy Protection Rule Goes Into Effect Today," FTC.gov, July 1, 2013; "The Ripple Effects of Stricter Privacy Rules for Kids," by Bryon Acohido, USA Today, July 1, 2013; "Fan Sites for Pop Stars Settle Children's Privacy Charges," by Natasha Singer, New York Times, October 3, 2012; "FTC Announces First-Ever COPPA Enforcement Action Against Mobile Apps," by David Silverman, Privsecblog.com, August 17, 2011; "FTC Fine on App Developer Prompts Calls for Updated Privacy Policies," by Josh Smith, National Journal, August 15, 2011; "Marketing to Kids Gets More Savvy with New Technologies," by Martin E. Klimek, USA Today, July 27, 2011; "FTC: Disney's Playdom Violated Child Protection Act," by Don Reisinger, News.cnet.com, May 13, 2011; "Watchdog Group Calls For Stronger Online Child Privacy Law," by Mike Sachoff, Webpronews.com, April 29, 2010; "Virtual Worlds and Kids: Mapping the Risks. A Report to Congress," Federal Trade Commission, December 2009; "Ad It Up: Kids in a Commercial World," Federal Trade Commission, March 12, 2009.

from telephoning or texting friends, to listening to music, watching videos, and using the Web to shop and purchase goods. The more phones can do, the more people rely on them in daily life. More than 246 million Americans are now using mobile devices, while 140 million of these use smartphones (eMarketer, Inc., 2013d). One report found that people look at their mobile devices at least 40 times a day. Most mobile phone users keep the device within arm's length 24 hours a day. For many, it's the first thing they check in the morning, the last thing they check at night, and the first tool to use when there's a question of where to go, what to do, and where to meet up.

OVERVIEW: M-COMMERCE TODAY

It's a short number of steps from owning a smartphone or tablet, to searching for products and services, browsing, and then purchasing. The resulting mobile commerce is growing at over 50% a year, significantly faster than desktop e-commerce at 12% a year. The high rate of growth for mobile commerce will not, of course, continue forever, but analysts estimate that by 2017, mobile commerce will account for 18% of all e-commerce. **Figure 7.6** describes the expected growth of mobile commerce to 2017.

A study of the top 400 mobile firms by sales indicates that 73% of mobile commerce is for retail goods, 25% for travel, and 2% for ticket sales. **Figure 7.7** lists the top ten companies in terms of mobile sales in 2012. Not surprisingly, the giant is Amazon, with more than $4 billion in sales through its mobile Web site and Amazon

FIGURE 7.6   **THE GROWTH OF MOBILE COMMERCE**

Mobile commerce is expected to grow to over $100 billion by 2017.

SOURCE: Based on data from eMarketer, Inc., 2013e

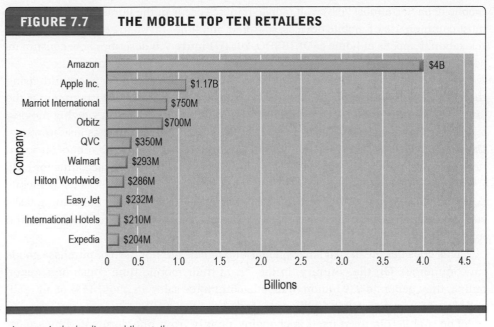

| FIGURE 7.7 | THE MOBILE TOP TEN RETAILERS |

Amazon is the leading mobile retailer.

SOURCE: Based on data from Internet Retailer, 2013.

app (Walmart is ranked #7 with $293 million in sales). Apple is second, primarily due to music and app sales for mobile devices. Hotels and travel companies play a surprisingly large role in the remaining top ten.

Increasingly, consumers are using their mobile devices to search for people, places, and things—like restaurants and deals on products they saw in a retail store. The rapid switch of consumers from desktop platforms to mobile devices is driving a surge in mobile marketing expenditures. Currently, about 25% of all search engine requests originate from mobile devices. Because search is so important for directing consumers to purchase situations, the mobile search advertising market is very important for search engines like Google and Bing. Desktop search revenues are slowing for both. While 25% of Google's searches come from mobile devices, mobile search ads generate only about $8 billion a year, only 16% of its overall ad revenue. Google's mobile ad business is growing rapidly, but the prices it can charge for mobile ads are far less than for desktop PC ads. The challenge facing Google and other mobile marketing firms is how to get more consumers to click on mobile ads, and how to charge marketers more for each click. And the answer lies with the consumer who decides what and when to click.

How People Actually Use Mobile Devices

If you plan a mobile marketing campaign, it's important to understand how people actually use their mobile devices (which may be different from what you do or think others do). For instance, most of us think people use their mobile devices on the go, moving about the city; but in fact, according to one of the very few studies of actual mobile behavior, almost 70% of all mobile minutes occur in the home. Over 75% of the most common use of mobile devices, so-called "me time" involving entertainment and relaxation, happens at home (AOL/BBDO, 2012). **Figure 7.8** describes how consumers actually use their mobile devices in terms of broad categories of activity.

On average, U.S. mobile users spend an estimated 1660 minutes per month using their devices (excluding phone calls, text messages, and e-mail). Entertainment is the largest single use, at 52% of user time (860 minutes). This includes viewing movies, television shows, shorter videos, or reading a gossip column, as well as just browsing. Users spend 25% of their mobile time (410 minutes) socializing with others on social network sites or blogs. Shopping (looking for specific goods to buy) accounts for only 7% of users' time (126 minutes). Actual purchasing of goods and services using mobile devices involves an estimated 3% of user time. Other uses include performing tasks such as online banking and investing (8%), planning trips (4%), reading news and magazines (3%), and hobbies (1%).

This does not mean that smartphones and tablets are not used to purchase goods (m-commerce). On the contrary, in the 7% of their mobile time consumers spend online, they generate $39 billion in mobile-commerce sales, or about 15% of all retail and travel e-commerce ($395 billion) (eMarketer, Inc., 2013f).

The mobile platform itself is changing rapidly from one dominated by smartphones to one dominated by tablets. The number of tablet users, once the newcomer to the mobile platform, is growing faster than the number of smartphone users in the

| FIGURE 7.8 | **HOW PEOPLE USE THEIR MOBILE DEVICES** |

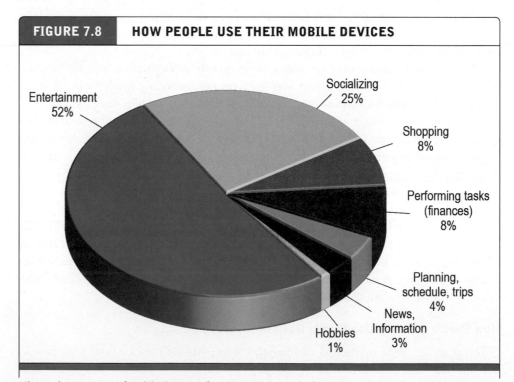

The predominant use of mobile devices is for entertainment and relaxation.

Source: Based on data from AOL/BBDO, 2012.

United States: 123 million Americans use tablets, about 50% of the Internet population, and their use is growing at about 30% annually although it will slow down to single digits by 2015. Tablets, with their larger screens, are the fastest growing and largest source of mobile commerce revenues (**Figure 7.9**)

In-App Experiences and In-App Ads

You may think that using a browser to access the Web on your smartphone is a typical mobile activity. In reality, however, mobile users spend over 80% of their mobile minutes using apps, and only 20% using their browsers. On average, users have downloaded about 40 apps, and regularly use about 15. There may be millions of apps on the iOS and Android cloud servers, but just a tiny handful are actually generating sufficient user traffic to be of interest to advertisers. Game and entertainment apps account for about 42% of user time, while social networks (Facebook and Twitter) take up about 31% of time). The remaining 25% of time is split among discovery and search apps (such as Google Search and apps for Yelp, Orbitz, and TripAdvisor) and apps by brands (Nike, RedBull, Jeep Mobile, Macys, and Amazon).

The implications for marketers are quite clear: if consumers are primarily using apps rather than browsing the Web on their mobile devices, marketers need to place ads in apps where most of the action is for attracting consumers. Second, if mobile consumers only use, on average, 15 apps, then marketers need to concentrate their marketing in these popular apps, let's say, the top 100. Niche marketers, on the other

FIGURE 7.9   **M-COMMERCE REVENUES BY DEVICE**

Tablet computers are the largest source of mobile commerce revenues.

SOURCE: Based on data from eMarketer, Inc., 2013h.

hand, can concentrate their ads in apps that support that niche. A distributor of diving equipment, for instance, could place ads in apps devoted to the diving community.

The implication for marketers is that rather than focus on mobile display ads that are difficult to read, the best ad may be an app that directly serves customer interest or an ad in an app that is precisely targeted to the consumer's current activities and interests. Highly targeted News Feed ads also benefit from relevance to users' current activities, which in part explains their effectiveness.

How the Multi-Screen Environment Changes the Marketing Funnel

Along with the growth of smartphones and tablets comes a multiscreen world: smartphones, tablets, desktops, and television. The reality, and the future, of computing devices is that consumers will be multi-platform: using desktops and laptops at work and home, and smartphones and tablets at home as well as when moving about. Television will be available all the time, both at home and on the go via tablets and smartphones. Consumer purchasing behavior changes in a multi-screen world. Consumers will often be using two or more screens at once, tweeting when watching a TV show, or moving seamlessly from a TV ad, to a mobile search for more information, to a later tablet purchase screen. Several research studies have found that 90% of multi-device users switch among screens to complete tasks, for instance, viewing an ad on TV, searching on a smartphone for the product, and then purchasing it with a tablet. Consumers move seamlessly among devices, either sequentially or simultaneously. Also, the more screens people use, the more shopping and purchasing they do. One conclusion is that the more screens consumers have, the more consumer touchpoints or marketing opportunities exist (Google, Inc., 2012).

The implications of the multi-device platform, or "screen diversity" environment, are that marketing needs to be designed for whatever device the consumer is using, and consistent branding across platforms will be important. Screen diversity means that one ad size, for instance, will not fit all situations, and that branding images will need to be adjusted automatically based on the device the consumer is using. From a design perspective, graphics and creative elements will appear differently depending on the screen. This is called "responsive design" or "responsive creative design." Responsive design is a Web design process that allows your marketing content to resize, reformat, and reorganize itself so that it looks good on any screen. You can see responsive design in action if you look at any portal on a desktop, and then compare the screen to that same portal viewed on a smartphone or tablet. You are likely to find there are three versions of the screen, one for each platform (IAB, 2012).

But even beyond screen adaptability, a multi-screen world means merchants need to be on all platforms, and to be integrated across platforms, in order to send a coherent message and to create a convenient consumer platform. The marketing environment today is much more complex than placing banner ads on pages or on search engine results pages on the Web.

Are Mobile Devices a Good Marketing Platform?

The answer is "Yes," but with some qualifications. Because consumers are so tightly coupled to their mobile devices, and the platform itself can support so many different types of media, it is a nearly ideal marketing environment. Fully 75% of mobile users are more likely to take action after seeing a relevant local ad; those who research products on their mobile devices are ready to buy; 70% take action within an hour, while 70% of people on desktop PCs take action within a week (Microsoft, 2011). What's more, 79% of shoppers use their mobile device to shop, and 70% of them use mobile devices in stores for price comparison and showrooming (Google/IPSOS OTX MediaCT, 2011).

BASIC MOBILE MARKETING FEATURES

As millions of consumers adopt mobile devices, mobile marketing expenditures have rapidly grown and in the next five years will equal marketing on desktop PCs. **Figure 7.10** illustrates how rapidly mobile marketing expenditures have grown, while marketing on desktops is slowing and will eventually decline.

In 2013, mobile marketing will be about 20% of all online marketing, which is extraordinary given that smartphones appeared only six years ago, in 2007, and tablets not until 2010. Analysts believe that if current mobile marketing growth rates continue, by 2017 mobile marketing will be 84% of all online advertising.

Mobile advertising is dominated by Google, with about $3.9 billion (54%) of mobile ad revenues generated by its search engine and YouTube. On the mobile platform, Google is king of search, garnering around 85% of all mobile searches. Google is also the largest video distributor on the mobile platform because of YouTube, earning about

| FIGURE 7.10 | MOBILE VERSUS DESKTOP MARKETING EXPENDITURES 2011–2017 |

Spending on mobile marketing is growing much more rapidly than spending on advertising aimed at desktop computers.

SOURCE: Based on data from eMarketer, Inc. 2013i.

75% of video play on mobile devices. Facebook is a very distant second with $1.1 billion (15%) of mobile ad revenues. Facebook is the leading display ad site on mobile devices, accounting for more than 80% of all mobile display ads. Unfortunately for Facebook, these ads sell for a fraction of what display ads sell for on desktop devices. In part this is because Facebook users do not respond well to advertising and marketing, and therefore do not have a high click rate. The problem is compounded by mobile Facebook users who have even less tolerance (and less screen space) for ads than is true of desktop Facebook users. Despite these difficulties, Facebook mobile ads have begun to gain traction, and generated significant revenues in the second quarter of 2013.

Other players in the mobile marketing marketplace are YP (5%) (previously known as the Yellow Pages, an AT&T telephone directory and online marketing business), the music service Pandora (5%), and Twitter, Apple, and Millennial, with less than 4% (see **Figure 7.11**).

The Technology: Basic Mobile Device Features

Everybody knows the capabilities of smartphones and tablets. But what is it about mobile platforms that make them any different from desktops? Are there any features that make them especially suitable for marketing? **Table 7.13** describes these basic features.

Smartphones today play a much more central role in the personal life of consumers than desktops and laptops in large part because smartphones are always physically with us, or close by. In this sense, they are more personal, and almost "wearable." The

FIGURE 7.11   THE TOP MOBILE MARKETING FIRMS BY REVENUE

Google: $3.9B
Facebook: $1.1B
Other : $981M
YP - $378M
Pandora: $375M
Twitter: $266M
Apple (iAd): $213M
Millenial: $94M

Mobile advertising is dominated by Google.
SOURCE: Based on data from eMarketer, Inc. 2013j.

TABLE 7.13	FEATURES OF MOBILE DEVICES
FEATURE	DESCRIPTION
Personal communicator and organizer	Telephone plus calendars and clocks to coordinate life on a personal scale.
Screen size and resolution	Resolution of both tablets and phones is high enough to support vibrant graphics and video.
GPS location	Self-locating GPS capability.
Web browser	Standard browsers will operate all Web sites and applications.
Apps	Over a million specialized applications running in native code and extending the functionality of mobile devices.
Ultraportable and personal	Fits into a pocket, or a briefcase for tablets, able to be used anywhere and on the go.
Multimedia capable: video, audio, text	Fully capable of displaying all common media from video to text and sound.

"always on, always with us" nature of smartphones has several implications for marketers. Because they are perceived as "personal appendages," consumers are less tolerant of commercial intrusion. Have you ever had a telephone conversation interrupted by an advertisement? You probably have not, and if so, you most likely would be annoyed at the interference with a personal conversation. These attitudes extend to any use of the phone or tablet, from reading e-mail, visiting Facebook, or watching a video. Consumers are simply less tolerant of advertising on the small screens of smartphones. Second, the around-the-clock physical proximity of smartphones to our persons greatly expands the time available for marketing materials and increases the supply of screens for marketing materials. This excess supply decreases the price of mobile marketing messages. In turn, there is a tension between marketers and consumers: marketers want to increase the number of mobile ads, while consumers want to see fewer ads, not more, on their mobile devices. Ads inside apps are treated differently by consumers: in return for a free game, consumers are more accepting of ads.

But perhaps the most unique feature of smartphones is that they know users' precise location by virtue of their built-in GPS. This allows marketing messages to be targeted to consumers on the basis of their location, and supports the introduction of location-based marketing and local marketing (described in Section 7.4). While Web sites may know a desktop's general location, it is a very imprecise fix, and the position of the desktop does not change as the user moves about.

MOBILE MARKETING TOOLS: AD FORMATS

Unlike social marketing, mobile marketing does not require much of a new marketing vocabulary. All the marketing formats available on the desktop are also available on mobile devices. With few exceptions, mobile marketing is very much like desktop marketing—except it is smaller. The major marketing opportunities in mobile market-ing are search ads, display ads, videos and rich media, messaging (SMS/MMS/PPS), and some familiar other formats like e-mail, classified, and lead generation. **Figure 7.12** illustrates the relative size of mobile marketing expenditures by format. The marketing formats on mobile devices are search ads, display, video, text/video mes-saging, and other (including e-mail and sponsorships).

In 2013, search engine advertising was the most popular mobile marketing format, accounting for 52% of all mobile ad spending, not surprising given that search is the second most common smartphone application (after voice and text communication). Search engine ads can be further optimized for the mobile platform by showing ads based on the physical location of the user. Display ads are the second leading ad format, accounting for about 37% of mobile ad spending. Display ads can be served as a part of a mobile Web site or inside apps and games. Ad networks such as Google's AdMob, Facebook, Apple's iAd, and MillennialMedia are the largest providers of mobile display advertising. Video and rich media ads are only 7% of mobile marketing, but are a fast growing segment because of their very high click rates. Most desktop video ads can be resized for use on mobile phones and tablets. Mobile messaging generally involves SMS text messaging to consumers, with coupons or flash marketing messages. Messaging is especially effective for local advertising because consumers can be sent messages and coupons as they pass by or visit locations (see Section 7.4).

Social networks such as Facebook, Twitter, and Pinterest have generally brought their desktop advertising techniques over to the mobile platform, with some alterations of the interface for use on small-screen smartphones. In the process, social networks

| FIGURE 7.12 | U.S. MOBILE AD SPENDING BY FORMAT |

Display $2.86B · Video $518M · SMS $216M · Others $100M · Search $3.95B

Search engine advertising is the most popular mobile marketing format.
SOURCE: Based on data from eMarketer, Inc. 2013k.

TABLE 7.14	SELECTED MOBILE MARKETING CAMPAIGNS
COMPANY	CAMPAIGN
Walmart	Company-wide mobile strategy using mobile applications, mobile Web, augmented reality, mobile advertising, mobile bar codes, social media, location-based services, and push notifications.
eBay	Multiple apps for deals, clothing, and flagship brand app eBay Mobile. $10 billion in mobile sales and $10 billion in mobile PayPal transactions.
OfficeMax	Uses iPhone and Android platforms for loyalty marketing and daily deals.
RueLaLa	Flash sales site for luxury clothing using SMS and Facebook mobile ads saw mobile sales increase to 40% of all online sales.
Ikea	Uses the Apple iAd platform to display banner ads promoting the Ikea catalog.
Starbucks	Early adopter of mobile marketing, now using a number of apps (company app, augmented reality app, and the Square Wallet mobile payment app) along with SMS and QR code campaigns to reach out to customers.

have brought real innovation to the mobile marketing experience, including Sponsored Stories and News Feed posts on Facebook, and Promoted Tweets in Twitter. **Table 7.14** provides selected examples of mobile marketing campaigns and techniques used by several well-known firms.

Mobile marketing is uniquely suited for branding purposes, raising awareness through the use of video and rich interactive media such as games. Read the *Insight on Business* case, *Mobile Marketing: Land Rover Seeks Engagement on the Small Screen*, for a further look.

STARTING A MOBILE MARKETING CAMPAIGN

As with all marketing campaigns, start by identifying your objectives and understanding just how a mobile marketing campaign might help your firm. Are you a new unknown start-up seeking to develop a brand image, or an already existing brand looking to strengthen your presence and sell products? Is there something about your products that makes them especially attractive to a mobile audience? For instance, if you sell to local customers walking by your shop, then you might want to use the GPS capabilities of smartphones to target consumers who are nearby.

Next, consider the target demographic for your campaign and products. The most active purchasers on smartphones are men (45% vs. 34%), and they are more likely to buy consumer electronics equipment and digital content. Women are more likely to cash in coupons and respond to flash sales and deals. Younger consumers are more likely to research products and price on mobile devices, and more likely to share experiences using social media. Mobile shoppers and buyers are more affluent than the online population in general. These demographics are averages, and mobile marketing campaigns do not need to restrict themselves to these averages. Find out where your mobile customers are congregating. Are your mobile customers likely to be using apps,

INSIGHT ON BUSINESS

MOBILE MARKETING: LAND ROVER SEEKS ENGAGEMENT ON THE SMALL SCREEN

Why is mobile marketing any different from ordinary online marketing? In one sense, it isn't. The same kinds of ad formats you find on Web sites are also used on smartphones—in order of importance, search, display, video, and text messages. In another sense, mobile marketing can be very different from other types of online marketing because of the unique features of the smartphone, which include a built-in GPS, a gyroscope, and an accelerometer. This means marketers can know the location of the user, and they can present rich media and video ads where the user can control the action in a way not possible with an ordinary PC. Smartphones use a touch interface, which increases user involvement. Mobile ads can therefore be more engaging and interactive than traditional PC ads. Location information can be used to market local businesses at the very point of consumer purchase, namely, on the street or in the store while browsing. Other unique smartphone features are that people almost always carry them and keep them turned on while moving about. This means that smartphone users can be exposed to marketing messages throughout the day (and sometimes the night). Of course, smartphones have limitations as well. The screens are much smaller than tablets and laptops, making it difficult to squeeze ads onto the screen when the user is looking at other content. Expectations are important as well: unlike "free" advertising-supported Web sites, consumers pay for cell phone service and may not wish to be annoyed by bothersome ads interrupting their service and consuming valuable screen real estate.

Mobile devices are used by consumers throughout the purchase cycle: over 50% of smartphone users research products before entering a store and 36% use their phones in retail stores. The use of mobile devices to actually purchase products online (as opposed to just shopping and browsing online) is also growing commensurately. U.S. mobile commerce grew by more than 55% to $39 billion in 2013, and is expected to grow to around $110 billion by 2017.

About 60% of the 118 million mobile online shoppers buy something using their devices, compared to more than 80% of desktop PC shoppers who purchase online. In part, the lower percentage of mobile purchasers reflects the novelty and comfort level of consumers, as well as the fact that many online retailers still do not have fully mobile Web sites or apps, and instead offer only their standard Web pages to mobile users. Many consumers feel the small screens on smartphones prevent them from examining retail products closely, and using a credit card with a smartphone is difficult. But this situation will change in the next few years as mobile commerce equals and exceeds desktop commerce. For certain goods that the consumer is familiar with, for sites that have an easy-to-use one-click shopping capability, and for purchases of content like books and movies, mobile purchasing can be convenient. Also, for local marketing, mobile is an ideal platform for merchants to attract consumers in the neighborhood. Restaurants, museums, and entertainment venues are ideal candidates to use mobile marketing aimed at local consumers. What attracts users to mobile purchasing is the ability to access product information now, find deals, and buy all with the swipe of a finger. But mobile is also good for introducing new

(continued)

products and building brand recognition, with sales taking place elsewhere and offline.

A good example of the use of mobile devices for marketing is Land Rover's use of Apple's iAd platform to introduce the Range Rover Evoque to a new audience in 2012 and 2013. The Range Rover Evoque (pronounced e-voke) is a compact SUV aimed at young urban buyers. Land Rover is known for its line of very luxurious and expensive SUVs that appeal to an older consumer. The Evoque is a smaller, more fuel-efficient, less-polluting SUV than its much larger luxury SUV cousins. Land Rover wanted to introduce the car to an entirely new demographic: young affluents. The problem was how to introduce this new concept for Land Rover to an audience that most likely never intended to buy a Land Rover.

Land Rover worked with Mindshare (an Internet marketing firm), Y&R Group (a New York-based marketing firm), and Apple's iAd Network team to build an immersive and engaging interactive app that would allow consumers to explore and configure the interior and exterior of the car using the finger gestures of the iPhone. Users are shown a mobile ad on their cell phones, and tapping the ad, they are taken to the Land Rover app to explore the car. iAd used iTunes-based targeting to pinpoint the right audience based on the kinds of music they liked to listen to. The music people listen to on iTunes, or select as favorites, provides clues to their age, personal tastes, passions, and interests. Demographic data was also available. The ad could be shown at several points, but the most effective was showing the ad when consumers were using their favorite apps. When using apps, a person's attention and engagement is quite high.

Using Land Rover's configuration app, customers can change the Evoque's body style, color, and wheels. They can take a photo of the car and send it to others by e-mail or SMS. There's an immersive 360-degree view of the interior that puts viewers inside the car. Using the iPhone's built-in gyroscope and accelerometer, viewers can tilt and turn the device to see a 360-view of the interior.

According to Land Rover, the iAd mobile marketing effort has been a success. As one Land Rover marketer noted, there's a difference between looking at a 30-second TV commercial, and someone using their iPhone to explore a new product. With the mobile ad, people are more engaged, in control, and attentive to the message. On average, people spent on average nearly 80 seconds whenever they engaged with the ad, nearly three times longer than a typical TV commercial.

In 2013, Land Rover built on its mobile platform by adding a mobile application called The Trail Less Traveled to showcase its new Range Rover through an interactive online journey using four synced camera angles. Users can select their own route through an interactive map, advance to different stages of the journey, and even pause the experience to explore pictures and videos of the latest engineering advancements in the vehicle. The app allows users to take a journey with the Range Rover, explore its on-road and off-road capabilities, and experience the vehicle's interior and exterior features. The app takes the driver through scenery, then switches instantly from wide camera angles to tight close-ups and even the driver's point-of-view, all to provide an authentic Range Rover driving experience.

SOURCES: : "Land Rover Flaunts New Range Rover Vehicle via Interactive Mobile App," by Rimma Kats, Luxurydaily.com, May 6, 2013; "Social Media Marketing on Mobile Devices," by Debra Aho Williamson, eMarketer, Inc.; January 2013; "Retail Mobile Commerce Forecast," by Cathy Boyle, *eMarketer, Inc.,* January 2013; "Twitter's Mobile Ads Begin to Click," by ShiraOvide, *Wall Street Journal,* June 28, 2012; "Land Rover Reaches New Audience with iAd for Brands," Apple Inc., 2012; "Land Rover iAd Campaign Delivers Highest Engagement Levels," by Chantal Tode, *Mobile Marketer,* August 8, 2012; "Majority of US Smartphone Owners Use Devices to Aid Shopping," eMarketer, Inc., April 12, 2012; "The Effect of Mobile On the Path to Purchase," eMarketer, Inc., February 29, 2012.

and if so, what are they? Are your customers likely to be on Facebook or use Twitter? Or are your customers most likely to find you on a Google mobile search page?

Finally, consider the marketspace where you hope to succeed. What are your competitors doing on the mobile platform? Is their presence effective? Where do they place their marketing efforts: display ads on Web portals, or display ads in Google search results? Or can they be found as in-app ads? What apps are they advertising in? How are they represented on Facebook Mobile? Do they also have a Twitter and/ or Pinterest brand page? Do your competitors have an app that users can easily download? You'll want to be able to meet your competitors on each of the platforms they have adopted. Once you've developed an initial vision for your marketing campaign, you can develop a timeline and an action plan of how to meet the milestones identified in your timeline.

Once you have envisioned your marketing campaign and identified your market, it is time to start implementing your mobile campaign. Here are some steps to follow:

- Develop a mobile Web site so mobile consumers can see and buy your products. Make your mobile Web site social by including Facebook, Twitter, Pinterest, and other social site links.

- Develop a Facebook brand page so your social and mobile marketing efforts are integrated.

- Develop a Twitter brand page so customers can follow your posts.

- If you already use a display advertising program like Google's AdWords or a Facebook display ad account, you can create a new campaign using the same ads designed specifically for mobile platforms.

- Consider opening an iAd account and using Apple's iAd network or Google's AdMob in part because these ad networks can publish and track your ads on multiple platforms simultaneously.

- Develop marketing content that is aimed specifically at the mobile user, with videos and high levels of interactivity designed for the mobile screen.

- Measure and manage your campaign. iAd and AdWords, along with many other ad networks, will host and manage your mobile campaigns. In addition, they can provide you with a host of campaign measures that will allow you to see which mobile ads and techniques are attracting the most followers, comments, and social activity concerning your brand. With this basic data you can start to manage the mobile marketing campaign by reducing expenditures on ads that do not work and increasing the budget of ads that do work.

MEASURING MOBILE MARKETING RESULTS

There are many different mobile marketing objectives, and therefore different types of mobile marketing campaigns. Some campaigns are sales-oriented, based on display and search ads, offering coupons or discounts, and taking users directly to a Web site where they can buy something. Measuring the results of these mobile campaigns follows similar campaigns launched on desktops. Other campaigns focus on branding, where the objective is to engage consumers in a conversation, acquire them as fans, and spread the word among their friends. You can use the framework from Figure 7.5 on page 419 to measure the results of these campaigns. The key dimensions to measure for mobile social campaigns are fan acquisition, engagement, amplification, community, brand strength (center of conversation), and sales.

Figure 7.13 illustrates how a brand-oriented marketing campaign utilizing the mobile platform and social marketing might present its effectiveness measures over a six-month period. In a branding campaign, the object is not so much sales as it is strengthening consumers' engagement with the brand. In the example provided in Figure 7.13, acquiring fans is measured by the number of unique visitors. Here you can see that over six months, visitors have risen over 60%. Engagement is reflected in the time on-site (in thousands of minutes); amplification is measured by the number of Likes, and this has expanded threefold. Community is measured by the number of posts, suggesting fans are actively engaging with one another and the brand. Posts have risen eightfold in the period. Brand strength is best summarized in this figure as the composite picture of fan acquisition, engagement, amplification, and community measures. Measuring the impacts of this mobile campaign on ultimate sales requires going a step further and measuring which sales can be attributed to this mobile campaign.

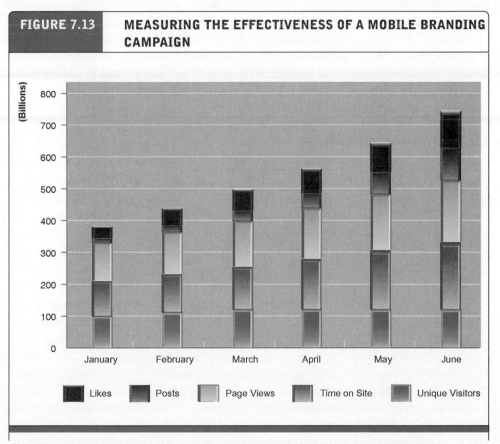

FIGURE 7.13 | **MEASURING THE EFFECTIVENESS OF A MOBILE BRANDING CAMPAIGN**

The effectiveness of a branding campaign utilizing the mobile platform and social marketing can be measured by examining the number of Likes, posts, page views, time on site, and unique visitors.

7.4   LOCAL AND LOCATION-BASED MARKETING

location-based marketing
targets marketing messages to users based on their location

location-based services
involve providing services to users based on their location

Location-based mobile marketing is the newest and fastest growing segment of the digital marketing universe. **Location-based marketing** targets marketing messages to users based on their location. Generally, location-based marketing involves marketing of location-based services. **Location-based services** involve providing services to users based on their location. Examples of location-based services are: personal navigation (How do I get there?), point-of-interest (What's that?), reviews (What's the best restaurant in the neighborhood?), friend-finder (Where are you? Where's the crowd?), and family-tracker services (Where is my child?). There is a connection of course: the more people use their mobile devices to search for and obtain local services, the more opportunities there are for marketers to target consumers with messages at just the right moment, at just the right location, and in just the right way—not too pushy and annoying, but in a way to improve the consumer experience at the moment of local shopping and buying. This is the ideal in any event. Location-based marketing can take place on a desktop as well because browsers and marketers know your approximate location. But in this section we focus on mobile location-based marketing, which is where the greatest growth and opportunities lie.

Experience and market research suggest that consumers want local ads, offers, information, and content. Consumers have a high likelihood of acting on local ads and purchasing the products and services offered. Because it has evolved so rapidly in the last five years, experience and research with respect to location-based marketing is a work in progress with many different platforms, providers, and techniques. Measures of effectiveness and returns on investment are being developed.

THE GROWTH OF LOCAL MOBILE MARKETING

Prior to the release of Google Maps in 2005, nearly all local advertising was non-digital and provided by local newspapers, radio and television stations, local yellow pages, and billboards. Of course, some was digital, involving the Web sites of local merchants. Today, total media ad spending in the United States is $170 billion, and approximately $130 billion of this is local media spending by both national and local brands. An estimated one-quarter of this local advertising (about $42 billion) involves truly local firms like restaurants, grocery stores, theaters, and shoe stores marketing to their local audience. The remaining three-quarters of local media marketing involves large national firms marketing to local audiences, such as an ad for Coca Cola in a local newspaper or Web sites created for local auto dealers by national firms.

After the introduction of Google Maps in 2005 and smartphones in 2007, online local marketing began to rapidly expand. Google Maps on desktop computers enabled the targeting of ads to users based on a general sense of their IP address and enabled merchants to display ads to users based on the general location of potential customers, usually within a several square-mile radius. IP addresses can be used to identify a city, and a neighborhood within the city, but not a zip code, street, or building. Google Maps helped users answer the question "Where can I find an Italian restaurant" in a city or section of a city from their desktop. The arrival of smartphones in 2007, and Google's mobile maps app, took this one step further. The GPS receivers in second-generation smartphones introduced in 2008 (Apple's 3G iPhone), along with other techniques, meant that a user's location (latitude and longitude) could be fairly well known by cell phone manufacturers, marketers, service providers, and carriers like AT&T and Verizon. These developments opened an entirely new growth path for local online advertising that heretofore had been confined to the desktop. In this new world, a local food market could shout out to mobile phone users as they walked by the store, offering discounts to responders, and users in turn could search for specific retail stores nearby, even checking their inventory before walking into the store.

THE GROWTH OF LOCATION-BASED MOBILE MARKETING

Location-based mobile marketing is currently a very small part of the online marketing environment, but it is doubling in the next two years, far faster than any other form of digital advertising. **Figure 7.14** helps put the location-based mobile market in perspective. In 2013, total online marketing is $42 billion and local online marketing is a healthy and surprisingly large $27.6 billion. The part of local online that is mobile (referred to as mobile local marketing) is $5.4 billion, and the part of local mobile that is targeted by location (location-based marketing) is $2.3 billion.

While small in an absolute sense, as mobile devices replace PCs and become the dominant location where consumers spend their time, mobile marketing and

---

FIGURE 7.14 | **LOCAL, MOBILE LOCAL, AND LOCATION-BASED MOBILE MARKETING**

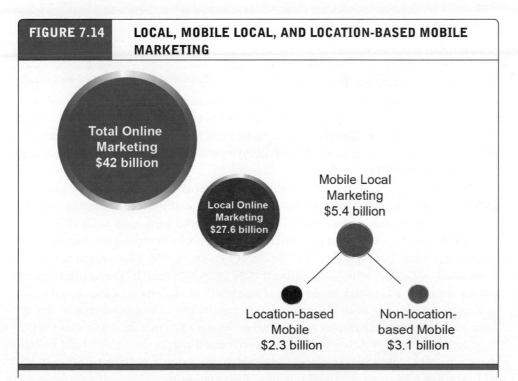

Local online marketing accounts for $27.6 billion in marketing expenditures in 2013, with mobile accounting for $5.4 billion of that amount..

FIGURE 7.15 THE GROWTH OF LOCATION-BASED MARKETING

Both location-based marketing and nontargeted, nonlocation-based marketing are expected to grow rapidly from 2013 to 2017.

SOURCE: Based on data from eMarketer, Inc., 2013l.

location-based mobile marketing will expand at a torrid pace. **Figure 7.15** illustrates the future trajectory of mobile local and location-based marketing. Location-based marketing in 2013 is $2.3 billion, but is expected to increase four times to $9 billion by 2017. Nontargeted, nonlocation-based mobile will also grow rapidly, to $7.7 billion. At that point, local mobile marketing of all types will be 30% of all online marketing (up from 12% in 2013).

The ad formats used in local mobile marketing are familiar—search ads, display, SMS text messages, and videos. A very large percentage of these local mobile ads will be delivered by search engines such as Google and social sites such as Facebook.

Search ads displayed as a part of user search results comprise the largest local mobile ad format, generating $1.3 billion in 2013. The mobile local search market is dominated by Google, which accounts for 80% of mobile search. The second largest format is display ads, which might appear as a result of clicking on a Sponsored Story in Facebook's News Feed or a Promoted Tweet on Twitter. Facebook accounts for an estimated 34% of mobile display ads. Videos are expected to increase their share of the local mobile market, but they still will remain a small part of the overall local mobile market in 2017. The primary platform for video ads today is YouTube. SMS text ads will continue to play a very small role in mobile marketing.

LOCATION-BASED MARKETING PLATFORMS

The key players in location-based mobile marketing are the same giants who dominate the mobile marketing environment described in a previous section, namely, Google, Facebook, Apple, Twitter, YP (formerly Yellow Pages), Pandora, and Millenial. **Figure 7.16** illustrates the annual location-based revenues by firm. Google generates 50% of the $3 billion in location-based marketing revenue in the United States and even more worldwide. Google is clearly the leading location-based marketer largely because of its widely used Google Maps app on smartphones. When a consumer searches for a location on Google Maps, it is an ideal marketing moment to pop an ad before the consumer's eyes. Google Places is a simple but effective service that provides short business profiles when users search for a specific business. Google's Android operating system has location functionality built into the system, and Google apps, like Google Maps, continuously update the user's location. Google purchased a mobile advertising firm called AdMob in 2009 and claims to be the world's largest mobile advertising firm for both Android and Apple's iOS operating systems. App developers use AdMob to provide their apps with consumer and user location information. Google also sells location information to independent marketing firms. Marketing firms use AdMob to develop full-screen rich media ads. Google's main revenue stream comes from its AdWords service, where marketers bid for keywords on Google's search engine. AdWords used to be the same whether displayed on a PC or a mobile device. Google has upgraded its AdWords service to optimize ads for user contexts and devices, and

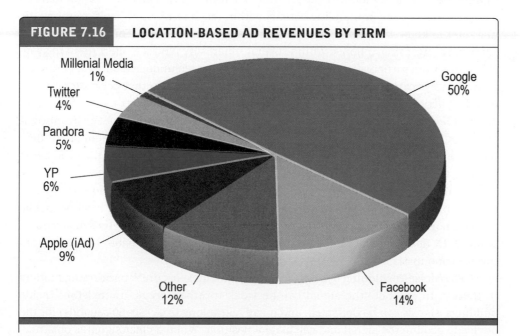

FIGURE 7.16   LOCATION-BASED AD REVENUES BY FIRM

Millenial Media 1%
Twitter 4%
Pandora 5%
YP 6%
Apple (iAd) 9%
Other 12%
Facebook 14%
Google 50%

Google dominates location-based mobile marketing.

SOURCES: Based on data from various company reports, 2012 and 2013; eMarketer, Inc., 2013m.

to provide management of campaigns across all mobile and desktop devices. The new service is called Enhanced AdWords. For instance, if a customer searches for "pizza" on a desktop PC from work at 1 PM, he or she would be shown restaurants nearby and a quick order form. If the customer searched for "pizza" at 8 PM on a smartphone within a half-mile of a pizza restaurant, he or she might be shown a click-to-call phone number and directions to the restaurant. Pizza restaurants pay Google for the chance to show up in these searches.

Google and Apple have advantages in the location-based market: they both have developed extensive maps of Wi-Fi networks throughout the world, allowing them to develop much more precise location information than competitors.

Apple's mobile platform iAd provides location data to iOS app developers and mobile marketing firms. Like AdMob, when users click on an iAd ad, a full-screen ad appears within the app they are using. The ad can be targeted to the user's location. Facebook was late to the mobile marketing but in two years it has gone from zero mobile advertising to $2 billion worldwide and $1.1 billion in the United States in 2013. Around 40% of Facebook's users access the site using mobile devices. Facebook's strength is showing display ads to its over 1 billion users worldwide.

LOCATION-BASED MOBILE MARKETING: THE TECHNOLOGIES

Location-based services and marketing require marketers and local service providers to have a fairly precise idea of where consumer mobile devices are located. There are two general types of location-based marketing techniques: geo-aware and geo-fencing. **Geo-aware** techniques identify the location of a user's device and then target marketing to the device, recommending actions within reach (which, in itself, requires the marketer to know where relevant things like stores are located). For instance, a marketer may target smartphones within several square city blocks to alert them to available offers from participating merchants. **Geo-fencing** techniques identify a perimeter around a physical location, and then target ads to users within that perimeter, recommending actions possible within the fenced-in area. The perimeter can be from hundreds of feet (in urban areas) to several miles (in suburban locations). For instance, if users walk into the geo-fenced perimeter of a store, restaurant, or retail shop, they will receive ads from these businesses. Both of these techniques utilize the same locating technologies.

Ad networks, local-mobile marketing firms, providers of devices and services like Google and Apple, as well as phone companies use several methods for locating mobile devices, none of which are perfect, and all of which have varying degrees of accuracy. **Table 7.15** describes the major locating technologies used to enable location-based services and marketing.

GPS (Global Positioning System) location is the most accurate positioning method in theory. In practice, the signal can be weak in urban areas, nonexistent inside buildings, signals can be deflected, and it can take a long time (30–60 seconds) for the device to acquire the signal and calculate a position. When a clear signal is obtained, GPS can be accurate to within 3–10 meters under ideal conditions, but more frequently, a cell phone's GPS is accurate only to within 50 meters—half a football field. Also, users have to activate the feature, and many do not for privacy reasons. Assisted

Geo-aware

techniques that identify the location of a user's device and then target marketing to the device

Geo-fencing

techniques that identify a perimeter around a physical location, and then target ads to users within that perimeter, recommending actions possible within the fenced-in area

TABLE 7.15	MAJOR LOCATING TECHNOLOGIES
TECHNOLOGY	DESCRIPTION
GPS	The user's device downloads GPS data from a GPS satellite. First introduced with the Apple 3G in 2008. Today, cellphones are required to broadcast their GPS location for emergency assistance purposes.
Wi-Fi	Estimates user's location within a radius of a known Wi-Fi access point.
Geo-search	Uses location information based on the user's search queries.
Cell tower	AT&T, Verizon, and other carriers are in constant contact with their devices, which allows approximation of location by triangulation and refinement of the unit's GPS location. Wireless carriers use a cell phone's MAC address to identify the phone and the location.
Sign in/registration	Estimates users' location when they self-identify their location using sign-in services or social network posts.

GPS (A-GPS) supplements GPS information with other information from the phone network to speed up acquisition. Nearly all smartphones use A-GPS. In Apple's iOS, users can decide whether to turn Location Services on or off. When turned on, the iOS uses GPS, cellular, and Wi-Fi networks to determine the user's approximate location to within 10 meters (30 feet). The user's iPhone continuously reports its position and reports to Apple servers.

Cell tower location is used by wireless telephone carriers to track the location of their devices, which is required to complete phone calls as devices pass from the range of one tower into the range of another. Cell tower location is also the basis of the wireless emergency response system in the United States. The FCC's wireless Enhanced 9-1-1 (E9-1-1) rules require wireless carriers to track cellphone locations whether or not the user has turned on location services in order to assist emergency responders in locating users who make 911 calls.

Wi-Fi location is used in conjunction with GPS signals to more accurately locate a user based on the known location of Wi-Fi transmitters, which are fairly ubiquitous in urban and suburban locations. Apple, Google, and other mobile service providers have developed global databases of wireless access points simply by driving cars around urban areas in much of the world. Google uses Street View cars to build a global database of wireless access points and their geographic location. Android applications can use this database to determine the approximate location of individuals based on the Wi-Fi networks detected by their mobile devices. All Wi-Fi devices continuously monitor the presence of local Wi-Fi networks, and mobile devices report back this data to Apple and Microsoft, along with other device manufacturers, who use similar methods. The goal of these technologies is to provide consumers and marketers with "micro-location data" accurate to within a few feet to support truly real-time, accurate, local marketing at the personal level. For instance, if you are looking at a rack of dress shirts in a retail store, an accurate positioning system could detect this, and direct you to appropriate accessories like socks and ties on surrounding shelves.

WHY IS LOCAL MOBILE ATTRACTIVE TO MARKETERS?

Consumers who seek information about local businesses using mobile devices are much more active and ready to purchase than desktop users. In part this is because desktop searchers for local information are not in as close proximity to merchants as are mobile searchers. Three-quarters of mobile users are more likely to take action after seeing a relevant local ad (Microsoft, 2011). Almost half of all mobile searches are for location-aware information. The percentage of smartphone users who have used their phones for proximity searches on information (e.g., local weather), products, and services is even higher: 95%. Over 69% have contacted a business after accessing that information and 36% have made a purchase on that connection (Google/IPSOS OTX Media CT, 2011). Research from comScore indicates that around 40% of U.S. Internet users search for local businesses at least once a week, so it's no surprise that search engine advertising is the most popular local mobile advertising format (comScore, 2012).

LOCATION-BASED MARKETING TOOLS

Location-based digital marketing, like social marketing, presents students of digital marketing with a confusing array of new services, platforms, and firms that provide these services. While some local-based marketing techniques, like placing ads on Google's AdSense platform aimed at mobile customers, are relatively easy to establish for the small business owner, others require the help of mobile marketing provider firms.

A New Lexicon: Location-Based Digital Marketing Features

Location-based services involve providing services to users based on their location. Examples include personal navigation, point-of-interest, reviews, friend-finder, and family-tracker services. **Table 7.16** describes how some of these features can be used for marketing.

Local Marketing Ad Formats

While location-based marketing is unique because it is targeted to individuals based on their location, the same types of ad formats used in desktop marketing are also used in location-based marketing. **Figure 7.17** illustrates the types of ads that are used and the percentage of revenue that each type generates.

Of the estimated $2.3 billion in location-based marketing spending in 2013, nearly 60% ($1.3 billion) is for Google search ads. The most common use of mobile devices is to search for directions or locations of places, and Google's Map app dominates this market. Display ads will constitute about 32% ($700 million) of location-based ads. Here the main players are Facebook and Google. With over 200 million users in the United States, and more than 40% of this audience using mobile devices (although not exclusively) to access the service, Facebook is the dominant mobile display ad provider, delivering three times as many display ads as Google. However, this dominance in

TABLE 7.16	LOCATION-BASED MARKETING TOOLS AND CAMPAIGNS
LOCATION-BASED MARKETING TOOLS	DESCRIPTION
Geo-social-based services marketing	Users share their location with friends. Can be used for check-in services like Foursquare; friend finders; transportation services.
Location-based services marketing	Provides services to consumers looking for local services and products.
Mobile-local social network marketing based on users' location	Facebook expands local offerings of deals by local firms, display ads using News Feed. Discount offers from a Gap store when claimed are broadcast to friends.
	Google+ Local. Connecting users with local businesses. Users can conduct searches within a local area and get Zagat reviews.
	Upgraded Foursquare app focuses on social updates but also recommendations and deals.
	Social network monitoring: sends messages within an app based on mentions of interest in products in Facebook and Twitter posts. Used by H&M.
	Intent marketing: scanning social networks for indications of real-time consumer interest in specific products. H&M partnered with LocalResponse to promote clothing inspired by the movie "Girl With the Dragon Tattoo."
Geo-fencing/Geo-targeting	Send messages to consumers in the area of a store or outlet to generate sales using a virtual fence around a retail location (could also be an airport, train station, or arena). Generally opt in. Miller Coors created a geo-fence around 28 US airports to alert Blue Moon beer fans on where it could be purchased.
In-store messaging	Messaging consumers while entering or browsing in a store. Retailers collect, analyze, and respond to customers' real-time shopping behavior.
Location-based app messaging	American Express MyOffersapp presents cardholders with personalized deals based on their location.

display is changing as Google's AdMob program gains ground, and over time challenges Facebook. Together, Google and Facebook account for 70% of location-based mobile marketing.

Text messaging generated 5% of mobile marketing spending, but it has not achieved credible market share, and consumer resistance to "text spam" has made the ads very ineffective and of little market value. Videos generate 4% ($100 million) of mobile ad spending, and this format is growing rapidly. Once again, Google dominates this ad format with its YouTube service.

STARTING A LOCATION-BASED MARKETING CAMPAIGN

As with all marketing campaigns, start by identifying your objectives and understand just how a location-based mobile marketing campaign might help your business.

FIGURE 7.17   **LOCATION-BASED MOBILE AD FORMAT SPENDING**

Search is the leading location-based mobile ad format.
SOURCE: Based on data from eMarketer, Inc., 2013n.

Location-based marketing is generally much more action-oriented than other forms of online marketing. A person is in a given location only for a short time, measured in minutes and hours, rarely days or weeks. If you want the consumer to do something, it's now. Does your product or service have this quality? Is there something related to a person's location that fits with your product? Is there something about your products that makes them especially attractive to a mobile audience at a specific location and time? There are very few products and services that don't have a location connection.

Next, consider the target demographic for your campaign and products. Location-aware consumers (those with mobile devices and familiar with location-based services) tend to be a younger, more educated, and wealthier demographic. They have many of the same characteristics as all mobile shoppers.

A strategic analysis of your marketspace is very important. The same questions that you would seek to answer if you were doing a nonlocation-aware mobile marketing campaign apply to a location-based marketing effort, such as examining what your competitors are doing. See page 457 for further issues you should consider.

Once you have envisioned your marketing campaign and identified your market, it is time to start implementing your mobile campaign. The same steps that you would follow in implementing a mobile campaign apply to location-based marketing as well. Note that you can't do everything at once—mobile-centric and location-based. Start by doing something simple like local search. Then consider more sophisticated local-based marketing tactics.

MEASURING LOCATION-BASED MARKETING RESULTS

There are a great many ways to measure the success of a mobile location-based campaign, some very sophisticated. The measures of success will vary depending on the objective of the campaign, which might be to raise the awareness of your brand among consumers, to bring customers to your retail store, or a click-to-call campaign where you want people to make reservations for a concert.

Because mobile local campaigns use the same marketing ad formats as both traditional and mobile Web marketing, the basic measures of effectiveness are similar (see Figure 7.13). For instance, the number of impressions (people who see an ad), click-through rate, and unique visitors are basic measures for a mobile local campaign. But mobile location-based marketing is much more personal and social than traditional Web marketing or even simple mobile marketing: it's a marketing message directed to a consumer's personal mobile device based on that person's location. Local mobile marketers hope consumers will take follow-on action almost immediately—inquire, reserve, click-to-call, friend, and ultimately purchase. **Table 7.17** describes some of the basic dimensions and metrics to use when evaluating a mobile marketing campaign. The nature of the location-based campaign makes a difference for how you measure success. For instance, in a click-to-call campaign, you want to measure the volume of calls, duration of call, new versus existing customers, and the number of accidental or hostile calls.

TABLE 7.17	MOBILE LOCATION-BASED MARKETING EFFECTIVENESS
SOCIAL MARKETING PROCESS	MEASUREMENT
Acquisition	Impressions; click-through; unique visitors to a mobile or desktop Web site; pages viewed; time on site.
Engagement	Inquire; reserve; visit a physical store; click-to-call; check maps for directions; register; request more information; posts and comments; responders to offers; Likes generated per visitor; click-to-call rate.
Amplification	SMS to friends; notify friends of location; share location or offers with friends.
Community	Content generated by visitors or responders; reviews; posts; positive comments generated.
Sales	Purchases; percentage increase in sales due to local mobile campaign; percentage of customers from local mobile.

ExchangeHunterJumper.com:
Building a Brand with Social Marketing

The Internet and Web have enabled thousands of business ideas to become online realities. The Internet has reduced the costs of starting a small business, and allowed small players to effectively use the same marketing and selling tools as major corporations. Small businesses usually occupy a market niche not occupied by big players or corporations. One such market niche in America, comprising about 10,000 to 30,000 players, is the high-end horse show circuit. These are people who are willing to drop $200,000 on a horse that can jump a five-foot fence with ease. This may be a very small market, but its members are highly motivated to both buy and sell horses, and they are willing to spend in the process. ExchangeHunterJumper.com is one example of how a small business focusing on a tiny niche market was able to successfully build an online brand.

According to Dagny Amber Aslin, founder and owner of ExchangeHunterJumper. com (The Exchange), a Web site created to help owners and professional trainers

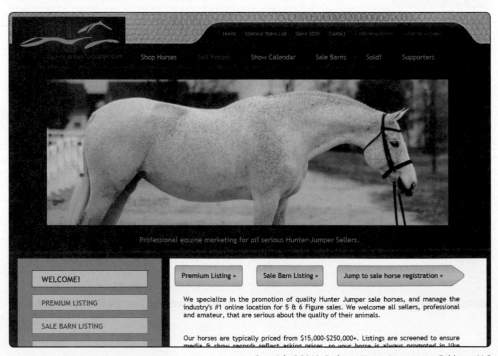

sell high-end competition horses, it's hard to "get rich" or even make money on the Internet. She adds, "There are a lot of preconceived notions … I beat down a path previously unplowed. It cost us a lot of money and we suffered many setbacks from our mistakes." Yet the site is still growing and has succeeded where others failed. How did Aslin break through and develop a site that works for professionals buying and selling alike? How did she build trust? How did she market her services?

Experience helped. Aslin started with applicable experience—in the horse world and in the world of Internet marketing. In addition to riding and competing as a child, Aslin spent several years working as a professional trainer. Working six-day weeks, including weekends, and spending most of her time outdoors riding, teaching, and competing, she saw first-hand the challenges facing professional horsemen, and she gained valuable credibility with those who would become her audience.

While working in the horse business, and learning how difficult it was to make a living, she took a part-time job as an assistant to a top California real estate agent, helping him market and sell high-end real estate in the Santa Barbara area. Among other activities, she helped him develop and expand his Web site. Through that experience, she realized that "selling six-figure horses and seven-figure houses are ridiculously similar—both tend to be overpriced, have emotional strings attached, require vettings and exhaustive negotiations, involve agents, and the list goes on." In 2005, when she moved from California back to the Midwest, where she had spent her childhood, The Exchange was born. Seven years later, the equine marketing model she has built is "a customized copy" of the real estate program she assisted with in Santa Barbara.

Aslin knew that busy horse professionals needed a high-quality, reliable source of suitable mounts for their clients, but their day-to-day business lives left them little time to thoroughly search the market, and they often lacked a good grasp of modern media technology. The same dilemma applied when it came to selling high-end horses. In response, she created an organized, professional process for preparing online horse sale advertisements. It included detailed forms for sellers to fill out, and she insisted that quality photos and video be provided for each horse advertised, enabling her to turn the descriptions into accurate portrayals of each animal and its capabilities. She created a fee structure that was reasonable and affordable, and she developed a multi-channel marketing program.

Aslin understood that her business plan needed to be a living document, evolving over time based on what the market was telling her. This helped her make inroads in a traditional industry that is very resistant to change. Most horse professionals spend their days outside, and tend to do business only with those they know personally—the level of trust is very low. Most existing horse sale Web sites were little more than online classifieds cluttered with unreliable information. Although professional horsemen have been slow to use computers and the Internet, the rise of smartphones and tablet computers has helped increase their comfort level with technology.

The Exchange took all of these things into account, and Aslin went further. In order to remain true to her business goal of providing a *reliable* service to professionals in the horse industry that would become a source of good horses described accurately, Aslin personally reviewed all potential advertisers. In some cases she went back to sellers and insisted on higher quality photographs and video, and in other cases where she determined the horse was not as represented, she turned down their business. The initial business plan process involved strict screening, and it meant turning away money and valuing quality over quantity in every area—horses, buyers, traffic, and ads. It was a hard and expensive premise to adhere to when building a reputation from scratch, but through persistence and dedication it has worked, and today, The Exchange's reputation and "brand" has become one of its most valuable assets.

In discussing some of the obstacles she faced in getting The Exchange up and running, Aslin starts with education—her own or lack thereof, specifically in the areas of graphic design and Web technology. While she knew what professional horsemen needed, she did not know how to translate that into graphic design or onto the Web. She says that looking back on the original logo and print designs is "a painful exercise," but she is happy with the current direction.

The budget was also an initial obstacle, as there wasn't a lot of money to spend up front. However, in hindsight, she believes that gave her an advantage because she had to learn what her market wanted and was able to do so without breaking the bank. Conversely, her main competitor took an opposite track, spent big up front, missed the mark with customers, and is now defunct.

In addition, she faced the negative perception among industry professionals and prospective buyers that equine Internet advertising was "worthless." Further, much of her target audience barely knew how to use a computer, didn't have e-mail addresses, and had been doing business in the same old-school manner for decades. For a few key players this worked very well, but it left a void for those outside that inner circle to move horses. Through a combination of knowledge of the marketplace, on-the-job training, perseverance, and listening to what the market was telling her, The Exchange has successfully begun to fill that void.

Here's how it works. The Exchange handles advertising for sellers and trainers across the country. In 2013, show horses advertised on The Exchange are typically priced from $15,000 to $250,000. The recession caused prices to fall significantly, but in 2012–2013, the prices in certain parts of the market have started to rebound. The Exchange specializes strictly in hunter-jumper show horses, and specifically those suited for high-level competition.

Trainers/sellers who sign up for a premium listing pay a flat $250 fee for the initial advertisement and a subscription fee of $35/month, which includes a listing on The Exchange's Web site featuring the horse's details, photos, show record, lineage, and videos. The Exchange provides copy-writing services and professionally edits all videos supplied by sellers, hosting them on its private server and making them available to download, embed, and share. Each listing typically takes 8–10 hours to prepare. In 2012, The Exchange added a second listing alternative—a Sale Barn listing for $300 a month or $3,000 a year, that allows for listing of up to 10 horses. A three-month commitment is required, but there are no initial or other fees. Aimed at high-volume operations with frequent turnover, the Sale Barn page can link to the seller's Web site,

YouTube, Facebook, and Twitter feeds, if available, with the goal of increasing overall brand awareness for the seller's business. Aslin designed the Sale Barn as an affordable option for professionals who might otherwise be reluctant to spend on marketing. International sellers are given a slight additional discount. The Sale Barn is beginning to take off, with 25 returning clients this year.

Statistics show that a horse's first month online is most successful in terms of the number of Web page visits. With the addition of monthly campaign management, The Exchange helps keep each horse's marketing fresh and up to date. Updates can immediately escalate a horse's popularity as much as 30% and attract new potential buyers. Sellers are encouraged to provide updates as frequently as possible. Online videos add to the brand of the horse for sale and are especially important for young horses or those "growing into" their price tags. Updates are added to the Web site and promoted through various media outlets including Facebook and e-mail campaigns.

Sellers currently fill out two separate forms: a credit card registration form and an equine fact sheet. The fact sheet includes a long series of checkboxes from which sellers select preworded traits, coupled with space for additional written descriptions. This saves some production time, although writing the actual copy is still a major part of the value that The Exchange provides. To implement this option, Aslin spent time investigating form-building tools. Custom-built form solutions were likely to be too expensive, so she played with numerous online form generators and ultimately was able to find some that offered great functionality at a relatively low cost. So, for example, a seller can indicate that the horse is a "jumper" and questions specific to jumpers will be displayed.

The Exchange develops a specific marketing strategy for each horse listed. This includes reviewing information submitted, combing through a horse's official show record, considering impartial impressions, and identifying the most likely buyers. If The Exchange thinks that the photos or videos don't help to sell the horse, they advise the seller on how to improve them. This advice stems from experience in marketing all types of horses from coast to coast, and an understanding of varied buyer profiles and geographic trends that exist in the market.

Social marketing forms the core of the Exchange's marketing efforts. Starting in 2009, The Exchange began experimenting with social media including RSS feeds, YouTube, Facebook, Twitter, and now, Pinterest. Aslin notes that when she began The Exchange, social media was not yet the phenomenon that it is today, but when its significance started to became apparent, she had no choice but to jump in and begin using it, learning as she went. The Exchange has experienced varying success with social media. For instance, The Exchange runs multiple RSS feeds through the free service, FeedBurner, although thus far, the equestrian set does not appear to be particularly interested in RSS feed subscriptions. The company's YouTube channel has been largely supplanted by a professional video management system from Vzaar that hosts all of its videos, serves to most smartphones, and provides more control, branding, and flexibility than YouTube without any annoying advertisements. Facebook has been the most resounding social media success. For the first six months of 2013, Facebook generated almost 30,000 visits to The Exchange's Web site. About 17% of visitors from Facebook's desktop site were new visitors, while 40% of the visitors coming from Facebook's mobile site were new visitors. The Exchange has more than 4,600 Likes on Facebook. In addition, Aslin's personal Facebook friends, which number over 1,100, extend her cumulative Facebook reach to almost 6,000 friends and fans, and make her online marketing efforts even more personal. Aslin's Twitter account has more than 1,600 followers, and links with both The Exchange's Facebook page and its YouTube channel. The YouTube channel has over 275 subscribers, and more than 25,000 views. The latest social media platform now in The Exchange's sights is Pinterest, which Aslin believes may be very beneficial, since visuals such as photos and video play such an important role in the marketing of show horses. Because every business is different, The Exchange's experience suggests it's important for e-commerce sites to experiment with social media to determine which outlets are most effective in reaching their specific target audiences. The Exchange's successful use of social media in the equestrian industry was recognized when it was named one of 10 finalists for the 2012 PagePlay Equestrian Social Media Awards for best use of social media in North America.

To track the effectiveness of her social marketing efforts, Aslin uses various tracking systems. For instance, Google Analytics allows her to track exactly how many people are on the ExchangeHunterJumper site in real time and how they got there. Aslin has found that focusing solely on Likes is not sufficient. For example, she notes that a photo she posted advertising a horse on Facebook generated only 10 Likes, but that actually almost 150 people followed the link associated with the photo to the ExchangeHunterJumper Web site. She also uses a short URL service, bit.ly, to create unique URLs associated with Facebook and other social media posts that have built-in click trackers. This enables her to quickly see the collective success of her social marketing efforts; in a good month, bit.ly stats show around 5,000 click-throughs to the ExchangeHunterJumper site.

Another challenge is developing the actual social media content, which needs to be presented in such as way as to attract attention, and determining the optimal amount and timing of new content to post each day. Aslin notes that if she posts too many times a day, or posts too much content too close together, the reach of her posts seems to drop off.

Although Facebook is currently the primary social marketing platform for ExchangeHunterJumper, the firm also has loyal followers on Twitter. Although Aslin doubts that many of these followers are actual buyers or sellers at this time, she notes that in the future they probably will be. Her site has grown up along with her clientele, and children who once drooled over ponies on her site are now, 7 years later, soon-to-be adults and, possibly, young professionals.

The firm's Web site is also a key element of its e-commerce presence. Aslin continually reviews the design of the Web site with an eye to making it the most effective marketing tool possible. She built the original site herself in 2005 and updated it almost yearly in response to her target market's needs. In 2012, Aslin relaunched the site for a fifth time, and for the first time ever hired a professional Web development team to convert the static HTML site into a dynamically driven content management system on the Expression Engine platform. While she was able to keep costs low by designing and developing the site's CSS layout, the advanced functionality that was desired, such as the sale horse filter that enables shoppers to sort horses based on price, location, gender, type, and size, still required a hefty five-figure investment. Aslin believes the ability to get to know the market and update the site accordingly has kept The Exchange fresh and innovative. Every iteration of the Web site has been focused on meeting the target market's needs. For instance, she has also spent considerable time and expense to make sure The Exchange's Web site, including video, works just as well on mobile devices as it does on a traditional laptop or desktop computer. That said, Aslin believes her next major effort will be to create a mobile site that is even easier for mobile consumers to use. And possibly on the horizon—browser-friendly 30-inch TV screens! Although potentially representing a whole new environment that would need to be designed for, Aslin believes it would actually be a great tool for her particular industry, given that it is so video reliant.

In addition to the Web site, The Exchange uses a variety of other marketing strategies, including e-mail campaigns, magazine advertising, and word of mouth. It recently ceased distributing its four-color, printed National Sales List booklet due to its high cost, and now relies almost totally on various types of online marketing. Aslin has found it has been extremely helpful to have the Web development experience she has honed over the years. Here are some of her words of wisdom: She feels that entrepreneurs don't necessarily have to know how to build sites, but do need to be familiar with what is and what is not possible in site construction. It is important to understand which functions are complicated and which are not, so that overly complicated add-ons that don't really add to the user experience can be eliminated from tight budgets. It's also important to know what technology is popular now and what technology is just around the corner. Even if you think you are proficient in all the tasks you will need to launch your business, with the rapid pace of technology, you inevitably spend much of your time learning something totally new, whether you want to or not.

By paying attention to these words of wisdom, as well as to detail at every step of the marketing process, The Exchange has managed to build a successful brand, one the horse community has come to rely upon.

SOURCES: Exchangehunterjumper.com, accessed September 1, 2013; Interview with Amber Aslin, founder of ExchangeHunterJumper, September 2013 and September 2012.

Case Study Questions

1. Find a site on the Web that offers classified ads for horses. Compare this site to exchangehunterjumper.com in terms of the services offered (the customer value proposition). What does The Exchange offer that other sites do not?

2. In what ways were social media effective in promoting The Exchange brand? Which media led to the highest increase in sales and inquiries? Why?

3. Make a list of all the ways The Exchange attempts to personalize its services to both buyers and sellers.

| 7.6 | **REVIEW** |

KEY CONCEPTS

■ **Understand the difference between traditional online marketing and the new social-mobile-local marketing platforms.**

Social, mobile, and local marketing have transformed the online marketing landscape. The major trends and concepts include:

- The emphasis in online marketing has shifted from exposing consumers to messages towards engaging them in conversations about your brand.
- Social marketing means all things social: listening, discussing, interacting, empathizing, and engaging the consumer.
- Social marketing and advertising is not simply a "new ad channel," but a collection of technology-based tools for communicating with shoppers.
- In the past, businesses could tightly control their brand messaging and lead consumers down a funnel of cues that ended in a purchase. This is no longer the case. Instead, consumer purchase decisions are increasingly driven by the conversations, choices, tastes, and opinions of the consumer's social network.
- Social, mobile, and local marketing are the fastest growing forms of online marketing.

■ **Describe the size and growth of social, local, and mobile marketing.**

- Social, mobile, and local marketing are the fastest growing forms of online marketing.
- By 2012, spending on mobile marketing had already overtaken social marketing. In 2013, mobile marketing spending is almost twice as much as spending on social marketing.
- While social marketing is growing at around 30% a year, mobile is growing at around 50% a year. Local marketing, estimated to be about $2.2 billion in 2013, is growing at nearly 100% a year.
- Traditional online marketing (browser-based search and display ads and e-mail) still constitutes the majority of all online marketing, but it is growing much more slowly than social-mobile-local marketing.

■ **Understand the relationships between social, mobile, and local marketing.**

- Social, mobile, and local digital marketing are self-reinforcing and connected.
- As mobile devices become more powerful, they are more useful for accessing Facebook and other social sites.
- Around 25% of all Facebook visits are from mobile devices, and 30% of its ad revenue is generated by its mobile audience.
- Local and mobile marketing are highly related: local advertisers most often target mobile devices.
- The strong ties among social, mobile, and local marketing have significant implications for managing a marketing campaign in this new environment. When you design a social marketing campaign, you must also consider that

your customers will be accessing the campaign using mobile devices, and often they will also be looking for local content.

■ **Understand the social marketing process from fan acquisition to sales.**

- Social marketing differs markedly from traditional online marketing.
- In social marketing, the objective is to encourage your potential customers to become fans of your company's products and services and engage with your business by entering into a conversation with it.
- Encourage your business's fans to share their enthusiasm with their friends, and in doing so, create a community of fans online.
- Facebook is the dominant social site, but LinkedIn, Twitter, Pinterest, Tumblr, and Instagram have more combined unique monthly visitors than Facebook.
- Pinterest and Instagram are among the fastest growing sites in Web history, and Tumblr is not far behind.
- There are five steps in the social marketing process model: fan acquisition, engagement, amplification, community, and brand strength and sales.
- Fan acquisition involves using any of a variety of means, from display ads to News Feed and page pop-ups, to attract people to a Facebook page, Twitter feed, or other platform like a Web page.
- Engagement involves using a variety of tools to encourage users to interact with content and brands located on a Facebook or Web page.
- Amplification involves using the inherent strength of social networks.
- Community involves building a more or less stable group of fans who are engaged and communicating with one another over a substantial period of time of months or years.

■ **Identify the marketing capabilities of social marketing platforms such as Facebook, Twitter, and Pinterest.**

- Facebook is a social network with over 1 billion members. Facebook is designed to encourage people to reveal as much personal information about themselves as feasible, including activities, behavior, photos, music, movies, and purchases. It describes itself as having three pillars: News Feed, Timeline (Profile), and the recently added Graph Search.
- Facebook's features are built to maximize the connections among people in the form of notifications, tagging, messaging, posting, and sharing. In many instances, the movement of personal information is so widespread that it is beyond the understanding of users.
- Social density refers to the number of interactions among members of a group and reflects the "connectedness" of a group, even if these connections are forced on users.
- Facebook has many basic marketing capabilities, which include Marketplace Ads, socially enabled ads, Promoted Posts, Sponsored Stories, brand pages, the Like button, mobile ads, and Facebook Exchange.
- The effectiveness of Facebook ads can be measured using five stages of social marketing model: fan acquisition, engagement, amplification, community, and ultimately brand strengthening and sales.
- Twitter is a micro-blogging social network site that allows users to send and receive 140-character messages.

- Twitter marketing tools include Promoted Tweets, Promoted Trends, Promoted Accounts, Enhanced Profile Pages, the Twitter Amplify program, television ad retargeting, and Lead Generation Cards.

- Measuring the results of Twitter marketing is similar to measuring the results of Facebook and other social marketing platforms, with some minor changes to account for the unique qualities of Twitter.

- Pinterest is the social network site that provides users with an online board to which they can "pin" interesting pictures. The success of Pinterest is based in part on a shift in consumer behavior enabled by new technologies: people talk about brands using pictures rather than words.

- Pinterest marketing tools include adding a Pin It logo to your Web site; pinning photos to Pinterest and direct users to your Web site; creating theme-based Pin It boards; placing URLs to stores that you support and receive lead generation fees from; integrating your pins and boards with other social sites; networking with users and followers.

- Pinterest campaigns can be measured using the same procedures as for Facebook and Twitter. The key dimensions to measure are fan (follower) acquisition, engagement, amplification, community, and sales.

- One downside of social marketing is that brands lose a substantial amount of control over where their ads appear in terms of other content and what people say about their brands on social sites.

■ **Identify the key elements of a mobile marketing campaign including app and in-app marketing.**

- Although still in its infancy, mobile marketing involves the use of mobile devices such as smartphones and tablet computers to display banner ads, rich media, video, games, e-mail, text messaging, in-store messaging, QuickResponse (QR) codes, and couponing.

- Mobile devices represent a radical departure from previous marketing technologies simply because the devices integrate so many human and consumer activities from telephoning or texting friends, to listening to music, watching videos, and using the Web to shop and purchase goods.

- Mobile commerce is growing at over 50% a year, significantly faster than desktop e-commerce at 12% a year.

- 70% of all mobile minutes occur in the home. Over 75% of the most common use of phones, so-called "me time" involving entertainment and relaxation, happens at home.

- The mobile platform itself is changing rapidly from one dominated by smartphones to one dominated by tablets. The number of tablet users, once the newcomer to the mobile platform, is growing faster than the number of smartphone users in the United States.

- Mobile users spend over 80% of their mobile minutes using apps, and only 20% using their browsers. On average, users have downloaded about 40 apps, and regularly use about 15.

- Marketers need to place ads in apps where consumers spend most of their time.

- Mobile devices create a multi-screen world: smartphones, tablets, desktops, and television. The reality, and the future, of computing devices is that consumers will be multi-platform: using desktops and laptops at work and home, and smart-phones and tablets at home as well as when moving about.

- The implications of the multi-device platform, or "screen diversity," environment are that marketing needs to be designed for whatever device the consumer is using, and consistent branding across platforms will be important.
- Unlike social marketing, mobile marketing does not require a great deal of new marketing vocabulary. All the marketing formats available on the desktop are also available on mobile devices. With few exceptions, mobile marketing is very much like desktop marketing—except it is smaller, mobile, and with the user all the time.
- The major marketing opportunities in mobile marketing are search ads, display ads, videos and rich media, messaging (SMS/MMS/PPS), and other familiar formats like e-mail, classified, and lead generation.
- The effectiveness of mobile marketing can be measured using the dimensions of the social marketing process model: fan acquisition, engagement, amplification, community, brand strength, and sales. Traditional Web-browser based metrics also can be used when measuring mobile campaigns.

- ■ **Understand the capabilities of location-based local marketing including in-store messaging, geo-fencing, geo-social-based services, and geo-targeting**

- Location-based marketing is the targeting of marketing messages to users based on their location. Generally, location-based marketing involves marketing of location-based services.
- Examples of location-based services are personal navigation, point-of-interest, reviews, friend-finder, and family-tracker services.
- Location-based marketing is dependent on two technologies: accurate mapping software and mobile device geo-positioning technologies like GPS and Wi-Fi network location data.
- Location-based mobile marketing is currently a very small part of the online marketing environment, but is expected to double over the next two years, and is growing far faster than any other form of digital advertising.
- The ad formats used in local mobile marketing are familiar—search ads, display, SMS text messages, and videos. A very large percentage of these local mobile ads will be delivered by search engines such as Google, and social sites such as Facebook.
- The key players in location-based mobile marketing are the same giants of advertising who dominate the mobile marketing environment: Google, Facebook, Apple, Twitter, YP (formerly Yellow Pages), Pandora, and Millenial.
- Geo-aware techniques identify the location of a user's device and then target marketing to the device, recommending actions within reach.
- Geo-targeting of ads involves sending ads based on the user's location.
- Geo-fencing techniques identify a perimeter around a physical location, and then target ads to users within that perimeter, recommending actions possible within the fenced-in area.
- In-store messaging involves messaging consumers while entering and browsing in a retail store. This requires a very precise calculation of location.
- Consumers who seek information about local businesses using mobile devices are much more active and ready to purchase than desktop users.

- The most common use of mobile devices is to search for directions or locations of places, and Google's Map app dominates this market.
- Measuring the effectiveness of location-based mobile campaigns involves using the same techniques used for browser-based search and display ads (impressions), but also should include the dimensions of the social marketing process model such as acquisition, engagement, amplification, community, and brand strength and sales.

QUESTIONS

1   Describe the two factors that make social, local, and mobile marketing different from traditional online marketing.
2   Why are social, mobile, and local marketing efforts interconnected?
3   Why is the connection between social, mobile, and local marketing important to marketers?
4   What are the objectives of social marketing?
5   What are the major social network sites?
6   What are the five elements of the social marketing process?
7   What are the three most important features of Facebook for marketers to consider?
8   List and briefly describe the basic Facebook marketing tools.
9   How can you measure the results of a Facebook social marketing campaign?
10   List and briefly describe Twitter marketing tools.
10   How can you measure the results of a Twitter social marketing campaign?
11   In what way are Pinterest postings similar to display ads?
12   List and briefly describe some of Pinterest's marketing tools.
13   Why is mobile marketing different from desktop marketing?
14   What is the fastest growing mobile commerce platform and why?
15   Why are in-app ads so important to marketers?
16   What is the multi-screen environment and how does it change marketing?
17   What kinds of ad formats are found on mobile devices?
18   What accounts for the growth of local mobile marketing?
19   Why is location-based marketing so attractive to marketers?
20   List and describe some basic location-based marketing tools.

PROJECTS

1.   Visit the Web sites of at least two different online companies. Make a list of the social, mobile, and local marketing efforts you see on the Web site. Do their pages display Like it! plug-ins, and/or Google +1 logos? Do they have a Facebook page? If so, visit the pages to see how they use their Facebook pages. Is it different from their Web site pages? Can you identify how the firms use mobile marketing? Use your smartphone or tablet to access their Web sites. Are their Web sites designed specifically for each platform? In conclusion, compare and critically contrast these firms, and make recommendations for how you, as a marketing manager, would improve their effectiveness.

2.   Visit your Facebook page and examine the ads shown in the right margin. What is being advertised and how do you believe it is relevant to your interests or

online behavior? Make a list of ads appearing in your News Feed. Are these ads appropriately targeted to you in terms of your demographics, interests, and past purchases? Go to at least two Web sites, and Like it or Like a product. In the next 24 hours, do you see marketing messages on Facebook related to your Likes?

3. Visit two Web sites of your choice and apply the social marketing process model to both. Critically compare and contrast the effectiveness of these sites in terms of the dimensions of the social marketing process. How well do these sites acquire fans, generate engagement, amplify responses, create a community, and strengthen their brands? What recommendations can you make for these sites to improve their effectiveness?

4. Identify two Pinterest brand pages. Identify how they use Pinterest marketing tools described in this chapter. Are there some tools they are not using? What recommendations can you make for these sites to improve their Pinterest marketing campaigns?

CHAPTER 8

Ethical, Social, and Political Issues in E-commerce

LEARNING OBJECTIVES

After reading this chapter, you will be able to:

- Understand why e-commerce raises ethical, social, and political issues.
- Recognize the main ethical, social, and political issues raised by e-commerce.
- Identify a process for analyzing ethical dilemmas.
- Understand basic concepts related to privacy.
- Identify the practices of e-commerce companies that threaten privacy.
- Describe the different methods used to protect online privacy.
- Understand the various forms of intellectual property and the challenges involved in protecting it.
- Understand how governance of the Internet has evolved over time.
- Explain why taxation of e-commerce raises governance and jurisdiction issues.
- Identify major public safety and welfare issues raised by e-commerce.

Free Speech on the Internet:
Who Decides?

© kentoh / Shutterstock

Now that nearly all of our public and private life has moved online, who determines whether what we choose to say can be disseminated to the rest of the world via the Internet? There seem to be several possibilities here. One is that the private companies that now dominate and control the primary communication channels on the Internet, namely Google (including YouTube), Facebook, and Twitter, are actually the ones who can and do control what can be distributed with the click of a mouse. The second possibility is that governments are the ones that make the determination. As powerful as some private companies are, they are totally dependent on the good will of the governments of the countries in which they operate, which, if deemed necessary, could pull the plug on those firms or make their life difficult in other ways. There now also seems to be a third possibility: any group that is powerful enough to threaten the social order appears to be able to influence what is disseminated on the Internet.

Nearly all developed countries, and many developing countries, have laws that prohibit "hate speech." Hate speech is defined in most of these laws (as it is in Google's Terms of Service) as speech that may promote or incite hate or violence against a group or individual. These laws often identify protected groups by disability, ethnicity, religion, gender identity, nationality, race, or other characteristic. Hate speech is prohibited in England, Germany, France, the Netherlands, and other European countries. Europe has prohibited Neo-Nazi speech and banned materials that are offensive to various religious and ethnic groups, long before the Internet existed. Generally, Google, Facebook, and Yahoo follow the requirements of local laws. For instance, Google has removed videos that ridiculed Pakistani officials and blocked access to videos that exposed private information about Turkish officials, in both instances because the content violated local laws.

In contrast, hate speech is not prohibited in the United States. The United States has a more absolutist view of the right to freedom of speech because of the First Amendment to the Constitution which declares "Congress shall make no law respecting an establishment of religion; or abridging the freedom of speech, or of the press; or the right of the people peaceably to assemble, and to petition the Government for a redress of grievances." Like all rights, there are limitations in the United States with respect to the right to free speech. Speech can be prohibited if there is an imminent and immediate likelihood that there will be violence in close proximity to the speech in time and space. This situation has occurred when speakers are addressing crowds face-to-face, for instance. Incitement to riot, and the use of "fighting words," which by their very utterance inflict injury or tend to incite an immediate and violent breach of the peace, can lead to criminal arrest. Although more than 350 colleges and universities in the United States, along with many local governments, have policies or laws that prohibit hate speech, these policies and laws have not withstood judicial challenge. Secondary school systems attempting to limit off-campus speech of students, especially that involving criticism of teachers or administrators, bullying of other students, and vulgar behavior, have received scant support from courts in the United States.

In September 2012, the Obama administration requested that Google remove links on the Google search engine and refuse to answer search queries with respect to a video that had created public unrest in Muslim countries, as well as remove the video from YouTube. The government argued that the video constituted "hate speech," which Google prohibits under its Terms of Service. Google disagreed, saying the video did not clearly violate its Terms of Service. However, a day after refusing to remove the video from YouTube, Google did block access to it in two countries because, it said, the situation in those countries was exceptional and the ban was temporary. It did continue to allow the video to circulate elsewhere. Strong advocates of free speech criticized Google. Will freedom of speech on the Internet be determined by mobs in the street? Civil libertarians warned that to allow Google, a private corporation, to determine what is or is not published on the Web is a worrisome development. Freedom of speech is guaranteed in the Constitution, and they question whether or not Google has the right to regulate a "public speech platform." For instance, the *New York Times* has editorialized that nobody should be banned from the Internet because it is a fundamental tool for enabling free speech. Yet few of these critics would deny the editorial right of the *New York Times,* or any other newspaper, to refuse to publish any material, for whatever reason. Indeed, this happens all the time. On the other hand, Google does not believe it is a publisher that potentially can be held liable for failing to monitor content. Google believes it is a utility carrier, like a telephone company, and that therefore it cannot be held liable for content, or conspiracies, that users distribute and create on its various services.

Others question Google's administration of its own content policies: surely Google managers knew, or should have known, that distributing this video on YouTube would be a violation of local laws in some countries, and that they should have, and could have, anticipated the public unrest that ensued. In this view, the right to freedom of speech has limits, and one of them is imminent danger to violence. However, in this case, there was a long gap between distribution of the video and the resulting violence. Violence was not imminent, immediate, or proximate in physical space. If there are to be limits to the freedom of speech on the Internet because of the potential for violence, then new criteria may be needed to replace imminence, immediacy, and proximity because these conditions are rarely met on the Internet.

Many of today's most popular Web sites, Facebook and Twitter in particular, are popular because they encourage personal expression and provide a public forum. In 2013, Twitter, while promoting itself as a protector of free speech for more than 200 million people who use the service to broadcast their lives, loves, and passions, increasingly found itself in trouble with the laws and standards of various lands. Twitter was variously characterized as a censor, an enabler of hate speech, a tool of Big Brother, and as an inciter of riots and public anarchy. In July 2013, French prosecutors required Twitter to turn over information on users who tweeted anti-Semitic messages. In the U.K., which has strong child pornography laws and which has proposed that ISP broadband providers install filters on their network services, prosecutors have criticized Twitter for allowing pornographic images and tweets to be widely disseminated. In China, Twitter is not available because it won't comply with Chinese government censorship; in Germany, Twitter has blocked accounts at government request because of Neo-Nazi content. In the United States, Twitter reluctantly complied with prosecutors' demands to turn over the Twitter posts of Malcolm Harris, one of the Occupy Wall Street protestors, who was accused of disorderly conduct.

Twitter allows users to post anonymously, and most governments oppose anonymity because it makes it difficult to hold people accountable for their actions and for what they say. Anonymity leads to an explosion of "trolls," people who post inflammatory and abusive comments. In the U.K., Stella Creasy, Labor member of Parliament, was threatened with rape and received death threats on Twitter for supporting the retention of images of women on British Bank notes. After complaining to Twitter, Twitter blocked her account! After a public outcry against Twitter, the company reversed course and added a button to its interface that allows users to alert Twitter employees to malicious or abusive tweets. Creasy and others in Parliament are calling for a much more aggressive stance involving police scrutiny of people who post abusive, threatening, misogynistic Tweets.

Critics of Twitter's lackadaisical approach believe the company does not restrict hate speech at all. They argue that Twitter, by allowing anonymity and refusing to aggressively identify and restrict known, repeat trolls, has led to binges of harassment against minority groups, violent speech, and threats against women. Twitter's policy is that users cannot "publish or post direct, specific threats of violence against others." But Twitter admits it does not have the staff to implement this policy, and the service is literally filled with threats and abusive language.

As "expression services" like Facebook, Tumblr, WordPress, Twitter, Pinterest, and many others achieve scale and success, encouraging their users to reveal their inner thoughts, they are also providing a public forum for the expression of violent, threatening, and abusive messages from anonymous subscribers. As a result, they are increasingly the target of government concerns, pressured to self-censor content, and open to government requests for personal information on their users. In so doing, they are difficult to tell apart from government agencies seeking to suppress political expression.

Today, what speech should be protected on the Internet, and who should protect it, is suddenly not clear at all. Ironically, the very technology that was supposed to bring people together into one big global community, can have just the opposite impact, dividing nations, religions, and peoples. The Internet can become a platform for wicked individuals to sow violence with their user-generated content. Like bringing the extended family together for holidays, bringing the world's diverse populations together on the Internet can have unexpected, and even dangerous, consequences.

SOURCES: "Crackdown on Bloggers is Mounted by China," by Chris Buckley, *New York Times*, September 10, 2013; "A Political Star Rises in Britain, Helped by Twitter," by Katrin Bennhold, *New York Times*, August 20, 2013; "For Twitter, Free Speech is a High Wire Act," by Shira Ovide, *Wall Street Journal*, August 4, 2013; "Twitter's Free-Speech Problem," by Emily Greenhouse, *The New Yorker*, August 1, 2013; "Held Dear in the U.S., Free Speech Perplexing Abroad," National Public Radio, September 19, 2012; "State of the Web: Online Speech Is Only as Free as Google Wants It to Be," by Andrew Couts, Digitaltrends.com, September 18, 2012; "On the Web, a Fine Line on Free Speech Across the Globe," by Somini Sengupta, *New York Times*, September 16, 2012; "As Violence Spreads in the Arab World, Google Blocks Access to Inflammatory Video," Claire Cain Miller, *Wall Street Journal*, September 13, 2012; "Google Groups Content Policy," Google Inc., http://support.google.com/groups, September 2012; "Free Speech and the Internet," *New York Times*, July 3, 2011; "Supreme Court Plays Hooky, Leaves Student Online Free Speech Rights Murky," by David Kravets, *Wired*, November 1, 2011; "The Role of Telecommunications in Hate Crimes," National Telecommunication and Information Administration, U.S. Department of Commerce, December 1993.

Determining how or whether to regulate behavior on the Internet is just one of many ethical, social, and political issues raised by the rapid evolution of the Internet and e-commerce. For instance, as described in the opening case, whether U.S. principles of free speech should govern on the Internet, or the principles of other nations, has not been determined. These questions are not just ethical questions that we as individuals have to answer; they also involve social institutions such as family, schools, business firms, and in some cases, entire nation-states. And these questions have obvious political dimensions because they involve collective choices about how we should live and what laws we would like to live under.

In this chapter, we discuss the ethical, social, and political issues raised in e-commerce, provide a framework for organizing the issues, and make recommendations for managers who are given the responsibility of operating e-commerce companies within commonly accepted standards of appropriateness.

8.1 UNDERSTANDING ETHICAL, SOCIAL, AND POLITICAL ISSUES IN E-COMMERCE

The Internet and its use in e-commerce have raised pervasive ethical, social, and political issues on a scale unprecedented for computer technology. Entire sections of daily newspapers and weekly magazines are devoted to the social impact of the Internet. But why is this so? Why is the Internet at the root of so many contemporary controversies? Part of the answer lies in the underlying features of Internet technology itself, and the ways in which it has been exploited by business firms. Internet technology and its use in e-commerce disrupt existing social and business relationships and understandings.

Consider for instance Table 1.2 (in Chapter 1), which lists the unique features of Internet technology. Instead of considering the business consequences of each unique feature, **Table 8.1** examines the actual or potential ethical, social, and/or political consequences of the technology.

We live in an "information society," where power and wealth increasingly depend on information and knowledge as central assets. Controversies over information are often disagreements over power, wealth, influence, and other things thought to be valuable. Like other technologies, such as steam, electricity, telephones, and television, the Internet and e-commerce can be used to achieve social progress, and for the most part, this has occurred. However, the same technologies can be used to commit crimes, despoil the environment, and threaten cherished social values. Before automobiles, there was very little interstate crime and very little federal jurisdiction over crime. Likewise with the Internet: before the Internet, there was very little "cybercrime."

Many business firms and individuals are benefiting from the commercial development of the Internet, but this development also exacts a price from individuals, organizations, and societies. These costs and benefits must be carefully considered by those seeking to make ethical and socially responsible decisions in this new environment. The question is: How can you as a manager make reasoned judgments

TABLE 8.1	UNIQUE FEATURES OF E-COMMERCE TECHNOLOGY AND THEIR POTENTIAL ETHICAL, SOCIAL, AND/OR POLITICAL IMPLICATIONS
E-COMMERCE TECHNOLOGY DIMENSION	**POTENTIAL ETHICAL, SOCIAL, AND POLITICAL SIGNIFICANCE**
Ubiquity—Internet/Web technology is available everywhere: at work, at home, and elsewhere via mobile devices, anytime.	Work and shopping can invade family life; shopping can distract workers at work, lowering productivity; use of mobile devices can lead to automobile and industrial accidents. Presents confusing issues of "nexus" to taxation authorities.
Global reach—The technology reaches across national boundaries, around the Earth.	Reduces cultural diversity in products; weakens local small firms while strengthening large global firms; moves manufacturing production to low-wage areas of the world; weakens the ability of all nations—large and small—to control their information destiny.
Universal standards—There is one set of technology standards, namely Internet standards.	Increases vulnerability to viruses and hacking attacks worldwide, affecting millions of people at once. Increases the likelihood of "information" crime, crimes against systems, and deception.
Richness—Video, audio, and text messages are possible.	A "screen technology" that reduces use of text and potentially the ability to read by focusing instead on video and audio messages. Potentially very persuasive messages that may reduce reliance on multiple independent sources of information.
Interactivity—The technology works through interaction with the user.	The nature of interactivity at commercial sites can be shallow and meaningless. Customer e-mails are frequently not read by human beings. Customers do not really "co-produce" the product as much as they "co-produce" the sale. The amount of "customization" of products that occurs is minimal, occurring within predefined platforms and plug-in options.
Information density—The technology reduces information costs, and raises quality.	While the total amount of information available to all parties increases, so does the possibility of false and misleading information, unwanted information, and invasion of solitude. Trust, authenticity, accuracy, completeness, and other quality features of information can be degraded. The ability of individuals and organizations to make sense out of this plethora of information is limited.
Personalization/Customization—The technology allows personalized messages to be delivered to individuals as well as groups.	Opens up the possibility of intensive invasion of privacy for commercial and governmental purposes that is unprecedented.
Social technology—The technology enables user content generation and social networking.	Creates opportunities for cyberbullying, abusive language, and predation; challenges concepts of privacy, fair use, and consent to use posted information; creates new opportunities for surveillance by authorities and corporations into private lives.

about what your firm should do in a number of e-commerce areas—from securing the privacy of your customer's clickstream to ensuring the integrity of your company's domain name?

A MODEL FOR ORGANIZING THE ISSUES

E-commerce—and the Internet—have raised so many ethical, social, and political issues that it is difficult to classify them all, and hence, complicated to see their relationship to one another. Clearly, ethical, social, and political issues are interrelated. One way to organize the ethical, social, and political dimensions surrounding e-commerce is shown in **Figure 8.1**. At the individual level, what appears as an ethical issue—"What should I do?"—is reflected at the social and political levels—"What should we as a society and government do?" The ethical dilemmas you face as a manager of a business using the Web reverberate and are reflected in social and political debates. The major ethical, social, and political issues that have developed around e-commerce over the past 10 years can be loosely categorized into four major dimensions: information rights, property rights, governance, and public safety and welfare.

Some of the ethical, social, and political issues raised in each of these areas include the following:

- **Information rights:** What rights to their own personal information do individuals have in a public marketplace, or in their private homes, when Internet technologies make information collection so pervasive and efficient? What rights do individuals have to access information about business firms and other organizations?
- **Property rights:** How can traditional intellectual property rights be enforced in an Internet world where perfect copies of protected works can be made and easily distributed worldwide in seconds?
- **Governance:** Should the Internet and e-commerce be subject to public laws? And if so, what law-making bodies have jurisdiction—state, federal, and/or international?

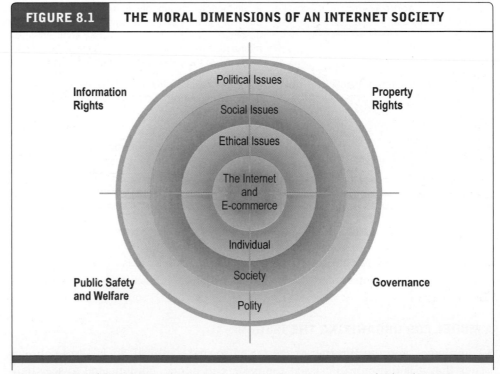

FIGURE 8.1   **THE MORAL DIMENSIONS OF AN INTERNET SOCIETY**

The introduction of the Internet and e-commerce impacts individuals, societies, and political institutions. These impacts can be classified into four moral dimensions: property rights, information rights, governance, and public safety and welfare.

- **Public safety and welfare:** What efforts should be undertaken to ensure equitable access to the Internet and e-commerce channels? Should governments be responsible for ensuring that schools and colleges have access to the Internet? Are certain online content and activities—such as pornography and gambling—a threat to public safety and welfare? Should mobile commerce be allowed from moving vehicles?

To illustrate, imagine that at any given moment, society and individuals are more or less in an ethical equilibrium brought about by a delicate balancing of individuals, social organizations, and political institutions. Individuals know what is expected of them, social organizations such as business firms know their limits, capabilities, and roles, and political institutions provide a supportive framework of market regulation, banking, and commercial law that provides sanctions against violators.

Now, imagine we drop into the middle of this calm setting a powerful new technology such as the Internet and e-commerce. Suddenly, individuals, business firms, and political institutions are confronted by new possibilities of behavior. For instance, individuals discover that they can download perfect digital copies of music tracks from Web sites without paying anyone, something that, under the old technology of CDs, would have been impossible. This can be done, despite the fact that these music tracks still legally belong to the owners of the copyright—musicians and record label companies. Then, business firms discover that they can make a business out of aggregating these digital musical tracks—or creating a mechanism for sharing musical tracks—even though they do not "own" them in the traditional sense. The record companies, courts, and Congress were not prepared at first to cope with the onslaught of online digital copying. Courts and legislative bodies will have to make new laws and reach new judgments about who owns digital copies of copyrighted works and under what conditions such works can be "shared." It may take years to develop new understandings, laws, and acceptable behavior in just this one area of social impact. In the meantime, as an individual and a manager, you will have to decide what you and your firm should do in legal "gray" areas, where there is conflict between ethical principles but no clear-cut legal or cultural guidelines. How can you make good decisions in this type of situation?

Before examining the four moral dimensions of e-commerce in greater depth, we will briefly review some basic concepts of ethical reasoning that you can use as a guide to ethical decision making, and provide general reasoning principles about the social and political issues of the Internet that you will face in the future.

BASIC ETHICAL CONCEPTS: RESPONSIBILITY, ACCOUNTABILITY, AND LIABILITY

Ethics is at the heart of social and political debates about the Internet. **Ethics** is the study of principles that individuals and organizations can use to determine right and wrong courses of action. It is assumed in ethics that individuals are free moral agents who are in a position to make choices. When faced with alternative courses of action, what is the correct moral choice? Extending ethics from individuals to business firms and even entire societies can be difficult, but it is not impossible. As long as there is a decision-making body or individual (such as a board of directors or CEO in a business firm, or a governmental body in a society), their decisions can be judged against a variety of ethical principles.

ethics
the study of principles that individuals and organizations can use to determine right and wrong courses of action

responsibility

as free moral agents, individuals, organizations, and societies are responsible for the actions they take

accountability

individuals, organizations, and societies should be held accountable to others for the consequences of their actions

liability

a feature of political systems in which a body of law is in place that permits individuals to recover the damages done to them by other actors, systems, or organizations

due process

a process in which laws are known and understood and there is an ability to appeal to higher authorities to ensure that the laws have been correctly applied

If you understand some basic ethical principles, your ability to reason about larger social and political debates will be improved. In western culture, there are four basic principles that all ethical schools of thought share: responsibility, accountability, liability, and due process. **Responsibility** means that as free moral agents, individuals, organizations, and societies are responsible for the actions they take. **Accountability** means that individuals, organizations, and societies should be held accountable to others for the consequences of their actions. The third principle—liability—extends the concepts of responsibility and accountability to the area of law. **Liability** is a feature of political systems in which a body of law is in place that permits individuals to recover the damages done to them by other actors, systems, or organizations. **Due process** is a feature of law-governed societies and refers to a process in which laws are known and understood, and there is an ability to appeal to higher authorities to ensure that the laws have been correctly applied.

You can use these concepts immediately to understand some contemporary Internet debates. For instance, consider the 2005 U.S. Supreme Court decision in the case of *Metro-Goldwyn-Mayer Studios v. Grokster, et al.* MGM had sued Grokster and other P2P networks for copyright infringement. The court decided that because the primary and intended use of Internet P2P file-sharing services such as Grokster, StreamCast, and Kazaa was the swapping of copyright-protected music and video files, the file-sharing services should be held accountable and shut down. Although Grokster and the other networks acknowledged that the most common use of the software was for illegal digital music file-swapping, they argued that there were substantial, nontrivial uses of the same networks for legally sharing files. They also argued they should not be held accountable for what individuals do with their software, any more than Sony could be held accountable for how people use VCRs, or Xerox for how people use copying machines. Ultimately, the Supreme Court ruled that Grokster and other P2P networks could be held accountable for the illegal actions of their users if it could be shown that they intended their software to be used for illegal downloading and sharing, and had marketed the software for that purpose. The court relied on copyright laws to arrive at its decisions, but these laws reflect some basic underlying ethical principles of responsibility, accountability, and liability.

Underlying the *Grokster* Supreme Court decision is a fundamental rejection of the notion that the Internet is an ungoverned "Wild West" environment that cannot be controlled. Under certain defined circumstances, the courts will intervene into the uses of the Internet. No organized civilized society has ever accepted the proposition that technology can flaunt basic underlying social and cultural values. Through all of the industrial and technological developments that have taken place, societies have intervened by means of legal and political decisions to ensure that the technology serves socially acceptable ends without stifling the positive consequences of innovation and wealth creation. The Internet in this sense is no different, and we can expect societies around the world to exercise more regulatory control over the Internet and e-commerce in an effort to arrive at a new balance between innovation and wealth creation, on the one hand, and other socially desirable objectives on the other. This is a difficult balancing act, and reasonable people will arrive at different conclusions.

ANALYZING ETHICAL DILEMMAS

Ethical, social, and political controversies usually present themselves as dilemmas. A **dilemma** is a situation in which there are at least two diametrically opposed actions, each of which supports a desirable outcome. When confronted with a situation that seems to present an ethical dilemma, how can you analyze and reason about the situation? The following is a five-step process that should help:

dilemma
a situation in which there are at least two diametrically opposed actions, each of which supports a desirable outcome

1. **Identify and clearly describe the facts.** Find out who did what to whom, and where, when, and how. In many instances, you will be surprised at the errors in the initially reported facts, and often you will find that simply getting the facts straight helps define the solution. It also helps to get the opposing parties involved in an ethical dilemma to agree on the facts.

2. **Define the conflict or dilemma and identify the higher-order values involved.** Ethical, social, and political issues always reference higher values. Otherwise, there would be no debate. The parties to a dispute all claim to be pursuing higher values (e.g., freedom, privacy, protection of property, and the free enterprise system). For example, supporters of the use of advertising networks such as DoubleClick argue that the tracking of consumer movements on the Web increases market efficiency and the wealth of the entire society. Opponents argue this claimed efficiency comes at the expense of individual privacy, and advertising networks should cease their activities or offer Web users the option of not participating in such tracking.

3. **Identify the stakeholders.** Every ethical, social, and political issue has stakeholders: players in the game who have an interest in the outcome, who have invested in the situation, and usually who have vocal opinions. Find out the identity of these groups and what they want. This will be useful later when designing a solution.

4. **Identify the options that you can reasonably take.** You may find that none of the options satisfies all the interests involved, but that some options do a better job than others. Sometimes, arriving at a "good" or ethical solution may not always be a balancing of consequences to stakeholders.

5. **Identify the potential consequences of your options.** Some options may be ethically correct but disastrous from other points of view. Other options may work in this one instance but not in other similar instances. Always ask yourself, "What if I choose this option consistently over time?"

Once your analysis is complete, you can refer to the following well-established ethical principles to help decide the matter.

CANDIDATE ETHICAL PRINCIPLES

Although you are the only one who can decide which ethical principles you will follow and how you will prioritize them, it is helpful to consider some ethical principles with deep roots in many cultures that have survived throughout recorded history:

- **The Golden Rule:** Do unto others as you would have them do unto you. Putting yourself into the place of others and thinking of yourself as the object of the decision can help you think about fairness in decision making.

- **Universalism:** If an action is not right for all situations, then it is not right for any specific situation (Immanuel Kant's categorical imperative). Ask yourself, "If we adopted this rule in every case, could the organization, or society, survive?"

- **Slippery Slope:** If an action cannot be taken repeatedly, then it is not right to take at all. An action may appear to work in one instance to solve a problem, but if repeated, would result in a negative outcome. In plain English, this rule might be stated as "once started down a slippery path, you may not be able to stop."

- **Collective Utilitarian Principle:** Take the action that achieves the greater value for all of society. This rule assumes you can prioritize values in a rank order and understand the consequences of various courses of action.

- **Risk Aversion:** Take the action that produces the least harm, or the least potential cost. Some actions have extremely high failure costs of very low probability (e.g., building a nuclear generating facility in an urban area) or extremely high failure costs of moderate probability (speeding and automobile accidents). Avoid the high-failure cost actions and choose those actions whose consequences would not be catastrophic, even if there were a failure.

- **No Free Lunch:** Assume that virtually all tangible and intangible objects are owned by someone else unless there is a specific declaration otherwise. (This is the ethical "no free lunch" rule.) If something someone else has created is useful to you, it has value and you should assume the creator wants compensation for this work.

- **The New York Times Test (Perfect Information Rule):** Assume that the results of your decision on a matter will be the subject of the lead article in the *New York Times* the next day. Will the reaction of readers be positive or negative? Would your parents, friends, and children be proud of your decision? Most criminals and unethical actors assume imperfect information, and therefore they assume their decisions and actions will never be revealed. When making decisions involving ethical dilemmas, it is wise to assume perfect information markets.

- **The Social Contract Rule:** Would you like to live in a society where the principle you are supporting would become an organizing principle of the entire society? For instance, you might think it is wonderful to download illegal copies of Hollywood movies, but you might not want to live in a society that does not respect property rights, such as your property rights to the car in your driveway, or your rights to a term paper or original art.

None of these rules is an absolute guide, and there are exceptions and logical difficulties with all of them. Nevertheless, actions that do not easily pass these guidelines deserve some very close attention and a great deal of caution because the appearance of unethical behavior may do as much harm to you and your company as the actual behavior.

Now that you have an understanding of some basic ethical reasoning concepts, let's take a closer look at each of the major types of ethical, social, and political debates that have arisen in e-commerce.

8.2 PRIVACY AND INFORMATION RIGHTS

Privacy is the moral right of individuals to be left alone, free from surveillance or interference from other individuals or organizations, including the state. Privacy is a girder supporting freedom: Without the privacy required to think, write, plan, and associate independently and without fear, social and political freedom is weakened, and perhaps destroyed. **Information privacy** is a subset of privacy. The right to information privacy includes both the claim that certain information should not be collected at all by governments or business firms, and the claim of individuals to control the use of whatever information that is collected about them. Individual control over personal information is at the core of the privacy concept. Implicit in the claim to control one's own personal information is the claim to be able to edit and even delete personal information from the Web. This is often called "**the right to be forgotten**" (Rosen, 2012).

Due process also plays an important role in defining privacy. The best statement of due process in record keeping is given by the Fair Information Practices doctrine developed in the early 1970s and extended to the online privacy debate in the late 1990s (described later in this section).

There are two kinds of threats to individual privacy posed by the Internet. One threat originates in the private sector and concerns how much personal information is collected by commercial Web sites and how it will be used. A second threat originates in the public sector and concerns how much personal information federal, state, and local government authorities collect, and how they use it. While these threats are conceptually distinct, in practice they are related as the federal government increasingly relies on Internet companies to provide intelligence on specific individuals and groups, and as Internet records held by search engine companies and others (like Amazon) are sought by legal authorities and attornies.

Privacy claims—and thinking about privacy—mushroomed in the United States at the end of the nineteenth century as the technology of photography and tabloid journalism enabled the invasion of the heretofore private lives of wealthy industrialists. For most of the twentieth century, however, privacy thinking and legislation focused on restraining the government from collecting and using personal information. With the explosion in the collection of private personal information by Web-based marketing firms since 1995, privacy concerns are increasingly directed toward restraining the activities of private firms in the collection and use of information on the Web. Claims to privacy are also involved at the workplace. Millions of employees are subject to various forms of electronic surveillance that in many cases is enhanced by firm intranets and Web technologies. For instance, the majority of U.S. companies monitor which Web sites their workers visit, as well as employee e-mail and instant messages. Employee posts on message boards and blogs are also coming under scrutiny.

In 2013, the public discussion of privacy has broadened from a concern about tracking the behavior of individuals while they use the Internet, especially on social networks, to include the impact of mobile devices for tracking the location of people via their smartphones, and collecting information on their personal behavior including the shops, churches, political rallies, bars, and other locations they have visited.

privacy
the moral right of individuals to be left alone, free from surveillance or interference from other individuals or organizations, including the state

information privacy
includes both the claim that certain information should not be collected at all by governments or business firms, and the claim of individuals to control the use of whatever information that is collected about them

right to be forgotten
the claim of individuals to be able to edit and delete personal information online

These concerns about tracking and surveilling people throughout their daily lives have been heightened by the revelation that the federal government's National Security Agency has been logging virtually all cell phone calls of all residents for many years. Smartphone apps that tap user information have also received critical attention. The falling costs of personal tracking technology like mobile cameras, the ubiquitous use of always-on smartphones fitted out with GPS, and the growth of powerful storage and analytic capabilities, has resulted in a torrent of data, referred to as "Big Data," pouring into marketing and law enforcement databases. Private and government investigations have found both Apple and Google are collecting personal location and behavior data, and potentially sharing this information with marketers and government agencies. The cell phone carriers receive more than a million requests each year from law enforcement agencies for call data (Maass and Rajagopalen, 2012). Apart from smartphone surveillance, new wireless cameras mounted on cars (a kind of remote sensing device) have led to a new industry of license plate tracking, resulting in hundreds of millions of license plate photos collected by private firms and police forces, regardless of whether or not the car's owners have done anything wrong (Angwin and Valentino-Devries, 2012).

In general, the Internet and the Web provide an ideal environment for both business and government to invade the personal privacy of millions of users on a scale unprecedented in history. Perhaps no other recent issue has raised as much widespread social and political concern as protecting the privacy of 243 million Internet users in the United States alone. The major ethical issues related to e-commerce and privacy include the following: Under what conditions should we collect information about others? What legitimates intruding into others' lives through unobtrusive surveillance, online tracking programs, market research, or other means? Do people have a right to be informed when Web sites are collecting data about them? The major social issues related to e-commerce and privacy concern the development of "expectations of privacy" or privacy norms, as well as public attitudes. In what areas of life should we as a society encourage people to think they are in "private territory" as opposed to public view? The major political issues related to e-commerce and privacy concern the development of statutes that govern the relations between record keepers and individuals. How should both public and private organizations—which may be reluctant to remit the advantages that come from the unfettered flow of information on individuals—be restrained, if at all? In the following section, we look first at the various practices of e-commerce companies that pose a threat to privacy.

INFORMATION COLLECTED AT E-COMMERCE SITES

personally identifiable information (PII)
any data that can be used to identify, locate, or contact an individual

anonymous information
demographic and behavioral information that does not include any personal identifiers

As you have learned in previous chapters, e-commerce sites routinely collect a variety of information from or about consumers who visit their site and/or make purchases. Some of this data constitutes **personally identifiable information (PII)**, which is defined as any data that can be used to identify, locate, or contact an individual (Federal Trade Commission, 2000a). Other data is **anonymous information**, composed of demographic and behavioral information, such as age, occupation, income, zip code, ethnicity, and other data that characterizes your life such as Web browsing

TABLE 8.2	PERSONAL INFORMATION COLLECTED BY E-COMMERCE SITES		
Name	Gender	Education
Address	Age	Preference data
Phone number	Occupation	Transaction data
E-mail address	Location	Clickstream data
Social security number	Location history	Device used for access
Bank accounts	Likes	Browser type
Credit card accounts	Photograph	

behavior without identifying who you are. **Table 8.2** lists some of the personal identifiers routinely collected by online e-commerce sites including mobile sites and apps. This is not an exhaustive list, and in fact many Web sites collect hundreds of different data points on visitors.

Advertising networks and search engines also track the behavior of consumers across thousands of popular sites, not just at one site, via cookies, Web beacons, tracking software, spyware, and other techniques

Table 8.3 illustrates some of the major ways online firms gather information about consumers.

SOCIAL NETWORKS AND PRIVACY

Social networks pose a unique challenge for the maintenance of personal privacy because they encourage people to reveal details about their personal lives (passions, loves, favorites, photos, videos, and personal interests), and to share them with their friends. Social networks have greatly enlarged the depth, scope, and richness of information collected by private corporations. While Google's search engine is a massive database of personal intentions, Facebook has created a massive database of friends, preferences, Likes, posts, and activities. An Austrian researcher was able to obtain his Facebook file (possible under European laws) and received a 1,222 page document of messages, photos, posts, and friends (Sengupta, 2012a). Some social networkers share these personal details with everyone on the social network. On the face of it, this would seem to indicate that people who participate in social networks voluntarily give up their rights to personal privacy. How could they claim an expectation of privacy? When everything is shared, what's private?

But the reality is that many adult (18 or over) participants in social networks have a very keen sense of their personal privacy. Every time a leading social network has sought to use the personal information provided by participants as a method of monetizing social networks by displaying ads and targeting individuals, it has been vociferously rejected by many members of the networks. Facebook is a prime example of senior management pushing the envelope of privacy, and experiencing a number of public relations reversals and growing government concern. In a recent gaffe,

TABLE 8.3	THE INTERNET'S MAJOR INFORMATION-GATHERING TOOLS AND THEIR IMPACT ON PRIVACY
INTERNET CAPABILITY	**IMPACT ON PRIVACY**
Smartphones and apps	Used to track location and share photos, addresses, phone numbers, search, and other behavior to marketers.
Advertising networks	Used to track individuals as they move among thousands of Web sites.
Social networks	Used to gather information on user-provided content such as books, music, friends, and other interests, preferences, and lifestyles.
Cookies and Super Cookies	Used to track individuals at a single site. Super Cookies are nearly impossible to identify or remove.
Third-party cookies	Cookies placed by third-party advertising networks. Used to monitor and track online behavior, searches, and sites visited across thousands of sites that belong to the advertising network for the purpose of displaying "relevant" advertising.
Spyware	Can be used to record all the keyboard activity of a user, including Web sites visited and security codes used; also used to display advertisements to users based on their searches or other behavior.
Search engine behavioral targeting (Google and other search engines)	Uses prior search history, demographics, expressed interests, geographic, or other user-entered data to target advertising.
Deep packet inspection	Uses software installed at the ISP level to track all user clickstream behavior.
Shopping carts	Can be used to collect detailed payment and purchase information.
Forms	Online forms that users voluntarily fill out in return for a promised benefit or reward that are linked with clickstream or other behavioral data to create a personal profile.
Site transaction logs	Can be used to collect and analyze detailed information on page content viewed by users.
Search engines	Can be used to trace user statements and views on newsgroups, chat groups, and other public forums on the Web, and profile users' social and political views. Google returns name, address, and links to a map with directions to the address when a phone number is entered.
Digital wallets (single sign-on services)	Client-side wallets and software that reveal personal information to Web sites verifying the identity of the consumer.
Digital Rights Management (DRM)	Software (Windows Media Player) that requires users of online media to identify themselves before viewing copyrighted content.
Trusted Computing Environments	Hardware and software that controls the viewing of copyrighted content and requires users identification, e.g., Amazon Kindle.

Facebook deployed facial recognition technology without any previous notice, which compromised its users' privacy by allowing them to be tagged in photos without their consent. Researchers at Carnegie Mellon found that it is possible to identify people, even their social security numbers, based on a single Facebook photograph and using facial recognition programs (Angwin, 2011; Acquisti, et al., 2011). After consumer uproar and challenges from various state attorneys general, Facebook reversed course and made it easier for users to opt out of the technology. In 2012, Facebook began pushing ads on its users based on their use of apps, and offering advertisers the ability to serve ads to Facebook users even while not using Facebook. In August 2013, Facebook announced a new privacy policy that it claimed clarified its use of personal information. In the new policy, Facebook claimed it could use any personal information for any purpose it wanted to. After howls of protest from users, privacy groups, and congressmen, the policy was temporarily withdrawn. For a review of Facebook's various positions on online privacy over the years, and public and congressional reaction to these issues, refer back to the *Insight on Society* case, *Facebook and the Age of Privacy*, in Chapter 1.

The result of these conflicts suggests that social network participants do indeed have a strong expectation of privacy in the sense that they want to control how "their" information is used. People who contribute user-generated content have a strong sense of ownership over that content that is not diminished by posting the information on a social network for one's friends. What's involved are some basic tenets of privacy thinking: personal control over the uses of personal information, choice, informed consent, participation in formulation of information policies, and due process. Some of these ideas are foreign to managers and owners seeking to monetize huge social network audiences. As for members who post information to everyone, not just friends, these should be seen as "public performances" where the contributors voluntarily publish their performances, just as writers or other artists do. This does not mean they want the entirety of their personal lives thrown open to every Web tracking automaton on the Internet.

MOBILE AND LOCATION-BASED PRIVACY ISSUES

As the mobile platform becomes more and more important, issues about mobile and location-based privacy are also becoming a major concern. In 2012, investigators discovered that iOS and Android apps were funneling location information to mobile advertisers, along with users' address books and photos (Bilton, 2012). In April 2012, Congress opened an investigation into the privacy policies of smartphone manufacturers, along with Facebook, Pinterest, Yahoo, Google and 30 others in the app marketplace. Twitter announced that anyone using its "Find Friends" feature on smartphones was also sending every phone number and e-mail address in their address books to the company (Sarno, 2012).

In April 2011, a furor erupted over news that Apple iPhones and iPads and Google Android smartphones were able to track and store user location information. In July 2012, Facebook launched a new mobile advertising service that tracks what apps people use on their smartphones, and what they do while using the apps. The tracking starts when users sign on to Facebook Connect with their smartphones. Apple and

Google track users' apps also. Apple disclosed that it can target ads based on the apps that a person has downloaded, while Google does not currently do this. Google and Apple do not track what users do on apps, while the Facebook program goes this additional step. For instance, Facebook can target a frequent player of Zynga games with ads using the player's Facebook News Feed, which is a major channel for Facebook ads (the other being display ads on the user's page) (Raice, 2012). Apps on both Android and Apple smartphones share user information with advertisers seeking to target their ads by location, time of day, and personal data shared with the app. Apple and Google have not settled on industry standards defining how mobile user data should be used, and what kinds of notice to users are required to protect users. In June 2011, a bill was proposed in the U.S. Senate that would require mobile companies to obtain a user's consent before collecting location-based data and before sharing that data with third parties. In 2012, investigators discovered that some cell phone companies had installed tracking devices inside phones to improve customer service. This ignited a flurry of criticism. In 2012, Congressman Ed Markey introduced the Mobile Device Privacy Act. The Act requires any firm performing consumer data collection on cell phones, other devices, or on Web sites, to inform consumers, and the Federal Trade Commission. However, the Act has not yet been passed by Congress.

According to a 2012 TRUSTe/Harris Interactive survey, 42% of smartphone users said privacy and security are their top concerns. Only 31% said they would exchange personal information in return for free apps. Amazon's use of personal information was twice as likely to be "acceptable" to respondents as was Facebook (68% vs. 33%) (TRUSTe, 2012; Harris, 2012). Refer back to the *Insight on Society* case, *Foursquare: Check Your Privacy at the Door*, in Chapter 2, for more discussion of some of the issues associated with mobile and location-based privacy.

PROFILING AND BEHAVIORAL TARGETING

On an average day, around 212 million Americans go online (Pew Internet & American Life Project, 2013). Marketers would like to know who these people are, what they are interested in, and what they buy. The more precise the information, the more complete the information, and the more valuable it is as a predictive and marketing tool. Armed with this information, marketers can make their ad campaigns more efficient by targeting specific ads at specific groups or individuals, and they can even adjust the ads for specific groups.

profiling
the creation of digital images that characterize online individual and group behavior

anonymous profiles
identify people as belonging to highly specific and targeted groups

personal profiles
add a personal e-mail address, postal address, and/or phone number to behavioral data

Many Web sites allow third parties—including online advertising networks such as Microsoft Advertising, DoubleClick, and others—to place "third-party" cookies and Web tracking software on a visitor's computer in order to engage in profiling the user's behavior across thousands of Web sites. A third-party cookie is used to track users across hundreds or thousands of other Web sites who are members of the advertising network. **Profiling** is the creation of digital images that characterize online individual and group behavior. **Anonymous profiles** identify people as belonging to highly specific and targeted groups, for example, 20- to 30-year-old males, with college degrees and incomes greater than $30,000 a year, and interested in high-fashion clothing (based on recent search engine use). **Personal profiles** add a personal e-mail address, postal address, and/or phone number to behavioral data.

Increasingly, online firms are linking their online profiles to personal offline consumer data collected by database firms tracking credit card purchases, as well as established retail and catalog firms. In the past, individual stores collected data on customer movement through a single store in order to understand consumer behavior and alter the design of stores accordingly. Also, purchase and expenditure data was gathered on consumers purchasing from multiple stores—usually long after the purchases were made—and the data was used to target direct mail and in-store campaigns, in addition to mass-media advertising.

The online advertising networks such as DoubleClick and 24/7 Real Media have added several new dimensions to established offline marketing techniques. First, they have the ability to precisely track not just consumer purchases, but all browsing behavior on the Web at thousands of the most popular member sites, including browsing book lists, filling out preference forms, and viewing content pages. Second, they can dynamically adjust what the shopper sees on screen—including prices. Third, they can build and continually refresh high-resolution data images or behavioral profiles of consumers. Other advertising firms have created spyware software that, when placed on a consumer's computer, can report back to the advertiser's server on all consumer Internet use, and is also used to display advertising on the consumer's computer.

A different kind of profiling and a more recent form of behavioral targeting is Google's results-based personalization of advertising. Google has a patent on a program that allows advertisers using Google's AdWords program to target ads to users based on their prior search histories and profiles, which Google constructs based on user searches, along with any other information the user submits to Google or that Google can obtain, such as age, demographics, region, and other Web activities (such as blogging). Google also applied for a second patent on a program that allows Google to help advertisers select keywords and design ads for various market segments based on search histories, such as helping a clothing Web site create and test ads targeted at teenage females. In 2007, Google began using behavioral targeting to help it display more relevant ads based on keywords. According to Google, the feature is aimed at capturing a more robust understanding of user intent, and thereby delivering a better ad. Google's Gmail, a free e-mail service, offers a powerful interface, and more than 7 gigabytes of free storage. In return, Google computers read all incoming and outgoing e-mail and place "relevant" advertising in the margins of the mail. Profiles are developed on individual users based on the content in their e-mail. Google's Chrome browser has a Suggest feature that automatically suggests related queries and Web sites when the user enters search terms. Critics pointed out this was a "key logger" device that would record every keystroke of users forever. Google has since announced it will anonymize the data within 24 hours. In 2010, Google began "personalizing" search results without asking users. Opt-in is the default option. Google uses your past personal search history to influence the ads you see on the page. It also can track the pages you subsequently visit if you have the Google toolbar turned on.

In 2013, both American and European regulators are objecting to Google's integration of personal information from all of its services into a single personal profile, and second, failing to let users know what it is doing with their personal information (Charlton, 2013). Google is claiming that people who send mail to a friend's Gmail account do not have an expectation of privacy, and that anyone who sends information to a third party does not have an expectation of privacy.

Facebook's photo recognition tools add a new dimension to profiling and behavioral targeting by posting the photos of users next to ads for products that they Liked. In this case, photo images and behavioral profile data is used directly to pitch products in the Facebook News Feed without the user's permission or even knowledge. Facebook claims that users opt into this use of their personal information in the initial registration, and that permitting Facebook to use any photographic information for any purpose is a condition of using the service (Goel and Watt, 2013).

deep packet inspection

a technology for recording every key stroke at the ISP level

Deep packet inspection is another technology for recording every keystroke at the ISP level of every Internet user (no matter where they ultimately go on the Web), and then using that information to make suggestions, and target ads. While advertising networks are limited, and even Google does not constitute the universe of search, deep packet inspection at the ISP level really does capture the universe of all Internet users. The leading firm in this technology was NebuAd. After testing the hardware and software with several ISPs, the outcry from privacy advocates and Congress caused these ISPs to withdraw from the experiment, and NebuAd withdrew the product from the market and subsequently closed its doors. In 2013, deep packet inspection is not used in the United States by advertising firms because of it is likely a violation of the Electronic Communications Privacy Act of 1986. It is used as network management and law enforcement tool (Kuehn and Mueller, 2012).

Network advertising firms argue that Web profiling benefits both consumers and businesses. Profiling permits targeting of ads, ensuring that consumers see advertisements mostly for products and services in which they are actually interested. Businesses benefit by not paying for wasted advertising sent to consumers who have no interest in their product or service. The industry argues that by increasing the effectiveness of advertising, more advertising revenues go to the Internet, which in turn subsidizes free content on the Internet. Last, product designers and entrepreneurs benefit by sensing demand for new products and services by examining user searches and profiles.

Critics argue that profiling undermines the expectation of anonymity and privacy that most people have when using the Internet, and changes what should be a private experience into one where an individual's every move is recorded. As people become aware that their every move is being watched, they will be far less likely to explore sensitive topics, browse pages, or read about controversial issues. In most cases, the profiling is invisible to users, and even hidden. Consumers are not notified that profiling is occurring. Profiling permits data aggregation on hundreds or even thousands of unrelated sites on the Web. The cookies placed by ad networks are persistent, and they can be set to last days, months, years, or even forever. Their tracking occurs over an extended period of time and resumes each time the individual logs on to the Internet. This clickstream data is used to create profiles that can include hundreds of distinct data fields for each consumer. Associating so-called anonymous profiles with personal information is fairly easy, and companies can change policies quickly without informing the consumer. Although the information gathered by network advertisers is often anonymous (non-PII data), in many cases, the profiles derived from tracking consumers' activities on the Web are linked or merged with personally identifiable information. Anonymous behavioral data is far more valuable if it can be linked with offline consumer behavior, e-mail addresses, and postal addresses.

From a privacy protection perspective, the advertising network raises issues about who will see and use the information held by private companies, whether the user profiles will be linked to actual personally identifying information (such as name, social security number, and bank and credit accounts), the absence of consumer control over the use of the information, the lack of consumer choice, the absence of consumer notice, and the lack of review and amendment procedures.

The pervasive and largely unregulated collection of personal information online has raised significant fears and opposition among consumers. Contrary to what the online advertising industry has often said, namely, that the public really does not care about its online privacy, there is a long history of opinion polls that document the public's fear of losing control over their personal information when visiting e-commerce sites. A 2012 survey by TRUSTe and Harris Interactive found that 94% of online consumers think privacy is an important issue, with 55% saying online privacy is really important to them. Targeted advertising makes 40% of those surveyed uncomfortable. More than 75% do not allow companies to share their personal information with a third party. More than two-thirds say they have stopped doing business with an online company because of privacy concerns (TRUSTe, 2012). A Pew Internet survey found that 68% of Internet users disapprove of Web sites that track their behavior for the purpose of ad targeting (Pew Internet, 2012). The actual amount of lost sales due to online privacy concerns is not known. This deep-seated and well-documented concern with respect to online privacy provides support for a steady stream of legislation seeking to redress this concern.

THE INTERNET AND GOVERNMENT INVASIONS OF PRIVACY: E-COMMERCE SURVEILLANCE

Today, the online and mobile behavior, profiles, and transactions of consumers are routinely available to a wide range of government agencies and law enforcement authorities, contributing to rising fears among online consumers, and in some cases, their withdrawal from the online marketplace. 2013 has not been a good year for advocates of privacy with revelations that federal government agencies have been routinely gathering cell phone call data on Americans and foreigners in the United States for a period of several years with scant judicial oversight. Working closely with private Internet firms like Google, Facebook, Twitter, and phone companies like Verizon and AT&T that operate the Internet, there seemed to be no limits on the reach of federal law enforcement agencies in pursuit of terrorists and terrorist conspiracies. Advances in technology for storing, processing, and analyzing unimaginable quantities of personal data, referred to as "Big Data" and "Business Analytics" (data mining and representation software), further heightened perceptions that privacy was increasingly difficult to define and protect in the age of e-commerce and social networks (Kakutani, 2013; Mayer-Schonberger and Cukier, 2013). Striking a balance between security and liberty is at the center of the privacy debate (Ford, 2013). While the Internet used to be thought of as impossible for governments to control or monitor, nothing could be actually further from the truth. Law enforcement authorities have long claimed the right under numerous statutes to monitor any form of electronic communication pursuant to a court order and judicial review and based on the reasonable belief that a crime is being committed. This includes the surveillance of consumers engaged in e-commerce. In the case of the Internet, this is accomplished by placing sniffer software and servers at the ISP being used by the target suspect, in a manner similar to pen registers and trap-and-trace devices used for telephone surveillance. The Communications Assistance for Law Enforcement Act (CALEA), the USA PATRIOT Act, the Cyber Security Enhancement Act, and the Homeland Security Act all strengthen the ability of law enforcement agencies to monitor Internet users without their knowledge and, under certain circumstances when life is purportedly at stake, without judicial oversight. The Patriot Act designed to combat terrorism inside the borders of the United States permits nearly unlimited government surveillance without court oversight, according to several senators (Savage, 2012).

There have been several Congressional initiatives to strengthen the privacy protections for electronic communications and personal location data. In 2013, Senators Patrick Leahy and Mike Lee introduced the "Electronic Communications Privacy Act Amendments Act of 2013," which would require a probable cause warrant for access to e-mail and other electronic communications no matter how long they were saved or where they were saved, whether on a personal computer or an online storage system. Under current law, there is no warrant requirement after an e-mail has been stored for 180 days. The bill also applies warrant requirements to the use of some location data. Also in 2013, Senator Ron Wyden and Representative Jason Chaffetz reintroduced the Geolocation Privacy and Surveillance Act (GPS Act) to protect location privacy. The bill requires law enforcement to get a warrant based on probable cause before accessing location information and also regulates the use of this information by businesses. With location tracking cases rising all over the country, this would provide a strong and clear national standard for law enforcement. Neither bill has yet passed as of October 2013.

Government agencies are among the largest users of private sector commercial data brokers, such as ChoicePoint, Acxiom, Experian, and TransUnion Corporation, that collect a vast amount of information about consumers from various offline and online public sources, such as public records and the telephone directory, and non-public sources, such as "credit header" information from credit bureaus (which typically contains name, aliases, birth date, social security number, current and prior addresses, and phone numbers). Acxiom is the largest private personal database in the world with records on more than 500,000 people and about 1,500 data points per person (Singer, 2012a). Information contained in individual reference services' databases ranges from purely identifying information (e.g., name and phone number) to much more extensive data (e.g., driving records, criminal and civil court records, property records, and licensing records). This information can be linked to online behavior information collected from other commercial sources to compile an extensive profile of an individual's online and offline behavior.

In 2011, a U.S. House of Representatives committee approved a bill that would have forced ISPs to keep logs of their customers' activities for one year and store information on customers' names, addresses, phone numbers, credit card numbers, bank account numbers, and temporarily assigned IP addresses. The logs would have been accessible to police investigating any crime and possibly to attorneys litigating civil disputes as well. Currently, ISPs typically discard log files that are no longer required for business reasons. However, the bill failed to pass the full House and Senate. The European Union's Data Retention Directive (DRD) is similar in nature but more limited in scope, requiring electronic communications providers to store usage and location data for a period of at least six months but for no longer than two years. The British government proposed in 2012 to permit intelligence and security services to monitor all of the communications of everyone in the country. However, the bill has not passed as of October 2013 and appears unlikely to become law (Cowell, 2012; Whittaker, 2012).

Retention of search engine query data is also an issue. Although the amount of time such data is retained is not governed by U.S. law, the European Union has indicated that it should not be retained for more than six months. The three major search engines (Google, Bing, and Yahoo) have varying policies. In 2010, Microsoft agreed to reduce the amount of time that it retains certain data, such as IP addresses, to six months to comply with the E.U. standard, although it retains other data, such as cookie IDs and cross-session IDs for 18 months. Google has refused, however, and retains search records for 18 months, claiming that this amount of time is necessary for it to improve services and prevent fraud. In 2011, Yahoo, which had previously prided itself for retaining search records for only three months, announced that it too would extend that time to 18 months, for competitive reasons.

LEGAL PROTECTIONS

In the United States, Canada, and Germany, rights to privacy are explicitly granted in, or can be derived from, founding documents such as constitutions, as well as in specific statutes. In England and the United States, there is also protection of privacy in the common law, a body of court decisions involving torts or personal injuries. For instance, in the United States, four privacy-related torts have been defined in court decisions involving claims of injury to individuals caused by other private parties: intrusion on solitude, public disclosure of private facts, publicity placing a person in a false light, and appropriation of a person's name or likeness (mostly concerning celebrities) for a commercial purpose (Laudon, 1996). In the United States, the claim to privacy against government intrusion is protected primarily by the First Amendment guarantees of freedom of speech and association, the Fourth Amendment protections against unreasonable search and seizure of one's personal documents or home, and the Fourteenth Amendment's guarantee of due process.

In addition to common law and the Constitution, there are both federal laws and state laws that protect individuals against government intrusion and in some cases define privacy rights vis-à-vis private organizations such as financial, educational, and media institutions (cable television and video rentals) (see **Table 8.4**).

Informed Consent

The concept of **informed consent** (defined as consent given with knowledge of all material facts needed to make a rational decision) also plays an important role in

informed consent
consent given with knowledge of all material facts needed to make a rational decision

TABLE 8.4	FEDERAL AND STATE PRIVACY LAWS
NAME	DESCRIPTION
GENERAL FEDERAL PRIVACY LAWS	
Freedom of Information Act of 1966	Gives people the right to inspect information about themselves held in government files; also allows other individuals and organizations the right to request disclosure of government records based on the public's right to know.
Privacy Act of 1974, as amended	Regulates the federal government's collection, use, and disclosure of data collected by federal agencies. Gives individuals a right to inspect and correct records.
Electronic Communications Privacy Act of 1986	Makes conduct that would infringe on the security of electronic communications illegal.
Computer Security Act of 1987	Makes conduct that would infringe on the security of computer-based files illegal.
Computer Matching and Privacy Protection Act of 1988	Regulates computerized matching of files held by different government agencies.
Driver's Privacy Protection Act of 1994	Limits access to personal information maintained by state motor vehicle departments to those with legitimate business purposes. Also gives drivers the option to prevent disclosure of driver's license information to marketers and the general public.
E-Government Act of 2002	Regulates the collection and use of personal information by federal agencies.
FEDERAL PRIVACY LAWS AFFECTING PRIVATE INSTITUTIONS	
Fair Credit Reporting Act of 1970	Regulates the credit investigating and reporting industry. Gives people the right to inspect credit records if they have been denied credit and provides procedures for correcting information.
Family Educational Rights and Privacy Act of 1974	Requires schools and colleges to give students and their parents access to student records and to allow them to challenge and correct information; limits disclosure of such records to third parties.
Right to Financial Privacy Act of 1978	Regulates the financial industry's use of personal financial records; establishes procedures that federal agencies must follow to gain access to such records.
Privacy Protection Act of 1980	Prohibits government agents from conducting unannounced searches of press offices and files if no one in the office is suspected of committing a crime.
Cable Communications Policy Act of 1984	Regulates the cable industry's collection and disclosure of information concerning subscribers.
Video Privacy Protection Act of 1988	Prevents disclosure of a person's video rental records without court order or consent.
Children's Online Privacy Protection Act (1998)	Prohibits deceptive practices in connection with the collection, use, and/or disclosure of personal information from and about children on the Internet.
Health Insurance Portability and Accountability Act of 1996 (HIPAA)	Requires healthcare providers and insurers and other third parties to promulgate privacy policies to consumers and establishes due process procedures.
Financial Modernization Act (Gramm-Leach-Bliley Act) (1999)	Requires financial institutions to inform consumers of their privacy policies and permits consumers some control over their records.

TABLE 8.4	FEDERAL AND STATE PRIVACY LAWS (CONT'D)
NAME	**DESCRIPTION**

SELECTED STATE PRIVACY LAWS

Online privacy policies	The California Online Privacy Protection Act of 2003 was the first state law in the United States requiring owners of commercial Web sites or online services to post a privacy policy. The policy must, among other things, identify the categories of PII collected about site visitors and categories of third parties with whom the information may be shared. Failure to comply can result in a civil suit for unfair business practices. Nebraska and Pennsylvania prohibit false and misleading statements in online privacy policies. At least 16 states require government Web sites to establish privacy policies or procedures or incorporate machine-readable privacy policies into their Web sites.
Spyware legislation	A number of states, including California, Utah, Arizona, Arkansas, and Virginia, among others, have passed laws that outlaw the installation of spyware on a user's computer without consent.
Disclosure of security breaches	In 2002, California enacted legislation that requires state agencies or businesses that own or license computer data with personal information to notify state residents if they experience a security breach involving that information; today, nearly every state has enacted similar legislation.
Privacy of personal information	Two states, Nevada and Minnesota, require ISPs to keep their customers' PII private unless the customer consents to disclose the information. Minnesota also requires ISPs to get permission from subscribers before disclosing information about subscribers' online surfing habits.
Data encryption	In October 2007, Nevada passed the first law that requires encryption for the transmission of customer personal information. The law took effect October 1, 2008.

protecting privacy. In the United States, business firms (and government agencies) can gather transaction information generated in the marketplace and then use that information for other marketing purposes, without obtaining the informed consent of the individual. For instance, in the United States, if a Web shopper purchases books about baseball at a site that belongs to an advertising network such as DoubleClick, a cookie can be placed on the consumer's hard drive and used by other member sites to sell the shopper sports clothing without the explicit permission or even knowledge of the user. This online preference information may also be linked with personally identifying information. In Europe, this would be illegal. A business in Europe cannot use marketplace transaction information for any purpose other than supporting the current transaction, unless of course it obtains the individual's consent in writing or by filling out an on-screen form.

There are traditionally two models for informed consent: opt-in and opt-out. The **opt-in** model requires an affirmative action by the consumer to allow collection and

opt-in
requires an affirmative action by the consumer to allow collection and use of consumer information

use of information. For instance, using opt-in, consumers would first be asked if they approved of the collection and use of information, and then directed to check a selection box if they agreed. Otherwise, the default is not to approve the collection of data. In the **opt-out** model, the default is to collect information unless the consumer takes an affirmative action to prevent the collection of data by checking a box or by filling out a form.

opt-out

the default is to collect information unless the consumer takes an affirmative action to prevent the collection of data

Until recently, many U.S. e-commerce companies rejected the concept of informed consent and instead simply published their information use policy on their site. U.S. businesses argue that informing consumers about how the information will be used is sufficient to obtain the users' informed consent. Most U.S. sites that offer informed consent make opting in the default option, and require users to go to special pages to request to opt out of promotional campaigns. Some sites have an opt-out selection box at the very bottom of their information policy statements where the consumer is unlikely to see it. On Yahoo's home page there is a link that takes users to an AdChoice page that allows users to opt out of interest-based advertising although the user has to allow cookies from Yahoo and sign into a Yahoo account before the choices take effect. Privacy advocates argue that many information/privacy policy statements on U.S. Web sites are obscure and difficult to read, and legitimate just about any use of personal information. For instance, Yahoo's privacy policy begins by stating that Yahoo takes the user's privacy seriously and Yahoo does not rent, sell, or share personal information about users with others or non-affiliated companies. However, there are a number of exceptions that significantly weaken this statement. For instance, Yahoo may share the information with trusted partners, which could be anyone that Yahoo does business with, although perhaps not a company that the user might choose to do business with. In its privacy policy, Yahoo also says it places web beacons on its Web pages and e-mails in order to track user clickstream behavior across the Web.

The Federal Trade Commission's Fair Information Practices Principles

In the United States, the Federal Trade Commission (FTC) has taken the lead in conducting research on online privacy and recommending legislation to Congress. The FTC is a cabinet-level agency charged with promoting the efficient functioning of the marketplace by protecting consumers from unfair or deceptive practices and increasing consumer choice by promoting competition. In addition to reports and recommendations, the FTC enforces existing legislation by suing corporations it believes are in violation of federal fair trade laws.

In 1998, the FTC issued its Fair Information Practice (FIP) principles, on which it has based its assessments and recommendations for online privacy. **Table 8.5** describes these principles. Two of the five are designated as basic, "core" principles that must be present to protect privacy, whereas the other practices are less central. The FTC's FIP principles restate and strengthen in a form suitable to deal with online privacy the Fair Information Practices doctrine developed in 1973 by a government study group (U.S. Department of Health, Education and Welfare, 1973).

The FTC's FIP principles set the ground rules for what constitutes due process privacy protection procedures at e-commerce and all other Web sites—including government and nonprofit Web sites—in the United States.

TABLE 8.5	FEDERAL TRADE COMMISSION'S FAIR INFORMATION PRACTICE PRINCIPLES
Notice/Awareness (core principle)	Sites must disclose their information practices before collecting data. Includes identification of collector, uses of data, other recipients of data, nature of collection (active/ Inactive), voluntary or required, consequences of refusal, and steps taken to protect confidentiality, integrity, and quality of the data.
Choice/Consent (core principle)	There must be a choice regime in place allowing consumers to choose how their information will be used for secondary purposes other than supporting the transaction, including internal use and transfer to third parties. Opt-in/opt-out must be available.
Access/Participation	Consumers should be able to review and contest the accuracy and completeness of data collected about them in a timely, inexpensive process.
Security	Data collectors must take reasonable steps to assure that consumer information is accurate and secure from unauthorized use.
Enforcement	There must be a mechanism to enforce FIP principles in place. This can involve self-regulation, legislation giving consumers legal remedies for violations, or federal statutes and regulation.

SOURCE: Based on data from Federal Trade Commission, 1998, 2000a.

The FTC's FIP principles are guidelines, not laws. They have stimulated private firms and industry associations to develop their own private guidelines (discussed next). However, the FTC's FIP guidelines are often used as the basis of legislation. The most important online privacy legislation to date that has been directly influenced by the FTC's FIP principles is the Children's Online Privacy Protection Act (COPPA) (1998), which requires Web sites to obtain parental permission before collecting information on children under 13 years of age.

In 2000, the FTC recommended legislation to Congress to protect online consumer privacy from the threat posed by advertising networks. **Table 8.6** summarizes the commission's recommendations. The FTC profiling recommendations significantly strengthened the FIP principles of notification and choice, while also including restrictions on information that may be collected.[1] Although the FTC supported industry efforts at self-regulation, it nevertheless recommended legislation to ensure that all Web sites using network advertising and all network advertisers complied.

In the last decade, the FTC's privacy approach has shifted somewhat, away from notice and choice requirements and into a harm-based approach targeting practices that are likely to cause harm or unwarranted intrusion in consumers' daily lives.

[1] Much general privacy legislation affecting government, e.g., the Privacy Act of 1974, precludes the government from collecting information on political and social behavior of citizens. The FTC restrictions are significant because they are the FTC's first effort at limiting the collection of certain information.

TABLE 8.6	FTC RECOMMENDATIONS REGARDING ONLINE PROFILING
PRINCIPLE	DESCRIPTION OF RECOMMENDATION
Notice	Complete transparency to user by providing disclosure and choice options on the host Web site. "Robust" notice for PII (time/place of collection; before collection begins). Clear and conspicuous notice for non-PII.
Choice	Opt-in for PII, opt-out for non-PII. No conversion of non-PII to PII without consent. Opt-out from any or all network advertisers from a single page provided by the host Web site.
Access	Reasonable provisions to allow inspection and correction.
Security	Reasonable efforts to secure information from loss, misuse, or improper access.
Enforcement	Done by independent third parties, such as seal programs and accounting firms.
Restricted collection	Advertising networks will not collect information about sensitive financial or medical topics, sexual behavior or sexual orientation, or use social security numbers for profiling.

SOURCE: Based on data from Federal Trade Commission, 2000b.

However, in recent years, the FTC has recognized the limitations of both the notice-and-choice and harm-based models. In 2009, the FTC held a series of three public roundtables to explore the effectiveness of these approaches in light of rapidly evolving technology and the market for consumer data. The major concepts that emerged from these roundtables were:

- The increasing collection and use of consumer data
- Consumers' lack of understanding about the collection and use of their personal data, and the resulting inability to make informed choices
- Consumers' interest in and concern about their privacy
- Benefits of data collection and use to both businesses and consumers
- Decreasing relevance of the distinction between PII and non-PII.

As a result of the roundtables, the FTC has now developed a new framework to address consumer privacy. **Table 8.7** summarizes the important aspects of this framework. Among the most noteworthy is the call for a "Do Not Track" mechanism for online behavioral advertising. The mechanism would involve placing a persistent cookie on a consumer's browser and conveying its setting to sites that the browser visits to signal whether or not the consumer wants to be tracked or receive targeted advertisements. A number of bills have been introduced in Congress to implement Do Not Track, but as yet none have been passed.

In response to growing public and congressional concern with online and mobile privacy violations, the FTC has begun taking a much more aggressive stance based on its new privacy policies developed over several years. In March 2011, the FTC reached

TABLE 8.7	THE FTC'S NEW PRIVACY FRAMEWORK
PRINCIPLE	APPLICATION
Scope	Applies to all commercial entities that collect or use consumer data; not limited to those that just collect PII.
Privacy by Design	Companies should promote consumer privacy throughout the organization and at every stage of development of products and services: • Data security • Reasonable collection limits • Reasonable and appropriate data retention policies • Data accuracy • Comprehensive data management procedures
Simplified Choice	Companies should simplify consumer choice. Need not provide choice before collecting and using data for commonly accepted practices: • Product and fulfillment • Internal operations, fraud prevention • Legal compliance • First-party marketing For all other commercial data collection and use, choice is required, and should be clearly and conspicuously offered at a time and in context in which consumer is providing data. Some types of information or practices (children, financial, and medical information, deep packet inspection) may require additional protection through enhanced consent. Special choice mechanism for online behavioral advertising: "Do Not Track."
Greater Transparency	Increase transparency of data practices by: • Making privacy notices clearer, shorter, and more standardized to enable better comprehension and comparison • Providing consumers with reasonable access to data about themselves • Providing prominent disclosures and obtaining express affirmative consent before using consumer data in a materially different manner than claimed when data was collected • Educating consumers about commercial data privacy practices

SOURCE: Based on data from Federal Trade Commission, 2010.

an agreement with Google concerning charges it used deceptive tactics and violated its own privacy policies when it launched its Google Buzz social network, forcing people to join the network even if they selected not to join. Under the settlement, Google agreed to start a privacy program, permit independent privacy audits for 20 years, and face $16,000 fines for every future privacy misrepresentation. This was the first time the FTC had charged a company with such violations and ordered it to start a privacy program (Federal Trade Commission, 2011). In August 2012, the FTC fined Google $22.5 million to settle charges that it had bypassed privacy settings in Apple's Safari browser to be able to track users of the browser and show them advertisements, and violated the earlier privacy settlement with the agency. This fine is the largest civil penalty levied by the FTC to date, which has been cracking down on tech companies for privacy violations and is also investigating Google for antitrust violations (Federal Trade Commission, 2012a). In August 2012, the FTC also reached a settlement with Facebook resolving charges that Facebook deceived its users by telling them they could keep their information on Facebook private, but then repeatedly allowing it to be shared and made public. The settlement requires Facebook to live up to its promises by giving consumers clear and prominent notice and obtaining their express consent before sharing their information beyond the user's privacy settings. It also requires Facebook to develop a comprehensive privacy program, and obtain independent biennial privacy audits for a period of 20 years (Federal Trade Commission, 2012b). In September 2012, the FTC also reached a settlement with Myspace for misrepresenting its privacy policies. The settlement bars Myspace from future misrepresentations, requires the company to implement a comprehensive privacy program, and calls for regular, independent privacy assessments for the next 20 years (Federal Trade Commission, 2012c).

In March 2012, the FTC released a final report based on its work in the previous two years. The report describes industry best practices for protecting the privacy of Americans and focuses on five areas: Do Not Track, mobile privacy, data brokers, large platform providers (advertising networks, operating systems, browsers, and social media companies), and the development of self-regulatory codes. The report called for implementation of an easy to use, persistent, and effective Do Not Track system; improved disclosures for use of mobile data; making it easier for people to see the files about themselves compiled by data brokers; development of a central Web site where data brokers identify themselves; development of a privacy policy by large platform providers to regulate comprehensive tracking across the Internet; and enforcement of self-regulatory rules to ensure firms adhere to industry codes of conduct. The report warned that unless the industry developed a Do Not Track button for Web browsers by the end of the year, and developed policies for reigning in rampant online tracking without user consent by data brokers, it would seek legislation to force these requirements on the industry (Federal Trade Commission, 2012d). The FTC report is supported by the White House, which in February 2012 issued its own framework for protecting online privacy. One provision of this framework is the development of a one-click, one-touch process by which users can tell Internet companies whether they want their online activities tracked. In July 2012, eight members of Congress launched an investigation of data brokers who collect both online and offline data on consumers.

Facing fines, congressional investigations, and public embarrassment over their privacy invading behaviors, with the potential loss of some business and credibility, the major players in the e-commerce industry in the United States are beginning to change some of their policies regarding the treatment of consumer data.

In 2013, large Internet firms that rely on personal information (Google, Facebook, Microsoft, and many others), along with privacy advocates, are calling on Washington to develop comprehensive consumer privacy protection legislation that would clarify for consumers and business firms the meaning of privacy in the current online commercial environment (Singer, 2013). The Obama administration has proposed a Consumer Privacy Bill of Rights that emphasizes transparency (how personal information is being used and distributed) and user control over personal information. This represents a change in the meaning of privacy from "leave me alone" to "I want to know and control how my personal information is being used."

The European Data Protection Directive

In Europe, privacy protection is much stronger than it is in the United States. In the United States, private organizations and businesses are permitted to use PII gathered in commercial transactions for other business purposes without the prior consent of the consumer (so-called secondary uses of PII). In the United States, there is no federal agency charged with enforcing privacy laws. Instead, privacy laws are enforced largely through self-regulation by businesses, and by individuals who must sue agencies or companies in court to recover damages. This is expensive and rarely done. The European approach to privacy protection is more comprehensive and regulatory in nature. European countries do not allow business firms to use PII without the prior consent of consumers. They enforce their privacy laws by creating data protection agencies to pursue complaints brought by citizens and actively enforce privacy laws.

On October 25, 1998, the European Commission's Data Protection Directive went into effect, standardizing and broadening privacy protection in the E.U. nations. The Directive is based on the Fair Information Practices doctrine but extends the control individuals can exercise over their personal information. The Directive requires companies to inform people when they collect information about them and to disclose how it will be stored and used. Customers must provide their informed consent before any company can legally use data about them, and they have the right to access that information, correct it, and request that no further data be collected. Further, the Directive prohibits the transfer of PII to organizations or countries that do not have similarly strong privacy protection policies. This means that data collected in Europe by American business firms cannot be transferred or processed in the United States (which has weaker privacy protection laws). This would potentially interfere with a $3.5 trillion annual trade flow in goods, services, and investment between the United States and Europe.

The U.S. Department of Commerce, working with the European Commission, developed a safe harbor framework for U.S. firms. A **safe harbor** is a private self-regulating policy and enforcement mechanism that meets the objectives of government regulators and legislation, but does not involve government regulation or enforcement. The government plays a role in certifying **safe harbors**, however. Organizations that decide to participate in the safe harbor program must develop policies that meet European standards, and they must publicly sign on to a Web-based register maintained by the Department of Commerce. Enforcement occurs in the United States and relies to a large extent on self-policing and regulation, backed up by government enforcement of fair trade statutes. For more information on the safe harbor procedures and the E.U. Data Directive, see www.export.gov/safeharbor.

safe harbor
a private self-regulating policy and enforcement mechanism that meets the objectives of government regulators and legislation but does not involve government regulation or enforcement

In 2012, the E.U. issued significant proposed changes to its data protection rules, the first overhaul since 1995 (European Commission, 2012). The new rules would apply to all companies providing services in Europe, and require Internet companies like Amazon, Facebook, Apple, Google, and others to obtain explicit consent from consumers about the use of their personal data, delete information at the user's request (based on the "right to be forgotten"), and retain information only as long as absolutely necessary. The regulations also give users the right to transfer text, photo and video files in usable formats from one online service provider to another. American consumers do not have such a national right to data portability, and have to depend on the largesse of companies like Google, which permits them to download their own YouTube videos or Picasa photo albums. The proposed rules provide for fines up to 2% of the annual gross revenue of offending firms. In the case of Google, for instance, with 2012 revenue of $50 billion, a maximum fine would amount to $1 billion. The requirement for user consent includes the use of cookies and super cookies used for tracking purposes across the Web (third-party cookies), and not for cookies used on a Web site. Like the FTC's proposed framework, the EU's new proposed rules have a strong emphasis on regulating tracking, enforcing transparency, limiting data retention periods, and obtaining user consent. The regulations are expected to be formally adopted in 2014 and take effect by 2016.

PRIVATE INDUSTRY SELF-REGULATION

The online industry in the United States has historically opposed online privacy legislation, arguing that industry can do a better job of protecting privacy than government. However, individual firms such as Facebook, Apple, Yahoo, and Google have adopted policies on their own in an effort to address the concerns of the public about personal privacy on the Internet. The online industry formed the Online Privacy Alliance (OPA) in 1998 to encourage self-regulation in part as a reaction to growing public concerns and the threat of legislation being proposed by FTC and privacy advocacy groups.

The FTC and private industry in the United States has created the idea of safe harbors from government regulation. For instance, COPPA includes a provision enabling industry groups or others to submit for the FTC's approval self-regulatory guidelines that implement the protections of the FIP principles and FTC rules. In May 2001, the FTC approved the TRUSTe Internet privacy protection program under the terms of COPPA as a safe harbor.

OPA has developed a set of privacy guidelines that members are required to implement. The primary focus of industry efforts has been the development of online "seals" that attest to the privacy policies on a site. The Better Business Bureau (BBB), TRUSTe, WebTrust, and major accounting firms—among them PricewaterhouseCoopers' BetterWeb—have established seals for Web sites. To display a seal, Web site operators must conform to certain privacy principles, a complaint resolution process, and monitoring by the seal originator. More than 5,000 companies subscribe to TRUSTe and more than 7,000 Web sites now display the TRUSTe seal, while more than 140,000 display the BBB's Accredited Business seal. Nevertheless, online privacy seal programs have had a limited impact on Web privacy practices. Critics argue that the seal programs are not particularly effective in safeguarding privacy. For these reasons, the FTC has not deemed the seal programs as "safe harbors" yet (with the exception of TRUSTe's children's privacy seal under COPPA), and the agency continues to push for legislation to enforce privacy protection principles.

The advertising network industry has also formed an industry association, the Network Advertising Initiative (NAI), to develop privacy policies. The NAI policies have two objectives: to offer consumers a chance to opt out of advertising network programs (including e-mail campaigns), and to provide consumers redress from abuses. In order to opt out, the NAI has created a Web site—Networkadvertising.org—where consumers can use a global opt-out feature to prevent network advertising agencies from placing their cookies on a user's computer. If a consumer has a complaint, the NAI has a link to the Truste.org Web site where the complaints can be filed. Consumers still receive Internet advertising just as before, but the ads will not be targeted to their browsing behavior (Network Advertising Initiative, 2010; 2011).

In general, industry efforts at self-regulation in online privacy have not succeeded in reducing American fears of privacy invasion during online transactions, or in reducing the level of privacy invasion. At best, self-regulation has offered consumers notice about whether a privacy policy exists, but usually says little about the actual use of the information, does not offer consumers a chance to see and correct the information or control its use in any significant way, offers no promises for the security of that information, and offers no enforcement mechanism (Hoofnagle, 2005).

PRIVACY ADVOCACY GROUPS

There are a number of privacy advocacy groups on the Web that monitor developments in privacy. Some of these sites are industry-supported, while others rely on private foundations and contributions. Some of the better-known sites are listed in **Table 8.8**.

TABLE 8.8	PRIVACY ADVOCACY GROUPS
ADVOCACY GROUP	FOCUS
Epic.org (Electronic Privacy Information Center)	Washington-based watch-dog group
Privacyinternational.org	Watch-dog organization focused on privacy intrusions by government and businesses
Cdt.org (Center for Democracy and Technology)	Foundation- and business-supported group with a legislative focus
Privacy.org	Clearinghouse sponsored by EPIC and Privacy International
Privacyrights.org	Educational clearinghouse
Privacyalliance.org	Industry-supported clearinghouse

THE EMERGING PRIVACY PROTECTION BUSINESS

As Web sites become more invasive and aggressive in their use of personal information, and as public concern grows, a number of firms have sprung up to sell products that they claim will help people protect their privacy. Venture capital firms have picked up the scent and are investing millions in small start-up companies based on the premise that people will pay to protect their reputations. For instance, Reputation.com has received over $67 million in funding as of 2013. Other firms in the business of reputation protection include Avira Social Network Protection and Abine. For as little as $14.95 a month, you can monitor what people are saying about you, or about your children, on social Web sites. A small number of firms are trying to help users put a price on their personal information, and sell it to the highest bidders if they want (Laudon, 1996). Personal.com and LockerProject are firms that create a personal data locker for users that stores all their online behavioral information in a single location. Users can then decide who they want to give access to, and how much to charge. The idea is to make it possible for people to control the uses of their information. Personal.com has raised over $8 million as of 2013. However, these types of firms can succeed only if people are willing to pay out of pocket for privacy protection. Economists studying this issue have found that people are not willing to pay much to protect their privacy (at most about $30), and are willing to give up their privacy for small discounts (Brustein, 2012; Acquisti, et. al., 2009).

TECHNOLOGICAL SOLUTIONS

A number of privacy-enhancing technologies have been developed for protecting user privacy during interactions with Web sites such as spyware blockers, pop-up blockers, cookie managers, and secure e-mail (see **Table 8.9**). However, the most powerful tools for protecting privacy need to be built into browsers. Responding to pressure from privacy advocates in 2012, browsers have a number of tools that can help users protect their privacy, such as eliminating third-party cookies. One of the most powerful browser-based protections is a built-in Do Not Track capability. Microsoft, Mozilla, Google, and Apple have all introduced a default Do Not Track capability. Microsoft ships its browser with the default set to "Do Not Track." Others may follow this precedent in time. Most of these tools emphasize security—the ability of individuals to protect their communications and files from illegitimate snoopers.

8.3 INTELLECTUAL PROPERTY RIGHTS

Congress shall have the power to "promote the progress of science and useful arts, by securing for limited times to authors and inventors the exclusive right to their respective writings and discoveries."

—Article I, Section 8, Constitution of the United States, 1788.

TABLE 8.9	TECHNOLOGICAL PROTECTIONS FOR ONLINE PRIVACY	
TECHNOLOGY	PRODUCTS	PROTECTION
Spyware blockers	Spyware Doctor, ZoneAlarm, Ad-Aware, and Spybot—Search & Destroy (Spybot-S&D) (freeware)	Detects and removes spyware, adware, keyloggers, and other malware
Pop-up blockers	Browsers: Firefox, IE, Safari, Opera Toolbars: Google, Yahoo, MSN Add-on programs: Adblock, PopUpMaster	Prevents calls to ad servers that push pop-up, pop-under, and leave-behind ads; restricts downloading of images at user request
Secure e-mail	ZL Technologies; SafeMessage.com, Hushmail.com, Pretty Good Privacy (PGP)	E-mail and document encryption
Anonymous remailers	Jack B. Nymble, Java Anonymous Proxy, QuickSilver, Mixmaster	Send e-mail without trace
Anonymous surfing	Freedom Websecure, Anonymizer.com, Tor, GhostSurf	Surf without a trace
Cookie managers	Cookie Monster and most browsers	Prevents client computer from accepting cookies
Disk/file erasing programs	Mutilate File Wiper, Eraser, Wipe File	Completely erases hard drive and floppy files
Policy generators	OECD Privacy Policy Generator	Automates the development of an OECD privacy compliance policy
Public Key Encryption	PGP Desktop	Program that encrypts your mail and documents

Next to privacy, the most controversial ethical, social, and political issue related to e-commerce is the fate of intellectual property rights. Intellectual property encompasses all the tangible and intangible products of the human mind. As a general rule, in the United States, the creator of intellectual property owns it. For instance, if you personally create an e-commerce site, it belongs entirely to you, and you have exclusive rights to use this "property" in any lawful way you see fit. But the Internet potentially changes things. Once intellectual works become digital, it becomes difficult to control access, use, distribution, and copying. These are precisely the areas that intellectual property seeks to control.

Digital media differ from books, periodicals, and other media in terms of ease of replication, transmission, and alteration; difficulty in classifying a software work as a program, book, or even music; compactness—making theft easy; and difficulty in establishing uniqueness. Before widespread use of the Internet, copies of software, books, magazine articles, or films had to be stored on physical media, such as paper, computer disks, or videotape, creating some hurdles to distribution.

The Internet technically permits millions of people to make perfect digital copies of various works—from music to plays, poems, and journal articles—and then to distribute them nearly cost-free to hundreds of millions of Web users. The proliferation of innovation has occurred so rapidly that few entrepreneurs have stopped to consider who owns the patent on a business technique or method that they are using on their site. The spirit of the Web has been so free-wheeling that many entrepreneurs ignored trademark law and registered domain names that could easily be confused with another company's registered trademarks. In short, the Internet has demonstrated the potential to destroy traditional conceptions and implementations of intellectual property law developed over the last two centuries.

The major ethical issue related to e-commerce and intellectual property concerns how we (both as individuals and as business professionals) should treat property that belongs to others. From a social point of view, the main questions are: Is there continued value in protecting intellectual property in the Internet age? In what ways is society better off, or worse off, for having the concept of property apply to intangible ideas? Should society make certain technology illegal just because it has an adverse impact on some intellectual property owners? From a political perspective, we need to ask how the Internet and e-commerce can be regulated or governed to protect the institution of intellectual property while at the same time encouraging the growth of e-commerce and the Internet.

TYPES OF INTELLECTUAL PROPERTY PROTECTION

There are three main types of intellectual property protection: copyright, patent, and trademark law. In the United States, the development of intellectual property law begins in the U.S. Constitution in 1788, which mandated Congress to devise a system of laws to promote "the progress of science and the useful arts." Congress passed the first copyright law in 1790 to protect original written works for a period of 14 years, with a 14-year renewal if the author was still alive. Since then, the idea of copyright has been extended to include music, films, translations, photographs, and most recently the designs of vessels under 200 feet (Fisher, 1999). The copyright law has been amended (mostly extended) 11 times in the last 40 years.

The goal of intellectual property law is to balance two competing interests—the public and the private. The public interest is served by the creation and distribution of inventions, works of art, music, literature, and other forms of intellectual expression. The private interest is served by rewarding people for creating these works through the creation of a time-limited monopoly granting exclusive use to the creator.

Maintaining this balance of interests is always challenged by the invention of new technologies. In general, the information technologies of the last century—from radio and television to CD-ROMs, DVDs, and the Internet—have at first tended to weaken the protections afforded by intellectual property law. Owners of intellectual property have often, but not always, been successful in pressuring Congress and the courts to strengthen the intellectual property laws to compensate for any technological threat, and even to extend protection for longer periods of time and to entirely new areas of expression. In the case of the Internet and e-commerce technologies, once again, intellectual property rights are severely challenged. In the next few sections, we discuss the significant developments in each area: copyright, patent, and trademark.

COPYRIGHT: THE PROBLEM OF PERFECT COPIES AND ENCRYPTION

In the United States, **copyright law** protects original forms of expression such as writings (books, periodicals, lecture notes), art, drawings, photographs, music, motion pictures, performances, and computer programs from being copied by others for a period of time. Up until 1998, the copyright law protected works of individuals for their lifetime plus 50 years beyond their life, and works created for hire and owned by corporations, such as Mickey Mouse of the Disney Corporation, for 75 years after initial creation. Copyright does not protect ideas—just their expression in a tangible medium such as paper, cassette tape, or handwritten notes.

In 1998, Congress extended the period of copyright protection for an additional 20 years, for a total of 95 years for corporate-owned works, and life plus 70 years of protection for works created by individuals (the Copyright Term Extension Act, also known as CTEA). In *Eldred v. Ashcroft*, the Supreme Court ruled on January 16, 2003, that CTEA was constitutional, over the objections of groups arguing that Congress had given copyright holders a permanent monopoly over the expression of ideas, which ultimately would work to inhibit the flow of ideas and creation of new works by making existing works too expensive (Greenhouse, 2003a). Librarians, academics, and others who depend on inexpensive access to copyrighted material opposed the legislation.

In the mid-1960s, the Copyright Office began registering software programs, and in 1980, Congress passed the Computer Software Copyright Act, which clearly provides protection for source and object code and for copies of the original sold in commerce, and sets forth the rights of the purchaser to use the software while the creator retains legal title. For instance, the HTML code for a Web page—even though easily available to every browser—cannot be lawfully copied and used for a commercial purpose, say, to create a new Web site that looks identical.

Copyright protection is clear-cut: it protects against copying of entire programs or their parts. Damages and relief are readily obtained for infringement. The drawback to copyright protection is that the underlying ideas behind a work are not protected, only their expression in a work. A competitor can view the source code on your Web site to see how various effects were created and then reuse those techniques to create a different Web site without infringing on your copyright.

copyright law

protects original forms of expression such as writings, art, drawings, photographs, music, motion pictures, performances, and computer programs from being copied by others for a minimum of 70 years

Look and Feel

"Look and feel" copyright infringement lawsuits are precisely about the distinction between an idea and its expression. For instance, in 1988, Apple Computer sued Microsoft Corporation and Hewlett-Packard Inc. for infringing Apple's copyright on the Macintosh interface. Among other claims, Apple claimed that the defendants copied the expression of overlapping windows. Apple failed to patent the idea of overlapping windows when it invented this method of presenting information on a computer screen in the late 1960s. The defendants counterclaimed that the idea of overlapping windows could only be expressed in a single way and, therefore, was not protectable under the "merger" doctrine of copyright law. When ideas and their expression merge

TABLE 8.10	FAIR USE CONSIDERATIONS TO COPYRIGHT PROTECTIONS
FAIR USE FACTOR	INTERPRETATION
Character of use	Nonprofit or educational use versus for-profit use.
Nature of the work	Creative works such as plays or novels receive greater protection than factual accounts, e.g., newspaper accounts.
Amount of work used	A stanza from a poem or a single page from a book would be allowed, but not the entire poem or a book chapter.
Market effect of use	Will the use harm the marketability of the original product? Has it already harmed the product in the marketplace?
Context of use	A last-minute, unplanned use in a classroom versus a planned infringement.

(i.e., if there is only one way to express an idea), the expression cannot be copyrighted, although the method of producing the expression might be patentable (*Apple Computer, Inc. v. Microsoft*, 1989). In general, courts appear to be following the reasoning of a 1992 case—*Brown Bag Software vs. Symantec Corp.*—in which the court dissected the elements of software alleged to be infringing. There, the Federal Circuit Court of Appeals found that neither similar concept, function, general functional features (e.g., drop-down menus), nor colors were protectable by copyright law (*Brown Bag vs. Symantec Corp.*, 1992).

Fair Use Doctrine

Copyrights, like all rights, are not absolute. There are situations where strict copyright observance could be harmful to society, potentially inhibiting other rights such as the right to freedom of expression and thought. As a result, the doctrine of fair use has been created. The **doctrine of fair use** permits teachers and writers to use copyrighted materials without permission under certain circumstances. **Table 8.10** describes the five factors that courts consider when assessing what constitutes fair use.

doctrine of fair use
under certain circumstances, permits use of copyrighted material without permission

The fair use doctrine draws upon the First Amendment's protection of freedom of speech (and writing). Journalists, writers, and academics must be able to refer to, and cite from, copyrighted works in order to criticize, or even discuss them. Professors are allowed to clip a contemporary article just before class, copy it, and hand it out to students as an example of a topic under discussion. However, they are not permitted to add this article to the class syllabus for the next semester without compensating the copyright holder.

What constitutes fair use has been at issue in a number of recent cases, including the Google Books Library Project described in the case study at the end of the chapter, and in several recent lawsuits. In *Kelly v. Arriba Soft* (2003) and *Perfect 10,*

Inc. v. Amazon.com, Inc. et al., (2007), the Federal Circuit Court of Appeals for the 9th Circuit held that the display of thumbnail images in response to search requests constituted fair use. A similar result was reached by the district court for the District of Nevada with respect to Google's storage and display of Web sites from cache memory, in *Field v. Google, Inc.* (2006). In all of these cases, the courts accepted the argument that caching the material and displaying it in response to a search request was not only a public benefit, but also a form of marketing of the material on behalf of its copyright owner, thereby enhancing the material's commercial value. Fair use is also at issue in the lawsuit filed by Viacom against Google and YouTube described further in the next section.

The Digital Millennium Copyright Act of 1998

The **Digital Millennium Copyright Act (DMCA)** of 1998 was the first major effort to adjust the copyright laws to the Internet age. This legislation was the result of a confrontation between the major copyright holders in the United States (publishing, sheet music, record label, and commercial film industries), ISPs, and users of copyrighted materials such as libraries, universities, and consumers. While social and political institutions are sometimes thought of as "slow" and the Internet as "fast," in this instance, powerful groups of copyright owners anticipated Web music services such as Napster by several years. Napster was formed in 1999, but work by the World Intellectual Property Organization (WIPO)—a worldwide body formed by the major copyright-holding nations of North America, Europe, and Japan—began in 1995. **Table 8.11** summarizes the major provisions of the DMCA.

Digital Millennium Copyright Act (DMCA)

the first major effort to adjust the copyright laws to the Internet age

TABLE 8.11	THE DIGITAL MILLENNIUM COPYRIGHT ACT
SECTION	**IMPORTANCE**
Title I, WIPO Copyright and Performances and Phonograms Treaties Implementation	Makes it illegal to circumvent technological measures to protect works for either access or copying or to circumvent any electronic rights management information.
Title II, Online Copyright Infringement Liability Limitation	Requires ISPs to "take down" sites they host if they are infringing copyrights, and requires search engines to block access to infringing sites. Limits liability of ISPs and search engines.
Title III, Computer Maintenance Competition Assurance	Permits users to make a copy of a computer program for maintenance or repair of the computer.
Title IV, Miscellaneous Provisions	Requires the Copyright Office to report to Congress on the use of copyright materials for distance education; allows libraries to make digital copies of works for internal use only; extends musical copyrights to include "webcasting."

SOURCE: Based on data from United States Copyright Office, 1998.

The penalties for willfully violating the DMCA include restitution to the injured parties of any losses due to infringement. Criminal remedies may include fines up to $500,000 or five years imprisonment for a first offense, and up to $1 million in fines and 10 years in prison for repeat offenders. These are serious remedies.

The DMCA attempts to answer two vexing questions in the Internet age. First, how can society protect copyrights online when any practical encryption scheme imaginable can be broken by hackers and the results distributed worldwide? Second, how can society control the behavior of thousands of ISPs, who often host infringing Web sites or who provide Internet service to individuals who are routine infringers? ISPs claim to be like telephone utilities—just carrying messages—and they do not want to put their users under surveillance or invade the privacy of users. The DMCA recognizes that ISPs have some control over how their customers use their facilities.

The DMCA implements the WIPO Copyright Treaty of 1996, which declares it illegal to make, distribute, or use devices that circumvent technology-based protections of copyrighted materials, and attaches stiff fines and prison sentences for violations. WIPO is an organization within the United Nations. Recognizing that these provisions alone cannot stop hackers from devising circumventions, the DMCA makes it difficult for such inventors to reap the fruits of their labors by making the ISPs (including universities) responsible and accountable for hosting Web sites or providing services to infringers once the ISP has been notified. ISPs are not required to intrude on their users. However, after copyright holders inform the ISP that a hosted site or individual users are infringing, they must "take down" the site immediately to avoid liability and potential fines. ISPs must also inform their subscribers of the ISP's copyright management policies. Copyright owners can subpoena the personal identities of any infringers using an ISP. There are important limitations on these ISP prohibitions that are mostly concerned with the transitory caching of materials for short periods without the knowledge of the ISP. However, should the ISP be deriving revenues from the infringement, it is as liable as the infringer, and is subject to the same penalties.

Title I of the DMCA provides a partial answer to the dilemma of hacking. It is probably true that skilled hackers can easily break any usable encryption scheme, and the means to do so on a large scale through distribution of decryption programs already exists. The WIPO provisions accept this possibility and simply make it illegal to do so, or to disseminate or enable such dissemination, or even store and transmit decrypted products or tools. These provisions put large ISPs on legal notice.

There are a number of exceptions to the strong prohibitions against defeating a copyright protection scheme outlined above. There are exceptions for libraries to examine works for adoption, for reverse engineering to achieve interoperability with other software, for encryption research, for privacy protection purposes, and for security testing. Many companies, such as YouTube and Google, have latched on to the provision of the DMCA that relates to removing infringing material upon request of the copyright owner as a "safe harbor" that precludes them from being held responsible for copyright infringement. This position is currently being tested in a $1 billion lawsuit originally brought by Viacom in 2007 against Google and YouTube for willful copyright infringement.

In the Viacom case, Viacom alleges that YouTube and Google engaged in massive copyright infringement by deliberately and knowingly building up a library of infringing works to draw traffic to the YouTube site and enhance its commercial value. In response, Google and YouTube claim that they are protected by the DMCA's safe harbor and fair use, and that it is often impossible to know whether a video is infringing or not. YouTube also does not display ads on pages where consumers can view videos unless it has an agreement with the content owner. In October 2007, Google announced a filtering system (ContentID) aimed at addressing the problem. It requires content owners to give Google a copy of their content so Google can load it into an auto-identification system. The copyright owner can specify whether it will allow others to post the material. Then after a video is uploaded to YouTube, the system attempts to match it with its database of copyrighted material and removes any unauthorized material. Whether content owners will be satisfied with this system is unknown, particularly since guidelines issued by a coalition of major media and Internet companies with respect to the handling of copyrighted videos on user-generated Web sites calls for the use of filtering technology that can block infringing material before it is posted online. In June 2010, the federal district court ruled against Viacom, on the grounds that YouTube had taken down more than 100,000 videos requested by Viacom, as required by the DMCA, and that YouTube was protected by the safe harbor provisions of DMCA. Viacom continued to appeal the case. In April 2012, a U.S. appeals court reversed the lower court decision, allowing the case to move forward. The court ruled that YouTube had specific knowledge or awareness of the infringing activity, and ample ability to prevent it. In April 2013, the lower court ruled against Viacom's claim that Google knew it was infringing copyrighted material, and encouraged infringement. The case is under appeal.

The entertainment industry continues to be aggressive in pursuing online copyright infringement. In 2011, in a suit brought by the Motion Picture Association of America, a federal judge ordered DVD-streaming service Zediva to shut down. Zediva had argued that its service was just like one person lending a physical DVD to another, but just using the Web to accomplish the task. The court did not agree and said that the service threatened the growing Internet-based video-on-demand market. In January 2012, the Department of Justice seized the domain megaupload.com, one of the largest cyberlockers on the Internet dedicated to storing and sharing copyrighted movies and music. A **cyberlocker** is an online file storage service dedicated to sharing copyrighted material (often movies) illegally. Megaupload's founder Kim Dotcom was arrested in New Zealand at his home, and $17 million in assets were confiscated, and later, $37 million in cash in Hong Kong was confiscated. Since the Megaupload case, other cyberlockers have restricted their activities to avoid a similar fate as Megaupload.

Refer to the case study at the end of Chapter 1, *The Pirate Bay: The World's Most Resilient Copyright Infringer?* for further discussion of copyright issues in e-commerce.

cyberlocker
an online file storage service dedicated to sharing copyrighted material illegally

PATENTS: BUSINESS METHODS AND PROCESSES

"Whoever invents or discovers any new and useful process, machine, manufacture, or composition of matter, or any new and useful improvement thereof, may obtain a patent therefore, subject to the conditions and requirements of this title."

—Section 101, U.S. Patent Act

patent

grants the owner an exclusive monopoly on the ideas behind an invention for 20 years

A **patent** grants the owner a 20-year exclusive monopoly on the ideas behind an invention. The congressional intent behind patent law was to ensure that inventors of new machines, devices, or industrial methods would receive the full financial and other rewards of their labor and still make widespread use of the invention possible by providing detailed diagrams for those wishing to use the idea under license from the patent's owner. Patents are obtained from the United States Patent and Trademark Office (USPTO), which was created in 1812. Obtaining a patent is much more difficult and time-consuming than obtaining copyright protection (which is automatic with the creation of the work). Patents must be formally applied for, and the granting of a patent is determined by Patent Office examiners who follow a set of rigorous rules. Ultimately, federal courts decide when patents are valid and when infringement occurs.

Patents are very different from copyrights because patents protect the ideas themselves and not merely the expression of ideas. There are four types of inventions for which patents are granted under patent law: machines, man-made products, compositions of matter, and processing methods. The Supreme Court has determined that patents extend to "anything under the sun that is made by man" (*Diamond v. Chakrabarty*, 1980) as long as the other requirements of the Patent Act are met. There are three things that cannot be patented: laws of nature, natural phenomena, and abstract ideas. For instance, a mathematical algorithm cannot be patented unless it is realized in a tangible machine or process that has a "useful" result (the mathematical algorithm exception).

In order to be granted a patent, the applicant must show that the invention is new, original, novel, nonobvious, and not evident in prior arts and practice. As with copyrights, the granting of patents has moved far beyond the original intent of Congress's first patent statute, which sought to protect industrial designs and machines. Patent protection has been extended to articles of manufacture (1842), plants (1930), surgical and medical procedures (1950), and software (1981). The Patent Office did not accept applications for software patents until a 1981 Supreme Court decision that held that computer programs could be a part of a patentable process. Since that time, thousands of software patents have been granted. Virtually any software program can be patented as long as it is novel and not obvious.

Essentially, as technology and industrial arts progress, patents have been extended to both encourage entrepreneurs to invent useful devices and promote widespread dissemination of the new techniques through licensing and artful imitation of the published patents (the creation of devices that provide the same functionality as the invention but use different methods) (Winston, 1998). Patents encourage inventors to come up with unique ways of achieving the same functionality as existing patents. For instance, Amazon's patent on one-click purchasing caused Barnesandnoble.com to invent a simplified two-click method of purchasing.

The danger of patents is that they stifle competition by raising barriers to entry into an industry. Patents force new entrants to pay licensing fees to incumbents, and thus slow down the development of technical applications of new ideas by creating lengthy licensing applications and delays. The *Insight on Technology* case, *Theft and Innovation: The Patent Trial of the Century*, examines these issues in the context of the Apple-Samsung lawsuit with respect to infringement of Apple's patents for the iPhone.

E-commerce Patents

Much of the Internet's infrastructure and software was developed under the auspices of publicly funded scientific and military programs in the United States and Europe. Unlike Samuel F. B. Morse, who patented the idea of Morse code and made the telegraph useful, most of the inventions that make the Internet and e-commerce possible were not patented by their inventors. The early Internet was characterized by a spirit of worldwide community development and sharing of ideas without consideration of personal wealth (Winston, 1998). This early Internet spirit changed in the mid-1990s with the commercial development of the World Wide Web.

In 1998, a landmark legal decision, *State Street Bank & Trust v. Signature Financial Group, Inc.*, paved the way for business firms to begin applying for "business methods" patents. In this case, a Federal Circuit Court of Appeals upheld the claims of Signature Financial to a valid patent for a business method that allows managers to monitor and record financial information flows generated by a partner fund. Previously, it was thought business methods could not be patented. However, the court ruled there was no reason to disallow business methods from patent protection, or any "step by step process, be it electronic or chemical or mechanical, [that] involves an algorithm in the broad sense of the term" (*State Street Bank & Trust Co. v. Signature Financial Group*, 1998). The State Street decision led to an explosion in applications for e-commerce "business methods" patents. In June 2010, the U.S. Supreme Court issued a divided opinion on business methods patents in the *Bilski et al. v. Kappos* case (*Bilski et al. v. Kappos*, 2010). The majority argued that business methods patents were allowable even though they did not meet the traditional "machine or transformation test," in which patents are granted to devices that are tied to a particular machine, are a machine, or transform articles from one state to another. The minority wanted to flatly declare business methods are not patentable in part because any series of steps could be considered a business method (Schwartz, 2010).

Table 8.12 on page 527 lists some of the better-known e-commerce patents. Some are controversial. Reviewing these, you can understand the concerns of commentators and corporations. Some of the patent claims are very broad (for example, "name your price" sales methods), have historical precedents in the pre-Internet era (shopping carts), and seem "obvious" (one-click purchasing). Critics of online business methods patents argue that the Patent Office has been too lenient in granting such patents, and that in most instances, the supposed inventions merely copy pre-Internet business methods and thus do not constitute "inventions" (Harmon, 2003; Thurm, 2000;

INSIGHT ON TECHNOLOGY

THEFT AND INNOVATION: THE PATENT TRIAL OF THE CENTURY

Imagine you have just bought the car of your dreams, one with an unmistakable, unique, look on the outside and with some very unique features on the inside. You drive the car home to show friends and relatives. Across the street, a neighbor has parked his newly purchased car in his driveway. It looks strikingly similar but was manufactured by a different firm. On the inside, you find that it has all the features that your car dealer claimed were unique to your car. Your neighbor bought the car for substantially less than you paid. You might feel "cheated" as a consumer, paying so much more for an identical product. How would you feel if you were the manufacturer?

Apple found itself in a situation similar to the one above when Samsung introduced its line of Galaxy smartphones in 2010, phones that Apple claimed were nearly identical in design and functionality to Apple's iPhone, right down to the icons that bounced when clicked and the polished metal band around the phone. Apple sued Samsung for violating its patents for iPhones, iPads, and iPods in 2011 and on August 24, 2012, a California jury in federal district court delivered a decisive victory to Apple and a stunning defeat to Samsung. The jury awarded Apple $1 billion in damages in what some have called the patent trial of the century because it established criteria for determining just how close a competitor can come to an industry-leading and standard setting product like Apple's iPhone before it violates its patents. The same court ruled that Samsung could not sell its new tablet computer (Galaxy 10.1) in the United States. This was not just a loss for Samsung, but a warning shot across the bow for Google, which developed the Android operating system, and all other makers of Android phones.

In January 2007, Apple introduced the first iPhone. The iPhone was a truly remarkable advance in design and technology. It was the first smartphone that combined, in a single device, the functionality of a phone with a music and video player and an Internet browser. The iPhone turned out to be wildly popular and quickly captured more than 70% of the smartphone market worldwide at its high point. Apple refused to license the iPhone iOS operating system to other manufacturers, and tied it closely to its iTunes store and its newly introduced App Store.

In the same year, Google introduced the Android operating system and licensed it without charge to smartphone manufacturers in return for retaining the rights to place mobile ads on Android devices and other considerations. Android is an open source operating system. Thousands of programmers around the world contribute to its development, which is led by the Android Open Source Project controlled by Google. The Open Handset Alliance was also formed in 2007 by 86 hardware, software, and telecommunications companies, led by Google, to advance open standards for mobile devices. Aside from Google, the Alliance included HTC, a Korean cell phone maker, and Samsung, the largest electronics component, consumer device, and cell phone manufacturer in the world. Samsung is also based in Korea. The Alliance was clearly a coordinated effort of the firms involved to develop a smartphone that was competitive with the iPhone. The iPhone had caught the world's other phone manufacturers completely flatfooted. The first HTC Android phones were sold in 2008, followed shortly by a Samsung Android phone. By 2013, over 1 billion people in the world used smartphones, a number that is expected to double by

(continued)

2015. Android phones have continued to swallow up market share, especially in developing countries, growing to 79.3%, with Apple falling to just 13.2%. For every iPhone sold, three Androids are sold in the global market. Nevertheless, Apple is the largest single manufacturer of smartphones, the most valuable company in the United States, and is expected to be the first company in history to attain a stock market valuation of $1 trillion dollars.

Samsung introduced the Galaxy S in September 2010. While the early Samsung smartphones of 2008-2010 did not look like Apple's iPhones or have the same functionality, the Galaxy S was clearly designed to compete against the iPhone, with similar functionality, and it looked strikingly like an iPhone so much so that Apple sued Samsung in June 2011 for trademark and patent infringement, unfair competition, and other violations of law.

Apple alleged in its complaint that Samsung had quite literally copied the functionality and design of the Apple iPhone. Apple claimed that Samsung violated Apple's so-called "utility patents" like the multi-touch interface (which enables gestures such as selecting, scrolling, pinching, and zooming); arrangement of text on screen; arrangement and actions of images (such as bounce-back when user scrolls down too far), and the movement of buttons when pressed. Apple had been granted patents for these "fundamental features" that the world has come to associate with Apple products.

Apple also claimed infringement of its "trade dress" patents. Trade dress patents cover non-functional design elements of physical devices such as the unique and ornamental appearance of the iPhone: the black face, bezel, a matrix of on-screen icons, a black thin rim surrounding a flat screen, a rectangular product with four rounded corners, a display screen under a clear glass surface, a thin metallic band around the outside edge, a row of small dots on the display screen, screen icons with evenly rounded corners, and a bottom dock of evenly rounded square icons.

In a counter-complaint, Samsung denied infringing any Apple patents, and questioned the integrity of the patents issued by the U.S. Patent Office on the grounds that the functionality of the utility patents had already been prior art that Apple itself had copied. Samsung simply denied the trade dress and trademark infringement claims. Samsung claimed as well that Apple had violated its patents on various electronic components that perform critical functions in cell and smartphones. Samsung asked for $422 million in damages. Usually patent and trademark cases are settled out of court after a fair amount of posturing. But in this case, the parties could not come to an agreement, and the case went to a jury trial, a rare, risky, and expensive endeavor.

The jury found in over 700 determinations that Samsung had violated Apple's utility patents covering things like the "bounce back" effect at the end of lists and the ability to distinguish between one-finger scrolling and two-finger scrolling. The jury also found that Samsung had violated Apple's trade dress patents protecting the physical design of the iPhone, and the trademarked icons as well. The $1.05 billion in damages awarded to Apple represented a crushing blow to Samsung, not only in the moment, but also to its future chances of winning similar court cases. The jury flatly denied Samsung's claims that Apple violated its patents on various components and rejected Samsung's claim for $422 million in damages. Samsung is appealing. Generally in these cases an out-of-court settlement is reached, but given the hostility between the firms, Apple may not settle if only as a warning to Google and other Android phone makers that they may not copy the design and functionality of the iPhone.

In 2013, the war between Apple and Samsung rages on. Although the federal appeals court ruled

(continued)

in Apple's favor in 2012, the judge in the case permitted Samsung to continue selling 26 different products that were found to infringe on Apple patents, and Apple has appealed that portion of the ruling. Apple was also the beneficiary of a U.S. trade agency ruling preventing Samsung from selling any devices infringing two particular patents covering the detection of headphone jacks and touchscreen operation. Still, Samsung was cleared of infringing on other Apple design patents, which according to Samsung, will prevent Apple from attempting to monopolize rectangles and rounded corners. Samsung also claims that more recent devices have features that differentiate them more clearly from Apple's offerings.

The Apple vs. Samsung case raises several issues for manufacturers of smartphones, consumers, and the development of the smartphone market. But it also raises ethical issues having to do with what's right and what's wrong. Few, if any, would argue that it's ethically acceptable to copy another person's work (their intellectual property), claim it is your own, and be well rewarded by the marketplace for the theft. In a society that respects property rights, this would seem to be a contradiction: people could take your house or car if they wanted and sell them. Nobody wants this outcome. Copycat designs challenge one of the foundations of intellectual (and other property) which argues that people (and companies) deserve the rewards of their investments and efforts—the "sweat of the brow" theory.

Business critics of the decision argue that innovation in the marketplace will be harmed and slowed down because the inventions of one firm cannot be built upon, but will have to be designed around, slowing the introduction of innovations. They also argue that some of the features Apple claims to own are part of the "standard design" of a smartphone without which a contemporary smartphone can't be built, or only built by the one firm that owns the patents. This would include features of Apple's multi-touch interface like pinching, zooming, and active icons. This is the "steering wheel" argument: you can't build a car without a steering wheel because it's become the standard design in the market. Owners of the steering wheel patent must therefore license the steering wheel patent for a reasonable fee. If smartphone makers could not use some of Apple's patented features, the smartphone market would become fractionated into a plethora of designs, and some phones would have missing features that consumers expect (like pinch to zoom).

Supporters of the decision argue that it provides incentives for firms to invest in design, and come up with new innovations, rather than just copy existing state of the art designs. They point to Windows Phone, Microsoft's operating system for smartphones, which looks nothing like the iOS interface and has received praise for its distinctive design. Moreover, innovative firms like Apple deserve to be rewarded for their research and successful designs and products. Without financial incentives, innovation will decline or disappear. Why should firms innovate if they cannot be rewarded in the marketplace?

SOURCES: Susan Decker, "Apple's Legal Wins Show No Clear Victor in Patent War," by Susan Decker, Bloomberg.com, August 11, 2013; Ashby Jones, "Apple-Samsung Patent Battle Heads for Next Round," by Ashby Jones, *Wall Street Journal*, August 8, 2013; "Number of Smartphones Around the World Top 1 Billion - Projected to Double by 2015," finance.yahoo.com, Oct. 19, 2012; United States Patent Office, "Intelligent Automated Assistant," Apple Inc., United States Patent Application, 20120245944, September 27, 2012; "Apple Seeks U.S. Samsung Sales Ban, $707 Million More in Damages," *Reuters*, September 22, 2012; "Samsung Fails to Defeat Galaxy Table Sale Ban in Apple Case," by Joel Rosenblatt, Bloomberg News, September 19, 2012; "Apple Did Not Violate Samsung Patents: U.S. Trade Judge," by Diane Bartz, *Reuters*, September 14, 2012; " Apple Case Muddies the Future of Innovations," by Nick Wingfield, *New York Times*, August 26, 2012; "Apple-Samsung Case Shows Smartphone as Legal Magnet," by Steve Lohr, *New York Times*, August 25, 2012; "Jury Awards $1 Billion to Apple in Samsung Patent Case," by Nick Wingfield, *New York Times*, August 24, 2012; "Apple v. Samsung: The Patent Trial of the Century," by Ashby Jones and Jessica Vascellaro, *Wall Street Journal*, July 24, 2012; Apple v. Samsung, Complaint, United States District Court, Northern District of California, Case No. 11-cv-01846-LHK, June 16, 2011.

TABLE 8.12	SELECTED E-COMMERCE PATENTS	
COMPANY	SUBJECT	UPDATE
Amazon	One-click purchasing	Amazon attempted to use patent originally granted to it in 1999 to force changes to Barnes & Noble's Web site, but a federal court overturned a previously issued injunction. Eventually settled out of court. In September 2007, a USPTO panel rejected some of the patent because of evidence another patent predated it, sending it back to the patent examiner for reconsideration. Amazon amended the patent, and the revised version was confirmed in March 2010.
Priceline	Buyer-driven "name your price" sales	Originally invented by Walker Digital, an intellectual property laboratory, and then assigned to Priceline. Granted by the USPTO in 1999. Shortly thereafter, Priceline sued Microsoft and Expedia for copying its patented business method.
Sightsound	Music downloads	Sightsound won a settlement in 2004 against Bertelsmann subsidiaries CDNow and N2K music sites for infringing its patent.
Akamai	Internet content delivery global hosting system	A broad patent granted in 2000 covering techniques for expediting the flow of information over the Internet. Akamai sued Digital Island (subsequently acquired by Cable & Wireless) for violating the patent and, in 2001, a jury found in its favor.
DoubleClick	Dynamic delivery of online advertising	The patent underlying DoubleClick's business of online banner ad delivery, originally granted in 2000. DoubleClick sued competitors 24/7 Media and L90 for violating the patent and ultimately reached a settlement with them.
Overture	Pay for performance search	System and method for influencing position on search result list generated by computer search engine, granted in 2001. Competitor FindWhat.com sued Overture, charging that patent was obtained illegally; Overture countered by suing both FindWhat and Google for violating patent. Google agreed to pay a license fee to Overture in 2004 to settle.
Acacia Technologies	Streaming video media transmission	Patents for the receipt and transmission of streaming digital audio and or video content originally granted to founders of Greenwich Information Technologies in 1990s. Patents were purchased by Acacia, a firm founded solely to enforce the patents, in 2001.
Soverain Software	Purchase technology	The so-called "shopping cart" patent for network-based systems, which involves any transaction over a network involving a seller, buyer, and payment system. In other words, e-commerce! Soverain filed suit against Amazon for patent infringement, which Amazon paid $40 million to settle. In 2013 a Federal District Court ruled Soverain's claims against Newegg in part invalid.
MercExchange (Thomas Woolston)	Auction technology	Patents on person-to-person auctions and database search, originally granted in 1995. eBay ordered to pay $25 million in 2003 for infringing on patent. In July 2007, a U.S. District Court in Norfolk, VA, denied a motion for permanent patent injunction against eBay using the "Buy It Now" feature. MercExchange and eBay settled the dispute in 2008 on confidential terms.
Google	Search technology	Google PageRank patent was filed in 1998 and granted in 2001. Became non-exclusive in 2011 and expires in 2017.
Google	Location technology	Google issued a patent in 2010 for a method of using location information in an advertising system.
Apple	Social technology	Apple applied for a patent in 2010 that allows groups of friends attending events to stay in communication with each other and share reactions to live events as they are occurring.

Chiappetta, 2001). The Patent Office argues, on the contrary, that its Internet inventions staff is composed of engineers, lawyers, and specialists with many years of experience with Internet and network technologies, and that it consults with outside technology experts before granting patents. To complicate matters, the European Patent Convention and the patent laws of most European countries do not recognize business methods per se unless the method is implemented through some technology (Takenaka, 2001).

TRADEMARKS: ONLINE INFRINGEMENT AND DILUTION

> A trademark is "any word, name, symbol, or device, or any combination thereof ... used in commerce ... to identify and distinguish ... goods ... from those manufactured or sold by others and to indicate the source of the goods."
>
> —The Trademark Act, 1946

trademark
a mark used to identify and distinguish goods and indicate their source

Trademark law is a form of intellectual property protection for **trademarks**—a mark used to identify and distinguish goods and indicate their source. Trademark protections exist at both the federal and state levels in the United States. The purpose of trademark law is twofold. First, trademark law protects the public in the marketplace by ensuring that it gets what it pays for and wants to receive. Second, trademark law protects the owner—who has spent time, money, and energy bringing the product to the marketplace—against piracy and misappropriation. Trademarks have been extended from single words to pictures, shapes, packaging, and colors. Some things may not be trademarked such as common words that are merely descriptive ("clock"). Federal trademarks are obtained, first, by use in interstate commerce, and second, by registration with the U.S. Patent and Trademark Office (USPTO). Federal trademarks are granted for a period of 10 years and can be renewed indefinitely.

Disputes over federal trademarks involve establishing infringement. The test for infringement is twofold: market confusion and bad faith. Use of a trademark that creates confusion with existing trademarks, causes consumers to make market mistakes, or misrepresents the origins of goods is an infringement. In addition, the intentional misuse of words and symbols in the marketplace to extort revenue from legitimate trademark owners ("bad faith") is proscribed.

dilution
any behavior that would weaken the connection between the trademark and the product

In 1995, Congress passed the Federal Trademark Dilution Act (FTDA), which created a federal cause of action for dilution of famous marks. This legislation dispenses with the test of market confusion (although that is still required to claim infringement), and extends protection to owners of famous trademarks against **dilution**, which is defined as any behavior that would weaken the connection between the trademark and the product. In 2006, the FTDA was amended by the Trademark Dilution Revision Act (TDRA), which allows a trademark owner to file a claim based on a "likelihood of dilution" standard, rather than having to provide evidence of actual dilution. The TDRA also expressly provides that dilution may occur through blurring (weakening the connection between the trademark and the goods) and tarnishment (using the trademark in a way that makes the underlying products appear unsavory or unwholesome).

Trademarks and the Internet

The rapid growth and commercialization of the Internet have provided unusual opportunities for existing firms with distinctive and famous trademarks to extend their brands to the Internet. These same developments have provided malicious individuals and firms the opportunity to squat on Internet domain names built upon famous marks, as well as attempt to confuse consumers and dilute famous or distinctive marks (including your personal name or a movie star's name). The conflict between legitimate trademark owners and malicious firms was allowed to fester and grow because Network Solutions Inc. (NSI), originally the Internet's sole agency for domain name registration for many years, had a policy of "first come, first served." This meant anyone could register any domain name that had not already been registered, regardless of the trademark status of the domain name. NSI was not authorized to decide trademark issues (Nash, 1997).

In response to a growing number of complaints from owners of famous trademarks who found their trademark names being appropriated by Web entrepreneurs, Congress passed the **Anticybersquatting Consumer Protection Act (ACPA)** in November 1999. The ACPA creates civil liabilities for anyone who attempts in bad faith to profit from an existing famous or distinctive trademark by registering an Internet domain name that is identical or confusingly similar to, or "dilutive" of, that trademark. The act does not establish criminal sanctions. It proscribes using "bad-faith" domain names to extort money from the owners of the existing trademark **(cybersquatting)**, or using the bad-faith domain to divert Web traffic to the bad-faith domain that could harm the good will represented by the trademark, create market confusion, or tarnish or disparage the mark **(cyberpiracy)**. The act also proscribes the use of a domain name that consists of the name of a living person, or a name confusingly similar to an existing personal name, without that person's consent, if the registrant is registering the name with the intent to profit by selling the domain name to that person.

Trademark abuse can take many forms on the Web. **Table 8.13** lists the major behaviors on the Internet that have run afoul of trademark law, and some of the court cases that resulted.

Cybersquatting and Brandjacking

In one of the first cases involving the ACPA, E. & J. Gallo Winery, owner of the registered mark "Ernest and Julio Gallo" for alcoholic beverages, sued Spider Webs Ltd. for using the domain name Ernestandjuliogallo.com. Spider Webs Ltd. was a domain name speculator that owned numerous domain names consisting of famous company names. The Ernestandjuliogallo.com Web site contained information on the risks of alcohol use, anti-corporate articles about E. & J. Gallo Winery, and was poorly constructed. The court concluded that Spider Webs Ltd. was in violation of the ACPA and that its actions constituted dilution by blurring because the Ernestandjuliogallo.com domain name appeared on every page printed off the Web site accessed by that name, and that Spider Webs Ltd. was not free to use this particular mark as a domain name (*E. & J. Gallo Winery v. Spider Webs Ltd.*, 2001). In August 2009, a court upheld the largest cybersquatting judgment to date: a $33 million verdict in favor of Verizon against OnlineNIC, an Internet domain registration company that had used over 660 names

Anticybersquatting Consumer Protection Act (ACPA)
creates civil liabilities for anyone who attempts in bad faith to profit from an existing famous or distinctive trademark by registering an Internet domain name that is identical or confusingly similar to, or "dilutive" of, that trademark

cybersquatting
involves the registration of an infringing domain name, or other Internet use of an existing trademark, for the purpose of extorting payments from the legitimate owners

cyberpiracy
involves the same behavior as cybersquatting, but with the intent of diverting traffic from the legitimate site to an infringing site

TABLE 8.13	INTERNET AND TRADEMARK LAW EXAMPLES	
ACTIVITY	**DESCRIPTION**	**EXAMPLE CASE**
Cybersquatting	Registering domain names similar or identical to trademarks of others to extort profits from legitimate holders	*E. & J. Gallo Winery v. Spider Webs Ltd.*, 129 F. Supp. 2d 1033 (S.D. Tex., 2001) aff'd 286 F. 3d 270 (5th Cir., 2002)
Cyberpiracy	Registering domain names similar or identical to trademarks of others to divert Web traffic to their own sites	*Ford Motor Co. v. Lapertosa*, 2001 U.S. Dist. LEXIS 253 (E.D. Mich., 2001); *PaineWebber Inc. v. Fortuny*, Civ. A. No. 99-0456-A (E.D. Va., 1999); *Playboy Enterprises, Inc. v. Global Site Designs, Inc.*, 1999 WL 311707 (S.D. Fla., 1999), *Audi AG and Volkswagen of America Inc. v. Bob D'Amato* (No. 05-2359; 6th Cir., November 27, 2006)
Metatagging	Using trademarked words in a site's metatags	*Bernina of America, Inc. v. Fashion Fabrics Int'l, Inc.*, 2001 U.S. Dist. LEXIS 1211 (N.D. Ill., 2001); *Nissan Motor Co., Ltd. v. Nissan Computer Corp.*, 289 F. Supp. 2d 1154 (C.D. Cal., 2000), aff'd, 246 F. 3rd 675 (9th Cir., 2000)
Keywording	Placing trademarked keywords on Web pages, either visible or invisible	*Playboy Enterprises, Inc. v. Netscape Communications, Inc.*, 354 F. 3rd 1020 (9th Cir., 2004); *Nettis Environment Ltd. v. IWI, Inc.*, 46 F. Supp. 2d 722 (N.D. Ohio, 1999); *Government Employees Insurance Company v. Google, Inc.*, Civ. Action No. 1:04cv507 (E.D. VA, 2004); *Google, Inc. v. American Blind & Wallpaper Factory, Inc.*, Case No. 03-5340 JF (RS) (N.D. Cal., April 18, 2007)
Linking	Linking to content pages on other sites, bypassing the home page	*Ticketmaster Corp. v. Tickets.com*, 2000 U.S. Dist. Lexis 4553 (C.D. Cal., 2000)
Framing	Placing the content of other sites in a frame on the infringer's site	*The Washington Post, et al. v. TotalNews, Inc., et al.*, (S.D.N.Y., Civil Action Number 97-1190)

that could easily be confused with legitimate Verizon domain names. Although there have not been many cases decided under the ACPA, that does not mean the problem has gone away. Impersonation of individuals and brands on social network sites adds another dimension to the problem. Both Twitter and Facebook make cybersquatting and impersonation a violation of their terms of service. ICANN's authorization of thousands of new top-level domains are also expected to make it harder for companies to track cybersquatters.

Cyberpiracy

Cyberpiracy involves the same behavior as cybersquatting, but with the intent of diverting traffic from the legitimate site to an infringing site. In *Ford Motor Co. v. Lapertosa*, Lapertosa had registered and used a Web site called Fordrecalls.com as an adult entertainment Web site. The court ruled that Fordrecalls.com was in violation of the ACPA in that it was a bad-faith attempt to divert traffic to the Lapertosa site and diluted Ford's wholesome trademark (*Ford Motor Co. v. Lapertosa*, 2001).

The Ford decision reflects two other famous cases of cyberpiracy. In the *Paine Webber Inc. v. Fortuny* case, the court enjoined Fortuny from using the domain name wwwpainewebber.com—a site that specialized in pornographic materials—because it diluted and tarnished Paine Webber's trademark and diverted Web traffic from Paine Webber's legitimate site—Painewebber.com (*Paine Webber Inc. v. Fortuny*, 1999). In the *Playboy Enterprises, Inc. v. Global Site Designs, Inc.* case, the court enjoined the defendants from using the Playboy and Playmate marks in their domain names Playboyonline.net and Playmatesearch.net and from including the Playboy trademark in their metatags. In these cases, the defendants' intention was diversion for financial gain (*Playboy Enterprises, Inc. v. Global Site Designs, Inc.*, 1999).

Typosquatting is a form of cyberpiracy in which a domain name contains a common misspelling of another site's name. These domains are sometimes referred to as "doppelganger" domains. Often the user ends up at a site very different from one they intended to visit. For instance, John Zuccarini is an infamous typosquatter who was jailed in 2002 for setting up pornographic Web sites with URLs based on misspellings of popular children's brands, such as Bob the Builder and Teletubbies. The FTC fined him again in October 2007 for engaging in similar practices (McMillan, 2007). Harvard Business School professor Ben Edelman conducted a study that found that there were at least 938,000 domains typosquatting on the top 3,264 ".com" Web sites, and that 57% of these domains included Google pay-per click ads. In July 2011, Facebook filed a lawsuit against 25 typosquatters who established Web sites with such domain names as Faceboook, Facemook, Faceboik, and Facebooki. In 2013, Facebook was awarded $2.8 milion in damages.

Metatagging

The legal status of using famous or distinctive marks as metatags is more complex and subtle. The use of trademarks in metatags is permitted if the use does not mislead or confuse consumers. Usually this depends on the content of the site. A car dealer would be permitted to use a famous automobile trademark in its metatags if the dealer sold this brand of automobiles, but a pornography site could not use the same trademark, nor a dealer for a rival manufacturer. A Ford dealer would most likely be infringing if it used "Honda" in its metatags, but would not be infringing if it used "Ford" in its metatags. (Ford Motor Company would be unlikely to seek an injunction against one of its dealers.)

In the *Bernina of America, Inc. v. Fashion Fabrics Int'l, Inc.* case, the court enjoined Fashion Fabrics, an independent dealer of sewing machines, from using the trademarks "Bernina" and "Bernette," which belonged to the manufacturer Bernina, as metatags. The court found the defendant's site contained misleading claims about Fashion Fabrics' knowledge of Bernina products that were likely to confuse customers. The use of the Bernina trademarks as metatags per se was not a violation of ACPA, according to the court, but in combination with the misleading claims on the site would cause confusion and hence infringement (*Bernina of America, Inc. v. Fashion Fabrics Int'l, Inc.*, 2001).

In the *Nissan Motor Co., Ltd. v. Nissan Computer Corp.* case, Uzi Nissan had used his surname "Nissan" as a trade name for various businesses since 1980, including Nissan Computer Corp. He registered Nissan.com in 1994 and Nissan.net in 1996. Nissan.com had no relationship with Nissan Motor, but over the years began selling auto parts that competed with Nissan Motor. Nissan Motor Company objected to the use of the domain name Nissan.com and the use of "Nissan" in the metatags for both sites on grounds it would confuse customers and infringe on Nissan Motor's trademarks. Uzi Nissan offered to sell his sites to Nissan Motor for several million dollars. Nissan Motor refused. The court ruled that Nissan Computer's behavior did indeed infringe on Nissan Motor's trademarks, but it refused to shut the site down. Instead, the court ruled Nissan Computer could continue to use the Nissan name, and metatags, but must post notices on its site that it was not affiliated with Nissan Motor (*Nissan Motor Co., Ltd. v. Nissan Computer Corp.*, 2000).

Keywording

The permissibility of using trademarks as keywords on search engines is also subtle and depends (1) on the extent to which such use is considered to be a "use in commerce" and causes "initial customer confusion" and (2) on the content of the search results.

In *Playboy Enterprises, Inc. v. Netscape Communications, Inc.*, Playboy objected to the practice of Netscape's and Excite's search engines displaying banner ads unrelated to *Playboy Magazine* when users entered search arguments such as "playboy," "playmate," and "playgirl." The Ninth Circuit Court of Appeals denied the defendant's motion for a summary judgment and held that when an advertiser's banner ad is not labeled so as to identify its source, the practice could result in trademark infringement due to consumer confusion (*Playboy Enterprises, Inc. v. Netscape Communications, Inc.*, 2004).

Google has also faced lawsuits alleging that its advertising network illegally exploits others' trademarks. For instance, insurance company GEICO challenged Google's practice of allowing competitors' ads to appear when a searcher types "Geico" as the search query. A U.S. district court ruled that this practice did not violate federal trademark laws as long as the word "Geico" was not used in the ads' text (*Government Employees Insurance Company v. Google, Inc.*, 2004). Google quickly discontinued allowing the latter, and settled the case (Associated Press, 2005). In July 2009, Rosetta Stone, the language-learning software firm, filed a lawsuit against Google for trademark infringement, alleging its AdWords program allowed other companies to use Rosetta Stone's trademarks for online advertisements without permission. In April 2012, the 4th Circuit Court of Appeals held that a jury might hold Google liable for trademark infringement, pointing to evidence that an internal Google study found that even sophisticated users were sometimes unaware that sponsored links were advertisements. In November 2012, Rosetta Stone and Google settled, which was seen as a strategic win for Google because it eliminated one of the last major cases challenging the legitimacy of its AdWords program. Currently Google allows anyone to buy anyone else's trademark as a keyword. In February 2011, Microsoft decided to follow this practice as well with Bing and Yahoo Search.

Linking

Linking refers to building hypertext links from one site to another site. This is obviously a major design feature and benefit of the Web. **Deep linking** involves bypassing the target site's home page and going directly to a content page. In *Ticketmaster Corp. v. Tickets.com*, Tickets.com—owned by Microsoft—competed directly against Ticketmaster in the events ticket market. When Tickets.com did not have tickets for an event, it would direct users to Ticketmaster's internal pages, bypassing the Ticketmaster home page. Even though its logo was displayed on the internal pages, Ticketmaster objected on the grounds that such "deep linking" violated the terms and conditions of use for its site (stated on a separate page altogether and construed by Ticketmaster as equivalent to a shrink-wrap license), and constituted false advertising, as well as the violation of copyright. The court found, however, that deep linking per se is not illegal, no violation of copyright occurred because no copies were made, the terms and conditions of use were not obvious to users, and users were not required to read the page on which the terms and conditions of use appeared in any event. The court refused to rule in favor of Ticketmaster, but left open further argument on the licensing issue. In an out-of-court settlement, Tickets.com nevertheless agreed to stop the practice of deep linking (*Ticketmaster v. Tickets.com*, 2000).

linking
building hypertext links from one site to another site

deep linking
involves bypassing the target site's home page, and going directly to a content page

Framing

Framing involves displaying the content of another Web site inside your own Web site within a frame or window. The user never leaves the framer's site and can be exposed to advertising while the target site's advertising is distorted or eliminated. Framers may or may not acknowledge the source of the content. In *The Washington Post, et al. v. TotalNews, Inc.* case, The Washington Post Company, CNN, Reuters, and several other news organizations filed suit against TotalNews, Inc., claiming that TotalNews's use of frames on its Web site, TotalNews.com, infringed upon the respective plaintiffs' copyrights and trademarks, and diluted the content of their individual Web sites. The plaintiffs claimed additionally that TotalNews's framing practice effectively deprived the plaintiffs' Web sites of advertising revenue.

TotalNews's Web site employed four frames. The TotalNews logo appeared in the lower left frame, various links were located in a vertical frame on the left side of the screen, TotalNews's advertising was framed across the screen bottom, and the "news frame," the largest frame, appeared in the center and right. Clicking on a specific news organization's link allowed the reader to view the content of that particular organization's Web site, including any related advertising, within the context of the "news frame." In some instances, the framing distorted or modified the appearance of the linked Web site, including the advertisements, while the appearance of TotalNews's advertisements, in a separate frame, remained unchanged. In addition, the URL remained fixed on the TotalNews address, even though the content in the largest frame

framing
involves displaying the content of another Web site inside your own Web site within a frame or window

on the Web site was from the linked Web site. The "news frame" did not, however, eliminate the linked Web site's identifying features.

The case was settled out of court. The news organizations allowed TotalNews to link to their Web sites, but prohibited framing and any attempt to imply affiliation with the news organizations (*The Washington Post, et al. v. TotalNews, Inc.*, 1997).

CHALLENGE: BALANCING THE PROTECTION OF PROPERTY WITH OTHER VALUES

The challenge in intellectual property ethics and law is to ensure that creators of intellectual property can receive the benefits of their inventions and works, while also making it possible for their works and designs to be disseminated and used by the widest possible audience. Protections from rampant theft of intellectual property inevitably lead to restrictions on distribution, and the payments to creators for the use of their works—which in itself can slow down the distribution process. Without these protections, however, and without the benefits that flow to creators of intellectual property, the pace of innovation could decline. In the early years of e-commerce, up to 2005, the balance has been struck more towards Internet distributors and their claim to be free from restrictions on intellectual content, particularly music. Since the development of the iTunes store, smartphones, and tablets, after 2005, the balance has swung back towards content owners, largely because Internet distributors depend on high-quality content to attract audiences, but also partly due to the effectiveness of lawsuits in raising the costs to Internet firms that fail to protect intellectual property.

8.4 GOVERNANCE

governance
has to do with social control: who will control e-commerce, what elements will be controlled, and how will the controls be implemented

Governance has to do with social control: Who will control the Internet? Who will control the processes of e-commerce, the content, and the activities? What elements will be controlled, and how will the controls be implemented? A natural question arises and needs to be answered: Why do we as a society need to "control" e-commerce? Because e-commerce and the Internet are so closely intertwined (though not identical), controlling e-commerce also involves regulating the Internet.

WHO GOVERNS THE INTERNET AND E-COMMERCE?

Governance of both the Internet and e-commerce has gone through four stages. **Table 8.14** summarizes these stages in the evolution of e-commerce governance.

Prior to 1995, the Internet was a government program. Beginning in 1995, private corporations were given control of the technical infrastructure as well as the process of granting IP addresses and domain names. However, the NSI monopoly created in this period did not represent international users of the Internet, and was unable to cope with emerging public policy issues such as trademark and intellectual property protection, fair policies for allocating domains, and growing concerns that a small group of firms were benefiting from growth in the Internet.

TABLE 8.14	THE EVOLUTION OF GOVERNANCE OF THE INTERNET
INTERNET GOVERNANCE PERIOD	DESCRIPTION
Government control, 1970–1994	DARPA and the National Science Foundation control the Internet as a fully government-funded program.
Privatization, 1995–1998	Network Solutions Inc. is given a monopoly to assign and track high-level Internet domains. Backbone is sold to private telecommunications companies. Policy issues are not decided.
Self-regulation, 1995–present	President Clinton and the U.S. Department of Commerce encourage the creation of a semiprivate body, ICANN, to deal with emerging conflicts and establish policies. ICANN currently holds a contract with the Department of Commerce to govern some aspects of the Internet.
Governmental regulation, 1998–present	Executive, legislative, and judicial bodies worldwide begin to implement direct controls over the Internet and e-commerce.

In 1995, President Clinton, using funds from the Department of Commerce, encouraged the establishment of an international body, the Internet Corporation for Assigned Names and Numbers (ICANN), that hopefully could better represent a wider range of countries and a broad range of interests, and begin to address emerging public policy issues. ICANN was intended to be an Internet/e-commerce industry self-governing body, not another government agency.

The explosive growth of the Web and e-commerce created a number of issues over which ICANN had no authority. Content issues such as pornography, gambling, and offensive written expressions and graphics, along with commercial issue of intellectual property protection, ushered in the current era of growing governmental regulation of the Internet and e-commerce throughout the world. Currently, we are in a mixed-mode policy environment where self-regulation through a variety of Internet policy and technical bodies co-exists with limited government regulation.

Today, ICANN remains in charge of the domain name system that translates domain names (such as www.company.com) into IP addresses. In 2012 ICANN approved 1,574 applications for new top-level domains, expanding from the previous 22 top-level domains like .com and .org. It has subcontracted the work of maintaining the databases of the domain registries to several private corporations. The U.S. government controls the "A-root" server. However, these arrangements are increasingly challenged by other countries, including China, Russia, Saudi Arabia, and most of the European Union, all of whom want the United States to give up control over the Internet to an international body such as the International Telecommunication Union (ITU) (a U.N. agency). In 2005, an Internet Summit sponsored by the ITU agreed to leave control over the Internet domain servers with the United States and instead called for an international forum to meet in future years to discuss Internet policy issues (Miller and Rhoads, 2005). The position of the United States with respect to international governance of the Internet changed significantly after the terrorist attacks of September 11, 2001. Currently, the United States has no intention of diminishing its role in control over the global or domestic Internet.

Can the Internet Be Controlled?

Early Internet advocates argued that the Internet was different from all previous technologies. They contended that the Internet could not be controlled, given its inherent decentralized design, its ability to cross borders, and its underlying packet-switching technology that made monitoring and controlling message content impossible. Many still believe this to be true today. The slogans were "Information wants to be free," and "The Net is everywhere" (but not in any central location). The implication of these slogans is that the content and behavior of e-commerce sites—indeed Internet sites of any kind—cannot be "controlled" in the same way as traditional media such as radio and television. However, attitudes have changed as many governments and corporations extend their control over the Internet and the World Wide Web (Stone, 2010).

In fact, as you learned in the Chapter 3 *Insight on Society* case, *Government Regulation and Surveillance of the Internet*, the Internet is technically very easily controlled, monitored, and regulated from central locations (such as network access points, as well as servers and routers throughout the network). For instance, in China, Saudi Arabia, Iran, North Korea, Thailand, Singapore, and many other countries, access to the Web is controlled from government-owned centralized routers that direct traffic across their borders and within the country (such as China's "Great Firewall of China," which permits the government to block access to certain U.S. or European Web sites), or via tightly regulated ISPs operating within the countries. In China, for instance, all ISPs need a license from the Ministry of Information Industry (MII), and are prohibited from disseminating any information that may harm the state or permit pornography, gambling, or the advocacy of cults. In addition, ISPs and search engines such as Google, Yahoo, and Bing typically self-censor their Asian content by using only government-approved news sources or, in the case of Google, exit the country altogether. Twitter is not planning any Chinese presence. China has also recently instituted new regulations that require cafes, restaurants, hotels, and bookstores to install Web monitoring software that identifies those using wireless services and monitors Web activity.

Following the outbreak of street demonstrations in June 2009 protesting a rigged election, the Iranian government unleashed one of the world's most sophisticated mechanisms for controlling and censoring the Web. Built with the assistance of Western companies like Siemens and Nokia, the system uses deep packet inspection to open every packet, look for keywords, reseal it, and send it on the network. In Great

Britain, Prime Minister David Cameron suggested that he might temporarily block social network sites such as Facebook and Twitter during periods of social unrest such as the rioting that hit the country in August 2011.

In the United States, as we have seen in our discussion of intellectual property, e-commerce sites can be put out of business for violating existing laws, and ISPs can be forced to "take down" offending or stolen content. Government security agencies such as the National Security Agency (NSA) and the FBI can obtain court orders to monitor ISP traffic and engage in widespread monitoring of millions of e-mail messages. Under the USA PATRIOT Act, passed after the World Trade Center attack on September 11, 2001, American intelligence authorities are permitted to tap into whatever Internet traffic they believe is relevant to the campaign against terrorism, in some circumstances without judicial review. Working with the large ISP firms such as AT&T, Verizon, and others, U.S. security agencies have access to nearly all Internet communications throughout the country. And many American corporations are developing restrictions on their employees' at-work use of the Web to prevent gambling, shopping, and other activities not related to a business purpose.

In the United States, as discussed in the opening case, efforts to control media content on the Web have run up against equally powerful social and political values that protect freedom of expression, including several rulings by the Supreme Court that have struck down laws attempting to limit Web content in the United States. The U.S. Constitution's First Amendment says, "Congress shall make no law … abridging the freedom of speech, or of the press." As it turns out, the 200-year-old Bill of Rights has been a powerful brake on efforts to control twenty-first-century online content.

Public Government and Law

The reason we have governments is ostensibly to regulate and control activities within the borders of the nation. What happens in other nations, for the most part, we generally ignore, although clearly environmental and international trade issues require multinational cooperation. E-commerce and the Internet pose some unique problems to public government that center on the ability of the nation-state to govern activities within its borders. Nations have considerable powers to shape the Internet.

TAXATION

Few questions illustrate the complexity of governance and jurisdiction more potently than taxation of e-commerce sales. In both Europe and the United States, governments rely on sales taxes based on the type and value of goods sold. In Europe, these taxes are collected along the entire value chain, including the final sale to the consumer, and are called "value-added taxes" (VAT), whereas in the United States, taxes are collected by states and localities on final sales to consumers and are called consumption and use taxes. In the United States, there are 50 states, 3,000 counties, and 12,000 municipalities, each with unique tax rates and policies. Cheese may be taxable in one state as a "snack food" but not taxable in another state (such as Wisconsin), where it is considered a basic food. Consumption taxes are generally recognized to be regressive because they disproportionately tax poorer people, for whom consumption is a larger part of total income.

Sales taxes were first implemented in the United States in the late 1930s as a Depression-era method of raising money for localities. Ostensibly, the money was to be used to build infrastructure such as roads, schools, and utilities to support business development, but over the years the funds have been used for general government purposes of the states and localities. In most states, there is a state-based sales tax, and a smaller local sales tax. The total sales tax ranges from zero in some states (North Dakota) to as much as 13% in New York City.

The development of "remote sales" such as mail order/telephone order (MOTO) retail in the United States in the 1970s broke the relationship between physical presence and commerce, complicating the plans of state and local tax authorities to tax all retail commerce. States sought to force MOTO retailers to collect sales taxes for them based on the address of the recipient, but Supreme Court decisions in 1967 and 1992 established that states had no authority to force MOTO retailers to collect state taxes unless the businesses had a "nexus" of operations (physical presence) in the state.

The explosive growth of e-commerce, the latest type of "remote sales," has once again raised the issue of how—and if—to tax remote sales. Since its inception, e-commerce has benefited from a tax subsidy of up to 13% for goods shipped to high sales-tax areas. Local retail merchants have complained bitterly about the e-commerce tax subsidy. E-commerce merchants have argued that this form of commerce needs to be nurtured and encouraged, and that in any event, the crazy quilt of sales and use tax regimes would be difficult to administer for Internet merchants. Online giants like Amazon claim they should not have to pay taxes in states where they have no operations because they do not benefit from local schools, police, fire, and other governmental services. State and local governments meanwhile see billions of tax dollars slipping from their reach.

In 1998, Congress passed the Internet Tax Freedom Act, which placed a moratorium on "multiple or discriminatory taxes on electronic commerce," as well as on taxes on Internet access, for three years until October 2001. Since that time, the moratorium has been extended several times, most currently until 2014.

The merger of online e-commerce with offline commerce further complicates the taxation question. Currently, almost all of the top 100 online retailers collect taxes when orders ship to states where these firms have a physical presence. But others, like eBay, still refuse to collect and pay local taxes, arguing that the so-called tax simplification project ended up with taxes for each of 49,000 zip codes, hardly a simplification. The taxation situation is also very complex in services. For instance, none of the major online travel sites collect the full amount of state and local hotel occupancy taxes, or state and local airline taxes. Rather than remitting sales tax on the full amount of the consumer's purchase, these sites collect taxes only on the basis of the wholesale price they pay for the hotel rooms or tickets. The states have not given up on collecting hundreds of millions of dollars from Internet merchants. The *Insight on Business* case, *Internet Sales Tax Battle*, provides further insight into the fight over e-commerce sales taxes.

INSIGHT ON BUSINESS

INTERNET SALES TAX BATTLE

Most people are happy when they discover they don't have to pay any sales tax on a purchase they make online. However, few stop to consider the implications that this may have. States in the last few years have been suffering a persistent budget crunch. Constitutionally bound to balance their budgets, starved for revenue, and simultaneously facing increased demand for public services, many of the 45 states that levy sales taxes have been eying the lost revenue from e-commerce sales, estimated at nearly $14 billion nationwide in 2013.

Internet sales tax policy has been dictated by the Supreme Court decision in *Quill v. North Dakota*, which held that retailers without a store or other physical presence (nexus) in a state could not be forced to collect state sales taxes. Citizens were supposed to be responsible for remitting unpaid sales tax along with their state income tax returns. This unsurprisingly proved to be unworkable, with nearly universal noncompliance. The rationale for not closing this loophole, which resulted from a MOTO (Mail Order/Telephone Order) case, was to provide protection for a nascent market. With total 2013 B2C e-commerce sales topping $419 billion in the United States, this argument had lost its punch.

Internet retail kingpin Amazon has been at the center of the political battle. Multiple states, frustrated by the lost revenue that could have been used to balance their budgets and prevent further layoffs, have taken Amazon on. In 2010, Texas levied a $269 million sales tax bill against Amazon covering a period of four years. In response, Amazon, which asserted that a warehouse did not constitute a nexus, shuttered its Dallas-vicinity warehouse. In 2011, Illinois, which estimated that the state had lost up to $170 million in sales tax revenue every year, enacted legislation requiring all retailers with a marketing affiliate in the state to collect sales taxes. Amazon retaliated by severing all ties to its Illinois affiliates. The Illinois law was fashioned after a New York law with which Amazon has complied while simultaneously challenging its constitutionality. It did not drop its New York affiliates, but when Rhode Island and North Carolina followed New York's lead, Amazon terminated its affiliate relationships in those states. California, which estimated that it lost $1.1 billion per year in uncollected sales tax, passed its legislation expanding the definition of nexus in September 2011, but delayed tax collection until September 2012.

Facing a continuing state-by-state assault, Amazon recognized that its former competitive advantage was ultimately going to come to an end. It devised a dual-pronged strategy. In the short term, it negotiated deals with states in which it planned to open distribution centers. These distribution centers were strategically located to support its long-term goal and what it hopes will become its new competitive advantage—same day delivery.

For example, in April 2012, Amazon settled its dispute with Texas when it agreed to create 2,500 local jobs over four years' time, pay an undisclosed amount to resolve its tax bill, and begin collecting sales tax from Texas residents. Similarly, in May 2012, Amazon reached an agreement with New Jersey that allowed it to build two distribution centers in the state. Amazon will also receive yet to be determined tax incentives from the state Economic Development Authority. In California, in exchange for the one-year tax reprieve, Amazon agreed to spend $500 million building new facilities, which also positioned it for same-day delivery in two major metropolitan areas.

(continued)

In November 2011, Amazon threw its support behind the Durbin-Enzi-Alexander bill, the Main Street Fairness Act. Under the terms of this bill, businesses with less than $500,000 in annual sales would not have had to remit sales taxes. States would have had to agree to the Streamlined Sales and Use Tax Agreement, which simplifies their tax policies so that it will be easier for Internet retailers to conform. The bill did not pass, however, in 2012, and in 2013, still continues to undergo tweaks. Now known as the Marketplace Fairness Act, the bill has finally cleared the Senate. The updated bill would put an end to tax-free shopping on the Internet and would create a uniform set of rules for collecting taxes from e-commerce sales. The exemption for small businesses was increased from $500,000 to $1 million. It's no surprise that Amazon, Wal-Mart, Best Buy, and other retailers are all lobbying hard in favor of the bill, which would eliminate a major advantage for many of their smaller competitors. In 2013, Amazon is on pace to spend approximately $3 million lobbying in favor of the bill in Washington D.C. Perhaps hedging its bets in case the bill does not pass, Amazon has continued to battle individual states on their rights to collect sales tax on e-commerce purchases, including in New York, where it appealed the issue to the Supreme Court in August 2013.

eBay still remains staunchly opposed to the bill. eBay and other online marketplaces have created unique environments in which lowered barriers to entry enable entrepreneurs to either work for themselves or start their own businesses and further, they present new opportunities to developing markets to offer their goods directly to buyers. eBay believes the bill will be a crippling blow for small online businesses, many of whom it claims won't survive if they are forced to collect taxes. A $1 million annual remote sales cap would give them a leg up, support innovation where government intervention is necessary to do so, and avoid unduly burdening small sellers whose contribution to state revenue is minor in comparison.

The big players such as Amazon are now operating in a mature market in which they must adapt and formulate new strategies for remaining competitive. Whether or not Amazon will succeed in its ambitious same-day delivery plan remains to be seen, but it is operating as all businesses must—evolving with changing circumstances in an ever-changing business environment. Clearly Walmart and the other big-box retailers are not suffering from lack of a level playing field. They are simply using their political clout to benefit themselves and erect barriers for smaller competitors. However, they do have a point vis-à-vis tax fairness and civic duty.

Sales taxes have been an established method for raising revenue at the state and local level for more than half a century. First adopted by Mississippi in 1932, the idea quickly caught on spreading to 22 additional states by 1940 and extending to 45 states and the District of Columbia by 1969 when Vermont was the final adopter. Alaska, Montana, Oregon, Delaware, and New Hampshire are the holdouts. We have all enjoyed purchasing online goods from out-of-state sellers and evading the sales tax, but this is not a new tax. It is a tax that we have enjoyed evading, and one which the states desperately need to pay for the services and professions we rely on every day.

SOURCES: "Amazon Lobbies Heavily for Internet Sales Tax," by Kyung M. Song, *Seattle Times*, September 7, 2013; "Impact of Marketplace Fairness on Select Jurisdictions," IHS Global Insight, May 2013; "Small E-retailers Mobilize to Lobby Against Online Sales Tax Collection," by Paul Demery, Internet Retailer, September, 14, 2012; "Coalition Launched to Oppose Internet Sales Tax Legislation," by Juliana Gruenwald, NextGov Newsletter, September 13, 2012; "Amazon, Forced to Collect a Tax, Is Adding Roots," by David Streitfeld, *New York Times*, September 11, 2012; "10 Surprising Facts About Online Sales Taxes," by Robert W. Wood, *Forbes*, September 11, 2012; "Durbin Still Hopeful for Action on Net Sales Tax Bill," by Juliana Gruenwald, " *National Journal*, June 12, 2012; "Amazon.com to Begin Collecting Sales Tax on N.J. Orders Next Year," by Matt Friedman and Jarrett Renshaw, NJ.com, May 30, 2012; "Tax Revenues Continue to Grow in Early 2012," by Lucy Dadayan, The Nelson A. Rockefeller Institute of Government State Revenue Report No. 88, August, 2012; "Durbin Gains Key Support for Revitalized Internet Sales Tax Bill," by Paul Merrion, *Crain's Chicago Business*, November 9, 2011; "Revenue Declines Less Severe, But States' Fiscal Crisis Is Far From Over," by Donald J. Boyd and Lucy Dadayan, The Nelson A. Rockefeller Institute of Government State Revenue Report No. 79, April, 2010.

The taxation situation in Europe, and trade between Europe and the United States, is similarly complex. The Organization for Economic Cooperation and Development (OECD), the economic policy coordinating body of European, American, and Japanese governments, is currently investigating different schemes for applying consumption and business profit taxes for digitally downloaded goods. The E.U. began collecting a VAT on digital goods such as music and software delivered to consumers by foreign companies in 2003. Previously, European Union companies were required to collect the VAT on sales to E.U. customers, but U.S. companies were not. This gave American companies a huge tax edge.

NET NEUTRALITY

"Net neutrality" is more a political slogan than a concept. It means different things to different people. Currently, all Internet traffic is treated equally (or "neutrally") by Internet backbone owners in the sense that all activities and files—word processing, e-mailing, video downloading, music and video files, etc.—are charged the same flat rate regardless of how much bandwidth is used. However, the telephone and cable companies that provide the Internet backbone (Internet Service Providers or ISPs) would like to be able to charge differentiated prices based on the amount of bandwidth consumed by content being delivered over the Internet, much like a utility company charges according to how much electricity consumers use. The carriers claim they need to introduce differential pricing in order to properly manage and finance their networks.

There are three basic ways to achieve a rationing of bandwidth using the pricing mechanism: cap plans (also known as "tiered plans"), usage metering, and "highway" or "toll" pricing. Each of these plans have historical precedents in highway, electrical, and telephone pricing. **Cap pricing** plans place a cap on usage, say 300 gigabytes a month in a basic plan, with more bandwidth available in 50-gigabyte chunks for, say, an additional $50 a month. The additional increments can also be formalized as tiers where users agree to purchase, say, 400 gigabytes each month as a Tier II plan. Additional tiers could be offered.

A variation on tier pricing is to offer **speed tiers**. Comcast offers its Xfinity Platinum Internet plan with download speeds of 300 megabits per second for $300, and Verizon offers its FiOS high-speed tier for $204 a month. An alternative to cap plans is metered or **usage-based billing**. Time Warner is testing usage plans that start at five gigabytes a month (the equivalent of two high definition movie downloads) and charge $1 for every additional gigabyte (much like an electric usage meter in a home). One variation on metering is **congestion pricing**, where, as with electric "demand pricing," the price of bandwidth goes up at peak times, say, Saturday and Sunday evening from 6:00 P.M. to 12 midnight—just when everyone wants to watch a movie! Still a third pricing model is **highway (toll) pricing** where the firms that use high levels of bandwidth for their business pay a toll based on their usage of the Internet. Highway pricing is a common way for governments to charge trucking companies based on the weight of their vehicles to compensate for the damage that heavy vehicles inflict on roadways. In the case of the Internet, YouTube, Netflix, Hulu, and other

cap pricing
Putting caps on bandwidth usage, charging more for additional usage in tiers of prices

speed tiers
charging more for higher speed Internet service

usage-based billing
charging on the basis of metered units of Internet service

congestion pricing
charging more for peak hour Internet service

highway (toll) pricing
charging service providers like Netflix for their use of the Internet based on their bandwidth use

heavy bandwidth providers would pay fees to the Internet carriers based on their utilization of the networks in order to compensate the carriers for the additional capacity they are required to supply to these heavy user firms. Presumably, these fees would be passed on to customers by the industry players by charging users a distribution expense. The only way to do this fairly is to charge fees to users based on how much they download, e.g., a short YouTube video might cost 10 cents, a feature-length movie might cost $1.

Plans to ration bandwidth are controversial, and in some cases bring legal, regulatory, and political scrutiny. For instance, in September 2007, Comcast, the largest ISP in the United States, began to slow down traffic and specific Web sites using the BitTorrent protocol not because the content was pirated, but because these video users were consuming huge chunks of the Comcast network capacity during peak load times. In this case Comcast was restricting certain file types. Comcast claims its policy was a legitimate effort to manage capacity. In August 2008 the Federal Communications Commission (FCC) disagreed and ordered Comcast to stop discriminating against certain Web sites. Comcast filed suit and in April 2010, a federal appeals court ruled against the FCC and for Comcast, arguing that Comcast had the right to manage its own network, including charging some users more for bandwidth or slowing down certain traffic such as BitTorrent files (Watt, 2010).

In 2009, the FCC began developing a national broadband strategy. In December 2010, the FCC approved "compromise" net neutrality rules (Schatz, 2010). The rules force ISPs to be transparent about how they handle network congestion, prohibit them from blocking traffic such as BitTorrent or Skype protocols on wired networks, and outlawed "unreasonable" discrimination on such networks. The regulations do not cover wireless cellular networks, nor do they prohibit "paid prioritization," in which broadband companies could enable premium customers to have access to higher-speed, higher-priced "fast lanes." For instance, telecommunications providers such as Verizon and AT&T, and Internet distributors such as Google, have reached a market-based compromise: maintain existing rules for landlines, but implement differential pricing for mobile wireless networks. Currently, for instance, for new wireless customers, AT&T no longer offers a flat-rate plan. Instead, consumers must choose between plans with different data limits, ranging from $15/ month for 200 MB/month of data to up to $45/month for 4 GB/month. In September 2011, Verizon sued the FCC to stop its net neutrality rules from going into effect (Wyatt, 2011a). In November 2011, the FCC implemented its new rules despite Verizon's law suit. In 2012, the U.S. Court of Appeals began consideration of the Verizon case, which will not be decided until late 2013 (Sasso, 2012).

How the net neutrality debate impacts the use of the mobile platform in the future is anyone's guess. Will consumers be less likely to want to use the mobile platform once they start to bump up against the data limits of their plans and pay additional fees? For instance, in 2012, AT&T restricted FaceTime calls on Apple's iPhones to customers signed up to a premium data plan. 4G networks in 2012 are already generating public criticism for their high monthly charges. This would put a big kibosh on the plans of content distributors, and they are not likely to be happy if that occurs. At the end of the day, both the content distributors and network providers need one another, and they are likely to work out a plan that is mutually beneficial (Stelter, 2012).

In the end, net neutrality is about generating revenue for content distributors and Internet service providers. Keep your eyes on the money.

8.5 PUBLIC SAFETY AND WELFARE

Governments everywhere claim to pursue public safety, health, and welfare. This effort produces laws governing everything from weights and measures to national highways, to the content of radio and television programs. Electronic media of all kinds (telegraph, telephone, radio, and television) have historically been regulated by governments seeking to develop a rational commercial telecommunications environment and to control the content of the media—which may be critical of government or offensive to powerful groups in a society. Historically, in the United States, newspapers and print media have been beyond government controls because of constitutional guarantees of freedom of speech. Electronic media such as radio and television have, on the other hand, always been subject to content regulation because they use the publicly owned frequency spectrum. Telephones have also been regulated as public utilities and "common carriers," with special social burdens to provide service and access, but with no limitations on content.

In the United States, critical issues in e-commerce center around the protection of children, strong sentiments against pornography in any public media, efforts to control gambling, and the protection of public health through restricting sales of drugs and cigarettes.

PROTECTING CHILDREN

Pornography is an immensely successful Internet business. Statistics with respect to revenues generated by online pornography range widely. However, it is probably safe to estimate that the online pornography industry in 2013 generates somewhere between $5–$10 billion in revenue in the United States. Adult Web sites reportedly attract around 75 million unique visitors a month and make up 12% of the Internet (Rosen, 2013).

To control the Web as a distribution medium for pornography, in 1996, Congress passed the Communications Decency Act (CDA). This act made it a felony criminal offense to use any telecommunications device to transmit "any comment, request, suggestion, proposal, image, or other communications which is obscene, lewd, lascivious, filthy, or indecent" to anyone, and in particular, to persons under 18 years of age (Section 502, Communications Decency Act of 1996). In 1997, the Supreme Court struck down the CDA as an unconstitutional abridgement of freedom of speech protected by the First Amendment. While the government argued the CDA was like a zoning ordinance designed to allow "adult" Web sites for people 18 years of age or over, the Court found the CDA was a blanket proscription on content and rejected the "cyberzoning" argument as impossible to administer. In 2002, the Supreme Court struck down another law, the Child Pornography Prevention Act of 1996, which made it a crime to create, distribute, or possess "virtual" child pornography that uses computer-generated images or young adults rather than real children, as overly broad (*Ashcroft v. Free Speech Coalition*). The Children's Online Protection Act (COPA) of 1998 met with a similar fate.

In 2001, Congress passed the Children's Internet Protection Act (CIPA), which requires schools and libraries in the United States to install "technology protection measures" (filtering software) in an effort to shield children from pornography. In June 2003, the Supreme Court upheld CIPA, overturning a federal district court that found the law interfered with the First Amendment guarantee of freedom of expression. The Supreme Court, in a 6–3 opinion, held that the law's limitations on access to the Internet posed no more a threat to freedom of expression than limitations on access to books that librarians choose for whatever reason not to acquire. The dissenting justices found this analogy inappropriate and instead argued the proper analogy was if librarians were to purchase encyclopedias and then rip out pages they thought were or might be offensive to patrons. All the justices agreed that existing blocking software was overly blunt, unable to distinguish child pornography from sexually explicit material (which is protected by the First Amendment), and generally unreliable (Greenhouse, 2003b). Other legislation such as the 2002 Domain Names Act seeks to prevent unscrupulous Web site operators from luring children to pornography using misleading domain names or characters known to children. A plan to create an .xxx domain for adult Web site content was approved by ICANN in June 2010, and in September 2011, limited registration for .xxx domains began. Trademark holders who do not wish their brand to be associated with an .xxx domain can block requests by other companies for domain names that include their brand name. The 2003 Protect Act is an omnibus law intended to prevent child abuse that includes prohibitions against computer-generated child pornography. Part of that statute was previously held to be unconstitutional by the Eleventh Circuit Court of Appeals, but in May 2008, the Supreme Court reversed the circuit court and upheld the provision (Greenhouse, 2008).

The Children's Online Privacy Protection Act (COPPA) (1998) prohibits Web sites from collecting information on children under the age of 13. It does permit such data collection if parental consent is obtained. Because COPPA does not interfere with speech or expression, it has not been challenged in the courts. However, since 1998, entirely new technologies like social networks, online tracking, advertising networks, online gaming, and mobile apps have appeared that are now being used to gather data on children and which were not specifically addressed in COPPA or FTC regulations. Responding to these changes in technology and public pressure, the FTC announced a new set of rules that are now in effect. The new rules prohibit online tracking of children across the Web with cookies or any other technology such as persistent identifiers; prohibit ad networks from following children across the Web and advertising to them without parental consent; make clear that mobile devices are subject to COPPA, including games and software apps; and make clear that third-party data collection firms that collect data on Web sites are responsible for any unlawful data collection. See the Chapter 7 *Insight on Society* case, *Marketing to Children of the Web in the Age of Social Networks*, for more information.

CIGARETTES, GAMBLING, AND DRUGS: IS THE WEB REALLY BORDERLESS?

In the United States, both the states and the federal government have adopted legislation to control certain activities and products in order to protect public health and welfare. Cigarettes, gambling, medical drugs, and of course addictive recreational drugs, are either banned or tightly regulated by federal and state laws (see *Insight on Society: The Internet Drug Bazaar*). Yet these products and services are ideal for distribution over the Internet through e-commerce sites. Because the sites can be located offshore, they can operate beyond the jurisdiction of state and federal prosecutors. Or so it seemed until recently. In the case of cigarettes, state and federal authorities have been quite successful in shutting down tax-free cigarette Web sites within the United States by pressuring PayPal and credit card firms to drop cigarette merchants from their systems. The major shipping companies—UPS, FedEx, and DHL—have been pressured into refusing shipment of untaxed cigarettes. Philip Morris has also agreed not to ship cigarettes to any resellers that have been found to be engaging in illegal Internet and mail order sales. However, a few off-shore Web sites continue to operate using checks and money orders as payments and the postal system as a logistics partner, but their level of business has plummeted as consumers fear state tax authorities will present them with huge tax bills if they are discovered using these sites. In 2010, President Obama signed the Prevent All Cigarette Trafficking Act. The law restricts the sale of untaxed cigarettes and other tobacco products over the Internet and bans the delivery of tobacco products through the U.S. mail.

Gambling also provides an interesting example of the clash between traditional jurisdictional boundaries and claims to a borderless, uncontrollable Web. The online gambling market, based almost entirely offshore—primarily in the United Kingdom and various Caribbean Islands—grew by leaps and bounds between 2000 and 2006, generating as much as $50 billion to $60 billion a year, and with much of the action (some estimate up to 50%) coming from customers based in the United States. Although the federal government contended online gambling was illegal under U.S. federal law (the "Wire Act" of 1961 prohibits use of wire communications for sports betting), they were initially unable to stop it, with various federal courts offering mixed opinions. However, in the summer of 2006, federal officials turned up the heat and arrested two executive officers of offshore gambling operations as they passed through the United States, leading their companies to cease U.S. operations. Then in October 2006, Congress passed the Unlawful Internet Gambling Enforcement Act, which makes it a crime to use credit cards or online payment systems for Internet betting. This effectively bars online gambling companies from operating legally in the United States, and shortly thereafter a number of the leading, publicly traded companies suspended their business in the United States. However, the bill has not eliminated all online gambling in the United States, with some smaller companies still offering offshore gambling. An association of online gambling groups challenged the law as unconstitutional, claiming that Internet gambling is protected by First Amendment privacy rights and that filtering technology exists to make sure that children and compulsive gamblers cannot access offshore betting sites. These arguments were rejected by the Third Circuit Court of Appeals in September 2009. Several countries are also seeking compensation from

INSIGHT ON SOCIETY

THE INTERNET DRUG BAZAAR

In June 2013, the US Food and Drug Administration working in tandem with other international law enforcement agencies shut down a crime ring of over 1,600 online pharmacies. Nearly 10,000 Web sites were warned or had their assets seized, accounting for $41 million in illegal drugs. Despite successes such as this, however, the Internet drug bazaar operated by rogue Internet drug outlets remains a continuing public health and safety issue. For instance, a Massachusetts General study found that the increase in Internet access parallels the growth in prescription drug abuse, and posits that increasing access to rogue online pharmacies and easy online availability of controlled drugs without a prescription might be an important factor behind the rapid increase.

According to a study done by the Treatment Research Institute at the University of Pennsylvania, addictive and potentially lethal medications are available without prescription from more than 2 million Web sites around the world, with many sites based in countries that impose little if any regulation on pharmaceuticals. A Google search on "drugs no prescription" returns more than 94 million results.

The International Narcotics Control Board, a U.N. narcotics watchdog agency, has provided guidelines and a framework for governments struggling to contain growing abuse of prescription drugs on the Internet. According to the report, only two of 365 so-called Internet pharmacies it surveyed were legitimate. In many countries, the report said, trafficking in illegal prescription drugs now equals or exceeds the sale of heroin, cocaine, and amphetamines. While properly regulated Internet pharmacies offer a valuable service by increasing competition and access to treatments in underserved regions, Web pharmacies are a long way from proper regulation.

The sale of drugs without a prescription is not the only danger posed by the Internet drug bazaar. Rogue online pharmacy sites may be selling counterfeit drugs or unapproved drugs. For instance, in the past, the FDA has issued warnings that a number of consumers who had purchased Ambien, Xanax, and Lexapro online from several different Web sites had instead received a product containing haloperial, a powerful anti-psychotic drug. Drug pushers on the Internet also include legitimate U.S. pharmaceutical firms who have discovered search engine advertising. Enter a search for "high cholesterol" on Bing or Google and you will be faced with multiple ads extolling the benefits of Lipitor (Pfizer's leading statin drug).

But despite these dangers, online pharmacies remain alluring and are one of the fastest growing business models, with, oddly, senior citizens— usually some of the most law-abiding citizens— leading the charge for cheaper drugs. The main attraction of online drug sites is price. Typically, online pharmacies are located in countries where prescription drugs are price-controlled, or where the price structure is much lower, such as Canada, the United Kingdom, and European countries, as well as India and Mexico. U.S. citizens can often save 50%–75% by purchasing from online pharmacies located in other countries.

Currently, a patchwork regulatory structure governs the sale of drugs online. At the federal level, the 1938 Food, Drug, and Cosmetic Act (FDCA) requires that certain drugs may only be purchased with a valid doctor's prescription and must be dispensed by a state-licensed pharmacy. To get around this requirement, some online pharmacies use questionnaires to diagnose disease and have these questionnaires reviewed by doctors who write the prescription. The Ryan Haight Online Pharmacy Consumer Act, which took effect in 2009, was designed to give the Drug Enforce-

(continued)

ment Agency authority to address rogue Internet pharmacies selling controlled substances without a valid prescription. The act bans the sale of prescription drugs over the Internet without a legitimate prescription issued by a medical practitioner who has examined the patient in person at least once. The act is named after teenager Ryan Haight, who died from a drug overdose using drugs purchased on the Internet. The act requires online pharmacies to comply with pharmacy licensing laws in every state where they do business, and to register with the FDA before beginning to sell drugs online. This requirement is virtually unenforceable because foreign online pharmacies can easily run their Web sites from an offshore location, making it difficult for federal and state authorities to exercise jurisdiction over them.

Another haven for online purveyors of illegal drugs is the "Dark" or "Deep" Web, which consists of sites that are not accessible by search engines and often feature security measures designed to allow complete anonymity or to mask illegal activity. In 2013, the most prominent online drug marketplace on the Deep Web is the Silk Road, which is estimated to attract as much as $45 million a year in illegal drug purchases. Run by a shadowy figure known only as the "Dread Pirate Roberts," the Silk Road requires users to run Tor anonymity software and accepts the virtual currency Bitcoin (see the *Insight on Society* case *Bitcoin* in Chapter 5), allowing online drug buyers an unprecedented level of protection. But the Silk Road and other competing

sites like Atlantis are now squarely in the crosshairs of the FDA and other national and worldwide law enforcement agencies.

The Silk Road is not so much a pharmacy as it is a sort of eBay for illegal drugs. Users can both buy and sell drugs, and the Silk Road takes as much as a 10% commission on all sales. Though 'Roberts' claims that the Silk Road exists as a libertarian challenge to the authority of government to limit personal freedoms, the rise in Bitcoin's value and growing popularity of his site have likely made him a millionaire many times over.

The implications for sites like the Silk Road are worrisome. If sites are able to use the Deep Web to traffic in illegal drugs, there's not much to stop them from using similar methods for illegal firearms, child pornography, or other much more undesirable commodities. And though many Bitcoin exchanges are forcing users to provide their identities, law enforcement agencies have not developed reliable methods for tracking virtual currencies. While law enforcement agencies grapple with sites like the Silk Road, traditional illegal pharmacies continue to proliferate. The FDA recommends that consumers look for the NABP Verified Internet Pharmacy Practices Sites (VIPPS) seal, which verifies that the site is legitimate with respect to conformance with state laws, and requires a prescription for controlled drugs. So far, 32 major Internet pharmacies have signed on, including Drugstore.com, Caremark.com, Walgreens.com, and many other U.S. online pharmacies.

SOURCES: "Meet the Dread Pirate Roberts, The Man Behind Booming Black Market Drug Website Silk Road" by Andy Greenberg, *Forbes*, September 2, 2013; "Over $41 Million Worth of Illegal Drugs Seized in Massive Online Pharmacy Bust," by Jacob Kastrenakes, Theverge.com, June 27, 2013; Legitscript. com, accessed October 4, 2012; "HSI Seizes 686 Websites Selling Counterfeit Medicine to Unsuspecting Consumers," U.S. Immigration and Customs Enforcement, October 4, 2012; VIPPS, National Association of Boards of Pharmacy, October 1, 2012; "The Wrong Way to Stop Fake Drugs," by Roger Bate, *New York Times*, April 22, 2012; "In Whom We Trust: The Role of Certification Agencies in Online Drug Markets," by Roger Bate et al, NBER Working Paper, March 2012; "UN Cracks Down on International Drug Fraudsters," by Natalie Morrison, In-pharmatechnologist.com, March 1, 2012; "Behind Google's $500 Million Settlement with the U.S.," by Peter J. Henning, *New York Times,* August 30, 2011; "Internet Drug Outlet Identification Program: Progress Report for State and Federal Regulators: July 2011," Nabp.net, July 11, 2011; "Drug Dealers on the Internet: Is the DEA Enforcing the Ryan Haight Act?", Legitscript.com, June 2011; "Increase in Internet Access Parallels Growth in Prescription Drug Abuse," Massgeneral.org, May 12, 2011; "Rogue Pharmacies Still a Problem For Search Engines," by Lance Whitney, CNET News, August 19, 2009; "FDA Warns Drug Firms Over Internet Ads," by Jerod Favole, *Wall Street Journal*, April 4, 2009; "U.N. Issues Guidelines on Illegal Web Pharmacies," by Reuters, *PC Magazine*, March 17, 2009; "Don't Put Your Health in the Hands of Crooks," Federal Bureau of Investigation, Headline Archives, March 3, 2009; "Ryan Haight Online Pharmacy Consumer Protection Act," H.R. 6353, 110th Congress, 2008.

the United States on the basis of a World Trade Organization ruling that American Internet gambling restrictions are illegal.

More recently, however, perhaps because of the recession which depleted state budgets, or the widespread use and popularity of state lotteries, the political climate in the United States seems to have shifted towards tolerance and even support for online gambling operations. In 2010, legislation was introduced in the House of Representatives calling for legalization of online gambling and taxation of gambling revenues by both states and the federal government, and in 2011, a bipartisan group of legislators introduced a more narrowly drawn bill that would legalize only online poker. Proponents argue that Internet gambling goes on anyway, so why not regulate and tax the activity? In the meantime, online gambling continues, as do prosecutions. For instance, in April 2011, federal prosecutors filed fraud and money laundering charges against the operators of three of the most popular online poker sites, Full Tilt Poker, PokerStars, and Absolute Poker, basing the suit not only on federal law but also New York state law. The three sites together have about 6 million monthly unique visitors.

By the end of 2011, however, the Justice Department reversed its stance against Internet gambling, removing a major obstacle for states like New York and Illinois that want to legalize online gambling so they can tax the proceeds (Wyatt, 2011b). In June 2012, the State of Delaware became the first state to legalize online gambling in all its forms (Berzo, 2012). With the promise of enormous profits, Amazon, Facebook, Apple, and Zynga are rumored to be developing online betting apps (Winkler, 2012). The ethical issues surrounding online gambling may have less influence on the public debate than the need for new tax revenues, and for firms, the hope for additional revenues.

In May 2013, Station Casinos, a local Las Vegas company, opened the nation's first legal, pay-to-play poker Web site. The site claims it can use geo-location technology to ensure that the players are in the State of Nevada and over the age of 21, a condition of its operation insofar as the federal government does not allow online poker whereas it is legal in Nevada and supported by the large casinos as an extension of their brands.

8.6   **CASE STUDY**

The Google Books Settlement:
Is It Fair?

In the Internet age, books are supposed to die off and go away. Who wants to read books when YouTube streams more than 4 billion videos every day, covering most topics known to man, and Google can provide online access to the world's information? Steve Jobs once noted in an interview about the Kindle e-book reader that people don't read anymore. However, in 2012, approximately 2.5 billion books were sold, generating around $27.1 billion in revenue. Although that represented a drop of just under 1% from 2010, e-book sales continued to grow rapidly, increasing by 44% to $3.04 billion, accounting for 20% of all trade sales in 2012. Books continue to be a very hot topic in 2013 as e-readers and tablets have exploded in popularity and Google battles the major heavy-hitter tech companies, authors, publishing firms, the United States Congress, the Department of Justice, and the European Commission over the future of online digital books.

© Cyberstock / Alamy

Google is on a tear to put everything digital on its servers and then, as the founders promise in ceaseless self-congratulatory announcements, provide access to "all the world's information" through its efforts. And make a buck, as it turns out, by selling ads aimed at you that are "relevant" to your searches. A problem arises, however, when what Google wants to put on its servers does not belong to them. We're all familiar with the copyrighted music and video situation, where firms often operate offshore, beyond the law (or so they think), and enable, induce, and encourage Internet users to illegally download copyrighted material without paying a dime for it, while in the meantime raking in millions of advertising dollars from companies willing to advertise on their networks.

But Google is no criminal organization. For a firm whose informal motto is "Don't be evil," it seems out of character for it to initiate a program of scanning millions of copyrighted books it does not own and then, without permission, providing its search engine users with access to those books without charge, while selling ad space and pocketing millions for its own account without sharing that revenue with publishers or authors. One major difference between Google and most file-sharing firms is that Google has very deep pockets filled with cash, and they are based in the United States, making it an excellent legal target.

It all started with Google's secret 2002 project to scan all the books in libraries and make parts ("snippets") available online, and of course, display ads next to the results of book searches, even on the pages of snippets. In 2004, Google announced a program it first called Google Print and now just calls Google Books. There are two parts to the project. Under the Partner Program, publishers give permission to Google to scan their books, or make scans available, and then make parts of the work, or simply bibliographic information (title, author, and publisher), available on Google's search engine. No problem there: publishers and authors get a chance to find a wider market, and Google sells more ads. Publishers may even choose to sell online editions of their books on their own Web sites. And publishers were promised a hefty 70% of the display ad revenues and book sales (far better than Amazon's cut of book sales, which is about 50%).

It's the second part of the project that became controversial. Under the Library Project, Google proposed to scan millions of books in university and public libraries, allow users to search for key phrases, and then display "relevant" portions of the text ("snippets"), all without contacting the publisher or seeking permission or paying a royalty fee. Google said it would "never show a full page without the right from the copyright holder," just the "relevant" portion. Google gave the publishing industry until November 2005 to opt out by providing Google with a list of books they did not want included. In addition, Google proposed to scan millions of books for which the copyright has lapsed and make those available on its servers for free. In these early days, Google's public stance towards authors and publishers was, "Stop us if you can."

Google has the backing of a number of prestigious libraries, such as the University of Michigan, Harvard University, Stanford University, the New York Public Library, and Oxford University. But not all librarians agree. Some believe this is a marvelous extension of public access to library collections, while other librarians fear it is harmful to book authors and publishers. A number of well-known libraries, such as the Smithsonian Institution and the Boston Public Library, as well as a consortium of 19 research and academic libraries in the Northeast, have refused to participate, in part because of restrictions that Google wants to place on the collection. Libraries that work with Google must agree to make the material unavailable to other commercial search services. Google claims it is performing a public service by making an index of books, and relevant portions, available to millions on the Internet, and perhaps even helping publishers sell new copies of books that currently sit on dusty library shelves. Google wants a monopoly on the books it has scanned (which is pretty much the universe of all books).

In 2005, the publishing industry struck back at Google's book-scanning program and two lawsuits were filed in federal court in New York, one a class-action suit by the Authors Guild and the second by five major publishing companies (McGraw-Hill, Pearson Education, Penguin Group, Simon & Schuster, and John Wiley & Sons), claiming copyright infringement. Patricia Schroeder, president of the publishers' consortium, the American Association of Publishers (AAP), alleged that Google was claiming the right to unilaterally change copyright law and copy anything unless somebody tells them "No." Schroeder noted that Google keeps talking about how what it is doing is good for the world, but that in her view, they are just stealing people's property. Or, as one commentator put it, it's like having a thief break into your house and clean the kitchen—it's still breaking and entering.

Google, on the other hand, claimed its use was "fair" under the "fair use" doctrine that has emerged from a number of court decisions issued over the years, and which is codified in the Copyright Act of 1976. The copying and lending of books by libraries has been considered a fair use since the late 1930s under a "gentleman's agreement" between libraries and publishers, and a library exemption was codified as Section 108 of the Copyright Act of 1976. Libraries loan books to patrons for a limited period, and must purchase at least one copy. Many people read books borrowed from libraries and recommend them to friends, who often buy the books rather than take the time and effort to go to a library. Libraries are also considered by many in the publishing industry as helping to market a book to a larger public, and libraries are believed to be performing a public service by increasing literacy and education.

In 2008, Google agreed to a settlement of the lawsuit with the authors and publishers. In return for the nonexclusive right to sell books scanned into its database, place advertisements on those pages, display snippets, and make other commercial uses of its database of scanned books, Google agreed to pay about $125 million to the parties. All books that Google digitizes will be listed in the central registry available to the public on the Internet. In 2009, a group of companies and organizations, including Microsoft, Yahoo, and Amazon, the American Association of Publishers, members of the Author's Guild, and publishers in the European Union all filed briefs with the court disputing the settlement. The technology companies formed the Open Book Alliance to oppose the settlement. They were joined by privacy protection groups who claimed that Google would be able to track whatever e-books people accessed and read. In September 2009, representatives of those groups spoke out at a hearing sponsored by

SOURCES: "Google Seeks Ruling Copying Books Without Permission Is Fair," by Don Jeffrey, Business-week.com, September 23, 2013; "Appeals Court Hints Strongly That Google Books Project Is Fair Use," by Emma Woollacott, Forbes.com, July 1, 2013; "Google Scanning Is Fair Use Says Judge," by Andrew Albanese, October 11, 2012; "Google Deal Gives Publishers a Choice: Digitize or Not," by Claire Cain Miller, *New York Times*, October 4, 2012; "Suit Over Google Book Scanning Delayed on Appeal," by Chad Bray, *Wall Street Journal*, September 17, 2012; "Book Sales Fell 2.5% in 2011," by Jim Milliot, *Publishers Weekly*, July 18, 2012; "Google Suit Gets Class-Action Status," by Jeffrey A. Trachtenberg, *Wall Street Journal*, May 31, 2012; "Authors Organizations File Fresh Lawsuit Challenging Google Library Scans and Pending 'Orphan Works' Access," by Michael Cader, PublishersLunch, September 13, 2011; "New Publishing Industry Survey Details Strong Three-Year Growth in Net Revenue Unit," by Andi Sporkin, Publishers.org, August 9, 2011; "Judge Rejects Google Books Settlement," by Amir Efrati and Jeffrey A. Trachtenberg, *Wall Street Journal*, March 23, 2011; "Judge Rejects Google's Deal to Digitize Books," by Miguel Helft, *New York Times*, March 22, 2011; "What Is Google Editions?" by Peter Osnos, Theatlantic.com, July 10, 2010; "11th Hour Filings Oppose Google's Book Settlement," by Miguel Helft, *New York Times*, September 9, 2009; "Congress to Weigh Google Books Settlement," *New York Times*, September 9, 2009; "Tech Heavyweights Put Google's Books Deal in Cross-hairs," by Jessica Vascellaro and Geoffrey Fowler, *Wall Street Journal*, August 21, 2009; "Probe of Google Book Deal Heats Up," by Elizabeth Williamson, J. Trachtenberg and J. Vascellaro, *Wall Street Journal*, June 10, 2009; "Justice Department Opens Antitrust Inquiry Into Google Books Deal," by Miguel Helft, *New York Times*, April 29, 2009; *The Authors Guild, Inc., Association of American Publishers, Inc., et al., v. Google Inc.*, Preliminary Settlement, Case

the European Commission against the proposed deal. They said it would give Google too much power, including exclusive rights to sell out-of-print works that remain under copyright, a category that includes millions of books.

The Justice Department is continuing its investigation into the antitrust implications of the settlement. Critics argue the settlement will create a de facto monopoly position for Google, make it difficult for competitors to enter the field, and give Google broad copyright immunity. The settlement provides that Google's access to publishers' books is "non-exclusive," but competitors would have to scan all the same books over again in order to establish a competitive position, something that experts believe is financially prohibitive. Google, they argue, would end up owning the digital book, which is like owning the libraries of the future. Google counters that the settlement will expand digital access to millions of books that are gathering dust on library shelves.

Currently, Google has reportedly scanned about 20 million of the estimated 130 million books in the world. About 2 million of those are in the public domain, and can be viewed for free through Google's Book Search. Google Book users can also view previews of another 2 million books that are in copyright and in print, under agreements with various publishers. The remainder of the scanned books are out of print but still in copyright. These are currently available only in short "snippet view." The settlement would have allowed users to preview longer parts of those works and potentially purchase them in their entirety, but in March 2011, Federal Judge Denny Chin rejected the settlement, throwing the project into legal limbo once again. Citing copyright, antitrust, and other concerns, Chin said that the settlement went too far, and agreed with critics that it would give Google a "de facto monopoly" and the right to exploit and profit from books without the permission of copyright owners, particularly the authors of "orphaned" works whose content owners Google could not identify. The judge said that he would consider a revised settlement that addressed these concerns, suggesting that copyright owners be given the right to "opt in" to the settlement rather than "opt out" as originally proposed. An "opt in" structure had previously been rejected by Google as unworkable.

In September 2011, in a related action, the Authors Guild filed a new lawsuit related to the Library Project, suing Google, the university consortium HathiTrust, and five universities that are participating in the book-scanning project. The suit charges that the scanning of 9.5 million works in the HathiTrust repository constitutes massive copyright infringement, and also takes issue with HathiTrust's planned October 2011 launch of its Orphan Works Project, which would make available scans of books it had concluded were available after failing to locate valid copyright holders. Interestingly, as soon as the list was made public, a crowdsourcing effort quickly located some of the authors that purportedly could not be found. In October 2012, the U.S. District Court for the Southern District of New York dismissed the Authors Guild case against HathiTrust, finding that HathiTrust's use of Google's scanning program was fair use under copyright law, and that in particular, the scanning of books for the purpose of indexing was a transformative act. The Authors Guild is appealing the decision and the suit must wind its way through the legal process.

In 2013, the legality of the Google Library project is still up in the air. In May 2012, Judge Chin granted class-action certification to the lawsuit, allowing authors to sue Google as a group. Google had argued that copyright claims needed to be brought individually by authors, which would have made things much more difficult for them in their fight against Google. After Google appealed Judge Chin's latest decision, the case was once again delayed. In July 2013, a federal Circuit Court of Appeals ruled that before the court can consider the Authors Guild's desire to convert the lawsuit into a class action, whether Google's actions constitute fair use must first be determined. The Authors Guild had suffered a previous setback in October 2012, when Google and the publishers reached an out-of-court settlement (after seven years of litigation) that allows the publishers to choose whether to permit Google to scan their out-of-print books that are still under copyright. If Google scans these permitted books, it must provide the publishers with a digital copy for their own use. The economic value of this victory for publishers is difficult to perceive. Google will be giving away the scanned books for free and receive revenue from ads displayed on some book pages or as pre-roll ads. It's unlikely the publishers will be able to sell these e-books if a free version is also available from Google.

1:05-cv-08136-JFS Document 56, Filed 10/28/2008; "Publishers Sue Google to Stop Scanning," by David A. Vise, Washington Post, October 20, 2005; *The McGraw-Hill Companies, et al., v. Google Inc.,* United States Southern District Court, Southern District of New York, October 19, 2005.

Case Study Questions

1. Who is harmed by the Library Project? Make a list of harmed groups, and for each group, try to devise a solution that would eliminate or lessen the harm.

2. Why is Google pursuing the Library Project? What is in it for Google? Make a list of benefits to Google.

3. If you were a librarian, would you support the Library Project? Why or why not?

4. Why have firms like Amazon, Yahoo, and Microsoft opposed the Library Project? Why would a firm like Sony support Google?

5. Do you think the Library Project will result in a de facto monopoly in e-books, or will there be other competitors?

8.7 REVIEW

KEY CONCEPTS

■ Understand why e-commerce raises ethical, social, and political issues.

Internet technology and its use in e-commerce disrupts existing social and business relationships and understandings. Suddenly, individuals, business firms, and political institutions are confronted by new possibilities of behavior for which understandings, laws, and rules of acceptable behavior have not yet been developed. Many business firms and individuals are benefiting from the commercial development of the Internet, but this development also has costs for individuals, organizations, and societies. These costs and benefits must be carefully considered by those seeking to make ethical and socially responsible decisions in this new environment, particularly where there are as yet no clear-cut legal or cultural guidelines.

■ **Recognize the main ethical, social, and political issues raised by e-commerce.**

The major issues raised by e-commerce can be loosely categorized into four major dimensions:
- *Information rights*—What rights do individuals have to control their own personal information when Internet technologies make information collection so pervasive and efficient?
- *Property rights*—How can traditional intellectual property rights be enforced when perfect copies of protected works can be made and easily distributed worldwide via the Internet?
- *Governance*—Should the Internet and e-commerce be subject to public laws? If so, what law-making bodies have jurisdiction—state, federal, and/or international?
- *Public safety and welfare*—What efforts should be undertaken to ensure equitable access to the Internet and e-commerce channels? Do certain online content and activities pose a threat to public safety and welfare?

■ **Identify a process for analyzing ethical dilemmas.**

Ethical, social, and political controversies usually present themselves as dilemmas. Ethical dilemmas can be analyzed via the following process:
- Identify and clearly describe the facts.
- Define the conflict or dilemma and identify the higher-order values involved.
- Identify the stakeholders.
- Identify the options that you can reasonably take.
- Identify the potential consequences of your options.
- Refer to well-established ethical principles, such as the Golden Rule, Universalism, Descartes' Rule of Change, the Collective Utilitarian Principle, Risk Aversion, the No Free Lunch Rule, the *New York Times* Test, and the Social Contract Rule to help you decide the matter.

■ **Understand basic concepts related to privacy.**

To understand the issues concerning online privacy, you must first understand some basic concepts:
- *Privacy* is the moral right of individuals to be left alone, free from surveillance or interference from others.
- *Information privacy* includes both the claim that certain information should not be collected at all by governments or business firms, and the claim of individuals to control the use of information about themselves.
- *Due process* as embodied by the Fair Information Practices doctrine, informed consent, and opt-in/opt-out policies also plays an important role in privacy.

■ **Identify the practices of e-commerce companies that threaten privacy.**

Almost all e-commerce companies collect some personally identifiable information in addition to anonymous information and use cookies to track clickstream behavior of visitors. Advertising networks and search engines also track the behavior of consumers across thousands of popular sites, not just at one site, via cookies, spyware, search engine behavioral targeting, and other techniques

■ **Describe the different methods used to protect online privacy.**

There are a number of different methods used to protect online privacy. They include:

- Legal protections deriving from constitutions, common law, federal law, state laws, and government regulations. In the United States, rights to online privacy may be derived from the U.S. Constitution, tort law, federal laws such as the Children's Online Privacy Protection Act (COPPA), the Federal Trade Commission's Fair Information Practice principles, and a variety of state laws. In Europe, the European Commission's Data Protection Directive has standardized and broadened privacy protection in the European Union nations.
- Industry self-regulation via industry alliances, such as the Online Privacy Alliance and the Network Advertising Initiative, that seek to gain voluntary adherence to industry privacy guidelines and safe harbors. Some firms also hire chief privacy officers.
- Privacy-enhancing technological solutions include spyware and pop-up blockers, secure e-mail, anonymous remailers, anonymous surfing, cookie managers, disk file-erasing programs, policy generators, and public key encryption programs.

■ **Understand the various forms of intellectual property and the challenge of protecting it.**

There are three main types of intellectual property protection: copyright, patent, and trademark law.

- *Copyright law* protects original forms of expression such as writings, drawings, and computer programs from being copied by others for a minimum of 70 years. It does not protect ideas—just their expression in a tangible medium. "Look and feel" copyright infringement lawsuits are precisely about the distinction between an idea and its expression. If there is only one way to express an idea, then the expression cannot be copyrighted. Copyrights, like all rights, are not absolute. The doctrine of fair use permits certain parties under certain circumstances to use copyrighted material without permission. The Digital Millennium Copyright Act (DMCA) was the first major effort to adjust copyright law to the Internet age. The DMCA implements a World Intellectual Property Organization treaty, which declares it illegal to make, distribute, or use devices that circumvent technology-based protections of copyrighted materials, and attaches stiff fines and prison sentences for violations.
- *Patent law* grants the owner of a patent an exclusive monopoly to the ideas behind an invention for 20 years. Patents are very different from copyrights in that they protect the ideas themselves and not merely the expression of ideas. There are four types of inventions for which patents are granted under patent law: machines, man-made products, compositions of matter, and processing methods. In order to be granted a patent, the applicant must show that the invention is new, original, novel, nonobvious, and not evident in prior arts and practice. Most of the inventions that make the Internet and e-commerce possible were not patented by their inventors. This changed in the mid-1990s with

the commercial development of the World Wide Web. Business firms began applying for "business methods" and software patents.

- *Trademark protections* exist at both the federal and state levels in the United States. The purpose of trademark law is twofold. First, trademark law protects the public in the marketplace by ensuring that it gets what it pays for and wants to receive. Second, trademark law protects the owner who has spent time, money, and energy bringing the product to market against piracy and misappropriation. Federal trademarks are obtained, first, by use in interstate commerce, and second, by registration with the U.S. Patent and Trademark Office (USPTO). Trademarks are granted for a period of 10 years and can be renewed indefinitely. Use of a trademark that creates confusion with existing trademarks, causes consumers to make market mistakes, or misrepresents the origins of goods is an infringement. In addition, the intentional misuse of words and symbols in the marketplace to extort revenue from legitimate trademark owners ("bad faith") is proscribed. The Anticybersquatting Consumer Protection Act (ACPA) creates civil liabilities for anyone who attempts in bad faith to profit from an existing famous or distinctive trademark by registering an Internet domain name that is identical or confusingly similar to, or "dilutive" of, that trademark. Trademark abuse can take many forms on the Web. The major behaviors on the Internet that have run afoul of trademark law include cybersquatting, cyberpiracy, metatagging, keywording, linking, and framing.

■ **Understand how governance of the Internet has evolved over time.**

Governance has to do with social control: who will control e-commerce, what elements will be controlled, and how the controls will be implemented. Governance of both the Internet and e-commerce has gone through four stages:

- *Government control (1970–1994).* During this period, DARPA and the National Science Foundation controlled the Internet as a fully government-funded program.
- *Privatization (1995–1998).* Network Solutions was given a monopoly to assign and track high-level Internet domain names. The backbone was sold to private telecommunications companies and policy issues remained undecided.
- *Self-regulation (1995–present).* President Clinton and the Department of Commerce encouraged creation of ICANN, a semi-private body, to deal with emerging conflicts and to establish policies.
- *Governmental regulation (1998–present).* Executive, legislative, and judicial bodies worldwide began to implement direct controls over the Internet and e-commerce.

We are currently in a mixed-mode policy environment where self-regulation, through a variety of Internet policy and technical bodies, co-exists with limited government regulation.

■ **Explain why taxation of e-commerce raises governance and jurisdiction issues.**

E-commerce raises the issue of how—and if—to tax remote sales. The national and international character of Internet sales has wreaked havoc on taxation schemes in the United States that were built in the 1930s and based on local commerce and local jurisdictions. E-commerce has benefited from a tax subsidy since its inception.

E-commerce merchants have argued that this new form of commerce needs to be nurtured and encouraged, and that in any event, the crazy quilt of sales and use tax regimes would be difficult to administer for Internet merchants. In 1998, Congress passed the Internet Tax Freedom Act, which placed a moratorium on multiple or discriminatory taxes on electronic commerce, and any taxation of Internet access, and since that time has extended the moratorium several times, most recently until November 2014. Federal legislation to implement a uniform set of rules for collecting taxes on e-commerce sales is currently pending in Congress.

■ **Identify major public safety and welfare issues raised by e-commerce.**

Critical public safety and welfare issues in e-commerce include:

- The protection of children and strong sentiments against pornography. Several attempts by Congress to legislate in this area have been struck down as unconstitutional. The Children's Internet Protection Act (CIPA), which requires schools and libraries in the United States to install "technology protection measures" (filtering software) in an effort to shield children from pornography, has, however, been upheld by the Supreme Court.
- Efforts to control gambling and restrict sales of cigarettes and drugs. In the United States, cigarettes, gambling, medical drugs, and addictive recreational drugs are either banned or tightly regulated by federal and state laws. Yet these products and services are often distributed via offshore e-commerce sites operating beyond the jurisdiction of federal and state prosecutors. At this point, it is not clear that the Web will remain borderless or that e-commerce can continue to flaunt national, state, and local laws with impunity.

QUESTIONS

1. What basic assumption does the study of ethics make about individuals?
2. What are the basic principles of ethics?
3. Explain Google's position that YouTube does not violate the intellectual property rights of copyright owners.
4. Define universalism, slippery slope, the *New York Times* test, and the social contract rule as they apply to ethics.
5. Explain why someone with a serious medical condition might be concerned about researching his or her condition online, through medical search engines or pharmaceutical sites, for example. What is one technology that could prevent one's identity from being revealed?
6. Name some of the personal information collected by Web sites about their visitors.
7. How does information collected through online forms differ from site transaction logs? Which potentially provides a more complete consumer profile?
8. How is the opt-in model of informed consent different from opt-out? In which type of model does the consumer retain more control?
9. What are the two core principles of the FTC's Fair Information Practice principles?
10. How do safe harbors work? What is the government's role in them?
11. Name three ways online advertising networks have improved on, or added to, traditional offline marketing techniques.

12. Explain how behavioral targeting is supposed to benefit both consumers and businesses.

13. How could the Internet potentially change protection given to intellectual property? What capabilities make it more difficult to enforce intellectual property law?

14. What does the Digital Millennium Copyright Act (DMCA) attempt to do? Why was it enacted? What types of violations does it try to prevent?

15. Define cybersquatting. How is it different from cyberpiracy? What type of intellectual property violation does cybersquatting entail?

16. What is deep linking and why is it a trademark issue? Compare it to framing—how is it similar and different?

17. What are some of the tactics that illegal businesses, such as betting parlors and casinos, successfully use to operate outside the law on the Internet?

PROJECTS

1. Go to Google and click the Advanced Search link at the bottom of the page. Examine its SafeSearch filtering options. Surf the Web in search of content that could be considered objectionable for children using each of the options. What are the pros and cons of such restrictions? Are there terms that could be considered inappropriate to the filtering software but be approved by parents? Name five questionable terms. Prepare a brief presentation to report on your experiences and to explain the positive and negative aspects of such filtering software.

2. Develop a list of privacy protection features that should be present if a Web site is serious about protecting privacy. Then, visit at least four well-known Web sites and examine their privacy policies. Write a report that rates each of the Web sites on the criteria you have developed.

3. Review the provisions of the Digital Millennium Copyright Act of 1998. Examine each of the major sections of the legislation and make a list of the protections afforded property owners and users of copyrighted materials. Do you believe this legislation balances the interests of owners and users appropriately? Do you have suggestions for strengthening "fair use" provisions in this legislation?

4. Visit at least four Web sites that take a position on e-commerce taxation, beginning with the National Conference of State Legislatures (Ncsl.org) and the National Governors Association (Nga.org). You might also include national associations of local businesses or citizen groups opposed to e-commerce taxation. Develop a reasoned argument for, or against, taxation of e-commerce.

E-commerce in Action

CHAPTER 9

Online Retail and Services

Blue Nile Sparkles

for Your Cleopatra

Men: looking for that special gift for your Cleopatra but don't want to spend a lot of time shopping? Want to give the "Big Rock" without spending a mountain of cash for the engagement experience? Not sure about the future value of diamonds? Then how about pearls, gold, or platinum?

Your answer has arrived: BlueNile offers you an online selection of over 80,000 diamonds for that special someone. You can buy them cut and polished, or put them into settings like rings, bracelets, earrings, necklaces, pendants, watches, and brooches that you choose online. All the dia-

© Ken Gillespie Photography / Alamy

monds are graded by the 4Cs: carats (size), cut, color, and clarity, and a report for each diamond prepared by the Gemological Institute of America is available online. To make it easier, the carats are translated into milligrams, and one carat is exactly 200 milligrams of mass (if that helps). Just ask her what size she wants, and then look in your wallet.

BlueNile.com started out as RockShop.com in March 1999 in Seattle, Washington. In November 1999, the company launched the Blue Nile brand and changed its name to Blue Nile Inc., opening up its Web site, BlueNile.com, in December 1999. In 2004, it went public. In 2007, Blue Nile sold the biggest item in Internet history, a $1.5 million single diamond of around 10 carats, a size that would cover your finger with a penny-size rock. In 2010, another diamond sold for $500,000.

Back in the early days of e-commerce, no one ever thought that the Internet would be a place where fine jewelry was sold. Typically, gifts of jewelry such as diamonds are associated with a significant emotional event, such as an engagement, marriage, or an anniversary. Generally, the event is shared with a significant other and often involves shopping together for the gem. Shopping on the Web (alone or together) hardly matches the emotional impact of walking into Tiffany's or another established retail store, with marvelous clear glass cases filled with brilliantly shining baubles, attended by a small army of unctuous perfumed sales clerks that make you feel so special. Diamonds represent a significant cost, and there is significant uncertainty about their value and pricing. Surveys show that most shoppers believe jewelry is highly overpriced, but they lack the knowledge and information to negotiate a better price or even judge the quality of what they are buying. Consumers generally have no rational way to compare diamonds, and face a limited selection at a single store, often in a high-pressure environment where sales employees are helping several customers at the same time. Most experts thought that, given the emotional significance and uncertainty of purchasing diamonds, few consumers would heighten the built-in anxiety by going to a strange Web site and plunking down $5,000 or more for a diamond they could not see or touch for several days.

But jewelry and high-fashion retailers are leading the second act of online retailing, bursting on the scene with high-growth rates and spectacular average sales transaction levels. As it turns out, the retail jewelry industry is an ideal candidate for Web sales. Here's why.

The $62 billion jewelry industry is a byzantine, fragmented collection of about 25,000 specialty jewelry stores and another 100,000-plus that sell jewelry along with other products. To supply this fragmented market, several layers of wholesalers and middle-men intervene, from rough diamond brokers to diamond cutters, diamond wholesalers, jewelry manufacturers, jewelry wholesalers, and finally, regional distributors. Oddly, the source of raw mined diamonds is monopolized by a single company, De Beers, which controls around half of the world market. The fragmented supply and distribution chains add to huge markups based on monopoly-set prices for the raw diamonds. Currently, the typical retail store markup for diamonds is between 50% and 100%. Blue Nile's markup is around 30%.

Blue Nile's 2012 revenues were $400 million, up around 15% from $348 million in 2011, and the company experienced a 20% increase in revenues in the critical fourth quarter, which accounts for the lion's share of its revenues. International sales (in more than 40 countries worldwide) grew from $56 million in 2011 to $62 million in 2012. However, profits declined by 26% to $8.4 million, in part due to less than expected sales of non-engagement jewelry during the holiday season and higher marketing and advertising costs. In the first half of 2013, Blue Nile's sales have continued to grow, increasing by almost 18% over 2012 totals. Net income for the first six months of 2013 is 75% higher than the same period in 2012, increasing to $3 million. International sales continued to grow as well.

Blue Nile's online competitors include Tiffany, Ice.com, Bidz, an online auction jewelry discount site, and even Amazon. Together, these companies are transforming the jewelry business. Blue Nile, for instance, has simplified the supply-side of diamonds by cutting out several layers of middlemen and instead dealing directly with wholesale diamond owners and jewelry manufacturers.

Blue Nile minimizes its inventory costs and limits its risk of inventory markdowns. On the sell side of distribution, Blue Nile has eliminated the expensive stores, sales clerks, and beautiful, but expensive, glass cases. Instead, Blue Nile offers a Web site at which it can aggregate the demand of thousands of unique visitors for diamonds and present them with a more attractive shopping experience than a typical retail store. The result of rationalizing the supply and distribution chain is much lower markups. For example, Blue Nile will purchase a pair of oval emerald and diamond earrings from a supplier for $850 and charge the consumer $1,020. A traditional retailer would charge the consumer $1,258.

Blue Nile has improved the shopping experience primarily by creating a trust- and knowledge-based environment that reduces consumer anxiety about the value of diamonds. In essence, Blue Nile and the other online retailers give the consumer as much information as a professional gemologist would give them. The Web site contains educational guides to diamonds and diamond grading systems, and provides independent quality ratings for each diamond provided by nonprofit industry associations. There's a 30-day, money-back, no-questions-asked guarantee. The company's focus is "empowering the customer with information." And empower they do. The average customer visits the Web site repeatedly over several weeks, views at least 200 pages, and typically calls Blue Nile's live customer service line at least once. Repeat business accounts for around 25% of revenue.

In 2009, Blue Nile rebuilt its Web site, strengthening its appeal to its mostly male customer base while attempting to draw more women to the site. The new site removed the left menu so common to older Web designs, enlarged the pictures, added visualization software so visitors can see the jewelry with shadows and sparkles, expanded the product detail, and improved the search engine. The site's "Build Your Own Ring" feature became easier to use. Another addition was the Recently Purchased Engagement Rings feature that showcases custom-ordered engagement rings. Blue Nile also added functionality that allows customers to transact in their local currency, and now supports 24 different currencies in addition to the U.S. dollar, helping fuel the increase in international sales. In 2010, it introduced a mobile Web site and iPhone/iPad app. The iPhone app provides users with a quick way to set specifications for a diamond and see the price. A Dream Box button allows users to view the latest rings being sold by Blue Nile and share selections with friends via e-mail or Facebook. The app also features a Call button that provides a direct link to the Blue Nile call center for phone orders. In 2012, 25% of Blue Nile's traffic came to it via smartphones. The average smartphone shopper spends more than the traditional Web shopper. The biggest smartphone sale to date: a $300,000 engagement ring! It has also dived into social media marketing, with a Facebook page that has over 500,000 Likes, a YouTube channel with over 475,000 views, a Pinterest page with over 50,000 followers, and a Twitter feed with 8,000 followers.

In 2012, Blue Nile began a shift in its strategy driven by the possibility that online retailers will have to begin collecting Internet sales taxes in most jurisdictions (see the *Insight on Business* case, *Internet Sales Tax Battle*, in Chapter 8). The company is moving towards fashion jewelry and higher price points and away from simply offering the lowest prices. Blue Nile has begun offering a proprietary line of high-end jewelry, and has added a design director and a new chief merchant to retool its product offerings. Still, even with additional sales taxes, Blue Nile's Internet-based distribution methods and lack of overhead from physical stores will allow them to continue to offer competitive prices.

So far, the "Blue Nile" effect of lower margins and Internet efficiency has mainly impacted the small mom-and-pop jewelry stores. About 3,000 small retailers have disappeared in the last few years for a variety of reasons. The big retailers, such as Tiffany, Zales, and others, sell more than Blue Nile, and continue to benefit from consumer interest in diamond engagement and wedding rings. Both Tiffany and Zales have active Web sites. Tiffany's site is primarily a branding site, but it has greatly improved its online graphics and online sales capabilities. The Zales site is a much more effective sales site than Tiffany's, with a marvelous build-a-ring capability, but still not quite up to the level of Blue Nile with respect to certification. Still, Blue Nile will have to keep a keen watch on its competitors, who are not far behind, to keep its edge online.

SOURCES: "Blue Nile Announces Second Quarter 2013 Financial Results," Bluenile.com, September 4, 2013; "Blue Nile Announces Fourth Quarter and Full Year 2012 Financial Results," Bluenile.com, February 12, 2013; "Top 500 Guide 2013 Edition," Internet Retailer, 2013; "Blue Nile's Cheaper Diamonds Need Not Threaten Tiffany. Here's Why." by Dina Wang. Blogs.hbr.org, December 5, 2012; "Blue Nile's New Direction, and What it Says about Our Industry," by Rob Bates, JCKOnline.com, September 7, 2012; "Blue Nile Carries the Week in the Internet Retailer Online Retail Index," by Thad Rueter, Internetretailer.com, August 6, 2012; "Customer Says 'I Do' To a $300,000 Mobile Transaction," by Bill Siwicki, InternetRetailer.com, September 15, 2011; "Blue Nile CEO: More Shoppers Saying 'I Do,'" by Christina Berk, Cnbc.com, November 29, 2010; "Shopping on a Phone Finds Its Customer," by Geoffrey Fowler, *Wall Street Journal*, November 26, 2010; "Blue Nile Works to Build Repeat Business," Internet Retailer, September 22, 2010; "Blue Nile's App Is a Girl's Best Friend (And Maybe a Boy's Too)," by Christina Berk, Cnbc.com, September 16, 2010; "Selling Information, Not Diamonds," by Kaihan Krippendorf, Fastcompany.com, September 1, 2010; "Blue Nile Sparkles," by Kaihan Krippendorf, Fastcompany.com, August 30, 2010; "Digital Bling: Diamonds For Sale Online," by Wendy Kaufman, NPR.org, February 14, 2010; "Blue Nile Gets Makeover to Please Ladies," by Geoffrey Fowler, *Wall Street Journal*, September 1, 2009; "New Blue Site Hits Web," *New York Times*, September 1, 2009; "Blue Nile Aims to Sparkle With Re-designed Web Site," Internet Retailer, September 1, 2009; "Blue Nile: A Guy's Best Friend," by Jay Greene, *Business Week*, May 29, 2008.

The Blue Nile case illustrates some of the advantages that a pure-play, start-up retail company has over traditional offline retailers, and some of the disadvantages. A pure-play consumer service company can radically simplify the existing industry supply chain and develop an entirely new Web-based distribution system that is far more efficient than traditional retail outlets. At the same time, an online pure-play retailer can create a better value proposition for the customer, improving customer service and satisfaction in the process. On the other hand, pure-play start-up companies often have razor-thin profit margins, lack a physical store network to bolster sales to the non-Internet audience, and are often based on unproven business assumptions that, in the long term, may not pan out. In contrast, large offline retailers such as Walmart, JCPenney, Sears, and Target have established brand names, a huge real estate investment, a loyal customer base, and extraordinarily efficient inventory control and fulfillment systems. As we shall see in this chapter, traditional offline catalog merchants are even more advantaged. We will also see that, in order to leverage their assets and core competencies, established offline retailers need to cultivate new competencies and a carefully developed business plan to succeed on the Web.

As with retail goods, the promise of pure-online service providers is that they can deliver superior-quality service and greater convenience to millions of consumers at a lower cost than established bricks-and-mortar service providers, and still make a respectable return on invested capital. The service sector is one of the most natural avenues for e-commerce because so much of the value in services is based on collecting, storing, and exchanging information—something for which the Web is ideally suited. And, in fact, online services have been extraordinarily successful in attracting banking, brokerage, travel, and job-hunting customers. The quality and amount of information online to support consumer decisions in finance, travel, and career placement is extraordinary, especially when compared to what was available to consumers before e-commerce.

The online service sector—like online retail—has shown both explosive growth and some recent impressive failures. Despite the failures, online services have established a significant beachhead and are coming to play a large role in consumer time on the Internet. In areas such as brokerage, banking, and travel, online services are an extraordinary success story, and are transforming their industries. As with the retail sector, many of the early innovators—delivery services such as Kozmo and Webvan and consulting firms such as BizConsult.com—are gone. However, some early innovators, such as E*Trade, Schwab, Expedia, and Monster, have been successful, while many established service providers, such as Citigroup, JPMorgan Chase, Wells Fargo, Bank of America, and the large airlines, have developed successful online e-commerce service delivery sites. In Sections 9.5–9.7 of this chapter, we take a close look at three of the most successful online services: financial services (including insurance and real estate), travel services, and career services.

9.1 THE ONLINE RETAIL SECTOR

Table 9.1 summarizes some of these leading trends in online retailing for 2013–2014. Perhaps the most important theme in online retailing is the effort by retailers—both offline and online—to integrate their operations so they can serve customers in the various ways they want to be served.

By any measure, the size of the U.S. retail market is huge. In a $16 trillion economy, personal consumption of retail goods and services accounts for about $11.4

TABLE 9.1	WHAT'S NEW IN ONLINE RETAIL 2013–2014

- Mobile commerce exploded, increasing from around $25 billion in 2012 to $39 billion in 2013. It is expected to continue growing significantly to over $50 billion in 2014.
- Continued rapid growth in social networks and user-generated content sites encourages "social commerce," where users pass on their opinions and recommendations to others in several online viral networks. Social commerce in the United States almost doubled, from $3 billion in 2012 to $5 billion in 2013, and is expected to almost double again, to $9 billion in 2014.
- Local commerce, headlined by daily deal sites such as Groupon and LivingSocial, continues to be popular with consumers, increasing to $4.4 billion in 2013.
- The number of online buyers increased to over 155 million in 2013, and the average annual purchase is up 10% to $1,663.
- Online retailers remain generally profitable by focusing on revenue growth, increasing the size of average purchase amounts, and improving efficiency of operations.
- Online retail remains the fastest growing retail channel.
- Buying online has become a normal, mainstream, everyday experience. Around 89% of Internet users in the United States are now online shoppers.
- The selection of goods for purchase online continues to increase to include luxury goods, such as jewelry, gourmet groceries, furniture, and wine, as customer trust and experience increase.
- Informational shopping for big-ticket items such as cars and appliances continues to expand rapidly to include nearly all retail goods (both durables and non-durables).
- Specialty retail sites show rapid growth in online retail as they develop customized retail goods and customer online configuration of goods.
- Online retailers place an increased emphasis on providing an improved "shopping experience," including ease of navigation and use, online inventory updates, interactive tools, customer feedback and ratings, and social shopping opportunities.
- Online retailers increase the use of interactive marketing technologies and techniques such as blogs, user-generated content, and video that exploit the dominance of broadband connections and offer features such as zoom, color switch, product configuration, and virtual simulations of households and businesses.
- Retailers become increasingly efficient in integrating multiple retailing channels, beyond "bricks-and-clicks" to "click-and-drive" and in-store Web kiosk ordering.
- More than half of online shopping and nearly a third of online purchases occur at work. However, growth of at-home broadband connections increases, making evening purchases from home the fastest growing time segment for retail purchases online and relieving some pressure on workplace purchasing.

trillion (about 71%) of the total gross domestic product (GDP) (Bureau of Economic Analysis, U.S. Department of Commerce, 2013).

THE RETAIL INDUSTRY

The retail industry is composed of many different types of firms. **Figure 9.1** divides the retail industry into seven segments: durable goods, general merchandise, food and beverage, specialty stores, gasoline and fuel, mail order/telephone order (MOTO), and online retail firms. Each of these segments offers opportunities for online retail, and yet in each segment, the uses of the Internet may differ. Some eating and drinking establishments use the Web to inform people of their physical locations and menus, while others offer delivery via Web orders (although this has not been a successful model). Retailers of durable goods typically use the Web primarily as an informational tool rather than as a direct purchasing tool, although this has begun to change.

The MOTO sector is the most similar to the online retail sales sector. In the absence of physical stores, MOTO retailers distribute millions of physical catalogs (their largest expense) and operate large telephone call centers to accept orders. They have developed extraordinarily efficient order fulfillment centers that generally ship customer orders within 24 hours of receipt. MOTO was the fastest growing retail segment throughout the 1970s and 1980s. It grew as a direct result of improvements in the national toll-free call system, the implementation of digital switching in telephone systems, falling long distance telecommunications prices, and of course, the expansion of the credit card industry and associated technologies, without which neither MOTO nor e-commerce would be possible on a large national scale. MOTO was the last "technological" retailing revolution that preceded e-commerce. Because

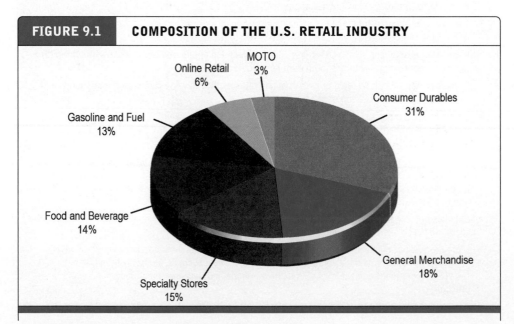

FIGURE 9.1 **COMPOSITION OF THE U.S. RETAIL INDUSTRY**

The retail industry can be grouped into seven major segments.
SOURCE: Based on data from U.S. Census Bureau, 2012.

of their experience in fulfilling small orders rapidly, the transition to e-commerce was not difficult for these firms.

ONLINE RETAILING

Online retail is perhaps the most high-profile e-commerce sector. Over the past decade, this sector has experienced both explosive growth and spectacular failures. Many of the early pure-play online-only firms that pioneered the retail marketspace failed. Entrepreneurs and their investors seriously misjudged the factors needed to succeed in this market. But the survivors of this early period emerged much stronger, and along with traditional offline general and specialty merchants, as well as new start-ups, the e-tail space is growing very rapidly and is increasing its reach and size.

E-commerce Retail: The Vision

In the early years of e-commerce, literally thousands of entrepreneurial Web-based retailers were drawn to the marketplace for retail goods, simply because it was one of the largest market opportunities in the U.S. economy. Many entrepreneurs initially believed it was easy to enter the retail market. Early writers predicted that the retail industry would be revolutionized, literally "blown to bits"—as prophesized by two consultants in a famous Harvard Business School book (Evans and Wurster, 2000). The basis of this revolution would be fourfold. First, because the Internet greatly reduced both search costs and transaction costs, consumers would use the Web to find the lowest-cost products. Several results would follow. Consumers would increasingly drift to the Web for shopping and purchasing, and only low-cost, high-service, quality online retail merchants would survive. Economists assumed that the Web consumer was rational and cost-driven—not driven by perceived value or brand, both of which are nonrational factors.

Second, it was assumed that the entry costs to the online retail market were much less than those needed to establish physical storefronts, and that online merchants were inherently more efficient at marketing and order fulfillment than offline stores. The costs of establishing a powerful Web site were thought to be minuscule compared to the costs of warehouses, fulfillment centers, and physical stores. There would be no difficulty building sophisticated order entry, shopping cart, and fulfillment systems because this technology was well known, and the cost of technology was falling by 50% each year. Even the cost of acquiring consumers was thought to be much lower on the Web because of search engines that could almost instantly connect customers to online vendors.

Third, as prices fell, traditional offline physical store merchants would be forced out of business. New entrepreneurial companies—such as Amazon—would replace the traditional stores. It was thought that if online merchants grew very quickly, they would have first-mover advantages and lock out the older traditional firms that were too slow to enter the online market.

Fourth, in some industries—such as electronics, apparel, and digital content—the market would be disintermediated as manufacturers or their distributors entered to build a direct relationship with the consumer, destroying the retail intermediaries or middlemen. In this scenario, traditional retail channels—such as physical stores, sales clerks, and sales forces—would be replaced by a single dominant channel: the Web.

Many predicted, on the other hand, a kind of hypermediation based on the concept of a virtual firm in which online retailers would gain advantage over established offline merchants by building an online brand name that attracted millions of customers, and outsourcing the expensive warehousing and order fulfillment functions—the original concept of Amazon and Drugstore.com.

As it turned out, few of these assumptions and visions were correct, and the structure of the retail marketplace in the United States, with some notable exceptions, has not been blown to bits, disintermediated, or revolutionized in the traditional meaning of the word "revolution." With several notable exceptions, online retail has often not been successful as an independent platform on which to build a successful "pure-play" Web-only business. As it turns out, the consumer is not primarily price-driven when shopping on the Internet but instead considers brand name, trust, reliability, delivery time, convenience, ease of use, and above all "the experience," as at least as important as price (Brynjolfsson, Dick, and Smith, 2004).

However, the Internet has created an entirely new venue for multi-channel firms that have a strong offline brand, and in some cases, the Internet has supported the development of pure-play online-only merchants, both general merchandisers as well as specialty retailers. As predicted, online retail has indeed become the fastest growing and most dynamic retail channel in the sense of channel innovation. The Web has created a new marketplace for millions of consumers to conveniently shop. The Internet and Web have continued to provide new opportunities for entirely new firms using new business models and new online products—such as Blue Nile, as previously described. The new online channel can conflict with a merchant's other channels, such as direct sales forces, physical stores, and mail order, but this multi-channel conflict can be managed and turned into a strength.

The Online Retail Sector Today

Although online retailing is one of the smallest segments of the retail industry, constituting about 5%–6% of the total retail market today, it is growing at a faster rate than its offline counterparts, with new functionality and product lines being added every day (see **Figure 9.2**). Due to the recession, online retail revenues were basically flat from 2008 to 2009, but they since have resumed their upward trajectory. When we refer to online retail, we will not be including online services revenues such as travel, job-hunting, or the purchase of digital downloads such as software applications and music. Instead, for the purposes of this chapter, online retail refers solely to sales of physical goods over the Internet. The Internet provides a number of unique advantages and challenges to online retailers. **Table 9.2** summarizes these advantages and challenges.

Despite the high failure rate of online retailers in the early years, more consumers than ever are shopping online. For most consumers, the advantages of shopping on the Web overcome the disadvantages. In 2013, it is estimated that around 73% of Internet users over the age of 14 (around 150 million people) will buy at an online retail store, generating about $259 billion in online retail sales. While the number of new Internet users in the United States is not growing as rapidly at it was, with about 77% of the U.S. population already on the Internet, this slowdown will not necessarily

FIGURE 9.2 THE GROWTH OF ONLINE RETAIL IN THE UNITED STATES

Online retail revenues will be an estimated $259 million in 2013, and are expected to nearly double, to $434 million by 2017.

SOURCES: Based on data from eMarketer, 2013a.

slow the growth in online retail e-commerce because the average shopper is spending more on the Internet each year, and finding many new categories of items to buy. For instance, in 2003, the average annual amount spent online by users was $675, but by 2013, it had jumped to about $1,700 (eMarketer, Inc., 2013a, 2005). Also, as noted in Chapter 6, millions of additional consumers research products on the Web and are influenced in their purchase decisions at offline stores.

The primary beneficiaries of this growing consumer support are not only the pure online companies, but also the established offline retailers who have the brand-name recognition, supportive infrastructure, and financial resources to enter the online marketplace successfully. Table 1.5 on page 39 lists the top online retail firms ranked by online sales. The list contains pure-play online retailers for whom the Internet is the only sales channel, such as Amazon (in first place) and Newegg (in 14th); multi-channel firms that have established brand names and for whom e-commerce plays a relatively small role when compared to their offline physical store channels, such as Staples (2nd), Walmart (4th), Sears (6th), Office Depot (7th), Best Buy (10th), OfficeMax (11th), and Macy's (12th), and manufacturers of computer and electronic equipment, such as Apple (3rd) and Dell (8th). The top 10 retailers account for about 50% of all online retail. For pure-play firms heavily dependent on Web sales, the challenge is to turn visitors into customers, and to develop efficient operations that permit them to achieve long-term profitability. For traditional firms that are much less dependent on e-commerce sales, their challenge is to integrate the offline and online channels so customers can move seamlessly from one environment to another.

TABLE 9.2	ONLINE RETAIL: ADVANTAGES AND CHALLENGES
ADVANTAGES	**CHALLENGES**
Lower supply chain costs by aggregating demand at a single site and increasing purchasing power	Consumer concerns about the security of transactions
Lower cost of distribution using Web sites rather than physical stores	Consumer concerns about the privacy of personal information given to Web sites
Ability to reach and serve a much larger geographically distributed group of customers	Delays in delivery of goods when compared to store shopping
Ability to react quickly to customer tastes and demand	Inconvenience associated with return of damaged or exchange goods
Ability to change prices nearly instantly	Overcoming lack of consumer trust in online brand names
Ability to rapidly change visual presentation of goods	Added expenses for online photography, video, and animated presentations
Avoidance of direct marketing costs of catalogs and physical mail	Online marketing costs for search, e-mail, and displays
Increased opportunities for personalization, customization	Added complexity to product offerings and customer service
Ability to greatly improve information and knowledge delivered to consumer	Greater customer information can translate into price competition and lower profits
Ability to lower consumers' overall market transaction costs	

Multi-Channel Integration

Clearly one of the most important e-commerce retail themes of 2013–2014, and into the future, is the ability of offline traditional firms such as Walmart, Target, JCPenney, Staples, and others to continue to integrate their Web and mobile operations with their physical store operations in order to provide an "integrated shopping customer experience," and leverage the value of their physical stores. **Table 9.3** illustrates some of the various ways in which traditional retailers have integrated the Web, the mobile platform, and store operations to develop nearly seamless multi-channel shopping. This list is not exclusive, and retailers continue to develop new links between channels.

Rather than demonstrate disintermediation, online retailing provides an example of the powerful role that intermediaries continue to play in retail trade. Established offline retailers have rapidly gained online market share. Increasingly, consumers are attracted to stable, well-known, trusted retail brands and retailers. The online audience is very sensitive to brand names and is not primarily cost-driven. Other factors such as reliability, trust, fulfillment, and customer service are equally important.

The most significant changes in retail e-commerce in 2013 are the explosive growth in social e-commerce, the growing ability of firms to market local services and products through the use of location-based marketing, and not least, the rapidly growing mobile

TABLE 9.3	RETAIL E-COMMERCE: MULTI-CHANNEL INTEGRATION METHODS
INTEGRATION TYPE	**DESCRIPTION**
Online order, in-store pickup	Probably one of the first types of integration.
Online order, store directory, and inventory	When items are out of stock online, customer is directed to physical store network inventory and store location.
In-store kiosk Web order, home delivery	When retail store is out of stock, customer orders in store and receives at home. Presumes customer is Web familiar.
In-store retail clerk Web order, home delivery	Similar to above, but the retail clerk searches Web inventory if local store is out of stock as a normal part of the in-store checkout process.
Web order, in-store returns, and adjustments	Defective or rejected products ordered on the Web can be returned to any store location.
Online Web catalog	Online Web catalog supplements offline physical catalog and often the online catalog has substantially more product on display.
Manufacturers use online Web site promotions to drive customers to their distributors' retail stores	Consumer product manufacturers such as Colgate-Palmolive and Procter & Gamble use their Web channels to design new products and promote existing product retail sales.
Gift card, loyalty program points can be used in any channel	Recipient of gift card, loyalty program points can use it to purchase in-store, online, or via catalog, if offered by merchant.
Mobile order, Web site and physical store sales	Apps take users directly to specially formatted Web site for ordering, or to in-store bargains.
Geo-fencing mobile notification, in-store sales	Use of smartphone geo-location technology to target ads for nearby stores and restaurants.

platform composed of smartphones and tablet computers. In retail circles, tablets are being called "the ultimate shopping machine," enabling consumers to browse media-rich online catalogs just like they used to do with physical catalogs, and then buy when they feel the urge.

Social e-commerce refers to marketing and purchasing on social network sites like Facebook, Twitter, Pinterest, Tumblr, and others. To date, these sites have not become major locations from which consumers actually purchase products. Instead they have developed into major marketing and advertising platforms, directing consumers to external Web sites to purchase products. In 2013, social commerce is expected to reach $5 billion and is predicted to almost triple, to $14 billion, by 2015. More than 2.5 million Web sites have integrated with Facebook and more than 250 million people engage with Facebook from other Web sites (Paglia, 2012). Facebook has around 275 million North American members, and getting the marketing message out on the social graph can happen very quickly. In the near future, it is likely that Facebook will develop on-site shopping, competing with Amazon for the role of largest online store.

Whereas in the past only large firms could afford to run marketing and ad campaigns on the Web, this changed radically with the development of local marketing firms like Groupon and LivingSocial, and dozens of others, who make it possible for consumers to receive discount deals and coupons from local merchants based on their geographic location. Using billions of daily e-mails, these so-called daily deal sites have sold millions of coupons to purchase local goods and services at steep discounts. For the first time, local merchants can inexpensively use the Web to advertise their products and services. In 2013, local commerce is estimated to generate about $4.4 billion in revenues, and this is expected to grow to around $5.5 billion by 2016 (eMarketer, Inc, 2012a).

Social and local e-commerce are enabled by the tremendous growth in mobile Internet devices, both smartphones and tablet computers. In 2013, mobile commerce is expected to generate around $39 billion overall. In 2013, over 50% of online purchasers are expected to make a purchase using a mobile device, and it is estimated that this percentage will grow to over 75% by 2017. (eMarketer, Inc., 2013b).

9.2   ANALYZING THE VIABILITY OF ONLINE FIRMS

In this and the following chapters, we analyze the viability of a number of online companies that exemplify specific e-commerce models. We are primarily interested in understanding the near-to-medium term (1–3 years) economic viability of these firms and their business models. **Economic viability** refers to the ability of firms to survive as profitable business firms during the specified period. To answer the question of economic viability, we take two business analysis approaches: strategic analysis and financial analysis.

economic viability
refers to the ability of firms to survive as profitable business firms during a specified period

STRATEGIC ANALYSIS

Strategic approaches to economic viability focus on both the industry in which a firm operates and the firm itself (see Chapter 2, Sections 2.2 and 2.5). The key industry strategic factors are:

- *Barriers to entry*: Can new entrants be barred from entering the industry through high capital costs or intellectual property barriers (such as patents and copyrights)?

- *Power of suppliers*: Can suppliers dictate high prices to the industry or can vendors choose from among many suppliers? Have firms achieved sufficient scale to bargain effectively for lower prices from suppliers?

- *Power of customers*: Can customers choose from many competing suppliers and hence challenge high prices and high margins?

- *Existence of substitute products*: Can the functionality of the product or service be obtained from alternative channels or competing products in different industries? Are substitute products and services likely to emerge in the near future?

- *Industry value chain*: Is the chain of production and distribution in the industry changing in ways that benefit or harm the firm?

- *Nature of intra-industry competition*: Is the basis of competition within the industry based on differentiated products and services, price, scope of offerings, or focus of offerings? How is the nature of competition changing? Will these changes benefit the firm?

The strategic factors that pertain specifically to the firm and its related businesses include:

- *Firm value chain*: Has the firm adopted business processes and methods of operation that allow it to achieve the most efficient operations in its industry? Will changes in technology force the firm to realign its business processes?

- *Core competencies*: Does the firm have unique competencies and skills that cannot be easily duplicated by other firms? Will changes in technology invalidate the firm's competencies or strengthen them?

- *Synergies*: Does the firm have access to the competencies and assets of related firms either owned outright or through strategic partnerships and alliances?

- *Technology*: Has the firm developed proprietary technologies that allow it to scale with demand? Has the firm developed the operational technologies (e.g., customer relationship management, fulfillment, supply chain management, inventory control, and human resource systems) to survive?

- *Social and legal challenges*: Has the firm put in place policies to address consumer trust issues (privacy and security of personal information)? Is the firm the subject of lawsuits challenging its business model, such as intellectual property ownership issues? Will the firm be affected by changes in Internet taxation laws or other foreseeable statutory developments?

FINANCIAL ANALYSIS

Strategic analysis helps us comprehend the competitive situation of the firm. Financial analysis helps us understand how in fact the firm is performing. There are two parts to a financial analysis: the statement of operations and the balance sheet. The statement of operations tells us how much money (or loss) the firm is achieving based on current sales and costs. The balance sheet tells us how many assets the firm has to support its current and future operations.

Here are some of the key factors to look for in a firm's statement of operations:

- *Revenues*: Are revenues growing and at what rate? Many e-commerce companies have experienced impressive, even explosive, revenue growth as an entirely new channel is created.

- *Cost of sales*: What is the cost of sales compared to revenues? Cost of sales typically includes the cost of the products sold and related costs. The lower the cost of sales compared to revenue, the higher the gross profit.

- *Gross margin*: What is the firm's gross margin, and is it increasing or decreasing? **Gross margin** is calculated by dividing gross profit by net sales revenues. Gross margin can tell you if the firm is gaining or losing market power vis-à-vis its key suppliers.

gross margin
gross profit divided by net sales

- *Operating expenses*: What are the firm's operating expenses, and are they increasing or decreasing? Operating expenses typically include the cost of marketing, technology, and administrative overhead. They also include, in accordance with professional accounting standards (see below), stock-based compensation to employees and executives, amortization of goodwill and other intangibles, and impairment of investments. In e-commerce companies, these turn out to be very important expenses. Many e-commerce firms compensated their employees with stock shares (or options), and many e-commerce firms purchased other e-commerce firms as a part of their growth strategy. Many of the companies were purchased at extremely high values using company stock rather than cash; in numerous instances, the purchased companies fell dramatically in market value. All these items are counted as normal operating expenses.

operating margin
calculated by dividing operating income or loss by net sales revenue

- *Operating margin*: What did the firm earn from its current operations? **Operating margin** is calculated by dividing operating income or loss by net sales revenue. Operating margin is an indication of a company's ability to turn sales into pre-tax profit after operating expenses have been deducted. Operating margin tells us if the firm's current operations are covering its operating expenses, not including interest expenses and other non-operating expenses.

net margin
the percentage of its gross sales revenue the firm is able to retain after all expenses are deducted; calculated by dividing net income or loss by net sales revenue

- *Net margin*: **Net margin** tells us the percentage of its gross sales revenue the firm was able to retain after all expenses are deducted. Net margin is calculated by dividing net income or loss by net sales revenue. Net margin sums up in one number how successful a company has been at the business of making a profit on each dollar of sales revenues. Net margin also tells us something about the efficiency of the firm by measuring the percentage of sales revenue it is able to retain after all expenses are deducted from gross revenues, and within a single industry can be used to measure the relative efficiency of competing firms. Net margin takes into account many non-operating expenses such as interest and stock compensation plans.

When examining the financial announcements of e-commerce companies, it is important to realize that online firms often choose not to announce their net income according to generally accepted accounting principles (GAAP). These principles have been promulgated by the Financial Accounting Standards Board (FASB), a board of professional accountants that establishes accounting rules for the profession, and which has played a vital role since the 1934 Securities Act, which sought to improve financial accounting during the Great Depression. Many e-commerce firms in the early years instead reported an entirely new calculation called *pro forma earnings* (also called EBITDA—earnings before income taxes, depreciation, and amortization). Pro forma earnings generally do not deduct stock-based compensation, depreciation, or amortization. The result is that pro forma earnings are always better than GAAP earnings. The firms that report in this manner typically claim these expenses are non-recurring and special and "unusual." In 2002 and 2003, the SEC issued new guidelines (Regulation G) that prohibit firms from reporting pro forma earnings in official reports to the SEC, but still allow firms to announce pro forma earnings in public statements (Weil, 2003). Throughout this book, we consider a firm's income or loss based on GAAP accounting standards only.

balance sheet
provides a financial snapshot of a company on a given date and shows its financial assets and liabilities

assets
refers to stored value

current assets
assets such as cash, securities, accounts receivable, inventory, or other investments that are likely to be able to be converted to cash within one year

A **balance sheet** provides a financial snapshot of a company's assets and liabilities (debts) on a given date. **Assets** refer to stored value. **Current assets** are those assets such as cash, securities, accounts receivable, inventory, or other investments that are likely to be able to be converted to cash within one year. **Liabilities** are outstanding obligations of the firm. **Current liabilities** are debts of the firm that will be due within one year. Liabilities that are not due until the passage of a year or more are characterized as **long-term debt**. For a quick check of a firm's short-term financial health, examine its **working capital** (the firm's current assets minus current liabilities). If working capital is only marginally positive, or negative, the firm will likely have trouble meeting its short-term obligations. Alternatively, if a firm has a large amount of current assets, it can sustain operational losses for a period of time.

liabilities
outstanding obligations of the firm

current liabilities
debts of the firm that will be due within one year

long-term debt
liabilities that are not due until the passage of a year or more

working capital
firm's current assets minus current liabilities

9.3 E-COMMERCE IN ACTION: E-TAILING BUSINESS MODELS

So far, we have been discussing online retail as if it were a single entity. In fact, as we briefly discussed in Chapter 2, there are four main types of online retail business models: virtual merchants, multi-channel merchandisers (sometimes referred to as bricks-and-clicks or clicks-and-bricks), catalog merchants, and manufacturer-direct firms. In addition, there are small mom-and-pop retailers that use eBay, Amazon, and Yahoo Stores sales platforms, as well as affiliate merchants whose primary revenue derives from sending traffic to their "mother" sites. Each of these different types of online retailers faces a different strategic environment, as well as different industry and firm economics.

VIRTUAL MERCHANTS

Virtual merchants are single-channel Web firms that generate almost all their revenue from online sales. Virtual merchants face extraordinary strategic challenges. They must build a business and brand name from scratch, quickly, in an entirely new channel and confront many virtual merchant competitors (especially in smaller niche areas). Because these firms are totally online stores, they do not have to bear the costs associated with building and maintaining physical stores, but they face large costs in building and maintaining a Web site, building an order fulfillment infrastructure, and developing a brand name. Customer acquisition costs are high, and the learning curve is steep. Like all retail firms, their gross margins (the difference between the retail price of goods sold and the cost of goods to the retailer) are low. Therefore, virtual merchants must achieve highly efficient operations in order to preserve a profit, while building a brand name as quickly as possible in order to attract sufficient customers to cover their costs of operations. Most merchants in this category adopt low-cost and convenience strategies, coupled with extremely effective and efficient fulfillment processes to ensure customers receive what they ordered as fast as possible. In the following *E-commerce in Action* section, we take an in-depth look at the strategic and financial situation of Amazon, the leading online virtual merchant. In addition to Amazon, other successful virtual merchants include Newegg, Netflix, Overstock.com, Ratuken.com (Buy.com), Gilt Group, Wayfair, Rue La La, Blue Nile (profiled in the opening case), Bluefly, Hayneedle, Net-a-Porter, and Shoebuy.

virtual merchant
single-channel Web firms that generate almost all of their revenue from online sales

E-COMMERCE IN ACTION

AMAZON.COM

Amazon, the Seattle-based pure-online merchant, is one of the most best-known names on the Web. Never suffering from modesty, Amazon's founder, Jeff Bezos, has proclaimed in the company's annual report that the objective of Amazon is to "offer the Earth's Biggest Selection and to be Earth's most customer-centric company where customers can find and discover anything they may want to buy." Exactly what these claims mean, and how it might be possible to achieve them, is a matter of speculation for both customers and investors. Yet this has not stopped Bezos and his team from becoming the Web's most successful and innovative pure-play, online retailer.

Few business enterprises have experienced a similar roller-coaster ride from explosive early growth, to huge losses, and then on to profitability. No Internet business has been both so widely reviled and so hotly praised. Its stock reflects these changing fortunes, fluctuating over the past 10 years, from an early high of $106 in 1999, to a low of $6 a share in 2001, and then bouncing back and forth between 2003–2009 between $50–$90, then climbing toward its current price of $312 in September 2013. While controversial, Amazon has also been one of the most innovative online retailing stories in the history of e-commerce. From the earliest days of e-commerce, Amazon has continuously adapted its business model based both on its market experience and its insight into the online consumer.

The Vision

The original vision of founder Jeff Bezos and his friends was that the Internet was a revolutionary new form of commerce and that only companies that became really big early on (ignoring profitability) would survive. The path to success, according to founder Bezos, was to offer consumers three things: the lowest prices, the best selection, and convenience (which translates into feature-rich content, user-generated reviews of books and products, fast and reliable fulfillment, and ease of use). Currently, Amazon offers consumers millions of unique new, used, and collectible items in a variety of different categories, both physical and digital. Its physical goods include books; movies, music, and games; electronics and computers; home, garden, and tools; grocery, health, and beauty; toys, kids, and baby; clothing, shoes, and jewelry; sports and outdoors; and auto and industrial. Its digital products include unlimited instant videos, digital games and software, MP3s and Cloud Player, Audible audiobooks, and Kindle e-book reader products. And if Amazon does not carry it, they have created systems for helping you find it at online merchants who rent space from Amazon, or even at other places on the Web. In short, Amazon has come close to becoming the largest, single one-stop merchant on the Web, a kind of combined "shopping portal" and "product search portal" that puts it in direct competition with other large online general merchants, eBay, and general portals such as Yahoo, MSN, and even Google. As Amazon succeeded in becoming the world's largest online store, it expanded its original vision to become one of the Web's largest suppliers of merchant and search services.

Business Model

Amazon's business is currently organized into two basic segments, North American and International. Within those segments, it serves not only retail customers but also merchants and developers. The retail component of the business sells physical and digital products that Amazon has purchased and then resells to consumers just like a traditional retailer. It also manufactures and sells a variety of versions of its Kindle e-reader and Kindle Fire tablet computer.

Another major component of Amazon's business is its third-party merchant segment. Amazon Services enables third parties to integrate their products into Amazon's Web site, and use Amazon's customer technologies. In the early years of its business, Amazon entered into partnerships with large merchants such as Toys"R"Us, Borders, and Target, and created storefronts for these companies within the larger Amazon site. Today, Amazon has increasingly left the enterprise-level business to competitors and instead it has focused its efforts on small and medium-sized retail merchants.

Thousands of these types of merchants have signed on with Amazon, offering products that in some instances even compete with those that Amazon itself sells. For instance, a single product on the Amazon Web site may be listed for sale simultaneously by Amazon, by a large branded merchant participant such as Target, and by a business or individual selling a new, used, or collectible version of the product through Amazon Marketplace or an Amazon Webstore created by the merchant. For these types of merchants, Amazon is not the seller of record, does not own these products, and the shipping of products is usually handled by the third party (although in some instances, Amazon provides fulfillment services as well). Amazon collects a monthly fixed fee, sales commission (generally estimated to be between 10% and 20% of the sale), per-unit activity fee, or some combination thereof from the third party. In this segment, Amazon acts as an online shopping mall, collecting "rents" from other merchants and providing "site" services such as order entry and payment.

In many respects, Amazon's third-party seller segment is an effort to compete directly with eBay, the Web's most successful third-party merchant sales platform. eBay has a registered trading community of over 130 million active buyers and sellers. Amazon has even developed its own version of PayPal: Checkout by Amazon. At the same time, eBay itself has moved closer to Amazon's business model by encouraging merchants to sell rather than auction goods on its sites.

Another major part of Amazon's business is Amazon Web Services (AWS). Through this segment, Amazon offers a variety of Web services that provide developers with direct access to Amazon's technology platform, and allow them to build their own applications based on that platform. The company launched the program in 2002. Bezos, however, was not satisfied with only a slew of cool new applications for his company's Web site. In 2006, Amazon introduced the first of several services that Bezos hoped would transform the future of Amazon as a business. With Simple Storage Service (S3) and, later, Elastic Compute Cloud (EC2), Amazon entered the utility computing market. The company realized that the benefits of the billions it had invested in technology could also be valuable to other companies. Amazon has tremendous computing capacity, but like most companies, only uses a small portion of it at any one time. Moreover, the Amazon infrastructure is considered by many to be among the most robust in the world. Amazon began to sell its computing power on a per-usage basis, just like a power company sells electricity.

S3, for example, is a data storage service that is designed to make Web-scale computing easier and more affordable for developers. New customers get a certain amount of storage and services for free. Therafter, customers pay for exactly what they use and no more. Working in conjunction with S3, EC2 enables businesses to utilize Amazon's servers for computing tasks, such as testing software. Other "infrastructure" Web services offered by Amazon include messaging services such as Simple Queue Service (SQS), Simple Notification Service (SNS), and Simple Email Service (SES); database services such as SimpleDB, Relational Database Service, and ElastiCache; content delivery services called CloudFront; deployment and management services such as Elastic Beanstalk and CloudFormation; monitoring services such as CloudWatch; and Elastic MapReduce, a Web service that enables users to perform data-intensive tasks.

In addition to these Web services, Amazon offers networking services such as Route 53 (a DNS service in the cloud enabling businesses to direct Internet traffic to Web applications), Elastic Load Balancing, Direct Connect, and Virtual Private Cloud (VPC), which can be used to create a VPN between the Amazon cloud and a company's existing IT infrastructure. Flexible Payments Service (FPS) provides a payments service for developers. DevPay is an online billing and account management service for developers who create Amazon cloud applications. Amazon Mechanical Turk provides a marketplace for work that requires human intelligence. Alexa Web Information Service provides Web traffic data and information for developers. Fulfillment Web Services (FWS) allows merchants to access Amazon's fulfillment capabilities through a simple Web services interface.

Amazon does not break out its revenues from AWS, but analysts believe it will generate $3.8 billion in revenue in 2013. Because AWS provides cloud computing to thousands of Web sites, one research firm concluded that one-third of all Internet users access an AWS cloud site once a day on average, and that 1% of all Internet traffic runs through AWS infrastructure. According to Gartner, AWS has more than five times the combined capacity of its next 14 rivals. These numbers place Amazon at the forefront of the "infrastructure as a service market."

Even with the success of AWS, Amazon still continues to generate revenue primarily by selling products. While Amazon started out as an online merchant of books, CDs, and DVDs, since 2002, it has diversified into becoming a general merchandiser of millions of other products. Amazon has turned itself into a major online media and content firm. In 2012, 33% of its revenue came from the sales of media (including MP3 tracks, CDs, DVDs, and books) and 63% came from sales of electronics and general merchandise

In addition to Amazon.com in the United States, Amazon also operates 10 different localized sites in Europe, Asia, and Canada. The success of its international business often does not attract much attention. For instance, in 2012, Amazon derived over $26 billion, or about 43%, of its $61 billion of gross revenue offshore, and international sales grew by 23% for the year. In 2012, Amazon, following its success with Kindle e-books, also made a strong move into the music and streaming video business, with its Cloud Drive, Cloud Player, and Instant Video services.

Financial Analysis

Amazon's revenues have increased from about $600 million in 1998 to an astounding $61 billion in 2012. From 2010 to 2012, Amazon's revenues have almost doubled (see **Table 9.4**). This is very impressive, explosive revenue growth. However, Amazon's growth strategies have made it difficult for the company from a net income perspective. Although it showed a profit of $1.1 billion in 2010, net income declined to $631 million in 2011, and in 2012, Amazon experienced a net loss of $39 million, in large part due to increased operating expenses, which have almost doubled during the period, from $33 billion in 2010 to $60 billion in 2012. Even though investors are unhappy with Amazon's poor earnings record, they have driven the price of the stock to over $300 a share in September 2013. What this means is that investors are betting that Amazon will keep growing for a long time and that ultimately, it will be able to show a significant profit.

At the end of December 2012, Amazon had about $11.5 billion in cash and marketable securities. The cash and securities were obtained from sales, sales of stock and notes to the public, venture capital investors, and institutional investors in return for equity (shares) in the company or debt securities. Total assets are listed at about $32 billion. The company emphasizes the strength of its "free cash flow" as a sign of financial strength, suggesting it has more than enough cash available to cover short-term liabilities (such as financing holiday season purchasing). Amazon's cash assets should certainly be enough to cover future short-term deficits should they occur.

Strategic Analysis—Business Strategy

Amazon engages in a number of business strategies that seek to maximize growth in sales volume, while cutting prices to the bare bones. Its revenue growth strategies include driving the growth of e-book sales by offering continuing enhancements of its Kindle e-reader and Kindle Fire tablet computer, both in the United States and internationally, as well as new e-book publishing initiatives; expanding into the music and streaming video business, with its Cloud Drive, Cloud Player, and Instant Video services, and a planned tablet computer to rival the iPad; expanding its Amazon Web Services offerings and extending their geographic reach; moving towards a broader trading platform by expanding the third-party seller segment; and moving towards greater product focus by grouping its offerings into major categories called stores. Amazon is still following Walmart's and eBay's examples by attempting to be a mass-market, low-price, high-volume online supermarket where you can get just about anything. To achieve profitability in this environment, Amazon has invested heavily in supply chain management and fulfillment strategies to reduce its costs to the bare minimum while providing excellent customer service and even free shipping.

Specific programs to increase retail revenues are the continuation of free shipping from Amazon Retail (a strategy that has increased order sizes by 25%), Amazon Prime (which for $79 a year provides free two-day shipping and one-day delivery upgrades for $3.99), greater product selection, and shorter order fulfillment times. Amazon offers

TABLE 9.4	AMAZON'S CONSOLIDATED STATEMENTS OF OPERATIONS AND SUMMARY BALANCE SHEET DATA 2010–2012

CONSOLIDATED STATEMENTS OF OPERATIONS (in millions)

For the fiscal year ended December 31,	2012	2011	2010
Revenue			
Net sales/products.	$ 51,733	$ 42,000	$ 30,792
Net sales/services	9,360	6,077	3,412
Cost of sales	$ 45,971	37,288	26,561
Gross profit	**15,122**	**10,789**	**7,643**
Gross margin	**24.8%**	**22.4%**	**22.3%**
Operating expenses			
Marketing	2,408	1,630	1,029
Fulfillment.	6,419	4,576	2,898
Technology and content.	4,564	2,909	1,734
General and administrative	896	658	470
Other operating expense (income), net. . .	159	154	106
Total operating expenses.	14,446	9,927	6,237
Income from operations	**676**	**862**	**1,406**
Operating margin	**1.1%**	**1.8%**	**4.1%**
Total non-operating income (expense) . .	(132)	72	91
Income before income taxes	544	934	1,497
Provision for income taxes.	(428)	(291)	(352)
Equity-method investment activity, net of tax	(155)	(12)	7
Net income (loss).	**(39)**	**631**	**1,152**
Net margin	**-0.06%**	**1.3%**	**3.3%**

SUMMARY BALANCE SHEET DATA (in millions)

At December 31,	2012	2011	2010
Assets			
Cash, cash equivalents and marketable securities.	11,448	9,576	8,762
Total current assets	21,296	17,490	13,747
Total assets.	32,555	25,278	18,797
Liabilities			
Total current liabilities	19,002	14,896	10,372
Long-term liabilities.	5,361	2,625	1,561
Working capital.	2,294	2,594	3,102
Stockholders' Equity (Deficit)	8,192	7,757	6,864

SOURCE: Amazon.com, Inc, 2013.

customers same-day shipping in seven major cities without charging additional fees. Internet customers have long been frustrated both by high shipping and handling charges as well as long delays in receiving goods. A ticking clock can be seen next to some Amazon sale items indicating the hours remaining for an order to make it to the customer by the next day.

Amazon made several strategic acquisitions in 2012, including its blockbuster acquisition of warehouse robot manufacturer Kiva Systems in March 2012. Amazon acquired Kiva Systems for $775 million with an eye towards automating its expensive fulfillment process.

Amazon has moved strongly into the mobile shopping space as well, with shopping apps for the iPhone, BlackBerry, Android, Windows Phone 7, and iPad. It also has Deals, Price Check, and Student apps for the iPhone and has opened an Appstore for Android applications. In 2012, Amazon earned around $4 billion from mobile commerce. Reports have also surfaced that Amazon is developing its own smartphone to better compete in the mobile content marketplace.

In 2012, Amazon continued to build on the rousing success of its Kindle e-book reader platform, which Amazon has touted as the best-selling product in its history, releasing the Kindle Fire HD, with prices as low as $200 for the 7-inch screen version. In September 2013, it introduced an all new version of the Kindle Paperwhite, with new higher contrast display technology, a 25% faster processor, a next generation built-in light, and new touch technology that allows the Kindle to respond more accurately. According to Amazon, it now sells more Kindle books than all print books combined.

In 2012, Amazon increased its efforts in the entertainment business, with an expanded content licensing agreement with NBC Universal to add content to Amazon's Instant Video library, and similar agreements with CBS, Viacom and nearly every major Hollywood studio. In 2013, Amazon continued these efforts, with further agreements with Viacom, PBS, A + E, Scripps Networks and FX. Prime Instant Video now includes over 40,000 titles.

On the cost side, Amazon increasingly uses "postal injection" for shipping, in which Amazon trucks deliver pre-posted packages to U.S. Postal System centers. In 2012, Amazon also began an aggressive strategy to build warehouses all across the country to improve its delivery speeds, which it has continued in 2013, opening new fulfillment centers in New Jersey and Texas. Many of Amazon's customers who had previously not paid sales taxes will soon be forced to pay them, so Amazon has prepared by seeking an insurmountable advantage in the entirely different area of delivery speeds. The ultimate goal for Bezos and Amazon: same-day delivery in many areas of the country.

Strategic Analysis—Competition

Amazon's competitors are general merchandisers who are both offline and online, and increasingly both. This includes the largest online competitor, eBay, and multi-channel retailers such as Walmart, Sears, and JCPenney. Amazon also competes with catalog merchants such as L.L.Bean and Lands' End in a number of product areas. As the Web's largest bookseller, Amazon is in competition with bookstores such as Barnesandnoble.com. Insofar as other portal sites such as MSN and Yahoo are involved in operating online stores or auctions, or selling their own products, Amazon also competes with these portals. In addition, Amazon competes with other firms who sell Web services such as hosting, shopping cart, and fulfillment services. Amazon has also engaged iTunes and Netflix in competition by offering video and audio downloads and Amazon Cloud Player, which allows users to store and play music on the Web. Amazon offers over 22 million DRM-free MP3 songs from all four major music labels and thousands of independent labels that can be played on virtually any hardware device and managed with any music software. Amazon also offers Amazon Instant Video, which offers over 150,000 movies and TV shows to rent or buy.

Strategic Analysis—Technology

The person who said that "IT doesn't make a difference" clearly does not know much about Amazon. Amazon arguably has the largest and most sophisticated collection of online retailing technologies available at any single site on the Web. Amazon has implemented numerous Web site management, search, customer interaction, recommendation, transaction processing, and fulfillment services and systems using a combination of its own proprietary technologies and commercially available, licensed technologies. Amazon's transaction-processing systems handle millions of items, a number of different status inquiries, gift-wrapping requests, and multiple shipment methods. These systems allow customers to choose whether to receive single or several shipments based on availability and to track the progress of each order. Amazon's technology extends to its employees as well. Every warehouse worker carries a shoehorn-size device that combines a bar code scanner, a display screen, and a two-way data transmitter. It continues to invest heavily in AWS and the new versions of the Kindle e-reader, and in consumer electronics, with the Kindle Fire tablet and reportedly, a new smartphone. In 2012, Amazon spent over $4.5 billion on technology and new content, and is on track to spend even more in 2013.

Strategic Analysis—Social and Legal Challenges

Amazon faces a number of lawsuits concerning various aspects of its business. One series of lawsuits alleges that Amazon wrongfully failed to collect and remit sales and use taxes for sales of personal property, and knowingly created records and statements falsely stating it was not required to collect or remit such taxes. Amazon historically has also faced a number of patent infringement suits, which it typically settles out of court. Currently, there are several pending patent suits, including some involving Amazon's Kindle.

In 2012, Amazon faced increased challenges from states who were eager to begin collecting sales taxes from Amazon's sales. In the past, only customers in five states were required to pay sales taxes, but at least 23 states have now enacted legislation that will force companies like Amazon to begin charging sales tax. Amazon has already lost several legal battles involving the imposition of sales taxes. Many states had offered Amazon sweetened deals with tax breaks several years ago to lure Amazon's business, perhaps not expecting that Amazon would grow so large that the untaxed sales amount to billions of dollars in lost tax revenue. As many of those deals expire, Amazon has already begun, as mentioned previously, an aggressive (and costly) expansion of its warehousing infrastructure across the United States.

Future Prospects

For the first six months of 2013, Amazon registered over $31 billion in sales, as opposed to $26 billion for the same period in 2012, paced by increases in third-party sales, retail, and mobile sales. Amazon believes the increased sales were driven largely by its continued efforts to reduce prices, including shipping offers, by increased in-stock availability, and by an increased selection of products. Still, net income in the first half of 2013 decreased from $137 million for the first half of 2012 to only $75 million, due primarily to increased spending on new technology initiatives, such as a smartphone and Kindle TV set-top box, new warehouses, buying up video content in competition with Netflix, and creating original programming, as well as introducing new product categories, opening up marketplaces in new territories such as India, and continuing to introduce innovations and new content on the Kindle platform. Amazon's leadership claims to be taking a long-term view, and believes significant profits in the future will result from the investments it is currently making.

MULTI-CHANNEL MERCHANTS: BRICKS-AND-CLICKS

Also called multi-channel merchants, **bricks-and-clicks** companies have a network of physical stores as their primary retail channel, but have also introduced online offerings. These are multi-channel firms such as Walmart, Macy's, Sears, JCPenney, Staples, OfficeMax, Costco, Target, and other brand-name merchants. While bricks-and-clicks merchants face high costs of physical buildings and large sales staffs, they also have many advantages such as a brand name, a national customer base, warehouses, large scale (giving them leverage with suppliers), and a trained staff. Acquiring customers is less expensive because of their brand names, but these firms face challenges in coordinating prices across channels and handling returns of Web purchases at their retail outlets. However, these retail players are used to operating on very thin margins and have invested heavily in purchasing and inventory control systems to control costs, and in coordinating returns from multiple locations. Bricks-and-clicks companies face the challenge of leveraging their strengths and assets to the Web, building a credible Web site, hiring new skilled staff, and building rapid-response order entry and fulfillment systems. According to Internet Retailer, in 2012, the chain retailers accounted for around $75 billion (around 35%) of all online retail sales. In addition, 8 out of the top 10 fastest-growing merchants over a 10-year period tracked by Internet Retailer from 2003 to 2013 were retail chains (Internet Retailer, 2013a).

Macy's is a prime example of a traditional merchant based on physical stores moving successfully to a multi-channel online store. Rowland H. Macy opened the first R.H. Macy & Co. store in New York City in 1858, and moved the flagship store (now the site of the famous Macy's Thanksgiving parade) to Herald Square at 34th Street and Broadway in 1902. Today, Macy's is one of the largest national department store chains, with around 800 Macy's department stores throughout the United States.

bricks-and-clicks
companies that have a network of physical stores as their primary retail channel, but have also introduced online offerings

Like many traditional retailers, Macy's has had to change its business model to accommodate the Internet. Macy's (then called Federated Department Stores Inc.) jumped into e-commerce in 1995 with the creation of the Macys.com Web site. In 1999, Federated bought Fingerhut, at that time a leading catalog and direct marketer, in part for its expertise in e-commerce fulfillment and database management. Although the Fingerhut acquisition did not prove to be a financial success, Macy's e-commerce efforts benefitted from the acquisition.

In 2012, Macys.com ranked 12th on Internet Retailer's list of the top 500 retail Web sites ranked by annual sales, with about $3.2 billion in online sales, representing over 40% growth over 2011, and a tripling since 2008. Growth of its physical store sales pales by comparison.

The Macys.com Web site receives around 13 million monthly unique visitors. Web site features and functions include an interactive catalog, enlarged product views, ability to see products in different colors and from alternate views, including via zoom, and videos. It also offers product comparisons, product ratings, and product recommendations, as well as a real-time inventory check system. Macy's ranked 8th in the 2013 National Retail Federation survey of companies with respect to the best e-commerce sites for convenience, safety, and customer service.

Macy's has jumped into social media as well, with a Facebook page that has over 12 million Likes, a Twitter feed with over 270,000 followers, a Pinterest page with 33 different boards, and a YouTube channel with almost 4 million views. A shopping widget allows shoppers to create polls on Facebook. Macy's gets about 3% of its referred traffic from social networks, with the majority of it originating from Facebook, and an estimated $30 million in social commerce sales.

Macy's ranks 21st on Internet Retailer's Mobile 400, with an estimated $66 million in mobile sales, double that of 2011. It has iPhone and Android apps and an HMTL5 mobile Web site powered by Usablenet. It has also tried QR codes, SMS marketing, and augmented reality. In a trial run into mobile game advertising, Macy's ran an ad in the Pandora iPhone application that encouraged users to play a game while listening to music. The top of the ad promoted a one-day sale, and after playing the game, users could click through to visit the Macy's mobile site, where the sale was promoted. Previously, Macy's had partnered with Spotify as one of Spotify's first mobile advertisers. Macy's ran audio ads inside Spotify's iPhone app to promote its MStyleLab, targeted at Millennials. The goals of the campaign were to increase awareness and brand affinity for MStyleLab and drive sales. Macy's has landed on Internet Retailer's 2013 Hot 100 list for its efforts in targeting a new generation of shoppers through e-commerce (Internet Retailer, 2013a, 2013b, 2013c, 2013d; Kats, 2013; Love, 2013; Johnson, 2012).

CATALOG MERCHANTS

catalog merchants
established companies that have a national offline catalog operation that is their largest retail channel, but who have recently developed online capabilities

Catalog merchants such as Lands' End, L.L.Bean, CDW Corp., PC Connection, Cabela's, and Victoria's Secret are established companies that have a national offline catalog operation, but who have also developed online capabilities. Catalog merchants face very high costs for printing and mailing millions of catalogs each year—many of which have a half-life of 30 seconds after the customer receives them. Catalog merchants typically have developed centralized fulfillment and call centers, extraordinary service, and excellent fulfillment in partnership with package delivery firms such as FedEx and UPS. Catalog firms have suffered in recent years as catalog sales growth rates have fallen. As a result, catalog merchants have had to diversify their channels either by building stores (L.L.Bean), being bought by store-based firms (Sears purchased Lands' End), or by building a strong Web presence.

Catalog firms are uniquely advantaged because they already possess very efficient order entry and fulfillment systems. However, they face many of the same challenges as bricks-and-mortar stores—they must leverage their existing assets and competencies to a new technology environment, build a credible Web presence, and hire new staff. Nevertheless, according to Internet Retailer, in 2012, catalog merchants generated combined Web sales of about $25 billion (Internet Retailer, 2013a).

Arguably one of the most successful online catalog merchants is LandsEnd.com. Lands' End started out in 1963 in a basement of Chicago's tannery district selling sailboat equipment and clothing, handling 15 orders on a good day. Since then it expanded into a direct catalog merchant, distributing over 200 million catalogs annually and selling a much expanded line of "traditionally" styled sport clothing, soft luggage, and products for the home. Lands' End was the first apparel retailer to have an e-commerce-enabled Web site, launching in 1995 with 100 products and travelogue essays. Located in Dodgeville, Wisconsin, it has since grown into one of the Web's most successful apparel sites.

Lands' End has always been on the leading edge of online retailing technologies, most of which emphasize personal marketing and customized products. In 2012, it was featured as one of Internet Retailer's Hot 100 E-Retailers of 2012, which recognizes e-commerce sites that offer innovative tools and services. Lands' End was the first e-commerce Web site to allow customers to create a 3-D model of themselves to "try on" clothing. Lands' End "Get Live Help" enables customers to chat online with customer service representatives; Lands' End Custom allows customers to create custom-crafted clothing built for their personal measurements. While customized clothing built online was thought to be a gimmick in the early years of online retailing, today, 40% of Lands' End clothing sold online is customized. In 2003, Lands' End was purchased by Sears (which itself was purchased by Kmart in 2004) but retains an independent online presence and catalog operation. In 2012, Lands' End took 7th place in the National Retail Foundation's ranking of best customer service. Features that garnered praise include live video chat, product recommendations that reflect a shopper's preferences, content display based on the shopper's location and referral source, and iPhone and iPad apps that deliver Lands' End catalogs to mobile users. The digital catalogs contain exclusive content, including stories written by Lands' End employees. Shoppers can also visit Lands' End on Facebook, where it has over 1 million Likes. Shoppers can send Lands' End e-gift cards directly from Facebook. Lands' End also has a Twitter presence, where it has over 13,000 followers, and over 40 different Pinterest boards. Sears has incorporated many of Lands' End's online techniques into its own Web site, Sears.com (Landsend.com, 2013; Demery, 2012; Wagner, 2011).

MANUFACTURER-DIRECT

manufacturer-direct
single- or multi-channel manufacturers who sell directly online to consumers without the intervention of retailers

Manufacturer-direct firms are either single- or multi-channel manufacturers that sell directly online to consumers without the intervention of retailers. Manufacturer-direct firms were predicted to play a very large role in e-commerce, but this has generally not happened. The primary exceptions are computer hardware, where firms such as Apple, Dell, Sony, and Hewlett-Packard account for over 70% of computer retail sales online, and apparel manufacturers, such as Ralph Lauren, Nike, Under Armour, Fossil, Crocs, Jones Retail, and Vera Bradley. Most consumer products manufacturers do not sell directly online, although this has started to change. For instance, in 2010, Procter & Gamble launched PGeStore.com, which carries over 50 different Procter & Gamble brands. Overall, according to Internet Retailer, consumer brand manufacturers account for about $25 billion in online retail sales (Internet Retailer, 2013a).

channel conflict
occurs when retailers of products must compete on price and currency of inventory directly against the manufacturers

Manufacturer-direct firms sometimes face channel conflict challenges. **Channel conflict** occurs when retailers of products must compete on price and currency of inventory directly against the manufacturer, who does not face the cost of maintaining inventory, physical stores, or sales staffs. Firms with no prior direct marketing experience face the additional challenges of developing a fast-response online order and fulfillment system, acquiring customers, and coordinating their supply chains with market demand. Switching from a **supply-push model** (where products are made prior to orders received based on estimated demand and then stored in warehouses awaiting sale) to a **demand-pull model** (where products are not built until an order is received) has proved extremely difficult for traditional manufacturers. Yet for many products, manufacturer-direct firms have the advantage of an established national brand name, an existing large customer base, and a lower cost structure than even catalog merchants because they are the manufacturer of the goods and thus do not pay profits to anyone else. Therefore, manufacturer-direct firms should have higher margins.

supply-push model
products are made prior to orders received based on estimated demand

demand-pull model
products are not built until an order is received

One of the most frequently cited manufacturer-direct retailers is Dell Inc., the world's largest direct computer systems supplier, providing corporations, government agencies, small-to-medium businesses, and individuals with computer products and services ordered straight from the manufacturer's headquarters in Austin, Texas. Although sales representatives support corporate customers, individuals and smaller businesses buy direct from Dell by phone, fax, and via the Internet, with about $3.9 billion in sales generated online in 2012 (ranking 2nd only to Apple among consumer brand manufacturers and 8th on Internet Retailer's list of top 500 online retailers) (Internet Retailer, 2013a).

When Michael Dell started the company in 1984 in his college dorm room, his idea was to custom-build computers for customers, to eliminate the middleman, and more effectively meet the technology needs of his customers. Today, the company sells much more than individual computer systems; it also offers enterprise systems, desktop, and laptop computers, as well as installation, financing, repair, and management services. By relying on a build-to-order manufacturing process, the company achieves faster inventory turnover (five days), and reduced component and finished goods inventory levels; this strategy virtually eliminates the chance of product obsolescence.

The direct model simplifies the company's operations, eliminating the need to support a wholesale and retail sales network, as well as cutting out the costly associated markup, and gives Dell complete control over its customer database. In addition, Dell can build and ship custom computers nearly as fast as a mail-order supplier can pull a computer out of inventory and ship it to the customer.

To extend the benefits of its direct sales model, Dell has aggressively moved sales, service, and support online. Each month, the company typically has about 10 million unique visitors at Dell.com, where it maintains an estimated 80 country-specific Web sites. Dell's Premier service enables companies to investigate product offerings, complete order forms and purchase orders, track orders in real time, and review order histories all online. For its small business customers, it has created an online virtual account executive, as well as a spare-parts ordering system and virtual help desk with direct access to technical support data. Dell has also continued to broaden its offerings beyond pure hardware product sales, adding warranty services, product integration and installation services, Internet access, software, and technology consulting, referring to them as "beyond the box" offerings. These include nearly 30,000 software and peripheral products from leading manufacturers that can be bundled with Dell products. Dell has also embraced social media. It has a corporate blog, called Direct2Dell, and a presence on Facebook (with over 6 million Likes), Pinterest (with 9 boards, including boards on entrepreneurship, infographics, and tech tips), and Twitter (with almost 200,000 followers). It posts Twitter-exclusive sales for those who follow Dell Outlet. It also has a channel on YouTube that it calls the Dell Vlog Channel, with around 20,000 subscribers and almost 25 million views. In 2011, it released mobile apps for the iPhone and Android that featured in-app purchasing, customer ratings and reviews, product comparison, order tracking, a Shopping Advisor, and easy access to various customer support options. Dell promoted the release of the app via both a standard e-mail campaign and one optimized for mobile viewing, and discovered that the open rate for the mobile e-mail was twice that of the standard version, and the clickthrough rate was more than five times higher. In 2012, Dell redesigned its two-year-old mobile site, with a new layout, updated HTML5 navigation, and a host of new functionalities, including shopping assistance, Dell's full product image gallery, social sharing, mobile live chat, a product comparison tool, and simpler, more intuitive purchase process (Dell, Inc., 2013; Internet Retailer, 2013a, 2013b; Dusto, 2012).

COMMON THEMES IN ONLINE RETAILING

We have looked at some very different companies in the preceding section, from entrepreneurial Web-only merchants to established offline giants. Online retail is the fastest growing channel in retail commerce, has the fastest growing consumer base, and has growing penetration across many categories of goods. On the other hand, profits for many start-up ventures have been difficult to achieve, and it took even Amazon eight years to show its first profit.

The reasons for the difficulties experienced by many online retailers in achieving profits are also now clear. The path to success in any form of retail involves having a central location in order to attract a larger number of shoppers, charging high enough prices to cover the costs of goods as well as marketing, and developing highly efficient inventory and fulfillment systems so that the company can offer goods at lower costs than competitors and still make a profit. Many online merchants failed to follow these fundamental ideas, lowering prices below the total costs of goods and operations, failing to develop efficient business processes, failing to attract a large enough audience to their Web sites, and spending far too much on customer acquisition and marketing. By 2013, the lessons of the past have been learned, and far fewer online merchants are selling below cost, especially if they are start-up companies. There's also been a change in consumer culture and attitudes. Whereas in the past consumers looked to the Web for really cheap prices, in 2013, they look to online purchasing for convenience, time savings, and time shifting (buying retail goods at night from the sofa). Consumers have been willing to accept higher prices in return for the convenience of shopping online and avoiding the inconvenience of shopping at stores and malls. This allows online merchants more pricing freedom.

A second common theme in retail e-commerce is that, for the most part, disintermediation did not occur and the retail middleman did not disappear. Indeed, virtual merchants, along with powerful offline merchants who moved online, maintained their powerful grip on the retail customer, with some notable exceptions in electronics and software. Manufacturers—with the exception of electronic goods—have used the Web primarily as an informational resource, driving consumers to the traditional retail channels for transactions. Leaving Amazon aside, the most significant online growth has been that of offline general merchandiser giant intermediaries such as Walmart, Sears, Costco, JCPenney, Macy's, Target, and Nordstrom. Many of the first-mover, Web pure-play merchants (online intermediaries) failed to achieve profitability and closed their doors en masse as their venture capital funds were depleted. Traditional retailers have been the fast followers (although many of them cannot be characterized as particularly "fast") and are most likely to succeed on the Web by extending their traditional brands, competencies, and assets. In this sense, e-commerce technological innovation is following the historical pattern of other technology-driven commercial changes, from automobiles to radio and television, where an explosion of start-up firms attracts significant investment, but quickly fail, and are consolidated into larger existing firms.

A third theme is that in order to succeed online, established merchants need to create an integrated shopping environment that combines their catalog, store, and online experiences into one. Customers want to shop wherever they want, using any device, and at any time. Established retailers have significant fulfillment, inventory management, supply chain management, and other competencies that apply directly to the online channel. To succeed online, established retailers need to extend their brands, provide incentives to consumers to use the online channel (which given the same prices for goods is more efficient to operate than a physical store), avoid channel conflict, and build advertising campaigns using online search engines such as Google, Yahoo, and Bing, and shopping comparison sites, as described further in *Insight on Technology: Using the Web to Shop 'Till You Drop*.

A fourth theme is the growth of online specialty merchants selling high-end, fashionable and luxury goods such as diamonds (Blue Nile), jewelry (Tiffany), and high fashion (Emporio Armani and Gilt.com) or selling discounted electronics (BestBuy.com), apparel (Gap.com), or office products (OfficeDepot.com). These firms are demonstrating the vitality and openness of the Internet for innovation and extending the range of products available on the Web. Many virtual merchants have

INSIGHT ON TECHNOLOGY

USING THE WEB TO SHOP 'TILL YOU DROP

Comparison shopping sites allow consumers to compare prices, features, consumer reviews of the actual product performance, and reputations of merchants. When visitors click on a product and price they like, they are taken to the merchant's Web site where they can make the purchase. The idea: Shoppers would not have to shop till they dropped, but instead could conveniently compare prices at one site, and then buy from the lowest-price merchant on the Web.

The top comparison shopping sites in 2013 include Nextag, PriceGrabber, Shopping.com (which also includes Epinions.com, and is owned by eBay), Shopzilla/BizRate (owned by Scripps), Pronto, TheFind, Become, and Smarter. Shopzilla reaches a global audience of more than 40 million shoppers each month. According to Channel Advisor, a leading e-commerce software and services provider, comparison shopping sites drive about 15% of e-commerce, making them an important channel for retailers. Shopzilla, PriceGrabber, Shopping.com, and Pronto, among others, are used by over 50% of Internet Retailer's top 500 online merchants.

General merchandisers such as Amazon and search engines such as Google and Bing have also developed their own comparison shopping capabilities. Shopping sites make money by charging participating merchants on a per-click basis regardless of whether a sale is made. A twist on shopping search engines is comparison shopping coupon systems. Sites like Valpak, CurrentCodes, FatWallet, and Bing Offers search the Web for deals and coupons.

Comparison shopping sites focused originally on tracking online prices for electronic consumer goods and computers. Consumer electronics are fairly commoditized products by a few branded manufacturers, with standard features, making it relatively easy to compare one product to another. Type in "digital camera," select the number of megapixels you want, enter the zoom range and price, press the Enter key on your keyboard, and you will receive a long list of cameras and dealers. You can refine your search as you move along the purchase process, and explore the reputations of dealers before you decide to purchase.

However, although a site such as Shopzilla connects shoppers to more than 100 million products from tens of thousands of retailers, originally not as many of these items were so-called "soft goods" purchased by women, who have risen to equal the purchasing power of men on the Web. In 1998, 65% of Web purchases were made by men, while today, over 60% are made by women who are much more likely to be looking for soft goods, such as apparel, jewelry, accessories, luggage, and gifts. In fact, these are among the fastest growing consumer product categories on the Web. For this reason, the shopping comparison sites are currently adding soft goods to their services.

But the process of comparison shopping for soft goods is not as simple as for hard goods such as digital TVs or digital cameras. The strength of a comparison shopping site is to present highly similar or identical items from different merchants at varying prices and reputation levels. Generally, these kinds of electronic goods have a limited number of suppliers (mostly solid brand names) and limited features. But in more complex product areas, such as apparel or jewelry, such standards do not exist. In fact, manufacturers of these products emphasize their uniqueness, not their similarity. One solution is to focus on the brands of soft goods and not the price: bags from Gucci, sweaters from Benetton, and mountain climbing gear from REI. Yahoo and search engines such as Bing and Google are moving closer to the brand model of comparison shopping

(continued)

as price becomes a less powerful factor in consumer purchases of soft goods.

As more attention focuses on comparison shopping sites, the sites themselves continue to innovate and add features, and they attempt to go beyond simply finding customers the lowest-price products. Shopping.com tracks its visitors to help consumers decide what to buy, and where to buy. It does this by showing visitors the most popular sites for each category of product selected. It has moved strongly into the mobile arena and has both iPhone and Android apps that allow consumers to research products and compare prices while they are in a store. Shopzilla has developed a data categorization technology that it calls Robozilla, designed to help expedite the shopping process. Shopzilla also redesigned its Web site seeking to enhance the customer experience by adding speed, a better search engine, and more product detail. Shopzilla was able to reduce the search time for products from 6 to 9 seconds, down to 1.2 seconds on average. PriceGrabber has added product tours and a local availability feature to its Web site, and more content, such as user and third-party reviews, and discussion boards. It also offers price alerts and local availability on its iPhone and iPad apps. Nextag also offers consumers e-mail price alerts and product price history charting, and for merchants, a data feed auto-import option. Most of the larger sites are adding user-generated reviews and opinions of products.

As the number of shoppers using mobile to make purchases continues to rise rapidly, comparison shopping on mobile has grown as well. Half of the U.S. respondents in a 2012 survey report using their mobile devices to compare prices while out shopping. Comparison shopping sites have adjusted accordingly. Shopping.com has moved strongly into the mobile arena and has both iPhone and Android apps that allow consumers to research products and compare prices while they are in a store. Nextag has introduced a mobile app for its Radar feature, which searches for products and alerts consumers to price changes. The mobile app allows users to add items to their Radar list by taking a photo of the item. Radar uses image recognition and is integrated with the core Nextag Mobile app. In 2013, Shopzilla acquired mobile commerce technology provider Zappli and plans to integrate Zappli's InstaBuy (one-click shopping) and MyShopian (a social shopping app) into Shopzilla's mobile sites and apps. Pricegrabber also announced upgrades to its iPhone app, which now features greater speed, larger product images, and a refined search function.

Perhaps the biggest recent news in comparison shopping came from Google when it announced in 2012 that its free Google Product Search service would become a paid service called Google Shopping. This was bad news to merchants who were used to receiving this service for free from Google, but Google's unbeatable amounts of eyeballs and potential traffic will likely be too much for most merchants to ignore, and Google Shopping should maintain its position as the most popular comparison shopping engine. Merchants will be able to have their products appear more frequently than competitors and be listed as a "Trusted Store" if they share data with Google that proves reliable shipping and quality customer service. Merchants will pay Google at a cost per click rate. Search engines like Google and Bing are in direct competition with the stand-alone comparison shopping sites for business.

SOURCES: "Shopzilla Acquires M-commerce Technology Provider Zappli," by Bill Siwicki, Internetretailer.com, July 16, 2013; "Comparison Shopping Site PriceGrabber Upgrades Its iPhone App," by Bill Siwicki, Internetretailer.com, April 18, 2013; "Survey: Younger Shoppers Increasingly Using Mobiles To Buy and Compare," by Natasha Lomas, TechCrunch.com, September 28, 2012; "The 10 Best Shopping Engines," by Andrew Davis, Searchenginewatch.com, June 19, 2012; "The New Google Shopping: 15 FAQs," by Mary Weinstein, Cpcstrategy.com, June 14, 2012; "Nextag's Radar Picks Up a Smartphone App," by Kevin Woodward, *Internet Retailer,* August 24, 2011; "PriceGrabber Adds Price Alerts and Local Availability to its Mobile Apps," by Katie Deatsch, *Internet Retailer,* January 5, 2011.

developed large, online customer bases, as well as the online tools required to market to their customer base. These online brands can be strengthened further through alliances and partnerships that add the required competencies in inventory management and fulfillment services. Virtual merchants need to build operational strength and efficiency before they can become profitable.

A final theme in 2013 is the continuing extraordinary growth in social commerce, local marketing and commerce, and mobile commerce. In the space of six years since the first iPhone appeared, the mobile platform has emerged as a retail marketing and shopping tool, which will greatly expand e-commerce, potentially driving e-commerce to 20% of all commerce in the next five years. Local merchants will be a major benefactor of the growing mobile commerce platform. In an equally short time, Americans have begun to spend an increasing amount of their Internet time on social network sites where they share attitudes and experiences about business firms, products, and services. In a few years, social sites may turn into large purchasing venues.

9.4 THE SERVICE SECTOR: OFFLINE AND ONLINE

The service sector is typically the largest and most rapidly expanding part of the economies in advanced industrial nations such as the United States, and many European and some Asian countries. In the United States, the service sector (broadly defined) employs about four out of every five workers and accounts for about 75% of all economic activity (Bartash, 2011). E-commerce in the service sector offers extraordinary opportunities to deliver information, knowledge, and transaction efficiencies.

The major service industry groups are finance, insurance, real estate, travel, professional services such as legal and accounting, business services, health services, and educational services. Business services include activities such as consulting, advertising and marketing, and information processing. Within these service industry groups, companies can be further categorized into those that involve **transaction brokering** (acting as an intermediary to facilitate a transaction) and those that involve providing a "hands-on" service. For instance, one type of financial service involves stockbrokers who act as the middle person in a transaction between buyers and sellers. Online mortgage companies such as LendingTree.com refer customers to mortgage companies that actually issue the mortgage. Employment agencies put a seller of labor in contact with a buyer of labor. The service involved in all these examples is brokering a transaction.

transaction brokering
acting as an intermediary to facilitate a transaction

In contrast, some industries perform specific hands-on activities for consumers. In order to provide their service, these professionals need to interact directly and personally with the "client." For these service industries, the opportunities for e-commerce are somewhat different. Currently, doctors and dentists cannot treat patients over the Internet. However, the Internet can assist their services by providing consumers with information, knowledge, and communication.

With some exceptions (for example, providers of physical services, such as cleaning, gardening, and so on), perhaps the most important feature of service industries (and occupations) is that they are knowledge- and information-intense. In order to provide value, service industries process a great deal of information and employ a highly skilled, educated workforce. For instance, to provide legal services, you need lawyers with law degrees. Law firms are required to process enormous amounts of textual information. Likewise with medical services. Financial services are not so knowledge-intensive, but require much larger investments in information processing just to keep track of transactions and investments. In fact, the financial services sector is the largest investor in information technology, with over 80% of invested capital going to information technology equipment and services.

Services differ in the amount of personalization and customization required, although just about all services entail some personalization or customization. Some services, such as legal, medical, and accounting services, require extensive personalization—the adjustment of a service to the precise needs of a single individual or object. Others, such as financial services, benefit from customization by allowing individuals to choose from a restricted menu. The ability of Internet and e-commerce technology to personalize and customize service, or components of service, is a major factor undergirding the extremely rapid growth of e-commerce services. Future expansion of e-services will depend in part on the ability of e-commerce firms to transform their customized services—choosing from a list—into truly personalized services, such as providing unique advice and consultation based on a digital yet intimate understanding of the client (at least as intimate as professional service providers).

9.5   ONLINE FINANCIAL SERVICES

The online financial services sector is a shining example of an e-commerce success story, but one with many twists and turns. While the innovative, pure-online firms such as E*Trade have been instrumental in transforming the brokerage industry, the impacts of e-commerce on the large, powerful banking, insurance, and real estate firms have been delayed by consumer resistance and the lack of industry innovation. For instance, online-only banks have not displaced or transformed the large national banks or even regional and local banks. But e-commerce has nevertheless transformed the banking and financial industries, as the major institutions have deployed their own online applications to service an increasingly connected online customer base. Insurance has become more standardized and easier to purchase on the Web. Although security is still a concern, consumers are much more willing to trust online sites with their financial information than in the past. Firms such as Mint.com (now owned by Quicken), SmartyPig, Credit Karma, Moven, and Simple continue to show growth. Multi-channel, established financial services firms—the slow followers—also continue to show modest gains in online transactions.

ONLINE FINANCIAL CONSUMER BEHAVIOR

Surveys show that consumers are attracted to financial sites because of their desire to save time and access information rather than save money, although saving money is an important goal among the most sophisticated online financial households. Most online consumers use financial services sites for mundane financial management, such as checking balances of existing accounts, and paying bills, most of which were established offline. Once accustomed to performing mundane financial management activities, consumers move on to more sophisticated capabilities such as using personal financial management tools, making loan payments, and considering offers from online institutions. The number of people using mobile devices for financial service needs is also surging. According to research from Mojiva, 70% of survey respondents used a mobile device to access a financial app or site four or more times a week. Over 70% accessed banks accounts, more than 50% used credit card apps and sites, over 40% looked at financial news and stock market information, 35% accessed budgeting apps or sites, and 27% brokerage accounts (Mojiva, 2013).

ONLINE BANKING AND BROKERAGE

NetBank and Wingspan Bank pioneered online banking in the United States in 1996 and 1997, respectively. Although late by a year or two, the established brand-name national banks have taken a substantial lead in market share as the percentage of their customers who bank online has grown rapidly. The top banks are all large, national banks that also offer online banking: Bank of America, JPMorgan Chase, Wells Fargo, and Capital One. The major direct banks (those that operate without a network of branches or branded ATMs), include Ally, Discover, Capital One 360, and USAA. These direct banks have seen customer deposits grow faster than regular banks, indicating their growing popularity, particularly with younger customers. Several start-ups have also moved into the online banking and financial services spaces. For instance, Moven offers checking account services linked with online and mobile financial management tools. Another start-up, Simple, provides checking accounts linked to debit cards in addition to financial management tools.

In 2013, around two-thirds of U.S. Internet users use online banking. It has become the primary banking channel for all age groups. According to comScore, U.S. banking Web sites have around 100 million monthly unique visitors in 2013, via both desktop and mobile devices (Bruene, 2013). Online banking via a mobile device is growing, with 34% reporting that they access their banking information via a mobile app on a smartphone, and 23% via a mobile browser. Research firm Aite Group estimates that there are about 50 million mobile banking users in the United States in 2013 and predicts that that figure will almost double to around 96 million by 2016 (eMarketer, Inc., 2013c). Top mobile banking activities include checking balances and bank statements, viewing recent transactions, transferring money from one account to another, paying bills, and depositing checks.

From the bank's perspective, online and mobile banking can provide significant cost savings. According to Javelin Strategy & Research, the average in-person transaction at a bank branch costs $4.25, while an online transaction costs 19 cents, and a mobile transaction, just 10 cents.

The history of online brokerage has been similar to that of online banking. Early innovators such as E*Trade have been displaced from their leadership positions in terms of numbers of online accounts by discount broker pioneer Charles Schwab and

TABLE 9.5	TOP ONLINE BROKERAGES, 2013
FIRM	NUMBER OF UNIQUE VISITORS (IN MILLIONS)
Fidelity.com	7.66
Charles Schwab	3.04
Vanguard	2.68
Scottrade	2.61
TD Ameritrade	1.65
Merrill Lynch (Ml.com)	1.65
E*Trade	1.41
Troweprice.com	1.02
ShareBuilder	0.55

SOURCES: Based on data from Compete.com, 2013

financial industry giant Fidelity (which has more mutual fund customers and more funds under management than any other U.S. firm).

According to Nielsen Net Ratings, approximately 29 million U.S. investors trade online in 2013. According to comScore, almost 10 million use a mobile device to access brokerage or stock information (comScore, 2012a). The top trading Web site among U.S. Internet users in 2013 is Fidelity Investments, with around 7.6 million monthly unique visitors (see **Table 9.5)**. The major online brokerage firms are investing significantly in search engine marketing, and are among the biggest spenders in the paid search market. They are also increasingly using social media to engage with customers, although they must be careful to comply with all regulations and rules as they do so. For instance, some brokerage firms use Twitter to deliver commentary, company information, marketing, and customer service (eMarketer, Inc., 2011).

Multi-Channel vs. Pure Online Financial Services Firms

Online consumers prefer to visit financial services sites that have physical outlets or branches. In general, multi-channel financial services firms that have both physical branches or offices and solid online offerings are growing faster than pure-online firms that have no physical presence, and they are assuming market leadership as well. Traditional banking firms have literally thousands of branches where customers can open accounts, deposit money, take out loans, find home mortgages, and rent a safety deposit box. Top online brokerage firms do not have the same physical footprint as the banks do, but each has a strong physical presence or telephone presence to strengthen its online presence. Fidelity has urban walk-in service center branches, but it relies primarily on the telephone for interacting with investors. Charles Schwab has investment centers around the country as an integral part of its online strategy.

Pure-online banks and brokerages cannot provide customers with some services that still require a face-to-face interaction.

Financial Portals and Account Aggregators

Financial portals are sites that provide consumers with comparison shopping services, independent financial advice, and financial planning. Independent portals do not themselves offer financial services, but act as steering mechanisms to online providers. They generate revenue from advertising, referral fees, and subscription fees. For example, Yahoo's financial portal, Yahoo Finance, offers consumers credit card purchase tracking, market overviews, real-time stock quotes, news, financial advice, streaming video interviews with financial leaders, and Yahoo Bill Pay, an EBPP system. Other independent financial portals include Intuit's Quicken.com, MSN's MSN Money, and CNNMoney. A host of financial portal sites have sprung up to help consumers with financial management and planning such as Mint.com (owned by Quicken), SmartPiggy, and Credit Karma.

> **financial portals**
> sites that provide consumers with comparison shopping services, independent financial advice, and financial planning

Account aggregation is the process of pulling together all of a customer's financial (and even nonfinancial) data at a single personalized Web site, including brokerage, banking, insurance, loans, frequent flyer miles, personalized news, and much more. For example, a consumer can see his or her TD Ameritrade brokerage account, Fidelity 401(k) account, Travelers Insurance annuity account, and American Airlines frequent flyer miles all displayed on a single site. The idea is to provide consumers with a holistic view of their entire portfolio of assets, no matter what financial institution actually holds those assets.

> **account aggregation**
> the process of pulling together all of a customer's financial (and even nonfinancial) data at a single personalized Web site

The leading provider of account aggregation technology is Yodlee. It uses screen-scraping and other techniques to pull information from over 12,000 different data sources. A smart-mapping technology is also used so that if the underlying Web sites change, the scraping software can adapt and still find the relevant information. Today, Yodlee has more than 40 million personal financial management (PFM) users worldwide and is used by 600 leading financial institutions and companies (Yodlee, 2013).

ONLINE MORTGAGE AND LENDING SERVICES

During the early days of e-commerce, hundreds of firms launched pure-play online mortgage sites to capture the U.S. home mortgage market. Early entrants hoped to radically simplify and transform the traditional mortgage value chain process, dramatically speed up the loan closing process, and share the economies with consumers by offering lower rates.

By 2003, over half of these early-entry, pure-online firms had failed. Early pure-play online mortgage institutions had difficulties developing a brand name at an affordable price and failed to simplify the mortgage generation process. They ended up suffering from high start-up and administrative costs, high customer acquisition costs, rising interest rates, and poor execution of their strategies.

Despite this rocky start, the online mortgage market is slowly growing; it is dominated by established online banks and other online financial services firms, traditional mortgage vendors, and a few successful online mortgage firms.

Many mortgage shoppers research mortgages online, but few actually apply online because of the complexity of mortgages. Most mortgages today are written by intermediary mortgage brokers, with banks still playing an important origination role but generally not servicing mortgages they originate.

Although online mortgage originations currently represent a small percentage of all mortgages, their number is expected to continue to grow slowly but surely over the next several years.

Consumer benefits from online mortgages include reduced application times, market interest rate intelligence, and process simplification that occurs when participants in the mortgage process (title, insurance, and lending companies) share a common information base. Mortgage lenders benefit from the cost reduction involved in online processing of applications, while charging rates marginally lower than traditional bricks-and-mortar institutions.

Nevertheless, the online mortgage industry has not transformed the process of obtaining a mortgage. A significant brake on market expansion is the complexity of the mortgage process, which requires physical signatures and documents, multiple institutions, and complex financing details—such as closing costs and points—that are difficult for shoppers to compare across vendors. Nevertheless, as in other areas, the ability of shoppers to find low mortgage rates on the Web has helped reduce the fees and interest rates charged by traditional mortgage lenders.

ONLINE INSURANCE SERVICES

In 1995, the price of a $500,000 20-year term life policy for a healthy 40-year-old male was $995 a year. In 2013, the same policy could be had for around $400—a decline of about 60%—while other prices have risen 15% in the same period. In a study of the term life insurance business, Brown and Goolsbee discovered that Internet usage led to an 8%–15% decline in term life insurance prices industry-wide (both offline and online), and increased consumer surplus by about $115 million per year (and hence reduced industry profits by the same amount) (Brown and Goolsbee, 2000). Price dispersion for term life policies initially increased, but then fell as more and more people began using the Internet to obtain insurance quotes.

Unlike books and CDs, where online price dispersion is higher than offline, and in many cases online prices are higher than offline, term life insurance stands out as one product group supporting the conventional wisdom that the Internet will lower search costs, increase price comparison, and lower prices to consumers. Term life insurance is a commodity product, however, and in other insurance product lines, the Web offers insurance companies new opportunities for product and service differentiation and price discrimination.

The insurance industry forms a major part of the financial services sector. It has four major segments: automobile, life, health, and property and casualty. Insurance products can be very complex. For example, there are many different types of non-automotive property and casualty insurance: liability, fire, homeowners, commercial, workers' compensation, marine, accident, and other lines such as vacation insurance. Writing an insurance policy in any of these areas is very information-intense, often necessitating personal inspection of the properties, and it requires considerable actuarial experience and data. The life insurance industry has also developed life insurance policies that defy easy comparison and can only be explained and sold by an experienced sales agent. Historically, the insurance industry has relied on thousands of local insurance offices and agents to sell complex products uniquely suited to the circumstances of the insured person and the property. Complicating the insurance marketplace is the fact that the insurance industry is not federally regulated, but rather is regulated by 50 different state insurance commissions that are strongly influenced by local insurance agents. Before a Web site can offer quotations on insurance, it must obtain a license to enter the insurance business in all the states where it provides quotation services or sells insurance.

Like the online mortgage industry, the online insurance industry has been very successful in attracting visitors who are looking to obtain prices and terms of insurance policies. While many national insurance underwriting companies initially did not offer competitive products directly on the Web because it might injure the business operations of their traditional local agents, the Web sites of almost all of the major firms now provide the ability to obtain an online quote. Even if consumers do not actually purchase insurance policies online, the Internet has proven to have a powerful influence on consumer insurance decisions by dramatically reducing search costs and changing the price discovery process. According to a 2013 survey by Accenture, 47% of respondents preferred to obtain auto and home insurance quotes online or via a mobile app. However, conversely, most still preferred to meet in person with an agent to set up and proceed with payment for such policies (Accenture, 2013). Another survey found that over 60% of consumers surveyed would use the Internet to conduct research if they were to make a life insurance purchase, although they ultimately would buy from an insurance agent, and an additional 23% said they would both research and buy life insurance online (LIMRA and Life and Health Insurance Foundation for Education, 2013). Other forms of insurance are more likely to be purchased online. For instance, according to a 2012 comScore study, online auto insurance policy sales grew by 6% to 3.1 million online policy sales in 2011. The survey also found that the online channel continues to be consumers' preferred method for shopping for auto insurance policies, with nearly 70% of shoppers getting an online quote (comScore, 2012b). Some of the leading online insurance services companies include InsWeb, Insure.com, Insurance.com, QuickQuote, and NetQuote.

ONLINE REAL ESTATE SERVICES

During the early days of e-commerce, real estate seemed ripe for an Internet revolution that would rationalize this historically local, complex, and local agent-driven industry that monopolized the flow of consumer information. Potentially, the Internet and e-commerce might have disintermediated this huge marketspace, allowing buyers and sellers, renters and owners, to transact directly, lower search costs to near zero, and dramatically reduce prices. However, this did not happen. What did happen is extremely beneficial to buyers and sellers, as well as to real estate agents.

At one point, there were an estimated 100,000 real estate sites on the Internet worldwide. Many of these sites have disappeared. However, the remaining online sites have started to make headway toward transforming the industry. In addition, most local real estate brokers in the United States have their own agency Web sites to deal with clients, in addition to participating with thousands of other agencies in multiple listing services that list homes online. Some of the major online real estate sites are Realtor.com, HomeGain, RealEstate.com, ZipRealty, Move.com, Craigslist, Zillow, and Trulia.

Real estate differs from other types of online financial services because it is impossible to complete a property transaction online. Clearly, the major impact of Internet real estate sites is in influencing offline decisions. The Internet has become a compelling method for real estate professionals, homebuilders, property managers and owners, and ancillary service providers to communicate with and provide information to consumers. According to a survey conducted by the National Association of Realtors, 90% of buyers surf the Internet to search for a home. Although buyers also use other resources, most start the search process online and then contact an agent, with about 85% purchasing through an agent. Almost 40% of buyers said that they first learned of the home that they ultimately purchased via the Internet (National Association of Realtors, 2010).

The primary service offered by real estate sites is a listing of houses available. In 2013, Realtor.com, the official site of the National Association of Realtors, is one of the top Web sites in terms of market share of visits. Realtor.com listed over 4 million homes and had over 11 million unique visitors in September 2013. The offerings have become sophisticated and integrated. Listings typically feature detailed property descriptions, multiple photographs, and virtual 360-degree tours. Consumers can link to mortgage lenders, credit reporting agencies, house inspectors, and surveyors. There are also online loan calculators, appraisal reports, sales price histories by neighborhood, school district data, crime reports, and social and historical information on neighborhoods. Some online real estate brokers now charge substantially less than traditional offline brokers who typically charge 6% of the sale price. They can do this because the buyers (and in some cases, the seller) do much of the work of traditional real estate agents, such as prospecting, choosing neighborhoods, and identifying houses of interest prior to contacting an online agent. For instance, Move.com (the parent company of Realtor.com) also offers a "Find a Neighborhood" feature that allows users to choose the type of neighborhood they want to live in by weighing factors such as the quality (and tax costs) of schools, age of the population, number of families with children nearby, and available social and recreational services. Move.com also offers mobile apps for the iPad and iPhone, Android, and Windows phones. For instance, the Area Scout function allows users to see the list prices of all homes in a neighborhood on the street level.

Despite the revolution in available information, there has not been a revolution in the industry value chain. The listings available on Web sites are provided by local multiple listing services supported by local real estate agents. Sometimes, addresses of the houses are not available, and online users are directed to the local listing agent who is hired by the seller. Traditional hands-on real estate brokers will show the house and handle all transactions with the owner to preserve their fees, typically ranging from 5% to 6% of the transaction.

9.6 ONLINE TRAVEL SERVICES

Online travel is one of the most successful B2C e-commerce segments. The Internet has become the most common channel used by consumers to research travel options, seek the best possible prices, and book reservations for airline tickets, hotel rooms, rental cars, cruises, and tours. Today, more travel is booked online than offline. Online travel services revenues are expected to reach almost $137 billion in 2013, and continue growing to almost $170 billion by 2017 (see **Figure 9.3**) (eMarketer, Inc., 2013d).

WHY ARE ONLINE TRAVEL SERVICES SO POPULAR?

Online travel sites offer consumers a one-stop, convenient, leisure and business travel experience where travelers can find content (descriptions of vacations and facilities),

FIGURE 9.3   ONLINE TRAVEL SERVICES REVENUES

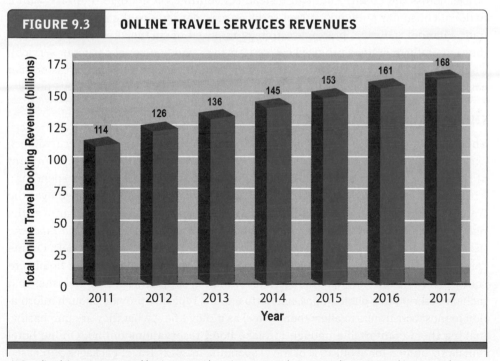

U.S. online leisure/unmanaged business travel service revenues has resumed growing and is expected to reach almost $170 billion by 2017.

SOURCE: Based on data from eMarketer, Inc., 2013d.

community (chat groups and bulletin boards), commerce (purchase of all travel elements), and customer service (usually through call centers). Online sites offer much more information and many more travel options than traditional travel agents. For suppliers—the owners of hotels, rental cars, and airlines—the online sites aggregate millions of consumers into singular, focused customer pools that can be efficiently reached through on-site advertising and promotions. Online sites create a much more efficient marketplace, bringing consumers and suppliers together in a low-transaction cost environment.

Travel services appear to be an ideal service for the Internet, and therefore e-commerce business models should work well for this product. Travel is an information-intensive product requiring significant consumer research. It is a digital product in the sense that travel requirements—planning, researching, comparison shopping, reserving, and payment—can be accomplished for the most part online in a digital environment. On the travel reservation side, travel does not require any "inventory": there are no physical assets. And the suppliers of the product—owners of hotels, airlines, rental cars, vacation rooms, and tour guides—are highly fragmented and often have excess capacity. Always looking for customers to fill vacant rooms and rent idle cars, suppliers will be anxious to lower prices and willing to advertise on Web sites that can attract millions of consumers. The online agencies—such as Travelocity, Expedia, and others—do not have to deploy thousands of travel agents in physical offices across the country but can instead concentrate on a single interface with a national consumer audience. Travel services may not require the kind of expensive multi-channel "physical presence" strategy required of financial services (although they generally operate centralized call centers to provide personal customer service). Therefore, travel services might "scale" better, permitting earnings to grow faster than costs. But these efficiencies also make it hard for reservation sites to make a profit.

THE ONLINE TRAVEL MARKET

There are four major sectors in the travel market: airline tickets, hotel reservations, car rentals, and travel packages. Airline tickets are the source of the greatest amount of revenue in online travel (in 2012, almost two-thirds of all online travel spending). Airline reservations are largely a commodity. They can be easily described over the Web. The same is true with car rentals; most people can reliably rent a car over the phone or the Web and expect to obtain what they ordered (see *Insight on Business: Zipcar Shifts into High Gear* for a different kind of car rental business model). Online car rentals accounted for about 9% of travel spending in 2012. Although hotels are somewhat more difficult to describe, hotel branding, supplemented by Web sites that include descriptions, photographs, and virtual tours, typically provide enough information to most consumers to allow them to feel as if they know what they are purchasing, making them comfortable enough to make hotel reservations online. Online hotel rentals accounted for about 19% of travel spending in 2012. Travel packages purchased online constituted the smallest percentage of travel sales, accounting for only 2%.

Increasingly, corporations are outsourcing their travel offices entirely to vendors who can provide Web-based solutions, high-quality service, and lower costs. Online

INSIGHT ON BUSINESS

ZIPCAR SHIFTS INTO HIGH GEAR

How would you like to have all the functionality of a car but not have to deal with any of the headaches typically associated with ownership of a car or even the hassles involved with renting a car from a traditional car rental agency? This might sound like an impossible dream, but it's not. In the late 1990s, a new car rental business model that leverages the power of the Web was imported from Europe by a group of environmentally conscious entrepreneurs. Today, Zipcar, and a number of smaller copycats, are using this model to propel their companies toward sustained growth.

Zipcar began in 1999 with a single lime-green Volkswagen Bug in Cambridge, Massachusetts, and slowly grew within the city. Members could pick up cars at any one of several parking spots around Cambridge, use them for as long as they wanted, and then return them to the same parking spot. Today, the combined company has over 12,000 cars and 800,000 members. The company operates in 21 major metropolitan areas in the United States, more than 300 college campuses, and in London, Toronto, and Vancouver.

Zipcar brings the Web 2.0 culture of sharing online videos and tweets to the car transportation market. An online application costs $25 and takes minutes to complete, and 94% of applicants are accepted. Zipcars are parked mostly in small clusters—between 2 and 20—in neighborhood garages, shoulder to shoulder with the owned and leased cars of the unenlightened. In Manhattan, a mix of Honda Civics, Toyotas, Volkswagens, Volvos, and Mini Coopers are available. Zipcar's predicate is that sharing is big business—bigger, potentially, than anyone can fathom. Its claim is that the winners in the new economy will be those

who crack the puzzle posed by scarce resources. In other words, in certain circles, using a Zipcar is cooler than owning a BMW!

In order to make the business work, Zipcar uses a lot of technology and tries to reduce human-customer contact as much as possible to keep expenses low. Here's how it works. Customers pay an annual subscription fee and are issued a Zipcard, a card subscribers use to lock and unlock Zipcars that they've reserved. Customers go online or call an automated central number to reserve a car. Rates start at a little over $7 an hour and vary depending on the vehicle, or a flat rate for a full day. Once a customer rents a car, a central computer activates the car's key card entry system to permit that customer to enter the car and start the engine. Customers return cars to the same locations and their credit cards are billed. Using wireless technology, the Internet, and automated voice recognition software at each city's central office, Zipcar is able to keep costs very low.

Zipcar is supported by universities and city governments looking for ways to discourage car ownership, encourage car sharing, and reduce pollution and congestion. Zipcar has exclusive arrangements with a number of major universities. In these deals, the universities promise the car will make a certain revenue level per year (usually about $100,000) and make up the difference if they do not hit that revenue target. In San Francisco, when the Bay Bridge closed for repairs in 2009, over 350 Zipcars were located near BART rapid transit terminals in the Bay Area so residents could take trains to stations and hop into Zipcars to drive to their final destinations. In an emergency, Zipcars can act as a reserve mini-mass transportation system.

Zipcar's customers are not Middle America, the people who own 200 million cars. Instead,

(continued)

most of Zipcar's customers are young urban professionals or college students, a market shunned by traditional car rental companies who typically will not rent to drivers under 21. The attraction for college students is that they save money compared to owning cars that sit idle while they are in classes. In urban areas, Zipcar users report they are saving over $500 a month on car operational and parking costs alone. Consider that in Manhattan, where studio apartments rent for $2,500 a month, garage parking for your personal four-wheeler will run another $300.

Car sharing is also green: national studies show that each shared car replaces up to 20 privately owned vehicles. Some corporations in major cities are thinking about eliminating their urban fleets and using car-sharing services.

However, it's unclear that Zipcar can expand beyond large cities and universities. The idea might not work as well in the suburbs, because customers would have to drive a car to pick up a Zipcar rental. On the other hand, Zipcar executives see an urban fleet of about 1 million cars in the future. This fleet would replace 20 million privately owned vehicles, one-tenth of the U.S. private fleet. Who needs the burbs? Traditional car rental companies have begun to respond to Zipcar by opening small neighborhood rental shops that make it much more convenient to rent cars. In 2009, Hertz started its own car-sharing service, Connect by Hertz, in New York, London, and Paris, with a fleet of Mini Coopers in each city. Hertz charges a flat hourly fee and its rates are lower than Zipcar's. In the New York area, Hertz has over 40,000 vehicles, many of which could ultimately be put into the program. Although

Hertz has been sidetracked by its 2012 acquisition of top competitor Dollar Thrifty for $2.6 billion, the company still represents Zipcar's biggest competitor moving forward. But these firms are not as Web-enabled as Zipcar, and currently still lack the technology infrastructure to compete effectively. Zipcar, for instance, spent over $500,000 on a fleet reservation system that connects users, its Web site, and the cars themselves.

So far, Zipcar is not worrying about the competition. In April 2011, Zipcar went public and raised almost $175 million to fuel its expansion. Although analysts have predicted that the car-sharing industry could grow into a multi-billion dollar industry by 2016, in 2012, Zipcar stock lost some ground. Valued at $1.2 billion at its opening price, Zipcar's market capitalization dipped to as low as $300 million. However, in 2013, rental car company Avis Budget Group purchased Zipcar for $500 million in cash. Although this represented an increase from its low, Zipcar shareholders believed that the sale price undervalued the company significantly, at least compared to its peak valuation. Nevertheless, the deal was completed in March 2013. Zipcar gets the benefit of a significant increase in fleet size with all of Avis' vehicles, and Avis gains the ability to offer car sharing as well as car rentals. Both benefit from cost savings through consolidation. Zipcar still operates as its own entity within Avis, and the market for car sharing is still growing. Zipcar's net income increased to $14.7 million, up $21 million from its $7.2 million loss the previous year. With Avis' resources at its disposal and with the car sharing market still growing, Zipcar's future is bright.

SOURCES: "Zipcar Reports Fourth Quarter and Full Year 2012 Results," zipcar.com, February 15, 2013; "Explaining the Avis Takeover of Zipcar," by Tim Worstall, Forbes.com, January 2, 2013; "Avis Budget Group to Acquire Zipcar For $12.25 Per Share in Cash," zipcar.com, January 2, 2013; "Zipcar Now Offers Campus Car Sharing With More Than 300 North American Colleges and Universities," Zipcar Inc., October 9, 2012; "Why Zipcar Is Worth $18," by Trefis Team, Forbes, June 15, 2012; "Is Zipcar as Bad as the Chart Suggests?" Seekingalpha.com, August 28, 2012; "Zipcar Expands 'Zipvan' Cargo Van Service to Boston and Washington D.C.," Zipcar.com, May 27, 2012; "Ford and Zipcar Join Forces," by Bill Vlasic, New York Times, August 31, 2011; Zipcar Quarterly Report on Form 10-Q for the period ended June 30, 2011, Sec.gov, August 5, 2011; "Zipcar Soars in Market Debut," by Evelyn M. Rusli, New York Times, April 14, 2011; "Car Sharing: Ownership by the Hour," by Ken Belson, New York Times, September 10, 2010.

vendors to corporations provide **corporate online booking solutions (COBS)** that provide integrated airline, hotel, conference center, and auto rental services at a single site.

ONLINE TRAVEL INDUSTRY DYNAMICS

Because much of what travel agency sites offer is a commodity, and thus they face the same costs, competition among online providers is intense. Price competition is difficult because shoppers, as well as online site managers, can comparison shop easily. Therefore, competition among sites tends to focus on scope of offerings, ease of use, payment options, and personalization. Some well-known travel sites are listed in **Table 9.6**.

The online travel services industry has gone through a period of consolidation with stronger offline, established firms such as Sabre Holdings (which now owns Travelocity, Lastminute, and Site59, among others) purchasing weaker and relatively inexpensive

corporate online-booking solutions (COBS)

provide integrated airline, hotel, conference center, and auto rental services at a single site

TABLE 9.6	MAJOR ONLINE TRAVEL SITES
NAME	DESCRIPTION
LEISURE/UNMANAGED BUSINESS TRAVEL	
Expedia	Largest online travel service; leisure focus.
Orbitz	Second-largest online travel service. Began as supplier-owned reservation system; now part of Orbitz Worldwide, a public company.
Priceline	Name Your Price model; leisure focus.
Travelocity	Part of global technology company Sabre Holdings. Leisure focus.
TripAdvisor	Travel shopping bot that searches for the lowest fares across all other sites.
CheapTickets	Discount airline tickets, hotel reservations, and auto rentals. Part of Orbitz Worldwide.
Hotels.com	Largest hotel reservation network; leisure and corporate focus. Owned by Expedia.
Hotwire	Seeks out discount fares based on airline excess inventory. Owned by Expedia.
MANAGED BUSINESS TRAVEL	
GetThere.com	Corporate online booking solution (COBS). Owned by Sabre Holdings.
Travelocity Business	Full-service corporate travel agency.

online travel agencies in order to build stronger multi-channel travel sites. Orbitz and Expedia have also been involved in the industry consolidation. Orbitz was initially an industry consortium, then went public, then was purchased by Cendant (along with other travel firms such as CheapTickets and Trip.com), then sold by Cendant to Blackstone Group, and finally went public again in 2007. Expedia, originally begun by Microsoft, was purchased by Barry Diller's conglomerate IAC/InterActiveCorp, but has now been spun off as an independent company once again, picking up IAC's Hotels.com, Hotwire, TripAdvisor, and TravelNow in the process.

In addition to industry consolidation, the online travel industry has been roiled by meta-search engines that scour the Web for the best prices on travel and lodging, and then collect finder or affiliate fees for sending consumers to the lowest-price sites. For instance, TripAdvisor has created a one-stop Web site where consumers can find the lowest price airfares and hotels by searching over 100 other Web travel sites and presenting the fares in rank order. Similar "travel aggregator" sites are Kayak, Fly.com, and Mobissimo. These sites, in the eyes of many industry leaders, commoditize the online travel industry even further, cause excessive price competition, and divert revenues from the leading, branded firms who have made extensive investments in inventory and systems.

Mobile devices and apps used for pre-trip planning, booking, check-in, and context and location-based destination information are also transforming the online travel industry (see also the case study on Orbitz's mobile strategy in Chapter 4). For instance, in 2013, almost 50 million are expected to use a mobile device to research travel, and that number is estimated to almost double, to about 93 million by 2017. Around 25 million are expected to actually book travel using a mobile device in 2013, and that number is expected to double as well, to over 56 million, by 2017 (eMarketer, 2013d). Most of the major airlines now have apps for a variety of mobile platforms to enable flight research, booking, and management. Apps from hotels and car rental companies are available from most of the major players such as Hertz and Avis for car rentals, and Best Western, Choice Hotels, Hilton, and Starwood for hotels. Apps may sometimes target specific consumer behavior. For instance, the Wyndham Hotel group discovered that about 70% of its mobile bookings come on the same day, in many cases within a few miles of the hotel (eMarketer, Inc., 2012b).

Social media is also having a big impact on the online travel industry. User-generated content and online reviews are having an increasing influence on travel-buying decisions. The *Insight on Society* story, *Phony Reviews,* examines some of the issues this presents for the industry.

9.7   ONLINE CAREER SERVICES

Next to travel services, one of the Internet's most successful online services has been job services (recruitment sites) that provide a free posting of individual resumes, plus many other related career services; for a fee, they also list job openings posted by

INSIGHT ON SOCIETY

PHONY REVIEWS

People used to rely on travel agents for professional recommendations about travel destinations and hotels. Today, however, that function has been largely usurped by sites like TripAdvisor, which aggregates consumer reviews. TripAdvisor has been a smashing success, with more than 100 million user-generated reviews, and is often one of the first places consumers go as they try to decide where to travel and what hotels to book. A good rating can be worth thousands of dollars in bookings. But are all those reviews for real? Can they be trusted?

In the United Kingdom, TripAdvisor is under investigation by the U.K. Advertising Standards Authority as a result of complaints that TripAdvisor's review problem has reached "epidemic levels." According to online reputation management firm KwikChex, as many as 10 million of the most current reviews on TripAdvisor could be fake. KwikChex alleges that hotels are paying people to create false identities and post favorable reviews on their properties, and also to slam competing venues. A *Times of London* investigation had previously found that hotel owners were paying thousands of dollars to companies that employ teams of writers to post hundreds of fake reviews. On various forums and classified sites, such as Craigslist, Fiverr, and Digital Point, ads can easily be found promising payment for positive feedback on various review sites. Some establishments offer guests future discounts for "honest but positive" reviews. In 2012, TripAdvisor was told by the ASA to remove wording on its site claiming that its reviews were "trusted and honest." In 2013, TripAdvisor continued to experience problems with fraudulent reviews, as a non-existent restaurant became one of the top rated establishments in Devon, England. A hotel in Quebec has also announced its intention to sue a customer who wrote a scathing review on TripAdvisor without any proof for his claims.

A disgruntled consumer with an axe to grind can do a lot of damage on online review sites. For instance, Dancing Deer Mountain, a small wedding venue in Junction City, Oregon, had steady business until one wedding went horribly wrong. The proprietors said that rules about bringing in outside alcohol were broken; the situation with the wedding-goers purportedly became combative as a result. Afterwards, five scathing online reviews were posted, including one that claimed "The owner is absolutely crazy and needs professional help," with another exclaiming "DO NOT USE THIS VENUE." As a result, business dropped off precipitously. The owners tried suing the reviewers but lost under Oregon's anti-SLAPP (Strategic Lawsuit Against Public Participation) legislation, which protects individual free speech, particularly speech that qualifies as an opinion. About half the states in the United States have an anti-SLAPP law, which many believe is vital to consumer free speech.

For sites like Yelp, which are primarily focused on business ratings and reviews, the growth in phony reviews presents a considerable challenge. The authenticity and accuracy of reviews are critically important to Yelp's success, but garnering a high review score is equally important to the businesses listed on the site. Studies have found that if a business can increase its Yelp rating by one star, its revenues will increase anywhere from 5 to 9 percent. If site visitors have no reason to trust Yelp's reviews, there isn't much incentive for those visitors to return in the future. With this in mind, Yelp has begun to remove suspect reviews from its site, including those from rings of businesses who work together to fraudulently increase the ratings of each business in the group. Yelp is also developing its own algorithms, which are intended to detect phony reviews. The

(continued)

company also conducts sting operations to infiltrate these rings, determines which businesses are working together, and outs those business publicly.

In 2012, Yelp introduced "Consumer Alerts," which inform readers when a review is likely to be fraudulent. The alerts are generated via an algorithm that monitors the site for suspicious posting patterns. While this helps to combat phony reviews, it also increases the risk that legitimate positive reviews will be flagged and removed, hurting both the reputation of the business and the reputation of the review. In 2013, Yelp released another round of Consumer Alerts for approximately 150 businesses. While this represents progress, analysts believe that for every 5 reviews posted on Yelp, one is fraudulent. This means that 150 businesses is likely only a fraction of the total number of businesses engaging in fraudulent activity on Yelp.

TripAdvisor also claims it uses an algorithm to help filter out false reviews, although it rejects requiring would-be reviewers to supply a reservation number in order to prove that they have actually stayed at the property that they are reviewing. According to TripAdvisor, it takes the authenticity of its reviews very seriously, and has numerous methods to ensure their legitimacy, including automated site tools and a team of review integrity experts. It also relies on the review community itself to identify suspicious content and trolls the sites where businesses advertise for fake reviewers. The fact that a nonexistent business could become one of the most positively reviewed places in an area casts serious doubt over the effectiveness of its methods, however.

There may soon be another tool in TripAdvisor's toolbox. Researchers at Cornell University have developed an algorithm that they say can identify language features specific to fake and truthful reviews. To train the algorithm, they created a database of 20 truthful and 20 fake reviews for 20 hotels, for a total of 800 reviews. According to the researchers, the algorithm accurately identified fake reviews 90% of the time. The truthful reviews tended to talk about the specific details, using specific nouns and adjectives as descriptors. Since those who wrote the fake reviews were not necessarily familiar with the physical location they were reviewing, the fake reviewers, not surprisingly, tended to talk more about themselves, reasons for the trip, and traveling companions. The algorithm has attracted the attention of a number of companies, including TripAdvisor, Hilton, and several specialist travel sites.

Will the days of phony reviews come to an end thanks to these advances? Probably not. But review sites and regulators are cracking down on phony reviews with increasing vigor. In 2013, 19 companies received fines from New York regulators totaling $350,000 for buying and selling fraudulent reviews. Investigators posed as a Brooklyn yogurt shop supposedly seeking help from reputation management firms to increase their rating. Other states are likely to follow suit. So it's best to take what you read with a grain of salt, discarding both the overwhelmingly positive and the unrelentingly negative reviews.

SOURCES: "Companies To Pay $350,000 Fine Over Fake Online Reviews," by Lance Whitney, CNETNews.com, September 23, 2013; "Give Yourself 5 Stars? Online, It Might Cost You," by David Streitfeld, *New York Times*, September 22, 2013; "TripAdvisor: Can Users Be Sued for Bad Reviews?" by Natalie Paris, telegraph.co.uk, September 12, 2013; "Why Yelp Will Never Be Rid of Phony Reviews," by Joshua Brustein, Businessweek.com, August 13, 2013; "Yelp Consumer Alerts: Letting You Know Before You Spend Your Dough," Yelp Official Blog, August 12, 2013; "TripAdvisor Fails to Spot Fake Restaurant," by Oliver Smith, telegraph.co.uk, July 25, 2013; "Deceptive Reviews: The Influential Tail," Eric Anderson and Duncan Simester, MIT, May 2013; "Buy Reviews on Yelp, Get Black Mark," David Streitfeld, *New York Times*, October 18, 2012; "Yelp Reviews: Can You Trust Them? Some Firms Game the System," by Jessica Guynn and Andrea Chang, *Los Angeles Times*, July 4, 2012; "TripAdvisor Told to Stop Claiming Reviews are 'Trusted and Honest,'" *Daily Mail*, February 1, 2012; "A Lie Detector Test for Online Reviewers," by Karen Weise, *BusinessWeek*, September 29, 2011; "Cornell Researchers Work to Spot Fake Reviews," by Emma Court, *The Cornell Daily Sun*, September 23, 2011; "Investigation Launched into TripAdvisor Following Claims up to 10 Million Reviews are Fake," News.com.au, September 5, 2011; "The Yelp Wars: False Reviews, Anti-SLAPP, and Slander — What's Ethical in Online Reviewing?", by Kathleen Miles, Scpr.org, August 25, 2011.

companies. Career services sites collect revenue from other sources as well, by providing value-added services to users and collecting fees from related service providers.

The online job market is dominated by two large players: CareerBuilder (which provides job listings for AOL and MSN), with about 20 million unique monthly visitors in August 2013, and Monster, with about 17 million. (Yahoo HotJobs, which had been the third large player, was acquired by Monster for $225 million in 2010.) Other popular sites include Indeed (26 million unique visitors), SimplyHired (4 million), and SnagAJob (5 million). These top sites generate more than $1 billion annually in revenue from employers' fees and consumer fees. Rising unemployment during late 2008 to 2010 has led to an increasing number of Americans seeking jobs and career opportunities online. A 2013 survey found that around 70% of U.S. Internet users surveyed had looked for jobs online, and that it was the primary form of job hunting for over 25% (ATYM Market Research, 2013). The professional social network site LinkedIn is also becoming an increasingly important player in this market (see the opening case in Chapter 11). In 2011, it added a plug-in, Apply with LinkedIn, that allows job seekers to easily submit their LinkedIn profile to an employer's Web site.

Traditionally, companies have relied on five employee recruitment tools: classified and print advertising, career expos (or trade shows), on-campus recruiting, private employment agencies (now called "staffing firms"), and internal referral programs. In comparison to online recruiting, these tools have severe limitations. Print advertising usually includes a per-word charge that limits the amount of detail employers provide about a job opening, as well as a limited time period within which the job is posted. Career expos do not allow for pre-screening of attendees and are limited by the amount of time a recruiter can spend with each candidate. Staffing firms charge high fees and have a limited, usually local, selection of job hunters. On-campus recruiting also restricts the number of candidates a recruiter can speak with during a normal visit and requires that employers visit numerous campuses. And internal referral programs may encourage employees to propose unqualified candidates for openings in order to qualify for rewards or incentives offered.

Online recruiting overcomes these limitations, providing a more efficient and cost-effective means of linking employers and potential employees, while reducing the total time to hire. Online recruiting enables job hunters to more easily build, update, and distribute their resumes while gathering information about prospective employers and conducting job searches.

IT'S JUST INFORMATION: THE IDEAL WEB BUSINESS?

Online recruitment is ideally suited for the Web. The hiring process is an information-intense business process that involves discovering the skills and salary requirements of individuals and matching them with available jobs. In order to accomplish this matchup, there does not initially need to be face-to-face interaction, or a great deal of personalization. Prior to the Internet, this information sharing was accomplished locally by human networks of friends, acquaintances, former employers, and relatives, in addition to employment agencies that developed paper files on job hunters.

TABLE 9.7	POPULAR ONLINE RECRUITMENT SITES
RECRUITMENT SITE	BRIEF DESCRIPTION
GENERAL RECRUITMENT SITES	
CareerBuilder	Owned by Gannett, Tribune, McClatchy (all newspaper companies), and Microsoft. Provides job search centers for more than 10,000 Web sites, including AOL and MSN, and 140 newspapers; 1.6 million jobs listed.
Monster	One of the first commercial sites on the Web in 1994. Today, a public company offering general job searches in 50 countries. Acquired Yahoo HotJobs in 2010 for $225 million.
Indeed.com	Job site aggregator
SimplyHired	Job site aggregator
Craigslist	Popular classified listing service focused on local recruiting
EXECUTIVE SEARCH SITES	
Futurestep	Korn/Ferry site, low-end executive recruiting
Spencerstuart.com	Middle-level executive recruiting
ExecuNet	Executive search firm
NICHE JOB SITES	
SnagAJob	Part-time and hourly jobs
USAJobs	Federal government jobs
HigherEdJobs	Education industry
EngineerJobs	Engineering jobs
Medzilla	Medical industry
Showbizjobs	Entertainment industry
Salesjobs	Sales and marketing
Dice	Information technology jobs
MBAGlobalNet	MBA-oriented community site

The Internet can clearly automate this flow of information, reducing search time and costs for all parties.

Table 9.7 lists some of the most popular recruitment sites.

Why are so many job hunters and employers using Internet job sites? Recruitment sites are popular largely because they save time and money for both job hunters and employers seeking recruits. For employers, the job boards expand the geographical reach of their searches, lower costs, and result in faster hiring decisions.

For job seekers, online sites are popular not only because their resumes can be made widely available to recruiters but also because of a variety of other related job-hunting services. The services delivered by online recruitment sites have greatly expanded since their emergence in 1996. Originally, online recruitment sites just provided a digital version of newspaper classified ads. Today's sites offer many other services, including skills assessment, personality assessment questionnaires, personalized account management for job hunters, organizational culture assessments, job search tools, employer blocking (prevents your employer from seeing your posting), employee blocking (prevents your employees from seeing your listings if you are their employer), and e-mail notification. Online sites also provide a number of educational services such as resume writing advice, software skills preparation, and interview tips.

For the most part, online recruitment sites work, in the sense of linking job hunters with jobs, but they are just one of many ways people actually find jobs. A survey by The Conference Board found that the majority (70%) of job seekers rely equally on both the Internet and newspapers to look for jobs, with about half relying on word-of-mouth leads, and about a quarter on employment agencies. Given that the cost of posting a resume online is zero, the marginal returns are very high.

The ease with which resumes can be posted online has also raised new issues for both job recruiters and job seekers. If you are an employer, how do you sort through the thousands of resumes you may receive when posting an open job? If you are a job seeker, how do you stand out among the thousands or even millions of others? Perhaps one way is to post a video resume. In a survey by Vault, nearly nine in 10 employers said they would watch a video resume if it were submitted to them, in part because it would help them better assess a candidate's professional presentation and demeanor, and over half said they believed video would become a common addition to future job applications. CareerBuilder became the first major online job site to implement a video resume tool for job candidates, following a previous launch for an online video brand-building tool for employers.

Perhaps the most important function of online recruitment sites is not so much their capacity to actually match employers with job hunters but their ability to establish market prices and terms, as well as trends in the labor market. Online recruitment sites identify salary levels for both employers and job hunters and categorize the skill sets required to achieve those salary levels. In this sense, online recruitment sites are online national marketplaces that establish the terms of trade in labor markets. For instance, Monster.com offers its U.S. Monster Employment Index. This index is based on a large, representative selection of corporate career sites and job boards, and calculates employment demand for the nation, regions, and specific occupations. The existence of these online national job sites should lead to a rationalization of wages, greater labor mobility, and higher efficiency in recruitment and operations because employers will be able to quickly find the people they need.

ONLINE RECRUITMENT INDUSTRY TRENDS

Trends for 2013–2014 in the online recruitment services industry include the following:

- **Consolidation:** The two major job services are CareerBuilder (owned by newspapers and Microsoft) and Monster (which now owns Yahoo HotJobs). In 2013, these two sites continue to dominate the market, and are expected to do so for some time to come.

- **Diversification:** While the national online market is becoming larger and consolidating into a few general sites, there is an explosion in specialty niche employment sites that focus on specific occupations. This is creating greater online job market diversity and choice.

- **Localization:** While local classified ads in newspapers remain a significant source of jobs, the large national online sites are also developing local boards in large metropolitan areas that compete more directly against local newspapers. The local newspapers themselves have responded by building Web sites that focus on local job markets, especially hourly and contract jobs that often do not appear on the large national job boards. Craigslist is another source of local job listings. Hence there is a growing focus on local job markets by all participants in the marketplace because this is where so many new jobs first appear.

- **Job search engines/aggregators:** As with travel services, search engines that focus specifically on jobs are posing a new threat to established online career sites. For instance, Indeed, SimplyHired, and Us.jobs "scrape" listings from thousands of online job sites such as Monster, CareerBuilder, specialty recruiting services, and the sites of individual employers to provide a free, searchable index of thousands of job listings in one spot. Because these firms do not charge employers a listing fee, they are currently using a pay-per-click or other advertising revenue model.

- **Social networking:** According to a survey of recruiters and executives in North America, 98% of recruiting professionals used social networks to find new employees in 2012, with over 97% of them using LinkedIn (eMarketer, Inc., 2013e). LinkedIn, probably the most well-known business-oriented social network, has grown significantly to over 225 million members representing over 170 different industries in over 200 countries as of September 2013. LinkedIn's corporate hiring solutions are used by 90 of the Fortune 100 companies, and more than 3 million companies have a LinkedIn page. Consumers are using sites such as LinkedIn to establish business contacts and networks. For instance, according to LinkedIn, its members did 5.7 billion professionally-oriented searches on LinkedIn in 2012. Employers are also using LinkedIn to conduct searches to find potential job candidates that may not be actively job hunting. For instance, LinkedIn offers companies a feature called LinkedIn Talent Advantage that includes tools that help corporate recruiters find "passive talent" (people who are not actively looking for a new job), as well as custom company profiles that are specifically designed for recruitment. CareerBuilder offers a job and internship matching application on Facebook that allows users to receive continuously updated listings based on the information found in their profiles. Social network sites are also being used by employers to "check up" on the background of job candidates. A study by Harris Interactive of 2,667 managers and human resource employees found that 45% are using social networks to screen job candidates, and 35% have rejected candidates because of content on a social site. Employers typically search Facebook, Twitter, and LinkedIn. Provocative photos were the biggest negative factor followed by drinking and drug references. Another survey found that 91% of employers surveyed used social network sites to screen applicants. Almost 70% reported rejecting a candidate because of what they saw.

- **Mobile:** As with other forms of services, career services firms have also moved onto the mobile platform. A 2011 study found that around 20% of job seekers who are 18 to 34 years old reported that they searched for jobs and researched companies using mobile devices. To reach this audience, CareerBuilder has a mobile Web site, as well as iPhone and Android apps that allow job seekers to create and upload resumes, search jobs by keyword, location, and company, e-mail jobs, browse and apply, and more. Monster offers similar functionality. CareerBuilder also has a mobile app for employers that allows them to sync directly to their existing CareerBuilder accounts and gain access to job applicants.

9.8 **CASE STUDY**

OpenTable:
Your Reservation Is Waiting

OpenTable is the leading supplier of reservation, table management, and guest management software for restaurants. In addition, the company operates OpenTable.com, the world's most popular Web site for making restaurant reservations online. In 14 years, OpenTable has gone from a start-up to a successful and growing public company that counts around two-thirds of the nation's reservation-taking restaurants as clients.

Today, more than 28,000 restaurants in the United States, Canada, Mexico, the United Kingdom, Germany, and Japan use the OpenTable hardware and software system. This system automates the reservation-taking and table management process, while allowing restaurants to build diner databases for improved guest recognition and targeted e-mail marketing. The OpenTable Web site, OpenTable for Mobile Web (its mobile Web site), and OpenTable Mobile (its mobile app), provide a fast, efficient way for diners to find available tables in real time. The Web sites and app connect directly to the thousands of computerized reservation systems at OpenTable restaurants, and reservations are immediately recorded in a restaurant's electronic reservation book.

Restaurants subscribe to the OpenTable Electronic Reservation Book (ERB), the company's proprietary software, which is installed on a touch-screen computer system and supported by asset-protection and security tools. The ERB software provides a real-time map of the restaurant floor and enables the restaurant to retain meal patterns of all parties, serving as a customer relationship management (CRM) system for restaurants. The software is upgraded periodically, and the latest version, introduced in April 2012, was designed to provide increased ease of use and a more thorough view of table availability to help turn more tables, enhance guest service, personalize responses to diners, coordinate the seating process, and maximize guest seating. The ERBs at OpenTable's customer restaurants connect via the Internet to form an online network of restaurant reservation books. For restaurants that rely less heavily on reservations, OpenTable offers Connect, a web-based service that lets restaurants accept online reservations.

OpenTable's revenue comes from two sources. Restaurants pay a one-time fee starting at $1,295 for on-site installation and training, a monthly subscription fee of $199 for software and hardware, and a $1 transaction fee for each restaurant guest seated through online reservations. The online reservation service is free to diners. The business model encourages diners to assist in viral marketing. When an individual makes a reservation, the site "suggests" that they send e-vites to their dinner companions directly from OpenTable.com. The e-vites include a link back to the OpenTable site.

OpenTable is a service-based (software as service, or SaaS) e-commerce company. In other words, customers don't buy software and install it on their computers, but instead go online and get the software functionality through subscriptions. OpenTable is also an online service that does not sell goods, but instead enables diners to make reservations, like social networking sites provide services.

The restaurant industry was slow to leverage the power of the Internet. This was in part because the industry was, and continues to be, highly fragmented and local—made up of more than 30,000 small, independent businesses or local restaurant-owning groups.

The founders of OpenTable knew that dealing with these restaurants as a single market would be difficult. They also realized that the Internet was changing things for diners by providing them with instant access to reviews, menus, and other information about dining options. And there was no method for making reservations online—we all know reserving by phone is time-consuming, inefficient, and prone to errors. In order to make the system work, reach and scale were very important. For diners to use an online reservation system, they would need real-time access to a number of local restaurants, and the ability to instantly book confirmed reservations around the clock. If customers were planning a trip to another city, OpenTable would need participating restaurants in those cities.

The company was originally incorporated in San Francisco in 1998 as Easy-eats.com, morphing into OpenTable.com, Inc. a year later. When the company was founded, most restaurants did not have computers, let alone systems that would allow online reservations made through a central Web site. OpenTable's initial strategy was to pay online restaurant reviewers for links to its Web site and target national chains in order to quickly expand its reach. This got the company into 50 cities, but it was spending $1 million a month and bringing in only $100,000 in revenue. Not exactly a formula for success. The original investors still felt there was a viable business to be built, and they made a number of management changes, including installing investor and board member Thomas Layton, founder of CitySearch.com, as OpenTable's CEO. Layton cut staff, shut down marketing efforts, and got the company out of all but four cities: Chicago, New York, San Francisco, and Washington, D.C.

The company retooled its hardware and software to create the user-friendly ERB system and deployed a door-to-door sales force to solicit subscriptions from high-end restaurants. The combination of e-commerce, user-friendly technology, and the personal touch worked. The four markets OpenTable targeted initially developed into active, local networks of restaurants and diners that continue to grow. OpenTable has implemented the same strategy across the country, and now includes approximately 28,000 OpenTable restaurant customers. In 14 years, the company has seated approximately 490 million diners, and it is currently averaging 12 million diners per month.

As the company grew, investors began making plans for it to go public. Layton stepped down from his position as CEO in 2007, though he remains a board member. He was replaced by Jeffrey Jordan, former president of PayPal. Jordan had some experience with public companies from working with eBay on its acquisition of PayPal. In 2009, he chose an aggressive strategy—going ahead with an initial public offering (IPO) despite a terrible economy and worse financial markets. So far, the gamble has paid off. On its first day of trading, OpenTable's shares climbed 59%. The share price at the end of September 2013 was in the mid-$70 range, nearly quadruple the $20 IPO price.

Despite the challenging economy, OpenTable's numbers at the time of the IPO were strong, and since then, it has continued to grow. In 2012, the company's total revenues were $161.6 million, up 16% from the $139.5 million recorded in 2011, with no signs of slowing in 2013. Revenues for the second quarter of 2013 increased by 15% to $45.6 million, and the company's earnings per share have continued to grow.

The company has benefited from having e-commerce revenue streams from subscription fees and per-transaction charges, rather than depending on advertising. Further, more than 50% of OpenTable's revenue comes from B2B subscriptions, which are typically part of long-term contracts. Restaurants that have invested in OpenTable's software package are less likely to want to incur the switching costs associated with changing to a different reservation management package.

Another reason for its success is that OpenTable has a large number of satisfied customers. Restaurant owners report that they and their staff members find the software easy to use, and it helps them manage their business better. Specifically, it streamlines operations, helps fill additional seats, and improves quality of service, providing a concrete return on investment. This has led to both high customer satisfaction and high retention rates.

OpenTable has also taken advantage of the interconnected needs of restaurants and diners. Restaurants want cost-effective ways to attract guests and manage their reservations, while diners want convenient ways to find available restaurants, choose among them, and make reservations. By creating an online network of restaurants and diners that transact with each other through real-time reservations, OpenTable has figured out how to successfully address the needs of both.

OpenTable's market is susceptible to network effects: the more people use it, the more utility the system delivers. OpenTable's growth continually provides diners with expanded choices. More diners discover the benefits of using the online reservation system, which in turn delivers value to restaurant customers, and helps attract more restaurants to the network. Diners serve as a source of viral marketing, as the OpenTable Web site encourages them to e-vite their dinner companions to the meal. When they do so, the e-mail provides links back to the OpenTable Web site. And the OpenTable link appears on the restaurant's Web site, linking directly to the reservation page. OpenTable has been able to improve its efficiency even as diners are staying home more often.

While OpenTable is the biggest, most successful online player in the restaurant reservations market, it does have competitors. MenuPages.com offers access to restaurant menus and reviews, but visitors to the site can't make reservations, and the site covers only eight U.S. cities. In 2012, OpenTable partnered with onetime competitor Urbanspoon, acquiring its reservation management system, Rezbook, and becoming Urbanspoon's reservation provider. Looming on the horizon is Google, which purchased online restaurant guide Zagat in September 2011, raising the specter that it might try to compete with OpenTable, although Zagat does not yet possess that functionality. Competitors such as Spain-based Restalo also pose a potential future challenge to OpenTable. Restalo, which has raised $10 million in funding in 2013, is poised to become the reservation leader in Spain and Italy, where OpenTable does not yet operate. Companies such as the Pittsburgh-based NoWait are gaining market share by targeting the casual dining market, which includes up to 270,000 restaurants, far higher than the 28,000 fine dining restaurants served by OpenTable.

While some may argue that there are better ways to make reservations that don't take visitors away from restaurant's Web sites (once someone clicks on the OpenTable link, they navigate away), restaurant owners like the OpenTable software, and diners have an enormous range of dining choices. Those two factors make this argument a relatively weak one.

The company is committed to shrewd technological investments to advance its position. It has a mobile Web site, mobile applications that work on just about every smartphone platform, and in 2012 it introduced an iPad app that fully integrates with its ERB software. GPS enables mobile users to locate and make reservations at nearby venues. What's more, a new addition, scheduled for release at the end of 2013, will allow users to pay for meals with a credit card directly from its apps. OpenTable also launched Facebook Connect, allowing users to share their reservations on Facebook, as well as a Facebook application called Reservations, which allows partner restaurants to book reservations directly from Facebook.

OpenTable has employed its tried-and-true business model, combining technology with old-fashioned door-to-door sales, to expand its North American markets over time. Growth is projected to continue in the United States, Canada, and Mexico despite considerable market penetration. Selective international expansion is planned beyond its current operations in Germany, Japan, and the United Kingdom. OpenTable supports each of these locations with a direct sales force servicing approximately 1,000 restaurants.

SOURCES: "European OpenTable Competitor Restalo Raises $10M Series B Led By Seaya Ventures," by Steve O'Hear, TechCrunch.com, September 17, 2013; "OpenTable, Inc. Announces Second Quarter Financial Results," opentable.com, August 1, 2013; "Pittsburg Startup NoWait Could Overtake OpenTable's Volume in 2014," by Louis Bedigan, benzinga.com, August 20, 2013; "Forget Flagging the Waiter: OpenTable Testing App That Lets You Pay," by Teresa Novellino, Upstart.bizjournals.com, July 31, 2013; "OpenTable Partners with Urbanspoon; Acquires Rezbook," opentable.com, July 31, 2013; "OpenTable Releases New Electronic Reservation Book and iPad App for Restaurants," opentable.com, April 4, 2012; "OpenTable Inc. Announces Fourth Quarter and Full Year 2012 Financial Results," opentable.com, February 7, 2013; "OpenTable Shares Drop After Analyst Cuts Rating," Businessweek.com, September 17, 2012; "OpenTable Hits 15 million Restaurant Reviews," by Anita Li, Mashable.com, September 6, 2012; "Google Buys Zagat to View the OpenTable, Yelp," by Alexei Oreskovic, Reuters, September 8, 2011; "Behind OpenTable's Success," Kevin Kelleher, CNNMoney.com, September 23, 2010; "OpenTable Introduces the Next Generation of Its Electronic Reservation Book Software," RestaurantNews.com, August 17, 2010; "OpenTable: the Hottest Spot in Town," by Maha Atal, CNNMoney.con, August 14, 2009; "OpenTable Unveils Version 2.0 of its iPhone App," AppScout.com, August 14, 2009; "Gadgetell: Fight for Your Dinner: Urbanspoon vs. Open Table," NewsFactor.com, August 8, 2009; "Urbanspoon is Now Taking Online Reservations: Takes on OpenTable," by Frederic Lardinois, ReadWriteWeb.com, August 7, 2009; "What Media Companies Could Learn from OpenTable," The Media Wonk, May 20, 2009; Open Table S-1/A Amendment #6, filed with the Securities and Exchange Commission, May 19, 2009.

The company's international strategy is to replicate the successful U.S. model by focusing initially on building a restaurant customer base. OpenTable believes the localized versions of its software will compare favorably against competitive software offerings, enabling them to expand across a broad selection of local restaurants.

The company is well-positioned for future growth. Its size, track record of growth, and high customer satisfaction rates should continue to work in its favor.

Case Study Questions

1. Why will OpenTable competitors have a difficult time competing against Open-Table?

2. What characteristics of the restaurant market make it difficult for a reservation system to work?

3. How did OpenTable change its marketing strategy to succeed?

4. Why would restaurants find the SaaS model very attractive?

9.9 REVIEW

KEY CONCEPTS

■ **Understand the environment in which the online retail sector operates today.**

Personal consumption of retail goods and services comprise about 71% and account for about $11.4 trillion of total GDP. The retail industry can be divided into seven major firm types:
- General merchandise
- Durable goods
- Specialty stores
- Food and beverage
- Gasoline and fuel
- MOTO
- Online retail firms

Each type offers opportunities for online retail. The MOTO sector is the most similar to the online retail sales sector.

During the early days of e-commerce, some predicted that the retail industry would be revolutionized, based on the following beliefs:
- Greatly reduced search costs on the Internet would encourage consumers to abandon traditional marketplaces in order to find the lowest prices for goods. First movers who provided low-cost goods and high-quality service would succeed.
- Market entry costs would be much lower than those for physical storefront merchants, and online merchants would be more efficient at marketing and order

fulfillment than their offline competitors because they had command of the technology (technology prices were falling sharply).

- Online companies would replace traditional stores as physical store merchants were forced out of business. Older traditional firms that were too slow to enter the online market would be locked out of the marketplace.
- In certain industries, the "middleman" would be eliminated (disintermediation) as manufacturers or their distributors entered the market and built a direct relationship with the consumer. This cost savings would ensure the emergence of the Web as the dominant marketing channel.
- In other industries, online retailers would gain the advantage over traditional merchants by outsourcing functions such as warehousing and order fulfillment, resulting in a kind of hypermediation, in which the online retailer gained the upper hand by eliminating inventory purchasing and storage costs.

Today, it has become clear that few of the initial assumptions about the future of online retail were correct. Also, the structure of the retail marketplace in the United States has not been revolutionized. The reality is that:

- Online consumers are not primarily cost-driven—instead, they are as brand-driven and influenced by perceived value as their offline counterparts.
- Online market entry costs were underestimated, as was the cost of acquiring new customers.
- Older traditional firms, such as the general merchandising giants and the established catalog-based retailers, are taking over as the top online retail sites.
- Disintermediation did not occur. On the contrary, online retailing has become an example of the powerful role that intermediaries play in retail trade.

■ Explain how to analyze the economic viability of an online firm.

The economic viability, or ability of a firm to survive during a specified time period, can be analyzed by examining the key industry strategic factors, the strategic factors that pertain specifically to the firm, and the financial statements for the firm. The key industry strategic factors include:

- *Barriers to entry*, which are expenses that will make it difficult for new entrants to join the industry.
- *Power of suppliers*, which refers to the ability of firms in the industry to bargain effectively for lower prices from suppliers.
- *Power of customers*, which refers to the ability of the customers for a particular product to shop among the firm's competitors, thus keeping prices down.
- *Existence of substitute products*, which refers to the present or future availability of products with a similar function.
- The *industry value chain*, which must be evaluated to determine if the chain of production and distribution for the industry is changing in ways that will benefit or harm the firm.
- The *nature of intra-industry competition*, which must be evaluated to determine if the competition within the industry is based on differentiated products and services, price, the scope of the offerings, or the focus of the offerings and whether any imminent changes in the nature of the competition will benefit or harm the firm.

The key firm strategic factors include:

- The *firm value chain*, which must be evaluated to determine if the firm has adopted business systems that will enable it to operate at peak efficiency and whether there are any looming technological changes that might force the firm to change its processes or methods.
- *Core competencies*, which refer to unique skills that a firm has that cannot be easily duplicated. When analyzing the economic viability of a firm, it is important to consider whether technological changes might invalidate these competencies.
- *Synergies*, which refer to the availability to the firm of the competencies and assets of related firms that it owns or with which it has formed strategic partnerships.
- The firm's current *technology*, which must be evaluated to determine if it has proprietary technologies that will allow it to scale with demand and if it has developed the customer relationship, fulfillment, supply chain management, and human resources systems that it will need in order to be viable.
- The *social and legal challenges facing the firm*, which should be examined to determine if the firm has taken into account consumer trust issues such as the privacy and security of personal information and if the firm may be vulnerable to legal challenges.

The key financial factors include:
- *Revenues*, which must be examined to determine if they are growing and at what rate.
- *Cost of sales*, which is the cost of the products sold, including all related costs. The lower the cost of sales compared to revenue, the higher the gross profit.
- *Gross margin*, which is calculated by dividing gross profit by net sales revenue. If the gross margin is improving consistently, the economic outlook for the firm is enhanced.
- *Operating expenses*, which should be evaluated to determine if the firm's needs in the near interim will necessitate increased outlays. Large increases in operating expenses may result in net losses for the firm.
- *Operating margin*, which is calculated by dividing operating income or loss by net sales revenue, and is an indication of a company's ability to turn sales into pre-tax profit after operating expenses are deducted.
- *Net margin,* which is calculated by dividing net income or net loss by net sales revenue. It evaluates the net profit or loss for each dollar of net sales. For example, a net margin of -24% indicates that a firm is losing 24 cents on each dollar of net sales revenue.
- The firm's *balance sheet,* which is a financial snapshot of a company on a given date that displays its financial assets and liabilities. If current assets are less than or not much more than current liabilities, the firm will likely have trouble meeting its short-term obligations.

■ **Identify the challenges faced by the different types of online retailers.**

There are four major types of online retail business models, and each faces its own particular challenges:
- *Virtual merchants* are single-channel Web firms that generate all of their revenues from online sales. Their challenges include building a business and a brand name quickly, many competitors in the virtual marketplace, substantial costs to build and maintain a Web site, considerable marketing expenses, large

customer acquisition costs, a steep learning curve, and the need to quickly achieve operating efficiencies in order to preserve a profit. Amazon is the most well-known example of a virtual merchant.

- *Multi-channel merchants* (bricks-and-clicks) have a network of physical stores as their primary retail channel, but have also begun online operations. Their challenges include high cost of physical buildings, high cost of large sales staffs, the need to coordinate prices across channels, the need to develop methods of handling cross-channel returns from multiple locations, building a credible Web site, hiring new skilled staff, and building rapid-response order entry and fulfillment systems. Macys.com is an example of a bricks-and-clicks company.
- *Catalog merchants* are established companies that have a national offline catalog operation as their largest retail channel, but who have recently developed online capabilities. Their challenges include high costs for printing and mailing, the need to leverage their existing assets and competencies to the new technology environment, the need to develop methods of handling cross-channel returns, building a credible Web site, and hiring new skilled staff. Lands' End is an example of a catalog merchant.
- *Manufacturer-direct merchants* are either single- or multi-channel manufacturers who sell to consumers directly online without the intervention of retailers. Their challenges include channel conflict, quickly developing a rapid-response online order and fulfillment system; switching from a supply-push (products are made prior to orders being received based on estimated demand) to a demand-pull model (products are not built until an order is received); and creating sales, service, and support operations online. Dell.com is an example of a manufacturer-direct merchant.

■ **Describe the major features of the online service sector.**

The service sector is the largest and most rapidly expanding part of the economy of advanced industrial nations. The major service industry groups are financial services, insurance, real estate, business services, and health services. Within these service industry groups, companies can be further categorized into those that involve transaction brokering and those that involve providing a "hands-on" service. With some exceptions, the service sector is by and large a knowledge- and information-intense industry. For this reason, many services are uniquely suited to e-commerce and the strengths of the Internet.

The rapid expansion of e-commerce services in the areas of finance, including insurance and real estate, travel, and job placement, can be explained by the ability of these firms to:
- Collect, store, and disseminate high-value information
- Provide reliable, fast communication
- Personalize and customize service or components of service

E-commerce offers extraordinary opportunities to improve transaction efficiencies and thus productivity in a sector where productivity has so far not been markedly affected by the explosion in information technology.

■ **Discuss the trends taking place in the online financial services industry.**

The online financial services sector is a good example of an e-commerce success story, but the success is somewhat different than what had been predicted in the early days of e-commerce. Today, the multi-channel established financial firms are growing the most rapidly and have the best prospects for long-term viability. Key features of the online banking and brokerage industries include the following:

- Multi-channel firms that have both physical branches and solid online offerings have assumed market leadership over the pure-online firms that cannot provide customers with many services that still require hands-on interaction.
- Financial portals provide comparison shopping services and steer consumers to online providers for independent financial advice and financial planning.
- Account aggregation is another rapidly growing online financial service, which pulls together all of a customer's financial data on a single personalized Web site.
- During the early days of e-commerce, a radically altered online mortgage and lending services market was envisioned in which the mortgage value chain would be simplified and the loan closing process speeded up, with the resulting cost savings passed on to consumers. Affordably building a brand name, the resulting high customer acquisition costs, and instituting these value chain changes proved to be too difficult. Today, the established banks and lenders are reaping the benefits of a relatively small but growing market.

Key features of the online insurance industry include the following:

- Term life insurance stands out as one product group supporting the early visions of lower search costs, increased price transparency, and the resulting consumer savings. However, in other insurance product lines, the Web offers insurance companies new opportunities for product and service differentiation and price discrimination.

Key features of the online real estate services industry include the following:

- The early vision that the historically local, complex, and agent-driven real estate industry would be transformed into a disintermediated marketplace where buyers and sellers could transact directly has not been realized. What has happened has been beneficial to buyers, sellers, and real estate agents alike.
- Since it is not possible to complete a property transaction online, the major impact of the online real estate industry is in influencing offline purchases.
- The primary service is a listing of available houses, with secondary links to mortgage lenders, credit reporting agencies, neighborhood information, loan calculators, appraisal reports, sales price histories by neighborhood, school district data, and crime reports.
- Buyers benefit because they can quickly and easily access a wealth of valuable information; sellers benefit because they receive free online advertising for their property; and real estate agents have reported that Internet-informed customers ask to see fewer properties.

■ **Discuss the major trends in the online travel services industry today.**

The Internet has become the most common channel used by consumers to research travel options and book reservations for airline tickets, rental cars, hotel rooms, and tours. Some of the reasons why online travel services have been so successful include the following:

- Online travel sites offer consumers a one-stop, convenient, leisure and business travel experience where travelers can find content, community, commerce, and customer service. Online sites offer more information and travel options than traditional travel agents, with such services as descriptions of vacations and facilities, chat groups and bulletin boards, and the convenience of purchasing all travel elements at one stop. They also bring consumers and suppliers together in a low transaction cost environment.

- Travel is an information-intensive product as well as a digital product in the sense that travel requirements can be accomplished for the most part online. Since travel does not require any inventory, suppliers (which are highly fragmented) are always looking for customers to fill excess capacity. Also, travel services do not require an expensive multi-channel physical presence. For these reasons, travel services appear to be particularly well suited for the online marketplace.

- It is important to note that various segments of the travel industry fit this description better than others—for instance, airline reservations, auto rentals, and to a lesser extent, hotels. Cruises and tours are more differentiated with varying quality and a more complex level of information required for the decision-making process.

- Corporations are increasingly outsourcing their travel offices entirely to vendors who can provide Web-based solutions, high-quality service, and lower costs.

The major trends in online travel services include the following:

- The online travel services industry is going through a period of consolidation as stronger offline, established firms purchase weaker and relatively inexpensive online travel agencies in order to build stronger multi-channel travel sites that combine physical presence, television sales outlets, and online sites.

- Suppliers—such as airlines, hotels, and auto rental firms—are attempting to eliminate intermediaries and develop a direct relationship with consumers.

- Meta search firms, mobile devices and apps, and social media also are having a big impact on the online travel industry.

■ Identify current trends in the online career services industry.

Next to travel services, job-hunting services have been one of the Internet's most successful online services because they save money for both job hunters and employers. In comparison to online recruiting, traditional recruitment tools have severe limitations:

- Online recruiting provides a more efficient and cost-effective means of linking employers and job hunters and reduces the total time to hire.

- Job hunters can easily build, update, and distribute their resumes, conduct job searches, and gather information on employers at their convenience and leisure.

- It is an information-intense business process that the Internet can automate, and thus reduce search time and costs for all parties.

Online recruiting can also serve to establish market prices and terms, thereby identifying both the salary levels for specific jobs and the skill sets required to achieve those salary levels. This should lead to a rationalization of wages, greater labor mobility, and higher efficiency in recruitment and operations as employers are able to more quickly fill positions.

The major trends in the online career services industry are:

- *Consolidation*—The online recruitment industry is going through a period of rapid consolidation.

- *Diversification*—There is an explosion of specialty niche employment sites that focus on specific occupations.

- *Localization*—There is a growing focus on local job markets.

- *Job search engines*—New online job search engines that scrape listings from thousands of online job sites pose a threat to established career sites.
- *Social networking*—Many Internet users are beginning to use social networking sites to establish business contacts and find jobs; employers are also using them to identify and find out further information about job candidates.
- *Mobile*—As with other forms of services, career services firms have also moved onto the mobile platform.

QUESTIONS

1. Why were so many entrepreneurs drawn to start businesses in the online retail sector initially?
2. What frequently makes the difference between profitable and unprofitable online businesses today?
3. Which segment of the offline retail business is most like online retailing? Why?
4. Describe the technological retail revolution that preceded the growth of e-commerce. What were some of the innovations that made later online retailing possible?
5. Name two assumptions e-commerce analysts made early on about consumers and their buying behavior that turned out to be false.
6. Explain the distinction between disintermediation and hypermediation as it relates to online retailing.
7. Compare and contrast virtual merchants and bricks-and-clicks firms. What other type of online retailer is most like the virtual merchant?
8. What is the difference between a supply-push and a demand-pull sales model? Why do most manufacturer-direct firms have difficulty switching from the former to the latter?
9. What are five strategic issues specifically related to a firm's capabilities? How are they different from industry-related strategic issues?
10. Which is a better measure of a firm's financial health: revenues, gross margin, or net margin? Why?
11. What are some of the difficulties in providing services in an online environment? What factors differentiate the services sector from the retail sector, for example?
12. Compare and contrast the two major types of online services industries. What two major features differentiate services from other industries?
13. What is the biggest deterrent to growth of the online insurance industry nationally?
14. Define channel conflict and explain how it applies to the retail industry.
15. What is the most common use of real estate Web sites? What do most consumers do when they go to them?
16. How have travel services suppliers benefited from consumer use of travel Web sites?
17. Name and describe five traditional recruitment tools companies have used to identify and attract employees. What are the disadvantages of such tools compared to online career sites?
18. In addition to matching job applicants with available positions, what larger function do online job sites fill? Explain how such sites can affect salaries and going rates.

PROJECTS

1. Find the Securities and Exchange Commission Web site at Sec.gov, and access the EDGAR archives, where you can review 10-K filings for all public companies. Search for the 10-K report for the most recent completed fiscal year for two online retail companies of your choice (preferably ones operating in the same industry, such as Staples Inc. and Office Depot Inc.). Prepare a presentation that compares the financial stability and prospects of the two businesses, focusing specifically on the performance of their respective Internet operations.

2. Examine the financial statements for Amazon and Best Buy Co., Inc. What observations can you make about the two businesses? Which one is stronger financially and why? Which one's business model appears to be weaker and why? If you could identify two major problem areas for each, what would they be? Prepare a presentation that makes your case.

3. Conduct a thorough analysis—strategic and financial—of one of the following companies or another of your own choosing: Bluefly Inc., Fragrancenet.com, or 1-800-Flowers.com, Inc. Prepare a presentation that summarizes your observations about the company's Internet operations and future prospects.

4. Find an example not mentioned in the text of each of the four types of online retailing business models. Prepare a short report describing each firm and why it is an example of the particular business model.

5. Drawing on material in the chapter and your own research, prepare a short paper describing your views on the major social and legal issues facing online retailers.

6. Conduct a thorough analysis—strategic and financial—of one of the following Web sites: Progressive.com, Insure.com, or Insweb.com. Prepare a presentation that summarizes your observations about the company's operations and future prospects.

7. Choose a services industry not discussed in the chapter (such as legal services, medical services, accounting services, or another of your choosing). Prepare a 3- to 5-page report discussing recent trends affecting online provision of these services.

8. Together with a teammate, investigate the use of mobile apps in the financial services industries. Prepare a short joint presentation on your findings.

9. Find at least two examples of companies not mentioned in the text that act as transaction brokers and at least two examples of companies that provide a hands-on service. Prepare a short memo describing the services each company offers and explaining why the company should be categorized as a transaction broker or a hands-on service provider.

CHAPTER 10

Online Content and Media

After reading this chapter, you will be able to:

- Identify the major trends in the consumption of media and online content, and the major revenue models for digital content delivery.
- Understand digital rights management.
- Discuss the concept of media convergence and the challenges it faces.
- Understand the key factors affecting the online publishing industry.
- Understand the key factors affecting the online entertainment industry.

YouTube

and the Emerging Internet Broadcasting System (IBS)

I n 2013, YouTube is well along in implementing its $300 million initiative to create 150 YouTube channels devoted to a wide variety of topics, from sports to music, food, and news. Google (YouTube's owner) is providing seed funding of up to several million dollars each to independent, and in some cases, well-known celebrities such as rapper JayZ, and Hollywood directors and producers, to produce video content and develop their brands online. The idea is to enourage advertisers to move some of their TV ad dollars to the new YouTube channels.

The new channel experiment was so successful in its first eight months after it was announced in late 2011, that Google doubled down and put another

© Ingvar Björk / Alamy

$150 million into the experiment in July 2012. When completed, and assuming the audience appears, YouTube will be on its way to developing a new kind of television network, one based on the Internet. This new network will go head to head with cable and broadcast television giants competing for viewers, and of course, advertising dollars, which make it all happen. In addition to these Google-supported channels, there are one million other channels, which are self-supported by individuals, corporations, and even universities. Most YouTube channels are supported by advertising, and more than one billion people visit YouTube each month.

YouTube subscription channels, where viewers pay to subscribe to video content, are the newest wrinkle. Announced in 2013, the paid-subscription channels follow along the lines of music, movie, and TV online subscription services like Pandora and Netflix. Why wouldn't this work for YouTube as well?

When YouTube was launched in 2005, no one envisaged that within eight years it would grow into a possible alternative to the cable and broadcast television system. Starting out with 8 million videos streamed daily in 2005, YouTube today supports 6 billion hours of video each month, in some cases rivaling the audience sizes of cable and broadcast television, still the most popular source of video in the United States. According to Nielsen, YouTube reaches more U.S. adults in the valued 18–34 years of age demographic than any cable TV channel. Equally alluring to advertisers is that more than one-quarter of YouTube's global watch time involves using mobile devices (smartphones and tablets). Mobile is a fast growing advertising channel.

Despite this success in building a very large global audience of 1 billion monthly unique visitors (192 million in the United States), YouTube has only recently shown a profit, and advertisers are still not moving much of their $70 billion in television advertising to YouTube videos no matter how they get made or who supported them. Monetizing the audience is as much a problem for YouTube as it is for Facebook. There are a number of factors inhibiting YouTube from becoming a profitable commercial success that rivals television.

The most popular television shows in 2013 (NCIS, Sunday Night Football, The Big Bang Theory, and American Idol) routinely draw 15 to 20 million viewers each (this includes one week of DVR replays). The audience tends to stay for the full show. Reruns and syndication over the lifetime of the show can easily triple these numbers. Thus far, the highest number of concurrent live stream viewers that YouTube has ever drawn is the 8 million that watched Felix Baumgartner's record-breaking skydive from 24 miles above the earth in October 2012. However, many YouTube videos have more than 500 million total views. For instance, as of September 2013, the three most popular YouTube videos in history are music videos: Psy's Gangnam Style (over 1.7 billion views), Justin Bieber's Baby (over 900 million views), and Jennifer Lopez's On the Floor (over 690 million views). Unfortunately, no one knows how many views are generated by the same people, so the measures are not equivalent. Yet in comparison to television shows, YouTube videos do not attract as large a concurrent audience.

The average YouTube visitor stays for 14 minutes, hardly enough time to get a word in from advertisers whose ads appear next to the video, or are themselves videos pre-run before the real video you want to see. Television advertising in the United States generates $70 billion in revenues, dwarfing YouTube's expected $3.7 billion in revenue in 2013. In the last few years, rivals such as Netflix, Hulu, Apple, and Amazon have developed new Internet audiences for high-quality video, both from television series to movie downloads and streams. And there's the problem: While YouTube's overall unique audience in the United States is about 192 million a month in 2013, it cannot easily be "monetized" if that audience only stays for a few minutes. The YouTube audience lacks intense engagement.

YouTube has figured out a possible solution to this problem: improve the quality and length of videos so visitors stay longer than a five-minute music video, or worse, a few seconds to watch a dancing cat. While YouTube built its huge audience using amateur videos of less than professional quality, it cannot grow advertising revenues without substantially increasing the quality, length, and popularity of its videos. If Web 2.0 meant user-generated content, Web 3.0 means professional content that can generate ad revenues by engaging a national audience.

There are three sources of high-quality entertainment videos in the United States: Hollywood studios, broadcast and cable television networks (like HBO), and a small number of independent producers. While YouTube executives claim YouTube will never enter the media production business because it's too hard to get it right, YouTube is coming close to being both a producer of video content and the world's largest Internet video distributor. In reality, it is becoming a third platform, right alongside cable television and broadcast television. YouTube is being joined by other Internet juggernauts Apple, Netflix, and Amazon, all of whom are reshaping the television and movie video industry. Together, these new Internet broadcasters threaten to disrupt the highly successful 50-year-old cable television industry, reshaping television and movies with their Internet Broadcasting System.

Google has initiated a number of new projects to improve the quality and advertising potential of YouTube's videos. Like its rivals who hold dominant positions in Internet distribution (Apple, Facebook, Netflix, and Microsoft), YouTube has reached out to Hollywood movie and New York television producers to offer streaming movies and television series. It has struck deals with Sony, Lionsgate, television networks, and MGM to rent full-length movies and television series. YouTube and MGM struck a deal to bring 600 new rental titles to YouTube. Google is late to the streaming movie business, compared to Netflix and Amazon. All these Web broadcasters have to share ad revenues with the copyright owners of the content, reducing profitability. One possible solution to this profit-reducing situation is for Web broadcasters to create their own content designed specifically for the Web audience of 12- to 34-year-olds who are watching less TV on traditional television sets than 34+ year-old viewers, and instead, watching on their tablets and smartphones more.

Today, as a result of the Google/YouTube initiative mentioned at the beginning of the case, about 100 new channels are now online, running the gamut from the IGN Entertainment game channel, MyIsh (a channel for discovering new music), celebrity channels (Madonna), a slew of sports channels (ESPN for kids), to the Wall Street Journal's channel featuring Off Duty, a daily lifestyle show, and regular contributions from the Journal's name-brand reporters. Yes, that's right: the Wall Street Journal newspaper is a major new online source of video, along with the New York Times and other papers. Foodies don't despair: Bruce Seidel, who produced shows for the Food Network, including the Iron Chef, is working with a YouTube media company, Electus, to produce a food channel that will drive the Internet food conversation. YouTube is providing $5 million in seed money. Electus, a production studio, is not an amateur outfit, formed by Ben Silverman, former co-chairman of NBC Entertainment, and owned by Barry Diller's IAC Inc., a firm with 30 years of television and Internet content development.

While YouTube's channels are aimed at niche audiences (just like the hundreds of cable channels), collectively they will play to an audience of the one billion people worldwide, who are viewing 6 billion hours of video each month. The YouTube channel content will not require a monthly subscription fee (outside of an Internet connection), and content will be paid for by advertising (as in existing television systems). Moreover, the user determines the schedule for on-demand viewing and the device on which to view the show. What's not to like?

However, so far, the supported channels are not yet producing the kind of video that advertisers want. Despite the rise of Web video, revenue growth from the business has been slower than many in the industry expected, because advertisers have been resistant to shifting broadcast-TV ad dollars online. As a result, YouTube has changed some of its policies to help video creators generate more revenue from their videos, both on and off the site.

In May 2013 YouTube announced its version of a paid video subscription platform. Move over Netflix! Unlike Netflix, which charges $7.95 for unlimited access to several thousand streaming movies and TV shows (most several years old), the new subscription

SOURCES: "US Ad Spending Mid-2013 Forecast and Estimates," eMarketer ,Inc., July 2013; "Analyst Report: YouTube Revenue Like $3.7 Billion in 2013," by Dan Rayburn, SeekingAlpha.com, June 25, 2013; "YouTube Offers 'Sesame Street' and Martial Arts, for a Fee," by Brian Stelter, *New York Times*, May 9, 2013; "YouTube Unveils Paid Subscription Channels," by Amir Efrati, *Wall Street Journal*, May 9, 2013; "YouTube is Said to Plan a Subscription Option," by Brian Stelter, *New York Times*, May 6, 2013; "It's Getting Harder to Make Money on YouTube," by Anita Hamilton, Businessweek.com, April 22, 2013; "Felix Baumgartner Jump: Record 8m Watch Live on YouTube," by John Plunkett, *The Guardian*, October 14, 2012; "YouTube to Double Down on Its 'Channel' Experiment," by Amir Efrati, *New York Times*, July 30, 2012; "Wall Street Journal Launches Video Channel For YouTube," *Wall Street Journal*, February 1, 2012; "Hulu to Create More Original Shows," by Sam Schechner and Christopher Stewart, *Wall Street Journal*, January 17, 2012; "YouTube Announces Channels: Video Site Will Feel a Little More Like Cable TV," by D. M. Levine, *Adweek*, October 28, 2011; "New Layer of Content Amid Chaos on YouTube," by Ben Sisario, *New York Times*, March 12, 2011.

channels will allow individual video creators to charge viewers a monthly fee to watch some, or all, the content. Some of those who have signed up include Sesame Street, Ultimate Fight Championship (a wrestling show), the Jim Hensen Company (Muppets), National Geographic, The Laugh Factory, Gravitas Video on Demand, Baby First TV, and many others that are even less well known. These companies believe they can make more money off subscriptions from devoted followers than from advertising sold by YouTube. And this plan has the advantage of keeping Google and YouTube out of the content production business where it does not want to go.

YouTube executives explain that YouTube viewers will pay a la carte for access to special content using their credit cards, and will not be forced to pay a single monthly subscription fee like cable television's bundled approach. The creators of the channels, which could ultimately be Hollywood movie and TV studios, will keep 50% of the subscription revenue, and YouTube will keep the rest. For instance, National Geographic and Magnolia Pictures (a Hollywood production studio) are planning to charge $2.99 a month for their content. A minimum charge of 99 cents a month is planned for all the subscription channels. So far, about 30 video creators have signed up for the program designed to launch 50 subscription channels. It's possible that some of these channels will show live content, like rock concerts, while others will offer videos on demand.

At this point it is not clear if the new subscription service will do any better than Google's earlier channel-creation efforts, at least in terms of generating revenue. It is also not clear that the subscription service will produce the kind of engaging content that YouTube needs to monetize its video user base, which everyone agrees is very large. Some analysts believe the price point is too high considering that consumers can pay Netflix $7.95 a month and receive unlimited streamed movies. Google executives point out that Sesame Street's channel attracts intensely devoted, more educated viewers, willing and able to pay $2.99 a month. Comedy fans are especially willing to pay for live feeds or videos on demand.

Google has taken a path that is very innovative but also risky. It apparently is not able to cut deals with Hollywood studios for their movie content, in part, analysts explain, because of Hollywood studio mistrust of Google, which in the early years allowed YouTube to show copyrighted films and music videos, hurting Hollywood revenues. Google changed its algorithms in 2012 to push copyright-infringing sites lower in its rankings, and to work with copyright owners to lessen widespread infringement on Google's search platform. Google has decided not to produce its own TV shows to compete with cable television networks. Netflix, meanwhile, has struck deals in 2013 with major Hollywood movie studios in an effort to find exclusive content, and it has started producing its own, original, exclusive content in the form of TV shows like House of Cards and Arrested Development.

The opening case illustrates how online content distributors like YouTube are both moving into premium content production and sales, and also becoming Internet stores for traditional television and movie content, possibly rivaling existing cable and satellite distributors. If consumers can find their favorite television shows and movies online, then why should they pay for cable or satellite TV, especially when a variety of devices enable users to display their computer and phone screens on a home TV set? If consumers can watch their favorite shows on a smartphone or tablet, why should they buy a TV? As Internet users increasingly change their reading and viewing habits, spurred on by the growth of mobile media devices, they are challenging existing business models that worked for decades to support newspapers, books, magazines, television, and Hollywood movies. Clearly, the future of content—news, music, and video—is online. Today, the print industry, including newspapers, books, and magazines, is having a difficult time coping with the movement of their readership to the Web. Broadcast and cable television, along with Hollywood and the music labels, are also wrestling with outdated business models based on physical media. Established media giants are continuing to make extraordinary investments in unique online content, new technology, new digital distribution channels, and entirely new business models. Internet giants like Apple, Google, Amazon, and Facebook are competing to dominate online content distribution. In this chapter, we focus primarily on the publishing and entertainment industries as they attempt to transform their traditional media into Web-deliverable forms and experiences for consumers, while at the same time, earning profits.

10.1 ONLINE CONTENT

No other sector of the American economy has been so challenged by the Internet and the Web than the content industries. The online content industries are organized into two major categories: the print industries (newspapers, books, and magazines), and the online entertainment industries of television, feature-length movies, radio, video games, and music. Together, the online content industries are expected to generate revenues of about $24 billion in 2013 (including the online versions of print products).

As a communications medium, the Web is, by definition, a source of online content as well as a powerful new distribution platform. In this chapter, we will look closely at publishing (newspapers, books, and magazines) and entertainment (music, film, games, and television). These industries make up the largest share of the commercial content marketplace, both offline and online. In each of these industries, there are powerful offline brands, significant new pure-play online providers and distributors, consumer constraints and opportunities, a variety of legal issues, and new mobile technology platforms that offer an entirely new content distribution system in the form of smartphones and tablet computers.

Table 10.1 describes the most recent trends in online content and media for 2013–2014.

TABLE 10.1	WHAT'S NEW IN ONLINE CONTENT AND MEDIA, 2013–2014

BUSINESS

- The mobile platform of smartphones and tablets accelerates the transition to digital content.
- Vertical integration: Amazon, Google (YouTube), Hulu, and Netflix (owners of the distribution channel) enter the content production business for video, books, and online TV-like channels.
- Netflix transitions to a TV show distributor, along with Hulu, AOL, and Amazon, in order to capture television advertising dollars and find reliable high-quality content partners.
- YouTube launches over 100 entertainment channels offering TV-like amateur productions aimed at the twenty-something marketplace.
- Internet content begins to challenge cable TV for the home viewing audience.
- Music: digital music sales top physical sales.
- Radio: streaming music services such as Pandora and Spotify (Internet radio) are the fastest growing digital music segment.
- TV: the number of Americans watching TV online continues to grow, to over 120 million (about 50% of the U.S. Internet population).
- E-book sales continue to grow rapidly.
- Movies: Americans continue to spend more on online movies than for DVDs.
- Magazines experience a small comeback via high-resolution tablet displays and magazine apps like Flipboard and Zinio.
- Newspapers: online readership exceeds print readership. Print ad revenues continue to fall, while digital ad revenues increase. However, online ad revenues do not make up for lost print ad revenues. Online newspaper audience grows at double digits as newspapers implement paywalls.
- Gaming market: console game sales stagnate as mobile gaming soars.
- The four Internet Titans compete: Apple, Google, Amazon, and Facebook vie for ownership of the online entertainment and content ecosystem, selling experiences as well as content.
- Business models: content owners adopt a mixture of business models: advertising-supported (free), subscriptions, and a la carte payment.
- Paid content and free content coexist: the common notion of the Internet means free information is being replaced by consumer acceptance of paying for premium content.
- Revenues from online media are the fastest growing media revenues, reducing revenues from physical products such as DVDs, CDs, newspapers, magazines, and printed books.
- Content gets social: social network sites become a major source of content recommendations and content distribution partners for content.

(continued)

TABLE 10.1	WHAT'S NEW IN ONLINE CONTENT AND MEDIA, 2013–2014 (CONT.)

TECHNOLOGY

- Smartphones, tablet computers, and e-readers together create a totally mobile multimedia entertainment environment.
- Netflix remains the largest consumer of bandwidth, constituting about 35% of Internet traffic.
- With more than 1 billion now available, apps become the foundation for an "app economy" as they morph into content-distribution platforms that are proprietary, where users can be charged for content.
- Cloud storage services grow to serve the huge market for mobile device content. Apple launches iCloud video service that allows users to watch purchased videos on multiple Apple devices (iPhones, iPads, and Macs). Amazon and Google develop similar cloud services.

SOCIETY

- Media consumption: Americans spend around 4,500 hours a year consuming various types of media, more than twice as many hours as they work.
- Time spent using digital media exceeds time spent with television.
- Time spent on mobile exceeds time spent on PCs
- Internet time exposure continues to grow rapidly, surpassing newspapers and music, but is still behind traditional television.
- Content consumption goes increasingly mobile.
- Young adults watch more TV on the Internet, less on cable.
- Apple is found to have engaged in e-book price fixing.

CONTENT AUDIENCE AND MARKET: WHERE ARE THE EYEBALLS AND THE MONEY?

The average American adult spends around 4,500 hours each year consuming various media, twice the amount of time spent at work (2,000 hours/year) (see **Figure 10.1**). U.S. entertainment and media (E & M) revenues (both online and offline) in 2013 are estimated to be $526 billion, and they are expected to grow at a compound rate of 6% to a total of $632 billion in 2017 (PWC, 2013). Sales of tablets and smartphones have created new revenue streams for entertainment and media firms as consumer behavior changes in response to the new technologies. Content is no longer tied to physical products, and can be delivered over the Internet to multiple mobile devices, reducing costs for consumers. Currently, online digital E&M revenue is 31% of total E&M revenue, or $163 billion in 2013. Analysts estimate that by 2017, digital E&M revenue will be 43% of E&M revenue or about $268 billion (PricewaterhouseCoopers, 2013).

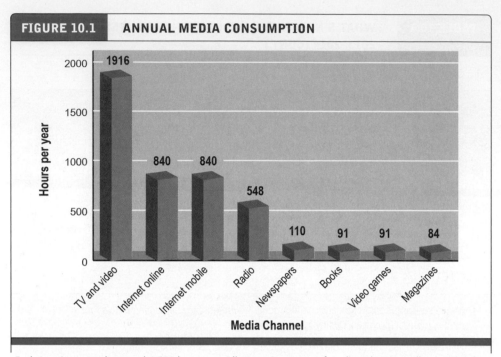

| FIGURE 10.1 | ANNUAL MEDIA CONSUMPTION |

Each American spends around 4,500 hours annually on various types of media. Television still consumes the most hours, but the time spent on the Internet, with mobile media, and playing video games, when added together, accounts for almost as many hours.

SOURCES: Based on data from eMarketer, Inc., 2013a; authors' estimates.

Media Utilization

The proliferation of new mobile media devices—tablets and smartphones—has led to an increase in the total amount of time spent listening to radio, watching TV and movies, and reading books, newspapers, and even magazines. An increasing percentage of this media engagement is digital. Although traditional TV and radio audiences have declined slightly, about 1.7% in the last few years, the actual amount of hours spent watching TV has not changed despite the advent of the Internet (Nielsen, 2013a). Television remains the most popular medium (5.3 hours a day on average), followed by the Internet, on desktops and laptops, mobile Internet, and then radio. Together, TV, the Internet, and radio account for more than 77% of the hours spent consuming various media. While the number of hours of TV viewing used to be far larger than Internet usage, since the development of mobile devices, total desktop plus mobile Internet is 4.6 hours, almost as much as television. In the next few years, total online usage is likely to exceed television. On the other hand, a great deal of Internet usage is watching time-shifted television shows! In 2013, 120 million people use their computers to watch television shows, about 40% of the population. Therefore, the distinction between Internet usage and television usage is not easy to make. The Internet, television, and movies are converging into a single digital stream. This convergence is described later in the chapter. Surveys report that 20% of online users read newspapers, books, and magazines less, but Internet usage does not reduce their television viewing (Nielsen, 2013a). Well over 50% of television viewers multitask while watching television, usually using a smartphone or tablet computer, texting with friends, reading e-mail, searching the Web, or visiting social network sites (eMarketer, Inc., 2012a, 2013b).

Internet and Traditional Media: Cannibalization versus Complementarity

Several studies reveal that time spent on the Internet reduces consumer time available for other media (Pew Research Center, 2013). This is referred to as cannibalization. The alternative argument is that the Internet and traditional media are complementary and mutually supportive rather than substitutive. True, there has been a massive shift of the general audience to the Web, and once there, a large percentage of time is spent on viewing content. Yet more recent data finds a more complex picture. Despite the availability of the Internet on high-resolution tablet computers, television viewing remains strong, video viewing on all devices has increased, and the reading of all kinds of books, including physical books, has increased. Total music consumption measured in hours a day listening to music has increased dramatically even as CDs decline, and movie consumption has increased dramatically even as DVD sales decline markedly. The impact of the Internet on media appears to be increasing the total demand for media, and even in some cases, stimulating demand for traditional products like books. It is also the case that content firms' physical products—printed newspapers, magazines, music CDs, and movie DVDs—are being replaced by digital versions.

Consumers are spending about 20% of their time online on social networks, 17% of their time doing e-mail, 13% of their time watching online video, 12% of their time searching, and 11% of their time playing online games. The remainder of the time is spent doing other activities, such as reading online newspapers, magazines, and blogs, and listening to online radio (eMarketer, Inc., 2013c). In general, Internet users spend 15%–20% less time reading traditional books, newspapers, and magazines, watching broadcast television and box office movies, talking on the phone, or listening to broadcast radio. On the other hand, Internet users consume more media of all types than non-Internet users. This reflects the demographics of the Internet user as more literate, wealthier, more technically savvy, and more media-aware. In addition, Internet users multitask when using the Internet, frequently listening to music, watching television, and using instant messaging while working on other tasks.

Multimedia use reduces the cannibalization impact of the Internet for some visual and aural media, but obviously not for reading physical books or newspapers. And even for these print media, the Internet is simply an alternative source; Internet users are increasing the time they spend online reading newspapers, magazines, and even books. Ironically, the new mobile media platform of smartphones and tablet computers has led to an explosion in reading of both newspapers and books, but digital versions, not the printed versions. Bottom line: the Internet is substituting for physical mediums, but it can be, and often is, supportive and complementary to content owned by traditional media firms, including newspapers, magazines, book publishers, television, and Hollywood movies. It's all about content regardless of the means of transmission.

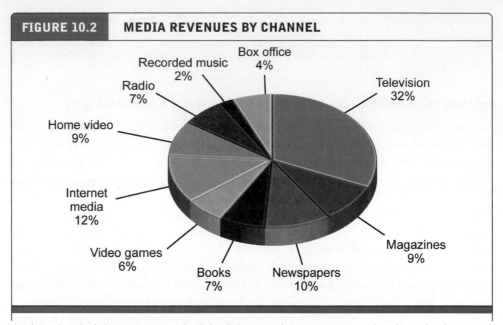

FIGURE 10.2 **MEDIA REVENUES BY CHANNEL**

Traditional media (television, print, and radio) still dominate the entertainment and media market, but Internet media (streaming videos, music, and content) is the fastest growing segment.

SOURCES: Based on data from industry sources; authors' estimates.

Media Revenues

An examination of media revenues reveals a somewhat different pattern when compared to media consumption (see **Figure 10.2**). In 2013, media of all kinds is expected to generate $209 billion in revenue (not including transmission fees for content). Television accounts for 32% of media revenues, print media (books, newspapers, and magazines) accounts for 26%, Internet media 12%, music media (radio and recorded music) 9%, box office 6%, and video games 6%. Internet media, while relatively small now, is growing at 12% annually, far faster than traditional media revenues.

Three Revenue Models for Digital Content Delivery: Subscription, A La Carte, and Advertising-Supported (Free and Freemium)

There are three revenue models for delivering content on the Internet. The two "pay" models are subscriptions (usually "all you can eat") and a la carte (pay for what you use). The third model uses advertising revenue to provide content for free, usually with a "freemium" (higher price) option. There is also completely free, user-generated content, which we will discuss later. Contrary to early analysts' projections that "free" would drive "paid" out of business ("information wants to be free"), it turns out that both models are viable now and in the near future. Consumers increasingly choose to pay for high-quality, convenient, and unique content, and they have gladly accepted "free" advertiser-supported content when that content is deemed not worth paying for but entertaining nevertheless. There's nothing contradictory about all three models working in tandem and cooperatively: free content can drive customers to paid content, as the recorded music firms have discovered with services like Pandora and Spotify.

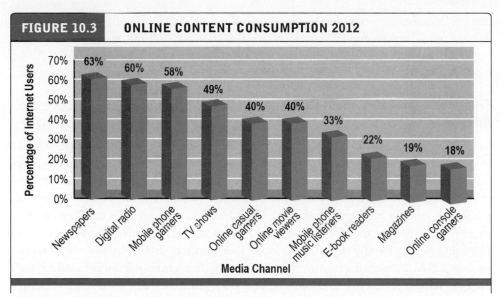

FIGURE 10.3 **ONLINE CONTENT CONSUMPTION 2012**

SOURCES: Based on data from eMarketer, Inc., 2013b; industry sources; authors' estimates.

Online Content Consumption

Now let's look at what kinds of online content Internet users purchase or view online (**Figure 10.3**). It may be a surprise to most that over 60% of Internet users read newspapers and 60% listen to digital radio, the two most popular activities. Newspapers and radio? Not what one might expect. Mobile phone gamers (58%) and TV shows (49%) are nearly as popular, followed by movies and mobile phone music listening. E-book consumption (22%) has grown at triple-digit rates since the Kindle was introduced in 2007 and the iPad in 2010. What this reveals is that Internet users retain their affinity to traditional formats—newspapers, radio, TV shows, books, and music tracks and albums—and bring these tastes to the Internet.

Figure 10.4 shows the estimated revenues from the online entertainment and media industries, projected to 2016. In 2013, total paid online entertainment content is estimated to be $15 billion, and to reach $26 billion by 2016. Online video (including premium movies), online TV, and music are the largest and fastest growing online segments.

Now let's look at the fastest growing paid content area: videos (which includes movies, short videos, and TV shows). This audience is huge and growing very rapidly. **Figure 10.5** shows the top online video sites in May 2013. The top 10 sites had over 182 million video viewers. The largest site remains Google (YouTube) with 156 million viewers, followed by Facebook, AOL, and the fast growing music video site, VEVO. The monetary value of all these videos is that they attract large audiences that can be shown ads.

The overall size of the online video audience (with more than 182 million monthly unique viewers in the United States) is about the same size as the traditional television audience. There are 115 million households with televisions, representing about

200 million individuals who tune in every month. However, major TV events tend to draw a much higher one-time viewership. For instance, 108 million people watched Super Bowl XLVII in 2013. No Internet video has drawn such a large audience during a single time period.

Free or Fee: Attitudes About Paying for Content and the Tolerance for Advertising

In the early years of online content, multiple surveys found that large majorities of the Internet audience expected to pay nothing for online content although equally large majorities were willing to accept advertising as a way to pay for free content. In reality, on the early Web, there wasn't much high-quality content. By 2013, attitudes towards paying for content had greatly changed. Until Internet services such as iTunes arrived in 2007, few thought the "fee" model could compete with the "free" model, and most Internet aficionados and experts concluded that information on the Internet wants to be free. Cable TV systems (networks themselves) offer a totally different history: they always charged for service and content, and cable TV experts never thought information wanted to be free. Neither did the Hollywood and New York media companies that paid for and provided the content to television and movie theaters. In 2013, millions of Internet users pay for high-quality content delivered on a convenient device such as a smartphone or tablet computer or using Internet TV services like Netflix or Amazon.

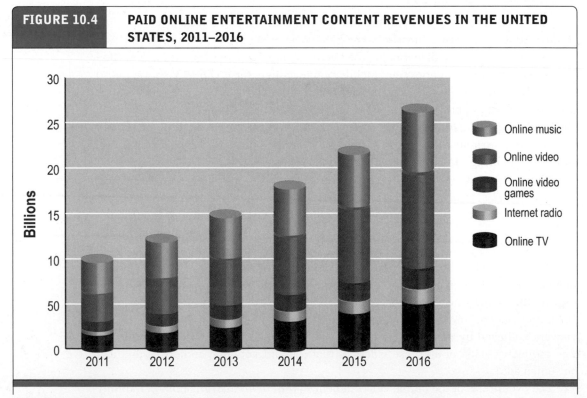

FIGURE 10.4 PAID ONLINE ENTERTAINMENT CONTENT REVENUES IN THE UNITED STATES, 2011–2016

SOURCES: Based on data from industry sources; authors' estimates.

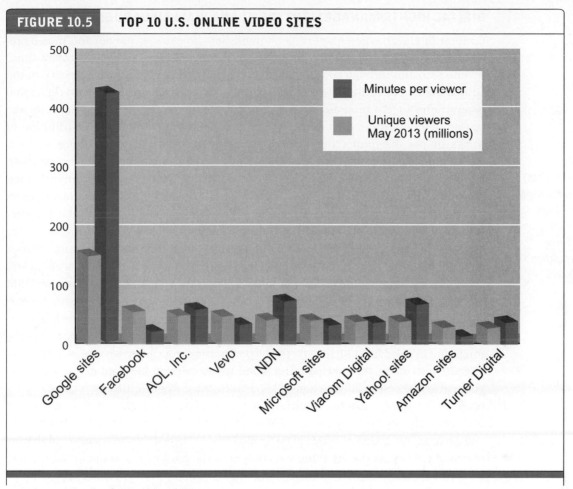

FIGURE 10.5 **TOP 10 U.S. ONLINE VIDEO SITES**

Legend:
- Minutes per viewer
- Unique viewers May 2013 (millions)

Sites: Google sites, Facebook, AOL, Inc., Vevo, NDN, Microsoft sites, Viacom Digital, Yahoo! sites, Amazon sites, Turner Digital

SOURCES: Based on data from comScore, 2013.

Like cable TV, Apple iTunes charges for service and content as well. In a demonstration of just how much quality online content is worth paying for, by 2013, Apple had sold 25 billion songs, 500 million TV shows, and more than 150 million movies (NPD Group, 2013a). Pandora, the second largest source of Internet music with 200 million subscribers, and the largest streaming service, has 70 million monthly unique visitors. While an estimated 21 million Internet users in the United States still download songs from illegal P2P sites (down from 33 million in 2005), 80 million buy music from legal sites in 2013, and over 150 million listen to online radio and streaming services, which are difficult to pirate, generating $4.1 billion in sales (eMarketer, Inc., 2013d). Worldwide, iTunes has more than 500 million customers with credit cards on file.

The culture of the Internet is beginning to change when firms such as YouTube (and its parent Google), which started out with a business model based on amateur videos and illegally uploaded music videos, begin cooperating closely with Hollywood and New York production studios for premium content. As it turns out, free content isn't worth very much and should be free, especially if producers give it away. Premium content is worth a great deal, and should be priced accordingly.

DIGITAL RIGHTS MANAGEMENT (DRM) AND WALLED GARDENS

Content producers—newspapers, book publishers, television, movie, and music producers—generate revenue and profits from their creations, and they protect these revenue streams through copyright. Created by Congress in Article I, Section 8 of the United States Constitution, Congress granted authors and inventors copyrights and patent rights to "the progress of science and useful arts." The first Copyright Act was passed in 1790. In the digital age, when exact copies and widescale distribution of works are possible, protecting the copyrights to content is a major challenge.

digital rights management (DRM)
refers to the combination of technical and legal means for protecting digital content from unlimited reproduction without permission

Digital rights management (DRM) refers to a combination of technical (both hardware and software) and legal means for protecting digital content from unlimited reproduction and distribution without permission. Essentially, DRM can prevent users from purchasing and making copies for widespread distribution over the Internet without compensating the content owners. While music tracks in the iTunes Store were originally protected by DRM, in 2009, Apple abandoned the practice because of user objections, and because Amazon had opened an online music store in 2007 without any DRM protections, with the support of music label firms, who came to realize that DRM prevented them from exploiting the opportunities of the Internet and perhaps encouraged an illegal market. Most music firms with subscription services use technologies that limit the time period that a song can be played without resubscribing. For instance, songs downloaded from Rhapsody, the largest music subscription service, will not play after 30 days unless the user pays the monthly subscription fee. And if you don't pay, you will lose access to all your songs. Movies streamed from Netflix are technically difficult for the average user to capture and share. Likewise, music streamed from Pandora is cumbersome to record and share. These newer digital services, including both Apple and Amazon, use a kind of DRM called "walled garden" to restrict the widespread sharing of content. They do this by tying the content to the hardware and operating system. E-books purchased from Amazon can only be played on Kindles or Kindle apps running on smartphones, tablets, computers, or browsers. Kindle books cannot be converted to other formats, like epubs or Adobe PDF files. By locking the content to a physical device, or a digital stream with no local storage, the appliance makers derive additional revenues and profits by locking customers into their service or device. Streaming any content from a cloud server also offers publishers protection from piracy.

While the issue of DRM is often cast as a moral contest between content owners and hackers bent on distributing and using free music, films, and books, the industry titans themselves are divided on DRM. The telecommunications and digital device industries directly benefit from the illegal and unfettered downloading of music and other content. For instance, Apple, Intel, Sony, and Microsoft all benefited from the explosion in illegal sharing of intellectual property simply because users will buy more devices. A mantra voiced first by Steve Jobs as "Rip. Mix. Burn" became an Apple advertising slogan and popular rationale for copying CDs and sharing or posting the music online for commercial purposes. [In subsequent interviews, Jobs said he did not intend this remark to encourage people to steal music, and in fact, he was a strong supporter of protecting the intellectual property rights of all artists and their production firms (Isaacson, 2011)]. Likewise, Verizon, SBC Communications, and Time Warner Cable (and the major Internet trunk line owners) also depend on their networks being kept as busy as possible. In 2013, an estimated 23% of global Internet bandwidth consists of unauthorized stolen material. BitTorrent traffic—mostly pirated video, but music and books as well—has fallen drastically from its high of 35% in 2005 to about 10% of Internet traffic in the United States. Netflix has replaced BitTorrent as the leading bandwidth user with 35% of all Internet traffic in the United States (Sandvine, 2013). Internet service providers, telecom providers, and even search engines like Google derive revenue from an environment where users can share any content whether or not it is legally obtained content. In contrast, content creators and owners often insist on DRM, and are supportive of walled gardens that make their content unusable on more general purpose platforms such as PCs, using Adobe Flash or PDF files. Content producers make nothing on the delivery devices or the telecommunications infrastructure. To understand all this, you need to keep your eye on the money.

In 2003, iTunes provided a partial but game-changing solution to illegal downloading and sharing by creating iTunes, and managed to make it a popular alternative to illegal file-sharing services like Kazaa, eDonkey, and Limewire. Of all the device makers, Apple has turned out to be the most friendly to artists and music labels. Google Play and Amazon's Store are closely following in the iTunes footsteps by providing an environment where users can conveniently download or stream legal content for a very low cost. By 2013, it is clear to the major online content distributors that more revenue can be generated from legal distribution of paid content than illegal distribution.

MEDIA INDUSTRY STRUCTURE

The media content industry prior to 1990 was composed of many smaller independent corporations specializing in content creation and distribution in the separate industries of film, television, book and magazine publishing, and newspaper publishing. During the 1990s and into this century, after an extensive period of consolidation, huge entertainment and publishing media conglomerates emerged.

The media industry is still organized largely into three separate vertical stovepipes: print, movies, and music. Each segment is dominated by a few key players. We do not include the delivery platform firms here, such as AT&T, Verizon, Sprint, Dish Network, or Comcast, because in general they do not create content but instead move content across cable, satellite, and telephone lines. The transmission industry is itself highly oligopolistic, with two dominant players in each distribution market. In telephony and wireless distribution, AT&T and Verizon dominate. In cable distribution, Comcast and Time Warner dominate. Generally, there is very little crossover from one segment to another. Newspapers do not also produce Hollywood films, and publishing firms do not own newspapers or film production studios. The purchase of the *Washington Post* in August 2013 by Jeff Bezos, the founder of Amazon, and an Internet mogul in his own right, was an anomaly. Even within media conglomerates that span several different media segments, separate divisions control each media segment. The competition between corporate divisions in mega-sized corporations is often more severe than with marketplace competitors.

While the commercial media industry is highly concentrated within each segment, the much larger media ecosystem includes literally millions of individuals and independent entrepreneurs creating content in the form of blogs, videos on YouTube and

VEVO, and music on indie sites like madeloud.com. At times, the viewership (or readership) of these much smaller but numerous players exceeds that of the media titans.

MEDIA CONVERGENCE: TECHNOLOGY, CONTENT, AND INDUSTRY STRUCTURE

Media convergence is a much used but poorly defined term. There are at least three dimensions of media where the term convergence has been applied: technology, content (artistic design, production, and distribution), and the industry's structure as a whole. Ultimately for the consumer, convergence means being able to get any content you want, when you want it, on whatever platform you want it—from an iPod to an iPad, Android phone, or home PC, or set-top device like Apple TV.

Technological Convergence

technological convergence

development of hybrid devices that can combine the functionality of two or more existing media platforms into a single device

Convergence from a technology perspective **(technological convergence)** has to do with the development of hybrid devices that can combine the functionality of two or more existing media platforms, such as books, newspapers, television, movies, radio, and games, into a single device. Examples of technological convergence include the iPad, iPhone, and Android ("smartphones") that combine print, music, pictures, and video in a single device.

Content Convergence

content convergence

convergence in the design, production, and distribution of content

A second dimension of convergence is **content convergence**. There are three aspects to content convergence: design, production, and distribution.

There is a historical pattern in which content created in an older media technology migrates to the new technology largely intact, with little artistic change. Slowly, the different media are integrated so that consumers can move seamlessly back and forth among them, and artists (and producers) learn more about how to deliver content in the new media. Later, the content itself is transformed by the new media as artists learn how to fully exploit the capabilities in the creation process. At this point, content convergence and transformation has occurred—the art is different because of the new capabilities inherent to new tools. For instance, European master painters of the fifteenth century in Italy, France, and the Netherlands (such as van Eyck, Caravaggio, Lotto, and Vermeer) quickly adopted new optical devices such as lenses, mirrors, and early projectors called *camera obscura* that could cast near-photographic quality images on canvases, and in the process they developed new theories of perspective and new techniques of painting landscapes and portraits. Suddenly, paintings took on the qualities of precision, detail, and realism found later in photographs (Boxer, 2001). A similar process is occurring today as artists and writers assimilate new digital and Internet tools into their toolkits. For instance, GarageBand from Apple enables low-budget independent bands (literally working in garages) to mix and control eight different digital music tracks to produce professional sounding recordings on a shoe-string budget. Writers of books are beginning to think about video and interactive versions of their books. Online newspapers are turning to live video as an enhancement to their stories.

On the production side, tools for digital editing and processing (for film and television) are driving content convergence. Given that the most significant cost of content is its creation, if there is a wide diversity of target delivery platforms, then it is wise to develop and produce only once using technology that can deliver to multiple platforms. Generally, this means creating content on digital devices (hardware and software) so that it can be delivered on multiple digital platforms.

On the distribution side, it is important that distributors and the ultimate consumers have the devices needed to receive, store, and experience the product. While for the most part technology companies have succeeded in giving consumers portable devices to receive online content, it has been more difficult for the content owners to come up with new, profitable business models.

Figure 10.6 depicts the process of media convergence and transformation using the example of books. For example, consider this book. In 2013, this book was written with a view to appearing on iPads and Kindle e-book readers, and is moving closer to the media maturity stage, in which the book will be available mostly as a purely digital product with substantial visual and aural content that can be displayed on many different digital devices. By that time, the "learning experience" will be transformed by greater use of interactive graphics, videos, as well as an integrated testing system that monitors student performance during the semester. Even the number of pages read by students, and the time on page, will be accounted for by this near-future digital learning system. Traditional bound books will probably still be available (books have many

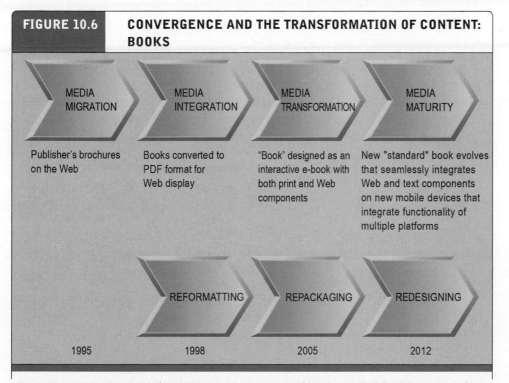

FIGURE 10.6 **CONVERGENCE AND THE TRANSFORMATION OF CONTENT: BOOKS**

MEDIA MIGRATION — Publisher's brochures on the Web

MEDIA INTEGRATION — Books converted to PDF format for Web display

MEDIA TRANSFORMATION — "Book" designed as an interactive e-book with both print and Web components

MEDIA MATURITY — New "standard" book evolves that seamlessly integrates Web and text components on new mobile devices that integrate functionality of multiple platforms

REFORMATTING — REPACKAGING — REDESIGNING

1995 — 1998 — 2005 — 2012

The Internet is making it possible for publishers and writers to transform the standard "book" into a new form that integrates features of both text and the Internet, and also transforms the content of the book itself.

advantages), but most likely, print editions will be printed on demand by customers using their own print facilities.

Industry Structure Convergence

industry convergence
merger of media enterprises into synergistic combinations that create and cross-market content on different platforms

A third dimension of convergence is the structure of the various media industries. **Industry convergence** refers to the merger of media enterprises into powerful, synergistic combinations that can cross-market content on many different platforms and create new works that use multiple platforms. This can take place either through purchases or through strategic alliances. Traditionally, each type of media—film, text, music, television—had its own separate industry, typically composed of very large players. For instance, the entertainment film industry has been dominated by a few large Hollywood-based production studios, book publication is dominated by a few large book publishers, and music production is dominated by four global record label firms.

However, the Internet has created forces that make mergers and partnerships among media and Internet firms a necessary business proposition. Media industry convergence may be necessary to finance the substantial changes in both the technology platform and the content. Traditional media firms who create the content generally do not possess the core competencies or financial heft to distribute it on the Internet. Technology companies that dominate the Internet (Google, Apple, Amazon, and Facebook) have the competency and wealth to pursue Internet channel strategies, but do not have the competencies needed to create content. Business combinations and partnerships are made to solve these issues.

While traditional media companies have not done well in purchases of Internet platform companies, the technology owners such as Apple, Amazon, Facebook, Microsoft, and Google have generally avoided merging with media companies, and instead rely on contractual arrangements with media companies to protect intellectual property rights and to create a business pricing model that both parties can accept. However, this pattern may be changing. For instance, in 2012, CBS Inc. produced a television show for Netflix; Netflix and Hulu have begun production and distribution of their own original TV shows; Google is producing original content designed for Internet distribution on YouTube. Amazon created its own book imprint, Amazon Books Publishing, and entered the book publishing business.

In the end, consumers' demands for content anywhere, anytime, and on any device is pushing the technology and content companies towards cooperation or outright purchases.

MAKING A PROFIT WITH ONLINE CONTENT: FROM FREE TO FEE

Despite the resistance of users in the early years of e-commerce, there is broad consensus that many online consumers, perhaps 25%, are increasingly willing to pay for high-quality content, at their discretion, and that sites offering a mix of free and fee content can be successful. In 2013, this is still an untested idea in some content areas, especially newspapers.

net value
that portion of perceived customer value that can be attributed to the fact that content is available on the Internet

There appear to be four factors required to charge for online content: focused market, specialized content, sole-source monopoly, and high perceived net value (see **Figure 10.7**). **Net value** refers to that portion of perceived customer value that can

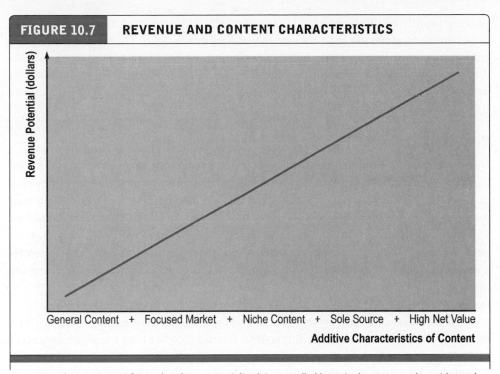

FIGURE 10.7 REVENUE AND CONTENT CHARACTERISTICS

As content becomes more focused and more specialized, is controlled by a single source, and provides real value to consumers for an Internet delivery (i.e., speed, searchability, and portability), the prospects for charging fees for access increase.

be attributed to the fact that content is available on the Internet. Net value derives from the ability of consumers to instantaneously access the information on the Web or mobile device, search large and deep historical archives, and move the online information to other documents or devices easily. Customer convenience is a large part of net value. For instance, Hoover's provides four different subscriptions ranging from $75 a month to $2,995 for a professional subscription. Hoover's content addresses a focused market (business analysts and executive search firms); it has specialized content (data gathered by its own reporters and other sources); it is the sole source for some of this information; and it has high perceived value because it can be quickly accessed, searched, and downloaded into other documents and made a part of business decision making. And the consumers are in a hurry to get the information. In general, the opportunity for paid content varies by the nature of the content and the audience.

10.2 THE ONLINE PUBLISHING INDUSTRY

Nothing is quite so fundamental to a civilized society as reading text. Text is the way we record our history, current events, thoughts, and aspirations, and transmit them to all others in the civilization who can read. Even television shows and movies require scripts. Today, the publishing industry (composed of books, newspapers, magazines, and periodicals) is a $92 billion media sector based originally on print, and now moving rapidly to the Internet. The Internet offers the text publishing industry an opportunity to move toward a new generation of newspapers, magazines, and books that are produced, processed, stored, distributed, and sold over the Web, available anytime, anywhere, and on any device. The same Internet offers the possibility of destroying many existing print-based businesses that may not be able to make this transition and remain profitable.

ONLINE NEWSPAPERS

Newspapers in 2013 are the most troubled segment of the publishing industry, troubles that result almost exclusively from the availability of alternatives to the printed newspaper, as well as a sluggish response by management to the opportunities on the Internet for news, if not newspapers. Also important is the failure of newspaper management to protect its valuable content from being distributed for free by headline aggregators such as Yahoo, MSN, and Google, as well as tens of millions of bloggers and tweeters. These search firms can index online newspaper content, and provide search results to users' queries (as they display ads to those same users and derive revenue). While these search firms do link to the actual newspaper articles, they have in the meantime generated revenue for themselves based on the newspaper article content. As it turns out, there wouldn't be a Google or Yahoo news functionality without traditional reporters and editors who work for newspapers and create the content. As you may have noticed, a single, original, high-quality newspaper article generates hundreds if not thousands of Internet knockoff articles on blogs, news aggregation sites, and content generator sites.

Over 60% of newspapers have reduced news staff in the last few years, and 61% report shrinking the size of the newspaper. Readership has been declining for 10 years, print edition advertising is down 15% a year, subscriptions are down, and old print readers are not being replaced by young readers, who instead get their news online. To make matters worse, in the slow growth period of 2010–2013, online ads declined another 16% (from $25 billion to $21 billion), and the amount spent on Internet advertising in general now equals that spent on newspaper advertising. Alternative online sources such as Yahoo, Google, and even blogs, have became major sources of news for many Americans. Much of this "news" is redistributed content generated by newspapers! Alternatives to newspaper classified ads like Craigslist have decimated newspaper classified revenues.

But there is some good news too. Online readership of newspapers is growing at more than 10% a year. New reading devices from smartphones to e-readers, iPads, and tablet PCs connected to wireless networks offer opportunities for online newspapers to be read everywhere. Newstand apps are growing in popularity. A new Internet culture is supportive of paying for quality content. Newspaper owners, faced with extinction, are exploring ways to protect their content, and are introducing "pay walls," paid "premium" news and views, a la carte purchase of articles, subscriptions to digital versions, and online apps for mobile devices. Pure Internet aggregators of news such as Google and Yahoo are beginning to recognize that if the newspaper industry disappears, there will be little news to aggregate, distribute, and place ads against. Amateur blogs and tweets may be wonderful for expressing opinions, or making instant reports on events as they occur, but they are no substitute for professional reporters and editors, and not a place for brand-conscious advertisers. Therefore, the Internet distributors are recognizing they have a vested interest in keeping the newspaper content industry in working order.

According to the Newspaper Association of America, in 2013, print newspapers have around 48 million paid subscribers, down from 62 million in 1990. Offline newspaper readership of physical papers has declined at about 2% a year for several years, while online readership is at an all-time high of about 114 million daily readers with online traffic growing at 10% annually in 2013. The important 21–34 age group is growing at 17%. Nearly 50% of all Web users on a typical day visit an online newspaper. The online audience increases the overall footprint of the newspaper media. Total print edition advertising in newspapers in 2013 is expected to be around $18 billion, and is declining at 10% a year. Since 2002, advertising revenues have fallen by 50%. Partially offsetting these negative trends is that subscription revenues produced by loyal daily readers have been stable over the decade at around $10 billion. However, online newspaper ad revenues in 2013 are expected to be about $3.6 billion, growing at 6% a year. Still, the online ad revenues represent only 13% of all revenues, not nearly enough to support current operations. In a nutshell, the problem confronting newspapers is how to grow online revenues fast enough so as to offset the losses from print advertising (Myers, 2012; Pew Research, 2013; Newspaper Association of America, 2013). To date, this has been an attractive but elusive target.

Audience Size and Growth

There are more than 10,000 online newspapers in the world. Globally, online newspaper readership is growing at 17% a year. According to comScore, online newspapers experienced very strong growth in recent quarters. (See **Figure 10.8** for a list of the top ten in the United States.) In Europe, half of all Internet users visit online newspaper sites, and the global newspaper audience is estimated at over 700 million! The online newspapers attract a wealthy and consumer-intense demographic, reaching 64% of 25- to 34-year-olds and 75% of individuals in households earning more than $100,000 a year on average throughout the quarter. The online newspaper audience is also highly engaged, generating 4.1 billion page views each month, spending nearly 3.4 billion minutes browsing the sites (comScore, 2011). The average online visitor stayed on the site for 35 to 45 minutes. Online newspapers are the dominant local Web site: 62% of Internet users look for local news on a local newspaper Web site. Given this huge online newspaper audience, it is clear that the future of newspapers lies in the online desktop and mobile market even as readership and subscriptions to the traditional print newspapers continue to decline at a steady pace.

Next to social networks, newspapers produce the largest online audiences of any media, and in that sense, contrary to popular opinion, are one of the most successful forms of online content to date. The Internet provides existing branded newspapers the opportunity to extend their brands to a new online audience, and also gives entrepreneurial firms the opportunity to offer services—such as classified job listings—on the Web that were previously delivered by newspapers. Online newspapers are the top choice for local news and information for Internet users in the United States. Unfortunately, newspaper management has not been able to monetize this very large online audience. The purchase of the *Washington Post* by Amazon founder, and media

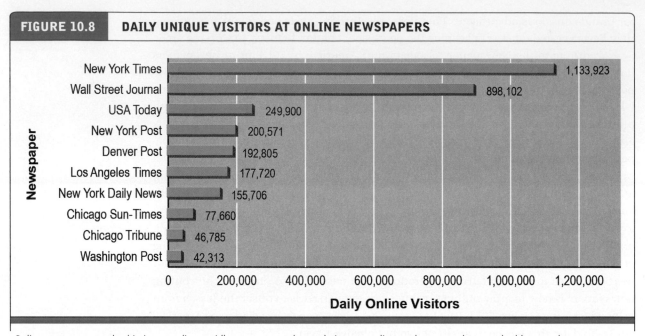

FIGURE 10.8   **DAILY UNIQUE VISITORS AT ONLINE NEWSPAPERS**

Online newspaper readership is expanding rapidly as more people get their news online, and as smartphone and tablet apps become more widespread.

SOURCES: Based on data from Alliance for Audited Media, 2013.

industry disrupter, Jeff Bezos in August 2013, has raised hopes among commentators that skilled e-commerce professionals can monetize the online newspaper audience. Keep reading until next year!

While newspapers have done an excellent job at increasing their Web presence and audience, few have reached break-even operations. Instead, online classified and advertising revenues have not kept pace with the fall in revenues from their traditional print editions. There are several reasons for this, including increased competition from general portal sites moving into the content aggregation business, loss of classified ads to online portals and job sites, and free listing services such as Craigslist. Craigslist is reported to have wiped out $50 million in classified ads for the *San Francisco Chronicle* alone.

The Web has provided an opportunity for newspapers to extend their offline brands, but at the same time it has given entrepreneurs the opportunity to disaggregate newspaper content—such as weather, classified ads, or current national and international news—and create stand-alone Web sites that compete with online and offline newspapers.

Newspaper Business Models

The online newspaper industry has gone through several business models, from fee to free, and most recently, struggling to return to a fee-based pay wall and subscription business model. In the past, a few online newspapers such as the *New York Times*, *Wall Street Journal*, and *Financial Times* (U.K.) charged for some or all online content, especially premium content. In the case of the *New York Times*, access to the *New York Times* archives was a paid service. Most newspapers did not charge for online content, and even the *New York Times* abandoned its Times Select subscription service for archived content. The result was that content generated by newspapers became freely available across the Web, where it could be indexed by search engines that redistributed the headlines and content. Newspaper headlines became the primary content on Google News and Yahoo News. Newspapers benefited from this because a Google listing brought readers to the newspaper, where readers could be exposed to advertising. In 2012, the threatened destruction of the newspaper industry is causing newspaper management to rethink free content supported by online ads placed at the newspapers' sites. The Associated Press has negotiated licensing agreements with Google, Yahoo, and other online news portals. The *Wall Street Journal* was prepared to abandon the fee model in 2008, but in 2009, the parent News Corp., the largest owner of newspapers in the world, announced plans to begin charging for all its online content across the world.

Starting in March 2011, the *New York Times*, the world's largest online newspaper, started charging for online access. Print subscribers pay $333 a year for seven days of home or business-delivered editions, and complete free access to any online editions from the Web to smartphone apps. Unlimited digital access is about $420 a year. Those who are not a print or digital subscriber are limited to 10 free articles a month, after which readers will have to become digital subscribers at $15 to $35 a month depending on the devices used to access the *Times*. In the first month of operation, the online edition had 100,000 paid subscribers, and in April 2013, the paper hit 640,000 paid subscribers. The *Times* online subscriptions produce more than $200 million in revenue, nearly 10% of its overall revenues. The *Times* print subscribers have free all-digital access, which helps drive sales of the 7-day a week home-delivered print edition. The print plus all-digital access costs less than the all-digital access alone.

The proliferation of e-reader devices such as smartphones, tablets like the iPad, and dedicated devices like the Kindle are greatly expanding the digital opportunities for consumers to read newspapers online. All the top digital newspapers have apps for readers to quickly access content.

These new reader devices offer newspapers an opportunity to connect directly with their readers anytime and anywhere. What has been missing is a kind of online newsstand, a newspaper version of the iTunes Store, where you can find newspaper content from any newspaper in the United States or the world. But this is changing with the appearance of Google and Apple newsstand apps, where newspapers can display their apps. Apple takes a 30% cut of sales, Google somewhat less. Newspaper-Direct is an online store that has same-day online editions of nearly 2,210 newspapers from 94 countries in 54 languages. Unlimited subscriptions are $29.00 a month, economy editions are $9.95 for 31 articles, and most individual articles cost 99 cents. See the *Insight on Society* case, *Can Apps and Video Save Newspapers?*

Challenges: Disruptive Technologies

The online newspaper industry would appear at first glance to be a classic case of disruptive technology destroying a traditional business model based on physical products and physical distribution. This may turn out to be the case, but it cannot

INSIGHT ON SOCIETY

CAN APPS AND VIDEO SAVE NEWSPAPERS?

In the past decade, Internet pundits have buried the newspaper industry several times, just as they did books and other print media. Rejected as a relic of the age of the Gutenberg press of 1467, published by old firms incapable of adopting new technology, newspapers would one day be replaced by free content from amateurs in the field and on the scene. Indeed, the newspaper industry has been disrupted by the Internet: ad revenues have been cut in half over the last 10 years, and classified ad revenue has been decimated by sites such as Craigslist and Angie's List.

The initial reaction of the newspaper industry to the Internet and Web was to build Web sites as a way to attract an Internet audience and advertisers. It didn't work. Newspaper executives now concede it was a terrible mistake to give away news content for free.

But the game is not over. Just the beginning is over. Because of the Internet, newspaper readership is actually up, not down. In 2013, more than half of newspaper readers get their news from an online edition. Online readership is growing: over 114 million people read newspapers online in 2013, nearly half of all adult users of the Internet, and readership is growing at 10% a year. Just as books rose from the ashes of technorati critical commentary, newspapers might be able to adapt to newer technologies and opportunities. The social, local, mobile platform driven by smartphones and tablet computers offers newspapers many new opportunities to attract subscribers and advertisers. There are four factors that might just keep newspapers around for a long time.

The first is the paid subscription business model. Newspapers are increasingly using a freemium business model and charging for online content. Typically, the freemium model gives readers the choice of some free articles (10 to 20) every day, or paying for a premium subscription to all the news, and then paying in addition for various platform choices (smartphones and tablet app versions). The *Wall Street Journal*, *New York Times*, *Minneapolis Tribune*, *Boston Globe*, *Dallas Morning News*, and the Gannett papers are just some of the major national and regional newspapers adopting online subscriptions.

Information wants to be expensive if it's current, relevant, accurate, and timely. The *Wall Street Journal* led the way in the United States with an online premium service: $260 a year for both the print and online editions, and $207 a year for the digital edition. Today, the *Journal* has nearly 800,000 online subscribers, over 80,000 of whom use tablets and smartphones. With over 2.4 million worldwide subscribers, roughly a third are now reading online. And the prices have gone up: $324 for both print and digital, and $276 for digital only. One key to the *Wall Street Journal*'s success is that a subscription gives users access to premium content in the form of 25,000 in-depth background reports on companies, an archive of news articles going back to 1996, and access to the Dow Jones Publication Library, which features current and past articles from 7,000 newspapers, magazines, and business-news sources. If you are a stock analyst or an individual investor looking for information on a specific company, this archive of material is worth the small annual subscription fee.

The *New York Times* led the pay revolution for general-purpose newspapers by announcing a paid subscription freemium service in 2011: everyone gets 20 free articles a day. While most experts predicted the pay model for general interest newspapers could not work in the Internet age, they were wrong. Today, the *Times* has approximately 650,000 online subscribers, although the ad revenue does not match the revenues lost from

(continued)

declining physical paper sales. In 2013, the Times announced that they would introduce a number of new offerings at lower price points as well as an enhanced product at a higher price point offering special benefits.

The second factor is the arrival of the mobile platform in the form of smartphones and tablets, which is proving to be a boon for online newspapers. In a survey by comScore, over 67% of online newspaper readers said they use multiple devices—PCs, tablets, and/or smartphones. It's a multiplatform world that plays to the strengths of newspapers. Apps enable the newspapers to charge a la carte for articles, develop different versions at different price points, personalize the content, and above all, protect the content from being copied without payment. Apps are a proprietary, walled garden where content cannot easily be copied, in contrast to the public Web where just about anything can be copied and distributed. From a customer experience point of view, high-resolution tablets are uniquely suited for the large format, pictures, and videos found in today's online newspapers.

The third factor is video content. If you visit online or app-based newspapers, you'll see that online newspapers are increasingly differentiated from traditional print newspapers because of extensive use of video. Online newspapers are redesigning themselves to be more like CNN or MSNBC television shows. For instance, in 2013, the *Wall Street Journal* produces over five hours of live video each day to accompany its text articles; the *New York Times* is running a live morning newscast, and a taped daily show called *TimesCast*. Newspapers are being helped in this transition to video on demand by Google, which is encouraging newspapers to establish YouTube channels. The attraction of extensive use of video by online newspapers is that ads displayed alongside videos pay over $50 per CPM (cost per thousand clicks), whereas ordinary display ads pay only $5 per CPM or less. For newspapers starved for revenue, the future is video, driven by a professional reporting and editorial staff.

The final factor is that news is predominantly local. While many wrote off the local town newspaper as advertising disappeared from their pages bound for Craigslist, Angie's List, and other locally oriented classified sites, and search engines like Google, instead they have proliferated. In 2013, an increasing number of small and mid-sized papers are finding success with digital pay plans, and investors like Warren Buffett are targeting small and mid-sized papers, believing them to be undervalued and capable of solid profits. While not as sophisticated in their use of video or apps, these local papers are building a strong local readership, and hopefully a successful business model.

Despite the downturn in all of newspapers' most basic indicators, investors like Buffett see reasons for optimism. Many of technology's elite companies and figures have begun to focus on reviving print journalism, perhaps in part due to a desire to reverse some of the erosion of the industry in which they were complicit. In 2013, no figure loomed larger than Amazon's Jeff Bezos, who finalized his acquisition of the *Washington Post* in a move that took many industry pundits by surprise. Bezos has not yet made his goals or plan for the newspaper abundantly clear, but his involvement has made the industry sit up and take notice. He's likely to use his technological savvy and focus on customer data and trends, not to mention his deep pockets, to help revitalize the *Post*.

■■■ **SOURCES:** "Jeff Bezos: My Plans for the Washington Post," by Paul Farhi, *The Independent*, September 3, 2013; "Technology Industry Extends a Hand to Struggling Print Media," by Nick Wingfield, *New York Times*, August 11, 2013; "New York Times Earnings: Digital Subscriptions Rise," by Tess Stynes and William Launder, *New York Times*, August 1, 2013; Rick Edmonds, Emily Guskin, Amy Mitchell, and Mark Jurkowitz, "Newspapers: Stabilizing, but Still Threatened," stateofthemedia.org, July 18, 2013; "Times Co. Profit Falls; New Subscription Model Is Set," by Christine Haughney, *New York Times*, April 25, 2013; "The American Newspaper Media Industry Revenue Profile 2012," www.naa.org, April 8, 2013; "Smart Devices Attract News Readers," eMarketer, April 11, 2012; "Papers Put Faith in Paywalls," by Russell Adams, *Wall Street Journal*, March 4, 2012.

be the final assessment just yet. The industry is changing rapidly. There are significant assets that newspapers have—excellent content and writing, strong local readership, strong local advertising, and a fragmented but huge audience of over 100 million readers that rivals Yahoo, Google, and Microsoft's audience. Content is still king: the thousands of blogs in the blogosphere depend on traditional reporting media like television and newspapers to create the content that blog writers can react to. Without the original content creators in the form of professional reporters and news organizations, the blogosphere would be a dull place. The people who read newspapers are very different from the people who visit YouTube: they are wealthier, more educated, and older. This is an ideal demographic for advertisers and a potential gold mine for newspapers. The online audience for newspapers will continue to grow in both sheer numbers and sophistication, demanding higher quality online delivery and more services. The industry has made significant investments in technology for Web content creation and delivery. The challenge is for newspaper owners and managers to invest heavily in the online editions even if they do not meet investment criteria at first. Jezz Bezos' purchase of the *Washington Post* in August 2013 could provide an example of how newspapers might be able to survive the transition to digital news content. Likewise, Warren Buffett's purchase of thirty local daily newspapers since 2011 is also a sign that local newspapers can be a good investment. If the newspaper industry has a future, it will be online. The challenge for newspapers is to create value by focusing on differentiated, timely, and exclusive content available nowhere else. And to make this content available anywhere, anytime, anyplace, on any device.

E-BOOKS AND ONLINE BOOK PUBLISHING

In April 2000, Stephen King, one of America's most popular writers, published a novella called *Riding the Bullet*. This novella was only available as an e-book. King was the first major fiction writer to create an e-book-only volume of a new work. King's publisher, Simon & Schuster, arranged for sales online through online retailers such as Amazon. In the first day, there were 400,000 downloads, so many that Amazon's servers crashed several times. More than 600,000 downloads occurred in the first week. While Amazon gave the book away for free in the first two weeks, when it began charging $2.50 for a 66-page novella—about the same price per page as a standard King hardcover novel—sales continued to be brisk.

Ten years later, on April 15, 2010, Amanda Hocking, an unknown and unpublished self-publisher from Austin, Minnesota, uploaded one of her vampire novels, *My Blood Approves*, to Amazon's self-publishing site, and later to Barnes & Noble e-book store. Her novels had been rejected by many of the publishing houses in New York. By March 2011, she had sold more than 1 million copies of her e-books, which generally sell for 99 cents to $2.99, and earned more than $2 million. Starting out with sales of 5 to 10 books a day, Hocking's sales have reached as many as 100,000 a day when she first publishes a novel. In the same month, she signed a traditional publishing contract worth $2 million with St. Martin's Press. In 2012, Hocking was listed as one of the Amazon 99 cent millionaires. In 2013, twenty-seven of the top 100 Kindle books are self-published independent books.

FIGURE 10.9   **E-BOOK SALES**

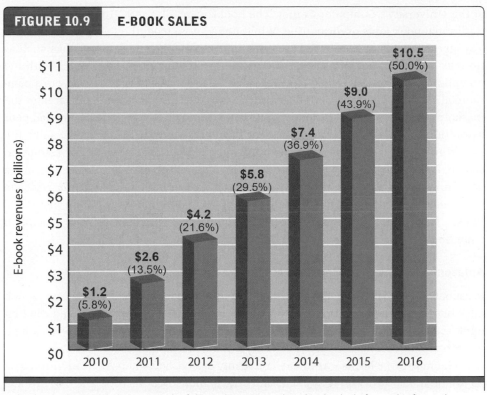

E-book sales have exploded as a result of the rival Amazon and Apple e-book platforms. This figure shows both total revenues and the percentage that e-books sales constitute of total book sales revenues.

SOURCE: Based on data from eMarketer, Inc., 2012b.

In the space of a decade, e-books have gone from an unusual experiment by a major author, to an everyday experience for millions of Americans, and an exciting new market for authors. Sales of e-books have exploded in a few short years, and the process of writing, selling, and distributing books has radically changed. E-book sales in 2013 are expected to be $5.8 billion dollars (see **Figure 10.9**). In 2013, e-book sales are expected to be 30% of all consumer book sales, and by 2016 to make up 50% of book sales. An entire new channel for self-published authors now exists, a channel not controlled by the major New York publishing houses and their professional editors. Bypassing professional editors and publishers, authors can now "crowdsource" the distribution of their books, relying on reader recommendations and social networks to market their books. Recognizing the booming self-publishing market, Penguin (the second largest trade book publisher in the world after Random House) purchased the self-publishing company Author Solutions in July 2012. Author Solutions has published 150,000 authors and more than 190,000 books. Other publishers have made similar purchases in the hope that successful books and authors will emerge from the burgeoning online author crowd (Bosman, 2012).

Little of this was supposed to happen. E-books have had a glorious history of birth, death, and rebirth, starting in the early 1970s when Project Gutenberg at the Materials Research Lab at the University of Illinois put more than 2,000 classic books online at the University's Computer Center. The books were all in ASCII plain text without traditional book fonts or formatting. While not a joy to read, they were free. In 1990, Voyager Company, a New York-based media company, began putting books such as *Jurassic Park* and *Alice in Wonderland* on CDs for reading on PCs. However, with the exception of encyclopedias and large reference texts, books on CDs never were a commercial success. They were expensive to produce and distribute, and appeared in the marketplace before most PC users had CD-ROM drives. PC screens of this era had poor resolution, making text characters appear fuzzy. Stand-alone reader devices like the Franklin Reader (1999–2002) met with a similar fate of poor design, low-resolution screen, lack of integration with the Internet, the absence of an online book store, and a very limited inventory of e-books. Many experts and commentators in the last decade believed e-books would never become a popular reading platform. They just could not see the new technologies that soon would be available to make reading a book on a handheld digital device a pleasurable experience.

Amazon and Apple: The New Digital Media Ecosystems

Prospects for e-books picked up in 2001 with the introduction of Apple's iPod, which later became a platform for e-books (iPod Touch). In 2004, Sony introduced the first e-ink reader (Sony Librie). In 2007, the iPhone smartphone was released with a high definition color screen that could be used to read books.

The future of e-books was finally and firmly established when Amazon introduced its Kindle in 2007 to a skeptical public and critical industry observers. The early Kindle readers used electronic ink technology, providing a higher resolution than PCs and a longer battery life than portable book readers. The early Kindle had 16 megabytes of memory and could store 200 books. More important, the reader was linked to the Internet through AT&T's cell network, permitting users to access Amazon's bookstore where they could browse, search, and purchase e-books. Amazon's bookstore is the largest online bookstore on the Internet. The first Kindle readers in 2007 sold out in a few days, and were on backorder for five months until Amazon caught up with demand. The Kindle is now available in a variety of different formats, such as the Kindle Fire, a small tablet computer with a 1-GHz processor, Android operating system, high-resolution IPS color touch screen similar to an iPad, and 8 gigabytes of memory to store 6,000 books, plus 10 movies or 800 songs. Storage of all content in the Amazon cloud is free (which means you can watch your movies either on the Kindle or your home TV, or tablet). The Kindle Fire is no longer simply an e-book reader, but rather a media and entertainment portable device connected to the Internet, competitive with tablet computers.

In 2013, Amazon's e-book and media store contains an estimated 1 million book titles. Although Amazon does not release Kindle sales numbers, it is estimated that more than 800 million Kindles of all types have been sold in the United States, and there are 51 million adults who use e-readers like the Kindle (and other e-book readers like the Barnes & Noble Nook, and tablet computers like the iPad). Industry analysts believe that Amazon is racking up Kindle unit sales of over 20 million units a year, and $7.96 billion in Kindle-related revenue (content and hardware sales). The Kindle ecosystem sales represent about 10% of Amazon's $61 billion in annual revenues, as e-book sales grow at 70% a year while its physical book sales grow at 17% a year. For every sale of

100 print books, Amazon sells over 115 e-books. Kindle users are avid readers and typically purchase a book a week. At one point in 2010, prior to the introduction of the iPad tablet computers, Amazon accounted for 90% of the e-book market. This did not last long: Apple's entry into the e-book marketspace temporarily reduced this share to 65%.

E-books received another large boost in 2010 when Apple introduced its first iPad tablet computer. With its large 11.7" screen and access to the iTunes Store of online music, video, TV, and book content, the iPad was an ideal media entertainment device. And with its high-resolution screen, the iPad was an even better e-book reader than the Kindle, albeit not easily slipped into a purse. While Amazon got the jump on Apple in dedicated e-book readers, Apple's approach from the beginning was a multipurpose device that could handle movies, music, magazines, and books, as well having a Wi-Fi connection to the Internet. Apple's iBookstore at launch in 2010 had 60,000 titles, and is estimated to have about 200,000 titles in 2013 (much smaller than Amazon's store). Apple has sold over 100 million iPads since 2007. It has a 60% market share of tablet computers in 2013, but only an estimated 20% of the e-book market, although it is gaining ground on Amazon's market share. The Barnes & Noble Nook had a 10% share when it was discontinued in 2013. The Google Play online store in 2013 is not a large book media and entertainment player yet, but is unlikely to challenge Amazon and Apple for the online e-book consumer, preferring to focus on a much more lucrative video-based entertainment market.

The result of the Amazon and Apple ecosystems, combining hardware, software, and online mega stores, is an explosion in online book content, readership, authorship, marketing, and at least a partial upending of the traditional book publishing and marketing channels. Increasingly, social networks play an important role in all book marketing as millions of social network members tell their friends about their favorite books. Traditional book publishing has similarly been altered. In the traditional process, authors worked with agents, who sold book manuscripts to editors and publishers, who sold books through bookstores, and at prices determined largely by the publishers. Because bookstores had a vested interest in selling books at a profit, there was only limited discounting during clearance sales. In the new publishing model, authors still write books, but then bypass traditional agent and publisher channels and instead publish their books electronically on the Amazon or Apple online stores. Prices are determined by the author, usually much lower than traditional books depending on the popularity of the author, and the digital distributor takes a percentage of the sale (usually 30%). New self-published authors typically give away their early works to develop an audience, and then, when an audience appears, charge a small amount for their books, typically 99 cents to $2.99. Marketing occurs by word of mouth on social networks, author blogs, and public readings. While a small percentage of all books are produced this way, it is a growing and popular form of publishing and striking it rich, sometimes. They're called "99 cent millionaires," and there's enough around to arouse the passions of thousands of potential writers of the great American novel, as well as lesser genres from police procedurals to paranormal romance writers.

The book publishing industry is generally comfortable with the security and intellectual property protections offered by the online distributors. Both Amazon and Apple offer publishers walled gardens and tight controls over proprietary formats, devices, and files, thus preventing the large-scale theft of copyrighted book content. This is very different from the music industry, where the MP3 files can be easily copied and distributed. Apple and Amazon e-books are difficult to copy and upload to cyberlockers or to distribute on the Internet. Amazon Kindle titles can be put on six devices, and the files are stored both in the Amazon cloud and on the Kindle reader. Likewise with Apple ebooks stored on iCloud servers. Kindles can be passed around, but that is thought to be a minor issue, much like lending a physical book to a friend. Consumers cannot access books purchased from other Amazon accounts, although family members can share accounts. Apple books can't be read on Kindle or B&N devices. Kindle apps allow iPad users to read and purchase Amazon e-books using their iPads. In all these ways, the e-book online stores offer a very secure environment for book publisher intellectual content. This environment also severely weakens the used book market, and virtually eliminates the sharing of books among friends. There is no used e-book market.

What Are the Challenges of the Digital E-Book Platform?

Despite, or because, of the rapid growth in e-books, the book publishing industry is in stable, even robust condition. There are two major challenges facing book publishers. Responses to these challenges will shape the future existence of the book publishing industry as we know it. These two challenges are cannibalization and finding the right business model.

cannibalization

when sales of new digital products replace sales of traditional products

Cannibalization in digital markets refers to the potential for new digital products to rapidly reduce the sales of existing physical products. This can be a threat to digital content firms insofar as the prices and profits available from selling digital products are lower than prices and profits from physical products. At $14.99 for an e-book, publishers are making as much profit or more than when they sell physical books to bookstores. At $9.99, they are gaining no profits. Sometimes the situation is complicated by large online digital distributors such as Amazon, who want to maximize their sales of physical devices by offering free or low-priced content, say, e-books below their cost at $9.99, and have little short-term interest protecting the profits of content owners and producers. Both the music and newspaper industries have suffered some cannibalization, with revenues declining by 50% or more over the last decade.

The evidence from book publishing is mixed so far. Overall, book publishing revenues in 2012 were $27 billion, about the same as the previous year. E-book sales made up nearly $1 billion or 20% of the total book revenue, growing at 15% a year. As digital revenues have expanded, print book sales have gone down about $1 billion from the previous year. The largest sales channel remains physical brick-and-mortar bookstores ($7.5 billion), and this has fallen 7% with the closing of Borders bookstore in 2011. Sales to online retailers grew 21% to $7 billion, reflecting in part the growth of e-book sales (Book Industry Study Group, 2013).

The overall picture that emerges is that the rapid growth of e-books and online sales has lowered sales of physical books in brick-and-mortar stores. However, much of this lost revenue is being made up by the growth in e-book sales online. Total readership has arguably increased with the popularity of e-books and the widespread adoption of Kindles and iPads. More than 40% of e-book readers use some kind of e-reader like Kindles and Nooks, 42% use a PC, 29% use cell phones, and 23% use tablet computers. In 2013, 21% of Americans have read an e-book (most using a PC or their smartphones) and 88% of e-book readers also read traditional books (eMarketer, Inc., 2012b; Pew Research, 2013).

E-Book Business Models

The e-book industry is composed of intermediary retailers (both brick-and-mortar stores and online merchants), traditional publishers, technology developers, device makers (e-readers), and vanity presses (self-publishing service companies). Together, these players have pursued a wide variety of business models and developed many alliances in an effort to move text onto the computer screen.

There are six very large publishers that dominate trade book, education, and religious book publishing. These traditional publishers have the largest content libraries for conversion to e-books. These large publishers started out using a **wholesale model** of distribution and pricing, in part because this is the same model they used with hard cover books. In this model, the retail store pays a wholesale price for the book and then decides at what price to sell it to the consumer. The retailer sets the price with, of course, some kind of understanding with the publisher that the book will not be given away for free. In the past, the wholesale price was 50% of the retail price. A retailer would pay the publisher a $10 wholesale price, and mark it up to $20 retail price. However, retailers could also determine to sell the book at a much lower sale price, say $5, as a way to attract readers to the store or as a close-out sale. Brick-and-mortar stores had a vested interest in selling most books above their wholesale cost. With e-books, publishers discovered that some online retailers like Amazon would gladly sell e-books below their own cost for a variety of reasons.

In the case of e-books, publishers sought to keep their prices high enough so as not to discourage hard cover sales. Generally, this meant publishers wanted e-books to sell at a retail price of $12.99 to $14.99, depending on the popularity of the book and the stage in the product life cycle (months since first publication). E-book distributors like Amazon were charged a wholesale price of about $9, and they were expected to mark up the product to around $12.99 to $14.99 or more. Instead, Amazon chose to sell e-books for $9.99, at or below cost, in order to attract buyers to its content store to buy Kindles, and to attract new customers to its online retail store. Amazon lost $1 to $3 on every e-book sold, but recouped the money by selling Kindles for hundreds of dollars, and from additional sales at its stores. With Amazon selling e-books at $9.99, the lowest prices on the Web, publishers were forced to sell their e-books on all other Web sites at the $9.99 Amazon price, as were local independent book stores just getting into e-book sales. Using this strategy, Amazon not only sold millions of Kindles but also sold 90% of all e-book titles on the Web in 2010 and 2011. Amazon had a near monopoly on e-books.

Publishers opposed Amazon's policy as debasing the perceived value of both physical and electronic books, and as a mortal threat to the publishers who could not survive if their e-books were priced at $9.99 across the Web. They claimed Amazon was engaging in "predatory pricing," designed to destroy traditional book publishers. In 2010, five of the largest publishers secretly met with Steve Jobs and Apple. They agreed to a new pricing model called "agency." In the agency model, the distributor is an agent of the publisher, and can be directed to sell e-books at a price determined

wholesale model
prices are determined by the retailer

agency model
the retailer is an agent and prices are set by the manufacturer

by the publisher, around $14.99 and higher for certain titles. In return for a 30% commission, Apple agreed to support this model, as did Google, neither of whom were comfortable watching as Amazon dominated one of the hottest areas of Web content sales. In these meetings, publishing executives discussed a common pricing strategy.

The **agency model** temporarily turned the tables on Amazon: it now had to charge whatever price the publishers wanted or the publishers would not sell Amazon any books (they would not choose Amazon as an agent for their products). A result of the agency model was that Amazon prices on e-books rose to the publisher desired levels, and its market share fell to 60% in 2012. Apple, Google, Barnes & Noble, and the five major publishers were delighted. The Justice Department was not delighted: it sued the five publishers and Apple for price fixing in violation of antitrust laws. All five of the publishers settled, but Apple refused to settle and asked for a trial before a judge. In July 2013, the United States District Court found that Apple had engaged in price fixing, not because of its agency pricing model, which is quite common throughout retail trade, but because of its "most favored seller" clause in its agreements with publishers that had the effect of discouraging other sites (like Amazon) from selling e-books for less than Apple's iBookstore price. Under the agreements, the publishers, not Amazon, would determine prices on Amazon. If publishers sold their books on Amazon for $9.95, then publishers would have to sell their e-books at iBookstore for $9.95. After the ruling, e-book prices on Amazon have largely remained in the $14 range, with limited discounting, and its market share rose to 65%. The government also wants to ban Apple from signing similar agreements with other suppliers of e-books, movies, music, and television content. In addition, the government wants Apple to allow other retailers like Amazon and Barnes & Noble to sell e-books directly from their iPhone and tablet apps, which they now cannot do now because of Apple's restrictions. Finally, the government has asked that Apple pay a court-appointed monitor to ensure compliance with antitrust law and the government's proposed remedies. While the ruling prevents Apple from fixing prices of e-books, it does nothing to solve the issues surrounding Amazon's dominance of the e-book marketplace.

Interactive Books: Converging Technologies

The future of e-books will also depend in part on changes in the concept of a book. The modern book is not really very different from the first two-facing page, bound books that began to appear in seventeenth-century Europe and had already appeared in the fourth century BCE in ancient China. The traditional Western book has a very simple, nondigital operating system: text appears left to right, pages are numbered, there is a front and a back cover, and text pages are bound together by stitching or glue. In educational and reference books, there is an alphabetical index in the back of the book that permits direct access to the book's content. While these traditional books will be with us for many years given their portability, ease of use, and flexibility, a parallel new world of interactive e-books is expected to emerge in the next five years. Interactive books combine audio, video, and photography with text, providing the reader with a multimedia experience thought to be more powerful than simply reading a book. In 2012, Apple released iBook Author, an app to help authors create interactive books. Hundreds of children's books are already built as interactive books. In 2012, Apple also introduced iBook Textbooks, a line of interactive textbooks created by several of the largest textbook publishing firms. Some experts believe that traditional print books will be curiosities by 2020. Yet by 2013 these newer all-digital textbooks have not yet been successful in the marketplace.

MAGAZINES REBOUND ON THE TABLET PLATFORM

Magazines in the United States reached their peak circulation in the early 1980s, with more than 40 million people reading some kind of weekly or monthly magazine. Most Americans got their national and international news from the three weekly news magazines, *Time, Newsweek*, and *U.S. News and World Report*. The "glossies," as general-interest magazines were known, attracted readers with superb writing, short-form articles, and stunning photography brought to life by very high-resolution color printing (Vega, 2012).

Circulation fell after 2000 in part because of the Internet. At first, the Internet and the Web did not have much impact on magazine sales, in part because the PC was no match for the high-resolution, large-format pictures found in, say, *Life* or *Time*. Eventually, as screens improved, as video on the Web became common, and the economics of color publishing changed, magazine circulation began to plummet and advertisers turned their attention to the digital platform on the Web, where readers were increasingly getting their news, general-interest journalism, and photographic accounts of events.

Magazine newsstand sales dropped from 22 million units in 2001 to 10 million in 2012 (Sass, 2011). Yet special-interest, celebrity, homemaking, and automobile magazines remained stable. The largest monthly subscription magazine for several decades has been the *AARP* magazine (American Association of Retired Persons), with a paid circulation of over 20 million readers.

Newstand sales are falling at 10% a year, and subscription sales are flat. Magazines have responded by developing "digital replica" magazines—fairly close copies of the physical magazine. Currently, there are about 300 digital replica magazines, and about 8 million units are sold each year. Unlike newspapers where digital advertising has not made up for the fall in print ad revenue, for magazines it has: digital revenues are expected to grow 10% a year to 2016, to $4 billion, just enough to make up for the loss in print ad revenues. Like newspapers, magazines are experimenting with different revenue models in an effort to monetize the rapidly growing tablet audience. Most magazines participate in Apple's iPad Subscription Service, which allows magazines to offer subscriptions from within their app and have the transaction processed by the App Store billing system. Publishers set the price, and customers can subscribe with one click. Apple keeps 30% of the transaction. Publishers can also direct app readers to their Web site for a subscription, in which case Apple does not make any fee. Virtual storefronts such as Apple's iOS Newstand and Google Play have helped publishers grow their digital subscriber base.

Despite the shrinkage of print subscription and newsstand sales, the growth of digital magazine sales has been extraordinary. Almost one-third of the Internet population in the United States (about 74 million people) read magazines online. More than 35% of tablet computer owners read magazine content once a week, and there are an estimated 1,200 magazine apps for mobile readers (eMarketer, Inc., 2013b).

Popular Web sites like Pinterest, an image-collecting site that attracts millions of women, and Facebook, Yahoo, and Twitter are among the largest drivers of traffic to digital magazines (Vega, 2012). The widespread adoption of tablet computers has helped create the "visual Internet," where glossy magazine publishers, who are inherently oriented to richly detailed color photography, can display their works and advertisements to great advantage. Social reader apps are another way magazines are trying to engage digital readers. Social reader apps allow Facebook users to share with their friends what they read in online newspapers and magazines. However, using these apps requires readers to share their personal information with Facebook, and many have decided they do not want their reading habits that widely distributed.

With hundreds of popular online magazines to choose from, magazine aggregators like Zinio, Flipboard, and Pulse make it possible for customers to find their favorite magazines using a single app. A **magazine aggregator** is a Web site or app that offers users online subscriptions and sales of many digital magazines. See the *Insight On Business* case, *Read All About It: Rival Digital Newsstands Fight.*

magazine aggregator
a Web site or app that provides subscriptions and sales of many digital magazines

10.3   THE ONLINE ENTERTAINMENT INDUSTRY

The entertainment industry is generally considered to be composed of four traditional, commercial players and one new arrival: television, radio broadcasting, Hollywood films, music, and video games (the new arrival). Together, these largely separate entertainment players generate $122 billion in annual revenue. This includes both digital and traditional format revenues. **Figure 10.10** illustrates the estimated relative sizes of these commercial entertainment markets as of 2013. By far, the largest entertainment producer is television (broadcast, satellite, and cable), and then motion pictures, followed by music, radio, and video games (both stand-alone and online games). While online, computer, and console

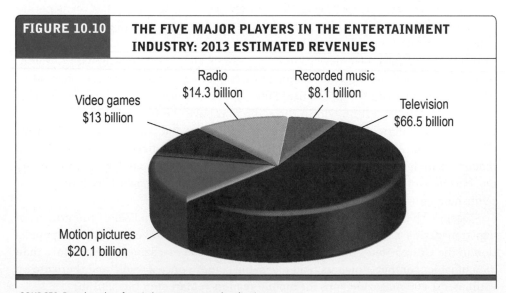

FIGURE 10.10   THE FIVE MAJOR PLAYERS IN THE ENTERTAINMENT INDUSTRY: 2013 ESTIMATED REVENUES

Radio $14.3 billion
Recorded music $8.1 billion
Video games $13 billion
Television $66.5 billion
Motion pictures $20.1 billion

SOURCES: Based on data from industry sources; authors' estimates.

INSIGHT ON BUSINESS

READ ALL ABOUT IT: RIVAL DIGITAL NEWSSTANDS FIGHT

Newsstands, the street shop on the corner hawking magazines, newspapers, soda, candy, cigarettes, and chewing gum in the downtowns of major cities, airports, train stations, and malls, are a pillar of magazine sales. In 2012, more than 10 million copies of magazines were sold at newsstands. That's an impressive number, but it's less than half of what it was in 2001. The other pillar of magazine sales is paid subscriptions. Over 110 million readers have paid subscriptions to magazines, down about 10% from 2001. The most popular subscriber magazine is *AARP The Magazine* (American Assocation of Retired Persons) with over 20 million subscribers; the most popular newsstand magazine is *Woman's World,* with around 1.1 million monthly sales. Despite declines in magazine advertising dollars and circulation, despite the threatened and actual digital disruption of new digital platforms for news and photos, magazines still attract a huge monthly audience of over 120 million readers. This is an audience worth fighting for—it's a more educated, wealthier, and aspirational audience than television or newspapers attract.

What really made magazines such a popular form of mass communication in the past was high-resolution photography, resulting in stunning, often full-page photos. In addition, magazines had longer, in-depth articles, written by some of the best writers in the business. Personal computer displays didn't stand a chance against the color photography available in magazines. But with the introduction of high-resolution tablet computers, connected to an online content store, it was a short hop to the idea of a "digital newsstand," where high-quality photography and long-form magazine articles could easily be presented and consumed. This short hop has turned into a fight among several start-ups, the owners of the content stores and devices (Apple, Google, and Nook), and the magazine publishers themselves.

In 2012, the largest digital newsstand, Zinio, rose to 13th on the AppData list of the top-grossing apps for iOS devices (iPad and iPhone), and 5th on the list of top-grossing news apps, behind giants like the *New York Times, Macworld,* and the *Economist.* In 2013, Zinio is still going strong. Zinio is an online magazine newsstand where users can find over 5,500 magazine titles, 2,500 of them exclusive to the platform. Among the available titles are *Rolling Stone, Road & Track, Seventeen,* and the *Economist.* In addition to iOS devices, Zinio is available on Android devices and Kindle. Zinio has partnerships with nearly all the largest magazine publishers including McGraw-Hill Companies, Wiley, Ziff Davis, Hearst Corporation, and Playboy Enterprises, Inc. The advantage of using Zinio, the company claims, is that a single app provides interface consistency across all the different magazines, and makes it easier for consumers to manage their subscriptions at one site. In August 2013, Zinio introduced a subscription model that it calls Z-pass, that allows users to access any three of the magazines available on its platform for just $5 a month.

Notably absent from Zinio's list is Time Inc., the largest U.S. magazine publisher with titles like *Time, Fortune,* and *People;* Condé Nast; the New York Times Company; and Wall Street Journal/Dow Jones. These publishers have their own proprietary apps available to consumers on the two largest mobile platforms, Apple's iOS and Android tablets and smartphones. Their

(continued)

message is clear: why sell to digital news-stand distributors at a discount when they can sell directly to the consumer using apps available for tablet computers? This works for readers who want to buy single issues (as a traditional newsstand), and pay the same price as they would for the physical magazine. Digital doesn't mean cheap. According to Hearst Publications, readers are willing to pay more for a tablet version than a physical version of its magazine simply because of its greater ease of use, portability, high resolution, and the inclusion of videos in some issues.

Adding to the competition for tablet magazine readers, the five largest publishers have launched their own newsstand called Next Issue Media with some of the most popular magazine titles in the United States, including *Better Homes and Gardens, Condé Nast Traveler, Esquire, Elle, Fortune, Glamour, Parents, People, Popular Mechanics, Real Simple, Sports Illustrated, Time, The New Yorker, Vanity Fair,* and many more. The top five publishers are Condé Nast, Meredith, Hearst, News Corp., and Time. Next Issue has developed a single app where, initially, 32 magazines will be available. For $9.99 per month, readers have unlimited access to 92 monthly and biweekly magazines. For $14.99 a month, an additional 102 magazines, including weeklies such as *Time* and *Sports Illustrated,* are available. With Next Issue, like Hulu in the television and film industry, the major publishers are building their own digital distribution platform rather than cede the customer relationship and revenues to start-up intermediaries like Zinio. Apple and Google are another matter.

The third player in the fight for the digital newsstand is the owners of the distribution platform (the tablet), and that means Apple and Google. Each has its own newsstand. Apple's Newsstand organizes magazine and newspaper subscriptions into a single app, provides a point of purchase for new subscriptions on iTunes, and sends the user notices as new issues become available. Google plans a similar service, as does Yahoo. Publishers are wary of Apple because it wants a 30% cut of subscription revenue, and worse, will not allow publishers to send users outside the Apple iOS sandbox to purchase subscriptions. Everything has to be purchased through the iTunes Store, and Apple retains ownership and personal data on the customer. The publishers and Apple are working on a compromise solution. Both need each other: Apple's Newsstand without magazines is a loser, and magazines want to sell digital subscriptions to iTunes' millions of users.

Whether or not digital newsstands can produce enough revenue to overcome the decline in physical magazine sales and advertising is not clear at this time. Although the unique features of tablets offer opportunities for publishers and writers, some industry predictions suggest that by 2017, the U.S. consumer magazine market will be worth $23 billion, down from $25 billion in 2012. The increase in digital advertising is unlikely to keep up with the decline in print advertising. In the short term, magazines have rebounded from recession-year lows, but the industry has more work to do to continue their growth in the future. Nevertheless, the tablet is a friend of magazines by enhancing the consumer experience of reviewing high-quality photos and videos.

SOURCES: "Zinio: App Now Offers Any 3 Magazines for $5 a Month," by Marc Saltzman, *USA Today*, August 22, 2013; "Magazine Newsstand Sales Plummet, but Digital Editions Thrive," by Christine Haughney, *New York Times*, August 6, 2013; "Consumer Magazine Market Predicted to Shed $1.3B by 2017," Adweek.com, June 4, 2013; "eMarketer: Magazines to See Positive Ad Spending Growth in 2012," eMarketer, Inc., September 25, 2012; "Hearst Hails the Age of the Tablet, Says Readers Are Willing to Pay More for Tablet Editions," by Doug Drinkwater, *Editor & Publisher*, May 15, 2012; "A Buffet of Magazines on a Tablet," by David Pogue, *New York Times*, April 11, 2012; "Zinio Makes the iPad a Viable Magazine Platform," by Jason O'Grady, ZDNet, April 4, 2012; "Magazine Newsstand Sales Suffered Sharp Falloff in Second Half of 2011," by Tanzina Vega, *New York Times*, February 7, 2012; "For the First Time, the Atlantic's Online Ad Revenue Exceeds Print," by Anna Heim, Thenextweb.com, November 21, 2011.

games have grown to be larger than film box office revenues (about $10 billion), total Hollywood film revenues dwarf the game industry when DVD sales and rentals, licensing, and ancillary products are added. Radio remains a strong revenue producer aided in part by the growth of Internet radio services like Spotify and Pandora, but is still largely reliant on FM and AM broadcast technologies, especially in automobiles. Recorded music is the smallest of the major players at $8 billion, half of its size ten years ago.

Along with the other content industries, the entertainment segment is undergoing a transformation brought about by the Internet. Several forces are at work. Accelerated platform development such as the iPhone/iPad video and music platform, other smartphones and tablets, the Amazon music and video platform, not to mention the Netflix streaming platform, have changed consumer preferences and increased demand for music, video, television, and game entertainment delivered over Internet devices whether in subscription or a la carte pay-per-view forms. Social network platforms are also spurring the delivery of entertainment content to desktop and mobile devices. Their role is not content delivery, but rather social interaction with friends while watching or listening to online content. The iTunes store and Amazon have demonstrated successful download music services where users pay for tracks and albums. Music subscriptions services like Pandora, Spotify, and Rhapsody have never made a profit and bleed cash despite having millions of subscribers. Both kinds of services—download and streaming—have demonstrated that millions of consumers are willing to pay reasonable prices for high-quality content, portability, and convenience. The growth in broadband has obviously made possible both wired and wireless delivery of all forms of entertainment over the Internet, potentially displacing cable and broadcast television networks. The development of high-quality customer experiences at online entertainment sites has in many cases eliminated the need for digital rights management restrictions. Closed platforms, like the Kindle and iBooks, also work to obviate the need for DRM. Subscription services for streaming music and video are inherently copyright-protected because the content is never downloaded to a computer (similar to cable TV). All of these forces have combined in 2013 to bring about a transformation in the entertainment industries.

The ideal Internet content e-commerce world would allow consumers to watch any movie, listen to any music, watch any TV show, and play any game, when they want, where they want, and using whatever Internet device is convenient. Consumers would be billed monthly for these services by a single provider of Internet service. This idealized version of a convergent media world is many years away, but clearly this is the direction of the Internet-enabled entertainment industry. It is the direction that large players like Apple, Amazon, and Google are moving towards.

When we think of the producers of entertainment in the offline world, we tend to think about television networks such as ABC, Fox, NBC, HBO, or CBS; Hollywood film studios such as MGM, Disney, Paramount, and Twentieth Century Fox; and music labels such as Sony BMG, Atlantic Records, Columbia Records, and Warner Records. Interestingly, none of these international brand names have a significant entertainment presence on the Internet. Although traditional forms of entertainment such as television shows and Hollywood movies are now commonplace on the Web, neither the television nor film industries have built an industry-wide delivery system. Instead, they are building alliances with players like Yahoo, Google, Amazon, Facebook, MSN, and Apple, all of whom have become significant players in media distribution.

While industry titans waiver, online consumers are redefining and considerably broadening the concept of entertainment. We refer to this development as "nontraditional" entertainment or what most refer to as user-generated content, which also has entertainment value including user videos uploaded to YouTube, photos uploaded to Photobucket, as well as blogs. User-generated content reflects some of the same shifts in consumer preferences experienced by traditional media: people want to participate in the creation and distribution of content.

ONLINE ENTERTAINMENT AUDIENCE SIZE AND GROWTH

Measuring the size and growth of the Internet content audience is far less precise than measuring a television audience. In fact one of the issues facing television producers is an inability to count Internet viewing, or time-delayed viewing. Recognizing the difficulties of measuring an Internet audience, let's first examine the use of "traditional" entertainment content, such as feature-length movies, music, online TV, online radio, and games. **Figure 10.11** shows the current and projected growth for commercial online entertainment revenues for the major players: music, Internet

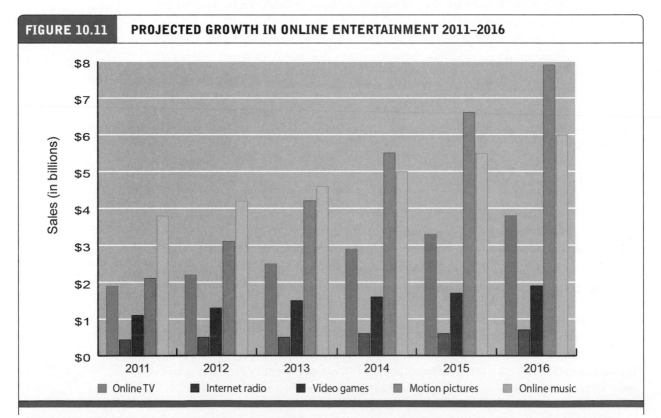

FIGURE 10.11 | **PROJECTED GROWTH IN ONLINE ENTERTAINMENT 2011–2016**

Legend: Online TV | Internet radio | Video games | Motion pictures | Online music

Among commercial forms of mass entertainment, online music downloads engage the largest number of people and generate the largest revenues on the Web in 2013. However, online movies and television revenues will grow dramatically in the next four years, with movies becoming larger than music in 2016 revenues.

SOURCES: Based on data from industry sources; authors' estimates.

radio, online TV, online games, and online video. Music leads the list of commercial entertainment revenues in 2013, followed by motion pictures, online TV, online games, and Internet radio.

There will be some interesting changes by 2016. Movies surpass music as the largest form of online entertainment. Online TV grows very rapidly (greater than 15% annually), while online games and radio remain relatively smaller generators of revenue, declining in significance when compared to movies, music, and TV.

User-Generated Content: Where Does It Fit?

Whereas traditional commercial entertainment is produced by professional entertainers and producers, user-generated entertainment involves all those other activities that people voluntarily engage in to have fun, such as shooting videos, taking pictures, recording music and sharing it, and writing blogs. We have extensively documented the user-generated phenomenon in previous chapters. One question for this chapter is, "How does this content fit into the overall entertainment picture?"

The answer appears to be that user-generated content is both a substitute for as well as a complement to traditional commercial entertainment. As people spend more time consuming user-generated content, one might think they would spend less time consuming commercial content. But this does not seem to be the case. Consumer-generated content seems to increase the acceptance of the Internet as a content channel, and consumption of all content seems to expand. **Figure 10.12** characterizes different types of Web entertainment experiences along two dimensions: user focus and user control. Sites that offer nontraditional user-generated forms of entertainment are unique not only because they afford access to large digital archives,

| FIGURE 10.12 | USER ROLE IN ENTERTAINMENT |

USER CONTROL

	HIGH	LOW
USER FOCUS HIGH	Internet programming Music download networks Auction sites	Reality TV shows TV game shows
USER FOCUS LOW	Traditional fan clubs MTV music shows	Traditional media programming

Popular Internet entertainment sites offer users high levels of control and user focus. Traditional media programming content is determined by programmers and has a celebrity focus. Traditional media has moved to become more participatory and more user-focused, but cannot match Internet levels of interactivity and user contribution to content.

promote fine-grained searching, and enable users to create their own archives, but also because they permit users high levels of control over both the program content and the program focus. For example, social network sites like Facebook or Google+ offer user-generated content that is viewed by others as "entertaining." The hypothesis is that sites that offer both high user focus and high user control will have the fastest rates of growth. Facebook is a good example of a site where user control is near absolute, and the focus is highly user centric.

TELEVISION AND PREMIUM VIDEO

In TV land, cable systems are challenged as the Internet offers alternative, unbundled, a la carte access to TV programs. Contrary to expectations, the big TV screen in the home is as popular as ever, supported by social networks that buzz with chat about what's on TV right now. In 2013, about 121 million Americans watch TV online, about 50% of the Internet population (eMarketer, Inc., 2013e). Increasingly, the TV household is a cross-platform phenomenon. Every week, Americans watch about 35 hours of TV on traditional TV sets, but nearly 6 hours using a computer, 2.5 hours watching time-shifted TV using a digital video recorder or cable system with cloud storage, and 7 minutes watching video on a smartphone. While teens continue to spend more time texting than ever, 70% of college students ages 18 to 30 report watching streamed television shows (eMarketer, Inc., 2011). The largest online movie download distributor is Apple's iTunes (which provides downloads or cloud storage and rentals, but not streaming). iTunes has 67% of the digital TV download market and 65% of the movie download market. No competitor comes close to producing Apple's combined TV plus movie download revenue of $1.75 billion annually (NPD Group, 2013a). It's a different story with streaming video: Netflix is the market leader in streaming movies and TV shows, producing an estimated $3.6 billion in revenue in 2013. While streaming has not replaced downloading (either purchasing or renting), it has grown faster and today produces more revenue. Netflix is close to exceeding iTunes video revenues.

The television industry, the major source of premium video on the Internet, is beginning a transition to a new delivery platform, the Internet and mobile smartphones and tablet computers. This transition closely follows an earlier but related transition to digital video recorders and "time-shifting" by consumers who no longer were constrained by television executives' programming and scheduling decisions. The current transition to Internet delivery of television is not leading to a decline in traditional television viewing, which has in fact increased slightly. The new platform is just changing how, when, and where consumers can watch TV. Cloud computing, the storage and streaming of content from large Internet datacenters rather than on individual personal devices, has created a large shift away from ownership of content, and a focus instead on access to content anywhere, anytime, from any device. Social networks have enabled a new kind of "social TV" where consumers share comments while viewing television shows. The most important activity in today's television household may not be what's on screen, but instead what's being said about what's on screen. Television rating agencies today do not have a methodology for measuring this kind of engagement.

Expansion of broadband networks, especially those serving mobile devices such as Wi-Fi and high-speed cellular networks, and the growth of cloud servers, has enabled the growth of a whole new class of television distributors. Cloud distributors, like Apple's iCloud service, allow users to purchase video and movies, store them in iCloud, and view the entertainment from any device, anywhere. Whereas the dominant way consumers obtained a TV signal in the past was from over-the-air broadcasters, cable TV, or satellite distributors, a new "over-the-top" channel has developed led by powerful technology companies such as Apple, Google, Hulu, VUDU, Netflix, and many others, all of whom offer consumers access to television shows and some full-length feature movies. **Over-the-top (OTT)** entertainment services refers to the use of the Internet to deliver online entertainment services to the home. "Over-the-top" refers to the fact that the entertainment service rides "on top" of other network services like cable TV and telephone service. It's as if we have a new Internet Broadcasting System with many new players. This new network is obviously a threat to cable television and the other distributors, who, in turn, have their on-demand services for television series and movies. In addition, the leaders in the new Internet-based networks are at odds with the content producers over how the content-generated revenues are divided. In some cases, the new distributors like Apple are so powerful, they can dictate the terms. When content producers want to charge very high prices, Apple, Google, and others, including Hulu, have begun to move into the content production business by creating their own TV shows. The marketplace is very fluid, and filled with conflicts.

The largest content provider in the United States, and most of the world, is television. In terms of audience size, ad revenue generated, and hours watched per day, the biggest screen in the house dominates the entertainment landscape in all countries. While the print industries struggle to attract customers to their traditional products, and the music industry struggles to generate revenues from streaming and downloaded music tracks, the television industry faces a nearly insatiable demand for its traditional products—sports, drama, and news—on both traditional platforms and the new Internet platforms.

While the Internet has not diminished TV viewing, it has transformed how, when, and where TV shows are watched. Alongside traditional television viewing, and the traditional "TV household," is a whole new "digital household" with broadband connections to the Internet, and new mobile viewing devices: the smartphone, tablet, and game console (Carr, 2011). While TV might be the biggest screen in the house, it has to compete or share with other digital devices. Increasingly, the television industry is providing high-quality content in the form of older versions of television series and some sporting events. These three factors—broadband penetration, new mobile platforms, and a willing industry that wants to monetize its library of high-quality content—are the leading factors in changing the television industry.

The Internet and the new mobile platform have also changed the viewing experience. The best screen when commuting or traveling is the smartphone and tablet. More importantly, Internet-enabled social networks like Facebook and Twitter have made TV viewing a social experience shared among neighbors, friends, and colleagues. In the past, television was often a social event involving family and friends in the same

over-the-top (OTT)
use of the Internet to deliver entertainment services to the home on cable TV or FiOS networks

room watching a single TV show. In 2013, the social circle has expanded to include Facebook and Twitter friends in different locations, changing television from a "lean back and enjoy" experience into a "lean forward and engage" experience. Reality television shows encourage viewers to tweet while watching, and run a scrolling bar of viewer tweets. About 20% of viewers start watching a TV show after hearing about it on a social network. TV viewers are multitasking: co-viewing shows while texting, commenting, and chatting on line while the show unfolds. Around 32% of Internet users will use social media while watching TV, and this jumps to 64% for users who own smartphones and tablets (eMarketer, Inc., 2012c). Nearly 60% are watching TV show clips on social networks.

While the Internet so far has had an expansive and positive impact on the television industry, challenges lie ahead. The largest providers of television in virtually all countries are cable television systems that charge consumers a monthly service fee for providing service, often accompanied by Internet and/or telephone service. This service in the United States costs, on average, about $125 per month per household. Cable systems also generate advertising revenues from local and national advertisers. The revenues generated are used to maintain the physical cable network, and pay program producers (often called "cable networks") for their content. For instance, HBO (Home Box Office network) creates a variety of television shows for the nearly 11,000 local cable systems in the United States, and collects fees from the local cable systems and their subscribers. ESPN, the largest sports network on TV and the Internet, charges local and national cable systems per-viewer fees. But with so much video available online for "free," many users are thinking about "cutting the cable cord" and just relying on the Internet for their video entertainment. Other viewers are "cord shavers," who have reduced their subscriptions to digital channels. Likewise, the improvement in over-the-air digital broadcasting of television signals has resulted in a slight increase in over-the-air viewers (about 15% of all television viewers). So far, cord cutting and shaving has been very limited, but the high service fees for cable television service, and expanding Internet capabilities, suggest the future of traditional cable systems, and their ungainly set-top boxes, may be challenged. In July 2013, the CEO of Comcast, the largest cable firm in the United States, noted that in the next five years Comcast may no longer offer cable TV, but instead distribute everything over the Internet. Cable companies, of course, happen to be the largest Internet networks so they will retain that connection with the consumer. However, they will be forced to deliver shows a la carte rather than bundled into packages where consumers are charged for cable television shows regardless of whether they watch them or not.

One response of the television production industry has been to set up their own online streaming services, the most popular of which is Hulu. Hulu is a joint venture of the Walt Disney Company, the News Corporation's Fox Broadcasting unit, Comcast's NBC Universal unit, and Providence Equity Partners. The original idea was that the movie and television studios would develop their own streaming and downloading service to counter the growth of online leaders like Apple, Netflix, and Amazon. The original plan called for advertising-supported "free content." While it has had its ups and downs, today Hulu has 30 million monthly visitors, and about 3 million subscribers to its $8 a month subscription. In 2012, Hulu began selling several self-produced television series, making it appear more like a traditional cable TV network (Cheney, 2012). Wall Street analysts believe Hulu has a confusing business model with conflicting interests. Other Internet distributors such as Apple, Google, and Netflix have all indicated they will begin producing their own "television" content for exclusive distribution on the Internet, as a way to obtain low-cost, current content (Sharma and Connect, 2013). If cable networks do not move fast enough, they may lose out to Internet distributors like Netflix, which is successfully moving into production of television series. In 2013, Netflix launched four critically acclaimed and popular series: House of Cards, Hemlock Grove, Arrested Development, and Orange is the New Black.

MOVIES

In Hollywood, box office is up, DVDs are down but not out, and Internet downloading and streaming is way up, offering many different and competing online distribution alternatives. As a result, prices for movie content charged by Hollywood are rising, pinching the profitability of distributors like Netflix, Amazon, Apple, and Google. For the first time in a decade, both box office theater receipts and attendance is up. Global consumer spending on movies hit $62 billion in 2012, up 2% from the year before, as recession-weary consumers went to the movies for relief (IHS iSuppli, 2013). Home movie sales in the United States increased for the first time in seven years to $18 billion (up .23%). This is down 20% from its peak on 2004, but at least it is improving. Overall sales of packaged physical goods (DVDs and Blu-ray disks) continued their slide, falling %6. Online spending soared with streaming sales (Netflix, Hulu, and others) rising 45%, and download sales of movies (Apple and Amazon) rising 35%. Total digital movie spending was up 28% in 2013, and accounted for $5.4 billion, 30% of the home entertainment market (Orden, 2013). Still, DVD and Blu-ray constitute a vital source of revenue: 61% of home movie revenue comes from DVDs (about $11 billion). On average, Hollywood receives 50 cents from every streamed movie, about $2 for each downloaded movie, and $4.50 for each DVD/Blu-ray sale. The challenge for Hollywood is that its fastest growing sales are its least profitable, and its most profitable products are declining in sales (NPD Group, 2013b).

The Hollywood movie industry is going through a difficult transition from a reliance on DVDs, its primary revenue generator over the last decade, to a new marketplace where consumers want to watch movies on their PCs, tablet computers, and their smartphones. In 2013, Americans spent more money on online videos (both streaming and purchased films) than they did on DVDs. Consumers are expected to download or stream 4 billion movies in 2013, versus renting or purchasing 2.4 billion DVDs (IHS iSuppli, 2013). A little over 91 million Americans watch movies online in 2013 (see **Figure 10.13**). Digital preferences are changing: consumers increasingly want access to cloud-stored movies rather than downloading entire movies to their devices. There are many parallels with the television industry: a very rapid growth in the mobile platform, expansion of cloud computing to support instant streaming of movies, and a change in consumer behavior in which movie viewing becomes both

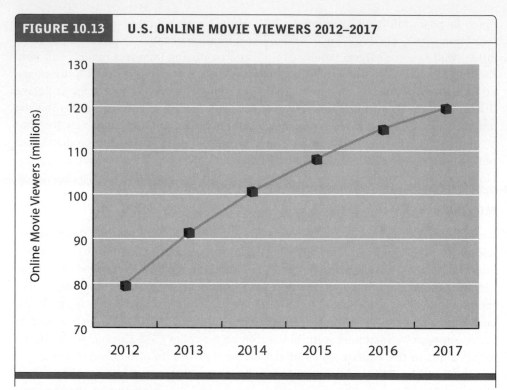

FIGURE 10.13   **U.S. ONLINE MOVIE VIEWERS 2012–2017**

SOURCE: Based on data from eMarketer, Inc., 2013f.

more individualized (watch whatever you want on your phone) and more social (let's text or tweet as we watch the movie). Both the television and movie industries are concentrated oligopolies with little competition. Pundits may write about the "indie" television movement, along with indie films built for the Internet, and the hundreds of millions of nonpremium movies on YouTube. But these subpremium efforts produce subpremium revenues or no revenues at all.

Hollywood is weathering the digital onslaught far better than is the music industry. Hollywood has a potent weapon in its corner: no one goes online to see zeroes and ones. Instead, they download or stream movies to be happy, sad, awed, romantically stimulated, or agitated. The future of online movies is very bright: it is expected to rise continuously worldwide through 2016 (IHS, 2012b). Hollywood has few competitors. Global sales of Hollywood movies are soaring: 60% of movie revenues are coming from foreign markets, especially developing markets. Also, movies are far larger than music tracks and much more difficult to illegally download and move around the Web without detection. And unlike the music labels, who allowed a single distributor (Apple iTunes) to dominate online sales, the movie producers have Apple, Google (YouTube), Amazon, Netflix, Hulu, VUDU, and others competing for distribution rights.

Major studios and production groups in Hollywood and New York still dominate profit-making movie and television content production. But the movie industry faces a more challenging environment than does television because, unlike TV, it heavily depended for several decades on physical DVDs, which are rapidly losing favor with consumers who want to watch movies they can download or stream on any of several digital devices. DVD sales were cut in half from 2006 to 2012.

In 2012, for the first time, consumers will view more and pay more for Web-based movie downloads, rentals, and streams than for DVDs or related physical products (eMarketer, Inc., 2012d). As with television, the demand for feature-length Hollywood movies appears to be expanding in part because of the growth of smartphones and tablets. In addition, the surprising resurgence of music videos, led by VEVO, is attracting millions of younger viewers on smartphones and tablets. Online movies began a growth spurt in 2010 as broadband services spread throughout the country. In 2011, online movie viewing doubled in a single year. In 2013, about 91 million Internet users are expected to view movies, more than one-third of the adult Internet audience. Online movie viewing is growing faster than all video viewing (which includes TV shows) (IHS iSuppli, 2012a; eMarketer, Inc., 2013a).

The size of the online movie business is difficult to ascertain because TV show rentals and movies are often lumped together. Nevertheless, industry observers estimate the total digital online movie market at about $5.4 billion in 2013. To put this in perspective, the total annual revenues of Hollywood studios when all revenue streams are combined is about $70 billion. So at this point, the Internet and online distribution is a small part of the overall picture, but one that is growing very rapidly. Netflix is the largest Internet video distributor (44% of online video and movie revenues), followed by Apple, and then a host of smaller services (Chen, 2013; NPD Group, 2013a) (see **Figure 10.14**).

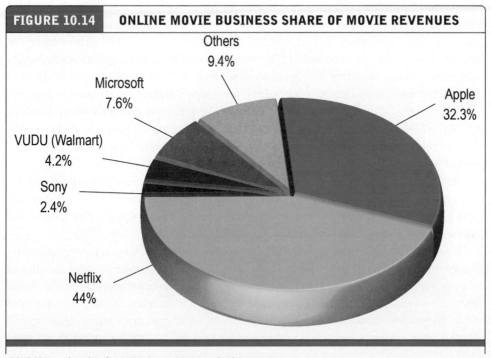

FIGURE 10.14   **ONLINE MOVIE BUSINESS SHARE OF MOVIE REVENUES**

Others 9.4%

Microsoft 7.6%

VUDU (Walmart) 4.2%

Sony 2.4%

Apple 32.3%

Netflix 44%

SOURCE: Based on data from NPD Group, 2013a, and industry sources.

iVOD (Internet video on demand)
streaming video to consumers for a subscription fee

EST (electronic sell-through)
downloading movies to consumers for home or cloud storage

There are two kinds of online movie sales and business models: **iVOD (Internet video on demand)**, and **EST (electronic sell-through)**. Netflix is the leading example of iVOD, with a business model of streaming video and movies to consumers for a subscription fee. iTunes is the leading example of EST, with a business model of consumers downloading movies to their home storage devices or to a cloud server where they can be watched at any time, from any device.

The online movie industry is a complex web of competing forces with conflicting interests. The existing Hollywood movie industry, which creates the products that produce the revenues, is threatened by the piracy of its products, loss of control over its traditional and very profitable distribution channels (largely movie theaters, television networks, and sales retailers of its DVD products), and the growth of powerful technology players such as Apple, Google, and Amazon, who own online movie stores and also sell the physical devices used to watch movies.

Piracy remains a threat to the movie and television industry despite years of effort by the industry and government to reduce piracy. Nevertheless, industry studies find that 24% of Internet traffic worldwide involves infringing content (illegal copies of movies and music), and about half of this involves bit torrent traffic (Envisional, 2013). In the United States, only 17% of Internet content is infringing. These numbers have declined in the last five years. BitTorrent is the most common illegal file transfer system. Other forms on Internet piracy include cyberlockers/file hosting sites (like Megaupload.com, now shut down), and third-party portals like MovieWatch and Movie2k, which link users to illegitimate streaming video and movie sites.

In the past, the movie industry estimated that it lost over $6 billion a year in pirated movies distributed over the Internet, copied from DVDs, early production copies, and in-theater videoing (Bialik, 2013). More recent academic research now estimates the loss is closer to $2 to $3 billion in the United States, roughly 10% of the $30 billion movie industry in the United States (Danaher et al., 2013). Critics argue the industry has exaggerated the losses. The emergence of multiple legitimate sources for streaming and downloading movies in a convenient and safe manner appears to have reduced the overall amount of piracy, both for movies and music. A Google research paper found that searches for pirated movies peaked in 2008, and have been dropping steadily, while searches for online rentals and streaming are up (Google, 2011). Insofar as searches are an indicator of consumer interest and intent, the public interest in pirated movies is declining.

In countries like France, which has passed strong laws to protect artists and discourage illegal downloading (the HADOPI laws), once the laws were implemented, sales of movies on DVDs and legitimate downloading sites increased by 25% in the following twelve months (Danaher et al., 2013).

Government actions to close down cyberlockers also can have a powerful impact on movie sales. In a natural experiment testing the impact of cyberlockers on sales of movies, in January 2012, the U.S. government, along with other governments, closed down the world's largest cyberlocker, Megaupload.com. In a few days, 25 petabytes of music and movies disappeared from the Internet. In 12 countries where Megaupload was the most widely used, digital revenues for two movie studios in the study were

6–12% higher in the 18 weeks following the shutdown (Danaher and Smith, 2013; Fritz, 2013). With few exceptions, the academic literature produced since 2000 shows that piracy causes a significant reduction in sales of legitimate movies (Danaher et al., 2013)

In 2013, the movie and Internet industries are both cooperative and competitive, with an explosion in alliances and agreements, many at cross purposes with one another. In 2012, Apple, the leading digital-movie downloading site, reached an agreement with five movie studios that allows consumers to buy their films on Apple's iTunes Store on one Apple device, store them on Apple's iCloud movie service, and then watch the same film on any Apple device (Vascellaro et al., 2012). The revenue split was not announced but movie studios much prefer users to own movies rather than rent because ownership generates more revenue. Meanwhile, 70 movie studios spent three years coming up with a cyberlocker service called Ultra-Violet that performs many of the same functions as iCloud. **UltraViolet** is a proof-of-purchase system where users enter a code into their UltraViolet online account attached to purchased DVDs, or online-purchased movies, which gives them access to that movie from any device, including Android and Apple smartphones. Walmart is offering its customers in-store assistance in setting up UltraViolet accounts, and storing their DVDs in the cloud (Kung, 2012). In the last year, Hollywood studios have avoided setting up their own Internet distribution sites, and Silicon Valley giant distributors have decided not to make movies. Instead, cooperation and alliances are the order of the day.

UltraViolet
movie industry proof of DVD purchase program that allows playback of DVDs to any digital device

MUSIC

In the music industry, revenues have stabilized and started to grow again, albeit at a slow pace. CDs are declining but still a strong profit center. Digital revenues are up strongly. And even vinyl is making a return. Global music industry revenues have stabilized at $27 billion for the first time since 2009, when they started falling from $35 billion. The U.S. music industry generates about $7.1 billion and has started to head up slightly for the first time in a decade. Digital music now accounts for over half of music revenue in the United States, about $4 billion (Nielsen, 2013a). The other half of music revenues derives largely from the sale of CDs—still a mainstay of the industry since they first appeared in 1982, over thirty years ago. Consumer tastes in music change much more slowly than is commonly thought. Vinyl record sales hit a new high of 5 million units in 2012, expanding at 30% a year, but are still a niche product with 2% of the industry revenues, enough to sustain growth in what remains of independent record stores (eMarketer, Inc., 2013g, 2012e).

While the classic bundled CD album was supposed to disappear in the digital age, replaced by unbundled single tracks, albums have made a comeback. For the second year in a row, the top-selling CD album was Adele's 21 with more than 10 million units sold since release. It was also the top-selling digital download album, with 3.8 million units sold in the last year. Both were a record in terms of sales for any album since 2004. After 12 years of bad digital news, with some predicting the record industry would collapse and albums were dead, the music industry is staging a steady comeback from the abyss created by new technology, and, in part, its own obstinacy. Great artists and their music can still sell traditional CDs albums as well as digital albums.

More than any of the other content industries, the recorded music industry has suffered the most from the onslaught of digital devices and Internet distribution. For most of its history, the music industry depended on a variety of physical media to distribute music—acetate records, vinyl recordings, cassette tapes, and finally CD-ROMs. At the core of its revenue was a physical product. Since the 1950s, that physical product was an album—a collection of bundled songs that sold for a much higher price than singles. The Internet changed all that when, in 2000, a music service called Napster begin distributing pirated music tracks over the Internet to consumers using their PCs as record players. Despite the collapse of Napster due to legal challenges, hundreds of other illegal sites showed up, resulting in music industry revenues falling from $14 billion in 1999 to an estimated $7.1 billion in 2013. The appearance of powerful mobile media players beginning in 2001 that could be connected to the Internet, like Apple's iPod, and later iPhone and iPad, further eroded sales of CD albums.

The music industry initially resisted the development of legal digital channels of distribution, but ultimately and reluctantly struck deals with Apple's new iTunes Store in 2003, as well as with several small subscription music services, for online distribution. Today, digital downloads of tracks from albums are widely perceived as the saviour of the music industry. Nevertheless, revenues from the sales of digital downloads of individual songs from iTunes selling for 99 cents pale in comparison to revenues produced by CD albums.

Clearly the future of music is digital. **Figure 10.15** shows consumer spending on digital music (both downloads and streams), which is expected to reach $5.5 billion in 2016, up from $4 billion in 2013 (RIAA, 2012). In 2013 there will be an estimated 50 billion streams and sales of 27 million digital and track downloads.

There are two kinds of digital music services, each with a different business model: digital download and streaming subscription services. Digital download services (also known as "download to own") are exemplified by iTunes, Amazon, and Google Play, where users download tracks and albums a la carte and pay a fee for each song. Increasingly, the songs are stored on a cloud server as well as the user's device so users can listen to the music from any of several personal devices. All revenue derives from the sale of music tracks.

Streaming subscription services (also known as Internet radio) like Pandora, Lastfm, iHeart, and Spotify allow users access to free streamed music for a limited number of hours per month and rely on advertising to generate revenue for the free streams. The music is delivered to users from a cloud server and is not stored on user devices. Users can also subscribe for a monthly fee, but fewer than 10% of stream listeners pay for subscriptions, relying instead on the free service with ads. Sites like Pandora are curated sites where users select an artist they want to listen to, and then the site uses experts and algorithms to build a list of artists similar to the artist selected by the user. Users do not control what they hear and cannot repeat a selection. Users

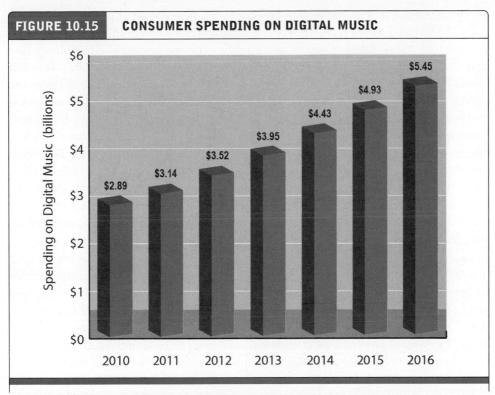

FIGURE 10.15   CONSUMER SPENDING ON DIGITAL MUSIC

SOURCE: Based on data from the Recording Industry Association, 2013; eMarketer, Inc., 2012e.

in this sense do not own the music or control it. While most subscription services use freemium business models, some like Rhapsody.com offer only a subscription service for a monthly fee ($10) that gives users access to millions of songs stored on the site's servers. Users can select specific artists and specific tracks, as if they owned the tracks. The music can be downloaded to user devices, and the user can have access to whatever songs they select using any device. However, once a user's subscription lapses, access to the music disappears (eMarketer, Inc., 2013h).

Digital download is the largest part of the digital music industry, producing 90% of the revenue in digital music, or about $3.6 billion annually. The largest players are iTunes and Amazon, followed by Google Play. While illegal pirated file sharing and downloads of music were the leading edge of a digital tide that deeply disrupted the music industry beginning in the 1990s, iTunes and similar legal download sites have saved the music label firms by generating solid revenues and profits, albeit not as generous as in the heyday of CDs. While music labels might make $7 on a CD sold at $16, they only make about 32 cents for a single track downloaded from iTunes for 99 cents. Digital albums produce about $3.00 for the music labels, roughly half of a CD album sale. Artists are similarly impacted, facing a halving of their incomes in the digital environment.

While digital downloads to own constitute the largest part of digital music revenues, the fastest growing segment is the streaming music services. The leading players are Pandora, Yahoo Music, Last.fm, and Spotify. With the growth of cloud computing and cloud-based music services, the very concept of "owning" music began to shift instead to "access" to music from any device, anywhere. Streaming music services are adding new listeners at a growth rate of 47.5% in 2013. Unfortunately, while streaming services are growing listeners at a torrid pace, they have not managed to earn a profit because of infrastructure costs, the costs of acquiring music content from the music labels, and freemium business models supported by advertising revenues. For artists and music label firms, streaming services have little to offer. While music labels might receive 32 cents for every iTunes track they sell, they receive only .63 of a penny on a streamed version of the same song. This revenue is split with the artists who receive .32 of a penny. Rolling Stone calculated that a very popular song selling one million streams would produce revenue of $3,166 for the artist and a similar amount for the music label. For this reason, many artists and groups refuse to allow streaming of their music; studios release only limited tracks of their popular musicians, and charge a fee for even free songs broadcast by the sites. Digital streaming for the music labels and artists is similar to traditional broadcast radio, which pays very little for the music it plays. Music labels allow the streaming services to stream music in the hope of interesting listeners to purchase a CD or download a track from iTunes. In fact this model does work somewhat, and a site like Pandora does receive referral fees from sites like Amazon for directing traffic to them.

Streaming subscription services are expected to generate about $1.22 billion in revenue in 2013 (Accustream, 2013). Pandora in 2013 has 71 million users (unique visitors) in August 2013, up 30% in the last year. Pandora users listened to 3.88 billion hours of music in the second quarter of 2013, up about 18% over last year. Revenues rose 55% in the quarter to $157 million. Pandora also provides one of the most popular mobile apps, and its mobile ads revenue was $116 million. As impressive as these numbers are, Pandora lost $7.8 million in the second quarter, up from a $5.4 million loss a year earlier. Less than 10% of listeners become paying subscribers. None of the streaming subscription services has ever shown a profit. It is unclear if streaming music is a viable business model. Pandora and the other streaming services demonstrate negative scale: the bigger they become, the more money they lose. Investors have nevertheless poured money into Pandora and Spotify hoping that their large audiences can be monetized. And Apple has announced its new iTunes radio service for the Fall of 2013 (eMarketer, Inc., 2013h). A direct competitor with Pandora, iTunes Radio has both free ad-supported options and a subscription service for $25 per year, undercutting Pandora's annual fee of $36. The music never stops.

GAMES

No Internet media content form has grown as explosively as online games. Well over 125 million Internet users play some kind of game online in the United States, and that number swells to over 300 million worldwide (NPD Group, 2013c). There are four types of Internet gamers. Casual gamers play games on a PC or laptop computer. Social

FIGURE 10.16	ONLINE GAMING AUDIENCE

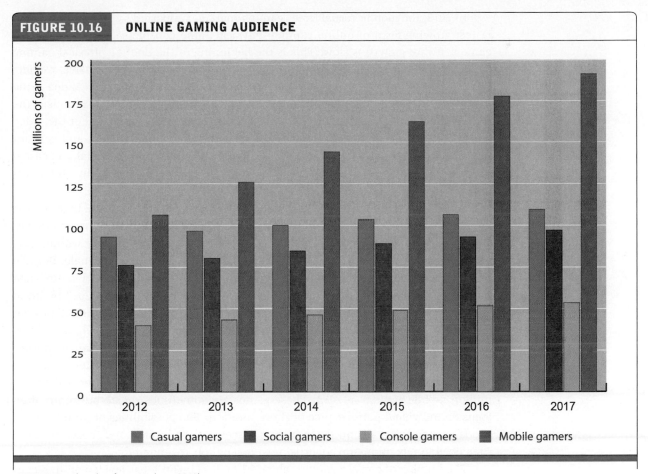

SOURCE: Based on data from eMarketer, 2013b.

gamers play games using a Web browser on a social network like Facebook. Mobile gamers play games using their smartphones or tablet computers. Console gamers play games online (or offline) using a console like Xbox, PlayStation, or Wii. Often, console gamers are connected over the Internet to enable group play. **Figure 10.16** illustrates the relative size of these four online gaming audiences and their future growth prospects. Because people play games in a variety of different venues, the total number of online gamers is on the order of 125 million, about 50% of all Internet users. Estimates vary, but in 2013, industry analysts peg annual sales of console games (hardware and software) at around $15 billion, and sales of subscriptions, virtual goods, and services on social, mobile, and casual gaming platforms at around $5 billion. One of the most widely played mobile casual games is *Angry Birds*. In *Angry Birds,* players launch birds at green pigs hiding inside buildings using a sling shot to blast away the pig and the building. As mindless as this sounds, *Angry Birds* was released in 2009, and had been downloaded in various editions more than 1.8 billion times by 2013 (Anderson, 2012).

In 2013, the mobile casual "free" gaming market, supported by advertising, is the fastest growing form of online gaming; physical game console sales are down, and game software growth is slow. This is the beginning of the end for physical gaming consoles and expensive software cartridges, and the rise of less expensive, mobile, online alternatives. Video game sales shrunk in July 2013 nearly 20%. Video game titles fell 20% (Sher, 2013). Nevertheless, like DVDs in movies and CDs in music, the sale of video game hardware and boxed software generates nearly 70% of the video game industries revenue. The challenge for the video game console and content market is to move onto the mobile platform and still make profits. Social and casual gaming—often lumped together in a single number—is growing at 10% in 2013, but is expected to slow over time to about 5% in 2017.

Social gaming on sites like Facebook grew very rapidly in 2010–2012 in large part due to the success of Zynga games like *Farmville*, *CityVille*, and *Words With Friends*. Online social gaming enlarged the demographic of gamers to include women and older people, compared to console gamers who tend to be young and male. But like other game platforms, consumers tire of current games and are attracted to the latest market entrants. Users of various Zynga "ville" games have fallen in 2013 by up to 50%, down to 39 million active users (Rusli, 2013). In 2013, the high flying Zynga cut its staff by 20% and its stock sank to $3 a share after reporting large declines in audience. Zynga had failed to make the move to mobile gaming, and its reliance on sales of virtual goods becomes more difficult in the mobile environment. Mobile gamers are the largest segment of the online gaming audience. There will be more than 126 million mobile gamers in 2013. These games are sometimes social, but more often focus on individual performance of short duration. The possibilities of selling virtual goods or displaying ads on these mobile games is very limited and therefore these sites need to rely on in-app advertising to make their revenue targets.

The number of console gamers, about 43 million in 2013, has leveled off in recent years. In part this is due to the age of the platforms. The Xbox, PlayStation, and Wii are old, have not been able to expand much beyond the young male demographic, and the games typically have large initial sales that wane quickly.

While casual and social gaming rapidly grows, nearly all these online and mobile games are free and users do not stay in the games very long. These two features make it difficult for gaming firms to monetize their user base by showing advertisements and charging for services. The business model of social and casual gaming is still not settled. Marketers have just recently begun to build video marketing campaigns that increase a brand's engagement and interaction with customers who are playing at social mobile gaming sites (Olsen, 2012).

THE ONLINE ENTERTAINMENT INDUSTRY STRUCTURE

The most likely development in industry structure will be the movement of Internet channel owners like Google and Apple into the content creation business. By creating their own content, distributors can reduce their costs of content and develop entertainment that is uniquely suited to the Internet, not just copies of the Hollywood and television styles of content. The existing online entertainment industry value chain is

FIGURE 10.17   ENTERTAINMENT INDUSTRY VALUE CHAINS

highly inefficient and fractured. For the entertainment industry to survive and prosper on the Web, there needs to be a reorganization of the value chain either through corporate mergers, strategic alliances, or both. In the process of reorganization, traditional distributors (like cable TV and broadcast television) most likely will experience severe disruptions to their business models as Internet power houses like Google, Apple, and Amazon replace them as a distribution media for video and movies.

Figure 10.17 illustrates the existing players and industry value chains and three alternative arrangements. The entertainment industry has never been a neat and tidy industry to describe. There are many players and forces—including government regulators and courts—that shape the industry. In the existing model, creators of entertainment such as music labels or television producers sell to distributors, who in turn sell to local retail stores or local television stations, who then sell or rent to consumers.

In the film industry, court decisions in the 1930s and 1940s forced production studios to give up ownership of local theaters on antitrust grounds, fearing the large Hollywood production studios would monopolize the film industry. One possible alternative to this fractionated industry is the content owner direct model. The Internet offers entertainment content producers (the music labels, Hollywood studios, and television content producers) the opportunity to dominate the industry value chain by eliminating the distributors and retailers and selling directly to the consumer. This has not yet been a successful model to date because the content producers have not independently developed large Internet audiences and have not been successful on the Internet. A second possibility is the Internet aggregator model. In this model, Web-based intermediaries such as Yahoo, Google, Amazon, and MSN that aggregate large audiences enter into strategic alliances with content owners to provide content to the aggregators.

A third possible model is the Internet innovator model, in which successful Internet technology companies that develop the technology platforms (such as Apple, Google, Facebook, and Amazon, as well as Internet communications platform providers like Verizon and Comcast) move back into the value chain and begin creating their own content for exclusive distribution on their proprietary platform or channels. So far, Internet distributors have not chosen this path, but they might if the content owners refused to license their works on favorable terms for online distribution.

Insight on Technology: Hollywood and the Internet: Let's Cut a Deal describes how Hollywood studios and Internet distributors are cutting deals to provide more video and movie content online.

INSIGHT ON TECHNOLOGY

HOLLYWOOD AND THE INTERNET: LET'S CUT A DEAL

In tough times, people go to the movies. All things considered, 2012 was a good year for the movie industry. Despite the continuing effects of the recession, or because of it, box office receipts were $10.8 billion in North America, up 6% from the previous year. Global box office sales were also up, to $34.7 billion in 2012, a record, and 6% higher than the previous year. Even more important, in 2012, admissions were actually up for the first time since 2009, reaching 1.3 billion in the United States, and ticket prices were stable. The number of films released in 2012 was up 10% to 677 new films. And online revenues from downloading and streaming exploded to $5.4 billion (about 30% of the home entertainment market). In 2013, Apple says users are downloading 800,000 TV shows and 350,000 movies a day. By any measure, the Hollywood money machine has been transformed by the Internet as DVD physical unit sales declined to half of what they were in 2005. But, unlike the music business, it has not been substantially disrupted. Hollywood is still in control of its fate.

The year also boasted the continuing success of the highest-grossing movies of all time. *Avatar* (2009) had grossed over $3 billion in global box office receipts by the end of the year. *Avatar's* budget was estimated at $300 million. Continuing sales of DVDs, and revenues from online streaming services and sales at the iTunes Store, drove revenues for even older movies. The second highest grossing movie, *Titanic,* hit $2.2 billion in revenue since its release in 1997. More recent blockbusters include *The Avengers* (2012), generating $1.5 billion, and *Harry Potter and the*

Deathly Hallows—Part 2 (2011), generating $1.3 billion. If only all movies could produce results like these, Hollywood would be golden again. One impact of the Internet on Hollywood revenues is that consumers can easily and inexpensively watch older movies that they did not see or that they want to revisit years after their release. The Internet is making Hollywood's backlist much more valuable.

But all is not well in Tinseltown. Once movies are shown in theaters, where Hollywood generates only 20% of its revenue, they move on to less-profitable venues, from DVDs (which are very profitable) to cable television video-on-demand services, and then to Internet distributors like Netflix and Apple for either purchase, rental downloads, or streaming. Internet streaming services like Netflix pay the least, and therefore, Hollywood does not sell current content to Netflix, preferring to deal with Apple, who charges its customers $5–$10 for recently released movies for download. Eventually, movies end up with broadcast television stations years after they were released. This "release window" differs for various films based on the studio's estimate of the revenue potential for each film. A very popular film will be delayed all along the release window.

Hollywood is facing several problems moving forward to a world where most people will be watching movies on the Internet, either at home, or on the go, using tablet computers and smartphones. One problem is that the fastest growing segment of its business, the Internet, is also the least profitable. A second problem is that Hollywood does not control its own Internet distri-

(continued)

bution network, but instead is forced to rely on the likes of Netflix, Apple, Amazon, and Google, each of whom attract large online audiences. Likewise, the big Internet distributors face a content problem: they cannot attract large audiences without recently made movies. Old movies and movie libraries on Netflix have a limited appeal, and consumers are looking for the latest releases.

Initially, Hollywood was highly dependent on Amazon's sales of DVDs as rental revenue from physical stores declined. iTunes is still the largest downloading service of movies a la carte (so-called electronic sell-through, or EST). In the last two years, the market dynamics have changed, in large part because of Netflix's success with its streaming video model. Why download to own when you can subscribe to anything you want? Hollywood is in the enviable position of being pursued by Internet distributors who are short of high-quality content. This is so different from what happened in the music business over the last decade. Multiple buyers of movies have appeared, not just Amazon or iTunes. Google is developing its own home TV device (like Apple TV) that may be a platform for movie streaming. Hulu is ramping up again as a studio-owned distribution platform.

Netflix continues to dominate online movie revenues, with a 44% market share compared to Apple at 32%. At one time, Apple had a 70% share of Internet movie revenue, and Hollywood studios feared Apple would be able to dominate Internet distribution and dictate prices. Now with Netflix dominating the streaming market, Hollywood fears it will be forced to sell its product for a pittance compared to DVD prices. For this reason, Hollywood has been restricting the release of movies to Netflix, doling out access to recent movies very carefully. Meanwhile, both Apple and Google are planning streaming services to compete with Netflix, which can only raise prices that Hollywood studios charge for recent movies.

More and more large firms are entering the premium video downloading and streaming market, and competing with one another for Hollywood movies, and driving up prices. Google is expanding its movie service beyond rentals to include sales of digital movies; Walmart's VUDU, and Best Buy's CinemaNow are promoting their movie rentals and sales. VUDU cut a deal with several major studios to supply rentals of movies on the same day they are released on DVDs, months before they become available on Netflix. Amazon is seeking to strike deals with the studios for digital a la carte purchases and streaming of recent movies. In 2012, Amazon struck a deal with Viacom to purchase TV episodes and movies to stock its forthcoming streaming service. In May 2013, Amazon announced it would produce five original TV series for streaming to its Amazon Prime subscribers for no additional cost. Amazon produced 14 pilot series, and allowed user feedback to determine which to finally produce. Amazon may not charge for these series in the future, seeing the investment as a way to sell diapers and other other consumer goods on its retail site, or to populate its growing Kindle library and a future Kindle movie store.

In late 2011, Google's YouTube announced the expansion of its movie rental service by adding 3,000 new films. YouTube finally signed deals with the major Hollywood studios including Warner Brothers, Sony, Universal, and Lionsgate. Most movies will be priced at $2.99. No subscriptions are required, it's a la carte. Hello Netflix and Hulu! In addition, Google is spending $300 million to produce its own content, making deals with Hollywood and New York production companies as a way to avoid hefty commissions

(continued)

paid to these same studios for their content. Imagine, "The Google Comedy Hour!"

One result of all this competition for Hollywood content is rising prices paid by the distributors, and a feeling in Hollywood that they can maintain some semblance of control over their fate, unlike the music industry. In fact, the prices being paid by Netflix and others exceed those paid by cable television video-on-demand services. For instance, Netflix cut a multi-year deal with the Weinstein Company for exclusive display of *The Artist* (an Academy Award–winning movie), and other films, before the films are released to leading pay-TV channels. The estimated size of this deal is over $200 million. Dreamworks, a Hollywood studio, has signed a deal with Netflix for exclusive access to films for $30 million a movie. Netflix spent nearly $2 billion in 2012 for content to stream to its 30 million subscribers. As a result, its profits fell significantly in 2012. Netflix may be the leading streaming movie site now, but it may be the equivalent of Blockbuster video stores in a few years given the strength and number of its main competitors.

The movie industry itself has launched a new movie service that would possibly give new life to DVDs. The new service is called UltraViolet. Designed to cut down on piracy, and make it possible for consumers to watch their movies on multiple devices, customers will purchase DVDs in retail stores and register the DVD serial number at the same time on the UltraViolet service. Once registered, consumers can watch a digital version of their movies stored on Walmart cloud servers streamed to their smartphones, tablets, or PCs. Apple's iCloud movie service avoids DVDs altogether. Can you imagine Steve Jobs wanting to preserve DVDs? iCloud offers a cyberlocker that allows consumers to purchase digital movies at iTunes and play them on other Apple devices, including Macs. Apple has struck deals with five major studios (Lionsgate, Sony Pictures, Walt Disney, Paramount, and Warner Brothers).

In the end, Hollywood and the Internet need each other, and the only question is how to find the price, define the terms of trade, and cut a deal where both parties come out winners. The flurry of deals in 2013 bodes well for consumers, and probably for both Internet distributors and Hollywood studios. Consumers are finding multiple services that will allow them to watch movies on whatever device is convenient, and move from one device to another with a lot less effort than in the past. Given the shift of eyeballs to online entertainment, Hollywood is expanding its audience while taking a haircut on pricing. With lots of Internet distributors competing, Hollywood gains in power from the competition among alternative distributors. And Internet companies are coming up with even more reasons why consumers should forget about cable TV and watch the Internet, which means more ad revenues for Internet distributors. How all these calculations will work out remains to be determined. Tune in next year on the same channel.

SOURCES: "How the New iPhone Helps Hollywood," by Andy Lewis, *Hollywood Reporter*, September 6, 2013; "Amazon Invests Millions In Original TV Shows To Get You To Buy More Diapers," by Timothy Senovac, *Huffington Post*, May 31, 2013; "Google Goes Hollywood with the 'Internship," by Ronald Grover and Alexei, Oreskovic, Reuters.com, May 28, 2013; "Netflix Passes Apple to Take Lead in Online Movie Business," by Dan Graziano, BGR.com, June 6, 2012; "Hollywood Studios Warm to Apple's iCloud Effort," by Jessica Vascellaro and Erica Ordern, *Wall Street Journal*, March 12, 2012; "Theatrical Market Statistics," Motion Picture Industry Association, March 2012; "Walmart to Give Hollywood a Hand," by Michelle Kung, *Wall Street Journal*, February 28, 2012; "Web Deals Cheer Hollywood, Despite Drop in Moviegoers," by Brooks Barnes, *New York Times*, February 24, 2012; Netflix Secures Streaming Deal With DreamWorks," by Brooks Barnes and Brian Stelter, *New York Times*, September 25, 2011; "For Wal-Mart, a Rare Online Success," by Miguel Bustillo and Karen Talley, *Wall Street Journal*, August 20, 2011; "Painful Profits From Web Video," by Sam Schechner, *Wall Street Journal*, August 15, 2011; "YouTube Is Said to Be Near a Major Film Rental Deal," by Brooks Barnes and Claire Cain Miller, *New York Times*, April 26, 2011; "YouTube Recasts for New Profits," by Jessica Vascellaro, *Wall Street Journal*, April 7, 2011.

Netflix:
The Next Blockbuster?

N etflix is one of those Silicon Valley stories that might make a good movie, or even a television series, because of its potential for disrupting the American television and movie landscape (or what's called "premium video"). Netflix started a video rental business as a small suburban firm with 30 employees, eventually expanding to a national and international powerhouse. Widely popular, the company disrupted and nearly eliminated the video rental store industry led by giants like Blockbuster and Hollywood Video, now among the departed. Sensing that the future was not physical DVDs, but broadband streaming to homes, the company moved aggressively in 2011 to dump its DVD business into a separate firm called Quickster, and focus on streaming, charging $8 for unlimited streaming, and an additional $8 for those who wanted to also rent DVDs. A consumer rebellion unique in Internet history ensued, commonly thought of as the worst public relations incident on the Internet. Subscribers dropped the service in droves, and the company barely recovered from consumer resistance, giving Wall Street investors a colossal headache. After assuaging DVD customers by retaining its rental service at $8, Netflix rapidly returned to profitability and popularity as the largest Internet video streaming service on Earth. But it's not in the clear yet: truly large Internet lions Apple and Google, not to mention the existing cable TV industry, want to dominate the online TV and movie market.

In one possible ending scenario for the Netflix movie, the company challenges the much larger cable television industry, which is based on an entirely different technology and business model, namely, selling expensive bundles of hundreds of TV channels that few people watch. Given Netflix's large national audience of streamers, the company makes new friends in Hollywood and New York that are looking for ways to distribute their shows to a new online, mobile, and social world. Hollywood bends the distribution window so that Internet distributors like Netflix get the same treatment as cable systems by allowing them to show the latest movies and shows at about the same time as cable systems. And the cable television industry is forced to retreat from its bundling background, and offer customers the ability to select just those channels they actually watch. In this dream scenario, Netflix goes on to challenge the cable networks like HBO by producing its own original TV dramas, and adds comedy to the mix.

Clouds on the horizon? You bet. Apple, Amazon, and Google all have their own plans for bringing premium TV series and movies to the millions of Americans who are now streaming videos. Amazon offers free streaming to Amazon Prime customers. Hollywood and New York studios like this competition and fear becoming too dependent on Netflix. So another possible ending for the Netflix movie is that ultimately it can't compete with Apple, Google, and Amazon, and is purchased by one of these firms. Apple's 2012 revenue is a staggering $156 billion, fifty times larger than Netflix, and it has a cash reserve of $145 billion.

No one really knows how this movie ends, certainly not Wall Street, where Netflix's stock has had a yo-yo pattern: starting out in 2002 with its IPO at $15 a share, then idling at $50 a share for many years until July 2011 when it shot to $286 on the strength of its DVD rental business, then falling off a cliff in October 2011 to $50 a share again as it tried to make the transition to a streaming video company. DVD customers started dropping accounts, and streaming customer growth slowed. By the third quarter of 2013, despite a slowing in subscription growth, Netflix appears poised to go head-to-head with the Internet lions who are still working out their services and strategies for entering the emerging Internet TV and film market place. Today, 33% of the Internet's traffic is used by Netflix's streaming service.

Netflix' strength in 2013 is that it is the leading DVD rental and Internet video streaming business in the world. Its 2012 annual revenues hit $3.6 billion, a growth of 12% over the previous year, and up considerably from $2.1 billion in 2010. Its second quarter 2013 revenue of $1 billion was up 20% from the previous year and its profit was $29 million, also up from the previous year, but still meager for $1 billion in revenue. It's possible that Netflix does not scale and that the more subscribers it has, the less profit it makes.

Netflix has nearly 30 million domestic subscribers to its DVD and streaming services, and it has added 680,000 new customers so far in 2013. Netflix delivers one billion movies or TV shows every month, and has a DVD and streaming catalog (which is much smaller) of about 150,000 titles. Only about 2,000 titles are ready for streaming. Netflix generates over 30 million daily rentals of both DVDs and streaming content (compared to Apple's iTunes' 15 million media downloads daily). iTunes has a 65% annual growth rate of downloads. On a market-share basis, Netflix accounts for over 90% of digital movie streaming, while its chief streaming competitors, Amazon and Hulu, make up the remaining market. DVD subscribers, who are more profitable and pay an $8 a month subscription fee, continue to shrink, down to less than 15 million, and shrinking at about 1 million a year. Only 20% of new subscribers sign up for the DVD plan.

In 2011, at the low point of its stock and the high point of subscriber rebellion, a number of factors were preventing Netflix from becoming a more powerful challenger to cable television networks and achieving a better bargaining position with Hollywood and New York studios. Netflix from the beginning was a general-purpose online DVD rental business, and a nascent repository of streaming older movies from the backlists of major studios like MGM, Time Warner, and 20th Century Fox. Netflix had few television shows to stream at a time when viewers were rediscovering older TV shows that could be downloaded or purchased as an entire series, permitting viewers to "binge view" an entire multi-year series in a few evenings. What Netflix needed to attract more subscribers was high-quality, current, contemporary content. It needed more TV shows, even if dated, and original content TV shows that would be fresh and contemporary.

In late 2011 the company set off on a new strategy with three major thrusts: drop thousands of movies that cost dearly, but did not have a large following; pivot towards streaming TV shows; and create new TV show content itself similar to the HBO cable network. In February 2012, it severed its three-year relationship with Starz network, which had supplied older movies like Scarface and a few hits like Toy Story 3. It also allowed to lapse agreements for older movies from MGM and Warner Brothers. In all,

Netflix dropped over 2,000 streaming movie titles, leaving many subscribers without their favorite movies.

Netflix started bulking up on older TV series that no longer were of interest to cable networks, but still had a popular following among key demographics. The strategic pivot to TV shows away from movies reflected the fact that Netflix subscribers were much more interested in TV shows than in feature-length movies: only 10% of Netflix streaming involves movie watching. In fact, this is true across the board of Internet movies, including Apple and Hulu. In addition, Hollywood studios, fearful that Netflix would become too powerful and too popular, challenging Hollywood's control over the release window, for instance, began charging much higher prices for contemporary movies. As a result, Netflix profits were being squeezed by the need to pay billions of dollars to Hollywood for movies. To replace 2,000 movies, Netflix added full seasons of Mad Men, Breaking Bad, and Lost, or what Netflix executives call "26 hour movies." Other less well-known series were added as well, including several reality shows.

The next step was to start producing its own content. In March 2011, Netflix announced it would produce House of Cards, a new TV series starring Kevin Spacey, an award-winning actor, and directed by David Fincher. In a twist, Netflix guaranteed the producers two years of production, and proposed to publish all episodes at once rather than on a week-by-week schedule. This would allow viewers to see the entire 26 hours of House of Cards over a weekend, or several nights, a form of binge viewing that was growing more popular. Later in 2011, Netflix struck a deal with Fox Television Network to make a fourth season of Arrested Development, a series about a dysfunctional family in California, that had aired on Fox Television for three seasons. It received critical acclaim, including six Emmy nominations, but it was not a popular success. Fifteen episodes of the Netflix revival were released in May 2013. There are no Nielsen ratings for Netflix TV shows (or any digital TV shows or DVR viewing of shows). Although Netflix refuses to say how popular these shows are with its subscribers, analysts believe that both series are exceptionally popular. House of Cards went on to become one of the more popular TV shows of the 2012–2013 season, receiving critical acclaim, and 9 Emmy nominations, including one for Best Drama. This was the first time that a digital TV series had been nominated for Best Drama. Arrested Development received four nominations.

In 2013 Netflix finally broke into the Big Leagues of TV show production and distribution (except in this case it was Internet distribution, not cable TV). To boost its TV show inventory, in June 2013 Netflix announced a deal with DreamWorks Animation for over 300 hours of original television programming in an effort to bring Hollywood-caliber content to the Web before its competitors. DreamWorks is attempting to reduce its reliance on feature-length movies, and to focus on developing its animation franchises such as Shrek and The Croods and other characters it owns like Casper the Ghost, Lassie, and Mr. Magoo. DreamWorks left its cable distributor HBO and opted instead to go with Netflix for its movies and TV specials. In August 2013, Netflix began streaming original comedy shows like Aziz Ansari's stand-up comedy, Buried Alive. Netflix' algorithms for recommending movies and TV shows to viewers are a big plus, making it easier for viewers to find shows they want, as well as shows they might not even know they want but are recommended by the algorithms.

To boost its library of contemporary movies, in August 2013 Netflix announced a deal with Weinstein Co., a major American film studio and producer of ten Academy Award films, to become the exclusive subscription TV home for the film studios' content, beginning in 2016. Weinstein chose Netflix over its long-time cable network distributor Showtime. This move puts Netflix into the same league of "premium channel" distributors and in direct competition with other cable networks like HBO, Starz, Showtime, and A&E for the rights to show movies about eight months after their theater run is complete.

In 2013 Netflix is the leading streaming distributor of online TV and movies with 90% of the market. It is competing against Apple, which is the top movie and TV download player with 70% of the download market, a far more lucrative market when consumers pay $5–$10 for a much more current movie or show. Studios like Apple because it is more profitable for them: they get to keep 66% of the download, and have no DVD physical media costs. So Apple, like pay-to-view cable TV, has the most recent movies and TV shows on the Web.

What's different now are three things. First, Internet players (primarily Netflix and Apple, but also Google) are challenging cable networks in the TV and movie distribution market. Second, they are challenging cable systems like Comcast and Time Warner in the distribution market. Just as cable displaced broadcast technology, systems, and owners, so now Internet players like Netflix and Apple are threatening to displace cable distribution systems. Why should consumers pay for hundreds of channels they do not watch? Most cable consumers watch fewer than ten channels, but are forced to pay for a bundle of over a hundred channels. Third, the Internet players are beginning to challenge cable in the production of original content. Fourth, consumers don't like the rising expense of cable TV monthly fees, and don't like paying for unused channels. They are much more comfortable paying a monthly Internet access fee, and then choosing and purchasing a la carte just what they want. The resistance is so strong that Congress has considered several pieces of legislation that would force cable to unbundle its services. In the meantime, a small but growing group of Americans is unplugging cable TV and using the Internet exclusively for entertainment.

How will Netflix compete in the Internet marketspace with Apple and Google, both of whom are developing streaming services? Amazon may also be developing a streaming service. How well will Netflix be able to compete in the larger Internet TV space in terms of producing new and original content, versus, or as well as, striking profitable deals with existing production studios? Amazon, Google, and Apple have their own giant cloud infrastructures that possibly can be less costly than Netflix's business model of renting infrastructure from its potential competitor, Amazon. In an ominous development in August 2013, company insiders are cashing in their stock options and heading for the exits.

If Netflix wins this competition, bundled cable TV will go into a decline because people don't need to buy bundles from cable providers, and because Netflix will have the audience size to provide a new channel for distributing video that is not controlled by cable companies. It will open the doors for Apple TV, Google TV Network, and others, and spell the end of the cable TV business model. This movie is not over till the last episode is finished. Stay tuned.

SOURCES: "Video Streaming Beats DVR and Video On Demand Viewing," eMarketer, Inc., September 6, 2013; "The Comedy Lineup Expands on Netflix," by Brian Stelter, New York Times, August 29, 2013; "Netflix Insiders Take the Money and Run," by Adam Levin-Weinberg, Motley Fool, August 29, 2013; "Netflix Expands Content Deal with Weinstein Co.," Amol Sharma and Ben Fritz, Wall Street Journal, August 20, 2013; "Form 10-Q Netflix Inc.," United States Securities and Exchange Commission, July 25, 2013; "Media Journal: Netflix Profit, Subscribers Rise, but Wall Street Underwhelmed," by William Launder, Wall Street Journal, July 23, 2013; "The State of Streaming TV, According to Netflix," by Tom Gara, Wall Street Journal, July 22, 2013; "Original Content Ever More Important to Netflix," Brian Fitzgerald, Wall Street Journal, July 22, 2013; "Inside Netflix's Historic 'House of Cards' Emmy Nods," Maria LaMagna, July 18, 2013; "How Netflix Is Shaking Up Hollywood," by Amol Sharma, Wall Street Journal, July 7, 2013; "Apple and Netflix Dominate Online Video," by Brian Chen, New York Times, June 19, 2013; "DreamWorks and Netflix in Deal for New TV Shows," by Brooks Barnes, New York Times, June 17, 2013; "Form 10-K Netflix Inc.," United States Securities and Exchange Commission, February 1, 2013; "Once Film Focused, Netflix Transitions to TV Shows," by Brian Stelter, February 27, 2012; "Will Qwikster, a Netflix Spinoff DVD-by-Mail Service, Damage Brand?," Washington Post, September 19, 2011; "Netflix Raises Price of DVD and Online Movies Package by 60%," by Brian Stelter and Sam Grobart, New York Times, July 12, 2011; "Amazon Adds Streaming-Video Service For Prime Members," by Nat Worden and Stu Woo, Wall Street Journal, February 23, 2011.

Case Study Questions

1. What were the most important weaknesses of Netflix's market position in 2010 and 2011?

2. What were the key elements of Netflix's new strategy?

3. What are the implications of Netflix's new strategy for the cable television systems like Comcast and TimeWarner?

4. Why is Netflix in competition with Apple, Amazon, and Google, and what strengths does Netflix bring to the market?

10.5 REVIEW

KEY CONCEPTS

■ **Identify the major trends in the consumption of media and online content, and the major revenue models for digital content delivery.**

Major trends in the consumption of media and online content include the following:
- The average American adult spends around 4,500 hours per year consuming various media. The most hours are spent viewing television, followed by using the Internet and listening to the radio.
- Although several studies indicate that time spent on the Internet reduces consumer time available for other media, recent data reveals a more complex picture, as Internet users multitask and consume more media of all types than do non-Internet users.
- In terms of revenue, television accounts for the most revenue (32%), followed by print media (books, newspapers, and magazines) (27%), and then Internet (12%).
- The three major revenue models for digital content delivery are the subscription, a la carte, and advertising-supported (free and freemium) models.
- Online newspapers, digital radio, mobile games, and online TV are the top four categories of online content.
- The fastest growing paid content area is videos.

■ **Understand digital rights management**
- Digital rights management (DRM) refers to the combination of technical and legal means for protecting digital content from reproduction without permission.
- Walled gardens are a kind of DRM that restrict the widespread sharing of content.

■ **Discuss the concept of media convergence and the challenges it faces.**

The concept of media convergence has three dimensions:

- Technological convergence, which refers to the development of hybrid devices that can combine the functionality of two or more media platforms, such as books, newspapers, television, radio, and stereo equipment, into a single device.
- Content convergence, with respect to content design, production, and distribution.
- Industry convergence, which refers to the merger of media enterprises into powerful, synergistic combinations that can cross-market content on many different platforms and create works that use multiple platforms.
- In the early years of e-commerce, many believed that media convergence would occur quickly. However, many early efforts failed, and new efforts are just now appearing.

■ **Understand the key factors affecting the online publishing industry.**

Key factors affecting online newspapers include:
- *Audience size and growth.* Although the newspaper industry as a whole is the most troubled part of the publishing industry, online readership of newspapers is growing at more than 10% a year, fueled by smartphones, e-readers, and tablet computers.
- *Revenue models and results.* Online newspapers predominantly rely upon an advertising model. Some also supplement revenues by using a subscription revenue model.

Key factors affecting e-books and online book publishing include:
- *Audience size and growth.* E-book sales have exploded, fueled by the Amazon Kindle, Barnes & Noble Nook, and Apple iPad. The mobile platform of smartphones and tablets has made millions of books available online at a lower price than print books. The future of the book will be digital although printed books will not disappear for many years.
- *Challenges.* The two primary challenges of the digital e-book platform are cannibalization and finding the right business model.
- *Competing business models.* E-book business models include the wholesale model and the agency model.
- *Convergence.* The publishing industry is making steady progress toward media convergence. Newly authored e-books are appearing with interactive rich media, which allow the user to click on icons for videos or other material.

Key factors affecting online magazines include:
- *Online audience and growth:* Digital magazine sales have soared, with almost a third of the Internet population now reading magazines online.
- *Magazine aggregation:* Magazine aggregators (Web sites or apps) offer users online subscriptions and sales of many digital magazines.

■ **Understand the key factors affecting the online entertainment industry.**

There are five main players in the entertainment sector: television, motion pictures, music, video games, and radio broadcasting. The entertainment segment is currently undergoing great change, brought about by the Internet and the mobile platform. Consumers have begun to accept paying for content and also to expect to be able to access online entertainment from any device at any time.

Key factors include the following:

- *Audience size and growth.* While music downloads generate the most revenue in 2013, online movies and television are growing dramatically.
- *The emergence of streaming services and the mobile platform.* In the movie and television industries, two major trends are the move to consumers purchasing streaming services, from Amazon, Apple, Hulu, and other channels and the continued increase in online purchases and downloads. Although physical sales of products (DVDs) are dropping significantly, more and more consumers are purchasing movies and television episodes on new mobile devices, such as smartphones and tablets. The music industry is experiencing similar trends as the movie industry: the growth of streaming services, or Internet radio, the continued expansion of online purchases, and increased downloads on mobile devices. However, the unbundling of a traditional music product, the album, into individual songs, has decimated music industry revenues. Of the four types of gamers—casual, social, mobile, and console—the greatest growth is anticipated for mobile gamers, as the mobile market is rapidly expanding along all e-commerce fronts.
- *Industry structure upheaval.* The online entertainment industry structure faces upheaval. The current structure is inefficient and fractured, with Internet channel owners, such as Google and Apple, owning advanced distribution technologies, and content producers and owners, such as television and movie studios, forced to find profitable distribution channels. Concurrently, Internet channel owners are moving into the content creation business.

QUESTIONS

1. What are the three dimensions in which the term "convergence" has been applied? What does each of these areas of convergence entail?
2. What are the basic revenue models for online content, and what is their major challenge?
3. What are the two primary e-book business models?
4. What effect is the growth of tablet computing having on online entertainment and content?
5. What techniques do music subscription services use to enforce DRM?
6. What type of convergence does the Kindle Fire represent?
7. How has the Internet impacted the content that newspapers can offer?
8. What changes have occurred for newspapers in the classified ads department?
9. What are the key challenges facing the online newspaper industry?
10. What are the advantages and disadvantages of e-book content?
11. How has the Internet changed the packaging, distribution, marketing, and sale of traditional music tracks?
12. How has streaming technology impacted the television industry?
13. Why is the growth of cloud storage services important to the growth of mobile content delivery?
14. Has the average consumer become more receptive to advertising-supported Internet content? What developments support this?
15. What factors are needed to support successfully charging the consumer for online content?

16. Why are apps helping the newspaper and magazine industries where Web sites failed?

17. What alternatives do magazine publishers have to using Apple and Google newsstands as distribution channels?

PROJECTS

1. Research the issue of media convergence in the newspaper industry. Do you believe that convergence will be good for the practice of journalism? Develop a reasoned argument on either side of the issue and write a 3- to 5-page report on the topic. Include in your discussion the barriers to convergence and whether these restrictions should be eased.

2. Go to Amazon and explore the different digital media products that are available. For each kind of digital media product, describe how Amazon's presence has altered the industry that creates, produces, and distributes this content. Prepare a presentation to convey your findings to the class.

3. Identify three online sources of content that exemplify one of the three digital content revenue models (subscription, a la carte, and advertising-supported) discussed in the chapter. Describe how each site works, and how it generates revenue. Describe how each site provides value to the consumer. Which type of revenue model do you prefer, and why?

4. Identify a popular online magazine that also has an offline subscription or newsstand edition. What advantages (and disadvantages) does the online edition have when compared to the offline physical edition? Has technology platform, content design, or industry structure convergence occurred in the online magazine industry? Prepare a short report discussing this issue.

CHAPTER 11

Social Networks, Auctions, and Portals

After reading this chapter, you will be able to:

- Explain the difference between a traditional social network and an online social network.
- Understand how a social network differs from a portal.
- Describe the different types of social networks and online communities and their business models.
- Describe the major types of auctions, their benefits and costs, and how they operate.
- Understand when to use auctions in a business.
- Recognize the potential for auction abuse and fraud.
- Describe the major types of Internet portals.
- Understand the business models of portals.

Social Network Fever

Spreads to the Professions

When social networks first appeared a decade ago, it was widely believed the phenomenon would be limited to crazed teenagers already captive to online games and video game consoles. Most of the technorati in Silicon Valley and Wall Street felt this was a blip on the horizon, and their full attention was occupied by search engines, search engine marketing, and ad placement. But when the population of social network participants pushed past 50 million and on to 75 million, even the technical elite woke up to the fact that these huge audiences were not just a bunch of teenagers. Instead, a wide slice of American society was participating. Steve Ballmer, CEO of Microsoft, expressed the conviction as early as September 2007 that social networks would have some staying power, although he tempered that outlook with reservations about just how long that would be, given their youthful appeal and faddish nature. This was just before Microsoft paid $250 million for a small stake in Facebook, which valued the company at $15 billion. Trying to sound convincing, the month before his company spent $1.65 billion for YouTube, Google CEO Eric Schmidt asserted his belief that despite prevailing opinion, social networks were a bona fide business opportunity.

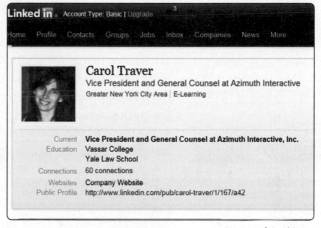

Courtesy of Carol Traver

By October 2013, Facebook had grown to over 1.1 billion members worldwide, challenging Google and Yahoo for face time with the Internet audience. The social network craze obviously has awakened the technology giants, but they focus mostly on the really huge audiences attracted to general social network sites such as Facebook, Twitter, and YouTube. However, in the background there is a fast-growing collection of social networks that are aimed at communities of practitioners or specific interest groups.

Take LinkedIn, for example, probably the best-known and most popular business network site. LinkedIn is an online network with more than 225 million worldwide members in over 200 countries, representing 170 different industries. Two new members join LinkedIn approximately every second. LinkedIn allows a member to create a profile, including a photo, to summarize his or her professional accomplishments. Members' networks include their connections, their connections' connections, as well as people they know, potentially linking them to thousands of others. How members use LinkedIn depends somewhat on their position. Top executives use the site mainly for industry networking and promoting their businesses. Middle managers use LinkedIn primarily to keep in touch with others and also for industry networking. Lower-level employees typically use the site for job searching and networking with co-workers. In 2013, to increase the level of engagement and excitement (some have called the site "boring"), LinkedIn has started

SOURCES: "About Us," LinkedIn.com Press Center, accessed October 1, 2013; "LinkedIn Corporation Market Cap," YCharts.com, accessed September 28, 2013; "Marketing on LinkedIn: New Opportunities, But Old Issues Remain," eMarketer, Inc., August 23, 2013; "More Employers Finding Reasons Not to Hire Candidates on Social Media, Finds CareerBuilder Survey," Careerbuilder.com, June 27, 2013; "LinkedIn Builds Its Publishing Presence," by Leslie Kaufman, New York Times, June 16, 2013; "Number of Active Users at Facebook Over the Years," Associated Press, October, 4, 2012; "How Professionals Use LinkedIn," eMarketer, August 5, 2011; "LinkedFA Offers Social Network for Financial Advisors," by David F. Carr, *Information Week*, June 1, 2011.

to publish posts of CEOs on management topics. On May 18, 2011, LinkedIn went public in what was, at the time, the biggest Internet IPO since Google, raising more than $350 million and giving it a company valuation of $8.9 billion. The company priced its IPO at $45 per share. As of October 2013 its stock had risen to approximately $248 per share, making its market capitalization now well over $28 billion.

Those with a particular interest in the stock market can choose from a crop of Web sites aimed at stock investors who want to share their ideas with other investors. These social networks are not just bulletin boards with anonymous comments, but active communities where users are identified and ranked according to the performance of their stock picks. One network is Stockr. Stockr is a community where stock investors exchange ideas and track the performance of financial bloggers. Like the larger social network sites, the financial sites allow users to connect with other investors, discuss issues focused on the stock market, and sometimes just show off investing prowess. The Motley Fool, one of the best-known online stock investment services, started its CAPS stock-rating social network in 2006 and has around 180,000 members.

You can find similar social network sites for a variety of specific professional groups such as health care (DailyStrength.org), law (LawLink), physicians (Sermo), wireless industry executives (INmobile.org), advertising professionals (AdGabber), and financial advisors (LinkedFA). These social networks encourage members to discuss the realities of their professions and practices, sharing successes and failures. There are also general business social networks designed more to develop a network for career advancement, such as Ecademy and Ryze. The rapid growth of professional social networks, linked to industry and careers, demonstrates how widespread and nearly universal the appeal of social networks is. What explains the very broad attraction to social networks? E-mail is excellent for communicating with other individuals, or even a small group. But e-mail is not very good at getting a sense of what others in the group are thinking, especially if the group numbers more than a dozen people. The strength of social networks lies in their ability to reveal group attitudes and opinions, values, and practices.

Professionals who join social networks need to be careful about the content they provide, and the distribution of this content. As business social networks have grown, and as the number of participants expands, employers are finding them a great place to discover the "inner" person who applies for a job. A March 2013 survey by CareerBuilder, the most widely used employment site in the United States, found that 39% of employers use social networks to screen job candidates. The survey found that 43% of hiring managers who use social media to vet candidates reported they found information that led them not to hire an applicant. Among the reasons were that the candidate posted provocative material (50%), information about drinking or using drugs (48%), criticizing former employers (33%), poor communication skills (30%), and discriminatory comments (28%). On the other hand, 20% of managers found information that led them to hire someone: a professional image, good personality, well-rounded with many different interests, creativity, and communication skills. Based on this survey, it's wise to use Facebook's and other sites' maximum privacy settings, and release to the public only the most innocuous content. Likewise, be cautious of social network sites that do not provide "take down" policies, which allow users to remove embarrassing materials from their pages.

I n this chapter, we discuss social networks, auctions, and portals. One might ask, "What do social networks, auctions, and portals have in common?" They are all based on feelings of shared interest and self-identification—in short, a sense of community. Social networks and online communities explicitly attract people with shared affinities, such as ethnicity, gender, religion, and political views, or shared interests, such as hobbies, sports, and vacations. The auction site eBay started as a community of people interested in trading unwanted but functional items for which there was no ready commercial market. That community turned out to be huge—much larger than anyone expected. Portals also contain strong elements of community by providing access to community-fostering technologies such as e-mail, chat groups, bulletin boards, and discussion forums.

11.1 SOCIAL NETWORKS AND ONLINE COMMUNITIES

The Internet was designed originally as a communications medium to connect scientists in computer science departments around the continental United States. From the beginning, the Internet was intended, in part, as a community-building technology that would allow scientists to share data, knowledge, and opinions in a real-time online environment (see Chapter 3) (Hiltzik, 1999). The result of this early Internet was the first "virtual communities" (Rheingold, 1993). As the Internet grew in the late 1980s to include scientists from many disciplines and university campuses, thousands of virtual communities sprang up among small groups of scientists in very different disciplines that communicated regularly using Internet e-mail, listservs, and bulletin boards. The first articles and books on the new electronic communities began appearing in the mid- to late 1980s (Kiesler et al., 1984; Kiesler, 1986). One of the earliest online communities, The Well, was formed in San Francisco in 1985 by a small group of people who once shared an 1,800-acre commune in Tennessee. It is now a part of Salon.com, an online community and magazine. The Well (Whole Earth 'Lectronic Link) is an online community that now has thousands of members devoted to discussion, debate, advice, and help (Hafner, 1997; Rheingold, 1998). With the development of the Web in the early 1990s, millions of people began obtaining Internet accounts and Web e-mail, and the community-building impact of the Internet strengthened. By the late 1990s, the commercial value of online communities was recognized as a potential new business model (Hagel and Armstrong, 1997).

The early online communities involved a relatively small number of Web aficionados, and users with intense interests in technology, politics, literature, and ideas. The technology was largely limited to posting text messages on bulletin boards sponsored by the community, and one-to-one or one-to-many e-mails. In addition to The Well, early networks included GeoCities, a Web site hosting service based on neighborhoods. By 2002, however, the nature of online communities had begun to change. User-created Web sites called blogs became inexpensive and easy to set up without any technical expertise. Photo sites enabled convenient sharing of photos. Beginning in 2007, the growth of mobile devices like smartphones, tablet computers, digital cameras, and portable media devices enabled sharing of rich media such as photos, music, and videos. Suddenly there was a much wider audience for sharing interests and activities, and much more to share.

A new culture emerged as well. The broad democratization of the technology and its spread to the larger population meant that online social networks were no longer limited to a small group but instead broadened to include a much wider set of people and tastes, especially pre-teens, teens, and college students who were the fastest to adopt many of these new technologies. Entire families and friendship networks soon joined. The new social network culture is very personal and "me" centered, displaying photos and broadcasting personal activities, interests, hobbies, and relationships on social network profiles. In an online social network, the "news" is not something that happened somewhere else to other people; instead, the news is what happened to you today, and what's going on with your friends and colleagues. Today's social networks are as much a sociological phenomenon as they are a technology phenomenon.

Currently, social network participation is one of the most common usages of the Internet. About two-thirds of all Internet users in the United States—about 163 million Americans—use social networks, about 67% of all Internet users and 50% of all adults (eMarketer, Inc., 2013a, 2013b). Facebook has over 1.1 billion active users worldwide (about 230 million in the North America), and about 148 million monthly visitors per month in the United States (Facebook, 2013). There are only seven markets in the world where Facebook is not the leading social network. Twitter is growing exponentially, with an estimated 200 million users worldwide and around 40 million in the United States as of August 2013 (Twitter, 2013; eMarketer, Inc., 2013b; comScore, 2013a). Facebook may not always be the leading social network: the Google+ social network exploded to 25 million users in its first month (Facebook took three years to reach that level), and now has 500 million accounts worldwide, and between 135 to 300 million active users, making Google+ the second leading social network worldwide, ahead of Twitter. In the United States, Google+ has an estimated 30 million active monthly visitors (eMarketer, Inc., 2013c; Kosner, 2013). Facebook's mindshare trumps Google+ by a huge margin, however: the average user spends six minutes per visit on Google+ versus six hours on Facebook.

Social network user numbers are notoriously inaccurate when assessing what exactly is an "active user." Both Facebook and Google+ have integrated their various services, forcing users to be "active" even if they did not intend to be active. Both networks routinely cause people to share personal information even if they did not intend to. People who "Like" a Web site, for instance, are considered "active users" by Facebook. In 2013, Google began automatically adding users of Gmail and its other services as members of Google+. The objective at both sites, as well as others, is to maximize the reported number of active users, and encourage potential users to sign up with the most popular service (Efrati, 2013).

Worldwide, the social network phenomena is even stronger. Social networks are the top online destination in every country, accounting for the majority of time spent online, and reaching at least 60% of active Internet users. Nordic countries ranked highest in social network usage (over 65%), followed by Europe and North America at around 60% (eMarketer, Inc., 2013d). Although Facebook dominates the global social network marketspace, in some countries, more localized social networks are signficant, such as Orkut (owned by Google) in Brazil, Mixi in Japan, Qzone, TenCent Weibo and RenRen in China, Tuenti in Spain, and Vkontakte in Russia. There is an online social network for you to join almost anywhere you go! Unfortunately, there's very little, if any, communication across social networks.

WHAT IS AN ONLINE SOCIAL NETWORK?

So exactly how do we define an online social network, and how is it any different from, say, an offline social network? Sociologists, who frequently criticize modern society for having destroyed traditional communities, unfortunately have not given us very good definitions of social networks and community. One study examined 94 different sociological definitions of community and found four areas of agreement. **Social networks** involve (a) a group of people, (b) shared social interaction, (c) common ties among members, and (d) people who share an area for some period of time (Hillery, 1955). This will be our working definition of a social network. Social networks do not necessarily have shared goals, purposes, or intentions. Indeed, social networks can be places where people just "hang out," share space, and communicate.

It's a short step to defining an **online social network** as an area online where people who share common ties can interact with one another. This definition is very close to that of Howard Rheingold's—one of The Well's early participants—who coined the term *virtual communities* as "cultural aggregations that emerge when enough people bump into each other often enough in cyberspace." It is a group of people who may or may not meet one another face to face, and who exchange words and ideas through the mediation of an online social meeting space. The Internet removes the geographic and time limitations of offline social networks. To be in an online network, you don't need to meet face to face, in a common room, at a common time.

THE DIFFERENCE BETWEEN SOCIAL NETWORKS AND PORTALS

We describe portals in the last section of this chapter. Portals began as search engines and then added content, Internet, and e-commerce services. In order to survive, portals have added many community-building and social network features, such as chat groups, bulletin boards, and free Web site design and hosting, that encourage visitors to stay on the site and interact with others who share their interests. Yahoo, for instance, uses deep vertical content features to retain its audience on-site and maximize revenue opportunities. Portals have begun to measure their success in terms of their social network features. For instance, Yahoo has purchased several Web properties, such as Flickr (a photo-sharing site), which has social network features. Portals have moved toward becoming general community meeting places in an effort to enlarge and retain audience share and increase revenues. User-generated content on portals is one way to entice visitors to stay online at the site (and, of course, view more commercials).

Similarly, sites that began as narrowly focused content or affinity group community sites such as iVillage, a site devoted to women's issues, have added more general portal-like services, including general Web searching, general news, weather, travel information, and a wide variety of e-commerce services. Browsers such as Mozilla Firefox and Microsoft Internet Explorer include social network features as well. There

social network
involves a group of people, shared social interaction, common ties among members, and people who share an area for some period of time

online social network
an area online, where people who share common ties can interact with one another

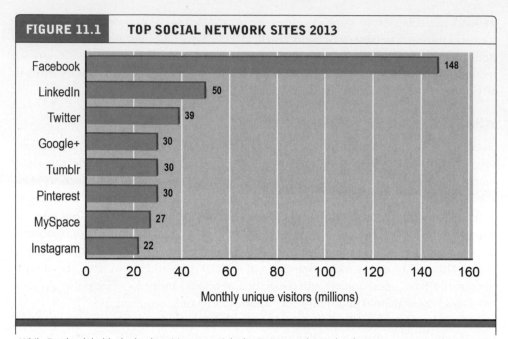

FIGURE 11.1 | **TOP SOCIAL NETWORK SITES 2013**

While Facebook holds the lead position now, LinkedIn, Twitter, and Google+ have stronger growth rates.
SOURCES: Based on data from comScore, 2013b.

is no reason why social networks have to be limited to self-proclaimed social network sites such as Facebook. Social networking is a functionality, not a Web site. For instance, many Web sites have online forums and blogs that are intended to create a sense of community and social network relationships. As a result, social networks and portals have moved closer together, and at times are indistinguishable from one another.

THE GROWTH OF SOCIAL NETWORKS AND ONLINE COMMUNITIES

Facebook, Twitter, LinkedIn, Google +, Pinterest, and Tumblr are all examples of popular online communities. **Figure 11.1** shows the top 10 social network sites, which together account for well over 90% of the Internet's social network activity.

While social networks originally attracted mostly young Internet users, social networks today are not just about teens and college students, but a much larger social phenomenon. More than 50% of Facebook's users are over 35. On Facebook, Twitter, and Google + 's networks, the fastest growing demographic is the 55–64 year-old bracket. While only 5% of the people 65 years of age and older use Twitter, 43% of this age bracket use Facebook (eMarketer, Inc., 2013e; Pew Internet, 2013).

While Facebook and Twitter dominate the news, a new kind of social network is appearing, and growing much faster than Facebook with respect to unique visitors and subscribers. These new sites are attracting marketers and advertisers as well. For instance, Pinterest, described in the opening case in Chapter 1, is a visually oriented site that allows users to curate their tastes and preferences, expressed in visual arts. You can think of Pinterest as a visual blog. Users post images to an online "pinboard." The images can come from any source. Users can also "re-pin" images they see on

TABLE 11.1	OTHER FAST-GROWING SOCIAL SITES
SOCIAL NETWORK	DESCRIPTION
Path	Personal journal for sharing photos, text
Stumbleupon	A search platform for sharing interests
Flickr	The original social photo-sharing site
Instagram	Social photo-sharing site (now owned by Facebook)
Ning	Platform for creating personal social networks
Polyvore	Topic-focused social network (fashion)
deviantART	Web site focused on art, sharing of images
Vevo	Video and music sharing site

Pinterest. Pinterest's membership has skyrocketed since its launch and now has more than 30 million monthly unique visitors in the United States in August 2013. Tumblr is an easy-to-use blogging site with tools for visual and text curating, sharing with others, and reblogging contents. Tumblr started in 2007 and has 30 million users in 2013.

Other new and fast growing sites are not necessarily competing with Facebook, but adding to the social network mix, and enlarging the total social network audience. Facebook's share of the total social market is declining. Facebook is not likely to be the sole place to meet your friends. **Table 11.1** describes some other social sites that are more focused.

It is easy to both overestimate and underestimate the significance of social networks. The top four social network sites in the United States (Facebook, LinkedIn, Twitter, and Tumblr) together have a total monthly unique audience of almost 270 million. In contrast, the top four portal/search engine sites (Google, Yahoo, MSN, and AOL) together have a total monthly unique audience of over 680 million. (Obviously, with 243 million people of all ages on the Internet in the United States, users are unique to more than one site.) Although Facebook's 148 million monthly unique U.S. visitors seems high, consider that Yahoo's various sites have around 196 million in the United States. Still, since 2008, Facebook has grown from a very small Internet audience of less than 20 million, to an Internet behemoth among the top three to four Web sites on the Internet.

The number of unique visitors is just one way to measure the influence of a site. Time on site is another important metric. The more time people spend on a site, called engagement, the more time to display ads and generate revenue. In this sense, Facebook is much more addictive and immersive than the other top sites on the Web. **Table 11.2** illustrates of the different levels of engagement with the top Web and social sites. In the United States, Facebook visitors spend almost seven hours a month on Facebook, compared to about 2.5 hours hours on Yahoo, and a hefty four hours on Google, Google +, and YouTube.

TABLE 11.2	TIME SPENT ON TOP WEB SITES
WEB SITE	MINUTES/VISITOR
Facebook	401
Yahoo!	152
AOL Media Network	129
Google	125
YouTube	117
MSN/WindowsLive/Bing	75
Microsoft	47
Twitter	39
Amazon	38
Pinterest	38
Wikipedia	24
LinkedIn	18
Ask Network	12
MySpace	5
Instagram	1

SOURCES: Based on data from eMarketer, Inc., 2013x, and Nielsen, 2013.

The amount of advertising revenue generated by sites is perhaps the ultimate metric for measuring the business potential of Web sites and brands. The top four search engine companies (Google, Yahoo, Microsoft, and AOL) are expected to generate about $22 billion in U.S. search and display advertising revenue in 2013 (eMarketer, Inc., 2013f, 2013g). In contrast, social network sites in the United States in 2013 are expected to generate about $4.45 billion in advertising revenue (eMarketer, Inc., 2013h). Social network sites are the fastest growing form of Internet usage, but they are not yet as powerful as traditional search engines/portals in terms of ad dollars generated. A part of the problem is that subscribers do not go to social network sites to seek ads for relevant products, nor pay attention to the ads that are flashed before their eyes (see Chapters 6 and 7).

TURNING SOCIAL NETWORKS INTO BUSINESSES

While the early social networks had a difficult time raising capital and revenues, today's top social network sites are now learning how to monetize their huge audiences. Early social network sites relied on subscriptions, but today, most social networks rely on advertising or the investments of venture capitalists. Users of portals and search engines have come to accept advertising as the preferred means of supporting Web experiences rather than paying for it. One important exception is LinkedIn, which offers free memberships to individual job seekers but charges professional recruiters and business firms for premium services. **Figure 11.2** shows the comparative amount of ad spending on various social networks.

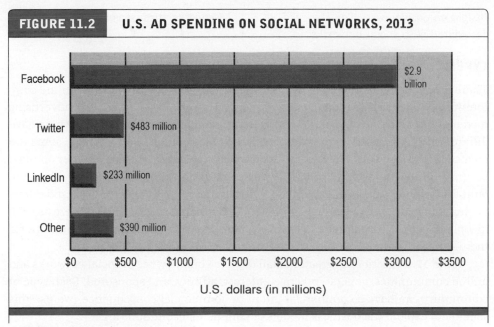

FIGURE 11.2 **U.S. AD SPENDING ON SOCIAL NETWORKS, 2013**

SOURCE: Based on data from eMarketer, 2013h.

Social networks have had a profound impact on how businesses operate, communicate, and serve their customers. The most visible business firm use of social networks is as a marketing and branding tool. More than 90% of the Fortune 500 have established Facebook pages, where "fans" can follow the business and its products and share opinions with the company and other fans. More than 80% of corporations have Twitter feeds for this purpose as well. A less visible marketing use of networks is as a powerful listening tool that has strengthened the role of customers and customer feedback systems inside a business. The software drink industry is a good example. Dr Pepper, for instance, has built up a fan base of 16 million people who Like it on Facebook and 80,000 people talking about the brand. Mountain Dew has about 8 million Likes, Coca-Cola more than 73 million, and Red Bull about 40 million. Twitter has attracted thousands of firms, from Fortune 500 companies to local stores, and over 200 million active users worldwide, 20% of whom follow tweets from brand name firms (Efrati, 2011).

Social networks are where corporate brands and reputations are formed, and firms today take very seriously the topic of "online reputation," as evidenced by social network posts, commentary, chat sessions, and Likes. In this sense, social network sites become an extension of corporate customer relationship management systems and extend existing market research programs. Beyond branding, social network sites are being used increasingly as advertising platforms to contact a somewhat younger audience than Web sites and e-mail, and as customers increasingly shift their eyeballs to social networks. Rosetta Stone, for instance, uses its Facebook page to display videos of its learning technology, encourage discussions and reviews, and post changes in its learning tools. Yet the business use of social networks does not always go well. The

Insight on Society case, *The Dark Side of Social Networks*, discusses some of the risks associated with social networks.

TYPES OF SOCIAL NETWORKS AND THEIR BUSINESS MODELS

There are many types and many ways of classifying social networks and online communities. While the most popular general social networks have adopted an advertising model, other kinds of networks have different revenue sources. Social networks have different types of sponsors and different kinds of members. For instance, some are created by firms such as IBM for the exclusive use of their sales force or other employees (intra-firm communities or B2E [business-to-employee] communities); others are built for suppliers and resellers (inter-organizational or B2B communities); and others are built by dedicated individuals for other similar persons with shared interests (P2P [people-to-people] communities). In this chapter, we will discuss B2C communities for the most part, although we also discuss briefly P2P communities of practice.

Table 11.3 describes in greater detail the five generic types of social networks and online communities: general, practice, interest, affinity, and sponsored. Each type of community can have a commercial intent or commercial consequence. We use this schema to explore the business models of commercial communities.

general communities

offer members opportunities to interact with a general audience organized into general topics

General communities offer members opportunities to interact with a general audience organized into general topics. Within the topics, members can find hundreds of specific discussion groups attended by thousands of like-minded members who share an interest in that topic. The purpose of the general community is to attract enough members to populate a wide range of topics and discussion groups. The busi-

TABLE 11.3	TYPES OF SOCIAL NETWORKS AND ONLINE COMMUNITIES
TYPE OF SOCIAL NETWORK / COMMUNITY	**DESCRIPTION**
General	Online social gathering place to meet and socialize with friends, share content, schedules, and interests. Examples: Facebook, Pinterest, Tumblr, and Twitter.
Practice	Social network of professionals and practitioners, creators of artifacts such as computer code or music. Examples: Just Plain Folks (musicians' community) and LinkedIn (business).
Interest	Community built around a common interest, such as games, sports, music, stock markets, politics, health, finance, foreign affairs, or lifestyle. Examples: E-democracy.org (political discussion group) and PredictWallStreet (stock market site).
Affinity	Community of members who self-identify with a demographic or geographic category, such as women, African Americans, or Arab Americans. Examples: BlackPlanet (African American community and social network site) and iVillage (focusing on women).
Sponsored	Network created by commercial, government, and nonprofit organizations for a variety of purposes. Examples: Nike, IBM, Cisco, and political candidates.

INSIGHT ON SOCIETY

THE DARK SIDE OF SOCIAL NETWORKS

ChapStick thought it had a great marketing idea when it decided to launch a new Facebook ad—a mildly provocative picture of a young woman on her disheveled sofa—derriere in the air—rummaging behind the couch. The ad proclaimed: WHERE DO LOST CHAPSTICKS GO? The subtitle—BE HEARD AT FACEBOOK.com/CHAPSTICK—invited user comment. Unfortunately, ChapStick had no social network advertising policy.

First, a blogger cited the ad in a post about the pervasiveness of sexist advertising. When she posted to ChapStick's Facebook page, her comment was deleted. Other Facebook posters followed suit. Their comments were also deleted. It wasn't long before a stream of comments mocking the "Be Heard" subtitle ensued.

ChapStick treated Facebook as simply another broadcast channel. But social networks are interactive. When your customers have an immediate and visible "voice," you cannot simply stay silent, delete dissent, and, as ChapStick did, hope the whole thing will just go away on its own. While negative posts that can be clearly identified as trolling can either be ignored or quickly deleted, criticisms that have merit must be responded to with candor, admission of guilt when appropriate, and by outlining the steps that will be taken to remedy the problem.

ChapStick had an opportunity to begin a conversation with its customers that would have demonstrated its cognizance of and sensitivity to sexist advertising. Even if it had chosen to defend its ad as comparatively mild in our sexual imagery saturated advertising environment, it would have demonstrated its willingness to hear and engage with its customers. If the controversy had not abated, it could have chosen to pull the ad

in deference to its most loyal customers. Rather than a public relations nightmare, it could have created a public relations coup, stamping itself as a company that cares about its most loyal fans. After all, if you have Liked ChapStick on Facebook, you are clearly a fan.

Finally, when it could no longer delete the negative posts quickly enough, ChapStick pulled the ad and responded. However, not only was its response anemic, it did not even fully own up to the mass deletions it had perpetrated. It offered regret if fans "felt" this had happened and essentially blamed posters for being uncivil or posting "menacing" comments.

When ChapStick finally tried to assure its fans that it valued them and was listening, it was hardly credible. In short, ChapStick presented us with a textbook case in how not to conduct social network advertising!

Shell Oil also learned the hard way that once an idea is unleashed online it is difficult to control, even if the idea is a hoax. In June 2012, Greenpeace, the environmental activist group, published a video on YouTube of a supposed Shell Oil drillship launch party at the Seattle Space Needle. Two drillships could be seen in the harbor heading off to the inaugural Arctic expedition. A model "oil rig" intended to dispense drinks malfunctioned, spraying Shell employees and the elderly widow of the rig's designer. Shell denied the authenticity of the event and threatened legal action. Next, a hoax Shell Web site went up—arcticready.com—proclaiming, "Let's Go! Shell in the Arctic." Users were invited to caption Arctic pictures. One user entered the slogan, "Our Money is Worth More than Any Animals Who Used to Live Here" atop a scene of melting, cracking Arctic ice. The Twittersphere erupted in posts criticizing the inappropriate slogans and Shell's silence. A hoax

(continued)

Twitter account, @ShellisPrepared, began tweeting overwrought messages threatening legal action and attempting to suppress the false ads. Twitter users, amused at the ineptitude of Shell's social media team, not only retweeted the messages, but also passed on the Arctic Ready and video URLs. With "friends" like these, who needs enemies?

Greenpeace had created a successful viral social media hoax garnering it new converts, 900,000 petition signatures, and a host of publicity for their anti-Arctic drilling campaign. Meanwhile, Shell was caught completely flat-footed. An authentic press release disavowing any association with the video, fake press release, Web site, and Twitter account was finally issued six weeks later. By that time the damage was done to Shell's brand.

Fast food giant McDonald's confronted the dark side of social networks when it began a public relations campaign on Twitter. Using the hashtag #meetthefarmers, it inserted promotional tweets into the streams of Twitter users and paid for premium search engine results. The Supplier Stories campaign encouraged users to share stories about the farmers who sold their meat and produce to McDonald's. All was proceeding nicely until McDonald's replaced the hashtag with #McDStories. Now encouraging users to share their general consumer stories, McDonald's almost immediately lost control of its advertising campaign. The Twittersphere exploded with tweets comparing McDonald's fare to dog food and diarrhea, sprinkled with barbs about Type II diabetes, obesity, and food poisoning. The best that can be said for McDonald's is that it was prepared to pull the plug on the campaign should anything go amiss. Within two hours, the promotion was halted.

The ChapStick, Shell, and McDonald's fiascos are instructive. Inadequate consideration and attentiveness can result in damage that is hard to ameliorate. ChapStick had no policies in place for how to respond to an ad campaign gone wrong.

Shell had no social media network monitoring in place so that it could form a rapid response. McDonald's failed to fully recognize the polarizing nature of its product, making soliciting general comments a risky proposition. Companies with controversial products need to tread carefully, and companies need to be prepared to handle negative comments appropriately and take responsibility for mistakes.

Companies do not seem to be learning from the experience of other firms. In 2013, supermarket chain Tesco suffered a public relations nightmare when it was discovered that horse meat had been found in burgers labeled as beef, and then it unwittingly tweeted from its corporate account, "It's sleepy time so we're off to hit the hay!" later that day. Allergy medicine Benadryl launched an initiative to crowdsource pollen count maps in users' neighborhoods; instead, the maps were defaced with vulgar language and images. Chrysler's social media account tweeted, "I find it ironic that Detroit is known as the #motorcity and yet no one here knows how to (expletive) drive"—clearly a case of an employee tweeting from the wrong account.

But marketing is not the only social media hazard. For employees, privacy protection for Facebook posts is still being determined in the courts. For example, Danielle Mailhoit was the manager of a Home Depot store in Burbank, California. After she was fired, she filed suit claiming gender and disability discrimination due to her vertigo. The defense attorney filed a broad request for all of Mailhoit's social media activity. In September 2012, a federal judge ruled this request overly broad and limited discovery to only communications between the plaintiff and current or former Home Depot employees. Stating that they were unlikely to be relevant unless they were directly related to the lawsuit or her former employment, she also denied Home Depot's request for photos.

Employers must be careful with personal information gleaned from social networking sites.

(continued)

If it can be proven that membership in a protected group was discovered during the hiring process and used to reject a candidate or later used to terminate an employee, a claim can be filed under one of the Federal Equal Employment Opportunity (EEO) laws. These include Title VII of the Civil Rights Act of 1964, the Age Discrimination in Employment Act of 1967 (ADEA), Title I and Title V of the Americans with Disabilities Act of 1990 (ADA), and Title II of the Genetic Information Nondiscrimination Act of 2008 (GINA), which prohibits employment discrimination based on genetic information about an applicant, employee, or former employee. GINA's regulations provide a distinction between whether genetic information is acquired purposefully or inadvertently. Inadvertent acquisition includes acquisition through social media sites, equating it to accidentally overhearing a conversation at work.

However, data on a social media site with privacy controls equipped should not be able to be "inadvertently" acquired. The Stored Communications Act (SCA) covers privacy protection for e-mail and digital communications. The latest court rulings on its application to social network communications have held that Facebook wall postings and other social media comments are protected as long as they have not been made public.

Facebook, to protect its business model, is speaking out against recent hiring practices that have come to its attention—and threatening legal action. According to both Facebook and the American Civil Liberties Union (ACLU), some companies have been asking new hires either to friend the hiring manager or to submit their password. Facebook's Privacy Page condemns this practice, stating that it violates both individual users' and their friends' expectations of privacy, jeopardizes security, and could reveal a user's membership in a protected group.

Legislators in a growing number of states have decided to be proactive. In May 2012, a bill prohibiting employers from asking prospective employees for their social media user names and passwords unanimously passed the California State Assembly and was on its way to the Senate. In 2013, New Jersey became the 12th state to restrict employer access to employee social media accounts, although New Jersey–based employers are still granted some rights in the cases of companies dealing with public safety and workplace investigations.

Carefully crafted policies can help companies to avoid the dark side of social networking. Advertising and hiring are but two of the areas that must be monitored. The Human Resources department must also develop policies regarding employee use of social networks. Employee education programs must be implemented to apprise employees of infractions that can be grounds for disciplinary action. IT departments must develop stringent policies to protect proprietary data and defend company networks from cyberscams. Social networking is an exciting new tool, but one which requires safeguards.

SOURCES: "NJ Passes a Business-Friendly Workplace Social Media Privacy Law," by Eric B. Meyer, Theemployerhandbook.com, September 3, 2013; "Top Social Media Mishaps of 2013," blueclawsearch.co.uk, August 24, 2013; "19 Companies That Made Huge Social Media Fails," by Arielle Calderon, Buzzfeed.com, May 22, 2013; "Judge: Home Depot Went Too Far in Seeking Worker's Social Posts, by Declan McCullagh, News.cnet.com, September 17, 2012; "Was Greenpeace's Shell Hoax Brilliant Or 'Villainous'? One of the Guys Behind It All Speaks," by Kashmir Hill, Forbes, July 19, 2012; "Shell's Fake Social Media Fiasco—What Would You Have Done?" by Vicki Flaugher, CommPro.biz, July 18, 2012; "California May Ban Employers from Asking for Facebook Passwords," by Jessica Guynn, Los Angeles Times, May 11, 2012; "N.J. Committee OKs Ban on Employers Seeking Passwords," by Doug Isenberg, GigaLaw.com, May 10, 2012; "Facebook Speaks Out Against Employers Asking for Passwords," by Doug Gross, CNN.com, March 23, 2012; "Why McDonald's Should Have Known Better," by Shelley DuBois, CNNMoney.com, January 31, 2012; "McDonald's Social Media Director Explains Twitter Fiasco," by Jeff John Roberts, paidContent.org, January 24, 2012; "Lessons from the ChapStick Social Media Fiasco," by Ted Rubin, Tedrubin.com, December 3, 2011; "ChapStick Gets Itself in a Social Media Death Spiral: A Brand's Silent War Against Its Facebook Fans," by Tim Nudd, Adweek, October 26, 2011; "The Social Media Pitfalls for Your Business: 10 Legal Issues Every Employer Should Consider," by Kevin Shook, FrostBrownTodd.com September 2, 2011; "The Dangers of Using Social Media Data in Hiring," by Gregg Skall, Radio Business Report, June 6, 2011; "Stored Communications Act Protects Facebook and MySpace Users' Private Communication," by Kathryn Freund, Jolt.law.harvard.edu, June 11, 2010.

ness model of general communities is typically advertising supported by selling ad space on pages and videos.

practice networks
offer members focused discussion groups, help, information, and knowledge relating to an area of shared practice

Practice networks offer members focused discussion groups, help, information, and knowledge relating to an area of shared practice. For instance, Linux.org is a non-profit community for the open source movement, a worldwide global effort involving thousands of programmers who develop computer code for the Linux operating system and share the results freely with all. Other online communities involve artists, educators, art dealers, photographers, and nurses. Practice networks can be either profit-based or nonprofit, and support themselves by advertising or user donations.

interest-based social networks
offer members focused discussion groups based on a shared interest in some specific topic

Interest-based social networks offer members focused discussion groups based on a shared interest in some specific subject, such as business careers, boats, horses, health, skiing, and thousands of other topics. Because the audience for interest communities is necessarily much smaller and more targeted, these communities have usually relied on advertising and tenancy/sponsorship deals. Sites such as Fool.com, Military.com, Sailing Anarchy, and Chronicle Forums all are examples of Web sites that attract people who share a common pursuit. Job markets and forums such as LinkedIn can be considered interest-based social networks as well.

affinity communities
offer members focused discussions and interaction with other people who share the same affinity

Affinity communities offer members focused discussions and interaction with other people who share the same affinity. "Affinity" refers to self- and group identification. For instance, people can self-identify themselves on the basis of religion, ethnicity, gender, sexual orientation, political beliefs, geographical location, and hundreds of other categories. For instance, iVillage, Oxygen, and NaturallyCurly are affinity sites designed to attract women. These sites offer women discussion and services that focus on topics such as babies, beauty, books, diet and fitness, entertainment, health, and home and garden. These sites are supported by advertising along with revenues from sales of products.

sponsored communities
online communities created for the purpose of pursuing organizational (and often commercial) goals

Sponsored communities are online communities created by government, nonprofit, or for-profit organizations for the purpose of pursuing organizational goals. These goals can be diverse, from increasing the information available to citizens; for instance, a local county government site such as Westchestergov.com, the Web site for Westchester County (New York) government; to an online auction site such as eBay; to a product site such as Tide.com, which is sponsored by an offline branded product company (Procter & Gamble). Cisco, IBM, HP, and hundreds of other companies have developed their internal corporate social networks as a way of sharing knowledge.

SOCIAL NETWORK FEATURES AND TECHNOLOGIES

Social networks have developed software applications that allow users to engage in a number of activities. Not all sites have the same features, but there is an emerging feature set among the larger communities. Some of these software tools are built into the site, while others can be added by users to their profile pages as widgets (described in earlier chapters). **Table 11.4** describes several social network functionalities.

THE FUTURE OF SOCIAL NETWORKS

Social networking in 2013 is one of the most popular online activities. Will it stay that way or grow even more popular? Today's social network scene is highly concentrated

TABLE 11.4	SOCIAL NETWORK FEATURES AND TECHNOLOGIES
FEATURE	**DESCRIPTION**
Profiles	User-created Web pages that describe themselves on a variety of dimensions
Friends network	Ability to create a linked group of friends
Network discovery	Ability to find other networks and find new groups and friends
Favorites	Ability to communicate favorite sites, bookmarks, content, and destinations
Games, widgets, and apps	Apps and games on the site, such as those offered by Facebook
E-mail	Ability to send e-mail within the social network site to friends
Storage	Storage space for network members' content
Instant messaging	Immediate one-to-one contact with friends through the community facility
Message boards	Posting of messages to groups of friends and other groups' members
Online polling	Polling of member opinion
Chat	Online immediate group discussion; Internet relay chat (IRC)
Discussion groups	Discussion groups and forums organized by topic
Experts online	Certified experts in selected areas respond to queries
Membership management tools	Ability of site managers to edit content, and dialog; remove objectionable material; protect security and privacy

with the top site, Facebook, garnering about 50% of the social network audience, which has declined from a few years ago when Facebook represented over 65% of the market. Relative to other sites then, Facebook's growth has slowed, while newer social network sites have grown explosively. There has also been an explosion of social networks that are more focused on specific interests that tie members together, not some diffuse sense of "friendship." It may be more fun to network on a site dedicated to your central interests. As a result, Facebook's growth rate has inevitably declined, and future revenue growth will depend on how well it can monetize its very large subscriber base either by selling ads, virtual goods, or other revenue sources. Moreover, the success of Facebook is likely to attract some powerful competitors with their own ideas of how to build online versions of the social graph, namely, Google, Apple, and Amazon. See the *Insight on Technology* case *Facebook Has Friends*.

Many Facebook users report "network fatigue" caused by spending too much time keeping up with their close and distant friends on many social networks. Fatigue grows as users increase the number of social networks to which they belong (Rosenblum, 2011). One result is avoiding Facebook (and other sites) or spending less and less time on the sites. A Pew survey found 42% of young users are spending less time on Facebook, in large part because they are bored. Over 60% of users said they had dropped using Facebook at one time or another; 20% of online adults used the site once, but

INSIGHT ON TECHNOLOGY

FACEBOOK HAS FRIENDS

In the ongoing battles between hype and substance, fantasy and reality, and hubris and humility on the Internet, Silicon Valley takes no prisoners and has no equals. Google wants to organize the world's information, Amazon wants to be the world's store, Apple wants to be the most beloved company, and now Facebook wants to be the social operating system for the Internet, connecting the world in one big social network (that it owns). Mark Zuckerberg, Facebook's founder, says he wants Facebook to connect everyone in what he calls the social graph. Facebook is built on the assumption that there is just one social graph, including you, your friends, colleagues, relatives, and their friends, and so forth. It's one big family.

So far, Facebook has been right in its strategy. In October 2013, Facebook has an estimated 1.1 billion users worldwide, with about 150 million unique visitors a month in the United States (about 40% of the entire U.S. social network audience). About 700 million of its users access the site every day to interact with 250 billion objects (posts to walls, photos, apps, and games) and 1.1 trillion Likes. According to Facebook, around 820 million people worldwide access Facebook using their mobile devices. Facebook is global: it's available in over 70 languages. Facebook seems to have attained social network dominance, but its growth rate has slowed (you can't get much bigger than 1.1 billion users), and minutes of engagement with the site have also begun to plateau. In America and Europe, Facebook may have reached a saturation point, and future growth in sheer numbers of visitors will have to come from emerging nations. One problem: Facebook's only source of revenue right now is advertising in advanced economies.

On May 18, 2012, Facebook went public in the largest IPO in Internet history, with its stock offered at $38 a share, and a total market value of $104 billion. As a public company, Facebook had to reveal its revenues and income. In 2011, Facebook had revenues of $3.7 billion, and revenues for 2012 were $5.1 billion, a hefty 35% growth rate, but much slower than the market anticipated. By September 2012, the stock had sunk to $20 a share amid questions about the efficacy of its ad business. Skeptics were also critical of Facebook's failure to develop a mobile application when nearly 40% of its visitors access the site with smartphones. A year later, investors are happier. Facebook stock is selling in the $30 to $50 dollar range, at more than 225 times its expected earnings! In 2013, it is expected to generate $7.5 billion, with 40% of that revenue coming from mobile advertising.

But there are other players and forces at work. While Facebook has around 150 million U.S. visitors, the other top nine social networks together have around 200 million, and some of them are growing much faster than Facebook. For instance, in late 2013, one of the fastest growing sites is Tumblr, with around 30 million visitors. Tumblr is a short form, or microblogging, site where users post text, images, videos, and links that other users can follow and share. Tumblr is growing at more than 100% a year. In 2013, Tumblr hosts over 110 million blogs, with over 50 billion posts. Tumblr's popularity is based on the idea of enhanced user control. Users control the look and feel of blog pages and can post anything, including documents as long as a book. Tumblr offers privacy controls that allow users to keep posts private. Users can create multiple groups of friends that include different people. Groups can create community-powered blogs to which anyone can contribute. Users own their own work (unlike Facebook), and Tumblr

(continued)

provides for automatic updates to Twitter and Facebook if users select that option. It's free, with no ads, forced banner ads, or logos (so far).

In September 2011, Tumblr raised $85 million from a group of venture capital firms. At that point, the firm was valued at $800 million. In May 2013, Tumblr was purchased by Yahoo for $1.1 billion. Yahoo believes Tumblr will help it appeal to a younger audience and also provides it with the possibility of monetizing the Tumblr user base by displaying ads.

While its rapid growth might be interesting to Facebook, Tumblr is, relatively speaking, a speck on the wall. Google is not. With annual revenues of $50 billion (96% comes from search and display advertising) and growth at about 30% a year, Google is one of the giants of the Internet. Facebook is a speck on Google's wall (no pun intended), albeit an irritant for all the press it receives and its huge, intense user base. After several failed efforts to enter the social network space, Google finally launched its Google+ site in June 2011, which is a serious worldwide competitor to Facebook. Google+ is based on the idea (similar to Tumblr) of sharing with multiple separate groups of friends who form the collection of real-world social networks that people participate in. Google+ assumes there are multiple social graphs—not just one. Google+ makes it really easy to have separate social networks for family, work colleagues, professional colleagues, fellow sports fanatics, and fashionistas who share your tastes, and to keep the messages separate. There's really no need for your parents to learn about your weekend parties. Rather than share with the entire online world, users share with their naturally formed groups called "circles," a much smaller audience. This is intended to eliminate "social network awkwardness" created when users post material on their walls that is embarrassing to some of their friends, or a real turn-off to their relatives (like Mom, Dad, or Aunt Bertha). It's called "oversharing" or "TMI" (too much information), and it's a major irritant to Facebook users (along with Facebook's privacy invading behavior).

Other features of Google+ include group video chatting (called "Hang Outs") and group mobile audio and video chatting (called "Huddles"). It is fully integrated with other Google products like Gmail, so you can drag and drop friends from your Gmail lists to request they join one of your circles. Gmail is used by an estimated 200 million users worldwide. The Google+ search feature now includes searching your friends' pages for relevant information, giving search a solid social quality and not just an algorithmic quality. "Sparks" is a feature that lets users declare what's interesting to them, and Google+ searches the Web for interesting news and stories on that topic, sort of like a personal research assistant. Google+ claims its solution to social networks is based on 100 new features not found on other sites. One feature found on Google+ (but not on Tumblr, for example) is Google's tracking of your interests and behaviors in all your circles so that it can, presumably, show you even better ads than it does now. Google+ is advertising-supported, you betcha!

Google launched Google+ to the public on September 20, 2011. By the end of September 2012, Google+ had rocketed to 27 million registered users. In 2013, Google+ has 30 million active users in the United States, but is much more successful globally, where it has an additional 300 million users, and is the second largest social network in the world after Facebook.

Google's social network strategy relies on the fact that it has multiple services like Gmail, Picassa, YouTube, Maps, and of course, search, which are being used by Google+ to become the hub of all things Google. Users of any of Google's services are encouraged to use Google+ to keep their friends abreast of their activities. Facebook does not have a similar capability at this point. However, while Google+ is a contender for social network power, it lacks the engagement of other sites like

(continued)

Facebook, Tumblr, and Pinterest. The average United States visitor to the social network spent 6 minutes 47 seconds on Google+'s site in March 2013, compared to 6 hours 44 minutes on Facebook. Facebook's numbers have declined from around 7 hours, while Google's have increased from 3 minutes in 2012. Google disagrees with this assessment because it does not include Google+ app visitors or activities on related Google sites like YouTube, Maps, and Picassa.

Of course, Microsoft wants to play in this new arena too. It invested $250 million in Facebook in October 2007 for a 1.6% stake. This valued Facebook at $15 billion, and was a sign of how desperate Microsoft was to play in this new field. However, Facebook and Microsoft have shared only a few technologies so far. Microsoft's search engine Bing is used by Facebook users. In May 2011, Microsoft purchased Skype, the Internet-based telephone service. Facebook needs Skype because it does not have a peer-to-peer network of its own that can handle video and voice services for users. In lending Skype's infrastructure to Facebook, Microsoft gains access to a huge audience. Google already has Google Voice, which performs these functions.

It's unlikely that Microsoft will be satisfied with its tiny slice of Facebook. In May 2012, Microsoft launched a social network called So.cl (pronounced "social"). So.cl combines elements of Facebook, Twitter, Pinterest, and Tumblr. While not clearly aimed at Facebook, Microsoft claims So.cl is designed to help students find and share interesting Web pages, combining social with Bing search. So.cl has developed partnerships with several universities, including New York University. So.cl is closely integrated with Facebook and appears to be aimed at competing with Google+ by combining search and social with other features like e-mail and visual pin-up boards. Apple is also rumored to be building a social network system based on iOS mobile devices. A recent patent application from Apple describes a proximity or location-based sharing and communication system where mobile devices share their users' interests with other cell phones in the area, seeking a match. For instance, users could search for people in their nearby location who had downloaded a particular movie, or song. Apple abandoned its Ping music social network in iOS 6.

While Facebook is the dominant social network site now, given the strength of its competitors, it is likely there will be many powerful social networks for users to join. One point competitors have already made is that there isn't "one social graph," but many social graphs that people want to keep separate. Journalists are already reporting a kind of "social network fatigue," where users are simply getting tired of following and updating their Facebook, Twitter, Tumblr, and LinkedIn networks. The next generation of entrepreneurs may solve this problem by creating an inter-network, an inter-operable system where users can participate in all their networks from one interface. But for now, the big players in this field are determined to build their own walls (pun intended).

▬ **SOURCES:** "Facebook CEO Defies Mobile Ad Skeptics as Sales Soar," by Douglas MacMillan and Brian Womack , Bloomberg.com, July 25, 2013; "Which Social Networks Are Growing Fastest Worldwide," eMarketer, Inc., May 13, 2013; "Twitter Now the Fastest Growing Social Platform in the World," GlobalWebIndex.net, January 28, 2013; "Apple Officials Said to Consider Stake in Twitter," by Evelyn Rusli and Nick Bilton, *New York Times*, July 27, 2012;"Microsoft Launches New Social Network to Compete With Google," by Kelly Clay, *Forbes*, May 21, 2012; "The Mounting Minuses at Google+," by Amir Efrati, *Wall Street Journal*, February 28, 2012; "Google Is Now in the Top Ten Social Networking Sites," by Matt Rosoff, *Business Insider*, September 26, 2011; "Google+ Traffic Floodgates Open," by Shira Ovide and Rolfe Winkler, *Wall Street Journal*, September 22, 2011.

no longer use it. The Facebook audience is highly fluid (Pew Internet, 2013b). An Associated Press poll found that 80% of users said they had never been influenced by an ad on the site, and 43% said Facebook would fade away as new platforms appear (Oreskovic, 2012; Murphy, 2012). The fears that many users have about the privacy of their posts and content is another factor in people either not joining Facebook, or pulling back from engagement.

The financial future of social networks hinges on becoming advertising and sales platforms. But social networks are not yet proven advertising platforms that drive sales. The relationship between Likes and sales is not clear yet. Response rates to display ads on Facebook are far lower than on portal sites like Yahoo, or search ads like Google. In part this reflects the sentiment of users who go onto social sites without the intention of purchasing anything.

11.2 ONLINE AUCTIONS

Online auction sites are among the most popular consumer-to-consumer (C2C) e-commerce sites on the Internet, although the popularity of auctions and their growth rates have slowed in recent years due to customers' preferences for a "buy now" fixed-price model. The market leader in C2C auctions is eBay, which has 130 million active users in the United States and over 350 million items listed on any given day within 18,000 categories. In July 2013, eBay had around 72 million unique visitors, placing it 13th on the list of top 50 Web properties (comScore, 2013a). In 2012, eBay had $6.1 billion in net revenues from its Marketplaces segment, a 12% increase from 2011, and the total worth of goods sold or auctioned was $75 billion (Gross Merchandise Value) (eBay, 2013). eBay is further discussed in the case study at the end of this chapter. In the United States alone, there are several hundred auction sites, some specializing in unique collectible products such as stamps and coins, others adopting a more general-ist approach in which almost any good can be found for sale. Increasingly, established portals and online retail sites—from Yahoo and MSN to JCPenney and Sam's Club—are adding auctions to their sites. Auctions constitute a significant part of B2B e-commerce in 2013, and more than a third of procurement officers use auctions to procure goods. What explains the extraordinary popularity of auctions? Do consumers always get lower prices at auctions? Why do merchants auction their products if the prices they receive are so low?

DEFINING AND MEASURING THE GROWTH OF AUCTIONS AND DYNAMIC PRICING

Auctions are markets in which prices are variable and based on the competition among participants who are buying or selling products and services. Auctions are one type of **dynamic pricing**, in which the price of the product varies, depending directly on the demand characteristics of the customer and the supply situation of the seller. There is a wide variety of dynamically priced markets, from simple haggling, barter-

auctions
markets in which prices are variable and based on the competition among participants who are buying or selling products and services

dynamic pricing
the price of the product varies, depending directly on the demand characteristics of the customer and the supply situation of the seller

ing, and negotiating between one buyer and one seller, to much more sophisticated public auctions in which there may be thousands of sellers and thousands of buyers, as in a single stock market for a bundle of shares.

In dynamic pricing, merchants change their prices based on both their understanding of how much value the customer attaches to the product and their own desire to make a sale. Likewise, customers change their offers to buy based on both their perceptions of the seller's desire to sell and their own need for the product. If you as a customer really want the product right now, you will be charged a higher price in a dynamic pricing regime, and you will willingly pay a higher price than if you placed less value on the product and were willing to wait several days to buy it. For instance, if you want to travel from New York to San Francisco to attend a last-minute business conference, and then return as soon as possible, you will be charged twice as much as a tourist who agrees to stay over the weekend.

fixed pricing
one national price, everywhere, for everyone

In contrast, traditional mass-market merchants generally use **fixed pricing**—one national price, everywhere, for everyone. Fixed pricing first appeared in the nineteenth century with the development of mass national markets and retail stores that could sell to a national audience. Prior to this period, all pricing was dynamic and local, with prices derived through a process of negotiation between the customer and the merchant. Computers and the development of the Internet have contributed to a return of dynamic pricing. The difference is that with the Internet, dynamic pricing can be conducted globally, continuously, and at a very low cost.

There are many other types of dynamic pricing that preceded the Internet. Airlines have used dynamic pricing since the early 1980s to change the price of airline tickets depending on available unused capacity and the willingness of business travelers to pay a premium for immediate bookings. Airline yield management software programs seek to ensure that a perishable item (an empty airline seat is useless after the plane takes off) is sold before flight time at some price above zero.

The use of coupons sent to selected customers, and even college scholarships given to selected students to encourage their enrollment, are a form of both price discrimination and dynamic pricing. In these examples, the price of the item is adjusted to demand and available supply, and certain consumers are discriminated against by charging them higher prices while others are advantaged by receiving lower prices for the same products, namely, a reduced price for an item or a college education.

trigger pricing
adjusts prices based on the location of the consumer

utilization pricing
adjusts prices based on utilization of the product

personalization pricing
adjusts prices based on the merchant's estimate of how much the customer truly values the product

Newer forms of dynamic pricing on the Internet include bundling, trigger pricing, utilization pricing, and personalization pricing. As discussed in Chapter 6, bundling of digital goods is the practice of including low-demand products in a bundle "for free" in order to increase total revenues. **Trigger pricing**, used in m-commerce applications, adjusts prices based on the location of the consumer—for example, walking within 400 yards of a restaurant may trigger an immediate 10% dinner coupon on a portable Web device. **Utilization pricing** adjusts prices based on utilization of the product; for example, Progressive Insurance Company adjusts the annual cost of automobile insurance based on mileage driven. **Personalization pricing** adjusts prices based on the merchant's estimate of how much the customer truly values the product; for instance, Web merchants may charge committed fans of a musician higher prices for the privilege of receiving a new DVD before its official release to retail stores. Higher-cost hardbound books sell primarily to committed fans of writers, while less-committed fans wait for cheaper paperback versions to appear.

Auctions—one form of dynamic pricing mechanism—are used throughout the e-commerce landscape. The most widely known auctions are **consumer-to-consumer (C2C) auctions**, in which the auction house is simply an intermediary market maker, providing a forum where consumers—buyers and sellers—can discover prices and trade. Less well known are **business-to-consumer (B2C)** auctions, where a business owns or controls assets and uses dynamic pricing to establish the price. Established merchants on occasion use B2C auctions to sell excess goods. This form of auction or dynamic pricing will grow along with C2C auctions.

Some leading online auction sites are listed in **Table 11.5**. Auctions are not limited to goods and services. They can also be used to allocate resources, and bundles of resources, among any group of bidders. For instance, if you wanted to establish an optimal schedule for assigned tasks in an office among a group of clerical workers, an auction in which workers bid for assignments would come close to producing a nearly optimal solution in a short amount of time (Parkes and Ungar, 2000). In short, auctions—like all markets—are ways of allocating resources among independent agents (bidders).

consumer-to-consumer (C2C) auctions
auction house acts as an intermediary market maker, providing a forum where consumers can discover prices and trade

business-to-consumer (B2C) auctions
auction house sells goods it owns, or controls, using various dynamic pricing models

TABLE 11.5	LEADING ONLINE AUCTION SITES
GENERAL	
eBay	The world market leader in auctions: 89 million visitors a month and millions of products.
uBid	Marketplace for excess inventory from pre-approved merchants.
eBid	In business since 1998. Operates in 18 countries, including the United States. Currently, the top competitor to eBay. Offers much lower fees.
Bid4Assets	Liquidation of distressed assets from government and the public sector, corporations, restructurings, and bankruptcies.
Auctions.samsclub	Sam's Club brand merchandise in a variety of categories.
SPECIALIZED	
BidZ	Live auction format for online jewelry.
Racersauction	Specialized site for automobile racing parts.
Philatelic Phantasies	Stamp site for professionals, monthly online stamp auction.
Teletrade	America's largest fully automated auction company of certified coins including ancient gold, silver, and copper coins. Also offers sports cards.
Baseball-cards.com	The Internet's first baseball card store. Offers weekly auctions of baseball, football, basketball, hockey, wire photos, and more.
Oldandsold	Online auction service specializing in quality antiques. Dealers pay a 3% commission on merchandise sold.

WHY ARE AUCTIONS SO POPULAR? BENEFITS AND COSTS OF AUCTIONS

The Internet is primarily responsible for the resurgence in auctions. Although electronic network-based auctions such as AUCNET in Japan (an electronic automobile auction for used cars) were developed in the late 1980s, these pre-Internet auctions required an expensive telecommunications network to implement. The Internet provides a global environment and very low fixed and operational costs for the aggregation of huge buyer audiences, composed of millions of consumers worldwide, who can use a universally available technology (Internet browsers) to shop for goods.

Benefits of Auctions

Aside from the sheer game-like fun of participating in auctions, consumers, merchants, and society as a whole derive a number of economic benefits from participating in Internet auctions. These benefits include:

- **Liquidity:** Sellers can find willing buyers, and buyers can find sellers. The Internet enormously increased the liquidity of traditional auctions that usually required all participants to be present in a single room. Now, sellers and buyers can be located anywhere around the globe. Just as important, buyers and sellers can find a global market for rare items that would not have existed before the Internet.

- **Price discovery:** Buyers and sellers can quickly and efficiently develop prices for items that are difficult to assess, where the price depends on demand and supply, and where the product is rare. For instance, how could a merchant (or buyer) price a Greek oil lamp made in 550 B.C. (to use just one example of the rare items that can be found on eBay)? How could a consumer even find a Greek oil lamp without the Internet? It would be difficult and costly for all parties.

- **Price transparency:** Public Internet auctions allow everyone in the world to see the asking and bidding prices for items. It is difficult for merchants to engage in price discrimination (charging some customers more) when the items are available on auctions. However, because even huge auction sites such as eBay do not include all the world's online auction items (there are other auction sites in the world), there still may be more than one world price for a given item (there are inter-market price differences).

- **Market efficiency:** Auctions can, and often do, lead to reduced prices, and hence reduced profits for merchants, leading to an increase in consumer welfare—one measure of market efficiency. Online auctions provide consumers the chance to find real bargains at potentially give-away prices; they also provide access to a very wide selection of goods that would be impossible for consumers to access physically by visiting stores.

- **Lower transaction costs:** Online auctions can lower the cost of selling and purchasing products, benefiting both merchants and consumers. Like other Internet markets, such as retail markets, Internet auctions have very low (but not zero) transaction costs. A sale at an auction can be consummated quickly and with very low transaction costs when compared to the physical world of markets.

- **Consumer aggregation:** Sellers benefit from large auction sites' ability to aggregate a large number of consumers who are motivated to purchase something in one marketspace. Auction-site search engines that lead consumers directly to the products they are seeking make it very likely that consumers who visit a specific auction really are interested and ready to buy at some price.

- **Network effects:** The larger an auction site becomes in terms of visitors and products for sale, the more valuable it becomes as a marketplace for everyone by providing liquidity and several other benefits listed previously, such as lower transaction costs, higher efficiency, and better price transparency. For instance, because eBay is so large—garnering close to 90% of all C2C auction commerce in the United States—it is quite likely you will find what you want to buy at a good price, and highly probable you will find a buyer for just about anything.

Risks and Costs of Auctions for Consumers and Businesses

There are a number of risks and costs involved in participating in auctions. In some cases, auction markets can fail—like all markets at times. (We describe auction market failure in more detail later.) Some of the more important risks and costs to keep in mind are:

- **Delayed consumption costs:** Internet auctions can go on for days, and shipping will take additional time. If you ordered from a mail-order catalog, you would likely receive the product much faster, or if you went to a physical store, you would immediately be able to obtain the product.

- **Monitoring costs:** Participation in auctions requires your time to monitor bidding.

- **Equipment costs:** Internet auctions require you to purchase a computer system, pay for Internet access, and learn a complex operating system.

- **Trust risks:** Online auctions are the single largest source of Internet fraud. Using auctions increases the risk of experiencing a loss.

- **Fulfillment costs:** Typically, the buyer pays fulfillment costs of packing, shipping, and insurance, whereas at a physical store these costs are included in the retail price.

Auction sites such as eBay have taken a number of steps to reduce consumer participation costs and trust risk. For instance, auction sites attempt to solve the trust problem by providing a rating system in which previous customers rate sellers based on their overall experience with the merchant. Although helpful, this solution does not always work. Auction fraud is the leading source of e-commerce complaints to federal law enforcement officials. One partial solution to high monitoring costs is, ironically, fixed pricing. At eBay, consumers can reduce the cost of monitoring and waiting for auctions to end by simply clicking on the "Buy It Now!" button and paying a premium price. The difference between the "Buy It Now" price and the auction price is the cost of monitoring. Also, most online auctions reduce monitoring costs by providing both a watch list and proxy bidding. **Watch lists** permit the consumer to monitor specific auctions of interest, requiring the consumer to pay close attention only in the last few minutes of bidding. **Proxy bidding** allows the consumer to enter a maximum price, and the auction software automatically bids for the goods up to that maximum price in small increments.

watch lists
permit the consumer to monitor specific auctions of interest

proxy bidding
allows the consumer to enter a maximum price, and the auction software automatically bids for the goods up to that maximum price in small increments

Nevertheless, given the costs of participating in online auctions, the generally lower cost of goods on Internet auctions is in part a compensation for the other additional costs consumers experience. On the other hand, consumers experience lower search costs and transaction costs because there usually are no intermediaries (unless, of course, the seller is an online business operating on an auction site, in which case there is a middleman cost), and usually there are no local or state taxes.

Merchants face considerable risks and costs as well. At auctions, merchants may end up selling goods for prices far below what they might have achieved in conventional markets. Merchants also face risks of nonpayment, false bidding, bid rigging, monitoring, transaction fees charged by the auction site, credit card transaction processing fees, and the administration costs of entering price and product information. We explore the benefits and risks for merchants later in this chapter.

Market-Maker Benefits: Auctions as an E-commerce Business Model

Online auctions have been among the most successful business models in retail and B2B commerce. eBay, the Internet's most lucrative auction site, has been profitable nearly since its inception. The strategy for eBay has been to make money off every stage in the auction cycle. eBay earns revenue from auctions in several ways: transaction fees based on the amount of the sale, listing fees for display of goods, financial service fees from payment systems such as PayPal, and advertising or placement fees where sellers pay extra for special services such as particular display or listing services.

However, it is on the cost side that online auctions have extraordinary advantages over ordinary retail or catalog sites. Auction sites carry no inventory and do not perform any fulfillment activities—they need no warehouses, shipping, or logistical facilities. Sellers and consumers provide these services and bear these costs. In this sense, online auctions are an ideal digital business because they involve simply the transfer of information.

Even though eBay has been extraordinarily successful, the success of online auctions is qualified by the fact that the marketplace for online auctions is highly concentrated. eBay dominates the online auction market, followed by eBid and uBid. Many of the smaller auction sites are not profitable because they lack sufficient sellers and buyers to achieve liquidity. In auctions, network effects are highly influential, and the tendency is for one or two very large auction sites to dominate, with hundreds of smaller specialty auction sites (sites that sell specialized goods such as stamps) being barely profitable.

TYPES AND EXAMPLES OF AUCTIONS

Auction theory is a well-established area of research, largely in economics (McAfee and McMillan, 1987; Milgrom, 1989; Vickrey, 1961). Much of this research is theoretical, and prior to the emergence of public Internet auctions, there was not a great deal of empirical data on auctions or consumer behavior in auctions. Previous literature has identified a wide range of auction types, some of which are seller-biased, and others of which are more buyer-biased. Internet auctions are very different from traditional auctions. Traditional auctions are relatively short-lived (such as a Sotheby's art auction), and have a fixed number of bidders, usually present in the same room. Online Internet auctions, in contrast, can go on much longer (a week), and have a variable number of bidders who come and go from the auction arena.

Internet Auction Basics

Before a business turns to auctions as a marketing channel, its managers need to understand some basic facts about online auctions.

Market Power and Bias in Dynamically Priced Markets Dynamically priced markets are not always "fair" in the sense of distributing market power to influence prices. **Figure 11.3** illustrates four different market bias situations that occur in dynamic markets.

In situations in which the number of buyers and sellers is few or equal in size, markets tend to be neutral, favoring neither the buyer nor the seller. One-on-one negotiations, barter markets, and stock exchanges all have this quality of neutrality, although specialists and market makers exact a commission for matching buy and sell orders. In stock markets, which are sometimes called a "double auction" because bids and offers are made continuously, many sellers and buyers call out prices for bundles of stock (of which there is a very large supply) until a deal is struck. In contrast, auctions such as those run by eBay and reverse auctions offered by companies such as Priceline have built-in biases. Usually on eBay, there is just one seller or a small number of sellers marketing goods that are in limited supply (or even rare goods) to millions of buyers who are competing on price. Priceline offers just the opposite bias and shares many features with a sealed-bid RFQ (request for quote) market. In Priceline's reverse auctions (described in greater detail later in this chapter), buyers post their unique needs for goods and services and a price they are willing to pay, while many sellers compete against one another for the available business. Of course, inherent bias in a marketplace does not mean consumers and merchants cannot find "good deals" and thousands of motivated customers willing to purchase goods at profitable prices.

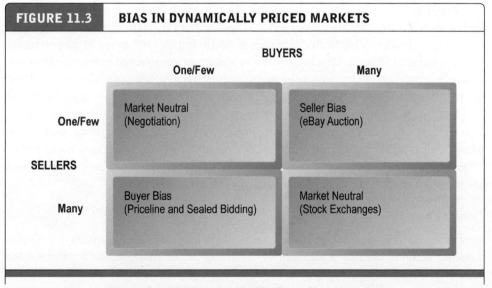

FIGURE 11.3 | **BIAS IN DYNAMICALLY PRICED MARKETS**

Dynamically priced markets can be either neutral or biased in favor of buyers or sellers.

However, the inherent biases should provide cautions to both merchants and consumers; namely, goods in auctions sometimes sell for far above their fair market value as they get bid too high, and sometimes for far less than their fair market value as merchants become too desperate for business. **Fair market value** could be defined here as the average of prices for that product or service in a variety of dynamic and fixed-price markets around the world. We explore other auction market failures in a later section.

fair market value
the average of prices for a product or service in a variety of dynamic and fixed-price markets around the world

uniform pricing rule
there are multiple winners and they all pay the same price

discriminatory pricing
winners pay different amounts depending on what they bid

Price Allocation Rules: Uniform vs. Discriminatory Pricing There are different rules for establishing the winning bids and prices in auctions where there are multiple units for sale, say, 10 Lenovo laptop PCs. With a **uniform pricing rule**, there are multiple winners and they all pay the same price (usually the lowest winning bid—sometimes called a market clearing price). Other auctions use **discriminatory pricing** in which winners pay different amounts depending on what they bid. See, for instance, Ubid.com, which typically auctions multiple units from manufacturers. Like so many other auction rules, price allocation can change bidding strategy in auctions. For instance, in a uniform pricing auction for 10 Lenovo laptops, you may bid a very high price for a few units, knowing that others will not follow, but you will only pay a price equal to the lowest winning bid needed to clear out the units from the market. The person who bid for the 10th unit may have only bid 75% as high as your offer. Nevertheless, that is the price you will actually pay—the price needed to "clear the market" of all units. However, under a discriminatory pricing rule, you would be forced to pay your high bid. Obviously, from a buyer's point of view, uniform pricing is better, but from a merchant's point of view, discriminatory pricing is much better.

Public vs. Private Information in Dynamically Priced Markets In some dynamic markets, the prices being bid are secret, and are known only to one party. For instance, a firm may issue a request for bid to electrical contractors for provision of electrical service on a new building. Bidders are requested to submit sealed bids, and the lowest bidder (subject to qualifications) will be the winner. In this instance, the bidders do not know what others are bidding, and must bid their "best" price. The danger here is **bid rigging**, in which bidders communicate prior to submitting their bids, and rig their bids to ensure that the lowest price is higher than it might otherwise be (which benefits the bidder, who in this instance is receiving the bid price as payment for services to be rendered). This is a common problem in sealed-bid markets. However, in auction markets, bid prices are usually public information, available to all. Here the risks are that bidders agree offline to limit their bids, that sellers use shills to submit false bids, or that sellers use the market itself as a signaling device, driving prices up. Open markets permit large players to signal prices or engage in **price matching**, where sellers agree informally or formally to set floor prices on auction items below which they will not sell. Generally such collusion exists on the sell side, where there are just a few sellers or auction houses in a position to fix prices.

bid rigging
bidders communicate prior to submitting their bids, and rig their bids to ensure that the lowest price is higher than it might otherwise be

price matching
sellers agree informally or formally to set floor prices on auction items below which they will not sell

Types of Auctions

Now that you have learned some basic auction market rules and practices, it's time to consider some of the major forms of dynamically priced markets and auctions, both online and offline. **Table 11.6** describes the major types of auctions, how they work, and their biases. As you can see in Table 11.6, aside from the different formats and rules, there are many other differences among auctions. As noted above, there are both discriminatory and uniform pricing rules, although the latter seem to be most common. Also, in some auctions, there are multiple units for sale, whereas in others, there is only a single unit for sale. The major types of Internet auctions are English, Dutch Internet, Name Your Own Price, and Group Buying.

TABLE 11.6	TYPES OF AUCTIONS AND DYNAMIC PRICING MECHANISMS	
AUCTION TYPE	MECHANISM	BIAS
Sealed-bid auction (B2B e-procurement—Ariba Sourcing; Elance)	Sealed-bid auction, RFQs. Winner is chosen from lowest bidders at acceptable quality levels.	Buyer bias: Multiple vendors competing against one another
Vickrey auction (private auction)	Sealed-bid auction, single unit; highest bidder wins at the second-highest bid price.	Seller bias: Single seller and multiple buyers competing against one another
English auction (eBay)	Public ascending price, single unit; highest bidder wins at a price just above the second-highest bid. Buyers can skip bidding at each price, but return at higher prices.	Seller bias: Single seller and multiple buyers competing against one another
Traditional Dutch (Dutch flower market)	Public descending-price auction, single unit; seller lowers price until a buyer takes the product.	Seller bias: Single seller and multiple buyers competing against one another
Dutch Internet (eBay Dutch auction)	Public ascending price, multiple units. Buyers bid on quantity and price. Final per-unit price is lowest successful bid, which sets a uniform price for all higher bidders as well (uniform price rule).	Seller bias: Small number of sellers and many buyers
Japanese auction (private auction)	Public ascending price, single unit; highest bidder wins at a price just above second-highest bid (reservation price) and buyers must bid at each price to stay in auction.	Seller bias: Single seller and many buyers
Yankee Internet auction (variation on Dutch Internet auction)	Public ascending price, multiple units. Buyers bid on quantity and price per unit. Bidders ranked on price per unit, units, and time. Winners pay their actual bid prices (discriminatory rule).	Seller bias: Single seller and multiple buyers competing against one another
Reverse auction	Public reverse English auction, descending prices, single unit. Sellers bid on price to provide products or services; winning bid is the lowest-price provider. Similar to sealed-bid markets.	Buyer bias: Multiple sellers competing against one another
Group buying (demand aggregators)	Public reverse auction, descending prices, multiple units. Buyers bid on price per unit and units. Groups of sellers bid on price; winning bid is lowest-price provider.	Buyer bias: Multiple sellers competing against one another
Name Your Own Price (Priceline)	Similar to a reverse auction except the price the consumer is willing to pay is fixed and the price offered is nonpublic. Requires a commitment to purchase at the first offered price.	Buyer bias: Multiple sellers competing against one another for an individual's business
Double auction (Nasdaq and stock markets)	Public bid-ask negotiation; sellers ask, buyers bid. Sale consummated when participants agree on price and quantity.	Neutral: Multiple buyers and sellers competing against one another. Market bias: trading specialists (matchmakers)

NOTE: "Public" means all participants can observe prices offered.

English auction

most common form of auction; the highest bidder wins

English Auctions The **English auction** is the easiest to understand and the most common form of auction on eBay. Typically, there is a single item up for sale from a single seller. There is a time limit when the auction ends, a reserve price below which the seller will not sell (usually secret), and a minimum incremental bid set. Multiple buyers bid against one another until the auction time limit is reached. The highest bidder wins the item (if the reserve price of the seller has been met or exceeded). English auctions are considered to be seller-biased because multiple buyers compete against one another—usually anonymously.

Traditional Dutch Auctions In the traditional Dutch auction in Aalsmeer, Holland, 5,000 flower growers—who own the auction facility—sell bundles of graded flowers to 2,000 buyers. The Dutch auction uses a clock visible to all that displays the starting price growers want for their flowers. Every few seconds, the clock ticks to a lower price. When buyers want to buy at the displayed price, they push a button to accept the lot of flowers at that price. If buyers fail to bid in a timely fashion, their competitors will win the flowers. The auction is very efficient: on average, Aalsmeer conducts 50,000 transactions daily for 20 million flowers. Dutch flower auctions are now conducted over the Internet. Buyers no longer have to be present at the market to bid, and sellers no longer have to have their flowers present in adjacent warehouses, but can ship directly from their farms (Kambil and vanHeck, 1996).

Dutch Internet auction

public ascending price, multiple unit auction. Final price is lowest successful bid, which sets price for all higher bidders

Dutch Internet Auctions In **Dutch Internet auctions**, such as those on eBay, OnSale, and others, the rules and action are different from the classical Dutch auction. The Dutch Internet auction format is perfect for sellers that have many identical items to sell. Sellers start by listing a minimum price, or a starting bid for one item, and the number of items for sale. Bidders specify both a bid price and the quantity they want to buy. The uniform price reigns. Winning bidders pay the same price per item, which is the lowest successful bid. This market clearing price can be less than some bids. If there are more buyers than items, the earliest successful bids get the goods. In general, high bidders get the quantity they want at the lowest successful price, whereas low successful bidders might not get the quantity they want (but they will get something). The action is usually quite rapid, and proxy bidding is not used. **Table 11.7** shows closing data from a sample Dutch Internet auction for a bundle of laptop computers. In Table 11.6, the bids are arranged by price and then quantity. Under a uniform pricing rule, the lowest winning bid that clears the market of all 10 laptops is $736 and all winners pay this amount. However, the lowest winning bidder, JB505, will only receive three laptops, not four, because higher bidders are given their full allotments.

Name Your Own Price auction

auction where users specify what they are willing to pay for goods or services

Name Your Own Price Auctions The **Name Your Own Price** auction was pioneered by Priceline, and is the second most-popular auction format on the Web. Although Priceline also acts as an intermediary, buying blocks of airline tickets and vacation packages at a discount and selling them at a reduced retail price or matching its inventory to bidders, it is best known for its Name Your Own Price auctions, where users specify what they are willing to pay for goods or services, and multiple providers bid for their business. Prices do not descend and are fixed: the initial consumer offer is a commitment to purchase at that price. In 2012, Priceline had more than $5.2 billion in revenues, and in 2013, attracts around 17.5 million unique visitors a month. It is one of the top-ranked travel sites in the United States. Today, it also arranges for the

TABLE 11.7	A MULTI-UNIT DUTCH INTERNET AUCTION

CLOSING AUCTION DATA

Lot number	8740240
Total Number of Units	10
Description	HP Envy Ultrabook Laptop; Win 7; Intel Core i5, 3 GHz, 14" widescreen; 5 GB memory; 500 GB hard drive
Reserve Price	None

BIDDER	DATE	TIME	BID	QUANTITY
JDMTKIS	9/30/13	18:35	$750	4
KTTX	9/30/13	18:55	$745	3
JB505	9/30/13	19:05	$736	4
VAMP	9/30/13	19:10	$730	2
DPVS	9/30/13	19:20	$730	1
RSF34	9/30/13	19:24	$725	1
CMCAL	9/30/13	19:25	$725	2

sale of new cars, hotel accommodations, car rentals, long distance telephone service, and home finance.

Table 11.8 describes the products and services available in Priceline's Name Your Own Price auctions. Clearly, a major attraction of Priceline is that it offers consumers a market biased in their favor and very low prices, up to 40% off. Brand-name suppliers compete with one another to supply services to consumers. However, it is unclear at this time if the Priceline business model can extend to other categories of products. Experiments to sell gasoline and groceries through Priceline failed.

But how can Priceline offer discounts up to 40% off prices for services provided by major brand-name providers? There are several answers. First, Priceline "shields the brand" by not publicizing the prices at which major brands sell. This reduces conflict with traditional channels, including direct sales. Second, the services being sold are perishable: if a Priceline customer did not pay something for the empty airline seat, rental car, or hotel room, sellers would not receive any revenue. Hence, sellers are highly motivated to at least cover the costs of their services by selling in a spot market at very low prices.

The strategy for sellers is to sell as much as possible through more profitable channels and then unload excess capacity on spot markets such as Priceline. This works to the advantage of consumers, sellers, and Priceline, which charges a transaction fee to sellers.

Group Buying Auctions: Demand Aggregators A **demand aggregator** facilitates group buying of products at dynamically adjusted discount prices based on high-volume purchases. The originator of demand aggregation was Mercata, formed in 1998, and

demand aggregators
suppliers or market makers who group unrelated buyers into a single purchase in return for offering a lower purchase price. Prices on multiple units fall as the number of buyers increases

TABLE 11.8	PRICELINE NAME YOUR OWN PRICE OFFERINGS
SERVICE/PRODUCT	DESCRIPTION
Airline seats	Brand-name carriers bid for individual consumer business—perishable items that airlines are motivated to sell at the last minute.
Hotel rooms	Brand-name hotels bid for consumer business—perishable services that hotels are motivated to sell on a last-minute basis.
Rental cars	Brand-name rental companies bid for consumer business—perishable services that rental companies are motivated to sell on a last-minute basis.
Vacation packages	Brand-name hotels and air carriers bid for consumer business—perishable services that providers are motivated to sell on a last-minute basis.
Cruises	Cruise ship companies bid for consumer business; especially active in off-season periods.

the Web's largest retail demand aggregator until it ceased operations in January 2001, when needed venture capital financing did not materialize. Mercata holds several patents covering online demand aggregation. The largest supplier today of demand aggregation software (what it now calls "social buying") is Ewinwin. Demand aggregation has also found a home in B2B commerce as a way of organizing group buying. Trade associations and industry buying groups have traditionally pursued group buying plans in order to reduce costs from large suppliers.

Online demand aggregation is built on two principles. First, sellers are more likely to offer discounts to buyers purchasing in volume, and, second, buyers increase their purchases as prices fall. Prices are expected to adjust dynamically to the volume of the order and the motivations of the vendors. In general, demand aggregation is suitable for MRO products (commodity-like products) that are frequently purchased by a large number of organizations in high volume.

Professional Service Auctions Perhaps one of the more interesting uses for auctions on the Web is eBay's marketplace for professional services, Elance. This auction is a sealed-bid, dynamic-priced market for freelance professional services from legal and marketing services to graphics design and programming. Firms looking for professional services post a project description and request for bid on Elance. Providers of services bid for the work. The buyer can choose from among bidders on the basis of both cost and perceived quality of the providers that can be gauged from the feedback of clients posted on the site. This type of auction is a reverse Vickrey-like auction where sealed bids are submitted and the winner is usually the low-cost provider of services. Another similar site is SoloGig.

WHEN TO USE AUCTIONS (AND FOR WHAT) IN BUSINESS

There are many different situations in which auctions are an appropriate channel for businesses to consider. For much of this chapter, we have looked at auctions from a consumer point of view. The objective of consumers is to receive the greatest value for the lowest cost. Now, switch your perspective to that of a business. Remember that the objective of businesses using auctions is to maximize their revenue (their share of consumer surplus) by finding the true market value of products and services, a market value that hopefully is higher in the auction channel than in fixed-price channels. **Table 11.9** provides an overview of factors to consider.

The factors are described as follows:

- **Type of product:** Online auctions are most commonly used for rare and unique products for which prices are difficult to discover, and there may have been no market for the goods. However, Priceline has succeeded in developing auctions for perishable commodities (such as airline seats) for which retail prices have already been established, and some B2B auctions involve commodities such as steel (often sold at distress prices). New clothing items, new digital cameras, and new computers are generally not sold at auction because their prices are easy to discover, catalog prices are high, sustainable, and profitable, they are not perishable, and there exists an efficient market channel in the form of retail stores (online and offline).

- **Product life cycle:** For the most part, businesses have traditionally used auctions for goods at the end of their product life cycle and for products where auctions yield a higher price than fixed-price liquidation sales. However, products at the beginning

TABLE 11.9	FACTORS TO CONSIDER WHEN CHOOSING AUCTIONS
CONSIDERATIONS	**DESCRIPTION**
Type of product	Rare, unique, commodity, perishable
Stage of product life cycle	Early, mature, late
Channel-management issues	Conflict with retail distributors; differentiation
Type of auction	Seller vs. buyer bias
Initial pricing	Low vs. high
Bid increment amounts	Low vs. high
Auction length	Short vs. long
Number of items	Single vs. multiple
Price-allocation rule	Uniform vs. discriminatory
Information sharing	Closed vs. open bidding

of their life cycle are increasingly being sold at auction. Early releases of music, books, videos, games, and digital appliances can be sold to highly motivated early adopters who want to be the first in their neighborhood with new products. Online sales of event tickets from music concerts to sports events now account for upwards of 25% of all event ticket sales in the United States.

- **Channel management:** Established retailers such as JCPenney and Walmart, and manufacturers in general, must be careful not to allow their auction activity to interfere with their existing profitable channels. For this reason, items found on established retail-site auctions tend to be late in their product life cycle or have quantity purchase requirements.

- **Type of auction:** Sellers obviously should choose auctions where there are many buyers and only a few, or even one, seller. English ascending-price auctions such as those at eBay are best for sellers because as the number of bidders increases, the price tends to move higher.

- **Initial pricing:** Research suggests that auction items should start out with low initial bid prices in order to encourage more bidders to bid (see "Bid increments" below). The lower the price, the larger the number of bidders will appear. The larger the number of bidders, the higher the prices move.

- **Bid increments:** It is generally safest to keep bid increments low so as to increase the number of bidders and the frequency of their bids. If bidders can be convinced that, for just a few more dollars, they can win the auction, then they will tend to make the higher bid and forget about the total amount they are bidding.

- **Auction length:** In general, the longer auctions are scheduled, the larger the number of bidders and the higher the prices can go. However, once the new bid arrival rate drops off and approaches zero, bid prices stabilize. Most eBay auctions are scheduled for seven days.

- **Number of items:** When a business has a number of items to sell, buyers usually expect a "volume discount," and this expectation can cause lower bids in return. Therefore, sellers should consider breaking up very large bundles into smaller bundles auctioned at different times.

- **Price allocation rule:** Most buyers believe it is "fair" that everyone pay the same price in a multi-unit auction, and a uniform pricing rule is recommended. eBay Dutch Internet auctions encourage this expectation. The idea that some buyers should pay more based on their differential need for the product is not widely supported. Therefore, sellers who want to price discriminate should do so by holding auctions for the same goods on different auction markets, or at different times, to prevent direct price comparison.

- **Closed vs. open bidding:** Closed bidding has many advantages for the seller, and sellers should use this approach whenever possible because it permits price discrimination without offending buyers. However, open bidding carries the advantage of "herd effects" and "winning effects" (described later in the chapter) in which consumers' competitive instincts to "win" drive prices higher than even secret bidding would achieve.

SELLER AND CONSUMER BEHAVIOR AT AUCTIONS

In addition to these structural considerations, you should also consider the behavior of consumers at auction sites. Research on consumer behavior at online auction sites is growing, but is still in its infancy. However, early research has produced some interesting findings.

Seller Profits: Arrival Rate, Auction Length, and Number of Units

The profit to the seller is a function of the arrival rate, auction length, and the number of units for auction. However, each of these relationships suffers a declining return to scale and rapidly falls off after an optimal point is reached (Vakrat and Seidmann, 1998, 1999) (see **Figure 11.4**). For this reason, in real-world auctions on eBay, sellers with a large number of units to sell, say, hundreds of PC laptops, usually have multiple concurrent auctions with about 10 units for sale in each auction, with a duration of three days. The auction is just long enough to attract most of the likely bidders, but not so long as to run up the cost of posting the auction beyond a profitable level. The more popular an auction (the more bidders who arrive), the longer an auction should be, up to the point where the costs of maintaining the auction listing outweigh the additional profit brought by the last bidder. These dynamics suggest a kind of bidding frenzy for popular items, in which the prices bid depend on the number of bidders, length of time, and units offered.

FIGURE 11.4	**AUCTION PROFITS**

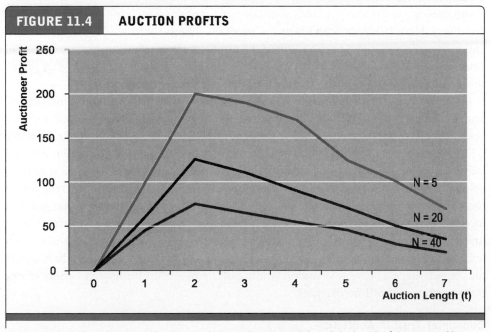

An auction's profit is determined by the arrival rate at the auction (N), and the length of the auction (t). Profitability rises rapidly at first, but then falls off rapidly as costs rise. Profits also rise with the number of units auctioned up to a maximum point, and then rapidly fall off.

SOURCE: Based on data from Vakrat and Seidmann, 1998.

Auction Prices: Are They the Lowest?

It is widely assumed that auction prices are lower than prices in other fixed-price markets. Empirical evidence is mixed on this assumption. Vakrat and Seidmann (1999) found auction prices were 25% lower on average than prices for the identical goods found in catalogs produced by the same retailers. Brynjolfsson and Smith (2000) also found that auction prices for CDs were lower than online store prices. Lee found, however, that auction prices for used cars in Japan on the AUCNET auction site were actually higher than fixed-price markets, in part because the quality of cars on the auction site was higher than cars found in car lots (Lee et al., 1999–2000).

There are many reasons why auction prices might be higher than those in fixed-price markets for items of identical quality, and why auction prices in one auction market may be higher than those in other auction markets. A considerable body of research has shown that consumers are not driven solely by value maximization, but instead are influenced by many situational factors, irrelevant and wrong information, and misperceptions when they make market decisions (Simonson and Tversky, 1992). Auctions are social events—shared social environments, where bidders adjust to one another (Hanson and Putler, 1996). Briefly, bidders base their bids on what others previously bid, and this can lead to an upward cascading effect (Arkes and Hutzel, 2000). In a study of hundreds of eBay auctions for Sony PlayStations, CD players, Mexican pottery, and Italian silk ties, Dholakia and Soltysinski (2001) found that bidders exhibited **herd behavior** (the tendency to gravitate toward, and bid for, auction listings with one or more existing bids) by making multiple bids on some auctions (coveted comparables), and making no bids at auctions for comparable items (overlooked comparables). Herd behavior was lower for products where there was more agreement and more objective clues on the value of the products—Sony PlayStations, for instance, compared to Italian silk ties. Herd behavior resulted in consumers paying higher prices than necessary for reasons having no foundation in economic reality.

The behavioral reality of participating in auctions can produce many unintended results. Winners can suffer **winner's regret**, the feeling after winning an auction that they paid too much for an item, which indicates that their winning bid does not reflect what they thought the item was worth but rather what the second bidder thought the item was worth. Sellers can experience **seller's lament**, reflecting the fact that they sold an item at a price just above the second place bidder, never knowing how much the ultimate winner might have paid or the true value to the final winner. Auction losers can experience **loser's lament**, the feeling of having been too cheap in bidding and failing to win. In summary, auctions can lead to both winners paying too much and sellers receiving too little. Both of these outcomes can be minimized when sellers and buyers have a very clear understanding of the prices for items in a variety of different online and offline markets.

Consumer Trust in Auctions

Auction sites have the same difficulties creating a sense of consumer trust as all other e-commerce Web sites, although in the case of auction sites, the operators of the marketplace do not directly control the quality of goods being offered and cannot directly vouch for the integrity of customers. This opens the possibility for criminal actors to

herd behavior
the tendency to gravitate toward, and bid for, auction listings with one or more existing bids

winner's regret
the winner's feeling after an auction that he or she paid too much for an item

seller's lament
concern that one will never know how much the ultimate winner might have paid, or the true value to the final winner

loser's lament
the feeling of having been too cheap in bidding and failing to win

appear as either sellers or buyers. eBay is the single largest source of consumer fraud on the Internet. Several studies have found that trust and credibility increase as users gain more experience, if trusted third-party seals are present, and if the site has a wide variety of consumer services for tracking purchases (or fraud), thus giving the user a sense of control (Krishnamurthy, 2001; Stanford-Makovsky, 2002; Nikander and Karnonen, 2002; Bailey, et al., 2002; Kollock, 1999). Because of the powerful role that trust plays in online consumer behavior, eBay and most auction sites make considerable efforts to develop automated trust-enhancing mechanisms such as seller and buyer ratings, escrow services, and authenticity guarantees (see the next section).

WHEN AUCTION MARKETS FAIL: FRAUD AND ABUSE IN AUCTIONS

Markets fail to produce socially desirable outcomes (maximizing consumer welfare) in four situations: information asymmetry, monopoly power, public goods, and externalities.

Online and offline auction markets can be prone to fraud, which produces information asymmetries between sellers and buyers and among buyers, which in turn causes auction markets to fail (see **Table 11.10**). In the past, according to the Internet Crime Complaint Center (IC3), Internet auction fraud was one of the top 10 types of fraud but in 2012 it represented only 10% of total Internet fraud in part because other Internet crimes had grown so rapidly. Auction-auto fraud scams were the most frequently reported, with more than $8.8 million in losses, and an average reported loss of more than $2,400 (National White Collar Crime Center/FBI, 2013).

eBay and many other auction sites have investigation units that receive complaints from consumers and investigate reported abuses. Nevertheless, with millions of visitors per week and hundreds of thousands of auctions to monitor, eBay is highly dependent on the good faith of sellers and consumers to follow the rules.

11.3 E-COMMERCE PORTALS

Port: From the Latin porta, an entrance or gateway to a locality.

Portals are the most frequently visited sites on the Web if only because they often are the first page to which many users point their browser on startup. The top portals such as Yahoo, MSN, and AOL have hundreds of millions of unique visitors worldwide each month. Web portal sites are gateways to the more than 100 billion Web pages available on the Internet. Millions of users have set Facebook as their home page, choosing to start their sessions with news from their friends. We have already discussed Facebook in Section 11.1. Perhaps the most important service provided by portals is that of helping people find the information they are looking for on the Web. The original portals in the early days of e-commerce were search engines. Consumers would pass through search engine portals on their way to rich, detailed, in-depth content on the Web. But portals evolved into much more complex Web sites that provide news, entertainment, maps, images, social networks, in-depth information, and education on a growing variety of topics all contained at the portal site. Portals today seek to be a sticky destination site, not merely a gateway through which visitors pass. In this respect, Web portals are very much like television networks: destination sites for content supported by advertising

TABLE 11.10	TYPES OF AUCTION FRAUDS
TYPE OF FRAUD	DESCRIPTION
FEEDBACK OFFENSES	
Shill feedback	Using secondary IDs or other auction site members to inflate seller ratings
Feedback abuse	Engaging in abuse in the feedback forum
Feedback extortion	Threatening negative feedback in return for a benefit
Feedback solicitation	Offering to sell, trade, or buy feedback
BUYING OFFENSES	
Transaction interference	E-mailing buyers to warn them away from a seller
Invalid bid retraction	Using the retraction option to make high bids, discovering the maximum bid of current high bidder, then retracting bid
Persistent bidding	Persisting in making bids despite a warning that bids are not welcome
Unwelcome buyer	Buying in violation of seller's terms
Bid shielding	Using secondary user IDs or other members to artificially raise the bidding price of an item
Nonpayment after buying	Blocking legitimate buyers by bidding high, then not paying
SELLING OFFENSES	
Shill bidding	Using secondary user IDs or bidders who have no actual intention to buy to artificially raise the price of an item
Seller nonperformance	Accepting payment and failing to deliver the promised goods, either at all, or delivering goods not as described in auction (counterfeit or poor quality)
Nonselling seller	Refusing payment, failure to deliver after a successful auction
Fee avoidance	Any of a variety of mechanisms for avoiding paying listing fees
Transaction interception	Pretending you are a seller and accepting payment
Contact Information/Identity Offenses	
Misrepresentation of identity	Claiming to be an employee of the auction site; representing oneself as another auction site member
False or missing contact information	Providing false information or leaving information out
Dead/invalid e-mail addresses	Providing false contact information
Underage user	A minor claiming to be 18 years old or older
MISCELLANEOUS OFFENSES	
Interference with site	Using any software program that would interfere with auction site operations
Bid siphoning	E-mailing another seller's bidders and offering the same product for less
Sending spam	Sending unsolicited offers to bidders

revenues. Portals today want visitors to stay a long time—the longer the better. For the most part they succeed: portals are places where people linger for a long time.

Portals also serve important functions within a business or organization. Most corporations, universities, churches, and other formal organizations have **enterprise portals** that help employees or members navigate to important content, such as human resources information, corporate news, or organizational announcements. For instance, your university has a portal through which you can register for courses, find classroom assignments, and perform a host of other important student activities. Increasingly, these enterprise portals also provide general-purpose news and real-time financial feeds provided by content providers outside the organization, such as MSNBC News and generalized Web search capabilities. Corporate portals and intranets are the subject of other textbooks focused on the corporate uses of Web technology and are beyond the scope of this book (see Laudon and Laudon, 2012). Our focus here is on e-commerce portals.

enterprise portals
help employees navigate to the enterprise's human resource and corporate content

THE GROWTH AND EVOLUTION OF PORTALS

Web portals have changed a great deal from their initial function and role. As noted above, most of today's well-known portals, such as Yahoo, MSN, and AOL, began as search engines. The initial function provided by portals was to index Web page content and make this content available to users in a convenient form. Early portals expected visitors to stay only a few minutes at the site. As millions of people signed on to the Internet in the early 2000s, the number of visitors to basic search engine sites exploded commensurately. At first, few people understood how a Web search site could make money by passing customers on to other destinations. But search sites attracted huge audiences, and therein lay the foundation for their success as vehicles for marketing and advertising. Search sites, recognizing the potential for commerce, expanded their offerings from simple navigation to include commerce (the sale of items directly from the Web site as well as advertising for other retail sites), content (in the form of news at first, and later in the form of weather, investments, games, health, and other subject matter), and distribution of others' content. These three characteristics have become the basic definition of portal sites, namely, sites that provide three functions: navigation of the Web, commerce, and content.

Because the value of portals to advertisers and content owners is largely a function of the size of the audience each portal reaches, and the length of time visitors stay on site, portals compete with one another on reach and unique visitors. *Reach* is defined as the percentage of the Web audience that visits the site in a month (or some other time period), and *unique visitors* is defined as the number of uniquely identified individuals who visit in a month. Portals are inevitably subject to network effects: The value of the portal to advertisers and consumers increases geometrically as reach increases, which, in turn, attracts still more customers. These effects have resulted in the differentiation of the portal marketspace into three tiers: a few general-purpose mega portal sites that garner 60%–80% of the Web audience, second-tier general-purpose sites that hover around 20%–30% reach, and third-tier specialized vertical market portals that attract 2%–10% of the audience. As described in Chapter 3, the top five portals/search engines (Google, Yahoo, MSN/Bing, AOL, and Ask.com) account for more than 95% of online searches. A similar pattern of concentration is observed when considering

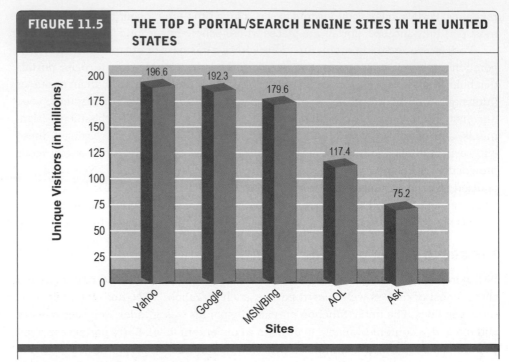

FIGURE 11.5 THE TOP 5 PORTAL/SEARCH ENGINE SITES IN THE UNITED STATES

SOURCE: Based on data from comScore, 2013a.

the audience share of portals/search engines as illustrated in **Figure 11.5**. However, this picture is changing as large audiences move to social network sites, and millions of users make these sites their opening or home pages.

For more insight into the nature of the competition and change among the top portals, read *Insight on Business: The Transformation of AOL*.

TYPES OF PORTALS: GENERAL-PURPOSE AND VERTICAL MARKET

There are two primary types of portals: general-purpose portals and vertical market portals. **General-purpose portals** attempt to attract a very large general audience and then retain the audience on-site by providing in-depth vertical content channels, such as information on news, finance, autos, movies, and weather. General-purpose portals typically offer Web search engines, free e-mail, personal home pages, chat rooms, community-building software, and bulletin boards. Vertical content channels on general-purpose portal sites offer content such as sports scores, stock tickers, health tips, instant messaging, automobile information, and auctions.

Vertical market portals (sometimes also referred to as destination sites or vortals) attempt to attract highly focused, loyal audiences with a deep interest either in community or specialized content—from sports to the weather. In addition to their focused content, vertical market portals have recently begun adding many of the features found in general-purpose portals. For instance, in addition to being a social network, you can also think of Facebook as a portal—the home page for millions of users, and a gateway to the Internet. Facebook is an affinity group portal because it is based on friendships among people. Facebook offers e-mail, search (Bing), games, and apps. News is limited.

general-purpose portals

attempt to attract a very large general audience and then retain the audience on-site by providing in-depth vertical content

vertical market portals

attempt to attract highly focused, loyal audiences with a deep interest in either community or specialized content

INSIGHT ON BUSINESS

THE TRANSFORMATION OF AOL

You have to give it to AOL; its corporate DNA must include a gene for tenacity. From its inauspicious beginnings as an online game server for the Atari 2600 video game console to its dizzying heights as the leading ISP in the United States—a time that even spawned a Meg Ryan/Tom Hanks movie entitled *You've Got Mail* after the ubiquitous greeting AOL users heard each time they signed on—to its equally staggering decline after its failed merger with Time Warner—somehow AOL has found a way to survive.

Started in the early 1980s as Control Video Corporation, it provided an online service called Gameline for the Atari 2600. The company didn't make enough money, and in May 1983, it was reorganized as Quantum Computer Services, providing a dedicated online service for Commodore 64 and 128 computers called Quantum Link. In 1988, the company added online services called Apple Link and PC Link, and in 1989, its name was changed to America Online.

In February 1991, AOL launched an online program for the DOS operating system (the early Microsoft operating system that used text commands) and one for Windows the following year. In contrast to CompuServe, which served the technical community, AOL positioned itself as the online service for people who weren't comfortable with technology, a shrewd move at the time. Initially, it provided proprietary software and charged users hefty hourly fees. In 1996, it switched to a subscription-based model, charging $19.99 per month. Mass distribution of AOL CD-ROMs through the mail spurred adoption—AOL was everywhere, giving over 10 million people their first exposure to the Web, e-mail, instant messaging, and chat rooms. However, the company was slow to provide access to the open Internet, and complaints erupted, in particular, about dropped connections and busy signals. Still, it continued to grow. In 1996, in

another boon to its brand, AOL signed a five-year agreement that it would be bundled with Windows on new PCs. The first major Web portal for the general public was on its way.

In 1999, CEO Steve Case said that Windows was in the past, and predicted that AOL would be the next Microsoft. This is not exactly how the story unfolded. When AOL tried to exploit its tremendous name recognition and brand prominence, it failed repeatedly. Its biggest failure, though not its only one, was not anticipating the broadband transformation. But that's getting ahead of the story.

In 2000, before the company's spectacular fall began, Time Warner bought AOL for $165 billion. Despite the media fanfare, there were problems from the start with what is now acknowledged by current CEO Tim Armstrong to be the worst merger in corporate history. In the first year, the merged company already had difficulty reaching growth targets, possibly because AOL had improperly inflated its pre-merger revenue. In 2002, advertising revenue declined sharply. The number of AOL ISP subscribers peaked in the fall of that year, at 26.7 million, and has been declining ever since. There are less than 2.7 million ISP subscribers today. However, these subscribers still generate approximately a third of the company's revenue. Incredibly, these core dial-up holdouts have substantially helped to keep the company afloat.

Some people believe the merger did not have to turn out that way. Marrying one of the foremost providers of "old fashioned" content to one of the largest distributors of "online" content might have made sense if it had been managed differently. But it wasn't. Key players at Time Warner resented the merger and thought it was a waste of time and money. To make matters worse, corporate leadership did little to persuade brand/division heads that it was their responsibility to make the merged company work.

And then came broadband. AOL underestimated just how attractive broadband would become. By

(continued)

2004, broadband adoption was gathering speed. At the same time, Google's search engine advertising took off and banner advertising with it. Yahoo was successful with banner display ads, and it added content that drew the broadband audience. AOL was quickly perceived as stodgy, slow, and uncool. Even when AOL made its subscriber-only content freely available, it was too little, too late.

Between 2002 and 2007 the company occupied various positions on the continuum between misstep and turmoil. Its stock price plummeted, it was investigated by the SEC for several unorthodox advertising deals, the Justice Department conducted a criminal probe, financial reports had to be revised downward, and the positions of CEO and VP of Marketing became revolving doors.

In 2007, AOL began pursuing a new strategy, creating more than a dozen niche content sites.

The following year, Time Warner negotiated with both Microsoft and Google in an attempt to sell AOL. When this was unsuccessful, it decided to spin off the company instead. First, it repurchased Google's 5% stake for $283 million. Google's purchase price in 2005 had been $1 billion.

When Tim Armstrong came on board in 2009, he added senior staff members from Google and Yahoo with an eye towards turning the company into the biggest creator of premium content on the Web and the largest seller of online display ads. Positioning AOL to be ready when the line between online and broadcast programming permanently blurred, he began assembling the infrastructure. Acquisitions included StudioNow, a provider of a proprietary digital platform that allows clients to create and distribute professional-quality videos; 5Min Media, which provided a syndication platform for instructional, knowledge, and lifestyle videos; Thing Labs, a Web-based software company specializing in social media applications; and Pictela, which enables AOL to scale its delivery of video, photos, and apps within advertising and generally across AOL. The real blockbuster acquisition was the Huffington Post in March 2011 for $315 million. Armstrong appeared to be betting big on its charismatic leader, Arianna Huffington,

and its 25 million unique monthly visitors. Around 20% of AOL's workforce was eliminated following the purchase.

It soon became clear that the big bet was actually on online video, with HuffPost Live as one significant part of the wager. Launched in the summer of 2012, HuffPost Live features live discussions on current events 12 hours a day, five days a week. The unique twist and perceived draw is user interaction. Viewers submit chat comments as programs are airing and can also tweet and submit their own videos. Viewers will also increasingly be included in programming, so that they can engage with the host and his or her guest, creating a "social video" experience. Rather than scheduling specific programs at specific times of the day, or even for a set period of time, topics are conversational, not bound by timeframe, and not bound by the hot topic of the day—a sort of freeform television. To which, Armstrong is of course hoping to add live advertising. Cadillac and Verizon are two of the main investors in the venture. Though Huff-PostLive is not yet profitable, the site is on track to show a profit by the end of 2014.

AOL also has teams of video producers in both New York and Los Angeles that are creating branded entertainment video. Sometimes working with celebrities, these teams, as well as video partners from around the world, are producing hundreds of videos a day of an informational, how-to, or entertainment nature. Sources include wholly owned properties such as TechCrunch, one of the most popular tech blogs on the Internet, with around 13 million unique monthly visitors. These videos will attempt to tread the line between branded infomercial and useful and sought after information.

Aiming to become a one-stop shop for consumers delivering the content they want when they want it, the AOL On Network debuted in April 2012. More than 420,000 videos are available on 14 channels divided into subject areas. In 2012, AOL had 55% more viewers than it had in the previous year, with a total of 71.2 million, enough to pass third-place Facebook. iOS and Android apps were released in October 2012. The opposite approach from HuffPost

(continued)

Live is embraced. Organized, selected, programmed content, much more like traditional TV, is offered here and syndicated out to different outlets.

AOL's second quarter 2012 financial report in July 2012 registered a turnaround from a loss of $11.8 million in 2011 to earnings of $970.8 million in 2012. This was mainly attributed to a one-time patent deal that was completed with Microsoft in June. In 2013, AOL continued to inch upward, posting earnings of $541 million in the second quarter. AOL's latest big bet is on programmatic advertising, an automated form of ad buying that promises to cut out advertising middlemen and allow content providers and advertisers both to make more money. AOL announced that it had already struck deals with major ad agencies to participate in these automated ad exchanges, which it believes will begin a seismic shift of TV advertising dollars to online video. To that end, the company also bought video ad company Adap.tv to bolster its position in online video. Many other companies are entering the programmatic ad exchange marketplace, however. Also, AOL's Patch community news venture continues to struggle, and in 2013 Armstrong planned to reduce the size and scale of Patch to improve its profitability.

AOL's strategy to focus on video, content, and display advertising is risky. Approximately one-third of the company's revenue is still derived from its dwindling dial-up subscriptions. But its online video and content initiatives are moving in the right direction, and time will tell if the company's big bet on programmatic advertising works out. Stay tuned.

SOURCES: "AOL CEO Leads Charge to Pry Ad Dollars From TV," by Keach Hagey, *Wall Street Journal*, September 24, 2013; "comScore: AOL Climbs to Second Place in Online Video Content Ranking," by Greg Jarboe, Clickz.com, September 24, 2013; "AOL Urges Industry to Embrace Programmatic Buying," by Mike Shields, *Adweek*, September 23, 2013; "AOL Q2 Comes In (Slightly) Above Estimates With $541M Revenue, $0.35 Earnings Per Share," by Anthony Ha, TechCrunch, August 7th, 2013; "AOL to Launch Programmatic Upfront During Advertising Week," by Mike Shields, *Adweek*, July 24, 2013; "Netflix's Amazing Growth and AOL's Dismal Decline," by Christina Warren, Mashable, May 9, 2013; AOL: You've Got Apps," *New York Business Journal*, October 4, 2012; "AOL," Wikipedia.com, accessed September 26, 2012; "AOL CEO Tim Armstrong: 'We Haven't Won Yet'," by Daniel Terdiman, News.cnet.com, September 11, 2012; "AOL's Triple-Pronged Approach to Online Video," by Troy Dreier, Streamingmedia.com, August/September 2012; "$1.1B Microsoft Patent Deal Done, AOL Buys Back $600M In Stock, Offers Dividend Of $5.15 Per Share," by Ingrid Lunden, TechCrunch.com, August 27th, 2012; "AOL Dialup Just Had Its 'Best' Quarter In A Decade, And Still Has 3 Million Subscribers," by Dan Frommer, SplatF.com, July 26, 2012; "AOL Says Patch Continues to Double Its Revenue from Last Year," by Steve Myers, Poynter.org, July 25, 2012; "AOL's Ad Revenue Up; Armstrong Bullish on Video," by Tanzina Vega, *New York Times*, July 25, 2012; "AOL Buys TechCrunch, 5Min and Thing Labs," by Jessica E. Vascellaro and Emily Steel, *New York Times*, September 29, 2010; "Eleven Years of Ambition and Failure at AOL," by Saul Hansell, *New York Times*, July 24, 2009; "Daring to Dream of a Resurgent AOL," by Saul Hansell, *New York Times*, July 23, 2009; "Before Spin-off, AOL Tries for that Start-up Feeling," *New York Times*, July 20, 2009.

The concentration of audience share in the portal market reflects (in addition to network effects) the limited time budget of consumers. This limited time budget works to the advantage of general-purpose portals. Consumers have a finite amount of time to spend on the Web, and as a result, most consumers visit fewer than 30 unique domains each month. Facing limited time, consumers concentrate their visits at sites that can satisfy a broad range of interests, from weather and travel information, to stocks, sports, and entertainment content.

General-purpose sites such as Yahoo try to be all things to all people and attract a broad audience with both generalized navigation services and in-depth content and community efforts. For instance, Yahoo has become the Web's largest source of news: more people visit Yahoo News than any other news site including online newspapers. Yet recent changes in consumer behavior on the Web show that consumers are spending less time "surfing the Web" and on general browsing, and more time doing focused searches, research, and participating in social networks. These trends will advantage special-purpose, vertical market sites that can provide focused, in-depth community and content.

As a general matter, the general-purpose portals are very well-known brands, while the vertical content and affinity group portals tend to have less well-known brands. **Figure 11.6** lists examples of general-purpose portals and the two main types of vertical market portals.

PORTAL BUSINESS MODELS

Portals receive income from a number of different sources. The revenue base of portals is changing and dynamic, with some of the largest sources of revenue declining. **Table 11.10** summarizes the major portal revenue sources.

The business strategies of both general-purpose and vertical portals have changed greatly because of the rapid growth in search engine advertising and intelligent ad placement networks such as Google's AdSense, which can place ads on thousands of Web sites based on content. General portal sites such as AOL and Yahoo did not have well-developed search engines, and hence have not grown as fast as Google, which has a powerful search engine. Microsoft, for instance, has invested billions of dollars in its Bing search engine to catch up with Google. On the other hand, general portals have content, which Google did not originally have, although it added to its content by purchasing YouTube and adding Google sites devoted to news, financial information, images, and maps. Yahoo and MSN visitors stay on-site a long time reading news, content, and sending e-mail. Facebook users stay on-site and linger three times as long as visitors to traditional portals like Yahoo. For this reason social network sites, Facebook in particular, are direct competitors of Yahoo, Google, and the other portals. General portals are attempting to provide more premium content focused on sub-communities of their portal audience. Advertisers on portals are especially interested in focused, revenue-producing premium content available on Web portals because it attracts a more committed audience.

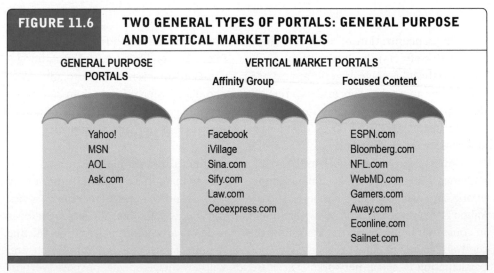

| FIGURE 11.6 | TWO GENERAL TYPES OF PORTALS: GENERAL PURPOSE AND VERTICAL MARKET PORTALS |

GENERAL PURPOSE PORTALS

Yahoo!
MSN
AOL
Ask.com

VERTICAL MARKET PORTALS

Affinity Group

Facebook
iVillage
Sina.com
Sify.com
Law.com
Ceoexpress.com

Focused Content

ESPN.com
Bloomberg.com
NFL.com
WebMD.com
Gamers.com
Away.com
Econline.com
Sailnet.com

There are two general types of portals: general-purpose and vertical market. Vertical market portals may be based on affinity groups or on focused content.

TABLE 11.10	TYPICAL PORTAL REVENUE SOURCES
PORTAL REVENUE SOURCE	DESCRIPTION
General advertising	Charging for impressions delivered
Tenancy deals	Fixed charge for guaranteed number of impressions, exclusive partnerships, "sole providers"
Commissions on sales	Revenue based on sales at the site by independent providers
Subscription fees	Charging for premium content
Applications and games	Games and apps are sold to users; advertising is placed within apps

For instance, financial service firms pay premium advertising rates to advertise on portal finance service areas such as Yahoo's Finance pages. As noted in Chapters 6 and 7, there is a direct relationship between the revenue derived from a customer and the focus of the customer segment (see **Figure 11.7**).

The survival strategy for general-purpose portals in the future is therefore to develop deep, rich vertical content in order to reach and engage customers at the site. The strategy for much smaller vertical market portals is to put together a collection of vertical portals to form a vertical portal network, a collection of deep, rich content sites. The strategy for search engine sites such as Google is to obtain more content to attract users for a long time and expose them to more ad pages (or screens).

FIGURE 11.7	REVENUE PER CUSTOMER AND MARKET FOCUS

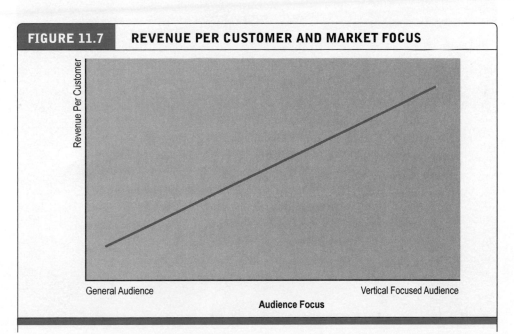

The more focused and targeted the audience, the more revenue can be derived per customer for an appropriately targeted product or service.

eBay Evolves

With the unveiling of its new, more reserved logo in 2012, eBay announced its arrival to the mainstream. Gone are the jaunty, incongruent block letters that characterized the offbeat startup auction site founded by Pierre Omidyar in 1995. In their place, the bold primary colors intact, is a symmetrical set of block letters staidly observing the same parallel bottom line. With eBay now deriving 70% of its revenue from traditional e-commerce, and peer-to-peer auctions taking a backseat, the time had come. Underscoring this change, which was by no means sudden, the 2012 Fall Seller Update announced that sales of tarot card readings, potions, spells, and psychic readings would no longer be permitted. And, in a progression from the previous Christmas when it provided a tool to allow customers to locate in-stock items at local bricks-and-mortar chains, eBay instituted a rewards program with Toys "R" Us, Dick's Sporting Goods, and Aeropostale in which customers who spend $100 either at one of these merchants' eBay storefronts or at their Web sites receive a $10 in-store coupon. Eccentric was out; conventional in.

© Iain Masterton / Alamy

The transformation began in November 2007, when former CEO Meg Whitman exited and was replaced by former Bain & Company managing director, John Donahoe. The company had already begun to stall, and the trend continued through 2009. For many buyers, the novelty of online auctions had worn off, and they were returning to easier and simpler methods of buying fixed-price goods from fixed-price retailers such as Amazon, which, by comparison, had steady growth during the same time period. Search engines and comparison shopping sites were also taking away some of eBay's auction business by making items easier to find on the Web.

Inheriting as he did one of the world's most recognizable and well-known Web sites perhaps made Donahoe's heretofore never accomplished task of turning around an Internet company more achievable, but his path was not easy or without controversy. His three-year revival plan moved eBay away from its origins as an online flea market, and at first it began to resemble an outlet mall where retailers sold out-of-season, overstocked, refurbished, or discontinued merchandise. From there it was a straightforward progression to partnering with firms such as Toys"R"Us to simply serve as another channel for current merchandise.

Small sellers were encouraged to shift away from the auction format and move toward the fixed-price sales model. The fee structure was adjusted, listing fees for fixed-price sales were lowered, improvements were made to the search engine, and rather than displaying ending auctions first, a formula was devised that took into account price and seller reputation so that highly rated merchants appeared first and received more exposure.

Unsurprisingly, the growing pains during this period included increasing complaints from sellers about excessive fees and eBay's favoritism toward big retailers. The hundreds of thousands of people who support themselves by selling on eBay and many millions more who use eBay to supplement their income often felt slighted. With its stock continuing to drop from its $58 high in 2004 to a low of just over $10 in early 2009, analysts' faith that Donahoe could turn things around had dwindled. Fearing that eBay had strayed too far from its original corporate culture and that competition from Amazon and Google Search presented serious threats, most forecasters were negative or neutral on eBay's chance of recovery. This pessimism discounted eBay's history of sensible growth marked by a number of canny purchases.

Its signature purchase is, of course, PayPal, whose payment services enable the exchange of money between individuals over the Internet. This acquisition was the key to eBay's endurance through the lean years and the propeller that pushed it towards the future. PayPal accounted for approximately 43% of eBay's revenues in 2012, and has been a significant factor in their growth. In 2013, PayPal propelled eBay's stock price back over $50 per share, and protected it from weakness in its retail business. PayPal has added 4.7 million active accounts, ending the second quarter with 132 million.

In 2012, a system was installed in 2,000 Home Depot stores so that PayPal card holders could either swipe their cards or use a PIN and their cell phone number to pay for purchases. Other bricks-and-mortar venues will be similarly equipped in the near future. Further expansion includes a credit card processing device called PayPal Here that allows small businesses to use smartphones and tablets to accept credit cards.

In direct competition with Square, eBay plans to enable consumers to "check in" so that they can be personally greeted, complete purchases without a mobile device or a credit card, and receive a text message as their receipt.

The 2008 addition of BillMeLater to the PayPal wallet, an instant credit product offered at checkout, has also proved, so far, to be farsighted. BML, which lets online customers pay several months after they have made purchases, logged 64% loan growth between 2010 and 2011, making it one of eBay's fastest growing business segments. BML can reduce funding costs for PayPal and help it to develop into a true financial product. Currently, more than 50% of PayPal purchases are funded using Visa and MasterCard credit and debit cards, which come with substantial fees. Reducing this cost would naturally increase profit margins. Now ranked the third most popular online payment service behind PayPal and Amazon's payment service, analysts expect BML revenue to exceed half a billion dollars in 2015.

One possible downside, however, is that as BML grows, it increases overall risk for the company putting downward pressure on stock price. Collecting fees for processing payments presents little in the way of risk. Expanding into the loan granting arena is coupled with the risk of default and with regulatory issues. Some analysts are worried that as eBay continues to expand its lending business, the company is sacrificing quality for quantity in its lending business, jeopardizing its future profitability. BML's continued expansion would likely mean that PayPal, which is already a bank in Europe, would have to become a chartered financial institution in the United States. This lengthy and expensive process has so far been forestalled by using WebBank as the lender and purchasing the receivables from them. This set-up has already been tested in a California district court case charging that the true lender is BML, and further, that it engages in usury lending practices because the loans carry close to a 20% annual interest rate. While the usury charges were dismissed, the remainder of the case was moved to a Utah district court. eBay will have to balance the risks and benefits of further BML expansion.

Still, with possible PayPal challenges in the future, its success gave the Marketplaces segment time to rebound. And recover it did. In 2012, it delivered double-digit growth, 11% annualized, and eBay stock rose to its highest level in six years, close to $50 in September. As impressive and encouraging as the Marketplaces turnaround was, it was another of eBay's astute investments that truly fueled its resurgence—mobile technology. eBay's mobile investments began in 2010 with RedLaser, a barcode-scanning mobile application. This was followed by Critical Path, an industry leading mobile app developer, doubling the size of eBay's mobile team. WHERE, a location-based media and advertising company with a local discovery mobile application, and Zong, a provider of mobile payments through mobile carrier billing, were purchased in 2011. PayPal was used to purchase Fig Card, a small mobile payment startup in April 2011. A year later, these outlays were bearing fruit, reportedly supporting $15 billion in mobile transactions over the preceding year. Approximately 50% of these transactions were mobile Marketplaces sales, while the other half was mobile PayPal transactions.

eBay recognized the coming mobile revolution even before the first iPhone or the establishment of the App Store, according to Olivier Ropars, senior director of Mobile

Commerce. This prescience resulted in two significant September 2012 milestones—the 100 millionth download of eBay mobile apps and the 100 millionth mobile listing. In 2013, eBay encountered increased competition in mobile commerce, and moved quickly to acquire mobile payment gateway Braintree for $800 million. Braintree's technology will allow eBay consumers to more easily make payments on smartphones and tablets, and the acquisition also eliminates a major competitor in that space for PayPal.

While many other acquisitions through the years have also helped to transform eBay from an online garage sale to a mainstream competitor with Amazon, its adoption of the "social, mobile, local" driving theme was central to its survival. Positioning itself at the center of the online—offline—mobile triangle by offering a wide variety of services that enable merchants to more easily integrate their cross-channel retailing is the key to its resurgence and to its continued success. Still, in a nod to its innovative origins, eBay built a new online tool called eBay Collect aimed at its original and still most active users—comic book and coin collectors. EBay Collect will enable avid collectors to compile and organize pictures of their treasures for display to other users and to create wish lists so that sellers can target market to them. iPhone and Android apps are in the works, and expansion to other collection categories will follow. eBay appears to be wisely adhering to two maxims for long-lived companies: Always be cognizant of your changing environment, and stay true to your core identity.

Case Study Questions

1. Contrast eBay's original business model with its latest proposed business model.

2. What are the problems that eBay is currently facing? How is eBay trying to solve these problems?

3. Are the solutions eBay is seeking to implement good solutions? Why or why not? Are there any other solutions that eBay should consider?

4. Who are eBay's top three competitors online, and how will eBay's new strategy help it compete? Will eBay be providing a differentiated service to customers?

SOURCES: "Behind eBay's $800M Buy: Braintree will Replace PayPal's Developer Platform," by Kevin Fitchard, GigaOm, September 26, 2013; "EBay to Buy Braintree to Boost PayPal's Mobile Presence," by Chandni Doulatramani, Reuters, September 26, 2013; "EBay 2Q Profit Slides; Europe Remains Weak Spot," Barbara Ortutay, Associated Press, July 17, 2013; "Amazon, eBay Lead Way as E-Commerce Sales Still Surge," by Brian Deagon, Investor's Business Daily, July 2, 2013; "Is eBay Reliant on Sub-Prime Lending?" by Bob Chandler, Motley Fool, April 22, 2013; "eBay Hits 100m Mobile App Download Mark," by Dervedia Thomas, Dailydealmedia.com, September 29, 2012; "With Setify, eBay Goes Back To Its Roots And Creates The Nerdiest Pinterest Ever," by Christina Chaey, Fast Company, September 25, 2012; "eBay: We Need to Behave More Like a Retailer," by Sarah Shearman, Tamebay.com, September 25, 2012; "eBay Logo Gets a Refresh; The Time Felt Right After 17 Years," by Mark Tyson, Hexus.com, September 14, 2012; "eBay Bans Magic Spells and Potions," by Katy Waldman, Slate.com, August 17, 2012; "Behind eBay's Comeback," by James B. Stewart, New York Times, July 27, 2012; "Bill Me Later, eBay's Credit Version of PayPal, Helps Company's Profits but Exposes It to Risk," by Alistair Barr, MercuryNews.com, July 12, 2012; "PayPal Strength Helps eBay Exceed Forecasts," by Somini Sengupta, New York Times, April 18, 2012; "eBay Favors Big-Box Retailers in Holiday Promotions," by Ina Steiner, eCommerce-Bytes.com, December, 16, 2011; "How Jack Abraham is Reinventing eBay," by Danielle Sacks, Fast Company, June 22, 2011; "Connecting the Dots on eBay's Local Shopping Strategy," by Leena Rao, Techcrunch.com, May 15, 2011; "eBay CEO Sees Opportunities in Online and Offline Commerce," by Scott Morrison, Wall Street Journal, February 10, 2011; "eBay Says Big Growth Is Not Over," by Verne G. Kopytoff, New York Times, February 6, 2011; "eBay Mobile Sales Rise to $2 Billion, Reach Top End of Forecast," by Joseph Galante, Bloomberg.com, January 5, 2011.

11.5 REVIEW

KEY CONCEPTS

■ **Explain the difference between a traditional social network and an online social network.**

Social networks involve:
*   A group of people
*   Shared social interaction
*   Common ties among members
*   A shared area for some period of time

By extension, an online social network is an area online where people who share common ties can interact with one another.

■ **Understand how a social network differs from a portal.**

The difference between social networks and portals has become blurred. Originally, portals began as search engines. Then they added content and eventually many community-building features such as chat rooms, bulletin boards, and free Web site design and hosting. Social network sites began as content-specific locations and added more general portal services such as Web searching, general news, weather, and travel information, as well as a wide variety of e-commerce services.

■ **Describe the different types of social networks and online communities and their business models.**

*   *General communities:* Members can interact with a general audience segmented into numerous different groups. The purpose is to attract enough members to populate a wide range of topical discussion groups. Most general communities began as non-commercial subscription-based endeavors, but many have been purchased by larger community portal sites.
*   *Practice networks:* Members can participate in discussion groups and get help or simply information relating to an area of shared practice, such as art, education, or medicine. These generally have a nonprofit business model in which they simply attempt to collect enough in subscription fees, sales commissions, and limited advertising to cover the cost of operations.
*   *Interest-based communities:* Members can participate in focused discussion groups on a shared interest such as boats, horses, skiing, travel, or health. The advertising business model has worked because the targeted audience is attractive to marketers. Tenancy and sponsorship deals provide another similar revenue stream.
*   *Affinity communities:* Members can participate in focused discussions with others who share the same affinity or group identification, such as religion, ethnicity, gender, sexual orientation, or political beliefs. The business model is a mixture of subscription revenue from premium content and services, advertising, tenancy/sponsorships, and distribution agreements.
*   *Sponsored communities:* Members can participate in online communities created by government, nonprofit, or for-profit organizations for the purpose of pursuing organizational goals. These types of sites vary widely from local government sites to branded product sites. They use community technologies and tech-

niques to distribute information or extend brand influence. The goal of a branded product site is to increase offline product sales. These sites do not seek to make a profit and are often cost centers.

■ Describe the major types of auctions, their benefits and costs, and how they operate.

Auctions are markets where prices vary (dynamic pricing) depending on the competition among the participants who are buying or selling products or services. They can be classified broadly as C2C or B2C, although generally the term C2C auction refers to the venue in which the sale takes place, for example, a consumer-oriented Web site such as eBay, which also auctions items from established merchants. A B2C auction refers to an established online merchant that offers its own auctions. There are also numerous B2B online auctions for buyers of industrial parts, raw materials, commodities, and services. Within these three broad categories of auctions are several major auction types classified based upon how the bidding mechanisms work in each system:

- *English auctions:* A single item is up for sale from a single seller. Multiple buyers bid against one another within a specific time frame, with the highest bidder winning the object, as long as the high bid has exceeded the reserve bid set by the seller, below which he or she refuses to sell.
- *Traditional Dutch auctions:* Sellers with many identical items sold in lots list a starting price and time for the opening of bids. As the clock advances, the price for each lot falls until a buyer offers to buy at that price.
- *Dutch Internet auctions:* Sellers with many identical items for sale list a minimum price or starting bid, and buyers indicate both a bid price and a quantity desired. The lowest winning bid that clears the available quantity is paid by all winning bidders. Those with the highest bid are assured of receiving the quantity they desire, but only pay the amount of the lowest successful bid (uniform pricing rule).
- *Name Your Own Price or reverse auctions:* Buyers specify the price they are willing to pay for an item, and multiple sellers bid for their business. This is one example of discriminatory pricing in which winners may pay different amounts for the same product or service depending on how much they have bid.
- *Group buying or demand aggregation auctions:* In the group-buying format, the more users who sign on to buy an item, the lower the item's price falls. These are generally B2B or B2G sites where small businesses can collectively receive discount prices for items that are purchased in high volumes.

Benefits of auctions include:

- *Liquidity:* Sellers and buyers are connected in a global marketplace.
- *Price discovery:* Even difficult-to-price items can be competitively priced based on supply and demand.
- *Price transparency:* Everyone in the world can see the asking and bidding prices for items, although prices can vary from auction site to auction site.
- *Market efficiency:* Consumers are offered access to a selection of goods that would be impossible to access physically, and consumer welfare is often increased due to reduced prices.
- *Lower transaction costs:* Merchants and consumers alike are benefited by the reduced costs of selling and purchasing goods compared to the physical marketplace.

- *Consumer aggregation:* A large number of consumers who are motivated to buy are amassed in one marketplace—a great convenience to the seller.
- *Network effects:* The larger an auction site becomes in the numbers of both users and products, the greater the benefits become, and therefore the more valuable a marketplace it becomes.
- *Market-maker benefits:* Auction sites have no inventory carrying costs or shipping costs, making them perhaps the ideal online business in that their main function is the transfer of information.

Costs of auctions include:
- *Delayed consumption:* Auctions can go on for days, and the product must then be shipped to the buyer. Buyers will typically want to pay less for an item they cannot immediately obtain.
- *Monitoring costs:* Buyers must spend time monitoring the bidding.
- *Equipment costs:* Buyers must purchase, or have already purchased, computer systems and Internet service, and learned how to operate these systems.
- *Trust risks:* Consumers face an increased risk of experiencing a loss, as online auctions are the largest source of Internet fraud.
- *Fulfillment costs:* Buyers must pay for packing, shipping, and insurance, and will factor this cost into their bid price.

Auction sites have sought to reduce these risks through various methods including:
- *Rating systems:* Previous customers rate sellers based on their experience with them and post them on the site for other buyers to see.
- *Watch lists:* These allow buyers to monitor specific auctions as they proceed over a number of days and only pay close attention in the last few minutes of bidding.
- *Proxy bidding:* Buyers can enter a maximum price they are willing to pay, and the auction software will automatically place incremental bids as their original bid is surpassed.

■ **Understand when to use auctions in a business.**

Auctions can be an appropriate channel for businesses to sell items in a variety of situations. The factors for businesses to consider include:
- *The type of product:* Rare and unique products are well suited to the auction marketplace as are perishable items such as airline tickets, hotel rooms, car rentals, and tickets to plays, concerts, and sporting events.
- *The product life cycle:* Traditionally, auctions have been used by businesses to generate a higher profit on items at the end of their life cycle than they would receive from product liquidation sales. However, they are now more frequently being used at the beginning of a product's life cycle to generate premium prices from highly motivated early adopters.
- *Channel management:* Businesses must be careful when deciding whether to pursue an auction strategy to ensure that products at auction do not compete with products in their existing profitable channels. This is why most established retail firms tend to use auctions for products at the end of their life cycles or to have quantity purchasing requirements.

- *The type of auction:* Businesses should choose seller-biased auctions where there are many buyers and only one or a few sellers, preferably using the English ascending price system to drive the price up as high as possible.
- *Initial pricing:* Auction items should start with a low initial bid in order to attract more bidders, because the more bidders an item has, the higher the final price will be driven.
- *Bid increments:* When increments are kept low, more bidders are attracted and the frequency of their bidding is increased. This can translate into a higher final price as bidders are prodded onward in small steps.
- *Auction length:* In general, the longer an auction runs, the more bidders will enter the auction, and the higher the final price will be. However, if an auction continues for too long, the bid prices will stabilize, and the cost of posting the auction may outweigh the profit from any further price increases.
- *Number of items:* If a business has a large quantity of items to sell, it should break the lot up into smaller bundles and auction them at different times so that buyers do not expect a volume discount.
- *Price allocation rule:* Because most buyers are biased toward the uniform pricing rule, sellers should use different auction markets, or auction the same goods at different times in order to price discriminate.
- *Closed vs. open bidding:* Closed bidding should be used whenever possible because it benefits a seller by allowing price discrimination. However, open bidding can sometimes be beneficial when herd behavior kicks in, causing multiple bids on highly visited auctions, while overlooked and lightly trafficked auctions for the same or comparable items languish. This generally occurs when there are few objective measures of a product's true value in the marketplace.

- ■ **Recognize the potential for auction abuse and fraud.**

Auctions are particularly prone to fraud, which produces information asymmetries between buyers and sellers. Some of the possible abuses and frauds include:

- *Bid rigging:* Agreeing offline to limit bids or using shills to submit false bids that drive prices up.
- *Price matching:* Agreeing informally or formally to set floor prices on auction items below which sellers will not sell in open markets.
- *Shill feedback, defensive:* Using secondary IDs or other auction members to inflate seller ratings.
- *Shill feedback, offensive:* Using secondary IDs or other auction members to deflate ratings for another user (feedback bombs).
- *Feedback extortion:* Threatening negative feedback in return for a benefit.
- *Transaction interference:* E-mailing buyers to warn them away from a seller.
- *Bid manipulation:* Using the retraction option to make high bids, discovering the maximum bid of the current high bidder, and then retracting the bid.
- *Non-payment after winning:* Blocking legitimate buyers by bidding high, then not paying.
- *Shill bidding:* Using secondary user IDs or other auction members to artificially raise the price of an item.
- *Transaction non-performance:* Accepting payment and failing to deliver.
- *Non-selling seller:* Refusing payment or failing to deliver after a successful auction.

- *Bid siphoning:* E-mailing another seller's bidders and offering the same product for less.

■ **Describe the major types of Internet portals.**

Web portals are gateways to the more than 100 billion Web pages available on the Internet. Originally, their primary purpose was to help users find information on the Web, but they evolved into destination sites that provided a myriad of content from news to entertainment. Today, portals serve three main purposes: navigation of the Web, content, and commerce. Among the major portal types are:

- *Enterprise portals:* Corporations, universities, churches, and other organizations create these sites to help employees or members navigate to important content such as corporate news or organizational announcements.
- *General-purpose portals:* Examples are AOL, Yahoo, and MSN, which try to attract a very large general audience by providing many in-depth vertical content channels. Some also offer ISP services on a subscription basis, search engines, e-mail, chat, bulletin boards, and personal home pages.
- *Vertical market portals:* Also called destination sites, they attempt to attract a highly focused, loyal audience with an intense interest in either a community they belong to or an interest they hold. Recent studies have found that users with limited time resources are interested in concentrating their Web site visiting on focused searches in areas that appeal to them. Vertical market portals can be divided into two main classifications, although hybrids that overlap the two classifications also exist.
- *Affinity groups:* Statistical aggregates of people who identify themselves by their attitudes, values, beliefs, and behavior. Affinity portals exist to serve such broad constituencies as women, African Americans, and gays as well as much more focused constituencies such as union members, religious groups, and even home-schooling families.
- *Focused content portals:* These sites contain in-depth information on a particular topic that all members are interested in. They can provide content on such broad topics as sports, news, weather, entertainment, finance, or business, or they can appeal to a much more focused interest group such as boat, horse, or video game enthusiasts.

■ **Understand the business models of portals.**

Portals receive revenue from a number of different sources. The business model is presently changing and adapting to declines in certain revenue streams, particularly advertising revenues. Revenue sources can include:

- *General advertising:* Charging for impressions delivered
- *Tenancy deals:* Locking in long-term, multiple-year deals so a company is guaranteed a number of impressions with premium placement on home pages and through exclusive marketing deals
- *Subscription fees:* Charging for premium content
- *Commissions on sales:* Earning revenue based on sales at the site by independent merchants.

The survival strategy for general-purpose portals is to develop deep, rich vertical content in order to attract advertisers to various niche groups that they can target with focused ads. The strategy for the small vertical market portals is to build a collection of vertical portals, thereby creating a network of deep, rich content sites for the same reason.

QUESTIONS

1. Why did most communities in the early days of e-commerce fail? What factors enable online social networks to prosper today?
2. How does a social network differ from a portal? How are the two similar?
3. What is an affinity community, and what is its business model?
4. What is personalization or personal value pricing, and how can it be used at the beginning of a product's life cycle to increase revenues?
5. List and briefly explain three of the benefits of auction markets.
6. What are the four major costs to consumers of participating in an auction?
7. Under what conditions does a seller bias exist in an auction market? When does a buyer bias exist?
8. What are the two price allocation rules in auction markets? Explain the difference between them.
9. What is a demand aggregator and how does it work?
10. What types of products are well suited for an auction market? At what points in the product life cycle can auction markets prove beneficial for marketers?
11. What three characteristics define a portal site today?
12. What is a vertical market portal, and how might recent trends in consumer behavior prove advantageous to this business model?
13. What are the two main types of vertical market portals, and how are they distinguished from one another?
14. List and briefly explain the main revenue sources for the portal business model.

PROJECTS

1. Find two examples of an affinity portal and two examples of a focused-content portal. Prepare a presentation explaining why each of your examples should be categorized as an affinity portal or a focused-content portal. For each example, surf the site and describe the services each site provides. Try to determine what revenue model each of your examples is using and, if possible, how many members or registered visitors the site has attracted.

2. Examine the use of auctions by businesses. Go to any auction site of your choosing and look for outlet auctions or auctions directly from merchants. Research at least three products for sale. What stage in the product life cycle do these products fall into? Are there quantity purchasing requirements? What was the opening bid price? What are the bid increments? What is the auction duration? Analyze why these firms have used the auction channel to sell these goods and prepare a short report on your findings.

3. Visit one for-profit-sponsored and one nonprofit-sponsored social network. Create a presentation to describe and demonstrate the offering at each site. What organizational objectives is each pursuing? How is the for-profit company using community-building technologies as a customer relations management tool?

CHAPTER 12

B2B E-commerce: Supply Chain Management and Collaborative Commerce

After reading this chapter, you will be able to:

- Define B2B commerce and understand its scope and history.
- Understand the procurement process, the supply chain, and collaborative commerce.
- Identify the main types of B2B e-commerce: Net marketplaces and private industrial networks.
- Understand the four types of Net marketplaces.
- Identify the major trends in the development of Net marketplaces.
- Identify the role of private industrial networks in transforming the supply chain.
- Understand the role of private industrial networks in supporting collaborative commerce.

Volkswagen

Builds Its B2B Platform

© Julian Clune / Alamy

Volkswagen AG is the world's third largest vehicle manufacturer, producing 9.2 million cars, trucks, and vans in 2012, and generating over $260 billion in revenue, up 26% from the year before. In addition to the Volkswagen brand, the Volkswagen Group also owns luxury carmakers such as Porsche, Audi, Bentley, Scania Bugatti, and Lamborghini, and family carmakers SEAT in Spain and Skoda in the Czech Republic. The company has almost 500,000 employees and operates plants in Europe, Africa, the Asian/Pacific rim, and the Americas. In the first half of 2013, Volkswagen Group continued its expansion. New investments in China, India, and Mexico, along with a strong American market, pushed sales revenues up 3.5%, and its share of the global passenger car market to 12.4%, making Volkswagen the second largest producer in the world, behind General Motors. VW entered the Chinese market in the 1980s long before other Western auto manufacturers, when the market was very small. Now it is the world's biggest car market and VW has 18% of it, more than any other vehicle manufacturer.

The various companies and 61 production plants in the Volkswagen Group annually purchase components, automotive parts, and indirect materials worth about 129 billion euros, or about $176 billion (which constitutes about 67% of Volkswagen's annual revenue). Obviously, the procurement process and relationships with suppliers are absolutely critical for Volkswagen's success.

Today, the Volkswagen Group manages almost all of its procurement needs via the Internet. It began building its Internet platform, VWGroupSupply.com, in 2000. The Volkswagen Group was looking for ways to create more efficient relationships with its suppliers and reduce the cost of paper-based procurement processes. However, the company did not want to automate procurement using a public independent exchange or an industry consortium because it would have had to adapt its own business processes to a common framework that could be used by many different organizations. Volkswagen hoped that by building its own B2B network, it could compete more effectively against other automakers. Volkswagen decided, for instance, not to participate in Covisint, the giant automotive industry consortium backed by major car manufacturers such as Ford, General Motors, and DaimlerChrysler, which provided procurement and other supply chain services for these companies, other automotive manufacturers, and their suppliers.

SOURCES: "Global Auto Production," by International Organization of Motor Vehicle Manufacturers, September 27, 2013; "Volkswagen Annual Report 2012," Volkswagen Group, March 14, 2013; "Volkswagen Half-Yearly Financial Report, January to June 2013," Volkswagen Group, July 30, 2013; "VW Conquers the World: Germany's Biggest Carmaker is Leaving Rivals in the Dust," *The Economist*, July 7, 2012; "Facts and Figures," Volkswagen Group Supply, September 2012; "e-Procurement within the Volkswagen Group," by Alex Smith, Littleknowhow.com, September 25, 2011; "Customer Specific Quality Requirements of the Volkswagen Group," IATF Global Certification Body Conference, February 10, 2011; "Automotive B2B Developments at Odette25," GXS.com, June 22, 2010; "Best Practices: VW Revs Up its B2B Engine," by Martin Hoffman, *Optimize*, March 2004.

Instead, Volkswagen opted for a private platform that would allow it to integrate its suppliers more tightly with its own business processes, and where it could control more precisely who was invited to participate. VWGroupSupply now handles over 90% of all global purchasing for the Volkswagen Group, including all automotive and parts components. It is one of the most comprehensive e-procurement systems in the global automotive industry. Volkswagen refers to it as the Group Business Platform. From an initial seven applications in 2003, the platform now offers over 60 different online applications, such as requests for quotations (RFQs), contract negotiations, catalog purchases, purchase order management, engineering change management, vehicle program management, and payments, among others. The Volkswagen Group developed the platform using technology from a number of vendors, including Ariba, IBM, and i2 Technologies.

Suppliers of all sizes can access VWGroupSupply with standard Web browser software. The Web site is limited to suppliers who have done business with one or more companies in the Volkswagen Group and potential new suppliers who go through an authorization process. Currently, over 45,000 suppliers are registered, and there are over 206,000 users. The system maintains a common data repository with details on each supplier concerning procurement, logistics, production, quality, technical design, and finance.

VWGroupSupply's online catalog currently contains about 2.5 million items from 590 global suppliers. There are 14,200 internal users of the online catalog who have conducted over 1.5 million transactions with a value totaling 380 million euros ($447 million). The catalog uses the eCl@ss standard for classifying its contents. All suppliers who participate in the catalog ordering process classify their products using this standard.

Online negotiations involve multiple bids by suppliers for various purchasing contracts. VWGroupSupply ensures that all participants meet its technical and commercial qualifications. Before an online solicitation begins, the system informs vendors about the data and precise rules governing negotiations. About 13,000 different vendors have taken part in online negotiations. In 2011, VWGroupSupply conducted around 2,500 online contract negotiations online, with a value of 2.6 billion euros ($3.3 billion).

Shifts in market demand have a drastic impact on Volkswagen's production activities and affect the ability of suppliers to deliver. Production bottlenecks can result if suppliers are unprepared for a sudden upsurge in demand. If suppliers stock too much inventory, they may incur excess costs from running at overcapacity. VWGroupSupply has an application called electronic Capacity Management (eCAP) to alert both Volkswagen and its suppliers to changes in trends in advance. eCAP enables suppliers to track Volkswagen's continually updated production plans and materials requirements in real time online. This capability captures information about participating suppliers' planned maximum and minimum capacities. If Volkswagen production requirements go beyond these limits, the system sets off an alarm so both parties can react quickly. eCAP maintains information on over 400 suppliers and 4,000 critical parts.

The VWGroupSupply case illustrates the exciting potential for B2B e-commerce to lower production costs, increase collaboration among firms, speed up new product delivery, and ultimately revolutionize both the manufacturing process inherited from the early twentieth century and the way industrial products are designed and manufactured. VWGroupSupply is an example of just one type of B2B e-commerce, but there are many other equally promising efforts to use the Internet to change the relationships among manufacturers and their suppliers. In the fashion industry, the combination of high-speed value chains coupled with equally high-speed trendy design not only clears shelves (and reduces the likelihood of clearance sales), but increases profits by increasing value to consumers (Zarroli, 2013; Cachon and Swinney, 2011). The success of VWGroupSupply and similar networks operated by the major automobile firms in the world stands in contrast to an earlier industry-sponsored Net marketplace called Covisint. Founded in 1999 by five of the world's largest automakers (General Motors, Ford, Chrysler, Nissan, and Peugeot), Covisint hoped to provide an electronic market connecting thousands of suppliers to a few huge buyers using auctions and procurement services. While initially successful, Covisint was sold in June 2004, although it continues as a B2B services firm in a number of industries. Its auction business was sold to FreeMarkets, an early B2B auction company, which itself was sold to another B2B e-commerce firm called Ariba later in 2004. In 2013, Ariba survives as a successful software firm focusing on the procurement process and the operation of a successful net marketplace.

The failure of Covisint (as well as Ford's AutoExchange) and the simultaneous growth in B2B e-commerce efforts such as VWGroupSupply illustrates the difficulties of achieving the broad visions established during the early days of e-commerce. From a high of 1,500 online B2B exchanges in 2000, the number has dwindled to less than 200 survivors today (Rosenzweig et al., 2011). Like B2C commerce, the B2B marketplace has consolidated, evolved, and moved on to more attainable visions. In the process, many B2B efforts have experienced extraordinary success. There are many failed efforts to consider as well; these provide important lessons to all managers.

In this chapter, we examine three different B2B e-commerce themes: procurement, supply chain management, and collaborative commerce. Each of these business processes has changed greatly with the evolution of B2B e-commerce systems. In Section 12.1, we define B2B commerce and place it in the context of trends in procurement, supply chain management, and collaborative commerce. The next two sections describe the two fundamental types of B2B e-commerce: Net marketplaces and private industrial networks. We describe four major types of Net marketplaces, their biases (seller, buyer, and neutral), ownership structure and accessibility (private versus public), and value creation dynamics.

Table 12.1 summarizes the leading trends in B2B e-commerce in the 2013–2014 period. Perhaps the most important themes are growing industry concern with supply chain risk and volatility, along with a growing public concern with the accountability of supply chains—in particular, violations of developed-world expectations of working

TABLE 12.1	MAJOR TRENDS IN B2B E-COMMERCE, 2013–2014

BUSINESS

- B2B e-commerce growth accelerates in 2013 to pre-recession levels as the global economy expands especially in commodities, mining, and manufacturing.
- Risk management: sophisticated global supply chains blindsided by the Fukushima Daiichi nuclear accident, and floods in Thailand; chaos in financial markets, rapid increases in fuel costs, rising labor and commodity costs in Asia, and a global recession.
- Regional manufacturing: risks of far-flung global networks lead to an increase in regional manufacturing and supply chains, moving production closer to market demand.
- Flexibility: growing emphasis on rapid-response and optimal supply chains rather than lowest cost supply chains, which typically carry great risks.
- Supply chain visibility: growing calls for more real-time data that would allow managers to "see" across not only their production, but also "see into" the production and financial condition of their key suppliers.
- Social commerce and customer intimacy: buyers, like consumers, are tapping into their tablets, smartphones, and social network sites for purchasing, scheduling, exception handling, and deciding with their B2B customers and suppliers in order to manage supply chain risk.
- Large firms begin splintering single, global B2B platforms into product and region-centered systems to achieve lower risk, greater adaptability, and lower complexity.
- Market ownership: private B2B markets proliferate, especially as Web services, while public B2B markets stabilize in selected industries.

TECHNOLOGY

- Big data: global trade and logistics systems are generating huge repositories of B2B data, swamping management understanding and controls.
- Business analytics: growing emphasis on use of business analytics software (business intelligence) to understand very large data sets.
- Cloud: migration of B2B hardware and software to cloud computing and cloud apps, away from individual corporate data centers, as a means of slowing rising IT costs. B2B systems move to Cloud computing providers like IBM, Oracle, Amazon, Google, and HP as their core technology.
- Mobile platform: growing use of mobile platform for B2B systems (CRM, SCM, and enterprise), putting B2B commerce into managers' palms.
- Social networking platforms increasingly being used by B2B managers for feedback from customers, strengthening customer and supplier relationships, adjusting prices and orders, and enhancing decision making.

SOCIETY

- Accountability: growing demands for supply chain accountability and monitoring in developed countries driven by reports of poor working conditions in Asian factories. Apple and others under fire for harsh working conditions in their supply chains.
- Sustainable supply chains: growing public demand for businesses to mitigate their environmental impact leads from local environmental optimization to consideration of the entire supply chain from design, production, customer service, and post-use disposal.
- Acceptance and growth of B2B platforms: Ariba, the largest Net marketplace, has 300,000 firms participating, 80% of the Fortune 500 firms.
- B2B firms discover social networks: 66% of B2B firms user Twitter along with other social network sites to build communities and enable collaboration among engineers, sales, and procurement personnel.
- The Dhaka fire in Bangladesh kills over 200 garment workers in the largest garment-industry accident in history. The garment supply chain comes under strong criticism in the EU and United States.

conditions in third-world factories that play a key role in the production of goods sold in more developed countries. What many firms have learned in the last decade is that supply chains can strengthen or weaken a company depending on a number of factors related to supply chain efficiency such as community engagement, labor relations, environmental protection, and sustainability. Yet many believe that all of these related factors are important to the long profitability of firms (Beard and Hornik, 2011). At the same time, in part because of the globalization of supply chains, B2B e-commerce systems are now used by nearly all of the American S&P 500 firms, where over half of all revenues are produced offshore. Thousands of smaller firms are now able to participate in B2B systems as low-cost cloud-based computing and software-as-a-service (SaaS) become widely available. The cost of participating in B2B e-commerce systems has fallen significantly, allowing smaller firms to participate along with giant firms. Taking advantage of the exploding mobile platform, more companies are using smartphones and tablet computers to run their businesses from any location. There are hundreds of iPhone and Android apps available from enterprise B2B vendors like SAP, IBM, Oracle, and others that link to supply chain management systems (Enright, 2013; Bolukbasi, 2011; Melnyk, 2010). Social network tools are pushing into the B2B world as well as the consumer world. B2B managers are increasingly using public and private social network sites and technologies to enable long-term conversations with their customers and vendors.

12.1   B2B E-COMMERCE AND SUPPLY CHAIN MANAGEMENT

The trade between business firms represents a huge marketplace. The total amount of B2B trade in the United States in 2013 is about $12.9 trillion, with B2B e-commerce (online B2B) contributing about $4.7 trillion of that amount (U.S. Census Bureau, 2013a; authors' estimates). By 2017, B2B e-commerce is expected to grow to about $6.6 trillion in the United States.

The process of conducting trade among business firms is complex and requires significant human intervention, and therefore, consumes significant resources. Some firms estimate that each corporate purchase order for support products costs them, on average, at least $100 in administrative overhead. Administrative overhead includes processing paper, approving purchase decisions, spending time using the telephone and fax machines to search for products and arrange for purchases, arranging for shipping, and receiving the goods. Across the economy, this adds up to trillions of dollars annually being spent for procurement processes that could potentially be automated. If even just a portion of inter-firm trade were automated, and parts of the entire procurement process assisted by the Internet, then literally trillions of dollars might be released for more productive uses, consumer prices potentially would fall, productivity would increase, and the economic wealth of the nation would expand. This is the promise of B2B e-commerce. The challenge of B2B e-commerce is changing existing patterns and systems of procurement, and designing and implementing new Internet-based B2B solutions.

DEFINING AND MEASURING THE GROWTH OF B2B COMMERCE

total inter-firm trade
the total flow of value
among firms

B2B commerce
all types of inter-firm trade

**B2B e-commerce
(B2B digital
commerce)**
that portion of B2B
commerce that is enabled
by the Internet

supply chain
the links that connect
business firms with one
another to coordinate
production

Before the Internet, business-to-business transactions were referred to simply as *trade* or the *procurement process*. The term **total inter-firm trade** refers to the total flow of value among firms. Today, we use the term **B2B commerce** to describe all types of inter-firm trade to exchange value across organizational boundaries. B2B commerce includes the following business processes insofar as they involve inter-firm trade: customer relationship management, demand management, order fulfillment, manufacturing management, procurement, product development, returns, logistics/transportation, and inventory management (Barlow, 2011). This definition of B2B commerce does not include transactions that occur within the boundaries of a single firm—for instance, the transfer of goods and value from one subsidiary to another, or the use of corporate intranets to manage the firm. We use the term **B2B e-commerce** (or **B2B digital commerce**) to describe specifically that portion of B2B commerce that is enabled by the Internet. The links that connect business firms in the production of goods and services are referred to as "the supply chain." **Supply chains** are a complex system of organizations, people, business processes, technology, and information, all of which need to work together to produce products efficiently. Today's supply chains are often global, connecting the smartphones in New York to the shipyards in Los Angeles and Quindow, and to the Foxconn factories that produce the phones. They are also local and national in scope.

THE EVOLUTION OF B2B COMMERCE

**automated order entry
systems**
involve the use of
telephone modems to send
digital orders

seller-side solutions
seller-biased markets that
are owned by, and show
only goods from, a single
seller

**electronic data
interchange (EDI)**
a communications standard
for sharing business
documents and settlement
information among a small
number of firms

B2B commerce has evolved over a 35-year period through several technology-driven stages (see **Figure 12.1**). The first step in the development of B2B commerce in the mid-1970s was **automated order entry systems** that involved the use of telephone modems to send digital orders to health care products companies such as Baxter Healthcare. Baxter, a diversified supplier of hospital supplies, placed telephone modems in its customers' procurement offices to automate reordering from Baxter's computerized inventory database (and to discourage reordering from competitors). This early technology was replaced by personal computers using private networks in the late 1980s, and by Internet workstations accessing electronic online catalogs in the late 1990s. Automated order entry systems are **seller-side solutions**. They are owned by the suppliers and are seller-biased markets—they show only goods from a single seller. Customers benefited from these systems because they reduced the costs of inventory replenishment and were paid for largely by the suppliers. Automated order entry systems continue to play an important role in B2B commerce.

By the late 1970s, a new form of computer-to-computer communication called **electronic data interchange (EDI)** emerged. We describe EDI in greater detail later in this chapter, but at this point, it is necessary only to know that EDI is a communications standard for sharing business documents such as invoices, purchase orders, shipping bills, product stocking numbers (SKUs), and settlement information among a small number of firms. Virtually all large firms have EDI systems, and most industry

FIGURE 12.1	THE EVOLUTION OF THE USE OF TECHNOLOGY PLATFORMS IN B2B COMMERCE

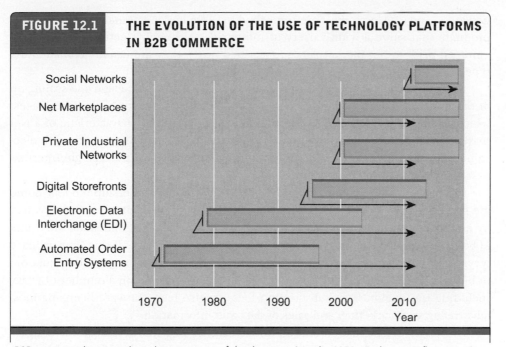

B2B commerce has gone through many stages of development since the 1970s. Each stage reflects a major change in technology platforms from mainframes to private dedicated networks, and finally to the Internet. In 2013, social networks—both private and public—are being used to coordinate decision-making in B2B commerce.

groups have industry standards for defining documents in that industry. EDI systems are owned by the buyers, hence they are **buyer-side solutions** and buyer-biased because they aim to reduce the procurement costs of supplies for the buyer. Of course, by automating the transaction, EDI systems also benefit the sellers through customer cost reduction. The topology of EDI systems is often referred to as a **hub-and-spoke system**, with the buyers in the center and the suppliers connected to the central hub via private dedicated networks.

EDI systems generally serve vertical markets. A **vertical market** is one that provides expertise and products for a specific industry, such as automobiles. In contrast, **horizontal markets** serve many different industries.

Electronic storefronts emerged in the mid-1990s along with the commercialization of the Internet. **B2B electronic storefronts** are perhaps the simplest and easiest form of B2B e-commerce to understand, because they are just online catalogs of products made available to the public marketplace by a single supplier—similar to Amazon for the B2C retail market. Owned by the suppliers, they are seller-side solutions and seller-biased because they show only the products offered by a single supplier.

Electronic storefronts are a natural descendant of automated order entry systems, but there are two important differences: (1) the far less expensive and more universal Internet becomes the communication media and displaces private

buyer-side solutions
buyer-biased markets that are owned by buyers and that aim to reduce the procurement costs of supplies for buyers

hub-and-spoke system
suppliers connected to a central hub of buyers via private dedicated networks

vertical market
one that provides expertise and products for a specific industry

horizontal markets
markets that serve many different industries

B2B electronic storefronts
online catalogs of products made available to the public marketplace by a single supplier

networks, and (2) electronic storefronts tend to serve horizontal markets—they carry products that serve a wide variety of industries. Although electronic storefronts emerged prior to Net marketplaces (described next), they are usually considered a type of Net marketplace.

Net marketplaces emerged in the late 1990s as a natural extension and scaling-up of the electronic storefronts. There are many different kinds of Net marketplaces, which we describe in detail in Section 12.2, but the essential characteristic of a Net marketplace is that they bring hundreds to thousands of suppliers—each with electronic catalogs and potentially thousands of purchasing firms—into a single Internet-based environment to conduct trade.

Net marketplaces can be organized under a variety of ownership models. Some are owned by independent third parties backed by venture capital, some are owned by established firms who are the main or only market players, and some are a mix of both. Net marketplaces establish the prices of the goods they offer in four primary ways—fixed catalog prices, or more dynamic pricing, such as negotiation, auction, or bid/ask ("exchange" model). Net marketplaces earn revenue in a number of ways, including transaction fees, subscription fees, service fees, software licensing fees, advertising and marketing, and sales of data and information.

Although the primary benefits and biases of Net marketplaces have to be determined on a case-by-case basis depending on ownership and pricing mechanisms, it is often the case that Net marketplaces are biased against suppliers because they can force suppliers to reveal their prices and terms to other suppliers in the marketplace. Net marketplaces can also significantly extend the benefits of simple electronic storefronts by seeking to automate the procurement value chain of both selling and buying firms.

Private industrial networks also emerged in the late 1990s as natural extensions of EDI systems and the existing close relationships that developed between large industrial firms and their trusted suppliers. Described in more detail in Section 12.3, **private industrial networks** (sometimes also referred to as a *private trading exchange*, or *PTX*) are Internet-based communication environments that extend far beyond procurement to encompass supply chain efficiency enhancements and truly collaborative commerce. Private industrial networks permit buyer firms and their principal suppliers to share product design and development, marketing, inventory, production scheduling, and unstructured communications. Like EDI, private industrial networks are owned by the buyers and are buyer-side solutions with buyer biases. These systems are directly intended to improve the cost position and flexibility of large industrial firms (Yoo et al., 2011; Kumaran, 2002). These private industrial networks have a much higher survival rate than other Net marketplaces (Rosenzweig, 2011).

Naturally, private industrial networks have significant benefits for suppliers as well. Inclusion in the direct supply chain for a major industrial purchasing company can allow a supplier to increase both revenue and margins because the environment is not competitive—only a few suppliers are included in the private industrial network. These networks are the most prevalent form of Internet-based B2B commerce, and this will continue into the foreseeable future.

Net marketplace brings hundreds to thousands of suppliers and buyers into a single Internet-based environment to conduct trade

private industrial networks (private trading exchange, PTX) Internet-based communication environments that extend far beyond procurement to encompass truly collaborative commerce

| FIGURE 12.2 | GROWTH OF B2B COMMERCE 2006–2017 |

Private industrial networks are the fastest growing form of online B2B e-commerce, which includes EDI, B2B Net marketplaces, and private industrial markets.

SOURCES: Based on data from U.S. Census Bureau, 2013a; authors' estimates.

THE GROWTH OF B2B E-COMMERCE 2012–2017

During the period 2012–2017, B2B e-commerce is projected to grow from about 40% to 42% of total inter-firm trade in the United States, or from $4.1 trillion in 2012 to $6.6 trillion in 2017 (see **Figure 12.2**).

Several observations are important to note with respect to Figure 12.2. First, it shows that the initial belief that electronic marketplaces would become the dominant form of B2B e-commerce is not supported. Second, private industrial networks play a dominant role in B2B e-commerce, both now and in the future. Third, non-EDI B2B e-commerce is the most rapidly growing type of B2B e-commerce, and EDI is still quite large but is declining over time.

Industry Forecasts

Not all industries will be similarly affected by B2B e-commerce, nor will all industries similarly benefit from B2B. Several factors influence the speed with which industries migrate to B2B e-commerce and the volume of transactions. Those industries in which there is already significant utilization of EDI (indicating concentration of buyers and suppliers) and large investments in information technology and Internet infrastructure can be expected to move first and fastest to B2B e-commerce utilization. The aerospace and defense, computer, and industrial equipment industries meet these criteria. Where the marketplace is highly concentrated on either the purchasing or selling side, or both, conditions are also ripe for rapid B2B e-commerce growth, as in the energy and chemical industries. In the case of health care, the federal government, health care providers (doctors and hospitals), and major insurance companies are moving rapidly towards a national medical record system and the use of Internet for managing medical payments. Coordinating the various players in the health care system is an extraordinary B2B challenge. Computer service firms like IBM, and B2B service firms like Covisint, are expanding the use of information ecosystems where health providers and insurers can share information.

POTENTIAL BENEFITS AND CHALLENGES OF B2B E-COMMERCE

Regardless of the specific type of B2B e-commerce, as a whole, Internet-based B2B commerce promises many strategic benefits to participating firms—both buyers and sellers—and impressive gains for the economy as a whole. B2B e-commerce can:

- Lower administrative costs
- Lower search costs for buyers
- Reduce inventory costs by increasing competition among suppliers (increasing price transparency) and reducing inventory to the bare minimum
- Lower transaction costs by eliminating paperwork and automating parts of the procurement process
- Increase production flexibility by ensuring delivery of parts "just in time"
- Improve quality of products by increasing cooperation among buyers and sellers and reducing quality issues
- Decrease product cycle time by sharing designs and production schedules with suppliers
- Increase opportunities for collaborating with suppliers and distributors
- Create greater price transparency—the ability to see the actual buy and sell prices in a market
- Increase the visibility and real-time information sharing among all participants in the supply chain network.

B2B e-commerce offers potential first-mover strategic benefits for individual firms as well. Firms that move their procurement processes online first will experience impressive gains in productivity, cost reduction, and potentially much faster introduction of new, higher-quality products. While these gains may be imitated by other competing firms, it is also clear from the brief history of B2B e-commerce that firms making sustained investments in information technology and Internet-based B2B commerce can adapt much faster to new technologies as they emerge, creating a string of first-mover advantages.

While there are many potential benefits to B2B e-commerce supply chains, there are also considerable risks and challenges. Often real-world supply chains fail to provide visibility into the supply chain because they lack real-time demand, production, and logistics data, and have inadequate financial data on suppliers. The result is unexpected supplier failure and disruption to the supply chain. Builders of B2B digital supply chains often had little concern for the environmental impacts of supply chains, the sensitivity of supply chains to natural events, fluctuating fuel and labor costs, or the impact of public values involving labor and environmental policies. The result in 2013 is that many Fortune 1000 supply chains are risky and vulnerable. Read *Insight on Society: Where's My iPad? Apple's Supply Chain Risks and Vulnerabilities* for a look at the impact the recent earthquake in Japan has had on global supply chains, as well as the reputational risk posed by supply chains.

THE PROCUREMENT PROCESS AND THE SUPPLY CHAIN

The subject of B2B e-commerce can be complex because there are so many ways the Internet can be used to support the exchange of goods and payments among organizations, efficient supply chains, and collaboration. At the most basic level, B2B digital e-commerce is about changing the **procurement process** (how business firms purchase goods they need to produce goods they will ultimately sell to consumers) of thousands of firms across the United States and the world.

procurement process
how firms purchase goods they need to produce goods for consumers

One way to enter this area of Internet-based B2B commerce is to examine the existing procurement business process (see **Figure 12.3**). Firms purchase goods from a set of suppliers, and they in turn purchase their inputs from a set of suppliers. The supply chain includes not just the firms themselves, but also the relationships among them and the processes that connect them.

There are seven separate steps in the procurement process. The first three steps involve the decision of who to buy from and what to pay: searching for suppliers of specific products; qualifying both the seller and the products they sell; and negotiating prices, credit terms, escrow requirements, quality, and scheduling of delivery. Once a supplier is identified, purchase orders are issued, the buyer is sent an invoice, the

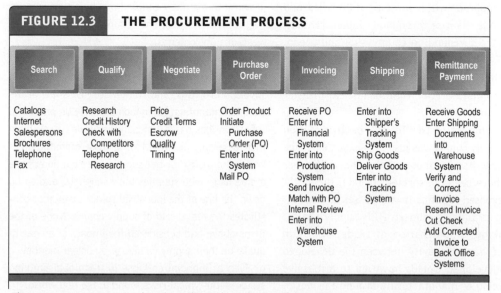

FIGURE 12.3   THE PROCUREMENT PROCESS

Search	Qualify	Negotiate	Purchase Order	Invoicing	Shipping	Remittance Payment
Catalogs	Research	Price	Order Product	Receive PO	Enter into Shipper's Tracking System	Receive Goods
Internet	Credit History	Credit Terms	Initiate Purchase Order (PO)	Enter into Financial System		Enter Shipping Documents into Warehouse System
Salespersons	Check with Competitors	Escrow	Enter into System	Enter into Production System	Ship Goods Deliver Goods	Verify and Correct Invoice
Brochures	Telephone	Quality	Mail PO	Send Invoice	Enter into Tracking System	Resend Invoice
Telephone	Research	Timing		Match with PO		Cut Check
Fax				Internal Review		Add Corrected Invoice to Back Office Systems
				Enter into Warehouse System		

The procurement process is a lengthy and complicated series of steps that involves the seller, buyer, and shipping companies in a series of connected transactions.

INSIGHT ON SOCIETY

WHERE'S MY IPAD? SUPPLY CHAIN RISK AND VULNERABILITY

On Friday, March 11, 2011, a magnitude 9.0 earthquake occurred offshore of northern Japan and the Oshika Peninsula of Tohoku. The Tohoku earthquake was the largest in recorded history and it immediately created a number of tsunami waves, some of which exceeded 100 feet in height and penetrated up to six miles inland. In their path were six coastal nuclear reactors in the Fukushima Prefecture near the town of Okuma, the largest nuclear power site in the world. The earthquake and tsunami combined to cut off the nuclear plant's electrical power, which caused the water pumps that keep the nuclear material from overheating and melting to stop. Backup diesel generators were swamped by the tsunami waves. Several of the nuclear reactors exploded and began leaking dangerous levels of radiation as fuel rods melted at temperatures exceeding 5,000 degrees. The government evacuated the entire population within a radius of 20 miles, and radiation levels rose throughout Japan, contaminating the surrounding countryside and ocean. Over 13,000 people lost their lives directly from the earthquake and tsunami, and the ultimate death and disease tolls from the nuclear disaster are still unknown.

The impact of the Tohoku earthquake on global supply chains was just as unexpected as the earthquake itself, although one wonders if either should have been unexpected. In fact, the earthquake exposed significant weaknesses and vulnerabilities in today's modern B2B supply chains. Technology, globalization of trade, and high levels of wage disparity between the developed and undeveloped worlds have led to a massive outsourcing of manufacturing around the world,

mostly to low-wage countries but also to countries with unusual expertise as well as low wages like Japan. Today, every component of every manufactured product is carefully examined by company engineers and financial managers with an eye to finding the lowest cost and highest quality manufacturer in the world. Production inevitably tends to concentrate at single firms that are given very high order volumes if they can meet the price. Large orders make lower prices easier to grant because of scale economies. Rather than spread production among multiple suppliers using small production runs, why not concentrate orders among one or two preferred global suppliers with huge production runs? The answer: when you concentrate production globally on a few suppliers, you also concentrate risk.

As a result, the world's manufacturing base is less redundant, flexible, and adaptive than older traditional supply chains. Interdependencies have grown into a tightly coupled machine that is quite fragile. Risk assessment in supply chains has been weak or nonexistent.

Computers, cell phones, Caterpillar earth movers, Boeing airplanes, and automobiles from Toyota, Ford, GM, and Honda are just a few of the complex manufactured goods that rely on parts and subassemblies made thousands of miles away from their assembly plants. Most of these manufacturers know who their first-tier suppliers are but don't have a clue as to who supplies their suppliers, and so on down the line of the industrial spider's web that constitutes the real world of supply chains. None of the firms above had considered the impact of an earthquake on their supply chains, or a nuclear meltdown, or even a financial collapse in the global banking system—all typical risks found in the real world.

(continued)

Take the Apple iPad. IHS iSuppli is a market research firm that tears apart consumer electronic devices to discover how they are made, who makes the components, and where they are made, in order to obtain market intelligence on producer prices and profits. In its teardown of the iPad 2, it identified at least five major components sourced from Japanese suppliers, some of whom are located in northern Japan: NAND flash from Toshiba Corp., dynamic random access memory (DRAM) made by Elpida Memory Inc., an electronic compass from AKM Semiconductor, the touch screen overlay glass likely from Asahi Glass Co., and the system battery from Apple Japan Inc. Not all of these suppliers were directly impacted by the earthquake, but some were, and many have subsuppliers of various hard-to-replace small components that were directly impacted. The iPad and iPhone's unusually shaped lithium batteries use a crucial polymer made by Kureha, a Japanese firm in the nuclear contamination zone. Kureha controls 70% of the global production of this polymer. Apple was not the only consumer product manufacturer hit hard: computer chips are built on silicon wafers, and 25% of the world's supply is made by two Japanese manufacturers, both of which have shut down wafer production.

Apple is especially susceptible to supply chain disruptions because its new products often experience huge surges in demand, stressing its supply chains in normal times, and causing 2–4-week delays in meeting orders. Apple's iPhone 5s and 5c, which sold more than 9 million units in the first month of their introduction in September 2013, are no different from previous Apple products. Over 90% of the parts, and the final assembly, originate from China and Mongolia (for the rare earths used in the batteries). In the first month, Apple was out of stock of a popular gold model, with a several-week backlog.

Apple has made some changes in its supply chain sourcing in order to lessen the risk of disruption. UBM TechInsights took apart several iPads and found that many of the components were made by two or more manufacturers when comparing different iPads. The retina display, for instance, was produced by three different manufacturers (Samsung, LG, and a third company not identified). Still, many of the major components were made by the same Asian companies that ran into difficulties with nuclear accidents and Asian floods. It's unclear if using multiple suppliers all from the same region mitigates Apple's supply chain risk, or if it is an effort to extract lower prices from competing suppliers.

Apple was not the only manufacturer that learned a lesson in supply chain risk from the Japanese earthquake: Boeing was without carbon fiber airframe assemblies made in Japan; Ford and GM closed factories for lack of Japanese transmissions; and Caterpillar reduced production at its factories worldwide as it attempted to secure alternative suppliers.

Supply chain risk involves more than disruptions in production, as Apple and many other companies have discovered. Supply chains can produce reputational risks when key suppliers engage in labor and environmental policies and practices that are unacceptable to developed world audiences. For instance, for much of 2012, Apple was under attack in the United States and Europe after an audit by the Fair Labor Association found that workers at several assembly plants operated by Apple contractor Foxconn were exposed to toxic chemicals and forced to work over 60 hours a week under dangerous work conditions.

For instance, in November 2012, a fire in a clothing factory in Dhaka, Bangladesh, killed 117 workers, mostly women and children. Well-known brands from Europe and the United States, among them Walmart and Spanish giant Inditex, were producing clothing in this factory. Walmart claimed a subcontractor was using this factory

(continued)

without Walmart's knowledge. The fire created a worldwide protest, and has led to government and industry efforts to certify factory safety in Bangladesh and hold firms responsible for working conditions.

One might think that in the so-called global and Internet economy, computer-based supply chains could quickly and effortlessly adjust to find new suppliers for just about any component or industrial material in a matter of minutes. Think again. New supply chains will need to be built that optimize not just cost but also survivability in the event of common disasters. They must also take into account efforts to reform labor and environmental practices of those involved in the supply chain.

SOURCES: "Gold iPhone 5S Backordered Online in US, Elsewhere," by Josh Lowensohn, Cnetnews.com, September 20, 2013; "Infographic Breaks Down Apple's iPhone Supply Chain," by Bryan Chaffin, MacObserver.com, August 6, 2013; "Bangladesh Factory, Site of Fire That Trapped and Killed 7, Made European Brands," by Julfikar Ali Manik and Jim Yardley, *New York Times*, January 27, 2013; "Disruptions: Too Much Silence on Working Conditions," by Nick Bilton, *New York Times*, April 8, 2012; "Audit Faults Apple Supplier," by Jessica Vascellaro, *Wall Street Journal*, March 30, 2012; "Under the Hood of Apple's Tablet," by Don Clark, *Wall Street Journal*, March 16, 2012; "In China, Human Costs Are Built Into an iPad," by Charles Duhigg and David Barboza, *New York Times*, January 25, 2012; "Japan: The Business After Shocks," by Andrew Dowell, *Wall Street Journal*, March 25, 2011; "Some Worry the Success of Apple Is Tied to Japan," by Miguel Helft, *New York Times*, March 22, 2011; "Crisis Tests Supply Chain's Weak Links," by James Hookway and Aries Poon, *Wall Street Journal*, March 18, 2011; "Caterpillar Warns of Supply Problems From Quake," by Bob Tita, *Wall Street Journal*, March 18, 2011; "Lacking Parts, G.M. Will Close Plant," by Nick Bunkley, *New York Times*, March 17, 2011.

goods are shipped, and the buyer sends a payment. Each of these steps in the procurement process is composed of many separate business processes and subactivities. Each of these activities must be recorded in the information systems of the seller, buyer, and shipper. Often, this data entry is not automatic and involves a great deal of manual labor, telephone calls, faxes, and e-mails.

Types of Procurement

Two distinctions are important for understanding how B2B e-commerce can improve the procurement process. First, firms make purchases of two kinds of goods from suppliers: direct goods and indirect goods. **Direct goods** are goods integrally involved in the production process; for instance, when an automobile manufacturer purchases sheet steel for auto body production. **Indirect goods** are all other goods not directly involved in the production process, such as office supplies and maintenance products. Often these goods are called **MRO goods**—products for maintenance, repair, and operations.

Second, firms use two different methods for purchasing goods: contract purchasing and spot purchasing. **Contract purchasing** involves long-term written agreements to purchase specified products, with agreed-upon terms and quality, for an extended period of time. Generally, firms purchase direct goods using long-term contracts. **Spot purchasing** involves the purchase of goods based on immediate needs in larger marketplaces that involve many suppliers. Generally, firms use spot purchasing for indirect goods, although in some cases, firms also use spot purchasing for direct goods.

According to several estimates, about 80% of inter-firm trade involves contract purchasing of direct goods, and 20% involves spot purchasing of indirect goods (Kaplan and Sawhney, 2000). This finding is significant for understanding B2B e-commerce.

direct goods
goods directly involved in the production process

indirect goods
all other goods not directly involved in the production process

MRO goods
products for maintenance, repair, and operations

contract purchasing
involves long-term written agreements to purchase specified products, under agreed-upon terms and quality, for an extended period of time

spot purchasing
involves the purchase of goods based on immediate needs in larger marketplaces that involve many suppliers

Although the procurement process involves the purchasing of goods, it is extraordinarily information-intense, involving the movement of information among many existing corporate systems. The procurement process today is also very labor-intensive, directly involving over 1.2 million employees in the United States, not including those engaged in transportation, finance, insurance, or general office administration related to the process (U.S. Census Bureau, 2012).

In the long term, the success or failure of B2B e-commerce depends on changing the day-to-day behavior of these 1.2 million people. The key players in the procurement process are the purchasing managers. They ultimately decide who to buy from, what to buy, and on what terms. Purchasing managers ("procurement managers" in the business press) are also the key decision makers for the adoption of B2B e-commerce solutions.

Although Figure 12.3 captures some of the complexity of the procurement process, it is important to realize that firms purchase thousands of goods from thousands of suppliers. The suppliers, in turn, must purchase their inputs from their suppliers. Large manufacturers such as Ford Motor Company have over 20,000 suppliers of parts, packaging, and technology. The number of secondary and tertiary suppliers is at least as large. Together, this extended **multi-tier supply chain** (the chain of primary, secondary, and tertiary suppliers) constitutes a crucial aspect of the industrial infrastructure of the economy. **Figure 12.4** depicts a firm's multi-tier supply chain.

The supply chain depicted in Figure 12.4 is a three-tier chain simplified for the sake of illustration. In fact, large Fortune 1000 firms have thousands of suppliers, who in turn have thousands of smaller suppliers. The complexity of the supply chain

multi-tier supply chain

the chain of primary, secondary, and tertiary suppliers

| FIGURE 12.4 | **THE MULTI-TIER SUPPLY CHAIN** |

Tier 3   Tier 2   Tier 1

SELLERS   **BUYER**

The supply chain for every firm is composed of multiple tiers of suppliers.

suggests a combinatorial explosion. Assuming a manufacturer has four primary suppliers and each one has three primary suppliers, and each of these has three primary suppliers, then the total number of suppliers in the chain (including the buying firm) rises to 53. This figure does not include the shippers, insurers, and financiers involved in the transactions.

Immediately, you can see from Figure 12.4 that the procurement process involves a very large number of suppliers, each of whom must be coordinated with the production needs of the ultimate purchaser—the buying firm. You can also understand how difficult it is to "manage" the supply chain, or obtain "visibility" into the supply chain simply because of its size and scope.

The Role of Existing Legacy Computer Systems and Enterprise Systems

legacy computer systems
older mainframe systems used to manage key business processes within a firm in a variety of functional areas

Complicating any efforts to coordinate the many firms in a supply chain is the fact that each firm generally has its own set of legacy computer systems, sometimes home-grown or customized, that cannot easily pass information to other systems. **Legacy computer systems** generally are older systems used to manage key business processes within a firm in a variety of functional areas from manufacturing, logistics, finance, and human resources. **Enterprise systems** are corporate-wide systems that relate to all aspects of production, including finance, human resources, and procurement. Many large Fortune 500 global firms have implemented global enterprise-wide systems from major vendors such as IBM, SAP, Oracle, and others. These enterprise systems have supply chain management modules designed to automate key B2B processes.

enterprise systems
corporate-wide systems that relate to all aspects of production, including finance, human resources, and procurement

With an enterprise-wide B2B system in place, incoming orders from customers can be translated into Bills of Material (BOM), production schedules, and human resource and financial requirements, including notifying the finance department to issue invoices to customers and pay suppliers. Similarly, enterprise systems automate the procurement process, including logistics, and track the delivery of parts from suppliers.

TRENDS IN SUPPLY CHAIN MANAGEMENT AND COLLABORATIVE COMMERCE

It is impossible to comprehend the actual and potential contribution of Internet-based B2B commerce, or the successes and failures of B2B e-commerce vendors and markets, without understanding ongoing efforts to improve the procurement process through a variety of supply chain management programs that long preceded the development of e-commerce.

supply chain management (SCM)
refers to a wide variety of activities that firms and industries use to coordinate the key players in their procurement process

Supply chain management (SCM) refers to a wide variety of activities that firms and industries use to coordinate the key players in their procurement process. For the most part, today's procurement managers still work with telephones, e-mail, fax machines, face-to-face conversations, and instinct, relying on trusted long-term suppliers for their strategic purchases of goods directly involved in the production process.

There have been a number of major developments in supply chain management over the last two decades that set the ground rules for understanding how B2B e-commerce works (or fails to work). These developments include just-in-time and lean production, supply chain simplification, adaptive supply chains, sustainable supply chains, electronic data interchange (EDI), supply chain management systems, and collaborative commerce (Supply Chain Digest, 2012a).

Just-in-Time and Lean Production

One of the significant costs in any production process is the cost of in-process inventory: the parts and supplies needed to produce a product or service. **Just-in-time production** is a method of inventory cost management that seeks to eliminate excess inventory to a bare minimum. In just-in-time production, the parts needed for, say, an automobile, arrive at the assembly factory a few hours or even minutes before they are attached to a car. Payment for the parts does not occur until the parts are attached to a vehicle on the production line. In the past, producers used to order enough parts for a week or even a month's worth of production, creating huge, costly buffers in the production process. These buffers assured that parts would almost always be available, but at a large cost. **Lean production** is a set of production methods and tools that focuses on the elimination of waste throughout the customer value chain. It is an extension of just-in-time beyond inventory management to the full range of activities that create customer value. Originally, just-in-time and lean methods were implemented with phones, faxes, and paper documents to coordinate the flow of parts in inventory. Supply chain management systems now have largely automated the process of acquiring inventory from suppliers, and made possible significant savings on a global basis. Arguably, contemporary supply chain systems are the foundation of today's global B2B production system.

just-in-time production
a method of inventory cost management that seeks to eliminate excess inventory to a bare minimum

lean production
a set of production methods and tools that focuses on the elimination of waste throughout the customer value chain

Supply Chain Simplification

Many manufacturing firms have spent the past two decades reducing the size of their supply chains and working more closely with a smaller group of "strategic" supplier firms to reduce both product costs and administrative costs, while improving quality. Following the lead of Japanese industry, for instance, the automobile industry has systematically reduced the number of its suppliers by over 50%. Instead of open bidding for orders, large manufacturers have chosen to work with strategic partner supply firms under long-term contracts that guarantee the supplier business and also establish quality, cost, and timing goals. These strategic partnership programs are essential for just-in-time production models, and often involve joint product development and design, integration of computer systems, and tight coupling of the production processes of two or more companies. **Tight coupling** is a method for ensuring that suppliers precisely deliver the ordered parts at a specific time and to a particular location, ensuring the production process is not interrupted for lack of parts.

tight coupling
a method for ensuring that suppliers precisely deliver the ordered parts, at a specific time and particular location, to ensure the production process is not interrupted for lack of parts

Supply Chain Black Swans: Adaptive Supply Chains

While firms have greatly simplified their supply chains in the last decade, they have also sought to centralize them by adopting a single, global supply chain system that integrates all the firm's vendor and logistics information into a single enterprise-wide system. Large software firms like Oracle, IBM, and SAP encourage firms to adopt a "one world, one firm, one database" enterprise-wide view of the world in order to achieve scale economies, simplicity, and to optimize global cost and value.

Beginning in earnest in 2000, managers in developed countries used these new technological capabilities to push manufacturing and production to the lowest cost labor regions of the world, specifically China and South East Asia. This movement of production to Asia was also enabled by the entrance of China into the World Trade Organization in September 2001. Suddenly, it was both technologically and politically possible to concentrate production wherever possible in the lowest cost region of the world. These developments were also supported by low-cost fuel, which made both transoceanic shipping and production inexpensive, and relative political stability in the region. By 2005, many economists believed a new world economic order had emerged based on cheap labor in Asia capable of producing inexpensive products for Western consumers, profits for global firms, and the opening of Asian markets to sophisticated Western goods and financial products.

As it turns out, there were many risks and costs to this strategy of concentrating production in China and Asia in a world of economic, financial, political, and even geological instability. For instance, in the global financial crisis of 2007–2009, relying on suppliers in parts of Europe where currencies and interest rates fluctuated greatly exposed many firms to higher costs than anticipated. Suddenly, key suppliers could not obtain financing for their production or shipments. In March 2011, following the earthquake and tsunami in Japan, key suppliers in Japan were forced to shut down or slow production because of nuclear contamination of the entire Fukushima region where, as its turns out, major Japanese and American firms had automobile parts factories. As a result, General Motors could no longer obtain transmissions for its Volt electric car, and had to shut down a truck factory in Louisiana due to a lack of parts from Japan. Japanese and other global firms could not obtain batteries, switches, and axle assemblies. Production lead times in the automobile industry were very short, and inventories of parts were intentionally very lean, with only a few weeks' supply on hand. Texas Instruments shut down several of its Japanese plants, as did Toshiba, putting a crimp on the world supply of NAND flash memory chips used in smartphones (Jolly, 2011; Bunkley, 2011). Caterpillar, Sony, Boeing, Volvo, and hundreds of other firms that are all part of a tightly coupled world supply chain also experienced supply chain disruptions. And then, in October of 2011, torrential rains in Thailand led to flooding of many of its key industrial regions, and the wiping out of a significant share of the world's electronics components from hard disk drives to automobile subsystems, cameras, and notebook PCs (Supply Chain Digest, 2012b; Hookway, 2012). In 2012 and 2013, the source of supply chain disruptions shifted to technology, with major disruptions due to failure of cloud-based services and cyberattacks (Gusman, 2013; Zurich Insurance, 2012).

By 2013, the risks and costs of extended and concentrated supply chains have begun to change corporate strategies. To cope with unpredictable world events, firms are taking steps to break up single global supply chain systems into regional or product-based supply chains, with some level of centralization, but substantial autonomy for the smaller systems. Using regional supply chains, firms can decide to locate some production of parts in Latin America, rather than all their production or suppliers in a single country such as Japan. They will be able to move production around the world to temporary "safe harbors." This may result in higher short-term costs, but provide substantial, longer term risk protection in the event any single region is disrupted. Increasingly, supply chains are being built based on the assumption that global disruptions in supply are inevitable, but not predictable (Simchi-Levi et al., 2011; Malik et al., 2011). The focus in 2013 is on "optimal-cost," not low-cost, supply chains, and more distributed manufacturing along with more flexible supply chains that can shift reliably from high-risk to low-risk areas. Regional manufacturing means shorter supply chains that can respond rapidly to changing consumer tastes and demand levels (Cachon and Swinney, 2011). There is some research indicating that when firms improve their B2B supply chains they open themselves up to greater disruption when compared to firms that did not improve their supply chains (Schmidt and Raman, 2013).

Accountable Supply Chains: Labor Standards

Accountable supply chains are those where the labor conditions in low-wage, under-developed producer countries are visible and morally acceptable to ultimate consumers in more developed industrial societies. For much of the last century, American and European manufacturers with global supply chains with large offshore production facilities sought to hide the realities of their offshore factories from Western reporters and ordinary citizens. For global firms with long supply chains, "visibility" did not mean their consumers could understand how their products were made.

Beginning in 2000, and in part because of the growing power of the Internet to empower citizen reporters around the world, the realities of global supply chains have slowly become more transparent to the public. For instance, for much of the past decade, beginning in 1997, Nike, the world's largest manufacturer of sporting goods, has been under intense criticism for exploiting foreign workers, operating sweat shops, employing children, and allowing dangerous conditions in its subcontractor factories. As a result, Nike has introduced significant changes to its global supply chain.

With the emergence of truly global supply chains, and political changes at the World Trade Organization, which opened up European and American markets to Asian goods and services, many—if not most—of the electronics, toys, cosmetics, industrial supplies, footwear, apparel, and other goods consumed in the developed world are made by workers in factories in the less developed world, primarily in Asia and Latin America. Unfortunately, but quite understandably, the labor conditions in these factories in most cases do not meet the minimal labor standards of Europe or America even though these factories pay higher wages and offer better working conditions than other local jobs in the host country. In many cases, the cost for a worker of not having a job in what—to Western standards—are horrible working conditions is to sink deeper into poverty and even worse conditions. Many point out that labor conditions were brutal in the United States and Europe in the nineteenth and early twentieth century when these countries were building industrial economies, and therefore, whatever conditions exist in offshore factories in 2013 are no worse than developed countries in their early years of rapid industrialization.

The argument results in a painful ethical dilemma, a terrible trade-off: cheap manufactured goods that increase consumer welfare in developed countries seem to require human misery in less developed countries. Indeed, these jobs would never have been moved to less developed parts of world without exceptionally low, even survival level, wages.

Notwithstanding the argument that having a job is better than being unemployed in low-wage countries, or any country, there are some working conditions that are completely unacceptable to consumers and therefore to firms in developed countries. Among these unacceptable working conditions are slave or forced labor, child employment, routine exposure to toxic substances, more than 48 hours of work per week, harassment and abuse, sexual exploitation, and compensation beneath the minimal standard of living leaving no disposable income. These practices were, and are, in some cases typical, and certainly not atypical, in many low-wage countries.

A number of groups in the last decade have contributed to efforts to make global supply chains transparent to reporters and citizens, and to develop minimal standards of accountability. Among these groups are the National Consumers League, Human Rights First, the Maquilla Solidarity Network, the Global Fairness Initiative, the Clean Clothes Campaign, the International Labor Organization (UN), and the Fair Labor Association (FLA). The FLA is a coalition of business firms with offshore production and global supply chains, universities, and private organizations. For member firms, the FLA conducts interviews with workers, makes unannounced visits to factories to track progress, and investigates complaints. They are also one of the major international labor standard-setting organizations (Fair Labor Organization, 2012).

In March 2012, the FLA released its investigation of Hon Hai Precision Industry Company (a Taiwan-based company known as Foxconn), which is the assembler of nearly all iPhones and iPads in the world. Foxconn operates what is alleged to be the largest factory in the world in Longhua, Shenzhen, where over 250,000 workers assemble electronics goods. The audit of working conditions at Foxconn was authorized by Apple, a member of the FLA, and was based on 35,000 surveys of workers at the Longhua factory. The report found over 50 legal and code violations (sometimes in violation of Chinese laws) including requiring too many hours of work a week (over 60), failing to pay workers for overtime, and hazardous conditions that injured workers (Fair Labor Association, 2012).

Sustainable Supply Chains: Lean, Mean, and Green

"Sustainable business" is a call for business to take social and ecological interests, and not just corporate profits, into account in all their decision-making throughout the firm. No small request. Since the United Nations World Commission on Environment and Development (WCED) published the first comprehensive report on sustainable business in 1987, firms around the globe have struggled with these concepts and in some cases ignored or resisted them as simply a threat to sustained profitability. The commission's report (*Our Common Future*) argued for a balance of profits, social community development, and minimal impact on the world environment, including of course, the carbon footprint of business. By 2013, the consensus among major firms in Europe, Asia, and the United States has become that in the long term, and through careful planning, sustainable business is just good business because it means using the most efficient environment-regarding means of production, distribution, and logistics. These efficient methods create value for consumers, investors, and communities.

Notions of sustainable business have had a powerful impact on supply chain thinking. In part, these efforts are good risk management: all advanced countries have substantially strengthened their environmental regulations. It makes good business sense for firms to prepare methods and operations suitable to this new environment.

For instance, all the major textiles brands and retailers have announced plans for a more sustainable supply chain in textiles. One of the world's truly ancient industries, textiles supports millions of workers while consuming extraordinary resources: it takes 1,000 gallons of water to make one pound of finished cotton (your jeans, for instance). While growing cotton has its issues (fertilizer), the subsequent dying, finishing, and cleaning of cotton makes it the number one industrial polluter on Earth (cKinetics, 2010). It's not a small matter then that Walmart, Gap, Levi's, Nike, and other large players in the industry are taking steps to reduce the environmental impact of their operations by improving the efficiency of the entire supply and distribution chains.

With the help of IBM, SAP, and Oracle, other firms and entire industries are working to develop sustainable supply chains. McKesson, North America's largest distributor of drugs, uses IBM's Supply Chain Sustainability Management Solution (SCSM) to minimize carbon dioxide emissions throughout its supply chain, while lowering its distribution costs. SCSM (a business analytics package that works with IBM's B2B software) can determine low-cost refrigeration alternatives for certain medicines (such as insulin and vaccines), identify the environmentally least harmful way to bring new products into its distribution network, and determine the best way to transport pharmaceuticals to customers (IBM, 2011a).

Electronic Data Interchange (EDI)

As noted in the previous section, B2B e-commerce did not originate with the Internet, but in fact has its roots in technologies such as EDI that were first developed in the mid-1970s and 1980s. EDI is a broadly defined communications protocol for exchanging documents among computers using technical standards developed by the American National Standards Institute (ANSI X12 standards) and international bodies such as the United Nations (EDIFACT standards).

EDI was developed to reduce the cost, delays, and errors inherent in the manual exchanges of documents such as purchase orders, shipping documents, price lists, payments, and customer data. EDI differs from an unstructured message because its messages are organized with distinct fields for each of the important pieces of information in a commercial transaction such as transaction date, product purchased, amount, sender's name, address, and recipient's name.

Each major industry in the United States and throughout much of the industrial world has EDI industry committees that define the structure and information fields of electronic documents for that industry. EDI communications at first relied on private point-to-point circuit-switched communication networks and private value-added networks that connected key participants in the supply chain. Estimates indicate that B2B e-commerce EDI transactions will total about $1.3 billion in 2013, about 30% of all

FIGURE 12.5 **THE EVOLUTION OF EDI AS A B2B MEDIUM**

EDI has evolved from a simple point-to-point digital communications medium to a many-to-one enabling tool for continuous inventory replenishment.

B2B e-commerce (U.S. Census Bureau, 2012a; authors' estimates). In this sense, EDI remains very important in the development of B2B e-commerce.

EDI has evolved significantly since the 1980s (see **Figure 12.5**). Initially, EDI focused on document automation (Stage 1). Procurement agents created purchase orders electronically and sent them to trading partners, who in turn shipped order fulfillment and shipping notices electronically back to the purchaser. Invoices, payments, and other documents followed. These early implementations replaced the postal system for document transmission, and resulted in same-day shipping of orders (rather than a week's delay caused by the postal system), reduced errors, and lower costs.

The second stage of EDI development began in the early 1990s, driven largely by the automation of internal industrial processes and movement toward just-in-time production and continuous production. New methods of production called for greater flexibility in scheduling, shipping, and financing of supplies. EDI evolved to become a system for document elimination. To support the new automated production processes used by manufacturers, EDI was used to eliminate purchase orders and other documents entirely, replacing them with production schedules and inventory balances. Supplier firms were sent monthly statements of production requirements and precise scheduled delivery times, and the orders would be fulfilled continuously, with inventory and payments being adjusted at the end of each month.

In the third stage of EDI, beginning in the mid-1990s, suppliers were given online access to selected parts of the purchasing firm's production and delivery schedules, and, under long-term contracts, were required to meet those schedules on their own without intervention by firm purchasing agents. Movement toward this continuous access model of EDI was spurred in the 1990s by large manufacturing and process firms (such as oil and chemical companies) that were implementing enterprise systems. These systems required standardization of business processes and resulted in the automation of production, logistics, and many financial processes. These new processes required much closer relationships with suppliers, who were required to be more precise in delivery scheduling and more flexible in inventory management. This level of supplier precision could never be achieved economically by human purchasing agents. This third stage of EDI enabled the era of continuous replenishment. For instance, Walmart and Toys"R"Us provide their suppliers with access to their store inventories, and the suppliers are expected to keep the stock of items on the shelf within prespecified targets. Similar developments occurred in the grocery industry.

Today, EDI must be viewed as a general enabling technology that provides for the exchange of critical business information between computer applications supporting a wide variety of business processes. EDI is an important industrial network technology, suited to support communications among a small set of strategic partners in direct, long-term trading relationships. The technical platform of EDI has changed from mainframes to personal computers, and the telecommunications environment is changing from private, dedicated networks to the Internet (referred to as Internet-based EDI, or just Internet EDI). Most industry groups are moving toward XML as the language for expressing EDI commercial documents and communications.

The strength of EDI is its ability to support direct commercial transactions among strategically related firms in an industrial network, but this is its weakness as well. EDI is not well suited for the development of electronic marketplaces, where thousands of suppliers and purchasers meet in a digital arena to negotiate prices. EDI supports direct bilateral communications among a small set of firms and does not permit the multilateral, dynamic relationships of a true marketplace. EDI does not provide for price transparency among a large number of suppliers, does not scale easily to include new participants, and is not a real-time communications environment. EDI does not have a rich communications environment that can simultaneously support e-mail messaging, sharing of graphic documents, network meetings, or user-friendly flexible database creation and management. For these features, Internet-based software has emerged (described below). EDI is also an expensive proposition, and a staff of dedicated programmers is required to implement it in large firms; in some cases, a considerable amount of time is also needed to reprogram existing enterprise systems to work with EDI protocols. Small firms are typically required to adopt EDI in order to supply large firms, and there are less-expensive, small-firm solutions for implementing EDI.

Supply Chain Management Systems: Mobile B2B in Your Palm

supply chain management (SCM) systems

continuously link the activities of buying, making, and moving products from suppliers to purchasing firms, as well as integrating the demand side of the business equation by including the order entry system in the process

Supply chain simplification, lean production, focusing on strategic partners in the production process, enterprise systems, and continuous inventory replenishment are the foundation for contemporary **supply chain management (SCM) systems**. Supply chain management systems continuously link the activities of buying, making, and moving products from suppliers to purchasing firms, as well as integrating the demand side of the business equation by including the order entry system in the process. With an SCM system and continuous replenishment, inventory is greatly reduced and production begins only when an order is received (see **Figure 12.6**). These systems enable just-in-time and lean-production methods. The growing use of smartphones has led software firms like SAP and Oracle to develop mobile apps for personal computers, smartphones, and other consumer devices to connect firms with their supply chain partners.

Hewlett-Packard (HP) is one of the largest technology companies in the world, with sales of $120 billion in 2012. With operations in 178 countries, sales in 43 currencies, and 15 languages, HP is truly a global firm with global supply chain issues that

FIGURE 12.6   SUPPLY CHAIN MANAGEMENT SYSTEMS

SCM systems coordinate the activities of suppliers, shippers, and order entry systems to automate order entry through production, payment, and shipping business processes. Increasingly customers, as well as employees working throughout the supply chain, are using smartphones and mobile apps to place and coordinate orders.

became even more complicated as HP expanded by making over 200 acquisitions in the last decade. To cope with one of the most complex supply chains in the world, HP turned to supply chain management software.

HP has a Web-based, order-driven supply chain management system that begins with either a customer placing an order online or the receipt of an order from a dealer. The order is forwarded from the order entry system to HP's production and delivery system. From there, the order is routed to one of several HP contractor supplier firms. One such firm is Synnex in Fremont, California. At Synnex, computers verify the order with HP and validate the ordered configuration to ensure the PC can be manufactured (e.g., will not have missing parts or fail a design specification set by HP). The order is then forwarded to a computer-based production control system that issues a bar-coded production ticket to factory assemblers. Simultaneously, a parts order is forwarded to Synnex's warehouse and inventory management system. A worker assembles the computer, and then the computer is boxed, tagged, and shipped to the customer. The delivery is monitored and tracked by HP's supply chain management system, which links directly to one of several overnight delivery systems operated by Airborne Express, Federal Express, and UPS. The elapsed time from order entry to shipping is 48 hours. With this system, Synnex and HP have eliminated the need to hold PCs in inventory, reduced cycle time from one week to 48 hours, and reduced errors. HP has extended this system to become a global B2B order tracking, reporting, and support system for large HP customers (Synnex Corporation, 2013; Hewlett-Packard, 2013). In 2010, HP began a simplification of B2B applications from over 300 applications down to 30. Many of these applications were inherited from acquired companies (Gardner, 2010).

It isn't just huge technology companies that use supply chain software. There's nothing quite so perishable as fashionable underwear given the rate of fashion change. Under Armour, which calls itself "the world's No. 1 performance athletic brand," uses software from SAP to predict sales, plan inventory, and coordinate suppliers (Booen, 2011). Prior to using these tools, Under Armour often missed sales because it did not produce enough of popular items, or overproduced items that were not selling.

Implementing an order-driven, Web-based supply chain management system is not always easy, however, as *Insight on Technology: RFID AutoIdentification: Giving a Voice to Your Inventory* illustrates.

Collaborative Commerce

Collaborative commerce is a direct extension of supply chain management systems, as well as supply chain simplification. **Collaborative commerce** is defined as the use of digital technologies to permit organizations to collaboratively design, develop, build, and manage products through their life cycles. This is a much broader mission than EDI or simply managing the flow of information among organizations. Collaborative commerce involves a definitive move from a transaction focus to a relationship focus among the supply chain participants. Rather than having an arm's-length adversarial relationship with suppliers, collaborative commerce fosters sharing of sensitive internal information with suppliers and purchasers. Managing collaborative commerce requires knowing exactly what information to share with whom. Collaborative

collaborative commerce
the use of digital technologies to permit organizations to collaboratively design, develop, build, and manage products through their life cycles

INSIGHT ON TECHNOLOGY

RFID AUTOIDENTIFICATION: GIVING A VOICE TO YOUR INVENTORY

It's 10 p.m. Do you know where your containers are? Wouldn't it be nice if your containers could talk to you, call home every now and then to report their progress towards your loading docks? Radio frequency identification (RFID) makes that possible today, and as of 2013, even your jeans will be given a voice inside, and maybe outside, the store where you purchased them.

If you're in business anywhere in the world today, and that business involves physical goods, then chances are quite good that your business depends on the movement of goods in containers. In fact, there are around 20 million sea cargo containers making over 200 million trips every year among the world's seaports, and nearly 50% of the value of all U.S. imports arrive via sea cargo containers each year. The containers are loaded onto ships, and stacked high on the deck. The containers also fit on the back of trucks and on railway carriages. So when the containers are unloaded from the ship, they continue their journey from the port on the back of trucks or trains. It is a fast and efficient way of moving cargo. A standard container is about 20 feet long, 8 feet wide, and 8 feet high, and can hold about 47,900 lbs of cargo.

Prior to the development of containers, all ocean-going cargo was loaded and unloaded onto ships in huge nets by dock workers, one package at a time. While the container revolutionized ocean shipping, vastly increasing productivity and reducing breakage, keeping track of 200 million cargo containers is difficult. While each container has its own permanent ID number painted on the side, as well as a bar code identification tag, this number must be entered manually by dock workers or scanned up close. Identification of containers is slow and prone to errors. If you had to find one container on a dock containing over 1,000 containers, you would have to read each ID number until you found the one you wanted. All by themselves, containers can't talk.

Tracking containers is just one part of the larger B2B product identification problem. Retailers such as Walmart, Target, and Amazon find it difficult and expensive to track millions of annual shipments into and out of their warehouses and sales floors; the automotive industry finds it costly and difficult to synchronize the flow of parts into its factories; the U.S. Department of Defense logistics system finds it difficult to track the movement of troop supplies; and the airline industry often loses bags in transit.

Thirty years ago, the development of the Uniform Product Code (UPC) and the ubiquitous bar code label was an initial first step towards automating the identification of goods. But the bar code technology of the 1970s still required humans or sometimes machines to scan products. The problem with bar codes is that they don't talk—they are passive labels that must be read or scanned.

Today, a technology to replace bar codes is being deployed among the largest manufacturing and retailing firms. RFID involves the use of tags attached to products or product containers that transmit a radio signal in the 850 megahertz to 2.5 gigahertz range that continuously identifies them to radio receivers in warehouses, factories, retail floors, or on board ships. RFID labels are really tiny computer chips and a battery that are used to transmit each product's electronic product code to receivers nearby.

RFID has several key advantages over the old bar code scanner technology. RFID eliminates the line-of-sight reading requirement of bar codes and

(continued)

greatly increases the distance from which scanning can be done from a few inches up to 90 feet. RFID systems can be used just about anywhere—from clothing tags to missiles to pet tags to food—anywhere that a unique identification system is needed. The tag can carry information as simple as a pet owner's name and address or the cleaning instructions on a sweater or as complex as instructions on how to assemble a car. Best of all, instead of looking at a warehouse filled with thousands of packages that can't talk, you could be listening to these same thousands of packages each chirping a unique code, identifying themselves to you. Finding the single package you are looking for is greatly simplified. RFID tags produce a steady stream of data that can be entered into Internet- and intranet-based corporate applications such as SCM and ERP systems.

The value of the global RFID market in 2012 was estimated to be $7.7 billion, with almost 4 billion RFID tags sold. The RFID market is expanding rapidly because of the growing use of RFIDs by governments and private industry, as well as the explosive growth in item-level RFID.

Walmart, the world's largest retailer, made RFID an important part of its supply chain strategy in the 2000s. The company mandated that its suppliers place RFID tags on all cases and pallets headed for its Dallas distribution centers, and RFID funding increased dramatically in the wake of its decision. Many thought that RFID had finally reached a tipping point and would become a mainstream technology used by the entire business world. When Walmart speaks, people listen. The problem was that the expense and extra hours required to switch to RFID was too heavy a burden on many of Walmart's suppliers, and the movement toward RFID stalled. However, RFID has made a comeback at the item level. Around 20 of the top 30 retailers in the United States, including Walmart, American Apparel, Macy's, and others, have implemented item-level RFID, with over 1 billion RFID labels sold worldwide in 2012. For instance, American Apparel, which has 254 stores and manufactures 1 million garments a week, has tagged 95% of all of the items in its stores. Antennas in the store ceiling allow it to scan 35,000 items an hour with 98% accuracy, enabling it to take inventory every day in all its stores and reduce out of stocks to less than 1%. Macy's is also moving aggressively into item-level RFID, with about 50% of its vendors now signed up to deliver RFID-tagged goods in the future.

Walmart has rolled out RFID in two non-apparel categories in 2012: tires and consumer electronics. The grocery industry is also starting to expand its use of RFID from the carton/pallet-level to the item-level, as well. As implementation costs for RFID continue to decrease, more companies will be able to tag their goods and use RFID to manage inventory. Analysts predict that the RFID retail market (including tags, readers, and software) will grow to around $3.2 billion in 2017.

As adoption of the technology increases, RFID will have a profound impact on B2B e-commerce by reducing the cost of tracking goods through industry supply chains, reducing errors, and increasing the chances that the right product will be sent to the right customer.

SOURCES: "RFID Forecasts, Players and Opportunites 2012–2022," Prweb.com, July 2, 2013; "Macy's Gives Updates on Its RFID Rollout and Plans, Connects RFID and Multi-Channel Commerce," Scdigest.com, July 2, 2013; "IS RFID Still a Disruptive Technology," Scdigest.com, May 15, 2013; "Item-level Tagging in the Grocery Industry—Are We There Yet?," by Hanna Ostman, Rfidarena.com, April 2, 2013; "Momentum Builds for Retail RFID in 2013," Rfid24-7.com, November 29, 2012; "Did Walmart Love RFID to Death?," by Matthew Malone, smartplanet.com, February 14, 2012; "Is the Tipping Point Really, Truly Here for Item Level RFID Tracking in Apparel Retail?," SCDigest.com, February 2, 2012; "RFID In Consumer Goods to Retail—A Comeback?," by Dan Gilmore, SCDigest.com, November 11, 2011; "Do JCPenney, Macy's Announcements Mean RFID to Finally Really Takeoff in Retail?," SCDigest.com, November 2, 2011; "Car2go Test Drive: RFID, GPS, and Mobile Apps Make for a Smarter Smart," by Tim Stevens, Engadget.com, March 14, 2011; "Walmart Will Track You and Your Undies With RFIDs," by Matthew Zuras, Switched.com, July 26, 2010; "Walmart Radio Tags to Track Clothing," by Miguel Bustillo, *Wall Street Journal*, July 23, 2010.

commerce extends beyond supply chain management activities to include the collaborative development of new products and services by multiple cooperating firms.

A good example of collaborative commerce is the long-term effort of P&G, the world's largest manufacturer of personal and health care products, from Crest toothpaste to Tide soap, to work with suppliers and even customers to develop 50% of its product line over time. In the past, for instance, P&G would design a bottle or product package in-house, and then turn to over 100 suppliers of packaging to find out what it would cost and try to bargain that down. Using Ariba's procurement network, P&G asks its suppliers to come up with innovative ideas for packaging and pricing. Taking it a step further, P&G's Web site, Pgconnectdevelop.com, solicits new product ideas from suppliers and customers. About 50% of P&G's new products originate with substantial input from its suppliers and customers (P&G, 2011; Vance, 2010). Other well-known companies using collaboration to develop and deliver products include Lego (DesignByMe), Harley Davidson, Starbucks, and GE's Ecomagination program (James, 2012; Esposito, 2012).

Although collaborative commerce can involve customers as well as suppliers in the development of products, for the most part, it is concerned with the development of a rich communications environment to enable inter-firm sharing of designs, production plans, inventory levels, delivery schedules, and the development of shared products (see **Figure 12.7**).

FIGURE 12.7	**ELEMENTS OF A COLLABORATIVE COMMERCE SYSTEM**

A collaborative commerce application includes a central data repository where employees at several different firms can store engineering drawings and other documents. A workflow engine determines who can see this data and what rules will apply for displaying the data on individual workstations. A viewer can be a browser operating on a workstation.

Collaborative commerce is very different from EDI, which is a technology for structured communications among firms. Collaborative commerce is more like an interactive teleconference among members of the supply chain. EDI and collaborative commerce share one characteristic: they are not open, competitive marketplaces, but instead are, technically, private industrial networks that connect strategic partners in a supply chain. Broadband video networks like Cisco's TelePresence Studios are beginning to play a role in enabling frequent, long-distance, collaboration among supply chain partners. TelePresence is one of several very high bandwidth video systems from different vendors that give users the impression they are sharing physical space with other participants who are in fact located remotely, sometimes on the other side of the globe. P&G has over forty TelePresence studios in its facilities around the world to encourage collaboration among its employees and suppliers (Cisco, 2013, 2011). Cisco's @CiscoLiveDesk's Twitter feed enhances the TelePresence experience by adding face-to-face support, scheduling assistance, and demos.

In Section 12.3, we discuss collaborative commerce in greater depth as a technology that enables private industrial networks.

SOCIAL NETWORKS AND B2B: THE EXTENDED SOCIAL ENTERPRISE

It's a short step from collaboration with vendors, suppliers, and customers, to a more personal relationship based on conversations with participants in the supply chain using social networks—both private and public. Here, the conversations and sharing of ideas are more unstructured, situational, and personal. Procurement officers, managers of supply chains, and logistics managers are people too, and they participate in the same social network culture provided by Facebook, Twitter, Tumblr, Instagram, and a host of other public social networks as we all do. Being able to respond to fast moving developments that affect supply chains requires something more than a Web site, e-mail, or telephone calls. Social networks can provide the intimate connections among customers, suppliers, and logistics partners that are needed to keep the supply chain functioning, and to make decisions based on current conditions (Red Prairie, 2012).

Participants in the supply chain network are tapping into their tablet computers, smartphones, and social network sites for purchasing, scheduling, exception handling, and deciding with their B2B customers and suppliers. In many cases, supply chain social networks are private—owned by the largest firm in the supply chain network. In other cases, firms develop Facebook pages to organize conversations among supply chain network members.

Some examples of social B2B include TradeSpace, a UK-based business social network where business people can share experiences and ideas, and buy and sell products. Cisco is using its Web site and Facebook pages to run new product campaigns for its business customers using social networks exclusively. Dell, like many businesses, uses its YouTube channel to engage suppliers and customers in conversations about existing products, and ideas for new products (Hird, 2011). While social networks have not yet had a large influence on B2B e-commerce, public social network sites like Facebook and Twitter are good listening posts for businesses involved in B2B trade.

FIGURE 12.8   **TWO MAIN TYPES OF INTERNET-BASED B2B COMMERCE**

There are two main types of Internet-based B2B commerce: Net marketplaces and private industrial networks.

MAIN TYPES OF INTERNET-BASED B2B COMMERCE

There are two generic types of Internet-based B2B commerce systems: Net marketplaces (which tend to be public) and private industrial networks (see **Figure 12.8**). Within each of these general categories are many different subtypes that we discuss in the following sections (Yoo et al., 2011).

Net marketplaces (also referred to as exchanges) bring together potentially thousands of sellers and buyers into a single digital marketplace operated over the Internet. Net marketplaces are transaction-based, support many-to-many as well as one-to-many relationships, and bear some resemblance to financial markets such as the New York Stock Exchange. There are many different types of Net marketplaces, with different pricing mechanisms, biases, and value propositions that will be explored in Section 12.2 (Kerrigan et al., 2001). Private industrial networks bring together a small number of strategic business partner firms that collaborate to develop highly efficient supply chains and satisfy customer demand for products. Private industrial networks are relationship-based, support many-to-one or many-to-few relationships, and bear some resemblance to internal collaborative work environments. There are many different types of private industrial networks, as discussed in Section 12.3. Private industrial networks are by far the largest form of B2B e-commerce and account for over 10 times as much revenue as Net marketplaces.

12.2 NET MARKETPLACES

One of the most compelling visions of B2B e-commerce is that of an electronic marketplace on the Internet that would bring thousands of fragmented suppliers into contact with hundreds of major purchasers of industrial goods for the purpose of conducting "frictionless" commerce. The hope was that these suppliers would compete with one another on price, transactions would be automated and low cost, and as a result, the price of industrial supplies would fall. By extracting fees from buyers and sellers on each transaction, third-party intermediary market makers could earn significant revenues. These Net marketplaces could scale easily as volume increased by simply adding more computers and communications equipment.

In pursuit of this vision, well over 1,500 Net marketplaces sprang up in the early days of e-commerce. Unfortunately, many of them have since disappeared and the population is expected to stabilize at about 200. Still, many survive, and they are joined by other types of Net marketplaces—some private and some public—based on different assumptions that are quite successful.

THE VARIETY AND CHARACTERISTICS OF NET MARKETPLACES

There is a confusing variety of Net marketplaces today, and several different ways to classify them. For instance, some writers classify Net marketplaces on the basis of their pricing mechanisms—auction, bid/ask, negotiated price, and fixed prices—while others classify markets based on characteristics of the markets they serve (vertical versus horizontal, or sell-side versus buy-side), or ownership (industry-owned consortia versus independent third-party intermediaries). **Table 12.2** describes some of the important characteristics of Net marketplaces.

TABLE 12.2	OTHER CHARACTERISTICS OF NET MARKETPLACES: A B2B VOCABULARY
CHARACTERISTIC	**MEANING**
Bias	Sell-side vs. buy-side vs. neutral. Whose interests are advantaged: buyers, sellers, or no bias?
Ownership	Industry vs. third party. Who owns the marketplace?
Pricing mechanism	Fixed-price catalogs, auctions, bid/ask, and RFPs/RFQs.
Scope/Focus	Horizontal vs. vertical markets.
Value creation	What benefits do they offer customers or suppliers?
Access to market	In public markets, any firm can enter, but in private markets, entry is by invitation only.

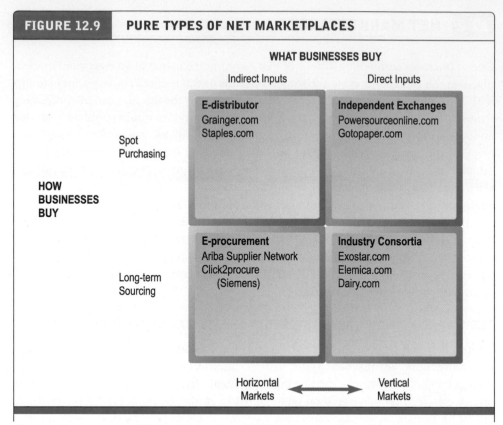

FIGURE 12.9 **PURE TYPES OF NET MARKETPLACES**

WHAT BUSINESSES BUY

Indirect Inputs Direct Inputs

HOW BUSINESSES BUY

Spot Purchasing

E-distributor
Grainger.com
Staples.com

Independent Exchanges
Powersourceonline.com
Gotopaper.com

Long-term Sourcing

E-procurement
Ariba Supplier Network
Click2procure
  (Siemens)

Industry Consortia
Exostar.com
Elemica.com
Dairy.com

Horizontal Markets ←→ Vertical Markets

There are four main types of Net marketplaces based on the intersection of two dimensions: how businesses buy and what they buy. A third dimension—horizontal versus vertical markets—also distinguishes the different types of Net marketplaces.

TYPES OF NET MARKETPLACES

Although each of these distinctions helps describe the phenomenon of Net marketplaces, they do not focus on the central business functionality provided, nor are they capable by themselves of describing the variety of Net marketplaces.

In **Figure 12.9**, we present a classification of Net marketplaces that focuses on their business functionality; that is, what these Net marketplaces provide for businesses seeking solutions. We use two dimensions of Net marketplaces to create a four-cell classification table. We differentiate Net marketplaces as providing either indirect goods (goods used to support production) or direct goods (goods used in production), and we distinguish markets as providing either contractual purchasing (where purchases take place over many years according to a contract between the firm and its vendor) or spot purchasing (where purchases are episodic and anonymous—vendors and buyers do not have an ongoing relationship and may not know one another). The intersection of these dimensions produces four main types of Net marketplaces that are relatively straightforward: e-distributors, e-procurement networks, exchanges, and industry consortia. Note, however, that in the real world, some Net marketplaces can be found in multiple parts of this figure as business models change and opportunities appear and disappear. Nevertheless, the discussion of "pure types" of Net marketplaces is a useful starting point.

Each of these Net marketplaces seeks to provide value to customers in different ways. We discuss each type of Net marketplace in more detail in the following sections.

E-distributors

E-distributors are the most common and most easily understood type of Net marketplace. An **e-distributor** provides an electronic catalog that represents the products of thousands of direct manufacturers (see **Figure 12.10**). An e-distributor is the equivalent of Amazon for industry. E-distributors are independently owned intermediaries that offer industrial customers a single source from which to order indirect goods (often referred to as MRO) on a spot, as-needed basis. A significant percentage of corporate purchases cannot be satisfied under a company's existing contracts, and must be purchased on a spot basis. E-distributors make money by charging a markup on products they distribute.

Organizations and firms in all industries require MRO supplies. The MRO function maintains, repairs, and operates commercial buildings and maintains all the machinery of these buildings from heating, ventilating, and air conditioning systems to lighting fixtures.

e-distributor
provides electronic catalog that represents the products of thousands of direct manufacturers

FIGURE 12.10	E-DISTRIBUTORS

E-distributors are firms that bring the products of thousands of suppliers into a single online electronic catalog for sale to thousands of buyer firms. E-distributors are sometimes referred to as one-to-many markets, one seller serving many firms.

E-distributors operate in horizontal markets because they serve many different industries with products from many different suppliers. E-distributors usually operate "public" markets in the sense that any firm can order from the catalog, as opposed to "private" markets, where membership is restricted to selected firms.

E-distributor prices are usually fixed, but large customers receive discounts and other incentives to purchase, such as credit, reporting on account activity, and limited forms of business purchasing rules (for instance, no purchases greater than $500 for a single item without a purchase order). The primary benefits offered to industrial customers are lower search costs, lower transaction costs, wide selection, rapid delivery, and low prices.

The most frequently cited example of a public e-distribution market is W.W. Grainger. Grainger is involved in long-term systematic sourcing as well as spot sourcing, but its emphasis is on spot sourcing. Grainger's business model is to become the world's leading source of MRO suppliers, and its revenue model is that of a typical retailer: it owns the products, and takes a markup on the products it sells to customers. At Grainger.com, users get an electronic online version of Grainger's famous seven-pound catalog, plus other parts not available in the catalog (adding up to around 900,000 parts), and complete electronic ordering and payment (W.W. Grainger Inc., 2013). Another example is McMaster-Carr.com, a New Jersey-based industrial parts mecca for manufacturers around the world.

E-procurement

e-procurement Net marketplace

independently owned intermediary that connects hundreds of online suppliers offering millions of maintenance and repair parts to business firms who pay fees to join the market

An **e-procurement Net marketplace** is an independently owned intermediary that connects hundreds of online suppliers offering millions of maintenance and repair parts to business firms who pay fees to join the market (see **Figure 12.11**). E-procurement Net marketplaces are typically used for long-term contractual purchasing of indirect goods (MRO); they create online horizontal markets, but they also provide for members' spot sourcing of MRO supplies. E-procurement companies make money by charging a percentage of each transaction, licensing consulting services and software, and assessing network use fees (Trkman and McCormack, 2010).

E-procurement companies expand on the business model of simpler e-distributors by including the online catalogs of hundreds of suppliers and offering value chain management services to both buyers and sellers. **Value chain management (VCM) services** provided by e-procurement companies include automation of a firm's entire procurement process on the buyer side and automation of the selling business processes on the seller side. For purchasers, e-procurement companies automate purchase orders, requisitions, sourcing, business rules enforcement, invoicing, and payment. For suppliers, e-procurement companies provide catalog creation and content management, order management, fulfillment, invoicing, shipment, and settlement.

value chain management (VCM) services

include automation of a firm's entire procurement process on the buyer side and automation of the selling business processes on the seller side

E-procurement Net marketplaces are sometimes referred to as many-to-many markets. They are mediated by an independent third party that purports to represent both buyers and sellers, and hence claim to be neutral. On the other hand, because they may include the catalogs of both competing suppliers and competing e-distributors, they likely have a bias in favor of the buyers. Nevertheless, by aggregating huge

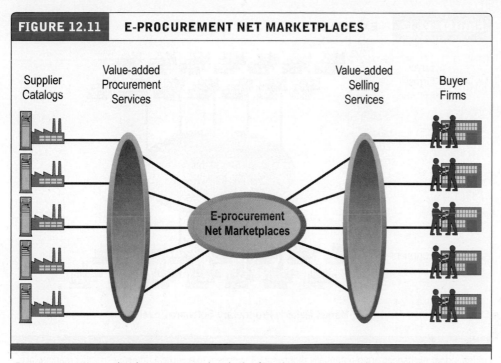

FIGURE 12.11   E-PROCUREMENT NET MARKETPLACES

E-procurement Net marketplaces aggregate hundreds of catalogs in a single marketplace and make them available to firms, often on a custom basis that reflects only the suppliers desired by the participating firms.

buyer firms into their networks, they provide distinct marketing benefits for suppliers and reduce customer acquisition costs.

Ariba stands out as one of the poster children of the B2B age, a firm born before its time. Promising to revolutionize inter-firm trade, Ariba started out in 1996 hoping to build a global business network linking buyers and sellers—sort of an eBay for business. With little revenue, the stock shot past $1,000 a share by March 2000. But sellers and buyers did not join the network in large part because they did not understand the opportunity, were too wedded to their traditional procurement processes, and did not trust outsiders to control their purchasing and vendor relationship. In September 2001, Ariba's share price tanked to $2.20. Ariba survived largely by selling software that helped large firms understand their procurement processes and costs. Finally, by 2008, large and small firms had become more sophisticated in their purchasing and supply change management practices, and Ariba's original idea of a global network of suppliers and purchasers of a wide variety of industrial goods came back to life. Today, Ariba is a leading provider of collaborative business commerce solutions (Ariba, 2013; Levy, 2010; Vance, 2010). Players in this market segment include Perfect Commerce, BravoSolution, A.T. Kearney Procurement & Analytic Solutions, and Emptoris. The very large enterprise software firms—Oracle, SAP, and JDA Software Group—now also offer procurement solutions to their customers and compete directly against the early entrants in this market.

FIGURE 12.12   EXCHANGES

Independent exchanges bring potentially thousands of suppliers to a vertical (industry-specific) marketplace to sell their goods to potentially thousands of buyer firms. Exchanges are sometimes referred to as many-to-many markets because they have many suppliers serving many buyer firms.

Exchanges

exchange

independently owned online marketplace that connects hundreds to potentially thousands of suppliers and buyers in a dynamic, real-time environment

An **exchange** is an independently owned online marketplace that connects hundreds to potentially thousands of suppliers and buyers in a dynamic, real-time environment (see **Figure 12.12**). Although there are exceptions, exchanges generally create vertical markets that focus on the spot-purchasing requirements of large firms in a single industry, such as computers and telecommunications, electronics, food, and industrial equipment. Exchanges were the prototype Internet-based marketplace in the early days of e-commerce; as noted previously, over 1,500 were created in this period, but most have failed.

Exchanges make money by charging a commission on the transaction. The pricing model can be through an online negotiation, auction, RFQ, or fixed buy-and-sell prices. The benefits offered to customers of exchanges include reduced search cost for parts and spare capacity. Other benefits include lower prices created by a global marketplace driven by competition among suppliers who would, presumably, sell goods at very low profit margins at one world-market price. The benefits offered suppliers are access to a global purchasing environment and the opportunity to unload production overruns (although at very competitive prices and low profit margins). Even though they are private intermediaries, exchanges are public in the sense of permitting any bona fide buyer or seller to participate.

Exchanges tend to be biased toward the buyer even though they are independently owned and presumably neutral. Suppliers are disadvantaged by the fact that exchanges put them in direct price competition with other similar suppliers around the globe, driving profit margins down. Exchanges have failed primarily because suppliers have refused to join them, and hence, the existing markets have very low liquidity, defeating the very purpose and benefits of an exchange. **Liquidity** is typically measured by the number of buyers and sellers in a market, the volume of transactions, and the size of transactions. You know a market is liquid when you can buy or sell just about any size order at just about any time you want. On all of these measures, many exchanges failed, resulting in a very small number of participants, few trades, and small trade value per transaction. The most common reason for not using exchanges is the absence of traditional, trusted suppliers.

While most exchanges tend to be vertical marketplaces offering direct supplies, some exchanges offer indirect inputs as well, such as electricity and power, transportation services (usually to the transportation industry), and professional services. **Table 12.3** lists a few examples of some current independent exchanges.

The following capsule descriptions of two exchanges provide insight into their origins and current functions.

Global Wine & Spirits (GWS) (Globalwinespirits.com) is somewhat unique among independent exchanges, not only as a start-up that has managed to survive, but also as a latecomer to the B2B e-commerce community. GWS opened in 1999, but did not begin to trade products online until May 2001. Based in Montreal, Quebec, GWS is operated by Mediagrif Interactive Technologies Inc., a Canadian company that operates a number of independent exchanges in a variety of industries. GWS offers a spot marketplace for wines, where wine and spirit producers offer wines for sale (recently, for instance, an Italian winery was offering 500 cases of Tuscan Chianti wine for $30 a case, with 20 days left on the offer); a "call for tenders" market, where members make offers to purchase wines and spirits; a trade database with listings of thousands of industry professionals; and a wine and spirits catalog with over 35,000 products and 6,700 companies (Globalwinespirits.com, 2013).

liquidity
typically measured by the number of buyers and sellers in a market, the volume of transactions, and the size of transactions

TABLE 12.3	EXAMPLES OF INDEPENDENT EXCHANGES
EXCHANGE	FOCUS
PowerSource Online	Computer parts exchange
Converge	Semiconductors and computer peripherals
Smarterwork	Professional services from Web design to legal advice
Active International	Trading in underutilized manufacturing capacity
IntercontinentalExchange	International online marketplace for over 600 commodities

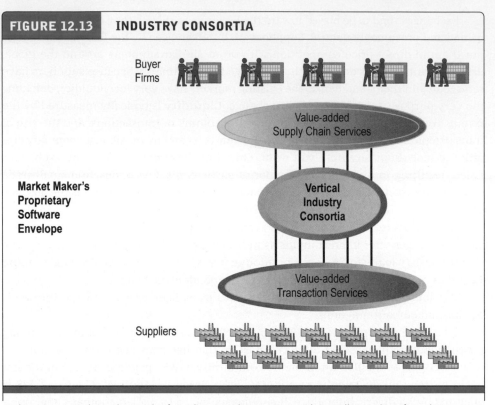

| FIGURE 12.13 | INDUSTRY CONSORTIA |

Industry consortia bring thousands of suppliers into direct contact with a smaller number of very large buyers. The market makers provide value-added software services for procurement, transaction management, shipping, and payment for both buyers and suppliers. Industry consortia are sometimes referred to as many-to-few markets, where many suppliers (albeit selected by the buyers) serve a few very large buyers, mediated by a variety of value-added services.

Inventory Locator Service (ILS) has its roots as an offline intermediary, serving as a listing service for aftermarket parts in the aerospace industry. Upon opening in 1979, ILS initially provided a telephone and fax-based directory of aftermarket parts to airplane owners and mechanics, along with government procurement professionals. As early as 1984, ILS incorporated e-mail capabilities as part of its RFQ services, and by 1998, it had begun to conduct online auctions for hard-to-find parts. In 2013, ILS maintains an Internet-accessible database of over 80 million aerospace and marine industry parts, and has also developed an eRFQ feature that helps users streamline their sourcing processes. The network's 23,000 subscribers in 93 different countries access the site over 65,000 times a day (Inventory Locator Service, 2013).

industry consortium
industry-owned vertical market that enables buyers to purchase direct inputs (both goods and services) from a limited set of invited participants

Industry Consortia

An **industry consortium** is an industry-owned vertical market that enables buyers to purchase direct inputs (both goods and services) from a limited set of invited participants (see **Figure 12.13**). Industry consortia emphasize long-term contractual purchasing, the development of stable relationships (as opposed to merely an anonymous transaction emphasis), and the creation of industry-wide data standards and synchronization efforts. Industry consortia are more focused on optimizing long-term supply relationships than independent exchanges, which tend to focus more on short-term transactions. The ultimate objective of industry consortia is the unification of supply chains within entire industries, across many tiers, through common data definitions, network standards, and computing platforms. In addition, industry consortia, unlike independent exchanges described previously, take their marching orders from the industry and not from venture capitalists or investment bankers. This means any profits from operating industry consortia are returned to industry business firms.

Industry consortia sprang up in 1999 and 2000 in part as a reaction to the earlier development of independently owned exchanges, which were viewed by large industries (such as the automotive and chemical industries) as market interlopers that would not directly serve the interests of large buyers, but would instead line their own pockets and those of their venture capital investors. Rather than "pay-to-play," large firms decided to "pay-to-own" their markets. Another concern of large firms was that Net marketplaces would work only if large suppliers and buyers participated, and only if there was liquidity. Independent exchanges were not attracting enough players to achieve liquidity. In addition, exchanges often failed to provide additional value-added services that would transform the value chain for the entire industry, including linking the new marketplaces to firms' ERP systems. A number of industry consortia now exist, with many industries having more than one (see **Table 12.4**).

The industries with the most consortia are food, metals, and chemicals, although these are not necessarily the largest consortia in terms of revenue. Many very large

TABLE 12.4	INDUSTRY CONSORTIA BY INDUSTRY (SEPTEMBER 2012)
INDUSTRY	**NAME OF INDUSTRY CONSORTIA**
Aerospace	Exostar
Automotive	SupplyOn
Chemical	Elemica
Food	Dairy.com
Hospitality	Avendra
Medical Services, Supplies	GHX (Global Healthcare Exchange)
Paper and Forest Products	PaperFiber
Shipping	OceanConnect
Textiles	The Seam (Cotton Consortium)
Transportation	Transplace

Fortune 500 and private firms are investors in several industry consortia. For instance, Cargill—the world's largest private corporation—invested in six consortia that exist at various points in Cargill's and the food industry's tangled value chain.

Industry consortia make money in a number of ways. Industry members usually pay for the creation of the consortia's capabilities and contribute initial operating capital. Then industry consortia charge buyer and seller firms transaction and subscription fees. Industry members—both buyers and sellers—are expected to reap benefits far greater than their contributions through the rationalization of the procurement process, competition among vendors, and closer relationships with vendors.

Industry consortia offer many different pricing mechanisms, ranging from auctions to fixed prices to RFQs, depending on the products and the situation. Prices can also be negotiated, and the environment, while competitive, is nevertheless restricted to a smaller number of buyers—selected, reliable, and long-term suppliers who are often viewed as "strategic industry" partners. The bias of industry consortia is clearly toward the large buyers who control access to this lucrative market channel and can benefit from competitive pricing offered by alternative suppliers. Benefits to suppliers come from access to large buyer firm procurement systems, long-term stable relationships, and large order sizes.

Industry consortia can and often do force suppliers to use the consortia's networks and proprietary software as a condition of selling to the industry's members. Although exchanges failed for a lack of suppliers and liquidity, the market power of consortia members ensures suppliers will participate, so consortia may be able to avoid the fate of voluntary exchanges. Clearly, industry consortia are at an advantage when compared to independent exchanges because, unlike the venture-capital-backed exchanges, they have deep-pocket financial backing from the very start and guaranteed liquidity based on a steady flow of large firm orders. Yet industry consortia are a relatively new phenomenon, and the long-term profitability of these consortia, especially when several consortia exist for a single industry, has yet to be demonstrated.

Exostar is one example of an industry consortium. Its founding partners include BAE Systems, Boeing, Lockheed Martin, Raytheon, and Rolls-Royce, all companies in the aerospace industry. Exostar has taken a slow but steady approach to building its technology platform. It has kept its focus on the direct procurement and supply chain needs of its largest members, and taken its time developing a portfolio of technology solutions that meet its needs. Its current products include Supply Pass, an integrated suite of tools that enables suppliers to handle buyer transactions via the Internet; SourcePass, which provides a dynamic bidding environment for buyers and sellers; and ProcurePass, which enables buyers to handle supplier transactions online, among others. As of September 2013, Exostar served a community of more than 70,000 trading partners (Exostar, 2012).

THE LONG-TERM DYNAMICS OF NET MARKETPLACES

Net marketplaces are changing rapidly because of the widespread failures of early exchanges and a growing realization by key participants that real value will derive from

B2B e-commerce only when it can change the entire procurement system, the supply chain, and the process of collaboration among firms. Several industry consortia have transformed themselves into industry data standards and synchronization forums. The consolidation of Net marketplaces has resulted in remaining firms that are much stronger and that are beginning to grow rapidly once again. In fact, B2B online transaction volumes are growing worldwide and within the United States at 20%–30% per year.

Figure 12.14 depicts some of these changes. Pure Net marketplace exchanges are moving away from the simple "electronic marketplace" vision, and toward playing a more central role in changing the procurement process. Independent exchanges are ideal buy-out candidates for industry consortia because they have often developed the technology infrastructure. In any event, consortia and exchanges are beginning to work together in selected markets. Likewise, e-distributors are securing admission to large e-procurement systems and also seeking admission to industry consortia as suppliers of indirect goods.

Other notable trends include the movement from simple transactions involving spot purchasing to longer-term contractual relationships involving both indirect and direct goods (Wise and Morrison, 2000). The complexity and duration of transactions is increasing, and both buyers and suppliers are becoming accustomed to working in a digital environment, and making less use of the fax machine and telephone. To date, Net marketplaces, as well as private industrial networks, have emerged in a

---

FIGURE 12.14   NET MARKETPLACE TRENDS

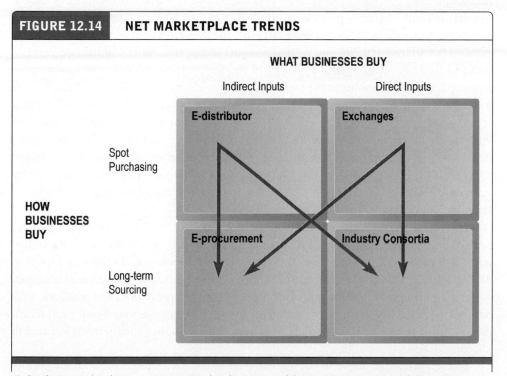

E-distributors and exchanges are migrating their business models toward more sustained, higher value-added relationships with buyer firms by providing e-procurement services and participating in industry consortia.

political climate friendly to large-scale cooperation among very large firms. However, the possibility exists that Net marketplaces may provide some firms with an ideal platform to collude on pricing, market sharing, and market access, all of which would be anti-competitive and reduce the efficiency of the marketplace.

12.3   PRIVATE INDUSTRIAL NETWORKS

Private industrial networks today form the largest part of B2B e-commerce, both on and off the Internet. Industry analysts estimate that in 2012, over 50% of B2B expenditures by large firms will be for the development of private industrial networks. Private industrial networks can be considered the foundation of the "extended enterprise," allowing firms to extend their boundaries and their business processes to include supply chain and logistics partners.

WHAT ARE PRIVATE INDUSTRIAL NETWORKS?

trans-organizational business process
process that requires at least two independent firms to perform

As noted at the beginning of this chapter, private industrial networks are direct descendants of existing EDI networks, and they are closely tied to existing ERP systems used by large firms. A private industrial network (sometimes referred to as a private trading exchange, or PTX) is a Web-enabled network for the coordination of trans-organizational business processes (sometimes also called collaborative commerce). **A trans-organizational business process** requires at least two independent firms to perform (Laudon and Laudon, 2012). For the most part, these networks originate in and closely involve the manufacturing and related support industries, and therefore we refer to them as "industrial" networks, although in the future they could just as easily apply to some services. These networks can be industry-wide, but often begin and sometimes focus on the voluntary coordination of a group of supplying firms centered about a single, very large manufacturing firm. Private industrial networks can be viewed as "extended enterprises" in the sense that they often begin as ERP systems in a single firm, and are then expanded to include (often using an extranet) the firm's major suppliers. **Figure 12.15** illustrates a private industrial network originally built by Procter & Gamble (P&G) in the United States to coordinate supply chains among its suppliers, distributors, truckers, and retailers.

In P&G's private industrial network shown in Figure 12.15, customer sales are captured at the cash register, which then initiates a flow of information back to distributors, P&G, and its suppliers. This tells P&G and its suppliers the exact level of demand for thousands of products. This information is then used to initiate production, supply, and transportation to replenish products at the distributors and retailers. This process is called an efficient customer response system (a demand-pull production model), and it relies on an equally efficient supply chain management system to coordinate the supply side.

Not surprisingly, there is not a great deal of detailed information about private industrial networks. Most companies that originate and participate in these networks

| FIGURE 12.15 | PROCTER & GAMBLE'S PRIVATE INDUSTRIAL NETWORK |

Procter & Gamble's private industrial network attempts to coordinate the trans-organizational business processes of the many firms it deals with in the consumer products industry.

view them as a competitive advantage, and therefore they are reluctant to release information about how much they cost and how they operate.

GE, Dell, Cisco Systems, Microsoft, IBM, Nike, Coca-Cola, Walmart, Nokia, and Hewlett-Packard are among the firms operating successful private industrial networks.

CHARACTERISTICS OF PRIVATE INDUSTRIAL NETWORKS

The central focus of private industrial networks is to provide an industry-wide global solution to achieve the highest levels of efficiency. The specific objectives of a private industrial network include:

- Developing efficient purchasing and selling business processes industry-wide
- Developing industry-wide resource planning to supplement enterprise-wide resource planning
- Increasing supply chain visibility—knowing the inventory levels of buyers and suppliers
- Achieving closer buyer-supplier relationships, including demand forecasting, communications, and conflict resolution
- Operating on a global scale—globalization
- Reducing industry risk by preventing imbalances of supply and demand, including developing financial derivatives, insurance, and futures markets

Private industrial networks serve different goals from Net marketplaces. Net marketplaces are primarily transaction-oriented, whereas private industrial networks focus on continuous business process coordination between companies. This can include much more than just supply chain management, such as product design, sourcing, demand forecasting, asset management, sales, and marketing. Private industrial networks do support transactions, but that is not their primary focus.

Private industrial networks usually focus on a single sponsoring company that "owns" the network, sets the rules, establishes governance (a structure of authority, rule enforcement, and control), and invites firms to participate at its sole discretion. Therefore, these networks are "private." This sets them apart from industry consortia, which are usually owned by major firms collectively through equity participation. Whereas Net marketplaces have a strong focus on indirect goods and services, private industrial networks focus on strategic, direct goods and services.

For instance, True Value is one of the largest retailer-owned hardware cooperatives with operations in 54 countries, 4,600 plus stores, and 12 regional distribution centers. The logistics are staggering to consider: they routinely process over 60,000 domestic inbound loads, and over 600 million pounds of freight. True Value imports roughly 3,500 containers through 20 international ports and 10 domestic ports. The existing inbound supply chain system was fragmented, did not permit real-time tracking of packages, and when shipments were short or damaged, could not alert stores. The supply chain was "invisible": suppliers could not see store inventory levels, and stores could not see supplier shipments. Using a Web-based solution from Sterling Commerce (an IBM company), True Value created its own private industrial network to which all suppliers, shippers, and stores have access. The network focuses on three processes: domestic prepaid shipping, domestic collect, and international direct shipping. For each process the network tracks in real time the movement of goods from suppliers to shippers, warehouses, and stores. So far, the system has led to a 57% reduction in lead time needed for orders, a 10% increase in the fill rate of orders, and an 85% reduction in back orders. If goods are delayed, damaged, or unavailable, the system alerts all parties automatically (True Value, 2013; IBM, 2011b).

Perhaps no single firm better illustrates the benefits of developing private industrial networks than Walmart, described in *Insight on Business: Walmart Develops a Private Industrial Network*.

PRIVATE INDUSTRIAL NETWORKS AND COLLABORATIVE COMMERCE

collaborative resource planning, forecasting, and replenishment (CPFR)

involves working with network members to forecast demand, develop production plans, and coordinate shipping, warehousing, and stocking activities to ensure that retail and wholesale shelf space is replenished with just the right amount of goods

Private industrial networks can do much more than just serve a supply chain and efficient customer response system. They can also include other activities of a single large manufacturing firm, such as design of products and engineering diagrams, as well as marketing plans and demand forecasting. Collaboration among businesses can take many forms and involve a wide range of activities—from simple supply chain management to coordinating market feedback to designers at supply firms (see **Figure 12.16** on page 791).

One form of collaboration—and perhaps the most profound—is industry-wide **collaborative resource planning, forecasting, and replenishment (CPFR)**, which involves working with network members to forecast demand, develop production plans, and coordinate shipping, warehousing, and stocking activities to ensure retail and wholesale shelf space is replenished with just the right amount of goods. If this goal is achieved, hundreds of millions of dollars of excess inventory and capacity could

INSIGHT ON BUSINESS

WALMART DEVELOPS A PRIVATE INDUSTRIAL NETWORK

Walmart is a well-known leader in the application of network technology to coordinate its supply chain. Walmart's supply chain is the secret sauce behind its claim of offering the lowest prices everyday. It's able to make this promise because it has possibly the most efficient B2B supply chain in the world. It doesn't hurt to also be the largest purchaser of consumer goods in the world. With sales of more than $466 billion for the fiscal year ending January 31, 2013, Walmart has been able to use information technology to achieve a decisive cost advantage over competitors. As you might imagine, the world's largest retailer also has the world's largest supply chain, with more than 60,000 suppliers worldwide. In the United States, Walmart has more than 4,600 retail stores (including Sam's Clubs). Internationally, Walmart has over 6,100 additional stores in 26 countries, giving it a total of over 10,500 retail units. The rapid expansion in Walmart's international operations will require an even more capable private industrial network than what is now in place.

In the late 1980s, Walmart developed the beginnings of collaborative commerce using an EDI-based SCM system that required its large suppliers to use Walmart's proprietary EDI network to respond to orders from Walmart purchasing managers. In 1991, Walmart expanded the capabilities of its EDI-based network by introducing Retail Link. This system connected Walmart's largest suppliers to Walmart's own inventory management system, and it required large suppliers to track actual sales by stores and to replenish supplies as dictated by demand and following rules imposed by Walmart. Walmart also introduced financial payment systems that ensure that Walmart does not own the goods until they arrive and are shelved.

In 1997, Walmart moved Retail Link to an extranet that allowed suppliers to directly link over the Internet into Walmart's inventory management system. In 2000, Walmart hired an outside firm to upgrade Retail Link from being a supply chain management tool toward a more collaborative forecasting, planning, and replenishment system. Using demand aggregation software provided by Atlas Metaprise Software, Walmart purchasing agents can now aggregate demand from Walmart's 5,000 separate stores in the United States into a single RFQ from suppliers. This gives Walmart tremendous clout with even the largest suppliers. Previously, Walmart's foreign location buyers relied on a mix of telephones, fax, and e-mail to communicate their spending forecasts. The Atlas system allows them to submit forecasts via the Internet. Walmart headquarters issues worldwide RFQs for all stores. The Atlas software helps Walmart purchasing agents select a winning bid and negotiate final contracts.

In addition, suppliers can now immediately access information on inventories, purchase orders, invoice status, and sales forecasts, based on 104 weeks of online, real-time, item-level data. The system does not require smaller supplier firms to adopt expensive EDI software solutions. Instead, they can use standard browsers and PCs loaded with free software from Walmart. There are now over 20,000 suppliers—small and large—participating in Walmart's network.

In 2002, Walmart switched to an entirely Internet-based private network. Walmart adopted AS2, a software package from iSoft Corporation, a Dallas-based software company. AS2 implemented EDI-INT (an Internet-based standard version of EDI), and the result was a radical reduction in communications costs. In 2007, Walmart's rapid

(continued)

growth, especially global operations, forced it to go outside for its financial services operation systems. Walmart hired SAP, an enterprise software management firm, to build a global financial management system for Walmart. Walmart had finally started to outgrow its homegrown systems.

By 2013, Walmart's B2B supply chain management system had mastered on a global scale the following capabilities: cross docking, demand planning, forecasting, inventory management, strategic sourcing, and distribution management. The future of Walmart's SCM lies in business analytics—working smarter—rather than simply making the movement and tracking of goods more efficient. For instance, in 2012 Walmart purchased Quintiq Inc., a supply chain management tool for improving load assignment and dispatch of trucks for large retailers. Quintiq's software will enable Walmart's managers to optimize the loading of its trucks and to reduce the time required to supply its retail stores.

Despite its success is building a world-class supply chain to support 4,600 plus stores, Walmart was not well prepared to deal with online sales, or to compete with the online champion, Amazon. From the beginning, Walmart separated out its fledgling e-commerce operation as a separate company with a much lower priority for investment than its physical stores. It was late to invest in an Internet supply chain because the separate companies could never agree on whether it was a good investment. Instead, Walmart's Internet supply chain is a work in progress, relying on employees at some of the stores to pick online orders and ship from the store, while other orders are handled by a few Internet order warehouses. Last year, Walmart had $7.7 billion in online sales (compared to Amazon's $66 billion),

and this represented less than 2% of its $466 billion in sales. In 2013, Walmart is creating a new inventory and logistics system that will combine the inventory information from 4,600 stores and 158 warehouses and then decide the most efficient way to pick and ship the order.

Like other large global firms, Walmart's global supply chain has been criticized for exploiting labor in underdeveloped countries where it buys products and in home markets where it sells them, bribing officials to look the other way, destroying environments, and wasting energy. In response to critics, Walmart has taken a number of steps. Walmart has set a goal of reducing carbon emissions in its supply chain by 20 million metric tons by 2015, and a goal of 100% renewable energy use in the United States. Walmart has made less progress in its labor policies: In January 2012, the ABP pension fund blacklisted Walmart for failing to comply with the United Nations' Global Compact principles. The Global Compact presents a set of core values relating to human rights, labor standards, the environment, and anti-corruption efforts. In April 2012 the Department of Justice opened an investigation into widespread allegations that Walmart had bribed Mexican officials to expand its stores and supply chain in Mexico.

Walmart's success spurred its competitors in the retail industry to develop industry-wide private industrial networks such as Global NetXchange (now Agentrics) in an effort to duplicate the success of Walmart. Walmart executives have said Walmart would not join these networks, or any industry-sponsored consortium or independent exchange, because doing so would only help its competitors achieve what Walmart has already accomplished with Retail Link.

SOURCES: "Wal-Mart's E-Stumble With Amazon," by Shelly Banso, *Wall Street Journal*, June 19, 2013; "The Trouble Lurking on Walmart's Empty Shelves," by Bill Saporito, *Time Business*, April 9, 2013; "Wal-Mart Toughens Supplier Policies," by Shelly Banjo, *Wall Street Journal*, January 21, 2013; "How Walmart is Changing Supplier Sustainability-Again," by Aran Rice, Renewablechoice.com, May 30, 2012; "Wal-Mart's Dirty Partners," by Josh Eidelson, Salon.com, July 6, 2012; "The Walmart Model and the Human Cost of Our Low Priced Goods," by Juan De Lara, *The Guardian*, July 25, 2012; "Supply Chain News: Walmart, Sustainability, and Troubles in Mexico," by Dan Gilmore, *Supply Chain Digest*, April 26, 2012; "Retail Giant Optimizes Supply Chain Processes With Quintiq Software," *Supply&Demand Chain Executive*, February 15, 2012; "Walmart Adds $7 Billion Through Acquisition in 2011," by Nate Holmes, Instore-Trends.com, May 11, 2012.

FIGURE 12.16   **PIECES OF THE COLLABORATIVE COMMERCE PUZZLE**

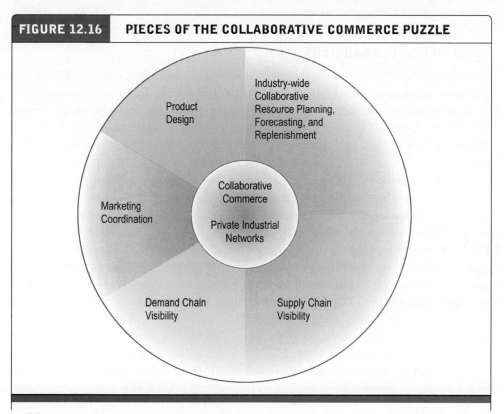

Collaborative commerce involves many cooperative activities among supply and sales firms closely interacting with a single large firm through a private industrial network.

---

be wrung out of an industry. This activity alone is likely to produce the largest benefits and justify the cost of developing private industrial networks.

A second area of collaboration is *demand chain visibility*. In the past, it was impossible to know where excess capacity or supplies existed in the supply and distribution chains. For instance, retailers might have significantly overstocked shelves, but suppliers and manufacturers—not knowing this—might be building excess capacity or supplies for even more production. These excess inventories would raise costs for the entire industry and create extraordinary pressures to discount merchandise, reducing profits for everyone.

A third area of collaboration is *marketing coordination and product design*. Manufacturers that use or produce highly engineered parts use private industrial networks to coordinate both their internal design and marketing activities, as well as related activities of their supply and distribution chain partners. By involving their suppliers in product design and marketing initiatives, manufacturing firms can ensure that the parts produced actually fulfill the claims of marketers. On the reverse flow, feedback from customers can be used by marketers to speak directly to product designers at the firm and its suppliers. For the first time, "closed loop marketing" (customer feedback directly impacting design and production, described in Chapter 6) can become a reality.

IMPLEMENTATION BARRIERS

Although private industrial networks represent a large part of the future of B2B, there are many barriers to its complete implementation. Participating firms are required to share sensitive data with their business partners, up and down the supply chain. What in the past was considered proprietary and secret must now be shared. In a digital environment, it can be difficult to control the limits of information sharing. Information a firm freely gives to its largest customer may end up being shared with its closest competitor.

Integrating private industrial networks into existing enterprise systems and EDI networks poses a significant investment of time and money. The leading providers of enterprise systems to Fortune 500 companies (Oracle, IBM, and SAP) do offer B2B modules, and supply chain management capabilities, that can be added to their existing software suites. Nevertheless, implementing these modules is a very expensive proposition in part because the procurement side of many Fortune 500 firms is so fragmented and out-of-date. For smaller firms, cloud computing and software as a service (SaaS) alternatives are appearing on the market, which offer far less-expensive supply chain management capabilities.

Adopting private industrial networks also requires a change in mindset and behavior for employees. Essentially, employees must shift their loyalties from the firm to the wider trans-organizational enterprise and recognize that their fate is intertwined with the fate of their suppliers and distributors. Suppliers in turn are required to change the way they manage and allocate their resources because their own production is tightly coupled with the demands of their private industrial network partners. All participants in the supply and distribution chains, with the exception of the large network owner, lose some of their independence, and must initiate large behavioral change programs in order to participate (Laudon and Laudon, 2012).

12.4 CASE STUDY

Elemica:
Cooperation, Collaboration, and Community

I t may seem unusual to refer to an entire industry as a "community," a word reserved typically for collections of people who more or less know one another. Trade associations are one example of an industrial community. Trade associations form in an effort to pursue the interests of all members in the community although usually they do not include customers in the community. Elemica is a B2B industry trading hub aiming to revolutionize the entire supply chain of the chemical, tire and rubber, energy, and selected manufacturing industries worldwide. Elemica's purpose is not just to foster cooperation on a one-to-one inter-firm basis, or just to foster collaboration on multi-firm projects, but instead to lift all boats on an industry tide by making all firms more efficient. Elemica is one of the few survivors of the early B2B e-commerce years. In 2013, Elemica connects over 5,000 companies to its network and clears over $200 billion in transactions a year. Clients include BASF, BP, Continental, The Dow Chemical Company, DuPont, The Goodyear Tire & Rubber Company, LANXESS, Michelin, Rhodia, Shell, Sumitomo Chemical, and Yokohama.

Copyright © 2013, Elemica, Inc.

Elemica is a global e-commerce company originally founded by 22 leading corporations in the chemical industry (including oil and industrial gases) to provide cloud-based order management and supply chain applications and services. A single platform provides one-stop shopping so that companies can buy and sell products to one another through their own enterprise systems or using a Web alternative. It also helps companies automate all of their business processes, creating efficiencies and economies of scale that lead to an improved bottom line.

How does Elemica achieve community among a diverse, global collection of firms where firms are often both customers and vendors to one another? It unites community members by linking together their enterprise systems. This is the "social glue" that sets Elemica apart. This "super platform" permits companies to communicate with one another electronically and to conduct transactions, handle logistics, and keep the books. The Elemica commerce platform has effectively standardized industry business transactions for all network members regardless of the type of enterprise system they have, and it's leveled the playing field for trade partners who are less technically sophisticated. This neutral platform facilitates millions of transactions for industry suppliers, customers, and third-party providers. In this sense, Elemica is one of the most sophisticated technology platforms in the B2B space.

One of the largest investments for a company is its enterprise system. Despite these investments, intercompany relationships—the backbone of their supply chain—are often left to outdated and unreliable processes. These shortcomings cost billions in lost productivity, revenue, and profit. Elemica's eCommerce platform changes that. It helps its clients leverage their enterprise system investment by incorporating transactions to external trade partners. Elemica's QuickLink ERP connectivity enables companies to link their internal IT systems through a neutral platform so that information is moved into each company's database while maintaining confidentiality and security. The chemical and oil industries were among the first users of enterprise systems (referred to in the early years as "manufacturing resource planning systems"). These large-scale systems were developed by single firms in order to rationalize and control the manufacturing process. They achieved this objective by identifying the outputs, inputs, and processes involved in manufacturing and automating key elements including inventory control and planning, process control, warehousing and storage, and shipping/logistics. If a company needed to produce 10 tons of polyethylene plastic, its enterprise system could tell it precisely how many tons of petrochemical inputs were required, when they should be delivered to manufacturing, the machinery and labor force required to manufacture the product, how long it would take, where it would be stored, and how it would be shipped. The systems can estimate the cost at any stage.

Elemica facilitates transactions of all types including order processing and billing, and logistics management. However, unlike some other companies in the field, Elemica does not buy, sell, or own raw material products. Instead it acts as an intermediary, or hub, linking companies together to automate confidential transactions. Like eBay or a credit card company, Elemica's revenue comes from charging transaction fees on a per-transaction basis. Its network of clients opens the door for companies to do business with all other connected buyers and sellers.

Elemica offers a variety of services for suppliers and customers, enabling them to automate both their business processes and internal purchasing. A modular, cloud-based solution simplifies sales, procurement, and financial processes; integrates supply chain partners to diminish communication barriers; and reduces overhead and errors.

Elemica integrates information flow among global trading partners using a cloud-based business process network. Each client needs only a single connection to Elemica, and Elemica manages the connections to that company's external trade partners. That means a company needs only maintain one connection to Elemica (important when it's time for enterprise system maintenance or upgrade) rather than maintain a variable number of connections and infrastructure to all its trade partners. Once a company connects to Elemica, it can have access to thousands of other customers. Clients are charged for the service based on volume of usage. This is much more efficient than older EDI solutions to inter-company transactions. Elemica provides the platform for collaborative commerce through a fully automated integrated network of suppliers, customers, and third-party providers.

Elemica offers cloud-based solutions for four areas: Logistics Management, Customer Management, Supplier Management, and Sourcing Management. Using these solutions, companies can automate ordering, invoicing, shipment tracking, and day-to-day business operations. Companies can sign up for one or more solutions depending on their needs.

Here's an example of how Elemica works. Let's say you need to order vinyl acetate from one of your suppliers. You put the order into your internal enterprise system, the order is automatically routed to Elemica, Elemica routes the order to your supplier's internal enterprise system, and you get a confirmed receipt of the order. Elemica's QuickLink Network ensures the accuracy of the item number and purchase order number and sends an alert if there's an issue. Once an order is confirmed, Elemica's platform can be leveraged to plan and coordinate delivery and automatically send an invoice and submit payment. For small or medium firms that may not have an enterprise system, Elemica has a Web portal with online software that allows firms to participate in the community with suppliers and customers. The platform offers a closed-loop process, end to end, from the purchase order, to acknowledgments, load tenders and responses, carrier status updates, and dock scheduling. All of this takes place in a few seconds with little or no human intervention. Elemica has even developed a solution that allows a customer to send a purchase order via e-mail or a print driver (alleviating fax processes) that is then routed to Elemica. The company then routes it to the supplier in its preferred format, integrated with its enterprise system as though it were a true electronic order. This holistic approach to order management allows suppliers to automate the process with both strategic and core customers, without asking its customers to change their processes. It's a win-win situation for suppliers and customers.

Unlike the automobile industry or the airline industry, where a few companies dominate, the $1.3 trillion chemical industry is made up of many companies of all sizes. The top 10 companies generate only 10% of the industry's annual revenue total, and the largest player, Dow Chemical, is responsible for 2%. In addition, unlike many other industries, chemical companies often buy the output from other chemical companies to use as raw materials for their products. Thus, chemical companies are often customers of one another as well as competitors.

Senior leaders at some of the larger chemical companies were aware of changes in technology that made the adoption of information technology and the tools of e-commerce more appealing. The questions were how to best use these advances to benefit their businesses and how to establish industry standards for electronic transactions to make them accessible and attainable for all. Leaders from companies such as Dow Chemical and DuPont began discussing this subject and determined that a cooperative alliance would be the most efficient way to move forward. They were met with initial skepticism by marketing and sales staff, worried that online procurement would negatively affect relationships. Further, senior corporate leadership wasn't sure that e-commerce would have any use in the chemical industry at all. And companies were cautious about the expense of investing in the infrastructure necessary for e-commerce.

However, there were compelling opportunities that were impossible to dismiss, including lowering costs, creating closer connections with customers and suppliers, and differentiating companies on something other than price. At the same time, new start-ups like e-Chemicals and PlasticsNet were making traditional chemical companies nervous. What would happen if their efforts to use information technology to streamline an inefficient supply chain helped them capture market share? In other words, if the more traditional companies didn't move forward, they might end up losing the revenue race.

When Dow began looking at start-ups that were using e-commerce and talking to their customers, they found that customers were concerned about making an investment to establish online connections with multiple firms. Dow and DuPont decided that the best and most economically efficient option was to offer customers the choice of a neutral one-to-one link. This would remove the obstacle of multiple connections. A strong, third-party network addressed the community concern about loss of control. The two companies decided to create and invest in a neutral e-commerce company, partnering with other companies to create the critical mass needed to make it viable.

In 1999, the corporate boards of Dow and DuPont agreed that there were major advantages to online transaction processing and additional online connections among buyers and sellers. Since time and cost considerations made multiple connections unattractive to customers, a "hub" concept was adopted. It was also decided that a neutral community was the best approach.

All participants shared the common goal of creating a neutral platform to facilitate inter-company transactions and enhance business processes. Dow and DuPont also reviewed the concept with the relevant regulatory agencies and received up-front approval. Ultimately, 22 global chemical companies were involved in the launch of Elemica.

When Elemica opened its doors in 1999, there were 50 start-up B2B e-commerce companies in the chemical industry. Nearly all of these B2B companies were third-party owned Net marketplaces suitable at best for short-term sourcing of some direct inputs. In 2013, only a handful of these Net marketplaces for the chemical industry remain. Elemica focuses on building longer-term business relationships by creating committed and contractual supply chains. The company acts only as a facilitator of business transactions and does not directly buy and sell chemical products.

Elemica's business model has been successful primarily because it addresses the needs of chemical, tire and rubber, energy, and selected manufacturing companies of all sizes. It does this by offering multiple options for connecting to its hub system, multiple products that can be used alone or in combination, and by ensuring that only one connection integrated with a client's enterprise system is needed for all transactions. Customers can use Elemica, and take advantage of the technology it offers, without purchasing an additional internal system.

With Elemica, companies benefit from improved operational efficiency, reduced costs due to elimination of redundant systems and excess inventory, and a much higher percentage of safe and reliable deliveries. The flexibility of Elemica's solutions and network combines simplification, standardization, and efficiency. And clients have increased their profitability and improved cash flow through faster payment.

A number of very large companies use Elemica's platform. In Europe, Shell Oil started using Elemica after recognizing that it had ongoing problems with the coordination of paperwork processing and deliveries. Truck drivers would arrive at delivery sites and wait up to two hours while paperwork was filled out. These delays were costing Shell money. Once Shell began using Elemica, things improved. Today, paperwork is processed 24 hours a day, and truck waiting time has been cut from an average of two hours to an average of 15 minutes. Given this success, Shell continues to expand its relationship with Elemica.

Dow Chemical began to transition to full procurement automation with Elemica in 2007. More than 300 of their MRO suppliers are now linked to Elemica's platform. Errors are down 75%, and Dow has achieved economies of scale that have led to meaningful financial savings. Elemica helped Dow unify multiple, disparate business processes, reduced the cost of getting contracted items from suppliers, and increased efficiency in procurement, operations, IT, and accounts payable.

Air Products & Chemicals, Inc. is a global provider of gases and chemicals with 22,000 employees worldwide, and $10 billion in revenue. A major customer asked them for online ordering, but the initial method proposed would have required considerable additional work for both parties. Since both companies were connected to Elemica, there was a better option—the Elemica Supply Chain Hosted Solution.

Elemica has also developed a sustainability program. In November 2011, Elemica received the Green Supply Chain Award from an industry group for incorporating sustainability goals into its supply chain services. Elemica says it has delivered more than 160 million messages since 2004, which equates to 1,666 cubic meters of landfill space, 18,160,002 liters of water saved in paper production, 17,434 trees, and 196,128 kilograms of CO_2 emissions. In February 2012, Elemica introduced a transportation management solution (ETM) powered by Oracle. Available as a cloud-based software-as-a-service (SaaS) on a subscription basis, ETM will enable Elemica member firms to optimize logistics and transportation business processes, resulting in supply chain savings and a reduction of carbon emissions.

SOURCES: "The Social Side of Supply Chain Management," by Adrian Gonzalez, *Supply Chain Management Review*, August 2013; "Next Generation Supply Chain Networks Enable More Robust Collaborative Workflows Across Trading Partners to Increase Value," Becky Boyd, *Market Wired*, July 2, 2013; "Elemica Named to Inbound Logistics Top 100 Logistics IT Provider Awards," *Wall Street Journal*, April 24, 2013; "About Elemica," Elemica.com, August 31, 2013; "Elemica Introduces Transportation Management Solution," Elemica Corporation, February 16, 2012; "Elemica Wins 2011 SDCExec Green Supply Chain Award for Helping Clients Incorporate Sustainability Within Their Supply Chains," Elemica Corporation, November 29, 2011; "Elemica Procurement Case Study: Dow," Elemica Corporation, September 2010; "Elemica Order Management Case Study: BP," Elemica Corporation, September 2010; "Elemica Case Study: LanXess," Elemica Corporation, September 2010; "Elemica and Rubber-Network Merge," SDCExec.com, August 25, 2009; "Case Study: Elemica," http://www.ebusiness-watch. org/studies, August 25, 2009; "Once Elemica Tackled the Hard Part, the Rest Was Easy," SupplyChainBrain.com, August 5, 2009; "Elemica Merger with Rubber Network," Philly.com, August 3, 2009; "Elemica Automates B2B Transactions Between Trading Partners—Speeding Up Orders by 78%," Softwareag.com, January 2009; "Top Chemical Company Selects Elemica's Business Process Network to Automate Global Procurement," Redorbit.com, December 18, 2008.

In May 2013 Elemica introduced a new network platform that it calls a Supply Chain Operating Network (SCON), which has built-in social collaboration tools. The idea is to give clients the ability to discover, create, and build social business networks—just as Facebook provides its users the ability to build online social networks. SCON provides its clients with a cloud-based network for establishing business relationships and SaaS (software as a service) applications to carry on trading once the relationship is established. Instead of creating hundreds of one-to-one EDI connections with partners, and then building their own software applications, firms can now more easily just connect to the network and find all the tools they need to trade with many partners.

Case Study Questions

1. If you were a small chemical company, what concerns would you have about joining Elemica?

2. Elemica provides a community for participants where they can transact, coordinate, and cooperate to produce products for less. Yet these firms also compete with one another when they sell chemicals to end-user firms in the automobile, airline, and manufacturing industries. How is this possible?

3. Review the concept of private industrial networks and describe how Elemica illustrates many of the features of such a network.

12.5 REVIEW

KEY CONCEPTS

- **Define B2B commerce and understand its scope and history.**

Before the Internet, business-to-business transactions were referred to simply as *trade* or the *procurement process*. Today, we use the term *B2B commerce* to describe all types of computer-assisted inter-firm trade, and the term *Internet-based B2B commerce* or *B2B e-commerce* to describe specifically that portion of B2B commerce that uses the Internet to assist firms in buying and selling a variety of goods to each other. The process of conducting trade among businesses consumes many business resources, including the time spent by employees processing orders, making and approving purchasing decisions, searching for products, and arranging for their purchase, shipment, receipt, and payment. Across the economy, this amounts to trillions of dollars spent annually on procurement processes. If a significant portion of this inter-firm trade could be automated and parts of the procurement process assisted by the Internet, millions or even trillions of dollars could be freed up for other uses, resulting in increased productivity and increased national economic wealth.

In order to understand the history of B2B commerce, you must understand several key stages including:

- *Automated order entry systems*, developed in the 1970s, used the telephone to send digital orders to companies. Telephone modems were placed in the offices of the customers for a particular business. This enabled procurement managers to directly access the firm's inventory database to automatically reorder products.

- *EDI* or *electronic data interchange*, developed in the late 1970s, is a communications standard for sharing various procurement documents including invoices, purchase orders, shipping bills, product stocking numbers (SKUs), and settlement information for an industry. It was developed to reduce the costs, delays, and errors inherent in the manual exchange of documents.

- *Electronic storefronts* emerged in the 1990s along with the commercialization of the Internet. They are online catalogs containing the products that are made available to the general public by a single vendor.

- *Net marketplaces* emerged in the late 1990s as a natural extension and scaling-up of the electronic storefront. The essential characteristic of all Net marketplaces is that they bring hundreds of suppliers, each with its own electronic catalog, together with potentially thousands of purchasing firms to form a single Internet-based marketplace.

- *Private industrial networks* also emerged in the late 1990s with the commercialization of the Internet as a natural extension of EDI systems and the existing close relationships that developed between large industrial firms and their suppliers.

Before you can understand each of the different types of Net marketplaces, you must be familiar with several other key concepts:

- *Seller-side solutions* are owned by the suppliers of goods and are seller-biased markets that only display goods from a single seller. Customers benefit because these systems reduce the costs of inventory replenishment and are paid for mainly by the suppliers. Automated order entry systems are seller-side solutions.

- *Buyer-side solutions* are owned by the buyers of goods and are buyer-biased markets because they reduce procurement costs for the buyer. Sellers also benefit because the cost of serving a company's customers is reduced. EDI systems are buyer-side solutions.

- *Vertical markets* provide expertise and products targeted to a specific industry. EDI systems usually serve vertical markets.

- *Horizontal markets* serve a myriad of different industries. Electronic storefronts are an example of a horizontal market in that they tend to carry a wide variety of products that are useful to any number of different industries.

■ **Understand the procurement process, the supply chain, and collaborative commerce.**

- The *procurement process* refers to the way business firms purchase the goods they need in order to produce the goods they will ultimately sell to consumers. Firms purchase goods from a set of suppliers who in turn purchase their inputs from a set of suppliers. These firms are linked in a series of connected transactions.

- The *supply chain* is the series of transactions that links sets of firms that do business with each other. It includes not only the firms themselves but also the relationships between them and the processes that connect them.

There are seven steps in the procurement process:
- Searching for suppliers for specific products
- Qualifying the sellers and the products they sell
- Negotiating prices, credit terms, escrow requirements, and quality requirements
- Scheduling delivery
- Issuing purchase orders
- Sending invoices
- Shipping the product

Each step is composed of separate substeps that must be recorded in the information systems of the buyer, seller, and shipper. There are two different types of procurements and two different methods of purchasing goods:
- *Purchases of direct goods*—goods that are directly involved in the production process.
- *Purchases of indirect goods*—goods needed to carry out the production process but that are not directly involved in creating the end product.
- *Contract purchases*—long-term agreements to buy a specified amount of a product. There are prespecified quality requirements and prespecified terms.
- *Spot purchases*—for acquisition of goods that meet the immediate needs of a firm. Indirect purchases are most often made on a spot-purchase basis in a large marketplace that includes many suppliers.

The term *multi-tier supply chain* is used to describe the complex series of transactions that exists between a single firm with multiple primary suppliers, the secondary suppliers who do business with those primary suppliers, and the tertiary suppliers who do business with the secondary suppliers.

Trends in supply chain management (the activities that firms and industries use to coordinate the key players in their procurement process) include:
- *Supply chain simplification,* which refers to the reduction of the size of a firm's supply chain. Firms today generally prefer to work closely with a strategic group of suppliers in order to reduce both product costs and administrative costs. Long-term contract purchases containing prespecified product quality requirements and prespecified timing goals have been shown to improve end-product quality and ensure uninterrupted production.
- *Supply chain management systems,* which coordinate and link the activities of suppliers, shippers, and order entry systems to automate the order entry process from start to finish, including the purchase, production, and moving of a product from a supplier to a purchasing firm.
- *Collaborative commerce,* which is a direct extension of supply chain management systems as well as supply chain simplification. It is the use of digital technologies to permit the supplier and the purchaser to share sensitive company information in order to collaboratively design, develop, build, and manage products throughout their life cycles.

- ■ **Identify the main types of B2B commerce: Net marketplaces and private industrial networks.**

There are two generic types of B2B commerce and many different subtypes within those two main categories of Internet commerce:

- *Net marketplaces,* which are also referred to as exchanges or hubs, assemble hundreds to thousands of sellers and buyers in a single digital marketplace on the Internet. They can be owned by either the buyer or the seller, or they can operate as independent intermediaries between the buyer and seller.
- *Private industrial networks* bring together a small number of strategic business partners who collaborate with one another to develop highly efficient supply chains and to satisfy customer demand for product. They are by far the largest form of B2B commerce.

■ **Understand the four types of Net marketplaces.**

There are four main types of "pure" Net marketplaces:

- *E-distributors* are independently owned intermediaries that offer industrial customers a single source from which to make spot purchases of indirect or MRO goods. E-distributors operate in a horizontal market that serves many different industries with products from many different suppliers.
- *E-procurement Net marketplaces* are independently owned intermediaries connecting hundreds of online suppliers offering millions of MRO goods to business firms who pay a fee to join the market. E-procurement Net marketplaces operate in a horizontal market in which long-term contractual purchasing agreements are used to buy indirect goods.
- *Exchanges* are independently owned online marketplaces that connect hundreds to thousands of suppliers and buyers in a dynamic real-time environment. They are typically vertical markets in which spot purchases can be made for direct inputs (both goods and services). Exchanges make money by charging a commission on each transaction.
- *Industry consortia* are industry-owned vertical markets where long-term contractual purchases of direct inputs can be made from a limited set of invited participants. Consortia serve to reduce supply chain inefficiencies by unifying the supply chain for an industry through a common network and computing platform.

■ **Identify the major trends in the development of Net marketplaces.**

- In the early days of e-commerce, independent exchanges were the prototype Internet-based marketplace and over 1,500 of them were created; however, most of them did not succeed. The main reason independent exchanges failed is that they did not attract enough players to achieve liquidity (measured by the number of buyers and sellers in the market, the transaction volume, and the size of the transactions).
- Industry consortia sprang up partly in reaction to the earlier development of independently owned exchanges that were viewed by large industries as interlopers who would not directly serve their needs. Industry consortia are profitable because they charge the large buyer firms transaction and subscription fees, but the rationalization of the procurement process, the competition among the vendors, and the closer relationship with the vendors are benefits

that more than offset the costs of membership to the firms. However, the long-term profitability of consortia has yet to be proven.

- The failure of the early exchanges is one reason Net marketplaces are changing so rapidly. Participants have come to realize that the real value of B2B e-commerce will only be realized when it succeeds in changing the entire procurement system, the supply chain, and the process of collaboration among firms.

■ **Identify the role of private industrial networks in transforming the supply chain.**

- Private industrial networks, which presently dominate B2B commerce, are Web-enabled networks for coordinating trans-organizational business processes (collaborative commerce). These networks range in scope from a single firm to an entire industry.

- Although the central purpose of private industrial networks is to provide industry-wide global solutions to achieve the highest levels of efficiency, they generally start with a single sponsoring company that "owns" the network. This differentiates private industrial networks from industry consortia that are usually owned collectively by major firms through equity participation.

- Private industrial networks are transforming the supply chain by focusing on continuous business process coordination between companies. This coordination includes much more than just transaction support and supply chain management. Product design, demand forecasting, asset management, and sales and marketing plans can all be coordinated among network members.

■ **Understand the role of private industrial networks in supporting collaborative commerce.**

Collaboration among businesses can take many forms and involve a wide range of activities. Some of the forms of collaboration used by private industrial networks include the following:

- *CPFR* or *industry-wide collaborative resource planning, forecasting, and replenishment* involves working with network members to forecast demand, develop production plans, and coordinate shipping, warehousing, and stocking activities. The goal is to ensure that retail and wholesale shelf space is precisely maintained.

- *Supply chain and distribution chain visibility* refers to the fact that, in the past, it was impossible to know where excess capacity existed in a supply or distribution chain. Eliminating excess inventories by halting the production of overstocked goods can raise the profit margins for all network members because products will no longer need to be discounted in order to move them off the shelves.

- *Marketing and product design collaboration* can be used to involve a firm's suppliers in product design and marketing activities as well as in the related activities of their supply and distribution chain partners. This can ensure that the parts used to build a product live up to the claims of the marketers. Collaborative commerce applications used in a private industrial network can also make possible closed loop marketing in which customer feedback will directly impact product design.

QUESTIONS

1. Explain the differences among total inter-firm trade, B2B commerce, and B2B e-commerce.
2. What are the key attributes of an electronic storefront? What early technology are they descended from?
3. List at least five potential benefits of B2B e-commerce.
4. Name and define the two distinct types of procurements firms make. Explain the difference between the two.
5. Name and define the two methods of purchasing goods.
6. Define the term *supply chain* and explain what SCM systems attempt to do. What does supply chain simplification entail?
7. Explain the difference between a horizontal market and a vertical market.
8. How do the value chain management services provided by e-procurement companies benefit buyers? What services do they provide to suppliers?
9. What are the three dimensions that characterize an e-procurement market based on its business functionality? Name two other market characteristics of an e-procurement Net marketplace.
10. Identify and briefly explain the anti-competitive possibilities inherent in Net marketplaces.
11. List three of the objectives of a private industrial network.
12. What is the main reason why many of the independent exchanges developed in the early days of e-commerce failed?
13. Explain the difference between an industry consortium and a private industrial network.
14. What is CPFR, and what benefits could it achieve for the members of a private industrial network?
15. What are the barriers to the complete implementation of private industrial networks?

PROJECTS

1. Choose an industry and a B2B vertical market maker that interests you. Investigate the site and prepare a report that describes the size of the industry served, the type of Net marketplace provided, the benefits promised by the site for both suppliers and purchasers, and the history of the company. You might also investigate the bias (buyer versus seller), ownership (suppliers, buyers, independents), pricing mechanism(s), scope and focus, and access (public versus private) of the Net marketplace.

2. Examine the Web site of one of the e-distributors listed in Figure 12.9, and compare and contrast it to one of the Web sites listed for e-procurement Net marketplaces. If you were a business manager of a medium-sized firm, how would you decide where to purchase your indirect inputs—from an e-distributor or an e-procurement Net marketplace? Write a short report detailing your analysis.

3. Assume you are a procurement officer for an office furniture manufacturer of steel office equipment. You have a single factory located in the Midwest with 2,000 employees. You sell about 40% of your office furniture to retail-oriented catalog outlets such as Quill in response to specific customer orders, and the remainder of your output is sold to resellers under long-term contracts. You have a choice of purchasing raw steel inputs—mostly cold-rolled sheet steel—from an exchange and/or from an industry consortium. Which alternative would you choose and why? Prepare a presentation for management supporting your position.

References

CHAPTER 1

Aguiar, Mark and Erik Hurst. "Life-Cycle Prices and Production." *American Economic Review* 97:5, 1533-1559. (January 1, 2008).

Alessandria, George. "Consumer Search, Price Dispersion, and International Relative Price Fluctuations." *International Economic Review* 50:3, 803-829 (September 1, 2009).

Bailey, Joseph P. *Intermediation and Electronic Markets: Aggregation and Pricing in Internet Commerce*. Ph. D., Technology, Management and Policy, Massachusetts Institute of Technology (1998a).

Bakos, Yannis. "Reducing Buyer Search Costs: Implications for Electronic Marketplaces." *Management Science* (December 1997).

Banerjee, Suman and Chakravarty, Amiya. "Price Setting and Price Discovery Strategies with a Mix of Frequent and Infrequent Internet Users." (April 15, 2005). SSRN: http://ssrn.com/abstract=650706.

Baye, Michael R. "Price Dispersion in the Lab and on the Internet: Theory and Evidence." *Rand Journal of Economics* (2004).

Baye, Michael R., John Morgan, and Patrick Scholten. "Temporal Price Dispersion: Evidence from an Online Consumer Electronics Market." *Journal of Interactive Marketing* (January 2004).

Brynjolfsson, Erik, and Michael Smith. "Frictionless Commerce? A Comparison of Internet and Conventional Retailers." *Management Science* (April 2000).

Buck, Stephanie. "The Beginner's Guide to Instagram." Mashable.com (May 29, 2012).

Bureau of Economic Analysis, U.S. Department of Commerce. "Table 3: Gross Domestic Product and Related Measures: Level and Change from Preceding Period." www.bea.gov (accessed May 10, 2013).

comScore. "comScore Releases April 2013 U.S. Online Video Rankings." (May 22, 2013a).

comScore. "comScore Media Metrix Ranks Top 50 U.S. Web Properties for May 2013." (June 24, 2013b).

eBay, Inc. "eBay Inc. Reports Strong Second Quarter 2013 Results." (July 17, 2013).

eMarketer, Inc. (Jeffrey Grau). "US Retail Ecommerce: 2013 Forecast and Comparative Estimates." (April 2013a).

eMarketer, Inc. "Internet Users and Penetration Worldwide, 2011-2017." (April 2013b).

eMarketer, Inc. (Krista Garcia). "Facebook Commerce: Reaching Shoppers Where They Socialize." (January 2012a).

eMarketer, Inc. "US Daily Deal Site Revenues, 2011–2016 (billions)." (September 17, 2012b).

Evans, Philip, and Thomas S. Wurster. "Getting Real About Virtual Commerce." *Harvard Business Review* (November-December 1999).

Evans, Philip, and Thomas S. Wurster. "Strategy and the New Economics of Information." *Harvard Business Review* (September-October 1997).

Forrester Research. "Forrester Research Web Influenced Retail Sales Forecast, 2011–2016 (US)." (August 3, 2012).

Ghose, Anindya, and Yuliang Yao. "Using Transaction Prices to Re-Examine Price Dispersion in Electronic Markets." Information Systems Research, Vol. 22 No. 2. (June 2011).

Internet Retailer. "Top 500 Guide 2013 Edition." (2013).

Internet Systems Consortium, Inc. "ISC Internet Domain Survey." (August 2013).

Kalakota, Ravi, and Marcia Robinson. *e-Business 2.0: Roadmap for Success, 2nd edition*. Reading, MA: Addison Wesley (2003).

Kambil, Ajit. "Doing Business in the Wired World." *IEEE Computer* (May 1997).

Levin, Jonathon. "The Economics of Internet Markets." Stanford University, Draft, February 18, 2011.

Mesenbourg, Thomas L. "Measuring Electronic Business: Definitions, Underlying Concepts, and Measurement Plans." U. S. Department of Commerce Bureau of the Census (August 2001).

Rayport, Jeffrey F., and Bernard J. Jaworski. *Introduction to E-commerce, 2nd edition*. New York: McGraw-Hill (2003).

Rosso, Mark and Bernard Janse. "Smart Marketing or Bait & Switch: Competitors' Brands as Keywords in Online Advertising." Proceedings of the 4th Workshop on Information Credibility. ACM (2010).

Shapiro, Carl, and Hal R. Varian. *Information Rules. A Strategic Guide to the Network Economy*. Cambridge, MA: Harvard Business School Press (1999).

Sinha, Indajit. "Cost Transparency: The Net's Threat to Prices and Brands." *Harvard Business Review* (March-April 2000).

Smith, Michael; Joseph Bailey; and Erik Brynjolfsson. "Understanding Digital Markets: Review and Assessment." In Erik Brynjolfsson and Brian Kahin (eds.) *Understanding the Digital Economy*. Cambridge MA: MIT Press (2000).

Tumblr.com. "About." (accessed June 3, 2013).

Tversky, A., and D. Kahneman. "The Framing of Decisions and the Psychology of Choice." *Science* (January 1981).

U.S. Census Bureau. "E-Stats." (May 23, 2013).

Varian, Hal R. "When Commerce Moves On, Competition Can Work in Strange Ways." *New York Times* (August 24, 2000a).

Varian, Hal R. "5 Habits of Highly Effective Revolution." *Forbes ASAP* (February 21, 2000b).

Wikipedia.org. "Wikipedia: About." (accessed June 3, 2013).

Wikimedia Foundation. "Wikipedia Celebrates 10 Years of Free Knowledge." (January 12, 2011).

YouTube.com. "Statistics." (accessed June 3, 2013).

CHAPTER 2

Arthur, W. Brian. "Increasing Returns and the New World of Business." *Harvard Business Review* (July-August 1996).

Bakos, Yannis. "The Emerging Role of Electronic Marketplaces on the Internet." *Communications of the ACM* (August 1998).

Barney, J. B. "Firm Resources and Sustained Competitive Advantage." *Journal of Management* Vol. 17, No. 1 (1991).

Bellman, Steven; Gerald L. Lohse; and Eric J. Johnson. "Predictors of Online Buying Behavior." *Communications of the ACM* (December 1999).

Bureau of Economic Analysis, U.S. Department of Commerce. "Table 3: Gross Domestic Product and Related Measures: Level and Change from Preceding Period." www.bea.gov (accessed May 10, 2013).

comScore, "comScore Releases July 2013 Search Engine Rankings." (August 14, 2013).

eBay, Inc. "eBay Inc. Reports Strong Second Quarter 2013 Results." (July 17, 2013).

Kambil, Ajit. "Doing Business in the Wired World." *IEEE Computer* (May 1997).

Kambil, Ajit; Ari Ginsberg; and Michael Bloch. "Reinventing Value Propositions." Working Paper, NYU Center for Research on Information Systems (1998).

Kanter, Elizabeth Ross. "The Ten Deadly Mistakes of Wanna-Dots." *Harvard Business Review* (January 2001).

Kaplan, Steven, and Mohanbir Sawhney. "E-Hubs: The New B2B Marketplaces." *Harvard Business Review* (May-June 2000).

Kim, W. Chan, and Renee Mauborgne. "Knowing a Winning Business Idea When You See One." *Harvard Business Review* (September-October 2000).

Magretta, Joan. "Why Business Models Matter." *Harvard Business Review* (May 2002).

Porter, Michael E. "Strategy and the Internet." *Harvard Business Review* (March 2001).

Porter, Michael E. *Competitive Advantage: Creating and Sustaining Superior Performance.* New York: Free Press (1985).

Rigdon, Joan I. "The Second-Mover Advantage." *Red Herring* (September 1, 2000).

Teece, David J. "Profiting from Technological Innovation: Implications for Integration, Collaboration, Licensing and Public Policy." *Research Policy* 15 (1986).

U.S. Census Bureau. "E-Stats." (May 23, 2013).

CHAPTER 3

Apple. "Apple Unveils New iTunes." (September 12, 2012).

Arstechnica.com. "Capitol Hill, The Internet, and Broadband: An Ars Technica Quarterly Report." (September 2010).

Berners-Lee, Tim; Robert Cailliau; Ari Luotonen; Henrik Frystyk Nielsen; and Arthur Secret. "The World Wide Web." *Communications of the ACM* (August 1994).

Bluetooth.com. "What Is Bluetooth Technology." (2013).

Brandt, Richard. "Net Assets: How Stanford's Computer Science Department Changed the Way We Get Information." *Stanford Magazine* (November/December 2004).

Burger, Andrew. "Report: Business Adoption Fuels Growth in VoIP Services." Telecompetitor.com (April 10, 2012).

Burger, Andrew. "Report: Mobile VoIP Users Up 550%, But Annual ARPU is $7.13." Telecompetitor.com (July 11, 2013).

Bush, Vannevar. "As We May Think." *Atlantic Monthly* (July 1945).

Cerf, V., and R. Kahn, "A Protocol for Packet Network Intercommunication." *IEEE Transactions on Communications*, Vol. COM-22, No. 5, pp 637-648 (May 1974).

comScore. "comScore Releases July 2013 U.S. Search Engine Rankings." (August 14, 2013a).

comScore. "comScore Releases July 2013 U.S. Online Video Rankings." (August 19, 2013b).

Deloitte. "Technology, Media, & Telecommunications Predictions 2013." (January 2013).

eMarketer, Inc. (Jeffery Grau). "US Retail Ecommerce: 2013 Forecast and Comparative Estimates." (April 2013a).

eMarketer, Inc. "Internet Users and Penetration Worldwide, 2011–2017." (April 2013b).

eMarketer, Inc. "Mobile Phone Users Worldwide, by Region and Country, 2011–2017." (May 2013c).

eMarketer, Inc. "Smartphone Users and Penetration Worldwide, 2011–2017." (May 2013d).

eMarketer, Inc. "US Mobile Phone Internet Users and Penetration, 2011–2017." (March 2013e).

eMarketer, Inc. "US Fixed Broadband Households, 2011–2017." (February 2013f).

eMarketer, Inc. "Mobile Phone Internet Users and Penetration Worldwide, 2011–2013." (May 2013g).

eMarketer, Inc. "US Blog Readers, 2012–2017." (February 2013; confirmed and republished August 2013h).

eMarketer, Inc., "US Bloggers, 2012–2017." (February 2013; confirmed and republished August 2013i).

eMarketer, Inc. (Cathy Boyle). "Retail Mobile Commerce Forecast—Shoppers Turn to Smartphones." (January 2013j).

eMarketer, Inc. (Catherine Boyle). "Tablet Computing Fuels 'Couch and Pillow' Commerce." (June 13, 2012).

Federal Networking Council. "FNC Resolution: Definition of 'Internet.'" (October 24, 1995).

Gartner, Inc. "Gartner Says Worldwide Public Cloud Services Market to Total $131 Billion." (February 28, 2013a).

Gartner, Inc. "Gartner Says Smartphone Sales Grew 46.5 Percent in Second Quarter of 2013 and Exceeded Feature Phone Sales for First Time." (August 14, 2013b).

Geni.net. "Global Environment for Network Innovations." (accessed September 2013).

Gross, Grant. "NSF Seeks Ambitious Next-Generation Internet Project." *Computerworld* (August 29, 2005).

IEEE Computer Society. "Top Trends for 2013." (2013).

Internet2. "Internet2 Planned 100 Gigabit Infrastructure Topology; Internet2 Network." Internet2.edu (September 2011).

Internet Corporation for Assigned Names and Numbers (ICANN). "ICANN Approves Historic Change to Internet 's Domain System." (June 20, 2011a).

Internet Corporation for Assigned Names and Numbers (ICANN). "Top-Level Domains (gTLDs)." (2011b).

Internet Retailer. "The Mobile 400 2013 Edition." (2013).

ISOC.org. "ISOC's Standards Actitivies." Internet Society (September 2010).

Internet Society. " World IPv6 Launch on June 6, 2012, To Bring Permanent IPv6 Deployment." (January 2012).

Internet Society. "RFC 2616: Hypertext Transfer Protocol-HTTP/1.1." (June 1999).

Internet Society. "RFC 0959: File Transfer Protocol." (October, 1985).

Kleinrock, Leonard. *1964 Communication Nets: Stochastic Message Flow and Delay*. New York: McGraw-Hill (1964).

Leiner, Barry M.; Vinton G. Cerf; David D. Clark; Robert E. Kahn; Leonard Kleinrock; Daniel C. Lynch; Jon Postel; Larry G. Roberts; and Stephen Wolff. "All About the Internet: A Brief History of the Internet." *Internet Society* (ISOC) (August 2000).

Marketshare.hitslink.com. "Top Browser Share Trend." (August 2013).

National Research Foundation. "NSP Leadership in Discovery and Initiative Sparks White House US Ignite Initiative." (June 13, 2012).

Netcraft. "August 2013 Web Server Survey." (August 2013).

Nielsen. "A Look Across Screens: The Cross-Platform Report." (June 2013).

Nielsen. "Mobile Apps Beat the Mobile Web Among US Android Smartphone Users." (August 18, 2011).

Pew Internet & American Life Project. "Daily Internet Activities." (September 2013).

Pfanner, Eric. "Ethics Fight Over Domain Names Intensifies." *New York Times* (March 18, 2012).

Radicati Group. "Email Statistics Report, 2013–2017." (April 2013).

Smith, Mat. "Apple Has Now Sold 600 Million Devices." Engadget.com (June 10, 2013).

Troianovski, Anton. "Optical Delusion? Fiber Booms Again, Despite Bust." *Wall Street Journal* (April 2, 2012).

U.S. Department of Commerce. "Letter to ICANN Chairman." http://www.ntia.doc.gov/comments/2008/ICANN_080730.html (July 30, 2008).

Visualware, Inc., "VisualRoute Traceroute Server." (September 2011).

Walsh, Mark. "eBay: Mobile Transaction Volume Hits $13 Billion." Mediapost.com (January 17, 2013).

Zakon, Robert H. "Hobbes' Internet Timeline v8.1." Zakon.org (2005).

Ziff-Davis Publishing. "Ted Nelson: Hypertext Pioneer." Techtv.com (1998).

CHAPTER 4

Banker, Rajiv D., and Chris F. Kemerer. "Scale Economies in New Software Development." *IEEE Transactions on Software Engineering*, Vol. 15, No. 10 (1989).

Doyle, Barry and Cristina Videria Lopes. "Survey of Technologies for Web Application Development." ACM, Vol.2., No. 3. (June 2005).

IBM (High Volume Web Sites Team). "Best Practices for High-Volume Web Sites." *IBM Redbooks* (December 2002).

Lientz, Bennet P., and E. Burton Swanson. *Software Maintenance Management*. Reading MA: Addison-Wesley (1980).

WebTrends, Inc. "WebTrends Analytics 10." (2011).

CHAPTER 5

Akamai. "The State of the Internet, 1st Quarter, 2013 Report." Volume 6, Number 1 (July 23, 2013).

Arbor Networks. "Worldwide Infrastructure Security Report 2012 Volume VIII." (2013).

Chirgwin, Richard. "Microsoft and FBI Storm Ramparts of Citadel Botnets." *The Register* (June 6, 2013).

Cisco. "2013 Cisco Annual Security Report." (2013).

Cybersource, Inc. "2013 Online Fraud Report." (2012).

Danchev, Dancho. "Exposing the Market for Stolen Credit Cards Data." DDanchev.blogspot.com (October 31, 2011).

Digital Transactions. "Online Volume Grows 13% as Mobile Traffic and Bill Me Later Surge." Digitaltransactions.net (December 11, 2012).

DMARC.org. "In First Year, DMARC Protects 60 Percent of Global Consumer Mailboxes." (February 6, 2013).

Dunn, John E. "Jailed Phishing Gang Targeted Banks in 14 Countries, Police Say." Techworld.com (June 18, 2013).

Federal Bureau of Investigation. "Romanian Citizen Involved in Phishing Scheme Sentenced to Four Years in Federal Prison." FBI.gov (January 9, 2013).

Finkle, Jim, "Virus Targets the Social Network in New Fraud Twist." Reuters.com (August 16, 2013).

Fiserv. "2012 Fiserv Billing Household Survey." (January 23, 2013).

Fiserv. "2007 Consumer Bill Payments Trends Survey: Volume of Electronic Payments." (2007).

Fox, Emily Jane and Greg Botelho. "5 Charged in Credit Card Hacking Scheme Feds Call Largest Ever Prosecuted in the U.S." Cnn.com (July 25, 2013).

Gartner. "Gartner Says Worldwide Security Market to Grow 8.7 Percent in 2013." (June 11, 2013).

GData SecurityLabs. "Malware Report. Half-Yearly Report July–December 2012." (2013).

Honan, Mat. "How Apple and Amazon Security Flaws Led to My Epic Hacking." Wired.com (August 6, 2012).

Javelin Strategy & Reseach. "2013 Identity Fraud Survey Report." (February 20, 2013).

Javelin Strategy & Research. "5th Annual Online Retail Payments Forecast 2012–2017." (November 2012).

Kaspersky Lab. "Kapersky Security Bulletin. 2012." (December 10, 2012).

Kirk, Jeremy. "Google to Lengthen SSL Encryption Keys in August." Computerworld (May 24, 2013).

Kolesnikov-Jessup, Sonia. "Hackers Go After the Smartphone." *New York Times* (February 13, 2011).

Microsoft. "Microsoft Security Intelligence Report Volume 14: July–December 2012." (2013).

Mitnick, Kevin. Ghost in the Wires. Little, Brown & Co. (2011).

Muncaster, Phi. "Citadel Botnet Resurges to Storm Japanese PCs." *The Register* (September 4, 2013).

Nilson Report. "General Purpose Cards—U.S. 2012." (February 2013).

PandaLabs. "PandaLabs Annual Report 2012 Summary." (2013).

PandaSecurity, "Cyber-Crime Files." http://cybercrime. pandasecurity.com/blackmarket/how_works.php (accessed September 15, 2012).

Ponemon Institute. "2012 Cost of Cyber Crime Study: United States." (October 2012).

Ponemon Institute. "2013 Cost of Data Breach Study: Global Analysis." (March 2013).

PWC. "Key Findings from the 2013 US State of Cybercrime Survey." (June 2013).

Rosenblatt, Seth. "Google Accelerates Encryption Project." News.cnet.com (September 6, 2013).

Santora, Marc. "In Hours, Thieves Took $45 Million in A.T.M. Scheme." *New York Times* (May 9, 2013).

Schwartz, Mathew J. "Another Java Zero-Day Vulnerability Hits Black Market." Informationweek.com (January 16, 2013).

Schwartz, John. "Fighting Crime Online: Who is in Harm's Way?" *New York Times* (February 8, 2001).

Software Engineering Institute. "Common Sense Guide to Mitigating Insider Threats, 4th Edition." Sei.cmu. edu (December 2012).

Stein, Lincoln D. *Web Security: A Step-by-Step Reference Guide*. Reading, MA: Addison-Wesley (1998).

Symantec, Inc. "Internet Security Threat Report 2013 Volume 18." (April 2013).

Symantec, Inc. "Internet Security Threat Report Volume XVII: May 2012." (May 2012a).

Symantec. "Symantec Intelligence Report: August 2012." (September 2012b).

Symantec, Inc. "Internet Security Threat Report: Trends for 2010, Volume 16: April 2011." (April 2011).

Symantec, Inc. "Internet Security Threat Report Volume XV: April 2010." (April 2010).

TrendMicro Incorporated. "TrendLabs 2012 Mobile Threat and Security Roundup: Repeating History." (2013a).

TrendMicro, Incorporated. "TrendLabs 2Q 2013 Security Roundup: Mobile Threats Go Full Throttle." (June 5, 2013b).

US-CERT. "Socializing Securely: Using Social Networking Services." (January 2011).

US-CERT. "Cyber Threats to Mobile Devices." TIP 10-105-01 (April 2010).

Vaughan-Nichols, Steven J. "Has the NSA Broken SSL? TLS? AES?" Zdnet.com (September 6, 2013).

Wakabayashi, Daisuke. "A Contrite Sony Vows Tighter Security." *Wall Street Journal* (May 1, 2011).

Wills, Amanda. "New Snowden Leak: NSA Program Taps All You Do Online." Mashable.com (August 1, 2013).

Wingfield, Nick. "Spam Network Shut Down." *Wall Street Journal* (March 18, 2011).

Zetter, Kim. "Top Federal Lab Hacked in Spear-Phishing Attack." *Wired* (April 20, 2011).

CHAPTER 6

AdAge.com "Google/Audience Buying Guide 2012." (2012).

Adjei, Mavis, and Stephanie Noble. "The Influence of C2C Communications in Online Brand Communities On Purchase Behavior." *Journal of the Academy of Marketing Science*, Vol. 38, No. 5 (2009).

Adomavicius, Gediminas, and Alexander Tuzhilin. "Using Data Mining Methods to Build Customer Profiles." *IEEE Computer* (February 2001a).

Adomavicius, Gediminas, and Alexander Tuzhilin. "Expert-Driven Validation of Rule-Based User Models in Personalization Applications." *Data Mining and Knowledge Discovery* (January 2001b).

Akerlof, G. "The Market for 'Lemons' Quality Under Uncertainty and the Market Mechanism." *Quarterly Journal of Economics* (August 1970).

Ba, Sulin, and Jan Stallaert, and Zhang. "Balancing IT with the Human Touch: Optimal Investment in IT-Based Customer Service." Information Systems Research (September 2010).

Ba, Sulin, and Paul Pavlou. "Evidence on the Effect of Trust Building Technology in Electronic Markets: Price Premiums and Buyer Behavior." *MIS Quarterly* (September 2002).

Bakos, J. Y., and Erik Brynjolfsson. "Bundling and Competition on the Internet: Aggregation Strategies for Information Goods." *Marketing Science* (January 2000).

Battelle, John. "The Database of Intentions is Far Larger Than I Thought." Battellemedia.com (March 5, 2010).

Battelle, John. "Search Blog." Battellemedia.com (November 13, 2003).

Baymard Reserach, "15 Cart Abandonment Rate Statistics." Baymard.com (July 17, 2012).

Belisle, Jean Francois. "The Battle of Web Analytics Solutions in 2013." Jfbelisle.com (January 21, 2013).

Bell, David R. and Sangyoung Song. "Social Contagion and Trial on the Internet: Evidence from Online Grocery Retailing." Unpublished paper. The Wharton School, University of Pennsylvania (May 12, 2004).

BIA/Kelsey. "Annual U.S. Local Media Forecast 2012–2017." (March 13, 2013).

Brightroll. "US Video Advertising Report." (June 7, 2012).

Brookings Institute. "Online Identity and Consumer Trust: Assessing Online Risk." (January 2011).

Chan, P. K. "A Non-Invasive Learning Approach to Building Web User Profiles." In *Proceedings of ACM SIGKDD International Conference* (1999).

Channel Advisor, "Through the Eyes of the Consumer: 2010 Consumer Shopping Habits Survey." (2010).

comScore. "2013 U.S. Digital Future in Focus." (February 14, 2013).

Corritore, C.L., B. Kracher, S. Wiedenbeck, "On-line trust: concepts, evolving themes, a model," *International Journal of Human-Computer Studies* (2006).

Cross, Robert. "Launching the Revenue Rocket: How Revenue Management Can Work For Your Business." *Cornell Hotel and Restaurant Administration Quarterly* (April 1997).

Direct Marketing Association (DMA). "Response Rate 2012 Report." (June 14, 2012).

Dyer, Pam. "Social Networks Have Little Influence on What You Buy Online." Pamarama.net (April 2011).

eMarketer, Inc. "US Time Spent with Media: The Complete eMarketer Forecast for 2013." (August 21, 2013a).

eMarketer, Inc. (Alison McCarthy). "US Mobile Users: 2013 Forecast and Comparative Estimates." (April 2013b).

eMarketer, Inc. "US Internet, by Age, 2012–2017." (August 2013c).

eMarketer, Inc. "US Internet User Penetration, by Age, 2012-2017." (August 2013d).

eMarketer, Inc. "US Fixed Broadband Households and Subscriptions, 2012–2017." (August 2013e).

eMarketer, Inc. (Alison McCarthy). "US Tablet Users: 2013 Forecast and Comparative Estimates." (May 2013f).

eMarketer, Inc. (Jeffrey Grau). "US Retail Ecommerce: 2013 Forecast and Comparative Estimates." (April 2013g).

eMarketer, Inc., "US Digital Ad Spending, 2011–2017 (August 2013h).

eMarketer, Inc. "US Digital Ad Spending, by Format, 2011–2017." (August 2013i).

eMarketer, Inc. "US Mobile Ad Spending, by Format, 2011–2017." (June 2013j).

eMarketer, Inc. (Lauren Fisher). "Email Benchmarks: Key Metrics and Trends for 2013." (August 5, 2013k).

eMarketer, Inc. (Jeffrey Grau). "Shopping Cart Abandonment." (January 2013l).

eMarketer, Inc. (Debra Aho Williamson). "Meeting the Needs for Speed: How Social Analytics Support Real-time Marketing." (February 2013m).

eMarketer, Inc. (Alison McCarthy). "US Ad Spending Forecast: Fall 2012 Update." (October 1, 2012a).

eMarketer, Inc. "US Social Network Ad Spending, 2012–2015." (September 2012b).

eMarketer, Inc. (Jeffrey Grau). "US Retail Ecommerce Forecast: Growth Opportunities in a Maturing Channel." (April 1, 2011a).

eMarketer, Inc. (Paul Verna). "Word of Mouth Marketing" (October 2010a).

eMarketer, Inc. "How Much Time People Really Spend with Ads." (August 24, 2009).

Evans, P., and T. S. Wurster. "Getting Real About Virtual Commerce." *Harvard Business Review* (November-December 1999).

Eyeblaster. "Trends of Time and Attention in Online Advertising." (July 22, 2009).

Farahat, Ayman and Michael Bailey. "How Effective is Targeted Advertising." International World Wide Web Conference Committee (April 26-20, 2012).

Fawcett, Tom, and Foster Provost. "Adaptive Fraud Detection." *Data Mining and Knowledge Discovery* (1997).

Fawcett, Tom, and Foster Provost. "Combining Data Mining and Machine Learning for Effective User Profiling." In *Proceedings of the Second International Conference on Knowledge Discovery and Data Mining* (1996).

Federal Communications Commission. "FCC Broadband Report Finds Significant Progress In Broadband Deployment, But Important Gaps Remain." (August 17, 2012).

Fireclick. "Fireclick Index/Top Line Growth." Index.Fireclick.com (accessed September 30, 2013).

Forrester Research. "US Cross-Channel Retail Forecast, 2011–2016." (July 23, 2012a).

Forrester Research. "Affiliate Marketing—The Direct and Indirect Values That Affiliates Deliver to Advertisers." (June 26, 2012b).

Forrester Research. (Sucharita Mulpuru). "Will Facebook Ever Drive eCommerce?" (April 7, 2011a).

Garg, Rajiv. "Peer Influence and Information Difusion in Online Networks: An Empricial Analysis." Carnegie Mellon University, School of Information Systems and Management, Working Paper, 2009.

Gigaom.com, "Survey: Percentage of Users Saying They Opt Out of Targeted Ads Has Nearly Doubled." Gigaom.com, (July 16, 2012).

Google, Inc. "What's Trending in Display for Publishers?" (May 29, 2012).

Guo, Stephen, M. Wang, and J. Leskovec. "The Role of Social Networks in Online Shopping Choice: Information Passing, Price of Trust, and Consumer Choice." Stanford University (June 2011).

Humphreys, Jeffrey M. "Buying Power: The Multicultural Economy 2013." The University of Georgia Terry College of Business Selig Center for Economic Growth (September 2013).

Interactive Advertising Bureau. "Mobile Rich Media Ad Definitions (MRAID)" (September 2012).

Interactive Advertising Bureau. "IAB Standards and Guidelines." Iab.net (September 2011).

Interactive Advertising Bureau (IAB)/PriceWaterhouse-Coopers. "IAB Internet Advertising Revenue Report: 2012 Full Year Results." (April 2013).

Iyengar, Raghuram, S. Han and S. Gupta. "Do Friends Influence Purchases in a Social Network." Harvard Business School. Working Paper, 2009.

Kim, D. and I. Benbasat. "The Effects of Trust-Assuring Arguments on Consumer Trust in Internet Stores," *Information Systems Research* (2006).

Kim, D. and I. Benbasat. "Designs for Effective Implementation of Trust Assurances in Internet Stores," *Communications of the ACM* (July 2007).

Kim, Dan, Donald Ferrin, and Raghav Rao. "Trust and Satisfaction, Two Stepping Stones for Successful E-Commerce Relationships: A Longitudinal Exploration." Journal of Information Systems Research (June 2009).

Kotler, Philip, and Gary Armstrong. *Principles of Marketing, 13th Edition*. Upper Saddle River, NJ: Prentice Hall (2009).

McKinsey & Company. "The Impact of Internet Technologies: Search." (July 2011).

MediaMind Inc. "The Rich and the Powerful." (March 2012a).

MediaMind Inc. "Consumers 27 Times More Likely to Click-Through Online Video Ads than Standard Banners."(September 12, 2012b).

Mishra, D. P., J. B. Heide, and S. G. Cort. "Information Asymmetry and Levels of Agency Relationships." *Journal of Marketing Research*. (1998).

Mobasher, Bamshad. "Data Mining for Web Personalization." Center for Web Intelligence, School of Computer Science, Telecommunication, and Information Systems, DePaul University, Chicago, Illinois. (2007).

National Conference of State Legislatures. "State Laws Relating to Unsolicited Commercial of Bulk E-mail (SPAM)." (February 10, 2010).

Nielsen Company. "December 2011—Top U.S. Web Brands." (January 25, 2012).

Nielsen Company. "Nielsen Receives MRC Accreditation for Nielsen Online Campaign Ratings." (September 7, 2011).

Nielsen Company. "Global Online Consumer Survey." (May 2011).

Opinion Research Corporation. "Online Consumer Product Reviews Have Big Influence." Opinion Research Corporation (April 16, 2009).

Oestreicher-Singer, Gail and Arun Sundararajan. "The Visible Hand of Social Networks." *Electronic Commerce Research* (2008).

Pavlou, Paul. "Institution-Based Trust in Interorganizational Exchange Relationships: The Role of Online

B2B Marketplaces on Trust Formation." *Journal of Strategic Information Systems* (2002).

Pew Internet & American Life Project, "Online Activities, Daily." http://pewinternet.org/Trend-Data-(Adults)/Online-Activities-Daily.aspx (accessed September 12, 2013a).

Pew Internet & American Life Project. "Demographics of Internet Users/Spring Tracking Survey, April 17-May 19, 2013." (Accessed September 15, 2013b).

Pew Internet & American Life Project. (Kathryn Zickuhr and Aaron Smith) "Digital Differences." (April 13, 2012).

PointRoll. "2012 Benchmark Report." (June 13, 2013).

Rayport, J. F., and J. J. Sviokla. "Exploiting the Virtual Value Chain." *Harvard Business Review* (November-December 1995).

Richtel, Matt. "Wasting Time is Divide in Digital Era." *New York Times* (May 29, 2012).

Screenwerk.com "Google: 50% of Mobile Search is Local." (October 1, 2012).

Shapiro, Carl, and Hal Varian. *Information Rules: A Strategic Guide to the Network Economy.* Cambridge, MA: Harvard Business School Press (1999).

Shapiro, Carl, and Hal Varian. "Versioning: The Smart Way to Sell Information." *Harvard Business Review* (November-December 1998).

Sinha, Indrajit. "Cost Transparency: The Net's Real Threat to Prices and Brands." *Harvard Business Review* (March-April 2000).

Socialmediatoday.com. "Mobile Apps: How Many People Use Apps?" (September 3, 2013).

Sterling, Greg. "Chitika: We Got Google's Local Search Number Wrong." Searchengineland.com (October 9, 2012).

Symantec. "Symantec Intelligence Report." (August 2013).

Takahashi, Dean. "Freemium Summit: Evernote Shares the Insider Secrets of Free Apps." Mobileventurebeat.com (March 26, 2010).

The Search Agency. "State of Paid Search Report—Q2 2013." (July 18, 2013).

Tobii/Mediative. "The Effectiveness of Display Advertising on a Desktop PC vs. a Tablet Device." (August 2012).

TRUSTe. "U.S. Consumer Privacy Attitudes and Business Implications." (July 16, 2012).

Van den Poel, Dirk and Wouter Buckinx. "Predicting Online Purchasing Behavior." *European Journal of Operations Research*, Vol. 166, Issue 2 (2005).

VINDICO. "2012 Annual Report." (June 1, 2013).

Wigand, R. T., and R. I. Benjamin. "Electronic Commerce: Effects on Electronic Markets." *Journal of Computer Mediated Communication* (December 1995).

Williamson, O. E. *The Economic Institutions of Capitalism.* New York: Free Press (1985).

Wolfinbarger, Mary, and Mary Gilly. "Shopping Online for Freedom, Control and Fun." *California Management Review* (Winter 2001).

CHAPTER 7

Aaker, D.A. "Measuring Brand Equity across products and markets." *California Management Review*, Vol 38, No. 3, pp 102–20. (1996).

Ailawadi, Kusum L., Donald R. Lehmann, and Scott A Neslin. "Revenue Premium as an Outcome Measure of Brand Equity." *Journal of Marketing*, 67 (October), 1–17 (October 2003).

AOL/BBDO/Insights Now. "Seven Shades of Mobile: The Hidden Motivations of Mobile Users." (October 2012).

BIA/Kelsey. "BIA/Kelsey Forecasts U.S. Mobile Local Ad Revenues to Reach $9.1 Billion in 2017." (April 4, 2013).

comScore. "U.S. Digital Future in Focus 2013." (February 2013a).

comScore. "comScore Media Metrix Ranks Top 50 U.S.Properties." (March 2013b).

comScore/Facebook. "The Power of Like: How Brands Reach and Influence Fans Through Social Marketing." White Paper (October 21, 2012).

eMarketer, Inc. "US Social Network Ad Spending, 2011–2017 (billions, % change and % of total media ad spending)"; "US Mobile Ad Spending, 2011–2017" (March 2013a).

eMarketer, Inc. (Krista Garcia). "Facebook Commerce: Evolving, Not Extinct." (April 2013b).

eMarketer, Inc. (Alison McCarthy). "US Social Network Users 2013." (April 2013c).

eMarketer, Inc. "US Smartphone Users and Penetration 2011–2017." (March 2013d).

eMarketer, Inc., "US Retail Mcommerce Sales, 2011–2017 (billions, % change and % of retail ecommerce)" (April 2013e).

eMarketer, Inc. "Smartphones, Tablets Drive Faster Growth in E-commerce Sales." (April 24, 2013f).

eMarketer, Inc. "US Tablet Users and Penetration, 2011–2017." (March, 2013g).

eMarketer, Inc. "US Retail Mcommerce Sales, by Device, 2011–2017 (billions and % change)." (April 2013h).

eMarketer, Inc. "US Digital Ad Spending by Channel, 2011–2017 (billions)." (June 2013i).

eMarketer, Inc. "US Net Mobile Internet Ad Revenues, by Company, 2011-2015 (millions)." (June 2013j).

eMarketer, Inc. "US Mobile Ad Spending by Format, 2011–2017 (millions)." (June 2013k).

eMarketer, Inc. "US Mobile Ad Spending, Local vs. National, 2012–2017." (April 4, 2013l).

eMarketer, Inc. "Net US Mobile Internet Ad Revenue Share, by Company, 2011–2015." (June 1, 2013m).

eMarketer, Inc. "US Local Mobile Ad Spending, by Format, 2012–2017." (April 4, 2013n).

eMarketer, Inc. "Time Spent on Social Network Sites by US Internet Users, Nov 2012 (millions of minutes)." (January 16, 2013x).

Google, Inc., "The New Multiscreen World." (August 2012).

Google/IPSOS OTX MediaCT. "The Mobile Movement: Understanding Smartphone Users." (April 2011). [Source for Figure 7.20]

Hof, Robert. "Mobile Ads Hit 30% of Facebook's Q1 Revenues." *Forbes* (May 1, 2013).

IAB (Interactive Advertising Bureau). "Response Design and Ad Creative: An IAB Perspective." (September 2012).

Internet Retailer. "The Mobile 400 2013 Edition." (2013).

Keller, K.L. (1993), "Conceptualizing, Measuring and Managing Customer-Based Brand Equity." *Journal of Marketing*, Vol 57, January, pp 1–22.

Microsoft. "Location Based Services Usage & Perceptions Study." (February 2011).

Simon, C.J., and M.J. Sullivan. (The Measurement and Determinants of Brand Equity: A Financial Approach, *Marketing Science*, Vol. 12, No 1, pg 28–52. (1993).

Vega, Tanzina and Leslie Kaufman. "The Distasteful Side of Social Media Puts Advertisers on Their Guard." *New York Times* (June 3, 2013).

CHAPTER 8

Acquisti, Alessandro, Ralph Gross, and Fred Stutzman. "Faces of Facebook: Privacy in the Age of Augmented Reality," Heinz College & CyLab Carnegie Mellon University (August 4, 2011).

Acquisti , Alessandro, Leslie John, and George Loewenstein. "What is Privacy Worth?" Twenty First Workshop on Information Systems and Economics (WISE) (December 14-15, 2009).

Angwin, Julia and Jennifer Valentino-Devries. "New Tracking Frontier: Your License Plates." *Wall Street Journal* (September 28, 2012).

Angwin, Julia. "Face-ID Tools Pose New Risk." *Wall Street Journal* (August 1, 2011).

Apple Computer, Inc. v. Microsoft Corp. 709 F. Supp. 925, 926 (N. D. Cal. 1989); 799 F. Supp. 1006, 1017 (N. D. Cal., 1992); 35 F. 3d 1435 (9th Cir.); cert. denied, 63 U. S. L. W. 3518 (U.S., Feb. 21, 1995) (No. 94-1121).

Ashcroft v. Free Speech Coalition, 535 U.S. 234 (2002).

Associated Press. "Google Settles Final Piece of Geico Case." BizReport.com (September 8, 2005).

Audi AG and Volkswagen of America, Inc. v. Bob D'Amato No. 05-2359, 6th Circuit (November 27, 2006).

Bernina of America, Inc. v. Fashion Fabrics Int'l., Inc. 2001 U. S. Dist. LEXIS 1211 (N. D. Ill., Feb. 8, 2001).

Berzo, Alexandra. "Delaware Lawmakers Clear Online Gambling." *Wall Street Journal* (June 27, 2012).

Bilski et al. v. Kappos, 177 L. Ed. 2d 792, 130 S. Ct. 3218, 561 U.S. _____(2010).

Bilton, Nick. "Apple Loophole Gives Developers Access to Photos." *New York Times* (February 28, 2012).

Brown Bag vs. Symantec Corp., 960 F. 2d 1465 (9th Cir. 1992).

Brustein, Joshua. "Start-Ups Seek to Help Users Put a Price on Their Personal Data." *New York Times* (February 12, 2012).

Charlton, Angela. "France Threatens Google with Privacy Fines." *New York Times* (June 20, 2013).

Chiappetta, Vincent. "Defining the Proper Scope of Internet Patents: If We Don't Know Where We Want to Go, We're Unlikely to Get There." *Michigan Telecommunications Technology Law Review* (May 2001).

Cowell, Alan. "Britons Protest Proposal to Widen Surveillance." *New York Times* (April 2, 2012).

Diamond v. Chakrabarty, 447 US 303 (1980).

E. & J. Gallo Winery v. Spider Webs Ltd. 129 F. Supp. 2d 1033 (S.D. Tex., 2001) aff'd 286 F. 3d 270 (5th Cir., 2002).

Eldred v. Ashcroft, 537 U.S. 186 (2003).

European Commission, "Commission Proposes a Comprehensive Reform of the Data Protection Rules." (January 26, 2012).

Federal Trade Commission. "Google Will Pay $22.5 Million to Settle FTC Charges It Misrepresented Privacy Assurance to Users of Apple's Safari Internet Browser." (August 9, 2012a).

Federal Trade Commission. "Facebook Must Obtain Consumers' Consent Before Sharing Their Information Beyond Established Privacy Settings." (August 10, 2012b).

Federal Trade Commission. "FTC Finalizes Privacy Settlement with Myspace." (September 11, 2012c).

Federal Trade Commission. "Protecting Consumer Privacy in an Era of Rapid Change." (March 26, 2012d).

Federal Trade Commission. "FTC Charges Deceptive Privacy Practices in Google's Rollout of Its Buzz Network." (March 3, 2011).

Federal Trade Commission. "Privacy Online: Fair Information Practices in the Electronic Marketplace." (May 2000a).

Federal Trade Commission. "Online Profiling: A Report to Congress." (June 2000b).

Federal Trade Commission. "Privacy Online: A Report to Congress." (June 1998).

Field v. Google, Inc. 412 F.Supp. 2nd 1106 (D. Nev., 2006).

Fisher, William W. III. "The Growth of Intellectual Property: A History of the Ownership of Ideas in the

United States." Law.harvard.edu/Academic_Affairs/coursepages/tfisher/iphistory.html (1999).

Ford, Paul. "Balancing Security and Liberty in the Age of Big Data." Businessweek.com (June 13, 2013)

Ford Motor Co. v. Lapertosa 2001 U. S. Dist. LEXIS 253 (E. D. Mich. Jan. 3, 2001).

Goel, Vindu and Edward Watt. "Facebook Privacy Change is Subject of T.T.C. Inquiry." *New York Times* (September 11, 2013).

Google, Inc. v. American Blind & Wallpaper Factory, Inc. Case No. 03-5340 JF (RS) (N.D. Cal., April 18, 2007).

Government Employees Insurance Company v. Google, Inc. Civ. Action No. 1:04cv507 (E.D. VA, December 15, 2004).

Greenhouse, Linda. "Supreme Court Upholds Child Pornography Law." *New York Times* (May 20, 2008).

Greenhouse, Linda. "20 Year Extension of Existing Copyrights Is Upheld." *New York Times* (January 16, 2003a).

Greenhouse, Linda. "Justices Back Law to Make Libraries Use Internet Filters." *New York Times* (June 24, 2003b).

Harmon, Amy. "Pondering Value of Copyright vs. Innovation." *New York Times* (March 3, 2003).

Harris Interactive ."Consumers Trust Amazon Twice as Much with Their Personal Data as They Do Facebook, Placecast Study Reveals." Prweb.com (July 20, 2012).

Hoofnagle, Chris Jay. "Privacy Self-Regulation: A Decade of Disappointment." Electronic Privacy Information Center (Epic.org) (March 4, 2005).

Kakutani, Michiko. "Watched by the Web: Surveillance Is Reborn." *New York Times* (June 10, 2013).

Kelly v. ArribaSoft. 336 F3rd 811 (CA 9th, 2003).

Kuehn, Andreas and Mueller, Milton,. "Profiling the Profilers: Deep Packet Inspection and Behavioral Advertising in Europe and the United States." Available at SSRN: http://ssrn.com/abstract=2014181. (September 1, 2012).

Mayer-Schonberger, Viktor, and Kenneth Cukier. *Big Data: A Revolution That Will Transform How We Live, Work, and Think.* Eamon Dolan/Houghton Mifflin Harcourt (2013).

Laudon, Kenneth. "Markets and Privacy." *Communications of the ACM* (September 1996).

Maass, Peter and Megha Rajagopalen. "That's No Phone. That's My Tracker." *New York Times* (July 13, 2012).

McMillan, Robert. "Porn Typosquatter Fined Again by FTC." *InfoWorld* (October 16, 2007).

Miller, John W. and Christopher Rhoads, "U.S. Fights to Keep Control Of Global Internet Oversight." *Wall Street Journal* (November 16, 2005).

Nash, David B. "Orderly Expansion of the International Top-Level Domains: Concurrent Trademark Users

Need a Way Out of the Internet Trademark Quagmire." *The John Marshall Journal of Computer and Information Law* Vol. 15, No. 3 (1997).

Nettis Environmental Ltd. v. IWI, Inc. 46 F. Supp. 2d 722 (N. D. Ohio 1999).

Network Advertising Initiative. "Network Advertising Initiative Releases 2010 Compliance Report." Networkadvertising.org (February 18, 2011).

Network Advertising Initiative. "Major Marketing/Media Trade Groups Launch Program to Give Consumers Enhanced Control over Collection and Use of Web Viewing Data for Online Behavioral Advertising." (October 4, 2010).

Nissan Motor Co., Ltd. v. Nissan Computer Corp. 289 F. Supp. 2d 1154 (C. D. Cal.), aff'd, 2000 U. S. App. LEXIS 33937 (9th Cir. Dec. 26, 2000).

PaineWebber Inc. v. Fortuny, Civ. A. No. 99-0456-A (E. D. Va. Apr. 9, 1999).

Perfect 10, Inc. v. Amazon.com, Inc. 487 F3rd 701 (CA 9th, 2007).

Pew Internet & American Life Project. "Daily Internet Activities." (September 2013).

Pew Internet & American Life Project. "Search Engine Use 2012." (March 9, 2012).

Playboy Enterprises, Inc. v. Global Site Designs, Inc. 1999 WL 311707 (S. D. Fla. May 15, 1999).

Playboy Enterprises, Inc. v. Netscape Communications, Inc. 354 F. 3rd 1020 (9th Cir., 2004).

Raice, Shayndi. "Facebook to Target Ads Based on App Usage." *New York Times* (July 6, 2012).

Rosen, Jeffrey. "The Right to be Forgotten." *Stanford Law Review,* 64. Stan. L. Rev. Online 88 (February 13, 2012).

Rosen, David. "Is Success Killing the Porn Industry." Alternet.org (May 27, 2013). Sasso, Brendan. "FCC Urges Court to Uphold Net Neutrality Rules." TheHill.com (September 10, 2012).

Sarno, David. "SmartPhone Apps dial Up Privacy Worries." *Los Angeles Times* (February 16, 2012).

Savage, Charlie. "Democratic Senators Issue Strong Warning About Use of the Patriot Act." *New York Times* (March 16, 2012).

Schatz, Amy. "Net Neutrality' Rules Set to Pass." *Wall Street Journal* (December 21, 2010).

Schwartz, John. "Justices Take Broad View of Business Methods Patents." *New York Times* (June 28, 2010).

Sengupta, Somini. "Europe Weighs Tough Law on Online Privacy." *New York Times* (January 23, 2012a).

Singer, Natasha. "Consumer Data, But Not For Consumers." *New York Times* (July 21, 2012a).

Singer, Natasha. "An American Quilt of Privacy Laws, Incomplete." *New York Times* (March 30, 2013).

State Street Bank & Trust Co. v. Signature Financial Group, 149 F. 3d 1368 (1998).

Stelter, Brian. "Sweeping Effects as Broadband Moves to Meters." *New York Times* (June 26, 2012).

Stone, Brad. "Scaling the Digital Wall in China." *New York Times* (January 15, 2010).

Takenaka, Toshiko. "International and Comparative Law Perspective on Internet Patents." *Michigan Telecommunications Technology Law Review* (May 15, 2001).

Thurm, Scott. "The Ultimate Weapon: It's the Patent." *Wall Street Journal* (April 17, 2000).

Ticketmaster v. Tickets.com. 2000 U.S. Dist. Lexis 4553 (C.D. Cal., August 2000).

TRUSTe, Inc.. "TRUSTe Releases U.S. Consumer Findings From 2012." (July 16, 2012).

United States Copyright Office. "Digital Millennium Copyright Act of 1998: U.S. Copyright Office Summary." (December 1998).

Washington Post, The et al. v. TotalNews, Inc., et al., S.D.N.Y., Civil Action Number 97-1190 (February 1997).

Watt, Edward. "U.S. Court Curbs F.C.C. Authority on Web Traffic." *New York Times* (April 6, 2010).

Whittaker, Zack. "UK's Web Monitoring Draft Bill Revealed: What You Need to Know." Zdnet.com (December 11, 2012).

Winkler, Rolfe. "Online Profits From Gambling in the Cards." *Wall Street Journal* (January 3, 2012).

Winston, Brian. *Media Technology and Society: A History From the Telegraph to the Internet.* Routledge (1998).

Wondracek, G. , Thorsen Holz, Christian Platzer, Engin Kirda, and Christopher Kruegel. "Is the Internet for Porn? An Insight into the Online Adult Industry." In *Proceedings (online) of the 9th Workshop on Economics of Information Security*, Cambridge, MA (June 2010).

Wyatt, Edward. "Verizon Sues F.C.C. to Overturn Order on Blocking Web Sites." *New York Times* (January 20, 2011a).

Wyatt, Edward. "Rule by Justice Department Opens a Door on Online Gambling." *New York Times* (December 24, 2011b).

CHAPTER 9

Accenture. "The Digital Insurer: Accenture US Personal-Lines Insurance Consumer Survey." (April 23, 2013).

Amazon.com, Inc. Amazon.com Inc. Form 10-K for the fiscal year ended December 31, 2012, filed with the Securities and Exchange Commission (January 30, 2013).

Bartash, Jeremy. "U.S. Service Sector Expands Faster in August." Marketwatch.com (September 6, 2011).

Brown, Jeffrey, and Austan Goolsbee. "Does the Internet Make Markets More Competitive? Evidence from the Life Insurance Industry." John F. Kennedy School of Government, Harvard University. Research Working Paper RWP00-007 (2000).

Bruene, Jim. "Metrics: Mobile Traffic at the 10 Largest U.S. Banks." Netbanker.com (March 27, 2013).

Brynjolfsson, Erik; Astrid Andrea Dick and Michael D. Smith. "Search and Product Differentiation at an Internet Shopbot," Center for eBusiness@MIT (December, 2004).

Bureau of Economic Analysis, U.S. Department of Commerce. "Table 3: Gross Domestic Product and Related Measures: Level and Change from Preceding Period." www.bea.gov (accessed May 10, 2013).

Compete.com. "Site Profiles: Fidelity.com, Sharebuilder, Scottrade, TDAmeritrade, E-Trade, Vanguard, Charles Schwab, Merrill Lynch, and Troweprice." (September 2013).

comScore. "2011 State of Online and Mobile Banking." (February 2012a).

comScore. "2012 Online Auto Insurance Shopping Report." (June 21, 2012b).

Dell Inc. Form 10-K for the fiscal year ended February 1, 2013, filed with the Securities and Exchange Commission (March 12, 2013).

Demery, Paul. "Amazon is Tops in Customer Service, an NRF Survey Finds." Internetretailer.com (January 18, 2012).

Dusto, Amy. "Dell Revamps Its Mobile Site." Internetretailer.com (September 19, 2012).

eMarketer, Inc. (Jeffrey Grau). "US Retail Ecommerce: 2013 Forecast and Comparative Estimates." (April 2013a).

eMarketer, Inc. "US Mobile Buyers, by Device, 2011–2017." (September 1, 2013b).

eMarketer, Inc. (Bryan Yeager). "Digital Banking Trends." (August 2013c).

eMarketer, Inc. (Dan Marcec). "US Digital Travel Sales." (May 2013d).

eMarketer, Inc. "Recruiters Rely More on Social Media for Talent." (February 26, 2013e).

eMarketer, Inc. "US Daily Deal Site Revenues, 2011–2016." (September 17, 2012a).

eMarketer, Inc. (Daniel Marcec). "The Mobile Traveler: How Smartphones Are Changing the Customer Journey." (August 7, 2012b).

eMarketer, Inc. "Online Brokerages Engage Clients Through Search and Social Media." (January 5, 2011).

eMarketer, Inc. (Jeffrey Grau). "E-commerce in the US: Retail Trends." (May 2005)

eMarketer, Inc., 2005 [p. 569]

Evans, Philip, and Thomas S. Wurster. *Blown to Bits: How the New Economics of Information Transforms Strategy.* Cambridge, MA: Harvard Business School Press (2000).

Internet Retailer. "Top 500 Guide 2013 Edition." (2013a).

Internet Retailer. "The Mobile 400 2013 Edition." (2013b).

Internet Retailer. "Social Media 300 2013 Edition." (2013c).

Internet Retailer. "Hot 100 Retailers of 2013." (2013d).

Johnson, Lauren. "Macy's Partners with Spotify to Further Mobile Advertising Stride." Mobilecommercedaily.com (August 1, 2012)

Kats, Rimma. "Macy's Exec: Mobile Amplifies Multichannel, Multiscreen Marketing." Mobilecommercedaily.com (May 13, 2013).

Love, Jack. "News Analysis: Big Store Sales Are a Tale of Two Channels." Internetretailer.com (August 19, 2013)

Lands' End, Inc. "About Lands' End." Landsend.com (accessed October 1, 2013).

LIMRA and Life and Health Insurance Foundation for Education (LIFE). "2013 Insurance Barometer Study." (April 16, 2013).

Mojiva. "Finance to Go: A Snapshot of Mobile's Role in the Lives of Financially Savvy American Consumers." (May 8, 2013).

National Association of Realtors. "NAR Home Buyer and Seller Survey Show Value of Long-Term Home Ownership." Realtor.org (November 5, 2010).

Paglia, Lou. "Facebook's Like Button—What's Not to Like." Loupaglia.com (July 23, 2012).

Pilon, Anne. "LinkedIn Survey: More Than One Third of Job Hunters Use Networking Site." Atym.com (January 14, 2013).

U.S. Census Bureau. *Statistical Abstract of the United States 2012* (2012).

Wagner, Mary. "Face to Face." Internet Retailer.com (November 30, 2011).

Weil, Jonathon. "Securities Rules Help to Close the Earning Reports GAAP." *Wall Street Journal* (April 24, 2003).

Yodlee, Inc. "About Us." (accessed October 1, 2013).

CHAPTER 10

AccuStream Research. "Streaming Radio, Curated Station And Track Play Programmers Recording $1.2 Billion In Revenue Alongside 35.9 Billion 2013 Listening Hours." (July 9, 2013).

Alliance for Audited Media. "Top 25 US Newspapers for March 2013." Auditedmedia.com (March 2013).

Anderson, Sam. "Just One More Game ..Angry Birds, Farmville and other Hyperaddictive 'Stupid Games'." *New York Times* (April 4, 2012).

Bialik, Carl. "Studios Struggle for Focus on Film Pirates Booty." *Wall Street Journal* (April 5, 2013).

Book Industry Study Group. "BookStats 2012." (April 2013).

Bosman, Julie. "Penguin Acquires Self-Publishing Company." New York Times (July 19, 2012).

Boxer, Sarah. "Paintings Too Perfect? The Great Optics Debate." *New York Times* (December 4, 2001).

Carr, David. "New Rules for the Ways We Watch." *New York Times* (December 24, 2011).

Cheney, Alexandra. "Hulu to Launch Three New Series, Seven Licensed Shows for Summer," *New York Times* (May 20, 2012).

comScore. "comScore Releases May 2013 U.S. Online Video Rankings." (June 14, 2013).

comScore. "Newspaper Websites Reach Nearly Two-thirds of all Internet Users in Fourth Quarter." (August 11, 2011).

Danaher, Brett, Michael D. Smith, and Rahul Tang. "Piracy and Copyright Enforcement Mechanisms," *Innovation Policy and the Economy*, Vol. 14 (May 3, 2013).

Danaher, Brett and Michael D. Smith. "Gone in 60 Seconds: The Impact of the Megaupload Shutdown on Movie Sales." Working Paper (April 2013).

eMarketer, Inc. "Average Time Spent per Day with Major Media by US Adults, 2013." (July 2013a).

eMarketer, Inc. (Alison McCarthy). "US Digital Content Users 2013." (March 2013b).

eMarketer, Inc. "Daily Time Spent with Digital Media According to US Consumers, 2010–2012 (hrs:mins)." (April 29, 2013c).

eMarketer, Inc. "US Digital Music Shipments and Revenues, by Format, 2011 & 2012 (millions and % change)." (April 2013d).

eMarketer, Inc. (Paul Verna). "Digital TV and Movie Streaming—A Rising Tide of Devices." (March 2013e).

eMarketer, Inc. "US Digital TV Viewers, 2012–2017." (February 2013f).

eMarketer, Inc. (Paul Verna). "Internet Radio." (February 2013g.)

eMarketer, Inc. (Paul Verna). "Digital Subscriptions: Essentials Revenue Streams Across a Wide Range of Content." (July 2013h).

eMarketer, Inc. (Mark Dolliver). "Time Spent With Media: Consumer Behavior in the Age of Multitasking." (March 22, 2012a).

eMarketer, Inc. (Paul Verna). "Book Publishing: The Price of Disruption." (August 2012b).

eMarketer, Inc. "TV Related Activities of US Internet Users, 2012." (January 2012c).

eMarketer, Inc. "Online Movies Set to Overtake DVDs and Blu-rays." (April 2, 2012d).

eMarketer, Inc. (Paul Verna). "US Digital Music Revenues, 2010–2016." (June 12, 2012e).

eMarketer, Inc. "TV Video Viewing: Beyond Cord Cutters." (July 2011).

Envisional, Inc. "An Estimate of Infringing Use of the Internet." (2013).

Fritz, Ben. "Movie Sales Increase With Shutdown of Piracy Site." *Wall Street Journal* (March 7, 2013).

Google. (Deborah Schwartz) "A Window Into Film." (April 2011).

IHS iSuppli. "Worldwide Consumer Spending on Movies Reached $62.4 Billion in 2012." Boxoffice.com (January 21, 2013).

IHS iSuppli. "Movie Consumption Revenue Expected to Rise Continuously from 2012 to 2015." (March 13, 2012a).

IHS iSuppli. "Netflix Surpasses Apple to Take Lead in U.S. Online Movie Business in 2011." (June 1, 2012b).

Isaacson, Walter. *Steve Jobs.* Simon & Schuster (2011).

Kung, Michelle and Miguel Bustillo. "Wal-Mart to Give Hollywood a Hand." *Wall Street Journal* (February 26, 2012).

Myers, Steve."Latest Numbers Indicate New York Times Traffic is Flat Since Paywall." Poynter.org (January 25, 2012).

Newspaper Association of America. "Annual Daily and Sunday Newspaper Circulation Expenditures." (September 30, 2013).

Nielsen. "The Cross Platform Report." (June 2013a).

Nielsen. "The Nielsen Company and Billboard's 2013 Music Industry Report." Nielsen SoundScan (July 18, 2013b).

NPD Group. "Apple iTunes Dominates Internet Video." (April 23, 2013a).

NPD Group, "DVDs Still Largest Revenue Source for Movies." (January 31, 2013b).

NPD Group. "Report Shows Increased Number of Online Gamers and Hours Spent." (May 2, 2013c).

Orden, Erica. "Home Movies Sales Log Rare Increase." *Wall Street Journal* (January 8, 2013).

Pew Research Center. "The State of the News Media 2013." (March 18, 2013).

PriceWaterhouseCooper (PWC). "Global Entertainment and Media Outlook 2013–2017." (June 4, 2013).

RIAA. "Global Entertainment and Media Outlook: 2012–2016." (June 12, 2012).

Rusli, Evelyn. "Zynga Business Erodes Further." *Wall Street Journal* (July 25, 2013).

Sandvine, Inc. "Global Internet Phenomena Report, 2013." (April 2013).

Sass, Erik. "Magazine Newsstand Sales Halved from 2001–2011." Mediapost.com (September 12, 2011).

Sher, Ian. "U.S. Videogame Sales Drop Again In July." *Wall Street Journal* (August 15, 2013).

Sharma, Amol and Christopher Connect. "Hulu Bids Depend on TV-Show Rights." *Wall Street Journal* (July 5, 2013).

Vascellaro, Jessica, Erica Order, and Sam Schechner. "Hollywood Studios Warm to Apple's iCloud Effort." *Wall Street Journal* (March 12, 2012).

Vega, Tanzina. "Marketers Find a Friend in Pinterest." *New York Times* (April 17, 2012).

CHAPTER 11

Arkes, H. R., and L. Hutzel. "The Role of Probability of Success Estimates in the Sunk Cost Effect." Journal of Behavioral Decisionmaking (2000).

Bailey, Brian P.; Laura J. Gurak; and Joseph Konstan, "Do You Trust Me? An Examination of Trust in Computer-Mediated Exchange," In *Human Factors and Web Development*, 2nd Edition. Mahwah, NJ: Lawrence Erlbaum (2002).

Brynjolfsson, Erik, and Michael Smith. "Frictionless Commerce? A Comparison of Internet and Conventional Retailers." *Management Science* (April 2000).

comScore. "comScore Media Metrix Ranks Top 50 U.S. Properties for July 2013." (August 21, 2013a).

comScore. "comScore Media Metrix Ranks Top 50. U.S. Properties for March 2013." (May 1, 2013b).

Dholakia, Utpal, and Kerry Soltysinski. "Coveted or Overlooked? The Psychology of Bidding for Comparable Listings in Digital Auctions." *Marketing Letters* (2001).

eBay, Inc. "Form 10-K For the Fiscal Year Ended December 31, 2012." Filed with the Securities and Exchange Commission. (February 1, 2013).

Efrati, Amir. "There's No Avoiding Google+." *New York Times* (January 2, 2013).

Efrati, Amir."Twitter Tests New Ad Types." *Wall Street Journal* (July 29, 2011).

eMarketer, Inc. "US Social Network Users and Penetration, 2012–2017." (August 1, 2013a).

eMarketer, Inc. "US Twitter Users and Penetration, 2012–2017." (August 1, 2013b).

eMarkter, Inc. "Google+ Users (% of Internet Users), United States, 2012–2013." (August 2013c).

eMarketer, Inc. (Mitchel Winkels). "The Global Social Network Landscape." (July 2013d).

eMarketer, Inc. "Twitter Use Rises Across US Age Groups." (August 9, 2013e).

eMarketer, Inc. "Net US Search Ad Revenues, by Company, 2011–2015." (August 1, 2013f).

eMarketer, Inc. "Net US Digital Display Ad Revenues, by Company, 2011–2015." (August 1, 2013g).

eMarketer, Inc. "Social Network Revenues by Venue, 2011–2015" (August 1, 2013h).

eMarketer, Inc. "Time Spent on Social Network Sites by US Internet Users, Nov 2012 (millions of minutes)." (January 16, 2013).

Facebook. "Newsroom/Key Facts." (accessed September 30, 2013).

Hafner, Katie. "The Epic Saga of The Well: The World's Most Influential Online Community (and It's Not AOL)." Wired (May 1997).

Hagel, John III, and Arthur G. Armstrong. *Net Gain: Expanding Markets Through Virtual Communities.* Cambridge, MA: Harvard Business School Press (1997).

Hanson, Ward, and D. S. Putler. "Hits and Misses: Herd Behavior and Online Product Popularity." Marketing Letters (1996).

Hillery, George A. "Definitions of Community: Areas of Agreement." Rural Sociology (1955).

Hiltzik, Michael. *Dealers of Lightning: Xerox PARC and the Dawn of the Computer Age.* New York: Harper Collins (1999).

Kambil, Ajit, and Eric van Heck. "Competition in the Dutch Flower Market." New York University, Stern School of Business, Center for Information Systems Research (1996).

Kiesler, Sara. "The Hidden Messages in Computer Networks." Harvard Business Review (January-February 1986).

Kiesler, Sara; Jane Siegel; and Timothy W. McGuire. "Social Psychological Aspects of Computer-Mediated Communication." American Psychologist (October 1984).

Kollock, Peter. "The Production of Trust in Online Markets" In Advances in Group Processes (Vol 16) edited by E. J. Lawler, M. Macy, S. Thyne and H. A. Walker. Greenwich, CT: JAI Press (1999).

Kosner, Anthony. "Watch Out Facebook, With Google + at #2 and YouTube at #3, Google Could Catch Up." *Forbes* (January 26, 2013).

Krishnamurthy, Sandeep. "An Empirical Study of the Causal Antecedents of Customer Confidence in ETailers." First Monday (January 2001).

Laudon, Kenneth C. and Jane P. Laudon. *Management Information Systems: Managing the Digital Firm. 13th edition.* Upper Saddle River, NJ, Prentice Hall (2012).

Lee, H. G.; J. C. Westland; and S. Hong. "The Impact of Electronic Marketplaces on Product Prices: An Empirical Study of Aucnet." International Journal of Electronic Commerce (Winter 1999-2000).

McAfee R., and John McMillan. "Auctions and Bidding." Journal of Economic Literature (June 1987).

Milgrom, Paul R. "Auctions and Bidding: A Primer." Journal of Economic Perspectives (Summer 1989).

Murphy, Samantha. "Is Facebook a Passing Fad? Nearly Half of Americans Think So." Mashable.com (May 15, 2012).

National White Collar Crime Center and the Federal Bureau of Investigation. "Internet Crime Complaint Center 2012 Internet Crime Report." (2013).

Nielsen "January 2013: Top U.S. Entertainment Sites and Web Brands." (March 22, 2013).

Nikander, Pekka, and Kristina Karvonen. "Users and Trust in Cyberspace." In the Proceedings of Cambridge Security Protocols Workshop 2000, April 3-5, 2000, Cambridge University (2002).

Oreskovic, Alexei. "Facebook Comments, Ads, Don't Sway Most Users." Reuters (June 4, 2012.)

Parkes, David C., and Lyle Ungar. "Iterative Combinatorial Auctions: Theory and Practice." *Proceedings of the 17th National Conference on Artificial Intelligence* (AAAI-00) (2000).

Pew Internet & American Life Project. "72% of Online Adults are Social Networking Site Users." (August 5, 2013a).

Pew Internet &American Life Project. (Lee Rainie). "Coming and Going in Facebook." (February 5, 2013b).

Rheingold, Howard. Hosting Web Communities. New York: John Wiley and Sons (1998). Also see Rheingold.com for more recent articles by Rheingold.

Rheingold, Howard. *The Virtual Community.* Cambridge MA: MIT Press (1993).

Rosenblum, Stephanie. "For the Plugged-In, Too Many Choices." *New York Times* (August 10, 2011).

Simonson, Itamar, and Amos Tversky. "Choice in Context: Tradeoff Contrast and Extremeness Aversion." *Journal of Marketing Research,* Vol. 20, 281-287 (1992).

Stanford Persuasive Technology Lab and Makovsky & Company. "Stanford-Makovsky Web Credibility Study 2002." Stanford Persuasive Technology Lab. (Spring 2002).

Twitter, Inc. "Twitter Stats," business.twitter.com/basics/ (accessed September 30, 2013).

Vakrat, Yaniv, and Abraham Seidmann. "Can Online Auctions Beat Online Catalogs?" *Proceedings of the 20th Conference on Information Systems* (December 1999).

Vakrat, Yaniv, and Abraham Seidmann. "Analysis and Design Models for Online Auctions." *Proceedings of the 4th INFORMS Conference on Information Systems and Technology.* (May 1998).

Vickrey, William. "Counterspeculation, Auctions and Competitive Sealed Tenders." Journal of Finance (March 1961).

CHAPTER 12

Ariba Inc. "About Us." (September 2013).

Barlow, Alexis. "Web Technologies and Supply Chains." Glasgow Calendonian University, Scotland. In *Supply Chain Management: New Perspectives*, edited by S. Renko. (2011).

Beard, Alison and Richard Hornik, "It's Hard to Be Good," *Harvard Business Review Magazine,* November 2011

Bunkley, Nick. "Lacking Parts, GM Will Close Plant." *New York Times* (March 17, 2011).

Bolukbasi, Hande. "Putting the Business in the Palm of Your Hand." SAPInsider.com (January 2011).

Booen, Brett. "The Under Armour Success Story: How SAP Improves the UA Supply Chain." SupplyChainDigital.com (March 10, 2011).

Cachon, Gerard, and Robert Swinney, "The Value of Fast Fashion: Quick Response, Enhanced Design, and Strategic Consumer Behavior." *Management Science* Vol. 57 778-795 (April 2011).

Cisco Systems, Inc. "Proctor & Gamble Revolutionize Collaboration With Cisco TelePresence." (March, 2011).

Cisco. "@CiscoLiveDesk." twitter.com/CiscoLiveDesk (accessed September 30, 2013).

Enright, Allison. "B2b E-commerce is Poised for Growth: More Than a Third of Business Buyers Plan to Spend More Online Next Year." InternetRetailer.com, May 31, 2013.

Esposito, Carl. "What Are the Best Examples of Crowdsourcing." Crowdsourcing.org (2012).

Exostar LLC. "About Exostar." (September 2013).

Fair Labor Association. "Independent Investigation of Apple Supplier, Foxconn Report Highlights." Fairlabor.org (March 30, 2012).

Gardner, Dana. "HP Shows Benefits From Successful Application Consolidation With Own Massive Global Supply Chain Project." Zdnet.com (May 20, 2010).

Globalwinespirits.com. "About GWS." Globalwinespirts.com (September 2013).

Gusman, Phil. "Most 2012 Supply-Chain Disruptions Were from Tech-Related Events, Not Weather." *Property Casualty Journal* (September 9, 2013).

Hewlett-Packard. "HP.com Business to Business." Hp.com (September 2013).

Hird, Jake. "25 Business-tastic B2B Social Media Case Studies." eConsultancy.com (October 11, 2011).

IBM Corporation. "No Resting Place." (July 2011a).

IBM Corporation, "True Value Company: True Value Optimizes Their Inbound Supply Process with IBM Sterling Supply Chain Visibility." (July 2011b).

Inventory Locator Service LLC. ILSmart.com "About Us." (September 2013).

James, Henry. "Crowdsourcing Trends in 2012." Crowdsourcing.org (April 9, 2012).

Jolly, David. "Long Pause for Japanese Industry Raises Concerns About Supply Chain." *New York Times* (March 16, 2011).

Kaplan, Steven, and Mohanbir Sawhney. "E-Hubs: The New B2B Marketplaces." Harvard Business Review (May-June 2000).

Kerrigan, Ryan; Eric Roegner; Dennis Swinford; and Craig Zawada. "B2B Basics." McKinsey Quarterly (2001).

Kumaran, S. "A Framework-Based Approach to Building Private Trading Exchanges." IBM Systems Journal (July 2002).

Levy, James. "Ariba: Sustained Profitable Growth in B2B Collaborative Commerce Solutions." Seekingalpha.com (June 7, 2010).

Melnyk, Steven, et. al. "Supply Chain Management 2010 and Beyond." APICS Educational & Research Foundation (2010).

Red Prairie, Inc. "The B2B SoLoMo Imperative." (September 2012).

Rosenzweig, et. al., "Through the service operations strategy looking glass: Influence of industrial sector, ownership, and service offerings on B2B e-marketplace failures." *Journal of Operations Management*, (29) (2011).

Schmidt, William and Ananth Raman,. "When Supply-Chain Disruptions Matter." Harvard Business School, Working Paper (November 13, 2012).

Supply Chain Digest. "Building the Supply Chain from the Shelf Back Research." (April 4, 2012a).

Supply Chain Digest. "Global Supply Chain: Toyota Taking Massive Effort to Reduce Its Supply Chain Risk in Japan." (March 7, 2012b).

Synnex Corporation. Form 10-K for the fiscal year ended November 30, 2012, filed with the Securities and Exchange Commission (January 28, 2013).

Trkman, P.; McCormack, K.; "Estimating the Benefits of Implementing E-Procurement," Engineering Management, IEEE Transaction, Volume 57, Issue 2 (May 2010).

True Value. Annual Report 2012. (March 2013).

U.S. Census Bureau. "eStats." (May 23, 2013).

U.S. Census Bureau. Statistical Abstract of the United States (2012).

Vance, Ashlee. "For an Online Marketplace, It's Better Late Than Never." *New York Times* (November 20, 2010).

Wise, Richard, and Dave Morrison. "Beyond the Exchange: The Future of B2B." *Harvard Business Review* (November-December 2000).

W.W. Grainger. Inc. Form 10-K for the fiscal year ended December 31, 2012, filed with the Securities and Exchange Commission (February 28, 2013).

Yoo, Byungjoon; V. Choudray; and T. Mukhopadhyay. "Marketplaces or Web Service: Alternate Business Models for Electronic B2B Commerce." *Proceedings of the 44th Hawaii International Conference on System Sciences* (HICSS) (2011).

Zarroli, Jim. "In Trendy World Of Fast Fashion, Styles Aren't Made To Last." National Public Radio (March 11, 2013).

Zurich Insurance. "Outsourcing Failures Now in Top 3 as Causes of Supply Chain Disruption." *Insurance Journal* (November 8, 2012).

Index

A

a la carte revenue model, 634–635
AAM (Alliance for Audited Media), 185
abandonment rate, 389, 390
Abbott Laboratories, 247
Abdulmutallab, Umar Farouk, 255
ACC files, 77
acceptance testing, 203
access controls, 292
accessibility
   design for, 227, 228–229
   features, 234
   rules, 227
Access (Microsoft), 372
account aggregators, 595
account numbers, 262
accountability, 490
accumulating balance payment systems, 298
ACLU (American Civil Liberties Union), 63, 703
ACPA (Anticybersquatting Consumer Protection Act), 529–532
acquisition rate, 389, 390, 469
active content tools, 223–225
Active Server Pages. See ASP
ActiveX (Microsoft). See Microsoft ActiveX
Acxiom, 366, 502
ad exchanges, 325, 351, 401, 402
   programmatic, 731
ad servers, 157, 212, 351
ad networks, 257–258, 401
ad targeting, described, 343–344
ADA (Americans with Disabilities Act), 228
Adap.tv ad exchange, 325
add-to-cart rate, 397
Adidas, 377
Adobe Systems, 86, 185, 257
Adobe Analytics, 398
Adobe Dreamweaver, 152, 198, 199
Adobe Flash, 42, 153
   cookies, 379–381, 400
   online marketing and, 348, 349, 379, 380, 381, 400
   streaming media and, 162
Adobe Omniture, 86
Adobe Reader, 271
Advanced Encryption Standard. See AES
Advanced Research Projects Agency Network. See ARPANET
advertising. See also online advertising; marketing; online marketing
   continued use of traditional print, 337
   cost of, 56, 395

e-commerce presence maps and, 191
   Foursquare and, 62–63
   Google Glass and, 109
   low-cost tools for, 215
   market segmentation and, 210
   mobile presences and, 231
   networks, described, 351
   online advertising and, comparison of, 343–344
   Pandora and, 98
   requiring users to use, 221
   revenue model, described, 60, 64, 73
   search engines and, 160
   "trust factor" and, 338
   Twitter and, 56
   USA Today and, 183–185
   video, 165
adware
   described, 260
   cookies and, 379
aerospace industry, 84
AES (Advanced Encryption Standard), 278, 287
affiliate marketing, 86, 355, 379
   cookies and, 379
   programs, 191
   revenue model, 61, 73
affinity communities, 695, 700, 704
affinity group portal, 728, 732
Africa, 56, 138, 745
African Americans, 330, 331
age, of Internet users, 330, 336
agency model, 656
aggregators, 76
Agha-Soltan, Neda, 138
AgoraCart.com, 215
A-GPS, 465
AIM (AOL Instance Messenger), 159
Air Products & Chemicals, 797
Airbnb, 33, 34, 435
Airborne Express, 769
airline industry, 36, 235–239, 373. See also travel industry
Akamai, 86, 172–176, 269
Al-Assad, Bashar, 265
Alcatel, 145
Alexander, Keith B.
algorithms, 97, 305–306, 347
   Akamai Technologies and, 174
   encryption and, 278–279
   WPA2 and, 287
Ali, Ben, 137
Alice in New York app, 202

C

C (high-level language), 171

C++ (high-level language), 171

C2C (Consumer-to-Consumer) e-commerce, 19, 20–21, 23, 72

auctions, 709, 711, 713

Cabir, 272

Cable Communications Policy Act, 504

cable modems, 118, 132, 133, 134, 288. *See also* modems

Cablevision, 133

CALEA (Communications Assistance for Law Enforcement Act), 270, 502

calendar software, 124, 167

California Online Privacy Protection Act, 505

Cameron, David, 537

campus area networks. *See* CANs

Canada, 363, 503

cannibalization, 633–634, 654–655

CANs (campus area networks), 130–132

CAN-SPAM Act, 294, 354

cap pricing, 541

capital
    raising, 68–69
    seed, described, 68–69
    working, 575

Capital Factory, 69

car rentals, 234, 235–239

Carbonite, 73, 81

carding forums, 255

Cargill, 784

career services, 604–611, 692

CareerBuilder, 608, 609, 611

Carroll, Lewis, 202

cart conversion rate, 389, 390

CAs (certification authorities), 248, 283–285, 292

Cascading Style Sheets. *See* CSS

case studies
    Akamai Technologies, 172–176
    eBay, 734–737
    Elemica, 793–798
    ExchangeHunterJumper.com, 470–475
    Google Books, 549–553
    Netflix, 682–685
    OpenTable, 612–616
    Orbitz charts, 235–239
    Pandora, 97–101
    payment systems, 311–316
    real time advertising, 399–404
    TPB (The Pirate Bay), 46–49

cash
    as payment system, 296–297
    digital cash, 305–306

catalog(s)

application servers and, 211–212
    databases, 197

catalog merchants, 36, 73, 584–585

Caterpillar, 757, 762

CBS Sports, 73, 75

CDA (Communications Decency Act), 543–544

CDMA (Code Division Multiple Access), 144

CDN (content delivery network), 174

cell towers, 465

cellular network Internet access technologies, 144

censorship, 137–138

Census Bureau (United States), 21, 82, 81

central processing units. *See* CPUs

CenturyLink, 130, 132, 200

CEOs (chief executive officers), 99, 290, 411, 489, 614

Cerf, Vint, 114

CERN (European Particle Physics Laboratory), 115, 148

CERT Coordination Center, 295

CGI (Common Gateway Interface), 199, 209, 223–225

Chaffetz, Jason, 502

Channel Advisor, 86

channel(s),
    conflict, 586
    management, 722

Chapstick, 701

Charles Schwab, 593–594

Charmin SitOrSquat Restroom Finder, 170

chat, 161, 162, 430. *See also* SMS (Short Message Service) texting
    rooms, 162
    servers, 212
    surveillance and, 255
    wiretapping and, 270

CheapTickets, 89

checking transfers, 297

checkout conversion rate, 389, 390

Chestnut, Ben, 99

chief executive officers. *See* CEOs.

Child Pornography Prevention Act, 544

children. *See also* COPPA (Children's Online Privacy Protection Act), 445
    marketing to, 444–445
    protecting, 445, 543–544

Children's Internet Protection Act. *See* CIPA

China, 136, 247, 301, 367, 535
    cyberwar and, 246
    e-commerce in, 7
    Five-Year Plan, 247
    Google and, 138, 247
    IoT and, 148
    mobile phone users in, 123
    social networks in, 695
    supply chains, 757, 762

G

gadgets, 167

gambling, 40, 545–548

game(s), 9, 60, 674–676
    collection of personal information from, 445
    online marketing and, 356, 357, 358
    security and, 259, 265, 272
    social-mobile-local marketing and, 444, 445
    statistics, 330
    viral marketing and, 356

Gannett, 183, 184, 402

Gap.com, 61, 64, 588, 765

gateways, 76, 288, 303

Gbps (gigabits per second), 130

GData Security Labs, 259

gender, 330, 483

General Electric, 787

General Motors, 367, 372, 745, 747
    supply chains and, 762

General Services Administration (United States), 151

Genealogy.com, 60

general communities, 700, 704

Generalized Markup Language. See GML

GENI (Global Environment for Network Innovations) initiative, 116, 142, 143

geo-aware techniques, 464

geo-fencing techniques, 464, 467

geo-location, 232

geo-search, 465

geo-social, 467

geo-targeting, 467

Geolocation Privacy and Surveillance Act. See GPS Act

Germany, 48, 139, 301, 483, 485, 503

gesture technology, 34

Gheorghe, Christian, 202

ghost web sites, 403

gigabits, 130

Gilt Group, 374, 575, 588

GIS (geographic information systems), 234

Glaser, Will, 98

Glassware, 109

Global Environment for Network Innovations. See GENI

Global Name Registry, 151

global positioning systems. See GPS

global reach, 13–14, 17, 87, 94, 95, 378, 487. See also reach

GML (Generalized Markup Language), 150

Goat Rodeo, 311–316

GoDaddy, 86

Gold Rush of 1849, 85

Golden Rule, 492

Goldman Sachs, 332, 413

Gondad exploit kit, 246

Gonzalez, Albert, 267

Goodyear Tire & Rubber Compay, 793

Google, 33, 160–161, 327. See also Android (Google), portals
    apps and, 7, 26, 27, 81, 124, 169–170, 359
    big data and, 385
    blogs and, 164
    business models and, 73, 79–81, 86
    censorship and, 138, 536
    click-through rates and, 392
    cloud computing and, 76, 77–78, 124, 431
    collection of private data by, 63
    cyberespionage and, 247
    ethical issues and, 483–484, 495, 497–500, 503, 509–510, 512
    FiOS and, 143
    Firefox and, 149
    founding of, 160
    free products offered by, 371
    global mission of, 3, 186
    instant ads and, 401
    intellectual property and, 9, 519, 521, 524, 531–533
    intelligent assistants, 167–168
    interest-based advertising and, 364–365
    local marketing, 462, 463, 465, 466–467
    local searches using, 359
    market share, 159
    mobile marketing and, 429, 451, 452, 454, 458, 474
    Music Manager app, 78
    NSA PRISM program and, 139
    online marketing and, 327, 345, 347, 357, 359, 365
    "open" app model, 274
    P2P networks and, 47
    payment systems and, 311
    phishing and, 263
    privacy and, 63
    ranking of companies by, 346–347
    RSS and, 164
    security and, 257–258, 274–275, 285
    small business and, 7
    social networks and, 691, 694, 695, 696, 706–708
    social search and, 346
    statistics on unique URLs, 24
    stickiness and, 390
    surveillance and, 139, 255
    Terms of Service, 483, 484
    text ads, 56
    top portal/search engine, 727, 728
    tracking files and, 400
    Twitter and, 57
    Web site optimization and, 222
    Web and, relationship of, 23
    widgets, 167

I

Credits

CHAPTER 1

p.3, Pinterest, © Blaize Pascall/Alamy; p.46, Pirate Bay, © Tommy (Louth)/Alamy.

CHAPTER 2

p.55, Twitter, © Kennedy Photography/Alamy; Figure 2.1, Ancestry.com, © Ancestry.com, 2012; p.97, Pandora.com, © NetPhotos/Alamy.

CHAPTER 3

p.107; Sergey Brin, © REUTERS/Carlo Allegri; Figure 3.10, © Visualware, Inc., 2012. Used with permission; Figure 3.14, from Internet2.edu, © 2012; p.172, Akamai.com © 2012 Akamai Technologies, Inc.

CHAPTER 4

Figure 4.12, screenshot of WebTrends Analytics 10, © WebTrends, Inc., 2012. Used with permission.

CHAPTER 5

p.245, CyberAttack, © Rafal Olechowski/Fotolia; Figure 5.4, © keith morris/Alamy; p.312, PayPal, © Ian Dagnall/Alamy.

CHAPTER 6

p.325, ExpoTV.com © EXPO Communications, 2012; Figure 6.1, adapted from Kotler and Armstrong, *Principles of Marketing*, 13e, 2009. Reprinted by permission of Pearson Education, Inc., Upper Saddle River, NJ; Figures 6.5 and 6.8, based on data from eMarketer, Inc.,© 2013, used with permission; Table 6.2, based on data from eMarketer, Inc. © 2011, used with permission; Table 6.4, based on data from eMarketer, Inc. © 2013, used with permission.

CHAPTER 7

p.411, Facebook © digitallife/Alamy. Used with permission; Figures 7.6, 7.9, 7.10, 7.11, 7.12, 7.15, and 7.17, based on data from eMarketer, Inc., © 2013, used with permission; p.470, ExchangeHunter-Jumper.com, © 2012 Eohippus, LLC.

CHAPTER 8

p.483, Free Speech, © kentoh/Shutterstock; p.549, Google books, © Cyberstock/Alamy.

CHAPTER 9

p.561, © Ken Gillespie Photography/Alamy; Figures 9.2 and 9.3, based on data from eMarketer, Inc., © 2013, used with permission.

CHAPTER 10

p.625, © Ingvar Bjork/Alamy; Figures 10.13, 10.15, 10.16, based on data from eMarketer, Inc., © 2013, used with permission.

CHAPTER 11

p.691, courtesy of Carol Traver; Figure 11.2, based on data from eMarketer, Inc., © 2013, used with permission; p.734, eBay, © Iain Masterton/Alamy.

CHAPTER 12

p.745, VW, © Julian Clune/Alamy; p.793, Elemica, © 2012, Elemica, Inc.